THE ASTROLOGY OF SAHL B. BISHR
Volume I

Principles, Elections, Questions, Nativities

TRANSLATED FROM THE ARABIC

TRANSLATED & EDITED BY
BENJAMIN N. DYKES, PHD

The Cazimi Press
Minneapolis, Minnesota
2019

Published and printed in the United States of America
by The Cazimi Press
515 5th Street SE #11, Minneapolis, MN 55414

© 2019 by Benjamin N. Dykes, Ph.D.

All rights reserved. No part of this publication may be reproduced, stored in or introduced into a retrieval system, or transmitted, in any form or by any means (electronic, mechanical, photocopying, recording or otherwise), without the prior written permission of both the copyright owner and the above publisher of this book.

The scanning, uploading, and distribution of this book via the Internet or via any other means without the permission of the publisher is illegal and punishable by law. Please purchase only authorized editions and do not participate in or encourage electronic piracy of copyrighted materials. Your support of the author's rights is appreciated.

ISBN-13: 978-1-934586-48-8

Acknowledgements

I would like to thank the following friends and colleagues, in alphabetical order: Steven Birchfield, Chris Brennan, Tania Daniels, Sharon Knight, Monadhl al-Mukhtār, John and June Peacock, and Mohammed Vaez.

Also available at www.bendykes.com:

Designed for curious modern astrology students, *Traditional Astrology for Today* explains basic ideas in history, philosophy and counseling, dignities, chart interpretation, and predictive techniques. Non-technical and friendly for modern beginners.

Dorotheus's *Carmen Astrologicum* is a foundational text for traditional astrology. Originally written in a lost Greek version, this is a translation of the later Arabic edition. It contains nativities, predictive techniques, aspect and house combinations, and a complete approach to elections or inceptions.

This excellent and popular introduction to predictive techniques by contemporary Turkish astrologer Öner Döşer blends traditional and modern methods, with numerous chart examples.

The first two volumes of this medieval mundane series, *Astrology of the World*, describe numerous techniques in weather prediction, prices and commodities, eclipses and comets, chorography, ingresses, Saturn-Jupiter conjunctions, and more, translated from Arabic and Latin sources.

Two classic introductions to astrology, by Abū Ma'shar and al-Qabīsī, are translated with commentary in this volume. *Introductions to Traditional Astrology* is an essential reference work for traditional students.

The classic medieval text by Guido Bonatti, the *Book of Astronomy* is now available in paperback reprints. This famous work is a complete guide to basic principles, horary, elections, mundane, and natal astrology.

This first English translation of Hephaistion of Thebes's *Apotelesmatics* Book III contains much fascinating material from the original Dorotheus poem and numerous other electional texts, including rules on thought-interpretation.

The largest compilation of traditional electional material, *Choices & Inceptions: Traditional Electional Astrology* contains works by Sahl, al-Rijāl, al-'Imrānī, and others, beginning with an extensive discussion of elections and questions by Benjamin Dykes.

The famous medieval horary compilation *The Book of the Nine Judges* is now available in translation for the first time! It is the largest traditional horary work available, and the third in the horary series.

The Search of the Heart is the first in the horary series, and focuses on the use of victors (special significators or *almutens*) and the practice of thought-interpretation: divining thoughts and predicting outcomes before the client speaks.

The Forty Chapters is a famous and influential horary work by al-Kindī, and is the second volume of the horary series. Beginning with a general introduction to astrology, al-Kindī covers topics such as war, wealth, travel, pregnancy, marriage, and more.

The first volume of the *Persian Nativities* series on natal astrology contains *The Book of Aristotle*, an advanced work on nativities and prediction, and a beginner-level work by his student Abū 'Alī al-Khayyāt, *On the Judgments of Nativities*.

The second volume of *Persian Nativities* features a The second volume of *Persian Nativities* features a shorter, beginner-level work on nativities and prediction by 'Umar al-Tabarī, and a much longer book on nativities by his younger follower, Abū Bakr.

The third volume of *Persian Nativities* is a translation of Abū Ma'shar 's work on solar revolutions, devoted solely to the Persian annual predictive system. Learn about profections, distributions, *fardārs*, transits, and more!

This compilation of sixteen works by Sahl b. Bishr and Māshā'allāh covers all areas of traditional astrology, from basic concepts to horary, elections, natal interpretation, and mundane astrology. It is also available in paperback.

Expand your knowledge of traditional astrology, philosophy, and esoteric thought with the *Logos & Light* audio series: downloadable, college-level lectures on MP3 at a fraction of the university cost!

Enjoy these new additions in our magic/esoteric series:

Astrological Magic: Basic Rituals & Meditations is a basic introduction to ritual magic for astrologers. It introduces a magical cosmology and electional rules, and shows how to perform ritual correctly, integrating Tarot and visualizations with rituals for all Elements, Planets, and Signs.

Available as an MP3 download, *Music of the Elements* was composed especially for *Astrological Magic* by MjDawn, an experienced electronic artist and ritualists. Hear free clips at bendykes.com/music.php!

Nights is a special, 2-disc remastering by MjDawn of the album GAMMA, and is a deep and powerful set of 2 full-disc MP3 soundtracks suitable for meditation or ritual work, especially those in *Astrological Magic*. Hear free clips at bendykes.com/music.php!

Aeonian Glow is a new version of the original ambient work mixed by Steve Roach, redesigned by MjDawn and Vir Unis from the original, pre-mixed files. This MP3 album is entrancing and enchanting: hear free clips at bendykes.com/music.php!

TABLE OF CONTENTS

Table of Abbreviations x
Table of Figures xi
EDITOR'S INTRODUCTION 1
  §1: Sahl's life and works 3
  §2: Overview of this volume 12
  §3: The use of Māshā'allāh by Sahl 22
  §4: Dorotheus and the *Bizidaj* in Sahl 23
  §5: The missing Rhetorius link: al-Andarzaghar 27
  §6: Angularity, whole signs, and quadrant division 32
  §7: Special vocabulary 35
  §8: Editorial principles 38
THE INTRODUCTION 41
  Chapter 1: Categories of the signs 41
  Chapter 2: The essences of the twelve houses *&* what each of them
    indicates 44
  Chapter 3: On the explanation of being *&* corruption 52
THE FIFTY APHORISMS 76
ON QUESTIONS 89
  Chapter 1: The sign of the Ascendant *&* what is in it 89
  Chapter 2: The second sign *&* what is in it, of questions 98
  Chapter 3: The third sign *&* what is in it, of questions 100
  Chapter 4: The fourth sign *&* what is in it, of questions 100
  Chapter 5: The fifth sign *&* what is in it, of questions 104
  Chapter 6: The sixth sign *&* what is in it, of questions 107
  Chapter 7: The seventh sign *&* what is in it, of questions 115
    Chapter 7.1: Marriage *&* relationships 115
    Chapter 7.2: Lawsuits 120
    Chapter 7.3: Buying *&* selling 122
    Chapter 7.4: Runaways *&* fugitives 122
    Chapter 7.5: Theft 125
    Chapter 7.6: Partnerships *&* meetings 135
    Chapter 7.7: War 136
  Chapter 8: The eighth sign *&* what is in it, of questions 147
  Chapter 9: The ninth sign *&* what is in it, of questions 148

Chapter 10: The tenth sign & what is in it, of the questions attributed to it.. 158
Chapter 11: The eleventh sign & what is in it, of questions 173
Chapter 12: The twelfth sign & what is in it, of questions 174
Chapter 13: On books & messengers 177
Chapter 14: On reports... 180
Chapter 15: On retaliation 183
Chapter 16: Questions about multiple options & topics 184
Chapter 17: Hunting & fishing.. 186
Chapter 18: On meals... 188

THE BOOK OF CHOICES **194**
Chapter 1: General principles 194
Chapter 2: The knowledge of the natures of the signs............................ 196
Chapter 3: The second sign from the Ascendant, & what types of choices are in it 202
Chapter 4: The fourth sign from the Ascendant, & what types of choices are in it 205
Chapter 5: The fifth sign, & what types of choices are in it 209
Chapter 6: The sixth sign, & what types of choices are in it 210
Chapter 7: The seventh sign, & what types of choices are in it.............. 216
Chapter 8: The eighth sign, & what types of choices are in it 220
Chapter 9: The ninth sign, & what types of choices are in it 220
Chapter 10: The tenth sign, & what types of choices are in it................. 225
Chapter 11: The eleventh sign, & what types of choices are in it.......... 227
Chapter 12: The twelfth sign, & what types of choices are in it............. 228
Chapter 13: Choices of what is not in the twelve signs........................... 231

ON TIMES **232**
Chapter 1: Introduction.. 232
Chapter 2: Aphorisms of times.. 235
Chapter 3: The explanation of the extraction of the indicator of time.. 236
Chapter 4: The house of life, the Ascendant 240
Chapter 5: The house of assets.. 241
Chapter 6: The house of children.. 242
Chapter 7: The house of illness... 242
Chapter 8: The times of wars... 243
Chapter 9: On travels, from the sayings of the ancients 245
Chapter 10: On receiving a book or report, from Māshā'allāh 248

Chapter 11: On the Sultan, from the statement of Māshā'allāh 248

ON NATIVITIES 255

Chapter 1: On life & the lifespan 255

   Chapter 1.1: On the knowledge of the distinctions among nativities 255

   Chapter 1.2: On the knowledge of the planets' management 257

   Chapter 1.3: What things the native resembles, & the management of the planets in his life 257

   Chapter 1.4: Two other perspectives 259

   Chapter 1.5: On the knowledge of rectifying the hour in which the native was born, & whether it was by night or day 260

   Chapter 1.6: On the knowledge of the Ascendant of the nativity, which is the *namūdār* for one established on that day, & one whose Ascendant is not found 263

   Chapter 1.7: On knowing of the degree of the Ascendant 264

   Chapter 1.8: On nativities of nine months & seven months, & the knowledge of how long the fetus's stay in the belly of its mother is, & one having four feet (or one whom people will be astonished by) 265

   Chapter 1.9: Another approach to the staying of the fetus in the belly of its mother 271

   Chapter 1.10: On the *namūdār* of the falling of the seed 272

   Chapter 1.11: On the *namūdār*, the increase of the hour & its decrease 283

   Chapter 1.12: The native who dies in the hour he is born 285

   Chapter 1.13: On looking into the matter of childbirth, its difficulty & facilitation 286

   Chapter 1.14: The work of Abū Sinīna concerning the *namūdār* & the claim that it is correct 287

   Chapter 1.15: On life, the releaser, & the house-master, from the statement of Nawbakht 287

   Chapter 1.16: The statement of Zādānfarrūkh al-Andarzaghar on that 290

   Chapter 1.17: On the superiority of the Moon as the releaser, & the quickness of the childbirth & upbringing, in corruption 291

   Chapter 1.18: On the testimonies of the Moon also indicating the shortness of the upbringing 293

Chapter 1.19: The statement of Dorotheus on short lives 297
Chapter 1.20: The testimonies of who is looking at the releaser, so it may be known which of them is stronger 298
Chapter 1.21: On the aspect of the planets to the house-master 300
Chapter 1.22: The easternness of the planets, & their westernness. 302
Chapter 1.23: The statement of Māshā'allāh on the lifespan & the releaser 307
Chapter 1.24: On the work of the lights & turning 319
Chapter 1.25: On looking at the mother's safety in childbirth 322
Chapter 1.26: On the knowledge of whether natives are of human kind or of beasts 324
Chapter 1.27: On the knowledge of whether the native is male or female 327
Chapter 1.28: On the knowledge of twins, & multiple children in a single belly 328
Chapter 1.29: On the native's upbringing 330
Chapter 1.30: The lifespan 335
Chapter 1.31: On those whose lives are ruined, & those who do not linger for more than a few days 344
Chapter 1.32 On the matter of survival for one who does not live ... 345
Chapter 1.33: On the knowledge of the native's image & his color . 350
Chapter 1.34: Looking at the positions of the planets in the months of pregnancy, & whom the native resembles 357
Chapter 1.35: On the dispositions of the native & his condition, & what it gives rise to, & his passion, & what type it is 359
Chapter 1.36: The knowledge of health, intelligence, foolishness, & other things pertaining to morals 360
Chapter 1.37: The positions of the Lot of Fortune in the signs 369
Chapter 1.38: Categories of the signs 374

Chapter 2: On assets, fortune, & livelihood 379
Chapter 2.1: Classes of good fortune & misery: al-Andarzaghar 380
Chapter 2.2: On those who always have the greatest good fortune, from al-Andarzaghar 380
Chapter 2.3: Other approaches for powerful good fortune 393
Chapter 2.4: On the positions of the planets in the signs, & what that indicates 398

Chapter 2.5: On the right-sidedness of the planets (& it is what is called the "spear-bearing" of the planets): what it indicates of good fortune & assets 400
Chapter 2.6: On the twelfth-parts of the planets 401
Chapter 2.7: The repelling of evil by the planets 402
Chapter 2.8: On the knowledge of nursing & its goodness 403
Chapter 2.9: On the positions of the lords of the glowing one, what it indicates 404
Chapter 2.10: On the positions of the luminaries, & what that indicates 404
Chapter 2.11: The statement of Theophilus on good fortune & assets 406
Chapter 2.12: The statement of Ptolemy about that 408
Chapter 2.13: The statement of Māshā'allāh & Abū 'Alī al-Khayyāt about that 409
Chapter 2.14: The lord of the second house according to its nature & in the houses 414
Chapter 2.15: The knowledge of the Lot of assets 416
Chapter 2.16: On those in the middle, from al-Andarzaghar 421
Chapter 2.17: On falling down from good fortune, from al-Andarzaghar 422
Chapter 2.18: More on falling from good fortune 423
Chapter 2.19: On those who rise after wretchedness, from al-Andarzaghar 424
Chapter 2.20: Those who are always miserable, from al-Andarzaghar 425
Chapter 2.21: On those whose earnings are from their own hands, or from force & injustice, from al-Andarzaghar 426
Chapter 2.22: More on good fortune, the Lot, & timing, from al-Andarzaghar 427

Chapter 3: On the matter of siblings, whether they are many or one **429**
Chapter 3.1: Whether he is the first-born or not 430
Chapter 3.2: On abundance & scarcity 431
Chapter 3.3: The agreement & hostility of the siblings 438
Chapter 3.4: The benefit of the siblings 440

Chapter 3.5: The number of the native's siblings from his own father & mother 443
Chapter 3.6: Whether the siblings are brothers or sisters 445
Chapter 3.7: On those born after the native 446
Chapter 3.8: On the death of the siblings from al-Andarzaghar 446
Chapter 3.9: How to interpret family members & their Lots 447
Chapter 3.10: On what the lord of the house of siblings indicates when it is in the twelve places, without the aspect of the fortunes & infortunes, from Māshā'allāh 450
Chapter 3.11: On the knowledge of the Lot of siblings 451
Chapter 3.12: On the positions of the Lot of siblings from Māshā'allāh 452
Chapter 3.13: The Roman *Bizidaj* on the knowledge of the rankings of the siblings, & their insignificance 454

Chapter 4: On the matter of fathers & mothers 458
Chapter 4.1: Paternity 458
Chapter 4.2: On examining the good fortune of the parents, & their suffering, from the statement of al-Andarzaghar 462
Chapter 4.3: The father according to the *Bizidaj* 465
Chapter 4.4: On the father from the statement of Māshā'allāh 468
Chapter 4.5: On examining the matter of the mother & her condition 471
Chapter 4.6: On the length of the mother's survival 474
Chapter 4.7: The good fortune or falling of the parents 475
Chapter 4.8: On aspects 479
Chapter 4.9: The shares of the planets' twelfth-parts 485
Chapter 4.10: Various statements about the father 485
Chapter 4.11: The lord of the fourth in the houses, from Māshā'allāh 486
Chapter 4.12: The statement of Abū 'Alī al-Khayyāt on directions for parents 489
Chapter 4.13: On looking into the lifespans of the parents, & its time 490
Chapter 4.14: The Lot of fathers 490
Chapter 4.15: The exaltation of the fathers & their suffering 495
Chapter 4.16: Background & relationship of the parents 497

Chapter 4.17: On the knowledge of the affection of the parents & the child, one to the other, & their enmity 499
Chapter 4.18: On inheritance 500
Chapter 4.19: Which of the parents will die first: al-Andarzaghar.... 501
Chapter 4.20: The lifespan of the parents 503
Chapter 5: On the matter of children 512
Chapter 5.1: The multiplicity of the children & their scarcity 512
Chapter 5.2: On sterility 523
Chapter 5.3: When a child will be born, & whether it is male or female
.... 525
Chapter 5.4: Which of his children will be more elevated, & what he will experience from them 528
Chapter 5.5: On the death of the children 530
Chapter 5.6: On the number of children 532
Chapter 6: On health, defects, & chronic illness 538
Chapter 6.1: On illness & ailments 538
Chapter 6.2: On chronic illness of the eyesight 542
Chapter 6.3: On the lords of chronic illness 552
Chapter 6.3.1: Seven items for illness, from al-Andarzaghar 552
Chapter 6.3.2: On making inferences from nativities: the lords of defects & misfortunes 555
Chapter 6.3.3: On those born in the signs, if one of the planets is in them, & the stink of their odor 559
Chapter 6.3.4: Knowing the place of the chronic illness 561
Chapter 6.3.5: The position of the Lot of chronic illness 563
Chapter 6.3.6: Natives who are deprived of their tongues & have defects in reason & language 565
Chapter 6.3.7: The nativities of those whose joints are severed & their bodies broken 565
Chapter 6.3.8: The nativities of those who fall from elevated places 566
Chapter 6.3.9: Nativities accompanied by gout & gangrenous sores
.... 568
Chapter 6.3.10: Nativities which are afflicted by leprosy, itching, & sparse whiskers 568
Chapter 6.4: On an apparent or hidden chronic illness, on the right or left 570
Chapter 6.5: When the chronic illness will be 572

Chapter 6.6: The knowledge of the insane & the deranged, & the losing of their minds.. 574
Chapter 6.7: Robbers & sorcerers from al-Andarzaghar.................... 578
Chapter 6.8: The nativities of eunuchs from al-Andarzaghar............ 578
Chapter 6.9: On short people from al-Andarzaghar 579
Chapter 6.10: On slaves & servants 580

Chapter 7: On marriage 583
Chapter 7.1: On the marriage of men & women 583
Chapter 7.2: On his marrying someone of the people of his house . 608
Chapter 7.3: The knowledge of the abundance of his women, & how much their number is, in the nativities of men & women 617
Chapter 7.4: The knowledge of the time of the marriage of men with women.. 618
Chapter 7.5: The knowledge of how the harmony is, of the woman to her husband & the husband to the woman................................... 621
Chapter 7.6: The knowledge of who will die before his partner, the man or the woman.. 624
Chapter 7.7: The statement on immorality & fornication, & passion & fornication in men & women 626
Chapter 7.8: The sodomite & the moral person.................................... 631

Chapter 8: On the causes of death 637
Chapter 8.1: Introduction.. 637
Chapter 8.2: On nativities in which their manner of death is by means of iron or something else, from an adversary or tribulation.......... 639
Chapter 8.3: Māshā'allāh on the lord of the Ascendant 648
Chapter 8.4: Death abroad 649
Chapter 8.5: The lord of the eighth in the houses, according to Māshā'allāh 651
Chapter 8.6: The Lot of death, according to Māshā'allāh 652
Chapter 8.7: Various statements 652

Chapter 9: On travels & religion 654
Chapter 9.1: Whether the native will travel or live abroad 655
Chapter 9.2: The knowledge of which direction his travel will be in, & at which time.. 663
Chapter 9.3: The knowledge of which direction is better for the native if he travels to it from al-Andarzaghar... 663
Chapter 9.4: Māshā'allāh on travel 664

Chapter 9.5: On looking into the matter of religion & fidelity 668
Chapter 10: Occupation, authority, & valor 679
   Chapter 10.1: On work & occupation 679
      Chapter 10.1.1: Overview 679
      Chapter 10.1.2: An explanation of the essences of the planets' works, & an enumeration of them & what they grant 684
      Chapter 10.1.3: The knowledge of the work from the position of the lord of the tenth in the signs, & the natures of every sign 690
      Chapter 10.1.4: The meeting & fullness before the nativity 693
      Chapter 10.1.5: On various occupations, from al-Andarzaghar 697
      Chapter 10.1.6: The knowledge of the native & his lowness, from al-Andarzaghar 699
   Chapter 10.2: On the nativities of kings 700
      Chapter 10.2.1: Overview 700
      Chapter 10.2.2: The statement of Māshā'allāh b. Atharī on the nativities of kings 702
      Chapter 10.2.3: On associating with authority & entering into it, according to Māshā'allāh 705
      Chapter 10.2.4: The lord of the tenth in the houses, from Māshā'allāh 707
      Chapter 10.2.5: The Lot of work 709
      Chapter 10.2.6: Hermes on the nativities of kings 711
      Chapter 10.2.7: Examples of spear-bearing 717
   Chapter 10.3: The lords of horsemanship & valor 724
Chapter 11: On friends & fraternity 727
   Chapter 11.1: What the friendships will be like 728
   Chapter 11.2: How friendships change, from al-Andarzaghar 733
   Chapter 11.3: The knowledge of when he will be hostile to his friend 734
   Chapter 11.4: Benefit & love between people 737
Chapter 12: On enemies & suffering 742
   Chapter 12.1: Enemies 742
   Chapter 12.2: Riding animals & livestock 748
APPENDIX A: THE 66 SECTIONS 750
APPENDIX B: CONNECTIONS OF THE LORD OF THE ASCENDANT .. 759
APPENDIX C: SAHL'S *NATIVITIES* & *THE BOOK OF ARISTOTLE* 766
GLOSSARY 771
BIBLIOGRAPHY 798

Table of Abbreviations

Works in This Volume	
Aphorisms	*Fifty Aphorisms*
Choices	*The Book of Choices*
Connections	*Connections of the Lord of the Ascendant* (App. B)
Introduction	*The Introduction*
Nativities	*On Nativities*
On Times	*On Times*
Questions	*On Questions*
Sections	*Sections on Ascendants & the Judgments of Nativities* (App. A)
Other Authors	
AW1 / AW2	Dykes, *Astrology of the World* Vols. 1-2
BA	*The Book of Aristotle* (in *PN1*)
Carmen	Dorotheus, *Carmen Astrologicum*
Excerpts	Dorotheus *Excerpts*, in *Carmen* Appendix C.
Gr. Intr.	Abū Maʾshar, *The Great Introduction to the Science of the Stars*
Heph.	Hephaistion, *Apotelesmatics III*
ITA	Dykes, *Introductions to Traditional Astrology*
JN	Al-Khayyāt, *On the Judgments of Nativities* (in *PN1*)
Judges	Various, *The Book of the Nine Judges*
Labors	Theophilus, *Labors Concerning Military Inceptions*
OVI	Theophilus, *On Various Inceptions*
PN1 – PN3	Dykes, *Persian Nativities* Vols. I - III
PN4	Abū Maʾshar, *Persian Nativities IV: On the Revolutions of the Years of Nativities*
RYW	Māshāʾallāh, *On the Revolutions of the Years of the World*, in *WSM*
Search	Hermann of Carinthia, *The Search of the Heart*
TBN	ʿUmar al-Tabarī, *Three Books on Nativities* (in *PN2*)
WSM	Dykes, *Works of Sahl & Māshāʾallāh*

CONTENTS xi

Table of Figures

Figure 1: Attributions to al-Andarzaghar by Sahl 30
Figure 2: Mars angular by sign, withdrawing dynamically 34
Figure 3: Crooked and straight signs 41
Figure 4: Triplicity lords 44
Figure 5: The 8-place system of good or suitable places (grey) 48
Figure 6: The 7-place system of good or suitable places (grey) 48
Figure 7: 7-place system rankings, in Sahl and *Carmen* 49
Figure 8: Signs configured to Jupiter in Sagittarius (white), ... 50
Figure 9: Advancing (gray) and retreating (white), ... 52
Figure 10: Transfer of light 55
Figure 11: Collection of light 55
Figure 12: Blocking #1 ("Cutting") 56
Figure 13: Blocking #2 ("Intervention") 57
Figure 14: Blocking #3 ("Nullification") 58
Figure 15: Conjunction nullifying a connection from another sign .. 59
Figure 16: Moon received by Mars (by house) 60
Figure 17: Saturn and Mars not accepting nor receiving the Moon .. 62
Figure 18: Five kinds of non-reception 62
Figure 19: The Moon in the empty course 63
Figure 20: Banished or wild Mars 63
Figure 21: Returning #1 64
Figure 22: Returning #2 64
Figure 23: Handing over power 65
Figure 24: Comparative table of planetary strengths and weaknesses 69
Figure 25: Enclosure or besieging by degree 72
Figure 26: Joys by house 74
Figure 27: Joys by sign 74
Figure 28: Joys in relation to Sun 74
Figure 29: Joys by quadrant 74
Figure 30: Fortunes relieving hardship (Aphorism #36) 84
Figure 31: Planets in eastern and western rising (*Aphorisms* #40) .. 85
Figure 32: Upright and falling Midheavens 95
Figure 33: Sahl's question about authority (MS values) 97
Figure 34: Sahl's question about authority (modern calculation) 97
Figure 35: Angles for buying land and cultivation 101

Figure 36: Angles for leasing 103
Figure 37: Angles for treating patients 108
Figure 38: Critical days 110
Figure 39: Angles for theft 126
Figure 40: Angles for partnerships 135
Figure 41: Houses for war (*Questions* Ch. 7.7, 90-101) 147
Figure 42: Angles for travel (*Questions* Ch. 9, 22-25) 150
Figure 43: Houses for meals (*Questions* Ch. 18, 36-61) 192
Figure 44: Timing by quarters and hemispheres 233
Figure 45: Timing by solar phase (*On Times* Ch. 1, 17-21) 234
Figure 46: Basic time units by sign and planet 236
Figure 47: Planetary years and other time units 238
Figure 48: Ptolemaic Ages of Man 258
Figure 49: Hephaistion's template, pre-conception lunation 267
Figure 50: Sahl's template, pre-conception lunation 268
Figure 51: Sahl's comparisons of pre-natal lunation and its ASC 269
Figure 52: Trutine of Hermes 274
Figure 53: Superiors' easternization and westernization 305
Figure 54: Inferiors' easternization and westernization (Sahl, al-Bīrūnī) ... 306
Figure 55: Years given by planets making Lot of Fortune unfortunate 373
Figure 56: Frequency of illness, from the Lot of Fortune (*Anth.* III.12) 374
Figure 57: Degrees of nobility and rank (*Nativities* Ch. 1.28, 41) 378
Figure 58: Death of mother (Dykes, from *Nativities* Ch. 4.14, 32-39) 494
Figure 59: Fixed stars harming eyes (Dorotheus, Rhetorius) 550
Figure 60: Years given by planets making Lot of Fortune unfortunate 573
Figure 61: Frequency of illness, from the Lot of Fortune (*Anth.* III.12) 574
Figure 62: Sahl's use of al-Andarzaghar in *Nativities* Ch. 8 637
Figure 63: Lots of action or work in Sahl's *Nativities* 709
Figure 64: Spear-bearing example #1 717
Figure 65: Spear-bearing example #2 718
Figure 66: Spear-bearing example #3 719
Figure 67: Spear-bearing example #4 721
Figure 68: Spear-bearing example #5 722
Figure 69: Spear-bearing example #6 722
Figure 70: Spear-bearing example #7 723
Figure 71: Three versions of Māshā'allāh's Lot of enemies 747

Editor's Introduction

When I first encountered the astrologer Sahl b. Bishr (fl. 810-825 AD) in Guido Bonatti's *The Book of Astronomy* (2007), I found him so interesting that I decided to translate as much of him as I could find. In 2008 I published five of his works from Latin manuscripts, in my *Works of Sahl & Māshā'allāh*. For part of his *Introduction* I also included a parallel translation from a partial Arabic edition by Stegemann (1942), translated by Terry Linder.

I was vaguely aware of other works by Sahl in Arabic, but at the time I only knew Latin and already had stacks of other manuscripts to translate. Many of my readers know that I planned an elaborate set of translations in all areas of traditional astrology (the *Essential Medieval Astrology* series), and while I made some changes along the way, I think I completed most of what I set out to do. As of 2019 I have translated major and minor works in all areas of traditional astrology, and the landscape for this field is much richer and fuller than it was when I published Bonatti and Sahl-Māshā'allāh.

Ten years later, I have returned to Sahl. This was partly because I have turned almost exclusively to Arabic translation, and I eventually wanted to do all of his works from Arabic. But the immediate reason is because this volume forms one of two textbooks for my forthcoming traditional natal course. The other textbook is Abū Ma'shar's complete *On the Revolutions of the Years of Nativities* from the original Arabic, which I am publishing as *Persian Nativities IV* (or PN4). (My translation of the incomplete Latin edition was *Persian Nativities III*).

Why should this be my textbook? Because after some research I realized that Sahl's *On Nativities* contains almost the entire natal portion of a book which came to be known in Latin as the *Book of Aristotle* (BA) which I had translated and published as *Persian Nativities I*. The Arabic original was put into Latin by Hugo of Santalla in the early 1100s, and in their 1997 edition Charles Burnett and David Pingree argued that it had been authored by Māshā'allāh; moreover, in their annotations they made it clear that Sahl's *On Nativities* contained many passages from it. The Latin *BA* is chock full of instructions and rules from Dorotheus and Rhetorius, along with some Ptolemy and others, and was carefully organized for the practicing astrologer: three of its books were on basic concepts and natal interpretation, and the fourth was on predictive techniques. So its use of early authors and careful organization made it an ideal course text—in theory.

The main problem with *BA* is its excruciating style, which I faithfully replicated from Hugo of Santalla's Latin instead of paraphrasing and simplifying. It can be difficult to understand, even for someone already familiar with traditional concepts and techniques. But as I looked more at Sahl's *On Nativities*, I realized two things: first, the so-called *Book of Aristotle* was not by Māshā'allāh at all, but by the earlier Persian astrologer al-Andarzaghar; second, Sahl's *On Nativities* had a whole lot more in it, including material from Valens and alternative translations of Dorotheus, Theophilus and others—including much from Māshā'allāh himself, none of which is part of *BA*. Put simply, I found that in addition to Sahl's excellent *Introduction* and *Aphorisms*, and his books on questions, elections, and timing techniques, his *On Nativities* had one of the most extensive and organized natal compendiums I had seen, and showcased the work of a hitherto neglected astrologer, al-Andarzaghar. This made a Sahl volume the obvious choice for a course book.

In sum, this volume represents a transmission of Hellenistic astrology via the Sasanian Persians, and newly translated for the 'Abbāsid Court in Baghdad, compiled and rearranged by an astrologer who actually worked for the 'Abbāsids and had access to manuscripts reaching back to Rhetorius and beyond, including Persian translations of Dorotheus and Valens. It contains the following six works and two Appendices (to be followed by Sahl's mundane work in Volume II):

1. *The Introduction*
2. *The Fifty Aphorisms*
3. *On Questions*
4. *On Choices*
5. *On Times*
6. *On Nativities*
7. *The 66 Sections on Ascendants and the Judgments of Nativities* (Appendix A)
8. *The Connections of the Lord of the Ascendant* (perhaps by Māshā'allāh: Appendix B)

§1: Sahl's life and works

Sahl's full name was Abū 'Uthmān Sahl b. Bishr b. Habīb[1] b. Hāni' al-Isrā'īlī al-Yahūdī,[2] which al-Nadīm says was sometimes shortened to Hāyā al-Yahūdī[3] (Hāyā the Jew). His precise dates are unknown, but he seems to have been most active in the years 811-825 AD (see below), and Sezgin calls him both an astrologer and mathematician.[4] In the Latin West his name is usually transliterated as *Zahel*, which sometimes causes confusion because the Arabic name for Saturn is *Zuhal*, and that name is sometimes assigned to magical treatises.

In my Introduction to *Astrological Works of Theophilus of Edessa*, I sketched the life and times of Theophilus (695-785), one of the last truly Hellenistic astrologers and the personal astrologer of the 'Abbāsid Caliph al-Mahdī (r. 775-785). The influence of Greek and Hellenistic culture was waning as Persian astrologers like Māshā'allāh, 'Umar al-Tabarī, Nawbakht the Persian, and others were introduced to the court at Baghdad in the 760s. Arabic-language and Persian-style astrology (especially well-organized horary and mundane astrology) was flourishing, and astrologers played important roles in politics.

Al-Mahdī's son al-Hādī reigned for only about a year before dying suddenly, putting his brother Hārūn al-Rashīd (r. 786-809) on the throne. This was a famous and prosperous Caliphate, and was the setting for the *1,001 Arabian Nights* stories. Our Sahl would have grown up during this time, but was most active (or perhaps, most politically connected) during the ensuing 'Abbāsid civil war of 811-819, when he worked for and around several key political figures. Because this period also involved influential astrologers, let us draw up a cast of characters in order to understand what kinds of intrigues Sahl would have observed. They chiefly involve two astrologer-viziers and two Caliphs: two sets of brothers.

First, we have two Persian brothers who were both astrologers and viziers or chief ministers—unfortunately for us, their names also include the name "Sahl." They were two of the "Sahlids," senior bureaucrats and scholars who

---

[1] Al-Nadīm omits this name.
[2] Sezgin p. 125.
[3] Al-Nadīm VII.2, p. 651.
[4] Sezgin p. 125.

were "originally Zoroastrian nobles from Sarakhs,[5] whose families dominated the top jobs in the ʿAbbāsid administration in the late eighth and early ninth centuries."[6]

The Sahlid brothers: astrologers and viziers
- Al-Faḍl b. Sahl (771-818),[7] originally one of the astrologers for Caliph Hārūn al-Rashīd (r. 786-809) and later a vizier and viceroy of the east for Caliph al-Maʾmūn (r. 813-833).
- Al-Ḥasan b. Sahl (782-851), a vizier for al-Maʾmūn in Baghdad (from 814-19), and father of the noted female astrologer Būrān (who married al-Maʾmūn in 817 or 818).[8] Our Sahl b. Bishr worked for him (see below).

In addition to these brothers, we must remember that Māshāʾallāh and ʿUmar al-Ṭabarī were said to have been alive up through part of al-Maʾmūn's Caliphate (which would have allied them first with Caliph al-Amīn in Baghdad). So depending on exactly when Sahl came to Baghdad, he may have known these older astrologers personally, although they would have been elderly and perhaps retired.

The Caliphs
- Hārūn al-Rashīd (r. 786-809), a famous Caliph who left the ʿAbbāsid empire wealthy and unified.
- Al-Amīn, his eldest son (r. 809-813), ruling from Baghdad.
- Al-Maʾmūn, a younger son born in the same year as al-Amīn, governing in the east and then proclaimed as a rival Caliph (r. 813-833).

The Generals
- Ṭāhir b. al-Ḥusayn, "the One-Eyed" (d. 822). A general of al-Maʾmūn's in Khurāsān; later governor there (821-822).

---

[5] A city in northeastern Khurāsān.
[6] Hoyland 2015, p. 221 and p. 274 n.17.
[7] In what follows, the dates are somewhat uncertain within about six months because the Islamic calendar's months do not completely match ours.
[8] Sezgin pp. 115 and 122-23; al-Ṭabarī Vol. 32, p. 82.

- Harthama b. A'yan (d. 816). A general from Khurāsān, serving Caliphs from al-Hādī through al-Ma'mūn.

The story begins like so many others in dynastic politics, with the father Hārūn al-Rashīd wanting to avoid any problems in the succession.[9] He made it very clear who was to rule, in what order, and what rights each son would have. The eldest brother al-Amīn was to succeed, with the younger al-Ma'mūn being allowed to rule Khurāsān somewhat separately. Khurāsān was the famous and wealthy homeland of the 'Abbāsids, and former province of the Sasanian Empire, which had remained largely intact during the Arab invasions: it covered parts of eastern Iran into modern Afghanistan. Unfortunately, political factions in Baghdad and Iraq were unhappy with the semi-independent status of Khurāsān and its wealth (this had been a problem for over 100 years), so when each son took his appointed position, some military and political figures began to pressure al-Amīn to take over Khurāsān and depose al-Ma'mūn, violating the succession rules.

Al-Amīn began to demand land and money from his brother, and al-Ma'mūn might have given in were it not for—his vizier and astrologer, al-Fadl b. Sahl. Under al-Fadl's influence, al-Ma'mūn created alliances with other regional players, to which al-Amīn responded by declaring his own son his successor (definitely violating the succession rules); in 811 he then assembled an army to march east and take Khurāsān by force and capture al-Ma'mūn. Al-Ma'mūn in turn sent a general named Tāhir b. al-Husayn (known as "the One-Eyed") to halt the invasion, and at the city of Rayy in western Khurāsān, al-Amīn's troops were totally defeated.

From this point on (811-812), al-Ma'mūn suddenly found himself declared Caliph by his own people, while al-Amīn was losing support from every direction. Across the empire many cities began to switch allegiance to al-Ma'mūn, until practically all that was left for al-Amīn was Baghdad—and even then, the military leadership had converted to al-Ma'mūn and Tāhir as well, leaving al-Amīn with practically no one to defend him but some of the citizenry (indeed, the lower classes). Tāhir and others laid a devastating siege to Baghdad in 812-813, and in 813 al-Amīn was captured and executed.

This matters for our story because al-Fadl's policy—partly driven by astrology—was guiding al-Ma'mūn's actions. Al-Fadl had inspired the alliance

---

[9] For the following, see especially Kennedy 2004, pp. 142-53.

which led to the victory and al-Ma'mūn's becoming sole Caliph, but in the tradition of similar thinking in Khurāsān, al-Fadl thought the capital and power center ought to be in the Persian east, in the city of Merv—not in Baghdad. In the end this turned out to be unworkable. Moreover, al-Fadl was jealous of others' influence, sending Tāhir into exile in Raqqa in 814, and having another general (Harthama b. A'yan) executed on suspicion of treason in 816. What is even more surprising is that this other general was helping al-Fadl's own brother, al-Hasan.

In 814 al-Fadl sent his brother al-Hasan to try to rule Baghdad as a similar astrologer-vizier. But al-Hasan was ill-equipped to do so, especially since he was seen as a Persian and Zoroastrian outsider by the Arab elites, so he turned to the general Harthama for help in crushing a rebellion (815-816). At the same time, al-Fadl also had al-Ma'mūn declare a western descendant of Muhammad his heir, in an attempt to unify both ethnic and regional halves of the empire. Unfortunately, this backfired because the real objection was that western and Arab people were being ruled from Khurāsān. Many provinces were revolting or at least not supporting al-Ma'mūn, and Iraq was devolving into civil war: the empire was disintegrating. In the event, Harthama presented a threat to al-Fadl's authority when he tried to alert al-Ma'mūn to the depth of the problems. Al-Fadl turned al-Ma'mūn against Harthama, and when al-Ma'mūn threw Harthama in prison, al-Fadl had him secretly killed (816).

The failed attempt to unify the empire while ruling from the east was the last straw for al-Ma'mūn, who was finally persuaded that the Sahlid brothers were deceiving him about how big the problem was. So, in 817-18 he left Khurāsān for Baghdad, had al-Fadl executed (818), and upon entering Baghdad in 819 he sent al-Hasan into retirement. Tāhir—who had refused to help al-Hasan—was brought back from exile and rewarded with the governorship of Khurāsān in early 821, dying in 822. Al-Ma'mūn continued to rule until 833.

Although we know little about his life, our Sahl was present and a witness for many of these events. According to al-Nadīm, he worked for the general Tāhir and later for al-Hasan, and indeed at least one of his mundane ingress charts seems to discuss the war between the Caliphs directly (albeit without names).¹⁰ Apparently he later retired to Khurāsān, where he was probably from, to write a compilation of his works (*The Tenth Book*, see below).¹¹

Al-Nadīm's statement means that Sahl (1) worked for Ṭāhir in Khurāsān, (2) probably followed him to Baghdad, and then (3) remained in Baghdad in 814 when Ṭāhir was exiled and al-Ḥasan took over. If so, then Sahl would have been part of the long tradition of Persian astrologer-bureaucrats who had advised the Sassanian Shahs, remained active in Khurāsān, and later began to manage affairs for the 'Abbāsid Caliphs in Baghdad in the 760s. We can only imagine what it might have been like for Sahl to come to Baghdad and meet other, establishment colleagues, and gain access to their work. On the other hand, there is no reason to suppose that Sahl was a country bumpkin. After all, he was not only part of the establishment in Khurāsān (with its deep historical roots), but his own writings show he had access to special astrological works perhaps already available to him in the east. For example, Sahl had a copy of al-Andarzaghar's *Book of Nativities*, which was a vehicle for transmitting Rhetorius to the Arabic-speaking astrologers. Since al-Andarzaghar-Rhetorius does not seem to have been transmitted at any great length by other astrologers of the time,¹² it is likely that Sahl was already in possession of this material *before* his term in Baghdad: he came prepared.

As for the rest of his career, we have a mixture of guesswork and inferences. In addition to al-Nadīm's statement about retiring to Khurāsān to write *The Tenth Book*, it is again possible that some of his mundane charts will turn out to be from later decades. But we can be certain that he was still active in 824, since in *Questions* Ch. 1, **53-66**, Sahl describes a horary chart about gaining a position of authority, which can be timed to July 5, 824 AD JC.¹³ Without knowing exactly what tables Sahl used, the Ascendant-Midheaven combination matches the location of Baghdad perfectly, as opposed to Merv or somewhere else, so it is reasonable to assume that Sahl was still active in Baghdad in the aftermath of the civil war. But in what capacity? The chart is cast for a querent who is looking for a position of power, and since Sahl says that the civil authority (or more simply, "the Sultan") will be responsible for problems or the breakdown in the position, Sahl was proba-

---

¹⁰ I am currently translating his *On the Revolutions of the Years of the World*, which contains many historical charts.
¹¹ Al-Nadīm, p. 652.
¹² More translations must be completed before we can be sure of this.
¹³ This uses the "Sassanian" zodiac, in the Janus astrology program.

bly working independently in elite circles as a consulting astrologer. We can only hypothesize, but perhaps al-Hasan's administration was broken up after his dismissal in 819, and Sahl had to make it on his own or find a new patron. Finally, Sahl had a student named Khurrazādh b. Dārshād, who wrote a *Book on Nativities* and a *Book on Choices*.[14] According to Sezgin, al-Rijāl quotes a fragment by him on the length of dynasties.[15]

Following are Sahl's named sources—which however do not include either al-Fadl or al-Hasan, perhaps for good political reasons. Note the heavy reliance on Persian astrologers, even when they are ultimately drawing on Rhetorius, Dorotheus, Valens, and Ptolemy (whom I omit here).

- **Hermes**, who is sometimes a pseudonym for Theophilus (or a similar military source),[16] or Rhetorius,[17] or the same source on Lot calculations used by Abū Ma'shar in his *Great Introduction*,[18] or Ptolemy,[19] or others.[20]
- **Buzurjmihr** (ca. early 500s – ca. 580).[21] A vizier or chief minister for the Sasanian Persian emperor Khusrau I (r. 531-579),[22] who according to al-Nadīm created a commentary on Valens's *Anthology* called the *Bizidaj*.[23] But Sezgin also points out that according to ibn Hibintā, Buzurjmihr had instead compiled the views of previous Persian astrologers, and made a commentary on *those*. Either way, it is clear from Sahl that there was plenty of Dorotheus in the *Bizidaj*, which may mean that it was compiled around the same time as the 6th Century revision and additions to the Persian version of Dorotheus. So whatever the original *Bizidaj* was, it was *not* simply a commentary on Valens. See below for more.
- **Zādānfarrūkh al-Andarzaghar** (active ca. 650?).[24] Al-Andarzaghar (which means "teacher of precepts")[25] wrote a *Book on Nativities*

---

[14] Sezgin p. 129; al-Nadīm, p. 655.
[15] Sezgin cites ff. 146-147a, but I am not sure what manuscript this refers to.
[16] *On Times* Ch. 8.
[17] *Nativities* Ch. 1.4, **6**; Ch. 5.6, **2**.
[18] *Nativities* Ch. 3.11, **2**; Ch. 5.1, **92**.
[19] *Nativities* Ch. 10.2.6, **1ff**.
[20] *Nativities* Ch. 1.10, the so-called "Trutine of Hermes."
[21] Sezgin, p. 80; Hoyland 2015, p. 221.
[22] Buzurjmihr was also a minister for the preceding and following emperors as well.
[23] Al-Nadīm, p. 641.
[24] Sezgin pp. 80-81.

which is quoted by many authors in short statements (such as in al-Qabīsī's *Introduction*), or in longer sections (such as in al-Dāmaghānī and Abū Ma'shar). But based on the explicit quotations by Sahl in his *Nativities*, I believe that al-Andarzaghar was the original author of what became the Latin *BA*. Put differently, Sahl's *Nativities* contains most of the Arabic for al-Andarzaghar's *Book on Nativities* (for the house topics), and al-Dāmaghānī and Abū Ma'shar contain most of its predictive material. I will argue for this viewpoint below.

- **Nawbakht the Persian** (d. ca. 775).[26] One of the famed astrologers (along with Māshā'allāh and others) who were commissioned by Caliph al-Mansūr to elect the founding of Baghdad in 762. He was apparently one of the chief astrologers and accompanied the Caliph in his travels. Sahl explicitly quotes him in *Nativities* Chs. 1.15 (longevity), 1.30 (upbringing), and 6.2 (illness).
- *Sibārmahnar* (سبارمهنر). Unknown (and perhaps a misspelling), but identified in *Nativities* Ch. 2.2, **6** as "the master of the scholars." The name evidently comes from Persian.[27]
- **Theophilus of Edessa** (ca. 695 – 785 AD). A Greek-speaking Christian astrologer and one of the "last" properly Hellenistic astrologers. He specialized in military astrology and adapted much of Dorotheus's work for those purposes. For many years he worked for 'Abbāsid rulers, and was the official astrologer to Caliph al-Mahdī. Sahl uses his material (explicitly or implicitly) in most of the works here, which must reflect great respect for him.
- **Māshā'allāh b. Atharī** (d. ca. 815).[28] A Persian Jewish astrologer from Basrah[29] and one of the most famous of the early 'Abbāsid era

---

[25] Burnett and al-Hamdi 1991/1992, p. 295.
[26] Sezgin p. 100.
[27] In their edition of *BA*, Burnett and Pingree believe this is Hermes, pointing to Arabic manuscripts of Zarādusht in which an older form of Sahl's star list is attributed to Hermes in the title. But the Latin *BA* of Hugo gives the name within the text as *Sarhacir*, and there is no way to mistake the Arabic spelling of the name in Sahl for the "Hermes" (هرمس). Moreover, Sahl does not use the title applied to Hermes in the other manuscript, "chief of the sages" (رأس الحكماء), but calls Sibārmahnar the "master of the scholars" (سيّد العلماء). Sahl is so keen to transcribe most of al-Andarzaghar, it is hard to believe he would change or mistake both the name and the title. Perhaps in the future we can find an Arabic al-Andarzaghar or other copies of Sahl, to check this.

(only overshadowed later by Abū Ma'shar), Māshā'allāh was part of the team which was commissioned by Caliph al-Mansūr to elect the founding of Baghdad in 762. He wrote numerous books on pretty much every subject (including one on astrolabes). Sahl liberally quotes Māshā'allāh in virtually every book, and can now be affirmed as an important preserver of Māshā'allāh's work (see below).

- Yahyā b. Jālib (or Ismā'īl b. Muhammad) **Abū 'Alī al-Khayyāt** (active in early 800s).[30] Al-Khayyāt was a student of Māshā'allāh and wrote works on many astrological subjects. Sahl explicitly cites al-Khayyāt in *On Times* (timing techniques), *Nativities* (on finances and parents), and shows some of the same source material as al-Khayyāt in *Questions* and *Nativities* (Ch. 9.5 on religion, and the material on eminence)—most likely, from Māshā'allāh.
- Al-Hasan b. Ibrāhīm/Muhammad al-Tamīmī **al-Abakh** (active ca. 813-833).[31] Al-Abakh was an exact contemporary of Sahl's, active during the Caliphate of al-Ma'mūn (but I am not sure where he lived). He wrote a *Book on Choices* for al-Ma'mūn, a *Book on Nativities*, and a *Book on Rain*. Sahl has an excerpt that must be from the *Book on Nativities*, on determining the date of conception.[32]
- A **Muhammad b. Bishr al-Khurāsānī** (unknown, but evidently from Khurāsān). Sahl quotes this unknown astrologer in *Nativities* Ch. 3.4, **5-6**, on the topic of siblings.
- An **Abū Sufyān** (unknown) on conception and rectification,[33] who apparently worked from an author or book called *Thayūghūrs*.[34]
- An **Abū Sinīna** (unknown), again on conception and rectification.[35]

---

[28] Sezgin p. 102.
[29] Many texts say "Egypt," because in Arabic this is spelled almost exactly like the word "Basrah."
[30] Sezgin p. 120; al-Nadīm p. 655.
[31] Sezgin p. 117; al-Nadīm p. 654. Actually, the *kh* at the end of the name is doubled, so it should read *al-Abakhkh*, but this looks very strange in English.
[32] *Nativities* Ch. 1.10, **57-61** (and perhaps more).
[33] *Nativities* Ch. 1.10, **75**.
[34] Unknown at this time (ثيوغورس). It resembles "Theophilus," but to my mind is too mangled, especially coming from a near-contemporary of Theophilus.
[35] *Nativities* Ch. 1.14.

Sahl is attributed with the following works by Sezgin; titles included in this volume are in boldface:[36]

1. A work which goes under many titles, but generally seems to include **The Introduction, The Fifty Aphorisms,** and **The Book on Questions.**[37]
2. **The Book of Nativities.**
3. **The Book of Choices based on the Twelve Houses.**
4. **The Book of Times.**
5. **The Sections on Ascendants and the Judgments of the Stars.**
6. *The Letter on the Lunar and Solar Eclipse.* I plan to include this in the next volume.
7. *The Book of the Revolutions of the Years [of the World],*[38] to appear in the next volume.
8. *The Book of Precepts.* I hope to translate this in the future.
9. *The Book of Questions and Judgments,* which may be an arrangement of *Questions* and *Aphorisms* above, but appearing as a separate title.

According to al-Nadīm (English edition)[39] and Sezgin,[40] he also wrote the following, which are not yet identified in any manuscript collections:

a. A small and large *Introduction.* I suspect that the *Introduction* in this volume is the large one, and the small one is something else.
b. *The Large Book on Questions.* This may be the same as #9 above, or the *Questions* in this volume (#1 above).
c. A small *Book of Nativities.*
d. *The Book of Organization*[41] *and the Science of Calculation.*
e. *The Book on Rains and Winds.*[42]
f. *The Book on the Time of Labor and Marriage.*[43]

---

[36] Sezgin pp. 125-28.
[37] This may be the work which also appears separately below as #9.
[38] In full, *The book of the revolutions of the years and what will happen in the world, and what will affect each clime and city, in terms of command, fear, wars, and adversities.*
[39] VII.2, pp. 651-52.
[40] Sezgin, p. 128.
[41] I follow Sezgin's transliteration, for the English version "astronomy."
[42] Not in Sezgin's list.
[43] Not in Sezgin's list.

g. *The Book of the Key of Judgment*, which al-Nadīm says was a small book on questions. He also lists a *Book of the Key*, which may be the same.
h. *The Book of the Meanings.*
i. *The Book of Considerations.* This might be the *Fifty Aphorisms* in #1 above.
j. *The Book of the Revolutions of the Years of Nativities.*
k. *The Book of the Two Lots.*[44]
l. *The Book of Construction.*
m. *The Tenth Book.* This was apparently a 13-part collection of the essentials of his writings, written in Khurāsān.
n. *The Book of the Releaser and the House-master.*[45]

§2: Overview of this volume

Although al-Nadīm lists numerous titles for Sahl's works, they are rarely found as independent titles in the manuscript collections. As I mentioned above, three of them in this volume typically appear together: *The Introduction, The Fifty Aphorisms,* and *On Questions.* They appear like this in Leipzig, Hathi, and London, with Leipzig calling the collection *The Book of Judgments on the Celestial Guideposts.* Yale contains all of these but adds *On Times,* which is otherwise found separately in other sources. None contains *The Book of Choices,* which I have mainly gotten from Crofts's critical edition. The *Book on Nativities* is a wholly separate work in only two manuscripts. Following is a brief description of each of the works, beginning with the primary Arabic manuscript abbreviations:

- **B:** Yale, Beinecke 523 (*On Times, Introduction, Aphorisms, Questions*).
- **BL:** London, BL Or. 12802 (*Introduction, Aphorisms, Questions*).
- **E:** Escurial Ar. 1636 (*Nativities* [partial]).
- **Es:** Escurial Ar. 919 (*On Times* [partial]; Māshā'allāh's *The Book of the Sultan*).
- **H:** Hathi Trust 1701 (*Introduction, Aphorisms, Questions*).
- **L:** Leipzig, Vollers 0799 (*Introduction, Aphorisms, Questions*).

---

[44] Although we might think this is Fortune and Spirit, Persian mundane astrologers also called Jupiter and Saturn the "two Lots," for reasons I do not fully understand.
[45] This is in Sezgin's list, but not the English version of al-Nadīm.

- **M**: Tehran, Majlis 6484 (*Nativities*).
- **N**: Istanbul, Nuruosmaniye 2785 (*On Times* [partial]).

This volume has many diagrams, tables, and figures in it, but in the Sahl manuscripts they only occur in *Introduction* Ch. 3 and *Questions* Ch. 1, the example scenarios and charts which Sahl actually describes with planetary positions and degrees. All others are my own creation. However, we can use these figures by Sahl to tentatively date this initial collection of three works. The chart example in *Questions* can be dated to July 5, 824 AD JC, well after the fraternal civil war. If we look for years in which the figures in *Introduction* could have occurred in the Sasanian zodiac (ignoring the degrees, as these might have been finessed for purposes of instruction), most of them can be assigned specific days in 822-825 AD, with two exceptions: the collection of light is either 817 or 828, and nullification is perhaps 811 or 832. But the nullification example uses very fast planets so it is hard to choose between them. Since we know from the question chart that Sahl was still active in 824 AD, I suggest that these two works were written around 825 AD, with Sahl leafing through recent years in his ephemeris to find most of his configuration examples, and then looking a bit later or earlier for the others.

1. The *Introduction*

Again, what I have called Sahl's *Introduction* is the first of three works which are commonly bundled together but not given standardized titles (see #1 above): here the text simply begins by quoting Sahl. It is probably either the small or large *Introduction* mentioned by al-Nadīm (#a above). The MSS used in this edition are:

- **B**: Yale, Beinecke 523, slides 2139-77.
- **BL**: London, BL Or. 12802, slides 15-29.
- **H**: Hathi Trust 1701, images 4-16.
- **L**: Leipzig, Vollers 0799, ff. 2b-9a.
- The Latin manuscripts, in Paris BN 16204 and Venice 1493.

In the long tradition of the *Tetrabiblos*, Dorotheus, Antiochus, Firmicus Maternus, and others, the *Introduction* defines things like the categories of signs, aspects, house meanings, planetary configurations, and so on:

Chapter 1 begins with categories of the signs and triplicity lords. The reader should compare these categorizations with *Nativities* Ch. 1.38, which contains more and sometimes has alternative views. My footnotes guide the reader to other lists and categories sprinkled throughout the book.

Chapter 2 deals with house significations, the places which are good or advantageous or "preferable," and aspects. There are several points of interest here. First, the *Introduction* is clearly designed more for the horary astrologer, because of its emphasis on questions as well as the processes of events coming to be and passing away (to be emphasized in its Ch. 3). Next, Sahl emphasizes the *signs* when speaking about the houses or places: his fundamental orientation is towards whole-sign houses, especially when he points out that these categories are related to configurations and aversion between signs: aversion makes no sense in houses based on quadrant divisions. On the other hand, Sahl is well aware of the difference between sign-based configurations, quadrant houses, and how planets move by primary motion past the axial degrees: so there is still some ambiguity when speaking of angularity in terms of signs, and in terms of motion through quadrant divisions. (See §6 below for more.) Finally, before describing aspects and aversion, Sahl outlines two schemes for the good or preferable places: an eight-place scheme that emphasizes the angular and succeedent regions, and a seven-place scheme emphasizing places configured to the Ascendant.

Chapter 3 contains the richest and most varied material, on planetary configurations and other planetary conditions: again, Sahl emphasizes how these affect the development of matters in horary questions. Of the configurations, what I find most interesting is the appearance of historical transition: that is, astrologers of Sahl's day were working through their new Arabic vocabulary, making older schemes more complicated but without the systematizing that we find in Abū Ma'shar's *Great Introduction*. For example, Sahl has many more ways of showing how a planetary connection may be hindered, as compared with previous books (such as Rhetorius). He even has three different terms for his three types of blocking (which I have not seen in other texts), and we can see different types of "handing over."[46] On the other hand, Sahl does not include all combinations of retrogradation and changing signs as we see later in Abū Ma'shar. In *Aphorisms*, Sahl even describes what Abū Ma'shar will later call "escape" (see below) but which

---

[46] دفع إلى. In previous translations I erroneously followed Burnett and others in calling this "pushing," but am now using the more accurate "handing over."

evidently did not have a formal name in Sahl's day.[47] So to my mind, his *Introduction* provides an interesting window into the transition from Persian astrology under the Sasanians, to Arabic-language astrology under the 'Abbāsids.

2. The *Fifty Aphorisms*

Aphorisms is a handy set of rules and keywords for common planetary conditions and chart configurations, most likely with questions in mind but certainly applicable to other branches of astrology. It is the second of the three works found together (#1 above), and might be identical to one of al-Nadīm's attributions, such as the *Book of Considerations* (#i above). Unlike the *Introduction*, this is given a title almost in passing, stating at the end of the *Introduction* simply that "this is the beginning of the aphorisms of judgment": so we could take the title to be the *Aphorisms of Judgment*. But I have followed the Latin tradition by calling it the *Fifty Aphorisms*. (Actually, the Arabic means something more like "anecdotes" of judgment, but that has a trivializing sound in English.) The four MSS used for this edition are:

- **B**: Yale, Beinecke 523, slides 2177-95.
- **H**: Hathi Trust 1707, images 18-23.
- **L**: Leipzig, Vollers 799, 9a-12a.
- **BL**: London, BL Or. 12802, slides 29-35.

The aphorisms are not meant to be "mathematically" precise in their use and interpretation, and their declarative style should not deceive us: sometimes elements of one aphorism might seem incompatible with another, and the practitioner will have to decide how much weight each one should be given. Some can be traced to Theophilus or Dorotheus, but I suspect many have come from Māshā'allāh.

At the beginning I have placed a table which identifies many of the aphorisms by topic. There are several which are notable. *Aphorism #25* is on the effect of a received infortune, which the text says will make it *stronger* for its

---

[47] On a related topic, Sahl uses the term "reflection" to describe a special configuration, but sometimes explains that it is the same as a transfer of light; but by the time of Abū Ma'shar the definition has been sharpened and changed somewhat.

harm: but in my footnote I give sources and reasons to believe that this is incorrect. And as I mentioned above, *Aphorisms* #16-17 describe a configuration called "escape" by Abū Ma'shar: here Sahl only describes it, which shows that it had not yet become part of the official set of named configurations. This is a nice indication that even in the early 9th Century there were still creative minds systematizing the astrology they had inherited from the Persian and Greek sources.

3. *On Questions*

The title of this work in the MSS is not actually given, but begins as "The first chapter, *On starting to look at things sought*." I have assigned it the title *On Questions*, following the Latin and al-Nadīm. The Arabic sources used are:

- **B**: Yale, Beinecke 523, slides 2195-2349.
- **BL**: London, BL Or. 12802, slides 35-101.
- **H**: Hathi Trust 1707, images 23-76.
- **L**: Leipzig, Vollers 799, 12a-41b.

In addition, I have referred to my translations of the Latin *The Book of the Nine Judges* by Hugo of Santalla, al-Rijāl's Arabic *The Book of the Skilled*, and the Latin version of *Questions* which I used in *Works of Sahl & Māshā'allāh*, which I had assumed was made by John of Spain but I will now simply call "the Latin" edition.

The questions in this book have had a long career since Sahl, because they were picked up and used by Bonatti and many other traditional astrologers. Many of them go back to Dorotheus, showing that the Persian astrologers were converting elections into questions: this was probably the primary way by which the formal books on questions began in the Sasanian period. But many questions can also be traced to other works on questions by Māshā'allāh, as I sometimes point out in the footnotes. (Sahl often abbreviates Māshā'allāh's versions.) But a quick comparison between Sahl and Abū 'Alī al-Khayyāt's book on questions suggests that perhaps the connection to Māshā'allāh was indirect, as Sahl was copying many things directly from al-Khayyāt. In the future I will translate those works and we will see more clearly what Sahl was doing. Finally, Sahl evidently either had a copy of

Theophilus's *Labors* in Greek or Arabic, or was copying from al-Khayyāt (whose book on questions also has at least some it), because he uses Theophilus extensively for the war material.

As a language note, there is occasionally evidence that some manuscripts were dictated to a scribe from other manuscripts. For example, in Ch. 10, **6** the word كوكبًا is written in **BL** as the *tanwīn* sounds, so appears to be a nominative dual (كوكبان); other manuscripts did not make this error but it would make sense for someone listening and writing quickly.

4. The Book of Choices

This edition of Sahl's *The Book of Choices according to the Twelve Houses* (or: *Choices*) was translated from the Arabic edition of Crofts (1985), which was made from three manuscripts: (1) Beirut, University of St. Joseph, 199,5; (2) Cairo, Dar al-Kutub, Tal'at, miqat 139/2; (3) Escurial 919/2. The Crofts edition also compared the Arabic with numerous Latin copies.

As the reader will see, many of the passages in *Choices* come from Dorotheus: a good example is the defects of the Moon in Ch. 2, **19-28**, which can be traced back to *Carmen* V.6. But as Pingree pointed out (2006, pp. 235-36), other sections are based on hitherto untranslated materials by Māshā'allāh on questions and elections:[48] indeed, we can see that Sahl's Ch. 4, **21ff** on planting trees comes from Leiden, Or. 891 f. 23b (lines 6ff). (I have added a few footnotes based on this Māshā'allāh manuscript but have not thoroughly translated it yet.) And sometimes Sahl draws on Theophilus, such as the treatment of the quadruplicities in Ch. 2, which can be well traced to *OVI*, or some of the war material on Ch. 7 (from *Labors*).

5. On Times

The manuscripts used for this edition are as follows:

- **B**: Yale, Beinecke 523, slides 2108-36.
- **Es**: Escurial 919/4, ff. 47b, 48a-51b (incomplete).

---

[48] See Istanbul, Suleymaniye (Laleli) 2022M, or Leiden Or. 891. (2022M is the current shelfmark for the Laleli manuscript; in earlier years it was 2122b, as Pingree has it.)

- **N**: Istanbul, Nuruosmaniye 2785, ff. 11b-13a (Chs. 1-3 only).
- Māshā'allāh, *The Book of the Sultan*, Escurial 919/3 (ff. 44b-46a), used only for Ch. 11.
- Theophilus of Edessa, *Labors*.
- The Latin versions, from Paris BN 16204 and Venice 1493.
- Al-Rijāl's *The Book of the Skilled*, from London, BL Add. 23399.

This short work is called simply *The Times* by **N**, and *The Letter on Times, Indicating Judgments* by **B**. It is a guide to methods of timing, both in general and for specific topics. Sahl explicitly draws on the following named sources: Māshā'allāh, al-Khayyāt, Theophilus, and Hermes. Unfortunately, certain parts of this work are choppy and confusing, and I do wish that we had more examples of the text.

As for the general approaches, in Chs. 1-3 Sahl provides several lists of what to look for:

First, in Ch. 1 he lists three primary ways that planets can show *changes* to a topic, in real time: their easternness and westernness relative to the Sun, their cycle of retrogradation (**7-9, 17-21**), and their changing in ecliptical latitude (**7, 16**).

To these real-time methods he adds conditions which can affect the expected quickness or slowness of the *effect*, to be used in symbolic timing: for example, based on what quarter or hemisphere the planet is in (Ch. 1, **7, 10-15**; Ch. 2, **5-6**), or the quadruplicity of its sign (Ch. 2, **2-4, 7**).

Then, in Ch. 3 he changes tack and turns to identifying a planetary "indicator of time," adding five ways in which such an indicator can show the timing of a topic—this seems especially suitable for questions and choices. First, the degrees between two applying planets can be turned into units of time, based on the symbolic quickness or slowness described above (**9**). Second, note when the real-time bodily connection between two planets occurs (**10**). Third, convert the degrees between them into days (**11**). Fourth, use a monthly profection between the Ascendant and the planet accepting the management (**12**). Fifth, use the lesser years (or similar numbers) of the planet as time-units (**13, 15-21**).

Finally, Sahl mentions primary directions (or directing by ascensions), pointing out that both Māshā'allāh and al-Khayyāt advocated taking latitude into account, and possibly using converse directions (Ch. 1, **24-25**).[49]

But throughout the rest of *On Times*, Sahl does mention other methods, notably the use of solar revolutions as described by Māshā'allāh in Ch. 11. The main idea in this chapter is that we can see when certain significators of an event chart are later burned or harmed in the angles—perhaps of the original chart as time goes on, but certainly in later solar revolution charts.

6. On Nativities

I call this *The Book on Nativities*, according to the *explicit* in **E**; but it might have been a *Book of Nativities*, or maybe *The Great Book of Nativities* mentioned by al-Nadīm. Certainly it is large enough to merit the latter name. It exists in only two known manuscripts, neither of which is fully complete (but there is enough in each to create the whole):

- **E**: Escurial Ar. 1636.
- **M**: Tehran, Majlis 6484.

Of these, **E** begins at *Nativities* Ch. 2.19, 7. **M** contains almost everything but is missing a few pages here and there, as well as its title page. Previous scholars have been puzzled by **M**, believing that it begins abruptly on f. 61a, and that the previous folios were by another author, "probably Abū Ma'shar."[50] But the puzzle is easily solved when we realize that the manuscript was dropped on the floor before it was bound: by turning pages around and piecing them together based on their contents, it is easy to see that it is the complete book by Sahl (again, minus whatever was on the initial page).

---

[49] I say "possibly," because one way to understand this passage is simply that directing backwards takes us backwards in time. So, let the Ascendant be at 15° Gemini, with two other planets at 1° and 29°. A direction between the Ascendant and 29° would represent a normal direction for a future event. But the planet at 1° could represent something that has *already* happened, because that planet has already arisen: in that case, the measurement between it and the Ascendant could show the time of that event *in the past*. This is different from some other ways of doing converse directions, in which significators and promittors are allowed to move back and forth in whatever way the astrologer wants.

[50] See Sezgin, pp. 126 and 485.

As I have already discussed, Sahl's book is valuable as a document of its time, due to its extensive use of ancient and contemporary sources, and simply due to its size. Probably only the natal section of al-Rijāl's *The Book of the Skilled* is longer. With it, we are getting a full dose of authentic Hellenistic astrology from Dorotheus up to the Persian astrologers of the late 700s. We could summarize its sources as follows:

1. Dorotheus and Rhetorius, as filtered through:
2. Al-Andarzaghar's *Book of Nativities* and Buzurjmihr's *Bizidaj* (which includes some Valens), with:
3. A lot of Māshā'allāh pasted strategically in the right places, and:
4. A few more authors, including Ptolemy.

So in terms of primary sources, apart from the very varied chapter on upbringing and longevity (which mainly shows Persian authors), the book is largely comprised of three ancient authors (Dorotheus, Rhetorius, Ptolemy), and one medieval one (Māshā'allāh).

But *Nativities* is also valuable to the student because Sahl adopts and adapts al-Andarzaghar's organization. Sahl typically structures his chapters around al-Andarzaghar's method of an expanding table of contents. He typically begins with al-Andarzaghar's brief table of contents, which lists multiple "topics" to be addressed for a particular house. Each of these topics is then expanded by listing at least one "item" which is used to find the answer for it, and then these items are elaborated with actual rules.

For example, in Ch. 5, **1-6** Sahl gives the six topics for children, such as how many children the native will have (**1**). (I tend to divide the chapter into sub-chapters in accordance with these topics.) But the topic of the number of children is judged via four items, listed in Ch. 5.1, **1-5**: Jupiter and his triplicity lords, the Lot of children, the Midheaven and its lord, and the fifth house. Then, Sahl follows up with al-Andarzaghar's rules for these items. But he also feels free to add material from Ptolemy, or Māshā'allāh, or others, either throughout or at the end. Thus, Ch. 5.1 is all about the number of children: after Sahl gives al-Andarzaghar's rules, he appends several passages by Māshā'allāh on the same topic (**61-110**). Then in Ch. 5.2 he moves to the next topic (sterility) and does something similar. When Sahl recreates al-Andarzaghar's tables of contents and item lists, I direct the reader to the corresponding passages later in the chapter; otherwise, the reader should consult Appendix C, which lists all Sahl sentences deriving from BA.[51]

Sahl's use of fixed stars is interesting, because although he clearly had a copy of al-Andarzaghar, who uses some Pahlavi names for the stars (and which Hugo transliterates in his Latin), Sahl instead uses Arabic terms: sometimes much older ones than we find today. So for instance Sahl's term for Spica, "The Defenseless One," is not classical Greek nor the Persian ("Ear of Corn").[52] But for the "Falling Vulture" (α Lyra), Sahl translates this classical Hellenistic name into Arabic.[53] So while al-Andarzaghar reflects the older Persian star list, Sahl was either able to draw on an updated one in Arabic, or translated it himself.

7. The 66 Sections

This short set of 66 statements appears in two manuscripts mentioned by Sezgin (p. 127, #5). The version here is based on Nuruosmaniye 2785/3, 13a-15a; the other manuscript (not yet seen by me) is Cairo, Tal'at 139/4, 62a-65a. They cover all areas of traditional astrology: questions, inceptions, nativities, and mundane.

It so happens that every one of these is reflected in the famous *Propositions of al-Mansūr*, one of several centiloquies popularized in the Latin Middle Ages. In some cases, the Latin helps clarify some readings in **N**. I have prefaced each of the sections with a "Sahl number" [S] and an "al-Mansūr number" [M] so that they may be compared.

8. The Connections of the Lord of the Ascendant

This appeared at the end of the twelfth house in Sahl's *Nativities*, in **M**. Although it does not name an author, I suspect it is Māshā'allāh. The combination of house lords is typical of his approach, as is his occasional grouping of houses by type, as in his treatise on Lots.

---

[51] Please note that I have changed some of the chapter numbers in BA since the first edition, and I refer to sentence numbers which I had omitted in it.
[52] *Nativities* Ch. 2.2, **8**.
[53] *Nativities* Ch. 2.2, **9**.

This short piece gives easy, cook-book style interpretations for connections between the lord of the Ascendant and the lords of other houses. The author focuses on the following principles of interpretation:

1. Whether the lord of the Ascendant hands the management over to the other lord, or *vice versa*.
2. Out of which house the management is handed over (i.e., where the applying planet is).
3. Whether the planet being handed over to (or applied to) is a fortune or infortune.

§3: The use of Māshā'allāh by Sahl

Although the search for Māshā'allāh in the Latin *BA* is a red herring (see below), Sahl does make extensive use of Māshā'allāh and frequently mentions him by name. Indeed, from Sahl's *Nativities* we can reconstruct large portions of otherwise rare or lost works by the older astrologer. Following are the primary references, which explicitly cite Māshā'allāh or can be shown to be from him:

- A translation of most of the *Book of Lots*,[54] apart from Māshā'allāh's Arabic chart example (in *Nativities*).
- Interpretations for the lord of the Ascendant with the lords of most other houses (in *Nativities*).
- Complete interpretations for the lord of each house in all houses, distributed throughout *Nativities*. (This is probably the Arabic original for the Latin work I translated in *WSM*, titled *On the Significations of the Planets in a Nativity*.)
- Excerpts on many natal topics from a book of nativities. Two of these (in Chs. 2.13, 10.2.3) obviously form the basis of al-Khayyāt's *JN*, Chs. 11 and 31, but others do as well. I also suspect that most of

---

[54] Sezgin p. 105, #12. I have used two Arabic versions of this in editing Sahl: (1) Tehran Dānishgāh, Nafīsī 429 (67b-74b); (2) Tehran, Majlis 17490 (130-43). The Lot of Spirit material missing in the Arabic is preserved in a Latin translation, Vatican Pal. lat. 1892, ff. 99v-100r; a version is also in the Latin Abū Bakr II.1.10. Sahl also preserves the Lot of chronic illness, again missing in the Arabic but found in Vat. Pal. lat. 1892, f. 102r.

Ch. 9.5 on religion is by Māshā'allāh, as it is also the basis of al-Khayyāt's treatment in *JN*'s Ch. 29.
- Material on questions and inceptions or elections (in *Questions* and *Choices*), taken from Māshā'allāh's books on the same topics.[55]
- Some comments on planetary configurations, in *Introduction* (and probably in *Aphorisms*, from a *Book of 85 Proverbs*).[56]
- All or most of the short *Book of the Sultan*,[57] on the accession of kings (in *On Times* Ch. 11).

Again, *none* of these Māshā'allāh passages appear in the Latin *BA*.

The material on the lords of the houses in the houses, and in combination with the lord of the Ascendant (applying, separating, and so on), suggests that Māshā'allāh's approach represents a separate Persian tradition highly linked to horary astrology.

Throughout Sahl's book we can see that Māshā'allāh's astrology is notable for several recurring themes: (1) frequent reference to retrogradation, (2) constant use of reception, (3) casting the solar revolution for years in which time lord techniques indicate some event, (4) referring to the tenth place as the eighth from the third, indicating problems for siblings, and (5) a heavy reliance on derived houses.

§4: Dorotheus and the *Bizidaj* in Sahl

Even more so than his other works, Sahl's *Nativities* shows how thoroughly a knowledge of Dorotheus had permeated Persian and Arabic astrology. But this is also the place to speak about the *Bizidaj* (a Persian work attributed to the astrologer Buzurjmihr or Burjmihr), for Sahl's quotations from it show that it was more complicated than we normally think. To put it simply: (1) Sahl had multiple avenues for reading Dorotheus, (2) his sources sometimes had better readings and may supply sentences missing from 'Umar's transla-

---

[55] I am in the process of translating several "new" works by Māshā'allāh on questions and inceptions, from Arabic and Greek. Hopefully these will shed more light on Sahl's sources.
[56] Sezgin p. 104, #4.
[57] Sezgin p. 105, #9.

tion in *Carmen*, and (3) his use of the *Bizidaj* shows that it had also been a conduit of Rhetorius, in addition to al-Andarzaghar.[58]

The Hellenistic astrologer Dorotheus of Sidon (fl. late 1st Century AD) wrote an extremely influential poem in five parts (the *Pentateuch*), which included basic concepts in astrology, natal interpretation, predictive techniques, longevity calculations, and elections or inceptions. Our most extensive knowledge of it in Greek is in the *Apotelesmatics* by Hephaistion of Thebes (fl. early 5th Century AD), who often quotes the poem verbatim or puts long sections in prose paraphrase. In the 3rd Century the Sasanian Persian King Shapūr I commissioned a translation of the *Pentateuch* into Pahlavi (Middle Persian), which was later changed by various insertions.

So by the 5th Century when Hephaistion of Thebes was still able to quote Dorotheus directly, there were only two complete versions: the original Greek *Pentateuch*, and the Pahlavi translation. But over the next few centuries, others were drawing on Dorotheus in their own compilations, especially the following four men: Rhetorius, Zādānfarrūkh al-Andarzaghar, Buzurjmihr or Burjmihr, and Theophilus of Edessa.

Rhetorius of Egypt is usually thought to have lived in the 7th Century, but as I argued in my Introduction to the recent edition of his works, he more likely lived in the late 5th or early 6th Century. His primary Greek work[59] shows the influence of Dorotheus, which means that anyone with a copy of Rhetorius, would indirectly have some Dorotheus.

The Persian astrologer al-Andarzaghar, who perhaps lived around the time of the 'Umayyad Caliphate's conquest of Sasanian Persia (651 AD), also used Dorotheus (and apparently, Rhetorius) to write his *Book on Nativities*, which has come down to us as the Latin *BA*. I will argue for al-Andarzaghar's authorship in the next section, but it's worth pointing out here that Sahl copies much of al-Andarzaghar's book in his own *Nativities*.

The Persian Buzurjmihr or Burjmihr wrote a book known in Arabic as the *Bizidaj* (a transliteration from the Pahlavi title), which we have been told is a partial translation and commentary on Valens, along with other things—but

---

[58] It is not known whether al-Andarzaghar himself had a copy of the *Bizidaj*, but it seems likely.
[59] This is often called the *Treasury* of Rhetorius, and is the fifth book in a manuscript version (of which the first four are Ptolemy's *Tetrabiblos*). The sixth book seems to be notes or passages attributed in part to Rhetorius, and is slated to be published by Stephan Heilen. See Pingree 1977, p. 210.

as we will see below, there must have been plenty of Dorotheus in it too, most likely from the Pahlavi translation.

Finally, Theophilus of Edessa (ca. 695 – 785 AD) had copies of both a Dorotheus (whether the *Pentateuch* or the Pahlavi edition, I am not sure) and Rhetorius. As a military and political astrologer, he rewrote huge swaths of Dorotheus in the form of elections and questions for wars and military operations—but without actually identifying any of it as Dorotheus or Rhetorius. In this way, anyone using his books would not have known who the original sources were.

From this list of sources, we can derive four ways by which an astrologer of Sahl's time could have had access to Dorotheus, listed roughly in order of how direct and explicit their use of Dorotheus is:

1. *Direct quotation from the Pahlavi* (whether translated into Arabic for that purpose, or quoting from some other Arabic version). Sahl *does not* seem to have owned 'Umar al-Tabarī's translation, which is known as *Carmen*.
2. *Summaries and commentaries*, like the *Bizidaj*. As we will see below, Sahl explicitly identifies three of these passages, the fourth of which uses Rhetorius's version of a Dorothean text.
3. *Collations, rearrangements, and cut-and-paste jobs*. This would include Rhetorius and al-Andarzaghar, who reorganized Dorothean material while preserving the sense of the original sentences. Huge amounts of Sahl's *Nativities* is directly comprised of al-Andarzaghar.
4. *Repurposed passages for other contexts*. This includes many passages in Sahl's *Choices* and *Questions*, and Theophilus's own rewording of Dorotheus for military purposes.

Of these, (1) is probably found all over the place, and one sometimes does not know what the direct source is. As an example, *Choices* Ch. 2, **41** quotes or summarizes a passage from Dorotheus, but it is unclear whether Sahl is quoting directly (1), or is quoting someone such as Māshā'allāh (3). But consider *Nativities* Ch. 1.15, **5**, where Sahl pastes a passage by Nawbakht the Persian: Nawbakht is summarizing or quoting from his own Dorothean source.

Either way, these sources are all culturally and linguistically close to the Pahlavi edition and the *Bizidaj*, and sometimes the same passage shows up more than once, showing the influence of multiple authors and translators: see for example the treatment of siblings in the following three passages, all taken from the same section in Dorotheus: *Nativities* Ch. 3.1, **3-7**; Ch. 3.5, **2-6**; Ch. 3.13, **5-13**.

We can also say that some of the Dorotheus which Sahl had access to, had *more* information in it than the 'Umar al-Tabarī translation: the synastry material in the chapter on friendship (*Nativities* Ch. 11.4, **1-2**) can be confirmed as Dorothean, both from Hephaistion and the Greek prose Dorotheus *Excerpts*.[60]

At this point let me address the *Bizidaj*. Apparently, while the name of Valens is most associated with it (as a partial translation and commentary of the *Anthology*), ibn Hibintā points out that it drew on other ancient sages.[61] We now have confirmation of that. For one thing, al-Bīrūnī describes certain categorizations of the signs which we now know were in Dorotheus because of the Greek *Excerpts*—but which do not now appear in Valens.[62] But in *Nativities* Sahl explicitly quotes the *Bizidaj* in four places, once calling it the "Roman" *Bizidaj* (just as al-Bīrūnī did), and reveals more:

- Ch. 3.2, **37-47**, on siblings. Here, Sahl quotes "the *Bizidaj* and Dorotheus," a remarkable statement that either means he knew it was Dorotheus because the *Bizidaj* said so, or he had separate copies of both and had compared them.
- Ch. 3.13, on siblings. Sahl cites "the Roman *Bizidaj*," and certain elements of the passage are very interesting. For one thing, sentences like **2** echo Greek terminology;[63] **3** could be a missing Dorotheus sentence, and **5-13** reflects *Rhetorius's* version of the material, showing that the author of the *Bizidaj* had a copy of Rhetorius.
- Ch. 4.3, on the father. Sentences **1-2** reflect material in *Carmen*, but **3-4** do not, even though it seems they should: again, these could be missing Dorothean sentences. The rest is not Dorotheus (so far as I know) nor Valens.[64]

---

[60] Heph. III.20, **5**; *Excerpts* XVII, **3**; XVIII, **1-6**; XIX, **1**.
[61] See Pingree 1989, p. 231.
[62] See al-Bīrūnī 1959, p. 124; *Excerpts* XVIII.
[63] This passage uses the term "triangle" to mean a triplicity or trine, as with Greek.
[64] I add that in the Latin *BA*, the sentence corresponding to Sahl's *Nativities* Ch. 4.1, **4** is attributed to Buzurjmihr, showing that al-Andarzaghar had access to the *Bizidaj* as well.

- Ch. 6.2, **69-72**, on fixed star degrees harming the eyesight. The stars listed are from the beginning of Rhetorius Ch. 62—again showing that the author had access to Rhetorius.

Two of these passages from the *Bizidaj* show that Rhetorius was transmitted to the Arabic-speaking astrologers via it, and not just via al-Andarzaghar. Let us now turn to that.

§5: The missing Rhetorius link: al-Andarzaghar

At this point we must revisit a set of arguments from my Introduction to Theophilus of Edessa's works (2017). These involve David Pingree's claims about the transmission of Rhetorius to the Baghdad astrologers, as well as the original author of the Arabic source of *BA* (which I translated from its Latin edition and published in 2009, in *Persian Nativities I*).

Sahl's *Nativities* plays a key role in clearing up these misunderstandings. Put simply, Pingree condensed the transmission of Rhetorius's work to the Baghdad astrologers down to a personal transfer of one book between two men: namely, that Theophilus of Edessa handed his own copy of Rhetorius to Māshā'allāh, and Māshā'allāh used it to write the Arabic work known to us in Latin as *BA*.[65] Unfortunately, Pingree's claims are incorrect but have been widely accepted and are still influencing scholarly opinion about the history of astrology. I don't relish pointing this out, but it's important that we have the latest information as new translations emerge.

You might wonder why this puzzle about who transmitted Rhetorius even exists: don't books get passed on in all sorts of ways? Actually, what makes it a strange puzzle is that to my knowledge the Arabic-language astrologers do not mention the name Rhetorius at all, even when we can trace Arabic passages back to him. The bibliographer Fuat Sezgin does not even list any Arabic translation of Rhetorius as a stand-alone work (which you would expect there to be). So in one sense we could say there is no special puzzle to solve, because no Arabic-speaking astrologer seems to have been aware of the transmission in the first place. On the other hand, the thrust of the question is backwards: it seems that Pingree believed *first* that the original *BA* was

---

[65] The second part of Pingree's argument does not concern us: that some copy of Rhetorius was also passed on to Theophilus's colleague Stephanus, who later brought it to Constantinople.

written by Māshā'allāh, and *because* it has Rhetorian passages in it, he wanted to explain how Māshā'allāh—in Baghdad—could have gotten a copy of Rhetorius when no one else did. The obvious answer was Theophilus, who also seems to have had one and no doubt knew Māshā'allāh personally. So the question of transmission originated with Pingree's beliefs about *BA*, with Theophilus being used to justify the belief.

But as I argued in the Theophilus volume and will review here, Pingree's argument is wrong. Rather, with the help of Sahl's *Nativities* it is easy to show that al-Andarzaghar wrote the Arabic source of *BA*, so he was the primary but not sole transmitter of Rhetorius (recall from the previous section that the *Bizidaj* also contained some Rhetorius). Māshā'allāh is simply a red herring here, and we currently have no reason to suppose that anyone reading al-Andarzaghar had any idea who Rhetorius was, much less possessed his book. This raises the much more interesting question: how did al-Andarzaghar, a Persian astrologer from (perhaps) the early 'Umayyad Caliphate, get a copy of Rhetorius—especially since it seems the 'Umayyad Caliphs were not especially interested in astrology? Was it one of the spoils of the early Arab conquest of Alexandria? Or had it been copied much earlier and been brought to Damascus (the 'Umayyad capital) before Islam? Or was it already in circulation among the Persians, a collegial transfer between astrologers of two empires in conflict, the Roman and Sasanian? There are many possibilities, and perhaps in the future we will know.

Before addressing al-Andarzaghar himself, let me review the question of Māshā'allāh's relation to *BA*. Pingree had argued for Māshā'allāh's authorship of its Arabic original, on the basis of two points.[66] The first is that a medieval Greek book list attributed to Māshā'allāh, claims that he wrote a four-part natal compilation on the basis of the books in the list; and an almost identical Latin list, which does *not* mention Māshā'allāh, forms the introduction to the Latin *BA*. Second, one of the two surviving copies of *BA* occurs in a manuscript next to another work attributed to Māshā'allāh (in Oxford, Bodleian Savile 15).

This is a highly circumstantial case, and has several problems. Right away we can reject the second point: the fact that two works appear next to each other in a manuscript has no bearing on their authorship. And in this case, it's worth pointing out that *BA* nowhere mentions Māshā'allāh: not in the book list in its introduction, not anywhere in the text, and not at the end. If we did

---

[66] Pingree 1989, pp. 227-29.

not know about the Greek book list, there would be no reason to think that *BA* had anything to do with Māshā'allāh.

The claim which is based on the two book lists is more important. The first thing to note is that (again) the Latin *BA* never mentions Māshā'allāh, nor is it divided by Hugo into four parts: the division into parts was made by Pingree,[67] although the divisions seem reasonable. Nevertheless, this editorial decision has notionally converted a book list without the name of Māshā'allāh and a book without four parts, into a book list by Māshā'allāh and a book with four parts.

Second, and more importantly, neither version of the book list nor the text of *BA* itself, ever mentions Rhetorius. Since he is one of the two major sources of the text, we would expect him to be mentioned somewhere, along with everyone else: remember, Pingree's theory is that *the book of Rhetorius itself* was given to Māshā'allāh, who then wrote the Arabic *BA* using it. In the meantime, the book list mentions dozens of works which do not seem to be used, or do not exist at all (or not in the way they are listed), such as a thirteen-book edition of Dorotheus, with 89 chapters on historical astrology. This book list may have no meaningful relation to the Arabic version of *BA*.

Third, we already know that virtually every sentence of *BA* Book IV (on predictive techniques) already corresponds to sentences by al-Andarzaghar (and so are likely to have been written by him), as Burnett and al-Hamdi showed in their 1991/1992 translation of a compilation by al-Dāmaghānī. So even if we supposed that Māshā'allāh had written *BA*, and based its Book IV on a work by al-Andarzaghar, we would expect to see the latter on the extensive book list, too. But he is not there. If however al-Andarzaghar wrote the original *BA*, this would make perfect sense: he would not have cited himself.

Fourth, as Appendix C in this book shows, *most* of the natal interpretation material from *BA* Book III appears in Sahl's *Nativities*, sentence-by-sentence, often with intact blocks of text rearranged according to Sahl's desire. But *none* of these passages are identified by him as being by Māshā'allāh. As I pointed out above, Sahl has included perhaps several entire works by Māshā'allāh into *Nativities*, along with portions of others, and virtually goes out of his way to credit Māshā'allāh wherever he can. So it's not as though Sahl was trying to hide the role of Māshā'allāh. There is simply no overlap between Sahl's attributions to Māshā'allāh and *BA*. A nice example of this is *Nativities* Ch. 5.1,

---

[67] Burnett and Pingree 1997, pp. 7-8.

61-76, where Sahl inserts an entire passage by Māshā'allāh on the number of children, following numerous *other* passages from *BA* on the same topic, which contain a *different* method.

Now, there is a close parallel between Māshā'allāh's and al-Khayyāt's treatments of upbringing[68] and the *BA* passages in Sahl's *Nativities* Ch. 1.29, 15-23, but all this shows is that there was some common source, or even that Māshā'allāh had a copy of al-Andarzaghar. For one thing, Māshā'allāh and al-Khayyāt include many other rules and also add the triplicity lords of the prenatal lunation—which Sahl/*BA* do not. Also, in *BA* this passage follows directly after another one found in *Nativities* Ch. 1.25, 8—which Sahl affirms *is* by al-Andarzaghar.

	Sahl's *Nativities*	*Book of Aristotle*	Rhetorius
1	1.16, **1-6**	III.1.9, **3-16**	
	1.16, **7-11**	III.1.9, **25-30**	
2	1.25, **8-14**[69]	III.1.2, **1-7**	Ch. 55 (p. 41)
(3)	1.29, **15-23**[70]	III.1.2, **8-25**	
4	1.30, **36-50**	III.1.3, **1-17, 26-27**	
5	2.16, **1-5**	III.2.3, **1-5**	
6	3.2, **12**	III.3.3, **18-19**	
	3.2, **13**	III.3.3, **19-20**	Ch. 108 (p. 155)
	3.2, **14-16**	III.3.3, **22-23**	Ch. 108 (p. 155)
	3.2, **17-24**	III.3.4, **1-7**	
	3.2, **25-26**	III.3.4, **8-10**	Ch. 108 (p. 155)
	3.2, **27-31**	III.3.4, **11-13**	
7	3.4, **1**	III.3.6, **1**	
8	4.1, **4-5**	III.4.2, **1-4**	
9	4.2, **1-2**	III.4.1, **1-2** ; III.4.3, **7**	
	4.2, **3**		Ch. 97 (p. 146)
	4.2, **4-9**	III.4.3, **1-6**	
10	8.7, **5-6**	III.8.1, **28**	Ch. 77 (p. 127)
11	11, **5**	III.12.1, **1-2**	

Figure 1: Attributions to al-Andarzaghar by Sahl

---

[68] For Māshā'allāh, see the Latin *On Nativities*, in *WSM*.
[69] This could perhaps include **15**.
[70] Sahl does not name al-Andarzaghar here, but in *BA* they form a continuous passage with Sahl's Ch. 1.25, **8-14**, which he does say is al-Andarzaghar.

But the most important point is that Sahl explicitly names al-Andarzaghar as the author of eleven passages which match *BA*, and four of them can be sourced to Rhetorius. The table here lists them.[71]

We can see that in three separate chapters (*Nativities* 1.25, 3.2, 8.7), Sahl's attribution to al-Andarzaghar matches both *BA* and Rhetorius, sentence-by-sentence. In the fourth chapter (4.2), Sahl's sentence **3** matches Rhetorius precisely, in the middle of a parallel passage in *BA* (but which *BA* lacks). Not only is the phrasing and order of sentences striking, but in the case of Sahl's 1.25, Sahl-*BA*-Rhetorius contains three elements which other sources like *Carmen* I.3 and Heph. III's Appendix A do not. (1) The infortunes are in the Ascendant, unlike both *Carmen* and Hephaistion. (2) The Moon is besieged, which *Carmen* lacks but Hephaistion attributes to Manethō. (3) The Moon is in the straight signs, which *Carmen* lacks but Hephaistion has. So, only Rhetorius directly gives us this passage.

To all of these we may tentatively add *Nativities* Ch. 1.33, **17-20**: it is definitely reflected in *BA* I.1, **21-24**, and while Sahl does not assign it to al-Andarzaghar, the Latin Abū Bakr Ch. I.9 contains it and assigns it via Latin transliteration to an *Andoroar* or *Amdasoar*. Likewise, *Nativities* 5.6, **20** is partly reflected in *BA* III.5.4, **14-15**, and Abū Bakr Ch. II.6.4 definitely assigns this longer statement to al-Andarzaghar.

Also, in *Nativities* Ch. 2.2 (which almost completely matches *BA*), Sahl adds a sentence **71** about the Moon being with the fixed stars: it does not appear in the Latin *BA*, but *is* in Rhetorius. This is likely to reflect an error in the Latin *BA*.

Another interesting al-Andarzaghar connection is *Nativities* Ch. 3.11, **3**, on a Mercury-Jupiter Lot for siblings. This passage is shared between Sahl and *BA*, and both attribute it to Valens. But in his list of Lots, Abū Ma'shar (*Gr. Intr.* VIII.4, **48**) says that it was *al-Andarzaghar* who attributed it to Valens. So it makes perfect sense that Sahl, copying from al-Andarzaghar's own book, would have made this same attribution.

I would like to point out that *Nativities* 4.1, **4-5** in the table above is indeed attributed to al-Andarzaghar, but *BA* itself attributes it to Buzurjmihr. So it could well be that al-Andarzaghar had a copy of the *Bizidaj*, but Sahl, simply copying from al-Andarzaghar, only cited the latter.

---

[71] In my Introduction to the Theophilus volume, I divided some of these differently and omitted others, which now appear here.

I also note that according to Burnett and Pingree,[72] the passage which is shared between Sahl's Ch. 1.16, **1-5** and *BA* III.1.9, **3-13** (see Appendix C) is also reflected in Ch. 17 one of the Greek epitomes of Rhetorius, *Peri oikodespotou*. This may be the same as the chapter of the same name which Heilen will publish in the future, but I am not sure, nor am I sure it is even really by Rhetorius. But if authentic, it would be a fifth passage proving the transmission of Rhetorius by al-Andarzaghar.

In conclusion, unless by some fortunate miracle we discover an actual Arabic copy of *BA* with the name of the author at the top, we can conclude that its author was al-Andarzaghar. We can also assume that he was the primary conduit of Rhetorius to the Arabic-speaking astrologers in Baghdad—for remember, the table above only lists those passages which explicitly name al-Andarzaghar: Sahl's *Nativities* contains many other passages shared between *BA* and Rhetorius, without al-Andarzaghar's name. (An interesting example is in *Nativities* Ch. 3.13, **15-18**).

Given all of this evidence, it is possible (if not likely) that the reason no Arabic translation of Rhetorius exists, and that no one mentions him, is because no Persian or Arabic writer after al-Andarzaghar had a copy of his book or knew who he was: they only had the illustrious al-Andarzaghar. So while Pingree's theory was based on a false view of Māshā'allāh and *BA*, solving the problem with Sahl's *Nativities* thrusts al-Andarzaghar into a position of much greater importance and shines light on a little-understood Persian period in astrology as it transitioned over to the Arabic language.

§6: Angularity, whole signs, and quadrant division

The next topic is our ongoing understanding of whole-sign houses versus quadrant houses or divisions. It is well known that by the time of the Arabic period, astrologers were using both, to the extent that they called whole signs houses "by counting" (عدد), and quadrant divisions houses by "equation" / "calculation" (سواء) or "division" (قسمة).[73] In some cases astrologers used both at the same time, and it's easy enough to criticize them for simply throwing different houses' meanings into the same pot and seeing what hap-

---

[72] Burnett and Pingree 1997, p. 143.
[73] See for example Māshā'allāh's *Conjunctions* Ch. 7, **17** (in *AW2*), and *PN4* VI.2, **21-26**. See also the discussion in Brennan 2017, Ch. 11.

pens. There has been little information on why or how they distinguished their meanings in terms of angularity and dynamic power: for example, if a planet is in a cadent whole sign, but by quadrant division it is angular, what does that mean? Normally any cadent place or division is considered "weak," while an angular one is "strong." Unless we simply average them out into a mushy middle, what do we say in actual chart examples? This new translation of Sahl provides some answers that might revolutionize how we understand triads of signs around the angles, the meanings of houses, and signs versus quadrant divisions. I will say more in my course and perhaps other publications, but let me just draw your attention to the basics here.

First, recall that some terminology concerning whole signs and quadrant divisions is ambiguous: the word used for "angle" ("stake," وتد) sometimes seems to mean an angular whole sign, sometimes an axial degree, sometimes an angular quadrant division. The usual word for "cadent" ("falling," ساقط) likewise can mean a cadent whole sign or a cadent quadrant division. But these Arabic texts (and other, later ones) also establish a vocabulary that exclusively (or almost exclusively) refers to dynamical positions: "advancing" (مقبل) means moving by primary motion toward an axial degree, so it means being either angular *or* succeedent by quadrant divisions; "retreating" (مدبر) or "withdrawing" (زائل) means moving past it and being dynamically cadent. So we see an effort to distinguish signs and divisions astronomically, but not yet interpretively.

Second, in two passages Sahl emphasizes the importance of the axial degrees or stakes being "upright" (قائم): this has to do with whether the degree of the Midheaven falls in the expected tenth sign.[74] If it does then it is "upright," and the quadrant and whole-sign angles coincide; if not, then the next best is the eleventh sign; the worst is the ninth. Here Sahl enters interpretive territory. If the Midheaven is in the tenth sign, then the native's authority (the Midheaven) is more excellent; if in the eleventh, it is next best because that succeedent sign is at least advancing towards the tenth position; if in the ninth, his authority is little established because the sign is cadent. In other words, even though the Midheaven is by definition *dynamically angular*, it is affected by the *cadency* of its *sign*.

---

[74] *Questions* Ch. 1, **47**; *Nativities* Ch. 10.2.6, **57-60**.

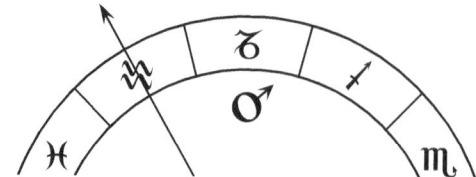

Figure 2: Mars angular by sign, withdrawing dynamically

If we apply the dynamic meaning of advancing-retreating to the three types of signs, this gives us six possibilities: a planet could be (1) angular-advancing or (2) angular-retreating, (3) succeedent-advancing or (4) succeedent-retreating; or (5) cadent-advancing or (6) cadent-retreating. We don't have the background theory for how all of these interact, but given the explicit vocabulary and knowledge of the problem we should be able to find *something* to say about them. And indeed, Sahl's texts give explicit interpretations for four of them: (1), (2), (3), and (5).[74] My impression is that angularity by sign (such as by angular triad) describes a kind of default assumption about that topic's expected benefit and manifestation in practical life; the goodness of the place (i.e., its configuration with the Ascendant) shows the worth and benefit of the topic; and the dynamic angularity shows the actual outcome, as against expectation or reputation. So if a planet indicating assets is in an angular sign such as the tenth, we can assume it will manifest assets and benefit the reputation (that is, people's impressions and expectations) because the tenth, being an angular, good sign related to fame, indicates that. But if the planet is there and dynamically retreating (so that the degree of the Midheaven itself is later in the sign or even in the eleventh sign), the assets he does get will be squandered. In this way the difference between whole sign and dynamic angularity largely concerns the contrast between expectations for an archetypally happy and practical life, and actual results: the quickness, presence, greatness, and disappearance of those expectations.

I have more to say about this, but this should suffice for now. I recommend that the student read the passages and consider how they might be applied in different circumstances.

---

[74] *Nativities* Chs. 9.5, **26**; 10.1.3, **16-19**; 2.3, **17-18**.

§7: Special vocabulary

As with most of my translations, this volume contains some new vocabulary and ideas to emphasize. The special terms found below all appear in the Glossary as well.

Easternization and westernization. Readers should already be familiar with "eastern" or "oriental" and "western" or "occidental," as well as the ambiguity in these words (see the Glossary). But the Arabic nicely adds two words based on Form II of these verbs, "easternize" (شرّق) and "westernize" (غرّب). These refer specifically to the process of making a solar phase: easternizing means actually coming out from under the Sun's rays, or at least being far enough away that one *will* do so in 7-9 days. Westernizing means actually going under the rays, or being close to doing so. (There may be some occasional ambiguity between superior and inferior planets, because Venus and Mercury can come out or go under on either side of the Sun.) See especially *Nativities* Ch. 1.22, and my *Comment* there.

Glow: sect and light. Another prominent word is "glow" (ضوء), which has three meanings. First, it is a synonym for "sect," so that a planet "in its own glow" is of the sect of the chart. Second, it simply refers to the amount of light given off by a planet, particularly the Moon: so if she increases in her glow, she is waxing. Third, another use of "in its own glow" means that a planet is out of the rays of the Sun so as to be visible on its own. Context should normally make it obvious which is meant.

Overlords and governors. Both of these terms refer to some principal planet with special rulership or influence. In Sahl, "overlord" (المسلّط) is used to describe either the primary triplicity lord over a place, or the domicile lord. A "governor" (المستولي) is a kind of overall victor over a place: in *Nativities* Ch. 1.7, it is specifically a Ptolemaic victor.

Owner (صاحب). This refers to the person who is the subject of a chart: the native is the owner of his or her own nativity, the querent is the owner of the question chart, etc.

Portions: degrees and bounds. In this book we see further how Arabic (and probably, Persian) reflects older sources in its vocabulary for degrees and bounds. Normally the Arabic for "degree" (درجة) means the same as the Latin *gradus*, a "step": a circle has 360 steps all around it. But sometimes a degree is called a "portion" (جزء), which matches the Latin *pars* and the Greek *moira*. When it does not mean a single degree, it usually means the degrees of a specific bound, such as the bound of the Ascendant or the bound in which the pre-natal lunation falls.

Position and place. First, the word "position" appears frequently, where we might normally expect "place": a suitable position in a chart, the position of a planet in the zodiac, and so on. Unless a particular degree is meant, in almost every case these two words mean exactly the same thing, normally a sign or house. There does not seem to be any reason for the Arabic to prefer "position" (موضع) to "place" (مكان), but I have distinguished them anyway.

Right-siding, paying honor, spear-bearing. The Hellenistic astrologers inherited a certain idea from the Babylonians (or perhaps, early Persians), called "spear-bearing" or "bodyguarding" (Gr. *doruphoria*). According to this idea, a native's social status is enhanced if his nativity contains a planet which can be treated as royal (normally, a luminary), and is also accompanied or protected in certain ways by a "spear-bearing" planet: different astrologers listed the various criteria which could show spear-bearing. In Arabic, this is commonly rendered as *dastūriyyah* (دستوريّة), derived from Persian words with military connotations. But Sahl's text also includes two new Arabic synonyms which I have invented translations for: "right-siding" or "being on the right" (ميمنة, تيامن), and "paying honor" or being in an "honor guard" (تكرمة). The notion of honor or an honor guard makes intuitive sense for an important person having an attachment of protective and status-enhancing guards. Being "on the right" refers to the fact that spear-bearing planets for the Sun are often preferred to be eastern, rising before him (on his right). See *Nativities* Chs. 2.5 and 10.2.7.

Share: dignity and sect. Sahl's Arabic frequently refers to dignity as a "share" (حظّ, *hazza*; but less often, نصيب, *nasīb*). So, a planet in its own exaltation is in one of its "shares." But occasionally Sahl uses this word when he really means sect, such as a planet being of the sect of the chart. Now, perhaps some Persians really thought of dignities and sect as all being part of a planet's "share," i.e., what belongs to it. But "share" in Arabic also sounds very much like the word for "domain" (حيّز, *hayyiz*), a sect-related condition which in Latin became *hayz* (and which sometimes simply means "sect");[75] so this might reflect an error in the copying process, or evolving vocabulary. Either way, I have added clarifying footnotes in the few cases where this happens.

---

[75] See *Nativities* Ch. 8.2, **35**.

Suitability: *advantage and goodness.* Readers will also know of the "good," "busy," or "advantageous" places, which are houses of the chart in which a planet is especially active or beneficial (whether for its own operation, or for the native): the best of these are typically the Ascendant, tenth, and eleventh places. Instead of using one of the normal words for "good," Sahl typically uses "suitable" and "suitability" (صالح, صلاح): these words contain a comparative meaning, indicating that these places are *suitable for* something, rather than just being good or suitable in their own right. I don't know if that's what the original translators intended, but it's a subtle distinction that I find interesting. Sahl also uses this word to denote a planet in a suitable *condition*, and in those cases he means it very broadly: being in a suitable place, or in a dignity, looked at by the fortunes, and so on.

Sultan, authority. In Arabic, the word for an individual called "the Sultan" can also mean "the government" or "the authorities": so one might read about the tenth house as "the house of the Sultan," or being on good terms with "the authorities." I have tried my best to choose between these as context allows; but the reader should keep an open mind about how narrowly the authority is meant in each case.

Turning and terminal points: *profection.* One nice surprise was to see the new word "turning" (إدارة) used for profections. This is instantly suitable because profections proceed sign-by-sign, just as the signs cross the horizon in order as the heavens turn. But it so happens that Dorotheus himself spoke of profections as "turning in a circle,"[76] so this kind of word has just about the best pedigree one could want. Interestingly, this Arabic noun also has management connotations, and the passing of something from hand to hand—which is precisely what happens when profections move from sign to sign and the management of a period is handed over from planet to planet. The sign which the turning or profection stops at, is the "terminal point" (انتهاء). See especially *Nativities* Ch. 1.24, and my *Comment* there.

---

[76] *Kuklōmenon*, quoted by Hephaistion from the original Greek poem (Heph. III.20, **3**).

§8: Editorial principles

In this volume I make use of both square and pointed brackets:

- Square brackets [ ] either add my own section divisions to help the reader, identify a new author, add a clarifying word, or indicate that something is illegible or uncertain. For example, if two planets are both referred to as "him," I may write [Mars] to identify which one is meant in a particular situation. If something is illegible or unclear, I put that in italics to indicate that the problem lies in the manuscript: [*uncertain*]. So, square brackets are always *my* way of alerting the reader.[77] To see which sentences in Sahl correspond to al-Andarzaghar in the Latin *BA*, see Appendix C.
- Pointed brackets < > *only* indicate words or passages which are actually omitted in the manuscripts but must be there. For example, if a sentence needs a "not," I will write <not>. (Sometimes we know a word is missing because we have other source texts that prove it.) If part of a sentence is missing or omitted, I write <*missing*> or <*omitted*>, again using italics to indicate that the problem is with the manuscript.

I have also begun to use boldface sentence numbers, to make it easy to find references. When I give references I will typically give the name of the work, the chapter number, and then the sentence: *Nativities* Ch. 1.28, **3**. Sometimes an italicized section title comes from the manuscripts and so has its own sentence number, but for aesthetic reasons I omit it when centering it on the page.

Sahl's books do not always have clear or consistent chapter breaks, and I occasionally have added my own chapter titles to break up the text more easily—again, in square brackets to show that they are my own insertion.

Finally, I make extensive use of flower symbols like ☙ to break up the text, either to separate an occasional *Comment* of my own from Sahl's content, or when it seems there is a clear thematic break in the text and I am not sure who the author is. For example, if I know that certain paragraphs come from Ptolemy but the text continues on with an unidentified source, I typi-

---

[77] However, when Sahl combines many authors in short sentences throughout long passages, I generally do not add bracketed titles to distinguish them, but use footnotes instead. I reserve bracketed and italicized titles for longer sections.

cally identify his portion by prefacing it with [Ptolemy], and add flowers at the end to separate it from what follows. Since Sahl does not always identify these breaks and transitions between authors, I cannot always be sure that I have inserted flowers in the correct space: treat them as helpful and aesthetic. I often indicate in footnotes how sure I am about these breaks.

THE INTRODUCTION

In the name of God, the Compassionate, the Merciful:

[Chapter 1: Categories of the signs]

2 Sahl b. Bishr the Israelite said: Know that six of the twelve signs are masculine, and six feminine. **3** So Aries is a masculine sign, diurnal, and Taurus a feminine sign, nocturnal; and likewise the masculine follows the feminine, and the feminine the masculine, up to the end of the signs.

4 And[1] of them are the signs straight in rising and crooked in rising. **5** Now the ones straight in rising are from Cancer to the end of Sagittarius: and it is that the breadth of each of these signs is greater than its length, and arises in more than two equal hours: so because of that they are called "straight in rising." **6** And those crooked in rising are from Capricorn to the end of Gemini: and it is that the breadth of each of these signs is shorter than its length, and arises in less than two equal hours: so because of that they are called "crooked in rising."

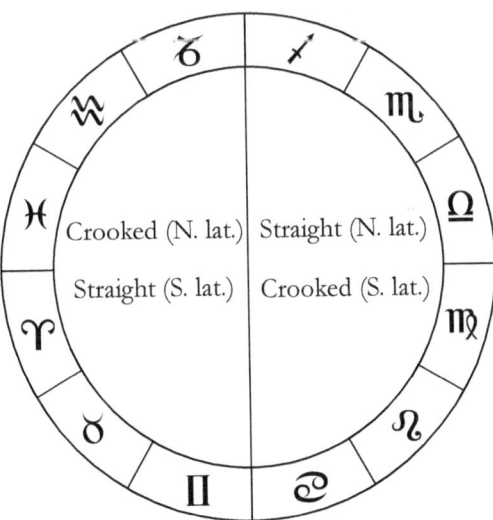

Figure 3: Crooked and straight signs

---

[1] For this paragraph, cf. *Carmen* V.2, **2-4**.

7 And² four of them are "convertible," and they are Aries, Cancer, Libra, and Capricorn. 8 And indeed, they are called convertible because when the Sun alights in the beginnings of these signs, the season is converted³ to the essence which follows it.

9 And four of them are "fixed," and they are Taurus, Leo, Scorpio, and Aquarius. 10 Because when the Sun alights in the beginnings of these signs, it fixes the season in one condition, and is not altered: if there was heat then it is hot, if it there was cold it is cold, if it was spring there is spring, and if there was autumn there is autumn.

11 And four of them have two bodies, and they are Gemini, Virgo, Sagittarius, and Pisces. 12 Because when the Sun alights in these signs, the season becomes mixed, so the first half becomes hot and the second one cold, [and vice versa].⁴

13 And of them are those having four feet: and they are Aries, Taurus, and the beginning of Capricorn, and the end of Sagittarius.⁵

14 And of them are the signs of fire, and they are Aries, Leo, and Sagittarius: and they are the triplicity of fire. 15 And of them is a triplicity indicating vegetation and everything that comes out of the earth, and they are Taurus, Virgo, and Capricorn. 16 And of them is a triplicity indicating the condition of humans and winds and everything which is in the atmosphere, and they are Gemini, Libra and Aquarius. 17 And of them is a triplicity indicating the water and everything which is in it, and they are Cancer, Scorpio, and Pisces.

18 And of them are signs which are said to be dark,⁶ and they are Libra and Capricorn.

19 And of them is a place called the "burned place,"⁷ and it is the end of Libra and the beginning of Scorpio.

20 And⁸ of them are signs which are said to have half a voice, and they are Capricorn, Aquarius, and Virgo. 21 And of them, signs having [full] voices,

---

² For **7-11**, cf. *Tet.* I.11 (Robbins pp. 65-67).

³ Following **B**, as it explains the name through a verb with the same root. **BL**, **H**, and **L** all say, "is shifted."

⁴ Adding on the basis of the Latin, as obviously the second half of every season does is not cold.

⁵ But see *Nativities* Ch. 1.38, **1**.

⁶ Lit., "have injustice" (لها مظلمة), but in both *Nativities* Ch. 1.38, **8** and *Carmen* V.6, **18** it is clear that these are "dark" (مظلمة). Without voweling, the noun "injustice" and the adjective "dark" look the same.

⁷ Usually called the *via combusta*, the burned "path" or "way."

and they are Aries, Taurus, Gemini, Leo, Libra, and Sagittarius. **22** And of them, signs which do not have a voice, and they are Cancer, Scorpio, and Pisces.

23 And[9] of them are signs of barrenness, few in children: and they are Aries, Leo, and Virgo. **24** And of them are signs of many children, and they are Cancer, Scorpio, and Pisces.[10]

25 And[11] of them are signs indicating mountains and difficult places, and they are Aries, Leo, and Sagittarius. **26** And of them are signs indicating cultivated, flat places, and they are Virgo, Taurus, and Capricorn. **27** And of them are signs indicating deserts,[12] and they are Gemini, Libra, and Aquarius. **28** And of them are signs indicating moist places, abundant in waters, and in proximity to water: and they are Cancer, Scorpio, and Pisces.

29 Now, the signs of fire indicate fire and what is produced in it, of jewels[13] and other things. **30** And the signs of vegetation indicate the earth and cultivation, and what comes to be from it. **31** The signs of people indicate people and winds and what is raised up from the earth. **32** The signs of water indicate places in which there is moisture, and every work with comes to be from moisture. **33** And the signs abundant in children indicate groups[14] of people.

34 And Aries and its triplicity are hot, dry: of natures they have yellow bile, and of regions the east. **35** The lords of this first triplicity are by day the Sun, by night Jupiter, and their partner by night and by day is Saturn. **36** And Taurus and its triplicity are cold, dry: of natures they have black bile, and of directions the south. **37** And the lords of this triplicity are by day Venus, by night the Moon, and their partner by night and by day is Mars. **38** And Gemini and its triplicity are hot, moist; of natures they have blood, and of regions the west. **39** And the lords of this triplicity are by day Saturn, by night Mercury, and their partner by night and day is Jupiter. **40** And Cancer and its

---

[8] For this paragraph, cf. also *Nativities* Ch. 1.38, **25-29**.
[9] For this paragraph, cf. also *Nativities* Ch. 1.38, **14-17**.
[10] The Latin adds an extra sentence, making Libra, Sagittarius, and Capricorn be sterile as well, and that Taurus, Gemini, and Aquarius are middling. See also *Nativities* 1.38, **14-17**; 3.0, **10**; 5.1, **8**; *Carmen* I.21, **3**; II.10, **12-13**.
[11] For this paragraph, cf. *Questions* Ch. 4, **16-18**.
[12] الصّحارى. Or, steppes and other sandy-type land.
[13] الجوهر, which can also refer generically to matter, substance, essence, etc.
[14] Or the "grouping" (حماعة), but reading the plural as it is more natural.

triplicity are cold, moist; of natures they have phlegm, and of regions the north. **41** And the lords of this triplicity are by day Venus, by night Mars, and their partner by day and by night is the Moon.

	Day	**Night**	**Partner**
♈ ♌ ♐	☉	♃	♄
♉ ♍ ♑	♀	☽	♂
♊ ♎ ♒	♄	☿	♃
♋ ♏ ♓	♀	♂	☽

Figure 4: Triplicity lords

[Chapter 2:] The essences of the twelve houses
& what each of them indicates

2 Know that we have found, for every desire and sought thing, that it is requested, sought, and proceeds in accordance with that, based on the good or bad which is in that question: namely from the ways that the scholars assigned the indication of the question and the sought things from the essences of the twelve signs, and from the natures of the seven planets, and the places from which the sought things are taken, just like what the planets have in terms of natures and the indications, and other things of the twelve houses, based on what I will explain, if God wills (be He exalted!).

The Ascendant and what is in it of questions,
and the other things of the twelve houses[15]

4 The[16] first of the houses [in] a question of the circle [arises] from the east: in the hour of a report[17] [or] one born, or the inception of a work, the

---

[15] After the Ascendant, the Arabic lists of house significations are extremely short, but the Latin ones are much longer. I believe that instead of having a separate, more detailed manuscript, the Latin translator used his knowledge of many of the topics Sahl handles later, to add to the Arabic lists here. He probably also added significations from other sources.

[16] I have read this sentence very freely, as its grammatical structure is bizarre to me in the Arabic, seeming to improperly mix definite and definite words. Nevertheless the gist is clear: the Ascendant is the most important or "first" (أوّل) of the houses, and forms the beginning of everything.

beginning is the Ascendant. **5** And it indicates life and death, because there arises the life of one who receives his lifespan through it in his coming out from the belly of his mother; and that sign arises from the darkness to the light, and from under the earth to above it, and the native's exit from the darkness of the belly to the openness of the air, and the questioner will reveal the question from the hiddenness of his heart, and it will shine forth and become clear after what was concealed inside. **6** It indicates the body and what comes from the contingent,[18] or every apparent thing and event, and what is set into motion, and speech,[19] and the beginning of a matter.

7 The second sign from the Ascendant is of what follows[20] the Ascendant; it does not look at the Ascendant. **8** It indicates assets,[21] assistants, profiting, and labor.[22]

9 The third sign from the Ascendant falls from the stakes.[23] **10** It indicates brothers and sisters, close companions,[24] travel, and relatives.

11 The fourth sign from the Ascendant is the stake of the earth. **12** It indicates the outcome, fathers, buildings,[25] lands, and everything which is hidden under the earth.

13 The fifth sign from the Ascendant is of what follows the stake of the earth, and it is the place of the Ascendant's affection and its delight. **14** It indicates children and all of what is hoped for with that.

15 The sixth sign from the Ascendant falls away from the Ascendant, not looking at it, and it is a place of evil. **16** It indicates illness and slaves.

---

[17] Tentatively reading this (الخِيَر) for "the good" (الخير). The "hour of the good" could be read as "the hour of the preferable," implying elections, but those are already dealt with later in the sentence.

[18] العرض. But this word also has connotations of something publicly presented, offered, etc.

[19] ناطق, which also has connotations of rationality.

[20] يلي. This verb means both to be adjacent to and to follow after something. This is what is normally called "succeedent."

[21] المال, which can mean both money and personal property, so it well captures the notion of "movable wealth," as opposed to the immovable wealth or real estate of the fourth.

[22] الكدّ. That is, earning one's daily bread; thus this is also the house of "livelihood" (Gr. *bios*, Ar. معيشة).

[23] Reading for "Ascendant," as with **35** below.

[24] ألفة, which has connotations of people one is close to, intimate with, likes, and spends time with.

[25] This word (الدور) can also mean "homes" or something as broad as "structures." B includes a reading from another MS, "wells" or "springs."

17 The seventh sign from the Ascendant is the stake of the west. **18** It indicates women, wars, lawsuits,[26] and every transaction between two people, and the seeker and the one sought (the fugitive, the thief, the missing person, and what is like that). **19** And this sign (and every planet which is in it) is the enemy of the Ascendant, for it is contrary to the Ascendant.

20 The eighth sign from the Ascendant is of what follows the stake of the west. **21** It indicates death, inheritances, and everything that has already perished, general evil, grieving, destruction, and something demanded back,[27] and the allies of one who is sought.

22 The ninth sign from the Ascendant falls from the stakes.[28] **23** It indicates travel, religion, the knowledge of God and the matter of the hereafter, invisible things, piety, and what has already transpired of matters, and withdrawing, and what is distant, and the man who has already been dismissed from his work.

24 The tenth sign from the Ascendant is the stake of heaven. **25** It indicates the Sultan,[29] and the property which was already stolen and disappeared,[30] magistrates and those in charge,[31] and works and professions.[32]

26 The eleventh sign from the Ascendant is of what follows the stake of heaven. **27** It indicates friends,[33] hope, good fortune, the assets of the Sultan and his land tax, and his assistants,[34] and the governor who is installed over the work after the first governor.[35]

---

[26] Or, "quarrels" (الخصومة).

[27] المطالبة, which might more generically be understood as "a demand." The eighth indicates something possessed by someone else, which one might want back.

[28] Reading for "Ascendant," with **35** below.

[29] Or, the political "authority" in general.

[30] That is, in questions and elections pertaining to theft. See for example *Questions* Ch. 7.5, 1.

[31] This word also has connotations of guardians or people who help (الوالي).

[32] Or, "calling," "vocation," "craft" (الصناعات).

[33] In Arabic, this kind of friend (الأصدقاء) implies not so much intimacy and affection (see the third house), but people whom one trusts and has mutual consent: the original root of this verb has to do with telling the truth and keeping promises, so there is a bit of the contractual involved here.

[34] This can include minor officials and even bodyguards.

[35] That is, the current authority mentioned in **25**.

28 The twelfth sign from the Ascendant falls away from the Ascendant, not looking at it. **29** It indicates enemies, downfalls, travel, the wicked,[36] prison, and riding animals.

[The 8-place system of good or suitable places]

30 Now[37] as for the preferability[38] of some of the places of the circle over others in power, the circle is divided into twelve signs:

31 Four of them are called the "stakes," and they are the sign of the Ascendant, the fourth, the seventh, and the tenth. **32** And these stakes indicate what is already present[39] of matters, and what there is in them, and the power in every thing. **33** And four of them are said to be what follows the stakes (that is, rising up to them), and they are the second from the Ascendant, the fifth, the eighth, and the eleventh. **34** And they indicate what is coming to be of matters. **35** And four of them are said to be falling from the stakes, which have already withdrawn and fallen away from the stake: and they are the third sign from the Ascendant, the sixth, the ninth, and the twelfth. **36** And they indicate what has already elapsed and passed away of matters, by the permission of God.[40]

37 And the strongest of the places of the circle is the Ascendant, and it is the most preferable of the signs; and the planet which is in it is the strongest of the planets, and especially if it was in its own house or its exaltation, triplicity, bound, or face. **38** Then the Midheaven follows that in power (and it is the tenth).[41] **39** Then the stake of the west follows that, and it is the seventh from the Ascendant. **40** Then the stake of the earth follows that, and it

---

[36] As it is, the Arabic reads "the bad/wicked journey," treating "wicked" as an adjective modifying "travel/journey." But this does not really make sense to me, so I have added the Arabic equivalent of a comma to separate them (since the twelfth does indeed indicate wicked people and things). But it is possible that Sahl really does mean something like "bad travel" or a "bad journey."

[37] Here we begin with the "other things" of the houses, which Sahl mentioned in **3**. The phrase, "the preferability of some of the places of the circle over others" is a direct reference to *Carmen* I.5, which uses the same places but in a slightly different order. Sahl first identifies the angular and succeedent places (eight of them), which have to do with presence, and then the preferability of the places by goodness and power (seven are the most preferable).

[38] This word (فضل) also implies superiority and moral goodness.

[39] Or, what has "already appeared" (حضر).

[40] See also Ch. 3, **4-5**.

[41] This parenthetical remark only in **B**.

is the fourth from the Ascendant. **41** Then the eleventh sign from the Ascendant follows that in power. **42** Then[42] the ninth sign follows that, because it is the house of the joy of the Sun. **43** Then the fifth sign from the Ascendant follows that. **44** And these seven places are praised, powerful; and the first one [mentioned] is better than the second one, and the second one better than the third one.

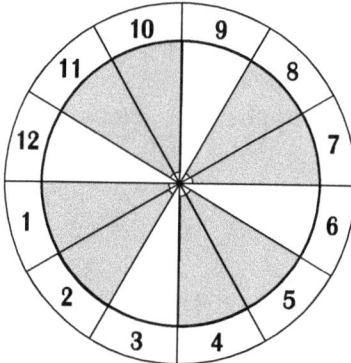

Figure 5: The 8-place system of good or suitable places (grey)

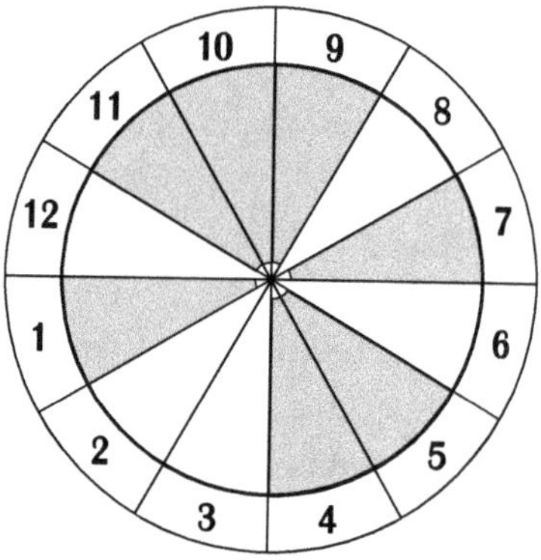

Figure 6: The 7-place system of good or suitable places (grey)

---

[42] **42-43** is a construction from **H** and **L** (which read alike), and **B**, and follows on the discussion of the relative superiority of the places earlier in the chapter. **B** has the fifth followed by the ninth, with the explanatory note about the Sun's joy (which no other manuscript has). **H** and **L** have the ninth, followed by the fifth. (**BL** does not mention the ninth at all, so can be ignored.) The decisive points here are two: (1) the note about the Sun's joy, and (2) Sahl's earlier decision to prioritize all of the angles, in contrast to *Carmen* and the two reports of Māshā'allāh's ranking (*Search* I.3.4 and III.1.1). (1) If the ninth were in last place, then the note about the Sun would not make sense, since being the Sun's joy should speak in its favor, not to its detriment. But also, below Sahl justifies making the third the best of the other places, *because it is the joy of the Moon* (see *Carmen* I.5, **3-4**, which makes precisely this point). Indeed, the reason Sahl needs to explain prioritizing the third, is because it is a falling or cadent place, violating his general preference for (2) the angles. Therefore, by putting the ninth before the fifth, and adding the explanatory statement about the Sun, we have a perfect symmetry. In both cases, the joy explains the prioritizing of the cadent place over the succeedent one: the ninth is better than the fifth because of the Sun's joy, and the third is better than the second because of the Moon's joy.

[The 7-place system of good or suitable places]

45 After that, of the signs which are recognized as being good, the third sign from the Ascendant is preferred because it is the place of the Moon's joy; then the second place from the Ascendant, because it rises up toward the Ascendant.

46 Now as for the eighth sign from the Ascendant, indeed intense misfortune is in it, because it is the sign of death, and does not look at the Ascendant. **47** And as for the remaining two signs of the circle (and they are the sixth and the twelfth from the Ascendant), they are the most bad of the places and the most evil of them, and every planet in these two places has no benefit. **48** And that is because the sixth sign from the Ascendant is a place of illness and defects, and it falls away from the Ascendant, not looking at it, <and it is the joy of Mars>.[43] **49** And the twelfth is the place of prisons, diseases, sorrows, and tribulation,[44] and it falls away from the Ascendant, not looking at it, and it is the place of the joy of Saturn (and indeed, his joy is in sorrow and weeping and tribulation).

	Good							Middle		Bad		
Sahl	1	10	7	4	11	9	5	3	2	8	6	12
Carmen I.5	1	10	11	5	7	4	9	3	2	8	6	12

Figure 7: 7-place system rankings, in Sahl and *Carmen*

[On aspects, or "looking"]

50 "Looking": and that is the union, sextile, square, trine, and opposition.

51 As for the union (and it is the assembly), indeed that comes to be if two planets were in one sign, the heavy one in front of the light one, and between the two of them in terms of degrees are 12° and what is less than that: for that is the limit of the assembly.[45]

---

[43] Adding with the Latin version, and in parallel with **49**. We have already seen Sahl use the joys as justifications for the relative preferability of the houses, in **42** and **45**.

[44] In Arabic, this word also has the specific meaning of a trial – and of the glory that one wins by surviving it. This inadvertently provides an Arabic-language justification for the 12th signifying labor and childbirth: the trial the infant experiences before being fully born.

[45] Sahl could simply be reporting 12° dogmatically. But in Ch. 3, **14** he points out that the Moon's body (or in modern parlance, her "orb") is 12° on either side. Since she has the

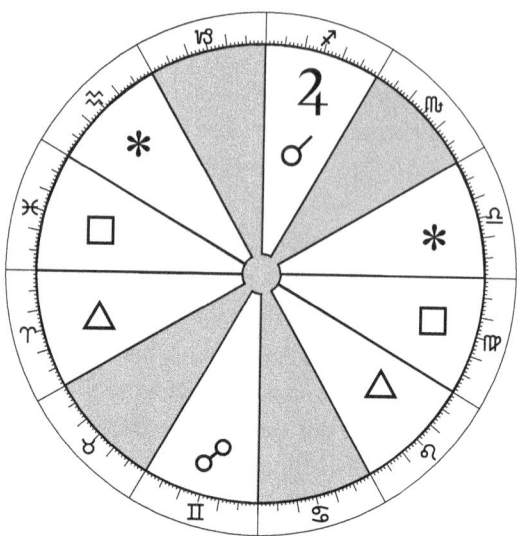

Figure 8: Signs configured to Jupiter in Sagittarius (white), and in aversion to him (gray)

52 And[46] as for the aspect of the sextile (and it is one-sixth of the circle), it is if a planet looks at a planet from the third sign in front of it (and it is called the aspect of the first sextile), and it looks at it from behind it, from the eleventh sign (and it is called the aspect of the second sextile).

53 And as for the aspect of the square (and it is one-fourth of the circle), it is if a planet looks at a planet from the fourth sign in front of it (and it is called the aspect of the first square), and it looks at it from the tenth sign, from behind it (and it is called the aspect of the second square).

54 And as for the aspect of the trine (and it is one-third of the circle), it is if a planet looks at a planet from the fifth sign in front of it (and it is called the aspect of the first trine), and it looks at it from the ninth sign (and it is called the aspect of the second trine).

---

second-largest body besides the Sun (15°), the largest distance between two planets whose bodies *both* touch each other is indeed 12°—all others will be "what is less than that."

[46] In the following paragraphs, Sahl distinguishes "first" and "second" aspects. A "first" aspect is a right or "dexter" aspect cast backwards in the order of signs, such as from Leo backwards to Taurus; a "second" aspect is a left, "sinister" aspect cast forwards in the order of signs, such as from Leo forwards to Scorpio. But the texts are not always consistent. For example, in Sahl's mundane example in *Scito* Ch. 95 (in *AW1*), Mercury is in Aries, and Sahl says he casts his "second" trine backwards to Sagittarius; according to the definition here, that should be Mercury's "first" trine.

55 And as for the aspect of the opposition (and it is the "confrontation"),⁴⁷ it is one-half of the circle: it is if a planet looks at a planet from the seventh sign; [and] it is called the aspect of the opposition, and it is the confrontation.

56 So, the aspect of the sextile is from the third sign and the eleventh, the aspect of the square from the fourth sign and the tenth, the aspect of the trine from the fifth sign and the ninth, and the aspect of the opposition from the seventh sign.

57 And the strongest of these aspects is the assembly and the opposition—and [the opposition] is the more intense by place, and the more extreme, and this aspect indicates enemies and fighters, and contrariety and contention. **58** And the aspect of the square is the middle of the aspect [of the opposition], not openly proclaiming hostility.⁴⁸ **59** And the aspect of the second sextile is stronger than the first, and the second square is stronger than the first square, and the second trine is stronger than the first trine (and this aspect is called "superiority").⁴⁹

60 And as for the signs which do not look at each other, and if a planet was in them it does not look at [another] planet, they are the second sign, the sixth sign, the eighth sign, and the twelfth sign, and what is equivalent to these four: for they are adversarial.⁵⁰

---

⁴⁷ In this paragraph, Sahl is equating two Arabic words which are linked by their root, and are almost indistinguishable. The first word is مقابلة (*muqābalah*, here "opposition"), the second is استقبال (*istiqbāl*, "confrontation"): both mean to stand opposite someone, confront, encounter, etc. From now on, I will translate each as simply "opposition."

⁴⁸ L adds in a marginal note: "The trine and sextile indicate the easiness of the matter and the pleasantness of the mind. The square and opposition indicate difficulty and hindering."

⁴⁹ الاستعلاء, which has connotations of height (and indeed, this is the "superior trine"); but it also has connotations of mastery and taking possession of something, and indeed the superior aspects do have a more controlling and dominating effect upon the "lower" planet they are superior to. See Overcoming in the Glossary.

⁵⁰ Or, "similar" (مناظرة). That is, aversion occurs between any signs which have the relationship of being in the second, sixth, eighth, and twelfth from each other: see Ch. 3, **26**.

Chapter [3:] On the explanation of being & corruption[51]

2 Know that the whole of what the stars indicate concerning what comes to be and is corrupted, is based on 16 approaches. **3** And they are: [1] advancement, [2] retreat, [3] connection, [4] separation, [5] transfer, [6] collection, [7] blocking, [8] reception, [9] <non-reception>,[52] [10] emptiness of the course, [11] returning, [12] handing over power, [13] handing over management and nature, [14] strength, [15] weakness, and [16] the conditions of the Moon.

4 As for [1] **advancement**, it is if a planet was in a stake or what follows a stake.

5 And [2] **retreat** is if a planet was falling from the stakes.

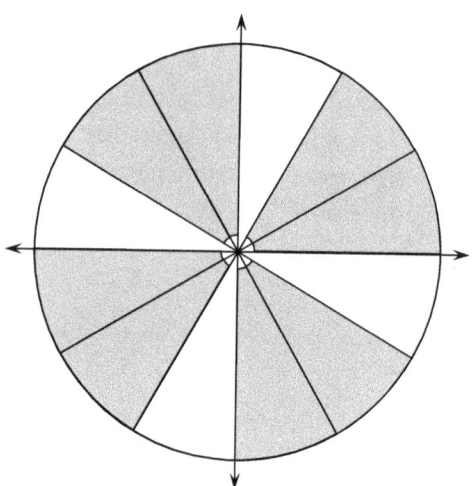

Figure 9: Advancing (gray) and retreating (white), understood dynamically

6 And [3] **connection** is if a light, quick star is going straightaway to a heavy star, and the light star is fewer in degrees than the heavy one, as long as the [light] planet is going towards the [heavy] planet, until it touches it and comes to be with it by degree, to the minute: and then it is said to be con-

---

[51] In Greek philosophy, this phrase would be "coming-to-be and passing away," or "generation and corruption."

[52] All manuscripts omit this, but it is clearly discussed later and is the only way to reach 16.

nected. **7** And as for when it comes to be with it to the minute, its connection has come to an end, and then it is in the position of two men under a single blanket. **8** And the connection in [such a] position is a thread extending from the middle of the body of the light planet to the middle of the body of the heavy planet.[53] **9** And the planet does not cease to be counted as being connected until it separates from the planet by a full degree.

10 Now as for when the two planets are united in one sign, a planet is not considered to be separated from a planet until the light one departs from the heavy one by one-half of its body—and that is its light, because every one of the planets has a body, and a light, and individual parts, and one-half of those parts are in front of the planet, and one-half of them behind it.[54] **11** And when it passes beyond it by what I mentioned to you,[55] then indeed it is sundered from it.

12 A section on the knowledge of the lights of the seven planets. **13** Know that the body of the Sun is 30°, so one-half of them are in front of him and one-half of them behind him: so if there was from a degree to 15° between the Sun and one of the planets, then he has already shone his light,[56] and he is connected with [the planet]. **14** And the light of the Moon is 12°, in front of her and behind her. **15** And[57] the light of Saturn and Jupiter (each one) is 9° in front of him and likewise behind him. **16** And Mars is 8° in front him and likewise behind him. **17** And Venus and Mercury (each one of them) is 7° in front of it and likewise behind it. **18** So by the extent of these lights, they are connected one to the other.

19 And if a planet looked at a planet [from another sign], and it already struck with its own light upon its degree, then it is connected with it; and if it is not striking with its own light, then it is moving toward the connection until it is connected.

20 And if a planet was at the end of a sign, not connecting with anything, and it has already struck into the next sign with its own light, then whatever

---

[53] This imaginary "thread" must be vertical, stretching up and down between the two planets' spheres in the heavens (i.e., one above the other) *not* laterally in the zodiac.

[54] That is, for astrological purposes a planet's body, light, and the degrees they encompass, are considered to be the same thing: see the rest of the section.

[55] That is, by one-half of the planet's "body" or "light" mentioned in **10**. Next Sahl will define what those sizes are for each planet.

[56] That is, upon the planet.

[57] For **15-17** I have followed the other manuscripts, as **B** puts them in the order of the planets (from Saturn down to Mercury) rather than in the order of the size of their bodies.

planet was the first in that light, it is connected with it. **21** And if it was not in the sign, then it will not see it.[58]

22 Now as for the explanation of [4] **separating**, it is if the degree of the light planet separates from the degree of the heavy one, and the light planet is in more degrees than the heavy one. **23** So, looking is from sign to sign, and connecting is from degree to degree: and this is the statement of Māshā'allāh.

24 And as for the explanation of [5] **transfer** [or] the **transfer of light**, it is if the light planet separates from the heavy planet, and is connecting with another: it forms an equivalence[59] between them, and it transfers the nature of the first to the second one which it has already connected with. **25** An example of that is if the Ascendant was Virgo, and the question about marriage; and the Moon in 10° of Gemini, and Mercury in 8° of Leo, and Jupiter in 13° of Pisces. **26** Now Mercury (who is the lord of the Ascendant and the indicator of the one asking) is not looking at Jupiter (who is the lord of the sign of marriage), because he is in the eighth sign from him.[60] **27** So I looked at the Moon, and I found her separating from Mercury and connecting with Jupiter, so she transferred the light between them: it indicated victory in the matter based on the assistance of messengers and people going back and forth.[61]

---

[58] This sentence simply seems to mean that if the first planet is still at the end of its sign, it will not see, *but will still be connected with*, the planet in the next sign: for the next sign is in aversion to it. In other words, the sentence is emphasizing the existence of out-of-sign conjunctions by body. But it does not support out-of-sign aspects. On the other hand, Abū Ma'shar in *Gr. Intr.* VII.5 uses this very scenario to say that such planets may "mix their natures" together because of their overlapping orbs, but they are not properly *connected* or *conjoined.*

[59] وازى.

[60] That is, Jupiter is in the eighth sign from Mercury, and so in aversion to him. See Ch. 2, **60**. Because they are in aversion, this could be considered a case of "reflection," which is described in *ITA* III.13. Reflection is essentially "transfer from aversion," and some authors insist that the reflecting planet also see the place signifying the topic: in this case, the Moon does see the seventh (marriage).

[61] Such people are especially indicated by the Moon.

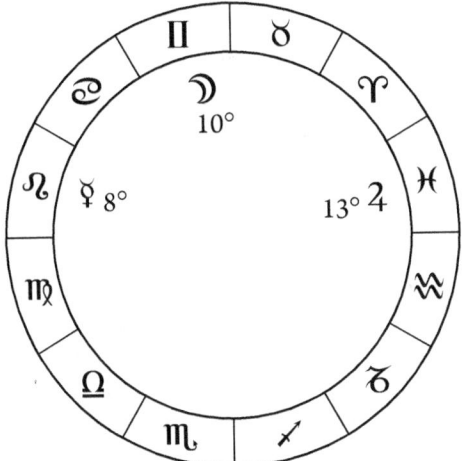

Figure 10: Transfer of light

28 And [6] **collection of light** is if the lord of the Ascendant and the lord of the sought thing are connecting with a planet heavier than they, so it collects their power and takes their light and their natures.[62]

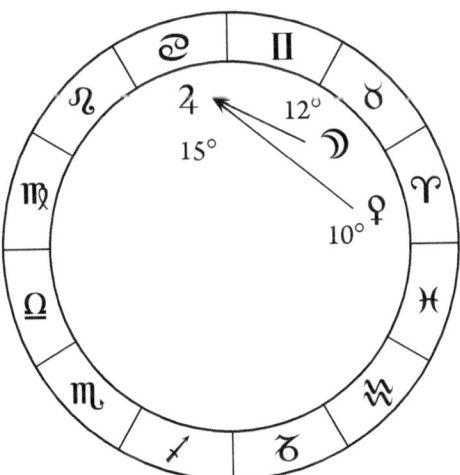

Figure 11: Collection of light

---

[62] See also *Questions* Ch. 1, **27**, which recommends that the collecting planet look at the place of the topic.

29 An example of that is a question about the Sultan: and the Ascendant was Libra, and Venus (who was the lord of the Ascendant and the indicator for the one asking) was in 10° of Aries, and the Moon (who was the lord of the Midheaven and the indicator for the Sultan) in 12° of Taurus, so they were not looking at each other; and Jupiter was in 15° of Cancer, in the stake of the Midheaven, and the Moon and Venus connecting with him. **30** So Jupiter was collecting their light in the stake, in the place of the sought thing: it indicated victory based on the assistance of a sage[63] or man entering between them, [and] they will come to terms through him.

31 And [7] **blocking** is based on three approaches.[64] **32** Of them, [the first] is **"cutting the light"**: and it is if there was a planet between the lord of the Ascendant and the lord of the sought thing, in fewer degrees than one of them, so the connection with it is before the connection [of the lord of the Ascendant] with the lord of the sought thing.

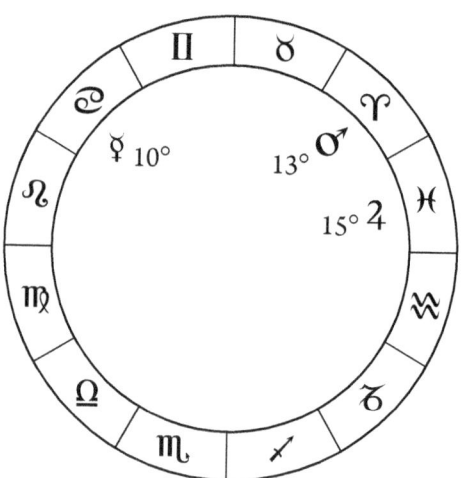

Figure 12: Blocking #1 ("Cutting")

33 And an example of that is a question about marriage: and the Ascendant is Virgo, and Mercury (who is the lord of the Ascendant and the indicator of the one asking) in 10° of Cancer, and Jupiter (who is the lord of

---

[63] Such people are signified by Jupiter.
[64] Based on the language used by Sahl, we can say that connections by aspect "cut" each other, conjunctions "intervene" (lit., "come in between"), and a conjunction "nullifies" an aspect.

the seventh and the indicator of the woman) in 15° of Pisces, and Mars in 13° of Aries. **34** So Mars was cutting the light of Mercury from Jupiter; and Mars was in the eighth from the Ascendant, in the sign of the woman's assets: it indicated that any corruption of this matter would be in relation to the dowry.

35 The second way is if there is a light planet and another, heavy one, and they are both in one sign, and the light one is connecting with the heavy one, and if another planet connected, in [their] union, with the heavy one, and it is less than the light one [by degree],[65] then the former has already **intervened** between [the light planet] and the connection [with the heavy one]. **36** And an example of that is if the Ascendant was Cancer, and the question about marriage, and the Moon in 8° of Gemini, and Mars in 10° of Gemini, and Saturn in 12° of Gemini, in front of Mars. **37** So Mars had intervened between the Moon and the connection with Saturn: it indicated the corruption of the sought thing.

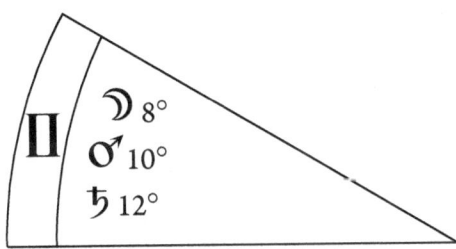

Figure 13: Blocking #2 ("Intervention")

38 And the third way is if a planet is united to a planet heavier than it, connecting to it, and another one connects to the heavy one by an aspect, and [by degree] it is less than the light one that is uniting. **39** So the uniting planet blocks the planet that is looking, from the connection.[66] **40** And if it goes beyond that, its connection is valid. **41** And this type blocks the sought things, and repels them, just like the other two types. **42** An example of that is if the Ascendant was Cancer, and the question about marriage, and the

---

[65] That is, there are fewer degrees between the cutter and the heavy one, than between the light planet and the heavy one.
[66] This is confusing, but in the example below the Moon is the "light" planet, Mars is the "heavy" planet, and Saturn is the "heavier" planet.

lord of the Ascendant is the Moon (and she is the indicator of the one asking), in 10° of Scorpio, and Mars in 15° of Taurus, and Saturn in 23° of Taurus. **43** Now Mars was greater in degrees than the Moon, and he is cutting the aspect between the Moon and Saturn, because Mars is uniting with Saturn, and a uniting is stronger than an aspect.[67] **44** And[68] a connection does not nullify a uniting, but a uniting does **nullify** a connection, while an aspect does not cut an aspect [but] hands over[69] the sought thing, and a uniting cuts an aspect.

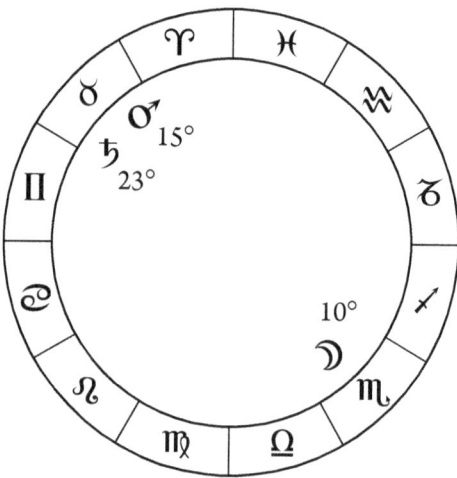

Figure 14: Blocking #3 ("Nullification")

45 And should a planet already be uniting with a planet in a sign, and it was handing over *its* management to *another* planet (that is, it is connecting with it), and then *after* that it comes to the planet which it is uniting with,

---

[67] In this example, the Moon wants to connect by aspect with Saturn (because he is the lord of the seventh), but because Mars is already connecting with Saturn by body, his conjunction "nullifies" what the Moon is trying to do.

[68] In this sentence, Sahl is prioritizing three things: (1) "uniting" or a conjunction by degree, (2) a connection by degree from another sign, and (3) an aspect by sign. In other words, while degree-based connections can cut each other as in type #1, aspects by sign do not cut each other. See also **48** below and *Aphorism* #17.

[69] يدفع. This is ambiguous, because this verb can mean either to urge on, propel, etc. (as I have read it here), or to shove aside and cancel. I believe Sahl is saying that if there are two whole-sign aspects impinging upon some planet, they do not cut off its activity, but they are competing influences which will affect the matter in their own, possibly contradictory way.

then indeed the effect will be ascribed to the planet being united to.⁷⁰ **46** And an example of that is if the Moon is in 10° of Taurus, and Mars in 20° of Taurus, and the Moon is connecting with Venus (and Venus is in 15° of Cancer). **47** So her connection with Venus is prior to her uniting with Mars, but⁷¹ the Moon is uniting [with Mars], and that is stronger than an aspect and a connection.⁷² **48** And this is an elucidation of what I have described, of [the fact that] a connection does not nullify a uniting, but a uniting nullifies a connection.

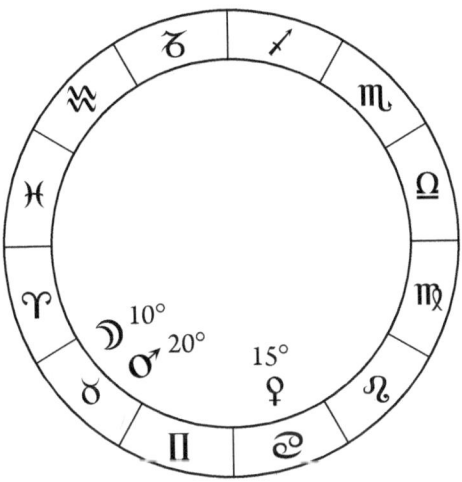

Figure 15: **Conjunction nullifying a connection from another sign**

---

⁷⁰ In other words, *even though* the connection by aspect may perfect first, the planet it is connecting to by body will still be the dominant one.

⁷¹ Reading لكنّ for "because" (لأنّه).

⁷² The Latin version finishes the thought using the language from **45**, that *therefore* "the judgment would be referred to Mars." In this example, the Moon and Mars seem to be the primary significators, and they are already uniting by body. But because a conjunction nullifies a connection from another sign, it does not matter that she must connect with Venus before her conjunction with Mars is complete: the Moon-Mars conjunction is still operative and valid. Note that this is *not* a case of "cutting," which only involves a connection from different signs; it is not a case of "intervention," because they are not all in the same sign; and it is not exactly a case of blocking by nullification, because Venus is not one of the significators we want to join.

49 And as for [**8**] **reception**, truly the reception of the planets is when a planet is connected with it from its exaltation or its house: for then it has perfect reception, with truthful intention. **50** And below this reception is if it is connecting with a planet from the triplicity of that planet being connected with. **51** And what is contrary to this, the astrologer has nothing to do with, and he does not acknowledge it, he does not accept it, and does not see it as fit for anything.[73] **52** And an example of that is if the Moon is in Aries and she is connecting with Mars: then he receives her because [Aries] is his house; or she connects with the Sun, because he is the lord of the exaltation. **53** Or, [if] she is in Taurus and connecting with Venus, or in Gemini and she is connecting with Mercury: for that is perfect reception.

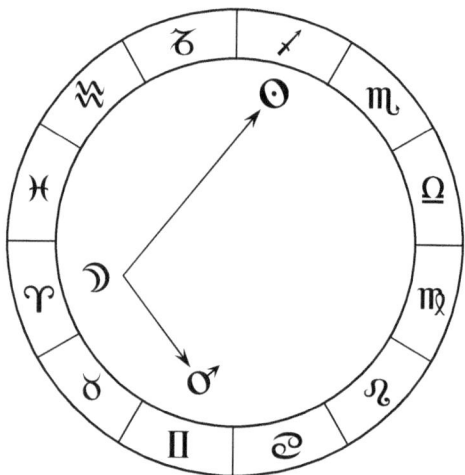

Figure 16: Moon received by Mars (by house) and the Sun (by exaltation)

54 And as for the reception of triplicity and bound, it is if the Moon in a question is in the bound of Venus, and [the Moon] is connecting with her, and Venus is the lord of the triplicity of the Moon as well as the lord of her bound; or, the Moon is in Gemini in the bound of Saturn, and she is connecting with Saturn, and Saturn is the lord of the triplicity and bound. **55**

---

[73] See non-reception in **58** below. However, I do not understand why Sahl speaks about the *astrologer* as rejecting this, when clearly it should be the *planets* accepting or not accepting the light from each other. Sahl might mean that the astrologer should not guarantee *success* to the *client* without proper reception.

And when the Moon is like that, then she is received: and this is the statement of Māshā'allāh on the reception of triplicity and bound.

56 And if the Moon was connecting with a planet and that planet was connecting with the lord of the house of the Moon or its exaltation,[74] then the Moon is received.[75]

57 And if the Moon was empty in course,[76] and then she passed over into the next sign and connected with the lord of her first sign (or its exaltation), it is just like reception; and if she connected with a planet other than the lord of her first sign or its exaltation, it undermines her.[77]

58 And as for the positions in which there is [9] **no reception**[78] nor recognition,[79] if the Moon or the lord of the Ascendant connected with a planet, [and] that planet did not have testimony in the position of the Moon or the lord of the Ascendant, it will not recognize it nor receive it. **59** And likewise if the Moon or lord of the Ascendant connected with a planet from [the other planet's] fall, it would be like one who comes to it from the house of its enemies, not accepting it nor approaching it. **60** And an example of that is if the Moon is in Aries and she is connecting with Saturn, or in Cancer and she is connecting with Mars, or in Virgo and she is connecting with Venus, or in Capricorn and she is connecting with Jupiter, or in Libra and she is connecting with the Sun.[80]

---

[74] That is, the exalted lord of the sign in which the Moon is.

[75] This is like a transfer of light which indirectly allows for reception.

[76] See also **63** below.

[77] This is a version of "escape" (see *Aphorisms* #16-17), which like many configurations here is geared towards the fluid situations of horary or question charts. In "escape," planet A seeks to connect with planet B, but B crosses over into the next sign. Normally that would be the end of the matter, because sign boundaries define the current situation. But if A can cross over and connect with B *before* there is a connection with another planet, it can complete the *original* situation which had been left behind. Here Sahl is saying that we *wanted* the Moon to connect with the lord of her sign (and so be received), but she is empty in course; however, if she can connect with it after entering the next sign, then it is "just like" the original reception we wanted. See also *Questions* Ch. 6, **44-45**, where it makes a big difference whether a connection with that planet was indeed desired.

[78] This could also be read as "no acceptance," here and at the end of the sentence ("nor accept it").

[79] See **51** above, and *Questions* Ch. 1, **40-42**.

[80] The only combination missing here is Pisces-Mercury, which is included in the Latin edition. And again, **B** suggests that its editor was consulting multiple manuscripts, as it says "and in one copy" right before the phrase "or in Virgo."

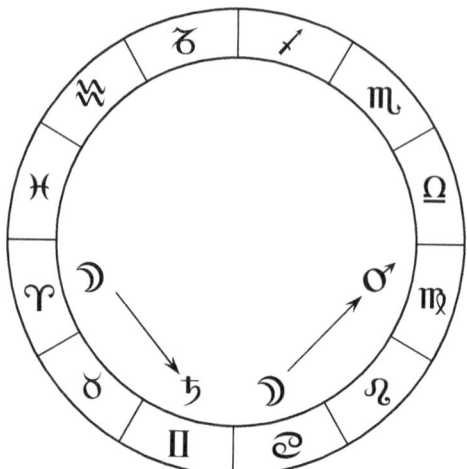

Figure 17: Saturn and Mars not accepting nor receiving the Moon

61 Now if the indicator[81] was in its fall, and it is connecting with a planet [and] that planet did not have a share[82] in the position of the indicator (that is, by house or exaltation), it will not see it as fit for anything, as though the one asking is offering defeat,[83] and it will not be recognized.

62 And if a star connected with a planet in its own fall, or [in] the fall of the planet handing over to it,[84] it brings it down and diminishes what comes to it from that.

Ch. 3:	Description: A → B	Model: ☽ → ♄
58	B is alien in A's sign	☽♍ → ♄
59-60	A in B's fall	☽♈ → ♄
61	A in its own fall, B alien in A's sign	☽♏ → ♄
62	B in its own fall	☽ → ♄♈
62	B in A's fall	☽ → ♄♏

Figure 18: Five kinds of non-reception

---

[81] In *Aphorisms* #1, 2 Sahl says that the Moon is the indicator, but I do not see why he wouldn't simply say "the Moon" here. Perhaps he means to include the lord of the Ascendant, which is a default indicator in pretty much every chart.

[82] That is, a dignity (نصيب).

[83] Or, "[only a] sliver" (كسرة).

[84] For example, if the Moon connected with a Saturn who was in Aries (his fall) or with a Saturn in Scorpio (her fall).

63 And as for the explanation of [10] **the emptiness of the course**, that is when the Moon is not connecting with any of the planets, and not uniting with one: indeed, that is called the emptiness of the course of the Moon and of her body, making it ineffective.[85]

64 And the banished[86] planet is the planet which none of the planets connects to.

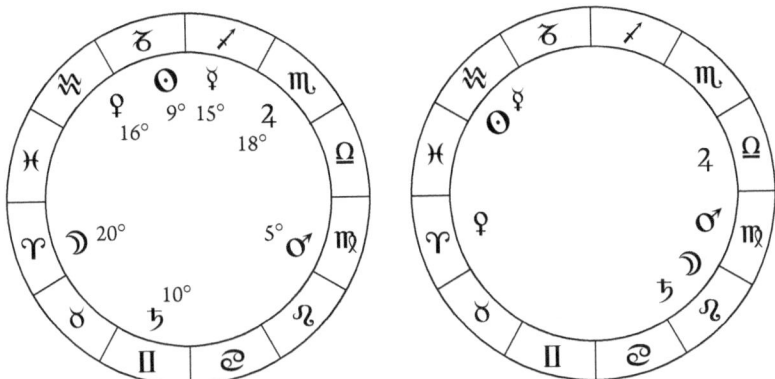

Figure 19: The Moon in the empty course

Figure 20: Banished or wild Mars

65 And as for the explanation of [11] **returning**, it is if a planet or the Moon is connecting with a retrograde planet or one under the rays: for it returns to it what it accepted from it, and has already corrupted its management, and indicates that the question does not have a beginning nor end.[87]

66 And[88] another manner of returning is that the light planet (and it is the one handing over) is in a stake, and connecting with a planet falling away

---

[85] See also *Aphorisms* #6. In Abū Ma'shar's *Gr. Intr.* this is sharpened so that she does not complete a connection with any planet while in her current sign. See also **111** below.

[86] المطرود. This seems to be an early form of "wildness," described in *ITA* III.10 as a state in which a planet lacks any planets even *looking* at it (i.e., it is in aversion to all other planets). I have designed the figure here to reflect this later, clearer definition. See also **111** below.

[87] The word for "beginning" here (اوَلِيّة) also means something that lacks a real foundation. The word for "end" here (آخريّة) may be coined by Sahl but is grammatical: it also connotes not having any sequel (the management does not go anywhere). But the two together would mean "neither beginning nor end."

[88] In all manuscripts, there follows here a chart example which really illustrates the second type of returning, below (**68**). There seems to have been some kind of recognition by the scribes that something was wrong, because in **H** and **L** the example is titled as though it is

from the Ascendant:[89] so that sought thing has a beginning because the one handing over (which indicates the beginning of the matter) is in a stake, but it does not have an end because the accepting one (which indicates the end of the matter) is falling. **67** And the one handing over is the light planet, in which the beginning is, and the accepting one is the heavy planet: and it is called "the one accepting the management," and the light one handing over is called "the one handing over the management." **68** And an example of that is if the Ascendant is Cancer, and the Moon in Sagittarius in the sixth, falling away from the Ascendant, connecting with Mars, and he is in Gemini in the twelfth from the Ascendant, falling. **69** So that indicates the corruption of the beginning of the question, and of its end.

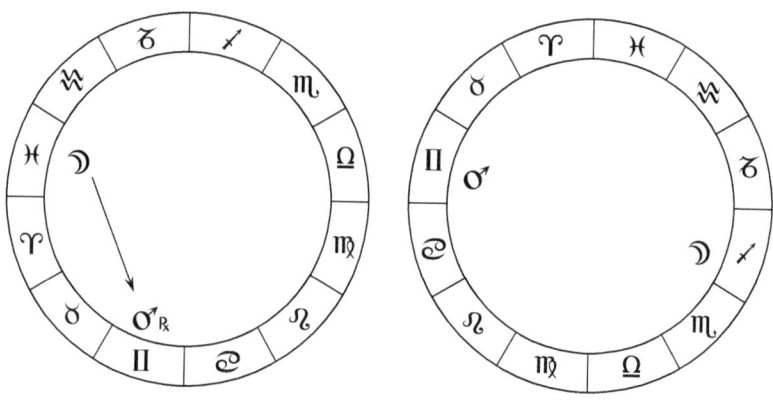

Figure 21: Returning #1   **Figure 22: Returning #2**

70 And as for the explanation of [12] **handing over power**, it is if a planet is connecting with a planet from its own house, exaltation, or triplicity. **71** And an example of that is if the Moon is in Cancer or Taurus, and she is connecting with Jupiter or [any] one of the planets: she hands over power to him because she is handing over the management to him from her house or her exaltation. **72** And likewise the remainder of the planets, if they handed over the management from their house or exaltation.

---

the second kind, and the second kind as though it is the example. I have put the sentences in what seems to be their proper order here.

[89] That is, in aversion to it. That makes sense only if we require the final planet to see the Ascendant. But perhaps this should be understood as "stake," so that the planet accepting the management is too weak to keep it, and gives it back. The problem is that in **68**, the planet returning the management is *both* in aversion to the Ascendant and falling from the stake of the Ascendant.

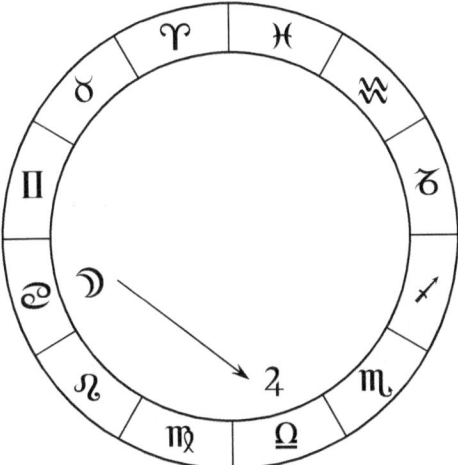

Figure 23: Handing over power

73 And as for the explanation of [13] **handing over management and nature**,[90] it is if a planet is connecting with a planet from its house or from its exaltation: for it hands over its management and its nature to it. 74 And an example of that is if the Moon or any of the planets is in Aries and is connecting with Mars, or it is in Gemini and is connecting with Mercury (that is, in reception). 75 And if the Moon was in Taurus or Cancer, she hands over power and management. 76 And in signs other than these two, she only hands over management.

77 And as for the explanation of [14] **the strength of the planets**, such that they do not have a deficiency at the time of judging[91] the sought thing, when they accept [the management] and make a promise, that is in eleven ways:

---

[90] Adding "and nature" with **H**. This definition seems simply to give names to three ways in which a planet may hand over to another, when we consider the dignities involved. In **76**, Sahl says that any application or connection hands over management, such as if the Moon is in neither her own dignity, nor does she hand over to any of her lords. The next step up would be handing over her *power and* management (**75**), if she connects while in her own house or exaltation. A related step would be connecting to her own lord, or management *and nature*—but this is the same as reception (**74**). Unfortunately, this does not tell us how to interpret them: what is the real difference between the Moon applying while in her own dignities, versus applying to one of her lords?

[91] This word (قضاء) can also refer to the "effecting" or "fulfillment" of the matter.

78 Of them, the first is that a planet is in an excellent place from the Ascendant: that is, in the stakes or what follows them, of the places which look at the Ascendant.[92]

79 The second is that a planet is in something of its own share: that is, in its house or its exaltation, triplicity, bound, face, or joy.

80 The third is that it is direct in course.

81 The fourth is that there is not an infortune with it in its sign, connecting[93] with it, or looking at it from a square or opposition.[94]

82 The fifth is that it is not connecting with a star that is falling away from the Ascendant, or with a star in its fall, or [that] it is itself in its own fall.

83 The sixth is that it is advancing.[95]

84 The seventh is that a masculine planet (and they are Saturn, Jupiter, <and Mars>) is eastern, arising at dawn.[96]

85 The eighth is that the planets are in their own glow: that is, a masculine planet in the day, and a feminine planet in the night.[97]

86 The ninth is that a planet is in fixed signs.[98]

---

[92] Cf. Ch. 1, **30ff**. The definition here allows only six good places, by leaving out the ninth place (because it is a falling place).

[93] This should perhaps be "assembling," so that this sentence contains only sign-based configurations, and contrasts with **94** below (which contains degree-based ones).

[94] Strictly speaking then, this would allow an infortune to be in the same sign, so long as they were far away or separated from each other.

[95] مقبل, the participle of Form IV, and *not* the passive participle of Form I ("received"), as Stegemann and the Latin have it. This means that it is dynamically angular or succeedent, i.e. by primary motion with respect to the angular axes, and not by whole sign.

[96] See **130**, which is better by including the nocturnal planets. Mars is the questionable one here, because while he is masculine, what makes it important that he rise before the Sun is that he is a *superior* planet (**131** below).

[97] This is an error, and Sahl should have said a *diurnal* planet in the day, and a *nocturnal* planet in the night. The reason for this confusion in the tradition is always Mars, who is a masculine, nocturnal planet.

[98] See *Choices* Ch. 2, **6**.

87 The tenth is that the planets are in the heart of the Sun (that is, when they are with him in one degree): for indeed at that time the fortunes increase good fortune, and the infortunes decrease their evil.

88 The eleventh is that, of the quarters of the circle, the masculine ones are in the masculine quarters of the Ascendant (and they are from the Midheaven to the Ascendant, and from the fourth to the seventh), and the feminine planets are in a feminine quarter (and they are from the seventh to the Midheaven, and from the Ascendant to the fourth), and the masculine planets are in masculine signs, and the feminine planets in feminine signs.

89 So these are the testimonies which, [when] planets are in them, they are strong, and they do not have a deficiency at the time of judging the sought thing, when they accept [the management] and make a promise.

90 And as for [15] **the weakness of the planets**, and their harms in nativities and questions, indeed that is in ten ways:

91 Of them, [the first is] if a planet was falling from the stakes and not looking at the Ascendant: and that is in the sixth and the twelfth.

92 The second is if the planet was retrograde.

93 The third is if the planet was under the rays of the Sun.

94 The fourth is if it was connecting with the infortunes from an assembly, opposition, or square.

95 The fifth is if a planet was enclosed between two infortunes, and that is if it is separating from [one] infortune and connecting with [another] infortune.

96 The sixth is if a planet was in its fall.

97 The seventh is if it is connecting with a planet falling away from the Ascendant, and it is separating from a planet receiving it.[99]

---

[99] I am not sure that these conditions must *both* exist at once.

98 The eighth is if a planet was in a house in which it did not have testimony (neither house nor exaltation nor triplicity).[100] **99** And, if a planet was western, the Sun having already overtaken it (that is, if it was in front of[101] the Sun).[102]

99 The ninth is if a planet was with the Head or Tail, if it does not have latitude.[103]

100 The tenth is if they were inverted,[104] and that is when they are in the contrary[105] of their house: that is, when they are in the seventh from their own house, and that is called "unhealthiness."[106]

101 And these are the situations in which there is a corruption of the planets in nativities and questions and the rest of actions: so beware of these conditions in the encountered star,[107] who is arranging[108] the thing sought.

---

[100] That is, it is alien or "peregrine."

[101] This word (قَدَام) is not Sahl's usual word for "in front of" (أمام), which suggests that perhaps he is copying his list from an older source.

[102] This seems to mean that the planet is in a later degree than the Sun, and already sunk under the rays so as to be invisible in the evening. This could hold good for any of the five planets.

[103] If the Moon's Nodes are meant (since every planet has a Node), this should be exceedingly rare: that is, being both in the *Moon's* Node, and in *its own* Node (so as to have no latitude). But in all likelihood only the Moon's Node is meant.

[104] مضادة, which also means to be antagonistic or contradictory.

[105] ضد (from the same root as in the previous footnote).

[106] الوبال, which also connotes bad air (such as in miasma theory). The sum total of these ideas is that a planet in detriment is in a situation antagonistic to its interests or even to itself, being disunified and unhealthy. This sense of internal contrast and conflict should be compared with the sense of unity and comfort a planet has when in its own house. See also *Aphorism #50*, **107**.

[107] المقابل. That is, the one accepting the management: see *Questions* Ch. 1, **18-19**, **31-32**.

[108] Reading المواعد with the majority of manuscripts for **B**'s الواعد ("the one promising"), with the idea that "promising" sounds more final and affirmative, whereas setting up the arrangements is more uncertain and complicated—a more suitable concept for planets in a bad condition

Strength of planets	Weakness of planets
(78) In excellent place	(91) Falling and in aversion to Ascendant
(79) In its own dignity	(98, 100) Alien; in detriment
(80) Direct	(92) Retrograde
(81) Not in whole-sign angles of infortune	(94) Connecting with infortunes from whole-sign angles
(82) Not connecting with planet in aversion to ASC	(97) Connecting with a planet in aversion to ASC
(82) Not connecting with a planet in its own fall	*Connecting with a planet in its own fall*
(82) Not in its own fall	(96) In its own fall
(83) Advancing	*Retreating*
(84) Diurnal planets eastern	*Diurnal planets western*
(85) Of the sect	*Contrary to sect*
(86) In a fixed sign	*In a convertible sign*
(87) In the heart of the Sun	(93, 99) Under the rays
(88) In quadrant of own gender	*In quadrant contrary to gender*
Besieged by fortunes	(95) Besieged by infortunes
Applying to planet receiving it	(97) Separating from a planet receiving it
Away from Nodes	(99) With the Nodes

Figure 24: Comparative table of planetary strengths and weaknesses[109]

---

[109] In this table I have paired the strengths and weaknesses from above. Conditions in normal typeface with sentence numbers represent items mentioned by Sahl, and italics show my own suggested contraries where Sahl has not listed them.

102 Now as for [**16**] **the defects of the Moon**, especially the badness of the Moon's condition in every question and every inception, indeed that is in ten ways.

> **103** Of them, [the first is][110] if the Moon is burned, within 12° of the Sun, not going past him, and likewise after him.
>
> **104** The second is if the Moon is in the degrees of her fall in Scorpio, or she is connecting with a star in its[111] fall.
>
> **105** The third[112] is if she is opposed to the Sun, within 12° of him [but] not having reached the opposition.
>
> **106** The fourth[113] is if she is assembled with an infortune or looking at it from a square or opposition, or she is enclosed between two infortunes, separating from [one] infortune and connecting with [the other] infortune.
>
> **107** The fifth[114] is if she is with the Head or Tail in [one] sign, there being less than 12° between them.[115]
>
> **108** The sixth[116] is if she is in the twelfth sign from her own house (and that is Gemini), or[117] the last degrees of the signs (because they are the bounds of the infortunes).
>
> **109** The seventh[118] is if she was falling from the stakes or connecting with a planet falling from the stakes.
>
> **110** The eighth[119] is if she is in the burned path, and that is at the end of Libra and the beginning of Scorpio.[120]

---

[110] Cf. *Carmen* V.6, **4**.

[111] This could either be the Moon's own fall, or the fall of the other planet, as explained in **62** above. See also *Questions* Ch. 1, **40-42**.

[112] See *Carmen* V.6, **8**.

[113] See *Carmen* V.6, **32**.

[114] See *Carmen* V.6, **3**.

[115] That is, between her and the Node.

[116] See *Choices* Ch. 2, **27**.

[117] See *Carmen* V.6, **13**.

[118] Cf. *Carmen* V.6, **14**.

[119] See *Carmen* V.6, **12**.

111 The ninth[121] is if she was wild: and that is empty of course, not connecting with any of the planets.[122]

112 The tenth[123] is if she is slow in course (and that is when the equation is subtracted from it),[124] or she is decreasing in light (and that is [at] the end of the [lunar] month).

113 So these are the defects of the Moon, and her misfortunes, in which work should not be undertaken, and they are not praised in a birth nor one making a journey.

114 And understand too the **harm of the Moon in the increase of the crescent and its decrease.** **115** For indeed if the Moon was increasing in her glow, and Mars was with her or looked at her from the fourth or seventh,[125] it does violence to the Moon: because if the Moon was increasing in light (that is, the beginning of the month) so that she is hot, Saturn will not harm her because he is cold, while Mars will harm her because he is hot. **116** And if she was decreasing in light (that is, the end of the month) so that she is cold, Mars will not harm her, while Saturn will harm her because he is cold.

117 And know that Saturn, in nativities of the day and questions whose hours are by day, and at the beginning of the month, and in the masculine signs, decreases harm; <and at night and at the end of the month and in feminine signs, he increases harm>.[126] **118** And Mars in the night, and at the end

---

[120] But some authorities put it between 19° Libra (the fall of the Sun) and 3° Scorpio (the fall of the Moon): see *ITA* IV.3, the excerpt from Abū Ma'shar's *Great Introduction*.
[121] See *Choices* Ch. 2, **30**.
[122] But the later Arabic definition of wildness is more coherent as an intensification of emptiness: namely, that she is in aversion to all other planets (see *ITA* III.10).
[123] See *Carmen* V.6, **11**.
[124] The simple meaning here is that she is moving more slowly than her average daily speed. In Ptolemaic astronomy, an "equation" is a correction added to the expected position of a planet, to account for its moving faster or more slowly than normal. So, if she is moving more slowly than normal, then she is behind, or in an earlier position than, her expected one: therefore, the correction must be subtracted from the expected position, to yield her slower position earlier in the zodiac.
[125] That is, the square or opposition.
[126] Adding based on the Latin.

of the month, and in the feminine signs, decreases harm; and by day and at the beginning of the month, and in the masculine signs,[127] he increases harm.

119 And neither a planet, the Moon, nor a sign is called "**unfortunate**" until an infortune is with it, or looks at it from the fourth, seventh, or tenth.[128] **120** And a planet is not called "**fortunate**" until the fortunes are in[129] the stakes of that planet, or the planet is in the stakes of the Ascendant.

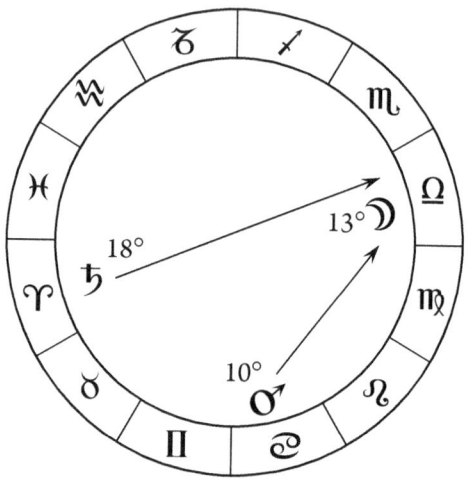

Figure 25: Enclosure or besieging by degree

121 And as for the explanation of an **enclosed**[130] [planet], that is if a planet is between the two infortunes, separating from one of them [and] connecting with the other, without another planet casting its rays between the two; and more powerful than that, and more unfortunate, is if the separation and the connection is at 7° and what is below that. **122** An example of that is if Mars is in 10° of Cancer, and Saturn in 18° of Aries, and the Moon in 13° of Libra. **123** So the Moon is separating from Mars from [his] second

---

[127] Not because Mars is feminine, but because he is nocturnal and the feminine signs are nocturnal: so by being in masculine or diurnal signs, he has some contrariety to his own nature. It would have been better for Sahl to have spoken of diurnal and nocturnal signs rather than their gender.
[128] That is, in its whole-sign angles.
[129] I have read the rest of the sentence based on the Latin, for "in the stakes or the planets [are] in the stakes of the Ascendant."
[130] Otherwise known as "besieged."

square,¹³¹ connecting with Saturn from the opposition: at this time she is enclosed due to her separation from the light of Mars and her connection with the light of Saturn.

124 And as for the explanation of a planet **in its own glow**, it is if Mars was shining bright by night:¹³² [he is] in his own glow because he is nocturnal; and Saturn by day is in his own glow because he is diurnal.¹³³

125 And as for the explanation of his¹³⁴ statement that a planet is in a sign in which it has **testimony or a share or friendship**, indeed that is a planet when it is in its house, exaltation, triplicity, bound, or face. 126 And the towering¹³⁵ planet is a planet in a sign in which it has testimony.

127 And as for the explanation of the **rejoicing of the planets**, indeed that is of four types:

128 The first type is their joy from the circle: and that is that Mercury rejoices in the Ascendant, the Moon rejoices in the third, Venus rejoices in the fifth, Mars rejoices in the sixth, the Sun rejoices in the ninth, Jupiter rejoices in the eleventh, and Saturn rejoices in the twelfth.

129 And they have a second joy, of their alighting in their houses: for Saturn rejoices in Aquarius because it is a masculine¹³⁶ sign, Jupiter rejoices in Sagittarius, Mars rejoices in Scorpio,¹³⁷ the Sun rejoices

---

¹³¹ See the footnote to Ch. 2, **52** above.
¹³² This suggests that he must be visible above the horizon. This definition for Mars is equivalent to *ḥalb*, at least in nocturnal charts; but it does not equate to this for Saturn, who is only required to belong to the sect of the chart.
¹³³ See also *Nativities* Ch. 1.23, **17** (attributed to Māshā'allāh). Indeed, this may refer to exactly that sentence, because **125** below follows directly upon it: *Nativities* Ch. 1.23, **18**.
¹³⁴ This is most likely Māshā'allāh: see the footnote to **124** above.
¹³⁵ المتطاول, which has connotations of being or feeling tall, being proud, etc. I am not sure of its precise meaning here, but Steven Birchfield helpfully suggests it is like the English idiom, "standing tall," in which someone shows courage, honesty, honor, and strength.
¹³⁶ Or rather, a diurnal sign, since Saturn is diurnal.
¹³⁷ Again, it would be better if Sahl pointed out that Scorpio is the *nocturnal* sign of Mars, since Mars is nocturnal. See my footnote to **118** above.

in Leo, Venus rejoices in Taurus, Mercury rejoices in Virgo, and the Moon rejoices in Cancer.

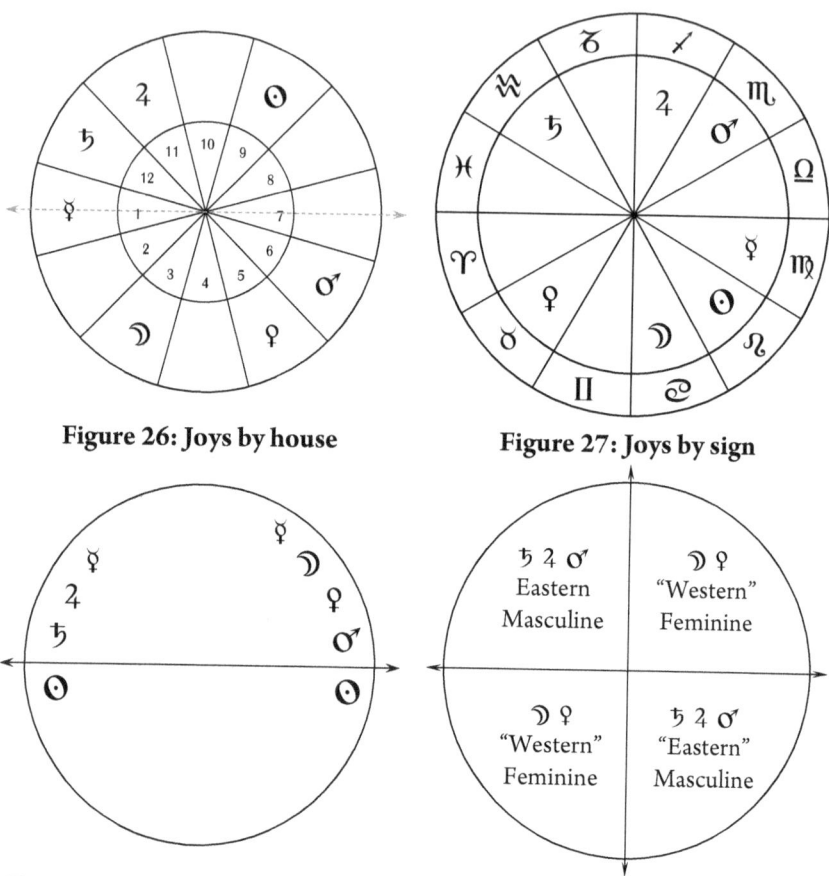

Figure 26: Joys by house

Figure 27: Joys by sign

Figure 28: Joys in relation to Sun

Figure 29: Joys by quadrant

130 And they have a third joy, and that is that the planets of the day rejoice when they are in the east (and that is when they are arising at dawn); and the planets of the night rejoice by night (and that is when they are arising in the evening from the horizon of the west).[138]

---

[138] As usual, the tricky planet is Mars: is the operative point really that he is nocturnal, or should he rise *before* the Sun because he is a superior planet? See **84** above.

131 And[139] they have a fourth joy, and that is that Saturn and Jupiter and Mars rejoice when they are in a masculine region (which is from the Midheaven to the Ascendant, and from the fourth sign to the seventh), and the Moon and Venus rejoice when they are in a western, feminine region (which are from the seventh to the Midheaven, and from the Ascendant to the stake of the earth). **132** And Mercury rejoices in both regions together: when he is with masculine planets he rejoices in the masculine region, and when he is with feminine planets he rejoices in the feminine region, due to the difference between these planets and their houses.[140]

---

[139] The mixing of signs and regions between the axes here may be an example of the growing tension between whole-sign houses and quadrant houses.
[140] I am not sure what this last clause means.

THE FIFTY APHORISMS

Comment by Dykes. This handy set of aphorisms connects many basic astrological principles with keywords and concrete interpretation—primarily in questions and choices or inceptions. Most of these are probably taken or adapted from some work of Māshā'allāh's, and many ultimately from other sources (several can be pretty reliably traced to Theophilus). However, it is not always clear that all of the aphorisms are mutually compatible; and some of them have absolute language that needs to be softened or moderated by others, or by experience.

Following is a handy guide for finding aphorisms by topic:

Topic	Aphorism #
Angularity	24, 27, 31, 37, 44, 45, 49
Aspects and connections	2, 4-5, 19, 22-23, 31, 36
Dignities	9, 18, 20, 21, 26-30, 32, 37, 41, 50
Direct/retrograde motion, stations	10, 11, 13, 18, 20, 24, 38, 41, 48
Easternness/westernness, Sun's rays/burning	18, 29, 38, 39, 40, 42
Fortunes and infortunes	2-5, 12, 18-20, 22-36, 43
Good/bad places	41
Moon, her motions and conditions	1, 6, 7, 8, 14, 49, 50
Other	15
Quadruplicity	46, 47
Reception	19, 25
Sect	32, 33
Special configurations	16, 17

1 This is the beginning of the *Aphorisms of Judgment,* and in it are 50 items.

2 *The first:* Know that the indicator (that is, the Moon) is the nearest of the planets of the celestial circle to the earth, and is the most similar of the planets to the affairs of the world. **3** Do you not see that man appears small, then grows big, and then is made complete? **4** Likewise the Moon: so take her as the indicator for every affair. **5** And her health is the health of every thing, and her corruption the corruption of every thing. **6** And she hands her management over to the first one she encounters and is connected to, because it accepts what she has handed over to it. **7** And she is the bearer for these planets, and the conciliator between two of them, and the transferor from one of them to another.

8 *The second:*[1] And the infortunes indicate corruption and evil by their excessiveness and their essence. **9** But if a planet was in the house of an infortune (or its exaltation), it would receive it and restrain its evil from it;[2] or [if] there was the aspect of the infortunes from a trine or sextile,[3] then indeed they would also restrain [their evil] from that, because they looked from friendship, without hostility. **10** And as for the fortunes, they are balanced by nature, mixed of heat and moisture, so they are useful whether they receive or do not receive (and [a planet] received by them is ideal and better).

11 *The third:* The stars are in two categories, the good and the bad: so wherever you see the infortunes, say bad; and wherever you see the fortunes, say good.

12 *The fourth:* And a planet is not said to be unfortunate until the infortune casts rays upon its light, according to what I described to you of their lights.[4] **13** When it goes beyond the boundary of the light, it is said to be "looking at" the infortune, and it does not have power over corruption. **14**

---

[1] See *Tet.* I.5 (Robbins p. 39).

[2] قد قبله وكفّ عنه شرّه. But simply being in the house of a planet does not mean reception exists, as Sahl has pointed out elsewhere. I suggest that this should read, "*and* it would receive it, *then* it would restrain its evil from it": وقد...فكفّ. In Arabic this is a small change to make.

[3] I take this to mean: "if they are *not* in the house or exaltation of the infortune *but they do* look at them by a trine or sextile."

[4] See *Introduction,* Ch. 3, **12-18**.

And when the planet goes beyond the infortune by one full degree, it introduces anxieties which do not assault the body, and the infortune does not have power over more than that, because it is separating. **15** And likewise a fortune, if it goes beyond the planet and separates from it by one full degree, it strives but does not complete the matter. **16** And every infortune makes unfortunate, but [if it is] falling,[5] it introduces anxieties and does not harm: and likewise the fortunes, if they were falling away from the Ascendant, he strives but does not complete the matter.[6]

17 *The fifth*: And if a planet was in the stakes of an infortune (that is, if it was with it or in the fourth from it, or the seventh or the tenth), it is like one being fought by his own soul, during the time it stays [there].[7] **18** And if it went beyond the infortune and separated from it by one full degree (like what I mentioned),[8] then surely the harms of the infortunes will pass away, and the infortunes will not have the power to introduce more than anxieties. **19** Bear these topics in mind, for they are of the secrets of questions and nativities.

20 *The sixth*: If the Moon was empty in course, not connecting with any of the planets, it indicates emptiness, idleness,[9] and returning from that situation with scanty [results], and the corruption of all of [one's] purposes.

21 *The seventh*: The connection of the Moon indicates what is going to be and what is hoped for of matters, in accordance with the nature of the planet accepting the Moon's management: if it was a fortune, then it is good fortune, and if it was an infortune, then it is misfortune.

22 *The eighth*: The separation of the Moon from the planets indicates what has elapsed of matters, and has gone away, in accordance with the nature of that planet the Moon has separated from.

23 *The ninth*: When a planet is in its own fall, it indicates misfortune, worry, and confinement.[10]

---

[5] This is ambiguous, because we would normally expect this to simply mean being dynamically "cadent." But later in the sentence the aphorism speaks clearly about the fortunes falling *away from* (i.e., being in aversion to) the Ascendant. Falling, and falling away from, are not the same thing. Preserving symmetry between the statements would make both a case of aversion, but it would have been easy to do that if that's what Sahl wanted.

[6] This could also be read as, "the matter is desired, but not completed."

[7] That is, by transit.

[8] See *Aphorism #4*.

[9] Or perhaps, "nullity" (البطالة).

[10] Or perhaps, "depression" or "oppression" (الضيق).

24 *The tenth:*[11] A retrograding planet indicates disobedience, collapse,[12] repetition, and disagreement.

25 *The eleventh*: A stationary planet indicates misfortune and hardship, and what is in it has already abated.

26 *The twelfth*: The infortunes indicate deviation[13] and hardship in the deed.

27 *The thirteenth*: If a planet was slow, it postpones its promise, be it good or bad. **28** And[14] likewise if it was in the houses of Saturn and Jupiter. **29** And in the light houses,[15] it hastens.

30 *The fourteenth*: If the Moon was connecting with a planet and she completed her connection (that is, if she was with it in one minute), then look for what there is going to be in that question, from the planet which the Moon is connecting to after that.

31 *The fifteenth*: If a planet came to be in the last degree of the sign, then its strength has already gone away from that sign, and its strength is in the next sign. **32** And it is in the position of a man putting his foot on the threshold of [his] door, and on the verge of departing: so if the house falls, it will not harm him. **33** And if a planet was in the twenty-ninth degree, then indeed the strength of the planet is in that sign. **34** For every planet has three degrees in which its strength is diffused: in the degree it is in, and the degree in front of it, and the degree behind it.[16]

35 *The sixteenth*: [Suppose] a planet is seeking a connection,[17] [but] then does not reach it in its sign, so that the planet shifts [into the next sign] due to its speed. **36** If it reaches it in the next sign and it does not connect with a different one, it accomplishes the thing sought. **37** And if it shifts over, but

---

[11] Cf. Theophilus, *OVI* Ch. 1.28, **18**.

[12] Or, "revolt" (الانتقاض). **L** has الانتقاص ("impairment"), which also makes astrological sense.

[13] الفسق, which in everyday speech usually means "sinfulness" and "wickedness." But I take Sahl to mean this in an operational sense, not moral. **BL** reads (from the same root) "outrage, iniquity," which is unambiguously moral.

[14] For **28-29**, see also *On Times* Ch. 2, 2-3.

[15] That is, in the houses of the light *planets*.

[16] This is reminiscent of Valens III.3, (Schmidt p. 41; Riley p. 61), who speaks of the 3° interval defining a connection by body or aspect. But Valens, like other Hellenistic astrologers, uses 3° on either side. Thanks to Steven Birchfield for pointing this out.

[17] That is, by aspect; the next paragraph describes a bodily conjunction.

then it connects after that with a different one, the thing sought will not be accomplished, because it is already mixing with the light of a planet other than [the original one].[18]

38 *The seventeenth*: Should a planet want to unite [by body] with a planet in a sign, but it does not reach it in that sign (so that it goes out into the next sign), then the thing sought is accomplished unless it[19] unites with another prior to it.[20] **39** And if connected with another [by aspect], it will not harm it, [like] when I described to you that a connection does not nullify a uniting, while a uniting does nullify a connection, and an aspect does not cut off an aspect:[21] understand.

40 *The eighteenth*: If an infortune was eastern (that is, arising in the early morning from the east), in its own house or its exaltation, and it is not connecting with an infortune corrupting it, then it is better than a retrograde benefic turning back.[22]

41 *The nineteenth*: If the infortunes were the lords of the things sought, and the lord of the Ascendant or the Moon connected with them from a square or opposition (I mean, from the fourth or seventh or tenth sign [from them]), they make the matters hard and undermine them (unless it was their house).[23] **42** Now [if] the infortunes at that time were the ones handing over (that is, the ones connecting), it is better than their being the ones accepting the management (that is, [that] it would be handed over to them and connected to them).[24]

---

[18] This is an example of "escape": see *ITA* Ch. III.22.

[19] I believe this is the planet which changed signs first.

[20] This is an example of "escape": see *ITA* Ch. III.22.

[21] See *Introduction* Ch. 3, **44-48**.

[22] منكوس. This passive participle has specifically to do with suffering reversals, relapses, setbacks, tottering, etc., so Sahl probably means that it is retrograde, and/or suffering some other problem. (This word is used three times in *Nativities* to simply denote a situation that is reversed: Ch. 2.5, **9**; Ch. 4.2, **12**; and Ch. 10.3, **7**. It is used twice in *On Times* to denote a planet which is coming back around or turning back towards something via astronomical motions: Ch. 1, **12**, **13**, and **22**.)

[23] By "their" (هم-), Sahl means the malefics: this would be a case of reception, as L points out parenthetically (قبول).

[24] Since the planet which accepts the application dictates what happens next, it is better that the malefics apply to other planets, than that the other planets apply to them. See **66-67** below. However, unless Sahl means this only loosely as an observation about the nature of infortunes, it would only be possible for Saturn to be the one handing over if he is retrograde, and one would have to overlook the rules for "returning light" (see *Introduction* Ch. 3, **65**).

43 *The twentieth*: If[25] an infortune was in its own house or its exaltation, it refrains from evil, unless it was retrograde in the Ascendant: for if it was retrograde, its misfortune intensifies and its disagreement[26] grows.

44 *The twenty-first*: If a planet was in its own type[27] of the signs, then it would be suitable for it (that is, that Saturn would be in his own house or his exaltation, or in a cold sign, and Mars would be as I described[28] or in a hot sign). **45** Now if it was the contrary of its nature, then it would be bad for it, just like water and oil, which are mixed but not blended. **46** And[29] if it was in a sign resembling it, it would blend in the manner of water and milk.

47 *The twenty-second*: If the fortunes looked at the infortunes, they take away from their evil.

48 *The twenty-third*: If the infortunes looked at the fortunes from a square or opposition, they take away from their good fortune.

49 *The twenty-fourth*: If the fortunes were falling away from the Ascendant, or retrograde, they will be corrupting in the manner of the infortunes.

50 *The twenty-fifth*: If a planet was received and it was a fortune, it would be stronger for it; and if it was an infortune, it would be stronger for its harm.[30]

51 *The twenty-sixth*: If the infortunes were in an alien sign (that is, if they were not in their own house nor exaltation nor triplicity), then indeed they will increase in evil and their misfortune will become mighty. **52** And if they

---

[25] Cf. *Carmen* I.6, 3.

[26] Reading اختلافه for اختلاطه ("mixture, confusion").

[27] Or, what is "like" it (شكله).

[28] That is, in his house or exaltation.

[29] This should probably read "but," and refer back to **45**. I take this to mean that when a planet is in its own dignity or elemental quality (like Saturn and cold signs), it will blend like water and milk: two different substances, but compatible. But if it is in something contrary, it is like water and oil. But a question is: for whom is it "suitable"? It may be suitable for Saturn to be in a cold sign, but for a native, or in terms of medical astrology, it might be awful. This is the sort of thing that shows the limits of aphorisms.

[30] I believe this is in error, and that received infortunes are *weaker* for harm. The Latin version reads, "[if the fortune were received] their good will be stronger; and if they were malefics, their impediment will be *less*" (my emphasis). This matches a marginal note in L: "A retrograde or burned fortune is too weak for good fortune, and a received infortune *refrains from evil*" (my emphasis). For similar views about received infortunes being improved, see Sahl's *Questions* Ch. 9, **58**; *Nativities* Ch. 1.23, **37** (from Māshā'allāh); *Nativities* Ch. 5.1, **64** (also Māshā'allāh).

were in signs in which they have testimony, they refrain from evil but there is no escaping their harm.

53 *The twenty-seventh*: If an infortune was in its own house or its exaltation, triplicity, or bound, and it was in the stakes or what follows the stakes, then indeed its strength is like the strength of the fortunes: understand what I have described to you.

54 *The twenty-eighth*: If the fortunes were in a sign in which they did not have testimony, they take away from their good fortune and their goodness. **55** And if they were in a sign in which they did have testimony (that is, by house, exaltation, triplicity, or bound), their good fortune becomes mighty, and the matter is accomplished, and they increase the good.

56 *The twenty-ninth*: If the fortunes and the infortunes were in a bad place (that is, in one of the houses which I described to you) or under the rays, burned, they indicate that the matters are base and small, and the planets would not be able to indicate good nor evil because of the weakness which is in it. **57** Because if a planet was under the rays, burned, or in the opposition of the Sun, then it would be weak because this place is not good for the fortunes to be in, nor the infortunes: because the fortunes indicate a scarcity of good if they were under the rays, and likewise if the infortunes were under the rays it would be less for their evil.

58 *The thirtieth*: And every planet, whether a fortune or infortune, if it was in its own house, exaltation, or triplicity, converts what is in it of evil into good: so take heed of what I have described to you, and draw your conclusion based on that.[31]

59 *The thirty-first*:[32] If the infortunes were in the stakes of the Ascendant or they made the lord of the Ascendant[33] unfortunate from a square or opposition, then indeed they are wicked, strong for evil, and they are the mightiest that it could be for disaster – and especially if they were overpowering to the planets which they make unfortunate (that is, if they were stronger than the planets).[34] **60** And as for if they were separating from a trine or sextile, they refrain from evil and take away from their misfortune.[35]

---

[31] This is perhaps based on *Carmen* I.6, **2-3**.
[32] Cf. Theophilus, *OVI* Ch. 1.28, **31**.
[33] Only **H** adds "the lord of the Ascendant," but it makes sense and adds the direct object.
[34] Nevertheless, I think this "overpowering" might be a synonym for overcoming.
[35] Both **H** and **L** contain the following marginal note: "Know that the stakes of the Ascendant are known, but as for the stakes of the lord of the Ascendant, it is that the indicator is

61 *The thirty-second:*[36] A fortune never indicates anything except for fortune, and an infortune never indicates anything except for evil (due to its excess in its nature and the core[37] of its mixture). **62** But it is necessary that one look at the position of the planet (that is, at its position relative to the Ascendant), and [at] the sign in which it is: for [even][38] if it was an infortune, and it was in its own glow[39] or in its own house, exaltation, or triplicity, or an excellent place relative to the Ascendant, it indicates good.

63 *The thirty-third:*[40] And if a fortune was not in its own glow (that is, that it would be of the planets of the night and it is an indicator by day, or of the planets of the day and it is an indicator by night), or it was in an alien sign, or falling away from the Ascendant or under the rays, then indeed it harms and is not beneficial.

64 *The thirty-fourth*: And if Jupiter looked at an infortune, he converts its nature to the good. **65** And Venus does not have power over the conversion of a mighty thing, except that she is comparable to Jupiter: Jupiter loosens what Saturn binds up (that is, that if Jupiter was connecting with Saturn, he breaks [Saturn's] misfortune and removes it), and Venus loosens what Mars binds up.[41]

66 *The thirty-fifth*: If there was an infortune handing over to an infortune, then indeed it transfers an evil to an evil; and it was an infortune handing over to a fortune, it is converted from an evil to good. **67** And if there was a fortune handing over to a fortune, it transfers a good to a good; and if a fortune was handing over to an infortune, after the good he will encounter evil. **68** Mix the matters in this way.

69 *The thirty-sixth*: If the Moon or the lord of the Ascendant was made unfortunate from an assembly, square, or opposition, and the fortunes at that time are connecting with it from the square, then indeed it will dissolve the

---

being connected with the lord of the Ascendant from a square or opposition, with their enmity: it is [also] called 'the stakes.'"

[36] Cf. Theophilus, *OVI* Ch. 1.28, **27-29**.

[37] Or perhaps, "heart," "center" (جوز), but the verb has to do with overstepping limits and permissiveness, which draws on the notion of excess.

[38] Adding with the sense of the Latin.

[39] See below.

[40] Cf. Theophilus, *OVI* Ch. 1.28, **27-29**. See also the *Introduction* Ch. 3, **124**, and *Nativities* 1.23, **18**.

[41] For an example of this, see *Carmen* I.16, **8-9**.

hardship which strikes the man and free him from it. **70** And likewise, if it connected with the infortunes from a square, and the fortunes were looking at it from a trine, then indeed that man will escape from the hardship he encountered, and will fall into another hardship.⁴²

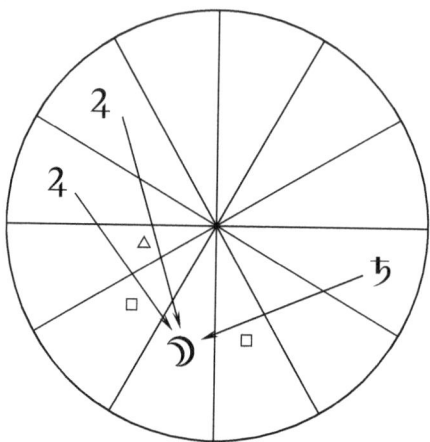

Figure 30: Fortunes relieving hardship (Aphorism #36)

71 *The thirty-seventh*: If a planet is not in its own house, nor its exaltation, nor its triplicity, nor in its own bound, nor in its own joy, nor in its own face, and it is falling from the stakes, then indeed that is a bad indication, with no good in it and no good in that planet.

72 *The thirty-eighth*: If a planet was under the rays, making its way towards the west⁴³ (that is, if it was arising in the evening), then indeed its strength is feeble, and there is no strength for it nor for its light—and it would be less for its evil if it was an infortune. **73** And if it was retrograde, then it will be difficult in all matters.

---

⁴² This *Aphorism* seems to be based on *Carmen* V.6, **33-34**. Under normal circumstances, this does not seem right: it would make more sense to say that the benefic trine (**70**) would free him, and the benefic square (**69**) would only save temporarily. But since the malefic in **70** is in a *square specifically* (and not in an assembly or opposition), then a trining benefic would be *in aversion to the malefic and be unable to affect it*. This could help to explain the reason why Sahl (or rather Māshā'allāh) speaks so often of aspects not cutting off aspects: the trine from the benefic saves the man at first by providing a liberating influence; but the malefic influence is not *specifically* being counteracted by the trine, since the benefic is in aversion to the malefic. If only the benefic could see the malefic, it could directly affect the malefic and perhaps permanently remove the evil after it has hit, as in **69**.

⁴³ نحو المغرب. That is, "westernizing."

74 *The thirty-ninth*: If planets were under the rays they would be weak in the whole of affairs: and it is like that if there were less than 12° between them and the Sun – unless a planet was in the degree of the Sun, for then it would be strong.

75 *The fortieth*:[44] If a planet was at a distance from the Sun by 12° in its rising from the east in the early mornings, then indeed it is strong in every inception and work. **76** And if it was at a distance of 15°, then at that time the planet would be the strongest it [could] be. **77** And if the planet was in front of the Sun in the direction of the west (that is, if it is arising in the evenings in the west), and there were from 7° to 15° between it and the Sun, then indeed it commences with weakness.[45] **78** And from 7° until it is in the heart of the Sun, the planet will be the weakest it [could] be. **79** And if it was in the heart, it is strong (by "the heart" I mean that it is with the Sun in one degree).[46]

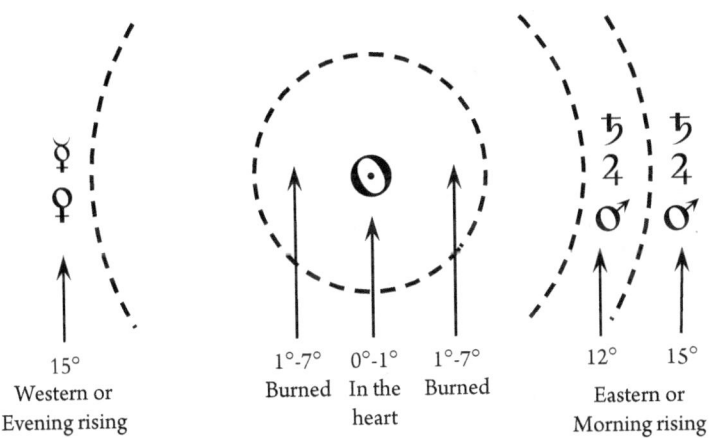

Figure 31: Planets in eastern and western rising (*Aphorisms* #40)

---

[44] See Heph. III.4, **5**, which seems to be the model for this *Aphorism*, except that Hephaistion does not include being in the heart. Compare this with the version in *Nativities* Ch. 1.22.

[45] This seems to mean *both* that the planet begins to be seriously weakened, *and* that inceptions or actions undertaken will be weak (compare **75**).

[46] This may be based on Rhetorius Ch. 1 (p. 4), who defines being in the heart as either being in the same degree as the Sun (as here) or in either adjacent degree.

80 *The forty-first*: If a planet was in exile, that makes it and its nature bad. 81 And if it was in something other than its own house or exaltation, but direct in course and [in] an excellent place (of the Ascendant or the Midheaven or the eleventh),[47] then it is also excellent.[48]

82 *The forty-second*: If the one accepting the management was western (that is, in front of the Sun),[49] it would be weak, defeated, not completing what it decrees. 83 And if it was eastern, it would be lively, strong, concluding the issue. 84 Because the corrupted[50] planet is as the example of a building if it is torn down: if it is built [again], it would be improved and become good.[51]

85 *The forty-third*:[52] If a planet was in the eighth from the Ascendant, and it is a fortune,[53] it does not give out either good or bad. 86 And if the infortunes were there, it makes their evil mighty.

87 *The forty-fourth*: Every planet which is at the beginning of a sign, is weak until it is firmly established in it and comes to be 5° within it. 88 And the planet will not be falling from[54] the stake unless it was 5° distant from its rear: I mean, if the stake was 10° of Aries, then indeed every planet which has[55] less than 5° between it and the stake,[56] is truly counted as being in the

---

[47] This could also be read as an excellent place from "the Ascendant or the Midheaven or the eleventh"; but a good place from all of them would include virtually every house; and because the Midheaven and the eleventh are commonly included in the excellent places from the Ascendant, they cannot really be separated from it. So, Sahl must mean "in an excellent place," of which these are the three he wants.

[48] At this point the Latin version includes the following statement about the Moon, which does not fit thematically here: "If the Moon is joined to some planet, the one to whom she is joined is said to be the acceptor of the Moon's management, and thus the accepting [of it] proceeds up to Saturn (because above Saturn there is no other who would accept the management)."

[49] That is, in a later degree than the Sun, so as to set after him.

[50] Reading as a passive version of Form III, rather than the active participle "corrupting."

[51] The "corrupting planet" here seems to be the western one, going under the rays: because after its great weakness and harm it emerges on the eastern side, just as the building is first torn down and then emerges new. But Sahl could also be making a kind of philosophical statement, namely that destruction is sometimes necessary and good, and precedes a better *construction*.

[52] Cf. Theophilus, *OVI* Ch. 1.28, **26**.

[53] Following **B**, but **H** and **L** read "fortunate" (which still makes astrological sense but does not contrast as obviously with "infortunes" in the next sentence).

[54] Lit., "falling away from."

[55] Lit., "is."

stake. **89** And every planet which was in more than 5° [from it] is not counted as being in the stake.

90 *The forty-fifth*: And every planet which is [distant] from the stake in what follows it, by 15°, is in the situation of one who is in the stake; and if it increases [beyond that], then it does not have strength.[57] **91** An example of that is if the stake was 10° of Aries, then up to 25° of it, it is indeed in that stake.[58] **92** And if it exceeded 15°, not.

93 *The forty-sixth*: If the planets were in the fixed signs, they indicate the stability of the matter which is being asked about. **94** And if they were in the signs having two bodies, they indicate upheaval[59] one time after another, and it attaches another object to that object, and a matter other than that matter. **95** And if they were in the convertible signs, they indicate the speed of the transformation to good or evil.

96 *The forty-seventh*: A fixed sign indicates the stability of the matter asked about, and every fixed matter, and it is an excellent assistant for the question. **97** And a sign having two bodies indicates a matter which is not single, and every affair will return a second time. **98** And a convertible sign indicates the speed of the transformation of that affair into something else.

99 *The forty-eighth*: If a planet was stationing towards retrogradation, it indicates collapse[60] in the matter, and disobedience. **100** And if it was stationing towards direct motion, it indicates forward movement in that matter, with no difficulty. **101** And every planet which was an indicator and wanted to go direct, indicates the suitability of the affair, and its strength, and its forward movement. **102** And if it was stationing towards retrogradation, it indicates corruption, difficulty, and collapse.

---

[56] This might also be put: "in less than 5° *of Aries*." This is the famous 5° rule of Ptolemy, where the power of the stake or angle extends by 5° beyond the cusp—as measured in diurnal motion, hence Sahl's reference to the "rear" of the stake.

[57] Or perhaps, it does not have *full* strength, but rather declines in strength from there. This statement is based on *Carmen* I.28, **1-7** (and is repeated correctly in Sahl's *Nativities* Ch. 2.13, **48-51**), but is misstated here. The range of 15° is measured in *ascensions*, not in zodiacal degrees: so the region of greatest power would reach to a different degree depending on the latitude of the chart and the type of sign rising (crooked or straight).

[58] The Arabic reads more literally, "if the stake was 10° of Aries up to 25° of it, then indeed it is in that stake."

[59] انتقاض. That is, the matter will not remain in one condition but will alter back and forth.

[60] Or, "rebellion" (الانتقاض).

103 *The forty-ninth*: Know that on the day the Moon is made unfortunate, everyone who asks on that day will be unfortunate, unless it is a place from the Ascendant which alters[61] that in increase and decrease: because if it made the Moon unfortunate and she was falling away from the Ascendant, it introduces anxieties. **104** And if she was in the stakes and the places which follow them, fear will occur in the body.[62]

105 *The fiftieth*: Know that the planet to which the Moon is connecting indicates what will be faced [in the future], so if she is connecting with the fortunes, it indicates that the future will be for the good. **106** And if she is connecting with an infortune, it indicates that the future will be for the bad. **107** And know that if the lord of the Ascendant (or the Moon) was in the seventh from its own house,[63] the owner of the sought matter will be reluctant about the sought matter which he asks about, and it will weigh heavily upon him.

---

[61] Reading يغيّر for بغير ("which is not that").
[62] Since the stakes and what follow them pertain to what is more immediate and present, they indicate the body; but falling or cadent places indicate what is more distant and peripheral: so, anxieties and fear, but not direct harm.
[63] That is, in detriment.

ON QUESTIONS
ON BEGINNING TO LOOK AT SOUGHT MATTERS

[Chapter 1]: The sign of the Ascendant & what is in it

3 If you were asked a question, begin looking based on what I will explain to you; and I have explained, for every thing sought, an approach you should take for it: so do not let it be changed to something else.

4 And do not take up a sought matter you are *not* asked about, in a matter which you have *already* been asked about, for you will introduce confusion into your soul: for example, one who asks about marriage, [and] when you looked into it, he asked you about another matter that came to him [at that moment]. **5** And if it is concealed [by him] prior to the judgment on different matters,[1] then it is all right that you take each sought matter from its own heading.

6 And it is not allowed that you ask [about] two matters for any inquiry, when their approach is one [and the same].[2]

7 And do not look except for one who comes to you or seeks or sends for you [when] strongly desiring, in need, or filled with sadness. **8** And as for one coming to you with a purpose in mind or to make fun, do not [do it]: for indeed the sought matter emerges in proportion to the concern of the one asking: so you should be mindful of these rules.[3]

9 And the most appropriate that a question could be is if a man asks about himself, or he sends someone to ask, of those concerned about his matter.[4] **10** So understand the intentions of people, for indeed the judgment and work is based on the intention of the one asking.

11 Should someone ask, and his concern is in a question about his destiny,[5] then the positions of those planets at the hour he asked indicate the condition of his whole struggle [through life]. **12** And likewise if it was his

---

[1] In other words, if he *already* has another topic in mind, as opposed to the sudden, new question in **4**.
[2] This seems to mean several unrelated questions that pertain to the same house.
[3] Or perhaps, "topics" (الأبواب): that is, the possible ways questions may be asked, as described above.
[4] This could possibly be read as one who is "affected by" the question, or perhaps one of the people "meant" by or involved in the question (ممّن يعنيه أمره).
[5] That is, over his lifetime (الدّهر).

concern to ask about a matter in his years or his months or in his day[s]:[6] it is [also] that.

13 So try to understand their intentions[7] before the assessment, because every questioner asks about good fortune and misfortune through what has power over him (of the nature of the heavenly circle), along with the situation he asks about (of the mixture of the circle): for indeed they are the branches and portions.[8] **14** For, someone to whom the good fortune of the lord of his Ascendant and the Moon corresponds, is made fortunate; and one to whom their misfortune corresponds, is made unfortunate. **15** And it is that no one asks, in a situation of the misfortune of the indicator (that is, the Moon) and of the lord of the Ascendant at the hour of the question or the nativity, unless he is an unfortunate, distressed man or a man whom misfortune ought to strike; and likewise good fortune: one does not ask in that [situation] unless it is a fortunate man or a man whom good fortune ought to affect.[9]

16 And do not let it frighten you if you were asked about different questions under a single Ascendant: for if the sought matters differ, then if their enumeration[10] was in conformity with a condition of misfortune or good fortune, it will be that for them. **17** And indeed one sees people [both] in good fortune, and what is just like that in misfortune: so understand.[11]

18 And if you were asked about a sought matter, and it was in the nature of advancing,[12] then look in the connection of the lord of the Ascendant with the lord of the sought thing, and the advancement of the one accepting [it] (that is, the heavy planet which is accepting the management), whether it was the lord of the Ascendant or the lord of the sought thing – the heavy one

---

[6] That is, a question about something with a shorter time frame.

[7] This actually means "understandings," which fits awkwardly with "try to understand." It could also be read as "So ask about their understandings."

[8] Or, "lots," "allotments" (سهام). This is a confusing sentence, but Sahl seems to be talking about the fundamental good or bad in one's life, and the particular situation one is in: these would be shown by the natal chart and the transits at the time of the question chart.

[9] In other words, the chart reflects the client's current or future fortune or misfortune, based on the situation he is actually in.

[10] That is, each one listed separately.

[11] This means that multiple questions should pertain to different houses, and each should be properly reflected in the description of the chart's features.

[12] That is, will it increase, move forward, be lasting, etc. Astrologically, this term (إقبال) is one of a few that refers to being angular or succeedent, hence Sahl says to look at the advancement of the planet accepting the management.

of them. **19** So look for its being free from what I mentioned to you of the misfortunes of the planets.[13] **20** But if the question was about the nature of retreating, such as travel, moving, a detained person's exit from his prison, and being released from sorrows,[14] then look for these matters from the place of retreat and withdrawal.[15]

ஐ ೂ ೫

21 And if you were asked about one of the sought matters which are in the twelve signs (for example, if a man asked about himself, or his assets, or his brothers) based on what I described to you of the natures of the twelve signs, then make the Ascendant and its lord and the Moon be the indicators for the man who is asking you, and the sign of the sought matter and its lord belong to the sought matter which he is asking about.

22 Then, look at the lord of the Ascendant and the Moon, the stronger one of them (that is, the one in a stake) and the one looking at the Ascendant: begin with it. **23** For if one of them connected with the lord of the sought thing, then indeed the sought thing will be accomplished by the seeking of the one asking; and if you found the lord of the sought thing connecting with the lord of the Ascendant, that sought thing would be accomplished in ease and the desire of the one asking, [but] apart from seeking it and without beseeching.[16]

24 And if you found the lord of the Ascendant or the Moon in the place of the sought thing, or you found the lord of the sought thing in the Ascendant, then indeed it will be accomplished, unless the Ascendant was the fall of the lord of the sought thing, or it was burned up in it: for indeed that will not come to be.

25 And if you found the lord of the Ascendant or the Moon connecting with a planet [which is] in the place of the sought thing, and that planet had

---

[13] *Introduction* Ch. 3, **90-101**.

[14] This is an interesting point because usually being cadent (falling, retreating, etc.) is associated with something failing, weak, and so on. Moreover, people often ask about something they want to take place and occur—but here, Sahl is reminding us that sometimes we want to know about something disappearing and going away. See for example Ch. 6, **39-40** below.

[15] That is, cadent or falling. See *Questions* Ch. 6, **39-41**, Ch. 9, **67-77**, and *Sections*, **63**.

[16] Or, "urgency" (إلحاح).

testimony in it (of its house, its exaltation, or its triplicity), it will also be accomplished.

26 And if there was not anything of what I mentioned, then look for a transfer of light from the Moon or one of the light planets: for if you found it separating from the lord of the Ascendant and connecting with the lord of the sought matter, or separating from the lord of the sought matter and connecting with the lord of the Ascendant, the sought matter will be accomplished by the hands of messengers and one who goes back and forth between them.

27 And if you do not find a planet between them [which is] bearing the light of one of them to the other, then look for a collection of light: for if you found the lord of the sought matter and the lord of the Ascendant both joining together with one planet heavier than them both, and that planet is looking at the place of the sought thing, or it is in the Ascendant or Midheaven, the sought thing will be accomplished by the hand of a judge or a man he has confidence in.

28 So from these three approaches comes the judgment[17] of all sought matters. **29** The first, the connection of the lord of the Ascendant, the Moon, and the lord of the sought thing; the second, if there is a planet transferring between them (that is, separating from one of them and connecting with the other), then the sought thing is accomplished in the hands of messengers; and the third is the collection of light (that is, if there is a planet heavier than them both, with which they are both connecting), so that it collects the light of them both or takes up their strength and they come to terms through a judgment [made] between them or through a man he has confidence in. **30** So from these topics comes a judgment of the sought things.

31 Then, after what I mentioned to you, look at the one accepting the management from one of the two (and that is the heavy planet, whether it was the lord of the Ascendant or the lord of the sought thing), or a planet which is collecting the light: for if it was free of the infortunes,[18] in the stakes and what follows them, and it is not retrograde, burned, nor falling from the stakes, that sought matter will be accomplished. **32** And if it was made unfortunate, the sought matter will be corrupted after he has attained it; and if the

---

[17] Or, "accomplishment" (قضاء), here and in **30**.
[18] **B** adds, "or." But Sahl seems to be giving a best-case scenario, so he probably means that it is *both* free *and* angular or succeedent.

one accepting [the management] was retrograde, it will be terminated after he believed he has already attained it.

33 And if you were asked whether the attainment would be with ease or difficulty, then look: for if the connection of the lord of the Ascendant and the lord of the sought matter was from a trine or sextile, the attainment will be with ease; and if the connection was from a square or opposition, then truly the attainment will be after difficulty, beseeching, and delay.

34 And if you were asked whether the attainment would be through the seeking of the one asking, or would it come to him spontaneously[19] [and] not through seeking by him, then if the lord of the Ascendant and the Moon were both connecting with the lord of the sought matter, or the lord of the Ascendant or the Moon were in the place of the sought matter, then indeed that will be with the seeking and desire of the one asking, with difficult straits or something else. **35** And if the lord of the sought matter was the one connecting with the lord of the Ascendant, or the lord of the sought matter was in the Ascendant, then truly he is wanted in that sought matter, and it will be handed to him spontaneously. **36** And if the question was about a governorship which would come to him in [his] status, [it will be] without him coming to the door of the Sultan in this.

37 And if the attainment of the sought matter was in relation to a transfer of light, then that will be in relation to messengers and those who go back and forth between them. **38** And if the Moon or the one transferring was separating from the lord of the Ascendant and connecting with the lord of the sought matter, then the messengers' starting-point will be from the one asking; and if the Moon was separating from the lord of the sought matter and connecting with the lord of the Ascendant, then the messengers will come to him and will want him in this.

39 And if the attainment of the sought matter was from the collection of light, the victory over the owner of the sought matter will indeed be from an authority who enters between the two, or a man through whom they will come to terms, until he attains the sought matter.

---

[19] Not so much spontaneously (عفوًا), because other people are involved; but without him having to do much about it (see also **23** and **35**).

40 And[20] know that the lord of the Ascendant and the Moon, if they connected with a planet from its fall (such as if the lord of the Ascendant is connecting with Mars from Cancer or with Jupiter from Capricorn), it indicates the corruption of the sought matters, and it will not turn out well. **41** And[21] likewise if they were connecting with a planet from their own fall:[22] it does not accept them, it indicates the vexation[23] of the owner of the question in what he wants to do with it, and that his sought matter will not be accomplished. **42** And an example of that is if the Moon is connecting with a planet from 3° of Scorpio (which is her fall), or the lord of the Ascendant is Mars and he is connecting from the end of Cancer (which is his fall).

43 And know that if an infortune was the lord of the sought thing, and the lord of the Ascendant or the Moon was connecting with it from a square or opposition, then it will not accept them, and indeed the one asking about that sought matter will want it not to exist at the time when its evil and disaster enters upon him. **44** And if the connection was from a trine or sextile, it will refrain from this.

45 And if the lord of the Ascendant and the lord of the sought matter were a single planet, and it was received (that is, it connected with the lord of its house or its exaltation), free of the infortunes, the sought matter will be accomplished; and if it was other than that, it will be corrupted. **46** And likewise, if the Moon connected with it and it[24] was safe from defects, it will be accomplished.

47 And know that the testimony of the signs in the accomplishment of the sought matters, is if the Ascendant is a fixed sign or one having two bodies, and the stakes are upright:[25] that is, if the Midheaven is the tenth sign, and the Midheaven is not the ninth sign nor the stake of the earth the third [sign]: for this is the meaning if the stakes are upright.

---

[20] For this first example, see *Introduction* Ch. 3, **59-60**.
[21] This example is similar to *Introduction*, Ch. 3, **61**.
[22] In *Introduction* Ch. 3, **61**, this also requires that the other planet not have any dignity in the connecting planets' sign—otherwise this would be a case of reception.
[23] Or, "badness" (سوء).
[24] Or perhaps, "she," but I think this refers to the other planet.
[25] Or, "standing up": in that case, we could undoubtedly allow the Midheaven to be in the eleventh sign, for that sign is moving up towards being the tenth sign.

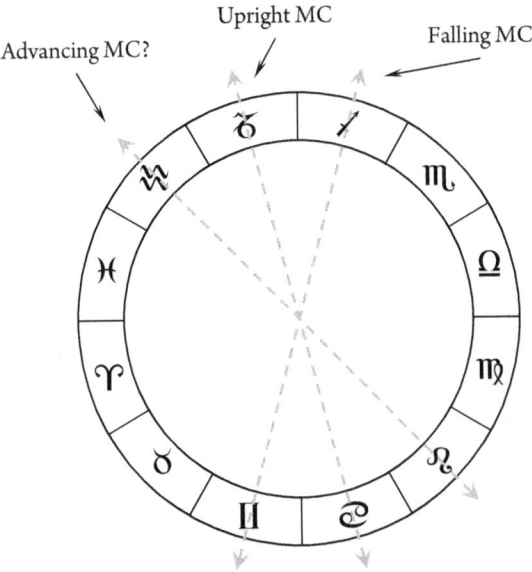

Figure 32: Upright and falling Midheavens

48 The testimony of the stars in the accomplishment of the sought matters, is [in] three testimonies from which the accomplishment is sought: and they are the lord of the Ascendant, the lord of the sought matter, and the Moon. **49** Now when the two indicators encountered [each other] (that is, the lord of the Ascendant and the lord of the sought matter), and one of the two is safe, he will attain to one-third of what he sought of that matter. **50** And if it was two testimonies (that is, they were both safe together), he will attain to two-thirds of what he sought. **51** And if all of the testimonies met together (that is, that the lord of the Ascendant, the lord of the sought matter, and the Moon were safe from retrogradation, burning, the infortunes, and falling), he will attain to all of what he sought. **52** And if along with their testimonies they were received, and the one receiving them was also received, then truly it will add good on top of that: so be acquainted with these questions, for they belong to all sought matters.

53 And an example of that is a question about authority, whether he would attain it or not. **54** And the Ascendant was Gemini, 20°; and the Midheaven Pisces, the first degree; and the Sun in Cancer, 12°; and the Moon in Virgo, 17°; and Mercury in Gemini, 27°; and Mars in Taurus, 8°; and Venus in Leo, 3°; and Jupiter in Pisces, in 20°, stationing toward retrogradation; and Saturn in Gemini, in 6°.

55 I looked in this question at the Ascendant, its lord, and the Moon (and they are the two indicators of the one asking), and at the sign of the Midheaven and its lord (and they are the two indicators of the authority about which he asks). **56** And the Ascendant was Gemini, the house of Mercury, and he was in the Ascendant, at the end of the sign; and Jupiter, who was the lord of the house of the sought matter, [was] in the Midheaven, in 20°: so I found the lord of the Ascendant separated from the lord of the sought matter. **57** So I looked at the Moon, and found her in the stake of the earth, connecting with Jupiter from an opposition: it indicated the attainment of the sought matter with beseeching, in trouble, and that is because the both of them were connecting from an opposition. **58** And if they had connected from a trine or sextile, it would have indicated attainment with ease. **59** And the Moon was the one connecting with the lord of the sought matter, so it indicated that that would be with the seeking and craving of the one asking. **60** And if the lord of the sought matter had been the one connecting with the Moon, he would have attained the sought matter spontaneously from the one who was put in charge of it, without the seeking and beseeching of the one asking.[26]

61 And I looked at Jupiter, and he was the one accepting the management, and I found him in the Midheaven, stationing towards retrogradation: it indicates the breakdown of what I mentioned, and its quick corruption; and that will be from the authority (and that is the tenth), on the part of Jupiter (who was the indicator of the authority). **62** And if the acceptor of the management had been the lord of the Ascendant, and it was corrupt, I would have said the corruption of this sought matter was on the part of the one asking, and from his own action.

63 And because the lord of the Ascendant was shifting over from his house to the house of assets, it indicated the quick shifting over of the one asking, and his moving (in the seeking of money) to a place in which he would stay; and he would not accept that, because when [Mercury] went out from his sign, he was connecting with Mars, and he does not accept [Mercury]:[27] it indicates that he will do work in his departure from which disturbance and anxiety will enter upon him.

---

[26] The Moon cannot be applied to—Sahl is simply trying to employ the rule mentioned in **22-23**.

[27] Mercury would be connecting to Mars from the sign of Mars's fall (see **40** above).

ON QUESTIONS

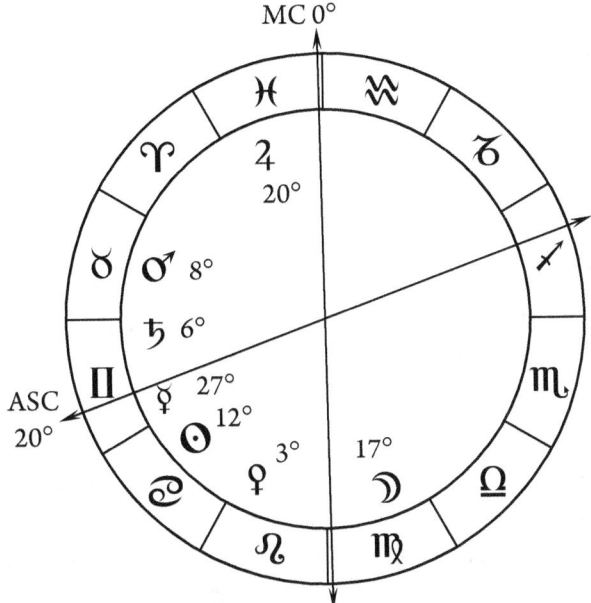

Figure 33: Sahl's question about authority (MS values)

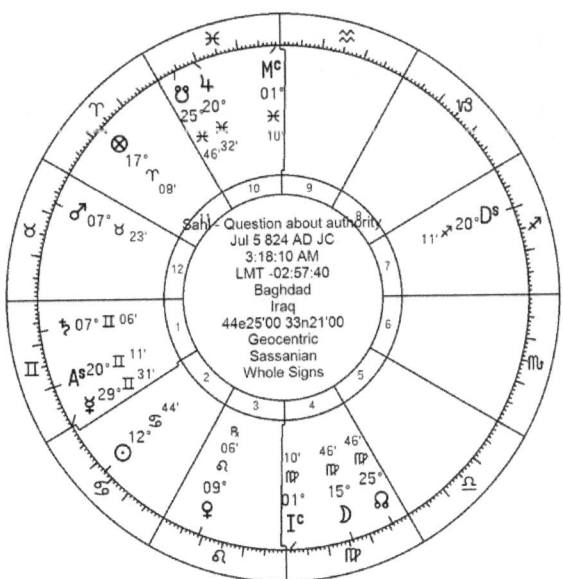

Figure 34: Sahl's question about authority
(modern calculation, "Sassanian" zodiac)

64 And because Mars is the lord of the sixth from the Ascendant, which is the house of slaves and illness, it indicated that what I described will be in relation to slaves, the underclass, and illness. **65** And because Jupiter is the lord of the sought matter, seeking the breakdown [of it],[28] and he is with the Tail, it indicated the shift comes upon the man from the one from whom he is seeking the sought matter, and the abundance of confusion [coming] over him. **66** And the separation of Mercury from the lord of the sought matter indicated that the one asking had indeed desired this matter before that, but at the time he separated from the lord of the sought matter, he lost hope of it; and likewise in all sought matters.

Comment by Dykes. At this point the 1493 Latin version (Bonatus Locatellus, Venice) has a short paragraph "On the corruption of the Ascendant," which is attributed to Māshā'allāh and describes the use of some kind of victor in questions. But it evidently did not appear in the Arabic manuscripts of Sahl. Bonatti seems to have used a MS which was part of this 1493 lineage, because he inserts his own version into *The Book of Astronomy* Tr. 6, Part 2, Ch. 5.

We might expect Sahl to insert questions pertaining to the first house in this chapter, but apparently he does not. The reader may see a question on the length of life in *On Times* Ch. 4, and similar questions in *Judges* §1.

[Chapter 2]: The second sign & what is in it, of questions

[Whether he will get assets]

2 And if you were asked about assets hoped for, or whether one who asked you would get assets or not, then look at the lord of the Ascendant and the Moon (and they are the two indicators of the one asking), and at the sign of assets and its lord (and they are the two indicators of the assets you were asked about). **3** For if the lord of the Ascendant or[29] the Moon connected with the lord of the house of assets, or the lord of the house of assets con-

---

[28] See **61** above.
[29] Some MSS read "and."

nected with the lord of the Ascendant, or you found the Moon transferring from the lord of the house of assets to the lord of the Ascendant, or from the lord of the Ascendant to the lord of the house of assets, then truly he will attain the assets. **4** And [it is] likewise if Jupiter or Venus (who are the two fortunes) were in the house of assets.

5 And if there was not anything of what I mentioned, then truly he will not attain it. **6** And if the infortunes were in the house of assets (and it is the second from the Ascendant), then it indicates the decline[30] of the owner of the question. **7** And if the Moon was empty in course, then the one asking will not leave that condition which he is in, until he dies.

[What kind of assets?]

8 And if you were asked of what kind the gotten [wealth] will be, then look at the acceptor of the management, whether it was the lord of the Ascendant or the lord of the sought matter (and it is the heavy planet). **9** And if it was in the Ascendant or the second, he will get and provide [it] from the work of his own hands; if it was in the third, in relation to brothers and sisters; if it was in the fourth, in relation to fathers, family, and lands; if it was in the fifth, in relation to children; if it was in the sixth, in relation to illness, slaves, and the lower class; if it was in the seventh, in relation to women (if the sign was feminine) or in relation to wars and quarreling (if it was masculine); if it was in the eighth, in relation to inheritance; if it was in the ninth, in relation to travels, religion, and mosques; if it was in the tenth, in relation to the Sultan, his workers, and his nobles;[31] if it was in the eleventh, in relation to friends and commerce; and if it was in the twelfth, in connection with enemies (and if this sign was one having four feet, in relation to riding animals; but if it was of the human signs, in relation to prisons and their people).

10 So these are the natures of the twelve signs: when you find fortunes, the attaining [of the wealth] will be in relation to the fortunes and the essence of that house; and where there are infortunes, the harm and corruption will be in relation to the essence of that house. **11** And look likewise in all

---

[30] إدبار, which is Sahl's usual word for "retreating."
[31] Some MSS read "works and nobles."

sought matters, so you may know from what direction the easiness is, and from what direction the scattering[32] is.

[Chapter 3]: The third sign & what is in it, of questions

2 If you were asked, concerning a brother, what his condition is, then look at the third sign (which is the sign of siblings), and you see the fortunes and infortunes, and their aspect to it. **3** If you found the lord of the third from the Ascendant in the sixth (which is the house of illness) or connecting with the lord of the sixth, then report that his brother is ill; and likewise if the lord of the sixth was in the third. **4** And if the lord of the third was in the fifth or eleventh, then truly his brother is absent.[33] **5** And if you found the lord of the third made unfortunate,[34] then his brother has grief and illness. **6** And if it was entering into burning, then truly he will not recover[35] from that illness; and likewise report based on the essence of the sign.

7 And if you were asked about his father or his mother, that is from the fourth; and about his child, from the fifth; and about his slaves, from the sixth; and about his women, from the seventh, based on what I described to you.

[Chapter 4]: The fourth sign & what is in it, of questions

[Will he obtain the land or property]

2 If you were asked about a home or real estate which a man was seeking, as to whether he would obtain it or not, then look at the lord of the Ascendant and the Moon (which are the two indicators of the one asking), and the fourth sign and its lord (and they are the two indicators of the land). **3** For if the lord of the Ascendant or the Moon connected with the lord of the fourth, or the lord of the fourth connected with the lord of the Ascendant, or the

---

[32] Or perhaps, "separation" (التّفريق). In financial terms this should refer to the dispersal of wealth, but I am not sure how to generalize it to other questions, as Sahl seems to want.

[33] The fifth is the third (travel) from the third, and the eleventh is the ninth (also travel) from the third. Thus, Sahl is suggesting we look at derived houses from the third.

[34] The Latin version has "in the twelfth," which makes sense here as well. In the previous sentence it also mentions the second, which would be the twelfth from the third.

[35] Lit., "be turned around" (منقلب من).

lord of the fourth was in the Ascendant, or the lord of the Ascendant or the Moon was in the fourth, then truly he will obtain it. **4** And if the Moon was transferring from one of them to the lord of the other, then it will be obtained at the hands of [other] men.

[The condition of the land]

5 And[36] if you were asked about a landed estate being bought, as to what its condition is, and the condition of its vegetation and what is on it, then erect the Ascendant at the hour you are asked, and make it an indicator for the leasing [of the land] and those of the farmers who work on it. **6** And the fourth sign indicates the condition of the land and what is on it, and the seventh sign indicates what is on it (of vegetation shorter than trees), and from the Midheaven is what is on it (of trees).

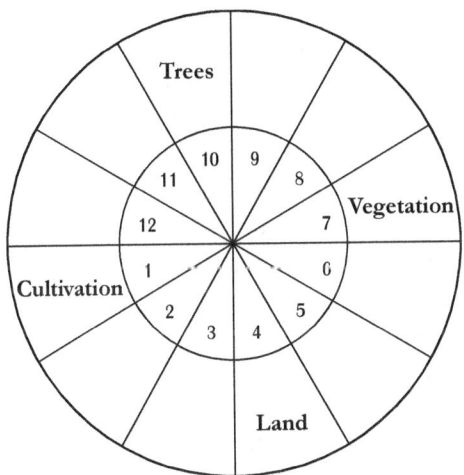

Figure 35: Angles for buying land and cultivation

7 And[37] if an infortune was in the Ascendant, then the renters are robbers and deceivers; and the infortune was direct they will stay on it, while if it was retrograde they will flee from it. **8** And if it was a fortune in the Ascendant,

---

[36] Cf. *Carmen* V.11, **1**. For this question (**5-18**), cf. also Māshā'allāh's version in Leiden Or. 891, ff. 24b-25a.
[37] For this paragraph, cf. *Carmen* V.9, **2-3**.

then truly the renters are morally upright, of good faith; and if the fortune was direct they will not leave from the land, while if it was retrograde they will leave.

9 And if there was a fortune in the Midheaven, direct in course, then the trees will be strong, abundant in fruits; and if it was retrograde, they will be middling except that he will begin to sell, and sell all of the trees from it. **10** And if there was an infortune in the Midheaven it indicates a scarcity of trees; and if it was retrograde, then he will sell what remains on [the land].

11 And if there was not a planet in the Midheaven, then look at the lord of the Midheaven: for if it was looking at the Midheaven, then truly there will be trees on it. **12** Now if it was eastern, then the trees will be planted just then, and if it was western then the trees planted will be the original ones or ancient. **13** And if it was direct in course its trees will remain; and if it was retrograde then they will not remain (so that they will be spoiled). **14** And if the lord of the Midheaven was not looking at its place, and it was in the twelfth from it (or the sixth, eighth, or second),[38] then the land will be without trees.

15 Then look at the vegetation from the seventh sign, based on what I mentioned to you about the Midheaven.

16 And[39] as for the essence of the land, you look at the fourth sign from the Ascendant: for if it was Aries, Leo, or Sagittarius, then that land will be one of mountains, and a hard land, dusty, abundant in heat.[40] **17** And if it was Taurus, Virgo, or Capricorn, then the land will be flat; and if it was Gemini, Libra, or Aquarius, the land will be of two types, between a mountain and a plain; and if it was Cancer, Scorpio, or Pisces, then the land will be jungle, and near the water. **18** And if the fourth sign was one having two bodies (I mean Virgo, Sagittarius, Pisces, and Gemini), the land will be two types: on it will be [both] deserts and mountains.

---

[38] That is, if it is in aversion to the Midheaven.
[39] For this paragraph, cf. *Carmen* V.11, **2**.
[40] "Heat" is a tentative reading, as multiple manuscripts give either unintelligible or unlikely readings for this word.

[Leasing land]

19 And[41] if you wanted to accept a land or let it out for hire, or settle it, or anything of leasing, then see the matter of the one advancing [the matter] <from the Ascendant>, and the matter of the one accepting [it] from the seventh, and the fee of the thing and its accomplishment from the Midheaven, and the outcome of that from the fourth sign.

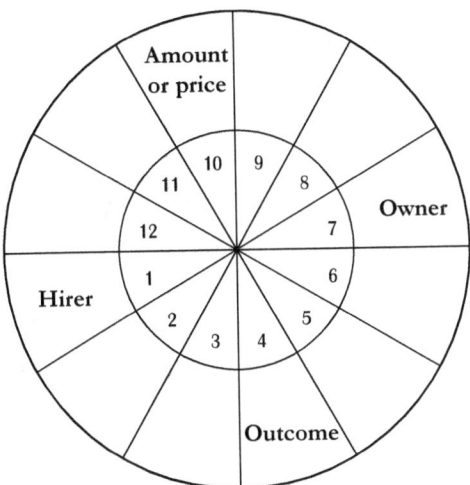

Figure 36: Angles for leasing

20 And if there was a fortune in the Ascendant, then the one advancing [the matter] is suitable and eager; and if there was an infortune in it, then the one departing from it or accepting it has deception, and it will not be accomplished by him.

21 And if there was an infortune in the seventh, then the one accepting it will return on a following day and he will not give him anything; and if he did give [something], adversity and damage will enter into it, and it will not be accomplished by him; and if there was a fortune in it, the one accepting will be suitable.

---

[41] For this whole question, cf. *Carmen* V.9, and the Māshā'allāh version in Leiden Or. 891, f. 25a.

22 <And if there was an infortune in the Midheaven or it was looking from hostility, the business will not go forward.>[42]

23 And if you found an infortune in the fourth or looking from hostility, then the outcome will [tend] towards tribulation, evil, and his death; and if it was a fortune, the outcome will be put in order, if God (be He exalted!) wills.

[Chapter 5]: The fifth sign & what is in it, of questions

[Whether he would have children: particular]

2 If a man asked you whether he would have a child from this woman or not, look at the lord of the Ascendant and the Moon: for if they connected with the lord of <the house of> children (and it is the fifth from the Ascendant), or you found the lord of the house of children in the Ascendant, or the lord of the Ascendant and the Moon in the house of children, or you found a planet reflecting the light between the lord of the Ascendant and the lord of the house of children, then truly he will have a child. 3 But in the reflection of light, look after that at the one accepting the management (and it is the heavy planet): for if it was free of the infortunes (that is, it is not connecting with them and they are not connecting with it), and it is not falling away from the Ascendant, and not burned under the Sun, then it will be accomplished. 4 If it was made unfortunate, or was falling away from the Ascendant or burned, then it will come to be [but] then be corrupted. 5 And if you found Jupiter in an excellent place, and he is not made unfortunate nor under the rays, it indicates pregnancy. 6 And if the infortunes were with Venus, it does not indicate pregnancy. 7 And if the Moon connected with an infortune, then judge that she will not become pregnant. 8 And if you found a fortune in the fifth (which is the house of children), then the woman will become pregnant. 9 And if the infortunes were in it, or looking at it from an opposition, it does not indicate pregnancy.

---

[42] Adding based on the Latin text; the Arabic MSS do not include it.

[Whether he would have children: general]

10 And if you were asked by a woman or man whether or not she would have a child [at all], then look at the Ascendant: for if the fortunes were in it, or the lord of the Ascendant was in the Ascendant, tenth, eleventh, or fifth, and Jupiter in a suitable place, one will be born to him. **11** And if the lord of the Ascendant was in the fourth or seventh, and Jupiter in an excellent place, then one will be born to him with a delay after the original question. **12** And if you found an infortune in the Ascendant or looking at it from an opposition or square, and the lord of the Ascendant in a place not excellent but rather bad, and Jupiter falling or in the house of death, or under the rays, then it indicates a scarcity of children and the smallness of their growth, if there were any.

13 And do not omit to look at the fifth from the Ascendant (which is the sign of children): for if the fortunes were in it, he will have a child quickly. **14** And if the infortunes were in it, and you saw something good in the matter of the question, then he will have a child but it grants the death of his child. **15** And if you found Jupiter in a stake, eastern, he will have a child quickly; but if he was western in a stake (that is, he arises from the west in the evening), and the lord of the Ascendant in a suitable place, one will be born to him after a delay.

[Whether she is pregnant]

16 And if you were asked concerning a woman as to whether she is carrying [a child] or not, and if she will give birth and it will be completed or not, then look at the lord of the Ascendant and the Moon (and they are the indicators of the woman), and at the fifth sign and its lord (and it is the indicator for the child). **17** And if you found the lord of the Ascendant or the Moon in the house of children, and[43] the lord of the house of children was in the Ascendant (and it is free of the infortunes), she has a pregnancy. **18** And if the lord of the Ascendant or the Moon handed over its management to a planet in a stake, then truly there is a pregnancy—and better than that if it was received. **19** And if they were both connecting with a planet falling away from the Ascendant, it indicates corruption, and that the pregnancy is futile; and

---

[43] **B** reads: "or."

more forcefully than that if the Ascendant was a convertible sign, or there was an infortune in a stake, or the Moon was connecting with an infortune: for all of these are what indicates its corruption.[44]

20 Now[45] if you were asked concerning the pregnancy as to whether it was true or would be false,[46] then look at the lord of the fifth: if it connected with the lord of the Ascendant, or with a planet in an excellent place from the Ascendant, in which it had testimony, then with that it indicates pregnancy. **21** And[47] if the lord of the Ascendant connected with a planet falling away from the Ascendant not receiving <it>, it indicates corruption.[48]

[Whether they would have twins]

22 And if you were asked about a woman carrying [a child] as to whether she would give birth to twins or to [only] one, then look at the Ascendant at the hour you were asked: for if it was a sign having two bodies, or in the Ascendant or the house of children there were two planets of the fortunes, then truly she is pregnant with twins; and likewise if you found the Sun or the Moon in signs having two bodies. **23** And if neither the Ascendant nor the sign of children was one having two bodies, and there was not in it what I mentioned of the fortunes, nor the luminaries in those having two bodies, then she is pregnant with one.

[Whether it is a boy or girl]

24 And if you were asked whether she would give birth to a boy or girl, then look at the lord of the Ascendant and the lord of the house of children: for if they were both in male signs, then the one which is in her belly is a boy; and if they were both in female signs, the one which is in her belly is a girl. **25**

---

[44] The Latin edition adds: "But if the acceptor of the management (that is, the heavier planet which accepts all of the management from the lord of the Ascendant or the Moon) was free of the infortunes (that is, if it was not joined to them nor they joined to it), and it was in a good place, the pregnancy will be perfected."
[45] This paragraph is rather jumbled in all of the MSS.
[46] باطل. This can also mean "in vain." This question seems to refer to a woman's belief that she is pregnant.
[47] This sentence only appears in **B** (with another partial version of **20**), and appears partially and embedded in **BL**'s **20**.
[48] The Latin adds, "unless the Moon was received, or the lord of the Ascendant was in a good place from the Ascendant: because then it signifies pregnancy."

And if one of them was in a male sign and the other in a female sign, then look at the sign in which the Moon is, and at the planet which she is connecting with: for if the Moon was in a male house or the one which she is connecting with was in a male house,[49] she will give birth to a boy; and if the Moon was in a female sign or she was connecting with a female planet, she will give birth to a girl. **26** And[50] know that if Mercury[51] was eastern (that is, arising before the Sun), it will be male; and if he was western (that is, arising after the Sun), it will be female.

[Chapter 6]: The sixth sign & what is in it, of questions

2 If[52] you were asked about a sick person, whether he would recover or die, then the Ascendant indicates the doctor, the Midheaven indicates the sick person, the seventh sign indicates the illness, and the fourth sign indicates the medicine.

3 And if an infortune was in the Ascendant, the doctors' medicine will not benefit him; <and if a fortune was there, the doctors' medicine and their treatment will benefit him>.[53]

4 And if an infortune was in the Midheaven, the sick person will not protect himself, but he will stir up the disease upon himself; and if a fortune was there, that sick person will treat himself with what benefits him.

5 And if an infortune was in the seventh, it will change from illness to illness; and if a fortune was there, the outcome will come upon him from something other than the treatment he is treated with.

6 And if an infortune was in the fourth sign, the medicine will increase the severity of the condition; and if a fortune was there, the medicines will benefit him.

---

[49] But see later in the sentence, when the gender of the planet is the deciding factor.
[50] For this sentence, cf. Theophilus (Appendix A, passage #3).
[51] That is, if Mercury is the planet she is connecting with.
[52] For **2-5**, cf. *Carmen* V.42, **33-38**.
[53] Adding the material in brackets, based on *Carmen* V.42.

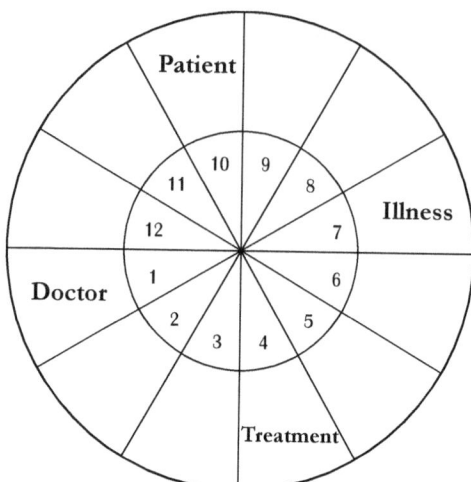

Figure 37: Angles for treating patients

7 Then look at the lord of the Ascendant and the Moon, and begin with the one of them which is in a stake and looks at the Ascendant. **8** And if it was free of the infortunes and not looking at the lord of the house of death (which is the eighth from the Ascendant), and not under the rays, then it indicates recovery. **9** And if it connected with the fortunes, it also indicates recovery. **10** And if that fortune was retrograde, it lengthens the illness in him, but he will recover.

11 And if the Moon was under the earth and she is connecting with a planet above the earth, it indicates recovery—unless the one accepting the management is entering into burning, for that indicates disaster. **12** And if the Moon was above the earth and she is connecting with a planetary infortune under the earth, then it indicates disaster.

13 And if the Moon connected with the lord of the Ascendant, and she is increasing in light and calculation, it indicates the quickness of his recovery, and the soundness of his body.

14 And if the lord of the Ascendant was under the earth, then if the Moon connected with a planet in the ninth from the Ascendant (wanting to fall), then he will perish.

15 And if the lord of the Ascendant connected with the lord of the house of death, and the Moon was corrupted, it indicates ruin. **16** And if she bore the light from the lord of the Ascendant to the lord of the eighth, then perishing is feared. **17** And if she was received, it lengthens the disease in him. **18** And if the lord of the Ascendant connected with the lord of the eighth from a trine, and the lord of the Ascendant is in a stake, then when the lord of the eighth reaches the degree of the Ascendant, it indicates disaster. **19** And if the lord of the house of death was in the Ascendant, and the lord of the Ascendant or the Moon was made unfortunate, it indicates disaster. **20** And if an infortune was accepting the management,[54] it indicates a relapse after the recovery.

21 And the presence of the lord of the eighth in the stakes is bad. **22** And if the lord of the Ascendant was above the earth, and it is connecting with a lord of the eighth in the fourth or in the house of death, it indicates disaster. **23** And if the lord of the eighth was not looking at the lord of the Ascendant, and a planet reflected their light, and the lord of the Ascendant was falling while the lord of the eighth was in a stake, it indicates disaster. **24** And if the lord of the Ascendant was entering into burning, and there was less than 12° between it and the Sun, he will die; and likewise if it was burned and it was <not>[55] received.

25 And if a planet was not handing over the management (that is, if it was a heavy planet), and it was free from burning, and the Moon safe, it indicates liberation.

26 And if the house of illness was a convertible sign, the disease will be light at one time, and burdensome at another; and if it was a sign having two bodies, it will shift from illness to illness; and if it was a fixed sign, his illness will be fixed in one condition.

27 And if the Moon separated from a western planet (that is, rising [out of the rays] in the evening in the west), that illness has already been a long time in him; and if the Moon separated from an eastern planet (that is, arising in the early morning from the east), then the illness is recent. **28** And if the Moon connected with an eastern planet, it indicates the quickness of his recovery; and if she connected with a western planet, the illness will last a long time in him.

29 And the best the lord of the Ascendant could be is, when it was made fortunate,[56] if the fortunes[57] look at it and it is in an excellent place from the

---

[54] With different voweling, this could be "and if the one accepting the management was made unfortunate."
[55] Adding on the basis of the Latin.
[56] Reading "fortunate" with the sense of the Latin, for "unfortunate." But it would indeed improve an infortune if it was in a good place and looked at by the fortunes.

Ascendant. **30** And the most wicked that the aspect of the infortunes could be, is if they look from a square, opposition, or assembly.[58]

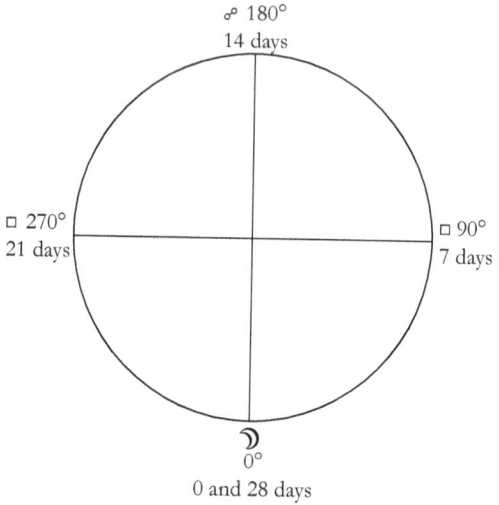

Figure 38: Critical days

[Critical days]

31 And[59] understand the position of the Moon on the seventh [day] from the beginning of his illness, and the fourteenth day, and the twenty-first day, and the twenty-eighth day. **32** For indeed if the Moon reached the infortunes on some day of these, it will inflame the illness on that day. **33** And if she reached the fortunes or they looked at her, a reprieve from that antagonism will happen to him. **34** And the seventh day adds 90° to the position of the Moon, and the fourteenth day adds 180° to her position, and the twenty-first day adds 270°, and the twenty-eighth day returns to her [original] position—[and] here repeats the statement of the positions.[60] **35** And whenever the

---

[57] Reading with the Latin for "infortunes."
[58] The Latin now adds: "And if the Moon were joined to a retrograde planet, it signifies the long-lastingness of the illness. And if she were joined to a slower planet, it signifies making [it] worse, and it will render him afraid."
[59] For this paragraph, cf. *Carmen* V.42, **10-17**. But notice that Dorotheus also allows the trines, at 9 and 18 days.
[60] This seems to mean, "if the patient is not yet cured, keep repeating the procedure for another lunar month."

Moon connects with fortunes in one of these positions, the sick person will find rest; and if she connected with infortunes, the illness will intensify for him.

[Whether he is sick or not]

36 And if you were asked about a man whether he is sick or not, then look at the lord of the Ascendant and the Moon—whichever one of them was the stronger of the two (that is, the one coming to be[61] in a stake or what follows the stake). **37** For if it was in the sixth from the Ascendant (which is the house of illness),[62] or was connecting with the lord of the sixth, or in its fall, or burned up under the rays, then he is sick; and if not, not.

[Emancipation: will it happen?]

38 And[63] if you were asked about someone being dominated, as to whether he would be emancipated or not, then look at the lord of the Ascendant and the Moon: for if you found one of the two separating from the lord of the Midheaven, or from the Sun, or from the infortunes, and it is not connecting with anything of what I mentioned, then say he will be emancipated; if not, not.

[Leaving for another master]

39 And if one being dominated asked you if he would leave the hand of his master for something else, be he sold or not, then look in that at the lord of the Ascendant. **40** For if it was in a stake and not connecting with a planet falling away from the Ascendant, then truly he will not leave; and if it connected with a planet in the ninth from the Ascendant or the third, it indicates leaving. **41** And if the lord of the Ascendant was in a stake made unfortunate by an opposition or assembly or square, or it is entering into burning, he will die before he leaves the slavery of his master.

---

[61] Lit. "being" (كائن).
[62] But according to **36**, it cannot be in the sixth because it must be in a stake or following it. The Latin omits the part about finding the stronger one, and so avoids this ambiguity.
[63] Cf. *Carmen* V.37, **1**.

[Which master is better?]

42 And if one under domination asked you, "Is my master better for me, or another?", and likewise if he was wanting to change to [another] master, or he wanted his master to transfer him to [another] (and this is his improvement too, referring to the statement of the writer),[64] then look at the lord of the Ascendant. **43** For if it was received in the sign it was in (that is, it is connecting with the lord of its house or its exaltation), then indeed his master and his [current] position is better for him; and if the lord of the seventh was the one received,[65] then the one whom he wants is better for him.

44 Then, look at the planet which the Moon is separating from and the one which she is connecting with: for if the one which the Moon is separated from is the one receiving her, then indeed his master is better for him; and if the one which the Moon is connecting with is the one receiving her, then the one he is thinking of is better for him.

45 And if it does not proceed in accordance with this, then look at the lord of the Ascendant and the Moon: for if one of the two was received in the sign it is in, or it is in a sign it owns (that is, if it is in its own house, exaltation, or triplicity), then indeed his master is better for him; and if it was received in the next sign,[66] then [the other] is appropriate for him, and the one he goes to is better for him than his own master.

46 And likewise advise a traveling man on the appropriateness of the land in which he is, and the appropriateness of the land he wants to move to.[67] **47** And look likewise when starting anew [in] every matter, and the switching of it [to something else], from his [current] station to another station, and from one homeland to another homeland, and from land to land,[68] and from work to work. **48** And whenever you were asked about two things, which of them is better, then look in this based on what I have described to you.[69]

---

[64] Reading somewhat uncertainly for: فهذا أيضًا إصلاحه رجع إلى قول الواضع. Unfortunately it seems to play no real role in the sentence, and is omitted in both the Latin and *Judges*.

[65] مقبولًا, but I believe this should read "was the one *accepting* [its application]" (مقبلًا), just as in **44**: namely, if the lord of the Ascendant is applying to the lord of the seventh.

[66] This seems to mean that we should move the planet into the next sign and see if it would be received there.

[67] See Ch. 9, **63-66**.

[68] Sahl has watered down his example by using three words which can all mean either "house" or "land," so I have tried to distinguish them.

[69] But see also Ch. 16 below, and Ch. 9, **63-66**.

[Will a slave be bought?]

49 And whenever you are asked about one under domination [by one] wanting to buy him, whether it would be completed or not, then look at the lord of the Ascendant, the Moon, and the lord of the sixth. **50** For if the Moon or the lord of the Ascendant connected with the lord of the sixth, or the lord of the sixth connected with the lord of the Ascendant, then indeed his purchase will be completed. **51** Or, should the lord of the sixth be in the Ascendant, or you found a planet bearing the light between the lord of the Ascendant and the lord of the sixth, then he will attain what he asks. **52** And if there was not anything of what I mentioned, then indeed he will not attain what he asks about.

[Will his servant be bought or hired?]

53 And[70] if you were asked about a man seeking a servant from him,[71] the Ascendant and its lord and the Moon belong to the one asking, and the seventh sign and its lord to the one being asked about the servant, and the eleventh sign from the Ascendant belongs to the servant. **54** Look in the connection of the lord of the Ascendant and the Moon with it, or the transferring of the planet between the two [significators] based on what I described to you before this chapter.

---

[70] To me, this question is ambiguous in several ways. First, it is unclear who the querent is. The opening sentence first makes it seem that the querent is the current owner, so the seventh is the one who wants the servant; but then it assigns the seventh to the one being asked about the servant, as though *he* is the owner. (An alternative is that he is the one "responsible for" the servant.) Then there is the issue of the eleventh and the gender of the servant. In terms of grammar, the word is masculine (الخادم), but the Latin texts always read it as referring to a female. If it is female, then it helps explain the choice of the eleventh: for the eleventh is the fifth from the seventh, implying sexual pleasure. But if we read the servant as masculine, there is nothing really to distinguish this question from the previous one.

[71] من قبله.

[Will he get his slave's inheritance?]

55 And if you were asked about the inheritance of a slave, whether [the owner][72] would attain it or not, then look at the lord of the Ascendant and the Moon. **56** For if they both connected with the lord of the seventh from the Ascendant (which is the second from the house of slaves), then indeed he will attain it. **57** And likewise, if the lord of the seventh connected with the lord of the Ascendant, or the lord of the seventh was in the Ascendant, or the lord of the Ascendant or the Moon in the seventh, or you found a planet transferring the light from one of them to its associate, then indeed he will attain it.

[Will he get the chattels?]

58 And if you were asked about some chattels,[73] as to whether they would reach the one who asked you about it or not, then look at the third sign from the Ascendant (which is <the tenth from>[74] the house of slaves). **59** For if you found the lord of the Ascendant or the Moon connecting with the lord of the third from the Ascendant, or you found the lord of the third connecting with the lord of the Ascendant, then indeed he will get the chattels. **60** And likewise, if its lord[75] or the Moon was in the third, or the lord of the third [was] in the Ascendant, or there was a planet transferring from one of the two to its associate (that is, from the lord of the Ascendant to the lord of the third, or from the lord of the third to the lord of the Ascendant), then indeed he will get the chattels through the hands of messengers.

---

[72] This is the only thing that makes sense to me, since if the slave were the querent (and the Ascendant), his inheritance would be the second place. But wouldn't the owner have access to the inheritance anyway?

[73] The word for "chattels" here (متاع) can mean a possession, but more broadly can have to do with enjoying something (see esp. Forms IV, V, X). Plus, the house of the sought matter is not the seventh (which would be the possessions of a slave, as in the previous question), but the *tenth* from the sixth, which indicates domination or control over a slave. I suggest that the question really has to do with what is called "usufruct" (lit., "using the fruits") in inheritance law: the ability to enjoy and use something, and gain profit from it, without actually owning it outright (for example, enjoying the interest income generated from a trust, without actually owning the trust). In this case, that might mean controlling a slave's labor on a temporary basis so as to gain profit, but how is this different from the other ways we have seen a querent want to buy or have a slave?

[74] Adding based on the Latin.

[75] The lord of the Ascendant.

[Chapter 7]: The seventh sign & what is in it, of questions

[Chapter 7.1: Marriage & relationships]

[Will they marry?]

2 If you were asked about marriage, whether it would be completed or not, and how the goodness of the relationship between them would be, and if it is not completed what would hinder [it], make the Ascendant and its lord and the Moon belong to the one asking, and the seventh sign and its lord belong to the woman. **3** For if the lord of the Ascendant or the Moon connected with the lord of the seventh, or the lord of the Ascendant was in the seventh, he will get the woman with ease. **4** And if the lord of the seventh connected with the lord of the Ascendant, or the lord of the seventh was in the Ascendant, it will be attained with ease, and the woman will be more eager than the man. **5** And if the Moon was transferring between the two of them, messengers will come between them, and the completion of the issue will be in their hands.

6 Then after that, look at the one accepting the management (and it is the heavy planet): for if it was made unfortunate from a square or opposition, or it was falling, the sought matter will be corrupted after their moving ahead with it.

7 And if you were asked from what [kind of] direction the corruption will be, then look at the infortune.[76] **8** For if it was <the lord of> the second from the Ascendant, or the eighth, the corruption will be in relation to the dowry; and if it was the lord of twelfth from the Ascendant, the corruption is from the estimation of the woman's stock;[77] and if it was the lord of the fourth, then the corruption is in relation to the fathers; and if it was the lord of the third, then in relation to the brothers; and you will likewise distinguish the signs according to their essence. **9** And if there was a planet cutting the connection between the two, the corruption is from the essence of its house. **10** And if it was the lord of the second or eighth, then in relation to the dowry: there will be a twist[78] [in it]. **11** And if it was the lord of the fifth, then indeed

---

[76] That is, the infortune which prevented the marriage at the end of the previous paragraph.
[77] The twelfth is the sixth from the seventh, suggesting that she is of low stock.
[78] Or, some kind of complication or absurdity (التواء).

the woman is a widow and has a child, and for that reason there is a twist. **12** And if it was the lord of the sixth, then in relation to illness or a defect in the body. **13** And if the corruption was from the transferring planet, it is in relation to the messengers.

[The quality of the relationship]

14 And as for the goodness of their relationship,[79] look at the connection which is between the lord of the Ascendant and the lord of the sought matter: for if they are looking at each other from the seventh sign (and that is the aspect of the opposition), it indicates the badness of [their] disposition, and an abundance of quarreling. **15** If the aspect is from a square, there is a goodness of disposition, but they will occasionally shout. **16** And if the aspect was from a trine or sextile, it indicates mutual love and the goodness of [their] disposition; and likewise if the Moon was received. **17** And if the lord of the Ascendant was in a stake, and it is a heavy planet (that is, it is the acceptor [of the management]), the man is the one elevated and [controlling][80] to the woman. **18** And that one of them which you found to be falling or handing over, that is the overpowered, subservient one (that is, the lord of the Ascendant or the lord of the sought matter). **19** And if they met in one sign, they indicate irritation.

20 And if the Moon was looking at the Ascendant and she was made unfortunate, it will be abominable between them. **21** And if the infortune[81] was in the Ascendant, that is from the direction of the man; and likewise the rest of the signs, based on their essences.

22 And if you saw the misfortune of <the Sun>,[82] the harm is to the man; and if Venus was unfortunate, she harms the woman; and if the Moon is harmed, it harms them both together.

---

[79] This word (إخلاق) really means "their moral qualities," "their character." But here we are speaking of how they relate to each other, not their intrinsic character, so I have opted for "relationship."

[80] Tentatively reading for الفا, which could possibly be الفا, but that means something along the lines of "devoted to" or "friendly to," whereas the logic of the passage (and as expressly stated by the Latin version) is that he should be controlling or ruling over her: see the next sentence.

[81] That is, the one making the Moon unfortunate.

[82] Adding with the Latin.

[The runaway wife]

23 And[83] if you were asked about a woman who has left her home out of anger at her husband, whether she would return or not, then look at Venus and the Sun (which are the two indicators of the man and the woman). **24** For if Venus was above the earth, in an excellent place from the Ascendant, and the Sun under the earth, then they report the woman's return to her home, with great difficulty.[84]

25 And if the Moon (at the hour she left her home, or at the hour of the question) had already passed beyond the opposition (that is, after the [first] half of the month), then indeed her return to her home will be quick. **26** And if the Moon was increasing in light (that is, [in] the first [half] of the month), then there will be a delay in her return.

27 And if Venus, when she left her home, was retrograde [and] western, then she will return to her home of her own accord, repenting. **28** And if she was eastern, going out from under the rays, retrograde, then she will return, and in her return she will be repentant over what there was of her returning—but she will not repent over what she did, like she repented in the previous case.

[Whether she is a virgin or widow]

29 And if you were asked about a woman as to whether she is a virgin or widow, then look at the Ascendant at the hour you are asked, and at its lord, and the Moon. **30** And[85] if it was in fixed signs, then she is a virgin, clear of what she is accused of; and if it was in convertible ones or those having two bodies, then she is a widow, having already been married. **31** And if the

---

[83] For this subsection, cf. *Carmen* V.18, **1-10**; also Heph. III.11.

[84] To my mind, this combination of Venus and the Sun suggests she will *not* come back; so perhaps Sahl is consoling the husband by saying that is possible, but very difficult. The problem is that all planets eventually come back to the Sun, so any planet indicating the wife will symbolically mean returning home; the key is to figure out what kinds of scenarios will be more pleasant and easy, and more difficult (see below).

[85] For the convertible signs, cf. *Carmen* V.17, **6-7**.

woman was a slave, claiming that she is a virgin, then [someone][86] has already acted immorally with her and her virginity was taken.

32 And if the Moon was in a sign having two bodies or a convertible one, and the Ascendant and its lord in a fixed sign, then she has already separated [from another person] and her virginity is not taken.

33 And if the Moon was with Mars in a convertible sign or one having two bodies, then indeed her virginity was taken in the friendship of men.

34 And if Saturn was in the Ascendant with the Moon, in a sign having two bodies, or a fixed one, then the one who was having sex with her was doing it in her rear, and her virginity is not taken. **35** And if Mars was in a stake of Venus, and the Moon was corrupted by Mars, and Venus in Scorpio, then the woman is not a virgin. **36** And if you found Mercury or Jupiter in Aries or Leo or Sagittarius, and Mars was falling away from them both and not looking at them, then indeed she is a virgin.

[Whether she already has a child]

37 And if you were asked about a woman as to whether she has a child or not, then look at Venus. **38** For if she was in Aquarius or Leo, and with her was Mercury, then she has never given birth to any. **39** And if Venus and Mercury were in Scorpio or Taurus, she does have a child.

40 And if the Moon and Mars or Venus were in signs having two bodies (except for Sagittarius), then she has a child; and as for Sagittarius, it indicates that the woman does not have a child, and will never give birth (and if she did give birth, it would die).[87] **41** And if the infortunes were in the convertible signs, then her child will be from what is forbidden, or companionship and immorality, and she is betraying her husband; and if the fortunes were in the convertible signs, her child is from what is permitted. **42** And if the fortunes and infortunes were mixed together in the convertible signs, then she[88] will be grieved over him.

---

[86] It would have been nice for Sahl to indicate the subject here; grammatically this could include anyone, including the querent himself; but because he is mentioning slavery, perhaps Sahl means her owner or master.

[87] Or perhaps, "has died" (ماتت).

[88] The Arabic (reading the masculine) seems to mean this impersonally, but Sahl's sense seems to be that the woman will grieve. But perhaps the *querent* will grieve over the situation with the children.

[Whether her child is legitimate]

43 And if you were asked about a pregnant woman, whether her child is from what is forbidden or from what is permitted, then look at the fifth sign from the Ascendant. **44** For if Mars, Saturn, or Mercury looked at it, then her child is from immorality. **45** And if the fortunes looked, then her child is from what is permitted.

[Whether she has a lover]

46 And if you were asked about a woman, whether she has someone whom she loves, or if a man loves her, then look at the lord of the Ascendant and the Moon. **47** For if one of them is with Mars in [the same] degree, then she has a friend with her in the home. **48** And if it was in one sign, and they were not in [the same] degree, then she has [someone] nearby. **49** And if one of them was separated from Mars, then she has already had someone she loved, and she has left him. **50** And if one of them was connecting with Mars, and he is in one of his houses, then indeed she has loved a man who seeks her, and she wants to follow him. **51** And if one of them is connecting with Jupiter, then she has loved a man who is more elevated than she, and she loves him. **52** And if it connected with Mercury, then she has already loved a youth younger than her husband, and he is a writer or merchant. **53** And if one of them connected with Venus, she has loved a woman infatuated with women.[89]

54 And if Jupiter was looking at it, her leaving him was due to [a sense of] decency which took place.[90] **55** And if it was the Sun, then a powerful man has already paid attention to her, and she has likewise left him. **56** And if Venus looked, then a woman has already become aware of her—and likewise the [whole] group of the planets based on their kinds.

57 And know that if Mercury and Saturn were both in one sign, and they were looking at the Moon or the lord of the Ascendant, then a gray-haired

---

[89] **B** adds "and she is," meaning that the woman who is the subject of the question is herself infatuated; but the majority of the manuscripts make the other woman infatuated, suggesting that this woman has only passing experience with women.

[90] Al-Rijāl makes this a little clearer: "repentance has already happened to her concerning what there was."

old man has become aware of her, whose white beard is dyed [so as to look] young. **58** And if the Moon connected with them both, she has already loved a man whose characteristics are as I described.

[Chapter 7.2: Lawsuits]

1 If you were asked about a lawsuit between two people, which of them will defeat the other[91] and be victorious, then make the Ascendant and its lord, and the Moon, belong to the one asking (the one who has asked you), and the seventh and its lord to the opposing party. **2** Then look: for if the two planets connected from a trine or sextile, they will make peace before the court appearance. **3** And if they connected from a square or opposition, they will not make peace except after the court appearance and lawsuit. **4** And if they met together in one sign, then the settlement between them will be without someone entering into what there is between them. **5** And if the lord of the Midheaven looked at them both, and there was a connection with it before one of them connects with the other, then they will not make peace until they bring it to the Sultan. **6** And if the Moon transferred the light between them both, the beginning of the settlement will be through the hands of messengers.

7 Then look at the position of the two planets (that is, the lord of the Ascendant and the lord of the sought matter, and that is the lord of the seventh), and their strength, for you will be guided in that by the stronger of the two opponents: and the stronger of the two is the one whose indicator is in a stake, and the one of them that is received will have more supporters. **8** And[92] know that the beginning of the settlement will be from the planet handing over (and it is the light one). **9** And know that <if> the lord of the seventh <was in the Ascendant, it indicates the strength of the one asking; and if the lord of the Ascendant was in the seventh>,[93] it indicates the strength of the one asked about.

10 And if one of the two significators was retrograde, it indicates the weakness, trickery, brokenness, and lying of the owner of that indicator: I mean, if the lord of the Ascendant was the retrograde one, the weakness be-

---

[91] Lit., "his associate."
[92] For this sentence, cf. *Labors* Ch. 2, **34**.
[93] Adding based on the Latin versions.

longs to the one asking; and if it was the lord of the seventh, the weakness belongs to the opposing party. **11** And if the lord of the Midheaven was looking at them both, and it was retrograde, it indicates the injustice of the judge, and indeed the lawsuit will last a long time; and likewise if one of the two indicators was separating from the other (by "the two indicators" I mean the lord of the Ascendant and the lord of the sought matter).

12 And know that if one of the luminaries connected with one of the two indicators or was in its house, then it is stronger and preferable.

13 And[94] if the lord of the Ascendant connected with the lord of the Midheaven, the owner of the question will seek help from the Sultan; and if the lord of the Midheaven connected with the lord of the Ascendant, the Sultan will aid him without his appealing to him [for it]. **14** And if the lord of the seventh connected with the lord of the Midheaven, the opposing party will boast[95] to the Sultan; while if the lord of the Midheaven connected with it, the Sultan will aid him. **15** And once you understood the strength of one of them over the other, and you knew that they were not going to make peace, then look at the authority who is looking between the two of them, from the lord of the Midheaven: then view it from that one of the two indicators it is looking at (that is, the lord of the Ascendant or the lord of the seventh): for the judge will be with the one it is looking at. **16** And if there was an alien planet in the Midheaven, and it was looking at them both while the lord of the Midheaven was not looking at them both, then truly they themselves will make use of justice in what is between them.[96]

17 And[97] if Saturn was in the Midheaven, and[98] he was the lord of the Midheaven, then the judge will not judge by means of truth; and if Mars made Saturn unfortunate, the judge will have a bad reputation[99] in that. **18** And if Mars was in the Midheaven, then the judge will be nimble,[100] keen, and quick. **19** And if it was Jupiter, there will be justice; and if it was Venus,

---

[94] For **13-15**, cf. *Carmen* V.34, **22-23**.
[95] تعزّز. That is, he will aggressively seek to get the Sultan or judge on his side.
[96] The alien or peregrine planet would then seem to indicate some third party—i.e., not part of the official judicial process.
[97] For this paragraph, cf. *Carmen* V.34, **8-10**.
[98] This should probably be "or."
[99] Or perhaps, "bad criticism" (سوء ثناء): in other words, he will be criticized.
[100] Or perhaps, "rushed" (خفيف).

he will be gentle, good in character, easy; and if it was Mercury, then he is sharp in perception. **20** And if the sign of the Midheaven was one having two bodies, then the first judge will not carry out their judgment until they raise it with another judge.

[Chapter 7.3: Buying & selling]

1 And if you were asked about a purchase or sale, then look in that at the lord of the seventh and the lord of the Ascendant. **2** For if they connected, then there will be a transaction between them; and if they did not connect, and you found another planet between them reflecting the light of one of them to the other, the transaction will be in the hands of a man entering into what there is between them. **3** <And if the lord of the Ascendant was in the seventh, the buyer will be in agreement with the seller>;[101] while if the lord of the seventh was in the Ascendant, the seller will be in agreement with the buyer. **4** And if there was a fortune in the Ascendant, it indicates the easiness of the buyer, and his truthfulness (and an infortune, the contrary of that).

5 And if the Moon was not separating from a planet, but she was connecting, then the seller will sell goods, [but the buyer] will not buy them, or he will inherit them, or he will not pay for anything of its value in cash. **6** And if she was separating but she is not connecting with a planet, then the one who does buy it will buy it by means of a lease. **7** And if the planet from which the Moon was separated, was entering into burning, then the seller will be dead before the assets return to him.

[Chapter 7.4: Runaways & fugitives]

[Will he be caught?]

1 And if you were asked about a runaway or stray, whether he would get him or not, then make the Ascendant and its lord and the Moon belong to the one asking, and the seventh and its lord to the slave and stray. **2** Then look: for if the lord of the Ascendant connected with the lord of the seventh from the Ascendant, the one seeking will get the runaway through searching

---

[101] Adding based on the Latin version.

and striving for him; and likewise if the lord of the Ascendant was in the seventh. **3** And if the lord of the seventh connected with the lord of the Ascendant, or was in the Ascendant, he will come [back] of his own accord before he leaves the lands. **4** And if you found the Moon separating from the lord of the Ascendant, and handing over to the lord of the seventh, the owner of the question will see someone who[102] points his servant[103] out to him. **5** And if she separated from the lord of the seventh and connected with the lord of the Ascendant, the slave will send someone to his master, seeking safety for him. **6** And if after that the lord of the seventh connected with the lord of the Ascendant, the runaway will return to his master of his own accord.

7 And if the lord of the seventh connected with an infortune in a stake, the runaway will be taken. **8** And if the lord of the Ascendant looked at the infortune or at the lord of the seventh, his master will get him after that and will labor in it. **9** And if one of the luminaries connected with the lord of the seventh, the location of the runaway will not be concealed. **10** And if the lord of the seventh was under the rays, it indicates the getting of the runaway; while if the lord of the Ascendant looked at it, it is more worthy.

11 And if the Moon connected with an infortune, it indicates the taking of the runaway; and if she connected with a fortune, he will not be taken unless that fortune was entering under the rays, or retrograde, or made unfortunate. **12** Now if it[104] was entering into burning, it indicates his death; and if it connected with an infortune and it was entering into burning, it indicates taking possession of his corpse.

13 And if the Moon connected with an infortune, he will get the runaway; and if she connected with a retrograde planet, he will return by himself; and if she connected with a stationary planet in a stake or what follows a stake, then the runaway or stray will not leave his place, and he will be in a good state until he is caught. **14** And if it was in the first station, and it was about to go retrograde, the runaway will be caught and be bound in chains, and returned to his master. **15** And if it was in its second slowness, and it was about to go direct, then he will be taken in part of his journey: he will be tied

---

[102] Reading with **B**; the other MSS read, "something which."
[103] Or, "boy" or "slave" (غلام): the runaway.
[104] I believe this is the fortune.

up, [but] then he will escape from that and [the master] will be able to [catch] him after that.[105] **16** And if the infortune which the Moon was connected to was direct in motion, then he will return after his chains. **17** And if the Moon was under the rays and connected with Mars, the runaway will be burned by fire; and if she connected with Saturn, he will die by water. **18** And if the Moon looked at the lord of her own house, then the assets of the runaway will be taken.

19 And[106] know that if the infortune was in the seventh, then the runaway will be caught; and if the fortunes were there, he will not be able to [catch] him, and he will run away.

20 And[107] the Moon increasing in calculation and light, slows down his capture; and in the Moon's decrease, he will be caught quickly.

[In which direction has he fled?]

21 And[108] if you were asked about the place of the runaway and the object of your search, or the place of what was stolen, then look at the position of the Moon: for if she was in the Ascendant, then the runaway is in the direction of the east; and if she was in the Midheaven, the runaway is in the direction of the south; and if she was in the seventh, then he is in the direction of the west; and if she was in the fourth, he is in the direction of the north. **22** And if the Moon was not in the direction of the stakes, then look at the region in which she is, and the direction of the sign in which she is,[109] and judge based on the region of the Moon and the sign in which she is.

[Is it better to flee or return?]

23 And[110] if the fugitive or outcast asked you, "is my return to my place which I fled from better, or where I want [to go]?", then look at the Moon. **24** For if she was separating from the infortunes, then returning to the place which he fled from is bad, and if she separated from the fortunes, then re-

---

[105] I believe this means that the master has a second chance to catch him.
[106] For the second half of this sentence, cf. *Carmen* V.37, **47-48**.
[107] Cf. *Carmen* V.37, **17**.
[108] For this paragraph, cf. *Carmen* V.37, **8-9**.
[109] That is, her direction by quadrant and the direction indicated by the sign. So, if she was in the northwest region of the chart, and in the sign of Taurus, then he would be either in the northwest or towards the south (as Taurus is an earthy sign).
[110] Cf. *Carmen* V.14 and V.35. See also a similar question in Ch. 6, **42-45**.

turning to the place he fled from is better for him. **25** And if she connected with the fortunes, then where he is going is excellent, and if she connected with the infortunes, then where he is going is bad.

[Chapter 7.5: Theft]

[Testimonies of recovery and getting the thief]

1 And if you were asked about stolen goods, whether their owner would get them or not, then make the Ascendant and its lord and the Moon belong to the one asking, and the seventh and its lord to the thief, and the Midheaven to the stolen thing, and the stake of the earth to the place of the stolen goods. **2** And if the lord of the Ascendant was connecting with the lord of the seventh, or the lord of the Ascendant was in the seventh, the one seeking will get the thief through searching for him and effort. **3** And if the lord of the seventh connected with the lord of the Ascendant, or the lord of the seventh was in the Ascendant, the thief will return what he stole. **4** And if, along with their connection, the lord of the second from the Ascendant (which is the sign of assets) was under the rays, he will get the thief and will not get the goods; and if it was coming out from burning, he will get [both] him and some of his goods.

5 And if the lord of the Ascendant connected with a planet in a stake (and better for that is the Midheaven), he will get the thief. **6** And if it connected with a falling planet not looking at the Ascendant, then he has left, showing [his] disappearance; and if the planet was looking at the Ascendant, then it is hoped for.[111]

7 And if the lord of the seventh was under the rays, it indicates getting the thief; and better than that is if the lord of the Ascendant was looking at it, for at that time it indicates that the owner of the goods will get the thief.

8 And if the lord of the seventh connected with the lord of the Midheaven, he will produce the goods due to the fear of the Sultan. **9** And if the lord of the Ascendant connected with it, the owner of the goods will threaten him

---

[111] In this second scenario, while the falling planet shows some distance and escaping, the aspect to the Ascendant shows there is still hope of finding him.

with the Sultan, and he will take his goods.¹¹² **10** And if they (that is, the lord of the Ascendant and the lord of the seventh) did not look at each other, the Sultan [himself] or another whom he asks about it,¹¹³ will take the goods.¹¹⁴ **11** And if the lord of the Ascendant connected with the lord of the Midheaven, the owner of the goods will be supported by the Sultan; and if the lord of the seventh connected with the lord of the Midheaven, the thief will be supported by the Sultan.

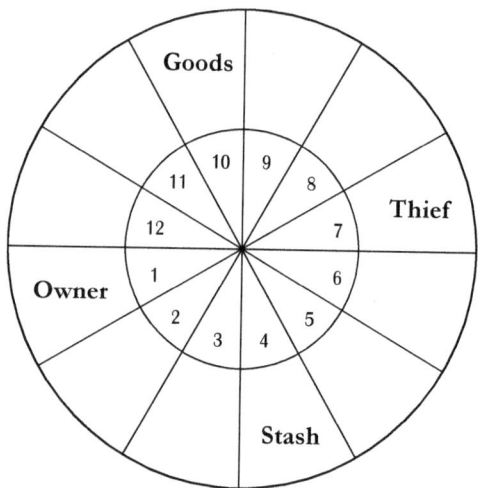

Figure 39: Angles for theft

12 And if the Moon connected the light between the two significators (that is, the lord of the Ascendant and the lord of the seventh), it indicates getting the thief.

13 And if the lord of the seventh connected with the lord of the third, the thief has left the lands. **14** And if it was in a stake of the Ascendant, then indeed the thief is not leaving his place.

15 And what the thief encounters is known from the aspect of the fortunes and infortunes to the lord of the seventh.

16 And if the Moon connected with the infortunes, it indicates the disappearance of the goods; and if she connected with a fortune, and that fortune

---

[112] This seems to mean that the Sultan (or authorities) will take the goods *on behalf of* the owner.

[113] This could also be read as, "another who asks about it."

[114] This seems to mean that the Sultan will take the goods *for himself*.

was under the rays or made unfortunate, it indicates the disappearance of the assets. **17** And if she connected with a planet in the Ascendant or the tenth, and the planet is free of the infortunes, it indicates the getting of the goods.

18 And[115] if the luminaries looked at each other from a trine or sextile, it indicates the getting of the stolen goods and what he has searched for (and better than that is if one of the luminaries was in the Ascendant or the Midheaven); and if they looked at each other from a square or opposition, the getting [of it] will be after losing hope and twists and turns.

19 And[116] if one of the luminaries looked at the Lot of Fortune or united with it in a sign, then the stolen goods will be taken quickly (and quicker for that is if the Sun looked). **20** And as for if the Moon looked at the Lot or united with it, its discovery will be difficult. **21** And if one of the luminaries is not looking at the Lot of Fortune, nor at the Ascendant, and the luminaries were not looking at each other,[117] then the stolen goods will not ever be found.

[Recovery, again]

22 And if you wanted to know whether he would get what was taken away or not, then look at the lord of the Ascendant and the Moon: for if one of them connected with the lord of the second from the Ascendant, or a planet reflected its light to it (that is, if it would transfer the light between them), it indicates getting [it], even if after some time; and likewise if the lord of the second connected with a planet in the second sign from the Ascendant.

23 And if the lord of the eighth from the Ascendant (which is the indicator of the thief's assets) was in the seventh, or the lord of the second (which is the indicator of the assets of the one asking) is in the eighth from the Ascendant, it indicates the disappearance of the assets. **24** And likewise, if the lord of the second from the Ascendant connected with the lord of the seventh (which is the indicator of the thief), or the lord of the seventh connected with the lord of the second, it indicates the disappearance of the goods.

---

[115] Cf. *Carmen* V.36, **1-2**.

[116] For this paragraph, cf. *Carmen* V.36, **11-13**.

[117] It would be impossible for all three of these conditions to exist at the same time.

25 And if the lord of the eighth (which is the indicator of the thief's assets) connected with the lord of the second (which is the indicator of what the one asking has lost, and his assets), he will find the goods and will take some of it from the thief—and better than that is if the lord of the Ascendant looks at them both, while if the lord of the Midheaven looked at it, the Sultan will take what I have mentioned. **26** If the lord of the eighth connected with the lord of the Midheaven (which is the indicator of the Sultan), the thief will bribe the Sultan.

27 And if the lord of the second from the Ascendant was not looking at the Ascendant nor at its[118] lord, the goods will disappear and no mention of it will be heard. **28** And if the lord of the second from the Ascendant connected with the lord of the third or ninth, or with a planet in them, or the lord of the second was in them, it indicates the departure of the goods to some market in town.

29 And know that if both of the luminaries were under the earth, he will never have power over the one who stole. **30** And if the Sun is looking at the Moon and the Ascendant, then the one who fled on that day or went astray or stole will be found and will return quickly. **31** And easier than that is if the aspect was from a trine.

[Who is the thief?]

32 If[119] you wanted to know whether the thief is foreign or not, then look at the luminaries. **33** For if they looked at the Ascendant, then the thief is from the family of the home;[120] and if one of them looked at the Ascendant and the other did not look, then he associates with them, [but] is not of the family of the home. **34** And likewise if you found the lord of the Ascendant in the Ascendant, or the lord of the seventh in the seventh, then the thief is of the family of the home. **35** And if the luminaries were in their own houses, looking at the Ascendant or its lord, then the thief is of the family of the home; and if they were in their own triplicities, then he is of the family, but he does not stay with them; and if they were in their own bounds or faces, then he is on friendly terms with the family of the home, and he claims that

---

[118] That is, the Ascendant.

[119] This paragraph is composed of two sources. Sentences **32-33** on the luminaries are from *Carmen* (V.36, **73-75**), and continue with **36** (*Carmen* V.36, **76**). But after each of these Sahl has inserted passages relating to the lord of the Ascendant: **34-35**, and **37-38**.

[120] Or, "the people of the region" (أهل الدّار), here and below.

there is kinship between him and them, and he visits them. **36** And if the luminaries were not in anything of what I have mentioned, [but] then they looked at the Ascendant and not at its lord, then he has not entered that house before that time—unless they were in a sign having two bodies: for if a luminary was in a sign having two bodies, then he has already entered it without the knowledge of the family. **37** Now if the luminary looks at the lord of the Ascendant and does not look at the Ascendant [itself], then he is known in the family of the home, but he has not entered the home before this. **38** And if the lord of the Ascendant was already falling away from the degree of the Ascendant, and there was another planet with it in the sign (it being closer to the degree of the Ascendant than it),[121] the thief is of the family of the house.

39 And if the lord of the seventh was in the ninth from its own house, then the thief is from a family outside the country. **40** (And[122] if the lord of the Ascendant was in the Ascendant, or in one of the stakes of the Ascendant, it indicates that the thief is the one asking.) **41** And if [the lord of the seventh] was in the sixth or eighth from its place, then it is a male or female slave. **42** And if it was in its own exaltation, then the thief is an eminent person; and if it was in its own house, then he is of the family of the house, known [to them]; and if it was in its own triplicity or its face or its bound, then he is not known in his country, but he is known among his own lineage and residence.

[Specific details about the thief]

43 And if you knew that the thief is of the people of the home, and the Sun was the indicator in that reasoning, then it is his father; and if it was the Moon, it is his mother; and if it was Venus, it is his wife; and if it was Saturn, he is a foreigner or slave; and if it was Jupiter, he is more eminent than those in the home, and one who will not acknowledge the theft; and if it was Mars, it is his daughter or his brother; and if it was Mercury, it was one of the friends who is on good terms with them. **44** And[123] if the thief was foreign,

---

[121] That is, the other planet is closer to the rising degree than the luminary is.
[122] This sentence is only in **B**. I have put it in parentheses, because **41** continues with the lord of the seventh, so **40** might be a mistake in any case.
[123] For this sentence, cf. *Carmen* V.36, **121**.

then look at the Lot of Fortune: for if it was free of the infortunes, then the thief did not steal before this time; and likewise if the lord of the seventh was free of the infortunes. **45** And[124] if Mars was separating from the lord of the seventh, he has already been punished before that.

[How was it stolen or lost?]

46 And[125] if Saturn was looking at the Moon or the Ascendant, then the one who stole did so by means of a ruse. **47** And if Jupiter was the one which signifies the thief (that is, the lord of the seventh), then he did not enter [while] wanting the theft: he entered for [reasons] other than that, so the theft happened to him, and he stole. **48** And if Mars was the one indicating [him], he did not come to the theft until he studied the house carefully or he bored through the wall of the house in which the goods are, or he broke the lock, or came into possession of the keys. **49** And if Venus was the indicator, then he entered by means of conversation or friendship, and by reason of a friend or traveler, then he stole. **50** And if Mercury was the indicator, then the thief entered the home through trickery, and he was deceptive and wicked.

[Age of the thief]

51 And[126] as for the Sun and Moon, if they looked at the Ascendant then the thief is of the family of the house.

52 And[127] if the indicator of the thief was a fortune, then he is a free man; and if it was an infortune, he is a slave. **53** And if Venus or Mercury was the indicator of the thief, then it is a maid or male servant (and Mercury is younger in age than Venus). **54** And if Mars was the indicator of the thief, then he is a grown youth; and Jupiter is greater in age than Mars. **55** And if it was Saturn, then an old man (and if he was eastern, then a middle-aged man). **56** And if the Moon was the indicator and she was in the beginning of the [lunar] month, then he is young; and in the middle of the month, in the middle; and at its end, an old man. **57** And if the Sun was the indicator and he was in what is between the Ascendant and the Midheaven, then the thief

---

[124] For this sentence, cf. *Carmen* V.36, **120**.

[125] Cf. *Carmen* V.36, **122-26**.

[126] Cf. *Carmen* V.36, **74**.

[127] For this paragraph, cf. *Carmen* V.36, **105-16**.

is young in age. **58** Then, it does not cease to increase until he reaches the stake of the earth: for that place is the end of old age.

[The place of the goods]

59 And[128] if you were asked about the place of the stolen goods, then look at the stake of the earth. **60** For if it was Cancer or its triplicity, the goods are buried near water. **61** And if it was Aries or its triplicity, then it is in a place of riding animals [or] in a place of fire. **62** And if it was Taurus or its triplicity, then for Taurus it is in a place of cattle, and for Virgo in a place of planting and food,[129] and for Capricorn in a place of sheep. **63** If it was Gemini or its triplicity, then it is in a shelf or box, or a high place, elevated from the ground.

64 And if the stolen goods are in the home, and you wanted knowledge of their position in the home, then look at the lord of the fourth or[130] the planet which is there. **65** For if it was Saturn, then the stolen goods are in the toilet of the home, and a distant or sunken, gloomy place. **66** And if it was Jupiter, it indicates the place of a garden or mosque. **67** And Mars indicates the kitchen and a place of fire. **68** The Sun indicates the courtyard and sitting-room of the master of the house. **69** Venus indicates the sitting-room of the women. **70** Mercury indicates a place of building, books, and wheat (especially in Virgo). **71** The Moon, at the well or a washroom.

72 And[131] know that if the fortunes were in the fourth, then the stolen goods are in a clean place, and have already been handed over to one who has prestige; and if the infortunes were in it, then in a filthy place, and they have already been handed over to one who does not have prestige.

[How many goods]

73 And[132] if you were asked concerning stolen goods or assets how much they are in number, then look at the signs which are between the Moon and Mercury: for if they were even, then what he asks about is bound together or

---

[128] For this paragraph, cf. *Carmen* V.36, **27-29**.
[129] This would probably apply especially to silos and other storehouses of grain and food. See also **180** below.
[130] Reading with **L**, but other MSS read "and."
[131] Cf. *Carmen* V.36, **29-31**.
[132] Cf. *Carmen* V.36, **72**.

more than one; and if [the number] between them was odd, then it is one thing.

[Is he the thief?]

74 And if you were asked about one accused man whether he is the thief or not, then let your examination be like what you look for in a report (whether it is true or false),[133] and also call upon the Moon. 75 For if she connected with an infortune, then he is the thief.

76 And if you were asked about a man whether he has stolen something [in the past] or not, then look at the lord of the Ascendant and the Moon (the stronger of the two). 77 For if it is taking something over from the infortunes (that is, separating from them), then he has already stolen—and that is more certain if it was separating from the lord of the house of assets (that is, the second from the Ascendant); but if it is not taking something over from the infortunes, then he has not stolen anything.

[The stolen goods: the bound of the Moon]

78 And[134] if you were asked what the stolen thing was, then look at the position of the Moon in the signs. 79 For if she was in the bound of Saturn, then the goods are of what is needed for the cultivation of the earth, and likewise if Saturn was in the Ascendant or the tenth, in Taurus or its triplicity; and if he was in the fourth from the Ascendant, then it is money.[135] 80 And if he was falling away from the Ascendant, and one of the luminaries did not look at him, or he was in Aries, it indicates the badness of the goods, and their filthiness. 81 And if Saturn was in Gemini or its triplicity, then the goods are a precious substance: if Jupiter was in the Midheaven, looking at Saturn, the substance is of gold, and if he was in the fourth from the Ascendant or the seventh, it is silver; and if he was falling from the stakes, then lead or what is like that.

82 Now if the Moon was in the bound of Jupiter, then look at her[136] condition and position, and who is looking at her. 83 And if it[137] was Aries or its

---

[133] See Ch. 14 below.
[134] For this subsection, cf. Carmen V.36, 44-56.
[135] Sahl is probably thinking of a strongbox with coins, buried somewhere.
[136] I take this to be the Moon, although grammatically this could be Jupiter.

triplicity, then the goods are gold or silver, and every thing worked by fire; and if Venus looked at Jupiter or he was in her bound, then it is a precious stone. **84** And if Jupiter was in Taurus or its triplicity, then it is garments suitable for kings or a jewel whose foundation is clothing.[138] **85** And if it was in Gemini or its triplicity, the goods are spiritual or something coming from what is spiritual. **86** And if it was in Cancer <or its triplicity> then they are of what comes from the water, such as pearls and [other] precious things.[139]

87 And if the Moon was in the bound of Mars, then those goods have already been processed by fire; and if the Moon looked at Venus, then they have been processed by dyes.

88 And if the Moon was in the bound of Venus, and [the Moon] was in Aries or its triplicity, then it is gold or silver. **89** And if it was in Taurus or its triplicity or Cancer and its triplicity, then it is adorned clothing or embroidered or painted fabric (and you will know the excellence of the goods and their beauty from the position of Venus in the signs). **90** Now if [Venus] was in Gemini or its triplicity, then the goods are worn [on the body], and in it is [something] of the substance of an animal. **91** And if Venus was going out of the rays, then the goods are new; and if she was retrograde or at the extremity of her course,[140] or decreasing in calculation, then the goods are money or [something] worked.

92 And if she was in the bound of Mercury, the goods are books. **93** And if she[141] was in Aries and its triplicity, then they are dinars or dirhams. **94** And if she was in Gemini or its triplicity, then those dinars and dirhams were taken from a sack or a box bound in red leather.

---

[137] Based on the model of **84**, this would be Jupiter—likewise for **85** and **86**. But in **88** this could only be the Moon. Throughout this passage in *Carmen* as well, it is sometimes unclear which planet has to be where.

[138] This probably means something worn on clothing, like a brooch.

[139] This word (الجوهر) very generally refers to something's "essence," or to precious gems and jewels.

[140] This probably means that she is about to station, at her furthest distance from the Sun.

[141] Grammatically this could be the Moon or Mercury.

[*The stolen goods: the sign of the Moon*]

95 Then[142] after that, examine the position of the Moon. **96** For if she was in Aries, then the goods are of what is put on the head and face.

97 And if she was in Taurus, then they are adorned or embroidered or painted, hung from the neck, or valuable goods.

98 And if she was in Gemini, then it is dirhams or dinars if Mercury looked at her; and if he is not looking, then the goods are of hide (that is, leather).

99 And if she was in Cancer, then the goods are of what comes out of the water or what has moisture.

100 And if she was in Leo and the Sun looked at her, then it is gold or silver; while if he is not looking at her, it is iron or brass.

101 And if she was in Virgo and Mercury looked at her, then it is dinars or dirhams; while if he does not look at her, it is clothing.

102 And if she was in Libra and Venus looked at her, then it is of what is sold and perfumed, and what women decorate themselves with; while if she is not looking at her, then it is an animal or [something] appropriate that there be blood in it.

103 And if she was in Scorpio and Mars looked at her, then it is gold or silver; and if he is not looking at her, then it is copper or what is worked by fire, and it gleams.

104 And if she was in Sagittarius and Jupiter looked at her, then it is of more than one substance, or manufactured goods; and if he is not connecting with her, then the goods are below what I mentioned, and they are not valuable.

105 And if she was in Capricorn, then the goods are old and shabby; and if Saturn looked at her, then it is of the substance of the earth and plants.

106 And if she was in Aquarius and its lord looked at her, then it is an animal or what comes from an animal; and if Jupiter looked at her then it is gold or silver; and if the Sun and Mercury looked at the Moon, then it is dinars or dirhams, and that will be in leather.

107 And if she was in Pisces and Jupiter looked at her, then it is pearls or ambergris, or something which comes out of the water; and if he is not looking at her, it is silk and of varied colors.

---

[142] For this subsection, cf. *Carmen* V.36, **57-69**.

[Chapter 7.6: Partnerships & meetings]

1 And[143] if you were asked about a partnership or association, look for the one asking from the Ascendant, and for his partner from the seventh, and for what there will be between them from the Midheaven, and the outcome of that from the stake of the earth.

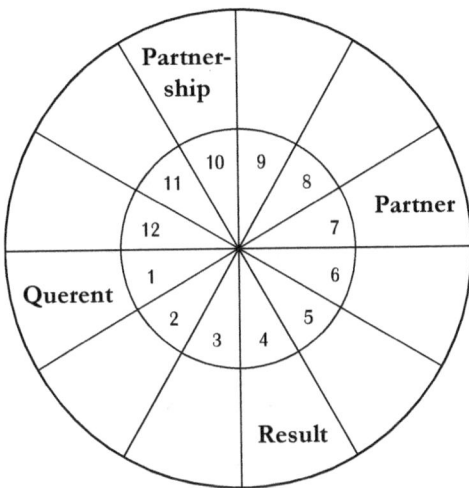

Figure 40: Angles for partnerships

2 Now[144] if the lord of the Ascendant and the Moon were in convertible signs, their partnership will not last; and if they were both in fixed signs, their partnership will have durability; and if they were both in those having two bodies, the partnership will be profitable, and their association will be with the loyalty and trust of each of them with his partner. **3** And if the infortunes were in the Ascendant, then disparity and lying and disunion will come from the one asking; and likewise if the infortunes were in the seventh, say that the disparity will be from his partner. **4** And if the Moon connected with the lord of her house, then they will separate with satisfaction and profit; and if she did not look at it, they will separate with an accusation[145] by one against the other. **5** And if the infortunes were under the earth, they will separate with

---

[143] For this question (**1-7**), cf. Māshā'allāh's version in Leiden Or. 891, f. 25a-25b.
[144] For this sentence, cf. broadly *Carmen* V.20, **1-13**.
[145] Or, "suspicion" (تهمة).

the mistrust of each one of them against his partner. **6** Now if the fortunes were in the Midheaven (and the infortunes outside of the Midheaven),[146] their profit will increase; and if the infortunes were there, their profit will decrease. **7** And if the Moon conjoined with the lord of her house, and they both connected together with an infortune, they will not separate except through death.

[Meeting with someone]

8 And if a man wanted to set out for a man and go to him, and he asked you if he would show up [and be in] his presence or not, then look at the lord of the seventh. **9** If it was in the stakes, then the man will be in his place where he is; and if it was in what follows the stakes, then he will be close to his place; and if it was falling away from the Ascendant,[147] the man will not be in his place.

[Chapter 7.7: War]

[General overview: war, its course, the commanders]

1 A question on war: if a commander asked you about travel to war (or someone worried about his matter and concern asked you), then make the Ascendant and its lord, and the planet from which the Moon is separating, belong to the one asking and the one initiating [the matter], and the seventh sign and its lord and the one the Moon is connecting to, belong to the enemy. **2** But if the Moon does not have a separation nor connection, then do not introduce her into this topic. **3** And know that the superior planets are stronger than the inferior planets in the topic of war.

4 So, look at the two indicators (that is, the lord of the Ascendant and the lord of the seventh): for if they connected from a trine or sextile, and one of them receives the other, it indicates reconciliation, and the initiation [of that] is from the one handing over (that is, the light planet of the two). **5** And if they connected from a square or opposition, and one of them receives the other, the reconciliation will be after contention. **6** Now if one of them is retrograde or in a bad place, and the one which receives it is not favorable

---

[146] This parenthetical remark is only in **B**.
[147] This should perhaps be "falling from the *stakes* [angles]."

(for instance, [in its] fall or the sixth, eighth, or twelfth),[148] he will be protected [but] then he will block him and he will encounter evil from him. **7** And if it was in the eighth, he will kill him and destroy him. **8** And if in addition to what I mentioned the lord of the seventh was retrograde, it indicates his fleeing after safety. **9** And if one of the two indicators separated from the other, the war between them will be prolonged.

10 And if you found one of the two indicators to be a superior planet, <and it was received in a stake, say that the owner of that indicator will triumph, unless it would be entering into burning.>[149] **11** <Now if the lord of the Ascendant was a superior planet>[150] and it is falling away from the Ascendant, and the lord of the seventh, an inferior,[151] is in a stake, then do not judge that the one asking is defeated until you see with whom the lord of the seventh is connecting: for if it connected with a star in a stake, receiving it, then the enemy will triumph over the one asking, and he will have the victory, strength, and triumph, according to the power of the planet which the lord of the seventh connected with. **12** And if the lord of the seventh was strong, and connected with a falling star making it unfortunate, then the enemy will still have the power so long as it is in an excellent place. **13** And if it changes out of that place, it is weak and does not cease to be weak until the lord of the seventh is made unfortunate or burned—and at that time, the enemy will be destroyed. **14** Now if it is not connecting with a planet [while] in the sign it is in, then change it over to the next sign, then look at its connection with a planet.

15 And you do not judge the course of the inferior planets except through the excellence of [their] place [relative to] the Ascendant, and its[152] safety from the [other] planets.

16 And if the lord of the Ascendant was in the seventh, it indicates the strength of the enemy, because it resembles one who is vanquished; and better than that is if the lord of the seventh is looking at it, for it indicates the

---

[148] Here the Latin versions point out that the effect will depend on which house is involved. For the second house, it seems that a cash payment might solve the problem; the sixth and twelfth each imply imprisonment.
[149] Adding with the Latin.
[150] Adding with Latin.
[151] **BL** and **L** omit this.
[152] I take this to mean the safety of the inferior planet, not the safety of its place.

victory of the enemy over the one asking. **17** And if the lord of the seventh was in the Ascendant, it indicates the strength of the one asking; and if the lord of the Ascendant looked at it, then the one asking will be victorious over the enemy.

18 And if the lord of the Ascendant was in the eighth, and the lord of the eighth connected with it, it indicates the destruction of the owner of the question. **19** And likewise the lord of the seventh: if it was in the second and the lord of the second connected with it, or it connected with the lord of the second, it indicates the destruction of the enemy. **20** And worse than that is if the lord of the house[153] was made unfortunate, and not accepting the one handing over.

21 And if the lord of the Ascendant connected with the lord of the Midheaven, or the lord of the Midheaven connected with it, and the lord of the Ascendant was in the Midheaven, it indicates the strength of the one asking, in his authority, and his victory over the one contending with him—and better than that is if the one accepting [the management] is in a stake: for then [the enemy][154] will neither endure nor covet his authority. **22** And likewise the lord of the seventh from the Ascendant: if it was in the fourth, and it connected with its lord or the lord of the fourth connected with it, and the acceptor was in a stake, then the enemy will[155] endure and one will fear for the authority of the one asking.

23 And if <one> of the two planets connected with a planet in a stake or the lord of a stake (and better than that is if it is in a stake), then it indicates the strength of the owner of that indicator. **24** And likewise, if one of the two indicators was in a stake, free of the infortunes, and it is in a convertible sign, then it indicates destruction soon after victory.[156]

25 And if the lord of the Ascendant was in the twelfth from the Ascendant, it indicates the fleeing of the owner of the question. **26** And likewise the lord of the seventh, if it was in the sixth or twelfth, it indicates the fleeing of the enemy.

---

[153] Lit., "houses": that is, the second and eighth.
[154] This seems to be the only possibility for what Sahl means: since the owner of the question is so strong, then the enemy must be the one who backs down. This is a little asymmetrical to the next sentence, which shows the enemy's power but explicitly says the enemy will *not* endure: so I have removed the "not" in **22**.
[155] Omitting "not"; see above footnote for **21**.
[156] The Latin version adds that a fixed sign would be much better, which makes astrological sense but is not explicit in the manuscripts.

27 And[157] if one of the two indicators was retrograde, it indicates the brokenness[158] and weakness belonging to the owner of that indicator.

28 And if the lord of the tenth is in the Ascendant, it indicates the assistance of the Sultan towards the one asking; and likewise if it was in the seventh from the Ascendant it indicates his assistance towards the enemy.

29 And if one of the luminaries handed over to one of the two indicators (that is, connects with it), it indicates the strength of the owner of that indicator, and assistance from the Sultan.

30 And if the Moon separated from the lord of the ninth[159] and connected with the lord of the seventh, the victory will belong to the enemy.

31 And know that if Saturn was in a stake at the question, when he did not have testimony, it indicates the prolonging of the war until [Saturn] withdraws,[160] and more powerful than that is if he was retrograde: for then the fighting will happen many times.

32 And if the Moon was with Mars, and the fortunes were falling away from her, then the one asking at that time will be killed or taken prisoner.

33 And if the Sun was with the Head or Tail at the time when he begins that fighting, there will be powerful slaughter from the two sides, and there will not be a reconciliation between them. **34** And if the lord of the Ascendant and the seventh were with the Tail, there will not remain but few of the two sides.

35 And for the violence of the fighting and its fear, look from Mars and his position relative to the Ascendant, and the one which is looking at him; and for the scarcity of the killing and its abundance, look from the perspective of the Moon, and her condition and her position.

36 And for the condition of the two commanders, and their ways or their condition, look from the two indicators.

37 And[161] look at the planet which Mars is separating from, and make it be the indicator of the one asking and the one initiating [the fighting], and [make] the one Mars is connecting with be the indicator of the enemy.

---

[157] Cf. *Labors* Ch. 2, **30-31**.
[158] In a military context, this word also means "being routed" (الانكسار).
[159] If this is correct, the ninth might indicate what is moral or religiously correct—i.e., God and the good are on that side.
[160] This probably means his transit into a cadent sign or quadrant division of the chart.
[161] See *Labors* Ch. 9, **2**.

38 Then, look at each one of the two indicators, for the weaker of them is the one which is in a convertible sign (for defeat is feared for him); and the one of them which was in a sign having two bodies indicates that its owner is belligerent; and a fixed [sign] indicates that he is self-reliant.[162] **39** Then, look for their strength based on what I will described to you. **40** If one of the two significators was in its exaltation, then it is stronger than if it was in its own house; and the house is stronger than the triplicity, and the triplicity is stronger than the bound, and the bound is stronger than the face. **41** And the more preferable of the planets is the one which has the lord of its house looking at it, for with that it will increase twofold in its strength. **42** And the most malignant which a planet could be is if it is in its own fall or a place of enmity,[163] and the lord of its house does not look at it. **43** If one of the two indicators was in its exaltation, then the owner of that indicator is a king; and if it was in its own house, then he is of the people of the king's house; and if it was in its triplicity, then he is of the children of the nobles; and if it was in its bound, he is below that. **44** And if the lord of one of the indicators is looking at it, it indicates the courage of the commander, and his endurance, and his sincere relationship[164] to the king; and if the lord of its house is not looking at it, he will not have a sincere relationship. **45** And whichever one of the two indicators was retrograde, made unfortunate, then it will bring forth what is deceptive;[165] and whichever of the two indicators was made fortunate, direct, then it will bring forth truth and religion.

[Mars as an indicator]

46 And look at Mars: if he was in his exaltation or the exaltation of the Sun, then the fighting will become powerful and spoken about. **47** Now if that was in the Midheaven, the fighting will be more violent until it is heard of in the east and west; and if it was in the Ascendant, it is lower than what I mentioned, and if it was in the west, there will be deception in it, and persistence, and the fighting will be increased in it. **48** And[166] if Mars was in a fixed

---

[162] مستقل (or, "independent"), which might make some sense for a fixed sign, but the Latin versions stay he will be stable or stand firm (which is better).

[163] This usually means it is in aversion to its own place.

[164] This word (مناصحة) also has connotations of giving advice: so the implication is that there is trust between the commander and his ruler, with earnest exchanges of advice.

[165] Or, what is "useless" or "false" (الباطل).

[166] For this sentence, cf. *Labors* Ch. 35, **5**.

sign and not in a stake, the fighting will be little; and if he was in a sign having two bodies, the fighting will be repeated and will increase; and if he was in a convertible sign, the fighting will be intense. **49** And if he was in his house or triplicity, the fighting will be middling; and if he was in his fall, it will not become powerful and [the fighting] will break off in a short time. **50** And report based on what you see of the strength of Mars and his weakness.

51 And know that if the Moon was in the Ascendant and Mars in the seventh, or Mars in the Ascendant and the Moon in the seventh, then the one going to the fighting, and the initiator, will be killed.

[Allies: Theophilus]

52 And[167] look for the abundance of the soldiers and allies from the aspect of the planets to the two indicators, and their[168] presence in the houses of both. **53** And make the second sign and its lord the two indicators of the soldiers of the one asking, and the eighth and its lord the indicators of the soldiers of the enemy, and the eleventh sign and its lord the indicators of the assistants of the king and his attendants, and the fifth and its lord the indicators of the assets[169] of his city and those who are in it. **54** Now if the fortunes were in the second sign from the Ascendant or are looking at it, or the lord of the second was in an excellent place, it indicates the strength of the soldiers of the one asking, and their sincere relationship and aid to him; and likewise in the eighth from the Ascendant it indicates the strength of the soldiers of the enemy.

55 And if the fortune which was in the second from the Ascendant was in a sign having two bodies, or in a sign of many children, or a convertible one, then tell him of the abundance of his soldiers. **56** And if the planet was eastern, in its own house, or the lord of the second was eastern, then the soldiers of the one asking will seek the truth; and if it was retrograde, then they are

---

[167] For **52-54**, see *Labors* Ch. 2, **9-13**.

[168] I have read this in the plural so as to refer to all of the other planets, which makes more sense; the manuscripts read this in the dual, as though it refers only to the presence of the two indicators in their own houses.

[169] Reading with **B**. The other manuscripts read "condition" (a difference of one letter), which makes some sense but the second sign (and its analogues in other parts of the chart) always has to do with support, means, assets, allies, etc., and "condition" does not capture this.

rebellious. **57** And if you found an infortune in the eleventh from the Ascendant, or [you found] the lord of the eleventh to be retrograde, then the attendants of the Sultan, his allies, and the powerful people of his deputies, will be dishonest—and especially if an infortune was in the second from the Sun, or Mercury,[170] and the Tail [is] with the Sun: for then the king too will have the great injustice of corruption,[171] along with[172] the majority of his friends.

[Intermediaries: Theophilus]

58 And[173] if you knew that the two commanders would reconcile, then look at the planet which indicates that.[174] **59** If it was in its own house, then the one entering between them is from they themselves; and if it was in its exile,[175] it is a foreigner. **60** And if it was Saturn, it is an old man; and if it was Jupiter, it is a powerful noble; and if it was Mars, then it is one of their own commanders, and he has already brought forth a lie; and if it was the Sun, then the head of a troop; and if it was Venus, then he does not have good breeding nor cunning; and if it was Mercury, then he is a household manager, writer, or scholar; and if it was the Moon, then a man arriving with goodness and impartiality in what is between them, or he will present it [before a proper authority].[176]

---

[170] It is unclear whether Mercury is in the second from the Sun, or an infortune in the second from Mercury.

[171] ذو جور كثير الفساد.

[172] This could be read simply as "with," as though he is bad to his friends but not the other way around; but since the sentence begins with a description of dishonest friends, it makes more sense to include them along with him.

[173] Cf. *Labors* Ch. 36, **11-17**.

[174] That is, a third planet transferring the light between them, or collecting or reflecting it. But see also **4-5** above.

[175] That is, a peregrine or alien planet.

[176] Reading قدّمه for قدمه ("he sent/sends it"). If this is correct, then maybe the Moon represents a legate from a higher authority, who is sent for this purpose. But the manuscript reading could also be understood as "he has done it before," suggesting ongoing rounds of talks or perhaps past experience: in this case, the astrological appeal is to the Moon's cyclical motion and phases.

[Deception]

61 And[177] in the matter of deception and cunning, look at Mercury. **62** If he was corrupted or under the rays, then the deception and cunning will be from both of the two sides, [each] toward his associate. **63** And if Mars was with Mercury, then that cunning and deception will appear and spread,[178] and not be covered up.

64 And[179] if the Moon and Saturn were testifying to the Ascendant, then judge betrayal, and it already has been or will be. **65** And likewise Jupiter, if he testified to the Moon and the Ascendant, it indicates <neither deception nor betrayal>.[180] **66** And if Venus testified to the Moon and the Ascendant, it does not indicate betrayal nor deception. **67** And if Mercury looked at the Moon or at the Ascendant, it indicates betrayal and deception.

[Spies: Theophilus]

68 And[181] as for the spy[182] who is between them, that is known from Mercury. **69** For if he was under the rays and the Moon [was] with Mars or with the planet Mars separates from, then the spy will be taken prisoner. **70** And if Mercury was eastern, then he will be escape. **71** And if Mercury was in a place having two bodies, then the spy who goes back and forth between them will not be [just] one [person]. **72** And if an infortune was looking down upon[183] Mercury, then punishment will afflict the spy or he will be tortured. **73** And if a fortune looked down upon him, he will escape. **74** And

---

[177] For this paragraph, see broadly *Labors* Ch. 35, **10-11**, which Sahl or his source seems to misunderstand; see the footnote for **68** below.
[178] Or, "be disclosed" (يفشو).
[179] For this paragraph, see *Labors* Ch. 17, **1-2** and **4-5**.
[180] Reading with Theophilus, *Labors* Ch. 17, **2**, for "it indicates what is hidden/an ambush."
[181] This paragraph is based on Theophilus, *Labors* Ch. 35, **10-14** (itself taken from Julianus of Laodikaia) although Sahl does not get **69** nor **74** right. **69** should read that *Mercury* being with the planet that Mars *connects with*, means that the enemy will get word of what the querent is doing. **69-70** should say that if Mercury is under the rays he will not be caught, but if eastern he will be found out. Finally, **74** should deal with planets that look at the *overcoming* planet, not the overcoming planet itself. Unfortunately, the Latin totally misreads the word for spy here (العين), treating it as "peacemaker"!
[182] This could also be read as "scout" or "lookout" (عين).
[183] Sahl is referring to overcoming, here and in the next sentence.

if his misfortune was from Mars, then the one who tortures him will be of the masters of wars; and if it was the Sun, then it is the king and the head of the troops.

[The cause of the war: Theophilus/Julianus]

75 And[184] as for knowledge of the cause of the war, look at the position of Mars: for if he was separating from the fortunes, then it is from the initiating person's search for what is right; and if he separated from an infortune, then it is from his search for what is not right; and if he connected with the fortunes, then the enemy[185] is the master of what is right, and if the infortunes connected with him then the enemy is the master of the injustice.[186]

76 And[187] if Mars was in the Ascendant, then the fighting is by reason of livelihood. **77** And if he was in the second, then it is by reason of assets. **78** And if he was in the third, then in relation to worship and religion. **79** And if Mars was in the fourth, then in relation to lands. **80** And if he was in the fifth, then it also indicates that the fighting is in relation to assets, or there is kinship between the two commanders (and perhaps they will make peace and give up the fighting), or in relation to women or a city; and especially, if you found the Moon connecting with Mercury from friendship, then the fighting at that time will be in relation to the city which they are traveling to out of a desire to conquer it. **81** And if he was in the sixth, the [reason for the] fighting is a weak matter, and killing and wounding will be increased in that. **82** And if he was in the seventh, then the fighting is based on an old enmity, and they will not[188] be seeking assets. **83** And if he was in the eighth, then it

---

[184] This paragraph is based on Theophilus, *Labors* Ch. 35, **1-2** (itself taken from Julianus of Laodikaia). But Sahl does not get the separations and applications correctly (or at least, not how Theophilus expresses it). Theophilus says that the planet from which Mars separates will indicate whether the outcome is fair (fortunes) or unfair (infortunes). Of course, this does not really make sense, since the planet Mars *separates* from should show origins, not outcomes. So I think that either Sahl is correct to impute motives to the separated planet, or else Theophilus really means the outcome is indicated by the planet Mars *connects* with.
[185] Reading for "spy."
[186] Reading for "Ascendant."
[187] This paragraph is taken from Theophilus, *Labors* Ch. 35, **7-8** (itself taken from Julianus of Laodikaia). Most of Sahl's list is close enough to Theophilus, except for the sixth house (**81**), which Theophilus says indicates mutilation and injustice as the source of the conflict.
[188] Theophilus says it will be about the means of living, which does sound a lot like assets: so, the "not" should probably be omitted.

concerns an ancient matter, and the seeking of blood; and if the Moon looked at the lord of the Midheaven, then that is because of assets, and the killing will be increased for both of the sides. **84** And if he was in the ninth, then they are fighting about religion. **85** And if he was in the tenth, then by reason of rulership.[189] **86** (And[190] if the Moon was in the Midheaven, and she connected with Mars from a square or opposition or assembly, then the killing will be about the boasting[191] of the king, and the seeking of authority.) **87** And if he was in the eleventh, <then it is about friends and those who are less than the king>.[192] **88** And if he was in the twelfth, then from an ancient enmity, and there will not be fighting, and they will listen to and yield to one who goes to them.

[The number of troops: Theophilus]

89 And[193] if you were asked about the troops, whether they are few or many, then take from the Moon to Mercury: for if there was an even number of signs between them, then the troops are many; and if there was an odd number between them, they are few.

[House analysis of war: Theophilus]

90 Then,[194] look for the whole of the matters of fighting in this section, for it unites all of the topics of fighting: and it is that you should know that the Ascendant is the indicator for the one initiating the fighting and its cause, and what is compelling it, and does he start it for what is true or what is false?

---

[189] Reading with Theophilus for what would normally be "king" (الملك), spelled the same but with different voweling.

[190] This sentence is not in *Labors* Ch. 35.

[191] Reading as فخير for the garbled readings of the manuscripts; but this could also be فخر, "honor." Another intriguing possibility is that **BL** is correct in its reading (مجير), "protector," suggesting that someone else associated with the king is seeking his throne.

[192] Adding based on the Latin (Hugo reads, "the riling up of friends, and royal patronage" in *Judges* 7.177), but Theophilus has "friendship and offspring" (which may explain the Latin's use of the word "younger" or "lesser."

[193] This paragraph is based on *Labors* Ch. 16. In Theophilus, the context seems to be that the commander has heard a rumor about troop levels, and wants to know whether the rumor is accurate (and how many more or fewer there really are).

[194] From **90-102**, see *Labors* Ch. 30.

91 And the second from the Ascendant also indicates fighting, [but] whether it will come to be or not, and whether it will be for benefit or for harm. **92** The third from the Ascendant indicates the weapons and what they are, and by what types of weapons there will be conquering and victory, and what kinds of weapons are not needed for it in that war. **93** The fourth from the Ascendant indicates the place in which the fighting is: is it rocks or mountains, or what it is, on the shore of a river or sea, big or small, or a ravine, or a place in which there are trees, or desert. **94** And the fifth indicates the eagerness of the soldiers or their mildness,[195] and their courage and their weakness. **95** The sixth indicates the animals[196] of the soldiers and what they are, be they horses, donkeys, mules, or camels. **96** The seventh indicates the enemy, and the construction of catapults, and the tools for fighting with cunning (or the contrary of that). **97** And the eighth indicates what occurs with respect to the wounded and prisoners, and the support,[197] and those who are routed, and the defeated. **98** The ninth indicates the spies and lookouts, and the secret thoughts of the enemies, and their communications[198] and stratagems. **99** And the tenth from the Ascendant indicates the marching[199] of the top commander, and the rest of the commanders who are under his banner. **100** The eleventh indicates mobilization[200] and how their ranks are, and their booklets, and how their promotion is, and how their battle lines[201] are, relative to the enemy. **101** And the twelfth indicates the city and those who are surrounded in it, and are attacked and remain in it.

102 So look at these twelve places, and the positions of their lords, and who (of the infortunes and the fortunes) is looking at them and at every house of them, and also those which are in them (be it a fortune or infortune), and those looking at the lord of every house of them, of the fortunes and infortunes. **103** Then, speak based on what you see of the fortunes and their strength and weakness: for if a fortune is looking, it indicates good fortune and the good for that sign. **104** And if the infortunes are looking from a

---

[195] Or even, "negligence" (تساهلهم).

[196] Or more specifically, the riding animals (دواب); for modern times, we could probably extend this to all types of transportation (both of troops and supplies).

[197] Probably that of the enemy (مؤيّد).

[198] Or, "reports" or "intelligence reports" (الخبر).

[199] Or, "attitude, demeanor, course [of action]" (سيرة).

[200] This would include recruitment or drafting.

[201] مصافاتهم. Reading this word tentatively with the meaning of Theophilus, as it seems to be equivalent to مصاف, but does not appear in Lane.

square or opposition, or one is in the sign, it introduces harm and corruption (by the permission of God, be He exalted), according to what is attributed to that sign, of what I have explained to you.

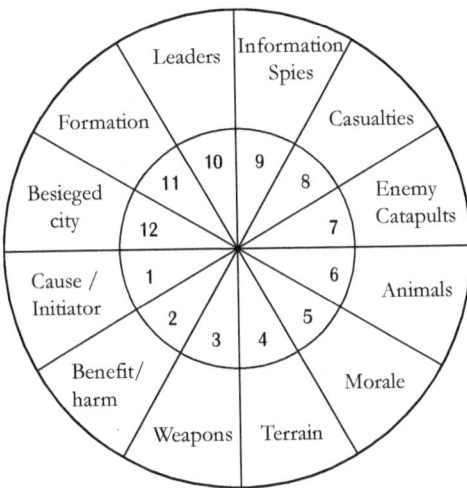

Figure 41: Houses for war (*Questions* Ch. 7.7, 90-101)

[Chapter 8]: The eighth sign & what is in it, of questions

2 If you were asked about an absent man (or someone else) whether he is living or dead, then look at the lord of the Ascendant and the Moon: for if it[202] was in the fourth from the Ascendant, or in the house of death (<which is the eighth> from the Ascendant), or they were both burned, in their falls, or with the lord of the house of death,[203] then he is dead. **3** And if you found one of the two like that, then look at the aspect of the infortunes and the fortunes to it.

4 Now if the lord of the Ascendant was retrograde in the fourth, or retrograde in [its] fall, or retrograde in the house of death, or separating from the lord of the house of death through retrogradation, then look: for if it was returning to the degree of burning, then he will be dead.

---

[202] This should probably be in the dual (referring to both planets), as later in the sentence.
[203] The Latin adds the lord of the fourth, but Hugo omits it.

5 And if the Moon connected with a planet under the earth, then he is dead; and if she connected with a planet above the earth, then he lives.

6 And[204] if you found the lord of the Ascendant in the twelfth with the infortunes (or the infortunes looked at it), and one of the luminaries was made unfortunate, then judge death.

7 And if the infortunes united with the luminaries, [but] without an aspect from the fortunes, they indicate death. **8** And [it is] likewise if the Lot of Fortune was with the infortunes in the fourth from the Ascendant, or the sixth or twelfth, and the fortunes are not looking at it. **9** And [it is] likewise if the Moon was in the fourth with Mars, and the fortunes are not looking at her.[205]

[Chapter 9]: The ninth sign & what is in it, of questions

[Travel and its outcome]

2 If you were asked about travel, whether it would come to be or not, and, if it would not be completed, what it is that cuts it off,[206] then look at the lord of the Ascendant and the Moon (and they are the two indicators of the one traveling), and at the sign of travel and its lord (and they are the two indicators of the travel).

3 Now if the lord of the Ascendant or the Moon were in the ninth, or one of them connected with the lord of the ninth, he will seek the travel of his own accord, not with distaste. **4** And if the lord of the ninth was in the Ascendant or connected with the lord of the Ascendant, then it will come to him such that he cannot avoid traveling.[207] **5** And if there was not what I mentioned concerning the situation of the lord of the Ascendant and the lord of the ninth, and a planet reflected the light of one of them to the other (that is, a transfer of light), it indicates travel. **6** And if there was not that, and

---

[204] Cf. Theophilus, *OVI* Ch. 8.7, **2** (Version 1).
[205] Both the Latin and Hugo now add an extra paragraph expressing the following points: (1) what is above the earth signifies life, and below it death; (2) if the lord of the Ascendant is burned and no fortune looked at it, and the Moon was under the earth in the third or sixth, then it indicates death; (3) this is especially so if the Moon is in the very degree of her fall (3° Scorpio), made unfortunate by Saturn.
[206] Or perhaps, interrupts or prevents it.
[207] Reading loosely for the awkward "there will come to him what does not change him from traveling for that reason."

you found the lord of the Ascendant and the lord of the ninth connecting with a heavy star, and that star is looking at the house of travel, it indicates travel; and if it did not look, he will not travel.

7 If the lord of the Ascendant was in a stake, and is connecting with a planet on the left of the Ascendant (that is, what is between the Ascendant up to the third), and it is free of the infortunes, it indicates travel. **8** And if the lord of the Ascendant and the Moon connected with a planet in a stake, he will not travel.

9 And if the two indicators connected with each other (that is, the lord of the Ascendant and the lord of the ninth), and there was an infortune in the Ascendant, in exile, and it is making the lord of the Ascendant or the lord of the ninth unfortunate, then the travel will not come to be, and that hindrance will be from the man [himself] or he will have someone who hinders him. **10** And if the infortune was in the seventh from the Ascendant, it will come to him from the land which he wants [to go to], and the thing which he is seeking will fill him with misgivings and hinder him. **11** And if the infortune was in the Midheaven, then a distraction will come to him from the Sultan or from one who is above [the one asking].

12 If the lord of the Ascendant connects with the lord of the house of travel, [but] then after that connects with an infortune from an assembly or opposition or square, then report what he finds of adversity after the travel, in accordance with the enmity of the planet. **13** If it was the lord of the sixth from the Ascendant, then illness; and if it was the lord of the fourth, confinement and griefs; and if it was the lord of the eighth, misfortune and ruin (and God is more knowledgeable); and if it was the lord of the twelfth or seventh, it indicates that the adversity is from robbers. **14** And if the aspect was from the Ascendant, killing should be feared for him. **15** And if the aspect to it is from the second from the Ascendant, it indicates the corruption of assets. **16** And likewise, the <first> square of the Ascendant indicates the corruption of the body, and the second square indicates the corruption of assets.[208] **17** If you found the lord of the Ascendant in the seventh or eighth, he will travel with hardship, and especially if it was an infortune.

---

[208] The "first" square is the dexter or right aspect, cast backwards in the order of signs. The "second" square is the sinister or left aspect, cast forwards in the order of signs. See *Introduction* Ch. 2, **53**.

18 And if the lord of the Ascendant had already begun its easternization,[209] or [its] release from the misfortune it was in, then the trip will be easy. **19** And if you found the lord of the Ascendant in the Ascendant or its other house, he will not set out, and especially if the sign was fixed.

20 And if you found [the Moon][210] received in the sign, it indicates ease; and if she was not received, it indicates difficulty and twists and turns, and indeed he will not be successful in anything in that purpose, and he will be severely hated in what he is responsible for. **21** And the lord of the Ascendant indicates likewise if it looked at her from the opposition.

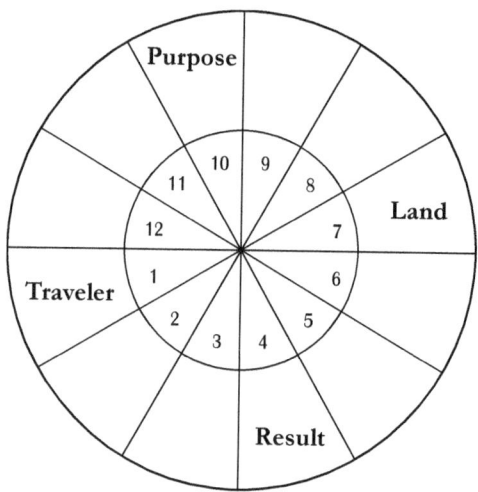

Figure 42: Angles for travel (*Questions* Ch. 9, 22-25)

22 Know[211] that the Ascendant indicates the traveler, and the Midheaven his sought matters, and the seventh from the Ascendant the land he is going to, and the fourth from the Ascendant the outcome of his matter. **23** If the fortunes were in the Ascendant, then his own body and soul will be safe; and if the fortunes were in the Midheaven, his sought matters will turn out well; and if the fortunes were in the seventh, in the country which he arrives at he

---

[209] That is, coming out of the rays so as to become a morning star, rising in the east before the Sun (تشريق).

[210] The Latin and Hugo read this as the Moon, which makes more sense given the reintroduction of the lord of the Ascendant in **21**. Most MSS read this as, "And if you found the *sign* received," which could be a misread for "if you found the *Moon* received in the sign."

[211] For this paragraph, cf. *Carmen* V.22, **1** and **5-7**.

will see everything he wants. **24** And if you found one of the infortunes in the Ascendant or the seventh, illness and hardship will afflict him, as well as decrease.²¹² **25** Now if you found the fortunes in the fourth from the Ascendant, the outcome of his matter will be to his liking.

26 And²¹³ if you saw that the travel would be completed, and you wanted to know to whom the traveler is going, then look at the Moon. **27** For if she connected with the Sun, then say he goes to kings and Sultans; and if she connected with Saturn, say he goes to the lower classes; and if she connected with Jupiter, then say he goes to the nobles; and Venus to women, and Mercury to writers, merchants, and scholars. **28** And if she was empty in course, then he leaves to search for one known [to him]. **29** And if with this she was separating from Saturn, then he leaves because of illness and blame,²¹⁴ or he seeks credit; and if she was separating from Mars, he is a runaway and like one who is on the run from the Sultan.

30 Then, look at the planet with whom the Moon connects: for if it was in its house, then the man to whom he goes is of the people of that land; and if it was in its triplicity, then he is not of that people, but he has already stayed with them and done business with them. **31** And if the lord of the house of the planet (with whom the Moon connects) is looking at it, then he is known in the country; and if it does not look at it, then he is unknown in the country. **32** Now if the aspect was from a square, then in the country he is between being praised and criticized; and if the aspect was from an opposition he is hated, a master of contentions. **33** And if the aspect was from a trine or sextile, he is loved. **34** And if it united to it, then he is of those who wrongfully take the people's money from them.

35 Then, look at the infortune which is making the lord of the Ascendant or the Moon unfortunate: for if it was in a sign of people (and that is Gemini or its triplicity), then he should beware of robbers and highway bandits. **36** And if it was in a sign of water, he should beware of drowning. **37** And if it was in a sign of livestock, he should beware of being thrown from riding animals, or catapults. **38** And if it was in a sign of vegetation, he should beware of trees and thorns, and a raised place, or food with poison in it. **39** And if it

---

²¹² Or, "need, want" (نقصان).
²¹³ Cf. generally *Carmen* V.15 and V.31, but also *Choices* Ch. 9, **12-18**.
²¹⁴ Reading with **BL** for "slave-girl" (**B**), "scholar" (**L**), "peace, security" (**H**).

was in Leo especially, the harm is in relation to lions or scorpions, or from pests. **40** And Pisces especially belongs to what resides in the water. **41** And Mars is greater in harm on land, and Saturn greater in harm on the sea.

[Entering a city]

42 When[215] the traveler enters the country he wants, see what the Ascendant is at the hour he enters. **43** For if the lord of the second from the Ascendant was retrograde, it indicates the quickness of [his] return, without the accomplishment of [his] sought matter, and he will not find good. **44** And if it was in its first station (and it is turning itself towards retrogradation), his stay will be prolonged, and he will return without accomplishing the sought matter. **45** And if it was in its second station (and it is turning itself towards moving direct), then he will return [somewhere] between quickness and slowness, and he will get his sought matter after being sad [about it]. **46** And if the lord of the second was in the Ascendant, the Midheaven, or the eleventh, the travel will be sound.[216] **47** And if it was in the seventh, then on his journey he will encounter hardship and contention. **48** And if it was in the ninth or third, then he will not linger in that land, until he heads out to another. **49** And if it was in the fourth, and an infortune looked at it or was with it, then he will delay his journey and death will be feared for him in that country, and he will in no way return.

50 Now if the Moon united with the lord of the second or looked at it, or she united with Mercury, or Mars looked at her, then wounds and the breaking [of bones] and something detestable will befall him. **51** And if in addition the Moon was in the stake of the earth, he will die from that. **52** But if she was in a stake other than that, the effect of the hardship and breaking will remain in him. **53** If the Moon looked at Mars and a fortune is not looking at her,[217] the affliction of the wound will be based on the essence of the sign he[218] is in. **54** And if with this the fortunes did look at the Moon, there will be a dispelling of what I mentioned of hardship, or a recovery from the

---

[215] For this subsection, cf. *Carmen* V.23, **7-15** (less close is Theophilus *OVI* Ch. 9.3, **5-9**). Compare also with *Choices* Ch. 9, **33-37**.

[216] This connotes healthiness and goodness (صحيح), and can also mean "complete," suggesting that the trip is completed; but normally Sahl uses تمّ for that.

[217] I take this to be the Moon because the fortunes do look at her in the next sentence.

[218] I take this to be Mars, but grammatically it could be the Moon as well.

illness and breaking and wounds. **55** And if the fortunes did not look, [the problems] will remain until he dies from them.

[The travel of kings and those left in his place]

56 If you were asked about the condition of the travel of kings and Sultans, and the condition of those who succeed [them], then look at the second: for if there was an infortune in it, not having testimony, then after his departure there will be corruption in what he leaves behind (of his family and his kingdom). **57** Now if it was Mars, then it is contention, fighting, and the burning of fire; and if it was Saturn, then [it is] robbers, and illness or drowning. **58** And if the infortune was received, it will not harm that, and it will be improved; and if it was in its fall, [the problems] will come to pass and become powerful, and more intensely than that if it was retrograde: for it indicates rebellion and corruption. **59** And likewise state suitability and the goodness of praise concerning the fortunes if they were in the second.

60 And know that when the lord of the Ascendant and the Moon are both corrupted, they indicate grief and hardship on the road. **61** Now if the infortune was above the earth, in what is between the Ascendant and the tenth, that will strike on his return; and if it was between the seventh and the tenth, then it is on his travel [towards his destination]. **62** And if it was under the earth, in what is between the Ascendant and the fourth, then it is in what he leaves behind, and that is [when] he goes; now if it was between the fourth and the seventh, then [it is] at his return, also in what he leaves behind.

[Which country is better?]

63 And[219] if he asked you, "Is the country in which I am better, or the country which I want [to go to] better," then look at the Moon: for if she was separating from an infortune, then departing is better; while if she separated from a fortune, then staying is better. **64** And if the lord of the Ascendant was good in condition, then staying is better, while if the lord of the seventh was, then travel is better.

---

[219] For this paragraph, cf. *Carmen* V.14, **1-3**. For this sentence, see also Ch. 6, **42-48** above.

65 And[220] if he asked, "Would you see for me if I should leave for this purpose, or should I do such-and-such," then look at the lord of the Ascendant and the Moon. 66 For if they were both separating from the infortunes, connecting with the fortunes, then instruct him that he should do what he wants; if they separated from the fortunes and connected with the infortunes, then he should not approach that.

[Prisoners]

67 And if you were asked about a prisoner, then look in this just as you look in the topic of travel, because they both focus on[221] departing from their [current] place[222]—except that [for] the topic of imprisonment, if the lord of the stakes are in the stakes and some of them are in the house of the others,[223] it indicates imprisonment in that year.

68 Then, after this begin with the lord of the Ascendant and its position: for if it was in a stake, his confinement will be prolonged (and the harshest of that is the stake of the earth). 69 Now if the lord of the twelfth or one of the infortunes looked at it, hardship will befall him along with the confinement. 70 And if the lord of the Ascendant was falling away from the Ascendant, and it is connecting with a star in a stake, then truly it prolongs his confinement after the hope of liberation.[224] 71 If it was in a stake and connected with a falling star, it indicates liberation after losing hope. 72 And if it connected with an infortune[225] in the stake of the earth (which is the fourth sign), and if the lord of the eighth was in the Ascendant (which is the sign of death), he will not leave the prison unless he is dead.

73 And if the lord of the Ascendant or the Moon connected with a planet in the third or ninth, it indicates liberation—and more easily than that if [the planet] was not the lord of one of the angles of the Ascendant. 74 And if one of them connected with the lord of the third or ninth, and the acceptor is on

---

[220] For this paragraph, cf. Theophilus *OVI* Ch. 9.8, **1-2**.
[221] Lit., "one puts effort on them both in" (يصرفهما في).
[222] Cf. *Questions* Ch. 1, **20**.
[223] Or perhaps more importantly, in *their own* houses.
[224] Here the falling lord of the Ascendant represents the hope of liberation, but because it hands over the management to an angular planet, he will stay in prison.
[225] Or literally, an "infortune planet" or "planetary infortune." This part of the sentence is unusual because "infortune" appears after the parenthetical remark, out of place in normal Arabic, which would normally place it just after "planet"—but this does seem to be what Sahl means.

the left of the Ascendant (that is, what is between the Ascendant up to the third), it indicates liberation, and that will be from what he does in his own matter, with none assisting him. **75** And if the lord of the third or ninth connected with the lord of the Ascendant, the work in his matter, and the rescue, will be without a demand from him. **76** And if the lord of the Ascendant connected with the lord of the twelfth, and it[226] is on the left of the Ascendant, it indicates escape from prison; and likewise the lord of the ninth (and third), if it was with the lord of the twelfth. **77** And if the lord of the Ascendant connected with the lord of the third or ninth, and the acceptor (that is, the heavy one) was in a stake, he will not leave until the acceptor leaves the sign and withdraws from the stakes; and if the lord of the house of the Moon connected with the lord of the Ascendant, it indicates difficulty as well as departure.

78 Then,[227] after you are done examining the lord of the Ascendant and its connection with the stars (and the connection of the stars with it), look at the place of the indicator (that is, the Moon). **79** Now[228] if she was in a convertible sign, it indicates liberation with quickness, except for Cancer (indeed it is slow, because it is her house; and Aries and Libra are slower for liberation than Capricorn), and he will remain in his confinement and find many allies there.[229] **80** And if she was in a fixed sign, it indicates the slowness of the departure, and the more difficult of them is Aquarius. **81** And as for if she was in a sign having two bodies, and he is not freed before the departure of the Moon from that sign, his confinement will be prolonged and become more harsh; and likewise the house of Jupiter, if he did not look at it. **82** And as for the house of Mercury, in that confinement he will see good and joy.

83 Then look at her connection: for if she was in a stake and connected with a star on the left of the Ascendant, and the lord of the Ascendant witnessed in that example,[230] it indicates liberation. **84** And if the Moon was

---

[226] I believe this is the lord of the twelfth.
[227] For this paragraph, cf. *Carmen* V.28, **1-12**; and the Māshā'allāh version in Leiden Or. 891, f. 16a. See also *Choices* Ch. 2, **1-11**.
[228] For this section on the convertible signs, cf. *Choices* Ch. 2, **5**.
[229] This must refer to Capricorn, indicating that there will be a delay.
[230] شهد صاحب الطالع على مثل ذلك. This could perhaps also be put as "in that manner," which is also awkward. At any rate, Sahl imagines that the lord of the Ascendant is witnessing.

falling, and connected with a star in a stake, it indicates the prolonging of the confinement, unless the planet is the lord of the third or ninth: for then he will be freed if that star was in a stake. 85 And if she was falling and connected with a falling star which owned one of the stakes of the Ascendant, then he will be in the hope of departing until that star enters one of the stakes of the Ascendant—for he will lose hope. 86 If the one with whom she connects was the lord of a stake and it is in the third or ninth sign, then truly that is better and easier for departing. 87 And if she connected with one of the lords of the stakes (and especially the lord of the Ascendant), it indicates difficulty.

88 And if the lord of the Ascendant was entering under the rays and an infortune was in the fourth sign,[231] then it diminishes his life. 89 Now if the infortune was Mars, he will be killed after he leaves the prison. 90 But if the lord of the Ascendant had already gone past burning, then he will become ill with a powerful illness, if the infortune was in a stake; and by however much you saw it to be farther from the degree of the Sun, it will be [that much] easier for his illness and faster for his recovery. 91 And if it connected with the lord of the eighth from the Ascendant, or an infortune in the stake of the earth, he will die in the prison. 92 And if it was with Saturn or he looked at it from strength, it indicates the long duration of the confinement, and grief, and harm in [his] assets and body. 93 And if it was with Mars, it indicates harm and chains. 94 If the Moon at that time was in her misfortune, then hardship has already[232] befallen him. 95 And if the Moon looked at her own house, it will be easy; and if she does not look, it will be difficult.

96 Then look for the adversary of the prisoner from the lord of the seventh from the Ascendant, and its situation relative to the lord of the Ascendant: for if they both look at each other from a trine or sextile, then indeed a companion of the truth[233] will undertake the effort and seek a conclusion and reconciliation. 97 And if the aspect was from a square or opposition, the companion of truth will be harsh in [his] effort, [and] insistent in his demands.

---

[231] In Māshā'allāh (Leiden Or. 891, f. 16b), this is Saturn: he is the lord of the Ascendant, burned, and in the fourth.

[232] Or, "will indeed" (قد).

[233] This phrase (صاحب الحقّ) must refer to a mutually agreed-upon arbitrator or perhaps a magistrate; it has the sound of an idiom.

[Absent people]

98 And if you were asked about the arrival of an absent person, then look at the lord of the Ascendant and its position. **99** If it was in the Ascendant or the tenth, or hands over its management to a planet in them,[234] it indicates the arrival. **100** And if the lord of the Ascendant was in the seventh or the stake of the earth, there will be difficulty in his arrival, and it indicates that the absent person is [still] in the [other] land which he is in, [and] he will not leave after that. **101** And if the lord of the Ascendant was in the ninth from the Ascendant or the third, and it is connecting with a planet in the Ascendant, then he is on the road and is intent on arrival. **102** And [it is] likewise if the lord of the Ascendant was in the eighth from the Ascendant or the second, and is connecting with a planet in the tenth. **103** Now if the lord of the Ascendant was falling, and not connecting with a planet in a stake, and not looking at the Ascendant, then it indicates a delay. **104** And if the lord of the Ascendant or the Moon connected with a retrograde planet, or the lord of the Ascendant was retrograde and it looks at the Ascendant, it indicates arrival. **105** And if the lord of the Ascendant was made unfortunate, it indicates the difficulty and prolonging of the arrival.[235]

106 Now if what I mentioned was not in the affair of the lord of the Ascendant,[236] then look at the indicator (and it is the Moon). **107** For if she handed over her management to the lord of the Ascendant, and it[237] was in the Ascendant or near the Ascendant, it indicates a quick return; and if it was in the seventh or what follows it, it prolongs that. **108** Now if the Moon separated from the lord of the fourth, seventh, third, and ninth, and she is connecting with the lord of the Ascendant, then truly it indicates the arrival. **109** And if she separated from a planet from the left of the Ascendant (that is, from under the earth), and connected with a planet from the right of the Ascendant (that is, above the earth), that also indicates the arrival. **110** If the Moon was falling, and she is connecting from the right of the Ascendant with a planet in the tenth, that indicates the arrival as well as delay, because the

---

[234] Reading with **B**. But **L** (and perhaps **BL** and **H**, which differ slightly in spelling) reads, "between them."
[235] Reading more naturally for "difficulty and prolonging and arrival."
[236] That is, if there were none of the above conditions showing his arrival.
[237] It is unclear whether this is the Moon or the lord of the Ascendant.

Moon is on the right of the Ascendant; and if she had been on its left, it would have been faster. **111** And if the Moon was made unfortunate, it indicates difficulty and being hindered from arriving.

[Chapter 10]: The tenth sign & what is in it, of the questions attributed to it

[Will he gain authority?]

2 If you were asked about authority, whether he would be successful in his sought matter or not, then look at the lord of the Ascendant and the Moon. **3** For if the lord of the Ascendant or the Moon connected with the lord of the tenth, and the acceptor [of the management] is looking at the Midheaven, it indicates the attainment of the sought matter, through the seeking of the one asking; and likewise if the lord of the Ascendant or the Moon is in the tenth, and it is not made unfortunate: for indeed he will be successful in his sought matter. **4** If the lord of the Midheaven is connecting with the lord of the Ascendant, or the lord of the Midheaven is in the Ascendant, he will be successful in what he desires, without seeking or pleading by him. **5** And likewise if the lord of the Midheaven connected with a fortune in the Ascendant, and the planet had testimony in it.

6 And if there was nothing of what I mentioned, and you saw a planet reflecting their light (that is, transferring from one of them to its associate),[238] then the one asking will not seek the authority by himself, but he will appeal to someone who will work for him in this. **7** And if the one accepting the management looked at the Midheaven, and it is free of the infortunes, then he will be successful. **8** And if it was made unfortunate, or is not looking at the Midheaven, then truly it will fail after it moves forward. **9** And know that if the infortunes made [it] unfortunate from a square or opposition, the owner of the question will refuse his associate with an ugly refusal;[239] and if it was from a trine or sextile, he will refuse with a good refusal.

10 And if a planet collected the light of the lord of the Ascendant and the lord of the Midheaven (that is, they are both connecting with it together),

---

[238] That is, the other lord.

[239] It seems to me that this is backwards: if the reflecting planet is being relied upon to bring about success, then if it is made unfortunate, *it* should refuse the owner of the question. But in any case, it will fail.

and that planet was in the Ascendant or Midheaven, then look with that at the Moon. **11** For if she connected with the lord of the Ascendant or with the lord of the tenth, it will come to be. **12** And if she is not connecting with one of them, and she was received, free of the infortunes, then he will be successful and he will turn to many people for help. **13** And if the Moon was not as we described, and the planet which collected the light was in the Midheaven or is looking at it, and it is not falling, nor is it going out from that sign before the lord of the Ascendant or[240] the lord of the tenth connects with it, and it is free of the infortunes, then truly he will be successful.

14 And the statement on [the matter] coming to be is not firm if you saw the lord of the Ascendant or[241] the lord of the tenth connecting, until the Moon is examined. **15** For if she handed over her management and her power to one of them, then it resolves [that it will] come to be. **16** And if she does not hand over to one of them, and she is received, it will also come to be; and if she is not received and not made unfortunate, then look at the one accepting the management (of the two of them):[242] for if it was free of the infortunes and looks at its own house, then he will be successful in part of what he sought. **17** But if it was made unfortunate, it indicates what I described of the corruption of the Moon, [namely] that he will not be successful. **18** And when[243] the lord of the Midheaven connected with the lord of the outcome, or[244] the lord of the outcome with the lord of the Ascendant, then he will be successful. **19** And if the lord of the Ascendant was connecting with the lord of the outcome, and the lord of the outcome connects with the lord of the Midheaven, then truly he will be successful after losing hope. **20** And if the lord of the Ascendant accepted the management of the Moon, the search of the one asking becomes easy. **21** And know that if the lord of the Ascendant was in its own house, he will be installed over the land in which he is; and if it was in its exaltation, he will be installed over

---

[240] Reading with **H** for "and."
[241] So the manuscripts, but this should probably be "and."
[242] This must mean the lord of the Ascendant and the lord of the tenth.
[243] To me this sounds like a description of a transit: that is, *if* we judge success, then it will occur *when* they connect. But this word (إذا) normally means "if," so it is possible that this is just another description of a set of conditions like any other. See also the next sentence.
[244] Two of the manuscripts read "and." To me it seems unlikely that Sahl needs both conditions to exist, as that would be very rare. But see the next sentence.

many lands, and an honored work of great seriousness will belong to him; and if it was in its own triplicity, it indicates a great work, but it will not be in his land in which he was born. **22** And if it did not have testimony in its position, then he will be unknown in the land in which he is and is in charge of.

23 And know that perhaps the lord of the Ascendant and the lord of the tenth will be one planet, such as if the Ascendant was Virgo and the tenth Gemini: now if it was like that, and the Moon was received and hands over her management and her power to [Mercury] from a stake, then he will be successful. **24** And if he was not received and the Moon was received, in an excellent position, looking at her own place, then indeed he will be successful in part of what he sought. **25** And if he was not received and the Moon corrupted as well, he will not be successful in what he sought.

26 And perhaps the lord of the Ascendant is not right for looking at[245] the lord of the Midheaven, such as if the Ascendant was Leo and the stakes upright: look in that at the position of the Sun and Venus individually, for truly if they were both received and looked at the Midheaven, they indicate their success. **27** And if one of them was received and the other not received, then look at the Moon: for if she handed over her power and her management to the one of them which was not received, he will be successful. **28** And if they were both not received, and the Moon corrupted, not received, and not looking at one of them, then truly he will not be successful; but if they were both not received and the Moon does hand over her management to one of them, and the one accepting the management does look at the Midheaven, and it is not at all made unfortunate, then he will be successful in part of what he sought. **29** And if a planet in a stake collected the light of both, [and] will not leave its place until they both connect with it, it indicates success and the attainment of what he asked about.

30 Then look at the Moon: for if she was received and is looking at the Midheaven, then certainly his good fortune and his power will be brought to completion. **31** And if she was the one connecting with the light of the lord of the Midheaven or transited it so that she connected with its body and she[246] looked at the Midheaven, he will be successful. **32** And if the lord of

---

[245] يستقيم أن ينظر. Given the example here, Sahl must mean "connect with." In the example, Leo is rising and Taurus on the Midheaven. But since Venus cannot be more than 48° from the Sun, they can look at each other from a whole-sign sextile, but not connect by degree.

[246] Or perhaps, "it," referring to the lord of the Midheaven; but if she was transiting it by body then they both would be looking anyway.

her house received her and they both looked together at the tenth, he will be successful in it. **33** And if the Moon does not encounter the light of a planet in the sign in which she is before she leaves it, then the one seeking the matter will not be successful in his affair, unless the lord of the Ascendant and the lord of the sought matter both have power and testimony, and they both look at the place of the sought matter.

34 And know that a defect in the Moon and the lord of the Midheaven will introduce diminishment in the work, and worse than that if the one accepting its management was made unfortunate: for with that, it indicates the corruption of the work. **35** And if the Moon connected with the lord of the Ascendant or with the lord of the Midheaven, it helps with the success. **36** And if the indicator[247] and the lord of the Midheaven handed over their power and their management to a planet receiving them, and it had testimony, and it was not looking at the Midheaven, then the sought matter will not be accomplished in the manner in which he is seeking it. **37** And if the indicator[248] was hostile to the lord of her house, it indicates difficulty and twists and turns in the seeking of the matter (and her hostility is if she was in the twelfth from it, or the second, sixth, or eighth).[249] **38** And if she looked at it from the seventh [sign from it], it indicates loathing and demands.

39 And know that the lord of the Ascendant is an indicator of what the owner of the authority encounters, of praise and blame, and other things from his own affair. **40** And the lord of the seventh is an indicator of the people of his work. **41** And the Midheaven and its lord are an indicator of what will come to be in his authority, of good and evil. **42** The eleventh sign and its lord are an indicator of what will come over his work after that. **43** The ninth and its lord are an indicator of what was before him. **44** And the fourth from the Ascendant and its lord are an indicator of the outcome of his command, and give information about his gains.[250] **45** His assets are from the second sign and its lord, and the Lot of Fortune and the excellence of its position, and the position of its lord. **46** And writing[251] is also from the second

---

[247] That is, the Moon.
[248] Again, this must be the Moon.
[249] In other words, in aversion to it.
[250] Or even, "affliction" (إصابته).
[251] Sahl might have in mind all sorts of record-keeping, and particularly financial records.

sign and its lord. **47** And the land-tax²⁵² is from the eleventh and its lord. **48** And friends are from the third and its lord. **49** And slaves are from the sixth and its lord. **50** And enemies are from the twelfth and its lord.

51 So look at the aspect of the fortunes and the infortunes towards these places: for wherever you found a fortune in it, there is good, joy, and profit in it; and wherever you found an infortune in it, there is evil, fear, and ridding one's hands of obedience, and fighting.

[His spending and future]

52 If you were asked on what he will spend the money he collects, then look at the lord of the house of assets. **53** For if it was Mars, he will scatter it in evil and sinfulness; and if it was Saturn, he will waste it on himself and consume the assets of others; and if it was Jupiter, he will give alms and bestow it [on others]; and if it was the Sun, he will ruin it by reason of fathers, and he will seek a high rank with it; and if it was Venus, he will pamper himself with every pleasure; and if it was Mercury, he will buy and sell and seek what is in excess; and if it was the Moon, he will seek based on the nature of the planet she connects with (and if she was empty in course, he will spend it until he consumes it [all]).

54 And the lord of the Ascendant indicates the outcome of his condition. **55** Now if you found the lord of the Ascendant in the twelfth, sixth, or eighth,²⁵³ it indicates the shamefulness of his deposing—and the most shameful it would be is in the sixth or twelfth, for with that it indicates that he will become angry about it, and be distressed, and the one who takes charge after him will gain mastery over him.²⁵⁴ **56** And if the lord of the Ascendant was received, then the evil will be extinguished and he will not be hindered nor put in chains; and if it was not received, and it was made unfortunate along with what I mentioned, then what he encounters after being deposed will be harder than the deposing [itself].

57 And if the lord of the twelfth connected with the lord of the Ascendant, and it is not receiving it, then the owner of the authority will be put in chains; and it is worse for that if it was in the stakes. **58** Now if it was in the Midheaven, then he will certainly be put in chains during his authority, be-

---

²⁵² In Islamic culture, the land-tax was a primary way of raising state funds.

²⁵³ Reading with the Latin for "second," which makes less astrological sense here.

²⁵⁴ But this could also be read as, "the one who takes charge after him will become angry at him and be distressed, and will overpower him."

fore the eyes of the people, and he will be presented to them; and if it was <in the Ascendant, then that will be>²⁵⁵ less than what I described; and if it was in the fourth, that will be in secret, but he will be in his authority;²⁵⁶ and if it was in the seventh, the people²⁵⁷ of his authority will be established as an authority over him, and he will encounter hardship from them. **59** And if it was falling from the stakes, and on the right of the Ascendant, and it associated with the lord of the twelfth, he will not be put in chains during his authority until he winds up in the earth when he is confined in it.²⁵⁸ **60** Now if it was on the left of the Ascendant, he will be put in chains [while] on the road. **61** If it connected with the lord of the eighth after its separation from the lord of the twelfth, it indicates his ruin and chains. **62** And if it connected with the lord of the Midheaven after that of the twelfth, he will attain the authority after the chains.

63 And know that Mars also indicates chains just as the lord of the twelfth indicates, if he was an enemy to the lord of the Ascendant (and that is if it was the lord of the second, eighth, sixth, fourth, or twelfth;²⁵⁹ <and the lord of the eighth>²⁶⁰ is worse because it indicates death in the chains). **64** And look at the infortune which makes the Ascendant unfortunate. **65** For if it was Saturn, it is like what I described of the hardship of punishment and confinement or beating with clubs. **66** And if the infortune was Mars, then it is from handcuffs and the pain of iron and beating with whips.

[Transition of power]

67 Now if you wanted to know his status²⁶¹ from the one who is installed over him, then look for the one asking from the Ascendant and its lord, and for the one who has authority over him from the seventh sign and its lord. **68**

---

²⁵⁵ Adding based on the Latin.
²⁵⁶ Or, "it will be in his authority." Meaning uncertain; it might mean that he will still remain the authority afterwards (perhaps a secret but failed coup?).
²⁵⁷ Or perhaps, "family"(أهل).
²⁵⁸ I take this to be a poetic way of saying, "when he is dead."
²⁵⁹ The Latin also adds the seventh.
²⁶⁰ Adding with the Latin.
²⁶¹ Or, "rank" (منزلة). But this question does not really seem to imply rank, but rather how peaceful the transition of power will be. It seems to me that something about the original context of this question got lost in the process of transmission and translation to Arabic.

For if the lord of the seventh was receiving[262] the lord of the Ascendant, or handed over its power to it, from a square or trine or sextile, then their matter will be connected [and] good.[263] **69** And if the Moon bore the light between the two of them, then between them there will be someone who will settle [things], if the one to which the Moon is handing over accepts [it] from a place it likes. **70** And as for the infortunes, they are harmful for every condition from a square or opposition, while the fortunes do perform in the square or opposition. **71** Now if the two indicators do not connect with each other, and a star does not bear [light] between them, there will not be someone between them in the way that is wanted.

[Where does a leader come from?]

72 And if you wanted to know from what land is the owner of that authority, then look at the planet which is in the sign of the Midheaven. **73** <For[264] if it was in its own house, then he is of the people of that land, the middle class of them>; and if it was in its exaltation, then from the nobility of the people; and if it was in its triplicity, then below that. **74** And if it was in something other than its own house or exaltation or triplicity, then he is a foreigner. **75** And if the planet was eastern,[265] then of the people of the east; and if it was western, then he is of the people of the west. **76** And if it was in the fourth from the Sun, then he is of the people of the north; and if it was in the tenth from the Sun, then he is of the people of the south. **77** And if the planet was alien in the sign in which it is, and it does not look at its own house nor its exaltation, then he has no worth. **78** And if there is not a planet in the Midheaven, you describe the lord of the Midheaven just as I have described to you.

---

[262] Or more simply, "accepting"; but since handing over power (in the next clause) also has to do with dignities, I favor reception here.

[263] متّصل حسن. Meaning unclear.

[264] Adding with the Latin.

[265] Normally the "eastern" and "western" here would refer to solar phase, but in **76** Sahl seems to use quadrants relative to the Sun, just as Ptolemy does in *Tet.* III.3 (Robbins pp. 239-41): this would make it possible to define 90° zodiacal quadrants from the Sun for all four of these directions.

[The length of his rule, from Theophilus]

79 Now²⁶⁶ look at the hour when that Sultan enters the seat of his power and takes his seat in which he carries out his authority, and commands and prohibits. **80** For if his entrance was in the day, and the Sun is with Saturn, then judge for him the quickness of [his] removal from that work. **81** And if the fortunes looked at the Sun, and you found the lord of the Ascendant and the Sun in an excellent place from the Ascendant and in a fixed sign, then his governorship will be lengthened and he will see what he loves. **82** And if the infortunes looked at the Sun and that infortune was Mars, and he is looking down upon [the Sun] from the Midheaven²⁶⁷ and the Sun is in the Ascendant in a convertible sign, then it is different: for one of the people of his work will frighten him repeatedly, and his end [will tend] towards killing and ruin. **83** And if you found Jupiter in the Midheaven²⁶⁸ and the Sun in a strong place, then his command will rise and increase and be renowned, and he will accumulate assets. **84** And if you saw the Sun in the eighth and sixth, and the lord of the Ascendant in the Ascendant or the Midheaven, and it is a fortune, then the work of that worker will be good, but it indicates ruin for the one who installed him.²⁶⁹

85 Now if that entrance was by night, then look at the Moon in accordance with what I explained to you about the Sun. **86** So, look at the safety of the Moon from the infortunes: for if she was cleansed, in an excellent place, it indicates the soundness of his body. **87** And if the infortunes were with the Moon or she connected with them, his removal from his work will be quick and he will complain of the worst grievance. **88** And if the Moon was with the Head or Tail, and there was 4° and what is less than that between them, then his command will not be suitable in that work. **89** And if there were more than 4° degrees between them, it will be less for her evil until she passes beyond 12°: for that is the time of her release from the evil. **90** And if the

---

²⁶⁶ For this whole subsection, see the version from al-Rijāl in Theophilus, Appendix A, passage #5. But the sentence order and structure is not always identical. Compare this whole topic with Māshā'allāh, in *On Times* Ch. 11.
²⁶⁷ Or more likely overcoming him from the superior square.
²⁶⁸ See footnote above.
²⁶⁹ فيمن استهمله. This is ambiguous, and could also be read as, "in the one whom he installs," i.e. *after* him. But the reading above is probably correct.

Moon and[270] the lord of the Ascendant looked to the lords of their houses, and the fortunes looked at them and at their lords, and the lords of both of them were in excellent positions, and the infortunes falling, and the fortunes were in the Midheaven, then the worker will see what he loves. **91** And if the Moon and the lord of her house were in bad places, evil will afflict him in those communities.[271]

92 Then, look at the Ascendant at the hour of [his] entrance: for if it was in the bounds of the infortunes and the infortunes were looking at the bound of the Ascendant, then he will be weak in that work, and ugly things will be spoken about him in it. **93** And if the degree of the Ascendant was of the bounds of the fortunes, and the fortunes looked at it, then that work will be completed and he will leave it while praise is upon him, along with favor which he will get from his work.

94 <And[272] if there was an infortune in the Ascendant, his work will be corrupted, for he will find difficulty in it, and perhaps he will die in his work.> **95** And if a fortune was in the Ascendant and an infortune in the fourth, the beginning of that work will be suitable <but its end bad>.[273] **96** <And[274] if there was an infortune in the Ascendant and a fortune in the fourth, the beginning of that matter will be corrupted and its end suitable>. **97** And if you found the Tail in the Ascendant and the lord of the Ascendant in a bad place, and an infortune in one of the stakes, and the Moon corrupted by the infortunes, then he will have assistants from the lower class who will corrupt his command, and he will not cease to be sad and frightened as long as he is in that work.

98 And if you found a fortune in the Ascendant at the hour of the entrance, and[275] you found the lord of the Ascendant in the Midheaven in a strong place, cleansed of the infortunes, it indicates the fineness of the one in charge and the length of his remaining [there]. **99** And if there was an infortune in the Ascendant and the lord of the Ascendant and the lord of the Midheaven in a bad place, then judge a quick removal for him. **100** But if you found the lord of the Ascendant to be Jupiter, eastern, and he is in the Ascendant or in the Midheaven, then nothing will make him leave.

---

[270] Some MSS read "or," but the rest of the sentence consistently mentions both of them.
[271] Or, "countries" (البلاد).
[272] Adding this sentence based on the Latin.
[273] Adding based on the Latin.
[274] Adding this sentence based on the Latin.
[275] B reads, "or."

101 Then, look at the sign of the Midheaven and its lord: where it is, and who is looking at it and at the Midheaven. 102 Now if it was in a stake, and the fortunes are looking at it, it indicates the fineness of his condition. 103 And if there was a fortune in the Midheaven, then in that work he will come to what is beyond his expectation and hope, and his work will be suitable for him, and his command will reach far, and his gains will be multiplied. 104 And if the infortunes were there, powerful hardship will afflict him in that work, and everything he gains will be taken away from him by means of punishment and chains, and being removed with displeasure in him by the authority over him. 105 And if the fortunes looked at the Midheaven, and there was not an infortune there, that work will be sincere and proper; and if an infortune looked at it, the work will be more corrupting for him. 106 And if a fortune and an infortune looked, then see which of them is stronger [and] which is greater in degrees, for it will defeat the other—except that the other will take over a portion from it.

107 And if Mercury was with Jupiter in the Midheaven, then his work will thrive[276] in knowledge, counsel, intelligence, and strength, and through that he will have a name, renown, and (based on what he is in charge of) he will increase the work or the extent[277] of the countries, especially if they both were looking at the Moon. 108 Now if the Sun was with the two of them in the Midheaven, without the lights of the infortunes, it indicates the extent of his fame[278] and his victory in what he wants, and the length of his lifespan in that work. 109 And it is likewise if you found Jupiter with the Moon in the Midheaven and Venus was in an excellent place. 110 And when you find one of the fortunes in the Midheaven, then judge for him the fineness of his behavior and his encountering the good. 111 And if the infortunes were there, and the lord of the Midheaven and the lord of the Ascendant both falling, there will be little time in his lifespan.

112 And when you find Mars in the seventh from the Ascendant, and there is not a fortune in the Ascendant, then he will die in that work as well. 113 Now if Saturn was there, and in the Ascendant or the seventh there was

---

[276] Or perhaps, "grow, increase" (يزكو).
[277] Or perhaps, "wealth" (سعة).
[278] Lit., "voice" (صوت).

a fortune, then he will not die nor be killed in that work. **114** And if there was a fortune in the seventh, then he will be removed in dignity and safety.

115 And if there was a fortune in the fourth, he will be healthy in his body, and his end will [tend] towards what he loves. **116** If there was an infortune there, evil and harm will befall him after he is removed from his work, along with imprisonment and punishment, and hardship in the length of [his] confinement. **117** But if a fortune looked at the fourth, then he will escape from that after the tribulation and hardship which will afflict him. **118** And if an infortune looked at that infortune which is in the fourth, then he will be shackled and tormented, and he will die in his confinement. **119** But if the lord of the fourth was in the Ascendant or Midheaven, or in the rest of the excellent places, cleansed of the infortunes, and the lord of the Moon likewise, it indicates the fineness of the outcome of that work.

[Will he step down?]

120 If[279] you were asked about the stability of an authority or his withdrawing, then look at the lord of the Ascendant and the lord of the tenth. **121** For if they connected and the acceptor of the management (that is, the heavy one of them) was in a stake, the lord of the authority will not depart nor leave his place; and if the acceptor of the management was on the left of the Ascendant (that is, under the earth), then he will go out from it and come back; and if the acceptor of the management was received, it indicates his quick return and his high esteem. **122** And if the lord of the Ascendant and the lord of the tenth had already left the light behind (that is, if they separated), they indicate the withdrawal of the authority.

123 Now if the Moon was handing over her management to a planet heavy in course [and] in a stake, then he will remain in his authority until that planet is burned or made unfortunate in its place, or withdraws: for with that, it indicates the disappearance of his authority.

124 And if the lord of the Ascendant connected with the lord of the sign of its fall, he will do a work in which he will be ruined. **125** And if the lord of the fall of the Ascendant connected with the lord of the Ascendant, he will be lied about, and things will be said about him which he did not do, until he

---

[279] Immediately before this, **B** inserts the view of a Sheikh Sulaymān 'Uthmān (currently unknown), on calculating the length of rule. It involves taking the degrees of the Ascendant that have risen, doubling them, and converting this number into years, months, and days.

is ruined. **126** And if the lord of the Midheaven connected with the lord of the house of its fall, then the worker will devastate his country. **127** And if the lord of the house of its fall connects with the lord of the Midheaven, it indicates the devastation of the countries.

128 And if the lord of the Ascendant was handing over its management to a planet in a stake, then the lord of the authority will be stable in his authority; and better than that is if the acceptor of the management was in one of the stakes (except for the stake of the earth). **129** Now if the lord of the Ascendant connected with a planet in the ninth or third from the Ascendant, there will be no doubt about his leaving his authority. **130** And if after that it connected with a planet in a stake, then he will return to his authority after his traveling.

131 Now if the lord of the Midheaven was in its place,[280] then the authority will not withdraw from his [position of] authority if the Moon connected with him.

132 If Jupiter was in a stake, and he or the lord of the Ascendant had a portion[281] of it, he will remain in his authority until an infortune corresponds to Jupiter,[282] or he is burned or withdraws from his place.

133 And know that if the lord of the Ascendant and the lord of the Midheaven were both connected, and the acceptor of the management was in an excellent position, not made unfortunate but *not* looking at the Midheaven, then the owner of the authority will be put in charge of what his not his authority;[283] while if it *did* look at the Midheaven, it indicates his stability in his authority.

134 And if the lord of the Ascendant and the Moon were in signs that are not convertible, and the Moon is not received, then the authority will withdraw.

---

[280] **H** adds in a marginal note: "the place of the lord of the Ascendant." But surely this refers to the place of the lord of the Midheaven itself, i.e., that it is in its own domicile.
[281] That is, some kind of dignity (مسه).
[282] This probably means "transits Jupiter by body," or perhaps even "transits the place Jupiter was at the time of the chart."
[283] At the least, this means he will be transferred or have authority over something unusual for him; the Latin reads this as being the authority over *someone else's* kingdom, which also makes sense.

135 Then, look at the Moon: for if she handed over her management to a planet in a stake, then the owner of the authority will not depart from his authority if the lord of the Midheaven looked at its[284] place. **136** And if the Moon connected with the lord of the Ascendant, and it is withdrawing from the stakes, and an infortune corresponds to the lord of the Ascendant before the Moon separates from it, then he will be removed from his authority. **137** And if the Moon connected with an alien planet from the ninth or third, or with their lords, and they both were in a place of exile,[285] he will travel away from his authority. **138** And if it[286] was in the fourth, in a convertible sign, the authority will withdraw. **139** And the most stable that it could be is if the Moon connected with the lord of the outcome (that is, the lord of the fourth from the Ascendant)—except that if it was the lord of her house, that would be ideal for her; and the worst that the Moon could be is if she connects with a planet in its fall or in the opposite of its own house.[287] **140** And if the Moon was strong in her place, and she was empty in course, it indicates the cutting off of [his] authority.

[Will he return to his position of authority?]

141 And if you were asked about a man who has departed from his position of authority, or about an absent authority, whether he would return to his position of authority or not return, then look in this just as I described to you in the first topic,[288] on the connection of the lord of the Ascendant and the lord of the Midheaven, one of them with the other. **142** For if they were connected and the one accepting the management from them is looking at the Midheaven, and the Moon is connecting with a planet in the Midheaven, then he will return. **143** And if the lord of the Ascendant was retrograde, then he will return to his authority; and if the Moon, along with what I mentioned, was in a convertible sign, it will be faster for him. **144** And if the lord of the Ascendant was not retrograde, and the Moon connected with a planet in the Ascendant or Midheaven, then he will return; and likewise if the Moon connected with the lord of the Ascendant. **145** And if she connected with the lord of the house of travel, he will seek travel of his own accord.

---

[284] I believe this refers to the angular planet accepting the Moon's management.
[285] That is, a peregrine or alien place.
[286] Either the Moon or the alien planet, but it is impossible to be sure based on the Arabic.
[287] That is, its detriment.
[288] Probably **120ff**, but perhaps also Ch. 1, **53ff**.

146 And if the lord of the Midheaven connected with the lord of its fall, it indicates the withdrawal of the authority. **147** And if they were both in two stakes,²⁸⁹ and if the lord of the stake of heaven was in its own place, then truly the traveler will return to his authority.

148 And if the lord of the Midheaven separated from the light of the lord of the outcome (that is, the fourth from the Ascendant), he will return; and if it connected with it, not. **149** And if the lord of the outcome connected with the lord of the Midheaven, he will maintain his authority as well as another authority.

150 And if the lord of the outcome connected with the lord of the Ascendant, he will not withdraw, and he will come to the position of the authority without striving. **151** And if [the lord of the Ascendant] separated from the lord of the outcome, it indicates concerning his authority that he will withdraw from it; and likewise the lord of the outcome if it separated [from the lord of the Ascendant].

152 And if the lord of the Midheaven connected with the lord of the Ascendant, it indicates the return of the owner of the authority. **153** And if the lord of the Midheaven is not looking at its own place, then he will pursue a different land than the one he is in charge of.

154 Then, look at the indicator (that is, the Moon): for if she connected with the lord of the Midheaven, and the lord of the Midheaven is not looking at its own place, then he will return; and better than that is if the Moon was in a convertible sign. **155** And if she handed over her management to a planet on the left of the Ascendant, alien in its position, he will depart. **156** And if the indicator was received, he will maintain his authority; and if she was not received, he will withdraw.

157 And if the Moon connected with a planet in the ninth from the Ascendant, then report the travel of that authority. **158** And if the planet²⁹⁰ was a fortune, and it was in a convertible or fixed sign, then he will return to his original authority. **159** And if it was one having two bodies, then he will go to a position of authority that is not his original authority. **160** And²⁹¹ he will

---

²⁸⁹ Or perhaps Sahl means, "in *the* two stakes," namely the Ascendant and Midheaven.
²⁹⁰ L adds a note: "that is, the one which is in the ninth."
²⁹¹ What Sahl seems to introduce in this paragraph is a kind of profection technique using the angular triad of the ninth-tenth-eleventh signs. The planet in the ninth indicates the first year of holding authority, the tenth sign the second year, and the eleventh sign the

work for three years (and that is because the acceptor of the management is not falling until it reaches the twelfth place from the Ascendant): it will be better for [his] work in the second year, and greater for his aspirations.²⁹² **161** Except²⁹³ that if an infortune reaches the Midheaven so that it recurs in it²⁹⁴ before what I mentioned of the time, then if the infortune reaches that place, it will corrupt his authority. **162** And if the Moon connected with the fortunes or she was received, he will be praised in his authority; and if she connected with the infortunes, he will be blamed.

163 And if she connected with a star in the eleventh, then he will work for this one year, if it did not coincide with an infortune in the Midheaven so that it recurs in it.

164 And if she connected with a star in the fifth from the Ascendant, then he will work for two years, and depart in the third one.²⁹⁵ **165** And if she connected with a star in the fourth, then he will work for one year and depart in the second one.

166 And if you found the Moon and the lord of the Midheaven made unfortunate at the same time, it does not indicate good, even if it was in the Midheaven. **167** And if you found the Moon and the lord of the Midheaven made fortunate, and they were both in signs having two bodies, then he will be advanced in his work [to] another work, and he will be strong in his own work. **168** And if he was leaving that work of his,²⁹⁶ then he will return to his own work.

---

third year. After that, the profection moves to a cadent or falling place, the twelfth (**160**), indicating change or decline. During these three years, the second year or tenth house (being an angular place) is the most powerful (**160**). But we must be careful lest, during those years, a transiting malefic should pass through the Midheaven (the tenth sign?): because at that time his authority will be weakened (**161**).

²⁹² Or, "security" (أمانه).

²⁹³ This is not really the grammatically proper place to break the Arabic sentences, but it makes more sense in English.

²⁹⁴ For more on this use of planetary recurrences, see below and *On Times* Ch. 11. The use of this term here suggests that Sahl is taking this passage from Māshā'allāh (the source of *On Times* Ch. 11).

²⁹⁵ Now Sahl or his source is reversing the order of the angular triad (in this case, the third-fourth-fifth). Normally, the triad would follow this order. But Sahl is imagining that the order is fifth-fourth-third, so that the time of the authority potentially begins with the fifth, and will expire after three years in the third sign.

²⁹⁶ That is, the common signs in the previous sentence not only indicate two types of work, but also repeating work after one has already left it.

[Will he gain authority, again]

169 And if the questioner asked you, "Will I come to a kingdom or position of authority, or not," then look at the lord of the Ascendant and the indicator:[297] for if they both connected with the lord of the Midheaven or with the Sun, and[298] they were both in the Midheaven, then say yes; and if not, then not.

[Chapter 11]: The eleventh sign & what is in it, of questions

[Will he get the thing hoped for?]

2 If you were asked about a matter hoped for, or [gaining] a position from kings, then look at the lord of the eleventh from the Ascendant. **3** For if it connected with the lord of the Ascendant, or the lord of the Ascendant connects with it, then he will be successful in that matter which he hopes for. **4** Now if the connection was from a trine or sextile, what I mentioned to you will be with ease; and if it was from a square or opposition, it will be after hardship.

5 If the lord of the eleventh was in a stake and the Moon received, then that matter will be completed for him in the way that he wants.

6 And if the one accepting the management from the Moon was in a sign having two bodies, he will easily be successful in something of that hope of his; and if it was in a convertible sign, then there will be folly in what I mentioned; and if it was in a fixed sign, he will be completely successful in his hope.

7 Now if you found the one accepting the management from the Moon to be made unfortunate, that matter will be corrupted after success in it. **8** And if the one accepting the Moon's management was received, he will be successful in the majority of what he hoped for. **9** And if the lord of the Ascendant was received, he will be successful in all that he wants.

---

[297] That is, the Moon.
[298] This is probably a best-case scenario, so this could be read as "or." On the other hand, if the querent were someone who would not normally expect authority anyway, it should probably be read as "and" so as to guarantee the otherwise unlikely result.

[Will we be friends?]

10 And if you were asked concerning a man of renown[299] if [he would] have him as a friend, and [the questioner] said, "Do you see that we will come together [in friendship] or not," then look at the lord of the Ascendant and the Moon. **11** For if they were connected with the lord of the eleventh from the Ascendant, then indeed they will come together. **12** And if the connection was from a trine or sextile, there will be joy and ingratiation in[300] their meeting; and if it was from a square or opposition, there will be contradiction and conflict in their meeting, and the irritation of each one of them with his associate (and the opposition with that is harsher for the conflict).

[Hoping for a matter]

13 And[301] if you were asked about a sought matter, and its owner <did not> name that sought matter, <and he said: "Do you see that I will be successful in the matter which I hope for or not," then look at the lord of the Ascendant and the Moon. **14** For if they connected with fortunes from the stakes or what follows the stakes, then he will be successful in it; and if they were not joined, then say no.

15 And if he> named that matter, then search for it from its position in the circle, based on what I have named for you of the essences of the twelve signs,[302] if God wills (be He exalted!).

[Chapter 12]: The twelfth sign & what is in it, of questions

[Which animal will win?]

2 If you were asked about a race, as to which riding animal will come in first, and the one asking has a riding animal or beast in the race [which is] one of those riding animals, then look at the lord of the hour in which he

---

[299] رجل ذكر. But perhaps this could be understood as رجل مذكور, "a stated man," meaning a *specific* man.
[300] Some manuscripts read, "from," referring to what will be the result.
[301] In this section, I have added material in brackets based on the Latin, using the style and vocabulary of the Arabic.
[302] **B** reads: "houses." In other words, if he states the topic, then it is no longer an eleventh-house topic, but seventh (for marriage), fifth (for children), and so on.

asks. **3** Now if it was in the Ascendant, then the animal which concerns him will beat [the other] animals; and if it was in the Midheaven, then it will come in second (and likewise in the eleventh); and if it was in the seventh from the Ascendant then it will be in the middle of them; and if it was in the fourth from the Ascendant, then it will be the last of them, with no animal after it. **4** And if the lord of the hour was in its own fall, then a wound will afflict the rider and he will fall from the animal. **5** And if, along with what I mentioned, the infortunes look at it, then the part of his body which the sign is an indicator of, will be broken. **6** And if an infortune looked at it from an opposition or union, and the lord of the hour is in the eighth from its own house, then the rider will die from his fall; and worse than that is if the lord of that house or the Moon is made unfortunate.

7 And if one who does not own one of the animals asked you, then look at the lord of the hour. **8** Now if it was in the Ascendant, or you found a planet in the Ascendant, Midheaven, or the eleventh, then the winner on that day will be the animal of the color of that star which is in one of these places.[303] **9** If the indicator of the winner is in its own <house or>[304] exaltation, triplicity, bound, or face, then the animal which comes in first will be known and pedigreed.[305] **10** And the more preferable of that is the house and exaltation; and what is other than that is not as powerful. **11** And if it is not in anything of what I mentioned to you,[306] then it is an outsider and unknown. **12** And if along with what I mentioned to you it was in its own fall, then along with being unknown it will be ugly and have a bad disposition. **13** And in the house and exaltation <it will be pedigreed, in the triplicity it will not be

---

[303] According to al-Qabīsī (Ch. 2, *passim*): Saturn is black, Jupiter dusty or green, Mars red, the Sun is transparent or shimmering, Venus whiteness, Mercury is motley or sky-blue, the Moon yellow. But according to ʿUmar's colors for robes in magical workings (Dykes 2018), Saturn is black or grey, Jupiter white or "bright," Mars red, the Sun bright, royal colors (probably including gold), Venus clean (probably white), Mercury silver, the Moon white or silver.

[304] Adding based on the Latin, and with **10**.

[305] منسوبة, which means that it can be "attributed" to some lineage.

[306] Thus, it is peregrine or alien.

known nor pedigreed, and in the bound or face>³⁰⁷ it will not be pedigreed [but will be] known in the country.³⁰⁸

14 And if you were asked what its age is, then look at the indicator. **15** For³⁰⁹ if it was eastern then it (that is, the riding animal) is two; and if it was western, then it is mature; and if it was in what is between those, then it is four.

16 And if you do not find what I mentioned to you, then look at the Ascendant. **17** Now if it was the house of the Sun, then the winner is of the animals of kings; and if it was a house of Saturn, then the animal belongs to an old man (and perhaps he will not have esteem, unless Saturn is in a stake or an excellent place); and if it was a house of Jupiter, then the winner is an animal belonging to some of the socially prominent people, of those who attend the Sultan; and if it was a house of Mars, then the winner belongs to one of the commanders and to one who wears weapons, and the masters of wars; and if it was a house of Venus and Mercury, then it belongs to one of the kings or to a woman or writer; and if it was the house of the Moon, then to one of the merchants, and to one involved in selling and buying.

[Enemies?]

18 Now if you were asked about enemies in general, <that is known> from the twelfth house and its lord:³¹⁰ look in what there is between them in terms of their connection, based on what I have explained to you.³¹¹

---

³⁰⁷ Adding with the Latin, taking the ما ("not") from **L** as a cue that something is missing in the Arabic (although ما is not normally used with the imperfect). Without this addition, it would simply say that the house and exaltation indicate being pedigreed and known.

³⁰⁸ The Latin now adds that the triplicity means being both unknown and not pedigreed; in the bound or face, it will be known but not pedigreed. But because these precise distinctions seem astrologically unclear to me (especially since one would expect the triplicity to be better), I omit them.

³⁰⁹ In this sentence, Sahl uses traditional Arabic terms for associating horses' teeth with their age, since the age of a horse may often be judged roughly based on the shape and type of teeth they have. "Two" here (ثني) refers to 2-3 years old, when the adult or "second" teeth (ثنية) begin to grow in (note that Lane pp. 358-59 seems to say that these teeth are *lost* then). "Mature" here (قارح) refers to teeth or a quality of teeth after a horse is about 6 years. "Four" (رباع) refers to the teeth at about four years old. Of course, if one is racing camels or other animals, the basic idea is that the animal is young, older (but not too old to race), or in the middle.

³¹⁰ This should probably include the lord of the Ascendant, too.

19 I have already explained the sought matters and questions in the twelve houses to you, and I will expound to you what is not in the twelve houses, lest you err: for indeed the scholars have erred in that. **20** And take what is not in the twelve houses from the essences of the planets, for there are more matters than can be comprehended[312] in a book one is proficient in.

Chapter [13]: On books & messengers

2 If you were asked about a book[313] or messengers, then look for the one who wrote the book from the Ascendant or the one from which the Moon separates; and for the one who wrote him the book, [look] from the sign of the seventh and its lord; and for what is hoped for, or what is feared, or what is in the soul of the two men, and their condition, [look] from the lord of the Ascendant and the lord of the seventh and their positions, based on the aspect of the fortunes and infortunes to them both. **3** For whichever one of them is in the stakes or in a position in which it is received, and is looking at its own place, that one is more mighty in rank.

4 And[314] if you found the planet from which the Moon separated to be a fortune or[315] in its own exaltation, then the book is from a companion of the Sultan. **5** Now if it was withdrawing from the stakes, then he has already had the authority, then he withdrew from it. **6** And if it was in its own house and it is in a stake, then it is from the people of a house of well-known people, and he is also from that house, and he has rank. **7** And the triplicity is below the house, and likewise the bound below the triplicity, and the face below the bound. **8** Now if it was in an excellent position relative to the Ascendant and is not received, then he does not have rank but [also] is neither praised nor in poor standing among the people of his house. **9** And if it was in its own fall,

---

[311] See *Nativities* Ch. 12.1, **24-34**, from Māshā'allāh (which suggests that perhaps this material is from him, too).

[312] Reading the rest of the sentence with **B**.

[313] "Book" (كتاب) can mean any type of writing; the Latin translations understand this as a letter, which is a valid translation. But I will stick to the normal translation, as "letter" also has its own particular word.

[314] For this paragraph, cf. Māshā'allāh's version in Leiden, Or. 891, ff. 17a-17b (which Sahl abbreviates here).

[315] This should be understood as "and," as with the following sentences.

and it is in a stake, then the one who wrote the book does not have esteem but he is with the authority and one who has prominence. **10** And if it was in its own fall and it is falling, he will not have esteem nor recognition among the people. **11** If it was not looking at the Ascendant nor looking at the lord of its own house, then the owner of the book has no power over anything except what he eats day by day. **12** And if with that a fortune looks at it, it will be from one who works and eats with his own hands. **13** And if the Moon separated from the infortunes, then it will be like what I have described, but along with that it is someone wicked in condition, concealing his heart.

14 <And[316] if the Moon was separated from a square or opposition or assembly, it signifies the hardness of the owner of the book; and more strongly than that if the Moon was in a stake and in her own sign, because it indicates that the one who wrote the book is of a good condition in his matter, but what disturbs him is in the book.

15 Then,[317] look for him to whom the book goes, from the planet with which the Moon is connecting, and report his condition according to what I described to you of the planet from which the Moon is separating. **16** And know that if the Moon separated from Saturn and Mercury was made unfortunate, there will be labor in the letter, and a hard matter; and if she separated from Jupiter, the letter will be from one of the nobility; and if from Mars, it will be a warrior who operates through blood and iron; and if from the Sun, it will be from the king; and if from Venus, then from a woman (but if it was from[318] Saturn, there will be a defect in her); and if it was from Mercury, it will be from a writer or merchant. **17** And if you were asked about the nature of the man to whom the book comes, then look at the Moon and her connection in this: if she is connecting with Saturn, the letter was sent to an old man; if Jupiter, to a noble; if Venus, to a woman; and it is likewise for the rest of the planets, according to their essences.>

---

[316] All four MSS now jump to the fifth house below (**25**). Unfortunately, I cannot locate the following sentences in *Judges* (under Sahl's name) or in al-Rijāl, so I have used the Latin version to rewrite them as sentences **14-17**, using the typical Arabic style. In **18**, I have adopted the reading of al-Rijāl's I.58, which is the same as that identified as al-Khayyāt in *Judges* 5.67 (Sahl and al-Khayyāt often have virtually identical readings in Hugo's Latin, and differ only in Hugo's style, not the content). Following that, I again reproduce the Latin's version of the first four houses before resuming with Sahl's Arabic.

[317] For this paragraph, cf. Māshā'allāh's version in Leiden, Or. 891, ff. 18a-18b.

[318] This should probably read, "if she was *with* Saturn." But if we compare it with Māshā'allāh I think it should read as follows: "but if it was from a man, then there is a defect in him." The words for "man" (رجل) and "Saturn" (زحل) are easy to mix up.

18 <If you were asked concerning the book, what is generally in it of good or bad, then look from the one Mercury or the Moon separated from: because writing[319] and reports[320] are from Mercury and the Moon (and the lord of the third and the ninth have a weak partnership in this). **19** For if the separation of them both was from a fortune, then there is good in the book; or, if the separation of them both was from an infortune, then it is the contrary of that.>

20 <Then,[321] look at the planet from which the Moon[322] separated, and at Mercury himself (that is, at the stronger of the two), and establish this one as the indicator. **21** For if it was in the Ascendant, there will be health and profit in it, and repayment. **22** And if it was in the second from the Ascendant, the book will be with assets (that is, in giving and taking them) and what is like this of assets. **23** And if it was in the third, it will be because of a brother or friend, and in the book he has described a journey which concerns him, or he is asking about its nature. **24** And if it was in the fourth from the Ascendant, in the book will be a mention of land, or perhaps the book will be from a relative of his who is greater than him in age, or it is about an ancient matter.> **25** And if it was in the fifth, then the book is about something he hopes for, and it is from a child or friend. **26** And if it was in the sixth, the book is from a slave; and if an infortune was looking at that place, the book is from a sick person or [is about] the affair of a sick person. **27** And if it was in the seventh, then the book is from a woman. **28** And if it was in the eighth, the book is about injustice[323] and inheritance. **29** And[324] if it was in the ninth, then the book is a sermon, and it mentions the Lord, and in it is mention of a journey or the withdrawal of the Sultan. **30** And if it was in the tenth, then the book is from the Sultan and it mentions kings and the mighty. **31** And if it was in the eleventh, then the book is from a friend and in his book is what

---

[319] Lit. "the book" or "the writing" (الكتاب) but treating as the verbal noun (الكتابة).

[320] Or, "communication" (read as إخبار).

[321] Again, I have adapted the following sentences concerning the first four houses, based on the Latin. Sahl's Arabic text resumes with **25**. But this is preserved well in Māshā'allāh, Leiden Or. 891, ff. 17b-18a.

[322] The Latin reads "Mercury," but the Māshā'allāh text is clear it is the Moon.

[323] Reading بغي with the Māshā'allāh text, for what looks like لعيا or لعبا. But an intriguing option is the verbal noun لقيًا, which would refer to something cast off or discarded.

[324] B reads: "And if it was in the ninth, then the book is from a journey or lecture, or the removal of one having an office."

delights him. **32** If it was in the twelfth, the book concerns a contention or it is from an enemy.

33 And if you wrote a book and you wanted to know its arrival and what [that] will be, then look for that from the first connection (and it is the indicator for what comes first), and from the second connection (the indicator for the arrival of the book).

34 If you were asked about a book, whether it is sealed or not, then look at the Moon. **35** For if she was connected with Mercury, then say it is sealed (and one does not want the Ascendant). **36** And if she was already separated and had gone past by the amount of 2° or 3°, then say it is sealed; and if not, then not.

37 And[325] if you were asked about a book, if it comes from the residence of the Sultan or not, then look at Mercury. **38** Now if you found him already separated from the Sun or from the lord of the Midheaven by a close separation, then say it does come [from there]; and if not, then not.

39 If you were asked about a book, if it will reach the Sultan or king or not, then look at Mercury. **40** For if he connected with the lord of the Midheaven or the Sun, then say it will arrive; and if not, then not.

Chapter [14]: On reports

[Whether the report is true or false]

2 If you were asked about a report, as to whether it is true or false,[326] then look at the lord of the Ascendant and the Moon, [namely] their being in the stakes, and begin with [the lord of the Ascendant].[327] **3** For if it was in a stake, free of the infortunes, not connecting with a falling star, then the report is true. **4** And if it was in a stake and was connecting with a falling star not receiving it, then there has already been mention of it, but it is not being spoken of and will not come to pass. **5** And if the lord of the Ascendant was not in a stake and it is connecting with a planet in a stake, then that report is

---

[325] **B** puts this paragraph (**37-38**) after the next (**39-40**).

[326] This word (باطل) also connotes what is empty or futile, so we can imagine a general getting a report that is not simply "false," but perhaps is of little value, or won't matter in the end, or is confused.

[327] The Arabic reads only "it," but the following sentences make it clear that Sahl means the lord of the Ascendant.

going to be true and appear—if it was a fortune; if it was an infortune, and it is not receiving the lord of the Ascendant, then the report is going to be false. **6** And if the lord of the Ascendant connected with a falling planet, then the report is a lie unless the planet was receiving the lord of the Ascendant.

7 And if the lord of the Ascendant connected with an infortune not receiving it, it indicates the corruption of the report, and that is going to be on the part of the owner of the question. **8** And if the infortune was the one which connects with the lord of the Ascendant, then the corruption will come from somewhere else, and the report goes on [from there].[328]

9 Then,[329] look at the Moon and call upon her testimony, along with the lord of the Ascendant. **10** And if <the lord of> the Ascendant is greater in testimony, <then call upon it>; and if the Moon was the powerful one, then call upon her (along with the lord of the Ascendant). **11** And if it was in a convertible sign or the Ascendant was convertible, and one of the infortunes looked at it, then the report is a lie. **12** And likewise if the Moon was empty in course, and likewise if the Moon connected with a retrograde planet, even if it was receiving her. **13** And likewise if the Moon connected with a falling planet, and more firmly than that is if it was an infortune: for then it indicates a lie (and likewise even if she was received). **14** And if she was in a stake and was made unfortunate, and that infortune is not receiving her, then it is false. **15** Now if she connected with a planet receiving her in a stake, it indicates the rightness and truthfulness of the report, and one should not seek additional testimony. **16** If she connected with a fortune in a stake (and the best of that is the Midheaven and Ascendant), it indicates that the report is true. **17** And if in addition the acceptor was safe from the infortunes and retrogradation, the report is sound. **18** Now if she was made unfortunate by a planet not receiving her or retrograde, it indicates corruption after moving forward.[330] **19** And likewise if the Moon connected with a planet receiving her in a stake or somewhere else, and the planet was made unfortunate, it indicates the corruption of the report. **20** And if she connected with a falling planet, it indicates a lie if she was not received.

---

[328] The Latin has it that the report is corrupted or destroyed, which could be possible if يتّصل should be read as يفسد. In certain handwriting (such as in **H**) this is easily imaginable.

[329] For this paragraph, cf. the Māshā'allāh version in Leiden, Or. 891, f. 18b.

[330] I take this to mean that *events* move forward, not that things will be corrupted when the *planet* moves forward.

21 And[331] if she handed over her management to a planet in a stake, then the report is true. **22** And if that planet was in the Midheaven, then the people already know of the report, and it is appearing. **23** Now if it was in the Ascendant, it has begun and will appear. **24** And if it was in the seventh, it has already become plain and appeared, and it will appear. **25** And if it was in the fourth, then it is kept secret.

[A report with fearful information]

26 And if a man asked you about a feared matter, then look at the lord of the Ascendant. **27** For if it was free of the infortunes, then that report is a lie and nothing of what he fears will reach him. **28** And if the lord of the Ascendant was in the bad places (and that is the second, the sixth, the twelfth, and the eighth), then the terror has already seized him in the respect which the owner of the Ascendant is afraid of, concerning the bad places.[332] **29** And if the infortunes witnessed, then it takes place; and if they do not witness, then it will recede and not go beyond what there is of the fear of it. **30** If it was in a stake and the infortunes looked at it from the stakes, then it is harsher for his condition. **31** If the infortune was the lord of the eighth from the Ascendant, then it indicates his death and ruin; and if it was <not>[333] that, hardships will afflict him. **32** And if the infortune was the lord of the twelfth he should dread punishment and chains. **33** And if it was the lord of the second, his assets will be taken.

34 And if the lord of the Ascendant was in the twelfth, and neither the lord of the seventh nor the lord of the twelfth looked at it, then he will escape and be rescued, and [the enemy] will not have power over him. **35** Now if the Moon connected with an infortune along with that, it indicates it[334] unless the infortune is the lord of her house (for then it indicates that he will encounter hardship in his escape). **36** And as for if it was not the lord of her house, then it is indicative of it.[335]

---

[331] This paragraph appears to be separate, as it deals with a different topic (public knowledge) but mixes it with the vocabulary of truth.

[332] This probably means that if it is in the second, the fears are about money; in the sixth, about illness or slaves, etc.

[333] Adding based on the Latin.

[334] I am not sure what Sahl means by "it." For we would expect the connection with an infortune to mean danger, except that Sahl seems to indicate that it means escape.

[335] See the previous footnote.

Chapter [15]: On retaliation

2 If[336] you were asked about someone killed (as to whether his companion would avenge him), or someone wronged (whether he would get power over the one who wronged him, or [he would] make restitution to him for his wrong),[337] then look at the Ascendant and the stake of the outcome (and that is the fourth from the Ascendant). **3** For if they were [both] convertible signs, and the Moon in a convertible sign, then he will not be able to do anything.[338]

4 Now if the lord of the Ascendant looked at the Ascendant,[339] he will be successful in his sought matter, quickly. **5** If it was just as I said, and the lord of the fourth looked at the seventh,[340] then he is going to be successful in his sought matter, and the blood of the killer will be shed, unless the Moon is connecting with the fortunes [and] then does not connect with an infortune: for then <it indicates that the associate of the one killed will accept a payment of blood-money; but if she did connect with an infortune after that fortune, then>[341] he will be killed after the reconciliation. **6** And if she did connect with an infortune, then he will be killed unless the connection is from a trine or sextile: for then it indicates that he will be punished and shackled with iron. **7** But if the infortune was in a fixed sign, then he will die in prison. **8** And if it was in a convertible sign, and its lord quick in course, and it is looking at the lord of its own house from friendship, then he will escape and be rescued. **9** And if the aspect was from a square or opposition, then he will escape by means of fighting and what is like fighting. **10** And if it

---

[336] For this chapter, cf. the Māshā'allāh version in Leiden Or. 891, f. 14a-15a.
[337] But with different voweling, "his wrong would be revisited upon him [in turn]."
[338] Or, "he would not have power over anything," linking this sentence with **2**.
[339] Here we see some abbreviation in the Sahl manuscripts, and that the Latin edition had a fuller account. In **3**, Māshā'allāh's version says that convertible signs mean he would not be successful, *and* that it is worse if the lord of the house of the Moon did not look at the Moon, nor the lord of the Ascendant the Ascendant. Then in **4**, the Latin edition contains some of the missing material: that if the lord of the Moon *does* look at the Moon, and the lord of the Ascendant the Ascendant, then he will be successful. But since we already know that Sahl does some abbreviations, I do not want to add more than I can justify
[340] This should be "the fourth," per the Māshā'allāh version.
[341] Adding material in brackets based on Māshā'allāh.

was from an assembly, then he will be released from it with harm or he will be terrified and disappear.³⁴²

11 And if you found a fortune in the Ascendant, then that anger will be extinguished on the part of his supporters. **12** <And³⁴³ if in addition [to the fortune being there] the Moon connected with an infortune and that infortune is powerful in its own place, then it indicates that that revenge [will not be] from his supporters>, for the Sultan will take revenge on him.³⁴⁴

13 And if there was an infortune in the Ascendant and the Moon is made fortunate, then his supporters will be able [to get] him, but the Sultan will be favorable to him and work hard for his removal.³⁴⁵ **14** Now if the lord of the Ascendant looked at the Ascendant, his supporters will be successful in it after laboring under the anger of the Sultan. **15** But if the lord of the Ascendant was not looking at the Ascendant, while the lord of the house of the Moon looked at the Moon, the Sultan will remove him after the supporters are satisfied.

16 And know that every punishment which Mars indicates, is with iron and whips; and Saturn is with clubs,³⁴⁶ a long confinement, and restriction.

[Chapter 16: Questions about multiple options & topics]³⁴⁷

1 If you were asked about the topic of alchemy, whether it³⁴⁸ is true or false, then look at the lord of the Ascendant and the Moon. **2** Now if they were both safe from the infortunes, then the matter is true [and] will come to be; and if they were infortunes, then the matter is false. **3** And if it was gold, then call upon the Sun as a witness; and for silver, the Moon.

---

³⁴² Māshā'allāh now adds the following related sentences, which fill out the interpretation: "But if the Moon was connecting with an infortune and then a fortune, and the infortune is weak and the fortune strong, then report that beating and punishment will afflict him, but then he will be released from it. And if the infortune was stronger, then it indicates killing."
³⁴³ Adding material in brackets from Māshā'allāh.
³⁴⁴ On the killer, that is.
³⁴⁵ Or, "expulsion" (إخراج). So, the Sultan saves him from death but does not allow him to stay in the area.
³⁴⁶ Lit., "wood."
³⁴⁷ For this chapter, cf. also Ch. 6, **42-48**.
³⁴⁸ Sahl probably means both the products of an alchemical process, and the process or instructions themselves.

4 And[349] if you were asked about one or two things, or three, as to which of them[350] will win, or [concerning] two men, which of them will be successful in his sought matter, then look at the lord of the Ascendant. **5** For if it was in the stakes, free of the infortunes, received, then the first thing of what he named is preferable, and he will be successful in it. **6** And if it was in the stakes [but] made unfortunate, then the first thing of what he named will come to be, [but] then it will be corrupted. **7** And if the lord of the Ascendant was in what follows the stakes,[351] free of the infortunes, received, then he will be successful in the second thing of what he named; and if it was made unfortunate, it will be completed [but] then it will be corrupted. **8** And if it was falling, free of the infortunes, received, then he will be successful in the third thing of what he named and asked [about]; and if it was made unfortunate, it will not be anything of what he mentioned, and the question will be corrupted. **9** And likewise too, when the Moon connects [with a planet].[352]

10 And if you were asked about several sought matters,[353] then make it the Moon and assign [her] to the one asking, and she is the indicator (that is, the Moon), and the stars are his sought matters: so assign it based on the number of those sought matters. **11** For the first connection is the indicator of the first question, and the second connection is the indicator of the second question, and likewise up to the number of the sought matters which he named for you. **12** And look concerning the power of every star in the stakes and what follows them, and its safety from retrogradation and the infortunes, then blend the planets in power, and speak according to that.

---

[349] This paragraph is also reflected in *Judges* 7.183 (method #6), where ʿUmar attributes it to Māshāʾallāh.

[350] **H** now adds: "is more worthy and better, and which of them true, or [concerning] one or two sought matters which of them he will be successful in, and concerning two [*unclear*] or three, which of them…".

[351] Reading with **B**. The other MSS read, "And if the lord of the Ascendant looked at the Ascendant, and the Ascendant was free…". This is indeed a good condition to have, but omits the essential point about being in a succeedent place.

[352] *Judges* 7.183 makes this sentence part of the next method, which makes more conceptual sense, but Sahl begins the next sentence as though the transition to the next method occurs after this sentence. If he had begun the sentence with ف, I would feel more comfortable assigning this to the next paragraph and method.

[353] That is, several *questions*, not a single question with several options to choose between (as the previous paragraphs address).

[Chapter 17: Hunting & fishing][354]

[Hunting on land]

1 And if you were asked about searching for game and how the catch will be, then look at the lord of the Ascendant and the lord of the hour (for it is powerful in hunting). **2** And understand the essence of the Ascendant (is it four-footed or not), then observe as well the essence of the seventh sign from the Ascendant when you head off towards the hunt or you are asked about it:[355] of which of the signs is it, and what is the position of its lord relative to the lord of the Ascendant? **3** For if they connected from friendship, it indicates success in what he seeks of the hunt, with ease; and if they connected from a square or opposition, he will be successful in the hunt [but] with hardship and toil. **4** And if they are not connecting, he will not get anything and will not be successful in what he seeks.

5 And if you found the seventh sign to be four-footed, and its lord and the lord of the hour are in it or in one of its stakes, he will get the prey. **6** And[356] if the lord of the hour was an infortune, and the fortunes fell away from it, he will inconvenience himself in the search and [it indicates] the scarcity of the prey, and pains will be feared for him in his body. **7** And in the hour of Jupiter or in one of the stakes,[357] [the prey] will be acquired in a pleasant way.

8 And if the lord of the seventh sign was an infortune, and the fortunes fell away from it, he will inconvenience himself in the search, and his catch will be small, and toil will be feared for him in his body if Saturn was in the seventh <or>[358] he was the lord of the seventh. **9** And if Mars was the lord of the seventh and was in a position in which he has power, then he will obtain the prey but one of those with him in the toil of hunting will cause frustration for him[359]—but he will be safe, because Mars has the essential quality of the hunt. **10** Now if Jupiter looked at Mars, and [Jupiter] was the lord of the hour or the lord of the Ascendant, he will be safe from everything he fears,

---

[354] For this chapter, see also *Choices* Ch. 12, **7-19**.
[355] This shows that Sahl would allow this to be either a question or an election.
[356] This sentence (not found in the Latin) is virtually identical to **8** except it deals with the lord of the hour, whereas **8** concerns the lord of the seventh. Nevertheless I hesitate to omit **6** as an error, since it pairs rather nicely with **7**, where the lord of the hour is a fortune.
[357] This probably means, "if Jupiter is in one of the stakes."
[358] Only **B** has Saturn in the seventh, but it makes sense.
[359] يفسد عليه, reading as Form IV.

and the hunt will be easy for him, and he will attain his sought goal without toil and trouble.

11 And if the seventh was of the signs of air or of the signs of earth, and a fortune was in them, and[360] its lord was an infortune or the lord of the hour was an infortune, he will be safe in his hunt but will not get all of what he wants, and the prey will escape from him, and his search will be hard on him, and he will inconvenience himself in it—unless Jupiter or Mercury were with the infortune which is the lord of the hour: for indeed that breaks the evil of the infortune and does not prohibit the hunt (because Mercury has a powerful partnership with Mars in hunting).

12 And as for the scarcity of the catch and its abundance, look at the Midheaven when he goes out to the hunt. **13** For if you found Mars to be the lord of the Midheaven, and he is there as well, and he is inspecting Mercury or Jupiter, or one of the two is the lord of the hour or lord of the Ascendant,[361] then he will obtain a great catch, and it will be safe for him, and he will be able to manage the prey with his two hands, and he will not have toil unless Saturn was inspecting Mars from a stake, or Saturn is in the Midheaven or he is its lord: for powerful distress will enter upon the master of the hunt in what he hopes for and desires. **14** Now if Jupiter fell away from him, and Saturn was as I described to you, and Mars in a stake, then disaster will befall the master of the hunt in his body and difficulty in his approach, and nothing of the prey will appear with it, because Saturn corrupts the hunt and delays its master—if it was a hunt by land.

[Fishing]

15 And as for fishing by sea, look at the lord of the Ascendant and the Moon, and the lord of the seventh. **16** For if the Ascendant was a watery[362] sign, and <the Moon>[363] connected with Mars, and the lord of the out-

---

[360] Reading with the Latin versions, for "or."
[361] This is a little ambiguous, because it makes it seem as though these conditions are separate. Probably Sahl means that he inspects one of them, *and at the same time* that same planet (or perhaps either one) is also the lord of the hour or lord of the Ascendant.
[362] All but **B** omit, and **B** reads, "convertible." I have read this with the Latin.
[363] Adding with the Latin.

come³⁶⁴ connected with Mars, and Venus fell away from the inspection of the Moon, then turn down that fishing trip as far as you can, because it will not have power nor last long unless it is with harm. **17** Now if the Moon connected with Saturn, and Venus looked at the Moon, then the catch will be much: for Saturn does not do violence to the Moon in fishing unless Mars was also inspecting the Moon along with that. **18** And <Mars> weakens Venus because Mars is an enemy of Venus.³⁶⁵ **19** If Saturn looked at her, then with that the owner [of the fishing trip] should fear drowning and what is like that, of moisture and wetness.

Chapter [18]: On meals³⁶⁶

[The meal itself]

2 If you were invited to a meal or were asked about a meal being arranged, and what they will eat, then look at the Ascendant. **3** Now if it was a convertible sign, then surely they will eat [many] dishes; if it was fixed, then one dish; and if it was one having two bodies, two dishes.

4 And if the Moon was in the Ascendant, then there will be saltiness in their meal. **5** And if Mars was in the Ascendant, then there is hotness in it; and Jupiter indicates sweetness, and the Sun what is hot,³⁶⁷ and Venus grease,³⁶⁸ and Mercury what is acidic³⁶⁹ and every mixed [dish], and Saturn what is unpleasant.

6 Then, look at the separation of the Moon and her connection: for if she separated from an infortune and connected with a fortune from a square or opposition, there will be no escape for the owner [of the question] from doing it—such as a marriage, circumcision, banquet, and what is like that of

---

³⁶⁴ That is, the lord of the fourth. But both Latin versions read "hour." These words can look similar in Arabic.
³⁶⁵ But recall that in *Aphorisms* #34, Venus is able to dissolve the problems of Mars.
³⁶⁶ Lit., "On food" (الطَّعام), but it is clear that something more extravagant like banquets is meant.
³⁶⁷ L reads "spicy," which seems good either for Mars or the Sun.
³⁶⁸ But see below, where Venus indicates sweetness. But perhaps Venus and Jupiter could be understood as "rich" foods, which could encompass both fat and sweetness.
³⁶⁹ Or, "sour" or "bitter" (الحامض).

what people do with some frequency.³⁷⁰ **7** And if it was from a trine or sextile, then the meal is for someone dear or making a connection,³⁷¹ and what is like that. **8** And if the one the Moon is connecting with is in a stake and it is a fixed sign, then their gathering will be one day; and if it was one having two bodies, then more than one day.

9 And if the lord of the house of the Moon is looking at her, then he will take pleasure in his seat and one should <not>³⁷² fear for him; now if it is not looking at her, then his seat will be inconvenient for him, and at [the gathering] will be someone he finds annoying, and he will leave and he will criticize his companions.³⁷³

10 If the Moon connected with Jupiter, it indicates the generosity of the gathering and the abundance of dishes. **11** And if she connected with the Sun, it indicates the cleanliness of the food <and the abundance of what is hot>.³⁷⁴ **12** <If she connected with Venus, it indicates the beauty of the food> and the abundance of its sweetness, with entertainment, listening, laughter, and fragrances. **13** And if she connected with Mercury, it indicates an abundance of crowding, and in that place there will be someone who speaks with wisdom, and there will be much conversation there, and in their food will be the meats of birds. **14** And if the connection was with Saturn, it indicates the impurity of their food, and oddities³⁷⁵ of food will be abundant there, and fish, and everything which comes from the water. **15** And if the connection was with Mars, it indicates mischief³⁷⁶ occurring among them, and they will eat every hot thing. **16** And if it was the Midheaven, it indicates what occurs among them.

---

³⁷⁰ Reading slightly loosely for ينوب. That is, the affair is important enough that he can't easily get out of it.
³⁷¹ صلة, which can also refer to kinship connections. The point seems to be that hard aspects imply obligation and not being excited about going, whereas easy aspects imply some advantage and fun.
³⁷² Added by Dykes.
³⁷³ Or perhaps, his "masters" or "lords" (أصحابه) in charge of the event. In this last part it is not absolutely clear to me who is finding whom annoying—nevertheless it suggests having a bad time.
³⁷⁴ Adding here and below with the Latin, using the attributions mentioned above. Again, an alternate reading in **5** above is "spicy."
³⁷⁵ This could also mean "rarities" (نوادر).
³⁷⁶ Or put more strongly, "disaster," "evil" (شرّ).

17 Now when you were invited to a meal, and the Moon was with Mars or connected with him from a stake, then you should not go to that meal, for indeed you will have regret in the outcome of that; and likewise with Saturn, for it indicates the impurity of the food, and its[377] stupidity. **18** (If you did go, you would not encounter what is pleasant at that time.) **19** And if she was with Mercury and Venus, then do go because you will see what you love. **20** And if she was with Jupiter it is likewise, and rice and grains will be abundant in that.

21 Then, look at the lord of the hour: for if it was in the Ascendant or in the Midheaven, then he will be served the food [and be among] the first of those who are seated; and if it was withdrawing from these two places, then he will already have eaten before he is served it, and he will not be served until that star withdraws. **22** And if it was in the seventh or fourth, then he will not be served food until it includes [everyone] there is.[378]

23 And whenever the Moon was connected with Mars, then the food will be hot.

24 And[379] if he summoned[380] you and the Moon was in a watery sign, looking at Saturn from a trine or sextile, he should[381] eat fish. **25** And if the Moon was in Libra, he should eat grains. **26** And if she was in Gemini[382] or Aquarius, then the meat of birds. **27** If she looked at Saturn from a square or opposition, he should eat cold meat. **28** And if the Sun connected with Mars,[383] then it will generally be burned. **29** If the Moon was in Libra or its[384] square, then you should not eat of the legumes, whether cooked or raw. **30** And in Virgo and Libra, you should not approach grains nor salad greens. **31**

---

[377] That is, the meal or gathering.

[378] Reading as يعمّه ما كان.

[379] In this paragraph, all of the MSS go back and forth between saying what "he" will or should (or will not or should not) eat, offering instructions in both the masculine singular and feminine plural. I have tried to follow the manuscript variants that are most consistent. Also, it is not always clear which malefic planets are in question which might spoil the food.

[380] Read with the prepositional complement, which is stronger than simply being "invited." Nevertheless Sahl might only mean an invitation.

[381] I have read this as a recommendation, even though it lacks the jussive particle that one might normally expect.

[382] Following the Latin. All manuscripts read "Pisces," but Pisces is not associated with birds and is dealt with in **34** below.

[383] But perhaps Sahl means that the Moon is *either* (1) burned by the Sun *or* (2) connecting with Mars, particularly from a bad aspect.

[384] Or perhaps "his," indicating Mars?

And if she was in Scorpio with the Tail, then beware of quail.³⁸⁵ **32** And if she was in Leo, beware of eating meat. **33** And in Sagittarius, do not approach wild meat,³⁸⁶ nor that of predatory animals. **34** And in Pisces, do not eat salted nor fresh fish. **35** So, beware of what I have mentioned of the positions of the Moon with the infortunes in these signs which I have named to you, for indeed they harm powerfully.

[House analysis of meals]

36 And³⁸⁷ know that the Ascendant indicates the reason for the event. **37** And if it was in a house of Venus, then it is a wedding; and if it was in a house of Mercury, then it is because of a child; and if it was in a house of Jupiter, then it is a friend who brings about that meal for him.

39 The second from the Ascendant indicates the vessels from which they drink, and the furnishings of the house. **40** Now if the second had two bodies, then their vessels will be of two types.³⁸⁸ **41** And if Mars was in it, then those vessels will be copper; and if Venus was in it, silver; and Jupiter [indicates] silver and gold; <and the Moon, glass>;³⁸⁹ and Saturn, wood and pottery. **42** And if the fortunes were in the second, they indicate the goodness of the linens of the house (and if the fortune was alien, then they are foreign;³⁹⁰ and if there was testimony in it, they belong to the people of the house).

43 And the third indicates those who witness the meal.

44 The fourth from the Ascendant is the place in which they sit. **45** If it was a sign having two bodies, then their supper will be on a porch.³⁹¹ **46** And

---

³⁸⁵ Or, "cooking butter" (سمّن).
³⁸⁶ That is, wild game.
³⁸⁷ For this list of houses, see the diagrams and discussion in Hephaistion III.36.
³⁸⁸ Reading for "many types," on the model of **3** above.
³⁸⁹ Adding based on the Latin.
³⁹⁰ Or more simply, that they belong to someone else.
³⁹¹ Reading with the Latin version, as a porch has a double quality: partly inside, partly outside. The Arabic (المخدم) generally refers to servants, which suggests a place with many servants; but a fancy meal would already have servants, and it does not make sense to hold such a meal in the servants' quarters or a kitchen.

if the sign of the Sun or Jupiter was in it, then their supper will be in the courtyard of the home, or in the south.³⁹²

47 The fifth from the Ascendant indicates their beverages. **48** Now if it has two bodies, then their drinks are of two types. **49** And if Jupiter or Mercury were in it, then their drink is date [juice].³⁹³ **50** And if Saturn was corrupted by Mars, <their drinks will be pungent>.³⁹⁴ **51** But if it was Mars, then it will already make their drinks acidic. **52** And if it was the Sun, then there will be bitterness in it, and acidity. **53** And if it was Venus, [then] date wine. **54** And if it was the Moon, then their drinks will be water.

55 The sixth from the Ascendant is the servants.

56 The seventh from the Ascendant belongs to one asking your opinion [on things].

57 The eighth and ninth, those who manage the kitchen.³⁹⁵

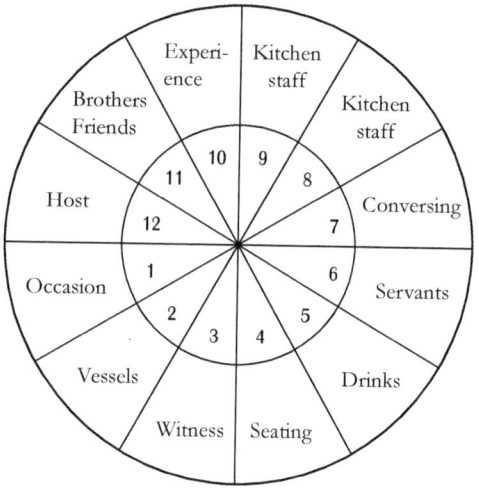

Figure 43: Houses for meals (*Questions* Ch. 18, 36-61)

---

³⁹² Or, "the prayer niche" (القبلة). I take it to be the south because (in the northern hemisphere) this is the direction which has the most light, indicated by the diurnal planets (the Sun and Jupiter).

³⁹³ L reads, "wine."

³⁹⁴ Some traditional Middle Eastern (and even Turkish) drinks are made from fermented juices that are extremely sharp and pungent (rather than being turned into wine).

³⁹⁵ Reading من يقوم على المطبخ with the sense of the Latin, for "those who go to the Ascendant" (من يقوم إلى الطالع). The Latin gives the eighth to bakers and cooks, and the ninth to those serving the dishes.

58 The tenth belongs to what is excellent in the meal,[396] and whether or not he will rejoice in that. **59** Now if the fortunes were in the Midheaven, he will rejoice in it; and if it was the infortunes, it will be bad and risky to life.[397]

60 The eleventh is the brothers and friends.

61 And the twelfth is the indicator of the owner of the house, whether he wants that[398] or not.

62 So, look at the position of the fortunes and infortunes in these twelve places, for every sign in which there is a fortune or its lord was made fortunate, judge joy and the good for what is attributed to the essence of that house. **63** And as for a sign in which there is an infortune or its lord was made unfortunate, it corrupts everything attributed to that house.

64 And God is more knowledgeable in what is true, and in Him is our refuge and return, and the prayer of God be upon our master Muhammad, and upon his family friendship and peace.

---

[396] But Sahl probably means "the excellence" of the meal, which would be the verbal noun instead of an adjective.

[397] استقتال, a verbal noun which appears ungrammatically here.

[398] Or more specifically, "has an appetite" (يشتهي).

THE BOOK OF CHOICES
ACCORDING TO THE TWELVE HOUSES

In the name of God, the Compassionate, the Merciful, and His prayers be upon the master of those who were sent as messengers, Muhammad.

The Book of Choices According to the Twelve Houses of Sahl b. Bishr the Israelite

[Chapter 1: General principles]

3 He said:[1] They have agreed that choices are weak[2] except for kings: for truly, even if their choice is weak, [kings] have a root[3] strengthening their nativities and strengthening every weak planet in the course.[4] **4** And as for the lowest people and the rabble who follow [upon them], do not choose anything for them unless it is based on their nativities and the revolution of their years, and the nativities of their children. **5** And for one who does not know that from [those charts], then let him ask a renewed question[5] about what he wants, and you will know the judgment of the thing sought from that: then, you choose based on that. **6** And if he asked about himself,[6] then

---

[1] From this somewhat confusing paragraph we can draw out four categories of clients or election charts, in decreasing levels of certainty and success: (**3**) wealthy people who know their nativities; (**4**) lower-class people who know their nativities; (**5**) someone without a known nativity but who has a successful question chart; and (**6**) someone without any chart at all, who simply wants an election taken by itself.

[2] As we will see, this means "choices taken *by themselves*," as Sahl prefers elections that have another, root chart as their basis.

[3] Normally this would mean a nativity. But if the root *is* the nativity, how can it strengthen the nativity? So by "root" or "foundation" (أصل), Sahl might mean that there is already a real-word foundation for their success: namely, because they are at the top of the social hierarchy. Even a weak choice by a king will have consequences much more powerful than that of an average person.

[4] "The course" here seems to mean "the arrangement of the planets in the election chart."

[5] مسئلة مستأنفة. That is, he should ask a horary question.

[6] سأل عن نفسه. This sentence seems to contradict or conflict with previous ones. I suggest that it refers to the lowest and most uncertain kind of chart: an election for someone without any nativity or question chart at all: in this case, there is nothing to ground the election in, and so Sahl recommends we do not take it. The key here may be in the word "himself," which in Arabic also has connotations of something done of one's own accord, in one's own

from his birth he has already reached the good or bad, because he is the one who is asking you: so you do not choose anything for him. **7** And if the sought thing cannot be carried out, or the man who asks you (or the one heading out toward fighting) is doomed, then how will it be chosen for one whose root is corrupted, when it is the first beginning and the old root which one depends on?

8 And beware of choosing for one whose root of his nativity or his question indicates something detestable, for truly [even] if you put all of the fortunes in the stakes and made the infortunes and every planet not agreeing with the lord of his Ascendant fall away from it, it would not benefit that man anything—and especially for low people and the middle class, because you do not know if perhaps you are choosing a star or Ascendant which is an enemy to him in the root, or there is an infortune in that Ascendant which you chose for him.

9 And one is already warned of that based on the group of people who sail on the sea or head out on a journey at one [and the same] hour: for of them, one sinks and another is safe, one gets money and another does not get anything, and the condition of some does not resemble that of others. **10** And I have already tested that many times in a group: they went out from a place at one time, and reached a country at one time: one of them is quicker in returning with fine assets, and one is slower in that, while another of them perishes on [the journey] before he left for his home: and in truth, that comes from their nativities and their distribution from those years. **11** And we already see people too, rejoicing and drinking on a bad, reprehensible day with great corruption, while they come together and evil enters upon them on a good, praiseworthy day.

12 And perhaps you have seen the indicator[7] being connected to an infortune from a square, assembly, or opposition, and someone had gains: that infortune was good for him, because the infortunes are perhaps more fitting for him, since [one] may be the lord of the original[8] Ascendant, and the lord of the distribution, or the lord of the Ascendant of the year. **13** And as for when you choose based on an Ascendant you knew, or the Ascendant of a

---

right—so it could be that Sahl means the election is taken alone, out of context, etc.: that is, without a supporting chart.

[7] This is probably the Moon.

[8] That is, "natal."

nativity you knew, or the lord of his year, it is preferable for your choice because you know what of the stars is consistent with it, and what his Ascendant is: so be cautious about this topic, and let your action be like your choice.

14 And know that God (be He blessed and exalted!) made Creation and what is in it from the four natures, and he connected the earth and what is on it (of the voiceless and the voiced, and what is set in motion and what is at rest) to the heavenly circle, and between it and them he put subtle things which the people of knowledge know, such as the subtle cause which he put between the magnet and iron, and the cause which is between a father and son, and the cause which is between what provides nourishment and the one nourished by it: so know that and understand it. **15** And from the conformity between the higher essences and the lower ones, things are balanced, while from [their] disagreement they are corrupted.

16 The fortunes are balanced and tempered in nature, while the infortunes are unjust in nature, and they want injustice: so beware of them. **17** For if they accepted [the management], there is no escape from their injustice and the wickedness of their disagreement; and they are in the position of thieves, and people of evil among men, and from them comes disagreement, evil, and alteration.

[Chapter 2]: The knowledge of the natures of the signs

2 Know[9] that the convertible signs indicate the quick transformation of matters, and nothing is made fixed by them, nor does its period of time last long. **3** They are suitable for sowing, buying and selling, and betrothals, and the sick person will recover quickly in them, and a lawsuit does not last long in them, and the runaway returns quickly, and travel is suitable in it, and one who makes a promise in them will not keep what he promised, and talking and visions and reports in them are worthless, and a doctor should not treat [a patient] in them, and a plant should not be planted in them, and a foundation should not be laid them: for truly it would be bad. **4** And every matter you begin in them whose fixity you wanted, will not last long; but every

---

[9] Most of the items in **3** derive from Theophilus, *OVI* Ch. I.1, which itself is based on Orphic material.

work you want to do, *begin* that in them.¹⁰ **5** And the quickest of the convertible [ones] are Aries and Cancer, and [they are] the most intense in crookedness and the greatest of them in changeability; and Libra and Capricorn are the more powerful and balanced of them.¹¹

6 And¹² as for the fixed signs, indeed they are appropriate for every work whose endurance, length, and fixity its owner¹³ wishes. **7** And building is suitable in them, and marriage (after there was an engagement in the convertible ones), and if a woman divorces in them she will not return to her husband, and there will not be contentment after a judgment and inception in them unless the testimonies of the fortunes are many, and [for] one who was imprisoned in them his imprisonment will be long, and one who became angry in them will not have control [over himself],¹⁴ and contract stipulations and legal claims are more suitable in them, and [laying a] foundation and building in them is excellent. **8** And Scorpio is the lightest of the fixed ones, Leo the most powerful in fixedness, Aquarius the most sluggish, and Taurus more even.

9 And¹⁵ as for the embodied signs,¹⁶ indeed they are suitable for a partnership and acting as brothers, and what is done of something will recur often, and buying and marriage in them will not last long, and there will be deception and trickery in them, and one who was accused of something in them will be freed and cleared of what is alleged against him, and he who was im-

---

¹⁰ Emphasis mine. That is, you should begin in them *only if* you might later go on to a new stage, or you want something to happen quickly but not last. See **7**.

¹¹ In terms of crookedness and straightness (that is, ascensional times), this is not true. Aries and Capricorn are crooked (and therefore faster), and Cancer and Libra are straight (and therefore slower). But Aries and Cancer could be viewed as faster because they are ruled by Mars and the Moon, who often indicate change. Libra is ruled by Venus, so is a straight sign ruled by a somewhat faster planet, and Capricorn is a crooked sign ruled by the slowest planet: so perhaps these mixtures create balance. See *Questions* Ch. 9, **78-79**, where the Māshā'allāh version of that passage confirms that the quickness of the lord contributes to it.

¹² Most of the items in **7** derive from Theophilus, *OVI* Ch. I.3, which itself is based on Orphic material.

¹³ That is, the person undertaking the act (such as the astrologer's client)

¹⁴ Or, "one cannot control him."

¹⁵ Most of the items in **9-11** derive from Theophilus, *OVI* Ch. I.2, which itself is based on Orphic material.

¹⁶ That is, the common or mutable signs, having two bodies.

prisoned in them will not remain [there] unless it is in Pisces[17] (especially because of the shortness of its appearance and emergence),[18] and one who was let out of prison will return to it, and if a runaway was taken in them he will return to his escape a second time, and [for] one who goes to the judge in them, neither the opinion nor judgment will be firm for him, and a ship should not be boarded in them, for one who does so will transfer from it to another one, and [for] one who is promised something in them, it will be violated and not fulfilled for him, and one who is sick in them will be freed, and then will relapse. **10** For everything of good and bad that befalls a man in them, will be doubled upon him, and [for] one who died in them, truly another close person[19] will die in that place. **11** Emigration, and washing the head and beard, and the purification of gold and silver in them, are [all] suitable, as well as sending youths to school.

12 Now if you wanted the inception of something (of what I mentioned to you), then make it be [when] both the Moon and the Ascendant are in those signs appropriate to them and to what you want, and connect the Moon with fortunes receptive to[20] her in that sign.

13 The[21] signs of the day and a work of the day, are stronger by day; and [so] you should make the Ascendant be diurnal, and [make] the Moon be in the diurnal signs.

14 And the watery signs are suitable for hunting by land and sea, and the signs of kings are suitable for kings, and the signs which have voices are suitable for one who plays the nay and the oud, and singing, and the fiery signs are suitable for everything that is worked with fire.

15 And the equinoctial[22] signs (in which night and day are equal), are suitable for what is right and being truthful, and for one who works with

---

[17] Reading with al-Rijāl VII.3.2, for variants such as "truth" (الحقّ) or "fear" (الخوف). Nevertheless I do not understand why Pisces would indicate this, except that Pisces has a reputation for trickery that might play a role here (see Ch. 6, **33**).

[18] Pisces and Aries are the shortest and most crooked signs (in the northern hemisphere).

[19] قريب, which can mean both a relative and something close by.

[20] القابلة له. This does not seem to mean "receiving" her, as that would not require the preposition; this phrase means being susceptible and well-disposed to her, but in an astrological sense I'm not sure if Sahl has something specific in mind.

[21] See *Carmen* V.5, **4**.

[22] Lit., "equality, evenness" (الاعتدال). That is, Aries and Libra. This probably also includes the end of Pisces and Virgo.

scales. **16** And the solstitial signs[23] (and they are the ones in which day and night begin [their] alteration) are suitable for change,[24] and for one who wants a shift from one thing to another thing.

17 Now[25] for every work you want to begin, look at what the nature of that sign is in the heavenly circles, and connect the Moon and the lord of the Ascendant to that essence, and the root of that nature, and its strength, in the hour of the inception. **18** So if you wanted what has to do with kings, authorities, chiefs, the mighty, the administrators of cities and their subordinates, and the lords of killing and sparing life, then make use of the Sun; and for what has to do with the nobles, make use of Jupiter; and for plowmen and the rabble, make use of Saturn; and for commanders and the masters of wars, make use of Mars; and for what has to do with women, make use of Venus; and for buying and selling, and a lawsuit, and matters of the book, and merchants, make use of Mercury; and for an association with ladies[26] and seeking what has to do with them, make use of the Moon.

19 If[27] you wanted to begin some work, then make the Ascendant suitable, and its lord, and the Moon, and the lord of the matter, and beware of the evil condition of the Moon, based on what Dorotheus and other scholars said in the inception of works—and there are ten types:[28]

20 The first[29] is that the Moon is burned, less than the Sun by 12° [before him], or after him by a similar [amount]—and that is less significant than being behind him.[30]

21 The second is that she is in the degree of [her] fall.

---

[23] Lit., "altering, changing" (المتغيّرة). That is, Capricorn and Cancer. This probably also includes the end of Sagittarius and Gemini.
[24] Or, "alteration."
[25] For this paragraph, cf. *Carmen* V.31.
[26] Lit. "the ladies from/among women," indicating a higher social class.
[27] Cf. *Carmen* V.6, **31**.
[28] Cf. *Introduction* Ch. 3, **102-12**, and *Carmen* V.6, **1-14**.
[29] See *Carmen* V.6, **4**.
[30] By "before" (or "less than") and "behind," Sahl means "in an earlier degree of the zodiac." By "after," he means "in a later degree of the zodiac. In other words, it is worse for the Moon to be burned while she is still moving towards the Sun, than when she has passed him and is moving away.

22 The third[31] is that she is in the opposition of the Sun.

23 The fourth[32] is that she is assembled with the infortunes or in the light of their square, or in their opposition.

24 The fifth[33] is that she is with the Head or Tail, from a degree up to 12° (which is the boundary of an eclipse).

25 The sixth[34] is that she is in the last degrees of the signs, which are the bounds of the infortunes.

26 The seventh[35] is that she is falling from the stakes, or in the burned path (which is the end of Libra and the beginning of Scorpio): and that is the worst of the misfortunes of the Moon, and especially if it was the inception of a marriage or anything of the matters of women, or buying or selling, or travel.

27 The eighth[36] is that she is in a twelfth-part with an infortune,[37] or she is in the contrary of her house[38] or absent from[39] it.

28 The ninth[40] is that the Moon was slow in course (and that is what the scholars call being "like the course of Saturn"), so that her travel in a day and a night is less than 12 [degrees], even if it was by a single minute. **29** (And that is when your calculation for the Moon is in the first of her *kardajas*, so that the *kardaja* is from a degree up to 15°.)

---

[31] See *Carmen* V.6, **8**.
[32] See *Carmen* V.6, **32**.
[33] See *Carmen* V.6, **3**.
[34] See *Carmen* V.6, **13**.
[35] See *Carmen* V.6, **12** and **14**.
[36] See *Carmen* V.6, **6**.
[37] This is ambiguous. It could mean that she is in the same sign as an infortune (since "twelfth-part" is sometimes, but rarely, used in Greek to mean a sign). It could also mean that the Moon's twelfth-part *corresponds to* a sign with an infortune in it. But if we compare this with *Introduction* Ch. 3, **108**, it could be a confusion for two thoughts: (1) being in the twelfth place from her own house, namely being in Gemini; (2) being in the bound of an infortune. Then again, *Carmen* V.6, **6** has the Moon "in the twelfth-part *of*" an infortune.
[38] That is, in detriment.
[39] That is, in aversion to it (غائب). This may be equivalent to Sahl's *Introduction* Ch. 3, **108**, which has the Moon in Gemini: because then she would indeed be in aversion to Cancer.
[40] See *Carmen* V.6, **11**.

30 The tenth type is what Māshā'allāh and the people of our time have mentioned, and that is that the Moon is empty in course.

31 Make the Moon suitable as much as you can, and do not make her be waxing[41] in the Ascendant, for indeed that is blameworthy due to the pain which will afflict its owner in his body—unless the lord of the Ascendant and the lord of the house of the Moon are both looking at the Ascendant. **32** For truly the position of the planet which does not look at its own house is the position of the man who is absent from his home, so he is not capable of repelling [anyone] from it nor blocking [anyone]. **33** And if the planet did look at its own house, it would be in the position of the owner of the home which he protects, so one who is in the home is wary of him, and one who is outside the home is afraid of going to it. **34** And if the lord of the Ascendant was an infortune, then make it inspect [the Ascendant] from a trine or sextile. **35** And beware of making the lord of the Ascendant or [lord of] the Moon (if they were infortunes) inspect the Moon from a stake; and you make it be from the stakes of the Ascendant.[42]

36 And in all inceptions or questions, the Lot of Fortune should not be falling away from[43] the inspection of the Moon or [her] assembly; and you do not pay attention to the lord of the Lot, and you do not take into account if the Lot is falling away from the Ascendant, when the Lot is looking at the [lord of the][44] Ascendant and the Moon. **37** And strive to make the lord of the Ascendant be with the Lot, for indeed it is more suitable and greater for the benefit [of the inception]; and never put the Moon in the second, sixth, eighth, or twelfth from the Lot, for indeed that is something detestable.

38 In[45] all inceptions, always make the Ascendant and the Moon be in signs that are straight in ascension, for indeed they indicate ease and success;

---

[41] زائد, which might mean "advancing," i.e., angular, moving by diurnal motion towards the Ascendant.

[42] I believe this means the following: do not make these malefic planets look at her from one of *her* whole-sign angles, but make them look at her by a trine or sextile (**34**) from one of the angles of the Ascendant.

[43] Reading عن ("away from") for من ("from"). That is, "in aversion to."

[44] Adding so as to make astrological sense; if the Lot were falling away from the Ascendant, it would already be in aversion to it and so could not see it; but since the lord of the Ascendant and the Moon are the key planets here, it makes sense to add "the lord."

[45] See generally *Carmen* V.2.

and you do not put it in signs crooked in ascension, for they indicate unevenness and difficulty.

39 The Ascendant and the fourth sign from it (and its lord) both[46] indicate the outcome of that inception.

40 See the fortunes and infortunes, the strong and weak ones of them, and you will speak about the beginning of that matter, and its end, in terms of [their] strength and weakness.

41 And Dorotheus said:[47] If you saw the Moon corrupted, and before you was present a matter you could not escape from, and you do not have the power to delay it, then do not make the Moon have a share in the Ascendant, and make her fall away from the Ascendant, and make a fortune be in the Ascendant, and strengthen the Ascendant and its lord.

[Chapter 3]: The second sign from the Ascendant, & what types of choices are in it

[Loans]

2 When[48] you wanted to choose a time in which to ask to borrow money, then let the Moon be in Leo, Pisces, Scorpio, Sagittarius, or Aquarius, and let the Moon be decreasing in light, and the two fortunes be decreasing,[49] both looking at the Moon or the Ascendant. **3** And[50] let Mercury be cleansed of Mars, and the Moon be with Jupiter or Mercury, and beware lest the Moon be corrupted by one of the two infortunes, or that Mercury be assembled with them or in their square, and the fortunes falling: for truly if the Moon was with Mars, troublemaking and evasion and a dispute will occur in it, and if she was corrupted by Saturn, there will occur delay and [then] relief after the adversity and disagreement and trouble.

---

[46] It is unclear who the "both" refers to here, since three things are mentioned. I believe we should read the connected pronoun in the dual, to read "the Ascendant and the fourth sign from it *and the lord of each of them* both indicate…". Certainly the fourth and its lord do indicate the outcome.

[47] See *Carmen* V.6, **15**.

[48] For this sentence, see *Carmen* V.21, **7**.

[49] My sense is that this means decreasing in speed, which suggests a longer time before one has to repay the loan.

[50] For this sentence, see *Carmen* V.21, **2-4**.

4 And[51] if you wanted to hide the loan for the debt and that no one be informed about it, then let the Moon at the time of your taking and requesting it be under the rays, going towards a connection with the fortunes after her departure from the Sun: for truly that is more hidden for the owner [of the action], and it will not become known. **5** And as for if the Moon was going out to a connection with Mars upon her exit from burning, truly that will become known, and it will fall into the mouths of the people and the mouths of one whom he does not wish to inform. **6** And[52] take care lest the Moon be in the belt of the signs[53] or in the burned path, for indeed that is something detestable. **7** And Dorotheus said:[54] do not loan anything to anyone when the Moon is in the beginning of the degrees of Leo, Gemini, or Sagittarius, or these signs were rising, for indeed that is detestable for a loan especially.

[Partnerships]

8 And[55] if you wanted to enter into a partnership with someone for money or work, then an excellent time for that is if the Moon is cleansed of the infortunes, connected to the fortunes, and they are in the signs having two bodies, so that it may increase and be completed, or [if] the Moon is in Leo or Taurus. **9** And they certainly detested that the Moon be in the lower signs:[56] and the worst of them is Libra (because the burned path is in it), and likewise Aquarius (for indeed it is reprehensible).

10 Let[57] the Moon be received from a trine or sextile so that their parting will be good, because the aspect of the square and opposition [indicate that] there will be words between them at their parting, and an aspect of friendship indicates the goodness of their parting, and loyalty and satisfaction.

---

[51] For this sentence, cf. *Carmen* V.21, **5**.
[52] For **6-7**, cf. *Carmen* V.21, **6**.
[53] That is, with 0° ecliptical latitude, so that she is directly on or about her Node.
[54] Omitting "do not ask for a loan and," in order to be more faithful to Dorotheus. These signs are bad for *loaning out* money but not for asking for or taking on a loan, as confirmed in Heph. III.28, **5**. Dorotheus then says (by direct quotation from the *Pentateuch*) that one should take on debt when the Moon (and perhaps the Ascendant) is in Aquarius, Scorpio, Leo, and also Pisces and Sagittarius, waning in light and decreasing in number.
[55] Cf. *Carmen* V.20, **1-13**.
[56] That is, the signs of southern declination.
[57] For this sentence, cf. *Carmen* V.20, **18-19**.

11 And beware of the presence of an infortune in the stakes, because the Ascendant belongs to the one initiating the partnership (or the younger of the two), and the seventh belongs to the other partner, and the tenth indicates what there will be between them, as well as the abundance of profit and its scarcity; and from the fourth you will understand the outcome of their matter.

12 And beware lest the lord of the Ascendant not be looking at the Ascendant, or the lord of the house of the Moon not be looking at the Moon: because if it was like that, each one of the two will ridicule his partner, and their matter will become bad at [their] parting.

[Investing]

13 If you wanted to channel money, seeking an excess of it,[58] then make the Moon and Mercury suitable, and the lord of the house of assets, and the degree of the house of hope. **14** And let the Moon be connected to Mercury, and make Mars fall away entirely from them both, as much as you can; and make Mercury suitable and cleanse him of defects. **15** And if he was retrograde, then make the Moon suitable as well as the degree of the house of hope, and make the light of Mars fall away from Mercury; and you should not make him[59] fall away from the inspection of Venus and the lord of the eleventh. **16** And in the channeling of money and the seeking of profit, let your confidence always be in Mercury, the Moon, and the degree of the house of hope, and their lords, and make Mars and his light fall away from them both.

[Buying and selling]

17 And if you wanted the choice of a time for a purchase, then make the Lot of Fortune suitable, and let it be in the houses of Jupiter, connected with the fortunes: for that is better for the buyer than the seller. **18** And[60] if the Moon was in the signs straight in ascension,[61] increasing in light and number,

---

[58] "Channel" here (توجّه) seems to be a synonym for "invest," and the excess sought is the great profit hoped for from it.
[59] That is, Mercury.
[60] For this sentence, cf. *Carmen* V.44, 2.
[61] But compare with *Carmen* V.44, and Hephaistion III.16, **13**, which refer to the Moon increasing in northern ecliptical latitude, not being in signs of straight ascension.

connected to the fortunes, then whatever is bought at that time, its owner will lose it, and it is superior for the seller than the buyer. **19** And let Mars be falling away from the Moon and Mercury, for in buying and selling Mars is the one who indicates troublemaking and disputes. **20** Likewise, make the Tail fall away from the Moon especially (and it is below Mars [in its harm]).[62]

21 And[63] if you wanted a sale, then make the Moon be in her exaltation or her triplicity, separated from the fortunes and looking at the infortunes (but not being connected to them).

[Alchemy]

22 And[64] if you wanted a work of alchemy or a treatment[65] whose repetition you wanted, then let that be when the Moon is in the signs having two bodies, cleansed of the infortunes, and let the Ascendant be likewise, and make it suitable: and if the treatment was in gold, then strengthen the Sun and make him suitable at the inception of the work.

23 What there is of choices in the third sign occurs partly in the ninth, and partly in the house of friends,[66] which we will describe in that [place], if God (be He exalted!) wills.

[Chapter 4]: The fourth sign from the Ascendant, & what types of choices are in it

[Building and tearing down]

2 If you wanted a choice for building a home, then make the Moon suitable as well as her lord, and the Ascendant and its lord, and the Lot of Fortune, and Mercury. **3** Make Mars fall away from these indicators which I

---

[62] Crofts reads, "*when*" it is below Mars, but my reading makes more astrological sense.
[63] Cf. perhaps *Carmen* V.10, **2-3**.
[64] For this topic, cf. *Questions* Ch. 16, **1-3**.
[65] علاج. This normally refers to medical treatments, and some alchemy was designed to produce medicine. But it also refers to technical processes, suggesting any complicated chemical process that must be repeated.
[66] That is, the eleventh, because the third can also signify close companions and friends, and those elections are given below.

named for you, and especially do not ever grant him an allotment in anything of the building of homes. **4** And if you did not find a way out of him having a share, then make Venus strong in her position, and make her have strength over Mars, and connect her to him from a trine or sextile: for indeed Mars will scarcely be able to corrupt the matter of Venus due to her friendship towards him. **5** And make Saturn fall away from Venus as much as you can (as well as Mars),[67] and [make her be] with the Moon, if [the Moon] looks at her from friendship.

6 And[68] let the Moon be increasing in light, connected to Jupiter from a square, for that is preferable to the opposition and indicates the goodness of that building and its completion. **7** And beware lest the Moon be with Saturn or the Tail, or that Saturn be in the Ascendant or the fourth, for that indicates slowness and trouble, and indeed [the building] will not go up; and if it did go up and was inhabited, its people will still be struck by fears and illnesses, and robbers, and misfortunes from death, and the building will crack and perhaps fall down. **8** And if Mars is looking at her, and he is rising,[69] burning and razing will be feared for it; and in that [situation] let the Moon be increasing in light, for truly that will be a blessing upon its owner.

9 And let the lord of the house of the Moon be looking at her, and likewise the lord of the Ascendant,[70] and let it[71] be looking at the Ascendant, and both of them cleansed of the infortunes; but if they did not look, the owner will not live in that building.

10 And[72] if you wanted to raze a building, then let the Moon be declining from the rising,[73] separated from the infortunes, connected with the for-

---

[67] I believe this means that Saturn should be in aversion from Mars as well as from Venus; I have divided this sentence up a little speculatively, as in the Arabic it seems to need a few more markers to indicate who is doing what to whom.

[68] For this paragraph, cf. *Carmen* V.7.

[69] صاعد. This probably means that he is succeedent or angular and moving by primary motion towards the degree of one of the stakes. (Alternatively, it could mean rising towards the apogee.) *Carmen* V.7 has Mars being with her or looking at her "from a strong place," which is most likely a succeedent or angular position.

[70] The Arabic does not indicate whether the lord of the Ascendant should be looking at her, or the lord of the Moon looking at the lord of the Ascendant.

[71] The lord of the Ascendant.

[72] For **10**, cf. *Carmen* V.8. Cf. also the Māshā'allāh version in Leiden, Or. 891, ff. 24a-24b.

[73] In Hephaistion III.7, **11**, this means moving down from the "northern heights," namely either northern latitude or northern declination.

tunes, and let that fortune be eastern or rising,⁷⁴ direct. **11** Or, the Moon should be connecting with the lord of her house from friendship (that is, from a trine or sextile), so that it will be easier for its demolition. **12** And as for the aspect of the square and the opposition, its demolition will certainly be more violent.

[Buying and working land]

13 And if you wanted the purchase of lands and entering into them with someone, and you wanted to obtain land or receive it from someone, then let Saturn be in his exaltation, triplicity, or bound, and let Jupiter be in his inspection from a stake or a trine, and make Mars be falling away from both of them. **14** And let the Moon be at the beginning of the month, looking at Saturn from friendship, increasing in calculation, looking towards Jupiter:⁷⁵ for indeed that indicates the flourishing of that land, and its growth. **15** And if you were not able to have the aspect of Jupiter with Saturn, then make it be Venus instead of Jupiter, and make the signs of water fortunate: for indeed if you made them fortunate with the fortunes, they would be superior to the signs of air. **16** And let the Moon be in her exaltation or the Midheaven, and the lord of the Ascendant looking at her, and the Moon and the Ascendant cleansed of the infortunes and defects.

[Digging]

17 If⁷⁶ you wanted to channel a river⁷⁷ or dig a canal, then let that be when Saturn is eastern⁷⁸ and the Moon under the earth in the third or fifth, free of the infortunes, made fortunate, received. **18** And beware lest one of the two infortunes be in the Midheaven, for indeed with that it will be feared that the canal will collapse or the river drain out.⁷⁹ **19** And let Saturn be in the eleventh sign from the Ascendant, and let the fortune which the Moon connects

---

⁷⁴ Again, this probably means being succeedent or angular, moving towards an axial degree.
⁷⁵ مناظرًا للمشتري.
⁷⁶ Cf. the Māshā'allāh version in Leiden, Or. 891, f. 23b.
⁷⁷ تجري نهرًا. Or perhaps, "make a river flow," but the pairing with digging a canal makes rerouting or channeling water more likely.
⁷⁸ The Māshā'allāh version in Leiden reads, "fast."
⁷⁹ Or, "decline, decrease."

to, be in a fixed, rising[80] sign. **20** And the more excellent of the fortunes is Jupiter: but if you were unable to have [the Moon apply to] him, then make Jupiter be [in] the Midheaven, for that is more durable for the river and more stable for the canal.

[Planting and sowing]

21 And[81] if you wanted the planting of palms and [other] trees, let that be when the Moon is in a fixed sign, and the lord of her house looking at her from the signs of water. **22** And let the Ascendant be a fixed sign, or double-bodied, and the lord of the Ascendant rising,[82] eastern. **23** For if it was rising[83] and it was not eastern, it would be quick in [its] growth but there would be a delay in its bearing [of fruit]. **24** And if it was eastern [but] declining, it would be slow in growth [but] quick in bearing [fruit]. **25** And if it was western [and] declining, it would be slow in growth and slow in bearing [fruit]. **26** And let the lord of the Ascendant and the lord of the house of the Moon be looking at the two of them,[84] and [let] them both[85] be free of the infortunes and burning.

27 And[86] if you wanted to sow seed or anything which you do not want ever to lose, then let the Ascendant be in a sign having two bodies, and its lord in a convertible sign, looking at the lord of its house,[87] and [let] it be free of the infortunes: because if an infortune was looking at it, disease will strike the vegetation. **28** And let the Moon be increasing in light and number: because if the Moon was under the rays and she is decreasing in calculation, then that seed will be carried away and nothing will grow from it. **29** And if it was just as I explained about the Moon ([namely under the rays but] increas-

---

[80] صاعد. This could mean that it is succeedent or angular, but perhaps even of northern declination.
[81] For this paragraph, cf. the Māshā'allāh version in Leiden, Or. 891, f. 23b (which Sahl has abbreviated).
[82] صاعداً. See above, but this probably means being succeedent or angular.
[83] صاعداً. See above, but this probably means being succeedent or angular.
[84] Namely, the Ascendant and the Moon.
[85] This is probably still the lord of the Ascendant and lord of the Moon's house.
[86] For this paragraph, cf. the Māshā'allāh version in Leiden, Or. 891, f. 23a.
[87] The Māshā'allāh version says, "and the *Moon* in a convertible sign, with the lord of *her* house looking at her."

ing in calculation), it will bring forth thin vegetation, in accordance with what its nature[88] produces.

[Chapter 5]: The fifth sign, & what types of choices are in it

[Conceiving children]

2 If you wanted the choice of a time for sexual intercourse, so that you may make the sperm masculine, then let the time of intercourse—the Ascendant and its lord, the Moon, and the lord of the house of children—be in male signs or a masculine region of the circle, and do not put a planet in the Ascendant of that hour, nor in the sign of children, unless it is a masculine one. **3** And if you wanted a feminine one, then let these indicators which I named for you be in the female signs and a feminine region of the circle. **4** And if you were not able to do that, and these indicators differed in the masculinization of the signs as well as their feminization, then make the lord of the hour, and the planet accepting the management of the Moon, and the one greatest in testimony in the male signs and masculinized regions, [all] be partners: the child will be in the manner of that, if God (be He exalted!) wills.

[Miscarriage and abortion]

5 And[89] if a child died in the belly and you wanted to remove it, then let that be when the Moon is decreasing in light, declining from the belt[90] toward the seventh sign from the Ascendant (that is, from the Midheaven to the seventh),[91] and she is looking at the fortunes from a trine, or a square

---

[88] نفسه, which also means "it itself" or "itself," as Crofts has it ("as much as it itself can send forth"); but to me this seems uninformative, and I think the point is that it will be thin or sparse, compared to whatever kind of lushness that plant normally has. The Māshā'allāh text is undotted and unclear.

[89] For this paragraph, cf. *Carmen* V.19.

[90] That is, declining in ecliptical latitude towards or in southern latitude (see *Carmen* V.19 and Heph. Ch. III.12, **1-2**).

[91] Sahl's parenthetical comment is incorrect, because it implies that "the belt" (the zodiac or ecliptic) indicates the Midheaven. This phrase should read: "declining from the belt toward *the south*" (الجنوب), as *Carmen* has it (and Hephaistion confirms).

from the inspection of Mars.⁹² **6** And the most preferable thing for that is if the sign of the Moon and the Ascendant are of the feminine signs, direct in ascensions, and not in the crooked signs.

[Educating children]

7 And⁹³ if you wanted to hand a child over to school or a place in which he may study a trade or calculation, then let your choice for that be when the Moon is looking at Mercury, and they are both free of the infortunes. **8** And let the Ascendant be Gemini or Virgo, and let Mercury be eastern, rising up,⁹⁴ and he should not be declining⁹⁵ nor retrograde, and not lingering in his fall, and not made unfortunate, and let the lord of the house of Mercury be likewise. **9** And you do not make the Moon be declining, nor decreasing in light, for that would slow down the learning. **10** And let the lords of both their houses⁹⁶ be looking at them.

[Chapter 6]: The sixth sign, & what types of choices are in it

[Exorcism]

2 If⁹⁷ in a place or house there was a devil or inhabiting [spirit] or a female spirit following a woman, or anything feared or showing itself, and you wanted its disappearance from its place or from anyone by a spell or entreaty or trick, then beware lest the Moon or Ascendant be in these signs: Leo, Cancer, Scorpio, or Aquarius, and let the Moon be in signs other than these, separating from the infortunes, connecting to the fortunes.

---

⁹² Hephaistion has it that both Venus and Mars should be with her or looking at her from a trine or square.
⁹³ For this paragraph, cf. *Carmen* V.16, **7-8**. Cf. also the Māshā'allāh version in Leiden, Or. 891, f. 23b-24a (which is more extensive).
⁹⁴ صاعدًا.
⁹⁵ إمنحدرًا, here and in **9**.
⁹⁶ That is, of the Moon and Mercury.
⁹⁷ Cf. *Carmen* V.38.

[Medicine for bowels and digestion]

3 And[98] if you wanted a choice for taking medicine of the bowels or taking medicine for a stomachache, or an injection,[99] then let that be when the Ascendant or the Moon is in Libra or Scorpio, connecting to the fortunes; and do not put anything of the infortunes in the stakes of the Moon. **4** Now if you could not find a way out of that, then let that be from a trine or sextile but not the assembly nor an encounter with the two rays.[100] **5** Now if she was entering under the rays, it produces colic.[101]

[Medicine for different parts of body]

6 And[102] if you wanted a treatment for the head and what comes down from it (such as gargling and vomiting), then let that be when the Ascendant and the Moon are in Aries and Taurus, and she is decreasing in light, connecting to the fortunes; and beware of the aspect of the Sun from the square and the assembly in Aries especially, due to the heat of the Sun.

7 And as for medicine introduced through the nose,[103] let that be when the Ascendant is Cancer, Leo, and Virgo, and the Moon is connected to the fortunes, not connected to the infortunes nor to a retrograde planet, nor to a corrupted one.

8 And if you wanted a treatment for the body and pain of the hands and legs, then let that be when the Ascendant and the Moon were in Capricorn, Pisces, and Aquarius, connected with the fortunes.

---

[98] For this sentence, cf. *Carmen* V.39. **2**.

[99] حقنة, which can also include enemas (appropriate here because of the parts of the body involved).

[100] This sounds like being besieged or enclosed by the malefics. Crofts does not end the sentence here, but that would make **5** logically related to or consequent upon, this condition; so I have separated them.

[101] That is, muscular contractions due to blockage, to try to expel the medicine.

[102] For this sentence. Cf. *Carmen* V.39, **1**, and Māshā'allāh's Ch. 45 in Laleli 2022.M (ff. 25a-25b), which however reads somewhat differently.

[103] السّعوط. But in *Carmen* this is done in Aries and Taurus, which makes more sense than these signs which rule parts of the chest and trunk.

[Curing old diseases]

9 And if you wanted a treatment for an old malady, then let your choice for that be when the Moon is in Taurus and its triplicity (and the best of those is Taurus), because it is of the pains of the earth:[104] and let the Moon be cleansed of the infortunes and the fortunes be in the stakes of the Moon from Taurus,[105] and let it[106] be stronger. **10** And take care that the old disease goes away and does not return to its sufferer,[107] and beware lest the Moon be connecting with Saturn especially, for he is the indicator of the long length of the illness.

[The Moon in signs and regions indicating limbs of the body]

11 And Māshā'allāh said:[108] Look, for every treatment you wanted, at its position in the body. **12** For if it was in the region of the head, throat, and chest, then treat it when the Moon is in Aries, Taurus, and Gemini: and it is the highest region. **13** If the malady was in the region of the belly and what is lower than the navel, then treat it when the Moon is in Cancer, Leo, and Virgo: and it is the middle region. **14** And if the malady was in the lower region, such as the buttocks and the lower part of the body, then treat it when the Moon is in Libra, Scorpio, and Sagittarius, and let the Moon be connecting to the fortunes, increasing in light and number. **15** <And[109] if the malady was in what is between the knees and the feet, then treat it when the Moon is in Capricorn, Aquarius, and Pisces.>

16 And[110] it has already been said as well: treat every pain from the head to the navel when the Moon is in what is between the stake of the earth, so rising up to the Midheaven due to the rising of the circle: and it is the place which is called the highest region of the circle. **17** And if the malady was from the navel to the bottom of the foot, then treat it when the Moon is in

---

[104] أوجاع الأرض. I believe this means that chronic or old illnesses are of the nature of earth, and since Taurus is the fixed sign, it especially indicates old, chronic illnesses.
[105] I am not sure what the "from Taurus" means here.
[106] Grammatically this could refer to either the Moon or Taurus.
[107] Lit. "its owner," referring to the lord of the Ascendant.
[108] For this election (**11-18**), cf. the Māshā'allāh version in Leiden, Or. 891, f. 26b (which Sahl has abbreviated).
[109] I have supplied this sentence based on the Latin; it is missing in Sahl's Arabic as well as in Leiden.
[110] For this paragraph, cf. *Carmen* V.28, **26**.

what is between the tenth, declining towards the stake of the earth: and that is the lowest part of the circle. **18** And let there be a fortune in the Ascendant, for truly that indicates health.

[Eyes, touching with iron, cupping, and bloodletting]

19 And[111] if there was a pustule in the eye, or what needs to be touched by iron or by a lancet, or there was a film over [the eye], or it was in a place of the body other than that which needs to be touched by iron (such as the opening of a vein),[112] let that be when the Moon is increasing in light and calculation—except for cupping, for indeed [in that case] you make the Moon be decreasing in light and calculation—connecting to the fortunes, and let Jupiter be above the earth, in the Ascendant or eleventh or tenth. **20** And beware the connection with Mars when the Moon is increasing in light and calculation. **21** And if you were unable to make Jupiter be in those positions, then let him be looking at the Ascendant; and beware lest the Moon and the Ascendant be in earthy signs and the Node mixed up with Mars.

22 And[113] along with that, beware when the New Moon appears until the Moon goes past the Sun by 12°, and likewise the opposition, or that Mars would be in the Ascendant when that [vein] is cut, and likewise Saturn (unless it was Saturn at the beginning of the month, and the Moon was increasing in calculation and glow): for if anything of the body is cut or lanced for pus, or veins opened, its owner[114] will not benefit by it.

23 And[115] beware of cutting a vein or extracting a tooth when the Moon is in a convertible sign or one having two bodies, [and] involved with the infortunes—unless the Moon is cleansed of the infortunes, or there is a strong fortune with the Moon or the Moon is connecting with it from a trine or sextile.[116]

---

[111] For **19-21**, cf. *Carmen* V.41 and V.40, **7**; and Māshā'allāh's version in Laleli 2022.M, Ch. 19 (f. 13b-14a).
[112] That is, bloodletting.
[113] Cf. *Carmen* V.40, **2-5**.
[114] Again, the sick person who is represented by the Ascendant and its lord.
[115] Cf. *Carmen* V.40, **9**.
[116] This sentence is stated a little awkwardly, but Sahl's point has to do with the movable and common signs: in other words, they are normally to be avoided if the Moon has any

24 And as for pains which are in the eye, such as swelling and leukoma,[117] and the rest of ailments which are treated with iron,[118] let that be at the increase of the Moon's glow and her calculation, based on what I mentioned to you before this chapter. 25 And let her be cleansed of Mars especially in the treatment of the eye, for truly his aspect becomes more violent in that; and as for the aspect of Saturn, indeed when the Moon is increasing in calculation and glow at the beginning of the month, it is less for his damage. 26 And if she was withdrawing from the opposition, then make the Moon be inspecting Mars from a trine, and he connecting with the fortunes. 27 And you do not grant Mars strength in anything of treating pain of the eyes, because the scholars agreed on the harm of Mars for the head. 28 And[119] they did say as well that for everything treated by iron, look at its authority over the body: do not put the Moon and the Ascendant in that sign, and you do not touch anything with iron with the Moon in a sign having two bodies or a convertible sign.

[Removing hair]

29 And if you wanted the shaving of hair by means of depilatory cream or something else, let that be when the Moon is in feminine signs, decreasing in light. 30 And if you cannot do that, then do not put her in signs which have hair, such as Aries, Leo, and others of the bestial signs, and let the lord of the Ascendant be declining from the Midheaven toward the stake of the earth.

[Slaves]

31 And[120] if you wanted to buy a slave, then beware lest the Moon be connecting with the infortunes or that a malefic be under the earth, or the Moon in a convertible sign: for that indicates that he will be deceitful to his masters, and will not remain fixed in [that] condition, or he will be a runaway if the Moon was separating from the infortunes—except for Libra, for

---

connection with the infortunes, but they will be all right *if* some of these other conditions hold.

[117] Any kind of white opaqueness in the eye.
[118] Or rather, any metal instrument.
[119] Cf. *Carmen* V.40, **8-9**.
[120] For this paragraph, cf. *Carmen* V.12.

indeed it is suitable for that [kind of purchase].¹²¹ **32** And as for the fixed signs, he will be a steadfast worker, of noble character for his masters—except for Scorpio, for he will be a slanderer, weak in speech; and in Leo he will be a voracious eater, and stomachache will afflict him for that reason, and he will be a robber¹²² [and] thief. **33** And if the Moon was in the signs having two bodies, truly he will be praised—except for Pisces, for he will conceal within himself his deception toward his masters and his slander towards them. **34** And be on guard against the connection of the Moon with the infortunes, for when she connects with an infortune it signifies that the slave will be sold. **35** Now if you wanted to gain something from slaves, from the existence of the Moon in the twelve signs, that is in the fifth book of Dorotheus.

36 And¹²³ if you wanted to emancipate a slave, then let that be when the Moon is cleansed of defects, increasing in light and number, connected to the fortunes. **37** And let that fortune be eastern, increasing: for if it was increasing [but] western, he will achieve good but pains will befall him, and he will not cease to be worn out until he dies. **38** And at the increase of the Moon's light he will be healthy in body, and at the increase of [her] calculation it indicates the attainment of wealth. **39** And¹²⁴ let the Sun and the sign of the Midheaven be cleansed of the infortunes, because if they were unfortunate, disaster will befall the master based on the essence of the sign. **40** And let the time of the emancipation be when the luminaries are looking at each other from a trine or sextile, so that there is friendship and agreement between the slave and the master, and he will get what is good from him. **41** And as for the aspect of the square, that is middling; and the aspect of the opposition indicates that the slave will argue with¹²⁵ his master. **42** And for one who emancipates with the Moon being made unfortunate, slavery and dominion will be better for him. **43** And make the Moon be of the fixed signs.

---

¹²¹ Sahl has jumbled several things together, but I believe he means that the malefics indicate deceit, while the convertible signs (except for Libra) show instability and running away.
¹²² Or perhaps simply, "stealthy" (لصّ).
¹²³ For this paragraph, cf. generally *Carmen* V.14, **1-3**.
¹²⁴ For this sentence, cf. *Carmen* V.37, **19**.
¹²⁵ This term also has connotations of lawsuits (يخاصم).

[Chapter 7]: The seventh sign, & what types of choices are in it

[Betrothal and marriage]

2 If[126] you wanted a choice for marrying, beware lest the Moon be in the twelfth, and beware lest she be in the signs which are not suitable for that (and those are Aries, Cancer, Capricorn, and Aquarius), and beware of the signs in which the two infortunes and the Tail are. **3** And let that[127] be when the Moon is connecting with a fortune, and she is in a convertible sign (and the best of them is Libra).

4 At[128] a betrothal, beware lest the Moon be in a fixed sign.

5 And[129] as for the marriage – at the time of entering women and consummating it with them – beware lest it be in a convertible sign, or one having two bodies; and let that be when the Moon is in a fixed sign (and the best of them are Leo and Taurus; as for Scorpio and Aquarius, truly they are not useful for the woman). **6** And the middle of Taurus is better than its beginning and its end, and the first half of Gemini is worse and its last [half] better, and Aries and Cancer are bad, and Leo is praiseworthy (except that each one of the two will not preserve the wealth of his partner, [and] will waste it).[130] **7** And Virgo is suitable for a woman and a widow,[131] but as for a virgin, not; and Libra is bad, and the beginning of Scorpio is suitable, but its end bad because it indicates that their partnership will not last long. **8** And Sagittarius is bad, and likewise the beginning of Capricorn (while its middle and end are excellent), and Aquarius is bad, and likewise Pisces.

9 And[132] it is not good in marrying if Venus is inspecting the infortunes, so let that be when Venus is in the houses of the fortunes and their bounds, connected with the lord of her own house (and if it was an infortune, then let

---

[126] For this paragraph, cf. *Carmen* V.17, **8-20**.

[127] This sentence cannot be right, or it refers to another election, because the convertible signs are *not* recommended for marriage (see especially the prohibition against Libra in **7** below). This is probably meant to be paired with **4**, referring to the betrothal: there, we want convertible signs because we want the betrothal to be fast, while for the marriage itself we want the fixed signs (so that it lasts). See Ch. 2, **3** and **7**.

[128] See also Ch. 2, **3** and **7**.

[129] For this paragraph, cf. *Carmen* V.17, **8-20**.

[130] Compare this with Ch. 6, **32**, where Leo also shows someone eager to consume.

[131] Or perhaps, "divorcee" (ثيّب).

[132] For this paragraph, cf. *Carmen* V.17, **21-23**.

her be separating from it). **10** And <let> Jupiter look down upon her,[133] or let Venus be connecting [to him] from the trine; and[134] let the Moon and Jupiter and Venus be looking, each of them, at the other from a trine or sextile (and the more preferable is the trine, especially the triplicity of water).

11 And[135] let the Moon be increasing in calculation and light, free of the infortunes, and let Venus always be in her exaltation, house, triplicity, or joy, or the conjunction of Jupiter or Mercury (and Mercury [should be] made fortunate, strong).

12 And[136] likewise make the Sun suitable based on what I described, because from the Sun and the Ascendant is known the condition of the man,[137] and from Venus and the Moon and the seventh sign is known the condition of the woman. **13** So, beware the aspect of the infortunes to them from the conjunction, square, or opposition.

14 And if it was a woman, then let the Moon be in a sign having two bodies,[138] and [let] the work be based on what I described to you.

15 And let the Ascendant at the hour of consummation be of the signs which I described such that the Moon should be in them, and do not put anything of the infortunes in the Ascendant, and they should not look at it from enmity.

16 And let one of the fortunes be in the Midheaven,[139] for[140] Dorotheus said[141] in that case they will be blessed with a child in that year in which they come together [sexually]. **17** Now, if the Midheaven was a watery sign, then truly the woman will become pregnant on the first [day] when they come together in it.

---

[133] That is, overcoming her.
[134] This should be understood as "or."
[135] Cf. *Carmen* V.17, **5, 21,** and **35.**
[136] For this paragraph, cf. *Carmen* V.17, **1.**
[137] Reading with Heph. III.9, 1 (quoting the *Pentateuch*), for Sahl's "child."
[138] I am not sure why this should be.
[139] That is, let a fortune in one person's chart be in the Midheaven of the other (see Heph. III.9, **19-20**). Hephaistion also mentions fortunes by transit. This should be at the time of the wedding, but I could understand it being at the consummation as well.
[140] Reading ف for و, which would have introduced a new sentence: but Dorotheus uses the following to explain *why* we want fortunes in the Midheaven.
[141] Cf. *Carmen* V.17, **25-26.**

[War]

18 Knowledge[142] of the times in traveling to war: you ought to make the Ascendant one of the houses of the superior planets, and the strongest of them is the house of Mars, when he is in the sextile of the Ascendant or its trine. **19** And let the lord of the Ascendant be in the Ascendant or the eleventh, and beware of the fourth, seventh, and eighth, <and> lest it be burned, falling, or connecting to a falling planet not receiving it. **20** And make the lord of the seventh be connecting with the lord of the Ascendant, or in the Ascendant, or in the second.

21 If you sought that they should meet, Mars [should] be placed in the stakes (so that there would be an encounter and war would take place), and join a fortune which has a share in the Ascendant, to Mars (it will block him from the Ascendant).

22 And do not ever travel to war unless Mars has governorship in his travel,[143] so that he would be the lord of the Ascendant, and strong, in an excellent place, not with corruption, and not burned; and let him be in signs straight in rising. **23** And watch out in placing him unless he is in the domain[144] of the Ascendant, and you bring about his assistance for the one whom you are sending forth to the war, and sending the soldiers: for indeed they will be safe, by the permission of God (be He exalted!).

24 And[145] make the second and its lord suitable for the assistants of the one beginning [the action], and the eighth and its lord for the assistants of the enemy; and you do not put the lord of the eighth in the seventh nor in the eighth, but put the lord of the eighth in the second.

25 And[146] place the Lot of Fortune and its lord in the Ascendant or in the second, and keep them both away from the seventh and the eighth.

26 And do not make the Ascendant and the lord of its house be corrupted until[147] he begins the matter, and likewise the share of the twelfth-part of the Moon.

---

[142] For the first part of this sentence, cf. *Labors* Ch. 24, **1**. See also *Sections*, **45**.

[143] I believe that "his" refers to the human client (rather than Mars's own course), so that Mars rules his travel.

[144] حيّز. This might simply mean that he is on the eastern side of the chart: see *On Times* Ch. 8, **19**.

[145] Cf. *Labors* Ch. 2, **9-12**.

[146] For this sentence, cf. *Labors* Ch. 2, **20-21**.

27 And truly, in the matter of wars there is no avoiding it but that you make the stars of fighting suitable: and they are Mars, Mercury, the Moon, and the lord of her house: so look in the suitability of these, and do not neglect them.

28 And know that on the whole[148] if the two armies' departures to the fighting were both strengthened in the way we described, that one of them will win who was born by night, and the one whose nativity had Mars in charge of it:[149] because he will be the master of wars and put in charge of them. **29** And perhaps they will come to an agreement or abandon their war: and that is if the place of the departure of each to the fighting is wholly favorable.

30 And if you wanted the purchase of weapons and instruments of war, then let that be when Mars is in his house, exaltation, or triplicity, at the end of the month: because the scholars have warned of the Moon being with Mars in the beginning of the month; while at its end it is suitable.

31 And if you wanted the demolition of fortresses, let the inception of that be when the Moon is made unfortunate [and] does not have strength.

32 And if you wanted the corruption[150] of something of the instruments of war, begin with that when Mercury is made unfortunate [and] does not have strength.

33 And if you wanted to spoil the fighting, let that be when Mars is made unfortunate [and] he does not have strength.

34 And if you wanted the spoiling of land, start when the Moon is made unfortunate [and] does not have strength.

---

[147] حتّى: if so, maybe this means "until *after*" he begins. But one of the Sahl MSS reads حين, "when," which makes more sense.

[148] جميعًا, which can also mean "wholly" or "entirely" (as in **29**), but this seems to be less redundant and also allows for the exception in **29**.

[149] Crofts reads, "the one who had Mars in his nativity," which does not make astrological sense (and is otiose, because everyone has a natal Mars). Therefore I am reading ولي ("ruling," "the one in charge") for ولد ("was born").

[150] Or better, "destruction" (فساد).

[Destroying idols]

35 And if you wanted the corruption of a place of idols and of religious beliefs that lack God, then begin that when Venus is made unfortunate [and] does not have strength.

[Chapter 8]: The eighth sign, & what types of choices are in it

2 If[151] a man wanted to make a will, he should not begin that when the Ascendant and the sign of the Moon are convertible: for that indicates that the will is going to be changed. **3** And let him make it when the Moon is decreasing in calculation, increasing in light.

4 And the Moon should not be connecting with a planet under the rays: for that is what indicates a quick death. **5** And worse than that is when the Moon is with Mars or in his square or his opposition, or Mars is in the Ascendant or looking at it from hostility: for truly that indicates that that will is not going to be changed, and the sick person will die from that illness of his, and that will is not going to be executed after his death, or it will be stolen.

6 And if Saturn was like that relative to the Moon and the Ascendant, there will be a prolonging of that man's lifespan, and that will is going to be executed after it, and it will not be rejected in his life nor after his death.

7 And if Venus and Jupiter were like that relative to the Moon and the Ascendant, then truly for the owner of that will, his lifespan will last a bit longer, and he is going to change that will.

[Chapter 9]: The ninth sign, & what types of choices are in it

[Travel in general]

2 Do not cease to send people on their journeys based on their nativities, according to the Ascendant of every birth and its stakes. **3** And let the Moon be in its Ascendant or its Midheaven, and make suitable the lord of the sought thing which he is searching for, and make the lord of the year suitable, as well as the lord of the rooted Ascendant and of the year.[152]

---

[151] For this chapter, cf. *Carmen* V.43.

[152] That is, the natal, profected, and solar revolution Ascendants.

4 And if you do not know what I mentioned, then look for the one who comes to you from the lord of the sought thing which he is seeking: where is its position relative to the lord of the Ascendant? **5** Then, choose for him an hour which agrees with his nativity or his question: and that is that you do not make the Ascendant of the question and its lord fall away from[153] the Ascendant of the departure, and let the Ascendant of the departure be the tenth of the Ascendant of the question or birth (if he was seeking the Sultan), and if he sought commerce [it should be] the eleventh from the Ascendant of the question—and likewise for every sought thing which he seeks, make that sign be rising for him. **6** And let the Moon be in the stakes and what follows them if she was free of the infortunes, and let her be looking at the Ascendant; while if she was made unfortunate, then make her fall away from the Ascendant. **7** And let the lord of the Ascendant and the lord of the house of the Moon be in the stakes, and the Moon looking at the lord of her house.

8 And[154] beware of putting the Moon with the infortunes or [making her] inspect them from a square or opposition, because the infortunes' looking at the Ascendant is easier than their looking at the Moon. **9** And that goes especially for travel, because her connection with Mars at the beginning of the month indicates robbers or the Sultan[155] or fire.

10 And beware lest you ever put the Moon in the fourth, but put her in the fifth, so if she is made fortunate in this position it will be shorter for the traveler's absence, and more successful for his sought matters, and greater for his profits,[156] and less for the weakening of his body, and more secure for what is with him, and easier for his path.

11 And also detested is the presence of the Moon in the Ascendant at the entrance or departure,[157] because illness will be feared for its owner, or a powerful burden[158] in the body.

---

[153] That is, "be in aversion to."

[154] For this sentence, cf. *Carmen* V.22, **10**.

[155] Crofts reads, "tyrant," which seems apt in this context: a powerful, destructive authority figure.

[156] This word also connotes benefit in general (فوائد).

[157] This view, that the Ascendant should not have the Moon in it during journeys, is the view of Māshā'allāh (see my *Choices & Inceptions* I.2.8). Now, **3** above seems to want the Moon of the inception to fall in the *natal* Ascendant, while **11** seems to say that she should *not* be in the Ascendant of the *inception*: so perhaps there is no contradiction here. See *On*

[Travel to particular people]

12 And[159] if the travel was to kings, then make the Moon be connected to the Sun or the lord of the Midheaven from a trine or sextile, and let the Sun be in an excellent place, in the Ascendant, eleventh, or tenth. **13** And if he was falling, you will not get good from that; but if he was in the ninth, third, or fifth, it indicates hardship and a scarcity of benefit, and likewise the stake of the west and the fourth indicate a scarcity of benefit, hardship, and prolonging [the trip]. **14** And if your seeking and departure was for nobles, judges, and masters of religion, then let the connection of the Moon be with Jupiter from the stakes or in an excellent place from the Ascendant. **15** And if your departure was to the masters of wars and fighting, then let the connection of the Moon be with Mars from a trine or sextile, and beware of the stakes and the assembly, and let Mars be in what follows from the stakes. **16** And if your departure was to mature people or to one who has no esteem,[160] then let the connection of the Moon be with Saturn from friendship, and let Saturn be in what follows the stakes. **17** And if your departure was to women, then connect the Moon to Venus, and [let Venus be] in a male sign;[161] and if you were able to [have her be] in the places which I mentioned to you for Jupiter,[162] then do it. **18** And if your departure was to writers, merchants, and scholars, then let the connection be with Mercury, and beware lest Mercury be under the rays at that time, or retrograde, or that the infortunes look at him.

19 And[163] whenever the star with which the Moon (or the planet which is in the opposite of the Ascendant, or the lord of the seventh) is connecting, is slow or retrograde or made unfortunate, it indicates twists and turns[164] and difficulty in that objective.

Times Ch. 9, 7, which explains that the Moon in the inception Ascendant will prolong the journey.
[158] Or, "exhaustion" (تعب).
[159] For this paragraph, cf. *Carmen* V.15 and V.31.
[160] لا حسب له, but reading as ليس له حسب.
[161] This seems odd: one would expect a feminine sign.
[162] Reading للمشتري with al-Rijāl, for "partnership" (للشركة).
[163] Cf. perhaps *Carmen* V.22, 7-8.
[164] This can also refer to detours, etc.

[Travel by water]

20 If[165] the travel was in the water, then let the Moon be in a sign of water, and in travel by water beware of the connection of the Moon with Saturn from a stake, and beware the malice of Saturn if he is in signs of water, having mastery over the Ascendant of the departure or over the Moon. **21** And if you did not find a way out of that, then let the Moon be connecting, along with him, to a strong fortune from a trine or sextile, or from a stake, so it may repel the malice of Saturn from sinking, beating, or violent wind.

22 And[166] as for traveling by sea, do not make the luminaries unfortunate, because both of them, if they are suitable and safe from the infortunes, and the fortunes are not making them fortunate,[167] indicate safety. **23** And if they were unfortunate, then truly that man will be put to death[168] or perish on the journey.

24 And do not sail when it is moonless, for truly that is detestable.

25 And[169] if his travel by sea was for commerce, then make Mercury suitable or the Moon especially, and let him[170] be looking at Jupiter from Cancer or Pisces. **26** And as for Scorpio, it is definitely detested in travel by sea due to [it being] the place of Mars and his[171] hostility to one who travels by sea.

27 And[172] be on guard against the bounds of the infortunes in travel by sea, for indeed by land and mountains they are less harmful than they are in travel by water.

[Land versus sea travel]

28 And[173] if the journey was by land, let the Moon be in signs not of water, cleansed of the infortunes, and beware the aspect of Mars on a journey by

---

[165] Cf. perhaps *Carmen* V.26, **16-18**.

[166] For this paragraph, cf. *Carmen* V.26, **35-36**.

[167] This seems counterintuitive, but Heph. III.30, **63** *does* have them (or rather the Moon) unconnected to the fortunes as well.

[168] Reading ميّت in the passive, or else the text would read "will die or perish," which does not express a real difference.

[169] For this sentence, cf. *Carmen* V.23, **20**.

[170] Or the Moon, as the case may be.

[171] But Saturn is usually the worse infortune for sailing (see **28**), so perhaps this should be "it," referring to Scorpio.

[172] Cf. *Carmen* V.26, **43**.

land, just as I warned you of Saturn in traveling by sea. **29** And watch out lest the journey in any way take place when the Moon is in Scorpio.

30 And[174] know that the safety of the earthy signs is for one who wants travel by land, and the safety of the watery signs is for one who wants travel by water. **31** And Saturn is stronger for harm on the sea, and more intensely for that if Jupiter was not inspecting him. **32** And beware travel on the land or sea if the Moon is in the last image[175] of Libra.

[Entering a city]

33 And[176] know that you ought to make suitable the town which you are entering, and that is that you make suitable the second from the Ascendant at your entrance, for every town you wanted: and when you have done that, you have already adjusted[177] for the town. **34** So the adjustment of the Ascendant is necessary for you, as well as its lord, and the Moon, and the lord of the second if you were able: make it be a fortune, and let it be above the earth, in the ninth, tenth, or eleventh. **35** And do not ever put it under the earth in the fourth, fifth, or sixth, for that is detestable in the journey and the work which you are seeking in that city: so let it be above the earth, whether it is a fortune or infortune. **36** And strive so that the lord of the house of the Moon is with the lord of the second, above the earth, and do not put it under the earth: for that is to be criticized—unless in that city he is seeking a matter which he does not want to be evident until he is done with it: [in that case], let the Moon at that time be with the Sun <in> what is between 12° up to 15°; and that is better for the Moon, until she goes out from under the rays up to 3°, made unfortunate; for that is more excellent and praiseworthy for what he needs in the concealment. **37** And if you sought authority in that city, then make the Midheaven and its lord suitable, along with the second from the Ascendant or [from] the Moon.

---

[173] Cf. *Carmen* V.26, **39-40** and **42**.
[174] Cf. *Carmen* V.26, **39** and **42**.
[175] Or, "face" (الصّورة). Crofts reads "paranatellonton," which would mean other constellations co-rising with Libra.
[176] For **33-36**, cf. *Carmen* V.23, **7-12**. Less close is Theophilus, *OVI* Ch. 9.3, **5-9**. Cf. also *Questions* Ch. 9, **42-49**.
[177] That is, made the right calculation of it, for the time (أصلحت).

On Choices

[The Moon in the signs for travel]

38 Then,[178] in journeys look at the position of the Moon in the signs, based on what Dorotheus said about journeys by water. **39** For if she was in the first face of Aries, whether the planets looked or not, it indicates that their[179] matter becomes easy. **40** And if she was in Taurus, then state damages for him; and if Saturn was looking, he will be restricted and it sinks him; and in the second face of Gemini it indicates slowness [but] then safety; and in Cancer, safety from all injury. **41** And in Leo state harm (and it is more intense for him if an infortune was looking), and in Virgo state safety, and it slows his return; and in Libra, if she went beyond 10° you should not set out by land nor by sea; and in Scorpio state anxiety. **42** And in Sagittarius, state that it will take away his refuge;[180] in the beginning of Capricorn there is no harm in it, and in Aquarius state slowness and safety; in Pisces state illness and hardship. **43** And if an infortune was looking, the corruption increases, and if a fortune was looking it dissolves the corruption and strengthens the suitability.

[Chapter 10]: The tenth sign, & what types of choices are in it

[Traveling with a king or prince]

2 If you wanted to set out with a king or Sultan to a district he is already in charge of, then let that be when Jupiter is in the Ascendant or the seventh: for indeed that indicates that the one traveling will find good and joy in that objective of his, and he will see what he likes. **3** And beware lest you put Jupiter in the fourth, for that is detestable, and let the Moon be testifying to him from one of the stakes, and Venus;[181] and beware of Saturn and Mars lest they be in the Ascendant or in one of the stakes. **4** And do not put the Moon

---

[178] For this paragraph, cf. *Carmen* V.26, **1-13**.
[179] This probably refers to the journeys, not the planets.
[180] Reading لواذها for Crofts's ألوانها ("colors"), which is ungrammatical (and flagged by her as questionable). This reading is closer to 'Umar as well as Hephaistion's quotation of Dorotheus (III.30, **47**).
[181] I believe this means that Venus, too, should be testifying to Jupiter from one of the stakes.

under the rays, and beware lest she be with the Tail or the infortunes, for indeed that is not good in it: if he leaves he will not return, and if he is sick he will die, and if he sets out to war he will be killed or defeated.

[Attaining a dignity]

5 And if you wanted to enhance your reputation with the Sultan, let that be when the Ascendant is Leo, and the Sun in Taurus (the Midheaven), and the Moon in the Ascendant, connecting with the fortunes or with the lord of the Midheaven.

[Accession to throne]

6 And if you wanted to introduce a Sultan to the seat of his authority, then let the Ascendant be a fixed sign, and likewise the sign of the outcome,[182] and the lord of the Midheaven free of the infortunes, and the lord of the Ascendant in an excellent place, received, and the lord of the tenth not looking at the eleventh from hostility. **7** And let the Moon be looking at the lord of her house from friendship, and the lord of the fourth sign looking at the fortunes. **8** And if you could not do what I described to you, then let the Moon be received and the lord of the fourth be in a strong place, looking at the fortunes. **9** And if you could not [do that], then make her be falling away from the Ascendant and her aspect to it, and make the fortunes be looking at the sign of the outcome and at the Midheaven.

[Particular dignities]

10 And if you wanted to choose a time for governing the collection of the land tax, let the Moon be connected to Saturn from friendship in the beginning of the month, and let her be in the houses of Saturn, and the fortunes looking at her (for indeed that indicates endurance), and let the Midheaven be a fixed sign so that the work will be one.

11 And if you wanted the summoning of the [military] standards, let the Moon be in the houses of Mars, made fortunate, and let her be looking at Mars from friendship, along with the fortunes, at the end of the month, connected to them. **12** And the most preferable thing there could be for the

---

[182] That is, the fourth: this means that the IC will be on the fourth sign, and the angles "upright."

standards which are below [the rank of] the king, is that the Moon be cleansed, not in the houses of the infortunes, nor in Cancer—unless that standard belongs to a master of war, [in which case] let her be in the houses of Mars (and the best of those is Scorpio, because of the strength of Mars in it and its fixity).

[The enmity of kings]

13 And if you wanted to incite [the enmity] of the Sultan, and you yourself were the aggressor, then let that be when the Moon is increasing in light, and let the Moon and the Ascendant both be cleansed of the infortunes, and the lord of the Ascendant in an excellent place from the Ascendant, in one of its shares, direct, safe from the infortunes (whether it was a fortune or an infortune). 14 And let the lord of the seventh be in a bad place from the Ascendant, neither the fortunes nor the luminaries looking at it.

15 And if he was inciting you, then do not appear before him unless the Moon is decreasing in glow, and let the Ascendant and its lord and the Moon be made unfortunate, and let the lord of the seventh be made fortunate in an excellent place from the Ascendant, so that it will be stronger for what you seek.

[Chapter 11]: The eleventh sign, & what types of choices are in it

[Making friendships]

2 If you wanted to befriend someone, let the Moon be cleansed of the stakes of the infortunes, and let the lord of the eleventh be looking at the Ascendant from friendship. 3 And make the Moon be connected to the essence of the planet which you seek: for example, Venus for women, and Mercury for writers, and all of the circles based on what that [planet] brings.

[Seeking something hoped for]

4 And[183] if you wanted to ask a man for something you need, then let the lord of the Ascendant be looking at the Ascendant from friendship, and let the Ascendant be a fixed sign or one having two bodies, and let the Moon be in the Ascendant or in its trine or its square.[184] **5** And beware of the opposition or that she be connected with the infortunes, or lest she not be looking at the lord of her own house: for truly if the Moon is not looking at the lord of her own house, that sought thing will not be fulfilled. **6** And always seek things you need when the Moon is increasing in light and number, and the lord of the Ascendant is direct, and the Moon connected to the fortunes: for if the fortune is direct and the Moon connected to increasing fortunes, [the outcome] will increase. **7** And beware lest Mercury be in a bad condition, for truly if he was made unfortunate and he was received, it indicates annoyance in the demand, and an ugly refusal. **8** And make the Moon be connected to the planet which is akin to the sought thing, such as for instance the Sun for the essence of kings, and Mars for commanders and the masters of wars, and likewise the lords of the [other] circles.

[Chapter 12]: The twelfth sign, & what types of choices are in it

[Buying animals]

2 If[185] you wanted the purchase of a riding animal, let that be when the Moon is connecting to the fortunes, and they are direct, rising,[186] eastern; and beware of the connection of the infortunes, for truly it will be feared for the animal. **3** And if it was tamed and already ridden, then choose it when the Ascendant is a sign having two bodies, and the Moon in a fixed sign (except for Aquarius and Scorpio). **4** And let the planet connecting with her be direct, rising, so that the animal will increase in price and bodily [size]: because if it was rising [and] retrograde, there will be a decrease in the body of

---

[183] For this election (**4-8**), cf. *Carmen* V.15. See also the Māshā'allāh version in Leiden, Or. 891, ff. 21a-21b, which Sahl has abbreviated.

[184] So says 'Umar's version of Dorotheus as well (*Carmen* V.15, **1**), but the corresponding passage in Hephaistion (III.25, **1**) has only the trine.

[185] For this election (**2-6**), cf. the Māshā'allāh version in Leiden, Or. 891, ff. 21b-22a.

[186] صاعدة. I am not sure if this means moving towards an angle, or rising in the circle of the apogee.

the animal, but with profit. **5** And if it was direct [but] declining, it will increase in body but the price will not be right for it. **6** And if the animal was unridden, then let the Ascendant be a sign having two bodies, and the Moon in a convertible sign, connecting with a fortune; then work just as I described to you in the first heading.[187]

[Hunting and fishing][188]

7 And if you wanted to go out to hunt, go out when the Ascendant is a sign having two bodies and the lord of the seventh decreasing, declining, and let it be in what follows the stakes: for indeed if it was falling, it indicates the escape of the quarry after he gets it.[189] **8** And let the Moon in every departure to the hunt be separating from Mars, and Mars being made fortunate, in an excellent place from the Ascendant. **9** And you do not leave for hunting when the Moon is at the end of the signs, nor empty in course, nor in a convertible sign. **10** And watch out if the lord of her house does not look at her, for truly if it does look at her, it indicates ease in that objective.

11 And make Mercury be cleansed of the infortunes in hunting on the water.[190] **12** And if you wanted a hunt in the mountains then let the Moon be in Aries and its triplicity. **13** And if it was a hunt for birds, then let the Moon be in Gemini and its triplicity, connecting with Mercury or separating from Mercury while he[191] is declining, for that is better.

14 And if you wanted a hunt on the sea, let that be when the Ascendant is a sign having two bodies, and its lord in one of the signs of water (and watch out lest the Ascendant be one of the signs of fire), and let the Moon be looking at the lord of her house. **15** And know that the corruption of the Moon with Mars in a hunt by sea is the most corrupting thing there is, and smaller for [any] benefit. **16** And guard against the misfortune of Mars in a hunt on

---

[187] Or, "chapter" (الباب). Sahl is referring to the rules in **2** and **4-5** above.
[188] For this topic, see also *Questions* Ch. 17.
[189] This probably means something like shooting an animal in a non-lethal place, so that it runs away and is not recovered.
[190] I retain the Arabic phrasing ("hunt on water," "hunt on the sea," etc.) rather than using "fishing," to emphasize that all of this is a version of hunting.
[191] Grammatically, this could refer to either Mercury or the Moon, but I take this to be Mercury.

the sea, and beware the misfortune of Saturn in a hunt on land.[192] **17** And if Venus and the Moon were suitable, and Mars did not corrupt them in a hunt on the sea, they will double the catch and it will be large, and its owner will get a great surplus from it, and that catch will be safe for its owner. **18** Let the Moon be connecting with Venus, and Mercury be with them as well; now if Mercury is corrupted by Saturn, it will not harm that. **19** And beware of Mars lest he be in one of the signs of water and the Moon connecting to him, or that Mars be conjoining with Venus.

[Fleeing, or performing concealed actions]

20 And[193] if you wanted an escape or you are working at some concealed matter, and for everyone wanting an escape and disappearance, let that be when the Moon is separating from the infortunes, connecting with the fortunes, and let the Moon be connecting with Saturn under the rays, and she[194] connecting with a fortune at her departure from the rays. **21** And[195] if the two luminaries were ascending over[196] a matter, they will reveal it and make it appear: so beware of their aspect in an example of this kind.

[Pursuing fugitives]

22 And[197] if you sought someone escaping, let that be when the Moon is connecting with the infortunes, or going out from under the rays and en-

---

[192] Compare with Ch. 9, **28**: this shows that traveling and hunting changes the role of the infortunes by land and sea. For travel, Mars is bad by land and Saturn is bad by sea (these suggests highway robbers and storms, respectively). But for hunting and fishing, Saturn is bad by land and Mars bad by sea (for Mars, to me this suggests lightning strikes on the ship).

[193] Cf. *Carmen* V.6, **4-5**.

[194] Grammatically this could be either the Moon or Saturn, but it makes more sense that the Moon would be connecting with (or rather, separating from) Saturn while under the rays and then connecting with a fortune afterwards. But the fact that Sahl emphasizes the pronoun makes me wonder whether he really means Saturn: in that case, the Moon would hand over management to Saturn under the rays, and when she leaves a *different* fortune like Venus or Jupiter would apply to Saturn—blessing, so to speak, the hidden action which the Moon now leaves behind.

[195] For this sentence, cf. *Carmen* V.36, **14**.

[196] طلعا على. In *Carmen* V.36, **14**, this means they are in the Ascendant; but generally in *Carmen*, the luminaries looking at the key places and planets shows recovery and discovery.

[197] For the first part of this sentence, cf. *Carmen* V.37, **10-14** and **22**.

countering an infortune from a square or opposition at her departure [from them], and do not ever make the Moon nor the planet accepting her management be in the fourth.

[Chapter 13]: Choices of what is not in the twelve signs

2 If[198] you wanted to write a letter,[199] then let that be when the Moon is connecting to Mercury, cleansed of the infortunes. **3** And let Mercury be strong, made fortunate, not retrograde, and let him and the Moon both be cleansed of the infortunes.

The account of choices is completed, and let it have praise and good will. And the prayers of God be upon our master Muhammad and his family, and his Companions.

---

[198] Cf. *Carmen* V.16, and Hephaistion III.27, **1**.
[199] Or even, "book" (كتاب).

ON TIMES

*In the name of God, the Compassionate, the Merciful:
The Book of Times by Sahl b. Bishr.*

[Chapter 1: Introduction]

2 Know that times vary according to the variety of motions, and every beginning of motion is in the celestial circle. **3** The finishing of the period which is between them is the time, [and] for every motion it begins until it is completed, according to the mixture appropriate to it. **4** And indeed *that* is also a time, indicative over good or evil. **5** And all of the motions are according to what I will describe to you of them.

6 Know that the alternation[1] of figures and the changing of [their] conditions in the celestial circle are all indicative for what they are consistent with, of good or evil. **7** And the changing of the figures is the shifting of the planets from the east to the west and from the west to the east, and from the north to the south and from the south to the north (and that pertains to latitude and longitude), as well as the circular motion which gets moving from the east to the west every day (and its night), one rotation.

8 And as for the explanation of their shift in longitude, indeed from the time the planets break away from the Sun, all of the superior planets and the Moon are eastern up to [where] they are distant from him by 180° (and that is where the point of the middle of the Sun's body is opposite to[2] them); and from that to the completion of 360°, they are western. **9** And this motion which I have mentioned to you as being from the east to the west, is accidental [to them], not essential.[3]

10 And the easternness of the planets is also related to the rotations of the highest heavenly sphere, so that a planet is in what is between the Ascendant and the Midheaven,[4] and what is opposite that (and that is what is between the setting and the stake of the earth): and this position of the circle indicates

---

[1] That is, from one condition to some contrary one, as explained in 7.
[2] محاذاتها, lit. "parallel to" them.
[3] Sahl means that their easternness and westernness is relative, a function of the Sun's position rather than pertaining solely to their own proper motion and qualities.
[4] **Es** reads, "the degree of the tenth."

quickness. **11** And their westernness is that a planet is in what is between the stake of the fourth and the Ascendant, and what is opposite that (and that is what is between the tenth and the seventh): and this position of the circle indicates slowness and delay, according to the statement of the ancients.

12 And as for Māshā'allāh, indeed he differs from them in that: he makes[5] the quick place of the circle be what begins its rise in the circle and hastens to [its] ascending and appearance (and it is what is from the degree of the fourth),[6] [then] turned back towards the Midheaven: and that is called "on the high side, belonging to the rotation of the circle in [its] rising." **13** Then, what is between the Midheaven and the fourth is called "turned back to the slow side, sloping, belonging to the beginning of the sloping of the circle and its decline, and the slowness of its appearance." **14** And that is the closest[7] of the two statements, in [its] analogy.

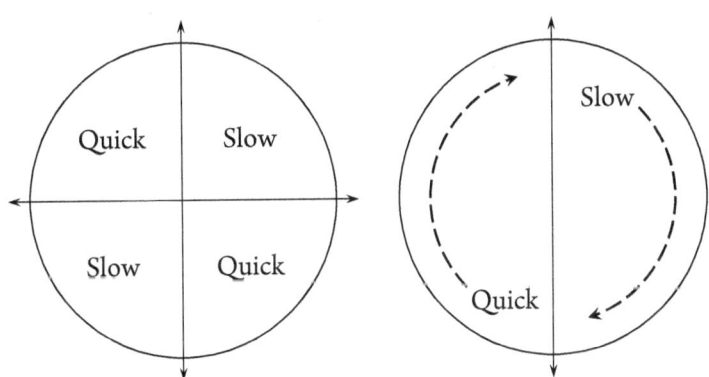

Figure 44: Timing by quarters and hemispheres
(*On Times* Ch. 1, 12-14)

15 And as for the point of the east, it is the portion of the Ascendant; and the point of the west is the portion of the seventh, and the point of the tenth[8]

---

[5] **B** has "he says," making the following a direct quote. This is a reference to passages such as *Carmen* V.28, **26**.
[6] **N** reads simply, "the fourth," while **B** reads, "the fourth sign" (which is probably a misread for "degree" here).
[7] That is, most appropriate, most resembling the truth.
[8] Or, "the right, the lucky side, the south" (**B**).

is the portion of the Midheaven, and the point of the fourth[9] is the portion of the middle of the earth.[10]

16 And as for the motion in latitude, it is that a planet is rising in the north and declining in the north, and rising in the south and declining in the south.

17 And as for the alternation of the planets' figures, [from] the assembly of a planet[11] with the Sun up to the moment of its easternization, that is a time. **18** And from that to the first station, is a time. **19** And from the first station to the extreme point of its retrogradation is a time.[12] **20** And the beginning of the second stay is a time, and the beginning of its direct motion is considered a time. **21** And from its direct motion to its assembly with the Sun, is a time.

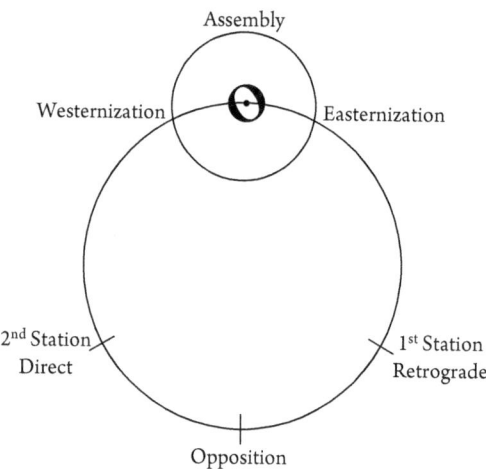

Figure 45: Timing by solar phase (*On Times* Ch. 1, 17-21)

22 And[13] from the motion of a planet with the highest sphere, being turned back towards the Sun in its transiting the degrees of the planets and signs, is a time.

---

[9] Or, "the warlike" side, the north (**B**).
[10] That is, the IC.
[11] Reading the singular to match the following pronoun.
[12] For this and the next time, adding "is a time" with **Es** and **N**, respectively.
[13] I do not really understand this sentence: this could refer to how a planet turns in its *epicycle*, from being opposite the Sun to moving back up towards him.

23 And from the motion of the highest sphere (which is from the east to the west), and its[14] shift to the positions of the planets by body and light, is a time.[15]

24 And from the direction of the degree of the Ascendant and the portions of the planets, for every degree a year and month and day and hour, in front or behind[16] to any of the planets and their rays, and any of the signs and the Lots, is a time. **25** And Māshā'allāh and Abū 'Alī al-Khayyāt have already mentioned that, and they said: the degrees are directed in longitude and latitude,[17] and in front and behind.[18]

26 And so, all of the motions of the circle from which time is known, are from these motions which I have made clear to you.

[Chapter 2]: Aphorisms of times

2 Know that the signs of the quick planets as well as the convertible signs are, in times, the quick ones: days and months.[19] **3** And the signs which belong to the heavy planets, and the fixed signs, are years and months.[20] **4** And in general, if the indicator of the time was in the fixed signs, it indicates years,

---

[14] Grammatically this seems to refer to the motion of the sphere, but the oddity of this sentence and the previous one suggests that it could refer to the *Sun's* motion.

[15] This might be a reference to primary directions.

[16] This may refer to a version of converse directions.

[17] This reference to latitude may be based on *Carmen* III.1, **71**, which says in particular that when planets are opposed by longitude but are in different regions of latitude (one being southern, the other northern), they may not really be considered opposed (at least for purposes of primary directions).

[18] In *Nativities* Ch. 4.12, **6** al-Khayyāt is said to endorse converse directions for retrograde planets, which may also be the intention here.

[19] I have omitted a parenthetical statement here which appears only in **B** and **Es**, that "in the sluggish times, [they indicate] months or years." So far we have no justification for this statement, and it is paralleled by a similar but redundant statement at the end of **3** which only appears in **Es** (see below). See also *Aphorisms* #13.

[20] See above: the parallel statement omitted here says, "and in the quick times, years and months." But years and months were already stated. It is possible that Sahl wants to be able to modify the basic time units, so that a normally quick indication can be slowed down by other factors (and vice versa), but that would more likely require the addition of "weeks," which do not appear here.

and if it was in the embodied signs they indicate months, and if it was in the convertible signs it indicates days.

5 And the quick places relative to the Ascendant indicate quickness in the time (and that is the elevated side), and the slow places of the circle (and that is the side sloping down) indicate slowness in the time.[21]

6 And the Ascendant and Midheaven both indicate quickness in the time, and the seventh indicates months (and that is slower), and the stake of the earth retards and indicates years.

7 And if the planetary indicator of the time was in an embodied sign,[22] then double the time.

Planets	Sign	Time units
Light	Convertible	Days, months
	Double-bodied	Months, doubled
Heavy	Fixed	Months, years

Figure 46: Basic time units by sign and planet

[Chapter 3]: The explanation of the extraction of the indicator of time

2 Know that it is not necessary for you to take the time from every planet, and indeed it should be a strong one if it does not [already] have testimony in the question, or it should have authority over something of it—except for the luminaries, for indeed they have a meaning in the time which the others do not.

3 You definitely take the time from the lord of the Ascendant, and the lord of the sought thing, [and] the one accepting the management from each of them, and the planet which one of them is being connected to (if they are not looking at each other), or the lights, or the one accepting the management of the Moon. **4** So, see which of these planets is stronger and more authoritative[23] in the question, and more victorious over it, and take it as the indicator of the time.

5 And if the indicator of the time was obscure to you, then make it be one of the luminaries (the one of them looking at the Ascendant). **6** And if you

---

[21] See Ch. 1, **12**.

[22] That is, a double-bodied or common or mutable sign.

[23] Or, "worthy" (أولى).

did know the indicator of the time, then it is more authoritative in the time than the lights are. **7** And of the lights, take the time from the one which is looking at the Ascendant.

8 Know that all of the times in questions are based on a number of ways:

9 And [the first way] is that you look at the degrees which are between the one handing over and the one accepting the light ([by aspect] or by body), and you make every degree be a year, month, day, or hour, in accordance with the swiftness of the position or its slowness.

10 The second way is that you see when the transferor reaches the one being transferred to, by body, to the degree and minute (that is, the light planet reaching the heavy one, by body).[24]

11 The third way is that you see how many portions [there are], by the number of signs:[25] what is between the one connecting and the one being connected to, you make into days.

12 The fourth way is that you count from the Ascendant to the position of the one accepting the management, or from the position of the one accepting the management to the Ascendant, a month for every sign.

13 The fifth way is that you look at the indicator of time and how many its lesser years are: for the time will be months or years, based on those.

14 And the time is not counted except from these five ways.

15 And[26] the time [when taken] from the Moon is often a month or two months, in the promise and the sought thing; and if she is in charge of the management, 25 months. **16** And the time of Venus and Mercury, if [either of them] promised the thing sought: to Venus, 10 months and 8 months, and

---

[24] This would be a "real-time" transit.

[25] **N** omits any mention of signs. I suspect (along with the Latin reading), that this should be "degrees." Thus, the number of degrees between them equals the number of days (which is in agreement with the reading of al-Rijāl). See also **27** below.

[26] This paragraph explains in more detail the lesser years (and other times) in **13** above. See also Ch. 11, **24ff**.

to Mercury belong 5 months, and 3[27] months too. **17** And if they were in charge of the management, then indeed Mercury (if a planet does not cut him off) indicates 20 months; and for Venus, 8 years. **18** And for the Sun, a year and[28] 19 months. **19** And for Mars, 18[29] months or 15 years. **20** And Jupiter, 12 months or 12 years. **21** And Saturn, 30 months or 30 years.

22 The knowledge of which of those five situations is of slowness and quickness, is based on what I will describe to you.

Planet	Lesser years	Other units (Sahl)
♄	30	
♃	12	
♂	15	18
☉	19	1 (year)
♀	8	10
☿	20	5, 10
☽	25	1 or 2 (months)

Figure 47: Planetary years and other time units

23 Know that if the planet handing over and the one accepting were, each of them, in the eastern region from the Ascendant [up to the Midheaven] (which indicates quickness), and they were both quick in course, then make the amount of what is between them (of the degrees of connection between them) an hour for every degree.[30] **24** And if the two planets were in what is between the Midheaven up to the seventh, they indicate months according to the amount of portions[31] which were between them. **25** And if the two planets were in what is between the seventh and the fourth and the Ascend-

---

[27] Source of this number unknown. Really, Mercury should have 20 months (the number of his lesser years) as below; perhaps Sahl or his source mistook this to be 30, and then decided that was too long for Mercury, reducing it by a factor of 10 to get 3 months. On the other hand, it could represent some number of days in Mercury's synodic cycle with the Sun. In **17** he correctly identifies Mercury's number as 20.

[28] This should be understood as "or." The tropical year (or solar year, in a sidereal zodiac) is the natural time span for the Sun, and 19 is the number of his lesser years.

[29] This should certainly be 15, as found in Ch. 11, **39** below. But again, perhaps these days represent something about a cycle of his.

[30] **B** and **N** read, "make every degree of the light which you find between them, an hour."

[31] That is, degrees.

ant, they indicate years and months, if the two planets agree in their own right [and] in the manner of their relationship to[32] the Ascendant. **26** If they are at variance, and the planet was eastern in itself, quick, and in relation to the Ascendant western, slow,[33] they indicate what is in the middle. **27** Now, the time of the portions which are between them is the amount of the signs, a day for every degree. **28** And if they went beyond that, then the portions which are between them in the connection are a month for every degree. **29** So mix based on what I have explained to you of the region from the Ascendant, and the essence of the planet and the sign in which it is, and the figure[34] of the planet. **30** Then, strive with your understanding in the quickness and slowness, and indeed you will not be mistaken, if God wills.

31 Know that these times are the foundations. **32** But perhaps the time would be separate from these foundations: and that is if the Moon was in the place of the sought thing (or[35] she is in a strong place resembling the character of the sought thing),[36] then she connected with the lord of the Ascendant or with the lord of the sought thing, and it[37] is looking at the place of the sought thing, it indicates the occurrence of the matter on that day (and if the question was quick, pertaining to that very day).[38] **33** And if the days of the connection encountered the last of the two planets,[39] the time is not made into a month until a cycle of the Moon passes by. **34** And know that perhaps the two planets would be separating, and the Moon would be passing be-

---

[32] Lit., "their agreement with" or "their agreement from" (اتّفاقهما من).
[33] E reads more simply: "and one planet was eastern from the Ascendant, and the other western...".
[34] This is the planet's position by solar phase, retrogradation, etc., as explained in Ch. 1, **6ff**.
[35] Reading for "and."
[36] Adding this parenthetical comment with **B**.
[37] I take this to be the lord of the sought thing, but it could be the Moon (or even the lord of the Ascendant).
[38] That is, either the matter happens on the future day indicated by her motion, or (if it is a question about something happening immediately), on the very day the question is asked. Sahl is trying to describe several scenarios in a somewhat cramped sentence. What he seems to mean is that the Moon is either (1) in the place of the matter or one like it, joined to the lord of the Ascendant, or (2) joined to the lord of the matter and she or it only *looks at* the place of the matter. The point is that she must have a relationship to the place of the matter and one of the two key lords.
[39] This seems to mean, "if the Moon reached the last of the two planets just mentioned, and the event has *not* happened yet."

tween them and be equidistant between the lord of the sought thing and the lord of the Ascendant,[40] or she would enter the Ascendant or the place of the sought thing: then it would be the time and the achieving of the sought thing on that day.

35 And perhaps the time would be from the degree of the more worthy [planet][41] up to the portion of the Ascendant, a day for every degree.

36 And perhaps the time will be from the Sun's entering the Ascendant or the place of the sought thing, or the position of the lord of the Ascendant, or the position of the lord of the sought thing: and the thing will be set into motion and bring forth its realization, similar to his activity in the periods of his entering the quarters [of the year]; and likewise they compare [the Sun] to the soul.[42]

37 Then look in the times of all twelve topics, based on what I will describe to you.

[Chapter 4]: The house of life, the Ascendant[43]

2 If you were asked about the time of a man's lifespan, from the sayings of the ancients, look at the Ascendant in the hour of the question, and its lord, and the luminaries, and the Lot of Fortune and its lord, and the meeting or[44] opposition which was before the question. 3 Take the stronger of these indicators, and the one of them greater in testimony, for it is the victor and the indicator of the time. 4 Direct it just like you direct the [longevity] releaser to the assembly of the infortunes and their aspect, a year for every degree by the ascensions of the signs in that city. 5 Now if the fortunes were not casting rays to that bound, the questioner will die in that year. 6 And the more forceful rays [of the infortunes], and the more deadly of them, are the square and opposition: indeed [in that case] perhaps it will kill even if a fortune casts rays to the bound.

---

[40] If this refers to midpoints, it is the only case I can think of in the traditional literature.
[41] Or, "more appropriate, authoritative," etc. (الأولى).
[42] In *Search* II.5.2, Hermann's version of this material adds that just as the *Moon* indicates changes in the body, so the Sun does in the soul. But this does not really help us understand the timing methods.
[43] Reading with **Es**. **B** has: "Lifespan, and it is the Ascendant."
[44] Reading for "and."

7 Now[45] if the victor was received, or if the releaser was [itself] ruling, then if the ruler was in a stake, eastern, it grants its greater years; or if it was in what follows the stakes, it grants its middle years; and if it was falling, it grants its lesser years.

8 And Māshā'allāh said:[46] Look at the lord of the Ascendant and the Moon, for indeed the lifespan is from the lord of the Ascendant, and calamities are from the Moon. **9** So if they both (or one of them) connected with the infortunes or burning, then know the amount of the degrees which are between it and the infortune or burning, and keep it in mind. **10** Now if the lord of the Ascendant was in a fixed sign, it is a year for every degree; and if it was in a sign having two bodies, it is a month for every degree; and if it was in a convertible sign, it is a day for every degree. **11** So what came out from the lord of the Ascendant is the amount of the lifespan, and what came out of what is between the Moon and the infortune and burning, is the amount [until] the calamities; and God is more knowledgeable.

[Chapter 5]: The house of assets

2 And as for the time of a question about assets, how [often] that will occur or he will be successful in them, you look at the degrees which are between the two significators: for it is known that the time of that is based on the amount of those degrees—days or months or years, according to the speed of that and its slowness. **3** And see also when the lord of the house of assets will enter into the Ascendant or into its own house, or the lord of the Ascendant enters into the house of assets, or the assembly of the two of them[47]—and I follow that.[48]

---

[45] This sentence expands the method to include the house-master, just like in a natal chart: the victor or longevity releaser in **2-3** may have a house-master (here called a "ruler") if one of its lords looks at it and so receives it, or it might itself be its own house-master. The house-master grants a certain "expected" longevity, which is compared to the actual primary direction of the releaser. See for example *Nativities* Chs. 1.15-1.16.

[46] The basic ideas of this paragraph can be found in the Māshā'allāh version, Leiden Or. 891, f. 22a, but Sahl has abbreviated it quite a bit.

[47] The Latin version includes the conjunction with the benefics, which makes astrological sense here but is not mentioned in **B** and **Es**.

[48] وإلى, omitted in **B**. But perhaps this could be read as وإلي, meaning "at that [time]."

4 The time of the third and fourth [houses] is included in the remainder of chapters.

[Chapter 6:] The house of children

2 And if you were asked about a pregnant woman, when she would give birth, then look at the lord of the house of children. **3** Make how much is between it and the house of children (in signs and degrees), a month for every sign and a day for every degree, for she will give birth towards that time. **4** And God (be He exalted!) is more knowledgeable.

[Chapter 7]: The house of illness

2 Do not[49] omit to call upon the Moon as a witness in all of the sick person's states. **3** And[50] as for the period of recovering from the illness, do not let the matter of the Moon fall down in course if she will not be looking at her own position.[51] **4** And if she was made unfortunate, then direct her to the degree of the infortune and to the degree of the lord of the house of death. **5** And if the Moon was uniting with the infortune before she reached the degree of the house of death, then indeed death will be feared for him upon the Moon's arrival at the house of death. **6** And if the infortune was Saturn, then every degree between the two of them is a month or year (and for Mars, a day or month), based on the strength and quickness of the position, and its slowness. **7** And do not neglect the degree of burning (and God is more knowledgeable).

---

[49] This sentence only in **Es**.
[50] This sentence only in **B**.
[51] Or, "place" (موضعه). This seems to mean (following the Latin), that one should not start treating the patient while the Moon is cadent, *unless* she aspects Cancer. Nevertheless, I do not quite understand it.

[Chapter 8]: The times of wars

2 From[52] the statement of Theophilus: if you wanted to know the time in which fighting will happen, then look ([in] the hour [when] you were asked), at the luminaries. **3** For if they were opposite[53] each other, they speed up the fighting.

4 And[54] if there were 20° between the Moon and the degree of the connection, they slow down the fighting. **5** And if the Moon was with any of the planets in her own house, the fighting will be quick,[55] and especially if the Sun was looking at her.

6 And[56] if the twelfth-part of the Moon was in the Ascendant or Midheaven,[57] or the place of the Sun or the lord of his house, or with a planet which has just arisen,[58] that indicates the quickness of the fighting.

7 And[59] he[60] also said: If you wanted to know the time of this fighting and when it will be concluded, then look at the luminaries. **8** For if they looked at each other from the trine,[61] and they both looked at the Ascendant, the fighting will be concluded quickly; and if they were looking [at each other] from the square, the fighting will not be concluded quickly, and the fighting will go on, and they will shift from place to place, and especially [at] the beginning. **9** And if they were looking from the opposition, the fighting will not be concluded quickly.

10 And[62] if the Lot of Fortune was in the Midheaven, the fighting will be concluded in the quarters.

---

[52] For this paragraph, cf. *Labors* Ch. 14, **1-2**. Sahl restates this more fully and accurately in **7-9** below. Broadly speaking, sentences **2-9** are from *Labors* Ch. 14, and ultimately from *Carmen* V.36, **1-6**.

[53] This should be "trine": see **7-9** below.

[54] For this paragraph, cf. *Labors* Ch. 14, **3-4**. For this sentence, *Labors* has only 8°, but the point is that she is not actively making a connection yet.

[55] Or perhaps, "hastened" (عاجلًا).

[56] See *Labors* Ch. 14, **5**.

[57] **Es**: "the tenth."

[58] شرق (but perhaps better شرَق). That is, "arisen from out of the Sun's rays."

[59] For this paragraph, see *Labors* Ch. 14, **1-2**.

[60] **Es** reads, "And *Hermes* said." But this is clearly Theophilus.

[61] **B** adds the sextile, but both **Es** and *Labors* omit it.

[62] Cf. *Labors* Ch. 2, **23**, which says instead that the war will be ended *quickly*. But the broader point is related to **11-12** below: whatever the relation between the Sun and Moon when

11 And[63] if the Sun at the question was in the square of the Ascendant or the square of the Moon, then indeed the cessation of the fighting is also in the quarters. **12** And if the Sun at the question was looking at what I mentioned from the opposition, the cessation of the fighting will be in the oppositions; and from the trine, in the triplicities. **13** And that is when Jupiter and the Moon both come to be looking at the Ascendant, in just the way that the Sun was looking at the question.[64]

14 And[65] look also at the Lot of religion[66] and at the planet which was with Mars or in his quarter.[67] **15** And if they were fortunes it will be over quickly; and if they were infortunes, the war will remain firm and intensify and be long. **16** And if the fortunes were mixed up with the lord of the Lot, one of the two sides will not hesitate to leave off and flee, based on what you see of the position of the fortune from the lord of the Lot.[68]

17 And Hermes said: Look, for the time of the cessation of all of the wars and things, at the luminaries and the Ascendant, and come to know[69] their degrees [relative to] to the fortunes and the infortunes. **18** And with that you will know the time of the things and their elapsing, in years and months and days.

19 And he also said: Look, in the slowness of the victory and its quickness, at the position of Saturn and Jupiter, for if they were quick in course, then indeed the victory will be quick for the one in whose region[70] Mars is,

---

the fighting starts, it will also stop when they recur in them. So for this sentence, if the Lot of Fortune is in the tenth sign, then by definition the Sun and Moon must be square to each other (in a lunar quarter): so, the fighting will end at some other lunar quarter.

[63] For **11-12**, cf. *Labors* Ch. 12, **38-39**, which is ultimately based on *Carmen* V.23, 1-3.

[64] This must refer to the transiting Jupiter and Moon, aspecting the Ascendant of the question chart.

[65] For this paragraph, cf. *Labors* Ch. 23, 7 and Ch. 37, 1.

[66] الدّين, although in Hermann's version (*Search* Ch. II.5.3) he reads "Fortune." To me Fortune makes more sense, but there is another possibility: the Lot of expedition, described in *Labors* Ch. 23.

[67] That is, square.

[68] **Es** omits "the lord of."

[69] Reading the imperative of خبر for a non-existent word (**B**) and "other" or "last" (**Es**).

[70] This is the usual word for "clime," but I think Hermes means it in one of two ways: (1) a region of the world ruled by the sign Mars is in, or (2) a general direction, such as east or west. Moreover, it is unclear to me who or what is meant by "it" later in the sentence, and how this should be understood: is it the solar phase of Mars, or something about the direction he is in in the chart? My feeling is that it means the quadrant or hemisphere of the chart Mars is in, indicates the winner. So if Mars is on the querent's side of the chart, the

be it eastern or western. **20** And if they were both slow in course, the victory will be slow and its matter drawn out, and will hardly end. **21** And truly, [if] the indicator of it (of Saturn and Jupiter) goes direct after Mars does, then indeed [the] separation [of the two sides][71] is in the land which is between the two engagements [of forces].[72]

22 And[73] if they were both in an embodied[74] sign, the fighting will be in all of the lands, and it will happen many times. **23** And if they were in a fixed sign, the fighting will diminish and become insignificant. **24** And if they were both in a convertible sign, the fighting will intensify and the matter of the world will be difficult, and affairs will be transformed just as they must for it.[75] **25** And this chapter is from the secrets of the statement of Hermes.

26 The eighth chapter, on death, was already presented in the chapter on life.

Chapter [9]: On travels, from the sayings of the ancients

2 Now,[76] if you wanted knowledge of the time of the traveler's return to his own people, then look at the Sun at the time of the commencement of the journey. **3** For if you saw the infortunes in [the Sun's] square or opposition,[77] his journey is long and he will slow down in his return. **4** And if [the Sun] connected with the fortunes, he indicates the speed of the return. **5** And if he connected with the fortunes after the infortunes, hardship will

---

querent will win; in an eastern quarter (such as between the Ascendant and Midheaven), the people of the east; and so on. In the mundane material I translated for *AW2*, the Persian astrologers like Māshā'allāh were primarily interested in whether people towards the west or east would win, as that was the primary preoccupation of their politics, as inherited from antiquity and the Muslim conquests: in Sassanian times, the west would have been the Byzantines, but in the Islamic period the Arabs; likewise the east would have been the Sassanians themselves or the eastern and northeastern peoples of the plains, or the Persian Muslims.

[71] Reading as صريمة (**B**). **Es** seems to read ضربته, "its striking."
[72] The meaning of this whole sentence is unclear to me.
[73] For this paragraph, cf. *Labors* Ch. 35, **5** and **9**.
[74] I.e., double-bodied. But in Theophilus, this is Mars throughout **22-24** here.
[75] كما كانت عليه.
[76] Sentences **2-10** are probably based on an alternative version of *Carmen* V.23, **1-5**.
[77] **Es** adds, "or his conjunction," which makes astrological sense.

reach him on his journey, [but] then he will be turned around from it and return to his country.[78]

6 And look at the Moon so that through her you may know the return and the staying. **7** For if you found the Moon in the Ascendant at the beginning of the journey, then indeed his stay on the journey will be lengthened, and especially if the Moon was in a house of Saturn or[79] his bound.

8 And when you find the Sun (at the beginning of the journey) not made unfortunate, then indeed when he comes around to his own square and own opposition, or he returns to his own position which he was in on the day he left, it indicates the return—*if* he is not made unfortunate in that sign. **9** And[80] likewise when the Sun is directed to his position in the root, or the trine of his place, or its square. **10** And if the Sun in the root was made unfortunate, then indeed his stay will be long, up to the departure of that infortune from the sign in which it is, and the arrival of one of the fortunes in the place of that infortune.

11 And likewise, know the strength of the rest of the planets, and their governance in the commencement [of the journey]: so speak in that manner about their period, in terms of years and months. **12** Because Saturn, if he was the lord of the Ascendant, or Saturn was in the house of travel, his jour-

---

[78] At this point **B** seems to begin a new sentence with "And the strength of the fortune and the infortune..." followed by the "so that...you may know," from **6**. To my mind this might have been part of a sentence or two that are missing but seem to be logical here: (1) what it means if he connects with the infortunes after the fortunes (that is, the reverse of what Sahl has just said), and (2) that the speed of the return and strength of the adversity depends on the relative strength of the benefic and malefic.

[79] **B**: "and."

[80] This is a somewhat difficult sentence. **B** reads: "And that [is] when the Moon is directed in her own position in the root or the trine of her place, or its square." **Es** reads, "And that [is] when the Sun is directed in his own position in the root, or the trine of his place, or its square." First, it makes more sense to direct the Sun or Moon *to* its place in the root chart, so I have made that change. Second, note that **B** reads the Moon throughout: this does not quite make sense, unless Sahl is suggesting a coordination of the Sun's transits and the direction of the Moon. Another option would be to read "And *likewise* when the Moon...", which would explicitly separate the techniques and only require adding one letter (كذلك instead of ذلك). But **Es** explicitly directs the Sun: this makes grammatical sense of the sentence, and suggests that by the Sun "coming around" (**8**) Sahl never meant a transit, but only the primary direction he explains here in **9**. But then why did he not also mention the trine in **8**? My own solution could be this: that we can look at the Sun's transits (**8**), and *likewise* (كذلك) certain primary directions (**9**).

ney will be long, in accordance with the period of Saturn.⁸¹ **13** And likewise, if you found Saturn and Jupiter in a stake, and they were both retrograde, then indeed the stay will be long. **14** And the rest of the planets are quicker in [their] marching along⁸² than these two planets.

15 As for the statement of Māshā'allāh on the time of the traveler's coming, he said:⁸³ Look at the Moon and the lord of the hour, whichever one was stronger. **16** Now if the stronger one was in what is between the tenth up to the fourth,⁸⁴ then take what is between the Ascendant and it. **17** And if the stronger one was the lord of the hour, then what comes out in degrees will be hours; and if the Moon was the stronger one, then the portions of what came out for you will be based on 13, and what comes out are days.⁸⁵ **18** And if it was in the opposite of what I told you of the circle,⁸⁶ and the lord of the hour was the stronger one, then count what is between it and the Ascendant, for what comes out is days.

19 And if that is not informative, and the lord of the Ascendant was the stronger one, then indeed he will arrive when the lord of the Ascendant enters the Midheaven or returns to the Ascendant. **20** And⁸⁷ if the Moon had much testimony [and] was strong, and the lord of the Ascendant was not looking at the Ascendant and not looking at the lord of its house, then indeed his return will be based on that.⁸⁸ **21** And if the lord of the house of the Moon was in a bad place and the Moon in an excellent place from the Ascendant, and she⁸⁹ was looking at her house, then count what is between her and her house in degrees, and that is the time of the arrival, if God wills.

---

⁸¹ Since Saturn's lesser years are 30, this probably means that he will indicate 30 years or months, based on whether the chart indicates something slower or faster.

⁸² Or perhaps, "operation," "propelling," "setting into motion" (تحريك).

⁸³ I do not currently find this in Laleli or Leiden.

⁸⁴ This probably means the eastern or rising half of the chart.

⁸⁵ Since the Moon's average daily motion is about 13°, this probably means we should divide the degrees by 13: the result would approximate the Moon's real-time motion to the degree of the Ascendant. Note that this statement by Māshā'allāh only makes sense for a short journey or someone who is already known to be close.

⁸⁶ This must be on the western, setting side of the chart.

⁸⁷ I am not sure if this continues the thought from the previous sentence, or should begin a new paragraph.

⁸⁸ By "that," I believe Māshā'allāh means the Moon.

⁸⁹ For the rest of this sentence, I assume Māshā'allāh means the Moon rather than the lord of her sign, but it is impossible to say based on the Arabic.

[Chapter 10]: On receiving a book or report, from [Māshā'allāh]

2 And he also said:[90] If you were asked concerning a book or report, when it would arrive, then look at Mercury. 3 Now[91] if he was in the Ascendant or in the twelfth (wanting entrance to the Ascendant), or the Moon was connecting with the lord of the Ascendant, or the Moon was connecting with Mercury, or Mercury was the lord of the Ascendant (or he had a claim in the Ascendant), then the time of that is when Mercury connects with the lord of the Ascendant: the book will come. 4 And if he was close to the Ascendant, then the time is his entrance into the Ascendant. 5 And if the Moon was connecting with Mercury, then the time of it is the meeting [between them] or the Moon's arrival at the Ascendant: the book will come. 6 And if the Moon was connecting from Mercury to the degree of the Ascendant (or the lord of the Ascendant), then the time is when the one transferring reaches the one transferred to.

7 And if you were asked about a book, how long ago it was written, then look at the degrees which are between the Moon and the planet the Moon is being separated from, and the book was written based on the number of those degrees.

8 And it is done likewise for the degrees which you find between the Moon and the planet she is connecting to: [that is] the time of the arrival of the book.

Chapter [11]: On the Sultan, from the statement of Māshā'allāh[92]

2 Look for the time of the Sultan's withdrawal,[93] for one whose entrance into power[94] (or the time of his taking the crown, or a question) you already knew: for from that you will know the extent of his remaining in power, and

---

[90] I do not currently find this in Laleli or Leiden.

[91] At first this sentence seems to be a grab-bag of possibilities, but Māshā'allāh will distinguish many of them in what follows.

[92] This chapter is Sahl's version of a short work by Māshā'allāh, *The Book of the Sultan*, called *The Chapter on Sultans and the Heart and the Soldiers and the Workers* in Escurial 919/3 (ff. 44b-46a). But see also the passage from Theophilus in *Questions* Ch. 10, **79ff**.

[93] This seems to be a euphemism by Māshā'allāh for "death" or "murder," as Sultans typically do not voluntarily give up power. But it might be appropriate in systems where leaders may be reelected for long periods of time, or may abdicate.

[94] Lit. "work," here and later in the sentence.

what his condition is in it. **3** And you will know the victory and might from the time of the founding.⁹⁵ **4** So when you found a star in the Ascendant having testimony in it, then when that star is burned up in the stakes of the Ascendant,⁹⁶ the Sultan will leave. **5** And if there is not a star in the Ascendant, then look at the house of authority:⁹⁷ for if you found a planet there having testimony in it, then when an infortune recurs there (or the lord of the fall of the house of authority), and it is looking at the star from which [the time] was inferred, the Sultan will leave.

6 And if you did not find a planet in these two positions, then look by day at the Sun, [to see] with whom he is being connected. **7** For if he connected with Saturn or with Mars, then indeed at that time when he reaches the degree of the one being connected with, in a stake, the Sultan will leave. **8** And if [the Sun] connected with Jupiter, his withdrawal will be upon Saturn's arriving at the place of the Sun, or his opposition or his square, or [when Saturn] recurs in these positions; and likewise if [the Sun] connected with Venus. **9** Now if the Sun was withdrawing from what I mentioned, or he was in the eleventh or the ninth and he had testimony, then when Saturn or Mars recurs in that place or its opposition, the Sultan will leave.

10 And work by night with the Moon just as you worked by day with the Sun, but do not look at the time of the Moon from her correspondence with the planets: but [rather], see if the Moon is being connected with the Sun. **11** And if she connected, or she was separated from him before she connects with an infortune, then indeed the time of that is from the Sun, in the way I described to you for his time. **12** And if she was not separating from the Sun nor connecting with him, then look in what I mentioned to you: there will not be completed for him [even] one year [of] his authority: so, work with that.

13 And know that the lord of the Ascendant and the lord of the tenth,⁹⁸ if they were burned in the stakes, they indicate [his] withdrawal.⁹⁹ **14** And if the lord of the exaltation of the Sun was made unfortunate, a year will not be completed for him, so look for his time before the year [is ended], and for

---

⁹⁵ Lit., "the fixing of the banners" (عقد اللواء), which suggests an official announcement.
⁹⁶ This may be at a later solar revolution, or perhaps during any later transit into that place.
⁹⁷ That is, the tenth.
⁹⁸ **B** reads, "the Midheaven."
⁹⁹ **Es** reads, "that [his] leaving is already at hand."

the burning of the lord of the Ascendant and the lord of the tenth, and the correspondence of the infortune with their positions. **15** And if the Moon was not the lord of the exaltation,[100] then see her connection with the planets. **16** For if she connected with Mercury, and he was in a fixed sign or one having two bodies, it indicates 20 months; and if the sign was convertible, then 10 months. **17** So look at the planet which she is connecting with, for if it was corrupted by the infortunes or burning, then see how many degrees are between it and the infortunes or burning: that is the time. **18** And[101] if the Moon and the lord of her exaltation were not made unfortunate, a year will be completed for him, so look in the second year, and revolve the years for him. **19** And know that the lord[102] is a blessing of the Moon if it was free of the infortunes, for indeed his authority will remain for more than a year. **20** And if the Moon was received, then look at the arrival of an infortune at the degree of the planet which received the Moon, or the lesser years of the lord of the Ascendant: combine it with the revolution of the year and [the year's] arrival.[103]

21 And if the Ascendant of the one entering [into power], and that of his commencement, was of the houses of the superior planets, while the lord of the blessing of the Moon indicated the completion of a year,[104] then revolve the years for him.

22 And if an infortune recurred in the Midheaven, or the burning of the lord of the Ascendant in the stakes, it indicates the corruption of the Sultan; and if the infortune recurred in the Ascendant, and the burning of the lord of the Ascendant in the Midheaven, there is destruction in his authority. **23** And if it recurred in the second, it indicates the corruption of his assets, and in the Midheaven the corruption of the work, and in the eleventh the breaking down of the land tax, and in the Ascendant the corruption of the body.

24 And look at the governing planets:[105] if they were in the stakes and they had strength, they grant the amount of their lesser years, in months or years. **25** So if Saturn was in the Ascendant or Midheaven, and he had testi-

---

[100] Reading the definite for the indefinite ("the lord of *an* exaltation").
[101] The next couple of sentences might now pertain only to nocturnal charts, forming a contrast with the Sun and the lord of his exaltation earlier in the paragraph.
[102] This seems to be the lord of her exaltation. See also **21** below.
[103] مبلغها. This seems to mean the profection from the Ascendant.
[104] Recall from **19** that this seems to be the lord of the exaltation of the Moon, *if* it is free of the infortunes.
[105] See Ch. 2, **15-21**.

mony, and he was received [and was] accepting the testimony of the planets, it indicates 30 years. **26** And if [those] were completed, revolve the year. **27** Now if the lord of the Ascendant or the indicator was burned up in the stakes, it corrupts that matter. **28** And if Saturn was strong, and the lord of that year assisted him, he will not cease to be firm [in his position] until the revolution is corrupted, and [then] his testimony and strength will go away. **29** And if Saturn did not have those testimonies, then revolve it for him in 30 months, for indeed the time is weak. **30** Then, look at the corruption of the year from burning and misfortune: for if the one which is governing the management was retrograde or at the end of its stake,[106] it corrupts that matter suddenly.

31 And if Jupiter was in the Ascendant or Midheaven, and he had testimony, it indicates 12 years.

32 And if Venus was in the Ascendant or in the Midheaven, and she had testimony, then calculate 10 months for her. **33** And if she was burned up in a stake, his authority will disappear. **34** Now if she was received, free of the infortunes, she indicates 8 years, and you revolve her years.[107] **35** If she corresponded to an infortune in the revolution before the eighth [year], and it recurred in her place,[108] it indicates the corruption of the Sultan, and his weakness, and the entering of distress upon him.

36 And if Mercury was in the Ascendant or Midheaven, and he had testimony and strength, and he was received, it indicates 20 months,[109] and you revolve his years. **37** And if he was weak [and] did not have testimony, then calculate it for him in five months. **38** Now if he was burned up in a stake, and an infortune or the light of an infortune corresponded to the stake of the Midheaven or the lord of the stake of heaven,[110] the Sultan will leave.

---

[106] This idiom seems to mean "at its greatest elongation" or near its station.

[107] That is, cast the revolution for 8 years in the future (her lesser years), which would be a Venus return.

[108] I take this to mean both that (a) she has returned to the sign she was in at his accession, and (b) that a malefic planet is transiting where her original position was.

[109] To me it seems better to read "years," along with the other planets in such a good condition. But in the next sentence we see Māshā'allāh insist on months.

[110] Māshā'allāh reads, "...corresponded to the stake of the lord of the tenth," namely the whole-sign angles from the lord of the tenth.

39 And if Mars was in the Ascendant or Midheaven, then see if he corresponds with burning within[111] 15 months: for indeed if he was burned in a stake, the Sultan will leave; so you revolve his years.

40 And if it was the Moon, and she was received, free of the infortunes, and she had testimony, it indicates 25 years; and if she did not have testimony, 25 months. **41** Or, you look at the planet which she is handing over the management to: for if it was burned up in a stake, he will leave. **42** And if it was not burned up in a stake, and it was received, it indicates the years of the planet, and its months.

43 And you look in this subject just as I informed you about the Sun in the arrival of an infortune at [the Sun's] degree. **44** And if the one in charge of the management is the Sun, and he was accepting the testimony of the stars, he indicates a year. **45** And if you calculated the year and the Sun was great in testimony,[112] he indicates 19 years, unless[113] an infortune corrupts the management at the beginning (corrupting the lord of the management or the Ascendant or the Midheaven);[114] and if [the Sun] was corrupted, he grants 19 months.

46 And know that if a planet indicated the number of the management, [but] then it was corrupted in a stake before that, then revolve that year for him. **47** Now if it was safe from burning and being made unfortunate, the matter will be safe until it reaches the number; but [then] corruption and diminishment will enter upon him. **48** Then, do in the revolution of the years for the Sultan with respect to the place where the rays fall, just as you do in nativities, for every sign a year.[115] **49** And you look from the lord of that sign: how is its position, and what is its condition, and what is in the sign (of the fortunes and the infortunes), and where is the position of the lord of the sign relative to the fortunes and infortunes, and where is its position, and is it received, made unfortunate (or not made unfortunate), and what is the situation of the lord of the Midheaven relative to the Ascendant of that year? **50** And let the revolution of your year be based on exact calculation[116] so that the Ascendant of the revolution is not corrupted.

---

[111] Or perhaps simply, "in."
[112] Or, "had much testimony" (كثيرة الشهادة).
[113] Reading with the sense of the Latin, for "then" (ثمّ).
[114] I understand this to be the lord *of* the Ascendant or *of* the Midheaven (rather than those places themselves), but it is impossible to say based on the Arabic.
[115] That is, an annual profection.
[116] الاستواء. That is, by calculating the ascensions instead of estimating by zodiacal degrees.

51 Then, look at the lord of the Ascendant and the lord of the Midheaven:[117] for if they were connecting, it indicates the endurance of the Sultan. **52** And if the Moon was free of the infortunes, and she was handing over her management to a planet in a stake, it indicates his endurance; and likewise the Sun by day, and likewise the lord of the Ascendant.

53 And if the lord of the Midheaven[118] was burned in the revolution, or an infortune recurred in the Midheaven,[119] it indicates the Sultan's withdrawing (and likewise the lord of the Ascendant). **54** And[120] if the lord of the Midheaven was eastern at the revolution, it indicates the establishment[121] of the work, and his staying. **55** And if it was western, it indicates its corruption and his ruin. **56** And if the lord of his Midheaven[122] connected to the lord of the outcome,[123] it indicates the Sultan's withdrawing; and if the lord of the outcome connected with it, it indicates the Sultan's enduring. **57** And the greater thing that indicates the Sultan's withdrawing, is if the Sun was going out from the stakes, and the Moon in the sixth or twelfth from the Ascendant of the year.

58 And seek help in this topic through the arrival of the lord of the year[124] at a sign in which there is a fortune or infortune. **59** And release[125] the planet which has the shift of the year,[126] and the planet alighting in the Ascendant of the year, and the lord of the Ascendant, and the lord of the tenth, one to the other. **60** And seek their testimonies based on what I explained to you, for

---

[117] Māshā'allāh reads, "the tenth."
[118] Māshā'allāh reads, "the tenth."
[119] Māshā'allāh reads, "the tenth."
[120] Reading this sentence with Māshā'allāh. **B** reads: "If it [who?] was in the Midheaven, eastern, it indicates...".
[121] Or more literally, the "defining" or "marking out" or "determination" (تحديد).
[122] Māshā'allāh reads, "the tenth."
[123] That is, the lord of the fourth or the IC.
[124] Reading with Māshā'allāh as a transit. But **B** reads "the arrival of the year," which would normally be a profection of the original Ascendant.
[125] This would seem to be an explicit (and rare) reference to primary directions (or directions carried out by ascensions), using the Arabic equivalent (Form IV, أفرج) of the Greek term (*aphesis*). I have read this sentence with Māshā'allāh. **B** reads: "And release between it and the lord of the year, and the planet which is in it, and the lord of the Ascendant, and the lord of the Midheaven, one to the other."
[126] That is, the sect light of the solar revolution: "shift" (*nawbah*, نوبة) refers to the shifting back and forth between night and day.

indeed you will be informed about the time and [his] removal. **61** And in God is success.[127]

---

[127] The work ends with a formulaic prayer and pious thanks, omitted here.

ON NATIVITIES

Chapter 1: [On life & the lifespan]

Chapter [1.1]: On the knowledge of the distinctions [among] nativities

1 Know[1] that the distinctions [among] nativities and other things is from the categories of creation, which will not be accurate nor can one do without [them] except after the knowledge of three things of the science of them, from the original roots and pre-existing arrangement:[2] and they are the origins, the countries, and food.
2 Now as for the origins, they are the differences in things such as [between] humans and animals. **3** And as for the countries, that is like Ethiopia and Rome in the difference of their expressions and their difference [according to] country. **4** And as for the food, that is like the Bedouins whose nourishment is dairy products and despised foods, while the rest of people are not like that.
5 And once you have understood these three things, the knowledge of it will be by means of what has come to it from [*uncertain*].[3] **6** Because[4] if the birth of animals had spread across the world, then it would not be necessary, and it would introduce errors, because he would say "this native will come to works, and his craft will be such-and-such"—and that does not come to be with the origin of riding animals and beasts. **7** And if he knew the origin [un-

---

[1] Much of the first 10 sentences is rather waterstained, making some of the following readings a bit tentative. But in **1-14** Sahl is following and elaborating upon *Tet.* IV.10 (Robbins pp. 439-41), which reminds us that real-life conditions must be taken into account before concrete interpretations can be made.
[2] Or more literally, "structure, physical constitution" (البنية القديمة). But Sahl is also speaking of cultural differences, so I am reading this more broadly.
[3] This waterstained word looks like القصاء or القساء.
[4] Between here and **13**, Sahl is speaking about understanding different peoples and cultures: if you don't have any real-world information about the native (such as his ethnicity, **10**), your judgments will not be tailored well to his situation, even though you have followed the rules properly. In this paragraph, Sahl seems to be imagining the nativities of *animals* (such as horses raised for racing): if you did not know it was an animal, you would misinterpret the chart as though it was a human (**6**); and if you knew it was an animal but not what type, you might not recognize the difference between a farmer's cow and a king's racehorse (**7**).

clear] riding animals, and he saw suitability, he would speak indeed of the riding animals of kings and nobles, and in [his] judgment would speak of what the origin of the thing resembles. **8** So, this concerns the origins and power of their difference.

9 And as for the countries, the knowledge of them should be sought before judging. **10** Because if Ethiopians had spread across the world, then [the nativity of an Ethiopian] would indicate *their* color and animals—so that a white philosopher would state errors, because perhaps he would find the positions of the planets to be excellent, and the Ascendant indicating whiteness and skill in things, and that [the native] is most intensely white of the people of his country, when [the native is really] the blackest in every sense, and he is skillful in the crafts of the people of *his* country, while among scholars he is ignorant.[5]

11 And as for foods, the knowledge of them should be sought before judging, lest the scholar err. **12** [For] perhaps he found the positions of the planets to be excellent, and the Ascendant indicating the best of foods (while the native is of the Arabs and his nourishment is curdled milk and what is like that of the foods of the people of his country), and he saw the strength of the planets, then he would not know its nature, so he would say his foods were horsemeat and noble foods—he would be in error. **13** But if he did know that, he would say it was the best food of his country, and the greatest of it in goodness.

14 And the root of this whole difference is from the distinction of natures [in] the celestial circle and the planets in it. **15** Because if the celestial circle was of one nature, neither colors nor countries would differ; but because of the difference in its natures, the majority [of people] in every distant land of the world come to be of the nature of what resembles[6] them, from the celestial circle and the fixed stars and its course.

---

[5] That is, the Ethiopian may be skilled in the crafts of Ethiopians, but not in the sciences and scholarship, because they are presumably not available in Ethiopia. So, one should not attribute characteristics to someone living in real-life conditions incompatible with them. The same idea is expressed concerning age, sex, and physical health and injury in Chs. 1.2-1.4.

[6] Lit., "imitates" (حاذاهم).

Chapter [1.2]: On the knowledge of the planets' management

1 And[7] it is also necessary before you introduce a judgment, that you look at another perspective, and it is from the first root, and that is that perhaps the young boy will come to the management of some of the planets indicating marriage, or the pursuit of works, or one of the matters which the young boy does not have power over, nor in that condition is he like men other than him who have power and pride; and like an old man of senility, if he came to be under the management of some planets indicative of children, one will not be born to him, nor will the power of youth come to him: so this is what you ought to know before determining a judgment.

Chapter [1.3]: What things the native resembles, & the management of the planets in his life

1 Know that at his going out from his mother's belly into the wide open air, the native resembles what image[8] arises from the earth, as well as the indicator[9] which is the cause of every thing and his beginning. **2** Then his support is from the four natures,[10] in moderateness and harmony, until he reaches maximum [development], unless an illness of the air (from cold and heat) afflicts him before that. **3** Then he will diminish until he returns [to being] as he began: small, wretched, and weak.

[The Ages of Man: Ptolemy]

4 So[11] the management of the beginning [of life] (and the cause of every motion) comes for four years to the indicator which is the Moon, [and] the power of the upbringing will be moisture and weakness: because from the

---

[7] For this paragraph, cf. *Tet.* IV.10 (Robbins p. 441). See Abū Ma'shar's nice discussion of this type of thing in *PN4* I.8, **1-8** and I.9.
[8] In Ch. 1.30, **1**.
[9] I am not sure which planet (or even degrees) Sahl is referring to; perhaps the Moon, which is the first time lord in the Ptolemaic Ages of Man below (**4**).
[10] That is, the four elements.
[11] For the rest of this chapter, cf. *Tet.* IV.10 (Robbins pp. 441-47), and compare with Abū Ma'shar's version in *PN4* I.8, **10-11**.

lowest sphere is known the upbringing, its corruption and its suitability, along with the lords of the triplicities of the Ascendant (which begins from the earth[12] at the beginning of the [exit of the] native from the belly into the breadth of the air and its natures. **5** So in accordance with her condition at the beginning, [such] will be the condition of the upbringing (and that is because the body of the child is of moisture and softness), and the quickness of the upbringing, and the weakness of the body, and the scarcity of knowledge and cleverness, and the soul's abstaining from work. **6** And [*unclear*] in what one is informed about, [is] that the Moon is the governor of his management in these four years, from the start of his years.[13]

Planet	# of Years	Ages
☽	4	0-3
☿	10	4-13
♀	8	14-21
☉	19	22-40
♂	15	41-55
♃	12	56-67
♄	30+	68+

Figure 48: Ptolemaic Ages of Man

7 Then, after the four years she hands over the management to Mercury for 10 years, and extends it to his sphere, which is the sphere of education and study, in accordance with the condition of Mercury at the beginning.[14]

8 Then Mercury hands over to Venus for 8 years, and Venus extends it to her own sphere, in passion and the love of women, singing, and pleasures.

9 Then Venus hands over to the Sun for 19 years, and he manages the degree of men's questing and looking for high rank, in accordance with his condition at the beginning.

10 Then the Sun hands over to Mars for 15 years, and in that is completed [his] courage and risk-taking, and the love of brotherhood.

---

[12] That is, which rises over the horizon.
[13] For the Moon and the triplicity lords of the Ascendant in upbringing, see for example Ch. 1.29.
[14] According to Abū Ma'shar (*PN4* Ch. I.8, **27**), we should look at both the natal condition of the planet, and its real-time condition at the solar revolution when it actually takes over.

11 Then Mars surrenders to Jupiter for 12 years, and that is the time of piety and goodness, in accordance with [Jupiter's] condition.

12 Then [Jupiter] hands it over to Saturn, and he extends it to his own sphere, which is that of old age and senility.

13 And if [the native] went past the management of Saturn, it returns to the management of the Moon, to weakness and an abundance of moisture, to the original management; and certainly diseases will have afflicted him before that.

14 Now, these two approaches[15] must come first in the examination, both of them, before the judgment of his resemblances.[16]

[Chapter 1.4: Two other perspectives]

1 As for the two topics which you look into before a judgment about the native,[17] likewise there are two other perspectives: so you ought to look into them both after these two topics.

2 Now as for the first perspective, before you judge you ought to understand whether the native is male or female: for if the native was a girl and you saw power in the Midheaven, [and] you say this native will be entrusted with governorships and works, you would be wrong, since that will not come to be in this region. **3** But if you saw power in the Midheaven, you will judge exaltation for this girl, and power over things needed at the doors of the Sultan, in relation to fathers and husbands.[18]

4 And[19] the second perspective is that you ought to know [whether] the native is safe from chronic illnesses and diseases or not. **5** Because if a chronic illness afflicts the native, it will hinder him from working (such as the cutting of the hand or leg,[20] and [what is] like that), [but if] then you looked

---

[15] So far, Sahl has mentioned several principles: the native's (1) geographical and cultural background, (2) Ascendant and temperament, (3) and age. I suspect he means (1) and (3), since he has not discussed the Ascendant yet, and will not until much later.

[16] That is, what his life will be "like."

[17] See **14** in the previous chapter.

[18] See also *PN4*, I.9, **30-31**, and numerous ways in Sahl's Ch. 7 below (on marriage) in which one ought to be sensitive to any differences between male and female natives.

[19] For this paragraph, cf. Rhetorius Ch. 82 (p. 134), who quotes the poem of Anubio.

[20] Sahl seems to mean amputations that *result from* some illness or injury.

into the topic of work and you said this native will be exalted, a warrior, [*illegible*] [or] he will be of those who do manual work with their hands, you would be wrong. **6** And Hermes has already mentioned that in his book; but if I saw chronic illness, and then I saw work, I would judge skill and refinement for him in that, but it would not be necessary that he work with his hands.

7 So looking into these two topics is necessary after the first two topics.

Chapter [1.5]: On the knowledge of rectifying the hour in which the native was born, & whether it was by night or day[21]

Comment by Dykes. This chapter has two problems. First, it is awkwardly placed by Sahl, because we should expect it after Ch. 1.10 on the Trutine of Hermes: this is evidenced both by sentence **1-2** (which assumes we have already done a rectification), and Hephaistion's account in his Book II.1 (pp. 5-6).[22] Second, Sahl's source has mixed up the instructions, assuming that we don't know whether the *nativity* was by day or night: really, it is the sect of the conception we want to find. Let me first explain Hephaistion's method, then show what Sahl's source has done.

Hephaistion assumes that we have used the Trutine of Hermes from Ch. 1.10 below to calculate a conception chart from the assumed (and rough) birth time. If the conception Ascendant is the same as the natal Moon, and the conception Moon the natal Ascendant, then the birth time was already correct and we can proceed with the chart interpretation: Sahl agrees in **1**. But if they do not agree, we need to make a correction based on whether the conception was by day or night (we need to know this in order to use Ptolemy's special table of ascensional times in *Almagest* II.8, pp. 99-103):[23]

- Compare the positions of the *natal* Moon and the *conception* Sun: if the Moon is later in the zodiac (up to 180° after the conception Sun), the conception was diurnal; if she is earlier in the zodiac (up

---

[21] Chapters 5-7 form a group: first determining night and day, and rough hour (5), then the sign (6), then the degree (7).
[22] However, Ch. 1.10, **3** shows that Sahl has a reason for doing this.
[23] The description of how to use Ptolemy's table is too confusing to describe here; the reader should use a modern astrology program to adjust the time back and forth. See Ch. 1.10, **51-54**, where Sahl's source again refers to these tables.

to 180° behind the conception Sun, or more than 180° after him), the conception was nocturnal.
- Use an astrology program to figure out how long each planetary hour is on that day or night, *in minutes*, and divide by 4: call this the "hourly times."
- If diurnal, count the ascensional times (AT) from that conception Sun to the natal Moon, and divide by the hourly times. If nocturnal, count the AT from the natal Moon to the conception Sun, and divide in the same way.
- The answer you get from dividing the AT between them by the hourly times, is the hour of the day or night when the conception happened. (I assume this is in planetary hours.)
- Calculate the conception Moon for that hour, and you have the natal Ascendant.

Why do we care about the conception Sun and natal Moon? Because in Hermes's theory, the natal Moon is on the conception Ascendant. So, if according to the Trutine the conception Sun was at 15° Gemini, and the rough natal Moon (or conception Ascendant) is later than him, at 20° Cancer, then the Sun had already arisen and the conception was obviously by day. If we can use the distance between them to tell what time it was, we can use that time to calculate the conception Moon—and voilà, we have the natal Ascendant. That is the theory.

Sahl's text takes a contrary approach, and seems to go seriously astray (and introduces a new theory). He does assume we have already done the Hermes rectification (**1**). But instead of finding the time of day or night for the conception, he does so for the *nativity*, and counts from the *natal* Sun to the *conception* Moon. Again, since the conception Moon is the natal Ascendant, measuring between them will tell us whether the nativity is by day or night (**2-3**).

At this point I suppose that we could still use this distance to get a better time. But now something different happens, and Sahl's source seems to introduce a different idea: that the *lunar phase* of the conception is related to the time of the nativity. First, he wants to find the pre-conception lunation (**4**), and count from it to the conception Moon—in other words, see how far the Moon has moved since the lunation—and convert that into ascensional times. Divide these times by 15, and this gives a number of civil hours or normal clock hours of 60 minutes. Finally, if the conception was after a conjunction, add these hours to local noon on the day of the nativity; but if the conception was after an opposition, add them to the previous midnight—I think (**5-6**). The resulting time is the correct time of birth.

ಌ ಐ ಐ

1 If the work of the calculation you carried out was accurate, then work based on that, and erect the stars and the stakes so that is accurate.

2 But if you have not got the rectification of the hour, so that it has passed by the [true] time of the nativity,[24] and the time in that is not known [as to whether] the nativity was in the night or day, then take from the degree in which the Sun is on the day of that nativity, to the degree in which the Moon was on the day of the planting of the sperm. **3** Now if what is between them is less than 180°, then the native was born by day; and if there was greater than 180° between them, he was born by night.

4 So when you know [whether] he was born [at] night or day, [and] then you wanted to know the hour in which the native was born, then take what is between the meeting or opposition belonging to[25] the day of the conception, and the Moon on the day of the conception, in degrees by ascensions (and let that be the stay [in the womb] apart from the average, for that is more correct):[26] so you divide that by 15, and what comes out are the hours; and what remains are the portions of an hour: preserve that.

5 Then look: for if the conception was after the meeting, then cast out what came out in hours, from the middle of the day to the middle of the night, and where it reaches, that is the hour in which the nativity was. **6** But if it was after the opposition, then cast out that hour by what is between one-half of the night to one-half of the day, and where it reaches, that is the hour in which the nativity was. **7** And likewise if you wanted to know from your day at the time it was in it, of nativities.[27]

---

[24] This simply means that the calculation using the Trutine does not exactly match the assumed natal positions.

[25] That is, the pre-*conception* lunation. If one has already used the Trutine to find the conception day, it is easy to find out when and where the pre-conception lunation was.

[26] "Apart from average" means "if the pregnancy is not the mean length of 273 days."

[27] من بومك لما فيه, من المواليد. I do not understand this sentence.

Chapter [1.6]: On the knowledge of the Ascendant of the nativity, [which] is the *namūdār*[28] for one established on[29] [that] day, & one whose Ascendant is not found

Comment by Dykes. This method assumes that the bound lord of the pre-natal lunation is the key to the natal rising sign. So for instance, if the native was born by day and the lord of the pre-natal lunation was Saturn, in Scorpio,[30] then the natal Ascendant will be one of the fixed signs (**1**). If by night, then it will either be Aquarius or Leo (**2**). But if Saturn was under the Sun's rays, then the natal Ascendant will be one of the signs which follow Aquarius or Leo, namely Virgo (the sextile behind Scorpio) or Pisces (the trine in front of it) (**3**).

1 If you wanted to know which sign is the Ascendant of the native, then take the lord of the bound of the meeting or opposition for that month, and see in which sign it is: for indeed the Ascendant of the native is that sign, or one of the stakes of that sign—and that is if it[31] was by day.

2 And if it was by night, then see the sign which is the square of the lord of the bound in front of it, and the other one which is its square behind it: for <the Ascendant of> the nativity will be the one which has passed or will occur, in one of the two signs which are the square of the sign of the lord of the bound.[32]

3 Now if the lord of the bound was in the rays [of the Sun], then do not take the signs of the square, but always take the signs which follow upon the two signs of the square: for in that case it will be the sextile behind [the lord] and the trine in front of it, and that is the sign of the Ascendant of the nativity.

---

[28] In Pahlavi, this means "indicator." Although I have stopped using transliterations wherever possible, I have retained it because it is only used for the rectification indicator, and would otherwise cause confusion when speaking of other indicators or significators.

[29] وفق على.

[30] I take this to be the position of Saturn in the nativity, not at the pre-natal lunation.

[31] I take this to be the nativity, not the pre-natal lunation.

[32] Without the added brackets, this would read: "…for the nativity which has already passed or will occur, will be in one of the two signs…".

Chapter [1.7]: <On> knowing of the degree of the Ascendant

Comment by Dykes. This chapter presents a version of the method of Ptolemy, in *Tet.* III.2 (Robbins pp. 231-35). First, we cast an assumed, rough natal chart, and determine whether the pre-natal lunation was a conjunction or opposition (**1**). For a conjunction, use that degree; for an opposition, whichever luminary had been above the horizon at the time of the lunation (**2**). (It cannot be the luminary above the horizon at birth, because many births will have both of the luminaries above or below the horizon, such as people born near a quarter Moon.)

Next, find the victor of that degree, according to the various types of dignity and good condition (**3-4**). If two or more seem to be roughly equal, then see which one is the best or becoming the best as it changes conditions (**5-7**). This is an elaboration on Ptolemy's instructions, as he only uses the planets closest to the assumed angles and more related "to the sect."

Finally, see where that victor is at the time of the assumed nativity, relative to the rough Ascendant-Descendant or MC-IC axes (**8**), because the degree of the victor in *its own* sign, will be the degree of that axis in the rough chart (**9-10**). So if the victor at the nativity is at 15° Sagittarius and is closer to the rough Ascendant-Descendant, then the true Ascendant will be 15° of whatever sign was rising. But if it is closer to the MC-IC, that degree will be the true degree of the MC-IC in those signs.

Of course the obvious flaw in this whole method is that the same planet is likely to be the victor for the entire two-week period. Let the lunation be at 15° Sagittarius: for the next two weeks, Jupiter will be the likely victor for all nocturnal charts, because he not only rules the sign but is the nocturnal triplicity lord. And because he moves so slowly, everyone born by night during that time would have their Ascendant or Midheaven at virtually the same degree of whatever sign was rising or culminating.

ಠ ಛ ಛ

1 Now if you knew [the sign of] the Ascendant, and you wanted knowledge of the degree of the Ascendant, then see whether the nativity is after the meeting or after the opposition. **2** If it was after the meeting, then look at the bound of the meeting, and if it was after the opposition, then take the portion[33] of whichever of the two luminaries was above the earth.

---

[33] That is, the degree.

3 Then, look at the planetary governor over the portion of the meeting or opposition: and you will know the one in charge of that portion from five things: the lord of the house, triplicity, exaltation, bound, and image, and the eastern one of them—if [one] had superior claims over the rest of them. **4** Then see which of them is stronger in its [own] place, and is direct in course, looking at the sign of the meeting or opposition, and understand it.

5 Then look: for if two planets or more were the governor, then the one in charge is the lord of the best. **6** And if there were two governors in what is best, then the one of them in charge will be the one which is changed more quickly from its condition into what is the superior one of them.[34] **7** And if they were both in power equally, [then] whichever of them was in a stake or in its own house, triplicity, bound, or exaltation, and had superiority over its associate in this respect, that is the governor.

8 Now once you knew the planetary governor, then look at which one of the stakes it is closer to by a calculation of the distance.[35] **9** If it was closer to the Midheaven, then make that the degree of the Midheaven, in accordance with the degree of that planet, then erect the Ascendant from that. **10** And if the governing planet was closer to the Ascendant, then make the degree of the Ascendant correspond to the degree of that planet.

Chapter [1.8]: On nativities of nine months & seven months, & the knowledge of how long the fetus's stay in the belly of its mother is, & one having four feet (or one whom people will be astonished by)

Comment by Dykes. The method described by Sahl here is also given, and more accurately, by Hephaistion (II.1, Schmidt pp. 6-7). The method compares features of two lunations (pre-natal and pre-conception), by laying them out on the *pre-conception* lunation chart. The purpose is to determine the length of the gestation, and also to identify viable and non- or less-viable births (and those with defects). When we read the instructions, the first question raised is, "if we already know the birth, why do we care how long the pregnancy was?" And more to the point, "Wouldn't it be obvious already if the infant had serious birth defects?" But perhaps there was some other

---

[34] This sentence reflects an adaptation by another author. See my comment above.
[35] That is, which of the assumed, rough angles it is closer to.

motivation. Valens (*Anth.* I.21) mentions that rectification was used to determine a conception date so as to accurately assign paternity to a child: so the methods for confirming the months of gestation might be ways of confirming or discounting the usual rectification. Thus after using the Trutine of Hermes to find the conception date (see Ch. 1.10 below), we might use this method to see whether it gives the right number of months, *knowing what we do about the infant already born*. If this method shows a shorter term, then we have to adjust the date and assume a different conception.

In order to understand what Sahl's source has done, we begin with Hephaistion. First, find the *pre-conception* conjunction,[36] and cast its chart so you have its Ascendant. Then, frame a right triangle from its Ascendant, by drawing lines at certain degrees from it in the zodiac. The first line is 150° "in the preceding direction," and called "the first subtending side." The second is 120° and called the "upturned side," and the remaining 90° is called the "right side" (i.e., the hypotenuse). The directions could frankly be clearer, but I believe my diagram below is correct. (Sahl's instructions are clearer, but different and perhaps wrong).

Now we have two possible procedures. One is to find out where the Ascendant of the *pre-natal* lunation falls in this chart: thus we are comparing the Ascendants of two different *lunations*. If the Ascendant of the pre-natal lunation is in region (1), it is a nine-month birth; if in (2), seven months; if in (3), the native is irrational or unusual (probably, having birth defects).

Hephaistion then says that some authorities "also" compare where the degrees of *both* conjunctions fall in this chart (the *pre-conception* and *pre-natal* lunation): thus we compare the lunations themselves. If they fall in a combination of (1) – (2), again it is nine months; if (2) – (3), seven months; if (1) – (3), irrational or unusual. Notice that Hephaistion does not give the option of both degrees being in the same region: this is because successive conjunctions or successive preventions are always about 30° apart. Therefore it's impossible for a healthy, viable birth to occur with both lunations in the same region. Suppose that the pre-conception lunation was in early Scorpio:

---

[36] Often in traditional astrology, sources use "conjunction" as shorthand so they do not always have to add "or prevention/opposition." But it could be significant that Hephaistion is specifying the conjunction, because the concern here is the number of (lunar) *months*, not half-months. So it really could be that *only* the conjunction is meant. Nevertheless I will just speak generally about the lunation.

the lunation of the sixth month will already in Aries, so cannot occupy the same division. This will be important when we look at Sahl below.

The chart below supposes that the Ascendant of the pre-conception lunation was at 0°, for the sake of simplicity. In the first method, suppose the Ascendant of the pre-natal lunation was in Gemini: this is region (2) and shows a seven-month birth. In the second method, let the pre-conception lunation be in Scorpio, and the pre-natal lunation be in Leo: this is a combination of (1) – (3), an irrational animal birth.

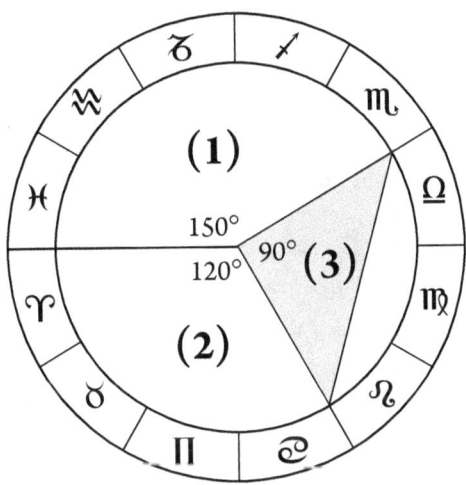

Figure 49: Hephaistion's template, pre-conception lunation
(Dykes, from Heph. II.1)

Now, Sahl's source differs in both the regions of the chart, and in what he compares. (It also omits to say in which chart the template is applied, but we will assume it is the pre-conception lunation, as with Hephaistion). But Sahl's source reads the instructions for the triangle in a different way, always moving clockwise: Hephaistion did not explicitly say that the 120° side had to be in the signs following the Ascendant, and to me he is not absolutely clear about the "subtending" and "upright" sides. So, Sahl divides them in order as we see below (3-4). (Note well that Sahl speaks of degrees of houses and the angle of the earth, which could add another distortion as compared with Hephaistion's intention.)

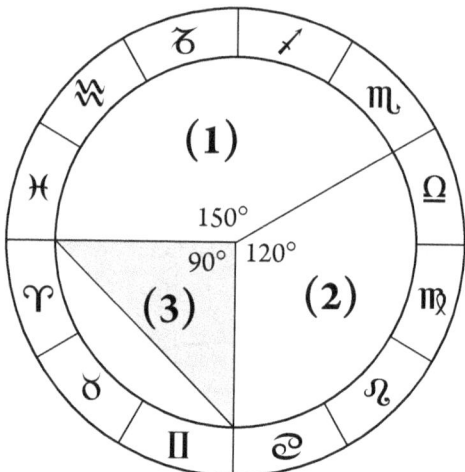

Figure 50: Sahl's template, pre-conception lunation

Then Sahl's source blends the two distinct methods in Hephaistion. He does put the Ascendant of the pre-natal lunation in the template (like Hephaistion), and but then *also* the *degree* of the pre-natal lunation (**5-6**). Therefore we are comparing two positions in the pre-natal lunation—its Ascendant and its degree—rather than the two lunations themselves (pre-conception and pre-natal). This means that Sahl's source can have two points in the same region, which Hephaistion could not.

The interpretation when both points are in the same region, are similar to Hephaistion's first method of looking at the Ascendant of the pre-natal lunation (**7-9**), but there are obvious mistakes, namely leaving out the irrational or unusual births and allowing two regions to be nine-month births. He should have made them be (1) nine months, (2) seven months, and (3) irrational, in order.

The interpretation when they are in different regions are likewise similar, but unlike Hephaistion Sahl's source wants to distinguish where the Ascendant is, from the degree (**10-13**). Unfortunately, this should give six permutations for the separate regions, but only three are mentioned, again showing that something has gone wrong with Sahl's source.

ASC and degree of pre-natal lunation	Months or unusual birth
Both in (1)	9
Both in (2)	9 (*should be: 7*)
Both in (3)	7 (*should be: unusual*)
One in (1), other in (2)	9
ASC in (3), degree in (2)	7
ASC in (3), degree in (1)	Unusual

Figure 51: Sahl's comparisons of pre-natal lunation and its ASC

1 Now indeed the indicators will be corrupted if the native was one of seven months (and likewise nativities having four feet):[37] the amount of the stay in the belly will not be adequate, because animals are those whose stay is one month, five months, and more than that and less, and the indicator will not be suitable unless for one born in nine months. **2** So before that you ought to begin and understand that, according to what I will explain to you.

3 Know that the degrees of the circumference of the circle are 360, and they are divided into three sections; you start with the first division from the degree of the Ascendant[38] up to the degree of the Midheaven, to the degree of the eighth,[39] [then] to the degree of the stake of the earth, [then] to the degree of the Ascendant. **4** And this dividing is made according to equal degrees which belong to the belt [of the zodiac]: so the first division is 150°, the second division 120°, and the third division 90°.

5 Then calculate the meeting[40] of the Sun and Moon which was before the native was born, in the month in which he was born, until you know in which sign it was, and which degree and minute. **6** Then erect the degree of the Ascendant for that hour, and the Ascendant of the meeting will be at that time.

---

[37] That is, an irrational or unusual birth, most likely one with birth defects.
[38] That is, of the pre-natal conception (according to Hephaistion).
[39] Reading for "seventh."
[40] Or rather the lunation, whether it was a conjunction or opposition (assuming that Hephaistion does not insist on only a conjunction).

7 Then look: for if the Ascendant of the meeting and the position of the meeting were both in the second division which is 120° (that is, from the region of the degree of the eighth to the stake of the earth), then the native will be of nine months.[41]

8 Now if the Ascendant of the meeting and the position of the meeting were in the first division (which is the 150° which are from the region of the degree of the eighth to the Ascendant), then the native will be a child of nine months.

9 And likewise if the Ascendant of the meeting is in the position of the meeting, in the third division (which is in the 90° which are from the degree of the Ascendant to the region of the stake of the earth), then the native will be a child of seven months.[42]

10 And if the Ascendant of the meeting was in the third division,[43] and the position of the meeting in the second division, then the native will be one of seven months.

11 And if the Ascendant of the meeting was in the first division and the position of the meeting in the second division, then the native will be one of nine months.

12 And if the Ascendant of the meeting was in the second division and the position of the meeting in the first division, then the native will be one of nine months.

13 And if the Ascendant of the meeting was in the third division, and the position of the meeting in the first division, then the native will have the four feet of a beast or something other than that, of what the people will be astonished at.

---

[41] This should be "seven months," to match Hephaistion.
[42] This should be an irrational or unusual birth, to match Hephaistion.
[43] Omitting "in the position of the meeting." If this phrase were retained, it would appear to be two sentences stuck together.

Chapter [1.9]: Another approach to the staying of the fetus in the belly of its mother[44]

1 Look at the Moon on the day the native was born, and erect her [position] by one year before that and a year after it;[45] then look at these three stakes:[46]

2 For if the past Moon and the renewed Moon are looking at the Moon of the nativity from the trine, then the native will be complete at nine months.

3 And if the two Moons are looking at the Moon of the nativity from a square, then the native will be born at the shorter period, which is 258 days.

4 And if the past Moon was in its trine and the renewed Moon in its square, then the nativity belongs to the middle period;[47] and likewise if [the situation] was reversed.[48]

5 And if the past Moon was in the square of the Moon of the nativity, and the renewed Moon is not looking at the Moon of the nativity, then the native will be one of eight months, and will not survive, and will come out dead.

6 And if the first Moon opposed it[49] and the second Moon was turned away from it, it indicates the shortness of [its] survival.

7 And if the two Moons were not looking at[50] the Moon of the nativity, then the native will come out dead, and harsh misfortune will afflict the mother.

8 And if each one of the two Moons were in the seventh from the Moon of the nativity, then the native will be one of seven months.

9 And if the past Moon was in the seventh from the Moon of the nativity, and the renewed one in the trine of the Moon or Ascendant [of the nativity], then it will also be one of seven months.

10 And[51] likewise [it is seven months] if the first Moon was in its trine or square, and the second Moon in its opposite.[52]

---

[44] The method in **1-11** is reported by Valens (*Anth.* I.22, Schmidt pp. 63-64), and so probably comes from the *Bizidaj*.
[45] This will yield three Moons: the rough Moon on the day of birth, the Moon exactly one year before, and the Moon exactly one year after (the "renewed" Moon).
[46] That is, these three fixed positions.
[47] Valens specifies 269 days.
[48] That is, if the past Moon squared and the renewed Moon trined.
[49] Valens has the trine here.
[50] That is, in aversion to.

11 And likewise if the Sun was in the seventh from the sign of the meeting of the conception.⁵³

☊ ☌ ☌

12 And know that a native whose stay in the womb is greater than the second stay, up to the third,⁵⁴ will be superior in his body and growth: for example, growing fleshier in the face and body. **13** And those whose stay is more than the first stay up to the second one,⁵⁵ their bodies will have decrease and weakness.

14 Now once you knew that the native was one of nine months, then you ought to know the day and hour in which the planting [of the sperm] takes place in the womb, and how long the stay is in the belly of its mother, by the day and hour; and the knowledge of that is according to what I will explain to you.

Chapter [1.10]: On the *namūdār* of the falling of the seed

[The Trutine of Hermes]⁵⁶

1 Know that Hermes and other scholars besides him all agreed that the position of the Moon at the hour of the nativity is the Ascendant of the falling of the seed, and the position of the Moon at the hour of the falling of the seed is the degree of the Ascendant of the nativity: so you ought to rectify that according to what I will explain to you, until there is no increase nor decrease in it. **2** So you should indeed erect the Ascendant based on the hour of its estimation by day and night, but there should not be more than an hour

---

⁵¹ In this sentence Sahl or his source has combined two thoughts in Valens that indicate seven months. The first has the past Moon opposing, the renewed Moon squaring the natal Moon and Ascendant (as a continuation of **9**). The second has the past Moon squaring, the renewed Moon opposing.

⁵² Valens then says "it will also be the same if it should be in a square," but he does not say which Moon that is.

⁵³ Valens does not specify which meeting it is, but this seems to be the only option.

⁵⁴ That is, between a normal term (273 days) and the greater term (288 days).

⁵⁵ That is, early term (258) to normal term (273).

⁵⁶ See my *Comment* to Ch. 1.5.

of error in the estimate:⁵⁷ for there should not have passed 3 hours of the day and night, so you state an hour has passed, or you state 5 hours have passed, unless one is ignorant of the hours and the estimate, [so] that you should be afflicted in what you estimated.

3 And⁵⁸ indeed you should know the rectification of the degree of the [natal] Ascendant *before* the hour in which the seed was planted in the womb—and *that* is known *after* your knowledge of how long the native's stay in his mother's womb is, with respect to the day and hour, from the hour the seed was planted in the womb, up to the hour in which the native was born.

4 And if you erected the degree of the native's Ascendant according to the hour which you presumed he was born in, and you estimated it [as being] of the night or day, then preserve that rising degree as well as the opposite of it from the seventh sign.⁵⁹ **5** Then, calculate for the Moon in that hour until you know which sign and degree she is, and preserve that, and preserve her middle⁶⁰ and the middle of her apogee which you adjusted according to it.

6 And know that in this the Moon has three positions, and they are the foundation [of the method]. **7** If the Moon was in the degree of the west itself at the hour in which the native was born, then know that the native stayed in the belly of his mother for 258⁶¹ days: and that is the smaller distribution. **8** And if the Moon was in the degree of the Ascendant itself, then the native stayed in the belly of his mother for <273 days:⁶² and that is the middle distribution. **9** And if she was under the earth in the west itself, then the

---

⁵⁷ The rest of the sentence is confusing, and I am not exactly sure what Sahl is trying to say beyond the fact that our estimate should not be too great. I am not sure if there is any significance in the periods of three and five hours.

⁵⁸ This sentence explains why Sahl has put Chs. 1.5 – 1.10 in the order he has: we need to know the length of the pregnancy (through various methods) and the rough natal Ascendant (through Ptolemy's *namūdār*), before we move to the Trutine of Hermes.

⁵⁹ This could refer to a point Hephaistion makes about Petosiris and others who promoted the Trutine theory: that the Moon of the nativity could be the Ascendant of the conception *or* the opposite sign (Heph. II.1, p. 1).

⁶⁰ Here and throughout this chapter, the "middle" (وسط) probably means "mean": the Moon's mean or average daily motion, and the mean position of her apogee. This is related to the complicated Ptolemaic theories of Lunar motion, and I do not fully understand how Sahl's source is using it: it depends greatly on the use of actual Ptolemaic tables.

⁶¹ Reading for 255.

⁶² Adding in brackets what must have been the equivalent of a missing line.

native stayed for> 288[63] days: and that is the greatest distribution, and that is the equivalent of the adjustment which you wanted to make. **10** And these distributions have an excess of 15 days, one over another.

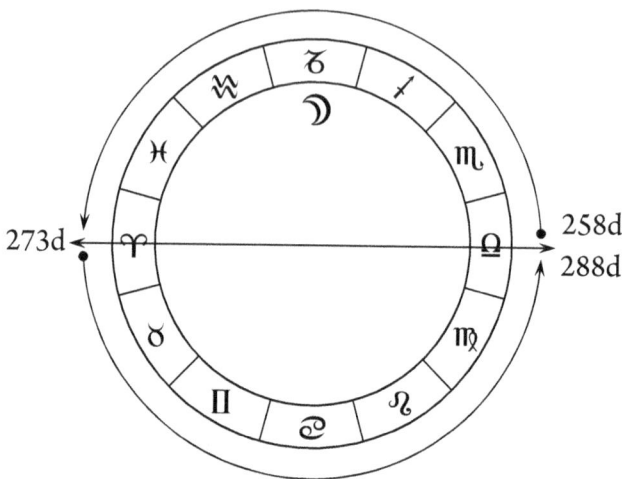

Figure 52: Trutine of Hermes

11 So if the Moon was in something other than these three positions, then you need an adjustment of the days, for these three positions have 15 days excess between them: so subtract that or add it according to these three positions which we have mentioned, based on what I will explain to you.

12 Look at the position of the Moon at the hour of the nativity. **13** For if she were above the earth (which is from the degree of the west, to the stake of heaven, to the Ascendant), then take from the degree of the west up to the degree in which the Moon is, by degrees of equality,[64] and divide that by 12, and what comes out are days.[65] **14** And double what remains, for that is the

---

[63] Reading for 280.
[64] That is, in zodiacal degrees rather than by ascensions.
[65] The reason for 12 is related to the Moon's average motion per day (about 13°) in relation to the Sun's (about 1°): since the Sun is also moving, the distance between them will be about 12° per day. And 180° / 12° = 15 days, the amount of days each hemisphere has. So this is not as exact as using her true mean value, and might be partly why the previous sentence spoke of "preserving the middle"—it might have something to do with her mean speed or her mean position. But it could also simply be that since each hemisphere (180°) is worth 15 days, the 12° is simply the result of dividing 180° / 15 = 12°. For a similar point, cf. Heph. II.1 (Schmidt p. 3).

exact⁶⁶ hours: so add that onto the 258 days which is the smaller distribution, and what it amounts to is what the native's stay was in the belly of his mother, from the hour in which the sperm was planted in the womb, up to the hour in which the native was born, [but] not [yet] adjusted. **15** And the adjustment of it is that you take these days and hours which you added to the 258; and if it was 15 days exactly, then take one day for that. **16** And if it was not a complete 15 days, then multiply the days by 24 until there are hours, and add to them the hours which they [already] had, and divide that by 15, and what comes out are the exact hours. **17** And what remains are the portions of 15, in hours, so add these hours and portions of the hour to the days which you added on top of what you added, and what it comes to is the native's stay in the belly of his mother, in adjusted days and hours: so preserve that.⁶⁷

18 And if the Moon was under the earth at the hour in which the native was born (which is from the Ascendant to the stake of the earth, up to the west), then take from the degree which is from the Ascendant up to the degree and minute in which the Moon is, by degrees of equality, then divide that by 12: and what come out are days. **19** And double what remains, and those are the exact hours: so add these days and hours onto the 273 days which are the middle distribution of the Ascendant, and what there was is the stay of the native in the belly of his mother but not adjusted; so preserve that. **20** And the adjustment of that is that you take the days and hours which you added to the middle distribution; now if there were 15 days, then take a day for that. **21** And if there were less than 15 days, then multiply them by 24, and add to that the hours which you have, and divide that by 15, and what comes out are the exact hours. **22** And what remains is the portions of 15, so subtract that from the days and hours which you preserved, and what remains is the stay of the native in the belly of his mother, from the hour the sperm was planted to the hour in which the native was born, and those are the adjusted days: preserve them.⁶⁸

---

⁶⁶ Lit., "equivalent" or "equated" or "civil" (مستويّة) hours, here and below.

⁶⁷ Although I do not fully understand the procedure here, the point of it is to convert fractional days into hours: a modern calculator could do this quickly. See a similar approach in Ch. 1.11, **4**.

⁶⁸ At this point a lot of Sahl's calculations are due to the nature of the tables he used and the need for hand calculation. A lot of these can be done quickly with a modern astrology program, for example by casting the assumed conception chart and using the animation

[Confirming the Moon]

23 Then, take these adjusted days and hours in which the native stayed in the belly of his mother (from whichever of the two approaches you worked on the course of the Moon and the course of her apogee), then subtract that from the middle of the Moon and her apogee which you derived for the hour of the nativity, and I instructed you to preserve), and adjust what remains until you know in which sign and in which degree and minute of that sign [it is], and that is the position of the Moon at the hour in which the sperm was planted in the womb.

24 Then, look at this degree in which you found the Moon at the planting of the sperm: and if it was like the rising degree in the hour in which the native was born, then the Ascendant is rectified, and the hour which you estimated is rectified, and you do not alter anything of your calculation.

[If the natal Moon is close to the horizon]

25 And if there is a difference of approximately 15° between them, then make the degree of the Ascendant for the native be like the degree in which the Moon was at the hour of the planting of the sperm. **26** And if between them there was a difference of the amount of 20° or more, then that has come about because of what I will mention to you, and that is that if the Moon at the hour in which the nativity was, was close to the degree of the west (whether before it or after it) by 15° under the earth, then the Moon has come to be where you estimated the hour under the earth, and in the rectification she is above the earth—there can be much difference in that.[69] **27** And if it was like that, then you ought to alter the degree of the Ascendant and the degree of the west which you worked out, and add a little bit to the degree of the Ascendant (or subtract from it), until the Moon falls into the difference which there was the first time [you estimated her position]; if the Moon was under the earth, then move her to be above the earth, but let her be close to the degree of the [provisional] Ascendant [of the conception].

---

function to move the chart back and forth in time until the Ascendant or other point is the one you want.

[69] I.e., if the assumed natal Moon is close to the Descendant, the danger is that you have put her above the earth when the true natal Moon is *below* the earth, which could yield a 30-day error in the conception.

28 Then derive the native's stay in the belly of his mother, according to what I have told you. **29** Then, with that derive the middle of the Moon and her apogee for these days, then subtract that from the middle which you derived for the hour of the nativity. **30** Then adjust it, and that is the station of the Moon at the hour of the planting of the sperm in the womb.

31 And if you found her to be close to the degree of the Ascendant by approximately 15°, then make the degree of the Ascendant be on the degree in which the Moon was at the hour of the planting of the sperm. **32** And if there was a great distance between them, of approximately 20° and more than that (whatever it amounted to), then know that you have definitely erred in your work the first time as well as the second one, so reckon your calculation and erect the degree of the Ascendant after the examination. **33** For there is no escaping [the fact that] the Moon is close to the degree of the Ascendant: so at that time you make the degree of the Ascendant be the degree in which the Moon was at the hour of the planting of the sperm.

[Comparing the Ascendants]

34 Then you ought to adjust the hours which you estimated, for they have passed from the day and night, and you have erected[70] the Ascendant for it, which you have rectified with the planting of the sperm, according to what I will explain to you. **35** Look at the first Ascendant which you erected by estimation, and the second Ascendant which you rectified with the planting of the sperm, whichever of them is before the other, and take from the one which was before, up to the one which was after the place, and divide that by the portions of the hours which are of the night and day [which] have passed on that day: and what comes out are the hours. **36** And multiply what remains by 60, then divide it by the portions, and what comes out are the minutes of the hour.

37 Then, look: for if the Ascendant which you adjusted for the planting of the seed was before the Ascendant you estimated [for the birth], then *subtract* these hours and portions of the hour which you estimated that have passed of the day and night, and what remains are the hours which have passed of the day and night when the native was born. **38** And if the Ascend-

---

[70] Or perhaps, "you should erect."

ant which you adjusted by estimate [for the birth] was before the Ascendant of the planting of the sperm, then *add* these hours and portions of the hours to the hours which you estimated, and whatever it was, that is what has passed of the day or night (of the crooked, adjusted hours) over the Ascendant.

39 Then, you ought to derive the middle of the Sun, Moon, and planets according to these hours which you have adjusted, then you equate[71] them[72] according to what I urged [to] you in their equating, and with that you will already have rectified the <first> approach which Hermes stated, [namely] that the position of the Moon at the planting of the seed is the Ascendant of the nativity.

[Confirming the conception Ascendant]

40 Now[73] as for the second approach he mentioned, [namely] that the position of the Moon at the nativity is the Ascendant of the planting of the seed, I will explain that to you. **41** Look at the stay of the native in the belly of his mother apart from the average,[74] how[ever] much it is in days, and subtract that from the years, months, days, and hours according to which you derived the Sun and Moon, and according to what remains you derive the middle of the Sun and Moon, and erect the Ascendant according to that. **42** And if you erected it and verified it, then it is the Ascendant of the planting of the seed: so preserve that. **43** Then look: for if you found the Ascendant of the planting of the sperm to be in the position of the Moon of the nativity,

---

[71] تسوي. Or, "equalize." I take this to mean what the Latin astronomers called "equating," which basically means "to correct." In Ptolemaic astronomy, the mean or average motions and positions were made more precise by "equations," which were corrections gotten from special tables. For a general explanation of how this worked, see my essays in my translation of Leopold of Austria's *Compilation*. But in **44** below, it seems that Sahl's source might mean this in a more general way, i.e., that they are more correct or exact without referring specifically to Ptolemy's tables of equations. But in **44** as well as **51-52**, the text might also be referring to "civil" hours, that is our normal hours of *equal length*, namely 60 minutes apiece: for it opposes these to "crooked" hours in **51**, which are the seasonal or "planetary" hours derived from dividing the period of daylight and nighttime into 12 "hours." At any rate, the mathematics here are attuned to Sahl's special tables.

[72] Omitting "that."

[73] So far, everything up until now has begun from the presumed nativity, and used the Moon's position in it to find the Ascendant of the conception. Now, Sahl's source uses this to go back to the conception and make sure that its Ascendant matches the natal Moon.

[74] That is, if it is not exactly the average term of 273 days.

then the Ascendant of the nativity which you erected by estimation is already verified.

44 And if you found the Ascendant of the planting of the seed to be different from the position of the Moon in the root of the nativity, then take from the degree of the Ascendant of the planting of the seed up to the degree of the Moon in the nativity, and what[ever] it comes to, divide it by 15, and what comes out is the exact hours. **45** And multiply what remains by 60, then divide it just as you divided it [before], and what comes out are the portions of the hours: so preserve them.

46 Then look: for if the position of the Moon in the root of the nativity was under the earth and the Ascendant of the planting of the seed (and that is what is between the degree of the Ascendant of the planting of the seed in front of it, up to the degree of the seventh coming from under the earth), then add those hours and portions of them to the years, months, days, and hours according to which you erected the Sun, Moon, and Ascendant, and what remains [is that] according to which you must derive the middle of the Sun, Moon, and Ascendant. **47** And where you found the Moon, that is the degree and minute of the Ascendant of the nativity, and the Ascendant of the planting of the seed which you erected will come to be in the corresponding degree of the Moon and its minute in the nativity.

48 And if the position of the Moon in the root of the nativity in that was above the earth and the Ascendant of the planting of the seed (and that is from the degree of the Ascendant, rising up to the Midheaven, up to the degree of the west), then subtract those hours from the years, months, and days according to which you erected the luminaries. **49** And what it amounts to, derive the Sun, Moon, and Ascendant according to it: and where you find the Moon, that is the Ascendant of the native, and the Ascendant of the planting of the seed will coincide with the position of the Moon in the nativity. **50** So with that, you will already have rectified at once the two approaches which Hermes mentioned, [namely] that the position of the Moon at the hour of the planting of the seed is the Ascendant of the nativity (and that is the first approach), and the position of the Moon in the nativity is the Ascendant of the planting of the seed (and that is the second approach).

51 And know that if you wanted to erect the Ascendant of the planting of the seed, you should take the hours of the planting of the seed according to which you erected the Sun, Moon, and Ascendant, from the exact[75] hours after half the night. **52** And if that hour was by night, adjust them to the crooked hours: and it is that you multiply them all together by 15, then you divide them by the portions of the hours of the opposite of the degree of the Sun, then the conception, then you erect[76] the Ascendant with that.[77] **53** And if those hours were by day, then understand how many portions of the hours of day belong to the degree of the Sun on the day of the conception, and convert those hours to crooked ones, and erect the Ascendant according to them, for at that time was the Ascendant of the planting of the seed. **54** And take what is between it and the Moon by degrees of ascensions, and work based on what I have explained to you.

55 And know that this work does not derive from the corruption of the Ascendant preceding or lagging behind its degree and minute, except in accordance with 6°, which is the motion of the Moon in one-half of a day, by six rising signs, and six signs altogether, and the Ascendant is not extracted by it except for one who is born at nine months: and there is rectified by it what we have taken [as] its model, if God wills. **56** And test out the stay of the native by the average, for at the adjusting of which[ever] of the two witnesses [it is], judge that whichever of them corresponds approximately to the Ascendant of the planting [of the seed], belongs to the position of the Moon in the nativity.

The statement of al-Abakh[78] on that:

58 Al-Abakh claimed that this indicator which I have explained to you is close to the indicator by which the planting of the sperm is rectified. **59** He said: see in which of the times the native was born ([that is,] night and day), and in which quarter [of the time] he was born, whether in the first quarter of the day or in the first quarter of the night, or in one of the [other] quarters

---

[75] As mentioned above, I take the "equal" and "crooked" hours in **51-52** to be the civil hours of 60 minutes apiece, and the seasonal or "planetary" hours, respectively. But this can also be "exact" (as I translate it here), in **14-21** above.

[76] Reading for "divide."

[77] This refers to the special use of Ptolemaic tables of rising times in *Almagest* II.8 (pp. 99-103): see my *Comment* to Ch. 1.5 above.

[78] الأبخ, taking the identification and pointing from Sezgin p. 117. Al-Abakh was active during the reign of al-Ma'mūn, and so was a contemporary of Sahl's. He wrote a book on choices (elections), nativities, and also on weather prediction. See al-Nadīm VII.2, p. 654.

of the day and night: for the hours of the nativities of males become odd, and the hours of females even.[79] **60** Then, multiply those hours by the portions of the hours of the degree of the Sun if it was day (and if it was night, then multiply the hours by the portions of the hours of the opposite of the degree of the Sun), and what it came to, project it from the opposite by ascensions, and understand the Ascendant. **61** Then see the hours according to which you erected the Ascendant, and convert them to exact[80] hours, and erect the Sun and Moon according to them, and understand their positions in the nativity.

62 And truly,[81] the luminaries are the souls of what is in the celestial circle, and they are the breath of the world, while an Ascendant is not known in the same way apart from the world: because [the luminaries] are the indicators of the Ascendants of the sons of Adam, since [God] granted to the luminaries superiority over the stars of the heavens, and that grants the sons of Adam superiority over all of what He created in the world; and the Ascendant of a native is not known, nor is it rectified, except through them.

63 Then look: for if the native was born by day, then look at the Sun (who is the ruler of the day and its luminary) and [see] if he was in his own exaltation, or in his own house, or in a male sign, or the Ascendant was his house or his exaltation—and that is four testimonies. **64** <And if the native was born by night, then look at the Moon>, and <see> if she was in her own house, exaltation, or a feminine quarter, or feminine sign.[82] **65** Now if you did not find anything of these four testimonies belonging to the Sun and Moon, then look: for perhaps you will find the Sun and Moon in a stake or in their own face (and those are weak testimonies).

66 Then see how much the Sun has moved in the sign he is in, in terms of degrees, and for every testimony take five of what the Sun has moved through in his sign, in terms of degrees. **67** Then, gather together what you have computed of the testimonies, and extract one-fifth, one-sixth, and one-

---

[79] For more on the male and female hours, cf. *Carmen* I.8, and Ch. 1.11, **7ff** below.
[80] Again, this could be "equal" or "civil."
[81] I believe this is still the view of al-Abakh, but cannot be sure.
[82] Note that Sahl's source has offered a different condition for one of the testimonies: for the Sun, he asks if the rising sign is his sign or exaltation; for the Moon, whether she is in a feminine quadrant. I am not sure whether this is intentional.

tenth,[83] and gather them together. **68** Then look: for if the meeting which was before the nativity was by day, then look at these one-fifth, and one-sixth, and one-tenth which you have gathered from the testimonies of the Sun and Moon, and subtract it from the degrees of the Ascendant which you erected from the odd and even hours. **69** And if the meeting was by night, then look at the one-fifth, one-sixth, and one-tenth which you have gathered from the testimonies of the Sun and Moon, and halve them: then add it to the degrees of that Ascendant which you erected from the odd and even [hours], and what it amounts to is the Ascendant of the nativity. **70** And work like that with the Moon just as you worked with the Sun.

71 And know that perhaps you will make the Ascendant be from sign to sign, and perhaps the hours of nativities will come to be odd from females, and even from males. **72** And if you erected the Ascendant after your addition to it or subtraction from it, then take what is between the degree of the Sun up to the degree of that rectified Ascendant, in the ascensions of that clime in which the native was born, and divide that by the portions of the hours of the degree of the opposite of the Sun: what comes out are the hours. **73** And multiply what remains by 60, and divide that by the portions of the hours, and what comes out are the portions of that in crooked hours at that time, so turn them back into exact[84] hours, and erect the Ascendant according to that.

74 And know that what is between the Ascendant up to the stake of the earth is a feminine quarter, and what is between the stake of the earth up to the seventh is a masculine quarter, and what is between the seventh up to the tenth is a feminine one, and what is between the tenth up to the Ascendant is a masculine quarter: understand that.

75 And Abū Sufyān expounded this topic from the writings of *Thayūghūrs*,[85] and he claimed that he tested it and found it to be appropriate for the calculation, and the most accurate calculation.

---

[83] I do not understand what these fractions mean, although 30° can be divided by 5, 6, and 10 without remainder.
[84] Again, this could be "equal" or "civil."
[85] Unknown at this time (ثيوغورس). It resembles "Theophilus" (ثوفيل), but is too long and unusual.

The statement of Māshā'allāh:

77 And if you are working with the planting of the seed, it is allowed that there be one, two, or three degrees between the Moon at the hour of the planting of the seed and the [natal] Ascendant which you erected by estimation: so see which one of them is increased over the other.[86] **78** So if the Moon was increased over the Ascendant which you estimated, make what[ever] is increased be according to one-half,[87] then add it to the Ascendant of the estimation, and where it comes to, there is the degree of the Ascendant. **79** And if the Ascendant of the estimation was the one increased over the position of the Moon, make what[ever] is increased be according to one-half, and then you decrease from the [estimated] Ascendant, and it is equally the Ascendant; and God is more knowledgeable.

Chapter [1.11]: On the *namūdār*, the increase of the hour & its decrease

Comment by Dykes. This chapter seems to cover two methods for determining the exact moment of birth, but I do not really understand the mathematics. Sahl's source seems to derive an almost-exact time in **1-6**, first using the ascensions between the Sun and Moon (**1**), and then the zodiacal degrees (degrees of equality, **4**). Next, he seems to refine this using the sex of the native and the sex of the hour (**7-13**). He then says that the work of conception and the natal time is done, so we must move to the condition of childbirth (**14**). Abū Ma'shar attributes a somewhat simpler version of this method to Valens in his *Book of the Judgments of Nativities* Ch. III.2 (Bodleian Hunt. 546).

ಜ   ಆ   ಆ

---

[86] This seems to mean, "which is in a greater degree."
[87] Reading somewhat uncertainly (here and in **79**) for جعل ما زاد على النصف. I believe Māshā'allāh is simply saying to divide the difference in half, i.e. to "split the difference," to get a better estimate. But why not simply say to divide in half?

1 Now if you knew the hour of the nativity and you wanted to calculate the hour,[88] then erect the Sun and Moon for whose judgment there is no doubt,[89] then take what is between the Sun and Moon by degrees of ascensions, and preserve it: for it is called the *namūdār* of the Sun. **2** Then, take the portions of the hours and multiply them by 12, then by the hours for whose judgment there is no doubt, and you do not multiply it [*by what fell*,[90] *for what was united of something*],[91] and subtract a [full] circle from that if there was more than one circle in what remains;[92] and it is the *namūdār* of the Ascendant. **3** Then look: for if the *namūdār* of the Sun is more than the *namūdār* of the Ascendant, then the hour is increasing; and if the *namūdār* of the Ascendant was more than the *namūdār* of the Sun, then the hour is decreasing.

4 Then, take what is between the Sun and Moon by degrees of equality: for if it was more than 180, then cast out 180 from it, and what remains [that is] less than that, divide by 12, and what comes out are days, and double what remains, and those are hours. **5** Then, see what is joined together in place of the days and hours, how much it is from 15,[93] and preserve it. **6** Now if the hour was increasing, then add that increase to the hours of which there is no doubt of their judgment; and if the hour was decreasing, then subtract that from the hours of which there is no doubt, and what remains is the hour in which the nativity was.

7 And[94] if you calculated for a male in an odd hour and the hour was increasing, then add what comes out for you to the even hour; now if it was decreasing from the odd hour then subtract it from the odd hour. **8** And if

---

[88] By "hour" in this sentence, I believe Sahl's source means "the rough hour," and "the exact moment" of birth, respectively.

[89] I believe this means, "if they are known rather precisely," subject to the further rectifications here.

[90] Or perhaps, "by what was subtracted."

[91] Reading rather uncertainly for what seems to be: ولا تضربه فيما سقطت فما اجتمع من شيء I. do not understand what kind of procedure Sahl's source means here.

[92] That is, if the result is more than 360°, then subtract 360°.

[93] Or perhaps, how many multiples *of* 15 it is?

[94] For 7-12, cf. *Carmen* I.8, which argues that that signs of the luminaries and Ascendant, and the sex of the hour, indicate male or female natives. By the sex of the hour, Dorotheus and Sahl's source seem to mean that odd-numbered hours from the beginning of the day are male, and even-numbered ones are female. But I am not sure if these are in civil hours of 60 minutes apiece, or the "planetary" hours derived by dividing the periods of daylight and nighttime by 12.

the nativity was [of] a girl, then add (if it was increasing) to the odd hour which was before it; and if it was decreasing then subtract from the even hour which you strove for, and erect the Ascendant according to that.

9 And if you found the native to be male, and the Ascendant and the luminaries were in female signs, then that native is born in an even hour and not born in an odd hour. **10** And if the native was a girl and the Ascendant and the luminaries in male signs, then she is born in an odd hour (and if they were in female signs, she was born in an even hour). **11** For those to whom what I mentioned does not happen, in general females are born in even hours, and males in odd hours. **12** Indeed, the conversion of the hours of males into even ones, and the hours of females into odd ones, is due to the luminaries and the Ascendant. **13** Then, erect the Ascendant which is nearest to your supposition, according to what I have explained to you.

14 So once you have erected the Ascendant of the native from the model which I adopted, or the *namūdār*, then begin by looking into the hardship of the mother and her difficulty, according to what I will explain to you.

Chapter [1.12]: The native who dies in the hour he is born

1 Know that if the native dies in the hour [of childbirth] at the hands of the midwives, it takes away his good and evil, and his misfortune and good fortune, from his parents and siblings;[95] and that amounts to the status of one who has going out of his mother's belly dead.

2 But if he lived for twelve hours (according to the course of the Moon in one day), then it creates fear[96] for his parents and siblings, and makes him be of those whose lifespan is short, and [so you should then] judge what he encounters of illnesses. **3** So as for the native, by the category of lifespan he will [have a] short one, then he will die.

---

[95] I believe this mean the native will not have a practical effect on the family, according to the questions that the astrologer usually investigates (the status of the parents, the relationship of the siblings to each other, etc.). But of course it might have an emotional effect on them (see **2**)—perhaps less so in earlier periods, where stillbirths were much more common.

[96] رعابة, not attested in this form in the lexicon but I can find no other reasonable alternative.

4 Then look in the matter of nativities and how the safety of the native and the mother is, in her labor.

Chapter [1.13]: On looking into the matter of childbirth, its difficulty & facilitation

1 Look at the two luminaries and the Ascendant: for if you found them both in a sign, then it hastens in that:[97] so look at the degrees which are between both [luminaries], and make them days. 2 And if the two testimonies were in the topic of upbringing, then make [the degrees] be days.[98] 3 Now if they were both in a single triplicity, then make [the degrees] months.

4 And if it[99] was withdrawing, not ruling anything of its own place, then revolve his year and call upon the Moon as a witness in that. 5 Now if *she* was the planet which indicates the shortness of the lifespan and the upbringing, it is faster for the native's ruin.

6 And call upon the lord of the Lot [of Fortune] as well as the Lot as witnesses in the upbringing, just as the Ascendant and its lord are called to witness, and look in the revolution of years for the corruption of the planet which indicates the native's upbringing, and the lord of the Ascendant of the year: and if it is corrupted, it indicates the native's ruin.

7 And know that the burning and retrogradation that would harm Mercury is small, because he is accustomed to that.[100] 8 And if Mercury was the lord of the Ascendant and was with the Tail, or made unfortunate while the Moon is with the infortunes,[101] or entering into burning, then the native will have a shorter life unless something of the lords of the triplicity of the As-

---

[97] I believe this means, "it will hasten the native's death," if there are *already* indications of a difficult birth or a short life.

[98] I believe this means, "If the two *luminaries* were like that in the matter of upbringing," assuming that a short life was *not* indicated. But even so, if the degrees were equivalent to days, it would amount to the same thing. There may be something missing from **M** which can only be supplemented from another source.

[99] Sahl's source might be referring to the longevity releaser, but without a source it is hard to say where this would have fit into the original text. But **5-6** suggest it is some planet which is somehow weak or made unfortunate, which ought to indicate life but is very weak.

[100] See also Ch. 1.18, **6**.

[101] بالقمر مع النحوس, reading القمر ("the Moon") for العمر ("the lifespan"). But the use of ب ("while, with") is a little strange to me here.

cendant witness it:[102] for if they witnessed, it indicates the native's upbringing, if the Moon was sound.

[Chapter 1.14]: The work of Abū Sinīna concerning the *namūdār* & the claim that it is correct

1 He[103] subtracts the time from the Ascendant of the meeting of the Sun and Moon, 8°: for that is a correct Ascendant of the nativity by day. **2** And by night he adds one-sixth to what comes out[104] from the Ascendant of the meeting of the Sun and Moon: for that is a correct Ascendant of the nativity, if God wills.

Chapter [1.15]: On life, the releaser, & the house-master, from the statement of Nawbakht

1 Scholars have already looked into the matter of life according to various ways, and I have already gathered topics from that, experiments with which are credible and for which there is testimony; then I have mentioned some of it from them, or a portion of it, and the more correct of it, and the more true.

2 So[105] you ought to look in the beginning of that at the house of children in the nativity of the parents, and what the indication is like concerning the condition of their children, then look after that at the topic of upbringing, and how the positions of the planets indicating the native's upbringing are, then especially the place of the Moon and how the infortunes conjoin with her, and what the position of the lord of the Ascendant is like, and what its strength is.

3 And know that in the length of natives' lifespans, perhaps a difficult obstacle akin[106] to death will afflict him, [but] then he will overcome it. **4** And that obstacle will certainly come to be when the releaser reaches the degree

---

[102] Grammatically this could be either the Moon or Mercury, but I suspect Mercury.
[103] I do not understand what exactly this method is doing, and something must be missing.
[104] فزاد سدس بالخرج, but sometimes manuscripts misspell a cardinal number as a fraction, so this could be سادس, "six."
[105] For this paragraph, cf. also Ch. 1.32, **21**.
[106] Reading more sensibly for "equivalent to."

of an infortune, or due to the distributor of time (and it is the distributor of life), and perhaps it will be in the revolution of years, and perhaps it will be in the transit of the planets, and perhaps it will be due to the direction of the releaser to the beginning of the Head, the bound of the infortunes.[107] **5** So, you ought to look in these matters with a subtlety in your examination, and you should not ever look nor incline to [just] one testimony, but you must turn to many testimonies and judge from them, and whichever of them was greater in testimonies, you approach the judgment based on that—apart from Dorotheus,[108] who mentioned that if the releaser was in the seventh, in a feminine sign, it is not fit because it will be feminized twice; and we have already tested that out, so we have exonerated that in practice.

6 Then look in nativities of the day at the Sun and the meeting: because if you found the Sun in the Ascendant, the Midheaven, the house of hope, or in the stake of the west, or in the eighth,[109] then he will have a releaser from which is taken the indication of life. **7** But if you do not find the Sun in any of these places, or he was in one of them but the lord of his bound was not looking at him, nor that of his house, exaltation, triplicity, or face, then the Sun will not be the releaser. **8** And with that you must look at the meeting, where it is: for if the meeting was in any of these five places, then the meeting is the releaser. **9** But if the meeting and the Sun were both falling, then the releaser at that time will be the Ascendant.

10 And in nativities of the night, begin by looking at the Moon, the fullness, and the Lot of Fortune. **11** Now if you found the Moon in a stake or what follows a stake, with the lord of the bound, house, exaltation, triplicity, or image[110] looking at her, then the Moon is the releaser. **12** But if the Moon was falling or none of these indicators is looking at her, then you must turn to the fullness: if it was in a stake or what follows a stake, and the lord of its bound looked at it (or its house, exaltation, triplicity, or image), then the portion of the fullness is the releaser. **13** (And that one—of any of these indicators—which is looking at the releaser, is the house-master.) **14** Now if the fullness was also falling, or the lord of its house, exaltation, bound, triplicity, or image was not looking at it, then the Lot of Fortune is the

---

[107] This might mean to the North Node, *if* it is in the bound of infortunes.
[108] *Carmen* III.1, **17**. Here *Carmen* is speaking specifically about the Sun (a masculine planet), so this consideration may not apply to the Moon.
[109] The inclusion of the eighth suggests that these are quadrant divisions, not whole signs.
[110] That is, the face.

releaser—unless the Lot of Fortune was not in a stake or what follows that, or it was in a stake or what follows a stake but the lord of its bound, house, exaltation, triplicity, or image, is not looking.

15 Now if you found the Sun, Moon, meeting, fullness, and the Lot of Fortune in the falling [places], or they were not falling but the lord of their bound is not looking at them (nor the lord of their house, exaltation, nor the lord of their triplicity, nor the lord of their image), then look at the Ascendant. **16** For if you found the Ascendant being looked at by the fortunes, and the lord of the Ascendant in its own <house or> exaltation, or in its own bound, triplicity, <or image>, in good places, <then the Ascendant is the releaser: and if there was nothing of what I have mentioned>, then know that the native does not have a foundation for his lifespan.

17 And look at the degree of the Ascendant, and direct from it by degrees of ascension in that city in which the native was born; but if it connects with any of the planets in opposition, and from the conjunction, square, trine, and sextile, then whenever it connected with the infortunes, judge evil and hardship for him; and if it connected with the fortunes, then judge life, delight, and the good for him. **18** And if it connected with the infortunes without the rays of the Sun, Jupiter, or Venus, then judge death or tribulation for him. **19** And if it connected with the fortunes and infortunes, then it is like that, and especially if the infortune was greater in degrees than the fortune.[111] **20** And it cuts off life if the Moon was in the bound of the infortunes, and that infortune in the nativity was of the enemies harming the Ascendant and the Moon; and worse than that is if the Moon in the revolution of that year was made unfortunate or with an infortune, or burned by the rays. **21** But if you found the degree of the Ascendant cleansed of the aspect of the infortunes, it indicates the soundness of life, and especially if a fortune looked.

22 And as for if you did find a releaser, then direct from it and from the degree in which it was, and let your examination be of the infortunes and fortunes according to what I explained to you: so where the two infortunes cast rays, state evil and hardship in it, and fear for [his] life; and wherever the two fortunes cast rays, state success and delight.

---

[111] In that case, the releaser or Ascendant would indeed meet with a fortune, but would then meet with an infortune later.

[Chapter 1.16:] The statement of Zādānfarrūkh al-Andarzaghar on that

1 Know that if the Sun was in Aries or Leo (or the Moon in Taurus or Cancer) in this situation, you must not seek his testimony from the house-master, for truly the Sun in these two signs becomes both the releaser and the house-master, since one of them is his house and triplicity, and the other his exaltation and triplicity. 2 And the Moon too is like that in these two signs.[112] 3 And <if> the Sun <and Moon are not in these two signs, then seek>[113] the testimony of the house-master in the manner I have described to you.

4 And know that the more excellent of the releasers are the Sun and Moon; so if one of them was the releaser and they were powerful in the places of the releaser which I have explained to you (even if a house-master is not looking, and it [itself] is not the house-master), then direct the Sun or Moon by the degrees of the ascensions in that city, and see when the releaser connects with a killer. 5 And if you found the releaser connecting with the infortunes, then it kills if the fortunes are not looking at its bound, and his obstacle will not be changed from that, even though they assist the days of that native.[114] 6 And look at that infortune which kills, [to see] in which bound it is, and what its strength is: and if it was falling and under the rays, or above the degrees of the Ascendant[115] when the releaser connects with it, it will not be capable of killing him, and he will overcome his obstacle.

7 (And know that even if the Moon is not the releaser, you should still direct her just as you direct the releaser: because if she connected with the infortunes, it points either at producing a harsh difficulty resembling death, or she will aid the killing infortune in killing.[116] 8 And if the Moon was the releaser and connected with an Ascendant made unfortunate in the root of the nativity, or with a Sun made unfortunate in the root of the nativity, then it kills.)

9 And also, if the Ascendant was the releaser and it connected with a Moon made unfortunate in the root of the nativity, then it kills. 10 And if the Ascendant connected with a degree of the meeting and opposition [that

---

[112] That is, in Taurus and Cancer.
[113] Adding and reading with *BA* III.1.9, 5 for "And the Sun the testimony...".
[114] That is, if fortunes look at the bound, they will save his life but not remove the obstacle altogether.
[115] Reading for "ascensions."
[116] Reading somewhat uncertainly for يعين النّحس القاتل على القتل.

was] made unfortunate, then it produces a difficulty resembling death. **11** And if the degrees of the meeting or opposition connected just as you direct the releaser, and it connected with the Head of the Dragon, then it kills, and especially if it reached the meeting and opposition which was on the day the sperm was planted in the womb; the Tail indicates [*illegible*].[117]

Chapter [1.17]: On the superiority of the Moon as the releaser, & the quickness of the childbirth & upbringing, in corruption[118]

1 If the Moon was in the sixth or twelfth, it indicates the bad condition of the native, and the hardship of his upbringing, unless she was received: for then it relieves that. **2** And if the Moon was free of the infortunes, it indicates the safety of the mother and native; and if she was received, it indicates the quickness of the childbirth and its safety.

3 And if the Moon mixed with the light of a planet under the earth, it buries the native and he will be mixed with the dirt.

4 And if there was a retrograde planet in the Ascendant, he will not have [*uncertain word*]...[119] **5** <Missing> ... amount of the year to that infortune or to its light or its degree; and look concerning the releaser and speak about that.

6 And if the Moon handed her management over to a retrograde planet, then look at the lord of the Ascendant: for if it was safe from retrogradation or a connection with a retrograde planet or burning, or from a planet harmful to it (and it is the lord of the sixth), free, <then that is good>[120] but he will not reach his [full] lifespan.

7 And if the Moon conjoined with an infortune and she is separated from an infortune,[121] then the child will emerge in the belly or come out, dead.

---

[117] This is probably something like "likewise," because BA includes both the Head and Tail in this.

[118] نطفة في, which normally would mean "in seed" but according to Hava can mean corruption or vice.

[119] M seems to read فوفه, but then seems to miss something before blending with the next sentence.

[120] Adding somewhat awkwardly to make the sentence make sense.

[121] That is, if she is besieged.

8 And if the Moon was in a stake and she connects with a retrograde planet, and the lord of the Ascendant connects with the lord of the eighth or with a retrograde planet, or the lord of the Ascendant was retrograde, then it diminishes [the amount] that he lives.

9 If the Moon hands over to an infortune in the Ascendant, and the lord of the Ascendant is close to the rays, or made unfortunate, the native will not live for [many] days.

10 And if the Moon was under the earth and she hands her management over to a retrograde planet above the earth, and it receives the Moon, and the lord of the Ascendant [was] free from burning and a planet harmful to it, then he will be brought up, but he will be weak, emaciated, with many illnesses. **11** And likewise if the Moon was above the earth and she connects with the lord of the Ascendant under the earth, then the native will not be harmed unless it is retrograde.

12 And if the Moon handed over to the lord of the eighth, and the lord of the Ascendant is made unfortunate, it indicates the shortness of life.

13 And[122] if the Moon by day was above the earth and she hands over her management to a planet under the earth, the native will not be harmed unless the planet is retrograde: for in that case he will be weak, fearful, and it will not harm him during the upbringing but it will harm him in [his] livelihood. **14** Now[123] if the lord of the Ascendant was in a bad condition, it indicates the native's ruin.

15 And if the Moon by night was under the earth and she hands over her management to a planet above the earth, it will be suitable; but if the planet was retrograde and it is received, it will not harm him in [his] upbringing but he will be weak, fearful. **16** And if it[124] was associated with what I mentioned, then it will be bad in [his] upbringing.

17 And if the Moon by night was above the earth and she is handing over her management to a planet above the earth, then it indicates the shortness of the upbringing.

---

[122] Cf. Ch. 1.18, **3** and 1.32, **37-38**.

[123] I take this sentence to be related to the previous one, i.e. if the lord of the Ascendant is in a bad condition *in addition to* her handing over to the retrograde planet. Moreover, after this the situation switches to the Moon by night.

[124] Grammatically this could be the Moon, but is probably the lord of the Ascendant, in parallel with **14**.

18 And likewise look at the diurnal and nocturnal planets in their management, according to what I described, for it is of what strengthens the upbringing and weakens it.

Chapter [1.18]: On the testimonies of the Moon also indicating the shortness of the upbringing

1 Her[125] connection with a retrograde planet not receiving her, is a testimony. **2** The handing over of her management to the lord of the eighth, or the eighth [from] her house, is a testimony. **3** The handing over of her management to a planet under the earth while she is above the earth by day, is a testimony. **4** The retrogradation of the lord of the Lot of Fortune, and the presence of an infortune in a stake, is a testimony, if it was inimical to the Ascendant or did not have a testimony in the Ascendant.

5 And know that the connection of the lord of the Ascendant with the lord of the eighth is equivalent[126] in its indication, and you do not seek a testimony with it; now if the lord of the eighth received the lord of the Ascendant, he will be brought up, but he will not reach [his full] lifespan.

6 And the retrogradation of the lord of the Ascendant inverts it,[127] unless it was Mercury. **7** And the connection of the lord of the Ascendant with a

---

[125] At least some of the following is from Māshā'allāh, as can be seen in Oxford Bodleian Savile 15, ff. 179va-b.) For **1-3**, see Ch. 1.32, **34** and **37**. For **5**, see Ch. 1.32, **31**. For **6-7**, see Ch. 1.32, **35-36** and **38**. Indeed, this entire chapter might be from Māshā'allāh, as he seems to be the one most interested in retrograde planets and the lord of the eighth.

[126] عدل. I believe this means that (1) it shows a short (or no) upbringing, like the scenarios in **1-4**, but (2) one does not need to count it as a possible testimony, because *by itself* it is decisive. Now, this could be عذل, which is how the last word of **7** seems to read, and which comes from a root meaning "to be blameworthy"; but I cannot find this listed as an actual adjective. See also **8** in Ch. 1.17 above, which has similar conditions.

[127] Reading as يكتفأ به, although I am not sure of the pairing of this preposition with this verb form. It may mean that retrogradation inverts or cancels any positive meaning, except for Mercury, who is often retrograde anyway (thanks to Steven Birchfield for this suggestion). But the inversion could refer to the harm from the lord of the eighth: as though the lord is backing out of the bad situation. In that case, Mercury would not be helpful because his frequent retrogradation would not matter. An alternative would be يكتفى به, "is content with it," but this does not make sense because retrogradation should make things worse, "invert," or "reverse" them, as I have read it.

<retrograde> planet, or one in its first slowness, inverts it[128] (unless it receives it): and it is equivalent.[129]

8 Now if in the nativity there was *one* of the testimonies which I mentioned concerning the shortness of the upbringing, the releaser will be weak and not fit, except through the reception of that releaser, [which indicates] fitness. **9** And if in the nativity there were *two* testimonies[130] of what I mentioned, and the native did not have a releaser, one will not know his lifespan except by revolving [his] years. **10** And if in the nativity there were *three* testimonies of what I mentioned, then he will not be brought up. **11** And if the fortunes were in the stakes, they will strengthen these testimonies.[131] **12** But[132] if it was the lord of the eighth and a retrograde planet [in the stakes], then it indicates the ruin of the native; <but> if it was from its own house, exaltation, or bound, then it kills.

13 And if the Moon was a releaser, and she connects by conjunction with a Sun that is made unfortunate, then it indicates tribulation and death at the connection of the degree of the Sun, and especially if the lord of the indication of the lifespan[133] is not in a stake. **14** And likewise, if you found the Moon in the fullness,[134] then it is bad. **15** But if the fullness and its lord were in a good position, and the fortunes looked, then judge for him both a releaser and completion.[135]

16 And know that if the releasers reached the beginning[136] of a bound of the infortunes, they kill, or they produce an obstacle like death.

17 And if the Sun was powerful in the root of the nativity, [and] then he came to the connection of that releaser with the infortunes, then [the Sun] will rescue him; and the Moon works like that as well.

---

[128] See the footnote above.

[129] See the footnote to **5**: reading what seems to be لاعذ as لاعد.

[130] Reading for "three testimonies," so that **8-10** have 1, 2, and 3 testimonies respectively.

[131] Or rather, they will give strength to the native *despite* the testimonies.

[132] The second part of the sentence suggests some kind of aspect which has not been mentioned yet, so there might be a fragment missing between **11-12** which provides some context.

[133] Reading العمر for القمر ("the Moon"). I take this to be the house-master.

[134] Probably, with a similarly unfortunate Sun opposing her.

[135] This probably means that the Moon—here understood as the releaser—no longer indicates a quick death by herself, but can be used in the full method of distributions through the bounds, as in a normal lifespan.

[136] رأس, lit. "head." But since this word can also mean "extremity," it is possible that the source means the end of the bound.

18 And know that the Moon is not more intense in power relative to the Ascendant,[137] and likewise the Ascendant [in relation to] the Moon; because I have already made it clear to you that if the Moon connected with the degree of the Ascendant it kills, and if the Ascendant connected with the degree of the Moon it kills; and[138] these two connections are very powerful, one to the other.

19 And[139] know that if there were 5° between a planet and the degree of the Ascendant from behind it (that is, if it was before the Ascendant by 5°), its strength will be in the Ascendant, and it will be fit for releasing; and likewise in all of the houses.

[Rules for distributions]

20 And look at the releaser (whichever is [the one] you ought to adopt as the releaser, for indeed the lord of <the bound of> that releaser is the distributor of time), and [look at] the one casting its rays upon it: because whenever an infortune casts its rays upon it and a fortune is not looking, it indicates fear for his person,[140] even if[141] it looked at the releaser in a bound of it. **21** Then how[ever] many degrees it traveled in the bound, and how many minutes,[142] direct the degrees from the degree in which the releaser is, by degrees of the ascensions of the signs in that city, for each degree (of the degrees of ascensions) a year, and for every 5' a month, and for every 1' six days, and for every 10" a day. **22** So direct them in this way until it goes out to the next bound, and the distribution will belong to the lord of that bound; draw it out in this way until it reaches the end of the native's life.

---

[137] ليس هو على شيء أشدّ قوّة على الطّالع.
[138] Reading somewhat loosely, as "these two connections" is in the wrong case in the Arabic.
[139] This is Ptolemy's 5° rule in *Tet.* III.10 (Robbins p. 273).
[140] Lit., "his soul" (النّفس).
[141] Reading وإنْ for فإن ("so if"). Read this way I believe this means, "even if [the infortune] looked at the releaser [while the releaser is] in the bound of [a fortune]," emphasizing that it is the aspect from the fortune that saves, not the rulership of the bound.
[142] Sahl's source seems to be referring to the natal position of the releaser, which will almost always fall partway into some bound.

23 Then see when the distribution of the distributor of time[143] comes to be in the bound of the infortunes: where is the infortune, and how is it looking at that bound? **24** For if that infortune looks at that bound with strength, and the fortunes are not looking at it, it kills the native: so look in this way from the distributor of time in the distribution of good and evil for the sons of Adam. **25** If the distributor of time was in the bound of the infortunes, and it is not looking at the fortunes, it kills. **26** Now if the fortunes did look at it, there will be illnesses and afflictions, [but] then he will be healed of them, because wherever the rays of a fortune are with the rays of an infortune, the fortune transforms what the infortune indicates. **27** Now if there was not a fortune here, nor its rays, it will definitely not take long before it destroys, for when you distribute to a planet, when it casts rays to the distribution, it mixes its power together with the power of the distributor, and it gives information about the condition of the native in that distribution in accordance with its [own] condition.

28 And if the distribution was in the bound of fortunes and the fortunes looked at it, it grants much good; and if the fortunes looked at the infortunes, it takes away from[144] that good.

29 And know that if the Moon's degree connected with the degree of an infortune, it indicates illness and tribulation—if a fortune is not looking. **30** And [it is] likewise if the luminaries were in the sixth or the twelfth, with the aspect of an infortune, if their degrees connected with the infortune without a fortune. **31** For if they were close, *not* made unfortunate, [then] upon their connection with the degrees of the infortunes it indicates illnesses as well as safety from them.[145]

32 And do not forget to look in the revolution of years (according to what I will explain to you) as well as the entry of the planets into the signs, and nothing of the matter of the native will be hidden from you.

33 And do not neglect to distribute from the Sun, Moon, Ascendant, the meeting, the opposition, and the Lot of Fortune. **34** For whenever an infortune looks at the Sun and Ascendant, then one should fear for his soul. **35** And if the aspect of the infortunes was to the Moon, there will be corruption

---

[143] At this point Sahl's source seems to be describing a direction or distribution of the house-master itself.

[144] This really means "abstains from," but it does not make astrological sense that it would prohibit *all* good.

[145] I believe this means that a *fortune* will show safety.

in the body. **36** And if it was to the Lot, then in [his] social status and good fortune. **37** And likewise if the distribution from one of them reached the fortunes, then state delight in it.

38 And if you found the releaser connecting with the degree of the Tail, then judge harm for the native from enemies and the introduction of evil upon him (and especially if Mercury and the Moon were with the Tail), along with distress afflicting him, until it connects with the Moon <or>[146] the degree of the Tail.

[Chapter 1.19]: The statement of Dorotheus on [short lives][147]

1 Know that if the native's releaser was not the Sun, Moon, nor Ascendant, the native will be short of life, poor in affairs, weak in strength. **2** And if the native did not have a releaser and house-master, then that will be worse, with no good in it, and he will not have strength. **3** And if the releaser and the house-master were in a weak place, made unfortunate or under the rays, then the native will have a short life. **4** Now if it occurred in a war or flood or crowd, there will be powerful danger, with no hope of life for him.

5 And likewise if the releaser was falling and did not have strength, disease will afflict him from sorcery or an epidemic, and some of the dreadful diseases which exist.

6 And if the Moon was under the rays, she will not be fit to take up [the role of the] manager[148] (and that is if there was 15° between her and the Sun, in front of him and behind him).

---

[146] Adding tentatively to make this part of the sentence grammatical in Arabic. Nevertheless I do not quite understand the meaning. Perhaps it should read, "until the degree of the Tail connects with the Moon"? That would be more like Greek grammar, which could be a source for this material.

[147] This does not seem to correspond well to anything in *Carmen*, except that **1-2** express ideas similar to *Carmen* III.1, **23-24**.

[148] This probably means, "releaser."

Chapter [1.20]: The testimonies of who is looking at the releaser, so it may be known which of them is stronger

1 Know that the more preferable of them is if it was eastern, and especially in nativities of the day and a male planet, and by night the female planets.

2 Now if you found all of the five indicators looking at the releaser, then the stronger of them is the lord of the bound, then the lord of the house, then the lord of the exaltation, then the lord of the triplicity, then the lord of the image. **3** And if you found one of them having two shares, then the one having two shares is stronger than the lord of [only] a single one. **4** And if you found the releaser in the bound of a planet, and that planet was in the Ascendant with the releaser, it is stronger than the others. **5** But if the house-master was under the rays, then it is deceptive, subtractive, corrupting.

6 And if you found the releaser in a good position, and its lord eastern and having a share in the Ascendant (even if it was in the second from it, not looking at it), then it will assume the responsibility of being the house-master with it, unless in that nativity there was a planet preferable to it.

[The years of the house-master]

7 And if you knew the house-master, then see where its position is, and whose house it is in, and whose exaltation, and whose bound, triplicity, and image. **8** For it is good if it is in its own house, exaltation, bound, triplicity, or image, eastern, direct, in a good position, and if the nativity was by day and it is looking at the Sun[149] (or it was by night and is looking at the Moon and the nocturnal planets). **9** And it is preferable if the house-master is of the share[150] in which the nativity is (if it was by day, then diurnal, and if it was by night, then nocturnal); and it is more preferable than that if it is a fortune.

10 So[151] <if> you found the house-master in the Ascendant or in the Midheaven, or in the sign of the west, or the eleventh, enhanced by what I explained,[152] then it indicates the native will live for the <greater> years of the house-master. **11** And likewise if you found it under the earth, eastern, in

---

[149] This should probably include "and the diurnal planets," in parallel with the Moon in the next clause.

[150] الحظ: that is, the sect.

[151] Sentences **10-11** are reflected in al-Ṭabarī's *TBN* Ch. 1.4.3. He then says that if they are in these places but alien (in exile) and western, they are reduced to the lesser years.

[152] See **7-9** above.

one of its shares, enhanced, then it also indicates its greater years (and by night in the fourth and fifth, it indicates the greater years). **12** And likewise, if you found it in the house of Good Fortune[153] and it is a diurnal planet in one of its places, eastern, then it indicates its greater years. **13** And likewise if you found Venus (and other planets besides her) in her own shares in the fifth, eastern, and she is the governor of the native, it indicates [*illegible*] greater [*illegible*] it grants the lesser ones.

14 Know[154] that exile, setting,[155] retrogradation, and burning do not stick to[156] the superior planets, but they do stick to the inferior planets. **15** And if a superior one was in the condition which sticks to it, it is corrupting, for it indicates its lesser years as months or days.

16 Now if you found the house-master in the second or eighth, then it indicates its middle years. **17** And if it was in the house of hope or the fifth, and was not in something of its shares,[157] and was not eastern, then it indicates its middle years.

18 And if it was under the rays of the Sun in a stake, then it indicates its middle years.

19 And if it was alien, westernizing in the places, then it indicates its middle years as months and days.

20 If the house-master was in the stakes, easternizing, or not easternizing so long as it is not retrograde and not burned, it indicates its middle years, by the permission of God.[158] **21** And if it was under the rays of the Sun, retrograde in a stake, then it indicates its lesser years. **22** And if it was alien, westernizing, retrograde, it indicates the lesser ones.

---

[153] That is, the eleventh.

[154] This paragraph is reflected in al-Tabarī's *TBN* Ch. I.4.3.

[155] Reading اغتراب for اعتراف, which normally means "emigration," "estrangement," but that would be redundant following "exile."

[156] يلزم, here and in **15**. Or, they do not "impose" upon them as they do the inferiors. The Latin version of this passage in al-Tabarī says these conditions do not "harm" them as much, but to me the meaning is still unclear. Since these difficult conditions are the typical ones that define corruption and harm, what other condition *would* adhere to or impose upon them?

[157] That is, its dignities.

[158] This probably means that it is *not* also in one of its dignities–otherwise we would expect an angular and eastern house-master to grant the greater years (as in **7-10**).

23 And if it was in the eleventh or fifth, retrograde, then it indicates its lesser years; and if it was under the rays of the Sun, then it indicates months. 24 And if along with that it was in its fall, then it indicates days and hours. 25 And if you found it in the second and eighth, retrograde, under the rays of the Sun, then it indicates months.

26 And if it was in the ninth, in one of its shares, eastern, then it indicates its middle years. 27 Now if it does not have a share nor easternization, it indicates its lesser years. 28 And if it was in the <other> [places] falling from the stakes, it indicates its lesser years. 29 And if it was under the rays of the Sun, retrograde, then it indicates months. 30 And if you found it in the third, [uncertain][159] in its house or share, then it indicates its middle years. 31 And if it does not have a share nor easternization, it indicates its lesser years. 32 And if it was retrograde, it indicates months. 33 And if it was retrograde under the rays, it indicates days. 34 And if with that it was in its fall, it indicates hours.

Chapter [1.21]: On the aspect of the planets to the house-master

1 See[160] who is looking at the house-master, because if you found a fortune or infortune looking from a stake or what follows a stake, [by] an aspect of trine or sextile, then it indicates an increase of the lesser years.[161]

2 So if a fortune was with the house-master, then it is preferable for that; and if it was eastern, then it is more powerful. 3 And if it looked from its own house, exaltation, or triplicity, then it is more powerful in the increase [of years], and especially if it was eastern. 4 And if it was enhanced by exaltation, house, triplicity, or easternization, and it is looking, and it is in the ninth place, then it increases it by its lesser years, and especially if the aspect was from a share of the house-master.

---

[159] **M** seems to read مريدًا.
[160] Sentences 1-7 are very close to statements in al-Ṭabarī's *TBN* I.4.3 – I.4.4, but **8-14** do match *TBN* I.4.4. Al-Khayyāṭ's *JN* Ch. 4, Māshā'allāh's Latin *On Nativities* §4, and al-Ṭabarī are very similar on all of this material.
[161] In these additions and subtractions, I take each planet to only be adding or subtracting the amount of *its own* years (i.e., the years it actually controls), rather than the house-master's. For example, Mercury's greater years are 76. If Jupiter is adding "the lesser years" to Mercury, I take this to mean *Jupiter's own* lesser years (12), not Mercury's lesser years (20).

5 But if you found an infortune with the house-master, or in its square or its opposition, then it subtracts from what the house-master indicates, in the lesser [years]; and worse is if that infortune was not in the sect[162] of the nativity, and there was no share[163] in it. **6** And if you found the infortune eastern, direct, and it had a share[164] in the nativity, and its position was good, and it is looking at the house-master from a trine or sextile, then it will add its own lesser years to it, and especially if the share[165] of the native has friendship with the house-master. **7** And [if] perhaps the infortune looked and its place was good, then it does not subtract years, but it subtracts months, days, and hours.

8 And if the fortunes looked from a square or opposition, or they were with the house-master, then they will <not> withhold years, but will even add the equivalent of its lesser years—if they were not retrograde nor burned: for if [the fortune] was retrograde or burned, it adds the equivalent of its lesser years, in months.

9 And if an infortune looked at the governor from the opposition or it conjoined with it or from its square, it subtracts the equivalent of its lesser years, whether it receives it or does not receive it. **10** And if it looked from a trine or sextile, then it resembles that: and that is if the infortune was with the house-master in the bound[166] and it had testimonies in the nativity, and was not removed[167] from it in longitude and latitude: for then it will not subtract the years but it will subtract months and days.

11 And if you found the Head with the house-master, and the house-master is a fortune, then it adds one-fourth of the years which the house-master indicates. **12** And if it was with the Tail, being distant from it by 12°,

---

[162] خظ, lit. "share."
[163] نصيب. I believe this means "dignity," so that the infortune is both contrary to the sect of the chart, and without dignity or significant rulership.
[164] حظ.
[165] خظ. But in this case I am not sure what Sahl's source means, whether simply "sect" or some planet with rulership, such as the lord of the Ascendant.
[166] Reading "the bound" for a slightly smudged word.
[167] يغيّب. This must mean "distant," especially when considering latitude (such as being on the other side of the ecliptic).

then it does not indicate a subtraction, especially if it had already separated from the Tail; and[168] at twelve [degrees] and what is less, it is worse.[169]

13 And if the house-master was burned, it will not indicate anything.

14 And[170] if Venus or Jupiter were in the Ascendant or Midheaven (or one of them) in the root of the nativity, then the equivalent of the lesser years of Venus of Jupiter should be hoped for, for the native.

[Chapter 1.22]: The easternness of the planets, & their westernness

Comment by Dykes. The text for **1-8** is very similar to two related texts, *BA* II.1-II.2 and *Carmen* III.1, 1-7 (so they should be read together). The main difficulty here is that the sentences are not ordered well for comprehension; another problem is that *BA* and *Carmen* read some things differently. The sentences here should be read in the following order, followed by **9-11** (which are on a different topic):

- Superior planets: their easternness, or being morning risers or morning stars (a 9-day allowance for Saturn and Jupiter): **1** and **6** (Saturn, Jupiter), and **3** and **6** (Mars).
- Superior planets: their westernness, or being evening setters, or going under the rays (a 7-day allowance): **2**, then **4**.
- Superior planets, on their eastern side up to retrogradation: **5**.
- Inferior planets: **7-8**.

This entire discussion is also reflected in al-Bīrūnī §§481-82. I have relied on al-Bīrūnī for the diagrams below, although his interval for being in the heart of the Sun is only 16', not 1°.

In context, the passage seems to be about whether or not a planet is "fit" to be the house-master of the nativity, based on its visibility relation to the Sun: when a superior planet is in such a position it can be, or simply is, the

---

[168] Reading the rest of this sentence somewhat loosely, for وفي الاثنى عشرة ما قلّ وقرب, فهو أردأ.
[169] That is, it *will* subtract one-fourth, *if* it is at or closer than 12°.
[170] Al-Khayyāṭ (*JN* Ch. 4, **17**) and al-Ṭabarī (*TBN* I.4.4) explain that this is if the nativity did not otherwise indicate a lifespan—so it is possible that this sentence belongs with **12**, for cases when the house-master is burned.

house-master of the nativity.[171] We may imagine that the same goes for an inferior planet, but on the other hand this entire discussion is reflected in al-Bīrūnī §§481-82 without reference to the house-master, and in a much more straightforward fashion. So I suggest that this is really a general theory of easternness and westernness, but is being applied here as a set of *fitness criteria* when finding the house-master. Since this has been alluded to in previous chapters and is part of *Carmen* III.1, it makes sense that Sahl would insert such basic concepts here.

As for whether or not this is genuinely Dorothean, that is harder to say. Hephaistion regularly draws on Dorotheus, but while Heph. III.4, **5-6** mentions some of these numbers, he does not distinguish between superiors and inferiors as our texts do here. So I tentatively suggest that Pingree is correct to view much of *Carmen* III.1 (including this extract) as a Persian interpolation.

At any rate, the passage is somewhat confusing and does not spell out every detail for every planet. The main idea is that while each planet has its official interval for being out of or under the rays (see diagram), planets are allowed to be closer or farther than that, depending on the interval and the kind of planet they are. By custom the planets are generally allowed seven days to be at their official interval. So for instance, the official interval for Saturn's evening occultation under the rays is 15°. But already when he is in a later zodiacal degree than the Sun by 22°, he can be considered western (**2**): this is because the Sun moves about 1° a day, so after seven days they will be 15° apart (22 − 7 = 15).

However, the text provides a special nine-day interval for the easternization of Jupiter and Saturn as morning risers (**1**), so they can be only 6° from the Sun on the eastern side, and still be considered eastern or fit to be eastern, because after seven days they will rise out of the rays (6 + 9 = 15). Why do they enjoy a special nine-day rule on the eastern side, and does this apply to the other planets? The text does not say. I also note that *Carmen* III.1 and *BA* II.2 differ in their intervals for Mercury and Venus (**7**): in *BA*, the intervals are 19°.

Following is a table showing the intervals between the superior planets and the Sun, when they are in the western and eastern zones, and at what

---

[171] *BA* II.1; *Carmen* III.1, **3**.

interval they actually westernize or easternize. (See the footnote for **3** below, as to why I assign 15° to Mars.) We cannot make a similar table for Venus and Mercury, because their daily motion and elongation from the Sun is highly variable and must be examined in the ephemeris.

Westernizes at:	Considered western		Considered eastern	Easternizes at:
15°	22°	♄	6°	15°
15°	22°	♃	6°	15°
18°	22°	♂	15°	18°

☋ ☊ ☋

1 And know that if there were 6° between Saturn and Jupiter and the Sun, then they are considered to be eastern, and they are powerful in the distributing of the lifespan and in every work, because in up to nine days the Sun will have passed them by 15°;[172] but if they were less than that, they will not be fit.

2 And [Jupiter and Saturn] are not considered western until there are 22° between them and the Sun: at that time they are fit to be considered western.[173]

3 And as for Mars, he does not easternize until there are 18° between him and the Sun.[174]

4 Now if they were not like that [in the west], these stars will <not> enter under the rays on the seventh day,[175] so they will not be fit at that time to be the house-master, nor for the distribution of life.

---

[172] Since the Sun moves about 1° per day (and these slow planets hardly at all), then if they are 6° or more degrees earlier then him in the zodiac, after nine days the Sun will have moved 9°, making a total of 15° between them and him.

[173] Again, since the Sun moves about 1° per day, then once they are at 22° from him on the western side, after seven days he will be 15° from them (22 − 7 = 15), and they will properly set under the rays.

[174] That is, Mars becomes *actually* eastern and visible at 18°. If so, then he would start to be in the range of the 7-day rule when around 15° from the Sun (just as Saturn and Jupiter are at 6°). Since Mars moves at about 31' per day, if he and the Sun were 15° apart, then after 7 days they would be about 18° apart. (The Sun would move forward by 7°, and Mars by 3.5°). But if the 9-day rule were applied to Mars as it is with Saturn and Jupiter, then he would be in the eastern zone at about 13.5° or 14°, and I have not heard of this number. So I think it is safe to say that he is considered eastern at 15° and then actually emerges or easternizes at 18°.

5 [But] then, [once eastern], the stars will increase in power and be fit until they go retrograde: for when they go retrograde they are corrupted. **6** And the power of easternization [for] Saturn and Jupiter is when 15° have passed them, and Mars 18°.

7 And Venus and Mercury are eastern [when] direct in course before rising, or in front of the Sun ([he being] in the west), and there are 12° between them and the Sun. **8** Now as for [being] in the west, if there were 15° between them and the Sun, they will have gone out of the rays and become western [risers].

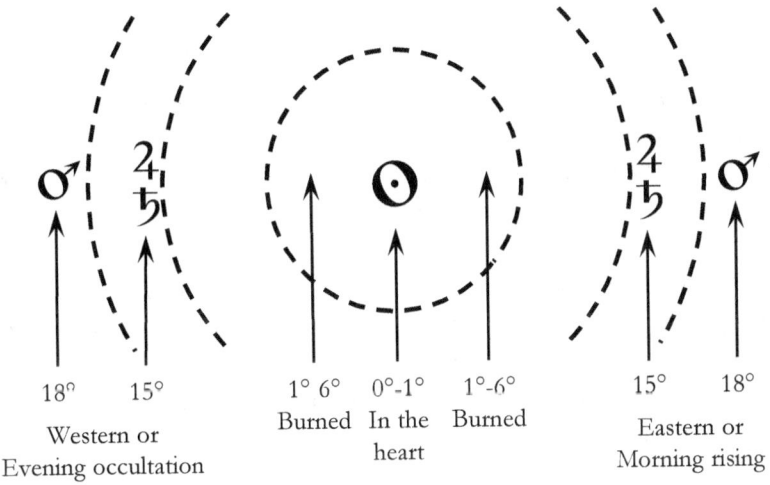

Figure 53: Superiors' easternization and westernization (Sahl, al-Bīrūnī)

---

[175] The "not" added by Dykes. The point is that we want the planets to westernize (go under the rays) *within* seven days, which makes their maximal distance be 22° (**2**). If Saturn and Jupiter are 22° from the Sun, then after 7 days the Sun will have traveled 7° (and them practically nothing), making the interval 15°. If Mars is at 22°, then after 7 days the Sun will have traveled 7° and Mars about 3.5°, making about 18° between them.

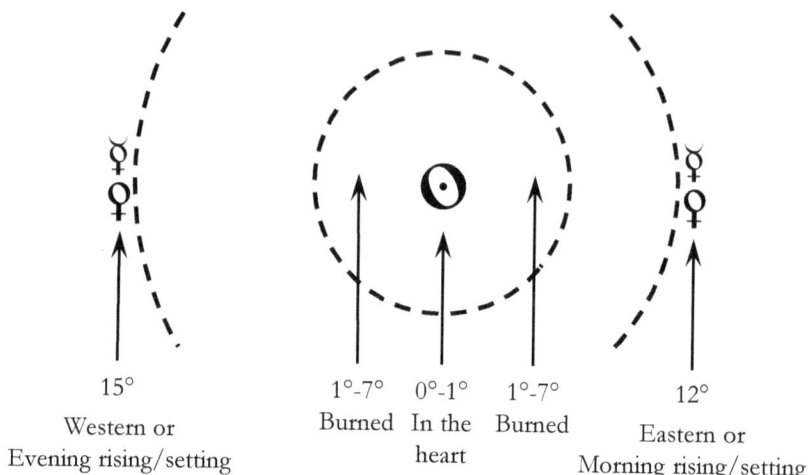

Figure 54: Inferiors' easternization and westernization (Sahl, al-Bīrūnī)

9 And[176] the planets will not fall from the stakes except after 5°, and the planets do not become powerful in the sign [they are in] until they travel 5° in it.

10 And[177] know that the planets, in the condition of their retrogradation, are not powerful (neither the fortunes among them nor the infortunes), even though they still do good and evil.

11 Now if the planetary fortunes were in their unhealthiness[178] or opposing the infortunes, then they do not distribute the good; and perhaps they will grant something, [which] will be unhealthiness upon their lord.[179] **12** And as for the infortunes, the worst is when [one] infortune opposes the other.

---

[176] This sentence represents Sahl's *Aphorism* #44.
[177] This is close to Sahl's *Aphorism* #38.
[178] That is, in their detriment.
[179] Or more likely, their "owner" (صاحب), namely the person signified by the planet. Thus in a question chart, if the lord of the Ascendant is in detriment, then the querent is harmed.

[Chapter 1.23]: The statement of Māshā'allāh on the lifespan & the releaser

Comment by Dykes. This is an extremely dense chapter, so allow me to sketch out its contents.

After reminding us that the house-master is the governor of the native's lifespan (**1**), in the first major section (**2-7**) Māshā'allāh suggests we direct its natal position to being burned by the Sun or harmed by an infortune (**2**). Then, we must cast the solar revolution chart for the year that corresponds to that burning, and see what it shows (**3**). Then follow a number of scenarios that show the native's death, *if* that directed house-master is *also* harmed in real time. If it is burned (or perhaps, just harmed) at the revolution or in one of its angles later in the year, the native will die (**4**). If the lord of the revolutionary Ascendant and the lord of the profected Ascendant are harmed, he will die (**5**). If the profected Ascendant reaches some natal infortune and the revolutionary Ascendant was on that infortune or its hard aspects, he will die (**6**). Sentence **7** seems to be an odd repetition of similar points. However, if the house-master is *not* harmed in these ways at the revolution, then we must consider the lord of the eighth and the lord of the eighth from the house-master,[180] and treat them as you did the infortunes (**8-9**). In the last resort, see if there are other harmful things described in **10-11**. All of this is supposed to be examined in the year indicated by the direction of the house-master.

The next section addresses charts in which the house-master is not really suited to grant years, or perhaps just not many (**12-14**). In those cases, it seems Māshā'allāh wants us to direct the lord of the Ascendant or the Ascendant itself to the degrees of burning or an infortune, just as we did above. If the house-master is not capable of bestowing life, then use the same methods as above.

Then Māshā'allāh considers nativities without a releaser and house-master (**15-21**), when we must rely on planets like the domicile lord or primary triplicity lord of the Ascendant, evaluating its fitness and then using it in directions and other techniques. Māshā'allāh proposes the novel idea that

---

[180] I'm not sure if these are taken at the nativity or in the revolution.

if this planet's ray falls close to the Ascendant, we can direct it from the degree of that ray, or from the Ascendant itself (**21**). (See also **38-39**.)

Then follow sections with general approaches to directions, distributions, and profections (**22-27**), and miscellaneous advice and comments (**28-39**).

After this Māshā'allāh returns to the subject of identifying the releaser (**40-47**), with advice on profections and directions or distributions (**48-52**), counting the years of the house-master and adding or subtracting years from it (**53-60**), and finally more rules on comparing the years of the house-master to the directed years of the releaser (**61-68**).

1 Māshā'allāh said concerning the lifespan that it is based on the two luminaries: and that is if one of them is looking at the Ascendant and at the lord of the Ascendant, and it is received by connection; for if it was in this manner, then the planet with which the luminary connects and does that, is the governor[181] of the native.

[Combining techniques with the direction of the house-master]

2 And with that, look at the position of the governor relative to the Ascendant and its lord, and its position relative to burning and the infortunes; then direct it to the conjunction of the infortunes and the degree of burning, and its[182] opposition and its square, a year for every degree of ascensions. **3** Then calculate for the revolution of that year in which the governor of the native corresponds to the degree of the infortune by union or opposition or its square, or the degree of burning. **4** For if your calculation of this [by direction] and the revolution both indicate burning, and then the governor is burned at the revolution, the native will be destroyed; and if it is not burned at the revolution but it is burned in one of the stakes of the Ascendant of the year,[183] it indicates that [as well]; and it is worse for that in the Ascendant [itself]. **5** And in accordance with what I have mentioned, call upon the lord

---

[181] That is, the house-master. Note that in **2-11**, Māshā'allāh directs the house-master (as apparently above in Ch. 1.18, **23-26**), a version of which is also described by Valens in *Anth.* III.3, **5**.

[182] That is, the degree of an infortune: see the next sentence.

[183] This must mean it is burned in one of them *later* in the year. For a similar approach by Māshā'allāh regarding kings, see Sahl's *On Times* Ch. 11, especially **24ff**.

of the Ascendant of the year[184] as a witness, as well as the lord of the year: for if their corruption existed along with the corruption of the governor, [he will die]. **6** Then, along with what I mentioned call as a witness the year's reaching[185] the sign in which an infortune[186] is: and if the revolution of your year was on the degree of the infortune, or its opposition or its square,[187] then <you look> at the infortune: if it coincides with it in the revolution as well, it indicates his destruction. **7** And according to what I have mentioned to you, call upon the Ascendant of the year as a witness, as well as the lord of the year, and the year's reaching[188] the position of the infortune or the planets which are contrary to[189] the lord of the Ascendant of the year.

8 But if the governor was not made unfortunate and not near burning, then examine the lord of the eighth from the Ascendant or the lord of eighth house from the governor. **9** And if they were both in the square of the governor (or its opposition), then work in that based on what I described in the matter of the infortune.

10 And if there was nothing of what I have mentioned, then look in the revolution of that year at the lord of the Ascendant of the root, and the lord of the Ascendant of the year: for if they both entered into burning or were made unfortunate by planets harmful to them, and the lord of the Ascendant of the year and the planetary governor are not looking at the Ascendant of the year, it indicates the native's ruin. **11** And if the year does not bear witness [to this], and his year is aided, that time [of death] will come when it reaches the position [in] which the year does bear witness to [it].

---

[184] That is, the lord of the revolutionary Ascendant.
[185] That is, by profection.
[186] It would be even more appropriate if it was the same infortune that was corrupting the lord of the profected or revolutionary Ascendant.
[187] This probably means that the solar revolution Ascendant is on the infortune's natal position, or the transiting infortune is actually on the revolutionary Ascendant at the time. In that case, the same infortune would be activated by profection as well as by revolution.
[188] That is, by profection.
[189] This verb in Sahl (ضدّ) usually has connotations of being "opposite" to.

[Unsuitable house-masters]

12 And perhaps one will not be able to be guided by the governor of the year[190] concerning the lifespan: and that is if the governor is one of the infortunes, or it is the lord of eighth [from] the Ascendant. **13** So if it was as I described, then look at the coinciding of the lord of the Ascendant with the degree of the infortune (or its square or opposition), or its entrance into burning;[191] and it is more pertinent for that if the infortune was the lord of the house of the lord of the Ascendant, or the infortune was the lord of the house of the eighth[192] [from] the Ascendant, if the corruption was from burning,[193] because the lord of the house of the lord of the Ascendant indicates the end of the matter just as the lord of the fourth does. **14** Now if there was nothing of what I have mentioned, then take[194] from the degree of the Ascendant to the positions of the infortunes, and their squares and oppositions.

[Nativities without releasers]

15 And know that the two luminaries are fit to be the releaser in all of the places, provided that they look at the Ascendant or at the lord of the Ascendant; now if they do not look at the Ascendant nor at the lord of the Ascendant, then see if the governor looks <at> the Ascendant or at the lord of the Ascendant: for if the governor is looking, it is fit.

16 But if the native does not have a releaser, and the indicator of the lifespan is the lord of the Ascendant or the lord of the triplicity of the As-

---

[190] To me this seems wrong, as there is no such thing as a "governor [house-master] of the year." Therefore, I take this to be the natal house-master, and "of the year" should be deleted. But what I find strange is that a house-master is not ruled out by being an infortune: so I think Māshā'allāh might mean one of two things. First, he could mean that an infortune as house-master is *unreliable* as a guide, because the infortunes do not naturally grant life. Or, he could mean that it is an infortune in a *bad condition*, so that it is unreliable for that reason.

[191] That is, just as we did with the house-master above.

[192] Reading with the sense of the preceding passage, for "lord" (which would have repeated the same phrase).

[193] I am not sure if the burning pertains to both of these planets, or just the lord of the eighth.

[194] This must be by primary directions.

cendant,¹⁹⁵ then look at that planet of these two which you are guided by: how is its position relative to the Ascendant, is it *strong* (or weak), or does it have *testimony* in its own place in which it is (or not)? **17** And the *strong* one is if it is in a stake or what follows a stake, and it is luminous in its own place, in its own glow (and that is if the planet was male, by day above the earth in a male sign, and by night under the earth in a female sign; and if it was feminine, by night it is above the earth and by day under the earth), far from the rays.¹⁹⁶ **18** And as for *testimony*, <that is> if it is in its own house, or in its exaltation, triplicity, or bound, or one of the luminaries is in its house, or the lord of its house receives it, or it is the lord of the house of the Lot of Fortune, or the lord of the Lot of Fortune is in its house. **19** For if it was like that, it indicates upbringing and the nativities of free people. **20** And if it was in the Ascendant, then the lifespan of the native will be from its degree, until it reaches the degree of an infortune (or its opposition or square). **21** And if it was not in the Ascendant, then look at the degree of its light [which is] in the Ascendant—if it was not withdrawing much, [and] if it was close to the Ascendant: for [then you should direct] from the position of its light; now if it was withdrawing much, then it should take place from the degree of the primary¹⁹⁷ Ascendant.¹⁹⁸

[General method of directions and profections]

22 Now¹⁹⁹ once you have calculated or reached²⁰⁰ the light of a star, then see what it is and what its condition is, and its power in its position, and

---

¹⁹⁵ Recall that these are important indicators in the topic of upbringing: so the native might not have a normal lifespan, but might have something of an upbringing.
¹⁹⁶ See also Sahl's *Introduction*, Ch. 3, **124-25**. Māshā'allāh's account of this rejoicing condition is at odds with later accounts. In later texts, *diurnal* (not male) planets should be above the earth during the day, and under the earth at night (and for *nocturnal* planets the reverse); and the planet should be in a sign of *its own* gender, not that of the chart.
¹⁹⁷ That is, "natal."
¹⁹⁸ So, suppose the natal Ascendant is at 15° Gemini, and a suitable planet is in the ninth, casting a trine ray to 18° Gemini: this degree is not withdrawing, and is close to the rising degree itself. In that case, we would direct from 18° Gemini. But if the planet's trine landed on 1° Gemini, this would be withdrawing and far from the rising degree, so we would have to use the rising degree itself, 15° Gemini. For a similar situation, see **39** below.
¹⁹⁹ For **22** and **24-26**, cf. Ch. 1.24, **9-12**. For **23**, cf. Ch. 1.24, **5**.
²⁰⁰ This probably means "calculated [by direction] or reached [by profection]."

which place it is relative to the Ascendant, and judge for him when the management of the light and the year reached it, and its position relative to the primary Ascendant. **23** (Now[201] if [the distribution] was in the light of a star[202] [which was] in an excellent position relative to the Ascendant, then if you came to the year of the turning before the departure of its light, it is preferable; and likewise the infortunes are worse.) **24** And if the governor of the management[203] from the light was Saturn, and he is in the house of travel relative to the primary Ascendant, in an excellent condition, then say he will gain good from travel, worship, and the Sultan. **25** And you should look likewise in every house, whichever position is that house in which the light is, and from where does that light arrive: if it was from the house of travel, and that star is in an excellent condition, you state the good about travel, and likewise the Sultan and friends. **26** And every planet to whom the management comes, and it is in a question and nativity (if the question was about [his] destiny), being in an excellent condition and [by its] position relative to the Ascendant, if the management reached it, it grants good.

27 So look on the day that the management reaches a star, [to see] what its condition on that day is: for if its condition on that day matched its condition in the root or the hour of the question, it has power over him, for good or evil; and if they differed, one of the two will defeat the other, inclining [to one of the two] between them.

[Comparing techniques in different charts]

28 And know that what the stars indicate in the roots is stable, and [their] course[204] increases and decreases a little bit, according to the power of the root.

29 And[205] know that if you directed the days from the degree of the Ascendant, the days will pass by the twelve signs; and if you directed the years,

---

[201] This sentence should not appear here, as is evident from its proper context in Ch. 1.24, **5**.

[202] Reading with the parallel sentence in Ch. 1.24, **5**, for an illegible phrase.

[203] This probably means the partnering planet in the distribution (in directions, the "promittor"). Abū Ma'shar likewise refers to partnering planets as "managers" in *PN4*.

[204] المسير. This word means any kind of later movement, direction, profection, etc.

[205] In this sentence, Māshā'allāh is comparing directions of the Ascendant of the solar revolution, and directions of the natal Ascendant. For the solar revolution, the Ascendant is directed around the whole chart (twelve signs) over the course of a single year, making it a direction of individual days. But for directing the natal Ascendant, a typical native will live

then what I mentioned [will pass] to the square[206] in accordance with his lifespan: <so> see what is in that square,[207] of the lights of the stars.

30 And[208] know that every beginning has an endpoint,[209] and every condition has strength and weakness due to the boundary[210] of the travel[211] of the turning, with injustice and justice (and they are the fortunes and the infortunes), whichever one of the two the [*uncertain*] [*uncertain*][212] began with, except for what the strength of the causes leaves behind[213] upon the turning of the beginning and the rotation of the circle [for the] cycles of nativities in the travel. **31** For indeed that will strengthen some of the power if the root

---

no more than about 90 years, an idealized one-fourth of the chart, between the Ascendant and the IC. Therefore, all directions that could happen to a typical native will be found by the bodies and aspects that fall in that quarter.

[206] الرّابع, normally "the fourth." Here Māshā'allāh seems to mean the theory that the normal human lifespan does not normally extend beyond the primary direction of a square, theoretically 90 years.

[207] الرّبع, normally "the quarter." See the footnote above.

[208] This paragraph is confusing, and feels like an early attempt to convert an existing Persian text into Arabic, as well as make a general statement about predictive techniques that also blurs the line between nativities and elections. I derive two broad ideas from it. First, Māshā'allāh is saying that profections ("the travel of the turning," "the turning of the beginning") and primary directions or distributions ("the rotation of the circle"), are marked by good and bad effects based on where they begin and end: namely, the profection or direction encountering a fortune or infortune. These profections and directions are evaluated every year when we do our suite of annual techniques, collectively called here the "cycle of nativities." Second, if a nativity or election or event chart has only middling qualities, then it can be strengthened when the techniques activate powerful (and most likely, benefic) planets; and if the chart had really great promise, like an election or event chart for a "powerful work," it will bring great increase to the effect indicated in the original chart. In the next paragraph he will directly connect this with charts for mundane astrology and political figures.

[209] منتهى, a common word for the place a profection reaches or "terminates at." I believe Māshā'allāh or his source is making a pun here, describing both the end of a process or phenomenon, as well as the endpoint of a timing technique (profections and directions or distributions).

[210] Or perhaps, "limit" (حدّ), the same word usually reserved for a "bound." Again, an irritating pun that simply makes things more confusing.

[211] This is not just the process of traveling, but can be the *distance* traveled.

[212] Two unknown (and possibly Persian) words, partially undotted: ارسامه طاقاه.

[213] Or, "bequeaths" (ترك).

was middling,²¹⁴ and will add a great increase if the root²¹⁵ was a powerful work.

32 So²¹⁶ do understand the work of turning for a king, dynasties, rulership, and nativities, in years, months, and days, because this travel lasts for every part it has ([for] whenever something shifts from the Ascendant, it produces something else from the second); but let your reliance be on directing the degree of the Ascendant or the releaser to the lights of the infortunes and their bounds.

33 And know that the lord of the distribution is like a tender [of sheep], and the lord of the year like a hireling; so if the tender committed himself to his sheep in a powerful way, the hireling would have not power over harming the sheep.²¹⁷

34 And²¹⁸ know that the lord of the distribution has authority over many years according to [the size of] its bound (and the lord of the rays is like that),²¹⁹ until its bound comes to an end. **35** And likewise the lord of the year, when it intends good or evil: a man will not cease to be in that matter until another planet has authority over the year, stronger in position than the first position, so it sends him forth in the management of the first one.

36 And some of the scholars of directing said [that] directing in nativities (as well as in the revolution of years) [should be] forward, from the Ascendant to the second [place]; but in recent things and what resembles that, from the Ascendant in reverse [fashion] to the twelfth, and especially if the Ascendant is convertible.²²⁰

---

²¹⁴ Reading as جوزا, lit. "the middle."
²¹⁵ Omitting a redundant "was middling and will add a great increase if the root was."
²¹⁶ Now Māshā'allāh concludes from the previous paragraph that profections are important and should be used to track the effects for many types of charts from period to period (such as when something profects or perhaps is directed from the Ascendant to the second place), because the effects change when the indicators shift like that. But in longevity, we should focus more on directions rather than profections.
²¹⁷ In other words, if the distributor and distribution indicates powerful good, then a single year of a bad profection cannot truly harm.
²¹⁸ For this sentence, cf. Ch. 1.24, **13-14**.
²¹⁹ This refers to the "partner" planet, any planet whose body or ray the releaser encounters while it moves through the bounds; this planet will remain the partner until the releaser encounters the next one.
²²⁰ On the one hand, this means that pre-natal (or in a horary question, pre-question) events are signified by things that the Ascendant has *already* passed through: the native or querent is not starting with an empty slate. This suggests that we could analyze earlier events by looking at those completed directions. On the other hand, the bit about converti-

37 And know that an infortune corrupts four signs, unless it is received; and if it was received[221] from an opposition, it does grant but then corrupts according to its position.

38 And know that if the star was advancing and had reception, it indicates good; and one retreating indicates corruption and falling,[222] [and especially if] the retreat from the Ascendant was great; [but if] it was close to the Ascendant, then [direct] from the position of its light. **39** Now if it was withdrawing greatly, then [direct] from the degree of the Ascendant by portions.[223]

[More on picking releasers and house-masters]

40 And certainly the planet which accepts[224] the Sun by day, and accepts the management of the Moon by night, does grant life—and it is the house-master. **41** Now if that accepting star was the lord of the house of the indicator, it is preferable for your work; and if it fell,[225] then make it be a partner to [the Sun][226] in the life. **42** But if they were not handing over [their management], then direct from the releaser or from degree of the Ascendant.

43 And know that the lord of the house of the Sun and the Moon each indicate life, and they are the house-master. **44** But as for the Sun and the

---

ble signs is related to Abū Ma'shar's claim in *PN4* that when we profect months for any given year, if the sign of the year is convertible, the months should be counted backwards.

[221] With different voweling (unfortunately absent in the manuscript), these instances of "received" could also mean that the infortune *is receiving* rather *being received*.

[222] Omitting "and advancing." This paragraph is rather garbled and could be the result of scribal errors.

[223] Tentatively reading for what seems to be اجر. Like **21**, this means that if the planet in the rising sign (or the degree of its ray there) is too far away, then use the degree of the Ascendant itself.

[224] This is the usual verb for "receive," but since Sahl speaks of the planet *accepting* the management of the Moon later in the sentence, I have rendered it as "accept." Also, since this still seems to be Māshā'allāh's view, in his mundane writings Māshā'allāh does pay special attention to the planet in an ingress which accepts the management of the sect light.

[225] Or, "occurred" (which makes the phrase incompleted). Reading a smudged word as بقي, which means "to fall" but is *not* any of the normal words referring to being cadent or in its fall. But perhaps it is دفع, "hand [over]," such as handing over to the Sun, just as the Sun handed over to a planet in **40**.

[226] The pronoun here may refer to the Sun as the standardly-approved releaser, but it can also indicate plurals.

Moon, they [can be] the releaser if they were not falling and the lord of each looks at them. **45** And if it is not looking, then they [cannot be] the releaser; and if [the luminaries] were both falling, then they are not the releaser. **46** So after that, look by day at the Sun, and direct from his light in the Ascendant, and by night the Moon, whichever of them both was stronger by aspect, and direct it from its light in the Ascendant. **47** But if the luminaries did not have light in the Ascendant, then [they] are not the releaser.[227]

[More on directing and profecting the releasers]

48 After that, work by the turning of the signs to the position of the fortunes and infortunes, and always by setting out[228] from the luminaries and the lord of the Ascendant, whichever of them was in the Ascendant or in the Midheaven (and that is primary);[229] so direct the light from it, from the position of its bound. **49** And if they fell from these two places, then look in the seventh, the fourth, the eleventh, and the fifth: and examine the stronger one of them in these positions, and project its light into the Ascendant, and direct from its light in the Ascendant.

50 And if you found a releaser, then direct from the position of the releaser and from the degree of the Ascendant to the lights of the infortunes, unless the years were just as I advised you concerning the light of the luminaries (because the position of the light of the luminaries in the Ascendant is more valid than the degree of the Ascendant). **51** So always direct from the degree of the Ascendant or from one of the luminaries (if it was close to the degree of the Ascendant), or from its light in the Ascendant, to the lights of the stars and their bounds. **52** Now[230] if the Sun was the releaser, he indicates the father and the native (for good and evil); and if he was not the releaser he indicates the father and his grandfather, and he indicates the beginning of life, and the lord of his house and triplicity indicate the end of life; and make the lords of his triplicity be partners (and likewise the Moon [indicates] the mother and the native).

---

[227] Māshā'allāh uses similar rules in his horary charts, in his *On Reception*.
[228] This is the usual word for "direction" (i.e. a primary direction), but Sahl's source seems to mean it here in terms of profections, as just suggested.
[229] This seems to mean that we *start with* the Ascendant and Midheaven, i.e. we prioritize them; in the next sentence Sahl provides other options.
[230] Reading more naturally for "because."

[More on the years of the house-master]

53 And know that if the governor granted something of years and that was confirmed, the infortunes would not be able to cut off [life] until the native completes those years; however, one should fear for the governor if it was retrograde or in its fall: for the infortunes will cut off years if it was like that. **54** And if the [*illegible*][231] affected the governor from the stakes, it will not decrease it, but will increase it. **55** And if they were looking at the governor from the stakes, and do not connect with it, they will not subtract [life] but they will create fears and risks to his life in those years. **56** And the fortunes increase from the stakes, the trine, and the sextile, and the infortunes do not increase from the stakes, unless the governor received them or they receive the governor; and they do not increase nor decrease except through a connection.

57 And if the governor was in a stake and the infortune falling, connecting to it, it does not have the power to decrease it. **58** And know that if the infortune in the nativity was falling or squeezed between the two fortunes,[232] it will have no power to harm, for they[233] are weak. **59** And [for] every infortune not in one of the stakes of the Ascendant in the root, neither the releaser nor the planets will be harmed by a connection of its degree with the degree of a harmful,[234] weak infortune, due to its being restrained from harm in the root.

60 And some of the scholars said that the Head does not increase and the Tail does not decrease, but the Head strengthens the governor and the Tail introduces illnesses into the body in that distribution, unless you see that he does not have a known quantity of years.[235]

---

[231] This word seems to be a plural (or a singular feminine), but since both fortunes and infortunes are mentioned in the next sentence, I am not sure what it could be.
[232] This is a rare example of besieging by the fortunes.
[233] This seems to be the infortune, even though it is in the plural (or perhaps feminine singular).
[234] Or perhaps, "harmed."
[235] Meaning of this last clause unclear; perhaps it means that if he does *not* have a known lifespan, then the Tail may kill instead of just introducing illnesses.

[Cutting off life]

61 Know that [with respect to] the degrees of the releaser or the degree of the Ascendant, perhaps the infortunes will cut off the years of the governor and the native will not reach what the governor indicates: and that is due to the weakness of the root of the nativity. **62** Now if the root of the nativity is strong, and the fortunes are in the stakes, and the Moon received in a stake, and the lord of the Ascendant (or a fortune) is strong, in a stake, and the lord of the Ascendant is in a stake,[236] then with that the governor will reach its years. **63** And if the root of the nativity is corrupted, it will be feared for him at every ray.

64 And know that every beginning in Creation proceeds according to the root of its beginning, and what is born proceeds from that into something else; and for every beginning is an essence which is its power. **65** So[237] if you saw the power extending the lifespan to the utmost limit[238] of the lifespan, [then] guide that period along, and the misfortune of the turning will not harm the positions of the infortunes in them,[239] and it will reach the lights of the infortunes until that power is done and the completing of the lifespan comes to an end. **66** And perhaps the lifespan will continue, and it will not be in anything of the positions of the infortunes: so pay close attention [and see] if it reached a year in which there was an infortune or the light of an infortune, for in that case the infortunes will be operative in destroying the essence of the power of the lifespan. **67** And if the infortunes did weaken the power of the lifespan in their positions in the turning and the course[240] of the lights, appoint[241] the releaser for that.

68 And if you saw one of the luminaries in the Ascendant or Midheaven, strong, then direct the lights from it and grant it the power of the lifespan;

---

[236] This is redundant, and something might be missing.

[237] Through "period along," this sentence does not seem to be structured like a proper Arabic sentence.

[238] Reading إقصاء for اقضاء.

[239] This should be read as "the misfortune of the turning will not *be harmed by* the positions of the infortunes." The point is that *if* a full lifespan is indicated, you can profect all the way to the end of life without worrying about death whenever the profection comes to the infortunes.

[240] سير. This should probably be "direction" (تسيير).

[241] وضع, but as this is not a proper imperative (which would be اوضع), reading as the Form II imperative وضّع. I am not sure how else to make sense of this phrase, especially since we are already supposed to find the releaser.

and if it handed over [to another], then take the lifespan from the one handed over to—its greater, middle, or lesser years, according to what I explained to you in the section on the house-master.

Chapter [1.24]: On the work of the lights & turning

Comment by Dykes. This chapter is a somewhat confusing blend of profections and distributions through the bounds. But if we overlook some oddities, the breakdown of the chapter is as follows.

In the first subsection, sentences **1-3** define monthly and annual profections, and give a short list of considerations for interpreting the profection: planets in the sign, looking at the sign, and the lord of the year. As for distributions, the text does use the usual term (قسمة), and further specifies that the "lord of the distribution" is the distributor, while the "lord of the rays" is the partnering planet. Sentence **4** points out the time-lord character of the distribution.

The first subsection also compares and combines profections and distributions. Sentence **2** says that profections ("turning") are stronger than the distributor, but I feel this is either a terminological error, or simply imprecise. On the face of it, it contradicts an earlier statement by Māshā'allāh (Ch. 1.23, **33**), some of whose statements are repeated in this chapter.[242] So I suggest two possible corrections: the first is that the *manager* or *partnering* planet is stronger than the distributor, for the purposes of longevity—which is true, in all versions of these methods. But he might simply mean that the profection is stronger than the distributor, *when examining a solar revolution*—and authors like Māshā'allāh do insist on looking at the lord of the year in this.[243]

Sentences **5-7** refer to a profection reaching some planet around the time when the *directed* Ascendant reaches or leaves the same or similar planet: for if a profection reaches the place of the partner while that partner is still in effect, it is more powerful for the effect (or perhaps, its timing). For example, let the partnering planet of the distributed Ascendant be Jupiter, and let him

---

[242] Māshā'allāh in Ch. 1.23, **22-26** match this chapter's **5** and **9-12**.
[243] See Ch. 1.23, **2-11**. I note that Abū Ma'shar also says profections are more powerful than the distributor, again in the context of solar revolutions, because they are more immediate in time (*PN4* II.1, **6** and **25**).

be the partner for 5 years, from the native's ages 47-51: if the profected Ascendant actually comes to the position of the natal Jupiter during those very ages, then Jupiter will be doubly activated, and his signification more powerful. This could be another reason for saying that a profection is more powerful, because it targets specific years, while a distributor or partner is generally active for many years.

The last section repeats sentences we have already seen in Māshā'allāh (Ch. 1.23, **22** and **24-26**). It includes more, general rules for profections and distributions. My footnotes there try to make sense of the instructions.

ಶ   ಐ   ಐ

1 Know that starting out from the Ascendant is a year or a month for every sign; then it returns every twelve months to the Ascendant, and every twelve years to the Ascendant.[244]

2 And know that turning is the foundation of the work of the stars and [their] appointed time, and it is stronger <than> the distributor of time:[245] so direct the degree of the Ascendant to the essences of the stars and their lights from the places, and in their natures.

3 Now when the turning reaches the position of a fortune or infortune, then it is in the nature of that star, except that the lord of the year alters the condition by itself,[246] whether it was good or bad, as well as the aspect of the fortunes and infortunes to that sign from the square.

4 And likewise the <management of>[247] years: if [one] reached the light or position of a star, it is in that nature until it reaches another. **5** And if it was in the light of a star with an excellent position relative to the Ascendant in the root, and the year of the turning reached it before the departure of its

---

[244] These are annual and monthly profections.

[245] But this seems to contradict Ch. 1.23, **33** above, which said that the distributor is stronger. This should probably read that it is stronger *when combined with* the distributor: see **5** below, and my *Comment* above.

[246] Reading وحده for حدّه, "of its bound." That is, the lord of the sign has a great influence even though the profection has reached a natal planet actually in that sign.

[247] Tentatively adding for clarity, because **5** speaks of the "year of the turning" (i.e., the profection) reaching the very planet mentioned here—which would not make sense unless **4** is speaking of a different technique, viz. distributions. In this case, reaching the "light or position" of a star refers to the partnering planet.

light,²⁴⁸ it is preferable; and likewise the infortunes will be worse. **6** And know that the light which it is in, and connects with, and separates from, is the matter which will come to be.

7 And if the year did reach the light, then look at the one which has departed that light: where is its position relative to the Ascendant, [is it] falling or upright, alien or in a good condition? **8** And look at its condition in the root and its condition in the year relative to the primary Ascendant, because those are the topics pertaining to the primary Ascendant.

9 Now²⁴⁹ if you calculated or reached the light of a star, then see who it is, and what is its condition and power in its position, and which place it is in from the Ascendant, and judge for him when the management of the light and the year reached it, and its position relative to the primary Ascendant. **10** Because if it handed over its management to Saturn, and it²⁵⁰ is in an excellent condition, and Saturn is in the house of travel relative to the primary Ascendant, then say he will gain good from travel, building,²⁵¹ and the Sultan. **11** And you look likewise for every sign at the position of that house in which the light is, and from where that light reaches: if it was from the house of travel, and that star is in an excellent condition, you state the good about travel, and likewise the Sultan, and friends. **12** And [for] every planet to which the management comes, if it is excellent in [its] position relative to the Ascendant in the root, when the management reaches it, it will grant good.

13 And²⁵² know that the lord of the distribution manages many years according to [the size of] its bound (and likewise the lord of the rays),²⁵³ until

---

²⁴⁸ The author means that if the distribution has a good partner by direction, *and* by profection we come to that same planet during those indicated years (before the distribution moves on), it is very good.

²⁴⁹ Sentences **9-12** parallel Ch. 1.23, **22** and **24-26**.

²⁵⁰ In context, this sounds like the previous time lord (e.g., the lord of the year from the previous sign). But in the parallel sentence in Ch. 1.23, **24**, this is Saturn.

²⁵¹ العمارة, but in Ch. 1.23, **24** it reads العبادة, "worship." Building is Saturnian, and worship is the ninth house, so either would make sense.

²⁵² For this paragraph, cf. Ch. 1.23, **34-35**. This paragraph is rendered very awkwardly by Sahl. The whole point is simply that, for each time lord, it only controls features of a person's life until the *next* time lord takes over. For the bound lord or distributor or "lord of the distribution," this is when the Ascendant enters the next bound; for the partnering planet or

its bound is completed. **14** And likewise the lord of the year, if it indicates good or evil, the man will remain in that situation until a planet stronger than it by [its] position relative to the position of the beginning, from the management of the beginning, governs the year.[254]

15 Then, see when the year reaches the one which mixes with that light: if its position relative to the Ascendant was falling or upright, alien or good in condition, and look at [its] condition in the root and at the condition of the year relative to the primary Ascendant, because truly they turn in direct ascension;[255] and in male <signs> in the nativities of males, they indicate the safety of the native and the mother (and likewise if it was the nativities of females and the signs were female).

Chapter [1.25]: On looking at the mother's safety in childbirth

1 If you found the fortunes looking at the Ascendant and the Moon, they indicate the healthiness of the childbirth; and likewise, if you found the Sun by day in the Ascendant and his own triplicity, it indicates what is like that.

2 And if in the nativities of females you found the Moon and Venus in female signs, they indicate the goodness of the condition of the mother and her child; and likewise in the nativities of males.

3 And[256] if the two luminaries, the Sun and Moon, were both meeting in a male sign, then they indicate health and safety.

4 And if the lord of the Ascendant was eastern, above the earth, then it is a suitable indication for that native.

5 And[257] if you found the two luminaries and the Ascendant in signs crooked in ascension, and in female ones in the nativities of males (or male ones in the nativities of females), it indicates difficulty; and that is worse if Saturn was in a stake (and especially in the Ascendant). **6** And likewise if you

---

"lord of the rays," this is when the Ascendant encounters the next partner or ray; for the lord of the year by profection, this is simply when the profection moves on to the next sign (and not, as Sahl says, when a "stronger" one comes along).

[253] That is, the partnering planet.

[254] This is extremely awkward, and should perhaps be rendered more loosely as something like "position by position, from that of the first management."

[255] يدورون مستقيمة الطُلوع. I think this simply means that they turn in the order of signs.

[256] Cf. *Carmen* I.3, **1**. That is, *if* the native is a male; if the native is a female, they should be in feminine signs to avoid trouble.

[257] For this sentence, cf. *Carmen* I.3, **5**, but also generally I.3.

found a retrograde planet in that, and the Ascendant a sign short in ascensions: for that indicates difficulty in childbirth. **7** And likewise if [the Moon] was going towards [her] fullness, and between her and the fullness are fewer than 12°, or she was empty in course: for then the mother will experience hardship in childbirth.

[Difficult births: al-Andarzaghar]

8 Al-Andarzaghar[258] said about this: If you found the native to be male, and the Sun and Moon <and the Ascendant>[259] in male signs, then the mother will be safe, cleansed of every pain and malady; and likewise her child. **9** And if the native was female, and the luminaries and Ascendant were in female signs, then speak likewise about her safety. **10** And if it was the contrary, then judge corruption based on what you see of its hardship and gentleness. **11** And if you saw them to be mixed, then make a judgment of it being mixed.

12 And if you found Saturn in the Ascendant, and especially in a female sign, then judge for him the hardship of the childbirth, and death and killing. **13** And if you found Mars in the Ascendant, and especially in a female sign, then judge for him the suddenness of the childbirth, and its coming upon the mother on the road or [in] a crowd, or places like that.

14 And if the Moon was enclosed between the two infortunes,[260] and especially in signs crooked in ascension, in one of the stakes, then [it will be painful][261] for that native and his mother, from hardship and tribulation.

15 And if Saturn was in the Ascendant, crying and scarring will afflict the one who gives birth.

---

[258] Sentences **8-14** are reflected in *BA* III.1.2. They are, precisely, taken from Rhetorius Ch. 55 (p. 41), and in turn from Dorotheus and Manethō, as both *Carmen* I.3, **1-4** and Heph. III, App. A show. First, *Carmen* and Hephaistion allow the infortunes to be in any stake or pivot, not specifying the Ascendant (as Rhetorius does). Second, *Carmen* does not contain the information about the Moon being besieged (**14**), which Hephaistion does but attributes to Manethō. Third, *Carmen* does not speak of the Moon being in the straight signs, while Hephaistion and Rhetorius do. So, this is a direct proof that al-Andarzaghar had access to Rhetorius.
[259] Adding with *BA* and Rhetorius.
[260] That is, besieged.
[261] Adding on the basis of Hephaistion, for a word that appears to be قوبك.

[Difficult births: Ptolemy]

16 Ptolemy said concerning this:[262] if you saw the infortunes in the twelfth of the stakes,[263] then the childbirth will be made difficult, and the body will be ill, and the mother will be taken by cutting, or chronic illness in the body, or a defect.

17 And if Jupiter was in the Ascendant, it will be easy for the mother's giving birth. **18** And if the Ascendant was a male sign, then his father will be superior to his mother in social value.

19 And[264] if the Moon was in a crooked sign, made unfortunate by an infortune with her or looking at her, then it will be difficult for the mother's childbirth, and harsher for that if the infortunes were in crooked signs, and they are looking from a stake.

20 And in addition you ought to look in the nativities of women, for when you see (in the nativity of a woman) the Moon with Saturn or in the house of Saturn, or inspecting[265] him, then it will be generally difficult for that woman's childbirth, and perhaps she will be sterile.

21 And if Mars was in a stake or with the Moon, it indicates the quickness of the childbirth, and especially if Saturn is not making Venus unfortunate.

Chapter [1.26]: On the knowledge of whether natives are of human kind or of beasts[266]

1 If you wanted to understand whether the native is of human kind or of beasts, look at the lord of the house of the Moon: for if it is not looking at the Moon, and you found the lord of the Ascendant not looking at the Ascendant, then that native will not be of human kind, or he will have four feet. **2**

---

[262] This does not seem to be Ptolemy, but see Heph. II.10 (Schmidt p. 23), attributed to Apollinarius and the Egyptians.

[263] That is, the twelfth. The sources in Hephaistion add that if an infortune is in the second place "after" the birth (I am not sure how long after), and succeeds the Moon or Sun, the native is short-lived.

[264] For this sentence, cf. *Carmen* I.3, **5-7**.

[265] يناظر ه. But this could also be understood as "opposing."

[266] Much of this chapter is from, or closely resembles, *Tet*. III.8 (Robbins pp. 261-65). This chapter is cast as a physical description of the baby, but could maybe be understood in terms of cognitive and emotional disturbances, imbalances in the brain, or birth defects. Compare with Heph. III.4, on the inceptions of irrational people.

Now if it was like that and the fortunes are looking at it, then he will have claws and the hair of dogs or predatory animals or cats, or virtually that. **3** And if the infortunes were in this manner from the stakes, and the fortunes are not looking, then the native will be a voracious beast.

4 Then, look at the share of the twelfth-part of the seven planets (and the more preferable is the Sun, Moon, and the Ascendant): in which place [each] is relative to the Ascendant, and who is looking at them. **5** For if they occurred in a sign having four feet, the native will have four feet, or will resemble [*uncertain*]:²⁶⁷ and it is likewise preferable if the Sun, Moon, and Ascendant were in that position, and especially if the Lot of Fortune and the lord of its house was like that. **6** Now perhaps it would be in that manner and he would be domesticated or be of those who raise dogs or beasts, and know the good, because the fortunes were testifying to it.

7 And if the third day of the Moon she reached a sign having four feet, and the infortunes are looking at her, then that is an indicator that the native will have four feet or what resembles that. **8** And likewise if the lord of the house of the meeting and fullness is not looking at its own house.

9 And if the luminaries were in the twelfth, and the infortunes in the stakes, and the fortunes not looking, then the native will be demonic.²⁶⁸

10 And²⁶⁹ if the luminaries had four feet or [were] in signs of predatory animals, and the infortunes were in the stakes, then the native will be bestial. **11** Now if the infortunes witnessed the luminaries, then he will be of a predatory animal or beasts; and if the fortunes witnessed, then he will be a dog or resembling that. **12** And if Mercury witnessed along with the fortunes, then chickens or cats or sheep, or will resemble that, in the manner of the nature of the signs.

13 And if the luminaries were in signs of people, and the positions of the planets according to what I described [above], and the fortunes not looking at those places, then the native will be of humankind. **14** Now if the native

---

²⁶⁷ **M** seems to read أوابه.
²⁶⁸ Reading as قطرب, a Persian word for an assortment of beings like goblins, bad spirits, wolves, etc.; but it can also indicate someone possessed or epileptic.
²⁶⁹ This paragraph is based on *Tet.* III.8 (Robbins pp. 261-63).

was male, he will be cut from or confined [in][270] the belly of his mother; and if it was a girl, she will be closed up.[271]

15 And[272] if Mercury was made unfortunate along with those things we have mentioned, he will be deaf and mute; but let your reliance be [on] looking at the meeting or the opposition which was before the nativity, and at the lords of their houses, and the lord of the house of the Moon and the Ascendant. **16** For[273] if you found these indicators, all [of them],[274] falling away from their lords, and you found the lord of the meeting or opposition not looking at that place, then know that the native will be changed.[275]

17 And[276] if these were according to what I mentioned, and the luminaries in signs having four feet or the signs of wild animals, and the infortunes in the stakes, then the native will not be of humankind. **18** And if the infortunes were looking at the luminaries,[277] then the native will be of harmful, corrupt wild animals. **19** And if Jupiter or Venus looked, then the native will have fangs[278] like a dog or cat, and what is like that. **20** And if Mercury looked, then he will be of those that humans need, like a bird or swine or goats or cattle, and what is like that.

21 And if the luminaries were in signs of the images of people, and they are in the condition which I mentioned before, then the native will be a human, or he will be humanoid,[279] and will be fond of them.[280]

---

[270] This sounds like a breech birth, which might also result in a caesarian.

[271] Reading as رتقًا. Meaning unclear, especially since the option of a caesarian was available earlier in the sentence. But this can also mean to be sewn up and repaired, suggesting a successful surgery. Nevertheless I do not understand the point of this sentence, and some context is missing.

[272] This is similar to *Tet.* III.8 (Robbins pp. 263-65).

[273] This is similar to *Tet.* III.8 (Robbins pp. 261-63).

[274] That is, the lords of the conjunction or opposition, and the luminaries, as well as the Moon and the Ascendant. Ptolemy wants them to be in aversion to the conjunction and opposition, but clearly Sahl's source has construed this differently.

[275] Lit., "exchanged," namely that they will have birth defects or be non-human.

[276] This paragraph is similar to *Tet.* III.8 (Robbins p. 263).

[277] In Ptolemy, this is rather that none of the fortunes are looking at them.

[278] ذو نابٍ. What is amusing is that Ptolemy originally referred to animals which were held as *sacred*, and it just so happens that this word for fang is close to the root verb that refers to prophecy (نبأ). So probably the meaning got garbled in transmission due to this linguistic coincidence. See also **24** below.

[279] Lit., "with humans."

[280] Or, he will be "accustomed" to them, or "tame" around them.

22 And the knowledge of looking with respect to those having the marks[281] and what their kind is, is from the types of signs in which are the infortunes which have governorship over the luminaries or the stakes. **23** Now if it was according to what I described, and nothing of the fortunes looks at anything of the places which I mentioned, then the native will be changed.[282] **24** And if Jupiter or Venus did look, then the native who has the mark will be honored in such a way that the Mercurial or Venusian image indicates;[283] but your reliance should be on the abundance of testimonies from these areas which I have described to you.

Chapter [1.27]: On the knowledge of whether the native is male or female[284]

[According to Ptolemy]

1 And[285] if you wanted to know whether the native is male or female, then look at the luminaries, the Ascendant, and the lords of these houses. **2** For if these indicators were masculine, then the native is male; and if they were feminine, she is female. **3** And look at their positions relative to <the Sun> and the Ascendant. **4** For if the stars were eastern,[286] they indicate males, and if they were western, then indicate females; and [it is] like that due to their positions relative to the Sun. **5** Then, also consult the testimony of the region relative to the Ascendant, and the masculinization of the signs and their feminization,[287] and you must [rely on] the majority of their testimonies.

---

[281] That is, those that exhibit strange shapes or qualities.
[282] Again, lit. "exchanged."
[283] For Ptolemy, this means having outstanding qualities like being hermaphroditic.
[284] For more on this, see Ch. 3.13, **19-22**.
[285] This paragraph is based on *Tet.* III.8 (Robbins pp. 255-57).
[286] For Ptolemy, this is being a morning star (i.e., rising before the Sun, but probably also out of his rays).
[287] That is, in the masculine or feminine quarters of the chart.

[*According to Dorotheus*]

6 And[288] if the Moon was in the share of the twelfth-part [which is] males, then a male will be born.

7 And if the hours were even and the share of the twelfth-part of the Ascendant in a male sign, and in the Ascendant is a male planet, then a male will be born.

8 And if you found a male planet in the Ascendant at [the time of] the question, and in the Ascendant a male,[289] and the two signs [were] masculine, it will be a male.

Chapter [1.28]: On the knowledge of twins, & multiple children in a single belly

1 Know[290] that this is known from the positions of the luminaries and the Ascendant. 2 Now if you found the luminaries in the stakes of the Ascendant[291] of the question, in signs having two bodies, it indicates the births of twins. 3 (And[292] if they were both in Pisces especially, then two or more than that will be born.) 4 And if they were all (or most of them) in signs having two bodies (and it establishes the indication for that if their lords were also in signs having two bodies), they indicate twins. 5 And if you found some of their lords in signs having two bodies, or you found two or more than two in a single sign, it also indicates <that>. 6 And if you found the lords of the luminaries and the Ascendant in signs having two bodies, and numerous planets looked at them, then likewise more than two will be born.

7 And the knowledge of the number [of them] is known from the position of the planets more numerous in testimony and governorship, and from them the number is made correct.

---

[288] These sentences seem to be a condensed version of *Carmen* I.8, with Sahl's **8** perhaps being adapted to a horary question.

[289] Since the text speaks of two signs in the next clause, it could be the Ascendant or fifth house of a querent's nativity and in a question chart; but it could also be a garbled form of Dorotheus, who speaks of several different planets in various signs.

[290] Sentences **1-13** are based on *Tet.* III.7 (Robbins pp. 257-61).

[291] Here and in **8**, Sahl or his source has either altered or misunderstood Ptolemy. For Ptolemy, it is not that the luminaries are "in" the Ascendant (or Midheaven), but it is the luminaries *and* the Ascendant (or Midheaven), just as stated in **1**.

[292] This sentence is not in Ptolemy.

8 Now if the luminaries were not in the Ascendant but in the Midheaven, then those mothers will be delivered of many children.

9 And if the three superior planets were in signs having two bodies and the luminaries looked at them, then she will give birth to three, <and they will be males; but if it was Venus, the Moon, and Mercury, then>[293] females.

10 And if Jupiter, Saturn, and Venus were in the places I described, and the luminaries looked, they indicate two males and one female. **11** And if Venus, the Moon, and Mars were in the same manner I described and they looked at the luminaries, then two females will be born, and one male.

12 And the infortunes[294] indicate the corruption of the constitution [of the fetus], by increasing [something of] the constitution, or by subtracting, or the desiccation[295] of some of his limbs, or it produces something detestable in the native's character: and that is if the granting planets joined, and in the indication [of this topic] they supervised the ways which I have described.

13 And you will know the males of them or the females, from the planets which are[296] looking at the luminaries and the degree of the Ascendant, so the information about males and females should be drawn from that.

☋   ♋   ♋

14 And if the two twins were male, they indicate the ruin of the father at first;[297] and if they were female, then the mother at first.

15 Now[298] if two twins were found, then know that they have two connections: the connection of the first belongs to the first native, and the second one [to] the second one in the condition, and apart from that; because the connection occurred so the indicator will be the indicator over the mother,

---

[293] Adding based on Ptolemy.
[294] Ptolemy does not specifically mention the infortunes, but says "in these cases," referring to the combinations in **10-11** above.
[295] Or perhaps, "rigidity" (يبس).
[296] Omitting a "not."
[297] Or, "at the beginning." I am not sure what this means or why the author would say this.
[298] I cannot understand what this paragraph means, nor am I completely certain of its translation (or even if something is missing; certainly its context is missing). This could be derived from a text on questions, in which the Moon is the indicator, and two planets indicate two children.

and the two twins by the two connections and [the] separation: so understand that.

Chapter [1.29]: [On the native's upbringing]

1 If[299] you wanted to know the upbringing of the native, then in the nativities of those who live, look at these things which I will explain do you. **2** Look, in the upbringing of the native, at the Ascendant and its lord, and the Moon, and the lords of the triplicity of the Ascendant. **3** For if they were safe from the infortunes, burning, and falling, then the native will be brought up and will reach [his] lifespan; and if they were corrupted, it destroys and he will not be brought up. **4** And if they differed and the Ascendant [itself] was safe from the infortunes and corruption, and a fortune was in the stakes, then the native will also be brought up. **5** But let the majority of your examination in the matter of upbringing be from the Moon and the lords of the triplicity of the Ascendant. **6** Now if you found the Moon cleansed of the infortunes, and the lords of the triplicities of the Ascendant in their own places and good positions, and not retrograde in their course, and not under the rays of the Sun, then that is a suitable sign of the goodness of the upbringing (and [this is] especially if they were in their exaltations). **7** And preferable to that is if the Moon was connected with the fortunes, increasing in light and number, and not made unfortunate by Mars: because Mars causes harm in upbringing, and especially in nativities of the day; and her being above the earth is the best there could be.

8 And if you found the lords of the triplicities of the Ascendant in the Midheaven, or in the place of Good Fortune,[300] or in the fifth, or in the Ascendant, it indicates the goodness of the upbringing; and if they were in the seventh, they indicate the badness of the upbringing, and then especially if that [lord] was an infortune.

9 And[301] if you found an infortune in the stakes, do not lose hope for the native, for from them is [also] one who lives.

---

[299] Most of **1-14** is a blend of upbringing material found in *Carmen* I.4, I.7, and I.12. I suspect that it represents Sahl's own views.
[300] That is, the eleventh.
[301] That is, provided that the triplicity lords of the Ascendant are in a good condition (*Carmen* I.4, **2ff**). See also **27** below.

10 And know that every planet which was eastern in nativities of the day, and was in a male sign, its strength is greater, and its testimony about upbringing more firm.[302]

11 And if you found the lords of the triplicities of the Ascendant in the stakes and what follows them, then the native will be brought up; now if the lords of its triplicity were corrupted and there was a fortune in a stake, and the third day of the Moon not corrupted,[303] then he will be brought up. **12** And if the two infortunes were in the Ascendant or seventh, and the third day of the Moon corrupted, he will not be brought up; and likewise if you found the two infortunes in the Ascendant and the seventh, and the lords of the triplicities [of the Ascendant] withdrawing from the stakes, and they are <not> looking at the Ascendant, he will not be brought up. **13** And if the lords of the triplicity of the Ascendant were corrupted and the Moon safe, as well as her third,[304] and the Lot of Fortune and the third lord of the triplicity, he will be brought up.

14 And if you found Mars in the second from the Ascendant, the native will resemble one who does not have an upbringing, and especially if the Moon was made unfortunate: for if Mars was in the second place it indicates ruin and fleeing from his country, and especially if he was in his own fall in nativities of the day.

[Upbringing according to al-Andarzaghar]

15 And[305] begin with the lord of the triplicity of the Ascendant, and of the triplicity of the Sun by day (and that of the Moon by night), and the lord of

---

[302] Al-Khayyāṭ (*JN* Ch. 1) confirms that the same is true for western planets in nocturnal nativities, in female signs.
[303] This could possibly also be translated as, "...in a stake, and not corrupted on the third day," in other words, it is the *fortune* which is not corrupted on that day. But it is more likely that the Moon's own condition is meant, as in *Carmen* I.12, and in Ch. 1.30, **28** below.
[304] This probably means her third day.
[305] In *BA* III.1.2, this subsection (**15-22**) directly follows the material on difficult births which Sahl attributed to al-Andarzaghar above in Ch. 1.25, **8-14**. A similar version is found in al-Khayyāṭ's *JN* Ch. 1, which he evidently took from Māshā'allāh (see the Latin *On Nativities* §1 in *WSM*). But the Sahl / *BA* version is shorter and does not include the triplicity lords of the pre-natal lunation.

the triplicity of the Lot of Fortune, [and] then look at Jupiter and Venus and their positions, <as well as the Moon with planets of the sect>.[306]

16 So if you found the lord of the triplicity of the Ascendant [to be] the lord of the triplicity of the Sun by day (or the lord of the triplicity of the Moon by night), and the lord of the triplicity of the Lot of Fortune, then in that case it will be powerful;[307] and if it was like this, the lord of the triplicity will be powerful in the distribution of life.

17 And if you found the lord of the triplicity of the Ascendant to be in an excellent position, cleansed of the infortunes and defects, then the native will live.

18 And if you found the lord of the triplicity [of the Ascendant] not cleansed of those defects, and the native was diurnal, then look at the lord of the triplicity of the Sun (and if it was by night, then look at the lord of the triplicity of the Moon): for if it was in an excellent position, cleansed of the infortunes and defects, then he will live.

19 And if you found this to be corrupted as well, then look at the lord of the triplicity of the Lot of Fortune: for if it was in an excellent position, cleansed of the infortunes, then he will live.

20 And if you found this to be made unfortunate as well, corrupted, then look also at Jupiter: for if you found him to be in an excellent position, cleansed of defects, and he was in the Ascendant or in the Midheaven, then judge that he will live. **21** Now if Jupiter was in the rest of the stakes or in what follows the stakes, and Venus looked at him, and she was cleansed of the infortunes and defects, in an excellent position, then he will live.

22 And if this was also corrupted, then look at Venus: for if you found her to be in an excellent position, and Jupiter looked at her, and he is cleansed of defects, and if Venus was in the 15° which are at the end of the sign of the Ascendant,[308] or in the Midheaven, or in the house of hope, <then[309] it indicates upbringing.>

---

[306] See **23** below: adding the material in brackets along with *BA* III.1.2, *JN* Ch. 1, and Māshā'allāh's Latin *On Nativities*.
[307] That is, because the same planet is taking responsibility for both roles.
[308] Or also in the 15° in ascensions which follow the Ascendant, as explained in *Carmen* I.7, **7-8** and I.28, **1-8** (and confirmed in *BA* III.1.2).
[309] I have added this material in brackets (including in the next sentence) on the basis of *BA* III.1.2, *JN* Ch. 1, and Māshā'allāh's Latin *On Nativities*, because Sahl has mangled and condensed the rules about Venus and the Moon with planets of the sect.

<23 But if she were corrupted, then look at the Moon: if she was cleansed of the infortunes and defects>, and the native is diurnal, and in <the Ascendant, Midheaven, or house of hope>[310] is a diurnal planet, then he will live; <and likewise if it was a nocturnal nativity, with a nocturnal planet in this way.>

 ൙ ൙ ൙

24 And know that if the lords of the triplicities of the Ascendant were in [a state of] advancement, and [nothing] that would bring them down[311] is looking at them, they indicate upbringing, whether they were fortunes or infortunes, provided that they do not have misfortune corrupting them due to the infortunes or falling.

25 And if you saw the lord of the Ascendant advancing[312] in the circle, or received and the one receiving it is advancing, it indicates upbringing; and likewise the Moon and the one receiving her.

26 And the fortunes are preferable to the infortunes in upbringing, because they are more balanced in [their] constitution; and the fortunes in the stakes indicate upbringing. **27** And if the infortunes did not have testimony and they were in the stakes, they create illness, and evil should be feared from them: see in which quarter of the circle it is, and if they were falling they undermine the upbringing and it reduces the lifespan.

28 And[313] even if you saw Saturn and Mars in the Ascendant, or both of them in one place, and the lord of the triplicities of the Ascendant in the powerful places, appearing from under the rays, then he will see light and be brought up.

29 And[314] if you found the lord[315] of the triplicities [of the Ascendant] under the rays, in the corrupting places, it subtracts from the native's life. **30**

---

[310] Reading for "it."
[311] يسقطهم. Or, "make them fall."
[312] مقبل. That is, moving toward the angular degrees by primary motion.
[313] For this sentence, see *Carmen* I.4, **7**.
[314] For this paragraph, see *Carmen* I.7, **9**.
[315] Reading the singular in this sentence, with *Carmen*, else the next one would not make sense.

But if both lords of the triplicity [of the Ascendant] were like that, then it is [even] clearer for the native.[316]

31 And[317] if Mars or Saturn were looking at the Moon from a square or opposition, then that is more cutting for the life; and if the Moon was in a stake, it increases that evil.

32 And[318] if you found the Moon in the seventh, and nothing of the fortunes is looking at her, and in one of the stakes is an infortune looking at her, that is more evil.

33 And know that if an infortune cast its rays upon the degree of the Ascendant, that native will not live except through the strength of the fortunes and the casting of their rays upon the rays of that infortune: so beware of that and watch for that in nativities, for perhaps the stars in the nativities will be sound, as well as the Moon and the lord of the Ascendant, but then the native will not live because the infortune will be laying a trap for the native, casting its light upon the rising degree. **34** Now if you were aware that there was an infortune casting its light upon the rising degree of the native, and you saw the Moon corrupted by the infortunes, without falling, then beware that he may not be brought up, and do not posit anything for him until the years of upbringing are past, and one turns through[319] twelve years so that one passes by the positions of the infortunes, then returns to the Ascendant, or the turning reaches the infortune and it does not kill him, until it reaches the fortunes [and] he is saved if there is not an infortune in [the] turning, until the turning returns to the Ascendant. **35** So beware of these two times: the completion of the upbringing, or the turning's reaching the other infortune: and that is up to the completion of twelve years.

36 And know that if the infortunes were harmful, and they were advancing,[320] then he will be brought up with illnesses.

---

[316] That is, it is a clearer sign of danger and a short life.
[317] See *Carmen* I.7, **10-11**.
[318] See *Carmen* I.7, **12**.
[319] That is, "profects."
[320] Again, dynamically angular, moving by primary motion towards the angular degrees.

Chapter [1.30]: The lifespan

1 Know[321] that if the native was born and came out of [his mother's] belly into the openness of the air, his nature will resemble the Ascendant which is rising from the earth with the celestial circle, by which is known [his] upbringing, both its suitability and its corruption, along with the lords of the triplicities of the Ascendant: so according to their condition at the beginning, [such] will be the condition of the upbringing. **2** And[322] what was before him of siblings is what you see above the earth, and what will be after him is what you see under the earth. **3** And the planets made fortunate bring safety, and those made unfortunate bring ruin.

4 And the separation of the indicator[323] indicates the condition which existed in his mother's belly, as well as his mother; and her connection indicates what will be, and what he will come to in [his] upbringing and future. **5** But if she is empty in her course, then his condition and outcome will be from the lord of her house.

6 And[324] know that the root of the native's good fortune in his childhood, the goodness of his character, and the abundance of his tender treatment, nursing, and love from the one embracing him, and his garment and finery—this affects him from the Lot of Fortune as long as he is [still] a child. **7** Now as for his good fortune, that belongs to his two parents until he grows up and needs that, so that [his own] good fortune will come to him.

[Nawbakht the Persian on upbringing]

8 Nawbakht said concerning this: For the upbringing, look at the Moon: for if she joined with an infortune in the ninth place or in its opposition or its square, then that is bad, corrupting for the condition of the upbringing, and especially if the infortune cast its rays to the degree of the Ascendant, and the lords of the triplicities of the Ascendant were in places that are not suitable: for that indicates that he will be raised, [but also] hardship and trouble in his

---

[321] For this sentence, see the similar one in Ch. 1.3, **1**.
[322] For **2-3**, see Ch. 3 on siblings.
[323] That is, the Moon.
[324] Cf. Valens, *Anth.* IV.4 (Schmidt pp. 5-6), who likewise says that the Lot of Fortune is more suitable for children, because choices and actions (which pertain to the Lot of Spirit) come later in life.

upbringing. **9** And if you found her in the sixth from the Ascendant or an infortune was there, it indicates illness. **10** And if she separated from the infortunes it indicates the goodness of the upbringing,[325] and good luck for the siblings and the health of the mother; and if she separated from the fortunes, it indicates travels for the native, and the badness of the upbringing, and harms, and the ruin of the siblings, and the badness of the mother's condition.

11 And[326] if the Lot of Fortune was with the Moon or the Moon looked at it, along with the aspect of Venus <by night>,[327] and Jupiter looked by day at the Lot, it indicates the goodness of the upbringing, and especially if the Lot was in a good position.

12 And if the indicator[328] was with Saturn or connected with him, and he did not have a lifespan, then watch out for him if the indicator reached <Saturn>, or the degree of the Ascendant reached him, or the year of the turning[329] reached him, unless Saturn receives the Moon and it[330] is under the earth, in an excellent position, having a share and testimony in the Ascendant. **13** For if it was under the earth, it corrupts, because if the indicator connected with Saturn and he was hostile, his life will be short. **14** And Mars is likewise, unless there was reception (and perhaps he will [even] kill[331] the one received).

15 And if you saw the Moon eclipsed at the hour of the nativity,[332] the native will have a short life; and likewise the Sun by day. **16** And if the Moon was with an infortune not receiving her, or she connected with it in the places of life, it corrupts the lifespan.[333]

---

[325] See **4**, where separation means the pregnancy and application the upbringing afterwards. Nawbakht is apparently imagining that she is separating from infortunes and applying to fortunes (so, a bad pregnancy but good upbringing), or separating from fortunes and applying to infortunes (a good pregnancy but a bad and unstable upbringing).

[326] Al-Khayyāt uses this sentence in his *JN* Ch.1 (as does Māshā'allāh in the Latin *On Nativities*).

[327] Tentatively adding to parallel the sect condition of Jupiter that follows.

[328] This may be the Moon, but in **35** it is explained that the indicator is the house-master.

[329] That is, the profection.

[330] I am not sure whether this is the Moon or Saturn, here and in the next sentence. I have a feeling this is Saturn.

[331] Reading يقبل for يقتل ("receive").

[332] This is probably in a nocturnal chart.

[333] Reading العمر for القمر ("the Moon").

17 And[334] know that the endpoint of the upbringing is four years, and it is from the Ascendant to the fourth, which is its end and terminal point, a year for every sign from the Ascendant to the fourth. **18** Now whichever of them [had] an infortune in it or looking at it from a square or opposition, then it makes his condition harsh in that year, and he will be ill, except that if the aspect to the sign of the year was from the opposition, it will virtually have the status of an infortune in the year.[335] **19** As for the aspect of the trine and sextile, that does not harm. **20** And every planet of the lords of the triplicities grants one and one-third years, so look into the upbringing star by star, in accordance with its condition, both its good fortune and misfortune. **21** And with that, look at the revolution of the year, and where it terminates,[336] and to what sign, and who is in it in the root, and who is in it at the revolution of the year, and direct the degree from the Ascendant in ascensions, [using] the ascension of the city in which the native was born.[337]

22 Then, look at the position of the Moon on the third day, the seventh, and the fortieth day. **23** For indeed from the third day is stated the matter of the native in the station he was born in, or he will be changed to, and the drinking of milk. **24** And the seventh day is the matter of the body and the scarcity or abundance of its defects, and [indicates] the goodness of its color; and[338] one considers it from the fortunes and infortunes. **25** And the fortieth day considers his infancy,[339] activeness, play, and the goodness of his soul. **26** And if the infortunes were victorious over these days, then judge for him and his upbringing [according to] what you see.

---

[334] In this paragraph, Nawbakht is combining the four years of the Ptolemaic Ages of Man (see Ch. 1.3 above), with profections (**17-19**), the triplicity lords (**20**), and solar revolutions (**21**).

[335] I am not exactly sure what this means; perhaps that the condition will not only be harsh generally, but something specific to the malefic and its placement will be relevant at the solar revolution.

[336] This could equally mean the profection as well as where the solar revolution Ascendant lands.

[337] Nawbakht may mean to direct the Ascendant of the solar revolution, so that he can track its directions around the chart for that year. If he means to direct the natal Ascendant, it would hardly be necessary because he has already said he is only looking at the first four years, and that involves hardly any distance or calculation at all.

[338] Reading for "or."

[339] Lit., the time of having "two teeth."

27 And look at the inclination of the Moon with the infortunes or with the fortunes: for if you found her made fortunate on the third day, then judge the goodness of the upbringing, and the continuation of milk and its abundance, and his being little cut off from it, and little resurgence of crying, and the goodness of [his] character, and love with the one who is in charge of his upbringing, and with those he sees. **28** But if you found the Moon made unfortunate on the third day, then in some of his upbringing it will introduce hardship and a bad character, and his tenderness will decrease in some of the periods, and he will drink from someone other than his mother, and his crying will increase, due to the place corrupting the Moon and her lord on the third day.[340]

29 And if the Lot of Fortune was corrupted, as well as the lord of the trine[341] of the Ascendant, along with the Moon—by the [same] infortune which undermines the Moon—it indicates the badness of his upbringing, and the abundance of his thirst, and the badness of his character, and he will be angry with the one who <is in charge of> his upbringing, being burdensome to [that person], and he will drink his milk from more than one place, and he will move from the place in which he was born to a place which is harsher than it, and he will thirst more than he says. **30** And if the sign in which the Moon was, and the infortune which corrupts the Moon as well as the Lot of Fortune, were both corrupted in a sign having four <feet>, then he will drink milk from <something> having four feet; and if he did not have a lifespan due to [having] strength from his releaser, he will die at once. **31** Because for some of those who are born miserable while a powerful planet governs his lifespan, it will take hold of his life until his food decreases and he comes into misery in the years of subsistence and changeability, until the infortune reaches the lord of his releaser and corrupts his life as well.

32 And likewise, look on the seventh day along with the second lord of the triplicity, and the fortieth day along with the third lord of the triplicity. **33** And look at the inclination of the Moon after that, and see to whom the bound of the Moon on the third day belongs, whether to a fortune or infortune, and how is her position relative to the Ascendant: for if the lord of that place was an infortune, it indicates [the native's] ruin,[342] unless the fortunes

---

[340] In line with **32-33** below, one should look at the first triplicity lord of the Ascendant along with the third day of the Moon.
[341] That is, "triplicity."
[342] This could also be read as "the ruin of his soul" (هلاك نفسه).

are in the Ascendant. **34** And if, of the stars, nothing of the two fortunes are in the Ascendant, and the Moon is made unfortunate, and the lords of its[343] triplicity are located in a bad place, then it corrupts, even if he had a manager or indicator: for he will not survive. **35** (And know that the releaser is the manager, and the house-master is the indicator.)

[al-Andarzaghar on those who do not survive]

36 Al-Andarzaghar said concerning that: And as for those who do not survive, look at this topic generally from the position of the Moon in nativities, and the position of an infortune.[344]

37 For[345] if the Moon was made unfortunate and the infortune in a stake (and the worst places are the Ascendant and the Midheaven), and nothing of the fortunes are looking at her, then if the Moon was like that, judge that he will definitively not survive. **38** And it is likewise worse if the Moon was in a stake, and harsher for her and worse if an infortune was with the Moon or with the Ascendant in its [very] degree, or looking from the opposition with its body and its degree, or looking from the square at the Moon or at the Ascendant with its body and its degree—and especially if the Moon or the Ascendant was in its degree: for if it was like that, he will not survive, even if the fortunes looked at it; but if a fortune looked and it is cleansed of defects and[346] it is in the degree of the Ascendant, then he will live.

39 And[347] if the Moon was in the house of marriage and an infortune looked at her from the opposition or from the square and a fortune is not looking at her, then it establishes concerning him that he will not live. **40** And if the Moon was in the house of fathers and the infortune was opposing her or with her, and especially if the other infortune was with the Moon, joining with her, then if this was like that, it will not entirely rescue the native and his mother together from death on the day he was born, unless the fortunes were in the Ascendant, or the Moon was in her triplicity or in

---

[343] I take this to mean the Ascendant.
[344] That is, the infortune making her unfortunate: see the next sentence.
[345] For this paragraph, cf. *Carmen* I.7, **10-11**.
[346] Reading with the sense of *BA* III.1.3, **4** for "or."
[347] For **39-40**, cf. *Carmen* I.7, **12-14**.

something of her shares,[348] or a fortune with strength is looking at that infortune from the trine. **41** For if it was like that, it rescues, because the fortunes in their triplicities[349] increase the power for good, and the infortunes in their triplicities subtract from evil, and especially if Mars was in a female sign and Saturn in a male sign.

42 And[350] if the Moon was enclosed between the two infortunes, and the fortunes are not looking at her, and the Moon is decreasing in glow, he will not be rid of misfortunes[351] until he dies, and he will have little understanding, and [his] discernment[352] will disappear before his death.

43 And[353] if an infortune was in the Ascendant and the other infortune was in the house of marriage, and the Moon in the house of fathers or in the Midheaven, and a fortune is not looking at her, [then] along with his death there will be distress, he will be thrown out of the house of his fathers before his death, and especially if the Moon was in a bound of the infortunes and the lord of the bound is in one of the stakes, and the fortunes are not looking at her[354]—for that is harsher for him and worse.

44 Now[355] if the planetary <fortunes> met in <the second, sixth, eighth>,[356] or twelfth, and they are not looking at the Ascendant, then judge that he definitely will not live. **45** Now if the two infortunes were in the stake of the Ascendant and the fortunes are not looking at them, <nor at> the sign in which the meeting or opposition was, and the fortunes are not looking at the Sun and Moon, while the infortunes did look at them, then [even if] the three lords of the triplicities are safe, then judge for him the shortness of life, and the mishap of his mother. **46** And[357] if Mercury was with that infortune,

---

[348] أنصبائه. That is, dignities.
[349] That is, "trines," here and in the next clause.
[350] Cf. *Carmen* I.7, **15-16**.
[351] Lit., "the infortunes."
[352] Or in a purely physical sense, his "vision" (بصر).
[353] Cf. *Carmen* I.7, **24-25**.
[354] Reading for the more generic "it," in accordance with *Carmen* I.7, **25**.
[355] For this paragraph, cf. *Carmen* I.7, **28-29**.
[356] Adding the houses in brackets based on *Carmen* I.7, **28**, which simply says there are no fortunes in the seven good places. This leaves the four places in aversion to the Ascendant, along with the third—which Sahl's text rules out by emphasizing that they do not see the Ascendant (while the third does). In Arabic, the word for "twelfth" begins with the word "second" (lit., "second-ten"), so it makes sense that a scribe would have mistakenly jumped to the word for "twelfth," thinking he had already written in the second house.
[357] *Carmen* does not mention Mercury, but it makes astrological sense.

it is harsher and worse. **47** And if Venus was made unfortunate along with that, then judge death for his mother, because the indicator of the mother is Venus as well as the Moon.

48 And if the Moon[358] was concealed under the rays, and Saturn looked at her from the square or from the opposition, then judge for him the shortness of life.

49 And if you found the Moon with Mars in Aries at the New Moon,[359] and the fortunes are not looking at her, then judge for him the shortness of life.

50 And know if that the lords of the triplicity of the Ascendant, apart from the Moon, were in the third from the Ascendant and[360] [if] they were made unfortunate by the harm of an infortune, then judge the shortness of life, unless the lord of the triplicity of the Ascendant was the Moon [herself]: for if she was in the third, she is powerful.

The statement of Ptolemy concerning that:[361]

52 He said: If you found one of the luminaries in the Ascendant with one of the infortunes, and the fortunes are not looking at the Ascendant, and the lords of the houses of the luminaries are falling, then he will not be brought up, and he will die at once.

53 And if the two infortunes cast their rays to the luminaries together, and the two infortunes are looking at the Ascendant, then the native will not live; and that is harsher from the stakes.

54 And if the Sun was in the Ascendant or the second, and Mars looking at them both, or he was with the Moon in these two places and Mars looked at her (and it is harsher than that if the aspect of each happened to be the two glowing ones and the Ascendant), then the native will not be brought up.

55 And if the two infortunes and the luminaries were in the stakes,[362] then he will come out of his mother's belly dead. **56** And if one of the luminaries joined with a fortune in this condition, or something of the fortunes looked

---

[358] Reading with BA for, "the infortune."
[359] That is, when she emerges from the rays and is visible.
[360] Reading for "or."
[361] For this subsection, cf. *Tet.* III.9 (Robbins pp. 265-71),
[362] For Ptolemy, the infortunes are opposing them.

at it, or cast its rays, then the native will live until the luminary reaches the portion of the infortune;[363] and every portion between them is a day (and if there were minutes, then they are hours).

57 Now[364] if the infortunes were with the luminaries in the seventh, and the infortunes were the lords of the houses of the luminaries or the Ascendant, then he will go out dead from the belly of his mother, and his birth will not be complete, and will be [*illegible*].

[*The infortunes in the stakes, with the Moon*][365]

58 And if you found Mars in the Ascendant and the infortunes are looking at the Moon from a square or opposition, then he will not live. **59** And if Mars was in the Midheaven, looking at the Moon, then the native will be afflicted by the burning of fire, and he will be on the verge of death from it. **60** And if he was in the seventh and is looking at the Moon, and the Ascendant is devoid of the fortunes and their aspect to it, then the native and his mother will die at the hour he is born. **61** And if he was in the fourth and the Moon looks at him from a square or opposition, then the child and mother will both die on that day, unless one of the fortunes is with them or they are both looking at them, for then the native will be rescued from[366] death.

62 And if you found <Saturn> with the degree of the Ascendant and the Moon is looking at him, then he will not survive. **63** And if Saturn was <in> the Midheaven, looking at the Moon, his mother will suffer a harsh complaint and will die quickly. **64** And if he was in the <seventh>, looking at the Moon and the Ascendant, devoid of the fortunes, then the native will come out dead from the belly of his mother. **65** And if he was in the fourth and the Moon looks at him, then the native will corrupt the assets of his father, and it will diminish what the native will live on.

---

[363] That is, by symbolic timing, converting the interval in degrees into units of time (greater or smaller, depending on the situation, according to Ptolemy).

[364] The relation of this sentence to *Tet.* is very ambiguous; if it is meant to summarize Ptolemy, it is a poor one and cannot really be pinned down to a specific sentence (Robbins pp. 269-71). But I do suspect that this scenario only refers to the sect light, and not both luminaries. Thanks to Steven Birchfield for pointing this out.

[365] This subsection reads like a systematic fleshing out of *Carmen* I.7, **24-25**, which deals generically with the angles instead of delineating each one.

[366] Tentatively reading for an uncertain verb, which could mean "conquer" (i.e., he will conquer or have victory *over* death), but the Arabic uses the wrong preposition in that case.

[Other considerations]

66 And³⁶⁷ if the Moon was in a stake or what follows a stake, with an infortune, looking <at> a fortune, he will be brought up unless his parents want to reject him. **67** Now if the Moon was made unfortunate, then his mother wants that, and if the Sun was unfortunate, then his father wants that; and if they were both unfortunate, then both of them [want it].

68 Now³⁶⁸ if there was not a fortune in a stake, nor in the house of good fortune,³⁶⁹ and not in the triplicity of the Ascendant, and an infortune looked at the Moon and the Sun or the meeting or fullness, then that is a mark of ruin.

69 And³⁷⁰ if the lords of the triplicities are corrupted, he will not be brought up. **70** And if a fortune was with them both, it indicates the repelling of disaster until its period completes.

71 And if the native did not have an illness harming his life which I described based on the infortunes, and the lords of the triplicities were in a bad place, and you found a blameworthy star or one of the infortunes³⁷¹ in the seven places (which are the stakes and the trines of the Ascendant, and the eleventh),³⁷² it indicates the shortness of his lifespan and survival. **72** And <it is like that> if the Moon was made unfortunate and the infortunes in the stakes (unless any of the infortunes is in the Ascendant, for then that [indicates] his survival is terminated). **73** And if the Moon and her lord were both made unfortunate, then <missing>, even if the fortunes were in the more preferable of them by place (except for the Ascendant), and he had a manager and indicator,³⁷³ for he will not have [any] survival. **74** And if one of the two fortunes, or one of the two luminaries, or Mercury, were in the Ascendant and the infortunes are not looking at them, then he will be brought up and survive with good and rank. **75** And if you found one of the two infor-

---

³⁶⁷ For this paragraph, see *Carmen* I.7, **18-21**.
³⁶⁸ See *Carmen* I.7, **28**.
³⁶⁹ The eleventh. This, plus the four angles and the trines to the Ascendant, are the seven good places described in Sahl's *Introduction* Ch. 2, **37-44**.
³⁷⁰ This paragraph resembles the ideas in *Carmen* I.25. But see also the incomplete sentences in *Carmen* I.7, **26-27**.
³⁷¹ Reading for "fortunes."
³⁷² That is, the seven good or advantageous places described in *Carmen* I.5.
³⁷³ Recall from above (**35**) that these are the releaser and house-master.

tunes in the Ascendant, looking at one of the luminaries, then that native will not be brought up and he will have few days, [being] chronically ill, sickly, and he will be an orphan.

Chapter [1.31]: On those whose lives[374] are ruined, & those who do not linger for [more than a few] days

1 If the Moon was conjoined with Saturn in the [same] degree, his life will be short; and if the other infortune was in her square or opposition, he will come out of his mother's belly by being cut out.

2 And if the Moon was in what is between Saturn and the Sun, his life will be short, and he will come out of his mother's belly one-eyed or blind, and that is if the fortunes are not looking at her. **3** And if the Moon was in what is between Mars and the Sun, his life will also be short, and he will come out blind and mute; and that is if the fortunes are not looking at her.

4 And[375] if the Moon and Mars were in the Ascendant, and Saturn setting opposite them in the west, then he will go out of his mother's belly by being cut out, and his mother will perish on that day. **5** And if the Moon and Mars were in the west, and Saturn is rising opposite them, then he will be destroyed on that day. **6** And if [the Moon] was setting in the west, and the infortunes are looking at her from the fourth and tenth, then the native and his mother will both be destroyed quickly. **7** And if the Moon and Mars were in the Midheaven and Saturn opposite them under the earth, then the native will be killed, and be crucified, and his body not buried. **8** And if the Moon was in the fourth and the infortunes opposite her <in> the Midheaven, then a house will fall on him. **9** And if the Moon was <in> the Midheaven, and <they> are opposite her under the earth, then he will be one losing both legs, <or> losing [his] eyesight.

10 And if the lord of the triplicity of the Ascendant was under the rays, in the preferable ones of the places, and the fortunes in a place below that,[376] and he did not have a manager nor indicator, then he will not survive. **11**

---

[374] Reading حيوتهم for بيوتهم ("houses").
[375] The configurations in this paragraph are very similar to *Mathesis* VII.2.
[376] I.e., in places not preferable.

And if[377] the sign of the native's life belonged to a fortune, and [that planet] occurred in a suitable place, and was under the rays, then he will not survive.

12 And know that the favorable stars are those of the nocturnal ones by night and the diurnal ones by day.

13 And if you found two planets in the Ascendant, one of them a fortune and the other an infortune, that one of them which is closer to the degree of the Ascendant is the stronger of the two, and you ought to look from it.

14 And if the lord of the triplicity of the Ascendant was in a suitable place and it is retrograde, then he will not survive, even if he has a manager and indicator;[378] and it is worse for that if the Moon was made unfortunate. **15** And if he does not have a manager and indicator, then he will be destroyed in the beginning: and the examination of it will be from the infortunes, unless there is something of the fortunes in the Ascendant.

16 And if one of the two infortunes is in the stake of the Midheaven, and the other in the stake of the earth, then even if the fortunes are in the place of the seventh or other places, with that he will not survive [except for] a short time; and God is more knowledgeable.

Chapter [1.32] On the matter of survival for one who does not live

[al-Andarzaghar]

1 Look <first> at the course of the Sun, Moon, Ascendant, and the house-master, if they reach the infortunes or the infortunes reach them. **2** And the second [is] if the Sun, Moon, and house-master of the nativity in the course reach their own square or opposition.[379] **3** And the third is the Lot of Fortune, the meeting, and the opposition, whichever of these the infortunes meet first.

---

[377] This can also be treated as "even if," which may be the case because both **10** and **11** seem to say that being under the rays prevents survival.
[378] That is, a releaser and house-master: see Ch. 1.30, **35**.
[379] This probably refers to a transit, since we are speaking about natives who do not live long. The same can be said for other sentences below.

4 And if the infortune was in a bad sign and under the rays, then it kills; and from the trine and sextile it <does not>[380] kill like the square and opposition, and is not an example of that.

5 And perhaps the Moon will kill the native if his planets were made unfortunate and the infortune in a stake: when it comes to be on itself or opposes itself, it kills.

6 And if the Moon was in the sixth, eighth, or twelfth, and she is in the square of the infortunes or in their opposition, then the first [time] that an infortune casts its rays to the Ascendant or Moon, it destroys, unless the indicator is in a powerful place. **7** And the Sun too, if he is in the sixth or twelfth in the nativity, and the infortunes looked at him, and likewise the infortune is in one of the stakes: for if the Sun overtakes[381] the infortunes, he kills.

8 And the house-master does likewise if it was made unfortunate, in a bad place, in the nativity of one who will not live: if it looked at its own triplicity or square, it kills.[382]

9 And if the nativity was corrupted by all of the planets, and the lord of the Lot of Fortune also made unfortunate, then judge that he will survive for this or that many hours, not adding anything [onto] it. **10** And if you saw the corruption of the nativity and the planets are middling, then judge days and months: it will less frequently make him complete a year.

11 And when neither the Sun, Moon, Ascendant, nor Lot are in the status of being the releaser, then you ought to direct whichever one of them that you find to be stronger, just as you direct the releaser to the infortunes, a year for every degree of ascensions. **12** For if you directed the Sun or Moon in their courses to the infortunes, or you directed an infortune to the degree of the Ascendant or to the Lot, then it kills, whichever of these four connects first with the infortune. **13** And [as for] the "stronger" one which is admitted

---

[380] Tentatively adding to make more astrological sense. But Sahl might indeed mean that even the trine and sextile in such a situation kill. In that case, the sentence should read, "…it kills like the square and opposition, even though [such aspects] are not like that." The problem is that the pronoun هو should not be used with plurals, so it strains Arabic grammar to read it without the negation.

[381] لحقت. This probably means that the Sun reaches it by transit. BA says an infortune is "followed by" the Sun. This Arabic verb can mean that, but requires the preposition بـ.

[382] Sahl might mean that the house-master will transit its own natal position from a trine or square.

(of these four places), the first of them is the Ascendant, then the Moon is the stronger of them.

14 Now if the releaser is not the Sun or Moon, then when the Lot[383] or Ascendant reaches the degrees of the infortune, it kills, if the fortunes are not looking at it.

15 And know that perhaps it will indicate years with respect to the lifespan, and perhaps it indicates that it is months, and perhaps it indicates that it is days. **16** Now if the indication for the lifespan was in years, then you ought to calculate <a year> for every degree of ascensions,[384] and direct from it. **17** And if it indicates that the lifespan is months, then you ought to calculate a month for every sign. **18** And calculate likewise for the amounts of days and hours, for every sign a day or for every sign an hour.

☙ ☙ ☙

19 And[385] certainly the infortunes are capable of destroying the native's life from four places: from the Ascendant, the two luminaries, and the Lot: so calculate from that place to the infortune which destroys life, in days, months, and years. **20** Now if the destruction of life was from the Sun, that will be [if] the Sun was falling from the stakes, and his misfortune was [from] Mars by day, and Saturn by night.

21 And[386] in the foundation of the upbringing you ought to look at the nativity of the two parents, and how they have Jupiter and the Lot of children, and the lords of their triplicities:[387] for when Mars does not look at anything of that, it will be less for [any] harm, and the upbringing for [that parent's] children will be more hopeful.

The statement of Māshā'allāh on that:

23 Māshā'allāh said: know that the universe [has] two worlds: a world in which the soul is before its mixture with the body (and it is the world [the

---

[383] Reading for "Moon," with BA III.1.7, **35**.
[384] Reading for "the Ascendant."
[385] Since this paragraph introduces the four places anew, I have set it apart as possibly being by another author.
[386] For this paragraph, cf. Nawbakht in Ch. 1.15, **2**.
[387] Reading the plural for "triplicity."

soul] returns to when it separates from the body), and the second world in which the soul is not known except by means of the body. **24** Now, a direct planet indicates upbringing and staying in that [second] world which [the soul] goes to, and a retrograde planet indicates death, returning, and disappearing to what it came from: for direct motion slopes down to the world below, and the retrograde one rises up to the world it came from. **25** So, the indication is based on its course.

26 And know that signs without stars [ruling them] are like bodies without souls, and stars without signs are like souls without bodies: so for every sign which is the Ascendant of a native, the lord of that sign is the indicator of his survival in the world [below], and his staying in it. **27** So if it was direct in course, it indicates staying and remaining; and if it was retrograde, the native will return to the world which he came from. **28** And likewise, if it was direct and connected with a retrograde planet, and it is received, it will be similar to one going out [and] wanting to travel, [but] he will encounter one returning him (because of that aspect) to his entrance into the second world, however it was for him at his exit from the belly [of his mother].

[Four testimonies of a short life: Māshā'allāh]

29 And I will make clear to you those who are not brought up, from the statement of Māshā'allāh.[388] **30** If the lord of the eighth was in the Ascendant, it indicates the shortness of the lifespan, and that is [one] testimony. **31** Now if along with what I mentioned it is connecting with the lord of the Ascendant, or[389] the lord of the Ascendant is connecting with it, and it is not receiving it, he will not be brought up; but if it did receive, he will be brought up, [so] seek out another testimony. **32** And if one of the two is not connecting with the other, and the lord of the eighth was in the Ascendant and the lord of the Ascendant was[390] connected with an infortune or a retrograde planet, the native will not be brought up; and the time is from the Ascendant.[391] **33** Now if the lord of the eighth is in the Ascendant and the lord of the Ascendant under the rays, entering into burning, he will not be brought up.

---

[388] Compare **30-33** with **47-52** below.
[389] Reading for "and."
[390] Omitting "not."
[391] See **36** for more on this.

34 Or, seek testimony about that from the Moon: for if she connected with a retrograde planet (or with the lord of the eighth [from] her house, or with the lord of the eighth [from] the Ascendant), and it <does not>[392] receive her, it indicates what I described of the shortness of the lifespan.

35 And if the lord of the Ascendant handed over its management to a retrograde planet or one in its first slowness,[393] and it is not receiving it, he will not be brought up. **36** And if it was received, he will be brought up but he will not reach [his full] lifespan, and the time is from the lord of the Ascendant: if it was received, then it is years, and if it is not received, then it is months.

37 And along with what I mentioned, seek testimony from the Moon: if she was above the earth, handing over her management to a planet under the earth not receiving her, and[394] to a retrograde planet, he will not survive, and the time will be days.

38 And know that if the lord of the Ascendant was retrograde, it indicates the shortness of the lifespan. **39** Now if the lord of the eighth was also retrograde, he will be brought up and it will not harm the native, because the activity of one of them will cancel out the other, so he will be brought up. **40** Now if along with the retrogradation the lord of the Ascendant the Moon is also connecting with a retrograde planet, he will not be brought up.

41 And if the lord of the Ascendant is entering into burning and the Sun is made unfortunate or is handing over his management to the lord of the eighth [from] the Ascendant, it indicates the shortness of the lifespan, and that he will die a bad manner of death.

42 If the lord of the Ascendant associated with the lord of the eighth with its own body, he will not benefit by the excellence of the Moon's position; and worse than that is if it was in the sign of the lord of the eighth,[395] for then he will not drink water; and it harsher for that if it is in a stake.

---

[392] Tentatively adding this negation, otherwise it would violate Māshā'allāh's reasoning above in **28** and **31**.
[393] That is, its first station.
[394] This should probably read "or" to a retrograde planet, which likewise does not receive her.
[395] This seems to mean, not just in any sign *with* the lord of the eighth, but in a sign actually *ruled by* the lord of the eighth.

43 And if the lord of the Ascendant was falling, not looking at the Ascendant, and the lord of the triplicity of the Ascendant is in one of the stakes, then work with that just as I explained about the lord of the Ascendant: because the lord of the triplicity will be more important for the Ascendant than the lord of the Ascendant [itself]. **44** Now if it was like that, then look at the lord of the triplicity: for if it handed over its management to a retrograde planet not receiving it, or to the lord of the eighth of the Ascendant, then concerning his situation it will be what I described about the lord of the Ascendant.

45 And if the lord of the Ascendant and the first lord of the triplicity of the Ascendant were both falling away from the Ascendant, then look at the Moon. **46** For if she connected with a retrograde planet or a planet under the earth, or with the lord of the eighth [from] the Ascendant or of the eighth [from] the house in which she is, then it indicates the shortness of the lifespan; and it is worse for that if the Moon was in a stake.

47 And I will make clear to you the summary of the testimonies of the lord of the Ascendant.[396] **48** The lord of the eighth in the Ascendant is a testimony. **49** And the connection of the lord of the eighth with the lord of the Ascendant is a testimony, and the connection of the lord of the Ascendant with the lord of the eighth is a testimony.[397] **50** And the connection of the lord of the Ascendant with a planet <not> receiving it, is a testimony. **51** And the burning of the lord of the Ascendant, or its retrogradation, is a testimony. **52** So these four testimonies pertain to the lord of the Ascendant.

Chapter [1.33]: On the knowledge of the native's image & his color

1 Now when you have finished with what I explained to you of the matter of upbringing, and it has become clear to you that he will be brought up and reach his lifespan, then look into the shape of the native and the variation in his conditions, according to what I will explain to you, if God wills.

2 If you wanted to understand the shape of the native and the pleasantness of his appearance, then look at the degree of the Ascendant, and who is

---

[396] Compare with **29-33** above.

[397] These should be understood as the same type of testimony, as **52** says there are four testimonies.

looking at the lord of the face,[398] and blend it with the planets which are looking at it.[399] **3** Because if you saw the quality of Venus, and Saturn connected with her from a square, he will blacken her with powerful blackness. **4** And if he looked at her from a suitable place, it will subtract from that blackness according to how he looks at her from conciliation and harmony. **5** And certainly the Sun will alter Saturn and reduce the blackness in Venus until she becomes brown or close to whiteness. **6** And the Moon does that, and Mars, until the blackness of Saturn disappears (except for some small bit one does not notice). **7** And Jupiter does that like the Moon does, except that he does not subtract like the Moon subtracts; and that is if these planets look at Saturn. **8** Now as for Mercury, he grants yellowness until Saturn turns to yellow so his resemblance comes to be yellow or [there is] whiteness in [the] yellow. **9** And perhaps the planets are looking along with Saturn so that he takes from their colors until they overcome the color of Saturn. **10** And[400] all of that is necessary for calculating their grouping until it is descriptive, when they are blended and associated with one another, for this is what they grant, of colors.

11 And as for the image,[401] it is the least of what one adds or subtracts from it, so you ought to blend the planets [in terms of] what they grant of their images; and I have already explained to you what every planet grants of its image, in the *Book of Natures*.[402] **12** So blend it according to that, with the planets which look at the lord of the face, and grant them based on their natures.

13 And see also who of the planets is looking at the degree of the Ascendant: for if the degree of the Ascendant is of the glowing degrees,[403] the native will be white, and more intensely for his whiteness if Venus, the Moon, or

---

[398] Perhaps this should be, "and look at the lord of the face."
[399] This is probably the lord of the face: see **12** below.
[400] Reading somewhat freely in this sentence, as the text seems to be referring this to Saturn, even though it is a general statement about all of the planets.
[401] This might mean the face or decan in which the Ascendant falls.
[402] This is not one of the works attributed to Sahl; it may be by al-Andarzaghar (see **17-20** below).
[403] That is, the bright degrees (as opposed to the dark degrees mentioned in **16** below). For a list of the bright and dark degrees, see for example *ITA* VII.7.

Jupiter is looking. **14** And if they were amiss,[404] and if the Sun and Mars are looking at the whiteness, they redden it;[405] and if Saturn looked, he blackens it. **15** And if you saw a mixture of the planets in the degree of the Ascendant, then mix it with the planets that are looking at the degree, along with the degree of the Ascendant.

16 And if the degree was dark, and the Moon looked, he will be brown; and if Venus and Jupiter looked too, it increases the whiteness; and if Mars looked, he reddens it, and if Saturn looked he blackens it: so always blend the planets with the degree of the Ascendant.

17 And[406] know that the image has variations due to the faces, and indeed that is not limited by the minutes:[407] because the ancient scholars said that in every hour from the east there arise 24,000 myriad points (and a myriad is 10,000) in which the colors differ, and apart from that Ascendants and bodies, and every point of them individually is a color, taste, constitution, and nature. **18** So the precision of that point and its fineness comes down to what no intelligent person nor spirit can grasp, and from here it is evident that there is nothing named, moving, nor living, nor anything which God has created, which does not have a familiarity with the seven [planets] and the twelve [signs]. **19** Then, the colors differ by country and parents, and the quarters of the day.[408] **20** And indeed one should pay heed to the properties of the stars, and I have already explained to you what every planet gives of images in the *Book of Natures* (and this section calls upon it as a witness) which I will explain to you.

[Bodily form, from Ptolemy]

21 Know[409] that the soul manages the affairs of the body, and that is because the body is dense, crude in mixture, and the soul is fine, active, a manager created with the seed when it fell: so it mixes with it, enters into it, and seizes victory over it in the womb; and after the native's departure from

---

[404] Reading somewhat uncertainly for ذوات ضلّ. This probably means they are in aversion or at least that the degree of their ray is far away.
[405] Reading حمّرته for خضّرته, "make it green."
[406] This paragraph is reflected in *BA* III.1, **21-24**, so is probably from al-Andarzaghar. See Abū Bakr I.9, whose Latin transliterates an author's name: *Andoroar, Amdasoar*.
[407] Reading for "by reality."
[408] See **44-52** below.
[409] For this subsection, cf. *Tet.* III.11 (Robbins pp. 307-13).

the womb, because of that the events of the body are known from the contemplation of what happens to the soul. **22** So,⁴¹⁰ you ought to look, in the image of the native and the mixture of his nature, at the Ascendant and its lord, and the luminaries, and the meeting and fullness which was before the nativity, and the Lot of Fortune, for these five things are greater in testimony. **23** And [the planet which is] more victorious over the native due to the abundance of its governance over these positions, is the governor for the native's image: so see what the nature of this planet is.

24 And if Saturn was the indicator for the image and he was eastern, then the native will be brown and tawny, gentle, strong, with black hair, in appearance fine, generally hairy, with black eyes tending towards yellow, good in body, round of face, serious, tending towards moisture and coldness. **25** And if he was western, he is delicate, short, tawny, with lank hair, black eyes and hair, stocky,⁴¹¹ it covers him with tawniness, some redness, his nature tending towards coldness and dryness. **26** And know that Saturn corrupts from the eyes and disfigures the face, and increases the hair on the head and body.

27 And if it was Jupiter and he was eastern, then the native will be white in color, the hair hanging down long, with powerful eyes, having authority and rank, handsome, having respect, and his nature tending towards heat and moisture. **28** And if he was western, he will be white, [but] not with pure whiteness, lank [of hair], his eyes different [colors], of medium stature, his nature tending towards greater moisture. **29** And know that Jupiter is round of face, powerful in the eyes and beard, and he increases the hair of the eyebrows.

30 And if it was Mars and he is eastern, then the native will be white with red, tall, easy of character, quick,⁴¹² much hair in the beard, his mixture tending towards heat and dryness. **31** And if he was western, he will be reddish, of medium stature, small eyes, lisping, with reddish hair, lank, short, quick, stocky,⁴¹³ reddish hair, his mixture tending towards greater dryness. **32**

---

⁴¹⁰ This sentence reflects a later approach: Ptolemy mentions only the Ascendant, planets in it and ruling it, and the Moon.

⁴¹¹ Reading as ازب, but this is somewhat redundant because his shortness was already mentioned. It could be أزب, "hairy," but Ptolemy says that a western Saturn shows little hair.

⁴¹² Or, "agile."

⁴¹³ See the footnote in **25**; likewise, Ptolemy says a western Mars has little hair.

(And[414] know that Mars brings the blood of the face to light, and reddens the eyes and corrupts them from the blood, and he is fine in strength, [tending] towards the [uncertain][415] of what he is.)

33 The Sun indicates brilliance and embellishment, and makes the eyes powerful, reddens the face, makes the forehead powerful and broadens it, and reduces the eyebrows, makes the head bald, thins the beard, and reddens the hair.

34 And if it was Venus and she is eastern, then she indicates what Jupiter indicates, but his hair will be full, beautiful, he will love beauty and clothing, being supple of body, his eyes laughing, tending towards the most beautiful and brilliance, and [his] form [having] a beautiful constitution [and] mixture, smiling, pleasant in soul, magnanimous, generous. **35** And if she was western, then she indicates a quality preferable to the eastern quality, in terms of beauty and brilliance. **36** And know that Venus increases the goodness and shine in the face, and she makes the eyes beautiful as well as the eyebrows and forehead, and she makes the cheeks smooth.

37 And if it was Mercury and he was eastern, the native will be brown, of medium stature, curly-haired,[416] with small eyes, handsome in stature,[417] his mixture tending towards heat. **38** And if he was western, he will be delicate, tending towards redness, small in the eyes, they being sunken, prominent, redness covering him along with tawniness, tending towards more dryness. **39** And know that Mercury is small in the face, is dry,[418] and makes the eyebrows thin, and he will be a big talker.[419]

40 And know that the Moon whitens the face and purifies it, and makes the eyes powerful, and indicates the ordaining of handsomeness and suppleness and calm, and that is according to the manner of her position relative to the Sun: if she was full, it makes her indication more powerful and grants according to her strength, and he will be quick in his speech and he will be boastful.

---

[414] This sentence is not reflected in Ptolemy.
[415] التّدوير.
[416] منحني, which means "curved" or "twisted," but Ptolemy is speaking about curly hair.
[417] Or, "proportion" (التّقطيع).
[418] يعرقه. Or thin, gaunt, etc.: in other words what one becomes when moisture is removed.
[419] طرمذار (from Persian); or more specifically a braggart.

41 And[420] if the planetary indicator was retrograde, in its first station, then it makes the body powerful and the native will be sturdy and strong, healthy in the body.[421] **42** And if it was in its second station, the native will be weak, with many pains and ailments. **43** And if it was under the rays, it indicates weakness and hardship.

[Temperament from quarters of the day, signs, and planets: al-Andarzaghar]

44 Then, look also at the differences of the quarters of the day, for the natures of hot, cold, soft,[422] and dry occur in trees and plants just as they occur in nativities, [but in the form] of blood, phlegm, air, and bile: because the sperm does not fall into the womb and plant that seed except according to what is rising [and] that planet which is the mixture of that hour:

45 So if the sperm fell or a native was born at the beginning of the three hours at the beginning of the day, <in an airy sign>,[423] and one of the planets was looking at it [which was] appropriate to it and harmonizing with it, then one born from that seed [will be like that]—and especially in the presence of the glow[424] of Venus, the native will be born according to the image of Venus and her likeness, in beauty and brilliance, laughing, with skill in stringed [instruments] and singing, and mocking, and an eagerness to pursue pleasures as well as good qualities, blood will be evident, being of a good character, loving ridicule and cleanliness, with much sexual intercourse, the pleasures

---

[420] Sahl's text is incomplete. In *Tet.* III.11 (Robbins p. 313), when a planet easternizes it shows a large body; at the first station, someone powerful and muscular; retrograde, badly proportioned; at the second station, weak; when westernizing, "without repute" (?) and able to bear hardship and oppression. This model is more appropriate to the superior planets but could be adapted for Mercury and Venus in the way that Dorotheus does for the age of a thief (see *Carmen* V.36, **116** and Heph. III.45, **15**): from the superior conjunction with the Sun to emerging as an evening star direct, young; from the first station retrograde to the conjunction with the Sun, adult; from the conjunction to being a morning star up to the second station, aging; from the second station to the conjunction, old.

[421] Or more concretely, the torso; for Ptolemy this indicates muscularity.

[422] Or rather, "moist" or "wet."

[423] Adding with BA and in harmony with the sentences below.

[424] See below, where this phrase becomes "the *degree* of the glow," i.e., by aspect or body. This latter formulation is probably more correct to the original text, especially as it requires only a small spelling change in Arabic: درجة \ وجه.

distracting him from what benefits him, and his temperament and constitution being according to that sign.

46 And if it was in the second portion of the day, so the settling of his water mixes with his dwelling[425] in those times and those fiery constellations (or a seedling was planted in them), and especially in the presence of the glow of Mars, the image of Mars and his likeness will cover him, and the appearance of vice too,[426] if it was fiery: for the nature of a native being born will be of red bile, and he will be brave, sharp, choleric,[427] not paying heed except for[428] what is to his own advantage in [matters of] frights, violence, and burning, not being a master of his own anger, with the [*uncertain*][429] of matters. **47** So, his character, color, health and illness, and activity, will all resemble Mars.

48 And one whose seed fell within the third portion, and especially in the degree of the glow of Saturn and signs of earth, the mixture of [such] a native born will be of black bile, his belly full of resentment and deceit, and working by means of evil; so his color, nature, health and illness, will be according to Saturn.

49 And one whose seed fell in the fourth portion (which is the end of the day), or a seedling planted in those hours, and especially in the degree of the glow of the Moon and signs of water, and a native born [then], will be large, with much flesh, huge, given to phlegm, [with] powerful eyes[430] in him. **50** So, his color, good qualities, and health and illness, will be according to the mixture of the Moon.

51 And[431] in the first portion of the night it is just as I described in the first portion of the day.

52 And [for] one whose seed fell in the glow of Mars, in the mixture of water, you ought to mix him according to what I described to you, a middle [ground] of that; except that if the times are concordant and the seasons di-

---

[425] فخالط استقرار مائه قراره, perhaps some strange idiom, but still referring to either the conception or (as in **44**) the nativity.

[426] Reading ونظر آفة as. But another possibility might be وبظرافة, "and with brilliance/wittiness too."

[427] Or, "irascible" (غضوبًا).

[428] Reading "except for" (إلّا) for "not" (لا).

[429] نابات or نابيات, an plural feminine word. I am not sure if the "with" here (عند) refers to his anger, or is a separate statement about his affairs.

[430] موق, which is both singular and describes the inner corner of the eye; it is related to crying, so perhaps with the emphasis on moisture and phlegm Sahl's source means that he has intense bouts of crying—or perhaps even watery eyes.

[431] This sentence is not reflected in *BA*, but probably should have been part of it.

verge as I explained, they differ: because if it was in the first and second portion, [and] the signs are watery and fiery, and the appearance of their color [is] what I described, then the child's condition and character will be blended of these two contrasting essences whose contrariety I described at the beginning of the book.[432]

[Seasonal effects on the body: Ptolemy]

53 And[433] of course they also differ from another perspective, and that is the changing of the four seasons. **54** Now if [there was] a native in what is between the spring up to the summer, then he will be full in body and color, keen of heart, handsome in the eyes, heat and moisture will be abundant in him. **55** And one born in what is between the summer and fall, will be middling in color and stature, keen of heart, handsome in the eyes, heat and dryness will be abundant in him. **56** And one born in what is between the fall up to winter, will be brown, delicate, keen of heart, middling in hair, handsome in the eyes, dryness and cold will be abundant in him. **57** And one born in what is between the winter up to the spring, will be of middling stature, lank in hair, slow of speech, soft, moisture and cold will be abundant in him.

Chapter [1.34]: Looking at the positions of the planets in the months of pregnancy, & whom the native resembles

1 Then, look at the positions of the planets in the months of pregnancy, because one looks for the native's character, body, shape, beauty, reason, and action, from the positions of the planets in the months of pregnancy.

2 So look for the character and his body from the position of the Sun in the fourth month: from his position in the signs, and his testimonies in the places, and the aspect of the stars to him. **3** Now if the planets were handing management over to him in the fourth month, it indicates a good character and strength. **4** And if the Sun is handing over the management, it indicates weakness in [his] strength and character: because if [the Sun] is accepting

---

[432] This is probably the *Book of Natures* described before.
[433] Cf. *Tet.* III.11 (pp. 313-15).

[the management], he will increase in his strength, and if he is the one handing over, it takes away from his strength.

5 And likewise look for his shape and beauty from the position of Venus in the fifth month from the placing of the seed, and you look for his reason and speech from the position of Mercury in the sixth month—looking for these two planets just as I explained in the matter of the Sun. **6** So from what I have mentioned is known the shape of the native and his character.

7 And as for the nativity, it does not indicate [that] he resembles the father or mother, or the paternal uncles or maternal uncles,[434] unless you speak about the lord of the native's Ascendant, the Sun, the Moon, the Lot of the father and the Lot of the mother (and the lords of them both), and the fourth house—if it was male, then the father, and if it was female, then the mother. **8** (And it is likewise in the topic of siblings.) **9** So look at the lord of the native's Ascendant, [then] secondly the planet of these indicators it connects [with], for whatever it is, he will resemble that.

10 And know that the lord of the house of the Sun indicates the family of the house of the father, and the lord of the house of the Mon indicates the family of the house of the mother.

11 And know that if the Moon connected with a male planet, then the native will resemble the father, and if she connected with a female planet then the native will resemble the mother. **12** Now if she connected with a female planet and it[435] is in a male sign, the native will resemble the family of the mother.

13 And know that the indicator of the character is the lord of the hour, and the indicator of the constitution is the Lot which is taken from the Sun to his foundation,[436] and you project it from the degree of the Moon (so seek information from the lord of that sign), and by night from the Moon to the degree of her foundation, and it is projected from the Sun. **14** So with these two together falling in the sign of a planet, the nature of the native will be according to that planet.

---

[434] Or in the case of a female native, the maternal and paternal aunts.
[435] I believe this refers to the other planet, and not the Moon.
[436] أسّ. This sounds like the fourth place from the Sun, but is perhaps 0° Leo (and likewise 0° Cancer for the Moon): Theophilus does something similar in his *On Cosmic Inceptions* Ch. 6, **18-20**. Thanks to Steven Birchfield for suggesting this.

15 And know that Jupiter is the indicator of the soul: if in the second month from the planting of the seed he was rising in the calculation of the atmosphere,[437] it indicates the native's intelligence and understanding, according to Jupiter's rising and his reception: he will do what is not heard of, and will be knowledgeable. **16** And if he was falling down in the calculation of the atmosphere from the middle of his course,[438] it indicates the conventionality[439] of the native and his thought, and it indicates that he will not work nor speak except for what he knows and hears, according to the declining of Jupiter. **17** And if in the second month he was rising in the stake,[440] it indicates what it indicates in the topic of the atmosphere. **18** And if he was falling down in the stake,[441] then he will scarcely remember [anything], and he will be slow in thought. **19** And if he was rising in the atmosphere as well as the stake, then he will be inspired, establishing the principles [of things] on his own, and he will speak with a wisdom like prophecy. **20** And if he was falling down in the atmosphere as well as the stake, then he will be stupid, not learning anything, and he will be like a beast, not understanding but [only] eating and drinking.

Chapter [1.35]: On the dispositions of the native & his condition, & what it gives rise to,[442] & his passion, & what type it is

1 Know[443] that if the convertible signs were the Ascendant of the native, they indicate that that native will love things involving other people, [be] a

---

[437] This probably means he is moving upwards towards his apogee, away from his perigee.
[438] Again, this probably means he is moving downwards from his apogee towards his perigee.
[439] نقل, which normally means "transfer" (as in the transfer of light), but can also mean something traditional that is handed down.
[440] Sahl's source is probably imagining a monthly solar or lunar return chart. "Rising" in the stake could either mean moving towards an axial degree, but also being anywhere from the IC up to the MC on the eastern, rising side of the chart.
[441] Again, this either means dynamically cadent, or specifically being in the western, sinking side of the chart, coming down from the MC towards the IC.
[442] Reading somewhat uncertainly for والتي ينشؤ عليها.
[443] This section is based on *Tet.* III.13 (Robbins p. 335); note that Ptolemy does not limit the following to the Ascendant, but makes it part of his general method (so probably pertains to Mercury and the Moon, too).

master of suitable intentions, desiring what is upright and the good, having determination in his religion, and the goodness of his conduct, concealing[444] the secrets he hears, generous, of good opinions, loving wisdom.

2 And if those having two bodies are rising, then that native will not be firm, having an opinion about one secret thought while not comprehending its depth, and his deception is easy, having two perspectives, loving women and impregnating, and comfort, and lazy in many things, desiring, quick to regret.

3 And if the fixed signs are rising, then that native will be hard, not retreating from what he wants, stubborn, patient, enduring hardship, spiteful, not yielding to anyone, self-controlled,[445] loving leadership, haughty in pride, desirous, eager, not being turned away from what he wants.

Chapter [1.36]: The knowledge of health, intelligence, foolishness, & other things pertaining to morals

1 If[446] the Ascendant of the native was the signs which resemble people, then the native will be gentle, dignified; and one born in the resemblances of something else of the signs will be virtually like those signs. **2** And if the native's Ascendant was Leo, Virgo, and Sagittarius, then he will be strong; and as for Pisces, Cancer, and Capricorn, one born with them will be weak. **3** And as for increase and decrease,[447] one born at the beginning of these signs which are Aries and <Taurus and>[448] Leo, will be increasing[449] because the beginnings of those signs are increasing, and their ends are decreasing.

4 Now as for health and ailments, one born at the beginning of Sagittarius, Scorpio, and Aquarius[450] will be healthy, and one born at their ends will be weak, ailing: because the beginnings of these signs are healthy, and their ends weak.

---

[444] Reading as يغشى, but its pairing with the preposition عن does not make sense to me.
[445] Tentatively reading محكوم ليفسه for مكوم لنفسه.
[446] Sentences **1-7** are based on *Tet.* III.11 (Robbins, pp. 315-17), which however is about body type, not character. So for example, in **5** Ptolemy discusses signs which have a balanced physical shape, while in Sahl these become balanced *personalities*.
[447] I am not sure whether this means bodily size, or the general course of the native's constitution.
[448] Adding with Ptolemy.
[449] That is, stronger in the upper body (Ptolemy).
[450] In Ptolemy, this is Gemini.

5 And as for temperateness and centeredness, Virgo, Libra, and Sagittarius are temperate, centered: so one born in them will be centered, temperate, intelligent.

6 And as for affection[451] and foolishness, Scorpio, Pisces, and Taurus indicate affection: so one born in them will be more foolish.

7 And these things I have described prove true in mixing.[452]

[The lord of the Ascendant]

8 Then,[453] look at the lord of the Ascendant and its conditions. **9** For if it was one of the superior planets, and it was eastern, in its own glow, free of the planets harmful to it, then the native will be healthy, quick in youth; now if it was received along with what I mentioned he will be praised, honored by his family, praised among the people, loved, attaining [what] he needs. **10** And if, along with what I mentioned, the sign it was in was of its own nature, he will be good of soul, fine in character. **11** Now if an infortune looked at it, anxieties and ailments will enter upon him, of the essence of the sign in which that infortune is. **12** And if the lord of the Ascendant was western, and the sign was of the infortunes, he will have little increase except that he will be safe from diseases. **13** Now if an infortune looked at it or a planet harmful to it (such as the lord of the sixth and the lord of the twelfth), he will have many diseases in relation to the essence of the sign in which the planet harmful to him is. **14** Now if it was received along with what I said, he will be honored in his family, loved among the people. **15** And if the sign in which it is, was of its own nature, he will be good of soul, fine in character. **16** And if the lord of the Ascendant was under the rays, he will be weak in his mind, and he will have a hidden illness. **17** Now if an infortune looked at it along with what I said, it will be worse for his condition and he will die a bad manner of death; and if a fortune [which was] appropriate for it looked at it, there will be a treatment for what it indicates of illness.

---

[451] مودة. This seems to mean that affection is linked to foolishness (not opposed to it) because affection and love can sway the mind that way. Thanks to Steven Birchfield for suggesting this.

[452] That is, combine this with all of the other planetary characteristics, to get a sense of the native's temperament and constitution (or here, personality).

[453] This subsection could be an adaptation of many statements in *Tet.* III.11 and *Tet.* III.13.

18 And if the lord of the Ascendant was of the inferior planets, then let there be a judgment in it in [its] easternness and westernness: because the inferior planets are the strongest they can be in the indication if they were in the west and they are coming out from under the rays without retrogradation, or when they come out from under the rays in the east and they are retrograde.

19 And as for the Moon, the fullness is her retrogradation; then [when] she is in other than that, the strongest she can be is in the west, for she is increasing in light, and in the east decreasing in light.[454] **20** Now if the Moon was received, it indicates the goodness of the upbringing and the native will be loved, having many friends.

[The governor of the Moon]

21 Then look at the Moon and who is looking at her, and in whose house she is, and whose bound, and whose triplicity, and whose image:

22 For if the Moon was in the house of Venus or with her, or looking at her, then the native will be a lover of entertainment and delights, and have a fine way of life, and a good character, a master of pleasures (and that will be according to the position of the Moon and the nature in which are the lords of the triplicities of the glowing one which has the indication of the testimony).[455]

23 Now if the Moon associated with Jupiter, then the native will be powerful in what he intends, elevated to [a position] of authority and integrity, uprightness and commendable action, he will be lucky for the people of his house, his siblings, and mother.

24 Now if the governor of that was Mars, then he will be wicked, bold, a master of toil and trouble, and labor and travels, a lover of fighting and the cavalry, and what is like that.

25 And if the governor of that was the Sun, and the Moon was looking at him by the aspect of a trine, then he will be of the powerful and kings, or of

---

[454] That is, when she comes out from under the rays so as to appear in the west in the evening, she is powerful; but when waning so as to appear before the Sun in the east in the morning, she is weaker.

[455] The "glowing one" means a luminary, and in this context of having the "indication of the testimony," this must mean the sect light. So, Sahl wants us to look at the triplicity lord of the sect light.

their friends, or of those associating with them, and it indicates good fortune as well as affliction in relation to his father.

26 And if the governor of that was Mercury, then it indicates hardship, wickedness, education and knowledge, contentions, and tricks.

27 And if the governor of that was Saturn, it indicates coldness, deceit, and toil in [his] way of life and acquisition; but if with that Saturn was eastern, then he will be of the masters of villages, contracts, and superb building.

[The lord of the Ascendant, again]

28 And know that if you found the lord of the Ascendant to be Saturn and he is in a stake, and Venus is with him or in <his>[456] stake, and Jupiter, Mercury, and the Moon are falling away from them, the native will emerge soft, resembling women, and love sweetness[457] with them, and their ways, and he will be feminized. **29** Now if Venus was inspecting Jupiter from a stake and Jupiter was also in a stake of Saturn, then the native will be eager for women and debauchery, and he will not be feminized, and that will be concealed.

30 And if Mars was the lord of the Ascendant and he is in a stake, and Venus with him or in his stake, and Saturn, Jupiter, and Mercury fell away from them both, then he will be an outstanding personality,[458] debauched, eager for debauchery, his interest appearing in that, and he will not care what is said about him in that. **31** Now if you found Mercury with Venus and they were both in a stake of Mars or his assembly, and Jupiter fell [away], he will emerge a sodomite, loving women as well as boys, and not eager for what is permitted; and the love of boys will predominate in him unless Mercury is retrograde or in his fall or under the rays: for [then] the love of women will appear and he will conceal the love of boys. **32** And if you found Mercury in a strong house, and he had a claim in it, and you found Venus retrograde or in her own fall or under the rays, then[459] the love of boys will appear and he will conceal the love of women.

---

[456] Adding based on **30** below.
[457] Reading الحلاوة for الحلوة.
[458] Or more concretely and perhaps to the point, a "stallion" (فحل).
[459] Reversing the order of "boys" and "women" in this sentence, as the scribe seems to have repeated the end of the previous sentence.

33 And if you found Jupiter to be the lord of the Ascendant and he is in a stake of the Ascendant or its triplicity, and Mercury was with him or had a partnership with him, and the two infortunes fell away from them both, then the native will emerge knowledgeable, God-fearing, a jurist, loving the search for knowledge, and enjoining the people to good, and studying much knowledge, and not loving debauchery, and seeking what is permitted. **34** Now if you found Venus with Jupiter and they were both devoid of the infortunes, then he will emerge eager for what is permitted and will seek women, and will not love what is forbidden. **35** Then, look at the Moon: for if you found her inspecting Jupiter in a male sign and in a masculine region, then he will emerge eager for women and will not remain with one woman.

36 And likewise the rest of the planets according to their kinds.

[Direction of motion and relation to Sun]

37 And know that the eastern planets indicate virtuousness and soundness, not deceiving anyone, prudent,[460] [with] the good appearing.

38 And[461] if a planet was retrograde, then the native will be rough, foolish. **39** Then especially, if that was Mercury from whom the matter of the soul and its burdens is known, he will have much endurance, patience, powerful in ambition, emerging rigorous. **40** And if he was in his second station[462] or western, then that native will not have a fixed view, and he will regret quickly, and be changed from thing to thing, and he will be weak, a coward, despised, vain about his own opinion. **41** And if he was under the rays of the Sun, it indicates love and equivocation.[463]

---

[460] Also, "discreet," "resolute," "judicious" (حازم).
[461] For **38-39**, see also **70-71** below.
[462] Lit., "second retrogradation."
[463] This should probably be understood as "the love *of* equivocation." See this repeated in **71** below.

[Mercury as intellect and knowledge][464]

42 Then,[465] look at Mercury, for he is the lightest of these planets. **43** For if you found him associating with a planet, then it will convert him to that essence and its indication: so if he was in a house of Mars, it indicates that the native will be effective, steadfast, knowledgeable, and especially if Mars was with him. **44** And if he was in a house of Saturn, it indicates that he will be spiteful, having depth, being secretive, an investigator, looking into religions and books. **45** And if he was in a house of Jupiter, then he will be praised, discerning in books and knowledge, received among the powerful. **46** And if he was in a house of Venus, then he will be a lover of crafts, charity, and gentleness, a master of amusement, women, and delights. **47** And if he was in the house of the Moon, then he will be one having knowledge in hidden, concealed things. **48** And you ought to look likewise at the planets which are in the house of Mercury and his bounds, for they will produce their own testimonies and power, and the native will incline towards their essences. **49** And if he was in the house of the Sun, it indicates writing and dignity.

50 And know that if Mercury was eastern, it indicates cleverness and intelligence, and greed in what the native wants of the goodness of education; and if he was western, it indicates he will reach it after trouble and a long time. **51** And[166] know that the benefit from the writing, education, and praise will not come to be unless Mercury is with Jupiter or inspecting him or mixing with him.

[Other planets indicating the mind]

52 And for the rest of the planets, if one of them was in the exaltation of another, or[467] the bound, house, or triplicity of another, then you ought to blend their power and make your statement based on that. **53** If Venus[468] was in a house of Mars or[469] his bound, it indicates the love of women and infamy

---

[464] For this subsection, cf. also Ch. 9.5, **5-16**.
[465] This paragraph may be based on *Carmen* II.36.
[466] See also Ch. 9.6, **46**.
[467] The text reads "and" here and later in the sentence, but I take it in the sense of "or."
[468] Sentences **53-57** read very similarly to *Carmen* II.35.
[469] Again, the text reads "and."

with them, and especially if Mars looked at her. **54** Now if Venus was in a house of Jupiter, it indicates abstinence. **55** And if she was in a house of Saturn, it indicates [*uncertain*][470] and the badness of the marriage, and especially in Capricorn. **56** And if she was in a house of Mercury, she indicates pairing up with slave girls and youths, and the masters of amusement. **57** And if she was in a house of Jupiter, she indicates the excellence of the marriage and the ugliness[471] of action. **58** And if she was in the house of the Moon, she indicates a desire for women. **59** And speak in that if the lord of the house is looking at her (I mean Venus), just as Jupiter looking at Venus indicates benefit from women; and likewise when she is in a house of Mars, you ought to impose her indication just as I picked from the essence of the planets.

60 And if Mars was in a house of Jupiter, it indicates sharpness[472] and steadfastness. **61** And if he was in a house of Venus, it indicates softness and infamy in sex. **62** And if he was in a house of Mercury, it indicates cleverness and knowledge. **63** And if he was in a house of Saturn, it indicates malice and reputation.[473] **64** And if he was in the house of the Moon it indicates illness and troubles. **65** And if he was in the house of the Sun it indicates harms as well as delights, and likewise one who is in[474] a house of Mars.

66 And if you found Jupiter in a house of Saturn or with Saturn, it indicates the love of architecture, building, and lands. **67** And if he was in a house of Venus, it indicates benefit from women. **68** And speak likewise for the rest of the houses in the manner of the essence of the lord of the house in which Jupiter is.

[*More considerations*]

69 And[475] if Mercury was with the Moon, he will have much contemplation, attention,[476] and contentions.

---

[470] الحدق.

[471] قبح. But this does not make astrological sense, so must be in error.

[472] الحدّة, which has a wide range of meanings pertaining to violence, anger, being impetuous, and so on.

[473] Or more likely, a "bad" reputation.

[474] Or perhaps, *if* he is in (reading إن for من).

[475] For this sentence, see also **75** below.

[476] This word (اهتمام) can also imply concern and anxiety; the sense is perhaps of someone who is obsessive or thinks too emotionally.

70 And if the planet was under the rays, it indicates love and equivocation.[477] **71** And[478] if the planet was retrograde, then the native will be rough, foolish, especially if it was Mercury from whom the matter of the soul and its actions are understood: because if Mercury was with the Moon or in her[479] house, he complements her indication and brings her essence to light.[480]

72 And[481] if the planet was retrograde, it indicates that he will be wild[482] in reason, infamous, angry, with many enemies, and especially by day. **73** Now if it looked at it,[483] pain and toil and beating will afflict the native, and likewise if it was in the seventh.

74 And if Mercury was in the seventh, and he is made unfortunate, then it will be bad, because evil gossip will be said about him, and it will be something of [*uncertain*];[484] and if a fortune looked, it will improve that. **75** And[485] if you found Mercury with the Moon he will have much contemplation, attention, and contentions. **76** And when you find Mercury with Mars or with Saturn, then speak about evil and tribulation in the nativity because of speech and contention. **77** And if you found Mars looking down upon Mercury, looking at the Moon, and Saturn is in a house of Mercury, tribulation and powerful misfortunes will afflict the native because of books, confinement, beating, and fighting, [and] whispering,[486] and especially if Mars was <in> the Midheaven or in the place of the seventh, eighth, or second.[487]

---

[477] See **41** above.
[478] For this sentence, cf. **38-39** above.
[479] Grammatically, this should be "his own" house (نفسه), but that does not make sense here because Sahl is speaking about combining them.
[480] This is still unclear to me, because both the Moon and Mercury are grammatically masculine in Arabic. I am reading the sentence as though Mercury draws out her essence, but she could equally be said to bring out his essence. Steven Birchfield suggests that since Mercury takes on other planets' characteristics, if he takes on the Moon he will highlight her characteristics, especially since they both pertain to the mind.
[481] See also **38** above.
[482] Tentatively reading واحشًا for واحسًا.
[483] It is unclear who is looking at whom in this sentence.
[484] The text seems to read النعال.
[485] For this sentence, cf. **69** above.
[486] Tentatively reading for وسوسا, which suggests the root وسوس ("to whisper"); but it might be a version of شوش, which implies confusion.
[487] Perhaps this should read "the twelfth," as the twelfth is a bad place and in Arabic is written as "second-ten," as though the "ten" was omitted by a scribe.

[Māshā'allāh on the lord of the Ascendant in the houses]

78 Then, look at the lord of the Ascendant and its course in the signs. **79** Now if the lord of the Ascendant was in the Ascendant, the native will be respected in his family. **80** And if it connected with a planet in the Midheaven, he will come to a powerful rank from the Sultan, if the planet which it connects with was in its own house; and if it was in its exaltation, he will gain status from the Sultan and kings. **81** And if it was in its fall, he will gain rank through the loss of his religion and honor. **82** And just as I described [to you] in the section on the Midheaven,[488] speak about all of the signs, [both] those beneficial to the Ascendant and harmful to it, for the native's condition is based on what happens to [his] indicator. **83** The lord of the Ascendant in the second: he will be a corruptor of assets; and if the lord of its house looked at it, and it was received, he will gain properly, and the gain will be from the essence of the sign the lord of the second is in. **84** The lord of the Ascendant in the third: he will have siblings suitable for him, [gaining] good from him, and he will be dependent upon them, and travel much. **85** And if a fortune looked at it, he will have good religion; and if an infortune looked at it, he will be wicked in his mind. **86** The lord of the Ascendant in the fourth: he will be reverent towards his parents, and he will experience hardship from the Sultan, and he will have a livelihood he is pleased with; and if it was received in its position, he will gain good or rank from [his] fathers. **87** The lord of the Ascendant in the fifth: he will be happy with children, and he will have many friends; and if an infortune looked, it undermines that. **88** The lord of the Ascendant in the sixth: he will be miserable, doing the work of slaves; now if it was received, illnesses will happen to him.[489] **89** And if the Moon was also corrupted, and connecting with a planet in a corrupt place, he will be a slave. **90** The lord of the Ascendant in the seventh: he will have many lawsuits, and will be deceptive, [and] subordinate to women in their speech. **91** The lord of the Ascendant in the eighth: he will have a wicked soul, much distress, be faint-hearted. **92** The lord of the Ascendant in the ninth: he will remain in a land that is not the one he was born in, and it multiplies [his] travels, and he will speak about knowledge; now if it was free of the infortunes, he will be knowledgeable and sensible. **93** The lord of the

---

[488] Reference uncertain.

[489] Since reception improves a situation, Māshā'allāh seems to be saying it's better to be sick than to be a slave.

Ascendant in the tenth: he will be at the doors of the Sultan, and will be known by him, make himself known [to him], and will live due to them. **94** The lord of the Ascendant in the eleventh: he will have a good character, many friends, [but] harsh towards children, having few children.[490] **95** The lord of the Ascendant in the twelfth: he will be miserable, with a bad livelihood, many enemies [who] will be victorious over him. **96** Now if it does not connect with a planet in a stake or in an excellent place from the Ascendant and the planet [is] in its nature, he will be miserable until he is ruined. **97** And if the planet which it connects with is an infortune or it has [something] harmful to it, enemies will kill him.

Chapter [1.37]: The positions of the Lot of Fortune in the signs

[Māshā'allāh on the Lot of Fortune][491]

1 The Lot of Fortune and its lord indicate the condition of the body just as the Ascendant and its lord do, because the Lot of Fortune is "the Ascendant of the Moon,"[492] just as <the Ascendant [itself]> is the Ascendant of the Sun. **2** And the knowledge of that is if you multiplied what has already passed of the day by what [is] the houses of the portions of its hours,[493] then you cast it out from the place of the Moon, [and] it will be cut off at the position of the Lot of Fortune. **3** And likewise the Lot of Fortune is the Ascendant of the Moon by night, and likewise the Lot of the Invisible by day is the Ascendant of the Moon.[494]

4 If the Lot of Fortune was <advancing>,[495] an infortune not associating with it, and it not under the rays, and its lord was also like that, it indicates

---

[490] This seems to be because the eleventh is opposed to the fifth; nevertheless this interpretation seems unlikely.

[491] Cf. Tehran, Dānishgāh, Nafīsī 429 (67b-68b); Majlis 17490 (130-32).

[492] See *Tet.* III.10 (Robbins p. 277).

[493] Reading as فيما بيوت أجزاء ساعاته, which is evidently some kind of calculation based on the time of day.

[494] Māshā'allāh now describes the usual formulas for the Lot of Fortune: by day from the Sun to the Moon and by night the reverse, the result being projected from the degree of the Ascendant.

[495] Adding with Māshā'allāh, here and below.

(by the permission of God) the soundness of the native and the goodness of his upbringing; now if it was made unfortunate or under the rays, it indicates the native's weakness and the hardship of his upbringing. **5** And if its lord was like that and they were both under the rays, he will encounter hardship from the Sultan. **6** Now if it was in the Ascendant, it will be harsher for his condition;[496] but if it was free of the infortunes and the rays, he will be sound, with a good form and body, flourishing, of a good character, generous in soul, wealthy.

7 The Lot of Fortune in the second from the Ascendant: if the lord of the Ascendant looked at it or at its lord, he will be fortunate, with much good, gaining assets without [his own] provisions; and if it does not look at it, but one of the luminaries looked at it or at its lord, and without harm to it, he will have a good livelihood, he will live by reason of the Sultan. **8** And if nothing of what I mentioned is looking at it, what he gains will [only] be what he eats day by day; and if it was made unfortunate, he will have a wicked way of life.

9 Now if it was in the third, it indicates the uprightness of the siblings and the goodness of their condition, if the lord of the third was looking at its own place and was received; and if the lord of the twelfth or tenth looked at it, he will have authority over prisons and the captured. **10** Now if an infortune was with it in the third, it indicates the ruin of the siblings; and if along with what I mentioned <the lord of the third> was made unfortunate or entering into burning, he will not have siblings.

11 And if it was in the fourth, free of the infortunes, and its lord likewise looking at it, it indicates the health of the native and it assists in wealth and respect among the people, and rank with [his] parents, and the goodness of their condition. **12** And if it was made unfortunate it indicates the badness of the parents' condition, and the difficulty of [his] upbringing.

13 Now if it was in the fifth, free of the infortunes and the rays, it indicates the goodness of the native's condition in that (if God wills), and likewise its corruption indicates the corruption of the children.

14 And in the sixth it indicates the badness of the native's condition; now if along with what I mentioned the lord of the Ascendant is not looking at the Ascendant, nor the lord of the Lot at the Lot, then <he will be expelled>[497] from his own land and will become a slave. **15** And if they were both in their own place, received, and the fortunes look at them both, he will

---

[496] That is, if it was in the poor condition just mentioned.
[497] Adding what seems to be the word from Māshā'allāh.

be released from slavery and will do the work of free people; <and if according to what I mentioned they were both made unfortunate or in a bad place, then he will be a miserable slave>. **16** And if they were both retrograde, he will not have an upbringing, <and likewise too if it connected with a retrograde star; while if [only] one of them was retrograde, he will have an upbringing but he will not be content and his upbringing is made harsh>.

17 And in the seventh, if the native had a lifespan, it indicates marriage. **18** Now if the lord of the seventh was free of the infortunes, looking at its own place, it indicates that he will gain what is good from women (if God wills), and joy, and they will love him very much. **19** If it was made unfortunate, he will not marry, and he will be embarrassed by what is said about him, and his sexual intercourse will be corrupted, and if it was under the rays he will associate with [women] in secret.

20 And in the eighth, if its lord was received, free of the infortunes, looking at the Ascendant and its lord, <he will be blessed with inheritances and because of the dead. **21** Now if it is not looking at the Ascendant and its lord>, and the lord of the second testifies to it, he will be separated from his assets and squander them; and if it was made unfortunate, he will have a humble soul, doing difficult work, and he will blame himself for the ruin he fears. **22** Now if along with what I mentioned the lord of the Ascendant was also corrupted, he will have a short lifespan; and if it was retrograde, he will not have an upbringing.

23 And in the ninth it indicates that the native will move house, and [it indicates] his travel; and if the lord of the Ascendant was in the ninth sign, he will remain abroad and not return to his own land, and he will be pious if it was free of the infortunes (and if it was made unfortunate, he will be weak [in his faith]).[498]

24 And in the tenth sign, it indicates that he will be known at the door of the Sultan, and his livelihood will be because of that. **25** Now if its lord was free of the infortunes, looking at the lord of the Ascendant or it is received, then he will gain authority; and if it was made unfortunate, he will have a bad livelihood and profit.

---

[498] Reading uncertainly for Sahl's "he will be effeminate." This phrase is not in Māshā'allāh and so cannot be checked against it.

26 And in the eleventh, its lord being received,[499] he will be respected, of a good upbringing, he will live because of the people, and will be devoted to God.

27 And in the twelfth, its lord being made unfortunate, it indicates the native's misery; and if the lord of the Ascendant was retrograde or entering into burning, he will not have a lifespan. **28** And if the lord of the Ascendant was free of the infortunes, and the lord of the Lot made unfortunate, and it is looking at it, and the one making it unfortunate is the lord of the eighth from the Ascendant (or the seventh or fourth), then the native will kill himself.

☵   ☙   ☙

29 And[500] if you found the Lot or its lord made unfortunate or burned, they indicate the native's sickliness and his misery.

30 And[501] if the Lot occurred in Capricorn, the native will be sluggish; and if it occurred in Aries, Leo, Taurus, or Scorpio, he will be keen, having bile.

31 And you ought to see what is the nature of the sign the Lot and its lord are in: because if the Lot was in a moist sign, and its lord likewise, then he will gain assets in relation to moisture, or a great matter.

32 And if the planets are not looking at the Lot, its lord, and the Ascendant, it indicates corruption at the beginning of his matter[502] and its end; and if they separated from the Ascendant but looked at the Lot and its lord, they indicate good at the beginning and corruption at the end.

33 And[503] if the Lot was looking at the Lot of religion or knowledge, where[ever] it is, they indicate the good. **34** And if they separated from it and from the stakes and from the eleventh, or from the Ascendant, where[ever] they were, it indicates downfall and weakness and indifference,[504] and especially in nocturnal [charts].

---

[499] Māshā'allāh has, "free of the infortunes."
[500] Compare this with Ch. 9.5, **70**, which concerns the Lot of religion.
[501] Compare this with Ch. 9.5, **72**, which concerns the Lot of religion.
[502] أمر ه. But this might better be read as عمر ه, "lifespan."
[503] Compare this sentence with Ch. 9.5, **69**, which concerns the Lot of Fortune and Lot of religion.
[504] Or, "flabbiness, slowness," etc.

[Valens on the Lot of Fortune]

35 And[505] if you found the Lot made unfortunate from an opposition, it indicates his chronic illness, up to 7 years; and if it was from the right triplicity,[506] then up to 9 years; and if it was from its right square, up to 10 years; and if it was from its left trine, up to 3 years;[507] and if it was from the twelfth from it, then up to 12 years; and if it was in the second from it, then up to 2 years—if a fortune is not looking.

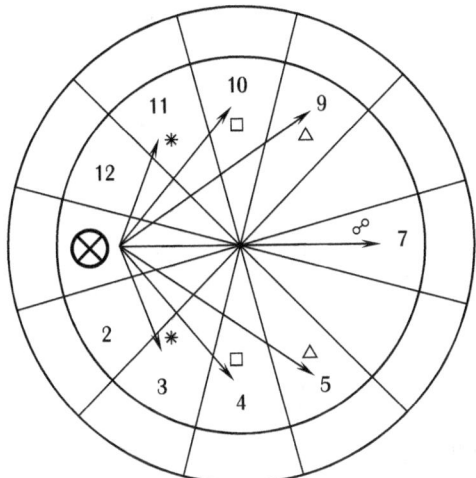

Figure 55: Years given by planets making the Lot of Fortune unfortunate (*Anth.* III.12)

36 And[508] if you found the Lot in Aries, then report that it will afflict him in 19 years; and if it was in Taurus, then in 25 years; and if it was in Gemini,

---

[505] The following material is based on Valens, *Anth.* III.12, and is probably from the *Bizidaj*. See also Sahl, *Nativities* Ch. 6.5, **4-5**. But note that in Valens, these positions show how often crises happen, not how long they last (as in Sahl). So if an infortune is in the fourth from the Lot, Valens says there will be a crisis "every four years," not one that will *last for four years*.

[506] That is, trine.

[507] This should be 11, at least in the fuller version according to al-Rijāl.

[508] This paragraph is also based on *Anth.* III.12 (and is probably from the *Bizidaj*), but note that Sahl's source uses the Lot itself instead of its lord, and gets many of the years wrong. See also Sahl, *Nativities* Ch. 6.5, **6-7**. In the Valens scheme, the triplicities are populated by

then in 10 years; and if it was in Cancer, then in 15 years; and if it was in Leo, then in 12 years; and if it was in Virgo, then in 8 years; and if it was in Libra, then in 30 years; and if it was in Scorpio, then in 15 years; and if it was in Sagittarius, then in 42 years; and if it was in Capricorn, then in 50 years; and if it was in Aquarius, in 30 years; and if it was in Pisces, 14 years – and that is if a fortune is not looking at it.

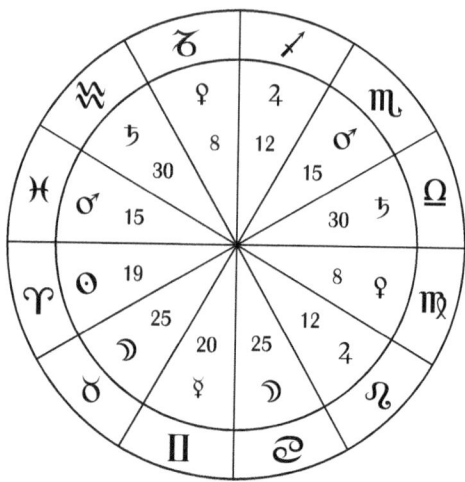

Figure 56: Frequency of illness, from the Lot of Fortune (*Anth.* III.12)

[Chapter 1.38: Categories of the signs]

1 The signs having two feet and four: Gemini, Libra, and Aquarius have two feet; Aries, Leo, Taurus have four feet; and the <first> half of Sagittarius has two feet, and the other has four feet.

2 The signs[509] having an ailment in the eyes if a native is born in them: Cancer (due to the position of the darkness which stimulates inflammation of the eye in it), Taurus (because of the position of the Pleiades), the mane of Leo, the stinger of Scorpio, Sagittarius (from the position of the arrowhead and the arrow), and the owner of the jug who pours out the water from Aquarius. **3** And some of the scholars said that these are signs of illnesses,

---

their two main triplicity lords; beginning with Aries, only the two main triplicity lords are used, with one of them taking up two signs. For fire, Sun-Jupiter-Jupiter; for earth, Moon-Venus-Venus; for air, Mercury-Saturn-Saturn; for water, Moon-Mars-Mars.

[509] See Ch. 6.2, especially **48ff**.

and [that] as for the signs of ailments, they are Aries, Taurus, Cancer, Scorpio, and Capricorn.

4 The signs having bellies are Sagittarius, Leo, Scorpio, Aries, and Taurus.

5 The signs of pleasures and passion are Aries, Taurus, Leo, and the faces[510] in the signs.

6 The signs of anxiety and sorrow are Leo and Scorpio.

7 The powerful signs are Taurus, Leo, and Virgo.

8 The signs of darkness are Libra, Capricorn.

9 And the burned place of the signs[511] is the end of Libra and the beginning of Scorpio.

10 The signs of deafness, muteness, and the sparseness of hair:[512] Aries, Cancer, Scorpio, Capricorn, Pisces, Sagittarius, and Aquarius.

11 What[513] resembles the image of people: Gemini and its triplicity, Virgo, and the beginning of Sagittarius (because, of its images, up to its head is an image of a man shooting, and from below that is the body of an archer). **12** Gemini belongs to powerful people, Libra to magistrates and to the masters of work,[514] Aquarius to the rabble, and one to whom one does not pay attention.[515]

13 The tranquil[516] ones of signs (and they are the ones having thought): Gemini, Virgo, Libra, and Scorpio.

14 The[517] signs of many children: Cancer, Scorpio, and Pisces are of many children. **15** A middling amount of children: Taurus, Gemini, Libra, Capricorn, Aquarius. **16** The barren ones: Leo, Virgo, and Sagittarius. **17** Some scholars said that Capricorn and Aquarius are barren, not having children.

---

[510] This may refer to the chapters in Rhetorius mentioned in Ch. 7.7. But surely the real source of this statement is Rhetorius Ch. 76, which lists: Aries, Taurus, Leo, part of Capricorn, and Libra (due to the rising of Capella with it). But see also **18-20** below.

[511] That is, the burned path or *via combusta*.

[512] Or more specifically, the beard.

[513] See also **46-47** below; Ch. 2.8, **4-9**; Ch. 4.5, **26-27**, and Ch. 6.10, **1**.

[514] That is, to everyone in the middle (see again below).

[515] See also Ch. 6.10, **1** for the slave classes (earthy signs).

[516] المخفضة, the same root used to mean "carefree" in **43** below. The use of "thought" here, and the combining of the humane signs with Scorpio, suggests that these are signs with much internal meditation or contemplation.

[517] For these, see also *Introduction* Ch. 1, **23-24**; *Nativities* Chs. 3, 10; 5.1, **8**; and *Carmen* II.10, **12-13**.

18 The[518] signs of much sexual intercourse: Aries, Taurus, Leo, and Pisces. **19** The signs of a middling amount of sexual intercourse: Gemini, Cancer, Sagittarius, and Capricorn. **20** The signs of little sexual intercourse: Virgo, Libra, Scorpio, and Aquarius.

21 The signs indicating yelling and lying if they were rising or the lord of the Ascendant was in them, or the Moon: and they are Gemini, Virgo, Libra, Scorpio, Sagittarius, and Pisces;[519] and they also indicate the generosity of the soul and its liberality, and a capacity for spending.

22 The signs indicating the chastity of women and their virtuousness: Taurus, Leo, Scorpio, and Aquarius. **23** The signs indicating their slackness and their corruption are Aries, Cancer, Libra, and Capricorn. **24** And the signs indicating the middle in their virtuousness are Gemini, Virgo, Sagittarius, and Pisces.

25 The signs[520] indicating the conditions of voices: indeed, the voiced signs with a powerful voice are Gemini, Virgo, and Libra. **26** And those with a balanced voice are those having half a voice: they are Aries, Taurus, Leo, and Sagittarius. **27** And those weak of voice are Capricorn and Aquarius. **28** And those which do not have a voice are Cancer and its triplicity. **29** So if Mercury was in a sign not having a voice and <*missing*>[521] is not looking at him with a suitable aspect, and he is made unfortunate, then the native's tongue will be corrupted, and his hearing; and perhaps he will be mute.

30 The[522] signs indicating itching, leprosy, muteness, baldness, stringy hair, and the armpit which does not have hair, are five: Aries, Cancer, Scorpio, <Capricorn>,[523] and Pisces.[524] **31** For if the Moon, the Lot of Fortune, or the Lot of the Invisible was in one of them, made unfortunate,[525] then it indicates that one of these ailments will afflict the native. **32** And when one of

---

[518] This is similar to the lecherous or licentious signs. In Rhetorius Ch. 5, these are Aries, Taurus, Capricorn, Pisces, and part of Pisces. But perhaps the more correct list is in his Ch. 76: Aries, Taurus, Leo, Capricorn (part), Pisces, Libra.
[519] But see **28**, as Pisces is a sign lacking a voice.
[520] Cf. *Introduction* Ch. 1, **20-22**.
[521] This is probably Saturn.
[522] For **30-31**, see Rhetorius Ch. 3. But for Rhetorius this has only to do with skin diseases, not baldness; the latter must have been added due to **32-33**.
[523] Adding with Rhetorius.
[524] Note that this is only four; also, what role does leprosy and itching play here? Maybe Sahl's source means any skin disease which makes the hair fall out. See also the use of signs in Ch. 6 below, and the repetition of this material below in **33**.
[525] In Rhetorius this is when *only* infortunes look at them.

these indicators is in one of these signs, and Jupiter is in the twelfth from the Ascendant, then the native will be bald; and likewise if the Moon was in them and she is under the rays.

33 Signs which indicate natives of baldness and [*uncertain*][526] if a native is born, [are if] the Moon is in Aries, Cancer, Capricorn, Scorpio, or Pisces: for they indicate that he will be bald, and especially if Jupiter was in the twelfth from the Ascendant, or the Moon or the lord of the hour was under the rays of the Sun.

34 And the signs of wickedness. **35** Now if the Moon was in Scorpio or Capricorn, and Saturn was looking down upon the Moon, and it was when she was departing from under the rays, then if she was in <this> state and governed something of the Ascendant, and the nativity was by night, and the lord of the sign diurnal, it indicates that he will have what belongs to men and women, and especially if Saturn was looking down upon Venus and the lord of the Ascendant was looking down upon Saturn. **36** And one whose planet (that is, the lord of the hour in which he was born) was male, and his Ascendant female, his inner mind and temperament will resemble men, but according to his [outward appearance],[527] females. **37** And one whose planet was female and his Ascendant male, his actions will be the actions of women, and his speech the speech of men. **38** And one whose planet and Ascendant were both male, his speech and actions will resemble men; and one whose planet and Ascendant were female, his speech and actions will resemble females.

39 A section on the knowledge of the degrees in which the native will reach nobility and rank (if God, be He exalted, wills). **40** If it happened that a native was born and his Ascendant was one of these degrees, or the Moon and Sun were in the equivalent of these degrees (and that is superior if it was

---

[526] The text reads الزمادة. But perhaps this could be a minority variation of الزمر, which means having little hair.

[527] Reading somewhat uncertainly for the unpointed سته or سه. An obvious reading would be "house," which suggests his outer build or construction but seems a bit of a stretch; less likely is هيئة, "appearance." One problem is that the following sentences speak of actions and speech (not the inner mind), and seem to apply them the other way around. My impression is that the planet ought to indicate character and thought, and the sign the outer appearance.

the Sun by day and by night the Moon), then he will reach exaltation and power, or he will rule many lands, by the permission of God:[528]

42 The signs which accumulate and squander, and grant and take [away]. **43** Aries, Leo, and Sagittarius accumulate, and they indicate a carefree life and comfort. **44** The signs which squander: Gemini, Libra, and Aquarius squander, and indicate squandering and extravagance. **45** The signs which take: Cancer, Scorpio, and Pisces take, and they indicate poverty unless they are made fortunate; Taurus, Virgo, and Capricorn grant, and they indicate ease and plenty.

♈	19°
♉	3°
♊	13°
♋	1°, 13°, 14°, 15°
♌	5°, 7°
♍	2°, 13°, 20°
♑	12°, 13°, 20°
♒	12°, 20°

Figure 57: Degrees of nobility and rank (*Nativities* Ch. 1.28, 41)

46 The[529] signs of the classes of people: the signs with reason indicate the types of people, and they are Gemini, Virgo, Libra, the first half of Sagittarius, <and Aquarius>. **47** Now as for Gemini, it belongs to the powerful and the nobles; and Virgo and Libra and the first half of Sagittarius to those in the middle; and Aquarius belongs to the lower class and those one does not pay attention to.

---

[528] The following is sentence **41**, put in the form of a table as it is simply a list of signs and degrees.

[529] See also **11-12** above, Ch. 2.8, **4-9**; Ch. 4.5, **26-27**; and Ch. 6.10, **1**.

Chapter 2: On assets, fortune, & livelihood

Comment by Dykes. In this chapter Sahl presents the seven classes of good fortune and misery from al-Andarzaghar. These are really clever cut-and-paste jobs from Dorotheus and others, which illustrate how (say) the triplicity lords of the sect light can show high prosperity, low-prosperity, and so on. However, Sahl's seven categories do not exactly match the neat organization of *BA*. Following is a table comparing the two:

Book of Aristotle	Sahl's Nativities
1. High: III.2.1	1. High: 2.2, 2.3, 2.5
2. High to low: III.2.2	2. High to low: *inserted below as #4*
3. Middling: III.2.3	3. Middling: 2.16
4. Low to high: III.2.4	4. High to low: 2.17-2.18
5. Low: III.2.5	5. Low to high: 2.19
6. Through own hands: III.2.6	6. Low: 2.20
7. Violence: III.2.6	7. Own hands, and injustice: 2.21

We can see in Ch. 2.1 that Sahl has inserted the "high to low" category (**4**) a second time (as **6**), off-setting the rest of the list by one category. But he also combines profiting from one's own hands and violence into one category (**9**) rather than splitting them as *BA* does. Of course, as usual Sahl also inserts material from Ptolemy, Māshā'allāh, and others in (2.6 - 2.15), so that his account is ultimately much richer than *BA*'s.

[Chapter 2.1: Classes of good fortune & misery: al-Andarzaghar]

1 In [their] books, the scholars have already and often dealt with, and established the topics in, good fortune and assets, from various areas; and I have already made comparisons in this whole subject, and have written for you powerful, correct sections. **2** And good fortune is based on seven approaches:

3 The first of them, on good fortune and how much that good fortune will come to.

4 Second, <on one who> falls from that good fortune.

5 Third, those whose livelihood is middling.

6 Fourth, the rabble [and] those who come down from an ascent to a downfall.

7 Fifth, those who rise up after wretchedness.

8 Sixth, the wretched who do not cease to be in wretchedness.

9 Seventh, those whose profit comes from their own hands.[1]

[Chapter 2.2: On those who always have the greatest good fortune, from al-Andarzaghar]

1 Now as for the greatest good fortune, and nobility and reputation, start by looking at the fixed stars:[2] for if you found one of them with the degree of the Ascendant or the degree of the Midheaven, or with the Sun or Moon, that will be more renowned for his nobility. **2** And when and where you found one of them with one of the seven planets (and the strongest of them is the Sun and Moon), you state approximately what their indication is when one of them happens to be in the Ascendant or in the Midheaven—but preferable to that is if the fixed star is with the planet which is more dominant for that native (and that is the lord of the Ascendant), for that indicates that native's elevation, and it makes his ability more powerful in what its sign resembles.

---

[1] And from violence and injustice, as we will see below in Ch. 2.21.

[2] See the end of the chapter for a table of these, and my comments. These stars are found in Rhetorius Ch. 58, but there are some mix-ups in Sahl. The most important one is that Sahl has followed al-Andarzaghar by inserting a Jupiter-Mercury category too early and with an extra, wrong star (**20-25**), but then added the correct Jupiter-Mercury category in its own place where Rhetorius does (**45-48**), with an interpretation not actually in Rhetorius.

3 And if the Moon conjoined with one of them, it indicates noble-heartedness in operation, and the greatness of [its] gift.

4 And if the fixed stars were of the complexion of the infortunes, then they likewise elevate but bring criticism[3] just as an infortune brings criticism.

5 And know that if all of the planets in the nativity were made unfortunate, falling, and one of these fixed stars was in the degree of the Ascendant or Midheaven, or was with the Sun or Moon, or the lord of the Ascendant, then they do elevate the native and he will reach [high] status, but none of the people of his house will wish nobility or social rank for him.

6 And if you found them too with the rest of the planets, and especially if those planets were northern or southern just like the latitude of the fixed stars,[4] and especially if they were in the bright degrees: for then, said *Sibārmahnar*,[5] the master of the scholars, the native will be an elevated lord, and astonishing the people from his height; and it is more excellent if it was with a fortune, in the house of a fortune, or in the bound of a fortune. **7** And I will explain to you the positions of the fixed stars in the northern <and southern> signs.

[Stars of Venus-Mercury]

8 Spica,[6] in Libra, in 20' of it, northern, of the first magnitude.
9 Vega,[7] in Sagittarius, in 24°, northern, of the first magnitude.
10 Fomalhaut,[8] in Aquarius, 12° 50', northern, of the first magnitude.[9]

---

[3] تتعقّب. This can also refer to repentance and doubt following an action (here, being raised up), or inflicting punishment.
[4] That is, if the planet is in northern ecliptical latitude, and so is the star.
[5] Unknown (سبار مهنر); see the Introduction for more on this name.
[6] α Virgo, lit. "the defenseless one" (الأعزل), because unlike its rough opposite Arcturus, it does not have a weapon near it.
[7] α Lyra, lit., "the Falling Vulture"; Sahl does not use the Persian name which Hugo used for BA, so he has converted al-Andarzaghar's Persian word to Arabic.
[8] α Piscis Austrinus, lit. "the following one" (الرّدف), but it also came to mean a star that rises in the east when its opposite sets in the west (in which case its associated star must be Regulus, another royal fixed star). The usual name Fomalhaut means "mouth of the fish."
[9] This list is incomplete. In order to follow Rhetorius (as described by Burnett and Pingree in their table in *BA*, p. 147), al-Andarzaghar should have added Alphecca (α Corona Borealis) as a fifth star, but he has put it below in **20** as one of the Jupiter-Mercury stars, with its description in **24**. He also should have added Deneb Adige (α Cygnus) as a fourth star, for

11 These three stars are of the first magnitude, of the complexion of Venus and Mercury.

12 If you found one of them in the degree of the Ascendant or the degree of the Midheaven, the native will be known, famous, fortunate, with much knowledge, elevated, a philosopher, a discusser of wisdom, having chemistry,[10] singing will impress him, having many servants,[11] a lover of amusement, pleased, delighted, ready to give answers, tending to get involved in matters, proficient in works, lucky in every work he does, truthful, studying knowledge by himself (but not doing things), and not speaking except with intelligence and knowledge, loving that he is praised because of the excellence of his speech,[12] serious, clean, sweet in speech and voice,[13] loving good health, stable in friendship, far from care, with much sexual intercourse, he will love women, a cultured man, loving worship and generosity, and inventing wonderful things in crafts, and especially if Mars is eastern, above the earth, and he is looking at Venus.

13 And if you found one of the three in the Ascendant, it increases [the chart's] owner in [his] search for knowledge and jurisprudence, unless Mars was in the Ascendant: for if he was in the Ascendant, it undermines that. **14** And if Mars was with one of them, it increases his passions, and especially if Mars was with the Sun in the Ascendant. **15** But if Venus or Mars were in the house of fathers or with one of the fixed stars which we mentioned, or one of the three was in the house of marriage, then his good fortune will be converted to tribulation, and he will be wicked or feminized, not able to do it with women, or all of his children will be females, because their indication will be for illnesses, harm, females, and depriving [him] of women and male children—because these fixed stars convert to what is bad if Venus and Mars were with them in the stakes. **16** Now if they[14] were in something other than the stakes, looking at one of the fixed stars, they indicate culture, and

---

a total of five Venus-Mercury stars, but it is totally omitted in both the Latin *BA* and in Sahl. (Note that the text in **11**, **13**, and **15** refers to "three" stars, so Sahl is not accidentally omitting something which al-Andarzaghar had included. Holden's Rhetorius also omits it, so perhaps not all of the copies of Rhetorius contained it.) See my table at the end of this chapter.

[10] Or rather, having chemical or alchemical knowledge.
[11] Reading الخدم for الحذم; but this might also be الحزم, "determination."
[12] Reading somewhat loosely, with the sense of Rhetorius.
[13] Reading صوتًا for صولًا. But perhaps it could be سؤلًا, "request, petition."
[14] But Rhetorius has Saturn here, looking at one of these stars while he is in the Ascendant.

knowledge in the secrets of books and eloquence, along with knowledge in medicine and what is useful.[15]

17 And if Jupiter witnessed one of these named stars, or looked at them, they increase his good fortune, nobility, and elevation, and they indicate luckiness and leadership, and certainly the wondrous things of the fixed stars.

18 And if you found Mercury with any of them in the Ascendant or in the Midheaven, he will speak with speech resembling prophecy, and he will be mighty in the eyes of the people, and will be elevated over them, and he will be a philosopher, of those who love knowledge, being proficient in [all] matters, and the knowledge of secrets, and especially one born in the clime of Babylon.

19 And[16] one born by night in this manner will be a worshipper of idols, speaking with speech resembling prophesy, feminine in manners, and he will be of those who have knowledge of magic spells, and work talismans and marvels with their own hands, and will be passionately fond of that until tribulation afflicts them.

[Stars of Jupiter-Mercury][17]

20 Also, a fixed star called the Northern Crown,[18] in Libra 15° 20', northern.

21 And another in Gemini (the rear head),[19] in 27°.

---

[15] Tentatively reading the verbal noun الترّفق.

[16] I am not certain if this is a general statement or continues the thought about Mercury in the previous paragraph.

[17] At this point something has gone wrong. Al-Andarzaghar should have continued on to the Jupiter–Mars stars at **26**, but instead he adds here an extra Jupiter-Mercury category. The first star is Alphecca (**20**, with its Rhetorian description in **24**), which should have appeared as the fifth star in the Venus-Mercury list above: so it is totally misplaced. The other two are Castor and Zuben Eschemali (**21-22**, with their Rhetorian description in **25**), which are indeed Jupiter-Mercury stars but are supposed to come later. Sahl may have recognized the mistake, because although he dutifully puts al-Andarzaghar's list here, later on he follows Rhetorius by inserting Castor and Zuben Eschemali where they appear in Rhetorius (**45-48**). Unfortunately, their description in **48** does not match Rhetorius: so the description is here (**25**), but they belong below (**45-46**).

[18] Alphecca, α Corona Borealis. Again, this and its description (**24**) should be included with the Venus-Mercury stars above.

22 And another fixed star in Libra,[20] 27° 50', northern.

23 These three stars are of the <second>[21] magnitude, <of the> complexion of Jupiter and Mercury.

24 And if you found one of these three in the Ascendant or in the Midheaven, and especially the one in Libra[22] (for that star is stronger than the other two, even though their complexion is one [and the same]), one born [like that, with] it being in the place which we mentioned, will be fortunate, experienced, friendly to the nobility, harsh [in using] violence, with a far-[reaching] voice, the family of his king love him, and he will be mighty, having superiority and leadership.

25 And [as for] these two other ones, one born with them will be a lover of knowledge, with many experiments, a preacher to the masses, with much general beneficence, a philosopher, loving God, deserving praise, thankful for[23] [his] gold and silver in the gathering of it, honored in his association with the people in [his] taking and giving, and especially one born by day; and nativities of the night will be famous, knowledgeable, intelligent, with many experiments,[24] pleasant.

[Stars of Jupiter-Mars]

26 And also, the Heart of Leo,[25] in Leo 6° 10', northern.
27 And the Heart of Scorpio,[26] in <Scorpio 16°> 20', northern.
28 And the one called the Dog,[27] in Gemini 21° 20', northern.
29 And a star[28] in Gemini 6° 30', of the second magnitude.

---

[19] Castor, α Gemini. This and its description (**25**) belong to the Jupiter-Mercury category, **46** and **48**.

[20] Zuben Eschemali, β Libra. This and its description (**25**) belong to the Jupiter-Mercury category, **45** and **48**.

[21] Adding based on Hugo.

[22] Alphecca (**20**).

[23] This seems to be the sense, although the text does not use the usual preposition.

[24] Not necessarily in the laboratory; this word means he has much experience, has tested his knowledge, etc.

[25] Regulus or *Cor Leonis*, α Leo.

[26] Antares or *Cor Scorpionis*, α Scorpio. Sahl (following al-Andarzaghar) also adds this incorrectly in the Mars-Venus category below (**66**).

[27] Sirius, α Canis Major.

[28] Menkalinan, β Auriga, which is a Jupiter-Saturn star and should have appeared within **33**-**38** below. Sahl (following al-Andarzaghar) has mistakenly put it here instead. The star which belongs here is Arcturus (α Bootes).

30 <And another[29] in Capricorn 7° 30'>.[30]

31 These stars are of the first magnitude, the complexion of Jupiter and Mars.

32 And if you found one of them in the Ascendant or in the Midheaven, one born like that will lead troops, be powerful in [his] significance, with a far-[reaching] voice, taking many lands and cities, his command being carried out in them and he being installed over them, and he will be very beneficial to the people, generous, resembling a king, proficient in his work, and not being under anybody, victorious, not submitting to anyone; and wherever he comes to he will be active, staunch, victorious, intelligent, revered, having plenty, with many assets, he will love to be commended and praised, and he will love money, and die a good manner of death, and he will be clean—because this star indicates the nativities of kings, and the masters of mighty affairs, and the leaders of troops, and those who are [held in] awe, and who do not submit to anyone, and victory over enemies, and valor, and the conquering of fortresses, and the goodness of [his] management, and he will become strong in raids and wars, and the initiatives of kings, and the power of princes, and what resembles that.

[Stars of Jupiter-Saturn]

33 And also a fixed star[31] in Taurus, 23° 50', southern, of the first magnitude.

34 And in Sagittarius another fixed star[32] in 20° 40', northern, of the first magnitude.

35 And in Taurus[33] another in 3° 50', of the second magnitude.

36 <And[34] in Taurus another fixed star,[35] 28° 40'>.

37 <And in Gemini another fixed star,[36] 1°>.[37]

---

[29] Altair, α Aquila.
[30] Adding based on Hugo and Rhetorius.
[31] Rigel, β Orion.
[32] Rukbat, α Sagittarius.
[33] Algol, β Perseus.
[34] Adding with Rhetorius.
[35] Capella, α Auriga.
[36] Alnilam, ε Orion.

38 These five stars are of the complexion of Jupiter and Saturn.

39 Now if one of them was in the Ascendant or Midheaven, one born with that will be wealthy, with many assets, of those who accumulate assets in lands and cities, mighty, loving agriculture, planting, and building. **40** And if the Moon looked at one of them and it[38] is in the Ascendant or Midheaven, he will be merciful, honored, fortunate, modest, patient, knowledgeable in everything, loving women; and if the one in Sagittarius was in this condition, then he will love birds and riding animals, and he will be of the more excellent of people, a rider of animals, in the status of a trainer and domesticator, and those whose work is with things having four feet, or of those who protect roads and bridges.[39]

[Stars of Mars]

41 And also a fixed star[40] in Cancer, in 20°, northern, of the second magnitude, the complexion of Mars alone.

42 Now if it was in the Ascendant or in the Midheaven, and especially in nativities of the night, then he will be a master of wars, a chief of chiefs, a practitioner of war, not wishing to be under the authority of anyone, irascible, mighty in his soul, and in no way being humble to anyone, harsh of soul; except that this star indicates the nativities of horseman, and the destructiveness[41] of those who are not subject to anyone, and who take from the people by force, and he will bring evil upon them.[42] **43** And one born by day <with this star in the Ascendant>[43] will be of those who do not have mercy, nor do they show human understanding, and you will never see him except [when] angry, banishing the people from [any] mercy, being contrary to people who are pious, seeking [to gain from] what is forbidden and calling [it] stupid, foolish in his understanding [but] speaking publicly, he will die a bad manner of death. **44** And if this star was in the Midheaven, it indicates eloquence

---

[37] Rhetorius added Menkalinan here, but Sahl (following al-Andarzaghar) includes it in **29** as a Jupiter-Mars star.

[38] Grammatically this could be either the Moon or the star, but it is probably the star.

[39] This last point about roads and bridges is not in Rhetorius at all.

[40] Pollux, β Gemini.

[41] This verbal noun (إبطال) usually simply means "destruction," but I take this to describe the *behavior* of such natives, not their own destruction.

[42] But this could also be read as, "but *it* [viz. this configuration] will bring harm upon them [viz. natives like this]."

[43] Adding based on Rhetorius.

and leadership, with a bad manner of death, he will have much speech [and] be a friend to kings.

[Stars of Jupiter-Mercury][44]

45 And also a fixed star in Libra,[45] in 25°, on the northern side, of the second magnitude.

46 And also another star[46] in the preceding head of Gemini, in 27°, and the second magnitude.

47 These two stars are of the complexion of Jupiter and Mercury.

48 Now if one of them was in the Ascendant or in the Midheaven, and the nativity is by day, it indicates a love of culture, and a good character, and worship and fidelity, and a love for sexual intercourse and speech, having many experiences, knowledgeable in the love of amusement, with much investigating, having an abundance of friends, fortunate from an abundance of taking and giving, and they indicate a good heart and condition, and a sound intention; and if the nativity was an indicator [of it], then wisdom, exaltation, leadership, wealth, and knowledge.

[Stars of Mars-Mercury]

49 And also another fixed star[47] in Cancer, in 4° 04', southern, of the first magnitude.

50 And in Gemini another star,[48] in 5° 40', southern, of the first magnitude.

51 And another star[49] in 21° 30' Pisces, northern, of the second magnitude.

---

[44] As I explained above, this is the correct Rhetorian place for the Jupiter-Mercury stars, which Sahl seems to have put here himself, because al-Andarzaghar had inserted it earlier with an extra, incorrect star (**20-25**). However, the description of these two Jupiter-Mercury stars in **48** is not very close to Rhetorius: **25** was actually much better. So we have here two correct stars in the right place, but with a bad description; earlier we had the two stars in the wrong place, but with a good description.

[45] Zuben Eschemali, β Libra.

[46] Castor, α Gemini.

[47] Procyon, α Canis Major.

[48] Betelgeuse, α Orion.

[49] Alpheratz, α Andromeda.

52 And a star[50] in Taurus, in 27° 40', southern, of the first magnitude.

53 And another star[51] in Pisces, in 5° 50', of the second magnitude.

54 And these five stars are of the complexion of Mars and Mercury.

55 And if one of them was in the Ascendant or in the Midheaven, and especially for one born by night, then the native will be a leader of troops, tending to get involved in matters, a powerful character, much intelligence, proficient in everything, a stern voice, gathering assets due to [his] passions, [having] many assets, a lover of male youths and virgins, often swearing false oaths, a loud voice, obstinate, a lover of culture. **56** And know that one born by day will be angry,[52] with little mercy, irritable, without a friend, a swindler, idle, [but] something of praise [is said] about him,[53] a master of falsehood, uniting with[54] every foul thing, conspicuous, a master of love and indecency and every foul thing, they love bloodshed, and the end of their affairs is bad.

[Stars of Venus-Jupiter]

57 And also another fixed star in 12° Scorpio,[55] southern, of the first magnitude.

58 And in Aries another star, in 3° 50',[56] of the first magnitude.

59 And these two stars are of the complexion of Venus and Jupiter.

60 And if one of these two stars was in the Midheaven or in the Ascendant, the native will be clean, accumulating many assets, beloved, loving God, intelligent, prominent, generous, modest, blessed by women and elevation by means of them, and success; but the majority of them will be redheads, weak-bodied, and especially if the Moon was looking at them.

---

[50] Bellatrix, γ Orion.
[51] Scheat, β Pegasus.
[52] حربًا. But this could also be جريئًا, "bold," "a risk-taker."
[53] Reading somewhat uncertainly for شيء الثناء عيله.
[54] This can also mean, "having sexual intercourse with."
[55] Toliman or Rigel Centaurus, α Centaurus.
[56] Θ Eridanus, known today as Acamar (and no longer a first magnitude star, hence it is only the θ star). Anciently it was at the end of Eridanus and first magnitude, but Eridanus was later extended and its new end was called Achernar (the new α Eridanus). See Kunitzsch and Smart, p. 36.

[Stars of Venus-Saturn]

61 And also in Leo another star[57] in 17° 18', northern, of the first[58] magnitude.

62 And another star[59] in Leo, in 3° of it, southern, in the second magnitude.

63 And also in Leo a star[60] in 28° 10', northern, of the first magnitude.

64 And these three stars are <of> the complexion of Venus and Saturn.

65 So if one of them was in the Ascendant or in the Midheaven, he will be happy, wealthy, his command being effective, notorious, known, having good, virtue, and high rank, and the knowledge of pleasures, but he will be a lisper,[61] foul, soft of speech, a lover of planting and building, debauched with women;[62] and <when he is older, he will be>[63] eloquent in orthodox practices, lead a devout life, and he will be knowledgeable in the stars and inner thoughts, darker in the eyes,[64] sweet, with a weakness of speech.

[Stars of Mars-Venus]

66 And also another star[65] in <Scorpio>, 16° 20', southern, of the first magnitude.

67 And another star[66] in Taurus, in 16° 20',[67] of the second magnitude.

68 And these two stars are of the complexion of Mars and Venus.

---

[57] Zosma, δ Leo.
[58] Reading with Rhetorius for "the second."
[59] Alphard, α Hydra.
[60] Denebola, β Leo.
[61] مصفرا, a somewhat tentative translation in accordance with the effeminacy suggested by Rhetorius. This word means to whistle or make strong sibilant sounds.
[62] Rhetorius emphasizes male homosexuality.
[63] Adding with Rhetorius.
[64] Rhetorius has "grey" or "bright" eyes. In Arabic, this word specifically pertains to using kohl around the eyes.
[65] Antares, α Scorpio. But this is incorrect, as it was already included among the Jupiter-Mars stars in **37** above. There is only one star in this category, Aldebaran (**67**). But al-Andarzaghar had good reason to associate Antares with this category, as it is mentioned below as a star *opposite* Aldebaran.
[66] Aldebaran, α Taurus.
[67] Reading with the statement below, and Rhetorius, for 27° 40'.

69 Now[68] if one of them was in the Ascendant or in the Midheaven, and especially the latter one of them which is in 16° 20' Taurus, then the native will be fortunate, the wealthiest of the wealthy, with much land in villages and cities, and he have many people at his service,[69] and his scribes and workers will be multiplied, and he will be a noble, a leader of troops, and conquer fortresses, and just as that star is [well] known in the heavens, so will he be known on earth, and famous for [his] character, and he will be powerful in his affairs, having good fortune and victory, and splendor, and [be the object of] awe, [and] he will affect lands and enemies. **70** And likewise the other star:[70] he will be fortunate, wealthy, famous among the people.

71 And[71] likewise for both, if one was with the Moon, in the degree of these two fixed stars, it doubles their power over the rest of the fixed stars: because these two stars, if they rose, the one which is in the west vanishes, and both of them are powerful in the heavenly circle, so [it is] likewise with them in the east, and they are elevated in power in all of the climes, because if this one was in the Ascendant, the one which was in the west will be in the

---

[68] This entire paragraph belongs to Aldebaran, but al-Andarzaghar splits it between Aldebaran (**69**) and Antares (**70**).

[69] Reading with the sense of Hugo and Rhetorius, for "and he will be at the service of many people."

[70] That is, Antares. Again, this is a misunderstanding by al-Andarzaghar.

[71] This paragraph is rather tortured in Sahl, and evidently Hugo decided to quietly drop the first part of **71** because it is missing in BA. In Rhetorius, (1) Aldebaran also indicates the grand things above when conjoined exactly with, and rising exactly with, the Moon, *because* it is twice as powerful as the other stars. But (2) the reason it is twice as powerful is because it is exactly opposite Antares: so when one is rising on the eastern horizon, the other is on western horizon. Such a native will therefore have two powerful fixed stars on the angles. Also, (3) Antares on the Descendant or western horizon will bring benefits and inheritance from marriage, because (4) those wives will be wealthy and illustries—but will die early due to the Martial star Antares setting. Finally, (5) *natives* with Aldebaran on the Ascendant will have powerful passions, because it is a Mars-Venus star. So we see that al-Andarzaghar has included these elements but in a changed way: (1) he accidentally included both Aldebaran and Antares as possibly rising with the Moon, but (2) correctly realizes that the doubling of power is because they are opposite each other. Again, (3) he accidentally allows both stars to possibly being on the Descendant, but correctly associates it with benefits from women. Then (4) he changes gears in **72** and assumes that all of the above also applies to *female nativities*, so that female natives will be rich but will die early, and (5) such female natives with either star will be passionate, etc. Now, I see no astrological problem applying the same rule to female nativities, but al-Andarzaghar or his translation of Rhetorius has garbled the reason for the interpretations.

house of his marriage, so the native will be one of those who gains many assets because of women.

72 And speak likewise for a woman born with these two stars, for she will be famous for the good, wealthy, her survival not being long, with a far-[reaching] voice, beautiful, held in awe, [mentally] keen, powerful in [her] passion for men until [her] foulness with men is consummated, and she is like the most graceful of women, and the most beautiful of them.

Scientific name	Common name	Rhetorius (Ch. 58)	Sahl	Nature (Rhetorius)
1. α Virgo	Spica	X	X	♀ – ☿
2. α Lyra	Vega	X	X	♀ – ☿
3. α Piscis Austrinus	Fomalhaut	X	X	♀ – ☿
4. α Cygnus	Deneb Adige	X[72]		♀ – ☿
5. α Corona Borealis	Alphecca	X	(X)[73]	♀ – ☿
6. α Leo	Regulus	X	X	♃ – ♂
7. α Bootes	Arcturus	X		♃ – ♂
8. α Aquila	Altair	X	X	♃ – ♂
9. α Scorpio	Antares	X	X[74]	♃ – ♂
10. α Canis Major	Sirius	X	X	♃ – ♂
11. β Orion	Rigel	X	X	♃ – ♄
12. ε Orion	Alnilam	X	X	♃ – ♄
13. β Auriga	Menkalinan	X	(X)[75]	♃ – ♄
14. α Sagittarius	Rukbat	X	X	♃ – ♄
15. β Perseus	Algol	X	X	♃ – ♄
16. α Auriga	Capella	X	X	♃ – ♄
17. β Gemini	Pollux	X	X	♂
18. β Libra	Zuben Eschemali	X	X	♃ – ☿
19. α Gemini	Castor	X	X	♃ – ☿

---

[72] Holden may have omitted this in his edition of Rhetorius, as Pingree and Burnett list it in their table in *BA*. But it is not in al-Andarzaghar or Sahl at all, so it might be missing in some versions of Rhetorius.

[73] Sahl (following al-Andarzaghar) classifies this as Jupiter-Mercury (**20, 24**).

[74] Sahl (following al-Andarzaghar) adds this again as a Mars-Venus star.

[75] Sahl (following al-Andarzaghar) classifies this with Jupiter-Mars.

20. γ Orion	Bellatrix	X	X	♂ - ☿
21. α Canis Major	Procyon	X	X	♂ - ☿
22. α Orion	Betelgeuse	X	X	♂ - ☿
23. α Andromeda	Alpheratz	X	X	♂ - ☿
24. β Pegasus	Scheat	X	X	♂ - ☿
25. α Centaurus	Toliman[76]	X	X	♀ - ♃
26. θ Eridanus[77]	Acamar	X	X	♀ - ♃
27. β Leo	Denebola	X	X	♄ - ♀
28. δ Leo	Zosma	X	X	♄ - ♀
29. α Hydra	Alphard	X	X	♄ - ♀
30. α Taurus	Aldebaran	X	X	♂ - ♀

Comment by Dykes. This ancient list of 30 fixed stars for eminence and prosperity is reflected in Anonymous of 379, Rhetorius (Ch. 58), and many other sources. Sahl has primarily copied directly from al-Andarzaghar, This table is organized according to the tables by Pingree and Burnett in their edition of *BA* (pp. 147-48), and compares Sahl's version to Rhetorius. Here are some differences:

- *Venus-Mercury stars.* There ought to be five, but Sahl has only three. He has omitted Deneb Adige (which some copies of Rhetorius might also have done), and assigns Alphecca to Jupiter-Mercury (see below).
- *Jupiter-Mars stars.* Sahl does have five, but instead of Arcturus, he has Menkalinan (which is a Jupiter-Saturn star), in **29**.
- *Jupiter-Saturn stars.* Sahl has only five stars, because he assigned Menkalinan to Jupiter-Mars in **29**.
- *Mars-Venus stars.* Sahl erroneously adds Antares to this category (**66**), after using it correctly as a Jupiter-Mars star earlier (**27**).
- Finally, note that in **20-25** Sahl has added an extra, redundant Jupiter-Mercury set which splits one star from its proper category and duplicates two others. Instead of adding Alphecca to Venus-Mercury, he has split it off and put it here (**20**), but does include the description from Rhetorius (**24**). Then he adds Castor and Zuben Eschemali (**21-22**) with their description from Rhetorius (**25**), but

---

[76] Today this is sometimes called Rigel Kentauri/Centauri.
[77] See the footnote to **58** above. Be sure you are using the correct star in your computer program, and not mistaking this for Achernar.

these are already correctly included later in their proper place (**45-48**), but with an unusual description that does not match either Rhetorius or the earlier version (**48**).

[Chapter 2.3: Other approaches for powerful good fortune]

[al-Andarzaghar]

1 Dorotheus said:[78] And when you have completed[79] the matter of the fixed stars in the topic of good fortune, look at the lords of the triplicities of the Moon by night, and the lords of the triplicities of the Sun by day, and the positions of them both[80] from the Ascendant. **2** For if you found the two lords of the triplicity cleansed of the infortunes and of defects, and you found them both in the stakes, then judge that the native will be happy for all the days of his life. **3** And[81] [this is] especially if the luminary was looking at them both from an excellent place, and the Moon was with them or looking at the Ascendant, and especially if they were both the lords of the house of the Lot of Fortune and the lords of the house of assets: for if it was like that, it will be more firm.

4 And Dorotheus said:[82] Then, look in the amount of good fortune from the lords of the triplicity which indicate good fortune: for if you found the lord of the triplicity in the first degree of the sign up to the end of [the first] half of it by ascensions, and it is in the stake,[83] he will be noble, happy, powerful, having followers and workers and secretaries, all of that under his authority (but you do not take it except as a chief).[84] **5** And if you found the

---

[78] For **1-2**, see *Carmen* I.24, **2-3**.
[79] Reading for an uncertain verb in the Arabic, which seems to be (عرفت من).
[80] That is, the primary and secondary triplicity lords.
[81] For this sentence, see perhaps *Carmen* I.27, **1-2**.
[82] For this paragraph, cf. *Carmen* I.28, **1-4**. The degrees here must be taken in ascensions as measured from the axial degree, not in zodiacal degrees, as is correctly reported in *Carmen*, and Ch. 2.13, **48-51**. But maybe it *would* be better if it was also in the first half of the sign.
[83] This shows that Sahl's source here did not quite understand the instructions. Rather, it is that the planet should be within the first 15° (by ascensions) of the region which begins with an axial degree (the stake), not the first 15° of the *sign*.
[84] *BA* says that he will never be deprived of that authority, so this probably means we should regard him as always being a chief once he attains high rank.

lord of the triplicity which indicates good fortune in the last half of the sign, then he will be below a chief or government ministers or a Caliph, and he will remain under the authority of [other] chiefs.

6 And[85] if you found the lord of the triplicity of the Sun[86] made unfortunate, then you must work with the Lot of Fortune. **7** For if you found it in the stakes or what follows them, and the lord of the Lot is eastern or[87] cleansed of the infortunes and the rays, and it looks at the Lot from a strong position, and a fortune is looking at them from a powerful position, and a fortune is looking at it as well, and the infortunes are not looking at it, then the native will be a king, or prominent, and a powerful noble, mighty, elevated, and especially if the Lot and its lord was with it.[88] **8** And for one born by night a nocturnal planet, and for one born by day a diurnal one, in its own triplicity, bound, or exaltation, it <is good if it>[89] looked at the <lord of the> Lot of Fortune. **9** Now if you found the lord of the Lot not looking at the Lot, and it occurred in the fifth or eleventh from the Ascendant, he will be happy; and more excellent than that is if it is looking at the Lot.

10 Now[90] if you found the Lot of Fortune and the lord of the Lot of Fortune made unfortunate, then look at the lord of the Ascendant or the lord of the Midheaven, or the lord of the house of hope. **11** For if these planets were cleansed of defects, in an excellent place, and they had the distribution of good fortune in the nativity, then he will also be happy.

12 And[91] look at the eleventh from the Ascendant: for if you found a fortune in it, it increases his good fortune; and if you found an infortune in it, it takes away from his good and increases in evil.

13 Then,[92] look at the Lot of assets and its lord. **14** For if you found them both in an excellent place, cleansed of the infortunes, it increases his good fortune and good.

15 And[93] if you found the Moon in the nativity [with] the fortunes looking at her, and she is in the second from the Ascendant, increasing in

---

[85] For this paragraph, cf. *Carmen* I.28, **10** and **12**, as well as the ideas suggested in **17, 19-20,** and **25**.
[86] Or the sect light, as *BA* has it.
[87] This should probably read, "and."
[88] I am not sure what this "it" refers to; perhaps the triplicity lord of the sect light?
[89] Adding with *Carmen* I.28, **19**, here and later in sentence.
[90] For this paragraph, cf. *Carmen* I.27, **5-6**.
[91] For this sentence, cf. *Carmen* I.28, **32**.
[92] For this paragraph, cf. *Carmen* I.29, **17-19**.

calculation and glow, and in the transit and [*uncertain*][94] she is connecting with a fortune, and looking at the Sun from a square,[95] and Saturn[96] is not looking at her, then he will be happy, a noble among elevated people.

ঙ   ৎ   ৎ

16 And among the most preferable things in the matter of good fortune and assets, is if the glowing luminary is in the Midheaven, in its own place, and the lords of its triplicity are in the stakes or in the place of good fortune or in the fifth (and the stronger of the stakes are the Ascendant and Midheaven).

17 Now if a planet was in one of the stakes by sign, and it was falling from the stakes by degrees, then it indicates for the native reputation, [but] it corrupts assets. **18** And if you found the planet in what follows the stake,[97] or it is falling in the sign, and is in the stake [by] degrees, it indicates assets and a fine condition, with difficulty in [his] reputation and no fame, and especially if the planet was western[98] [and] under the earth.

19 Now if you found the lord of the triplicity in the second and eighth, it indicates a decline of [his] condition in the matter which the planet likewise produces. **20** Now if that planet was a fortune, then his affairs will be set aright after their corruption. **21** And whenever you find Jupiter in one of these two places, (*if* he was not the governor of the triplicity) then it indicates a decline of [his] condition even though he will not provide injustice. **22** And the stronger of the lords of the triplicities is the first one, then the second, then the one partnering with them both.

23 And every planet, if you found it above the earth, then its indication is in the beginning of life; and if it was under the earth, then the end of life. **24** And it is preferable in the determination of that, if the one above the earth

---

[93] For this paragraph, cf. *Carmen* I.29, **15**.
[94] **M** seems to read وشنی. BA III.2.1, item 1.6 has her separating from the Node by at least 12° (i.e., coming out of the rays).
[95] In *Carmen*, this is a trine; see also Theophilus in Ch. 2.11, **15** below.
[96] In *Carmen* this is Mars, which is necessary because she is waxing. If she were waning, we would want this to be Saturn.
[97] This probably means being succeedent by sign.
[98] This might also be "alien."

was eastern, and the one under the earth western. **25** And[99] the Ascendant and the Midheaven indicate the beginning of life, and youth, and the seventh indicates adulthood, and the fourth indicates old age and the end of life.

26 And know that if you found the luminaries in the houses of the fortunes, without the aspect of the infortunes, they indicate comfort, gentleness, and the goodness of the livelihood. **27** And if Mars looked, it indicates travels, exertion, and he will devote himself to armies. **28** And if Saturn looked, it indicates illness, coldness, being idle from working, crime, and sorrow.

29 And know that when Jupiter looks at a planet, in whichever sect[100] it is, and which aspect it is, he will incline towards benefit. **30** For if he looked at the Sun, the benefit will be from chiefs, commanders, and the leaders of soldiers, and the powerful. **31** And if his aspect was to Mercury, then that benefit will be from writers and knowledge. **32** And if his aspect was to Mars, his benefit will be from cavalrymen, the leaders of soldiers, and the people of bravery,[101] and seizing by force. **33** And if his aspect was to the Moon, it indicates his healthiness in his body and his delight in his soul, and the benefit is because of devotion, females, the nobility, and friendship from them.[102]

34 And[103] look at the Lot of Fortune: for if it was in the exaltation of the Sun, in a stake, then the native will be of kings or those who associate with them. **35** And if it was in the exaltation of Jupiter, he will associate with nobles and the powerful. **36** And if it was in the exaltation of Mars, he will associate with commanders and cavalrymen, or he will be of them, and the cause of his good fortune will be from that. **37** And if it was in the exaltation of the Moon, then he will benefit from uprightness and the powerful and good fortune. **38** And work likewise with the house and bound in which the Lot is, and especially if its lord looked at it.

39 And of the preferable things in good fortune is if the Lot is in the Midheaven, or in the Ascendant, or in the eleventh, or in the fifth, inspecting the Sun and Moon (or one of them). **40** And the preferable of the two aspects is from the glowing luminary (from the Sun by day, and the Moon by night).

---

[99] Cf. *Carmen* IV.5,
[100] Tentatively reading حَيِّز for what also looks like حين ("time").
[101] البأس. But this word can also mean "injury, wrong," i.e. people who cause that.
[102] The last part of this sentence probably refers to Venus.
[103] For this paragraph, cf. al-Khayyāṭ's *JN* Ch. 50.

41 And every planet in its own exaltation or the exaltation of another (provided that it is not the place in which it has its fall), assists in the indication of good fortune and nobility, and according to the essence of that sign. 42 And the more preferable of that is if it was the Sun and Moon, for it is more excellent if they were in their exaltations or in the houses of Jupiter. 43 Now if you found them in the exaltation of Mars, they indicate that the native will be angry, steadfast, a cavalryman. 44 And if they were in the exaltation of Venus, then he will be generous, with a good character. 45 And if they were in the exaltation of Jupiter, then he will be mighty in [his] endeavors, at the far summit,[104] a master of authority and reputation. 46 And if they were in the exaltation of the Moon, then he will be content, praised. 47 And if they were in the exaltation of Saturn, they indicate patience.[105] 48 And if they were in the exaltation of Mercury, they indicate education. 49 And the intention in the determination of that is that one of these planets would be <in> the Ascendant, and the lord of that exaltation was in a stake or what follows a stake, of the beneficial places.[106]

50 And if you found the Sun rising, and the Moon setting, Jupiter southern, and Mars northern, all of them being in their exaltations and in the stakes,[107] they indicate the children of kings, commanders, and the powerful.

51 And if you found the house of the Head to be with the fortunes, he will be famous in nobility, leadership, and good fortune, and especially if with that it was in the Midheaven or in the Ascendant.

52 And likewise if you found the Tail by night to be with Mars,[108] then he will be powerful, wicked, an oppressor, angry, a shedder of blood, a destroyer of countries, leading both sexes into captivity, a squanderer of assets, and he will be of those without mercy, and especially if the Sun looked at him and they were both in one of the signs of kings or the exaltation of Mars. 53 And if they witnessed Mercury, it will be greater for his destruction and corrup-

---

[104] بعيد الغاية. This seems awkward to me.
[105] الحلم. This can also mean "mildness," "understanding," etc.
[106] This refers to a version of the 7-place system of good or suitable places: see *Introduction* Ch. 2, 37-45.
[107] But under these conditions that is not possible (for example, if the Sun is in Aries in the east, the Moon cannot also be in the west and in Taurus); perhaps Sahl's source means that these conditions can hold separately.
[108] Reading "Tail" with Ch. 10.2.1, **6**, for "Moon." it is the *Tail* which is with Mars, in a very similar sentence. See also Ch. 10.3, **18**.

tion, and more evil for his work. **54** And if you found the Moon with them, then it is more corrupting for what I mentioned, because the Moon indicates that the native will have his limbs cut and his bones broken, and his manner of death will be bad, and his end bad. **55** And likewise, if you found the Tail by day with Saturn, then it indicates something resembling what I mentioned of the gaining of assets without his losing his mind.[109]

56 Now if you found the Sun and Moon made unfortunate in nativities without an aspect from Jupiter, they indicate a scarcity of children and a scarcity of assets.

Chapter [2.4:] On the positions of the planets in the signs, & what that indicates

1 Now if you found all of the planets in good places, and you found Jupiter in the sixth or in the twelfth, not looking at the Sun and Moon, then the native will be of those who do not have good actions nor repute, and it will decrease what he has in the indication of the lords of the triplicities, and he will fall from his condition, and his enemy will be victorious over him and afflict him, and he will flee his country, and especially if Jupiter was in a female sign and not in his own house, and not in his own exaltation; and worse for that is if Jupiter is made unfortunate.

2 And if you found all of the planets in the nativity to be falling from the stakes, and Jupiter and his bound in the Midheaven or in the Ascendant, that indicates for the native the friendship of the powerful and of kings, and his entering into their houses, and the dignity he will obtain from them, and especially if Jupiter was in his exaltation and he had a share from the Moon.[110] **3** And if Venus in the nativity was in the Midheaven, and she had a share[111] in it, it indicates fertility, happiness, and leisure.

---

[109] حلّه العقد. This literally means "loosening the knot" and "dissolving a contract," but by analogy it refers to one's resolve or determination unraveling. Here, I take it to mean that he will not be out of control and corrupted, as described for Mars. See also Ch. 10.2.1, **9**.

[110] نصيب. Normally, "share" means a dignity, But perhaps this means that he is at least configured with the Moon, by contrast with **1**.

[111] حظ. That is, a dignity. But it could indicate the bound of the Midheaven, if not a dignity in her own position.

4 And[112] know that if Saturn was in the second, then the native will deceptive, greedy, a lover of assets, sociable,[113] falling from [his] condition and rank.[114] **5** And if Mars was in the second, then he will be accused of theft, a corruptor, or some of his assets will disappear, and the native will resemble one who did not have an upbringing: because if Mars was in this place, it indicates ruin and fleeing from his country, and especially if he was in his fall, in nativities of the day.

☜ ☙ ☙

6 And the most preferable that it could be in nativities of the night, is if the Moon was in the Midheaven, increasing in calculation and glow, and she is the governor of her own trine,[115] and looking at the lord of the trine[116] of the second, and the lord of that triplicity is a fortune. **7** And if it was as I described it, he will be wealthy, having plenty of assets, gold, and silver. **8** And if the Moon was as I described her [but] in her own exaltation or looking at her exaltation with a suitable aspect, and a fortune is looking at the Moon from its own exaltation or from the exaltation of the Moon, that will be more mighty and preferable for the native's good fortune. **9** And[117] if she was in a house of Venus, in a good place, it indicates increase because of women. **10** And if she was in a house of Mercury, then that will be by reason of writing and logic. <**11** And[118] if she was in a house of Jupiter, then it will be because of a noble man or the anger of kings, or because of the work of the Sultan or his country.> **12** And if she was in a house of Mars, then by reason of fear, blood, and evil. **13** And if she was in a house of Saturn, then he will inherit from his fathers and an ancient matter. **14** And if she was in the house of the Sun, then from kings and the leaders of groups. **15** And if she was in her own house, then that will be in relation to a craft.

---

[112] For this paragraph, see *Carmen* I.28, **30**.
[113] مستأنسًا, although this does not make sense in context.
[114] This is especially if Saturn is there by night (see **5** and the *Carmen* passage).
[115] That is, "triplicity."
[116] I.e., the triplicity. The use of the triplicity lords of the second suggests either Dorotheus or al-Andarzaghar as a source.
[117] The following list of planets seems to be drawn from *Carmen* I.29, **5-11**, which is about the lord of the second, not this complicated scenario with the Moon.
[118] Adding on the model of *Carmen* I.29, **7**, as Jupiter is the only planet missing and the order of planets here exactly parallels that chapter.

16 And the most preferable of good fortune in diurnal nativities is if the Sun is the governor of the native in the way that I mentioned about the Moon,[119] and he is in the Midheaven (and then especially in Aries), for he will indicate that the native is a king, a conqueror, or chief. **17** And if Mercury was with them both, then he will be a judge, knowledgeable in jurisprudence and orthodox procedures,[120] trustworthy in everything which comes to him, and especially if Jupiter was the lord of Mercury's bound or the lord of his house.

18 And know that if the lords of the triplicities of the glowing luminary were in the exaltation of the two glowing ones, and especially in the exaltation of the Moon, it indicates for the native the mightiness of [his] importance and the eminence of [his] name.

19 And if Leo was the house of his assets, it will be greater for his assets. **20** And if the sign was one having two bodies, it indicates the disappearance of part of it, and the remaining of some of it. **21** And if it was a convertible sign, it indicates the disappearance of all of it.

Chapter [2.5]: On the right-sidedness[121] of the planets (& it is what is called the "spear-bearing" of the planets): what it indicates of good fortune & assets

1 You should not neglect the knowledge of the right-sidedness of one of the planets toward another, for it is the summit of their good fortune in their indication, and especially if the diurnal planets were right-siding by day, and the nocturnal ones by night; and the explanation of right-sidedness is according to what I will explain to you.

---

[119] I.e., that he is his own triplicity lord.

[120] Lit., "the Sunnah."

[121] ميمنة. This word also has the metaphoric meaning of being "auspicious," a common relationship in many languages and cultures, between being "on the right and" being good. But here it is used to indicate "spear-bearing," a relationship that usually obtains between a luminary (considered as a royal planet) and another planet which acts as its protector. One of the typical relationships involves a planet to the right of the Sun so as to rise before him, or casting rays to degrees immediately to the right of the Sun. The discussion in **2-3** represents a version of the first definition of Antiochus (see Schmidt 2009, pp. 247ff). For more examples, see Ch. 10.2.7 for some examples that must derive from a Persian source, as well as the discussion in *ITA* III.28. In what follows, I will use variations such as "right-siding" to express the different forms of this noun in the passage below.

2 If you found one of the two planets in square or sextile to its companion, and they were both in their exaltations or their houses, or one of them was in its exaltation and the other in its house, or one of its shares, and each one of the two was casting rays upon its companion, then that is a strong right-sidedness. **3** And if they were not in their houses nor exaltations, but they were both of the sect[122] of the day or the sect of the night, then that is also called right-sidedness (though it is below [the first version]).

4 Now[123] if you found Mars right-siding for the Sun or Moon, then the native will be courageous, a deputized agent, a rider, rushing in on things, involved with the Sultan. **5** And if Venus was the one right-siding, she indicates that he will be handsome, of good speech, lucky, beloved, living a happy life, marriage will be easy for him, [and he will be] a lover of amusement. **6** And if Mercury was the one right-siding, then he will be intelligent, reasonable, having logic, an expert in jurisprudence, an administrator, capable, sensible. **7** And if it was Jupiter, then he will be a lover of honesty, faithfulness, fairness, generosity, of a good character, lucky, with many children. **8** And if it was Saturn, then he will have many assets and binding agreements, and he will inherit that from his fathers.

9 And if with that the glowing ones[124] were in the stakes, and the fortunes were in their right-sidedness, then that is more powerful and preferable, and more famous in the matter of good fortune; and if that was reversed,[125] it indicates the middle of what I have mentioned of [his] condition.

Chapter [2.6:] On the twelfth-parts of the planets

1 Look at the twelfth-parts of the planets and the Ascendant: for if you found the twelfth-part of the Sun, the Ascendant, and the Moon in a good place, with the fortunes, they indicate the health of bodies and the good fortune of the native and the parents.

---

[122] حظ, which normally means "share" or "dignity."
[123] For this sentence, cf. Theophilus, *Labors* Ch. 17, 7.
[124] The luminaries.
[125] I believe Sahl's source means that the fortunes are in the stakes, and the luminaries act as *their* spear-bearers.

2 And preferable to that[126] is if the twelfth-parts of the infortunes were not with the glowing ones nor in the Ascendant.

3 And preferable to *that* is if the twelfth-part of Jupiter and of Venus are with the luminaries and the Ascendant.

4 And preferable <to *that*> is if the twelfth-parts of the infortunes in the nativities of males were in the male signs, and in the nativities of females in female signs.

[Chapter 2.7: The repelling of evil by the planets]

1 And[127] if Jupiter was in a stake in a bad nativity, with bad planets,[128] it indicates the repelling of evil for twelve years; and if he was in what follows a stake, then [he will repel it] until he reaches a place in which he is unfortunate.[129] **2** <And if Venus was in a stake, she will repel that for eight years.>[130] **3** And if Saturn was like that, being the overlord (and that is if by day he was the lord of the triplicity of the Sun, and by night the lord of the triplicity of the Moon), it indicates the repelling of that for thirty years; and if he was not like that, he does not have an indication [for that]. **4** And if Mercury was in the status of Saturn, then for twenty years. **5** And if it was Mars, then fifteen years. **6** And if the Sun was in a stake by day or <in his own triplicity,[131] he will repel that>[132] for nineteen years; and he will not have [this] indication in nocturnal [nativities]. **7** And if the Moon was in a stake, in a female sign, then twenty-five years; and if she was in a male sign, those years will be months.

8 And[133] if one of the two infortunes was in the house of assets, they indicate poverty; and harsher for it is if it was not in its own sect.[134] **9** And

---

[126] This should probably be understood as "and *even more* preferable," i.e. as an extra condition, rather than being purely a stand-alone condition.

[127] For this paragraph, see *Carmen* I.25, **1-7** (entire). This probably only refers to these planets if they are the primary triplicity lords of the sect light, as is made clear in **3** (and also in *Carmen*'s **3**).

[128] I'm not sure if this means he is with the bad planets, or just that there are bad planets in the chart.

[129] I take this to be by transit.

[130] Adding based on *Carmen*.

[131] Again, this is by day.

[132] Adding with *Carmen*.

[133] For **8-9**, see *Carmen* I.28, **30-31**.

likewise if it was in the stake of the earth, and harsher for it is if the other [infortune] opposes it without an aspect from Jupiter: that indicates his flight and his death will be worse. **10** (And if the fortunes were like that, [they indicate] riches.) **11** And[135] likewise if the infortunes were in the square of the house of assets, or its opposition, then they indicate downfall, and the cause of the downfall will be according to the essence of the lord of the sign.

☋ ☊ ☍

12 Now if you wanted to know when he will gain his assets, then count from the Lot of assets to the lord of the house of assets by degrees of ascensions: and what it comes to in degrees between it and that, is the amount of time [after] which he will gain the assets.

Chapter [2.8:] On the knowledge of nursing & its goodness

1 And you ought to look at the Moon on the third day, where she is: for it is the indicator of nursing and travels. **2** And the Moon on the seventh day indicates youth and middle age, and the Moon on the fortieth day indicates old age. **3** Now if you found the Moon at these times in the houses of fortunes, and with fortunes, then judge good and fortune for that period; and if she was in the places of the infortunes, then state toil and difficulty in that.

4 And[136] you ought to look at the essence of the Ascendant and the sign in which the Moon is: for indeed among the signs are those suitable for kings and the nobility, and among them what corresponds to the subjects and the rabble. **5** The correspondence of Cancer, Aries, Leo, and Sagittarius is to kings and the nobility. **6** The correspondence of Capricorn and Scorpio is to the powerful. **7** The correspondence of Gemini, Virgo, and Libra is to writers, merchants, and the masters of crafts, knowledge, and the understanding. **8** The correspondence of Aquarius is to lords of lands and villages, and wetlands, and what is like that. **9** And the correspondence of Pisces and Taurus is to the middling ones of the people, and women, except that in Pisces <it

---

[134] حظ, which normally means "share" or "dignity."
[135] For this sentence, see *Carmen* I.29, **4ff** and *Excerpt* I.
[136] For these signs, cf. also Ch. 1.38, **11-12** and **46-47**; Ch. 4.5, **26-27**; Ch. 6.10, **1**.

includes> coarseness and lewdness, and especially the first image and the second of them.[137]

Chapter [2.9:] On the positions of the lords of the glowing one, what it indicates

1 Then, look at the lord of the triplicity of the glowing luminary.[138] **2** For if it was in a house and bound of Mercury, the craft of the native and his work will be from writing and thinking. **3** And if the lord of the triplicity was in a house of Jupiter, then it will be from the Sultan, and his livelihood from that. **4** And if it was in a house of Mars, then from cavalrymen and works pertaining to war. **5** And if it was in the house of the Sun, then from kings. **6** And if it was in the house of the Moon, then from mothers. **7** And if it was in a house of Saturn, then from detestable things and lamentation. **8** And if it was in a house of Venus, then from Venusian works, and his livelihood and work will be of her type.

9 The sum of that is that you should understand the place of the lord of the triplicity in the triplicity and bound, and the essence of the house and position, and the region[139] and countries, so that you speak according to that, if God (be He exalted!) wills.

Chapter [2.10:] On the positions of the luminaries, & what that indicates

1 And you ought to begin by understanding the sign and degree in which the Sun, Moon, Ascendant, Lot of Fortune, the meeting,[140] and the lords of their triplicities are, and you should understand the essence of the place in which they are, and especially that of the glowing luminary and the lords of its triplicity. **2** For if you found them in the signs of kings, then his affairs will be in relation to kings and authority. **3** And if they were in a watery sign, then from wetlands and moisture. **4** And if they were in what has four feet, then from riding animals. **5** And if they were in the earthy ones, then from the

---

[137] That is, in the first two faces or decans.
[138] That is, the sect light.
[139] النَّاحية. I believe this refers to the cardinal direction of the quarter.
[140] Or the opposition, whatever it is.

land and sheep.¹⁴¹ **6** And if they were in the signs of people, then his craft and work will be from people. **7** And if they were in the mountainous ones, then from mountains. **8** And if they were in the marine signs, then from the sea and [*uncertain*].¹⁴² **9** And if they were in the earthy ones, if it was Capricorn, then from the Sultan, and if they were in Taurus then from the Sultan and leadership and groups, and if they were in Virgo, then from the intellect, knowledge, and agriculture. **10** And if they were in Gemini, then from ideas, and the goodness of [his] estimation in relation to the contracting of accounts, or engraving¹⁴³ or what is like that of crafts (of what one needs eyesight for). **11** And if it was in Libra and Aquarius, then his livelihood will be from the rest of works; and preferable [to that] is if they were in their own places, free of the infortunes, for indeed that will be more in demand¹⁴⁴ for what he completes and what it indicates.

12 Then, look from the one governing the indication of assets,¹⁴⁵ and where its position is in <the circle>: for if it was in the Ascendant, it indicates the gaining of assets in youth and childhood, <in> his own country. **13** And if you found it in the second, then he will gain wealth from inheritance. **14** Now if it was in the third, then by reason of the stars, knowledge, friends, and siblings. **15** And if it was under the earth, <then from> a hidden matter, and he will gain from the father and mother. **16** And if it was in the fifth, then at the end of life, from the friendship of the powerful and leaders, and the acquisition of his assets will be from children. **17** And if it was in the sixth, then he will be despised, he will gain by reason of slaves and the rabble, he will be distressed and sad because of assets and seeking [them]. **18** And if it was in the seventh, then at the end of life, from inheritances and lawsuits, and towns and villages; and if it was a fortune, then that will be by reason of women. **19** And if it was in the eighth, then from inheritances and summoning [spir-

---

¹⁴¹ But voweled differently, this word can also mean "booty."
¹⁴² The text seems to read النكد.
¹⁴³ This includes sculpting (نقش).
¹⁴⁴ Reading أروج for أروح. But this might also be أزوج, which would suggest "doubling" something about what he does.
¹⁴⁵ In context, I should think that this is the triplicity lord of the sect light, or perhaps the best of the choices found in **1** above. But this would also apply to the lord of the second and planets in the second.

its].¹⁴⁶ **20** And if it was in the ninth, then from travels and houses devoted to the gods,¹⁴⁷ and that will be by reason of prophesying and the stars. **21** And if it was in the tenth, then in youth, in the corridors of power, and a craft which he is praised for, and he will be famous in it, of high reputation. **22** And if it was in the eleventh, then from government ministers and the followers of the powerful, and the friendship of kings and nobles, and the native will increase in good fortune and being honored in that. **23** And if it was in the twelfth, then he will be corrupt in work and soul, weak in livelihood, enslaved because of slaves, and his enemies will subjugate him, and he will be miserable on journeys, and his livelihood will be in confinement and by means of theft.

24 And if these planets which I have described were in a female sign and feminine region, then from females and because of females; and if it was in a male sign and masculine region, then from males. **25** And if it was in a sign of kings, then from kings. **26** And if it was in the rest of them, it will be in accordance with the essence of the sign in which it is.

[Chapter 2.11:] The statement of Theophilus on good fortune & assets

1 If¹⁴⁸ you found both of the two lords of the triplicity of the luminary to be strong,¹⁴⁹ they indicate high rank from the beginning of his life to its end. **2** And if one of the two was strong and the other weak, his benefit will be in the time of the strong one of them, and his baseness in the time of the one of them [that is falling]. **3** And if they were both falling, they indicate baseness from the beginning of his life to its end. **4** And the aspect of the fortunes and infortunes increases in that and subtracts from that, and the partnering lord of the triplicity supports them both in their elevation, through its strength (if it was strong), and brings [them] down (if it was a falling [place]).

---

¹⁴⁶ العقد. But this can also mean to conclude an agreement, which fits along with the eighth as indicating financial partnerships (or the money of partnerships).

¹⁴⁷ To me this reference to plural gods suggests a Hellenistic-type text as its source.

¹⁴⁸ For this paragraph, cf. *Carmen* I.24, **1-8**.

¹⁴⁹ By "strong," Theophilus might mean simply being "angular" or "pivotal" or "advancing," since he contrasts this in the next sentence with "falling," the usual term for being cadent. But since there are many ways to be "strong," and since this work for falling also has general connotations of being base, we might consider other conditions as well.

5 And[150] if the lord of the triplicity was under the rays, then it has no strength. **6** And if the luminaries testified to a planet in its own house, then it is an indication of good fortune.

7 And[151] every planet which is strong indicates assistance by reason of its essence. **8** If Jupiter was strong, it indicates wealth by reason of the powerful. **9** And if it was Venus, then in relation to women. **10** And if it was Mercury, then by reason of writing and commerce.

11 And[152] if there was a fortune in the eleventh, it indicates the acquisition of assets.

12 And[153] if the lord of the house of assets was a fortune, strong, not made unfortunate, it indicates riches and rank. **13** And if it was like that [but] in the aspect of an infortune, perhaps he will encounter tribulation; but if with that it was falling,[154] he will not leave [that] tribulation until he dies. **14** And if it was falling [but] not made unfortunate, then [it indicates] what is middling of assets; and if it was the reverse, then reverse it.

15 And[155] when you find the lord of the house of assets strong, in good order, and the Moon strong, increasing in her calculation and her glow, trining the Sun, it indicates what is most powerful of leadership and wealth. **16** And if the Moon was like that [but] decreasing in her calculation and her glow, it indicates decrease in that.

17 And[156] if the lord of the Lot of assets was a fortune, in its own house, exaltation, or bound, and the Lot made fortunate,[157] it indicates riches; and if it was the reverse, then reverse it. **18** And if it was eastern it will be preferable, and if it was western [but] arising within seven days, it indicates wealth without rank. **19** And if it and the Lot were both eastern, it indicates its duration and his good living.

---

[150] Cf. *Carmen* I.24, **8**.
[151] For this paragraph, cf. *Carmen* I.28, **24**. This situation has to do with the lord of the Lot of Fortune being unfortunate, but the native also having the fortunes in a good place, eastern, testifying to the Ascendant and the Moon.
[152] This is probably based on *Carmen* I.28, **32**.
[153] This paragraph bears a similarity to *Carmen* I.29, **12-14**.
[154] Perhaps this means being in its fall.
[155] For this paragraph, cf. *Carmen* I.29, **15-16**.
[156] For this paragraph, cf. *Carmen* I.29, **20-22** and **24**.
[157] Reading for "a fortune."

[Chapter 2.12:] The statement of Ptolemy about that[158]

1 He said: look at the Lot of Fortune and the lord of its house (and it is the overlord over it),[159] and what is the strength of those of the planets looking at it, and what kind of strength it has over those looking at it, and its weakness from them. **2** For if the planets looking at it were of its domain,[160] then the native will be wealthy, especially if the fortunes were looking at it from their own houses.

3 Now if Saturn was the overlord, the native's riches and his wealth will be from agriculture, building, and commerce on rivers and seas. **4** And if Jupiter was the overlord, his assets will be from things deposited in another's care, loyalties, and stewardships,[161] and from leadership in worship. **5** And if Mars was the overlord, from horsemanship and valor. **6** And if it was Venus, then from the gifts of the people or marrying them. **7** And if it was Mercury, then from wisdom, writing, and commerce. **8** And if it was the Moon, then from her own essence and the essence of the one mixed with her.

9 And if Saturn was the lord of the Lot, and Jupiter was looking at him, it adds him on top of what [Saturn] indicates. **10** And if Jupiter was in a sign having two bodies and the Moon assembling with him, then the children of that native will gain inheritances from foreigners.[162]

11 And if the planets which were testifying to it[163] were of its own domain,[164] what he acquires of wealth will be lasting, stable; and if they were not of its domain[165] and character, and there were infortunes in the second from it, there will not remain to him anything of what he acquired.

12 And the sum of what I have mentioned to you is from the stakes and the luminaries.[166]

---

[158] For this section, cf. *Tet.* IV.2 (Robbins pp. 373-77).
[159] In *Tet.* this seems to refer to the Ptolemaic victor.
[160] That is, its "sect" (حيّزه).
[161] Tentatively reading for القهرمة, on the model of قهارمة \ قهرمان, "steward, household manager."
[162] Or, "strangers" (الغرباء), which seems less likely.
[163] This seems to mean, "the planet which indicates Fortune."
[164] Again, "sect."
[165] That is, its sect.
[166] By the stakes, Ptolemy means that the *timing* of good fortune is judged via the relationship of the significating planets to the angles and the succedent places.

[Chapter 2.13:] The statement of Māshā'allāh & Abū 'Alī al-Khayyāṭ about that[167]

1 Look at the lord of the Ascendant and the lord of the second: for if the lord of the second connected with the lord of the Ascendant, the native will gain assets without toil or need in [his] seeking. **2** And if the lord of the Ascendant connected with the lord of the second, he will gain the assets with seeking and toil.

3 Then, look at the one of them accepting the management, in which position it is. **4** For if it was in the Ascendant he will gain from the work of his own hands; and if it was in the Midheaven he will gain because of the Sultan; and if it was in the seventh he will gain because of women and lawsuits; and if it was in the stake of the earth it will be from water, lands, and buildings; and what there is of it will[168] be from a known source, and he will bequeath to his children.

5 And if it was in a withdrawing place [but] looking at the Ascendant, then it will be below what I mentioned.

6 And if it was in the fifth or eleventh, his gain will be greater at the end of his life. **7** And if it was in the ninth and third, it will be greater at the beginning of his life. **8** And in these two areas[169] it indicates the goodness of the native's livelihood.

9 And if it was according to what I described to you and it was not looking at the Ascendant, in his profit there will be a mixture of what is not upright and not by means of work, or he will be stingy, tight-fisted.[170]

10 Then look: for if, along with what I described, there was a transit of the lord of the second to the lord of the Ascendant, it indicates many lasting, continuing gains which will come to him spontaneously from various directions. **11** And if it was a transit of the lord of the Ascendant to the lord of the

---

[167] For al-Khayyāṭ's contribution, cf. *JN* Ch. 11.
[168] Omitting "not" with al-Khayyāṭ, as the stakes or angles generally show things that are present and public.
[169] I have made this its own sentence, because I believe Māshā'allāh means these two axes: i.e., the fifth-eleventh and ninth-third—*not* merely the two houses, the ninth and third.
[170] The sentence ends with على نفسه, lit. "toward himself," but I am not sure of its precise meaning here; Sahl may mean that he will not allow himself to spend much money *on himself*, as opposed to refusing to spend money on others. The Arabic al-Khayyāṭ is a bit waterstained but ends with من النَفس, "of/from the soul."

second, it indicates eagerness in the search, and the corruption of what he receives.

12 If the indicator of the native's assets[171] was advancing in the stake, he will not gain anything from his father, and he will be the earner of the assets. **13** And likewise, if it was advancing in the two ways,[172] he will gain from his fathers, and he will earn. **14** And if it was decreasing in the two ways,[173] he will not gain anything from his father, and will not be <the earner> of the assets. **15** And you will seek the information like that from what I have mentioned to you about all of the ways.

16 Then, look at the lord of the second, in which of the places it is: for if it was in the stakes, he will be blessed and will be of those who are motivated[174] in works—if it was free of the infortunes. **17** And if it was withdrawing from the stakes, he will gain [only] what is appropriate, day by day. **18** And if it was not looking at the Ascendant, there will be hardship in his livelihood, and that is harsher if it was made unfortunate.

19 Then, look at the lord of the Ascendant: for perhaps it was connected with Jupiter (who is the indicator of assets), or Jupiter was connected with it: for if it was connected with it, it indicates wealth and accumulation.

20 Then, look at the position of the Lot of assets and its lord, and what is looking at them both (of the fortunes and infortunes). **21** For if it was with the lord of the Ascendant, and the lord of the Ascendant is looking at the Ascendant from a strong position, then the native will gain from the inheritance of [his] fathers.

22 If the lord of the second and[175] the lord of the Lot of assets[176] were made unfortunate or under the rays, entering into burning, it indicates the hardship of [his] condition.

23 If the Lot of Fortune was in an excellent place from the Ascendant, and its lord free of the infortunes, and it is looking at the Ascendant and its lord, it indicates the goodness of the native's livelihood.

---

[171] This may be the triplicity lord of the sect light, because it is distinguished from the lord of the second in **16**.

[172] This probably means that it is angular both dynamically (by quadrant division) and by sign (in an angular sign).

[173] Again, this probably means being cadent or falling both dynamically and by sign.

[174] يبعث. This verb generally means to incite, stir up, and provoke.

[175] The Arabic says "and," but then uses only the singular for being made unfortunate; so perhaps this should be read as "or."

[176] In the Latin and Arabic editions of al-Khayyāt, this is the Lot of Fortune, not assets.

24 And[177] look at the second from the Ascendant, its opposition, and its square, for perhaps one of the infortunes is inimical to the second: for if it was like that, it indicates the squandering of the native's assets, and their dispersal. **25** And you look likewise at the position of the Lot of assets.

26 And if the lord of the Ascendant and the second were not looking at each other, then see if perhaps a planet was reflecting their light. **27** For if a planet did reflect their light, it indicates the gain of assets, but it will be at the hands of the people, and he will be trained[178] in the gaining [of them].

28 If the Moon was received, looking at the Ascendant, then the native will be of a good livelihood, and that is better if the one receiving her was a fortune. **29** And if the Moon was in the second from the Ascendant, increasing in light and number, handing over her management and power to a fortune, and to the planet receiving her, then the native will increase in good the more that he advances in age.

30 And if the planet which gives information about the native's condition was in a convertible sign, it converts the native's condition often: hardship will afflict him as well as comfort, trouble, and ease.

31 And if the lords of the Ascendant and of the second were not looking at each other, and the lord of the Lot is not looking at the Ascendant, and the fortunes are falling away from the Ascendant and from the lord of the Ascendant, and the Moon is falling away from the Ascendant, and the Lot of Fortune and its lord made unfortunate, then he will be miserable in [his] life, in struggle and tribulation.

※ ※ ※

32 And[179] know that what I mentioned in the first section in the indication of assets, is more powerful and more lasting; then what follows it in the topics in succession is better and stronger than what follows that.

33 And understand the good fortune of the native from the position of the Moon and the one she connects with, and what is the strength of the planets which the Moon connects with, and the lord of the Ascendant and its strength.

---

[177] Cf. Ch. 2.7, **11** above.
[178] تلميذاً. Or, a "student, apprentice."
[179] This is no longer al-Khayyāt, and may be Sahl or something else (if not Māshā'allāh).

34 And understand [that there is] good fortune in nativities if the lord of the Ascendant was received (or the Sun by day or the Moon by night), and the acceptor [of the management] was powerful, in the degrees of the stakes, and not falling.

35 And in the matter of good fortune, make the Lot of Fortune and the Moon be partners, for they are partners in good fortune.

36 And know that the [types of] good fortune[180] in nativities, and the good and power the native has in his livelihood, is understood from the condition of the lords of the triplicities of the luminaries by night and day, and the condition of the lord of the Ascendant, and the indicator, and reception. 37 And if these were falling, the native will not have good fortune nor power in his livelihood, and then one will need the house of assets and its lord: and he will earn [assets] year by year, and day by day.

38 (And work likewise with the lords of the triplicities of siblings, and likewise the fathers, children, and women. 39 And[181] know that the condition of the father at the end of his life, and the condition of the native at the beginning of his life, since the <first> lord of the triplicity of the Sun and [the Sun's] lord both indicate the good of the father at the end of his life, [*uncertain*][182] the native; and likewise the Moon for the mother is made the end of her life for the native, because the first lord of the triplicity indicates the end of the father's life, and the beginning of the native's life.)

40 But for good fortune, let your reliance be on the Sun by day and the Moon by night, and their positions, and the positions of the lords of the triplicities of the luminaries in the excellent and bad places. 41 And certainly the native will be fortunate just as I have mentioned even if the lord of the Ascendant may be falling, for he will be minor in reputation, and he will have the reputation belonging to the position of the lord of the Ascendant, and he will not be fortunate in assets;[183] and the best that the lords of the triplicities could be is if they were not made unfortunate.

---

[180] Lit., "the good fortunes."

[181] This sentence is rather unclear. It seems to me that the *second* triplicity lord of the parent should indicate the *beginning* of the native's life, since the parent led a life before the native's birth.

[182] **M** seems to read سفى.

[183] What this seems to mean is that the triplicity lords of the sect light can show general good fortune, *even if* that good fortune is not really financial, due to the cadent state of the lord of the Ascendant.

42 And if the Moon and Sun were in the Ascendant, and an infortune is not looking at them, he will have a reputation among the people (and Jupiter is like that too).

43 And[184] the house of assets indicates earnings and work, and it is that you examine the lord of the house of assets, where it is: now if it was retreating[185] he will have bad work, being despised among the people of his work; and if it was received,[186] his work will be good, excellent, and he will gain good from it.

44 And know that people proceed in their works and good fortune according to their essences, from the lords of the triplicities of the luminaries. **45** And[187] as for the Midheaven, it indicates authority and high rank from authority, and in his work which is at the hands of the Sultan he will associate according to the example of the conditions of the people, because a retreating one retreats [and] falls, and an advancing one advances, indicating good in the revolution of years.

46 And know that if the star was in its strength and its nature,[188] in an excellent position, not made unfortunate, and not handing over its management to a star corrupting it and making it fall, and nothing is connecting with it, then he will live without his own earnings, and he will survive on the assets of the fathers and inheritance. **47** And if it was connecting [with another] or another was connecting with it, he will earn and gain in his own right.

48 And[189] of the more powerful indications of good fortune is if the first lord of the triplicity of the glowing one[190] is in a stake or what follows it, and that is the 15° which follows it, by degrees of ascensions: for if it was like that, it indicates praise and good fortune (and what is less [than that] in degrees is preferable). **49** Now if it was in the second 15°, it indicates his good fortune is below the first [type]. **50** And if it was in the third 15°, it indicates [what is

---

[184] This paragraph repeats in Ch. 10.1.1, **22-24**.
[185] Reading Form IV and with Ch. 10.1.1, **23-24** for the text's "manages," because Sahl is known for using Form IV to mean a cadent or retreating planet.
[186] مقبول. But Ch. 10.1.1, **24** reads "advancing" (مقبل), which makes a better contrast to retreating.
[187] See another version in Ch. 10.1.1, **25-26**.
[188] This most likely includes being of the sect of the chart.
[189] For this paragraph, cf. *Carmen* I.28, **1-6**.
[190] That is, the sect light.

in] the middle of assets. **51** And what is after that in degrees, up to the next stake, is of the nativities of the poor.

52 And[191] if you found one of the infortunes in the house of assets, it indicates poverty and obscurity.

[Chapter 2.14: The lord of the second house according to its nature & in the houses]

1 And you will understand the manner by which he will gain [assets] from the lord of the second (if it had testimony from its position relative to the Ascendant), and from its own nature according to the seven types, and the twelve <signs>.

2 And[192] as for the seven types, if the second was a house of Saturn, he will gain assets and a livelihood from the cultivation of lands, and water, and vegetation. **3** And if it was a house of Jupiter, then from the knowledge of uprightness and truth, and faith, from the nobles of the people. **4** And if it was a house of Mars, then in relation to war and weapons and the doors of the Sultan, and from the application of fire and blood. **5** And if it was the house of the Sun, then by reason of the Sultan, fathers, and ancestors.[193] **6** And if it was a house of Venus, then in relation to weights and measures and the like,[194] or because of women and medications.[195] **7** And if it was a house of Mercury, then in relation to writing, knowledge, and commerce. **8** And if it was the house of the Moon, then look at the planet which she is connecting with, for it is the indicator; and if she was empty of course, he will be a messenger, or [*uncertain*],[196] or of those who wander the lands, and he will transmit messages.

---

[191] See *Carmen* I.28, **30**; but there, Dorotheus says it will not indicate this if the infortune is of the sect of the chart.

[192] For this paragraph, cf. *Carmen* I.29, **5-11**; and *Excerpt* I.

[193] Or, "grandfathers," "forefathers" (أجداد).

[194] Probably due to Libra.

[195] الأدوية. But this seems wrong to me, and could be a misread for something like أدباء, "elegant people," "cultured people."

[196] The text seems to read فيجًا.

[The lord of the second in the houses, according to Māshā'allāh]

9 And as for the twelve signs, if the lord of the second was in the Ascendant, he will certainly work with his own hands, and he will be blessed without searching and need; and if it was received, it will be preferable.

10 And if it was in the second, then his livelihood will be from a known source.[197] **11** Now if the lord of the third looked at it, he will have suffering siblings whom tribulation will afflict; and if an infortune looked at it, it indicates the ruin of his assets and their scattering.

12 And if it was in the third, he will gain from travels and because of siblings; but if it was a fortune, he will have religion and will gain for that reason.[198]

13 And if it was in the fourth, then in relation to fathers and ancestors, and it indicates the goodness of the assets of the fathers, and the thriving of the house he was born in, and the goodness of their condition, and he will be devoted to his parents.

14 And if it was in the fifth, then in relation to women and the children he will have, or those known[199] at the door of the Sultan, and they will gain the good, or they will have importance among the people of their social class.

15 And if it was in the sixth, then in relation to slaves, riding animals, and medications. **16** Now if it was received, or the lord of the Ascendant looked at it, he will gain from medications and the illness of animals and slaves; but if it was not received, or made unfortunate, it ruins his animals (if there were [any]) and disaster will afflict him in his assets, and he will have a bad condition, and his livelihood will have toil, and labor, and hardship.

17 And if it was in the seventh, then from women and lawsuits. **18** And if neither a fortune nor infortune is looking at it, nor is it received, and the lord of the Ascendant is not looking at it, he will gather assets without the majority of it being from contention and lawsuits, and his women will die, and he will marry servant women. **19** And if the lord of the Ascendant did look at it, and it is an infortune, then he will waste his assets by reason of lawsuits and women, and he will encounter hardship from that.

---

[197] Another way of looking at this could be "self-employed."
[198] Note the subtle implication that siblings are troublesome, as though an infortune steers the house in the direction of siblings, while a fortune steers it towards religion.
[199] Reading for "not known."

20 And if it was in the eighth, then in relation to inheritance and the dead, and the native will be generous with [his] gains, not caring where he gets assets from and what he spends them on. **21** Now if it connected with the lord of the eighth, his assets will be taken by force, and he will be of those who impose taxes; now if the lord of the eighth connected with it, he will gain by reason of the dead and inheritances—then[200] speak about the aspect of the planets in accordance with what I described to you.

22 If it was in the ninth, then in relation to travels, piety, and religion. **23** Now if the lord of the Ascendant looked at it, his livelihood will be from travels and being away from home; and if it does not look at it, he will gain by means of kindliness in the travels.[201] **24** And if a fortune looked at it, and received it, his livelihood will be by reason of religion, piety, and devoutness; and if it was an infortune or it was inimical to it, he will be a master of magic and remedies, and will gain for that reason.

25 And if it was in the tenth, then at the doors of the Sultan and because of him.

26 And if it was in the eleventh, then in relation to friends and commerce. **27** And if the lord of the Ascendant looked at it, he will have a good condition and livelihood, and his acquaintances and friends will be in need of him; and if it does not look at it, he will be in need of his friends.

28 And if it was in the twelfth, then in relation to prisons and enemies, and he will be poor in soul, much distressed.

[Chapter 2.15:] The knowledge of the Lot of assets

[Māshā'allāh on the Lot of assets][202]

1 Then, look at the Lot of assets and its lord: and it is that you count from the lord of the second to the second place, and you add on top of that the degrees of the Ascendant, and cast out what there is from the beginning of the sign of the Ascendant, and where your calculation reaches, there is the Lot of assets.

---

[200] This last clause seems out of place to me.

[201] بالرَّأفة في الأسفار. Or perhaps, "pity in the travels." This could mean that because the lord of the Ascendant is in aversion, the native himself cannot create his own prosperity, but must rely on others.

[202] For this subsection, cf. Tehran, Dānishgāh, Nafīsī 429 (68b-69a); Majlis 17490 (132).

2 And look at its position and the position of its lord, and who is looking at them both, of the fortunes and infortunes. **3** For if you found the Lot of assets in the stakes, then it indicates the goodness of the native's condition, in the social class he is in, and his livelihood will be from a known direction. **4** Now if its lord was free of the infortunes or received, that good will increase the more he advances in years; and if it was made unfortunate, it indicates the corruption of that and its destruction. **5** If it was in the Ascendant, then from a work he does, and he will gain from it; and if it was in the fourth, then in relation to fathers and because of them; and if it was in the opposite [of the Ascendant], then from women and lawsuits; and if it was in the Midheaven, then from the Sultan.[203]

6 And if it was in the eleventh, fifth, ninth, and third, then it is below the first category, except that if its lord was in a stake or in an excellent place, then it makes it suitable. **7** And in the ninth house it indicates that it will be from travels, but it corrupts it after he collects it, or his condition will worsen at the end of his life. **8** And likewise in the third, and it [also] indicates that its corruption will be in relation to siblings. **9** And in the eleventh, he will gain authority in relation to friends, and he will gain assets from that. **10** And if it was in the fifth, then in relation to children.

11 The Lot of assets in the <second[204] sign: the power of the judgment proceeds from the lord of the second sign, because it has two testimonies by looking at the place and its lord, and you should not mix it with anything. **12** And in> the sixth, eighth, the twelfth, you mix it with the lord of the second. **13** Now if <the lord of the sixth> was greater in testimonies than the lord of the second, and it was in the sixth, and its lord looking at it, his livelihood will be from crops,[205] animals, <and servants>; and if it was not looking at it, it will be from remedies and medicine. **14** And if it was in the eighth, then look also at its testimonies and the testimony of the lord of the second: and if it was greater in testimonies <than the lord of the second, his livelihood will

---

[203] Māshā'allāh then adds: "Then, speak about the aspect of the fortunes and infortunes, based on what I have described to you of increase and decrease, and mix it with the second and its lord."
[204] Adding based on Māshā'allāh, here and below.
[205] Reading غلّات with Māshā'allāh for علّات ("illnesses").

be from a patron; and if the lord of the second was greater in testimony>,[206] he will be an author of lawsuits and contentions, with a difficult livelihood.

ಬಿ ಜ ಜ

15 And[207] if the lord of the Lot was inspecting the fortunes, it indicates riches; and if it was reversed, then reverse it. **16** And if it was easternizing, appearing, in its own place, then [it indicates] wealth; and if it was western [but] easternizing within[208] seven <days>, then [it indicates] wealth as well as obscurity.

17 And[209] count from Jupiter to Saturn by day, and by night the reverse of that, and cast it out from the Ascendant, and where it terminates, there is the Lot of assets. **18** And if a fortune coincided with it or looked at it from a square or opposition, the native will be blessed with assets. **19** Now if the sign was of the signs of animals[210] (Aries and others), then his assets will be from animals, and they will *be* animals. **20** And if it was Taurus and his triplicities, then from lands and vegetation. **21** And if it was in Gemini and its triplicities, it will be from knowledge and speech. **22** And if it was Cancer and its triplicity, then from waters and commerce [involving] travels. **23** And if this Lot was with an infortune or [one] inspected it from a square or opposition, the reason for the corruption of his assets will be from the essences of these triplicities which I have mentioned to you.

24 And look at the fortunes and infortunes, whichever of them are stronger: for truly the outcome in the indication of it is <from> the stronger of them.

---

[206] Adding from Māshā'allāh.
[207] This is now part of Dorotheus's discussion of the Lot of assets: *Carmen* I.29, **19-22**. Cf. also above. Ch. 2.11, **17-18**.
[208] Lit., "towards."
[209] This Lot is called the "Lot of life" by Abū Ma'shar, and may be the "Lot of livelihood" mentioned by name by Dorotheus in *Carmen* I.29, **29** but then abruptly abandoned without any information or instructions. This formula is identical to the generic Lot of children (see Ch. 5.1, **91**).
[210] Normally this word means *riding* animals, but one cannot ride sheep and similar animals indicated by Aries. There is ambiguity here because Sahl's source seems to want both the more concrete indications of the signs (e.g. animals for Aries), but also the broader classification by triplicity (e.g., the fiery triplicity as a whole).

25 Whenever you find the Sun and Jupiter (they being the lords of the triplicities of fire)[211] both in strength, he will gain authority and assets paid to him which he did not expect nor hope for. **26** And if Mars was the lord of its triplicity, blood will be on his hands. **27** And if Venus and the Moon were the two lords of its triplicity, he will gain authority without the shedding of blood, and he will not cease to rise in his authority. **28** And if it was Saturn, he will gain authority and rulership, and that will be in the nobility (so he will govern the people), and through the working of lands, and his authority will last; and if it was Mercury, he will gain authority and rulership by proceeding according to denial and deception,[212] and he will work with the Sunnah so that he will be good in the eyes of the people, and they will adorn him with praise. **29** And that is if these planets were in powerful positions of the circle; and if you found this one corrupted, [but] another one[213] of the indicators of assets is suitable, then he will gain assets but he will not have authority except a low authority.

30 And[214] look at the Lot of Fortune and its lord, just as you look at the Ascendant and its lord: now if the Sun was powerful by day and likewise his lord[215] (and the Moon and her lord strong by night), then you do not need[216] the Lot. **31** And if they were not powerful, then work with the Lot, for it will indicate [any] elevated rank and [his] condition in his position, so do not neglect it.

---

[211] النَيِّر, which normally means "luminary," viz. the sect light; but reading as النَّار, because I take Sahl to mean the triplicity lords of the Lot of livelihood in **17**, or the Lot of assets. But it is possible that he is reintroducing the triplicity lords of the sect light without saying so.

[212] But this could also be read as "...authority and rulership by punishing [people] for denial and deception." The key word is جريه ("[his] proceeding"), which could be read as جزية, the poll tax assessed primarily to non-Muslims, but which comes from a root that means to punish for wrongdoing.

[213] Or perhaps, "the other one," if the text is distinguishing the first triplicity lord from the second one.

[214] For this paragraph, cf. *Carmen* I.28, **10**.

[215] This is probably his triplicity lord.

[216] Reading for an uncertain word, but with the logic of the rest of the sentence.

[A three-tier system for assets]

32 Now as for those who reach extremes in the accumulation of assets and coffers until they bequeath them to someone after them, that is known from the Lot of Fortune: because Ptolemy says that all leadership and hope and benefit (or the majority of it) is from the Lot of Fortune.[217] **33** So if the Lot was connected with the Sun and Jupiter, and they are both falling away from the infortunes, and one of them is in its exaltation, and the Lot made fortunate by them both from the stakes, and the Moon connected with that fortune, then this native will have all of [his] profits remaining with him until he dies, [and] that will not dwindle.

34 And for those in the middle, if you found Mercury and Venus looking at the Lot and they were both made fortunate, and the degree of the Lot made fortunate, falling away from the infortunes, then that native will be of those in the middle, but he will be powerful in his assets and leadership, in relation to writing and commerce, and he will reach a limit after which there is no limit, especially in the abundance of assets. **35** And if you found the Moon connecting with Venus and Mercury and the Lot, or she connected with one of them, and she was made fortunate, then that native's assets will remain until he bequeaths them to one after him.

36 And if you found the two infortunes in the stakes or the Sun connected with them, then those assets will disappear from his hands during his life. **37** Now if that misfortune was from Saturn, it will disappear from theft[218] and being worn out. **38** And if it was from Mars, and he turns that away from Mercury[219] and the Lot, then the Sultan will take it from him by means of injustice; and if the Sultan ignored him and you found Mars in a powerful place, what he gathers will be taken by robbers or the burning of fire. **39** And He is more knowledgeable.

---

[217] Ptolemy would agree as far as material fortune goes, but this passage is not based on Ptolemy.

[218] Tentatively reading اللصوصية for الوصية.

[219] This probably means that he is in aversion to Mercury.

[Chapter 2.16: On those in the middle, from al-Andarzaghar]

1 Al-Andarzaghar said concerning this: As[220] for how the livelihood of those in the middle comes to be, look at the lord of the Lot of Fortune. **2** For if you found it made unfortunate, and you found a fortune looking at it from an excellent place, and it is eastern, then the good fortune of that native (as well as his good and wealth) will be in the middle, according to the distribution of that fortune.[221]

3 Now[222] if you found the lord of the triplicity of the Sun in the fifteenth[223] from the end of the [ascensional] sign of the stake, then his good fortune will be in the middle.

4 And[224] if the fortunes and infortunes were all looking together at the Lot of Fortune, then his livelihood will be in the middle.

5 And[225] look too at the lord of the Ascendant, the lord of the Midheaven, and the lord of the house of hope:[226] for if you found a motley mixture, [some] of them cleansed of the infortunes and [some] of them made unfortunate, then the good fortune of that native will be in the middle, sometimes with good, and sometimes with hardship.

<**6** If[227] the triplicity lord of the sect light is in a bad place, but that of the other luminary in a good place, it indicates someone in the middle.>

---

[220] For this paragraph, cf. *Carmen* I.28, **23**. *Carmen* also wants the fortune to look at the Ascendant and the Moon as well.

[221] That is, what kinds of things that planet doles out through its nature, not the predictive method called "distributions."

[222] Cf. *Carmen* I.28, **5**. Sahl's text is not as clear as it should be; a better, more faithful account of the method is in Māshā'allāh's version above (Section 2.13, **48**). In *Carmen* (I.28, **7**) one measures out 45° *in ascensions* out from the degree of an axis (not zodiacal degrees): the first 15° indicate high prosperity, the second 15° is next best, and the third 15° is middling (the rest are not powerful for this). So the measurement is not by normal zodiacal signs, but by *ascensional* "signs," which are so called because they are divisions of the celestial equator, *by analogy with* the zodiacal signs. Therefore, I have added "ascensional" in square brackets for clarity.

[223] Or rather, 15°.

[224] This could easily represent a missing sentence from *Carmen*.

[225] For this paragraph, cf. *Carmen* I.27, **5** and **7**. But this ought to be the second house, as Heph. II.18 (Schmidt p. 55) confirms.

[226] This might be the lord of the second, as Heph. II.18 confirms.

[227] Adding with *BA* III.2.3, **6**. *Carmen* I.28, **9** explains that the native's assets and condition will not rise beyond what he is able to manage by himself.

[Chapter 2.17: On falling down from good fortune, from al-Andarzaghar]

1 Because[228] good fortune and wealth do not last for any of the sons of Adam who are born, until the day they die, we ought to look at the topic of his falling (from wherever that [good] fortune falls): so work in that just as I have explained to you.

2 Look for one who is born by day at the lords of the triplicities of the Sun, and for one born by night at the lords of the triplicities of the Moon: for if they were in excellent places, [but] then the infortunes made them unfortunate, then he will fall from his good fortune.

3 And[229] if you found the Lot of Fortune or its lord in an excellent place, and the infortunes made them unfortunate, he will also fall from good fortune.

4 And[230] if you found the fortunes in the Ascendant or Midheaven, and the infortunes were in the house of marriage, then it indicates falling from good fortune.

5 And[231] if you found Mars or Saturn in the house of assets, and they were not powerful,[232] then it indicates falling from good fortune.

6 And[233] if they were both in the house of fathers (or one of them, and the other in the Midheaven), with Jupiter not looking at them, he will fall from good fortune; and worse for the fall [is that] he will be ejected from his land and country, and will fall after his good fortune [such that] he will never recover from it.

7 And[234] if you found Mars or Saturn in the eleventh from the Ascendant or in the eleventh from the Lot of Fortune, then it indicates a fall from good fortune.

8 And[235] if you found Saturn with the Moon in one of the stakes, even if he was a king, he will fall from good fortune; and that is worse if Mars looked

---

[228] Cf. Hugo's more flowery version of this simple statement in *BA* III.2.2.

[229] Cf. *Carmen* I.28, **25-26**.

[230] Cf. *Carmen* I.28, **28**.

[231] Cf. *Carmen* I.28, **30**.

[232] That is, not of the sect (see *Carmen* and *BA* III.2.2).

[233] Cf. *Carmen* I.28, **31**.

[234] Cf. *Carmen* I.28, **32** (which mentions only the eleventh from the Ascendant) and *Anth.* II.12 and Rhetorius Ch. 54 (p. 36), which discuss the infortunes (and other planets) in the eleventh from the Lot. However, *BA* adds that they are contrary to the sect (which makes more sense).

at it. **9** And if the nativity was like this and Jupiter looked at it, then judge a fall for him [anyway].

10 And[236] look also at the Moon: if you saw her separating from the fortunes[237] and connecting with the infortunes, then it indicates a fall.

11 And[238] likewise if the Sun was in the sixth or in the twelfth, and the infortunes looked at him, it indicates falling.

12 Now[239] if the luminaries were withdrawing from the stakes, and they are not looking at the Ascendant, and the infortunes were in the stakes, they indicate poverty.

13 And[240] look too at the lord of the meeting or fullness: for if it was in the house of the sixth or twelfth, it indicates a fall.[241]

14 And if you found the house-master of the nativity in a bad place, and the infortunes looked at it, then it indicates a fall from good fortune.

Chapter [2.18:] [More on] falling from good fortune[242]

1 And if Saturn looked at the meeting or fullness from a fixed sign, it indicates a lasting, steady fall. **2** Now if he was in one having two bodies, then occasionally. **3** And if he was in a convertible sign, then many times. **4** And if he was in a stake, then the fall will be from a great matter; and if he was in

---

[235] For this paragraph, cf. *Carmen* I.29, **1-3**.

[236] This follows logically from *Carmen* I.28, **27**, which has her separating from infortunes and connecting with fortunes (showing good fortune after difficulty).

[237] Reading for "infortunes." This is the contrary of (and is implied by) *Carmen* I.28, **27**; if it was read as "infortunes," it would not fit the category of falling fortune after previous success.

[238] Cf. *Carmen* I.28, **15**, which however uses the Lot of Fortune and its lord, not the Sun. *BA* III.2.2 adds that the fortunes are in aversion. But *BA* also connects this rule with the prenatal lunation. My sense is that this probably was originally about the Lot and its lord, as in *Carmen*; but somewhere along the way a similar consideration about the lunation and the Sun got blended with it. When Arabic is not written neatly the word for "Lot" and the word for "Sun" can look very similar.

[239] This sentence is not in *BA*.

[240] Cf. *Carmen* I.28, **15** and see the footnote to **11** above.

[241] **M** now repeats **10**, which I omit here.

[242] Sahl must have inserted this additional section on the same topic, because the text in *BA* ended at the equivalent of **14** above.

what follows a stake, then from the condition of men; and if falling, then in flight and scandal, pain, and sudden death.

Chapter [2.19:] On those who rise after wretchedness [from al-Andarzaghar]

1 As[243] for those who rise after wretchedness, if the infortunes were in the stakes and the fortunes in what follows them, it indicates falling down, then they will rise.

2 And[244] if you found the Moon separating from the infortunes and connecting with the fortunes, then he will rise after wretchedness.[245]

3 And[246] likewise also see if <only>[247] the nocturnal planets for one born by day (and for one born by night the diurnal planets) looked at the Lot of Fortune: he will be hidden in good fortune until it is the middle of his lifespan.

4 Look[248] also at the lords of the triplicities <of the luminary, if they were direct and safe from burning>:[249] for if their places were like that, then if one of them was in the house of the other, it is likewise. **5** And if the third lord of the triplicity was in the house of marriage, he will gain good fortune at the end of his lifespan.

6 And a native whose planets you find in the bad places from the Ascendant, and they are looking at the Lot of Fortune, and its lord in an excellent place, then at the end of his life he will have a good livelihood.

---

[243] Cf. *Carmen* I.28, **27**.
[244] Cf. *Carmen* I.28, **27**.
[245] Omitting a repetition of Ch. 2.17, **4**, which does not belong to this category.
[246] Cf. *Carmen* I.28, **36**.
[247] Adding with the sense of *Carmen*.
[248] Abū Bakr II.2.9 (in *PN2*) seems to supply the correct sense of this sentence. From the Latin: "If the lords of the triplicity were direct, in each other's domicile, and safe from burning, the native will be elevated from evil to good at the end of life." But it is not clear to me whether the two sentences are necessarily connected. This paragraph must have been garbled in many manuscripts of the source of *BA* as well, because in *BA* III.2.4, Hugo smooths it out so that the first two lords are simply in each other's houses *and also* the third lord is in the seventh.
[249] Adding with the sense of Abū Bakr.

7 And[250] likewise look at the Lot of Fortune and its lord: for the Lot indicates the beginning of the lifespan, and its lord the end of life.

8 And[251] if you found the Moon in the nativity going from the infortunes to the fortunes,[252] it indicates that the native will rise to good fortune from a fall.

9 And work likewise with the infortunes, if they were eastern, in the area[253] which is between the Ascendant up to the Midheaven, and the fortunes looked at them both from their opposition, and they have power in the nativity.

[Chapter 2.20: Those who are always miserable, from al-Andarzaghar]

1 As[254] for the miserable, the humble, and the poor who never cease to be with evil, look: if you found the lord of the triplicities of the Sun made unfortunate, or the Lot of Fortune unfortunate,[255] and you found it in the sixth and twelfth, if the infortunes were with it or they looked at it from a square or opposition, and you found the lord of the Lot in the house of its fall, or made unfortunate, powerful in misfortune (and you do not look at the Sun for one born by night, nor at the Moon for one born by day), and Mars for one born by day is with the Lot,[256] or opposing or in square to it, then that [native] will not cease to be miserable from the day he is born up to the day he dies.

2 And[257] look likewise at the lord of the Lot: if you found it in the sixth and twelfth, and you saw Jupiter and Venus made unfortunate in the sixth and twelfth, and they are both not looking at the Moon (and <worse is if>[258]

---

[250] Cf. Rhetorius Ch. 54 (p. 38).
[251] Cf. **2** above; **E** omits this sentence. In *BA* III.2.4, the Moon in the nativity does do this, in the equivalent of **2** above; for the sentence that occurs here in *BA*, she does this at the pre-natal lunation, not the nativity.
[252] Reading "from the infortunes to the fortunes" with *BA* III.2.4, for an unreadable phrase.
[253] Lit, "the bound, limit, border."
[254] Much of this paragraph is a combination of *Carmen* I.28, **9** and **15-16**.
[255] **M** omits this phrase about the Lot.
[256] **M** adds, "or with the Sun." In *Carmen*, this is the lord of the Lot.
[257] Cf. *Carmen* I.28, **21-22**.
[258] Adding with the sense of *Carmen*, here and later in the sentence.

you found the two infortunes in the stakes or what follows the stakes), <he will be miserable>.

3 And[259] if you found the lords of the four stakes and the lords of the second [places] from the stakes, all of them[260] corrupt, falling, then it makes him fall. **4** And you do not look at nativities of the day except from the Sun, nor for nativities of the night except <from> the Moon: so judge misery for him likewise.[261]

5 And[262] look likewise at the house of assets and its lord: if you found it in a bad place, and the infortunes looked at that house or they were in it, and the fortunes are not looking, and the planets powerful in good fortune are falling, then judge that he is wretched.

6 And[263] look at the Lot of assets and its lord: for if you found it in the sixth and twelfth, and the fortunes are not looking at it, then judge wretchedness for him.

[Chapter 2.21: On those whose earnings are from their own hands, or from force & injustice, from al-Andarzaghar]

1 And[264] if you found the first lord of the triplicity of the Lot of Fortune in the bound of the fortunes, and it is in an excellent position in the nativity, and it looked at the Lot of Fortune, his earning and livelihood will be from his own assets.

2 And[265] if you found <the two lords of the triplicity of>[266] the Lot of Fortune not looking at the Lot of Fortune, and the other fortune is not looking

---

[259] Cf. *Carmen* I.27, **5-9**.

[260] For the rest of the sentence, **E**: "leaving the stakes, it makes him fall." **M** omits the phrase about making him fall and jumps to the next sentence.

[261] What Dorotheus means is that we would prefer the lords of the angles and succeedents to be looking at the sect light.

[262] This may be a kind of mixture of *Carmen* I.29, **20** and **27**.

[263] This may represent a missing sentence from around *Carmen* I.29, **21**.

[264] Sentence **1-2** originally appeared at the beginning of the next chapter, but I have put them back here where they parallel *BA* III.2.6. For this sentence, cf. *Carmen* I.28, **33**. But in *Carmen*, this is the Lot itself, not its triplicity lord.

[265] Cf. *Carmen* I.28, **35**.

[266] Adding based on *Carmen*.

at the Lot of Fortune,²⁶⁷ his livelihood will increase in the good due to a foreign man, and good will be said about him.²⁶⁸

3 And²⁶⁹ as for those whose earnings are from their own hands, from force and injustice, if you found Saturn and Mars in the eleventh from the Lot of Fortune, and you found them both in their own houses, triplicity, or exaltation, his livelihood will be from force and injustice.

4 And if you found the first lord of the triplicity of the Lot of Fortune not looking at the Lot, while the second lord of the triplicity does look at the Lot, then judge for him that he will earn assets at one time and [then] destroy them at another,²⁷⁰ and will be of those who squander and are ruined.

[Chapter 2.22: More on good fortune, the Lot, & timing, from al-Andarzaghar]

1 And²⁷¹ if you wanted to know when the good fortune would be (or the middle of good fortune, and wretchedness), then look at [1] the course²⁷² of the planets and their connections, and [2] the stakes, and [3] the Lot of For-

---

²⁶⁷ *Carmen* has it that both fortunes are looking at the Lot. This makes sense in that for *Carmen*, the result is a good livelihood with strangers, while if both a fortune and infortune look, it will be mixed.

²⁶⁸ But *BA* III.2.6 more plausibly says simply that the native will be dependent on others. This is more appropriate since the text states there is no fortune configured with the Lot, so the statement about having a good reputation is out of place.

²⁶⁹ This is very close to *Anth.* II.21 (Schmidt pp. 31-32; Riley pp. 35-36), which does briefly consider the malefics in Fortune 11ᵗʰ and in a good condition, but does not mention violence. On the other hand, Rhetorius Ch. 54 (p. 36) does speak about violence but only when the malefics are in Fortune 12ᵗʰ. At any rate, the passage makes astrological sense and I have no problem believing it might have originated in *Carmen*.

²⁷⁰ For the rest, **M** reads: "through his deceit, and he will be ruined."

²⁷¹ Cf. Rhetorius Ch. 54 (p. 37). Sahl is sometimes clearer than Rhetorius. The list in Sahl seems to involve [1] primary directions, perhaps by ascensions, [2] ages of life based on planets in the quadrants (not in Rhetorius), [3] some method involving the Lots of Fortune and Spirit, perhaps profections (nor does Rhetorius explain), [4] the method of ascensions and planetary periods described at length by Valens in *Anth.* II.28 and VII.3, VII.5, and VII.6, [5] distributions, and [6] profections of the Ascendant.

²⁷² السّير, suggesting transits, but perhaps this should be التّسيير, "direction" (primary directions).

tune and the Lot of the Invisible, and [4] the ascensions of the signs[273] <and> from the periods of the planets (the greatest, the middle, and the least), and [5] the distributor of time and [6] the lord of the year, just as I described to you earlier in the book, if God wills.

---

[273] Reading with Rhetorius for "stars."

Chapter 3: On the matter of siblings, whether they are many or one

[al-Andarzaghar][1]

1 The first of [the topics]: if you would know the preferment of the native (is he the first-born child or not).[2]

2 The second: if you would know the abundance, middling amount, and scarcity of the siblings.[3]

3 The third: on the siblings' friendship with each other, and their enmity.[4]

4 The fourth: on the siblings' benefit to each other.[5]

5 The fifth: the number of siblings.[6]

6 The sixth: if you would know the sex[7] of the native's siblings, male or female.[8]

7 The seventh: if you would know who is born after him, male or female.[9]

8 The eighth: on the death of the siblings.[10]

9 Before everything in the subject of siblings, begin with the knowledge of the essences of the signs. **10** For[11] indeed the signs of many children are Cancer and its triplicity, and the signs hindering [them] are Leo, Virgo, and Capricorn; and the rest of the signs are middling.

11 And[12] know that the Sun and Saturn indicate the older brothers, Jupiter and Mars indicate the middle ones of them, and Mercury indicates the

---

[1] The following topics roughly track the order of chapters, but Sahl lists more topics than in BA does, which might have been in the Arabic original.

[2] See Ch. 3.1, esp. **1-10**.

[3] See Chs. 3.2 (esp. **12-31**), 3.5 (esp. **14-15**), and 3.11 (esp. **1-4**).

[4] See Chs. 3.3 (esp. **3-5**), 3.13 (esp. **14-18**).

[5] See Ch. 3.4 (esp. **1**).

[6] See Ch. 3.5.

[7] Reading جنس for خير ("good").

[8] See Ch. 3.6.

[9] See Ch. 3.7.

[10] See Chs. 3.2 (esp. **12-31**), and 3.8.

[11] See *Carmen* I.21, **3**; but also see the list in Ch. 5.1, **8**, Ch. 1.38, **14-17**, and *Introduction* Ch. 1, **23-24**.

[12] See *Carmen* I.23, **10**.

younger ones of them, and the Moon indicates the older sisters, and Venus indicates the younger ones of them.

[Chapter 3.1: Whether he is the first-born or not]

[al-Andarzaghar]

1 And[13] as for the knowledge of whether he is the first-born or not, if you found the lord of the triplicity of the Ascendant in the Ascendant, then the native is first-born; and if you found it in the Midheaven, then he is first-born or the fourth; and if you found it in the seventh, then he is first-born or the seventh. **2** Then,[14] look also at the fortunes and infortunes, how their aspect is, and where their positions are by union, opposition, or square: for indeed, the infortunes kill, and the fortunes save.

3 And[15] look also from the Midheaven to the Ascendant: for if you do not find a planet in what is between them, then say he is the first-born. **4** And if there was a child before him and you do not see anything [there], then judge for him that [the other brother] will die,[16] and [the native] will survive as the eldest of the siblings. **5** And if you found planets in what is between the Ascendant and the stake of the earth, then one will be born after him. **6** And if you do not see anything in what is between the Ascendant and the fourth except the infortunes, then judge for him that a sibling will not be born to him unless it is miscarried,[17] or the one who is born to him will come out dead or will die quickly. **7** And if the fortunes were in those places which I mentioned, then they will survive.

8 And look at the lord of the third: for if you found it in the Ascendant or in the seventh, then say that he will be an only child, not having a sibling. **9** And if you found it in the Midheaven, then he will have siblings older than

---

[13] For **1**, see *Carmen* I.19, **1-2**.
[14] For this sentence, see generally *Carmen* I.19, **4-11**.
[15] For this passage, see *Carmen* I.19, **4-12**, Rhetorius Ch. 103, and Sahl's Chs. 3.5, **2-8**, and 3.13, **5-13**.
[16] Or perhaps, "is dead" (يموت).
[17] سقط, the root of which literally means to "fall down"; to me this suggests broadly someone whose life somehow falls apart.

him. **10** And if you found it in the direction of the house of fathers,[18] then he will have siblings younger than him.

11 And[19] whenever you find the Moon separating from the infortunes, then speak about the disaster of ruin in the brothers which are before him. **12** And indeed it will be like that if the Moon was not in a separation from any of the planets. **13** And the worst separation is if it was from Saturn, for then if in addition Saturn is in a stake, then he is an only child. **14** Now if it was like that in births of the night, it indicates the death of the siblings.

15 And if you found the Sun or[20] Jupiter in a stake, then say that he is the first-born and will be the head of the people of the household he is from.

16 And[21] if you found Mercury in the Ascendant, it indicates that he will not have a brother older than him; and if there was one, then he has already died. **17** And if you found the Moon separating from Saturn by day, and by Mars at night,[22] it indicates the death of his older siblings.

Chapter [3.2]: On abundance & scarcity

1 Always[23] look at Mars: for if you found him in a sign of many children, and its lord eastern, then it indicates an abundance of the native's siblings—and especially if the Ascendant was not[24] Leo nor Sagittarius.

2 And if you found the lord of the house of siblings eastern, above the earth, it being a good place, then draw a conclusion about the uprightness of

---

[18] E: "in the fourth stake, in the direction of fathers."
[19] For this sentence, cf. *Carmen* I.23, **26-27**. But it does not make sense that this would always be bad.
[20] E: "and."
[21] For this paragraph, cf. *Carmen* I.23, **25-27**.
[22] This should be reversed, as Mars is more malefic by day and Saturn more malefic by night. This is the view of *Carmen* I.23, **26**, and *JN* Ch. 12.
[23] For this sentence, see al-Khayyāt Ch. 12.
[24] The Latin version of al-Khayyāt's Ch. 12 *recommends* both of these signs. But cf. *Carmen* I.20, **2**, which agrees with this sentence but also adds the Moon in Leo or Sagittarius.

the siblings and the goodness of their condition.[25] **3** And[26] if you found an infortune in the third from the Ascendant, then it is bad in the matter of siblings. **4** And likewise if you found the infortune in the second from the Ascendant, for it is not good for the brothers which are born after him, and especially if that infortune was in something other than its own share.[27]

5 And if you found the third place from the Ascendant to be a sign of many children, and in it a fortune, then he will be abundant in siblings, especially if you found the <first>[28] lord of the triplicity of Mars in a stake. **6** Now if you found the first lord of the triplicity of Mars in a bad place and the second one in a good place, eastern, then indeed the native's brothers will come about after he is grey. **7** And if Mars or[29] the lord of his triplicity were under the earth, it indicates a scarcity of siblings, and especially if it was under the rays. **8** If the lord of the triplicity of Mars looked at Mars from a good place, it indicates the goodness of the siblings.

9 If Saturn made Mars unfortunate, or he was in the eighth,[30] then it is bad in the matter of siblings, because it indicates the death of his siblings. **10** And if it was the Moon and Venus, then the disaster will be in the females among his siblings.

11 And the more preferable of the things in the matter of siblings is if the one in charge of his siblings (which is the one [most] abundant in testimonies) was above the earth, not below the earth.

[al-Andarzaghar]

12 Al-Andarzaghar said regarding this: If you found the lord of the triplicity of the sign in which Mars is, in a sign abundant in children, then there will be an abundance of siblings.

13 And if you found the Lot of siblings and its lord falling into one of those signs, <then he will have an abundance of siblings>.[31] **14** Now if you

---

[25] This is the exact phrase used by Māshā'allāh in Ch. 1.37, **9** above, suggesting that this is also by him.
[26] Cf. Dorotheus *Excerpts* XIV.
[27] حظ, which here probably means "sect."
[28] Added by Dykes for clarity.
[29] **E** reads "and" and the plural throughout this sentence, so that both planets are involved—certainly this would be worse.
[30] Reading with **M**, so that Mars is in the eighth. But **E** also plausibly reads: "or [Saturn] was in the second from [Mars]."
[31] Adding on the basis of *BA*.

found the two which are more indicative of siblings[32] in the sterile signs, then judge for him that he will not have siblings. **15** And if you found them in the middling signs, then judge for him a scarcity of siblings. **16** And look in this at the fortunes and infortunes, for the infortunes kill and the fortunes save.

17 And look at the positions of those planets strong in [the matter of] siblings. **18** Now if it was the Sun and Saturn, <and>[33] Mars looks at them from a square or opposition, then it kills the older brothers. **19** If Saturn made Jupiter or Mars unfortunate, it kills the middle brothers. **20** If Mercury was made unfortunate, it kills the younger ones. **21** If the Moon was made unfortunate, it kills the elder sisters. **22** If Venus was made unfortunate, it kills the younger sisters. **23** And if the fortunes assembled or looked from an opposition, square, trine, or sextile, they live; and if the infortunes looked, they will die. **24** And look at those signs, as to whether there are fortunes in them or looking from an opposition, square, or trine: for the siblings which are born after the native—if the Ascendant[34] was in those signs—will live; and those which are born in the unfortunate signs and those which the infortunes look at from a square or opposition will not survive.

25 And know that if the Moon and Ascendant of the native were in signs abundant in children, his mother will abound in children. **26** And if you found the Moon and her bound in Scorpio, and especially in the third degree of it (which is her fall), then she will not have children; and if there were [any], they are dead.

27 And[35] look at the flowing away of the Moon as well as her connection: for if you found the Moon flowing away from Saturn, then judge that he has siblings older than him; and likewise if she flowed away from Mars. **28** And if she flowed away from Venus, he has a sister younger than him, and in her youth she[36] was enthusiastic in the lesbianism of women. **29** Now if the Moon flowed away from Saturn and connected with Mars, the sister of his

---

[32] This probably is the triplicity lord of Mars and the lord of the Lot.
[33] Added by Dykes.
[34] This seems to mean the Ascendant of the *siblings'* nativities. If so, then let the native's Mars be in Aquarius: if a sibling born later has Aquarius rising, then that sibling is in danger, because of the previous connection with Mars in the native's chart.
[35] For **27-28**, cf. *Carmen* I.23, **26-28**.
[36] **M** reads "he." The text in *Carmen* says that the native will enjoy the acts of Venus. Clearly the male native assumed here cannot also be a lesbian unless perhaps the author means that he enjoys sex with multiple women.

who was older than him, has died.[37] **30** And if Saturn was in the house of fathers along with Venus, it kills the sisters, and perhaps they were killed in the wombs of their mothers and their limbs removed from the bellies of their mothers.[38]

31 And if you found the Sun, Saturn, and Mars in one of the stakes, then it corrupts the siblings.

[Theophilus]

32 Theophilus said: If you found the lord of the house of siblings in a sign of many children, [and] a fortune looking at it, and the infortunes were falling <away from it> or one of them looked by means of a weak aspect, then his brothers and sisters will be many, and children will be born to their mother based on what you see of the position of the lord of the house of siblings and the number of fortunes with it which assist it, and the position of the Moon. **33** So, speak about their scarcity and abundance in accordance with that, from the amount named for it.[39] **34** And if you found the lord of the house of siblings in a sign of few children, and you found one of the infortunes assembled with the lord of the house of siblings from a powerful position, and you found the fortunes weak in aspect, and you found the Moon made unfortunate by that infortune which made the house of siblings unfortunate by its influence over it, then judge that the child[40] has already been separated from its parents. **35** Except that if you find the house of siblings made fortunate by one of the fortunes and you find power for that fortune in its position, then you say that a child will be born to his father after him [*unclear*] survive.[41]

36 And[42] if you found the lord of the house of siblings in the twelfth, and you found Mars inspecting it from the stakes, with the strength of Mars and his claims in the position he is in, it introduces hardship and wounds upon him from his siblings, or grief from the Sultan, or intense quarrels.

---

[37] Tenses are sometimes imprecise in Arabic, so this could also be read as, "will die."

[38] This sounds like an abortion rather than miscarriage.

[39] This is awkward, but means the number of significators listed, and the number of planets involved.

[40] E reads, "the native" or "the one born," but in context this must refer to one of the siblings.

[41] Reading with **M**. **E** reads "a child... [*uncertain*] the powerful."

[42] Cf. Ch. 3.3, **9** below.

[The Bizidaj and Dorotheus]

37 The[43] *Bizidaj* and Dorotheus said: If you found the Moon in Leo or Sagittarius, or[44] one of these signs was the Ascendant of the native, it indicates a scarcity of siblings. **38** And if it was in Cancer, Scorpio, or Pisces, or these signs were rising, they indicate an abundance of them.

39 And[45] when the Sun is in the Ascendant, it is not good for siblings.

40 If[46] the lord of the triplicity of Mars was in the eighth or[47] bad places, it indicates a scarcity of siblings; now if one of the two [triplicity lords] was powerful and the other weak, then he will see the death of the siblings, or of some of them.

41 And if an infortune witnessed the lords of the triplicities of the Ascendant from an opposition or square, it indicates the scarcity of siblings; and if they[48] were in stakes, he will have none; but if he did have some, they were separated.

42 And if the Moon was in Sagittarius, it indicates the ruin of the eldest of the siblings.

43 And[49] if an infortune was in the Ascendant or Midheaven or in what follows them, it indicates the threats[50] of the siblings or their death, or he will be of those who do not have a sibling.

44 If Saturn was the lord of the house of siblings, and he was in one of his places, in a fearful position, then it will not be safe for that. **45** And if Jupiter was the lord of the house by day, it indicates siblings having religion; and if it was by night, western, it indicates siblings having false piety (and it indicates likewise if he was in the house of siblings). **46** And if Jupiter was in the house of siblings, in the bound of Mercury or in one of his places,[51] or Mercury

---

[43] For this paragraph, see *Carmen* I.20, **2-4**.
[44] **M** reads, "and."
[45] See *Carmen* I.23, **31**.
[46] See *Carmen* I.23, **11-13**.
[47] **E** omits the eighth; reading "or" for **M**'s "and."
[48] But perhaps this should be the infortune instead?
[49] See *Carmen* I.23, **32**.
[50] Or perhaps, "feuding" (تعادى).
[51] For example, one of Mercury's houses, or a place in which he has the primary triplicity rulership.

looked at him, it indicates their knowledge of secret things. **47** And if the two infortunes and the Sun were in the stakes, that damages the siblings.

The statement of Māshā'allāh on this:

49 He said: Look at the third sign and its lord, and the one which is in the third (of the fortunes and infortunes), and the one looking at that place from a square or opposition. **50** Now if an infortune was in the third sign, and it is alien, it indicates a scarcity of siblings, or the death of one who was before him. **51** And if it looked at it from a square or opposition, it indicates what I mentioned in the first section, and it will ruin those who are born after him (and more harsh for that is Saturn, because Mars has testimony in [the matter of] siblings). **52** And if a fortune looked at that place, it indicates the goodness of the condition of the siblings; now if the witnessing fortune was received, it indicates an abundance of siblings. **53** If it was at the beginning of the sign, it will be the older ones of his siblings; and if it was in the middle of the sign, it is the middle ones of them; and if it was at the end of the sign, it is in the last of them. **54** And if the fortune was the lord of the third and it is free of the infortunes, and one of the luminaries is looking at it, it indicates the goodness of the condition of the native, and an abundance of siblings.

55 Then, look at the lord of the third and its position relative to its own house, and its position relative to the Ascendant and its lord. **56** Now if it was under the rays, it indicates a scarcity of siblings; and it is worse for that if it is entering into burning. **57** And likewise if it was made unfortunate by an assembly or opposition or square, from a planet not receiving it: but if it was received, he will have siblings but they will be few, and there will be defects in them and they will be hostile to the owner of the Ascendant.[52]

58 If the lord of the third connects with a planet in its exaltation, the siblings will get a position from the nobles; and their condition is known from the planets it is connecting with.

59 Then, look at the position of[53] Mars (who is the indicator of siblings) and the essence of the sign in which he is: work with that, and with the lord

---

[52] That is, to the native.
[53] Up to the colon, I have rendered the sentence according to what makes astrological and textual sense. **M** reads: "the position of Mars (who is the indicator of siblings) in the essence." **E** reads: "the position of the sign of Mars, which has the essence." ("The sign of Mars" in **E** is written ungrammatically in the Arabic.)

of his house, based on what I described to you in the first section.[54] **60** Make his position in the sign be similar to the Lot,[55] and the position of the lord of his house be like the lord of the house of the Lot.

61 And if Mars was in what is between the Midheaven and the Ascendant, then his siblings which are older than him will be stronger and more steadfast, unless he is the first-born or Mars is in his fall (for indeed that situation indicates that he is better than his siblings). **62** Now if [Mars] was retrograde, they will have defects. **63** And if Mars was in what is between the Ascendant and the stake of the earth, then it indicates that there will be steadfastness and power in his siblings which are born after him, unless he is the last child of his mother or Mars is in his fall.

64 And the best that Mars could be is if he is eastern and has testimony in the sign which he is in, or he is received: for indeed that situation indicates steadfastness.[56] **65** <And if it was the contrary of this, it indicates>[57] corruption in the siblings and their disappearance and flight: and more wicked than that is if he is entering into burning. **66** And Mars [has more testimonies][58] if he was the lord of the third or the lord of the Lot, because [as] the lord of the third he would indicate their killing and ruin.

67 And the separation of the Moon indicates the one who was born before the native: so if she separated from a fortune and it receives her, then the one born before the native is alive and will be of a good condition. **68** And if she was received but did not have the fortune, or it was an infortune, it indicates [long] life, and he will not be in an unfortunate condition. **69** And if it was an infortune but she is not received, then the one who was born before him will not survive; and if with that the infortune looked at the Sun, <and> it was eastern in everything I mentioned,[59] it indicates the birth of these[60]

---

[54] I am not sure what Māshā'allāh is referring to; perhaps a missing portion of his book of nativities?

[55] This is undoubtedly the Lot of siblings.

[56] **M** now skips to the middle of Ch. 3.4, **3**. **E** omits this word, and jumps to "corruption" in the next sentence.

[57] Added by Dykes as it is the only way to make this sentence comprehensible.

[58] Reading very uncertainly: this sentence literally reads: "And Mars testimony and his testimony if he was...".

[59] Meaning unclear.

[60] This should be in the masculine plural, but is in the form that indicates a feminine singular or inanimate plural.

from the connection of the Moon. **70** And if the Moon separated from a planet in its exaltation or it is in a stake, then the one who was born before him is better than him; and you look likewise for the condition of one born after him, from the connection of the Moon.

71 And if you found the lord of the third in the eighth, then it indicates the badness of the siblings' condition. **72** And if it was in the tenth sign from the Ascendant, it indicates the shortness of their survival.

73 And in a revolution of years, if the lord of the third from the Ascendant of the year was in the tenth, the owner of the revolution will be oppressive to[61] some of his siblings; and if it was made unfortunate, it will be more harsh. **74** And if you found the lord of the third in a stake, in its own house or exaltation, then his siblings will attain nobility. **75** And if there was [nothing] of what I stated, and it was in a stake, the siblings will get [some other] position.

[Chapter 3.3: The agreement & hostility of the siblings]

[al-Andarzaghar]

1 And[62] as for the agreement of some siblings with each other, or their hostility, look at the Lot of siblings (both of them),[63] and the lord of each: if you found the lord of the Lot of siblings looking at the Lot from the trine, it indicates their safety and agreement with their whole heart. **2** And if it looked from the square, the love will be in the middle; and if it looked from an opposition, then their hatred will be deep; and a scarcity of interaction if one does not look at the other.

3 And[64] if you found Mars in the house of the glowing ones or in one of the stakes, then it is bad for siblings, and especially if the lord of the Ascend-

---

[61] خفيف على. Normally this adjective means "easy, light," but paired with this preposition it means "oppressive." The idea seems to be that the tenth of the revolution indicates the native's own exercise of authority, so if the lord of the third (of the revolution) is in the tenth (of the revolution), then he will have authority over a sibling.

[62] For this paragraph, cf. *Carmen* I.23, **36-38** and **40**.

[63] This must refer to the Saturn-Jupiter and Mercury-Jupiter Lots: see Ch. 3.11, **1-4** below. (But the Mercury-Jupiter Lot in Dorotheus is for the *number* of siblings.) Also note that Rhetorius Ch. 105 (see below, Ch. 3.13, **14ff**) compares the Lot of *friendship* or friends with the Lot of siblings.

[64] From the middle of **3** through the rest of the paragraph, cf. *Carmen* I.23, **33-35**.

ant and the lord of the Moon were with him or looked at him (and especially Mercury). **4** And it is more wicked for all of that if the lord of the Ascendant and the Moon were in the sign in which Mars was: for they themselves will speak of killing one another, and they will fight with each other and perhaps kill each other. **5** But if you found Mars with Mercury or Mercury looked at Mars, then they themselves will seek out a quarrel and disavow one another, and act in a pompous way towards one another, and perhaps that will rise in evil until there is killing—and especially if he looked at the Moon or at the Lot of siblings.

✺   ✺   ✺

6 And if you found the Head in the house of siblings, and you found \<it\> to be a house of Jupiter, and you found the Lot and the Moon both looking at the sign in which the Head is, then his siblings will be pleased with him and their hearts will rejoice.

7 Now if you found Mars in the sign of siblings or assembling with the lord of the house of siblings, then disaster will enter upon him in relation to his siblings, as well as sorrow, enmity, separation, hardship, [and] defeat.[65] **8** If you found Saturn in the house of siblings or assembling with the lord of the house of siblings, then evil will enter between them and him in relation to inheritance, and quarrels in that and in homes and real estate; then that will be prolonged between them due to the position of Saturn and his prolonging [of things], and his heaviness.

9 And[66] if you found the lord of the house of siblings in the twelfth and you found the Lot of Fortune made unfortunate, connecting with the lord of the house of siblings, and you found Mars inspecting them both from the stakes, with power from Mars, then hardship and wounds will enter upon him from his siblings, or grief from the direction of the Sultan, and intense quarrels.

10 Now if you found the lord of the third looking at the lord of the Ascendant from a trine or sextile, then the siblings will love one another or be interconnected; and if it was from an assembly or square, it is in the middle;

---

[65] غلبة. Really this word means "victory," (i.e., to defeat someone), but in context it seems the native is experiencing defeat with the siblings.
[66] See the other version of this in Ch. 3.2, **36**, attributed to Theophilus.

and if it was from an opposition, they will hate one another. **11** And if it was not looking at the lord of the Ascendant, see if it looks at the Ascendant: for if it does look, then speak on it based on what I described to you; except that the judgment regarding the lord of the Ascendant indicates what I pointed out about false piety (and if there was a judgment on the Ascendant, then it indicates false piety). **12** And if it did not look at the Ascendant nor at the lord of the Ascendant, then see if it looks at the Lot of Fortune or its lord: then judge on it just as I described to you in the section on the Ascendant and its lord. **13** Except that this is less than the first topic, unless the birth was by night: for indeed the Lot [of Fortune] and its lord are stronger in a birth by night.

[Chapter 3.4: The benefit of the siblings]

1 And[67] as for the benefit of the siblings, one to the other, look at the Lot of Fortune and its lord: for al-Andarzaghar <said> if it was with the Lot of siblings or the lord of the Lot of siblings, it indicates the benefit of one to the other, and perhaps they will gain much from their siblings. **2** And if the lord of the Lot of siblings was a fortune, and it is eastern, in one of the stakes, it indicates the benefit of the siblings, and especially if the Lot of Fortune was with the Lot of siblings, or the lord of siblings was the lord of the Lot of Fortune, or <the lord of>[68] the Lot of Fortune looks at the Lot of siblings and it is a fortune.

3 Now if you found the lord of the Lot of siblings in the place of Good Fortune,[69] the Ascendant, or the fifth, then state [that there is] agreement among the siblings; and likewise in the ninth. **4** And if you found the lord of the Lot of siblings with the Lot of Fortune or you found it looking at the Lot [of Fortune] with an aspect of friendship, or it itself was the lord of the Ascendant or the lord of the triplicity of the Ascendant, and it is a fortune, then he will have benefit and harmony with them; but if it was an infortune or it was outside of its own share,[70] it indicates corruption and shouting between them (and God is more knowledgeable, and in Him is success).

---

[67] For this paragraph, see *Carmen* I.23, **36-38**. Only **1** is in the Latin *BA*, but **1-4** fit well together and may have been in the original Arabic.
[68] Added by Dykes, because the Lot itself cannot be a fortune.
[69] That is, the eleventh.
[70] حظّه, which should probably be understood here as "sect."

5 Muḥammad b. Bishr al-Khurāsānī[71] said, concerning the day on which the second child is born: If the lord of the house[72] of siblings is in the house of a planet, he will be born after the native on the day of that planet, and in the hour of the lord of the house of siblings. **6** For example, if Jupiter was the lord of the house of children and he is in Aries, it indicates that after this native will be born a child on the day of <Mars>[73] (or the day of the other one [will belong] to the lord of the house or exaltation),[74] in the hour of Jupiter (who is the lord of the house of siblings).

The statement of Theophilus on this:

8 He said,[75] Look at the harmony of the Lot of Fortune with the lord of the house of siblings and the Lot of siblings, and the falling away of the infortunes from them: for that is what indicates that intense love and friendship and good will be bestowed upon him from his siblings.

9 And if you found the Moon assembled with the lord of the Lot of Fortune, or inspecting it with a connection, and it[76] is made fortunate, cleansed of the infortunes, then the native will be higher than his siblings, and he will overpower them, and they will seek his favor, and he will give preference to[77] them. **10** And if you found the Lot of Fortune made unfortunate, while you

---

[71] An astrologer currently unknown.

[72] **E**: "sign."

[73] Reading with the instruction above, for a word that seems to be a misspelling for "triplicities."

[74] This seems to mean that it could be on the day of the Sun, since the Sun is the exalted lord of Aries.

[75] For this paragraph, cf. *Carmen* I.23, **36-37**. This whole section by Theophilus is rather difficult in the Arabic, due to spelling differences and mismatches in the dotting of letters between the two manuscripts. My sense is that either Theophilus was very difficult for the original Arabic translator, or the source text was in poor condition. For example, in **10** the text repeats the phrase "and the Moon inspects" for both the fortunes and the Lot of Fortune whereas normally it would say it once and then list both of the objects in a row. Or in **12**, Sahl has both good and bad things happening at the beginning of the lifespan, when we would expect them to happen at different times.

[76] This is probably the lord of the Lot, not the Moon.

[77] يفضّل عليهم. Reading in Form II so as to avoid the redundancy of "be higher than" (Form I).

found the Lot of siblings and the house of siblings made fortunate, then the native will be in need of his fraternal relations, and he will seek their favor, and they will be higher than him: and he will not cease to rely on them[78] in his livelihood—unless you find the Moon inspecting the Lot of Fortune and the Moon inspecting the fortunes: for in that case, you will say that the native's livelihood will be taken away from him due to the corruption of the Lot of Fortune, but some of his circumstances in his livelihood will be suitable without his siblings, and he will disengage from them due to the suitability of the Moon with the fortune which helps her.

11 Now[79] if you wanted to know in which of the times of his lifespan that will be, whether its beginning or its end, then look first at the Moon and at the lord of the house of the native's assets:[80] for if you found them both made fortunate, then say that the suitability of his livelihood will be at the end of his lifetime.

12 Then, look at the Lot of Fortune, and due to the place of its misfortune it will indicate his suffering and the scarcity of his leadership; and what he encounters of the good will be at the beginning[81] of [his] lifespan, and that is due to the situation of the Lot of Fortune's misfortune at the beginning of his lifespan. **13** Then, see by which of the two infortunes the Lot of Fortune is made unfortunate: for if it was Mars, from [a situation of] power, and the fortunes fell away from him, then report that he will not cease to be miserable in his livelihood, subordinate to people of corruption and robbers and immoral living. **14** And if the infortune was Saturn, in his power, then he will become one of the underclass, and pimps, and porters, and what is like that of contemptible works, and he will remain in that [condition] (based on what you see of the Lot of Fortune) unless [that planet] manages the house of [the native's] assets.

---

[78] Reading with the sense of the previous sentence, for what seems to be "he will not cease to act with them" (lit., "be in their actions").

[79] At this point Theophilus turns to the *native's* livelihood and assets, presumably because he wants to know if and when the native will have to rely on his siblings.

[80] E has the house of his assets itself, not its lord.

[81] The timing in **11-12** does not make much sense to me. Sentence **11** says that if the Moon and lord of the second are in a good condition, then it will take time to develop and will only manifest later; but if they were in a poor condition would they likewise only show misfortune later? Likewise, **12** says that if the Lot is unfortunate, that will also only manifest later; so if it were good, would it manifest later or earlier? Something may be missing here. Normally, a sign or Lot indicates something earlier, and its lord something later.

15 And the good fortune of the Moon (which I explained to you) truly puts his condition in order after that corruption, [and] then he will rise out of these actions based on what you see of the position of the Moon and her condition, and the position of the infortunes relative to the house of his assets.

[Chapter 3.5:] The number of the native's siblings from his own father & mother

1 Now[82] as for the number of the native's siblings from his father (those which are before him and those after him), if you saw the lord of the Ascendant in the stake <of the Ascendant>,[83] then he is the first child; and if it was in the tenth, then he is second; and in the seventh, he is the third; and the stake of the earth [means] he is the fourth.

2 Another[84] way that is pertinent: see what is between the Midheaven up to the Ascendant, for what you find in it of stars already arisen, those are the siblings he has which were before him. **3** And what you find in what is between the Ascendant and the stake of the earth, that is the siblings which will be after him. **4** So, recognize those stars (and the ones made fortunate).[85] **5** And recognize what was before the native [from] what is above the earth, and what will be after him you will see from what is under the earth: because you will understand the siblings of the native from his own mother as being those of the stars which are rising in these signs, in what is between the Midheaven[86] up to the fourth, based on what I have reported to you. **6** And if there was nothing [in these regions], then look at the lord of the Ascendant and the lord of the house of siblings, and which of them is lighter in course:

---

[82] For this passage on the quadrants and number of siblings, see also Ch. 3.1, **1ff** (both based on *Carmen* I.19).

[83] That is, in the Ascendant itself.

[84] For this passage, see *Carmen* I.19, **4-12**, Rhetorius Ch. 103, and Sahl's Chs. 3.1, **3-7**, and 3.13, **5-13**.

[85] To me it seems that there should be something else to this, such as "for the fortunate planets indicate that ones that will survive."

[86] **E** reads "Ascendant" (and **M** omits this whole section), but I have read it as "Midheaven" because Sahl has made it clear several times that this entire eastern or rising hemisphere of the chart is what counts.

begin from it [and count] up to the other. **7** For[87] what there is between these two in terms of stars, that is the number of the siblings: because this approach is what is between the lord of the Ascendant to the lord of the house of siblings; and what is between the lord of the [house of] siblings up to the lord of the Ascendant, that is what there is. **8** But beware: for if you saw the star which was alighting [there] in a sign having two bodies, then that is more powerful.[88]

9 And the ancients have already said:[89] if the lord of the triplicity of Mars was above the earth, then count what is between them both[90] up to the Ascendant, for the number of his siblings is according to the number of the signs there are. **10** And if it was in what has two bodies, then double it. **11** Now if they were both under the earth, then count from the Ascendant to them both just as I reported to you. **12** If they were both eastern, then the first one is preferable.

13 And[91] [the ancients] also said, the number of what is above the earth in a birth of the day (of the diurnal planets), and in a nocturnal birth what is under the earth (of the nocturnal planets): the number of each will be his siblings.[92]

[Blood-siblings: al-Andarzaghar]

14 A section[93] on the knowledge of whether he has siblings from someone other than his mother or father, and whether his siblings are from one father or one mother. **15** Look at the sign of siblings: for if it was a sign hav-

---

[87] There may be something missing from the last half of this sentence, because Sahl repeats himself: since he has already said that one begins the counting from the lighter planet, there is no reason to duplicate the instructions to allow for counting from either one to the other.
[88] That is, it should count as two.
[89] That is, Dorotheus: this is taken from the chart example in *Carmen* I.23, **14-21**. In the example, both triplicity lords (Saturn and Mercury) are above the earth and in the same sign; but if they had not been in the same sign, one would prefer the one that is eastern and stronger.
[90] By "both," Sahl's source means "both triplicity lords": see **11** below.
[91] *Carmen* I.23, **22** refers generically to certain "scholars" as the source of this view; but he does not restrict the number only to the planets of the sect.
[92] I believe Sahl has got the nocturnal part of these instructions wrong. In a diurnal chart, it makes sense to take the diurnal planets that are above the horizon, since they rejoice there at that time; but in a nocturnal chart, the nocturnal planets *above* the horizon also rejoice, because they are in the hemisphere opposite the Sun.
[93] See Rhetorius Ch. 106.

ing two bodies, then indeed he has siblings from someone other than his father or mother, and especially if the lord of the house of siblings was in a convertible sign or one having two bodies, or two bodies such as Capricorn; and likewise if you found the sign of siblings to be convertible or its lord in a sign having two bodies, and especially if the Lot of siblings occurred in a sign having two bodies.

[Chapter 3.6: Whether the siblings are brothers or sisters]

1 And as for the knowledge of whether they are brothers or sisters, look at the sign of siblings and [that of] its lord, and the sign of the Moon. **2** For if you found these three signs to be male, then report that he has brothers but does not have sisters; and if you found all of these testimonies to be female, then judge that he has sisters but does not have brothers. **3** And call upon the Lot of siblings and its lord as witnesses, based on what I explained.

4 And if you found (of these testimonies) the sign of siblings to be male, and its lord male, and you found the Lot of siblings in a female sign, and the Moon in a female sign, then report that he has [both] brothers and sisters.

5 And if you wanted to know which of the sexes was more numerous, then look at these testimonies which I named for you. **6** Then, look at their lords together [with that], and look at the Moon and the lord of her house, along with which one of the two it connected with:[94] [is it] in a female sign or a male sign? **7** Then, speak according to what you see of the inclination[95] of the Moon. **8** For if you found these testimonies which I named for you to be split evenly in half, and the infortunes do not make one of these two [sides] unfortunate (for that corrupts and decreases due to the place of the infortunes), then make the brothers and sisters be half-and-half, unless the testimony of one of them happens to be more and you find the Moon inclining with the more numerous: then you make that one the greater of them.

9 And if you found Venus, Jupiter, and Mercury in suitable places, in male signs, they indicate the masculinity of the one born and the siblings; and if they were in female signs, they indicate females.

---

[94] The "it" here is probably the Moon, but I am not sure what "the two" are: I suspect that this should be لها ("them") instead of لهما ("the two").
[95] That is, to which of the genders she inclines according to her situation.

[Chapter 3.7: On those born after the native]

1 And as for the knowledge of one born after the native, whether male or female, look at the lord of the house of siblings. **2** For if it was in a male sign, a male is born after him; and if the lord of the house of siblings was male too, then it is a male; and if it was female, then it is a female.

3 And if the Moon connected with Venus or Saturn (due to his coldness), it indicates the birth of girls after the native, unless the native was the last child of his mother; and if she connected with a planet and that planet was received by Saturn, it is like that as well.

4 And the connection of the opposition with the planets and [their being] under the rays also indicates the birth of girls, because the connection of the opposition is an indicator of females, and the planets under the rays are subjugated[96]—and being subjugated in this situation is an indicator of the feminized and of females.[97] **5** And speak likewise for one born before the native, from the separation of the Moon. **6** And speak about the signs in which the one the Moon connects with, is, or the one she is separated from: if it was one having two bodies, then if it indicates girls, it is two girls. **7** And if it indicates boys, it indicates two boys.

Chapter [3.8:] On the death of the siblings [from al-Andarzaghar]

1 And[98] as for the death of the siblings, look in the sign of siblings: if it ought to be that the siblings are strong, then judge triumph[99] for them.

2 Now[100] if you saw Saturn with one of the two Lots of siblings[101] or opposing one of them or in its square, with no aspect of a fortune, then truly it indicates the death of the siblings, and especially if Mars was with it or looks at the Lot[102] from a square or opposition; and all of that is worse if the planet was in its first slowness, [about to be] retrograde, and especially if you found

---

[96] Or, "overwhelmed" (مقهورة).
[97] This may reflect Middle Eastern practices of veiling and secluding women.
[98] **M** omits this sentence.
[99] Reading for **E**'s "the majority."
[100] For this paragraph, cf. *Carmen* I.23, **39-42**, but also Ch. 3.11, **10** and Ch. 3.13, **23-29** below.
[101] This could be the Lot of siblings and the Lot of the number of siblings, or the Lots of siblings and Fortune (*Carmen*), or the Lots of siblings and friendship (Rhetorius Ch. 105).
[102] Reading السهم for الشمس ("Sun").

Jupiter not looking at the Lot of siblings. **3** So[103] direct the Lot to the infortunes, a year for every degree, by degrees of ascensions. **4** And if in the transformation of the year[104] Mercury was with the infortunes, it kills his siblings. **5** And if both of the infortunes (or one of them) in the root of the native was in the sign in which Mercury was, it kills the siblings; and if it[105] looked at the Lot of siblings from a square or opposition, it is likewise: so judge the death of the siblings. **6** And as for sisters, appoint Mercury and Venus.[106]

[**Chapter 3.9: How to interpret family members *& their Lots*]**

1 And look at the collection of Lots and the strength of the lords of the triplicities: for the father, from the Sun and the lords of his triplicity; for the mother, from the Moon and the lords of her triplicity; for the brothers, from Mars and the lords of his triplicity; and for sisters, from Venus and the lords of her triplicity.

2 Now, from the positions of the planets on the day the native is born is known the beginning of the matter and the rank in which he is on that day, and from the lords of the triplicities is the outcome and what they convert his matter to, of good and evil. **3** If the position of the Sun and the lords of his triplicities are excellent, the beginning of the matter and its end will be excellent. **4** And if the position of the planet is excellent and the position of the lord of the triplicity is corrupted, the beginning of the matter and his condition are good on the day the native is born, [but] then they convert his matter from the indication of that planet to hardship and destruction; and if it is the other way around, then turn it around.

5 Then, look at the Lots: for indeed from them one seeks information about the time in which he will encounter the indication of that evil (of the good and evil which you see), and from which direction he will experience that. **6** So if you found the Lot of the father (or another of the Lots) in a sign of kings, that good and evil will affect him in relation to kings and the Sultan.

---

[103] Sentence **3** is not in the Latin *BA*, but it was probably in the Arabic original.
[104] That is, the solar revolution.
[105] Perhaps this should be "he," meaning Mercury: see Ch. 3.13, **28**.
[106] This should be understood as "appoint Venus *instead of* Mercury."

7 And if it occurred in signs of vegetation, he will encounter that from vegetation, the earth, and trees. **8** If it occurred in signs of water, he will encounter it from a place with much water.

9 Then, see in which star's house the Lot occurred: for if it occurred in the houses of Mercury, that will affect him from a book or speech or merchants, or in something he attempts by using his own intelligence, viewpoint, and strategy. **10** And if it was in the houses of Venus, then in relation to women. **11** And if it was in the houses of Mars, then in relation to the cavalry, commanders, and works of fire. **12** And if it was in the houses of Saturn, then from the earth, settlements, and from a people having a long lineage.[107] **13** And if it was in the houses of Jupiter, then from prominent people, the nobility, and religion. **15** And if it was in the house of the Sun, then in relation to kings. **16** If it was in the house of the Moon, then from one who is likened to a king or it will affect him in relation to women.

17 And the most excellent position for the Lots, and the most powerful of them to occur in, is in the Ascendant, then the Midheaven, the eleventh, the fifth, the seventh, the fourth, then the ninth: for in these signs it is the most powerful the Lots could be, and the most excellent of them in everything in terms of place. **18** But as for that which does not have power [in itself] nor for anything happening in them (except for a small matter), those are the house of assets, siblings, and the house of death; but the most evil of all of them is the sixth and the twelfth. **19** Look at the Lots, where they are and where they occur, and where you find the lords of the houses[108] they occur in. **20** For if the position of both is excellent (as well as everything belonging to that Lot), then it is excellent (and especially if one of them looked at its own lord with good fortune),[109] and he will encounter excellence. **21** And if both were bad, then it is bad. **22** And if one of them was excellent, one-half of it is excellent, except that their lords are the more mighty of the two in [their] matter.

23 So, direct that Lot in the bounds of all of the signs, just as it is directed for the Moon. **24** Now if it looked[110] <and that Lot reached>[111] the fortunes, it produces good in relation to that Lot. **25** And if it looked and that Lot

---

[107] أسنان. But this might mean people who are very old themselves.
[108] **M:** "signs."
[109] This should perhaps be understood as "with [the Lot of] Fortune," but may simply mean "with a good aspect" and in a good condition.
[110] This could mean, "if it looked at it [by ray] *or* reached it [by body]."
[111] Reading on the model of the next sentence, for "and if it looked at the fortunes."

reached the infortunes, it produces evil in relation to that Lot. **26** So, whichever one that was, whether it reached [it] or cast its rays in it, see when that time was: for by how much it was after that time, will be what you saw, whether good or evil.

27 And[112] look into social classes, for the planets do indeed indicate every class in accordance with the class of that thing. **28** If they were both of the sons of kings and the wealthy, they will have a small amount of good fortune; it indicates abundant good.[113] **29** And if they were both of the middle class, then based on that [they will be] of the people of that level. **30** And if they were both of the poor, then it is that unless the time is one of upheaval. **31** Now if [it was] the lowest, they will rise in a similar time.[114]

32 And whenever you saw a planet arising from the east, they are young until they reach the Midheaven, and there they will be sons of 26 years. **33** Then they will increase in age until they reach the west, and there they will be sons of 42 years. **34** Then, they will increase in age until they are under the earth as old men. **35** Then they will increase in number until they are sons of 82 years. **36** Then, they will return to the Ascendant and be young.

37 Know that the lord of the Ascendant indicates the life of the man, and his work, and the lord of the face announces to you whether he has a reputation among the people or not. **38** And the lord of the bound indicates if the house which the native was born in, is high or of good construction, or of bad construction: and that is from the excellence of the bound and its lord, and the aspect of the fortunes and infortunes to them both. **39** For if the lord of the bound was in a high place, then the home in which he was born was high, of good construction. **40** And it is also the indicator of whether the

---

[112] This paragraph is opaque to me, for two reasons. First, it does not clearly have an astrological application. But if we compare it with the next paragraph, perhaps the author is relating social class to the quadrants in the chart (since there are four classes mentioned: the royal/wealthy, the middle, the poor, and the lowest). For example, perhaps beginning with the eastern quarter (from the Ascendant to the Midheaven), significators in that quadrant will indicate rising good fortune, or something like that. Second, the reader will note that the verbs are almost all in the dual ("they both"), but it is not clear what the two things are. Based on the previous discussion, it seems it could be the Lot and its lord.

[113] This does not make sense to me, but perhaps it means that *because* they are already wealthy, they will not need good fortune. If so, then the phrase should read, "*because* they *already* have abundant good."

[114] مثل ذلك الوقت. Meaning unclear.

native will move to another land, or never leave his people: because if the lord of the bound was in the ninth, he will go to another land and die away from the homeland; but if it was in the Ascendant, he will never leave his people.

Chapter [3.10:] On what the lord of the house of siblings indicates when it is in the twelve places, without the aspect of the fortunes & infortunes, [from Māshā'allāh]

1 Consider: if the lord of the third was in the Ascendant, it will be the good of his siblings, and they will encounter good from him and be sincere towards him. **2** If the lord of the third was in the second from the Ascendant, his siblings will contend with him in his assets, and sorrows will enter upon them, and they will seek him. **3** The lord of the third in the third: he will have siblings who are well-known, and they will go to him and protect him since he is loved. **4** The lord of the third in the fourth: the siblings will steal the assets of the parents, and the family will come to them and will recognize them [as the thieves]. **5** The lord of the third in the fifth: he will have siblings away from the homeland, and they will travel much, and be blessed with suitable children. **6** The lord of the third in the sixth: his siblings will be hostile to him and seek his calamity, and crave his ruin and corruption. **7** The lord of the third in the seventh: [either] his brothers will marry some of his women and be blessed with children from that, or else they will be hostile to him. **8** The lord of the third in the eighth: say that his brothers' women will not survive,[115] and they will get inheritances in relation to women. **9** The lord of the third in the ninth: his siblings will get married to foreign women [while] away from the homeland, and will reside with them and seek shelter with them.[116] **10** The lord of the third in the tenth indicates the death of the siblings and their ruin, and he will be jealous of them[117] and they will hate each other. **11** (And likewise in a revolution of years: if the lord of the third was there, it is feared for one of his siblings; if the lord of the revolution was

---

[115] The text uses a negation which is typically wrong for this tense. So, this translation is somewhat speculative, but it suggests that the brothers' (3rd) wives (9th) will be ill (8th).

[116] The ninth indicates foreignness; as the seventh from the third, it indicates marriage; because the lord of the third is in its own seventh, then siblings seek out the partner (rather than the other way around).

[117] This verb also means to begrudge someone something (تحاسد).

made unfortunate, it is more difficult.) **12** The lord of the third in the eleventh: he will have pious siblings who are renowned for that, and they will attribute [it] to him.[118] **13** The lord of the third in the twelfth: his siblings will be hostile to him, and will get his authority and be superior to him.[119]

14 Work in this chapter if the lord of the third and the third [itself] were free of the infortunes, and the fortunes do not witness.

Chapter [3.11]: On the knowledge of the Lot of siblings

[al-Andarzaghar]

1 Then, look at the Lot of siblings (and they are both applied). **2** One of them is just as Hermes,[120] the master of scholars, said: it is taken from Saturn to Jupiter, and projected from the Ascendant, and wherever it ends, that is the Lot of siblings: and that is for one who was born by day and night. **3** And another is one Valens put down, and indeed it is taken by night and day from Mercury to Jupiter,[121] and is projected from the Ascendant. **4** And both of the Lots are correct, so work with them both together.

5 Then,[122] look at the Lot of siblings: for if you found it in a sign abundant in children, with the fortunes, then that is a suitable omen in the matter of siblings; and if the Lot occurred in a sterile sign, it indicates a scarcity of siblings.

6 Now[123] if Venus and Mercury looked at it from a female sign, it indicates sisters; and if they looked from a male sign, then brothers. **7** And if one of

---

[118] Or perhaps, "they will be attributed / traced back to him." Meaning somewhat unclear.
[119] Or, "have power / influence over him."
[120] Or, Dorotheus (*Carmen* I.21, 1); I would recommend reversing it by night, as Valens does.
[121] This is in fact Dorotheus's Lot of *the number of* siblings (*Carmen* I.23, 1), which however is reversed at night. Abū Ma'shar *Gr. Intr.* VIII.4, 48 claims that this Lot is reported by al-Andarzaghar, and *he* related it from Valens. In any case, *Anth.* II.40 makes it clear that Valens only uses the Saturn-Jupiter Lot, and *does* reverse it by night.
[122] For this paragraph, cf. *Carmen* I.21, 3.
[123] For this paragraph, cf. *Carmen* I.23, 3-4.

them was in a male sign and the other in a female sign, then say brothers and sisters. **8** And if their[124] aspect was from places of evil, they indicate those having defects, and those from which there is no good in this.

9 And if Jupiter was with the Lot, looking at one of the luminaries, it indicates many siblings.[125]

10 If[126] Saturn conjoined with the Lot,[127] or opposed it, it indicates the death of the elder siblings; and it is harsher for that if Mars was looking along with that, and quicker for it if he was stationary, and more effective for that if Jupiter is not looking.

11 If an infortune witnessed[128] the Lot in the distribution of Mercury, it indicates the death of the brothers, and it is harsher for that if it was in the square of Mercury or his opposition.

12 And if the lord of the Ascendant connected with the lord of the third, [the native] will be in need of his siblings; and if the lord of the third connected with the lord of the Ascendant, his siblings will be in need of him.

Chapter [3.12]: On the positions of the Lot of siblings [from Māshā'allāh]

1 Māshā'allāh said:[129] if the Lot of siblings was in the stakes, he has siblings who are well-known, [and] they are preferred over the [other] people of their social class: and you mix that with the lord of the third. **2** Now if it was more numerous in testimony than the lord of the third, and it was in the Ascendant, the native will be preferred to his siblings; and speak likewise about the lord of the third sign. **3** And the lord of the Lot increases and decreases according to its position relative to the infortunes and the fortunes. **4** And if the Lot (or its lord) was in the Midheaven, they also indicate that they are talked about, but say they will not survive.[130] **5** And [it is] harsher for that if

---

[124] In *Carmen*, this refers to any planets looking at the Lot, not just Venus and Mercury.

[125] Instead of "many siblings," **M** contains an uncertain, unpointed word: "it indicates siblings [*uncertain*] from it/him."

[126] For this sentence, cf. *Carmen* I.23, **40-41**, but also Ch. 3.8, **2-6** and Ch. 3.13, **23-29**.

[127] **E** adds "or its lord." This should probably also include the square.

[128] **M** reads, "observed."

[129] **M** omits this attribution to Māshā'allāh. Cf. Tehran, Dānishgāh, Nafīsī 429 (69a-69b); Majlis 17490 (132-34).

[130] This is yet again the statement by Māshā'allāh that the tenth is the eighth from the third, and so indicates the siblings' death.

the lord of the third was in the Midheaven. **6** The Lot of siblings in the seventh from the Ascendant indicates that the native will be hostile to his siblings. **7** And if the lord of the house of the Lot or the lord of the house of siblings [was] in the fourth sign from the Ascendant, or its lord or the lord of the third were in the fourth, he will have siblings and they will have commerce and works, and they will be exalted above the parents, and they will appoint them as heirs, and they will have status among the people[131] and the parents—except that if the lord of the Ascendant was in the fourth sign, then he will be at [the same] status [as] the siblings.

8 If the Lot of siblings is in the eleventh, fifth, ninth, and third, or if its lord or the lord of the third were in these positions, it indicates that the siblings will show affection and support each other. **9** If it was in the eleventh it indicates that the siblings will travel much, and of them one will encounter the good during his absence from the homeland and will remain in it. **10** And if it was in the third it indicates a scarcity of siblings, and the scarcity of their needs. **11** If it was in the ninth they will marry during their absence and will have joy, unless there is an infortune in the ninth or its lord is made unfortunate: for indeed that indicates the corruption of religion, quarrels because of women, and contention in religion. **12** And if it was in the fifth it indicates that he will have siblings younger than him assisting him, and they will be under his authority. **13** Then, after that look at the lord of the Lot: for if it was free of the infortunes, received or in a stake, then the siblings will be worthy and rise; and if it was made unfortunate, it indicates their ruin.

14 If the Lot of siblings or the lord of the third was in the eighth, second, sixth, and twelfth, it indicates the bad condition of the siblings. **15** If it was in the second from the Ascendant, it indicates that his siblings will be his dependents, and their livelihood will be due to him. **16** If at the same time the lord of the Lot was made unfortunate, it indicates that they will be wretches, and one of them will be confined in prisons,[132] and some of them will be tortured.[133] **17** If it was in the eighth and had testimony, and its lord [was] strong but the lord of the Ascendant was corrupt, then it indicates that the siblings of the native will consume his inheritance; and if the lord of the Lot

---

[131] Or simply, "family" (اهل).
[132] Māshā'allāh has, "in the armed forces."
[133] Or perhaps more simply, "tormented, punished" (العذاب).

was corrupt, his siblings will have chronic illness and weakness. **18** And if it[134] was in the sixth and had testimony, and its lord was made unfortunate, his siblings will be slaves or be of those who do the work of slaves; then, chronic illness will afflict them. **19** And if it was free of the infortunes, they will have tricks and flattery, and will do contemptible labor that is hated.[135] **20** And if the Lot <or its lord>[136] was in the twelfth, and it had testimony and is[137] looking at its own place, then it indicates that his siblings are of those who do contemptible work at the doors of the Sultan, they[138] will be like a tax collector or the master of a prison. **21** And if it was in a stake, in an excellent position, it indicates the hostility of the owner of the Ascendant towards his siblings;[139] and you will know the [relative] power of each, and their weakness,[140] from the positions of their lords.[141]

[Chapter 3.13:] The Roman *Bizidaj* on the knowledge of the rankings of the siblings, & their insignificance

1 Saturn[142] and Jupiter indicate the greatness of the brothers'[143] rank, Mars indicates mediocrity, and Mercury indicates the insignificance of their rankings; the Moon indicates the greatness of the sisters'[144] rank, and Venus indicates the insignificance of their ranking.

---

[134] Māshā'allāh adds, "or its lord."

[135] Māshā'allāh reads, "work that is hidden."

[136] Adding with Māshā'allāh, else the phrase about looking at its place would not make sense.

[137] Omitting "not," with Māshā'allāh.

[138] Reading in the plural with Sahl, but Māshā'allāh only means for one (or maybe more) to be like this.

[139] Or perhaps, his "bad treatment" of his siblings (معاداة).

[140] Māshā'allāh reads, "victory."

[141] **M** now skips to the chapters on parents, indicating again that it is missing 1-2 pages; the rest is from **E**.

[142] Cf. *Carmen* I.23, **10**. The *Bizidaj* probably has this wrong, as according to *Carmen* these planets indicate siblings of different ages, not social rank.

[143] Reading the masculine instead of "siblings," because I have treated Venus and the Moon as indicating sisters below.

[144] Reading for "brothers/siblings."

2 And[145] if the lord of the triangle of the Ascendant was in the Ascendant, it indicates that the native is the first-born of his parents; and if it was in the Midheaven, then he was preceded by three siblings and he is the fourth of them (and that is if it is in a stake); and if it was in the setting, then he was preceded by six siblings. **3** And[146] if one of the infortunes was with the lord of the triangle of the Ascendant, or it was looking at it from a square or opposition, then that indicates the death of the siblings.

4 And if it was in the third, it does not indicate the number of siblings but it does indicate their absence from the homeland.

5 And[147] also, if the lord of the triangle of the Ascendant was in the half of the circle which is above the earth, then count from it to the Ascendant, for what there is of the number of signs, that amount is the number of siblings. **6** And if you came to a sign having two bodies, then double the amount for that. **7** And if the lord of the triangle of the Ascendant was in the half of the lower circle, which is under the earth, then count from the Ascendant to the lord of the triangle, for the amount of that is the number of siblings. **8** Now if the fortunes looked, it indicates that the siblings will survive (whichever ones do not die before they are born); and if the infortunes looked, it indicates their ruin. **9** And if there was nothing of the planets from the Midheaven to the Ascendant, then the native will not have a sibling before him; and if he did have a sibling before him, he will see [that sibling's] death. **10** And if one of the infortunes was from the Midheaven to the Ascendant, it indicates the death of that one of the siblings who was before him. **11** And if the lord of the triangle was between the Ascendant and the stake of the earth, and with it (or looking at it) was one of the fortunes, it indicates siblings which will be after him. **12** But if one of the infortunes was with it, then he will not have siblings <after him>. **13** And if he did have [any], they will not be strong.

---

[145] For this sentence, see *Carmen* I.19, **1-2**. The following text (and **7-11**) shows signs of its Greek source: for example, instead of "triplicity" (مثلّثة), this Arabic *Bizidaj* uses "triangle" (تثليث) just as Greek does (*trigon*)—normally, Arabic authors use تثليث to mean "trine." Likewise, instead of a planet being in the "west" (مغرب), it refers to "the setting" (الغارب) just as Greek does (*dusis*).

[146] This could well be a missing sentence from *Carmen*.

[147] For this paragraph see *Carmen* I.19, **4-12**, Rhetorius Ch. 103, and Sahl's Chs. 3.1, **3-7**; 3.5, **2-8**; and 3.13, **5-13**.

The mutual love of the siblings, and their hostility, [from al-Andarzaghar]:

15 If[148] the lord of the Lot of love[149] is looking at the Lot of siblings, one to the other, and[150] if Jupiter or Venus or Mercury is in the positions of the two Lots,[151] and in suitable places, in feminine signs, then they indicate sisters for the native (and if it was in masculine signs, then they indicate brothers), and that their affections will last. **16** And[152] <if those planets which look at the Lot are in bad places>, they will be hostile to each other, and illness will afflict <them>. **17** Now[153] if Saturn, Mars, and the Sun and Moon were in alien places, it indicates the ruin of the siblings. **18** And[154] if some of these planets were in <their own> house <and places>, then it indicates that they are not companions, and are not beneficial to each other, because the infortunes indicate evil.

---

[148] For this paragraph, see Rhetorius Ch. 105 (all). Al-Andarzaghar is following Rhetorius in this treatment of the relationship between siblings, whereas *Carmen* I.23, **36-38** follows Heph. II.6 (Schmidt p. 19) in using the Lot of Fortune and Lot of siblings.

[149] In Rhetorius this is the Lot of *philia*, which here may better be understood as the Lot of friends or friendship rather than love (which would be the Lot of *Erōs*).

[150] For the rest of this sentence, cf. *Carmen* I.23, **3-4**.

[151] In the version of *Carmen* I.23, **1-3**, this only concerns the Mercury-Jupiter Lot, which deals with the number of siblings.

[152] Cf. *Carmen* I.23, **3-7** and **37-38**. I have reconstructed **16** using *Carmen* I.23, **5**. The version in **E** reads (without corrections): "or they will be hostile to each other, and companions sickness, and especially if they were you reported them bad." 'Umar's version in *Carmen* reads: "And if those planets which look at the Lot were in bad places, then it indicates siblings in which there is no good, or who have emaciating illnesses—or enmity, evil, and the badness of opinion and thought will occur between them."

[153] Cf. *Carmen* I.23, **6-7**.

[154] I have reconstructed some of this sentence on the basis of the immediate source in *BA* III.3.5, **6** and the original reflected in *Carmen* I.23, **7**: "And if you found some of them in their own houses and their own places, then he will have siblings who do not love him, nor are they dear to him, or [they are] those who have no use for him, because what the infortunes indicate is not complete." **E**'s original (without corrections) reads: "Now if some of these planets were in their own house, then it indicates that they will not be companions sickness, but they themselves [are] an indication, and they will not [sic] be useful to each other because the infortunes indicate evil."

The knowledge of the one born, whether it is male or female:[155]

20 In a diurnal birth, calculate from the lord of the house of the Moon to the Moon, and by night the contrary of that, and add to that the portion[156] of the Ascendant, and it is projected from the Ascendant so that where the counting ends, there is the position of the Lot. **21** If this Lot occurred in a masculine sign and masculine quarter, and its lord was male, it indicates that the native will be male; and if it occurred in a female sign in the same manner as [before] with this characteristic, it indicates that the native will be female. **22** And if it was different from that and the indication was of many testimonies in masculinization but the feminization was greater, then multiply them in testimony.[157]

The time of the siblings' death:

24 If[158] Saturn was with the Lot of Fortune or the Lot of siblings, or he looked at them both from a square or opposition, it indicates the death of the siblings, and especially if Mars was with him. **25** And look at the Lot of siblings, for[159] it is harsher for that if they were both retrograde.[160] **26** And if Jupiter was turned around from the Lot of siblings (that is, not looking at it), it indicates the hardship of <the brothers of>[161] the native. **27** If[162] Saturn or Mars looked at the Lot of siblings, it indicates their death. **28** And if Mercury looked from a square or opposition, it indicates their death. **29** If Venus looked at Mercury, she indicates what we explained before.

---

[155] This should be read along with Ch. 1.27, as it pertains to the *native's* gender, not the siblings.

[156] That is, the degree.

[157] This must mean that we should take the gender that is greater in testimony. If this method works at all, perhaps it indicates something about the gender quality of the native's behavior as well.

[158] Cf. *Carmen* I.23, **39-42**, and Ch. 3.8, **2-6** and Ch. 3.11, **10** above.

[159] E reads "and," which would make this into two incomplete sentences.

[160] This must mean Saturn and Mars.

[161] Adding in accordance with *Carmen*; it does not make sense that the native alone would suffer in this situation.

[162] From here through **29**, see *Carmen*, which makes more sense: the malefics in the place of the Lot and looking at Mercury, kill the younger brothers, but if Venus the sisters.

Chapter 4: On the matter of fathers & mothers

[Chapter 4.1: Paternity]

1 Know[1] that the father has a share and allotment in every child born to him, and when another is born to him, his condition is changed over to that; and[2] likewise the children of men: the conditions of the fathers change over upon their heads[3] just as the years are changed over. **2** But[4] do not work for

---

[1] Sentences **1-3** are very difficult, because they blend general statements about the relationship between parents' and children's charts, with the topic of establishing paternity (the topic of the rest of the chapter). There is also terminological trickery. In the first place, at the beginning of **1** Sahl's source wants to establish a parallel between biology and astrology: that just as the father appears or "changes over" biologically in the children (due to what he transfers to them), so astrologically the father's situation should appear in or "change over" to the child's chart. But then the manuscripts diverge: **M** says that *due to* that, as the years go by the *children's* condition is reflected in the *father's* chart; but I have chosen **E**, which says that the *father's* condition is reflected in the *children's* charts. That is, (1) each person's chart will reflect the other, in an ongoing way: the father's fifth house will reflect his children, and the children's fourth house will reflect the father. But (2) a "change-over" (انقلاب) is not just an abstract notion, but is an astrological technique, one of the terms for a solar revolution: so the text is also instructing us how to look at one persons' revolution to understand the person. So the next question ought to be whose chart we revolve, and for what time: sentence **3** seems to say that we revolve each person's chart based only on their own nativity, not the other person's. For example, if the father asks about his own children, revolve the father's chart for his own birthday, not for the day of his children's birthdays: the reason seems to be that we only cast revolutions for things that are initiated and begun—but the father did not actually initiate anything on the child's birthday, and the father already has his own root chart. So, we use the father's chart. But the oddest thing about this passage is **2**, which suggests that the chart of the first-born has a weaker connection to the father than the second-born—which does not make sense to me. An option I could understand better is the following: if a father has a child sometime during his year, the *next year's* solar revolution will be more likely to reflect that change of life than the current one. But the text does not say that. Finally, what is frustrating is that most of this chapter is about establishing paternity and family traits: if the first child cannot be well matched to the father's chart, what good are the techniques? But perhaps **1-3** are not meant to address that yet. Hopefully in the future we can identify better sources. For more on this topic, see *PN4* I.9, **33** and a contrasting view in Sahl's *Sections* **37**.

[2] From here to "change over," reading with **E**. **M** reads, "and due to that, the conditions of men's children change over." Not only does **M** include something explanatory ("due to that"), but the readings are contrary: **E** has the conditions of fathers transfer to the children, and **M** has the conditions of children transfer to the fathers.

[3] على رؤوسهم.

anyone unless it is from the next child born to him, because the second one is more indicative and more excellent for examining than the first one is.

3 And[5] know that fathers do not have a revolution in nativities, nor do cities, nor does anything not[6] initiating a revolution;[7] but certainly a revolution and change-over does belong to everything one does initiate: understand that.

4 Al-Andarzaghar said:[8] Start at the beginning by looking [so you may] know the native, whether he belongs to his father or to another father. **5** Then look at the Lot of fathers: for if it looked at the Lot of the native[9] by any [kind of] inspection, the native will belong to his father; and if it does not look, then he [comes] from a deception.

6 And Theophilus said: Look at the Lot of exaltation, and it is that you take by day from the degree of the Sun to the degree of his exaltation, and it is cast out from the Ascendant, and where it terminates, that is the degree of Exaltation; and by night from the degree of the Moon to the degree of her exaltation, and projected from the Ascendant, and where it terminates, that is the degree of Exaltation.

7 So, look at the lord of the bound of this degree: now if it was Saturn and he was under the rays,[10] and you found Mercury connecting with Saturn, and you found the Moon made unfortunate by one of the two infortunes, and there was misfortune upon her from the position of the fall of the Sun (and

---

[4] Reading the first half of this sentence with **M**. **E** reads, "So do not work except for the next one born to him." If we ignore the question of who the client is, the point is that the father must be matched with the second child's nativity.

[5] I have read this sentence with **M**.

[6] **E** omits "not."

[7] I have added the indefinite accusative to "revolution," otherwise it would read, "nor does anything a revolution does not initiate."

[8] Cf. *BA* III.4.2, 3 where al-Andarzaghar attributes this to the Persian Buzurjmihr. See also Abū Bakr I.6.

[9] According to *BA* III.4.2, this is the Lot of Fortune.

[10] I believe Theophilus uses Saturn because he is one of the natural significators of the father, and being under the rays suggest a hidden or unknown father.

that is that the misfortune of the Moon is from the first degree of Libra to 19°, which is the fall of the Sun), or you found her made unfortunate as well from her own fall, or the fall of Saturn (who is the lord of the bound of the degree), then know that the mother has certainly committed a deed of wickedness in this birth, and this native is not of his father, and he will do works which will humiliate him if he was noble in his lineage and deeds.

8 Now if Jupiter was the lord of the bound of Exaltation, and the Moon was inspecting Jupiter, and the Sun was like that with Jupiter, inspecting him, then the native belongs to his father. **9** And if the Moon and Mercury were both made unfortunate, and Saturn was under the rays, then know that the mother has certainly committed a deed of wickedness in that birth. **10** Now if one of these three was cleansed of the infortunes, then know that the child is legitimate but the mother has committed an act of wickedness.

11 And if the Lot of exaltation was in the bound of a planet, then that planet is called the lord of the Lot of exaltation: and if it was made unfortunate, and Mercury and the Moon were both made unfortunate by whichever of the two infortunes it was, then the native is from another father; and God is more knowledgeable.

ಬ   ಞ   ಞ

12 And al-Khayyāt[11] said: If you saw the Sun in the trine of the Ascendant, then he belongs to his father, and likewise if the lord of the Ascendant was in the trine of the Sun. **13** Now if there was nothing of that and you saw the lord of the Ascendant and the Sun looking at each other but they were not connecting, then he belongs to his father; and likewise if the Sun was looking at the Ascendant. **14** Now if you saw the Sun in nothing of what I have mentioned, and not inspecting the lord of the Ascendant, then the native does not belong to his father. **15** And if there was a bearing of light between them,[12] then he will belong to his father; and if they connected together with a planet,[13] then he also belongs to his father. **16** And if the lord of the fourth and the lord of the house of the Sun fell away from the Sun, and the lord of the house of the Lot of the father [fell] away from the Lot, the

---

[11] **E** uses the name al-Hasan b. ʿAli al-Khayyāt, which is not the correct full name of al-Khayyāt according to Sezgin (p. 129). At any rate, this passage does not appear in the Latin version.

[12] That is, a transfer of light.

[13] That is, a collection of light.

native will not have a father known to him, and he will be a child of fornication.

17 A section on the knowledge of the life of the father, and his death. **18** Now if the native was born and you wanted knowledge[14] of the father, as to whether he is living or dead, then look at the lord of the Lot of fathers and the lord of the house of fathers. **19** For if they were both above the earth, eastern, then he lives; and if they both (or one of them) was under the earth, western, then he is dead.

20 A section on the presence of the father, and his absence. **21** And if it was said to you, "Was the father a witness at the birth of the native, or absent," then look at the indicator of the father. **22** For if it was not looking at the Lot of the mother nor at the Moon, then the native was born while the father was absent.

23 A section on the knowledge of whom the native resembles, the father or the mother, or the family of each, of the paternal and maternal uncles.[15] **24** So look at the lord of the native's Ascendant, the Sun, the Moon, the Lot of the father and of the mother, and the lords of each,[16] and the fourth house: if it[17] was male, then the father; and if it was female, then the mother; and likewise in the topic of siblings. **25** Look [at] the lord of his Ascendant, at whichever kind it was closer to: for whatever it was, the native will resemble that essence. **26** And the lord of the house of the Sun indicates the people of the house of the father, and the lord of the house of the mother indicates the people of the house of the mother. **27** Also, if the Moon connected with a

---

[14] At this point **E** is virtually unreadable until Ch. 4.2, **5**.
[15] Or aunts, for female natives: the words are given in the masculine, undoubtedly to match the assumption of a male native.
[16] I believe this refers to the two Lots. But this dual ("each") could be a misread for the plural ("their").
[17] I believe this refers to the gender of the sign on the fourth.

male planet, then the native resembles the father; now if the planet was in a <female> sign, <he resembles> the people of the father.[18] **28** And if she connected with a female planet, then the native resembles the mother; and if the planet was in a male sign, the native resembles the people of the mother;[19] and God is more knowledgeable.

Chapter [4.2]: On examining the good fortune of the parents, & their suffering, from the statement of al-Andarzaghar

1 Then,[20] in the matter of the father start by looking at the Sun and Saturn, because they are both partners in the matter of the father (especially the Sun by day and Saturn by night), as well as the lords of their[21] triplicities; look along with that at the Lot of the father and its lord, and the fourth. **2** And the first lord of the triplicity indicates the beginning of the father's lifespan after the birth of the native, and the second one the end of the lifespan.

3 And make a conclusion about the disasters of the fathers and their stock[22] by means of the luminaries (and Saturn and Venus)[23] and the lords of their triplicities, [as well as their] good fortune and assets.

4 Then,[24] after that begin by looking at the Sun and Saturn, because they are both partners: the Sun by day, and Saturn by night; and look along with that at the triplicity of the Sun, and the Lot of fathers and its lord. **5** For if you found the Sun in his exaltation, house, or triplicity, then say nobility and good concerning the birth, and especially if he was in a stake of a diurnal nativity: because the Sun indicates the nobility of fathers, and the lord of his

---

[18] This should probably be understood as, "the female relatives of" the father. (Material in brackets added on the model of **28**).

[19] This should probably be understood as, "the male relatives of" the mother.

[20] This paragraph seems to be adapted slightly from Rhetorius Ch. 97, the first paragraph.

[21] Sahl's Arabic reads "their," referring to whichever one we are using; but *BA*'s Latin has only the Sun.

[22] That is, their background and lineage.

[23] Saturn is the general significator of the father by night, while Venus is the general significator of the mother by day.

[24] For this paragraph, cf. *Carmen* I.13, **1ff**. But note that *Carmen* does not mention Saturn by night.

triplicities indicates their[25] good fortune and suffering. **6** Now if you found the lord of the triplicity of the Sun in a bad place, in its exile[26] or in its fall or in the house of its unhealthiness,[27] or falling from the stake, then his father will fall from his position and his assets will disappear. **7** And[28] if you also found the Sun along with the lords of his triplicities in a bad place, then report that his father is a slave or suffering, or condemned in status. **8** And if you found the Sun and the lords of his triplicities in this position which I mentioned to you, and the infortunes looked at him,[29] then judge a chronic illness for the father. **9** And[30] if you found the Sun in a bad place and the lord of his triplicities in an excellent place, then say that his father will be raised up after suffering and the falling of [his] status, and his elevation will be increased.

☋   ☍   ☍

10 And[31] if you found the Sun in a bound of the fortunes, then the father will be good, fine in his livelihood; and if he was in a bound of the infortunes, he will be unknown in influence, with a difficult livelihood, in need of what he does not have, especially if the Sun was in a feminine sign with an infortune or he connected with the Tail: for that is an indicator of servitude and abjectness.

11 And[32] if the Sun was in a fine place and his lord in a bad place, then the father of the native will be in a good condition at the beginning of the nativity, but then it will be changed and corrupted, and he will fall from his position. **12** And if that was the other way around, then say the contrary of it.

13 And if you found the Sun in the house of hope, then it is good in the livelihood of the father.

---

[25] Reading in the plural to make the sentence more comprehensible: that is, the fathers' good fortune.
[26] That is, peregrine or alien.
[27] That is, its detriment, the sign opposite its house.
[28] For **7-8**, see *Carmen* I.13, **5**.
[29] Or, "them" (لـ-), but probably the Sun.
[30] For this sentence, see *Carmen* I.13, **9**.
[31] For this paragraph, see *Carmen* I.13, **3-4**.
[32] For this paragraph, see *Carmen* I.13, **6** and **9**.

14 And whichever of the planets you found with the Sun, mix its essence with the power of the Sun, for it has indications for the father in accordance with its essence, and especially if you found it eastern: for if Jupiter was like that, and was in his house or one of his shares, then it is preferable in good fortune for the father; and if Mars was according to what I mentioned to you about easternization with the Sun, in the house of the Sun or with Saturn, then make a harsher statement about the father; and the rest of the planets are according to this. **15** But if the planet was under the rays then it is weak in power, and likewise if it was western it indicates a scarcity of power and the delaying of the indication.

16 And[33] whichever of the luminaries was in the fourth, speak evil about its owner; and if they met in it, then both of them.

17 And if the Moon was with the Sun in her own house or in her exaltation, western, it indicates the delight and good fortune of the parents, especially if an infortune is not looking at them, but a fortune is looking at them.

18 And[34] look at the twelfth-part of the Sun and Moon for the parents, and that one of the fortunes and infortunes [which are] in every one of them, and the one looking at them both, and speak good and evil according to the name of the place and its essence, and the essence of the planet.

19 Now,[35] it is not good if there is an infortune in the second place from the Sun, nor if it is in his opposition and square (and the harsher of the two squares is the one looking down upon[36] him); and better is if a fortune is in the place which one hates the infortunes being in.[37] **20** And if a planetary infortune or fortune was in the seventh from the Sun, it indicates lawsuits and something of error.[38] **21** And if you found an infortune in the eighth place from the Sun, it indicates fear and hardship, poverty, and the illness of the fathers, and a bad death.

22 And understand that if you found the fortunes in Cancer and Leo, they indicate the suitability of the parents' condition; and if the infortunes were there, it indicates the badness of their condition. **23** And it is worse for that if Saturn by night was in the house of the Moon, and Mars by day in the house

---

[33] See *Carmen* I.16, **21**.

[34] This paragraph is a version of Rhetorius Ch. 97, the last paragraph (p. 147).

[35] This sentence is a version of *Tet.* III.4 (Robbins p. 245); see also *Carmen* I.17, **3**.

[36] That is, overcoming or decimating him.

[37] That is, being with or in a square with the Sun, or the sign following his.

[38] But perhaps this should be only with malefics, not benefics?

of the Sun. **24** For if you found Saturn in the house of the Moon, it indicates the badness of the mother's condition, and likewise Mars in the house of the Sun for the father, along with sudden death while traveling. **25** And the Tail [is like this] too, so beware lest it be in one of these two houses; but if the Head was with the fortunes, it is an indicator of leadership and good fortune.

26 In the matter of the father, look at the meeting [of the luminaries] by day, and the fullness [of the Moon] by night. **27** And know that perhaps the meeting will be more powerful in testimony for the father, and the fullness for the mother, especially if the fullness was in a feminine sign.

28 And if you found the fourth from the Ascendant improved by the fortunes, and its lord was in a good place, eastern, then always say that the father will be praised and increase in the good. **29** And if the Sun and the lords of his triplicities were made unfortunate in the stakes,[39] then the father will encounter calamities and his assets will be confiscated; and judge likewise for the mother from the Moon. **30** And look also at the lord of the house of the luminaries, for if the infortunes looked at them both, then say likewise.

[Chapter 4.3: The father according to] the *Bizidaj*[40]

1 If[41] the Sun was falling and the two lords of his triplicity powerful, it indicates criticism of his standing and the rise of the father.[42] **2** And if the first one was powerful and the second one falling at the same time, it indicates the goodness of the condition of the father in the first [part of] the native's nativity, and the badness of the condition of its end; and if it is the other way around, then reverse it. **3** And if they were [both] falling at the same time, then state every difficulty about him and his father. **4** And the aspect of the fortunes and infortunes will increase and decrease [the judgment] about that.

---

[39] This could also be read as: "And if the Sun was made unfortunate, and the lords of his triplicities in the stakes," but the clearly negative interpretation here suggests that the triplicity lords are also made unfortunate.

[40] **M** omits this reference to the *Bizidaj*.

[41] For **1-2**, see *Carmen* I.13, **9-10**.

[42] That is, his lineage will be bad (Sun) but his livelihood good (triplicity lords).

5 And if the lord of the house of fathers was Saturn, then his exaltation is old.[43] **6** And if it was like that by day, then he is abundant with deals[44] and real estate; and if it was by night, it indicates the complications[45] his father will have, which will fall into his hands. **7** And if he was burned up, he will encounter the complications due to a lie. **8** And if Mars was the lord of the house, it indicates that he will encounter that in war[46] or from a sword, killing, or evil. **9** And if it was Jupiter, then say he will encounter that by means of hypocrisy and deception. **10** And if Mercury, then say he will encounter that from a treasure; and if it was Venus, then by reason of women and a lie.

11 And know that Saturn and the Sun are both partners in the matter of the father, the Sun by day and Saturn by night. **12** Now if Saturn was in the Midheaven or in the eleventh or the rest of the suitable places, then the father will have good fortune and rank, and especially by day if he is not made unfortunate by Mars. **13** And if the two partners looked at each other, it will be faster for the good of the father; and if their mutual aspect was received from [those] positions, that good of the father is doubled and faster. **14** And if they were not both looking at each other, then the good of the father will be delayed; and if the infortunes assisted, they increase in the slowness, and if the fortunes assisted they break much of that slowness. **15** And if Mars was inspecting one of the two from a square or opposition, the father will encounter injury and grief in accordance with what you see of the position of Mars. **16** Then, direct that degree to the light of Mars, for every degree of it a month; and if it went beyond that,[47] then make it years. **17** Except that if Mars was powerful in that misfortune through which he makes [them] unfortunate from his position and its essence, and weakens the indicator of the father in this place in which it is, then do not make that years nor months, but make it days when you direct that degree through the bounds; and the

---

[43] This must mean that his family has had a good condition for a long time.

[44] عقد. The *Bizidaj* may be making a play on words here. This verb root means to tie or bind up, and in this positive interpretation it means to complete an agreement or contract, like when we say we have "tied up the loose ends" or we have completed something and tied it up with a bow; but voweled differently as in the second part of this sentence, it means a complication or a bind one finds oneself in: see **6ff**.

[45] Again, عقد.

[46] **E** reads "fear," which is also plausible.

[47] That is, if the timing by months was completed but nothing had happened yet.

difficulty will be from fire, robbers, killing by kings,[48] soldiers, or something of the vices of Mars.

18 And if you found the two partners (that is, the Sun and Saturn) in one sign, and the birth was by night and Saturn is burned, then the burning of the father[49] will afflict him in relation to the Sultan. **19** And if it was by day and the Sun was inspecting Saturn from the stakes by means of a connection to him, and the fortunes fell away from Saturn, then with that Saturn will harm the father badly in his body, and difficulty will enter upon him in relation to the Sultan or in some of his assets, after experiencing the good which I mentioned about the inspection of Saturn and the Sun, each of them to its associate.

20 And look at Saturn and the Sun: for if [either] looked at the house of fathers and fell away from Mars, then report that the good of the father is on the increase, and the fulfillment of the good in what the father hopes for in that nativity. **21** Now if Mars did look at Saturn and the Sun and he was powerful, and he undermined the house of fathers, then he will subtract from the good of the father based on the position of Mars and what he undermines: so direct <that to his light>. **22** And if one of the fortunes was in the house of fathers or inspecting it from powerful places, then the father will encounter the good quickly, and there will not be a delay in it, and indeed he will be exalted [to a position] the likes of which have not been [before], and he will be sound in his body and his form strong—except that if Mars was inspecting the house of fathers from the stakes or an assembly, that will do violence upon the father with powerful force [because of][50] the hostility of Mars to Saturn and his hostility to the Lot of the father. **23** And if the fortunes were looking at the house of fathers along with Mars, or they approached[51] the house of fathers, then subtract from the evil of Mars based on what you see of the strength of the fortunes and their governorship.

---

[48] E reads, "or killing, or from kings."
[49] But perhaps this should be "Saturn"?
[50] Added by Dykes and omitting "the condition," as the sentence needs something to link it with the last part.
[51] Reading as تقارب. But perhaps this should be تقارن, "they conjoined with."

24 Then, gather together these four testimonies—from the position of Saturn, the Lot, the degree of the Sun, and the house of fathers:[52] for if these testimonies combined with the fortunes, and the infortunes are not looking at them, they grant many gifts. **25** And if two testimonies were made fortunate and one unfortunate, then make those two testimonies stronger in the good, and make use of the abundance of testimonies. **26** And if you found three of them made unfortunate, then misery will find the father, and injury and humility; and speak according to what you see of the falling away of the infortunes from that. **27** Now if you wanted to know what strength that infortune has, and how much[53] disaster that is, direct the degree of the infortune through the bounds to these degrees in which the four testimonies are: then distribute[54] based on that, for every degree a year; and God is more knowledgeable.

[Chapter 4.4: On the father] from the statement of Māshā'allāh

1 He said, begin by looking at the fourth sign: for if the infortunes were in it, then say evil. **2** But if the Sun had testimony in it, or he was the lord of the sign[55] or the lord of the triplicity, or the lord of the fourth was under his rays or in his house or his triplicity, or connects with him, then [the Sun] is more primary for the father than the lord of the fourth is.

3 And if there was nothing of what I mentioned, then look at the fourth and its lord. **4** Now if an alien infortune was in the fourth, or it looked at it from a square or opposition, then it indicates the badness of the condition of the father, and his distress. **5** And if the infortune was alien to the Ascendant[56] or not at all received, it is harsher for his condition. **6** Now if it was a fortune in the way I explained, it indicates the fineness of the condition of

---

[52] But below the text speaks of only three, which probably means that we do not use Saturn and the Sun together, but only the Sun by day and Saturn by night.
[53] The "how much" here seems to mean "how much *time*."
[54] **M** reads, "heap [them] together," which makes sense because the text is speaking of "how much," but this technique is called distributing, so I follow **E**.
[55] **M**: "house."
[56] **E** reads, "if the alien infortune was an enemy to the Ascendant." This latter phrase implies that it is in aversion to the Ascendant (as Māshā'allāh suggests in his *RYW* Prologue, **6-7**, in *AW2*), but that would make it less likely to square the fourth (unless Māshā'allāh means squaring the IC). In my preferred version from **M** here, it seems to mean that the infortune also lacks dignities in the Ascendant—so that it is alien to it.

the father; and if it was received, it is finer and more powerful for his rank. **7** And speak likewise about the lord of the fourth: for if it is in the rays and is entering into burning, it also indicates the distress of the father, and with that the Sun is more primary for the condition of the father than the lord of the fourth is: so look for [the Sun's]⁵⁷ condition. **8** And if an infortune looked at the lord of the fourth from an opposition or square, it also indicates the badness of the father's condition and his distress in relation to what the infortune or the planet harmful to it, is in. **9** And harsher for that is if the infortune or the planet harmful to it is alien or not at all received: for with that it indicates a scarcity of joy.

10 If the lord of the fourth was in a stake, it indicates that the father will be received and well known; and if it was the Midheaven it is preferable (and the Ascendant too is an example of that), and indicates the authority of the father. **11** Now if the Sun was the lord of the house of fathers or the lord of the Ascendant or Midheaven, and was in the Midheaven, it indicates that the fathers will be well known by the Sultan. **12** If the lord of the Lot of the father was in a stake as well, it indicates that the father will receive good and a rank; and preferable for that is the Midheaven (and the eleventh also indicates likewise). **13** And if it was falling, it indicates the badness of his condition in what he will receive; and it is harsher for that if, along with its withdrawal from the stakes and its falling away from the Ascendant, it was in its own fall or unhealthiness: for with that it indicates that he will encounter disaster, and enemies will conquer him. **14** Now if it was made unfortunate along with what I said, or it connects with an infortune, it is [even] worse for his condition.

15 If the Sun and the lord of his house were together in a stake, it indicates the fineness of the father's condition in what has [already] passed, and in what remains [in the future]; now if one of them looked at the lord of the Ascendant, then the native will inherit that. **16** So look with that at the lord of the Ascendant: for if it was in a stake as well, then the native will be like his father; and if it was in a stake, in its own exaltation, he will be superior to his father. **17** And if it was withdrawing or in its own fall, he will not be like his father, and he will undermine his position;⁵⁸ and it is worse for that if an in-

---

⁵⁷ Reading the appropriate gender for the Sun, against **M** (**E** omits).
⁵⁸ Or perhaps, "his position will be undermined."

fortune was looking at it, for indeed that indicates corruption from many directions.

18 And if the lord of the fourth was in a stake and the Sun withdrawing, it indicates that the fathers had dignity and rank, but their authority has already slipped away. **19** And if the lord of the house of the Sun was also withdrawing, then they will increase in evil and the badness of [their] condition. **20** If the lord of the fourth was under the rays, the father is more known than the people of his own house, and more powerful than them in rank, and they will need him and have fear for the father.

21 If the lord of the house of the Sun was in the ninth, the father is well known for knowledge, faith, and piety; and if an infortune looked at it, it undermines that. **22** Now if the Sun was received in the ninth, it indicates the father's knowledge and his perceptiveness.[59] **23** And if with that the lord of [the Sun's] house was in a stake, he will be well known in that knowledge; and the Midheaven is better for that as well as the Ascendant, for it indicates that he will be well known for that in [many] countries; or in the eleventh and in the ninth it indicates [this] as well. **24** Now if the lord of the house of the Sun was of the superior stars, that will be of obscure knowledge which verges on what one cannot put a name to; and if it was of the inferior stars, that will be in evident knowledge, of the knowledge of logic and tradecrafts. **25** And speak likewise about all of the signs, if the Sun was the indicator below[60] the lord of the fourth.

26 And[61] if the Sun was the indicator for the condition of the father, then look for the condition of the father from the lord of the fourth, and make the Sun be superior in[62] the condition of the father: so make a judgment about [the Sun] and the lord of his house.

27 And look for the condition of what the father receives of his lifespan, from the lord of [the Sun's] house and its place from the Ascendant, and the aspect of the fortunes and infortunes to it.

28 Then, mix the lord of the fourth with [the Sun], and what is in the fourth, and the one looking at it: and what[ever] there is, judge the family and the house in which he was born. **29** If the Sun was made unfortunate, it

---

[59] Or, his philosophical or reflective abilities (نظر).
[60] See **1-3** above.
[61] Reading this sentence with **M**. **E** reads: "And if the Sun was the indicator for the condition of the father, then look for the condition of the father from [the Sun's] position, and the aspect of the fortunes and infortunes to him."
[62] العالية على.

indicates the badness of the condition of the father; now if he was withdrawing and the lord of his house was made unfortunate, it indicates his ruin, along with what is in it. **30** And if the lord of his house was under the rays, entering into burning, then the father will ruin himself, and will do work in which his ruin is. **31** And when the Sun was made unfortunate from the sixth house or by the lord of the sixth, or by the lord of the twelfth or from the twelfth, and the Sun is in a stake or what follows a stake, and the infortune is in a stake,[63] there will be an evident defect in his father. **32** And if [the Sun] was made unfortunate just like I described him, and he was falling, in the sixth or twelfth, he will have a defect in a hidden place. **33** And if he was made unfortunate from the twelfth house or by its lord, it indicates an example of that, but it will be below what I mentioned, and he will encounter hardship from confinement and handcuffs. **34** Then you speak in all of that based on what we have described—except that the ugly defect and hard tribulation will not come to be except in these two areas.[64] **35** And concerning the eighth and its lord, it indicates the smallness of the lifespan.

36 And perhaps the Sun and the lord of his house are falling: they indicate the badness of the condition of the father. **37** Now, if they were received along with what I mentioned of falling, they indicate the fineness of the condition of the father, and he will achieve good or be very wealthy, well-known, [but] humble.

Chapter [4.5]: On examining the matter of the mother & her condition

1 Then, look in the matter of the mother from the Moon, for she is good in the matter of the mother—except that Venus [should] be in a stake by day, eastern,[65] or in what follows a stake (apart from the eighth), and by night the Moon [should] be in the Ascendant or in the Midheaven or in the rest of that (of the good places): because if in the birth the Moon was like that, it indicates rank and a good condition for the native and the mother, and especially

---

[63] Only **E** has this statement about the infortune.
[64] That is, "houses."
[65] Following **M**. Although **E** is very smudged here, it seems to read: "…if Venus by day was in an eastern stake, she being eastern."

if the Moon was in her own exaltation or in a female sign, cleared of the infortunes.

2 And if you found the Moon separating from Saturn, then it indicates for the mother the death of her husband and her brother, or for every condition of offspring that illness and coldness and difficulty will afflict her in pregnancy, as well as sorrow. **3** And likewise if the Moon connected with Saturn or she was in his opposition or square, for that indicates sadness for the mother and no good as well for the native in his assets and his good fortune, since that produces downfall. **4** And likewise if the Moon was with Mars or looking at him from the place which I mentioned,[66] because that produces hardship from what[67] I mentioned.

5 And look in the matter of the mother from the Moon and the lord of her house, just as you looked in the matter of the father from the Sun and the positions in which the fortunes and infortunes were. **6** And if you found the Tail with the Moon, and especially if the Moon was in a house of the infortunes, that indicates the baseness[68] of the mother and her lowness.

7 And if she looked at the Lot of the mother, then that is good if she was in a bound of the fortunes, devoid of the infortunes. **8** And recognize who of the fortunes and infortunes is looking at the Lot, and speak about that according to what I taught you about the Lot of the father. **9** If you found Saturn in the house of the Moon, it indicates the badness of the mother's condition; and whenever you found the Moon in something of her misfortunes, they are an indication of the badness of the mother's condition; and it is harsher for her if in addition to that an infortune looked at her. **10** And if in addition the Moon was falling, it indicates her lowness.

11 And[69] if she was in the stake of the earth, it indicates harm in her body or chronic illness will afflict her. **12** And likewise if she was in the seventh from the Ascendant,[70] in the bound of an infortune, it indicates along with that her error[71] and defects. **13** And if the Moon was in the stake of one of the two infortunes,[72] in its square or opposition, or she was connecting with it, it indicates that she will die a bad death.

---

[66] This probably means the opposition and square, as in **3**.
[67] ممّا. This probably should be understood simply as "along with."
[68] Or, her being depraved or despicable (نذالة).
[69] For this paragraph, cf. *Carmen* I.13, **13-15**.
[70] Or in the IC, as *Carmen* adds.
[71] زلّة, which more concretely means a lapse, slipping, a mistake.
[72] *Carmen* says she is in *a stake, and* in these aspects with the infortunes.

14 And if you found the twelfth-part[73] of the Moon in the twelfth, then report that the mother is fallen or a fornicator. **15** And likewise if the lord of the twelfth was with the Moon and they were both falling, then report that his mother is a slave. **16** And if with this the lord of her bound was falling, it indicates that she is a slave or resembles a slave. **17** And if the Moon was in a good position and an infortune looked at the same time, it indicates her poverty and her lowness. **18** And if the Moon was falling, looking at an infortune, it indicates her slavery. **19** And if the luminaries were not in their own houses nor in their places, falling, it indicates his poverty and the poverty of his parents. **20** And if an infortune witnessed the lord of the sign of the Moon, it indicates a bad death for his mother. **21** And if Saturn was the lord of the degree of the Moon by night, and the Moon was connecting with him, it indicates the shortness of the mother's survival. **22** If the Moon was in the bound of an infortune, and her lord was falling, it indicates slavery and suffering for her. **23** And if the infortune looked at her at the same time, she will die suddenly. **24** And if the Moon was in the seventh, in the bound of an infortune, it indicates separation and the disappearance of assets; and likewise if one of the luminaries was in the sixth and the other in the twelfth. **25** If the Moon and the Lot were made unfortunate, and the fortunes falling, and you found Venus weak, then indeed the mother will encounter tribulation from illnesses, and a powerful harm adhering to her until it kills her, and a defect [*unclear*] her to the native, and due to the father there will enter upon her a powerful anger about women.

26 Now if you wanted to know he that was from free women or from slave girls, then look at the position of the Moon or Venus, and the Lot of the mother: know whether it is in a house of slave girls or in a house of free women, and [if] the infortune which is making her unfortunate is in a house of slaves or in a house of free people. **27** Know that the signs of male and female slaves are Taurus and its triplicity: the harshest of them is Capricorn, and the middling one of them is Virgo, and the more elevated of them is Taurus.[74]

28 And[75] if Saturn was in the house of the Moon, it corrupts the mother's assets, and her character is from black bile, or an illness befalling her in her

---

[73] **M** reads, "the share of the twelfth-part."
[74] For more on such signs, see Ch. 1.38, **11-12** and **46-47**; 2.8, **4-9**; 6.10, **1**.
[75] For this paragraph, cf. *Carmen* II.37, **1** and **3**; also Sahl's Chs. 4.10, **2-3** and 4.20, **7-8**.

fear,⁷⁶ <and a> hidden <pain> due to coldness.⁷⁷ **29** And if you found Mars in the house of the Moon, then the mother will die suddenly or on a journey, and it corrupts her eyesight before her death.

30 And the Moon indicates the mother, and the lord of her house indicates what she will confront [in the future].

Chapter [4.6:] On the length of the mother's survival

1 Now⁷⁸ as for the length of the mother's survival, look at Venus and the Moon: for if you found Jupiter looking at the Moon and Venus, or Venus was in the friendship of the Moon⁷⁹ or her assembly, in good places, the mother will be long-lived. **2** And if Mars was looking at the Moon,⁸⁰ and he was rising after Venus⁸¹ or he was in her square or opposition, or Saturn was looking at the Moon from hostility and the Moon was in decrease or falling, then the mother will become thin and ill; and if the Moon was increasing in light, in the stakes and after the stakes, then the mother will be short in life. **3** If Mars looked at the Moon and the Moon is eastern,⁸² it indicates defects in the mothers and quickly ruins their eyesight; and if the Moon was after the meeting,⁸³ then her death will be from falling and it will afflict her from heat and fire.⁸⁴ **4** And if Mars looked at Venus, her death will be from fever. **5** And if Saturn looked at the Moon, it indicates the death will be sudden; and if the Moon was western, after the meeting, her death will be from pain of the uterus.⁸⁵

---

⁷⁶ Reading as خوفها, but this does not really make sense.
⁷⁷ Adding with the sense of *Carmen* II.37, **1**.
⁷⁸ The following paragraph is based on Ptolemy, *Tet.* III.4 (Robbins p. 247).
⁷⁹ That is, configured by a sextile or trine.
⁸⁰ Or Venus (*Tet.*).
⁸¹ Or the Moon, by implication.
⁸² That is, "waxing" (*Tet.*).
⁸³ This should be "the opposition," so that she is waning (*Tet.*).
⁸⁴ Ptolemy adds "abortions."
⁸⁵ Sahl's source has this sentence rather mixed up. For Ptolemy, Saturn looking at the Moon causes death and illness: if the Moon is in the east, then by chills and fever; if in the west, by cancer and uterine diseases.

The statement of Māshā'allāh on that:

7 He said: And as for the lifespan of the mother, look at the Moon. **8** For if she connected with a retrograde planet and the lord of her Lot was retrograde, it indicates the death of the mother, unless she is received: for if she was received, [the mother] should not be frightened. **9** And if she connected with a retrograde planet not receiving her, and the lord of the Lot was in the eighth sign[86] from its[87] house, then it indicates the death of the mother. **10** And if the Lot of the mother was with the Moon, and the Moon was made unfortunate, it indicates the ruin of the mother. **11** And if the lord of the house of the Lot connected with the lord of its eighth, or [the lord of its eighth] connected with it, it indicates the ruin of the mother.[88]

12 In[89] the matter of the mother, begin with the Moon: for if she connected with a retrograde planet, and the lord of her Lot was retrograde, it indicates the death of the mother unless the Moon is received: for if she was received, [the mother] should not be frightened.

[Chapter 4.7: The good fortune or falling of the parents]

1 Now[90] if you found the Sun in the fourth, it indicates the fall of the father. **2** But if the lord of the fourth and the lord of [the Sun's] exaltation looked down upon [the Sun], that is more suitable; and it is harsher for him if there was misfortune in it. **3** And it is worse if the fourth was not a house of Jupiter nor his elevation;[91] now if the fourth sign was Scorpio, <and Mars in>[92] a stake of the Sun, it indicates the baseness of the fathers. **4** Now if with that the lord of [the Sun's] sign was withdrawing from the stake, it indicates that he is a slave or resembles a slave, along with a bad death. **5** But if with

---

[86] **E** omits this, saying only "the eighth."
[87] This probably means the eighth from the Lot (which is the same as the lord being in its own eighth). Thus if the Lot was in Gemini, Mercury would be in Capricorn, the eighth from Gemini.
[88] For a restatement of these ideas, see also Ch. 4.14, **32-39**.
[89] Note that this virtually repeats **7-8**.
[90] For **1-2**, see *Carmen* II.26, **6**.
[91] That is, his exaltation. I take this to mean *Jupiter's* exaltation (i.e., Cancer).
[92] Adding because it makes astrological sense.

that he was eclipsed or his [*uncertain*]⁹³ was eclipsed, it indicates slavery for the native. **6** Now if the Sun was in the fourth with Saturn, he indicates poverty and the destruction of the home which he was born in, and the emigration of its people. **7** And if the Head was with him in the fourth, it indicates the nobility of his father. **8** And if with that an infortune was with him, they indicate misery and the destruction of the home, and the victory of enemies. **9** Now if he united with Mercury in the fourth along with an infortune, or saw it⁹⁴ without a fortune, it indicates poverty, immorality, chronic illness, injustice, and the destruction of the home, and the quick death of his father, along with the manner of his death being terrible for the native. **10** And if the Tail was in the fourth with the Sun or the Moon, it indicates blindness and the ruin of his parents, with the evil of their manner of death; and⁹⁵ likewise if he was alone in the fourth, the Sun indicates the hastening of the native's ruin and that of his father.

11 And⁹⁶ if the Moon was in the fourth and it is Scorpio, it indicates the baseness of the mother. **12** And if with that her lord was withdrawing, she will be a slave or will resemble a slave, with a bad death. **13** And if the Moon was in the fourth by night and the sign female, it indicates the nobility of the mother along with widespread good; and if it was by day, then speak about the baseness of the mother.

14 And if Saturn was in the fourth by night, it indicates the ruin of the two parents; and if Jupiter was in the fourth by day, cleansed of the infortunes, it indicates the suitability of the fathers, and their superiority, and their wealthiness.

15 And⁹⁷ whenever Saturn, Jupiter, and the Sun look at the fourth at the same time, it indicates the wealthiness of the native's father; and if Venus and the Moon looked with them, it indicates the wealthiness of his two parents at the same time.

16 And if a fortune was with the Head in the fourth, it indicates the purity⁹⁸ and the prosperity of the home, and the suitability of the two parents. **17**

---

⁹³ The text seems to read لرمها.
⁹⁴ This probably means, "or *Mercury* looked at the *infortune*."
⁹⁵ I believe the rest of the sentence should probably read that the *Tail* is alone in the fourth (and indeed **M** omits "the Sun" here); but the verb indicates a feminine subject, namely the Sun.
⁹⁶ For this paragraph, cf. **39-41** below.
⁹⁷ For this paragraph, see *Carmen* I.16, **17-19**.
⁹⁸ النَّقَاء. But this could also be read as "survival" (البقاء) with the change of one dot.

And if the two luminaries were in the third or withdrawing from the stakes, they indicate the travels of the parents, and the distance of kin.

18 And if the Sun was in the sixth and twelfth, he will be weak in good fortune, from the underclass of the people, along with the baseness of his father, or his chronic illness, and his need and emigration, and perhaps the quick ruin of his father. **19** And it is clearer for that if [the Sun's] lord or[99] the Lot of fathers or the share of the twelfth part of the Sun or the lord of his triplicity was in it, and the majority of them will be slaves and servants; and the Moon indicates likewise regarding the mother [that] she will be a lowly slave-girl, feeble [and] sickly: and perhaps it will ruin the mother quickly while the child will survive. **20** And if he was in the seventh, then the situation is difficult, troublesome, indicating travels and hostility and lawsuits. **21** And if the Sun was in the eighth, then he indicates toil in the matter of losing and acquiring things, and it indicates the death of his father and the confusion of his understanding based on the essence of [the Sun's] sign, or a planet if it testifies to [the Sun]. **22** And if he was in the ninth, he indicates the devotion of his parents, along with travel; and likewise the Moon is for the mother, along with amazement and being found pleasant.[100]

23 And[101] if you found Saturn in the Ascendant, and one of the luminaries in the west and the other in the stake of the earth, it indicates the death of the two parents, suddenly,[102] with a bad manner of death. **24** And whenever you find an infortune in the fourth or looking at it from an opposition, it indicates humiliation for his parents, and baseness, and tribulation. **25** And if Saturn was in the fourth, in the house of the Sun,[103] that is in his father; and if it was the house of the Moon, it is in his mother. **26** And Saturn especially indicates the corruption of the matter of fathers and the badness of their condition, and that is if he was not rejoicing in his own place, and he was alien.[104] **27** Now if he was in it at night, it indicates the ruin of the parents and

---

[99] E reads: "and."
[100] Reading "being found pleasant" (استطابة) with E (although this precise form does not appear in the lexicon) for M's استطالة ("boasting").
[101] Note the parallel with **33** below.
[102] Or perhaps, "quickly" (عاجلًا).
[103] Following E. M reads, "And if the fourth was the house of the Sun."
[104] Reading غريبًا, but it could equally be read غربيًّا, "western."

corrupts the assets of the fathers, and indicates travels and ailments along with fear for the father.

28 And if you found Mars in the tenth by day, it indicates the destruction of his father's assets and separating from his mother because of death or something else.

29 And if the infortunes met in the twelfth by night, it indicates the badness of the condition of the native's father and the retreating of his command along with the corruption of his body and vice coming from his slaves; and by day it is easier.

30 And if the Sun was in his own house by day, in a stake, it indicates leadership; and if he was not in the stakes, then it is lower than that. **31** Now if it was by night, then state the obscurity of the parents, and their emigration. **32** And if he was in the house of Mars, in Scorpio, by day, then state the death of the parents, entanglements, and a bad manner of death.

33 And[105] if Mars was in the Ascendant by day and the luminaries occurred in the seventh (or one of them was in the house of fathers and the other in the seventh), and Jupiter was falling, then indeed for those whose stars occur in this manner, a quick [and] horrible ruin will enter upon his parents. **34** And[106] if Mars was in the seventh and looked at the Sun or the Moon, then there will be a separation between him and his parents; and if the Moon was increasing, then it is worse.

35 And if Venus was with Mercury in the Ascendant, and Mars opposed them from the seventh, then he will also scatter the assets[107] of his parents. **36** Now if Venus was in the Ascendant and the sign female, then indeed the mother will be superior in condition to the father, and she will be longer in lifespan; and if Jupiter was in the Ascendant in a male sign, then the father will be superior and longer in lifespan.

37 And if the Moon was in the Ascendant and the sign feminine, it indicates the nobility of the mother; now if it was by day [and she was] in no way connected to a star, then she is[108] not praised. **38** And if she was made unfortunate, it indicates the baseness of the mother, and especially if the Tail united with her. **39** And[109] if she was in the fourth and it was Scorpio, it indi-

---

[105] Cf. *Carmen* II.29, **2**.
[106] Cf. *Carmen* II.29, **11-12**.
[107] For the rest of this sentence and the next, **E** reads: "of his parents, and the native will be superior in condition to his parents, and longer in lifespan."
[108] Grammatically, the Moon: but obviously this means that the *mother* is not praised.
[109] **M** omits this sentence. For **39-41**, cf. **11-13** above.

cates the baseness of the mother. **40** And if with this the lord of the fourth[110] was withdrawing, then say the mother will have a bad death.[111] **41** And if she was in it by night and the sign female, it indicates the nobility of the mother, along with the good; and if it was by day, then the baseness of the mother. **42** And in the sixth it indicates the baseness of the mother, while if she was made unfortunate it indicates the corruption of [her] condition. **43** And if she was in the seventh it indicates the speed of the mother's death; and the Sun in the seventh indicates the death of his parents.[112] **44** Now if with this [the Sun] was made unfortunate, then <it indicates> the disappearance of the assets along with poverty.

Chapter [4.8:] On aspects

[The aspect of the trine]

1 If[113] Saturn by night was in a trine of the Sun, it indicates the decrease of his father's assets, and a middling condition.

2 And[114] if Jupiter looked at Saturn from a trine, it indicates mutual respect between the parents and the children, and the exaltation of the parents.

3 And[115] if Saturn looked at the Sun by day, then it confers superiority on the father, and dignity in his country. **4** Now if they were both in male signs, it is more preferable. **5** But if he looked at the Sun by night, it indicates a decrease in his father's assets, and harm; and likewise the aspect of the sextile.

The aspect of the square

7 If[116] Saturn looked at Jupiter from a square, and [Saturn] was looking down upon him, it introduces vice and misfortune to the parents, and it un-

---

[110] **E**: "the Ascendant."
[111] Reading somewhat loosely with **M**; **E** has only one illegible word for this last clause.
[112] For the Sun, **E** reads: "the separation of the parents." But one would expect this to be, "the death of the father," to run in parallel with the statement about the Moon.
[113] Cf. *Carmen* II.14, **6**.
[114] Cf. *Carmen* II.14, **1**.
[115] Cf. *Carmen* II.14, **5-6**.
[116] Cf. *Carmen* II.15, **2-4**.

dermines their condition, and does violence to his siblings. **8** Now if Jupiter was the one looking down upon Saturn, it is less for the evil of Saturn, but his father will not have prominence among the people, nor importance, [although] attention will be paid to him.[117]

9 And[118] if Saturn was looking down upon Mars from the tenth sign, it ruins the assets of the parents. **10** Now if Mars was the one looking down upon Saturn, it indicates the death of his father before his mother, and it introduces corruption and ruin to his mother and her condition.

11 And[119] if Saturn looked down upon the Sun, it will afflict the native and his parents with leprosy and illnesses from cold, and the disruption of the work which is in their hands. **12** And if the Sun was the one looking down upon Saturn, he squanders what assets he has inherited, and it ruins his father because of coldness.

13 And[120] if Saturn was looking down upon the Moon, it undermines all of the parents' assets, and separates him, and the native will abandon his mother. **14** And if the Moon was the one looking down, it indicates a bad manner of death for the mother.

15 If[121] Jupiter was looking down upon the Sun, it indicates high rank for the father, and nobility, and being elevated in his station, and importance, and much good, and benefit, and high-mindedness, and the father will know many people. **16** And if the Sun looked down upon Jupiter, it indicates the nobility of his father, and the scarcity of his assets, and he will be afflicted by travel and exile, or enmity and envy will enter between him and the people of his land, and he will show hostility towards them, as well as warning[122] and power.

17 And[123] if Jupiter looked down upon the Moon, it indicates the goodness of his mother's condition. **18** And if the Moon looked down upon him, his mother will be blessed with a good livelihood, and dignity, and happiness.

---

[117] Reading as به يذكّر.
[118] Cf. *Carmen* II.15, **5-6**.
[119] Cf. *Carmen* II.15, **7-8**.
[120] Cf. *Carmen* II.15, **13-14**.
[121] Cf. *Carmen* II.15, **17-18**.
[122] Reading as the verbal noun إخطار, but this could also be the plural أخطار, in which case the father presents some kind of danger. To me the former makes more sense.
[123] Cf. *Carmen* II.15, **23-24**.

19 And if <omitted>[124] looked down upon Saturn or Saturn looked down upon it, it indicates the mutual attachment of the parents and children.

20 The square of Mars and Saturn indicates [unclear] [unclear] in [unclear] [unclear].[125]

21 And[126] if Mars was looking down upon the Sun, there will be wickedness in the affairs of the <father and>[127] child, harm and vice will enter upon him, as well as ruin; now if that was by day, then it is much worse. **22** And if the Sun was looking down upon Mars, then state violence for the father.

23 And[128] if Saturn and Mars were elevated over the Sun and he connected with them both, and they were both withdrawing from the stakes, or the Lot of fathers was like that, they indicate the emaciation of the parents. **24** Now if they were in the stakes and what follows them, or the Lot of fathers was like that, then state a scarcity of survival. **25** And if that was in the Ascendant or in the Midheaven or what follows them, then it is their chronic illness and their skinniness. **26** And if that was in the seventh or the fourth and what follows them, and Mars was the governor over the Sun or conjoined with him, then state the killing of the parents, or a severe defect is on their faces.

27 And[129] if Mars looked down upon the Moon, it indicates the death of his mother, and there will enter upon her and upon some of her relatives, strife, and corruption. **28** And if the Moon looked down upon him, his mother will be in a bad condition, low in significance, and harm will enter into her livelihood.

29 And[130] if the Moon looked down upon Venus, it indicates the beauty of his mother, and indeed she will fornicate with a slave[131] of her husband. **30**

---

[124] This is probably the Jupiter-Venus combination (*Carmen* II.15, **19-20**), but those passages do not mention parents. The other combinations are either unlikely or involve hostility.

[125] **E** omits this sentence, and **M** writes it in tiny, undotted script that is difficult to discern. But *Carmen* II.15, **5-6** says that the parents' assets will be destroyed (and if Mars overcomes Saturn, the father dies first).

[126] Cf. *Carmen* II.15, **25-26**.

[127] Adding with *Carmen*.

[128] See also **59-62** below.

[129] Cf. *Carmen* II.15, **31-32**.

[130] Cf. *Carmen* II.15, **36-37**.

And if Venus looked down upon her, his mother will be clean,[132] having superiority.

[The opposition]

31 And[133] if Saturn looked at Jupiter from an opposition, it indicates error[134] for his father.

32 And[135] if Saturn looked at Mars from an opposition, it indicates escape [through death][136] for his father.

33 And[137] if Saturn looked at the Sun from a square, opposition, or assembly,[138] it indicates poverty for the father and a bad manner of death, and the child will be bad, and he will be of those who needs the profit of his hands,[139] or he will be chronically ill or scatter all of his parents' assets, and be ruined, and after his death nothing will be left for the native's family but a little, and his death will be detestable, hideous—and that is if Jupiter is not looking at them. **34** And it is more dangerous for that if they were in feminine signs.

35 And[140] if the Moon looked <at Saturn> from an opposition, it indicates the corruption of his mother's assets, and pains and illnesses will afflict her in a hidden place. **36** Now if the fortunes did not look at them both, it introduces chronic illness and disease into the mother. **37** But if they both as well as their aspect were in a sign having four feet, trouble will afflict her from riding animals. **38** And if it was in signs of predatory beasts <or> people, illness will afflict her from vermin or people. **39** And if they were both in moist signs, disaster will afflict him from water and from mixtures [of water] and coldness, and every moist illness.

---

[131] Reading عبد for عند ("with, at"). This might mean "fornicate with her husband," but that seems likely; "fornicate at the home of her husband" makes more sense but is still expressed strangely.

[132] Reading متنظفة with the "Māshā'allāh" version of *Carmen* edited by Pingree 1999, for متيقظة ("vigilant").

[133] Cf. *Carmen* II.16, **1**.

[134] Reading غواية for عوايه. This word has connotations of sinfulness and temptation as well.

[135] Cf. *Carmen* II.16, **3**.

[136] Adding on the basis of *Carmen* II.16, 3. That is, the father will die.

[137] Cf. *Carmen* II.16, **10**.

[138] In *Carmen*, this is only the opposition.

[139] This suggests manual labor, or someone who lives "hand to mouth."

[140] Cf. *Carmen* II.16, **14-18**.

40 And[141] whenever you find Saturn opposing Mars, it indicates a cutting of relations between the fathers and the sons.

41 And[142] [Saturn] in the opposition of the Sun without a fortune indicates the separation of his parents in his childhood, and the loss of their assets; and perhaps he will live among them both, in a state of need. **42** And it is harsher for that if Saturn was in a stake, and worse for him if they were both in the seventh, and if Jupiter was not looking. **43** And Mars indicates likewise if he does not see Venus; and likewise if one of the luminaries was in the sixth and the other in its opposition.

44 If[143] Mars looked at the Sun from an opposition by day, it indicates a bad manner of death for his father, and tribulation by means of a detestable death, and disease will strike the father in his eyesight.

The assembly of the planets

46 If[144] Saturn was assembling with Mars, it indicates the death of his father, and an abundance of worry, and his father will be ruined before his mother, and the assets of the father will be destroyed and scattered.

47 Now[145] if Saturn assembled with the Sun, it indicates the loss of his father's assets, and the end of his affairs will [incline] towards corruption and evil. **48** Now if it was by night then it is much worse, for indeed if he was eastern or western then it will be very bad in the matter of the mother because there will enter upon his mother a detestable, violent death, along with his quick downfall from his station, and illnesses of his body and emaciation. **49** And if they were all in the house of one of the two, the father will be a respected noble, but [the native] will be hateful to his parents, [and] hostile.

50 And[146] if the Sun was with Jupiter, and [Jupiter] was eastern, the native will be mighty in good fortune over his parents, and there will enter upon him from his own child,[147] delight and joy.

---

[141] Cf. *Carmen* II.16, **3**.
[142] For this paragraph, see broadly *Carmen* I.16, **3** and **6-10**, but especially II.16, **10**.
[143] Cf. *Carmen* II.16, **26**.
[144] Cf. *Carmen* II.18, **2**.
[145] Cf. *Carmen* II.18, **4-6**.
[146] Cf. *Carmen* II.19, **4**.
[147] **E**: "...upon them both from his mother."

51 And[148] if Mars was with the Sun, it indicates the ruin of the father with sudden destruction and detestable death. **52** And if they were both in the stakes and what follows them, disease will afflict him in his eye, and the scattering of his father's assets, and disaster will strike him from iron or fire, and many of the people will slander him.

53 And[149] if Mars assembled with the Moon, it indicates the disease of the mother, and it introduces illnesses upon her, and sicknesses; and that is if Jupiter is not looking at them both.

54 And[150] if Mercury was with the Moon, his mother will be fine in intellect and cleverness, but she will be afflicted by being mixed up with a man <not>[151] good in power or importance. **55** And if the Moon was greater than Mercury in degrees, it will be preferable because one ought to look at the flowing-away of the Moon. **56** Now if she went beyond a star and she flowed away from it, it indicates the manner of the essence of the star which she is flowing away from, and that is because the Moon is the closest of the stars to the earth, so she mixes with every star which is with her or from which she flows, or connects with, in accordance with the essence of that star.

[*The illness or poverty of the parents*]

57 And[152] if you found the lord of the twelfth with the Sun, it indicates the wickedness of his father and the badness of his condition, and his poverty. **58** And if it was with the Moon, then [it is] the mother, or it will be an illness, or by means of it there will be a defect in her eye.

59 Now[153] if Mars or Saturn was elevated above the Sun, or he connected with them both, and they were both withdrawing from the stake, it indicates the emaciation of the parents. **60** And if that was in the stakes or what follows the stakes, or the Lot of fathers was like that, then [it indicates] illnesses and a scarcity of survival. **61** And if that was in the Ascendant or in the Midheaven or what follows them, then state the evil of their chronic illness or their skinniness. **62** And if it was in the stake of the west or the stake of the earth or what follows them, and Mars was the one elevated above the Sun or

---

[148] Cf. *Carmen* II.20, **1**.
[149] Cf. *Carmen* II.20, **9**.
[150] Cf. *Carmen* II.23, **1-3**.
[151] Adding on the basis of *Mathesis* VI.27.
[152] Cf. Rhetorius Ch. 98 (p. 148).
[153] Cf. **23-26** above.

assembling with him, it indicates the killing of the fathers or a powerful defect in their faces.

63 And if you found the lord of the fourth in the second, sixth, eighth, or twelfth, then indeed the native's parents will live in poverty, living in need. **64** Now if with that it was retrograde, it is harsher and more conclusive. **65** And if the sign was male, that will be in his father; and if it was female, then in his mother.

[Chapter 4.9:] The shares of the planets' twelfth-parts

1 Know that the share of the twelfth part of the degree of the Sun indicates the condition of the father, and the share of the Moon the mother. **2** Now if the share of the twelfth-part of Saturn was with the Sun, it indicates the scarcity of his father's assets. **3** If the share of the twelfth-part of Mars was with the Sun, it indicates disaster for his father from fire or a predatory beast. **4** And if the twelfth-part of the Sun was in a male sign, it indicates the nobility of his father, and it is more established for that if the Lot of fathers assembled with it.

5 Now if the share of the twelfth-part of the luminaries was the Midheaven, it indicates the superiority of the parents over the sons.

6 And the share of the twelfth-part of the Moon being in the twelfth indicates the bad condition of his mother and her lowness. **7** And if it was in the sixth, it indicates the corruption of the fathers and their ruin.

[Chapter 4.10: Various statements about the father]

1 And[154] if the opposition of Mars was by day, it indicates for his father a bad death and an illness in his eyesight.

2 And[155] if Saturn was in the house of the Moon, he will scatter the assets of his parents, and it introduces a bad manner of death upon them both, and humiliation in their lives, and it introduces illnesses upon them, and many

---

[154] Cf. *Carmen* II.16, **26**; also Ch. 4.8, **44** above.
[155] For this paragraph, cf. *Carmen* II.37, **1-2**; also Ch. 4.5, **28** and 4.20, **7-8**.

pains in hidden limbs, and cold illnesses, and pains from [black][156] bile, until she takes a solemn vow to make a votive offering because of that. **3** And if he was in the house of the Sun, the father will encounter a rise [in position], and the fineness of praise, and he will increase in his assets and livelihood—but certainly illnesses will enter upon him from coldness and moisture, and that will be followed by a bad, detestable death.

4 And[157] if Mars was in the house of the Sun, it introduces a bad condition upon his father, and the downfall of [his] station, and the scattering of [his] assets, and an illness will afflict him in his eye, and his work will be with fire and iron, or his profit and livelihood will be for that reason.

[Chapter 4.11: The lord of the fourth in the houses, from Māshā'allāh]

1 Now when you have made deductions from what I have described to you, then look at the lord of the fourth. **2** For if it was in the Ascendant, the native will be the master of his family, and their livelihood will be from him, and he will be charitable to his parents, and an authority to them. **3** Now if an infortune looked at it, hardship will afflict the parents in relation to authority.[158]

4 The lord of the fourth in the second: the parents will be prosperous, good in what they leave behind, and the native will inherit the parents' assets, and he will be the most distinguished of his brothers over the parents.[159]

5 The lord of the fourth in the third: he[160] will have siblings, and the parents will encounter hardship from them, and they will be hostile to them, and he will be better than his siblings in the opinion of his parents, and will seldom do them good.[161] **6** Now[162] if an infortune looked at it, it confines the parents in prisons, and they will encounter tribulation, and hardship in their

---

[156] Adding on the basis of *Carmen*.
[157] For this paragraph, cf. *Carmen* II.37, **4**.
[158] Here I believe the conflict is over the native's authority, not with the Sultan himself or government authority.
[159] This probably means that he will rise above his parents' station, more so than his brothers.
[160] Reading with **E**, but **M** reads "they," which would refer to the siblings of the parents.
[161] Reading أقلّهم خيرًا. The "them" seems to refer to the siblings.
[162] Reading with **M**, as **E** is largely illegible.

death, and he will be the better one of his siblings, and they will be most wretched.

7 The lord of the fourth in the fourth: the parents will be well known among the people, they will have importance and a reputation. **8** And if an infortune looked [at it], or it was made unfortunate by the Sun, it indicates the shortness of the parents' lifespan.

9 The lord of the fourth in the fifth: the parents will be prosperous, seeing children, and the children of their children, and they will come to [a full] lifespan[163] if an infortune is not looking while the fortunes do look; and they will increase in the good.

10 The lord of the fourth in the sixth: the parents will be unknown in the country which they are in, and their condition is seen from the planets connected with it. **11** For if an infortune looked, harm will happen to the parents from illnesses of the nature of the sign. **12** And if a fortune looked, they will attain good in what is not their own country, unless that fortune received it: for if it received it, they will also attain good in their own country, and the good in which they rejoice will be from the position of the fortune which is looking.

13 The lord of the fourth in the seventh: the native will get married to a woman somewhat greater than he, from his own family, and the fathers will be considered[164] base, and the father will be hostile to the native and will contend with him.

14 The lord of the fourth in the eighth diminishes the lifespan of the fathers, and it will be feared for the native, and the mother will die in childbirth, and it is harsher for that if the Moon was corrupted or connecting with a retrograde planet. **15** And if it was the Sun it is feared for the father, while if a fortune looked it will change some of what I mentioned.

16 The lord of the fourth in the ninth: the fathers will be unknown, moving from their homes, and [there will be] a defect in them, and they will die a bad manner of death, and pains will appear in them. **17** Now if the sign was in the image of what is four-footed, it will be from one who employs riding animals, and he will be a deceiver, and will not have piety.

---

[163] عمرًا. It makes a bit more astrological sense (since the fifth is the second from the fourth) that we should read عمران, "prosperity," but this would require an accusative *tanwīn* (عمرانًا), which does not appear in either MS.

[164] Literally, "traced back to" or "attributed to" something or someone base (القبيح).

18 The lord of the fourth in the tenth:[165] the fathers will be well known in the house of the Sultan, and he will increase [his] knowledge[166] with them, if the planet was received. **19** Now if an infortune looked, and it was not received, he will encounter hardship and tribulation and conflict from the Sultan because of that.

20 The lord of the fourth in the eleventh indicates the shortness of the father's lifespan, and the badness of their[167] condition, unless it was received by the lord of its house: for truly that dissolves [the problems] and improves their condition, and after that they will rise up [socially], and it is better for that if a fortune or beneficial planet looked at it.

21 The lord of the fourth in the twelfth: the fathers will be foreigners, having already left their own land due to the badness of their condition, and of them [is] one who is devoted [to God]. **22** Now if a fortune looked at it they will encounter good in the exile, while if an infortune looked, tribulation will afflict them. **23** And the better fortune is if it was receiving:[168] for if it received, he will encounter good in the exile, or an elevated status.

24 Then you look in this topic [to see] if the fourth and the lord of the fourth were free of the infortunes, while the fortunes are not testifying.

---

[165] Reading the rest of this sentence with **E**. **M** reads: "the parents will be well known in the house of the Sultan, and he will increase [his] knowledge with them, if the planet was received."

[166] Or perhaps, he will be better at being a well-known acquaintance (معرفة) of the Sultan, as they are.

[167] E reads "his," but it is good to remember that both parents are meant here, and are only distinguished by the natures of their planets and their respective Lots.

[168] I use "receiving" because Māshā'allāh seems to mean this in a stronger way than simply saying that it "accepts" (i.e., accepts the management from the lord of the fourth), just as in **12** and **20** above.

[Chapter 4.12:] The statement of Abū ʿAlī al-Khayyāt [on directions for parents][169]

1 He said,[170] the position of the Lot is fixed, and events always proceed in accordance with it when the fortunes and infortunes recur in the position of the Lot, and coincide with it.[171]

2 Now as for directing, look by day at the Sun and the Lot, namely which of the two was stronger by position relative to the Ascendant, and direct from it (and by night, Saturn and the Lot). **3** Indeed, you bring about[172] the direction from them together, the Lot [and] Saturn by night and the Lot and the Sun by day, for every degree a year and for every sign a year.[173] **4** Now if it reached the position of a fortune, then report good; and if it reached the position of an infortune, then report evil.

5 And know that if the luminaries connected their degrees in the root of the nativity with the degrees of the infortunes, death will be feared for the parents, and especially if they were both[174] falling from the stakes: and let your directing be by the bounds and not distributed, but direct them to the infortunes and the fortunes.[175] **6** Now if the planet was retrograde, then direct its rays conversely.[176] **7** And God is more knowledgeable.

---

[169] This little chapter is based on two texts, the first from **M** (slide 42/3, lines 4-13), which occurred at this place in the manuscript, and **E** (slide 31a, lines 10-19), which appeared much later, just before the beginning of the material on children. I have applied **E** here and deleted its instance below. However, I do not find this chapter in the Latin *JN*, so it might be from some other source, just as with the other al-Khayyāt in Ch. 4.1, **12** above.

[170] Translation somewhat free between "and events" and "when the fortunes." The sentence reads slightly differently between **E** and **M**, and in both cases oddly.

[171] That is, by transit.

[172] Reading tentatively as تسبّت.

[173] This last timing key could be a profection.

[174] This is probably the natal position of the luminaries, indicating that the life force is weak.

[175] Normally, directing through the bounds *is* distribution. But perhaps al-Khayyāt means that we are only focusing on the benefics and malefics, and not on a full-blown technique that uses the bounds and aspects of Mercury, nor the rays of the luminaries. Still, this is strange.

[176] مقلوبًا.

Chapter [4.13]: On looking into the lifespans of the parents, & its time

1 Look[177] concerning the times of the lifespans of the fathers (and others besides them), at the lord of the bound of the Lot, and the lord of the house of the Lot. **2** For if they were both corrupted, it indicates the death of the fathers; and the time of that is when Saturn passes over it[178] in his transiting, before he casts his light upon it—for at that time, [the parent] will die (and likewise if he cast his light upon it before he goes past it in his transit).[179] **3** And if one of the two is suitable and the other corrupt, then it also indicates [that parent's] death. **4** And if they were both suitable, then [Saturn] will not strive for his killing in his transit over it, but he will strive for his killing when one of the two infortunes casts its light upon it—unless Venus or Jupiter casts the light equally into the bounds. **5** And likewise the Lot of the mother and the lord of every Lot (of the mother, brother, and woman):[180] so look for them just as you have looked for the father.

Chapter [4.14]: The Lot of fathers

1 Then[181] look at the Lot of the father, and it is that you calculate by day from the Sun to Saturn and by night from Saturn to the Sun. **2** Now if Saturn was under the rays, then count from Mars to Jupiter, and project it from the Ascendant.

3 So[182] look at the position of the Lot, and who (of the fortunes and infortunes) is looking at it, and also look at the lord of its house and its position

---

[177] For this chapter, see an almost identical version in Ch. 4.20, **38-43**.

[178] This probably means the Lot.

[179] Normally in Arabic astrology, a transit is by body. The method here seems to be a combination of directions (or distributions through the bounds) and transits, so that Saturn would transit the sign of the Lot during the years when he is also a time lord for the directed Lot by distributions, when he has "cast his light" on it by direction.

[180] The Lot of "the woman" must be one of the marriage Lots.

[181] For this paragraph, see *Carmen* I.14, **1-2** and **5**.

[182] This paragraph is based on four passages. The first two are **M** (slide 42/4, lines 1-5) and **E** (slide 25b, lines 12-14), called here **M1** and **E1**, which appear in this place in the manuscripts. The others are in **M** (slide 45/3, lines 12-15) and **E** (slide 31a, lines 6-9), here called **M2** and **E2**. Passages M2 and E2 are shorter. I have applied them here and their instances later, where they would have appeared just after Ch. 4.14, **39**.

relative to the fortunes and infortunes, and its connection with the planets. **4** If an infortune was with the Lot, and it is alien, not received, it indicates the shortness of his lifespan, for he is a man of misfortune. **5** And likewise if the infortune looked at the Lot of the father from a square or opposition, then it is an indicator like the lord of the house of the Sun.

6 And if you found a fortune with the Lot, and it was not received, the father will be resolute,[183] not feeble, having a livelihood until, when he believes he has already been victorious, he will be destroyed. **7** Now if it was received he will be blessed, of a good condition, well known among the people; and likewise if it looked from a square or opposition. **8** And if you found it with the fortunes or looking at them, and its lord is eastern, and it is in a stake or in the house of hope or the fifth, it indicates nobility and good fortune for the father, and especially if numerous planets looked at the Lot, and the lord of the Lot was a fortune.

9 And recognize the lord of the bound of the Lot, and who is casting rays upon the Lot, so you assess the aspect of the planets and rays to the bound, and those inspecting the Lot: so, speak.

10 And if a planet of diurnality was with the Lot and the nativity was by day, or the nativity was by night and the planet a night one, then it is more excellent.

[*The Lot of the father in the houses, according to Māshā'allāh*][184]

11 And know that if the Lot was free of the infortunes, it indicates the healthiness of the father;[185] and if the lord of the house of the Lot was in the stakes, it indicates that the father will be mentioned among the people of his class. **12** Now if the lord of the fourth house was also in a stake, <it will be more powerful for the status of the fathers; and if the lord of the house of the Sun was in a stake>,[186] the parents will have authority, and status among them, and better than that is the Midheaven (and the Ascendant in this topic is better than the Midheaven).

---

[183] Tentatively reading and translating محروماً for محزوماً.
[184] Cf. Tehran, Dānishgāh, Nafīsī 429 (69b-70a); Majlis 17490 (134-35).
[185] Māshā'allāh reads "fathers," but like Sahl then uses the singular later in the sentence.
[186] Adding with Māshā'allāh.

13 If the Lot of the father was in the eleventh, fifth, ninth, or third, it indicates that the fathers are well known. **14** Then, look at the lord of the house of the Lot: for if it was free of the infortunes, in its own glow, then it indicates the fineness of their condition. **15** And if it was made unfortunate or under the rays, it indicates their bad condition: and in the eleventh, the shortness of the lifespan, and in the ninth a defect and illness, and in the fifth it indicates the fineness of the fathers' condition and their survival until they are blessed with the children of their children (unless the lord of the Ascendant indicates something other than that), and in the third it indicates the badness of the condition of the fathers relative to the social class they are in, because it indicates hostility from the people <of their class>.[187]

16 The Lot of fathers in the second sign, and the eighth, sixth, and twelfth, indicates that the parents will <not>[188] be well known. **17** Then, you look at the lord of the Lot and its position: for if it was free of the infortunes, it indicates the fineness of their condition; and if it was made unfortunate or under the rays, it indicates the badness of their condition. **18** And if it was in a stake, it indicates the prominence of the fathers, and their nobility. **19** And if it was in the twelfth sign, it indicates that the fathers will abound in travels. **20** Now if, along with what I mentioned, the lord of the Lot is not looking at the Ascendant, and[189] it is made unfortunate, it indicates that the parents will die abroad. **21** And if it was in the sixth, it also indicates the fathers' travel, but it is below what I mentioned. **22** And if its lord was made unfortunate, it indicates the defect of the fathers and their illness, and the father will not be friendly towards the native. **23** And if it was in the second and eighth, it indicates the advancement of the parents' condition, if the lord of the Lot was free of the infortunes, in its own glow; and if it was made unfortunate, it indicates the shortness of the parents' lifespan.

24 And the ancients said that if the Lots of the parents were in the houses which I described,[190] they signify the lowness of the parents.

25 And[191] if the Lot was in the twelfth with its lord, it indicates the enmity of the sons to the fathers.

---

[187] Adding with Māshā'allāh.
[188] Adding with Māshā'allāh.
[189] Māshā'allāh says, "or," but certainly this would be worse.
[190] See **16** above, but also *Carmen* I.14, **3**.

26 And[192] if you saw both Lots (or one of them) in the seventh, they will soon split up, with poverty and slavery or [something] resembling slavery.

27 And[193] if the lord of the opposite of the Lot was with the Lot, it indicates that the father will come to be with the family of the house of the mother.

28 And if the lord of [each of] the two Lots was strong, they indicate for both of them every good; and if they were to the contrary, then [say] the opposite of that.

29 And[194] if their two Lots met without a fortune, it indicates it indicates separation and need. **30** Now if they both are separated, and the infortunes do violence to them both, they indicate the occurrence of evil between them both.

31 And[195] if the lord of the house which opposes the Lot is looking at the Lot or at its lord from an opposition, from its own house, it indicates that the native will be imputed to[196] someone who is not his father.

☊   ☙   ☙

32 And[197] look in the matter of the Lot of the mother[198] just as I have explained to you in all of the positions. **33** For indeed whenever you see the Lot of the mother with the Moon, and the Moon is made unfortunate, it in-

---

[191] For this sentence, see Rhetorius Ch. 99 and Ch. 4.17, **3** below. Rhetorius has the Lot *or* its lord in the twelfth, whereas Sahl's version here makes it ambiguous whether the Lot is there with its own lord, or with the lord of the twelfth.

[192] For this sentence, see also Ch. 4.16, **15** below.

[193] This seems to be based on Rhetorius Ch. 97, in which the judgment is that the child is adopted (but Rhetorius's version of the sentence does not make much sense). See also my footnote to *Carmen* I.14, **6**. I believe the situation should be as follows: that either (1) the lord of the opposite of the Lot is on the Lot, or (2) the lord of the Lot is in the opposite sign. So, let the Lot be in Gemini: either (1) Jupiter should be in Gemini, or (2) Mercury should be in Sagittarius. For other versions, see **31** below, Ch. 4.16, **19**, Ch. 4.17, **10**, and Valens *Anth.* II.32.

[194] For this paragraph, cf. *Carmen* I.16, **12-15**.

[195] For this sentence, cf. *Carmen* I.14, **6**, and a similar rule for the Lot of marriage in II.4, **36**. See footnote to **27** above.

[196] يدعال. That is, be adopted by someone else.

[197] See Ch. 4.6, **10-11**, where these ideas are attributed to Māshā'allāh.

[198] The Lot of the mother is taken by day from Venus to the Moon (and by night the contrary), and is projected from the Ascendant.

dicates the ruin of the mother. **34** And likewise if the lord of the house of the Lot connected with the lord of its eighth, or the other way around:[199] it indicates the ruin of the mother. **35** And look likewise for the father from the Sun <and> the Lot of the two parents.

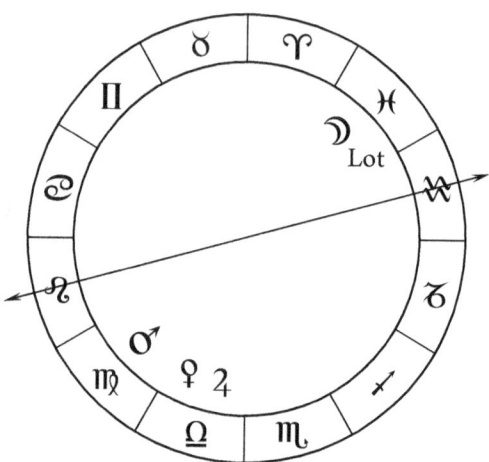

Figure 58: Death of mother (Dykes, from *Nativities* Ch. 4.14, 32-39)

36 So,[200] seek the testimony of the lifespan of the parents just as I described to you in the section on the native's upbringing:[201] and a single testimony indicates an average [amount] of the lifespan, and two testimonies indicate its shortness, and three testimonies indicate the quickness of death, based on what I explained. **37** And[202] an illustration of what I mentioned to you: so take it as a model.[203] **38** The Lot of the mother was with the Moon,

---

[199] Lit., "or it to it."

[200] This sentence is based on four texts. The first two are those of **M** (slide 43/2, lines 3-5) and **E** (slide 26b, lines 15-16), or **M1** and **E1**, which occurred in this place in the manuscripts. But it is also repeated in another place, in **M** (slide 45/3, lines 7-9) and **E** (slide 31a, lines 4-6), or **M2** and **E2**. I have removed these latter two instances and applied them here.

[201] See perhaps Ch. 1.18, **10**.

[202] This example (**37-39**) is based on three texts in the manuscripts. The first two are those of **M** (slide 43/2, lines 6-8) and **E** (slide 26b, lines 16-18), which occurred in this place in the manuscripts. But it is also repeated in a third place, in **M** (slide 45/3, lines 9-12). I have removed this third text from its later place and applied it here.

[203] Or more literally, "example," but I have tried to avoid the awkwardness of using the word twice in the same sentence. The figure below illustrates the situations described in **33-34**:

in the eighth, in Pisces; so the Moon and the Lot are two testimonies. **39** And the Moon connected with Mars from an opposition, and Venus connected with Jupiter in Libra: so, the mother died at that time.[204]

40 And[205] know that for each sought matter there are three pieces of evidence: the house, its lord, and the Lot. **41** Now, all of the Lots apart from the Lot of Fortune[206] are taken from two planetary significators, or the house and the planet:[207] so those are the roots and the Lots are the branches. **42** However, let your direction for the condition and time periods[208] of the parents be from the Sun and the Moon, and [their] misfortune from the Lot,[209] except that if the Sun is falling, weak, then let the direction for [the father's] condition and lifespan be from the Lot, because the Lot in that case is a proxy [for the luminary]. **43** And the scholars have already claimed that you should work with the Lots if the luminaries are falling, because the lord of the Lot is a proxy. **44** And God is more knowledgeable.

[Chapter 4.15: The exaltation of the fathers & their suffering]

[al-Andarzaghar]

1 As for the exaltation of the fathers and their suffering, look at the lord of the Lot of fathers. **2** For[210] if it was in an excellent place of the signs, in the stakes, then it indicates the exaltation of the father, and his goodness; and the

---

(1) The Lot is with the Moon, she is made unfortunate by opposing Mars, and (2) her lord (Jupiter) is with Venus, the lord of the eighth from his own position (Taurus).

[204] This phrase makes it unclear whether the example is simply a natal configuration, or a set of transits, or what. I have put the planets in the stated positions in the figure below. (Even if it is a natal configuration, it cannot be dated without more information.)

[205] I have a feeling this paragraph continues the author of **32-37** (most likely, Māshā'allāh), but cannot be sure.

[206] But the Lot of Fortune is also taken from two planets, namely the Sun and Moon, so I am not exactly sure what Sahl's point is here.

[207] For example, the Lot of assets or money is taken from the lord of the second to the second.

[208] Reading as مرّتيّة, which could also be translated as "timing," but seems to be a neologism invented for this purpose.

[209] **E** reads, "and the triplicity from the Lot." But this does not make much sense grammatically (using the preposition عن).

[210] For this and the next sentence, cf. *Carmen* I.14, **3-4**.

position of the Lot specifies his hardship and way of life. **3** And if you found the lord of the Lot of fathers in these bad places—the second, sixth, eighth, and twelfth—then his father will be disreputable[211] [and] wretched.

4 Look[212] at the spear-bearing of the Sun and Moon: for if the planets which are not [of the sect] have the spear-bearing of the luminaries, then the parents will not be fortunate, and especially if Mars is behind the Sun, and Saturn behind the Moon:[213] judge for both of the parents that they will be disreputable [and] low.

5 And[214] look at the lord of the twelfth from the Ascendant: for if you found it with the Sun, then state that his father will be a slave, [*uncertain*][215] the judgment upon him. **6** And if you found the portions of the twelfth-part of the Sun in the twelfth, then his father was an orphan, disreputable, [*uncertain*] the judgment upon him.

7 Then,[216] look at the meeting [of the luminaries] and the fullness [of the Moon]: for if Saturn and Mars looked at them[217] and the Moon was also connecting with the infortunes, then judge wretchedness and sorrow for the native and both of his parents. **8** And if you found one of the infortunes looking at the degree of the meeting or fullness, and the Sun or Moon were falling from[218] the stakes, then state that they will be sorrowful, then fate will induce them into slavery.

---

[211] Or, someone forgotten and unknown (ساقط).

[212] For this paragraph, cf. Rhetorius Ch. 99 (p. 148). Rhetorius prefers morning stars to spear-bear for the Sun, and evening stars the Moon.

[213] I believe this means different things for the Sun and Moon. For the Sun and Mars, it probably means that Mars is in an earlier degree than the Sun ("behind" him zodiacally), but so that he will rise before the Sun in the morning. For the Moon and Saturn, it probably means that Saturn is in a later degree than the Moon ("behind" her in diurnal motion), but so that she is applying to him. Some types of spear-bearing make these distinctions of diurnal motion and zodiacal degree, for the Sun and Moon respectively.

[214] For this paragraph, cf. Rhetorius Ch. 98 (p. 148). But *BA* III.4.3, **11-12** reads differently (and so must be due to Hugo's mistranslation): the Sun in the twelfth shows the father's slavery, and if the twelfth-part of the Sun is in the twelfth it also shows his ignobility and greed.

[215] Here and in the next sentence, the manuscripts read differently and uncertainly. But this is some kind of operational verb like وجب, "necessitating" the judgment—it does not concern the content of the delineation.

[216] For this paragraph, cf. Rhetorius Ch. 101 (pp. 149-50) and *Anth.* II.35.

[217] The luminaries, at the meeting or opposition before birth.

[218] Lit., "falling away from."

9 And if the Sun was falling, with the aspect of an infortune, it indicates the parents' slavery. **10** And if by day [the Sun] was in a stake, made unfortunate, and the lord of his bound falling, it indicates that he is a slave or resembles a slave. **11** And if the two lords of the triplicity of the Ascendant were falling, in the opposite of the Moon, or an infortune looks and the Sun is in the second, it indicates that his parents will be owned or will resemble being owned, and that the native will be a slave or just like a slave. **12** And if with that Jupiter looked, he will be emancipated or will purchase [freedom for] himself.

[Chapter 4.16: Background & relationship of the parents]

1 And as for what there is of good and evil between the parents, if the two luminaries were looking at each other from friendship, it indicates that there will be good between them. **2** And if they looked at each other from an opposition, they will be separated by death or life.[219] **3** And if it was an assembly, they will not be separated, and there will be boredom[220] between them. **4** Now[221] if they did not look at each other, it multiplies the absence of one of them from the other.

5 And[222] as for what I mentioned of the knowledge of fathers and mothers [being] of one nationality, look at the Sun, Moon, and Ascendant. **6** If you found them in convertible signs, then say that his parents are not of one nationality, especially if you found the Ascendant to be a convertible sign; and it is worse for that if the infortunes looked at it. **7** And if you found neither of the luminaries looking at its associate, nor at the Ascendant, then judge the same way for him.

---

[219] E adds about 10 more illegible words here.
[220] Or, "impatience" (ملالة).
[221] This sentence resembles *Carmen* I.16, **14**.
[222] For this paragraph, cf. *Carmen* I.16, **1-2** and **14**; Rhetorius Ch. 98 (p. 147). It is from al-Andarzaghar, as are **17** and **19**.

8 And likewise if one of the luminaries was in a stake above the earth, and the other under it, both being made unfortunate: it indicates distance, along with the cursing of his parents;[223] and likewise if one of the luminaries was separating from its associate. **9** And if the luminaries were turned away from the Ascendant, they indicate the emigration of one of the parents from the other.

10 And if the lord of the house of the Moon looked at the Moon from the trine or sextile, and she is connected with it, then the father will be powerfully in love with the mother.[224] **11** And if they connected from an opposition, the quarrels of both of them will be multiplied. **12** And if they were separated, they will separate. **13** And if the Moon was received, it indicates the kinship of the parents, and the length of their companionship. **14** And likewise the Sun for the father.

15 And if the Lot of fathers and its lord was in the seventh, they will soon split up, with poverty; and in the falling [places], it indicates baseness. **16** And if the Moon was opposing the Sun, then it indicates that the parents will separate by death or life, [and] then especially if the sign was convertible.

17 And[225] likewise if the Sun or Moon was in the seventh from the Ascendant, it indicates the separation of his parents. **18** Now if in addition to that it was in the bound of an infortune, it indicates need[226] along with the separation.

19 And if you found the lord of the opposite of the Lot of the father with the Lot, then the father will come to be with the family of the house of the mother.[227]

20 And[228] if the Lot of [each of] the two parents were separated, and the infortunes did violence to them, it indicates the occurrence of evil between them.

---

[223] دلّ على بعدٍ بسبّ.

[224] One would expect this to be the *Sun* and Moon being connected, but the pronoun used here rules the Sun out.

[225] For this paragraph, see *Carmen* I.16, **3-5**.

[226] That is, the squandering of the assets (*Carmen*).

[227] Reading with **E**. **M** reads, "the father will arrive at the origin of the mothers, and he the father will come to be with [*sic., wrong preposition*] the family of the house of the mother." See my footnote to Ch. 4.14, **27** above.

[228] Cf. *Carmen* I.16, **15**, which reads less coherently than the version here.

Chapter [4.17]: On the knowledge of the affection of the parents & the child, one to the other, & their enmity

[al-Andarzaghar]

1 Look[229] at the Sun for nativities of the day: for if you found him in the bound of Mars (but born by night in the bound of Saturn), or both infortunes are looking at the Sun, and Venus and Jupiter are not looking, then judge for the child that he will oppose his parents or will kill one of them, or will be destructive to his land or country. **2** And look at the Moon, and judge likewise for the mother that she will be cast off by her child.

3 And[230] if you found the Lot of fathers in the twelfth from the Ascendant, then the native will be an enemy to his father.[231]

4 And[232] if you found the Sun in a stake and Mars looking at him from the seventh,[233] then the fathers will hate the child.

5 And[234] if Saturn looked down upon Jupiter (and that is that he is on the side of the Midheaven),[235] then perhaps he will kill his parents, or one of them. **6** And if [Jupiter] was above Saturn, it indicates the harms of his father, and likewise if the Sun was looking down upon Saturn. **7** And if you found Saturn and Jupiter looking at each other from the opposition, then the fathers and child will fight, one with the other, and they will encounter violence and tribulation. **8** And if they were looking at each other from a trine, then that is love and friendship; and likewise the aspect of the sextile is different for that, weaker in strength than the trine.

9 And[236] if you found the Sun and the lord of his triplicity in a bad place of the nativity (and in nativities of the day), and the infortunes made them unfortunate by the meeting or opposition or square, then the fathers will hate the sons until they distance themselves from them.

---

[229] For this paragraph, cf. Rhetorius Ch. 99 (p. 148).
[230] For this paragraph, cf. Rhetorius Ch. 99 (p. 148).
[231] This should rather be that the father is an enemy to the native.
[232] For this paragraph, cf. Rhetorius Ch. 99 (p. 148).
[233] That is, from an opposition (per Rhetorius).
[234] For this paragraph, cf. Rhetorius Ch. 99 (p. 148), and compare with Ch. 4.8, **2, 7-8, 31**.
[235] That is, Saturn is overcoming Jupiter from a superior square.
[236] For this paragraph, cf. Rhetorius Ch. 97 (p. 147), and *Carmen* I.13, **16-17**.

10 And[237] if the lord of the sign which opposed the Lot of fathers is looking at the Lot and its lord from the opposition of its own house, then the native will be claimed as belonging to [someone] other than his own father.

11 And if the Sun connected with the lord of the Ascendant or it connected to him, it indicates the affection of the father toward the native (and likewise the Moon indicates the mother). **12** And if the lord of the Ascendant opposed the Sun, and one of them separated from the other, it indicates the native's hatred for the father, and the quarreling of his parents (and likewise the Moon indicates the mother). **13** And if they connected from an opposition, it indicates quarreling without hatred;[238] and the connection of the trine and sextile indicates friendship.[239]

[Chapter 4.18: On inheritance]

[al-Andarzaghar]

1 And[240] as for what I mentioned of inheritance, whether he will inherit from his parents or not, look at the Sun and Saturn for one born by day. **2** For if you found them both in an excellent position, strong, then the native will get the inheritance of his father, if Mars was not with them nor looking at them from a square or opposition, because if Mars looked he will scatter his assets in every direction. **3** But more excellent than that is if the fortunes looked at the Sun and Saturn (and especially the Sun), for then he will get the bulk of the assets of the father, and will inherit from his fathers. **4** And if you found Mars in the stake (and worse than that is if he is born by day), and you found Saturn not like that, then the assets of the father will be destroyed during the life of the father or after the father's death. **5** And likewise if you found the Sun in the sixth or twelfth, and Saturn just as I described to you: so judge like that. **6** And speak likewise for mothers from the Moon and Venus.

---

[237] Cf. *Carmen* I.14, **6**. Again, see the footnote to Ch. 4.14, **27** above.

[238] Sahl or his source seems to mean that a *separating* opposition means enmity with hatred (**12**), because they cannot even engage constructively; but a *connection* by opposition at least has them engaging.

[239] The texts now repeat **9** (omitted here).

[240] For this paragraph, cf. *Carmen* I.18, **1-8**.

7 And[241] if Saturn was opposed to Mars or[242] Mars was in the right square of Saturn, it indicates the disappearance of his father's assets. 8 And when Saturn terminates at that position,[243] it indicates the inheritance of the assets of his father.

[Chapter 4.19: Which of the parents will die first: al-Andarzaghar]

1 And[244] if you wanted to know which of the two parents will die first, then look at the Lot of fathers and mothers, which one of them the infortunes are closer to and looked at more quickly from an opposition, square, or union: judge for that one that he [or she] will die first.

2 And look at the lords of the Lot of fathers and the Lot of mothers, in which sign they are, and which of them is made unfortunate: judge death for the more unfortunate of the two. 3 And also look at the lord of the Lot of the father: for if you found it above the earth, and the lord of the Lot of the mother in the region of the house of fathers, then the mother will die before the father; and if it was the contrary, the father will die before the mother.

4 And[245] look at the two Lots,[246] which of them was faster in entering the stake of the earth through the rotation of the circle, whether an infortune looked or did not look: that one will be first.

5 And[247] look at the two luminaries, Saturn, and Venus: for if you found the Sun and Saturn more unfortunate than the Moon and Venus, then the father will die before the mother. 6 And if you found the Moon and Venus more unfortunate than the Sun and Saturn, then the mother will die before

---

[241] For this paragraph, cf. *Carmen* I.17, **11-13**, and Sahl's Ch. 4.8, **9-10** and **32**. It is probably from al-Andarzaghar, but I do not find it in *BA*.
[242] Reading for "and."
[243] In *Carmen* this is the Lot of the father, and a primary direction.
[244] For this paragraph, cf. *Carmen* I.17, **1**.
[245] Cf. *Carmen* I.17, **6-7**. This may represent a missing sentence in the Arabic al-Andarzaghar, because it is so close in meaning to the previous ones and comes from the same section of the Latin *BA*.
[246] In *Carmen*, we see which of the *luminaries* comes to the IC first, *if* both Lots are looked at by the infortunes and the fortunes are in aversion to the Lots.
[247] For this paragraph, cf. Rhetorius Ch. 102 (p. 150).

the father. **7** And if the four of them were unfortunate together, then say that the parents will die in an epidemic on the same day.[248]

8 And[249] if you found the Sun with Saturn in [one] degree, the father will die before the mother; and if the Moon was with [Saturn] in [one] degree, the mother will die before the father. **9** And if they were both just as I described, and Saturn was with the Moon, and Mars was looking, the mother will die in childbirth or a painful, hidden pain of the belly.

10 And[250] if Mars was in the square of the Sun from the direction of the house of fathers, the father will die a [*uncertain*][251] death before the mother, before the child knows his father. **11** And likewise if [Mars] was in the second sign from the Sun, judge death for him. **12** But if Mars looked by day, then he will die in an epidemic, and likewise if it was Saturn by night: so judge that he will die by means of an epidemic.

13 And[252] if the Sun was at the end of the sign in the last degree, then the father will die before the mother. **14** And if the Moon was empty in course, then the mother will die first.

15 Now[253] if you found Mars and Saturn in the house of fathers, the father will die in an epidemic.

16 And[254] if the Sun was in the Ascendant, not ascending,[255] and he was made unfortunate in the Ascendant, then the father <will die> first; and if the Moon was like that, then the mother will die first.

17 And if the Lot of the father connects with Saturn from a conjunction or aspect, then the father is first; now if it was the Lot of the mother, then the mother is first.

18 And calculate the meeting or fullness closest to the native, and multiply by 12, and add to it <the degrees of the Ascendant>: and where the calculation arrives, if the sign was male, the father will die before the mother; and if it was feminine, the mother will die before the father.

---

[248] Rhetorius says only that there will be bereavement—which I take to mean that they will both die early.

[249] Cf. Rhetorius Ch. 102 (p. 150).

[250] For **10-11**, cf. *Carmen* I.17, **2-3**; also Rhetorius Ch. 102 (p. 151). Rhetorius has Mars by day on the Sun of the conception.

[251] The text seems to read رحب. But *BA* III.4.9, **11** reads "sudden."

[252] See Rhetorius Ch. 102 (p. 151). Sahl's version makes more astrological sense.

[253] Cf. Rhetorius Ch. 102 (p. 151).

[254] This probably represents a missing sentence in the Latin *BA*.

[255] I am not sure what this means.

19 And[256] if the Moon was <in the opposition or square of the infortunes, the mother will die before the father>.[257]

20 And[258] if the two lords of their Lots were in one sign, then the stationary one, the westernizing one,[259] [and] the one entering under the rays, is first. **21** Now if they were both in one degree, then look from the lord of their sign: for if it was male, then the father is first; and if it was female, the mother is first.[260]

[Chapter 4.20: The lifespan of the parents]

[al-Andarzaghar]

1 Now as for the length of the lifespan of the parents, and its shortness due to harm, chronic illness, and a bad death, look at Mars and Saturn: for if he[261] looked at the meeting or fullness, then judge an ugly death for the parents.

2 If the Sun and the lords of his triplicity were made unfortunate in the stakes, then state he will be killed first, and his assets confiscated, and especially if the infortunes looked; and likewise the Moon for the mother.

3 And[262] look at the Sun: for if you found Mars elevated over him,[263] then the father will be killed by iron, or chronic illness will afflict him in his face and harm it. **4** Now if Saturn looked at Mars, then judge death or a destruc-

---

[256] This looks as though it should match *Carmen* I.17, **5**, which refers to the idea in **10** above about the Sun: in which case the missing portion should be, "as I mentioned for the Sun." However, within *BA* itself this sentence is *BA* III.4.9, **18**, which has the Moon in the opposition or square of the infortunes.

[257] At this point the manuscripts have the phrase, "the father will die before the mother," which seems to be a repetition of the same phrase in **18**, which is all part of the same passage in *BA*.

[258] For this paragraph, cf. Rhet. Ch. 102 (p. 150). It may represent something from the original al-Andarzaghar.

[259] For these first two conditions, Rhetorius simply has the one which is afflicted.

[260] In Rhetorius, this is rather (a) the lord of the *bound* they are in, and (b) what is the gender of the *sign in which* that bound lord is.

[261] I am not sure whether one or more is meant. *BA* III.4.6, **14** implies it is both.

[262] For this paragraph, see *Tet.* III.4 (Robbins pp. 245-47).

[263] That is, overcoming or decimating him from the superior square.

tive fever for him, or the cutting of some of his limbs, or burning[264] by fire or iron. **5** And if Saturn opposed the Sun, his death will be related to eyesight. **6** And judge likewise for the mother from the Moon and Venus.

7 And[265] if you found Saturn in the house of the Sun, then judge a bad, ugly death for the father; and if Saturn was in the house of the Moon, then the mother's character will be corrupted by black bile. **8** And[266] if Mars was in the house of the Sun, then his father will die a sudden death, or on a journey, and his eyesight will be corrupted before death; and likewise in the house of the Moon for the mother.

ᶳ ᴥ ᴣ

9 And if the Sun was opposed from a stake, in the aspect of an infortune (or its square), it indicates a bad death for the father; and likewise if the infortune witnessed the lord of the sign of the Sun.

10 And if Mars was the lord of the degree of the Sun by night, and the Sun was connected,[267] it indicates the shortness of the father's survival.

11 And if the lord of the house of fathers was falling, in the aspect of an infortune from a square or opposition or conjunction, it indicates a bad death for his father; and the time of that is when an infortune transits past the Lot of fathers in a stake, if a fortune is not looking.

12 And[268] whenever you found Mars looking down upon the Sun or rising after him, then judge a bad death for the father, or a chronic illness will happen to him in his face. **13** And if Saturn was in the square of the Sun or his opposition, it indicates a bad death and the length of an illness, and toil from moisture.[269]

[al-Andarzaghar]

14 And look at the lord of the house of the Sun: for if the infortunes looked at it, then the father will die an ugly death and his assets will be cor-

---

[264] This can include cauterization (كي).
[265] For this sentence, cf. *Carmen* II.37, **1-2**, and perhaps Rhetorius Ch. 102 (p. 151). Cf. also the other versions above in Chs. 4.10, **2-3** and 4.5, **28**.
[266] For this sentence, cf. Rhetorius Ch. 102 (p. 151), and perhaps *Carmen* II.37, **3-4**.
[267] Presumably, to Mars.
[268] For this paragraph, cf. *Tet.* III.4 (Robbins p. 245).
[269] This goes back to traditional associations of Saturn, such as waterside trades; Saturn also tends to indicate the accumulation of fluids in medical astrology.

rupted; and likewise if the infortunes looked at the Moon for the mother.[270] **15** And God is more knowledgeable.

16 As[271] for the length of the father's survival,[272] look at Jupiter and Venus: for if they[273] looked at the Sun and Saturn, and especially if it was from the left square, from the region of the house of fathers, and Saturn looked at them, [he being] with the Sun by a union or trine or sextile, and you found them both eastern in the stakes, then judge for the father his long survival. **17** And if you found them both under the rays, or retrograde, or decreasing, or falling from the stake, then [it indicates] an average survival; and if they were both exiled, falling, then it indicates the shortness of the survival.

18 And if Mars looked down upon the Sun from the side of the Midheaven, or upon Saturn, or Mars was in the second from them, rising after them, or the Sun was connecting with Saturn from a square or opposition, and they were falling from the stakes, then judge sickliness for the father, [but] not other than that. **19** But if you found them both in a stake or what follows a stake (and that is if what I mentioned was in the stakes and what follows them), then it indicates the shortness of the lifespan and chronic illness[274] for the father. **20** Now, if what I have described to you was in the Ascendant or Midheaven, or what follows these stakes, it indicates the shortness of the lifespan and survival. **21** And if this misfortune was in the seventh or fourth or in what follows these stakes, then judge for him sickliness and chronic illness.

22 The length of the parents' survival, and the knowledge of the years of the father and mother after the nativity. **23** Look at the Lot of fathers and mothers, and the aspect of the fortunes and infortunes to them both, and the course[275] of the two Lots by degrees of ascension to the lights of the assembly, and their squares, and their oppositions, until they connect with the infortunes, for each degree a year, until they reach the sign in which the two

---

[270] Or perhaps the lord of the Moon so as to parallel the statements about the Sun. But this could also refer to **12-13** as well, since Ptolemy does then turn to the mother with the same considerations.

[271] From here through **21**, cf. *Tet.* III.4 (Robbins pp. 243-45).

[272] **E**'s opening line reads: "The length of the father's survival: And as for looking at the lifespan of the father...".

[273] The text actually reads in the singular, and indeed Ptolemy allows either one.

[274] Ptolemy also includes injury.

[275] That is, by primary direction.

infortunes are; and also the course of the infortunes by the degrees and signs,[276] until in their transit they reach the place or sign in which the Lots are, by union or opposition or square. **24** For whichever one of these lights[277] was quicker in connecting with the infortunes, judge death for the parents from that one. **25** Now[278] if the two infortunes testified, then that is easier for rendering a judgment,[279] and especially if Jupiter was the lord of the year[280] of the nativity, and he is in a stake, eastern: for if it was like that, then the native will inherit the assets of his parents upon their death.

26 And look at the travel[281] of the Sun and Moon, whether it is with the fortunes or infortunes, and the course of the fortunes and infortunes to them.

27 And look at the more powerful period,[282] and the middle, and the lesser one in the signs, just as I informed you of in the chapter of his living or not living.[283]

28 Dorotheus said:[284] perhaps the infortunes will reach the place of the Sun and Moon in the nativity, so they kill the fathers and mothers: and that is when Saturn or Mars transits the sign in which the luminaries were in the root of the nativity. **29** And[285] [it is] likewise when Saturn or Mars transits the Lot from the stake of the earth.[286] **30** And he does not omit the revolution of years and the transit of the [malefic][287] planets over the Moon and Sun.

ಙ ಜ ಜ

---

[276] **E** omits "and signs."
[277] Based on *BA*, the "lights" are the aspects in the primary direction of the infortunes, not the luminaries themselves.
[278] Cf. *Carmen* I.17, **13-14**.
[279] Tentatively reading for what seems to be أجرى أن تفصل القضاء.
[280] Reading with **M**, but **E** reads, "lord of the *Lot*."
[281] Again, this would be through primary directions.
[282] That is, the planets' greater, middle, and lesser years.
[283] This might refer to Chs. 1.20 and 1.21.
[284] For this sentence, see *Carmen* I.17, **14**.
[285] For this sentence, see *Carmen* I.17, **13**.
[286] Reading with **E**; **M** has only, "in a stake," presumably meaning that Mars is in a stake.
[287] Adding with the sense of *Carmen* I.17, **14**.

31 And[288] know that if the nativity was by day, the infortunes which harm his Lot are Mars and Saturn (and Mercury, if he was unfortunate); and if it was by night, the infortunes which harm them are Mars and Mercury (if he was unfortunate).

32 Then, direct the degree of the Lot of the father and the Sun by day, and by night the Lot and Saturn. 33 And if you found an infortune casting its rays upon the Sun and upon the Lot, then look at this planet, to which of the two is it harsher in enmity in the root of the nativity: for it will kill the father when the direction reaches the infortune which casts the rays. 34 Now if you found one of the two infortunes casting its rays upon the Sun and the other upon the degree of the Lot, then look at these two infortunes, <whichever of them> was harsher in enmity in the root of the nativity [to] the Lot and the Sun: grant that one the power; and if they were each bad in enmity, then look at the more powerful of the two and grant it the matter. 35 Now if they were equal in power, then grant the matter to the one the luminaries are closer to. 36 And know that if Saturn looked at the degree of the Lot of the father from hostility, it is more harmful for some of the injuries, and that is a harm for the father resembling his whole self.

37 Now as for the mother, direct for her the Moon and the Lot by night, and by day the Lot and Venus,[289] and direct them both just as I described do you for the father.

38 And[290] see the lord of the bound of the Lot and[291] the lord of the house of the Lot: for if they were both corrupted, then it indicates[292] the death of the father. 39 And the time of that is when Saturn passes over it[293] in his course before he casts his light upon it: for at that time, the father will die;

---

[288] In this paragraph, we would expect Mars to be the primary malefic by day (along with Mercury), and Saturn to be the primary malefic by night (along with Mercury), since in both cases those malefics are contrary to the sect of the chart. But since Saturn is also used as an indicator for the father by night, he cannot also be the primary malefic. Hence, it seems Mars is the main malefic for both night and day (with some participation by Saturn by day), and Mercury as a possible malefic if he is made unfortunate.

[289] The texts assign the day to the Moon, and the night to Venus, which is incorrect; I have switched the designations here.

[290] For this paragraph, see the other version in Ch. 4.13.

[291] The texts say "or," but it is clear in the instructions below that we are to examine both.

[292] Reading يدل with Ch. 4.13, here and in 41, for برك.

[293] That is, "transits" it.

and likewise too if he cast his light upon it[294] before he crosses it in his course, for then he will also die. **40** And if one of the two was suitable and the other corrupt, then it also indicates his death. **41** And if they were both suitable, then it does not indicate his killing in [Saturn's] crossing over him in his course, but it does indicate his killing when one of the infortunes (Saturn or Mars) casts his light upon him,[295] unless Venus or Jupiter equally casts its own light into the bounds. **42** And likewise the Lot of the mother: look just as you examined the father. **43** And God is more knowledgeable.

The statement of Māshā'allāh:[296]

45 If the Sun was made unfortunate, it indicates the bad condition of the father, and his grieving. **46** And if [the Sun] was falling, and the lord of his house was in a stake, not free of[297] the infortunes, or the lord of the Lot was retrograde, it indicates the destruction of the father. **47** And likewise, if the Sun was made unfortunate by the lord of the eighth or by the lord of the eleventh from the Ascendant,[298] and the lord of the house of the Lot was retrograde, or the Sun connects with a retrograde planet not receiving him, then it indicates the shortness of the father's lifespan, and it will be feared for him the first time that an infortune sees from the conjunction, square, or opposition; or one[299] looks at the year in which the infortunes correspond to the position of the Lot or its square or its opposition: so revolve the year.

48 Now if the Sun or the lord of the house of the Lot was corrupted, it indicates the destruction of the father; and likewise the mother from Jupiter.[300] **49** And if the lord of the fourth was under the rays, entering into burning, it is feared for him that he will make a speech in which there is impoliteness; and that is harsher if it had testimony and if the lord of the fourth was the

---

[294] That is, by primary directions.
[295] That is, by direction or distribution.
[296] The text originally read, "and al-Khayyāt," but the passage attributed to him in **E** (which would have appeared below) actually matches the earlier passage, also attributed to al-Khayyāt, in Ch. 4.12 above. I have followed **M**'s pagination so al-Khayyāt does not appear here, but above.
[297] Reading as بري. But in the unpointed script of the manuscripts, this could also be يرى, "not *looked at/seen by*" the infortunes. But this latter would be a positive thing (i.e., being angular and with the infortunes in aversion), which does not match the interpretation.
[298] The eleventh is the eighth (death) from the fourth (parents).
[299] Reading as an instruction to the reader, instead of "it looks," referring to the infortune.
[300] This does not make sense, and should probably be "the Moon."

lord of the Lot. **50** And[301] know that the misfortune will hasten to the parents if the luminaries were in the stakes, and[302] they were made unfortunate from a stake, not received.

51 And[303] if you saw an infortune with the Lot of the father or in its square or opposition, connecting with it, then look in that at the Sun, [to see] when he connects his light with the light of the infortune: for indeed when he connected with its light, it will be feared for [the father]: so revolve his year. **52** And if you saw the Sun made unfortunate, or the lord of the Lot corrupted, it indicates the destruction of the father; and more harshly for that if the year reached the sign in which there was an infortune[304] in the root of the nativity, or the Ascendant of the revolution was in one of the stakes of the nativity, or the year reached an infortune or a sign in its stake.[305]

53 Then, look at the Lot of fathers: for if the Sun or Venus or Jupiter was with it, and neither Saturn nor Mars looks at the Lot, then his father will come to nobility and high rank, and he will mix with the powerful and find the good. **54** And if Saturn and Mars looked at the position of the Lot from a square or opposition, or one of them or both conjoined with it, then his assets and authority will disappear, and he will die poor.

55 And if Venus or Jupiter coincided with the Sun, or he looked at them both from a square, then the father and his siblings will be kings of their own places in which they are. **56** Now if along with this the infortunes were with him, it indicates a rebellion of its nature from that. **57** Now, look at the fortunes and infortunes, [to see] which of them is more powerful by place. **58** For if the fortunes were stronger <by place>, the outcome of his affair will [incline] towards good fortune; and if the infortunes were stronger by place, the outcome of his matter will [incline] toward evil.

---

[301] This sentence is based on three passages: **M** (slide 45/2 line 21 – 45/3 lines 1-2) and **E** (slide 30b, lines 12-13), here called **M1** and **E1**, and a few sentences later in **M** (slide 45/3, lines 14-15), here called **M2**. I have applied the later passage here and deleted it there, as it is not as complete as what appears here.

[302] **M2** reads "or."

[303] The "connecting" in this chapter is probably by primary direction, which is then followed by a solar revolution. But it is possible that Māshā'allāh is trying to pair two transits in time, and matching them to the solar revolution.

[304] Or perhaps, "*the* infortune," namely the one harming the Sun or the lord of the Lot.

[305] Reading with **E**. **M** reads, "the fourth sign, of the tenth or seventh," which is redundant.

59 And if the Sun was in the seventh, and with him Saturn or Mars, then the father[306] will waste all of his assets. **60** And if the Sun was looking at Mars from a square or opposition, it indicates his father's falling into evil and tribulation, until he destroys himself or turns himself towards distant travel, or is confined in prison, or chains afflict him. **61** And if nothing of that afflicts him, he will not remain except for something short, until he dies, and perhaps his death will be in fire. **62** And if the Sun was with Mercury and Mars, he will be hard-hearted to[307] the native, but he will not survive; and if he does not die, he will be miserable.

63 And if you found Jupiter in the Midheaven with the Sun, it indicates superior nobility, and that is if in addition Venus happens to be in a stake. **64** And if an infortune looked at them both like that from a square or opposition, it indicates the corruption of his father's assets, until he remains poor or dies poor. **65** And if Venus, where she was,[308] is inspecting the fortunes, that good fortune will belong to his mother; and if she was like that [but] falling, it indicates harm to his mother. **66** And if there was not an infortune looking at the Sun and Jupiter, it indicates the agreement of his parents, and his mother will die before his father. **67** And if Venus and the Moon happened to be in a good place without the aspect of an infortune, and the Sun and Jupiter were being looked at by an infortune (or its conjunction), the mother will be longer in lifespan than his father. **68** And if the Midheaven and the Moon were in their aspect, then the father is superior to the mother, and longer in lifespan.

69 Then, look at the sign of the father: for if the Tail coincided with it, and with it [was] an infortune, while his father is on the sea he will die by drowning; and if he was on the land, he will die a bad death, and he is apt to die of thirst.

70 Now if an infortune looked at the lord of the house of the Sun, it indicates the death of his father; and if the Moon was like that, his mother. **71** And if an infortune looked at them both, and likewise a fortune, it indicates [both] illness and safety.

72 And know that if the fourth sign was male, then it is the father along with the Sun; and if it was female, then it is the mother along with the Moon.

---

[306] **E** reads, "the native."
[307] Reading the rest of the sentence as a blend of **E** and **M**.
[308] This should probably be understood as her being in a stake (as in **63**), as later in the sentence this is contrasted with her falling.

73 And[309] know that the share of the degree of the Sun[310] indicates the condition of the father, and likewise the degree of the Moon indicates the condition of the mother. **74** So work with them both, because the degree of the Sun and the Moon both indicate the parents, by means of the status[311] of the Ascendant belonging to the native: so make the turning[312] from them both to the fortunes and the infortunes, and they indicate—through their positions from the Ascendant by day [for the father] and their aspects, and the one connected to [them]—the condition of the father along with the beginning of the [life of] the native; and the lord of [the Sun's] house indicates his end, because the start of his good fortune is from the place of the Sun, and the end of his good fortune is from the lord of his house. **75** And likewise the Moon by night indicates the mother. **76** And God is more knowledgeable.

---

[309] I am not sure whether or not this paragraph is still Māshā'allāh, but I think not due to the use of "And know that," which often shows a break or new topic.

[310] This probably means the bound of the Sun.

[311] بمنزلة. This seems to mean the quality and character of the Ascendant as it is profected through the signs (see later in the sentence).

[312] This would normally indicate only a profection, but I expect the source means primary directions from them as well.

Chapter 5: On the matter of children
And it has six topics

[al-Andarzaghar][1]

1 The first topic: begin by examining the multiplicity of the children, and their scarcity.

2 The second topic: whether he is sterile or not.

3 The third topic: see when one will be born to him, in which time period of his life, and will the children be male or female.

4 The fourth topic: which of his children will be more powerful and significant, or what will the father encounter from them.

5 The fifth topic: whether his children will die before him or not.

6 The sixth topic: what is the number of his children.

[Chapter 5.1: The multiplicity of the children & their scarcity]

[al-Andarzaghar]

1 As for the knowledge of the children, whether they are many or few, look at four items:

2 The[2] first of them is that you look at all of the lords[3] of the triplicities of Jupiter, or[4] Jupiter himself, [to see] in which position it is from the Ascendant, and its suitability, and see [if] perhaps it is under the rays, and in which category of sign Jupiter and the lord of his triplicity is in (whether it is many in children, or sterile, or middling).[5]

3 The second is, look at the Lot of children, [to see] in which sign it falls, and who is with it; and look at the lord of the Lot [to see] how it is from [the Lot].[6]

---

[1] Each of the topics in this list corresponds generally to each of the six chapters below, respectively.
[2] Cf. *Carmen* II.9, but especially **15**.
[3] In *Carmen* this is only the primary triplicity lord.
[4] This should be read as "and."
[5] This refers to **9-16** below (which *BA* abbreviates).
[6] See **33-41** and **91** (but cf. also **42-43**, which were probably in the Arabic *BA*).

4 And the third is, look at the Midheaven and its lord, and from the mixture of the sign which it is in, and who of the fortunes and infortunes is looking at it.[7]

5 The fourth is that you look at the fifth house from the Ascendant, and the fortunes and infortunes which are in it and looking at it from friendship and harmony.[8]

6 And[9] know that Jupiter, Venus, and the Moon are the planets indicating an abundance of children, and the Sun, Saturn, and Mars indicate a scarcity of children. **7** And as for Mercury, he partners with all of them: if he was eastern, he multiplies children; and if he was western, he diminishes them.

8 And[10] the signs of sterility are Gemini, Leo and its triplicity, Capricorn, Virgo, the beginning of Taurus, and the middle of Libra; and those abundant in offspring are Cancer and its triplicity (and Scorpio indicates an abundance of children as well as their death); and the rest of the signs are in the middle.

[The first item: Jupiter and his triplicity lords]

9 So let the beginning of your examination be [to look] at Jupiter, so you may know his condition in himself,[11] and his place in the signs. **10** And look at Mercury as well, and how his suitability is in himself. **11** And do not neglect to understand which of the planets is in the Midheaven.

12 Now if you found Jupiter in a sign abundant in children, in his own bound, and especially in Cancer, and the nativity was by day, and Jupiter was in a stake or what follows a stake, then judge an abundance of children for him—and especially if in addition Mercury was in the Midheaven, in a sign having several or an abundance [of children]. **13** And if you found the lord of Jupiter's triplicity in the stake of the Ascendant or in the Midheaven, or in the house of good fortune, or in the fifth house, then that is a mark of his suitability in the matter of children, because that indicates delight from the children, and especially if the lord of that triplicity was a fortune. **14** And if it

---

[7] See **46** below.
[8] See **47**, **51-52**, **58-59**, and Ch. 5.3, **6-7**.
[9] For his paragraph, cf. *Tet.* IV.6 (Robbins p. 409). Sentences **6-8** are not in *BA*.
[10] For this sentence, cf. *Carmen* II.10, **12-13**; for more on these signs, see *Introduction* Ch. 1, **23-24**; *Nativities* Ch. 3, **10**; 1.38, **14-17**.
[11] E reads, "in his body," for both Jupiter and Mercury.

was an infortune too, and it was in its own bound, direct in its course, it will not [*uncertain*];¹² and more excellent is if it was in its exaltation or own house, or any of his shares.

15 And¹³ if you found the lord of Jupiter's triplicity in a good place and the second one in a bad place, then in the beginning of his life he will have delight in children, and he will have children; but at its end he will be deprived with respect to them, with weeping and lamenting over his children through death or killing. **16** And if you found the lord of Jupiter's triplicity falling or under the rays,¹⁴ then he will not have children, and especially if Jupiter was under the rays.

17 And¹⁵ if one of the lords of the triplicities was in a good place or a bad one, it is an indication (in accordance with its essence) of the time period in which its governorship in it will come to it.

18 And the preferable one of the lords of the triplicities is the first one: for indeed when it is in a strong place, free of the rays, <*missing*>.¹⁶

19 And whenever you find Jupiter made unfortunate, and especially if his misfortune was from Mars, then state the ruin of his children, as well as what sorrow and tribulation will afflict him for that reason. **20** Now if the Tail was with Jupiter, then it is worse; and likewise if you found Jupiter in his fall, or burned by the rays, or in the sixth or in the twelfth (because these places are bad).

21 And if you found Jupiter in his own house, bound, or exaltation, then the native will have children. **22** And if you found Mercury with Jupiter, and not falling, it indicates several or an abundance, and delight from children; but if you found them in the second and eighth, it indicates sorrow, and especially if you found them in retrogradation or decreasing in their glow.¹⁷

23 And know that if you found Jupiter or the lord of his triplicity in their exaltation, and looking at the lords of their houses, then that is of the marks

---

¹² **M** is unpointed and too ambiguous. **E** seems to read: فلا يأثر به, which suggests "he will not be affected by it," except that meaning (with the use of the pronoun ب) requires Form V of the verb. At any rate, Sahl seems to be saying that it will not harm or prevent children.
¹³ For this paragraph, cf. *Carmen* II.8.
¹⁴ *Carmen* II.8, **4** implies it is falling *and* under the rays.
¹⁵ See *Carmen* II.8, **3**.
¹⁶ The missing statement here probably reads something like: "the native will have children in his youth" (i.e., young adulthood). But contrast this with *Carmen* II.9, **15**: if it is in a good place but under the rays, he will have children but they will not survive.
¹⁷ This might mean being under the rays.

of being delighted in children. **24** And if you found the lord of the house of Jupiter in its exaltation as well, then state [something] roughly like that too.

25 If the lord of the Jupiter's triplicity was a fortune, and he was with it, or if Jupiter was the ruler of that in his own right, then judge delight for him in children. **26** And if you found the lord of Jupiter's triplicity or the lord of his house to be an infortune, and it was not in its own house nor its own share, or it was a fortune and it was in a falling place, not looking at Jupiter, then judge sorrow for that native because of children.

27 And if you found Jupiter in the seventh or eighth from the Ascendant, and the lord of his triplicity was under the rays and not eastern, it indicates an abundance of children after obstruction and delay.[18] **28** And likewise if you found Jupiter and the lord of his triplicity in the fifth place, then truly he will delight in children at the end of his life, and especially if he was abundant in children. **29** And if you found Jupiter in his own share[19] or his exaltation, it indicates that he will see the children of his children,[20] and likewise if Mercury was in the house of Jupiter,[21] and he looked at him from a good place. **30** And if you found the lord of the Ascendant in a sign great in number, it also indicates that a child will be born to the native, and especially if the Moon was free of Saturn. **31** And if you found the lord of Jupiter's triplicity in a sign having two bodies, it indicates an abundance of children.

The second item: [the Lot of children]

33 Look[22] at the Lot of children:[23] for indeed if it was in the stakes or in an excellent place, it indicates an abundance of children and their suitability. **34** And if it occurred in the sixth or in the twelfth, then none will be born to him; and if [any] were born to him, they will die; and if they survived, they will be separated into every country, and no two of them will [ever] meet with their father. **35** And if you found the Lot empty, none being with it nor

---

[18] Or, "delay and slowness" (التَّأْخِير وَالإبْطاء).
[19] حظّ, which might be a synonym for "sect" here.
[20] Reading with **E** for **M**'s "children," as it seems that Sahl is trying to say something more than simply having his own children.
[21] **M** reads: "the Sun."
[22] For this paragraph, cf. *Carmen* II.10, **6-9** and **11**.
[23] This is calculated by day from Jupiter to Saturn (and by night the reverse), and projected from the Ascendant (*Carmen* II.10, **1**).

any of the planets looking at it, neither by a meeting nor by the aspect <of opposition>[24] nor by the square, then he will remain in need, sad over his children because of the emptiness of the Lot, and the first child born to him will die or come out miscarried. **36** And if you found a planet opposing the Lot or in its square, then judge that [children] will be born to him, and his children will be fit. **37** And if Saturn was with the Lot in a sign, he will be sterile or of few children.

38 And[25] if you found Venus made unfortunate by Saturn, and Jupiter not looking at her, then he will be sterile; and worse than that is if the Moon is unfortunate. **39** And see also if perhaps the Sun occurs in a sterile sign, for that indicates that he will be sterile or of few children. **40** And[26] if you found Venus, Jupiter, and Mercury turned away from[27] the infortunes in the root of the nativity, then he will be abundant in children, and his children will be sound. **41** And if they were in their unhealthiness,[28] he will not have children; while if they were raised, it will sadden their father because of them.

42 And if you found the Lot in a sign having a number [of children], it indicates an abundance of pregnancies, especially if its lord was a fortune and it was with the Lot in a sign having a number [of children] or having duplicates[29] or a convertible one, because it indicates an abundance of children. **43** And[30] whenever you find the Lot with the various planets or being looked at by them, then judge an abundance of children. **44** And judge likewise if the Lot was above the earth, in a good place, free of the infortunes and the rays and the Tail.

---

[24] Adding with *Carmen*.
[25] For this sentence, cf. *Carmen* II.12, **5-6** and **12**.
[26] For this sentence and the next, cf. *Carmen* II.12, **14-15**; however, Valens (*Anth.* II.39) attributes this view to Petosiris.
[27] That is, "in aversion to," reading أنحيا for what seems to be **E**'s أصحا. But if this is a different word, it must mean something like "free from," "unharmed by," and so on. **E** spells this almost as the scribe writes "lords" (أصحاب), but this is not the sense of *Carmen* nor *Anth.*
[28] This is a standard word for "detriment," although *Carmen* II.2, **15** refers to their "well or decline," suggesting being in fall or simply cadent.
[29] صور, which normally would mean "images," but can also mean copies or duplicates, and makes sense as a description of the common or double-bodied signs.
[30] This sounds very much like *Carmen* II.10, **14**, which is likewise preceded by a sentence about the fertility of the signs. But in *Carmen*, these planets must be in the Lot's angles (or with it, I'm sure), not just configured in any way at all.

The third item: [the Midheaven]

46 Then,[31] look at the Midheaven and who is looking at, its lord (where it is), and the fifth from the Ascendant and its lord: for if the fortunes were there, and it is a sign of many children, then it indicates an abundance of children along with suitability and his children will delight his eye.

[The fourth item: the fifth house]

47 Then,[32] look at the house of children: for if you found a fortune in it, and its lord in an excellent place, cleansed of defects and the infortunes, and looking at the Midheaven, it indicates an abundance of children and their suitability.

48 And if you found the lord of the house of children to be a fortune, and it was eastern, then say good about the children. **49** And if you found a fortune in the house of children, it indicates children and delight with them (and likewise for the opposition). **50** But if Mars was there it indicates the death of children; and if Saturn was there it indicates that a child will not be born to him; and if it was the Sun it indicates scarcity.

51 And[33] if you found the lord of the fifth house to be falling, and the two fortunes not looking at the fifth, and the infortunes did look at it, it indicates a scarcity of children; and if he did have children, their survival would be short. **52** And if one of the two fortunes looked at it, it indicates a middling amount of children.

53 And if the lord of the house was in <a sign> having two bodies, it indicates children from various women.

54 And if the fortunes were in the fifth, they indicate an abundance of births; and the Moon in the fifth indicates an abundance; and the infortunes there, not being in their own shares, [indicate that] they will die and his children will not survive.[34]

---

[31] Cf. *Carmen* II.12, **16-19**.
[32] For this sentence, cf. *Carmen* II.12, **19**.
[33] For this paragraph, cf. *Carmen* II.12, **17-18**.
[34] This last clause is redundant, so something might be missing.

55 And[35] the sum of the matter of children is that you look from the house of children and from the Lot of children, and the lords of their houses, and that you understand the essence of the sign and the essence of the planet which is in the sign, and the lords of the triplicities of Jupiter, and that you examine the lords of the twelve by place: because if you found any of them in the fifth place, then it will produce an example of its essence and the force of the indication of the place which it is lord of. **56** Because if the lord of the Midheaven or the lord of the Ascendant was in the fifth place, or the lord of the fifth place was in the Ascendant or Midheaven, it indicates an abundance of children and their suitability, especially if that was a fortune. **57** And if the lord of the fifth was in the twelfth or the lord of the twelfth in the fifth, it indicates the baseness of the children, and he will have children from slave girls.

58 And[36] look at the one which distributes [children] by the permission of God (and it is the lord of Jupiter's triplicity) and the lord of the Lot of children: for if you found them in the Ascendant or in the Midheaven, or in the house of hope, his children will be his youth. **59** Now if they were in the house of livelihood[37] or in the eighth,[38] he will have children in the middle of his life. **60** And God is more knowledgeable.

[*The method of Māshā'allāh*]

61 And Māshā'allāh said: If you found the lord of the house of children free of the infortunes and the planet repugnant to it (and it is the lord of the twelfth), and it is in a good place and the lord of the Ascendant connected with it, then it indicates an abundance of children, and their suitability, and the rise of their reputation. **62** And if they connected but they were not excellent in [their] position relative to the Ascendant, then they will be multiple but they will not be suitable nor famous. **63** And if they did not connect but the lord of the fifth was in an excellent place, free of the infortunes, then he will have a child.

64 And with that, look at the house of children and what is looking at it (of the fortunes and infortunes): for if a fortune looked at that position, it

---

[35] The following seems to be Sahl's own comment.
[36] For this paragraph, cf. *Carmen* II.9, **13-14**; note that it anticipates Ch. 5.3, **1** and **4-7** below.
[37] That is, the second.
[38] *Carmen* adds the seventh and the fourth: see also Ch. 5.3, **11-13** below.

indicates the safety of the children, and if an infortune looked it indicates their corruption and ruin—unless the infortune was received: because if it was received, it does not indicate their ruin, but there will be defects in them from the badness of their character and the corruption of [their] religion. **65** Now if the lord of the house of children was made unfortunate by the planet repugnant to it, he will not have children, or they will be miscarried and not survive.

66 Then, look at Venus as well: for if she owned the fifth sign from the Ascendant, then look at her position relative to the Ascendant, and the aspect of the infortunes and fortunes to her. **67** For if she was free from the infortunes then she indicates the power and testimony of the first one.[39] **68** And if she was made unfortunate, corruption will enter into her testimony of the first one; and if a fortune looked at her, she will increase in the testimony of the first house. **69** And if the lord of the house of Venus united with the fortunes, it indicates good health; now if it united with the infortunes, it indicates emaciation.

70 Then, look after that at the Lot of children, and who is looking at it (of the fortunes and infortunes): for it indicates the suitability of the children and their corruption. **71** Then look at the lord of the Lot and its position relative to the Ascendant, and the aspect of the fortunes and the infortunes to it, based on what I described to you about the lord of the fifth and the lord of the house of Venus, because they are both support for her.[40]

72 And if you found the lord of the house of children and the lord of the house of Venus to be with Saturn, or they looked at him from a square or opposition, they indicate distress because of the children. **73** And if Jupiter coincided with them, they indicate joy. **74** If the lord of the house of Venus <and the lord of the house of children>[41] were in the tenth from the Ascendant, they indicate a disease of lameness and the exhaustion of the body. **75**

---

[39] This may mean "the first house" or "the lord of the first house," as stated in **68**, but I do not really understand it.

[40] لها. This is the natural reading, but one would think this ought to be "it," meaning the topic of children.

[41] The texts only read the lord of the house of Venus, but then use the dual form of the verb, indicating the lord of the fifth (as was just mentioned); likewise in the next sentence the verb is only in the singular. So Māshā'allāh's view probably extends to each of them in isolation, but certainly if they are both in such a condition.

Now if they[42] were made unfortunate along with what I mentioned, there will be a chronic illness in them. **76** Now if it was in the twelfth from the Ascendant, it indicates their being killed; and if it was made unfortunate along with what I mentioned, he will survive his children.[43]

The lord of the house of children, if it was in the houses of the circle [according to Māshāʾallāh]

78 So, look at the lord of the house of children: for if it was in the Ascendant, he will be blessed with children in his youth, and his eye will be pleased, and he will be happy. **79** The lord of the fifth in the second from the Ascendant: he will have children blessed with a livelihood under their own authority,[44] and it[45] will be with the Sultan. **80** The lord of the fifth in the third from the Ascendant: he will have children named with the names of his siblings, successful in travels. **81** The lord of the fifth in the fourth: he will have children who are wretches, encountering hardship and enmity because of them.[46] **82** The lord of the fifth in the fifth: he will have well-known children, they being happy. **83** The lord of the fifth in the sixth: he will have children who are fortunate, but defects will appear in them. **84** The lord of the fifth in the seventh: his children will generally be from his maids and the women of his service, and they will be hostile to him, and he will deceive himself with respect to [the women]. **85** The lord of the fifth in the eighth: [*illegible*] they will survive and will be miscarried.[47] **86** The lord of the fifth in the ninth: he will get children while absent from his homeland, they will make him happy, and his eye will be pleased with them. **87** The lord of the fifth in the tenth: there will be illness appearing in his children, and a defect. **88** The lord of the fifth in the eleventh: his eye will be pleased with his chil-

---

[42] See previous footnote.

[43] Lit., "he will remain after the children." This seems redundant, but I think Māshāʾallāh means that instead of just one child dying, all of them will—so that the native will be left alone.

[44] Or more literally, "under their own protection."

[45] Or perhaps, "he," referring to one of the children.

[46] في سببهم. But if so, it seems to be it should be because *they* are suffering, since the lord of the fifth is in the twelfth *from the fifth*, indicating *their* problems.

[47] The word I have translated as "miscarried" (أسقاط) can also mean being very premature. The text here not only suffers the smudging found throughout E, but has a line from a faulty photographing process which runs directly across every word. Sahl probably means that his children will suffer or die, and those that do survive will be premature.

dren and the family of his house, and he[48] will be praised. **89** The lord of the fifth in the twelfth from the Ascendant: in his children there will have a defect or chronic illness, and they will die from that disease. **90** And if it was made unfortunate, he will not have children.

91 Know[49] that in this subject, if the lord of the fifth and the fifth are both free of the infortunes, and the fortunes do not witness[50] the Lot of children in the houses of the circle, then look at the Lot of children: and it is that you calculate for him by night and by day from Jupiter to Saturn,[51] and cast it out from the Ascendant, so where it terminates, there is the Lot of children, God willing. **92** And according to the method of Hermes, it is taken from Mercury to Saturn, and cast out from the Ascendant, and where it terminates, there is the Lot.

[*The Lot of children in the houses, according to Māshā'allāh*][52]

93 The Lot of children in the Ascendant: the native will be powerful in love for the children, and his children will remain absent <from> the land in which they were born. **94** Now if the lord of the Lot was in an excellent place, free of the infortunes,[53] his children will have piety in their religion; while if it was made unfortunate, it indicates the corruption of their religion. **95** The Lot of children in the second from the Ascendant: the native will have children who have a livelihood at the doors of the Sultan. **96** Now if its lord was free of the infortunes, in its own glow, they will have authority, will collect assets, and will inherit from their parents; but if the Lot and its lord were made unfortunate, they will inherit from the parents but will not collect assets. **97** The Lot of children in the third: he will have many children, on whom the good will be doubled, and they will gain from actions. **98** The Lot of children in the fourth: his children will have many <enemies>,[54] and will

---

[48] But this should probably be read as "they."
[49] I am not sure whether this is Māshā'allāh's or Sahl's comment.
[50] Tentatively reading يشهد, but **E** is virtually illegible here.
[51] According to Abū Ma'shar (*Gr. Intr.* VIII.4), this view belongs to Theophilus, whereas the usual calculation (from Jupiter to Saturn by day, and reversed by night) is that of Hermes.
[52] Cf. Tehran, Dānishgāh, Nafīsī 429 (70a-70b); Majlis 17490 (135-36).
[53] In Māshā'allāh, *both* the Lot and its lord are in good places and free of the infortunes.
[54] Adding based on Māshā'allāh, here and throughout the paragraph.

be named with the names of their <grandparents>⁵⁵ and uncles. **99** And if its lord was free of the infortunes, in its own glow, <his children> will get the inheritance of the grandparents; and if it was made unfortunate, his children will be of those who are incarcerated in prison and will encounter tribulation. **100** The Lot of children in the fifth: he will have well-known children; and the outcome will be from the lord of the fifth, because the testimony results in it.⁵⁶ **101** The Lot of children in the sixth, if its lord was free of the infortunes, in its own glow: the native will have children who will gain from the proceeds of animals⁵⁷ and servants, and of them will be one who is a physician; and that is known from the lord of the fifth, if it mixed with it;⁵⁸ and <if> it was made unfortunate, then <the native will have needy⁵⁹ children>. **102** The Lot of children, if it was in the seventh: the native will have children hostile to him and contending with him, and <the native> will marry someone who is in his own household <and belongs to him; and> if the lord of the fifth witnessed as well, he will marry his own child; and of them, one will marry the child of his woman, and with one who is in the household of his woman.⁶⁰ **103** The Lot of children in the eighth: if its lord was free of the infortunes and in its own glow, his children will inherit the assets of the native; now if it was made unfortunate, it indicates the scarcity of the native's children, and his children will quarrel with him and will litigate against him for his assets. **104** The Lot of children in the ninth, and its lord being free of the infortunes, in its own glow: the native will have children <having piety>, being well-known for good, blessed with suitable children. **105** But if it was made unfortunate, the native will have children lacking piety, doing work they suffer in. **106** The Lot of children in the tenth, and its lord being free of the infortunes, in its own glow, indicates that the native's children will be defective or will do a work in which there is no good; now if it was made un-

---

⁵⁵ Or more simply, "ancestors" (أجداد). Perhaps this does not really mean they will bear these names, but that they will take after them.

⁵⁶ In general, what something in a place means, is more immediate and comes first, whereas what its lord means is more indirect and comes last.

⁵⁷ So Sahl, but Māshā'allāh reads "households" (spelled similarly), referring to rents and revenues from crops and other things, including animals.

⁵⁸ Lit., "when its mixtures [or temperaments] are with it." Meaning unclear.

⁵⁹ مخل. This can also mean "disgraceful," but neediness contrasts nicely with their having resources from sixth-house topics.

⁶⁰ بمنزلة امرأته. But this could also be read as, "someone of the rank/status" of his woman. To me this suggests something like a concubine.

fortunate, it is worse for that. **107** The Lot of children in the eleventh: he will have children who are masters of contentions, of dubious morals; and it is harsher for that if its lord was made unfortunate: for then it indicates that they will be liars and immoral. **108** The Lot of children in the twelfth indicates a scarcity of children; now if its lord was free of the infortunes, in its own glow, and the lord of the fifth testified to the native,[61] then he will have children hostile to him; while if it was made unfortunate and the lord of the fifth corrupted, he will not have a child.

109 And[62] know that if an infortune looked at the Lot of children or united with it, it indicates the ruin of the one of the children who was prior. **110** If it was in the house of Mars and he looked at it, then [it indicates] the ruin of the one of the siblings who was before [him].[63]

[Chapter 5.2: On sterility]

1 And[64] as for the knowledge of the scarcity of children, and whether the native is sterile or not, look at Saturn: for if you found him with the Lot of children, and the fortunes not looking at him. **2** And the second [is], look at the sign in which the Lot of children is, [to see] whether it is sterile or not.

3 Whenever you find the Moon with Saturn in a sterile sign, it indicates a scarcity of children. **4** Now if the nativity was by night, then it is worse; and it is worse in the matter of the native's children if the Ascendant, the Moon, and Venus were made unfortunate by Saturn, because those things in nativities[65] [indicate he is] sterile or of few children. **5** But if Mars[66] was in a sign having two bodies or having a number [of children], and[67] he was in his own

---

[61] Reading with Māshā'allāh for Sahl's "the children"; this probably means that it is connecting with the lord of the Ascendant, and more likely from a difficult aspect or a conjunction.

[62] This is no longer Māshā'allāh (at least, not from his treatise on Lots).

[63] This is probably an adaptation from rules about siblings, but has been reworked to apply to children.

[64] Cf. *Carmen* II.10, **10-11** and **15-16**. That is, Saturn with the Lot in a sterile sign, indicates few or no children, with sorrow. Only **1-3** are from *BA*.

[65] Reading somewhat loosely for لأنّ أشياءه ذلك في المواليد.

[66] I take this to mean, "if it was Mars instead of Saturn."

[67] **M** reads: "or."

house or any of his places, and[68] he was the governor of the trine[69] of Jupiter, and the nativity was by night, then there is[70] security in that; and more excellent than that is if he was in a female sign.

6 And[71] if you found the Lot with Saturn, it indicates sterility.

7 And[72] if Jupiter and Mercury occurred in sterile signs, he will not have children.

8 And[73] if Venus was opposing Saturn, without the aspect of Jupiter, he will be sterile or of few children; and it is worse for him if he looked at the Moon like that.

9 And Māshā'allāh said: if you found the lord of the house of children entering into burning, and the lord of the eleventh also, by portions, he will be sterile: because if the lord of the house of children was entering into burning, the fortunes do not benefit him. **10** And if you found the Lot in a sign of few children, and the sign of children being of few children, and if you found the Sun in a sterile sign, he will be sterile or of few children. **11** If[74] you found the lord of the house of children falling, and the fortunes not looking at it,[75] and the infortunes are looking at it, he will die without children; and if he had children, their lifespans will be short, and they will die quickly. **12** And if the fortunes did look at it, then a child will remain to him. **13** And God is more knowledgeable.

---

[68] **M** reads: "or."

[69] That is, the triplicity.

[70] Omitting "not," contrary to the texts. For if Mars has all or most of these conditions, especially in a nocturnal chart, then indeed he would be much more supportive of children.

[71] For this sentence, cf. *Carmen* II.10, **11** and **16**.

[72] For this sentence, cf. *Carmen* II.10, **12**.

[73] For this sentence, cf. *Carmen* II.12, **5-6** and **10-12**.

[74] For **11-12**, cf. *Carmen* II.12, **17-18**.

[75] I take this to be the lord of the fifth, not the fifth itself.

[Chapter 5.3: When a child will be born, & whether it is male or female]

[al-Andarzaghar]

1 Now as for the knowledge of when one will be born to him, in which period of his life [it will be], look at the distributor of children: and that is the lord of the Jupiter's triplicity and the lord of the Lot of children—the more powerful of the two—[and see] in which place it is.

2 And[76] look at the Lot of [the timing of] children which is taken from Mars to Jupiter, [and see] where it falls, and who is with it (of the fortunes and infortunes).

3 So[77] see when the year reaches the sign in the root of the nativity in which Jupiter and Venus [each] are.

4 Then, look:[78] for if you found the distributor of children in the Ascendant or in the Midheaven, or in the house of hope, or Mercury or Jupiter was in these places, then one will be born to him in [his] ardent years and youth, and especially if the sign was many in [its] number [of children]. **5** And it is faster for that, and more hoped for, if the planets were eastern, and they are in their rising.[79]

6 And[80] if you found [the distributor of children] in the second from the Ascendant, or in the seventh or in the eighth, then one will be born to him in the middle of his life. **7** And if it was in the fifth or in the fourth, then he will rejoice in children at the end of his life.

8 And[81] take the Lot which is taken from Mars to Jupiter and cast out from the Ascendant, and see where this Lot falls: for when Jupiter reaches this Lot in his course and transit, or looks at it from an opposition or square,

---

[76] For this paragraph, cf. *Carmen* II.11, **2** and **5**. Most of the rest of the methods in *Carmen* II.11 are found below in **8-9**.

[77] See *Carmen* II.11, **5**.

[78] This paragraph is not in BA, but given the rest of the sentences here it probably was in the original Arabic.

[79] This probably means, "when they rise out of the Sun's rays."

[80] For this paragraph, cf. *Carmen* II.9, **13-14**. For children when he is young, the triplicity lord must be in the Ascendant, Midheaven, or sign of fortune (see **58-59** in Ch. 5.1 above).

[81] For this paragraph, cf. *Carmen* II.11, **2-4**. The text omits Saturn's transit to the Lot (or perhaps to the natal Jupiter or Venus), which is mentioned in *Carmen* II.11, **6**.

then one will be born to him in that year—after you see children for him in the root of the nativity. **9** And if Venus looked at the sign of the Lot, it is likewise.

[Māshā'allāh]

10 And Māshā'allāh said:[82] Look at Venus and at her position, and the position of the lord of her house. **11** For if they were eastern or in what is between the Midheaven and the Ascendant (and its opposite), then he will be blessed by children in his ardent years. **12** And if it was in what is between the west[83] and the Midheaven (or its opposite), then he will have children when he passes half of his lifespan. **13** [Do this] unless the lord of the fifth was more worthy than Venus, and that is if Venus was in [the lord of the fifth's] house or its triplicity: for if it was like this, then look at the lord of the fifth just as you looked for Venus.

14 And[84] whenever Jupiter transits where Mars was, or he looked at him from a square or opposition, it indicates pregnancy.

[al-Andarzaghar]

15 As for the knowledge of whether the children are males or females, look at the Sun, Moon, the house of children, and its lord: are they males or females?

16 And[85] look at the Lot of male children (and it is that you take from the Moon to Jupiter) and the Lot of female [children] (from the Moon to Venus), and they are cast out together from the Ascendant. **17** So look at the two lords of these Lots, and [see] who is looking at them both, and judge the children from the Lot and its lord.

18 And[86] look at the house of children and its lord: for if it was in a male sign, then they are males; and if it was in a female sign, then females.[87] **19**

---

[82] For **10-12**, cf. *Carmen* II.9, **13-14**, which however concerns Jupiter, not Venus.
[83] E: "from the stake of the west."
[84] Cf. *Carmen* II.13, **5-6**.
[85] For this paragraph, cf. *Carmen* II.12, **1-3**. But note that in *Carmen*, the Lot of male children is a *Sun*-Jupiter Lot, not Moon-Jupiter.
[86] For this paragraph, cf. *Carmen* II.13, **1-3**, and Heph. II.22 (Schmidt p. 71).
[87] At this point the manuscripts diverge between **19-21**. First, only E contains **19**, which says that if the sign and its lord diverge in gender, then both genders will be born. In **20-21**, the manuscripts consider which one will be more numerous. Sentence **20** has the sign fe-

And if you found the sign of children female and the lord male, or the sign male and its lord female, then males and females will be born to him. **20** And[88] if you found the house of children female and its lord male, the males of the children will be more numerous than the females. **21** And if it was a sign of males and its lord female, the females of the children will be more numerous.

ಬ ಞ ಞ

22 And[89] look at the two lords of the Lots of male and female children: for the stronger of the two indicates the sex and the abundance in its kind.

23 And if you found the Lot of children[90] in a male sign, and with it a male planet, then state that his children will be male; now if it was the reverse, then reverse it. **24** And if the fortunes looked, they increase,[91] and if the infortunes looked, they corrupt and decrease, especially the infortune opposing the Lot [which is] not in its own share[92] nor portion.

25 And if the planets in the matter of children were in a sign having one body, there will be [only] one child. **26** And if many of those more indicative of children were in signs having two bodies, and especially in Gemini and Pisces, the children will be twins or [even] more. **27** And if the masculine planets were in masculine signs, and likewise the lord of the Sun, the children will be males; and if it was the reverse, then reverse it. **28** But the more worthy one supports what the sign of children and its lord indicates, so speak

---

male and the lord male, and **21** (only in **M**, omitted by **E**) has the sign male and the lord male. But the two manuscripts differ in how they judge the more numerous of children. **E** makes the sign matter more, and **M** makes the lord matter more. I have followed **M** because it contains both **20-21**. But Heph. II.22 makes it clear that if all of the signs that provide children, and planets in them, are female, the children will be female; if male, male; if mixed, mixed. But neither *Carmen* nor Hephaistion address the issue of which is *more* numerous in this passage. But see **22** below, which is from Dorotheus and addresses this topic.

[88] **E**: "And if you found the house of children female and its lord male, the females of his children will be more numerous."
[89] For this sentence, cf. *Carmen* II.12, 3.
[90] This may be the Jupiter-Saturn Lot, and not the Lots of the two sexes.
[91] I believe this means they increase the *number* of the children or (if we are using the gendered Lots), namely the number of the children of *that* sex.
[92] حظّه. But this should probably understood as "sect."

about more abundant of the two in testimony, in males and females, and the genders of the planets (of the male and female).

29 And know that if Jupiter is strong, he will be more indicative of the births of males, and they will be more abundant in number than the females: and that is if he was in his exaltation or his triplicity, and[93] in his own sign, and especially nocturnal, because he is of those who rejoice by day, and are more mighty in power in births of the day.

[Chapter 5.4: Which of his children will be more elevated, & what he will experience from them]

[al-Andarzaghar]

1 As for the knowledge of which of his children will be more elevated, the males or the females, look at the Lot of male children and the Lot of female children, and their lords, and who is looking at them (of the fortunes and infortunes); then judge exaltation and rank based on that.

[Māshā'allāh]

2 And in sum, Māshā'allāh said: If you found the lord of the house of children in the second, his children will be lords of authority and provinces;[94] and likewise if the lord of the fifth connects with the lord of the second, or <the lord of> the second with the lord of the fifth: for then his children will be with the Sultan. **3** Now if it was received, it will be more powerful for their rank, and if it was not received, their condition with the Sultan will be weak. **4** And likewise, if you found the lord of the house of children in its exaltation or house, it indicates the power of their rank, and likewise in the stakes and what follows them (and the falling [places] are below that).

5 And[95] as for what the parents will experience from the children, and what benefit will be from them, if the lord of the Ascendant connected with the lord of the fifth, and the acceptor is in a stake, then the native will have

---

[93] This should probably be read as "or."
[94] This could also be read as "companions of a Sultan and [lords over] provinces," because of the ambiguity in سلطان between "Sultan" and "authority."
[95] I believe that most of this is still Māshā'allāh, as he usually compares the lord of the Ascendant with the lord of the house (as in **5-10**).

good from the children, or he will obtain a powerful rank because of them. **6** Now if with that the lord of the fifth was in its own exaltation or house, it will be more powerful because <in> this topic it indicates powerful exaltation. **7** [But] if the lord of the fifth was corrupt, then the native will corrupt his own assets because of his children; and it is harsher for that if the lord of the house of children was in its fall, and it is connecting with it from a stake or from its exaltation or house: for it indicates the ruin of the native and the disappearance of his assets because of his children.

8 And if the lord of the fifth connects with the lord of the Ascendant, and the acceptor was in a stake, then the native will be well known, [and] his children will have their livelihood from him. **9** But if they were both falling, they will not be well known and his children will <not>[96] have their livelihood from him. **10** And if the lord of the Ascendant was in its own fall or under the rays, entering into burning, and the lord of the fifth connecting with it, it indicates his ruin and the ruin of his children because of him.

11 And if the lord of the fifth was in the second, the children will be suitable, devoted to the fathers. **12** And if it was in the eighth, it corrupts his assets and his children, and diminishes what they provide, and they will be disreputable.[97]

[al-Andarzaghar]

13 And[98] if you found Saturn and Mars looking at the Moon from a stake,[99] then the parents will kick the children out of their house.

---

[96] The texts seem to read either "and" the children will have their livelihood from him, "or" the children will. But neither of these makes astrological sense given that both planets are falling or cadent.

[97] Or simply, obscure and forgotten (سقَاط).

[98] See *Carmen* II.13, **4**.

[99] Reading with *Carmen* for "trine." Evidently al-Andarzaghar had originally written "trine," because both the Latin *BA* and Sahl read it that way: but *Carmen* makes more astrological sense.

[Chapter 5.5: On the death of the children][100]

1 Now as for the death of the children,[101] look at the opposition of Saturn to Mercury[102] (if he was in a stake in the root of the nativity), then at the Lot of children, and who is with them both (of the fortunes and infortunes), and who is looking at them both.[103]

2 And look at the Sun and Saturn, and Mars and the Moon, how their positions are in the nativity, and who is looking at them both[104] (of the fortunes and infortunes).

3 And[105] if Saturn looked at Mercury from an opposition, and Mercury is in a stake, then it kills the children.

4 And if you found the two infortunes in the house of children or looking at it from a square or opposition, then judge for him the death of his children.

5 And[106] if the Lot occurred in the sixth or twelfth, it indicates the death of the children.

6 And if you found the Sun or[107] Saturn in a house of the infortunes,[108] then he will be sad about his children.

7 And if you found the Moon at the beginning of Scorpio, in the bound of her fall, it indicates the death of the children.

8 And if the lord of the fifth was an infortune, and looking at the house from a square or opposition, they will not cease to be ill.

9 And if the infortunes were in the house of children [but] not in their own shares, children will not survive him[109] and it indicates their death. **10**

---

[100] Sentences **1-6** and **13-15** are from al-Andarzaghar.
[101] In *BA* this is about sterility, not death; but I follow Sahl's lead here.
[102] E reads "look at Saturn and at Mercury," but as we will see below their opposition is what matters.
[103] This probably means Mercury and the Lot, but since the text has also mentioned Saturn it is unclear who they "both" are.
[104] Again, this is unclear. Sahl's text probably means the Sun and Mars in a diurnal nativity, and the Moon and Saturn in a nocturnal nativity (since these infortunes are contrary to those sect lights).
[105] Cf. *Carmen* II.12, **4**.
[106] Cf. *Carmen* II.12, **8**: in *Carmen*, Saturn must also be looking at the Lot.
[107] E reads "and."
[108] In *BA* III.5.5, **11** they are in the seventh; cf. **15** below, which is similar.
[109] Or, "will not remain to him" (لم يبق له).

And if Mars was there by day, it indicates their death, and what there is will be miscarried.

11 And if Saturn was in the stakes or in the house of children, it indicates the ruin of his children, and especially if Mercury was made unfortunate by Saturn, from the opposition. **12** And likewise, if Saturn conjoined with the Lot of male children or the Lot of female children, or looked at them from a square or opposition.

13 And[110] likewise if Jupiter was in the seventh or the stake of the earth with an infortune, or looking at it from a square or opposition, then it kills the children (and likewise if Jupiter was under the rays). **14** And[111] likewise if he was in the sixth or twelfth, looking at an infortune.

15 And[112] if the Sun conjoined with Saturn in a male sign, it indicates sorrow over the children.

16 And[113] likewise if Saturn harmed Venus without the aspect of Jupiter, and it is worse for him if in addition he looked at the Moon.

17 Now[114] if the lord of the fifth was falling, and the house of children made unfortunate, it indicates a scarcity of children, or their death. **18** And if one of the fortunes looked at it, then say [something] in the middle for the children; and if it was the reverse, then reverse it.

19 And if you found the indicator of children and Jupiter in a bad[115] place, under the rays, it indicates that the children will not flourish.[116]

20 And if you found the lord of the house of children under the earth, or in the second, sixth, eighth, or twelfth, it indicates the death of the children.

---

[110] For this sentence, see *Carmen* II.12, **9**.
[111] This closely resembles *Carmen* II.12, **11**.
[112] For this paragraph, cf. *Carmen* II.12, **10**.
[113] See *Carmen* II.12, **12**.
[114] For this paragraph, cf. *Carmen* II.12, **17-18**.
[115] **M**: "good."
[116] This could be read as "will not *live*," but the verb عاش has connotations of livelihood and flourishing, not simply being alive.

[Chapter 5.6: On the number of children]

[al-Andarzaghar]

1 And as for the knowledge of the number of children, know that the scholars have already spoken about the number of children in various ways.

2 And[117] Hermes said about that: You should not take too much trouble with the number of women, siblings, and children, for fear of the treachery of women, but [say] only that he will have "many" children, "many" siblings, or "many" women.

3 Dorotheus[118] said various things about this; I will explain it to you, God willing. **4** He said: Look at the lords of the triplicity of Jupiter, indeed the stronger of the two by position relative to the Ascendant and greater in testimony in the house in which it is, [provided that] it is above the earth. **5** So, calculate from it to the Ascendant, for what there is between them both in terms of signs, that is the number of children; now if you found a sign having two bodies in what is between them, then count two for it. **6** And if you found Jupiter or Venus in what is between that, then count for each of them another child. **7** Now if they were both there together, then they add two on top of that. **8** And[119] if you found the lord of the triplicity of Jupiter in a sign of many children, then say he will have many children. **9** And if you found Mars and Saturn in what is between that, they indicate death for the children, and especially if Mars and Saturn were in a bad place. **10** But if they were both in their shares, they indicate an increase [in the number] except that that child[120] will not have any good in it, and especially if that place was the stake of the west or under the earth. **11** And if you found the indicator of children (that is, the distributor of children) under the earth, then count from the Ascendant to it in the same way, and say he will have such-and-such many children, based on the number of signs. **12** And if you found the lord of the triplicity of Jupiter (which is the indicator of children) in the Midheaven,

---

[117] For this paragraph, cf. Rhetorius Ch. 104 (p. 152), who incidentally does not mention Hermes (while *BA* calls him the king of Egypt); also *BA* III.3.1 and III.5.4. The point of this passage is to say that it is not worth judging the exact number of siblings, children, or spouses, because of illegitimacy, affairs, remarriage, and so on: therefore it is better to keep the number general, such as "many" of them.

[118] For this paragraph, cf. *Carmen* II.9, **1-10**.

[119] **E** omits this sentence.

[120] Reading singular here, although Sahl regularly uses the singular to mean the plural, as I have followed him so far. It is unlikely that an infortune would mean this for every child.

then he will have four children or one,[121] or he will have no children. **13** And if it was in the stake of the west, then he will have seven or one, and especially if the seventh was Aries.

14 Now[122] if the lord of the triplicity was falling away from the Midheaven or the stake of the earth, then count from the Ascendant to it, so that what there is of the signs [between them], that is the number of the children; and double [a sign] with two bodies. **15** And also, if there were stars between that, they will increase [children]; and the infortunes looking among them [indicate] death. **16** And if the lords of the triplicities of Jupiter were in signs abundant in children, then report that the number of children will be more than what I mentioned.

17 And I will make their number clear to you from another section [of Dorotheus]:[123] If you found the Moon or Venus or Mars[124] in Taurus and its triplicity or in Cancer and its triplicity (due to their being the lords of these six houses),[125] look at these three, the more excellent one by position and the stronger: for it is the indicator of children, and calculate from it, for it is stronger than the lord of Jupiter's triplicity. **18** As for the rest of them,[126] look at the lord of the triplicity of Jupiter and judge just as I explained to you.

19 And[127] if you found the Sun or Moon or both of them looking at the Lot of children from a square or opposition, truly the Sun adds a male child, and the Moon adds a female child.

20 And[128] if you found an infortune in what is between [the Lot of children and its lord], it kills the child.[129]

---

[121] **E** omits the rest of this sentence.
[122] This paragraph is not in the Latin *BA*, but because it is part of this continuous *Carmen* passage, it was probably in the original Arabic.
[123] Cf. *Carmen* II.9, **11-12**.
[124] *Carmen* has "the Moon *and* Venus," which is a better reading. In the first place, both of these planets grant children, whereas Mars does not. Second, it must be both because we are supposed to choose between them.
[125] This parenthetical remark omitted in *Carmen*. These three planets, which are the triplicity lords for the earthy and watery signs, are also the domicile or exalted lords of these six signs – except for Virgo. But since Virgo is considered a sterile sign anyway, perhaps their presence there does not matter. On the other hand, Capricorn was also said to be sterile in Ch. 5.1, **8** above.
[126] That is, if they are in the other triplicities (the airy or fiery).
[127] See *Carmen* II.10, **4**.
[128] See *Carmen* II.10, **3**.

21 Look also at the sign of children: for if Pisces was the sign of children, and Jupiter in a suitable place, direct in course, then twelve children will be born to him. 22 And if Cancer was the house of children and the Moon in a suitable place, increasing in calculation and glow, then sixteen children will be born to him. 23 And if Scorpio was the house of children and Mars in a place looking at his elevation,[130] direct, then fourteen children will be born to him. 24 And if the lords of this triplicity were with the infortunes or the infortunes looked at them, then that native will experience sorrow with respect to the children.

25 And as for the signs of few children, if Leo was the sign of children and the Sun with the infortunes, then a child will never be born to him, and he will be sterile. 26 And if Sagittarius was the sign of children and Jupiter with the infortunes, then it testifies to[131] the death of his children; and if the fortunes looked at him,[132] they will be suitable. 27 And if Aries was the sign of children and Mars with the infortunes, then he will not have a child for thirty years, then after that two children will be born to him.

28 And if Gemini was the sign of children and Mercury with the infortunes, then a child will never be born to him. 29 If Libra was the sign of children and Venus with the infortunes, then many daughters will be born to him, and in them he will see some of what he detests. 30 And if Aquarius was the sign of children and Saturn with the infortunes, then a child will never be born to him.

31 If Virgo was the sign of children and Mercury with the infortunes, then a single child will be born to him, damaged or chronically ill. 32 And if Capricorn was the sign of children and Saturn with the infortunes, and the Moon looking at him, sorrow will afflict him concerning his children. 33 And if Taurus was the sign of children and Venus in her fall, he will have few children; and if [one] died, she adds a single child. 34 And God is more knowledgeable.

---

[129] Or, "the children."
[130] ارتفاعه. This may mean his "exaltation."
[131] Or, "he will witness" (يشهد).
[132] Or perhaps "it," indicating the sign.

35 And Dorotheus said:[133] Look at the sign in which the Lot of children is, [and] which planet is looking at it from its own house, bound, exaltation, or triplicity.

☋   ☍   ☌

36 Look at Jupiter and the lords of his triplicity, and how they are looking at Jupiter from these six places, which are the four stakes, the house of children, and the house of hope. **37** For if he looked at them from the Ascendant, from the square, it indicates the granting of four children, and from the trine three, and from the sextile two, and from the opposition three. **38** And he grants likewise from the Midheaven and the house of good fortune[134] and the house of children. **39** And from the house of marriage he subtracts one, and from the stake of the earth one, and from the house of assets two, and from the house of travel and the house of death and from the rest of the places (every one of them) one. **40** And from the house of his own exaltation, in the opposition of the places, in a strong place, he grants seven; and from the square and in a strong place, five; and likewise from the trine and sextile and a strong place, and from the place of the exaltation, three; and from the house of assets three, and from the eighth and the house of travel (every one of them) two, and from the rest of the places it indicates the granting of one.

41 Mars, from the Ascendant and from the square, grants three; and from the trine and sextile two, and from the opposition four. **42** And he grants likewise from the Midheaven and the house of hope. **43** And from the house of marriage and the stake of the earth (each one), he subtracts one. **44** And from the rest of the places (from each place) he grants one. **45** And from his own exaltation and from the square and sextile and trine (from each place of them), he indicates the granting of three; and from the opposition he indicates five, and from a strong place and from the rest of the places he grants one.

46 Saturn, from the Ascendant and from the square, looking at the Lot, indicates the granting two; and from the trine three, and from the opposition and sextile two. **47** And from the Midheaven and house of hope two, and

---

[133] This seems to be drawn generally from *Carmen* II.10.
[134] That is, the eleventh.

from the stake of the earth and the stake of the west (from each one of them) one. **48** And from the house of his own exaltation, from a strong place, from the square and trine and opposition, three; and from the sextile two. **49** And from the rest of the places he indicates the granting of one.

50 Venus, from the Ascendant from the square and trine, grants three; and from the sextile two, and from the opposition four.[135] **51** And from the house of marriage and the stake of the earth and the house of travel and the house of assets, she subtracts two; and from the eighth place and from the rest of the places, one. **52** And from her own exaltation, from a strong place [and] from the square, she grants four, and from the trine three, and from the sextile four,[136] and from the opposition seven, and from the rest of the places she grants one.

53 Mercury, from the Ascendant and from the square, grants one; and from the trine three, and from the sextile one, and from the opposition three. **54** And he grants likewise from the Midheaven and the house of hope. **55** And from the stake of the west and the stake of the earth he subtracts one. **56** And from the rest of the places he grants one. **57** And from his own exaltation, from a strong place [and] from the square and the trine, he grants three; and from the sextile two, and from the opposition five, and from the rest of the places he grants one.

58 And I will make clear to you what is granted from the house of enemies.[137] **59** Jupiter in the house of enemies grants, from a strong place and the square and trine, three; and from the opposition four, and from the sextile two. **60** Mars in the house of enemies grants, from the square and a strong place, three; and from the trine two, and from the opposition three, and from the sextile one. **61** Mercury, if he was in the house of enemies, grants from the square three,[138] and from the sextile and trine two, and from the opposition three. **62** The Moon in the house of enemies grants, in a strong place, from the square and opposition and trine, three; and from the sextile, one; and likewise Venus. **63** The Sun from the seventh and from the place of enemies, from a strong place, and from the square and trine and op-

---

[135] E reads, "two."

[136] E omits the sextile altogether, and says "from the trine, four."

[137] That is, the twelfth.

[138] This should probably add "from a strong place," as with the other planets.

position (from each one), three; and from the sextile two; and likewise Saturn.

64 And know that misfortune and harm will afflict those whom the infortunes grant; and likewise the luminaries and Mercury if they were with the infortunes and devoid of[139] the aspect of the fortunes.

65 And what there is from them in the houses of enemies [is] according to that I have described to you,[140] and they are likewise in the houses of exile.

---

[139] That is, in aversion to.
[140] Reading the rest with **M**. **E** reads: "and it likewise takes control of exile, if God wills."

Chapter 6: On health, defects, & chronic illness
And it has ten topics

[al-Andarzaghar][1]

1 The first topic: on illness and ailments.[2]
2 The second topic: on the chronic illness of the eyesight.[3]
3 The third topic: on the lords of chronic illness and defects.[4]
4 The fourth topic, on chronic illness: will it be apparent or internal, and on the right or left side?[5]
5 The fifth topic: when the chronic illness will be.[6]
6 The sixth topic: on the disappearance of their rationality, and the mentally unbalanced.[7]
7 The seventh topic: on short people.[8]
8 The eighth topic: on eunuchs.
9 The ninth topic: on sorcerers and robbers.[9]
10 The tenth topic: on what the native will be master of, among male and female slaves, and their abundance and scarcity.

[Chapter 6.1: On illness & ailments]

1 Now as for illness, recognize in which sign the Moon is, and in which degree, and who is looking at her from the aspects, and who is partnering with her and associating with her, and especially in the house of illness. 2 Then, see what the Ascendant is and what its nature is, and do not neglect to know the place of illness (and it is the sixth house), what it is and who of the planets is in it, and who is its lord, and know the Lot of illness. 3 Because

---

[1] The Latin *BA* only has **2-9** in the following list; the material on slaves (**10**) is reflected later in it.
[2] This corresponds to all of Ch. 6.1 below, which may not be by al-Andarzaghar because it does not appear in *BA* (but may have been omitted by Hugo).
[3] See Ch. 6.2, **1-8** (list of items) and **11-21** (most instructions).
[4] This refers to Ch. 6.3.
[5] See Ch. 6.4, **1-2** (but perhaps more).
[6] See Ch. 6.5, **1-2**.
[7] See Ch. 6.6.
[8] See Ch. 6.9.
[9] See Ch. 6.7.

whenever you find the Moon made unfortunate by the infortunes, or she is with the Tail, or with the Sun, or in the sickly degrees, then the native will become ill or sickly or ailing.

4 And if you found the Moon in the first degrees of Aries[10] and the last degrees of Capricorn,[11] then even if the fortunes looked at her, the native will be sickly. **5** And if you found the Moon in the sixth and twelfth, then it is bad in the matter of illness. **6** And likewise if you found her in Scorpio, then the native will be sickly. **7** And if you found the Moon in a house of Saturn, then the native will be cold in the body, moistening it (and likewise if you found the Sun in the house of Saturn), for the native will be sickly, and especially if the infortunes looked at her. **8** Now if both of the glowing ones were made unfortunate, that is bad in the matter of the body.

9 And if you found the Ascendant made unfortunate, then it is bad, and especially from a planet which is not of its essence (and that is that the share[12] of male [planets] is by day, and the share of female ones by night—except that Mars is by night, and the share of Saturn is by day).[13] **10** Because if you found an infortune in the Ascendant, then a defect will afflict the native in his head, and if you found it in the seventh, then that will afflict him below and in the lower [parts of] his body. **11** And if that infortune was Saturn, then his sickliness will be from moisture, and from hemorrhoids, and from a pain of the spleen, and kidneys, and the rest of illnesses which are from black bile or from phlegm, in accordance with the sign in which Saturn is in: because if he was in a moist sign, his indication in phlegm is greater; and if he was in a dry sign, then it is greater for what he indicates of black bile.

12 And if you found the Moon and the Ascendant both made unfortunate by Mars, then the native will be afflicted by breaking, cutting, and injuries, and his blood will flow from him, and the illness of jaundice will afflict him (which is from the blood and yellow bile).

---

[10] See **18** below, and Ch. 6.2, **73-75**.
[11] This could refer to stars in the spine of Capricorn.
[12] حظ, here and in the rest of the sentence: obviously, this is meant to be "sect."
[13] Note the implication that Saturn might be a feminine planet. This could be from a Persian or Indian tradition. I have also seen Theophilus explicitly say that Saturn denotes females (*OVI*, Ch. 5.5).

13 And whenever you find an infortune in the sixth place, then judge illness for the native.

14 And look at these twelve by place: for if [one] was made unfortunate and the Moon was in it, then judge illness and weakness for that member [of the body]. **15** And let your inspection be in the position in which the Lot of sickliness is (and this Lot is the Lot of illness):[14] if it was in a sign, corrupt in condition, then it indicates illness in that limb[15] of the body which belongs to it.

16 And if you found the Sun made unfortunate, or the Moon under the rays, then there is no good in it. **17** If the Moon was increasing, corrupt in misfortune, [then] if [the corrupter] is Mars, and if she is decreasing [and the misfortune] is from Saturn, and if the Moon is made unfortunate at her separation from the Sun, it indicates a powerful sickliness.

18 And[16] know that one of the illnesses which befall the body is if the Moon was corrupted in Aries, Cancer, Capricorn, Scorpio, or Pisces. **19** For[17] if the Moon was in the first degree of Aries, or the last degree of Capricorn, then even if the fortunes looked at her, the native will be sickly; and likewise if the Moon was in the middle of Taurus, or in the ninth degree of Cancer, or in the first degree of Sagittarius, due to darkness which will be in his eyes.

20 And know that if the infortunes were eastern, they multiply pains, and if they were western, they do the contrary of that.[18]

[The lord of the Ascendant and lord of the sixth: Māshā'allāh]

21 The statement of Māshā'allāh. He said: Look at the lord of the Ascendant and the lord of the sixth: for if they looked at each other from a conjunction, opposition, or square,[19] and the lord of the sixth was the transiting one, then the native will be sickly. **22** Now if that was in the stakes of the Ascendant, it is harsher; and the worst it could be is if the lord of the sixth was an infortune, for then along with what I mentioned there will be chronic illness.

---

[14] Reading with **E**. **M** simply has "this Lot." For the Lot of chronic illness, see Ch. 6.3.4, **2**.
[15] Reading for "sign."
[16] These are the same stars mentioned by Nawbakht in CH. 6.2, **73-74**.
[17] For this sentence, cf. Nawbakht in Ch. 6.2, **73-75**; perhaps much of **1-20** is from him.
[18] Westernness tends to mean chronic illness rather than injuries and pains: see Ch. 6.2, **12**.
[19] For the rest of this sentence, **E** reads: "it necessitates illness."

23 Now if the lord of the sixth was in the Ascendant and the lord of the Ascendant in the fourth, what I mentioned of defects and chronic illness will be due to the fathers,[20] [and] what I mentioned will be in his childhood. **24** If they were both in the Ascendant, it is harsher for the child's condition, because what I mentioned will afflict him in his infancy, and the treatments will not be beneficial.

25 Now if the lord of the sixth was in the Midheaven and the lord of the Ascendant in the Ascendant, then the native will be healthy in his childhood, but then what I mentioned will afflict him in his youth; and likewise if they were together in the Midheaven, but one fears that the chronic illness will be in a place in which part of his body will be broken.

26 Now if the lord of the Ascendant was in the Midheaven and the lord of the sixth was in the opposite,[21] what I mentioned will afflict him after youth, and a fall will be feared from him, from a place in which part of his body will be broken, and that will be from a branch or because of women.

27 And if they were both in the seventh, what I mentioned will afflict him after youth, and that will be from fighting or because of women.

28 And if the lord of the sixth was in the Midheaven and the Moon looks from the opposition, then what I mentioned will be in his childhood, and one fears for him that he will be afflicted by a physical disability.[22]

29 And if the lord of the sixth was in the opposite[23] and the Moon <looked> from the opposition, what I mentioned will afflict [him] from groups[24] or piercing.[25]

30 Now if they were both in the fourth, then he will be afflicted at the end of his life, and what I mentioned will also be from the fathers.

---

[20] This sounds like an inherited or genetic illness.

[21] This is most likely the seventh, which نظير usually designates: see also the end of the sentence, which specifically mentions women.

[22] Reading **M** as المعاواه (E omits). This word is unattested in Lane, but seems to derive from عوه, "to be afflicted by an ailment or disability."

[23] See the note above.

[24] Tentatively reading زمر for what seems to be زمن, which is the root of "chronic illness" and denotes a period of time; but this does not make sense to me. If the lord of the sixth is in the seventh here ("the opposite"), then it would make more sense for there to be attacks from other people or groups.

[25] This word (طعن) can also mean "defamation."

31 And if the transit of the lord of the Ascendant was over the lord of the sixth, the native will be a slave and do the work of slaves, and he will be safe from defects.

ஐ ෬ ෬

32 And[26] if the infortunes were not in the stakes of the Moon and the lord of the Ascendant, then the native will not cease to be healthy for the days of his life. **33** And if they were both made unfortunate, they indicate numerous illnesses, and he will be sickly until the end of his life.

34 And know that the Moon and Ascendant indicate the body, and the lord of the Ascendant and the lord of the house of the Moon indicate the soul. **35** So if the misfortune pertained to the lord of the Ascendant or the lord of the Moon, the body will be safe, and anxieties will enter into the soul; but if these two were safe and the Moon and Ascendant were unfortunate, tribulation and suffering will enter into the body.

36 And know the strength of the native is in the root of his nativity: for if it was strong, ailments will not harm him; and if it was weak, ailments will hasten to him,[27] unless he has power over the ailments due to his riches (and poverty which will ruin him if the ailments afflicted him, due to the scarcity of his assets and the badness of his condition).

Chapter [6.2:] On chronic illness of the eyesight

[Five items for eyesight: al-Andarzaghar]

1 Now as for the chronic illness of the eyesight, the scholars look for that from five items:

2 Begin by looking at the lord of the house of illness: in which house it is, and in which sign, and who is looking at it.[28]

3 Second, look at the besieging of the Sun and Moon between the two infortunes.[29]

---

[26] I do not believe the rest of this section is by Māshā'allāh due to the change in subject, but I could be wrong.

[27] I have rewritten the rest of this sentences as a combination of **M** and **E**, neither of which makes a lot of sense on its own in key spots, and has awkward grammatical structures.

[28] This refers to **11** below.

[29] This refers to **12** below.

4 Third, look at the Moon: in which sign she is, and which place, and who is with her, and who is looking at her from a square or opposition.[30]

5 Fourth, look at the Sun and Moon being with the infortunes in the stakes and the second from the stake, and from the opposition and square.[31]

6 Fifth, look at the degrees of chronic illness, if she was with them in the signs.[32]

7 And[33] know that the Sun indicates the right eye and the right side for nativities of the day, and the Moon indicates the left eye and the left side. **8** Now if the nativity was by night, then make the Sun belong to the left eye and the left side, and the Moon to the right eye and the right side.

[Items 1-4: al-Andarzaghar]

9 (And[34] Māshā'allāh said: If the two luminaries (or one of them) were made unfortunate, harm will afflict the native in his eyes, *if* they were above the earth. **10** Now if they were under the earth, the harm will afflict him in the stomach, brain, and lung.)

11 Then, look at the lord of the sixth: for if it was in the Ascendant, in a convertible sign, and the fortunes are not looking at it, <it damages>[35] the eyesight; now if Mars was the lord of that place, he will be blind.

12 And[36] if the Ascendant or the Sun (or the Moon), one of them, was enclosed by the two infortunes and the fortunes do not look, <it damages>[37] the eyesight or makes his face have a defect.

13 And[38] know that looking into chronic illness and sickliness is from the easternization of the planets, and their westernization: so if an eastern one

---

[30] This refers to **14** below.
[31] This refers to **15-21** below.
[32] This refers to **48-57** below.
[33] In *BA*, this is part of Item 4, and was placed after **21** below, but Sahl has moved it here.
[34] This is not in *BA*, but was added by Sahl.
[35] Reading with *BA* for a puzzling, partial phrase in the manuscripts that suggests either the two luminaries or the two benefics followed by "from," but then supplies no verb.
[36] Cf. Rhetorius Ch. 61 (p. 113).
[37] See footnote above.

was producing the misfortune, he will be chronically ill; and if it was western, he will be sickly.

14 And[39] if you found the Moon full or you found her in the sixth,[40] connecting with Mars himself or from an opposition or square, then he will be blind in his eyesight.

15 And if the infortunes were in the second sign from the Sun and the Moon, or with them both in one sign, and the Sun was greater in degrees (and especially [if it was] Mars), and the fortunes are not looking, then the eyesight will be chronically affected; and worse than that is if the Sun or Moon were in the Ascendant, and Mars in the second from the Ascendant. **16** And judge likewise if the degree of the luminaries was in the house of marriage,[41] and Mars was above it.[42] **17** And judge likewise for the Sun and Moon if one of them was falling and Mars was in the stake (and if you found the Moon increasing in glow then it is worse for him; and if she was decreasing in glow and Saturn looked at her, then it is worse and more awful). **18** And if Jupiter looked at them they will be prevented from [having] chronic illness of the eyesight, and his eyesight will not all disappear.

19 And if you found the two infortunes in the second from the Sun, and they looked at the Moon from the opposition and from the tenth[43] (and even if they do not look at her as well), and the fortunes do not look, then judge for him an ailment of the eyesight.

20 And[44] if the Moon was bodily with Saturn, then judge an ailment of the eyesight.

21 And[45] if one of the luminaries was in a stake and the other in the second, and Mars between them both, and the fortunes do not look, then the eyesight will be chronically ill, or the face will have a defect, and especially if

---

[38] This statement by al-Andarzaghar (*BA* III.6.3, **1-2**), taken from *Tet.* IV.2 (Robbins p. 321) was not originally part of this passage because it does not pertain to the eyes. It belongs better in Ch. 6.3.1 below.

[39] For **14-15**, see *Carmen* IV.2, **24**.

[40] In *BA* III.6.2, **5** and *Carmen* IV.2, **25**, this is the seventh.

[41] This must mean that they are on or very close to the Descendant itself.

[42] This probably means he is in a later zodiacal degree, so is somewhat elevated above the horizon, above the luminary.

[43] This is probably decimation.

[44] This is not in *BA*.

[45] In *BA* III.6.2, **11** this includes the infortunes by opposition and square, not just between them or in conjunction.

Saturn looked at the Moon decreasing in glow, by night (and also if <Mars> looked at the full Moon by day).

22 And do not omit knowledge of who is in the second: for if the infortunes were there, then they are bad in the matter of sickliness, and especially for the condition of the eyesight.

23 And[46] if Mars is in Leo without the aspect of a fortune, it indicates chronic illness and harm in the eyesight, along with harm in the stomach, spleen, and limbs.

24 And whenever you find the infortunes in the stakes and the luminaries falling, they indicate a pain of the eye.

25 And if the Moon was made unfortunate at her separation from the Sun [at] the meeting and fullness, it indicates damage to the eye.

26 And the worst it could be is if the luminary is falling[47] and the infortunes follow it in addition.

27 And whenever the fortunes look, then they rescue, and a defect does not become chronic.

28 And if an infortune looked at one of the luminaries or it was connected with the luminary, it indicates [flatulence?].[48]

29 And if an infortune ([itself] being made unfortunate) made the luminary unfortunate, they indicate the continuation[49] of that tribulation which will not be cut off except by death.

30 The[50] Moon in the eleventh, handing over her management to an infortune in the second, breaks the body of the native if the infortune was Mars; but if it was Saturn, he will fall from an elevated place.

---

[46] Cf. Rhetorius Ch. 61 (p. 116). See also Ch. 6.3.1, **28**.
[47] **E** reads this in the dual, indicating both luminaries (which would indeed be worse).
[48] The texts seem to read "the winds of a flood," and the verb for wind can indeed mean flatulence. Probably some kind of gastric disturbance is meant.
[49] Reading for **E**'s "termination." **M** simply says that the tribulation will not be cut off except by death. It may mean that it will *slowly* come to an end over time, but will never go away.
[50] Cf. *Carmen* IV.2, **21-22**, but also Sahl's Ch. 6.3.7, **5** below.

[Ptolemy]

31 And Ptolemy said:[51] If the Moon was made unfortunate in the Ascendant or the setting at the meeting or fullness, it indicates a defect in the eyesight. **32** And if the two infortunes were with both of the glowing ones, or one of them was with one of the luminaries and the other in the seventh from it, and they were both eastern from the Sun, western from the Moon, it indicates an illness in both of the pupils.

33 If[52] you found the sixth house and its lord with the infortunes looking at them, without the fortunes, he will be chronically ill and sickly just as I described concerning the east and west. **34** Now if you found the sixth house and its lord made unfortunate in the house of assets, and Saturn looked at it and the fortunes do not look, his sickliness and chronic illness will be from moisture or a veil will fall [over the eyes],[53] or his limbs will be chilled; and if Mars looked, then because of heat or the cutting of iron, or burning.

[Theophilus]

35 And[54] Theophilus said: Know that the harm of Mars is worse than the harm of Saturn, and the worst is [if] the luminary[55] is in the seventh and the infortunes follow it, and it is in the stake of the Moon;[56] and more unfortunate for that is if it is at the fullness of the Moon. **36** Now[57] if Jupiter looked at the Sun in that position,[58] his eyesight will not wholly disappear, but a little bit will remain. **37** And if Saturn and Mars met together above Jupiter[59] from the stakes, with an aspect and connection, so the position of the Sun and Moon is weakened, then all of his eyesight will disappear.

---

[51] For this paragraph, cf. *Tet.* III.12 (Robbins pp. 321-23). For **30**, Ptolemy has the Moon with one of the fixed stars damaging eyesight.

[52] Sentence **33** resembles *Tet.* III.12 (Robbins pp. 317-19), but not **34**.

[53] That is, cataracts.

[54] For this sentence, cf. *Carmen* IV.2, **25** and **27-28**.

[55] Theophilus seems to mean the Sun, because the next sentence presents a mitigating condition.

[56] In *Carmen* IV.2, **28**, this is Mars opposing the Moon ("from the seventh"), so he would indeed be in her whole-sign angle.

[57] For this sentence, cf. *Carmen* IV.2, **26**.

[58] من موضع نفسها, lit. "from [the Sun's] own place." But *Carmen* explains: this means that the Sun is in the position just described for the Moon, but Jupiter is looking at him.

[59] This must mean they are decimating him. But cf. generally *Carmen* IV.2, **27-29**.

38 And[60] if the Moon was with Saturn in Sagittarius, then that will afflict him in two places: one of them is his eye, and the other in the [*uncertain*][61] of the archer; and likewise, if she looked at Saturn from a square or opposition, judge the scarcity of the eyesight.

39 Now[62] if the nativity was by night and the Moon is made unfortunate by Saturn instead of the Sun, it is the left side and the left eye, and the left hand, and [*uncertain*][63] the chronic illness will afflict him in it, and [the treatments] will not benefit in his chronic illness, until he dies with his chronic illness—if the one in charge of the misfortune was Saturn.

40 And[64] if the Moon was made unfortunate from a square or opposition,[65] it indicates cataracts or an ailment in the eye; now if an infortune looked in addition,[66] then he will be blind. **41** Now if with that the Moon was full, then that is above[67] cataracts but below blindness. **42** And if the infortunes looked at her from a square or opposition, and the fortunes looked at her as well, there will be cataracts of both eyes, and a powerful dimness [of vision] will happen to him in his eyes, and that is because the Moon is unfortunate along with the misfortune of the two stakes, so that what I mentioned will afflict him in both eyes, but he will not be blind: for if something of the fortunes looked at her, then that chronic illness will be benefited by the treatments and remedies, and the chronic illness of the eyes will not be complete, and his eyes will change at times to fitness and times to corruption due to the aspect of the infortunes and fortunes.

---

[60] Cf. *Carmen* IV.2, 33-34.

[61] The MSS seem to read an undotted: بصب. *Carmen* says that the native will be harmed in *his* eye, but Theophilus seems to be identifying stars in Sagittarius itself. Ptolemy identifies a double-star nebula (ν¹ + ν² Sag.), called in Arabic "the eye of the Archer" (عين الرّامي), which may be what Theophilus means. (But normally the point of the arrow indicates damage to the eye: see **51** and the table below. I am not sure what the بصب is.

[62] Cf. *Carmen* IV.2, 40-41.

[63] **M** seems to read, "and his sickliness will afflict him in" the chronic illness, but the word for sickliness could also be the word above for cataracts. **E** has a few more words but they are illegible.

[64] For **39-40**, cf. *Carmen* IV.2, 43 and 51.

[65] But this is *only* if she is also on one of the fixed stars or clusters which indicate harm to the eyesight (see below).

[66] Perhaps Theophilus means that the *other* infortune is looking, along with the one which makes her unfortunate.

[67] That is, "worse than."

43 And[68] if the luminaries are corrupted in the Ascendant or the opposite, it indicates harm in the eye, and likewise if the luminaries were in one of these two places and the infortunes rise after them.

44 And[69] if the Moon was full, replete in [her] glow, and she connects with an infortune in a stake, it will harm his eyesight. **45** And if a fortune looked at her, [illegible].[70]

46 If the Moon was replete in [her] glow, and she is in the Ascendant and has testimony (or the nativity was by night), and Mars was with her in the sign, connecting with her, it indicates the disappearance of the native's eyesight. **47** And if,[71] along with what I mentioned, the twelfth-part of the Moon was with Mars, that chronic illness will afflict him in his childhood or from that year.[72]

[Item 5: al-Andarzaghar]

48 And[73] if you found the Moon in the degrees of chronic illness in the signs, and the infortunes looked at her and their bound, <it indicates> a defect of the eyesight generally, or in the rest of the body: because in the signs are positions which if the Moon is made unfortunate in them, or the lord of the Ascendant, it indicates the corruption of the eye; and that is:

49 If the Moon was in Leo, having already passed half [of it] until she completes 18°, and that is around the mane of the Lion, which is called al-Dafārah.[74]

50 And in Scorpio, in the eighth, ninth, and tenth degree (and in 23),[75] and it is the forehead of the Scorpion.

---

[68] Cf. *Carmen* IV.2, **24** and **27**.

[69] For this paragraph, cf. *Carmen* IV.2, **25-26** (and compare with **40-41** above).

[70] About seven words in **M** are largely erased due to water damage, and **E** is largely illegible for this half of the page. But *Carmen*, like **41** above, says that a fortune looking will allow him to see a little bit.

[71] For this sentence, cf. *Carmen* IV.2, **42**.

[72] Lit., "from his year" or "from her year." This suggests that perhaps the illness will begin after the lesser years of either the Moon or Mars.

[73] For **48-57**, see *Carmen* IV.2, **43-51**. But al-Andarzaghar has added two stars from Rhetorius Ch. 61, as **53-54** below.

[74] **M** spells this as الدَّوارة (**E** is illegible), "the rotation." However, as *al-dafārah* or *al-dhafārah*, it means something like "the stinking." However, Kunitzsch and Smart 2006 (p. 41) say that this name is *al-Dafīrah* (الضفيرة), "the lock of hair," an error for Coma Berenices in Cancer. At any rate, this is still the mane of Leo.

51 And in Sagittarius from 6° to 9°, and that is the place of the arrow.

52 And in Aquarius, the tenth, eighteenth, and nineteenth, and that is due to the place of the rope[76] which is in it.

53 And in Capricorn from 26° to 29°, and that is because of the spines.

54 And in Taurus from 6° to 10°, because of the position of the Pleiades.

55 And in Cancer the ninth degree to the fifteenth, and that is due to the place of the cloud.[77]

56 If[78] you found the Moon in something of these signs, decreasing in glow, made unfortunate from hostility, then the eyesight will be chronically afflicted. **57** And if she was increasing in glow, full, there will be water in his eyesight, and [uncertain] and [what] resembles that like [uncertain], and his eyesight will not be obscured.

58 Now[79] if Mars likewise testified by conjunction or an aspect of hostility, it indicates an abscess or burning by fire, or a blow from a group of people. **59** And if Saturn was the one testifying, he will have the action of coldness along with that, and an abundance of eating.

[Rhetorius][80]

60 The [degrees] indicative of chronic illness are:
    61 <In Leo>, 18° and 19° and 28°.[81]
    62 In Scorpio, in 19° and 29°.[82]

---

[75] This is the sting of Scorpio, as opposed to the others which form the forehead.
[76] Or rather, the Pitcher.
[77] That is, the cloudy cluster Praesepe.
[78] For this paragraph, cf. *Carmen* IV.2, **50-51**.
[79] This paragraph may not be from al-Andarzaghar as it does not refer to blindness and is not in *BA* nor in *Carmen*.
[80] See Rhetorius Ch. 61 (p. 114). Note that these overlap with, but are not identical to, the degrees harming the eyes.
[81] In Rhetorius Ch. 61: 18°, 27°, and 28°. These may include Denebola (β Leonis) and Zosma (δ Leonis)
[82] In Rhetorius Ch. 61: 19° and 25°. Identity uncertain.

63 And in Sagittarius the first degree, the seventh, eighth, 18, and 19.[83]

64 And in Taurus the sixth, seventh, eighth, and tenth.[84]

65 And in Cancer the ninth to the fifteenth degree.[85]

66 And in Capricorn the twenty-sixth to the twenty-ninth.[86]

67 Aquarius: the tenth, twelfth,[87] and in the nineteenth.[88]

68 And[89] in Libra the sixth, seventh, eighth, and tenth.

Fixed stars harming eyes (*Carmen* IV.2, 43-49)	
Description / common name	*Designation*
Coma Berenice (near Tail of Leo)	α-β-γ Coma Berenice
Sting of Scorpio	λ Sco., Shaula υ Sco., Lesath
Forehead, eyes of Scorpio	β Sco., Acrab/Graffias δ Sco., Dschubba π Scorpionis
Tip of Archer's arrow	γ² Sagitt., al-Nasl
Pleiades (in Taurus)	η Tauri, Alcyone[90]
Praesepe (in Cancer)	M44 or MCG 2632
Rhetorius Ch. 61 adds:	
Spine of Capricorn	ε, κ Capricorni?
Pitcher of Aquarius	ζ Aquarii?

Figure 59: Fixed stars harming eyes (Dorotheus, Rhetorius)

---

[83] These probably include the Sting of Scorpio and the Tip of the Arrow (see table below).
[84] These are probably the Hyades.
[85] These must be Praesepe (see table below).
[86] This must be a range of stars on the tail of Capricorn.
[87] In Rhetorius Ch. 61: the 18th.
[88] These may be stars around the Pitcher of Aquarius (see below) and Fomalhaut (α Piscis Austrinus).
[89] This may be an error, as it is not in Rhetorius Chs. 61-62 and has the same degrees as Taurus above. See **70** below, as well.
[90] Alcyone is only one of the Pleiades, but is the best known.

[The Bizidaj]

69 *The Bizidaj:* Now as for the degrees which indicate the corruption of vision especially, if the Moon was with them by night and the Sun by day, made unfortunate, that is in the conjunction of:

70 Libra, from 27° 36' to 28°.[91]

71 And likewise the first degree of Sagittarius, and the ninth and tenth <of Scorpio>.[92]

72 And likewise the blemish in Cancer, and it is from 15° to 19°.[93]

[Nawbakht]

73 And Nawbakht said:[94] If you found the Moon in the first degrees of Aries or the last degrees of Capricorn, then if the infortunes looked the child will be sickly. **74** And likewise if the Moon was in the middle of Taurus, or in the ninth degree of Cancer, or in the first degree of Sagittarius, for the native will have darkness in his eyes. **75** And it is likewise in the rest of these sickly degrees which I have described above.[95]

[Māshā'allāh]

76 And Māshā'allāh said: Look at the nature of the signs which I described, and the nature of the infortune corrupting the Moon: for if a mixture occurred between them, that is of less importance than if the Moon was in the nature of heat and being made unfortunate by Mars, or she is in the nature of cold and being made unfortunate by Saturn: so study this subject, for it [pertains to] the full scope[96] of the Moon.

77 And know that if you found that the one indicating misfortune and disease was Mars, the corruption of the eye will be from a blow, or an ailment

---

[91] In Rhetorius Ch. 62 this is the mane of the Lion, except that it ought to be Coma Berenices in Cancer, and not the mane of the Lion at all.

[92] The sting of Scorpio (1° Sagittarius), and the forehead (9°-10° Scorpio).

[93] That is, Praesepe or the nebula of Cancer, which in Rhetorius Ch. 62 is from 10°-15°.

[94] Cf. also Ch. 6.1, **19** above.

[95] I am not sure whose comment this is, Sahl's or Nawbakht; if Nawbakht, then he may be referring to the Rhetorian material in **60-68**.

[96] كمال.

of his eye, or iron, burning, fire, or heat. **78** And if it was from Saturn, then the corruption of the eye will be from water which falls into the eye, or from cold, or from moisture, or from snow.[97] **79** And if she was with Mercury, it is from a treatment, or struggle, or fighting, or robbers, or what resembles that.

[Chapter 6.3: On the lords of chronic illness]

[Chapter 6.3.1: Seven items for illness, from al-Andarzaghar][98]

1 Now as for the lords of chronic illness, look at the sixth house and its lord, and the aspect of the infortunes to it.[99]

2 Then, look also at the Lot which is called the Lot of chronic illness, and its lord, and the sign in which they both are, and who of the fortunes and infortunes is looking at them.[100]

3 Then, look at the second lord of the triplicity of the house of fathers,[101] and who of the fortunes and infortunes is looking at it.[102]

4 Then, look at the sign which is the house of chronic illness: over which limb (of the limbs of the body) does it have authority?[103]

5 Then, look at the Lot of Fortune and its lord, and the mixture of that planet and the sign in which it is.[104]

6 Then, look at the separation of the Moon, and her connection.[105]

7 Then, look at the Head of the Dragon: is it with the infortunes or with the fortunes?[106]

---

[97] Or, "ice."

[98] Compared with *BA*, this list is incomplete. *BA* lists nine items, and Sahl has put items 2-8 here. *BA*'s Item 1 is found below, as Ch. 6.4, **1-2**. *BA*'s Item 9 (at the end of III.6.1, **12**) refers to all of the planets, and the Lots of Fortune and Spirit (and their lords): it may refer to Sahl's Ch. 6.3.9, **1** below.

[99] This refers to **8-15** below.

[100] This refers to Ch. 6.3.4, **1-4** (and perhaps even the whole **1-11**), but as I suggest in my footnote there I believe Sahl has substituted a longer passage from another author (probably Māshā'allāh) there for the very short statement by al-Andarzaghar which would have appeared here (see *BA* III.6.3, **12-13**).

[101] This should perhaps be the IC itself.

[102] This refers to **16** below.

[103] This refers to **17** below.

[104] This refers to **18** below.

[105] This refers to **19-24** below.

[106] This corresponds to Ch. 6.3.8, **3** below.

8 Then[107] begin and look at the house of illness and its lord: for if they were both made unfortunate (the house and its lord), and Saturn looked at it and the fortunes do not look at it, his sickliness and chronic illness will be from moisture, or a veil will fall [over his eyes] or all of his limbs will be chilled, and a pain lasting a long time will afflict him. **9** Now if it was Mars then from burning or the searing[108] of fire or with iron, or burning with fire, or being pierced by a lance, or robbers will fall upon him, or wild animals will bite him and what is like that of what [makes him] chronically ill and sickly—and that is if he was glowing.[109] **10** But if he was under the rays, an obscure, subtle pain will afflict him in his belly so that he will die from that. **11** And if you found Jupiter to be the lord of the house of illness, and the infortunes looked at him, then his chronic illness will be from wine, and his liver will swell up from the wine. **12** Now if it was Venus, his chronic illness will be from a passion for women and sorrow concerning them, until the shame[110] of stupidity and madness takes him; and it is harsher for that if Venus was in a male sign. **13** And if it was Mercury, he will be deaf or mute, or confused in speech, or a lisper, so that the voice of that native is corrupted and hoarseness seizes him in his throat, and he will scarcely speak except with difficulty, and his hearing will decrease, and misfortune will seize him in his head, and evil will seize him in his throat; and Mercury produces [that] likewise if he was in the houses of Saturn or his bounds, without the aspect of the fortunes. **14** And if it was the Sun, then that chronic illness will be in the heart or his eyesight will be blind. **15** Now if it was the Moon, his sickliness will be in his spleen or his eyesight will be blind—and that is if the fortunes are not looking at her.

16 And turn your attention to the limb which it has power over, and if the infortunes looked at the second lord of the triplicity of fathers, and the fortunes do not look, and the lord of the Lot [of chronic illness] is in a bad place, then it will be sickly or chronically ill.

---

[107] For **8-15**, cf. *Carmen* IV.2, **2-10**; also Rhetorius Ch. 61 (pp. 115-16).
[108] Or "cauterization."
[109] That is, outside of the Sun's rays.
[110] كهئة, evidently from the rare root كهي.

17 And look at the infortune which makes it[111] unfortunate, [to see] over which of the limbs of the body it has authority: for if it was in Aries, then the head (and likewise all of the signs, according to the experience of them).

18 Look[112] also at the Lot of Fortune: for if an infortune looked at it and the fortunes are not looking, then he will be chronically ill or sickly in accordance with the type of planet and the authority of the signs over the body.

19 And[113] look too at the Moon, from which planet she flows away, and mix that according to the category of that planet and the sign in which the infortune is. 20 Then, mix her just as I described to you above. 21 For if you found her separating from the fortunes and connecting with the infortunes, then that native will be healthy at the beginning of his lifespan, [but] then at the end of his life he will be sick, chronically ill. 22 Now if the separation of the Moon was from Saturn, then a pain of the belly and the bowels will seize him, and coldness will seize him, and his pain will last a long time, and of them one whom asthma will seize, and a pain of the spleen, and sulphurous water[114] will occur in his belly, and coughing and tuberculosis. 23 And if her separation was from Mars, then blood will pour forth from his mouth and he will be cut by iron, and the treatments of doctors will not be beneficial. 24 And if it was a girl, she will be barren and no child of hers will survive, and her child will be cut [from] her belly and her womb will be distorted by the iron.

☋   ♌   ♋

25 And[115] if Saturn and Mars were in the twelfth and each of them looks at the Moon, and the fortunes are not looking at the Moon, then the native will be afflicted in his body by every tribulation.

26 And[116] if Saturn was with Venus in the tenth (or the Moon was in the tenth) and Mars was looking at them both, then he will not be able to have sex with women, and he will be a bad man.

---

[111] In **4** above and *BA* III.6.1, **11**, this is the sixth sign; but it could perhaps be generalized to all signs which show harm.
[112] Cf. Rhetorius Ch. 61 (p. 115), referring to Valens, *Anth.* II.37.
[113] For this paragraph, cf. *Carmen* IV.2, **62-66**.
[114] Lit. "yellow" or perhaps "bilious" water.
[115] Cf. *Carmen* IV.2, **67**.
[116] Cf. *Carmen* IV.2, **69**.

27 And know that if Mars was in the sixth, in a female sign, he will not have damage, because it is his joy (and especially if there was a fortune in the Midheaven or in the twelfth, or in the trine of the luminaries); but truly Mars will be corrupted in this sign if there was not a fortune in the Mid<heaven> or in the twelfth. **28** And[117] if the Moon was with Mars in Leo without a fortune, it indicates chronic illness and damage to the stomach and spleen. **29** And if the Moon was separated from an infortune, and the infortune was in a stake, it indicates the weakness of the body. **30** And[118] if the Moon was full in the sixth, and connects with Mars, <it indicates> muteness and chronic illness. **31** So take heed of what I have explained to you.

Chapter [6.3.2:] On making inferences from nativities: the lords of defects & misfortunes[119]

1 One born with both legs crooked indicates that his nativity was at the end of Aries, and in it Mars, and he was pierced[120] behind his ear at the beginning of his years.

2 And one who is leathery in the face, crooked in the nose, indicates that that afflicted him due to the presence of Saturn in Taurus, and the Moon in Aries, and Mars in what is between them.

3 And one whose beard is weak, that is because Saturn was in Scorpio, and Mars in the Archer, and the Moon in what is between that.

4 And one crooked in the mouth indicates that that afflicted him because of Venus being in the Archer, and Mercury in Scorpio,[121] and Mars in what is between them.

---

[117] Cf. Rhetorius Ch. 61 (p. 116), and Ch. 6.2, **23** above.

[118] Rhetorius Ch. 61 (p. 115) says that this condition indicates being lame or club-footed.

[119] This section is particularly atrocious, as **M** and **E** frequently give different readings, with unclear or unpointed spelling; the source is unknown at this time. It also largely lacks astrological context, in the sense that there are few rules being applied and the reasoning is unclear. And is it really true that anyone born in the hour of the Sun will have a bad knee (**6**)? Probably a lot of these aphorisms were taken from actual nativities and collated together without any rhyme or reason.

[120] بُثِر. I am not sure of the medical meaning of this. But perhaps it is بُثِر, "swelled."

[121] **E**: "Cancer."

5 And one whose knee is burst[122] indicates that that afflicted him because of the presence of Saturn in Scorpio, and Mars in the Archer, and the Moon in what is between them.

6 One born in the hour of the Sun indicates that he will be hobbled[123] in the knee.

7 And if Mars happened to be in Capricorn, and Saturn and the Moon[124] in Aquarius, it indicates nativities with crooked legs.

8 Now if Saturn happened to be in Pisces and Mars at the end of Aquarius, and Venus with him, it indicates nativities with multiple legs.

9 And if Saturn happened to be in Libra and Venus in Scorpio, it indicates a lisper or a mute.

10 If Venus and Mercury were in Scorpio and Pisces, or Venus and Saturn in Pisces, it indicates the nativities of physicians.

11 One who from birth is quick, restless, with small eyes,[125] indicates that Saturn and Mercury were in Capricorn, and that also indicates the shortness of the native's stature. **12** And one who was short, with large eyes, a long beard, serious, that indicates that Jupiter was looking at them, and he is direct in course.

13 Now as for those varied [in color], they are born at the end of Cancer, and that is if Mars and Mercury were in that place.

14 And the hairy are born in the Twins, if Saturn and Mercury were in it.

15 The blind <or those with?> bulging eyes are born at the end of Pisces, if Saturn and the Moon[126] were in it.

16 Those having leprosy and itching, and moist [*uncertain*] and ringworm are born in Pisces,[127] if Mars and Venus were in it, and that is more so if Saturn happened to be in Virgo.

17 And the lords of hernias,[128] and the streaming and retention [of urine] are born in Scorpio, if Saturn and Mars were in it.

---

[122] Tentatively reading متفقاً.
[123] Or, "limited" (**E**). **M** reads, "lengthened" or "stretched out."
[124] **E** only has Saturn, not the Moon. But in line with the previous examples, perhaps the Moon is between Saturn and Mars.
[125] Or, "subtle" (دقيق). Perhaps this should be understood as piercing and intelligent, which would make this close to the idiom "small/subtle of look," or "discerning."
[126] **M** reads, "Mars."
[127] **M** reads, "Libra."
[128] **E** reads an uncertain word.

18 One who has one eye (and it is the left one), indicates that his nativity was in Sagittarius, if Saturn and Mercury were in it; and one who has the right one indicates that he was born in Aquarius, and in it Saturn, Mars, and Venus.

19 And one whose [*uncertain*]¹²⁹ is lacking indicates that his nativity was between the Sun and Moon, at the end of the hour of Venus.

20 And one whose <hair> whitens suddenly before old age¹³⁰ indicates that his nativity was at the end of Virgo, and in it the Moon. **21** One whose hair does not whiten at all indicates that he was born at the end of Libra, and in it Saturn and Venus.

22 And one whose has bile multiplying in him indicates that his nativity was in Sagittarius (and perhaps it was in Pisces), and that is if Jupiter and Mercury were in it.

23 One dying in his bed from shivering,¹³¹ that is if his nativity was in Capricorn and in it Jupiter.

24 And one dying abroad indicates that his nativity was in Taurus, and more so for that if Mars was in it; now if Saturn and Mars were in it, it indicates that he will seek treatment.¹³²

25 One dying suddenly indicates that his nativity is at the end of Capricorn, and in it Venus.

26 Women who die at their divorce¹³³ indicate that their nativities are with the Moon under the rays.

27 One falling into a well or drowning in the sea or a river indicates that his nativity was in Aquarius, and in it Saturn.

28 One whom wild animals eat, indicates that his nativity was at the end of Aries or Capricorn, and in them Mars and Venus.

29 One dying in front of the Sultan indicates that his nativity was in Scorpio, and in it Mars, Venus, and Mercury.

30 One burning in fire indicates that his nativity was in what is between Pisces and Aries, and in them the Sun and Mars.

---

¹²⁹ The text seems to read بڡڡر.

¹³⁰ Reading somewhat loosely for a garbled and uncertain phrase.

¹³¹ Or more specifically, a kind of fever that produces shivering instead of one that feels hot (نافض).

¹³² Perhaps this means that it will be so bad, he will try to come home and be treated there.

¹³³ I am not sure what this means.

31 One who is afflicted by the effect of heat,[134] and he dies from it, indicates that his nativity was in[135] Aries, Taurus, and Capricorn, and in them Mars alone.

32 One on whom a house falls and buries him, indicates that his nativity was in Libra, and in it Saturn and Venus.

33 One falling from an elevated place indicates that his nativity was in Capricorn, and in it Venus and the Moon.

34 One afflicted by a collapse[136] or swelling[137] indicates that he was born in Virgo, Libra, or Pisces, and in them Venus, Saturn, and Mercury.

35 And one whose eyes are tinted [and] small, and their pupils red, that indicates that Saturn and Mars were in Pisces, or they look at them from Aquarius, so that these are wicked rebels, arrogant [in their] evil.

36 And one who has handsome pupils and a beautiful nose, that indicates that he had Venus and Mercury in Sagittarius.

37 One who is tolerant, patient, wise, not narrow-minded and not hasty, that indicates that his nativity was with the rising of Jupiter and the setting of Venus and Mercury; now if Saturn looked at them both, then it indicates that the native will be a leader of jurisprudence, of the imams who [*uncertain*].[138]

38 ... from Taurus and Aquarius and the nostril Jupiter[139] from Libra; now if there was a swelling in the nostril, then his nativity indicates that it was in Leo and Taurus.

39 One who has the edges of his ears inclined so as to resemble a curve,[140] that indicates that Saturn was in Capricorn or in Taurus.

40 One whose ears are big indicates that Jupiter and Mercury were in Aries.

---

[134] Or "iron," as **M** has it.

[135] **M** adds, "the end of."

[136] Or, a "collision."

[137] Or, "tumor."

[138] Here **M** and **E** give largely illegible and mutually incompatible readings, of about four or five words. But I believe that the word "eloquent" is used, and perhaps one of the manuscripts hints at double standards or hypocrisy. I have also ended the sentence here because immediately afterwards a statement about ears is made (**38**), which suggests that something is missing. (Since so little of this section is valuable anyway, it is hardly any loss.)

[139] This phrase does not make sense and is another indication that the sentences are mutilated and constructed improperly.

[140] I am not sure exactly what this means; perhaps that they stick out because of the size of the curvature in the back of the ear?

41 And one whose eyes are white, resembling stones,[141] indicates that the Moon and Jupiter in his nativity were in Leo and Venus in Virgo.

42 One who was cross-eyed indicates that he had Venus in Aquarius.

43 One born blind in his eyes, with one raised [above the other],[142] indicates that Mercury and Mars were in Taurus in his nativity, and Saturn in Aries.

44 One who has one of his limbs pierced, indicates that Mars and Saturn in his nativity happened to be in a sign corresponding to it.[143]

[Chapter 6.3.3:] On those born in the signs, if one of the planets is in them, & the stink of their odor

1 One born at the beginning of Aries indicates that his armpits will smell; and one born in the middle of it indicates the goodness of his odor; and one born at its end indicates the odor of his thighs.

2 And one born in Taurus indicates that he is stinking in the odor of his legs.

3 One born in Gemini indicates that their[144] odor is good, pleasant.

4 And one born in Cancer indicates the stench of the mouth.

5 And one born in the beginning of Leo indicates the stench of the mouth; now as for its end, it is good due to the waterskin[145] of Virgo and the place of Jupiter, who is the manager.[146]

6 And one born in Virgo will have a good odor, and likewise too one born in Libra.

---

[141] فصوص. This word has various meanings, but tends to focus on segments and joints of things, such as the segments of an orange or the stone of a ring. But I do not understand what Sahl's source means here.

[142] Reading somewhat speculatively for two different and incomplete phrases. I do not know why blindness should be associated with having eyes of uneven height.

[143] Reading somewhat loosely. The text reads, "happen to be in a sign of his nativity or one of them corresponding to it."

[144] That is, the natives (plural); this does not continue the thought about legs from the previous sentence.

[145] Reading قِربة. This must be a reference to Virgo's ε star Vindemiatrix ("the grape-gatherer"), from an alternative tradition in which Virgo carries a waterskin or wineskin.

[146] I do not understand what this means, here and below; probably some context is missing.

7 And one born in Scorpio indicates the stench of the odor of his genitals and thighs.

8 And one born in Sagittarius indicates the goodness of the odor, but perhaps their sweat will be excessive and [*uncertain*].

9 And one born in Capricorn indicates the offensiveness of the odor, and that is due to the stench of the goat when it is cooked in its milk.

10 And one born in Aquarius indicates the stink of the odor of the nostrils, and that is due to the place of the aquatic bird which plunges into the mud; now as for its beginning, it has a good odor due to the place of the manager.[147]

11 And one born in Pisces indicates the stench of the odor of their bodies.

12 And Māshā'allāh said: look for the position of the chronic illness and the defect from the place of the lord of the sixth and the nature of the sign in which it is; then count what it has traveled in the sign, and the place of its[148] transit in the signs. **13** For if its transit was in the beginning of the sign, then the defect is in the head; and in the middle of the sign it will be in the middle of the body, in the navel and what borders on it; and if it was at the end, it is in the legs.[149]

---

[147] المدبّر. Meaning uncertain.
[148] Both here and in the next sentence, "it" uses the feminine singular or non-rational plural, when we would expect the masculine singular. So there may have been some other consideration in the original Māshā'allāh.
[149] **M** now contains several sentences that are identical to Ch. 6.4, **3-4** (actually only the first half of **4**), but which are omitted in **E**. Since they do not really belong here, I omit them.

Chapter [6.3.4]: Knowing the place of the chronic illness[150]

[al-Andarzaghar?]

1 Take heed of these three things:[151] for whatever two [of the] things testify to, the position of the chronic illness is in that place. **2** So[152] look at the Lot of chronic illness, and it is taken from Saturn to Mars by day, and by night the contrary of that, and it is added to the degrees of the Ascendant: then see what is between them both in degrees, and project that from the Ascendant, and where it terminates, that is the sign from which the chronic illness is known, and his chronic illness will especially be in that sign. **3** Now if the lord of the Ascendant corresponded to that position, and an infortune looked at it, and the lord of the sixth is looking, it indicates a defect and chronic illness if that was in the root of the nativity: it indicates that. **4** If the Lot of chronic illness was in Aries, then the defect is in the head (and likewise the rest of the signs).

� ଔ ଔ

5 And[153] if the Moon was made unfortunate by an assembly, square, or opposition, and she looked at the Ascendant, it indicates the chronic illness of the native. **6** And if the Moon looked at one of these two planets which indicate work and profit,[154] his chronic illness will hinder him from working, and that is harsher if she was looking at them both together, for it indicates

---

[150] Lit., "A section from which is known as well the position of the chronic illness." Sentences **1-4** seem to correspond to al-Andarzaghar, *BA* III.6.3, **12-13** (and alluded to by Sahl in Ch. 6.3.1, **2**), but whose instructions about the Lot and its lord are rather vague. So my guiding assumption is that **1-4** are based on al-Andarzaghar, and maybe **5-11** as well. On the other hand, the instructions here to take two out of three testimonies is more typical of Māshā'allāh. So Sahl may have ignored al-Andarzaghar as being too vague, and is here substituting someone like Māshā'allāh, especially since the text in **12** seems to continue the thought of **11**.

[151] This may refer to the Lot of chronic illness, the Moon, and the sixth and its lord, all discussed below.

[152] For sentences **2** and **4**, cf. *Carmen* IV.2, **11-12**.

[153] It is possible that **5-11** are also from al-Andarzaghar, but the Latin *BA* is too brief to be sure.

[154] I am unsure what planets these are.

that he will not be useful to himself, and will be of need of [other] people for necessities, eating, and drinking.

7 Now if you found Saturn and Mars in the sixth or twelfth, then his chronic illness will be habitual and it will be with him, <and especially in?>[155] Cancer.

8 If the Moon was with an infortune and that infortune was direct and she had already separated from a retrograde infortune, or she connected with it and the lord of the Ascendant, it corrupts unless it[156] looks at the Ascendant: the native will be chronically ill unless God wills. **9** And if the infortune which is corrupting the Moon was in a sign having two bodies, his chronic illness will be from an increase in his body; and if it was convertible, it is from a decrease; and if it was fixed, it is not from increasing nor decreasing, but something other than that, of what prevents him from working. **10** Now if the Moon was where the corrupting infortune is, and both it and the Moon are in a sign having two bodies, then the native will have two types [of ailment].[157]

11 Now if an infortune does not testify to the lord of the sixth, nor a fortune, they indicate the changing of what the lord of the sixth indicates: so look in the place of the lord of the sixth in the signs.

[The lord of the sixth in the houses: Māshā'allāh]

12 If the lord of the sixth was in the Ascendant, he will have an illness of the essence of that planet, and it is the indicator of the death of his animals (if he had them) and his servants.[158] **13** The lord of the sixth in the second: he will make a livelihood from the produce[159] of slaves and the renting of animals, and he will be blessed from a lowly thing. **14** The lord of the sixth in the third: he will have siblings with defects or illness, or they will do the work of slaves, and it indicates the livelihood[160] of the siblings. **15** The lord of the sixth in the fourth: he will be of the children of slaves or of those who do the work of slaves. **16** The lord of the sixth in the fifth: the upbringing of his

---

[155] Reading tentatively for a partial phrase in **M**; **E** has skipped to **9**.
[156] I should think these are the professional significators, but I am not sure why Sahl specifies two of them here.
[157] صورتان.
[158] The Ascendant is the eighth (death) from the sixth (animals, servants).
[159] That is, what they produce and the profits from that.
[160] **E** reads "goodness," but neither word makes much sense or gives much guidance.

children will be hard, and his children will have a defect. **17** The lord of the sixth <in> its own place: the native will be healthy, *if* the lord of the Ascendant does not look at it. **18** The lord of the sixth in the seventh: he will associate with women who do not have social esteem, and bad words will be said about him. **19** The lord of the sixth in the eighth: the native will be healthy, *if* the lord of the Ascendant does not look at it. **20** The lord of the sixth in the ninth: the native will have excellent intentions, he will become ill while away from home, and will encounter hardship. **21** The lord of the sixth in the tenth: he will encounter hardship from the Sultan. **22** The lord of the sixth in the eleventh: he will befriend people who are not well known, and will associate with them. **23** The lord of the sixth in the twelfth: he will be hostile to people who <do not> have social esteem, and they will come[161] to harm.

24 Work this topic if the sixth sign and its lord are free of the infortunes and the fortunes do not testify to them.

Chapter [6.3.5]: The position of the Lot of chronic illness

[The Lot in the houses, according to Māshā'allāh][162]

1 Then, look at the position of the Lot of chronic illness in the signs, and it is that you take [it] by day from Saturn to Mars, and the converse of that for one born by night, and there is added to it the degrees of the Ascendant, and project it from the Ascendant, and where it terminates, that is the sign of the Lot;[163] and from it is known the position of the chronic illness.

2 And if this Lot was in the stakes, then see whether it belongs to an infortune or a fortune. **3** Now if it was an infortune, and it is looking at the Ascendant while not looking at its lord,[164] then the native will do work in which there is no good, or he will be a slave; now if it does look at the lord of

---

[161] **M**: "they will *not* come."
[162] That **1-9** is by Māshā'allāh from his original *Book of Lots*, is shows by the Latin translation in Vat. Pal. lat. 1892, f. 102r. The Arabic MSS contain only the calculation.
[163] **E**: "...that is the Lot."
[164] That is, the lord of the Ascendant (see later in the sentence).

the Ascendant, a visible chronic illness will afflict the native. **4** But if it was a fortune, he will be fit after his corruption.

5 If the Lot of chronic illness was in the eleventh, fifth, ninth, or third, if its lord was an infortune and it is looking at its place, then if it was in the ninth the native will be harmed by religion, and if it was in the eleventh he will be harmed by his friends,[165] and likewise say children and siblings in the fifth and third. **6** And what the infortune indicates, it converts it to that; and what[ever] the fortune indicates, will be fit after corruption.[166]

7 If the Lot of chronic illness [was] in the second, eighth, sixth, and twelfth, and it is an infortune, looking at the lord of the Ascendant or a planet in the Ascendant accepting its power, if it was in the second it will harm his assets; and if it was in the eighth it indicates a bad manner of death; and if it was in the sixth, it indicates the native's chronic illness; and if it was in the twelfth it indicates the power of the enemies over him, and evil entering upon him from them and because of them. **8** And if it was a fortune it indicates that what I explained to you will be less than what I mentioned, and he will have illnesses. **9** And if the lord of the Lot is not looking in these houses at the lord of the Ascendant or at a planet in the Ascendant, there will be nothing of what I mentioned, by the permission of God.

☋   ☋   ☋

10 If the planet was the indicator of the native[167] and it was made unfortunate, and it is rising up,[168] it indicates a spiritual illness; and if it was falling down,[169] made unfortunate, it indicates a bodily illness. **11** And if there was [both] a declining of the planet and its rising in the region[170] of a stake, it indicates that the illness will shift to something of misfortune;[171] in the re-

---

[165] This would more naturally be read as saying that his religion will be harmed, and his friends will be harmed; but it seems to me that this is backwards, since the Lot is supposed to harm the native, not others.

[166] Or perhaps, "whatever the fortune indicates, truly it will be made fit after corruption."

[167] E: "the indicator of excellence."

[168] This must mean either that it is rising towards its apogee (whether of the deferent or the epicycle), or is rising by primary motion toward the Midheaven.

[169] Again, this must mean moving down towards its perigee, or else by primary motion towards the IC.

[170] Or perhaps, "house" (باب).

[171] The rest of this sentence is uncertain, as **M** and **E** put their clauses in a different order and are hard to figure out.

gion of [*unclear*] it indicates an illness from rotten teeth not being extracted from him.

Chapter [6.3.6]: Natives who are deprived of their tongues & have defects in reason & language

1 That comes to be when the Moon connects with Saturn at [her] separation from the rays [and] then with Mercury, and Mercury is made unfortunate by Saturn: for then the tongue of that native will seize up so he will be incapable of speech. **2** Now if you found Saturn[172] inspecting Mercury and the Moon, then he will be halting and will not speak except with difficulty. **3** And if Saturn and Mercury were in the stakes (and especially in the stake of the west), then the native will be halting or mute. **4** And if Mars looked at them, it loosens that so that it makes him be a talker, and especially if the Moon connected with him.

5 And if the Moon was eclipsed and her lord was in a sign without a voice, it indicates a mute. **6** Now if it was in Leo, it indicates muteness and the chronic illness of the father.

7 And if Saturn looked at Mercury from a sign not having a voice, it indicates muteness.

8 And if Mercury was in the sixth,[173] made unfortunate, it indicates the corruption of [his] reason; now if the sixth was his house and he was in it, made unfortunate, it indicates muteness or blindness and stupidity; and it indicates likewise if he was in the conjunction of Saturn, and his bound.

[Chapter 6.3.7:] The nativities of those whose joints are severed & their bodies broken

1 So if you found the Lot of chronic illness with the Head, with the aspect of an infortune and a fortune does not look at it, it indicates the breaking of limbs and a fall from a height, or chronic illness.

---

[172] Reading for "Jupiter."
[173] E reads, "seventh."

2 And[174] if the Lot [of chronic illness] and the Moon were together in the second, they indicate the breaking of his limbs; now if Saturn testified to them along with that, it indicates falling from a height or something heavy will fall upon him.

3 And[175] if Mars was in the Ascendant or the seventh or the opposition of the Moon, and the Moon is decreasing in glow, and she is in a sign of cut limbs, it indicates the cutting of limbs from him.

4 And[176] if the Moon was in the eleventh, handing over her power to an infortune in the second, the native's body will be broken if it was Mars; but if it was Saturn, he will fall from an elevated place, so that what I mentioned will afflict him.

5 And[177] if the Moon and the Lot of chronic illness were in the eleventh and Mars in the eighth,[178] the body of that native will be broken, and all of them will be separated from him.

6 And[179] if you found the Moon in Taurus or in one of the signs of cut limbs, and Mars was looking at her from an opposition, then one of his limbs will be cut by iron, unless you find a fortune inspecting the Moon from strength, or the luminary[180] inspects it so that it repels the evil of Mars from her, so that the iron will affect him but that limb will not be broken from him, if God (be He exalted!) wills.

Chapter [6.3.8]: The nativities of those who fall from elevated places

1 Now if you found Saturn in the second and Mars and the Lot in the eleventh, then he will fall from a faraway, tall place.

2 And if the infortunes were with the luminaries or looked down upon them from the tenth, and the luminaries connected with them, then the native will fall from the cave of a mountain or an elevated place, or he will fall into the hands of robbers, and that will be the cause of his death.

---

[174] Cf. *Carmen* IV.2, **21-22**; but this has the Lot and Moon in the eleventh, not the second (see **4** below).

[175] Cf. *Carmen* IV.2, **52-53**.

[176] Cf. *Carmen* IV.2, **21-22**.

[177] Cf. *Carmen* IV.2, **21-22**.

[178] Reading for "second," with *Carmen* IV.2, **21**.

[179] Cf. *Carmen* IV.2, **53**.

[180] Reading النير for الثور ("Taurus"). This is probably the Sun.

3 And if you found the Head in the sixth and with it Mars and Saturn, then he will fall from an elevated place into a deep river and so will die in it, or he will escape but become chronically ill, or beating by iron will afflict him so he will become chronically ill.

4 And if Saturn was with the Sun and had testimony, then he will fall from an elevated place.

5 And if the Moon was connecting with Saturn, and Saturn in Aries and its triplicity, he will fall from an elevated place. **6** And if he was in Gemini and its triplicity, and he is in the Midheaven,[181] then a wall or building will fall upon him. **7** And if he was in the stake of the earth, he will fall from an elevated place.

8 And if the infortune was in the Midheaven, and it is in the fall of the lord of the Ascendant, and the lord of the Ascendant connects with it, then a building will fall on him and he will die under it.

9 And if the first parts of Gemini or Sagittarius were made unfortunate, he will be thrown down from a riding animal, or he will fall from a mountain or will be diminished in reason. **10** And if the last parts of Gemini or Sagittarius were made unfortunate, then the native will have his leg cut off, or his hand, or gout will afflict him, and what resembles that; but if the fortunes looked at these places, then he will recover.

11 And if the Moon was enclosed between the two infortunes (in whatever house it was), and a fortune is not looking at her, and the Moon is decreasing in glow, the infortunes will not consent to the death of that native until his eyesight disappears. **12** And[182] if an infortune was in the Ascendant and an infortune in the house of marriage, the infortunes will not consent to the death of that native until his eyesight disappears. **13** And if the infortune was in the Ascendant and it was made unfortunate in the house of marriage, they will not consent until his being thrown out of the house of his father before his death, especially if the Moon as in the bound of an infortune.

---

[181] **E** omits this statement about the Midheaven.

[182] In the next two sentences, it is unclear whether both infortunes must be involved (i.e. in the Ascendant and the seventh), or whether one infortune may be in *either* the Ascendant or the seventh.

[Chapter 6.3.9: Nativities accompanied by gout & gangrenous sores]

1 Now[183] as for nativities accompanied by gout and gangrenous sores, if you found the Lot of Fortune and the Lot of the Invisible and their lords made unfortunate in Sagittarius, Aquarius, Pisces, or Capricorn, then gout will make him chronically ill, or gangrenous sores will occur in his hand or leg (and especially if it was in Gemini or Cancer). **2** And the pains of itching[184] or chronic illness will afflict him in the limb which the sign[185] indicates, if it was in the aspect of Saturn.

3 And if you found Saturn in the sixth, the native will have gout, and his [*unclear*] will be confined, and an illness of black bile will afflict him.

4 And[186] if Capricorn, Cancer, or Pisces was rising, and it is made unfortunate, it indicates gangrenous sores and scrofula, and what is like that.

Chapter [6.3.10: Nativities which are afflicted by leprosy, itching, & sparse whiskers][187]

1 That will be from the Moon: if she was made unfortunate and she is in Aries, Cancer, Scorpio, Capricorn, or Pisces, and the Moon is not alone, that will be active. **2** But if the Lot of Fortune and the Lot of the Invisible were in these signs and the infortunes looked at them, then the native will have a sparse beard, not having an impediment, or he will have some of that defect.

3 And[188] if you found Saturn, Mars, and the Moon in Cancer and its triplicity, then the native will be mangy [or] leprous.

4 And[189] if Mars was in Scorpio, and especially in the Ascendant, it indicates the pain of ulcers in the intestines.

5 And if an infortune was with the Moon and[190] Venus in a sign of water, it indicates red pimples and ulcers, and hidden pains.

---

[183] For this paragraph, cf. Rhetorius Ch. 64, which however has gout and rheumatism, not sores.

[184] **M**: "pains of the body."

[185] In Rhetorius, this is the Lot of Fortune or Lot of Spirit, whichever is in the aspect of malefics.

[186] See Rhetorius Ch. 61 (p. 114), which however includes Scorpio.

[187] Reading this title largely with **E**; some of **M**'s title is uncertain, but then **M** repeats virtually the whole sentence the way **E** has it.

[188] Cf. Rhetorius Ch. 61 (p. 116), which however adds Venus.

[189] Cf. Rhetorius Ch. 61 (p. 116).

6 And if the Moon was made unfortunate in the convertible signs, it indicates what I will explain to you. **7** If she was made unfortunate in Aries, then the defect will be from leprosy or itching,[191] or what is like that. **8** If it was in Cancer, then it is from scabies and ringworm. **9** And if it was in Libra, then from black leprosy[192] and ulcers. **10** And if it was in Capricorn, then it is from cysts or a tumor[193] in the body.

12 And[194] if the Moon was in a sign and she is between the two infortunes, separating from one of them, connecting with the other, then look at the nature of the sign. **13** For if it was in Cancer and its triplicity, leprosy is feared for him; and if it was in Aries and its triplicity, disintegrative leprosy[195] is feared for him; and if it was in Gemini and its triplicity, an illness of the air will afflict him; and if it was in Taurus and its triplicity, excessive bile will afflict him. **14** This is if the connection was from an assembly, opposition, or square; and it is harsher for that if the separation was in this manner.[196]

15 If[197] you found the luminaries in the sixth with the infortunes and the Head, then the legs will become chronically ill. **16** And[198] if the Moon was increasing in glow or full, connecting with Mars in the sixth, it indicates corruption in the legs. **17** And[199] if you found the Head made unfortunate in the sixth, it indicates a defect in the legs and falling from a cave; now if an infortune looked he will be rescued, but there is no escaping a defect. **18** And if

---

[190] **M** reads, "or."
[191] Lit., "scratching."
[192] This (بهق أسود) is a mild form of leprosy in which the eruptions are black due to the mixture of black bile and blood (according to humor theory). The generic ailment (بهق) can also refer to herpetic eruptions.
[193] Or, "swelling."
[194] For this paragraph, cf. Rhetorius Ch. 59 (p. 109), which however only mentions the watery signs.
[195] جذام. This type of leprosy leads to the flesh of the limbs cracking and the extremities eventually falling off or being amputated.
[196] This probably means, "if it was *also* in this manner."
[197] **E** prefaces this sentence with the phrase, "The nativities of the effeminate," just as **BA** puts it in III.6.0; but like **BA**, the delineation is omitted.
[198] For this sentence, see Rhetorius Ch. 61 (p. 115).
[199] For this sentence, see Rhetorius Ch. 61 (p. 115).

the Moon was with the Head and Tail in a sign having a defect[200] (such as Aries, Taurus, Cancer, Scorpio, and Capricorn), then they will be born with these defects, mangy or crippled, or with flaccid bodies.

19 And[201] if the Sun and Moon were in the sixth or in the twelfth, and Mars and Saturn and Mercury were all in a stake or uniting in the stakes,[202] and neither Jupiter nor Venus looks at the Ascendant, the native will be [mentally] disordered, resembling devils.

[Chapter 6.4:] On an apparent or hidden chronic illness, on the right or left

[al-Andarzaghar][203]

1 Look at the eastern and western planets, and those under the rays or appearing from hiddenness:[204] for by that you will distinguish what appears from is hidden. 2 If the infortunes were eastern, the chronic illness will be apparent, and if they were western or under the rays, then hidden.

3 And[205] if you found the lord of the sixth where it indicates chronic illness, and it was in the stakes, then the chronic illness will be apparent (and worse for that is the Midheaven and Ascendant, for that indicates the face

---

[200] Lit., "ailment." These are the so-called defective signs, because something about their image is defective: for example, Aries has a broken neck, Taurus is missing most of its body, etc.

[201] See Rhetorius Ch. 59 (pp. 109-10).

[202] This seems to mean that they are all in the same stake, or connecting with each other in multiple stakes.

[203] I am not sure how much of the following is al-Andarzaghar: it definitely includes **1-2** (corresponding to BA III.6.1, 7), but I think probably **13-16** below as well.

[204] The manuscripts differ as to whether easternness and westernness are (1) identical to being out of or under the rays, or (2) distinct. In this sentence, **E** makes it seem that they are identical, whereas **M** does not, saying "*or* those under the rays." But in the next sentence, **E** has "*or*" under the rays, while **M** does not. Since each of the MSS contains an "or" in one of these sentences, I am assuming that they are not identical. If I am correct, then easternness and westernness are purely a function of the planet rising before the Sun or setting after him.

[205] This sentence, and the first half of **4**, also appeared in **M**, Ch. 6.3.3, as **14-16**—but they were omitted by **E** in that place so I omitted them here.

and a place which is not concealed). **4** And if it was falling, *not* looking at the Ascendant, then it is in a concealed place; but if it is in a place [that] *does* look at the Ascendant, then it will be in a place [in which] the matters will appear.

5 And know that if a planet was made unfortunate above the earth, the defect will be apparent, and if it was under the earth it will be hidden. **6** So if you found the luminaries made unfortunate above the earth, and they indicated chronic illness, the harm will afflict him in his eyesight; and if they were under the earth, then in the stomach and the brain and the lung, due to the condition of the Moon.

7 And if Saturn and Jupiter were made unfortunate and they were above the earth, the harm will afflict him in his ears: and the right ear belongs to Saturn, and the left ear to Jupiter. **8** But if they were under the earth, it will harm the spleen due to the condition of Saturn, and the heart due to Jupiter.

9 And if Mars and Venus were made unfortunate and they are above the earth, the harm will afflict him in the nose: the nostril on the right side belongs to Mars, and the left one to Venus. **10** And if they were under the earth, then to Mars belongs the liver, and to Venus the kidneys.

11 And if Mercury was made unfortunate and he is above the earth, the harm will afflict him in his tongue; and if he was under the earth it indicates the gallbladder.

12 So review this topic if the planets were above the earth or below it, for if a planet was made unfortunate under the earth, it indicates harm on the inside, in what does not appear; and if it was above the earth, then in what does appear.

13 Now[206] as for the knowledge of the chronic illness being on the right side and the left, look at the planetary indicator of the chronic illness: for if it was in what is between the Midheaven to the Ascendant and its opposite, the chronic illness and defects will be on the right half; and from the Ascendant to the stake of the earth and its opposite, the left side. **14** And[207] if you found the indicator of the chronic illness in any of these places, then it is on that side.

---

[206] For this paragraph, cf. *Carmen* IV.2, **15-16**.
[207] This sentence is redundant, and perhaps comes from a different source.

15 And if the sign in which the planet is, is male, the chronic illness and defect is in the upper [part] of the man, and if it was in a female sign, then in his lower [part].

16 Now if the nativity was by day, then on the right side, and if it was by night, then on the left.

17 And the female signs indicate every black defect, and the male every red or white one. **17** And know that the night is black, and the day white [and] red.

[Chapter 6.5:] When the chronic illness will be

[al-Andarzaghar]

1 And[208] know that if the planets which indicate chronic illness were in what is between the Ascendant and the Midheaven, then his chronic illness will be in his youth; and if it was between the Midheaven up to the house of marriage, it is in the middle of his life; and if it was from the house of marriage to the house of fathers, the chronic illness will be at his death and the extinction of his lifespan.

2 And[209] look at the planet which indicates chronic illness, whether it is eastern or western: for if it was eastern, then the chronic illness will be in childhood, and if it was western it will be at the end of his life (and if they were both[210] in the same manner, he will be chronically ill from the beginning of his lifespan up to its end).

3 Then[211] you look at the lord of the sixth: for if it was in the sixth, the chronic illness will be in his childhood; and if it was in the Midheaven, then in youth; and in the seventh, after youth; and if it was in the fourth, it will be at the end of his lifespan.

---

[208] For this paragraph, cf. *Carmen* IV.2, **78-80**.
[209] For this paragraph, cf. *Carmen* IV.2, **81-82**.
[210] I am not sure what two planets are meant.
[211] I am not sure if this sentence is from al-Andarzaghar, but it probably is.

[Two views from Valens]

4 Then,[212] look at the Lot of Fortune: for if it was made unfortunate from the opposite, it indicates a chronic illness at 7 years; if it was from the first sextile, then at 3 years; if it was from the second sextile, then at 11 years; if it was from the first square, then at 4 years; if it was from the second square, then at 10 years; if it was from the first trine, then at 5 years; if it was from the second trine, then at 9 years. **5** And if the infortune was in the second from it, then at 2 years, if it was in the twelfth from it, then at 12 years.

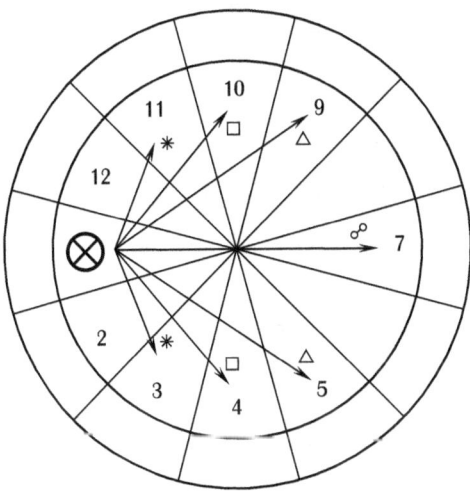

Figure 60: Years given by planets making the Lot of Fortune unfortunate (*Anth.* III.12)

6 And[213] if [the lord of the Lot] was in Aries, then in fifteen years; <and if it was in Taurus, then in twenty-five years>;[214] if it was in Gemini, then in twenty years; if it was in Cancer, then in twenty-five years; if it was in Leo, then in twelve years; if it was in Virgo, then in eight years; if it was in Libra, then in thirty years; if it was in Scorpio, then in fifteen years; if it was in Sagit-

---

[212] For this paragraph, cf. *Anth.* III.12, and Sahl, *Nativities* Ch. 1.37, **35** (and the footnote there).
[213] For this paragraph, cf. *Anth.* III.12, and Sahl, *Nativities* Ch. 1.37, **36** (and the footnote there).
[214] Adding with Valens.

tarius, then in forty-two years; if in Capricorn, then in fifty years; if it was in Aquarius, then in thirty years; and if it was in Pisces, then in fourteen years. **7** And all of that is if a fortune does not look at it.

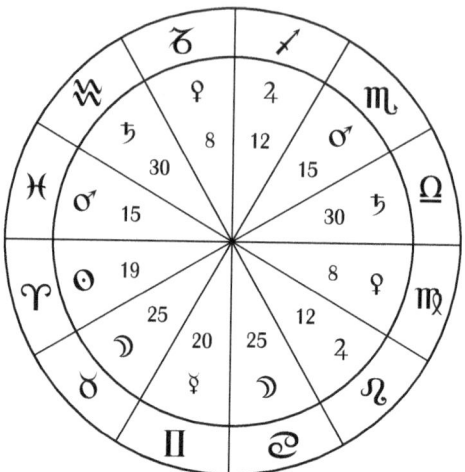

Figure 61: Frequency of illness,
from the Lot of Fortune (*Anth.* III.12)

[Chapter 6.6:] The knowledge of the insane[215] & the deranged, & the losing of their minds

[al-Andarzaghar]

1 Always look at the Ascendant, the Moon, and the stakes which the infortunes are in.[216]
2 Then, look at the Moon's flowing away in the meeting or opposition: from whom does she flow away?[217]
3 Then, look at the lords of the triplicity of the Sun by day and the Moon by night, along with the Ascendant and the Moon, and who is looking at them.[218]

---

[215] This word in Arabic also has connotations of spirit possession.
[216] This refers to **7-10** below.
[217] This refers to **11** and **14** below.
[218] This refers to **15-16** below.

4 And look at the besieging of Venus between the two infortunes; and the square of the Moon [and] Mercury; and Mars (who is[219] in the Ascendant), and Jupiter and Saturn (in the house of marriage); and the Moon (who is in the Ascendant), and Saturn, Mars, and Mercury in the house of fathers.[220]

5 Then, look at the meeting and opposition, and the aspect of the infortunes to their signs.[221]

6 Then, look at the Lot of Fortune and the Lot of the Invisible, and their lords, and who of the fortunes and infortunes is looking at them.[222]

7 Then,[223] begin with the Ascendant: for if you found Saturn and the Moon in the Ascendant, and Mercury opposing them, and the fortunes do not look at it, he will be insane, losing his mind. **8** And say likewise for one who has Saturn and Mercury in the Ascendant and Mars opposing them, that he is insane, losing his mind. **9** And likewise if the Moon and Mars were in the Ascendant and Mercury[224] opposing them. **10** And likewise if Saturn and Mercury were in the Ascendant, and Jupiter opposing them: he will be stupid, foolish, not learning nor understanding.

11 And[225] likewise if the Moon was flowing away from Saturn and she is full: he will be insane or lose his mind, or be confused, and perhaps he will be blind.[226] **12** And[227] if Mercury was in the eighth[228] with the Moon, he will

---

[219] Reading for "are," with *BA* and **27** below.
[220] This refers to **26-27**, maybe **13**, and maybe **24-25** below.
[221] This refers to **17-18** below.
[222] This refers to **28-29** and **19** below.
[223] For this paragraph (except for **9**), cf. Rhetorius Ch. 65 (p. 119).
[224] **M** reads "Jupiter," in line with *Carmen* IV.2, **55**; but that passage in *Carmen* appears below. This sentence does not appear in Rhetorius Ch. 65. The sentence here in Theophilus (*Apotel.* Ch. 21, 3) has the Sun and Moon in the Ascendant, and Saturn in the seventh (again, with the fortunes in aversion).
[225] For this sentence, cf. Rhetorius Ch. 65 (p. 120).
[226] **E** omits this statement about blindness.
[227] Sentence **12** does not appear in the Latin *BA*, but **13** seems to represent something in *BA*: see footnote to **13**.
[228] **M** reads, "the second."

be obsessed;[229] and it is harsher for that if an infortune looked. **13** And[230] if the infortune was under the earth in its degree,[231] he will be insane. **14** And[232] if the Moon at the opposition or <meeting> was flowing away from Mars (and if he was with her), then speak likewise.

15 And[233] if the lords of the triplicities of the Sun by day (and of the Moon by night) were opposing each other, and the infortunes looked at them both, and especially if the Ascendant and its lord were looking at the infortunes, he will be insane.

16 And[234] if Mercury does not look at the Moon nor at the Ascendant, and the fortunes do not look at it,[235] he will be insane; and if Saturn and Mars looked, he will be stupid.

17 And[236] if you found the meeting or opposition with Saturn looking at it, and the Moon decreasing in calculation, and the fortunes do not look at her, he will be insane. **18** And if the Moon was increasing in glow, and Mars alone looked at her, especially in Pisces or Sagittarius, he will be insane; but if Jupiter looked, <a treatment will benefit him>,[237] while if Venus looked, praying in the mosques will benefit him. **19** And[238] if you found Saturn and Mars with the Lot of the Invisible and Jupiter and Venus do not look at it, he will be insane or confused.

20 And[239] if Jupiter was in the seventh and the Moon with Mars in the Ascendant, spirits will seize him and he will not have [his own] mind; and it is likewise if it was Saturn in the Ascendant or the tenth, or Mars[240] in the seventh; and it is more unfortunate for him if the Moon was with Mars.

---

[229] Or, "delusional"; this verb primarily means to whisper or speak under one's breath, and by extension to be plagued by doubts and delusions.

[230] For this sentence, cf. Rhetorius Ch. 65 (p. 119). This may represent *BA* III.6.4, which has Saturn and Mars in the IC, accompanied by Venus (Rhetorius) or Mercury (al-Andarzaghar).

[231] I take this to be on the IC itself.

[232] For this sentence, cf. Rhetorius Ch. 65 (p. 120).

[233] For this paragraph, cf. Rhetorius Ch. 65 (p. 120).

[234] For this sentence, cf. *Tet.* III.13-14 (Robbins p. 363), which does not appear in the Latin *BA* so was probably added by Sahl.

[235] This is probably Mercury; this phrase does not appear in *Tet.*

[236] For this paragraph, cf. Rhetorius Ch. 65 (p. 120).

[237] Reading with Rhetorius for an uncertain and incomplete phrase in Arabic.

[238] See Rhetorius Ch. 65 (p. 121).

[239] For this paragraph, cf. *Carmen* IV.2, **55-56**.

[240] *Carmen* reads this as "the Moon."

21 And[241] if the Sun and Moon were in one sign, and Mars was between them, and Saturn looked at them and[242] arose after them, then he will not be in possession of his own mind.

22 Now if the fortunes[243] looked at them or arose after them, then it will be turned around from that.

23 And[244] if the Moon was under the rays and she is decreasing in glow, and it is her departure from the infortunes, and those infortunes are in the stakes, he will not have courage nor power;[245] and it is more unfortunate for that if the other infortune looked at her.

24 And if the Moon was in the Ascendant or in any of the stakes, and a planet made her unfortunate, then look at Jupiter: for if he had testimony or was in a stake of the infortune, the native will be insane. **25** Now if Mercury was according to what I mentioned of Jupiter, then the native will be corrupted by sorcerers and he will not be in possession of his own mind.

26 Now[246] if Venus was enclosed between Saturn and Mars in one sign, and the two infortunes looked at the Moon and Mercury from a square, he will be a worshiper of idols or what has to do with them. **27** And if Mars was in the Ascendant and Jupiter opposing him, and the rest of the planets are not looking at him, then he will be of the worshippers of idols.

28 And[247] if you found the Lot of Fortune or[248] the Lot of the Invisible in the ninth or third,[249] and the fortunes do not look at it but the infortunes do look at it from its unhealthiness,[250] then the native will be <prophetic>,[251] speaking wondrous things. **29** And if you found the lord of the Lot of Spirit-

---

[241] For this paragraph, cf. *Carmen* IV.1, **58** and **60**.
[242] Both this sentence and the next ought to be consistent, reading either "and arose" or "or arose."
[243] Reading with *Carmen* for "infortunes."
[244] See *Carmen* IV.2, **62**.
[245] Or rather, he will be emaciated and sick (*Carmen*). In *Carmen*, this is no longer about insanity.
[246] See Rhetorius, Ch. 65 (pp. 119 and 120, in separate statements). In both cases, the Islam-inspired text here focuses on idolatry, while the Greek speaks of being inspired by the gods, prophesying, etc.
[247] See Rhetorius Ch. 65 (pp. 120 and 121, in separate statements).
[248] Reading with Rhetorius for "and."
[249] In Rhetorius this is the *lord* of the Lot, not the Lot itself.
[250] That is, from the opposite sign.
[251] Reading with Rhetorius for an uncertain Arabic word.

uality looking at its own lord from its unhealthiness, he will have babbling speech, and will not speak except for the unsound[252] things which come over him.

Chapter [6.7]: Robbers & sorcerers [from al-Andarzaghar]

1 Before[253] everything begin with the Moon, Mercury, and Mars, [if] they are in the stakes. **2** For if you found them in a stake and the fortunes do not look at them, they will be wicked robbers. **3** And if you found Saturn in the region of the house of fathers and he looked at them from an opposition or square, they will be robbers and will bore into houses.

4 And if Saturn[254] and Mercury were in the house of marriage and the Moon looked at them from an opposition or square, they will be arrogant robbers, <who will> plunder him[255] [but] then they will be crucified so that the birds eat them.

5 And if you found both Mars and Mercury in a stake, in a single degree, he will be a liar, a writer of forgeries, swearing oaths with lies. **6** And if Saturn and the Moon looked at these two, he will be a communicator[256] with the dead, and of those who plunder the dead.

Chapter [6.8]: The nativities of eunuchs [from al-Andarzaghar]

1 If[257] you found Saturn elevated over Venus or a Moon made unfortunate,[258] and if it[259] was in the sixth or twelfth, he will be a eunuch; now if the

---

[252] Lit. "in unhealthiness," to match the fact that the lord is in its own detriment or unhealthiness.
[253] For this whole chapter, see Rhetorius Ch. 65 (pp. 119-20).
[254] In Rhetorius, this is Mars (in line with the previous statements).
[255] This is a confusing phrase which reads differently (and without much sense) in both manuscripts; part of the confusion is: who is this "him"? At any rate, Rhetorius simply says such natives are robbers and murderers.
[256] نقال. That is, a sorcerer.
[257] For this section, cf. *Carmen* IV.2, **69-74.**
[258] The manuscripts read the previous phrase in opposite ways. **M** has Venus overcoming (elevated over) Saturn, and **E** has Saturn overcoming Venus; in both cases, it is not exactly clear whether the Moon is overcoming or overcome. But it seems to me that Saturn should be overcoming the Moon or Venus, and I have read it this way (see also **4** below for a simi-

nativity belonged to a woman, she will be barren, not desiring men, and she will not have a husband nor children. **2** And if Mars also looked, then that man will have his manhood cut off by iron; and if it was a woman, she will be barren, not having children born to her; and it is worse for that if it was in the sixth or twelfth. **3** Now if Jupiter was looking at them, he will be a domestic servant to those who serve idols, and along with this tribulation he will have a long life, with a miserable livelihood. **4** And[260] if Saturn and Mars[261] harmed Venus, and the Moon was made unfortunate, it indicates the nativities of eunuchs; now if it was a female, then sterility, and especially if they both[262] were not in their shares.

5 And if Jupiter was in a house of Venus or in a house of Mercury, or Mercury was with him in a house of Venus (and her bound and her triplicity), in a sign having two bodies, and the planet which indicates chronic illness looked at them,[263] and he is in a bad place, then the native will be feminized or wicked; and God is more knowledgeable.

Chapter [6.9]: On short people [from al-Andarzaghar]

1 Begin[264] and look at the minutes of the Moon in the signs, and the house of fathers, and her presence with Saturn, and the fall of the Moon. **2** If you found the Moon in the first degree of the sign, not completing her course in that degree (or the thirtieth degree at the end of the sign, and she is not completing her minutes in that degree), and she is in the house of fathers, and with her Saturn, if the Moon was in her fall,[265] then those humble people will be short until they are ridiculed for [their] shortness.

---

lar sentence). Unfortunately, *Carmen* does not have as many details here so we cannot be sure.

[259] Here and in the next sentence, I am not sure who "it" refers to.

[260] This sentence repeats the essentials of **1**.

[261] **E** has only "Mars."

[262] I take this to be the Moon and Venus.

[263] Or "her," indicating Venus.

[264] Cf. *Carmen* IV.2, **75**.

[265] **M** adds an extra, undotted word that seems to be "on the right," but I am not sure of its application here.

3 And[266] if the Moon was at the end of the sign and she connects with a planet at the end of the sign,[267] then the native will be short. **4** Now if the planet was an infortune, then he will be a dwarf, because the longitude of the planet which the Moon connects, is cut short.[268]

[Chapter 6.10: On slaves & servants]

1 Now as for what the native will have of slaves and servants, begin with the knowledge of the signs of slave women, and they are Taurus and its triplicity (and the worse of them is Capricorn, and the middling one of them is Virgo, and the more elevated of them is Taurus).[269]

2 You look in the matter of them from the sixth place, and understand from its lord and how its position is, and who is in the sixth place, and where the Lot of slaves and servants is,[270] and how is the position of Mercury (from whom is the indication of slaves and servants). **3** Because it is good if Mercury was eastern,[271] in a sign having two bodies, or in a convertible sign, and[272] his position is in the Ascendant; but if he was retrograde or under the rays, then there is no good in him.

4 Now if you found Saturn in the sixth or twelfth, then state sorrow because of slaves. **5** And if you found the lord of the sixth in the seventh or under the earth, then [it indicates] that slaves will die because of him and he will be deprived of them. **6** And likewise if you found the Tail in the sixth place.

7 And if Jupiter was in the sixth or the lord of the sixth with Mercury in a stake, then the native will be abundant in slaves, and will benefit by them. **8** And when you find the fortunes looking at Mercury, then judge benefit for the native from slaves. **9** And if you found the Lot of slaves in a good posi-

---

[266] This paragraph virtually repeats the above and may represent Sahl's pasting of another source's version here.
[267] Or perhaps, any sign, not necessarily the one she is in.
[268] Translation of this last bit tentative, because I am not sure exactly what it means, nor what this has to do with being an infortune.
[269] See also Chs. 1.38, **11-12** and **46-47**; 2.8, **4-9**; 4.5, **26-27**.
[270] See the calculation in **20** below.
[271] Reading with **M**. **E** has "in his exaltation," but that could only be Virgo.
[272] **E**: "or."

tion, with the fortunes looking, then the native's slaves will be abundant (and judge like that in every case).[273]

10 And if the lord of the sixth and[274] the Moon handed over [their management] to the lord of the Ascendant, he will gain slaves and servants. **11** Now if the sign of slaves was male, then they are males; and if it was female, then females. **12** And if it was one having four feet, then it is a riding animal or resembles that.

13 And know that if you found the Moon in Capricorn[275] and looking at the Lot of Fortune from a trine or stake, then[276] those slave women he is master of will be lowly, from the region of the sea or a land of the sea, and what resembles that. **14** And if the Moon [in Capricorn] fell away from the stake of the Sun and Jupiter, the slaves he is master of will not be suitable for him, and they will not cease to hate his place, and it will intensify according to what he rules of them,[277] due to the position of the sign relative to Saturn. **15** Now if you found the Moon in Virgo and you found the Lot of Fortune with her or she inspected it from these two signs,[278] then see where the position of Mercury is relative to the Moon. **16** For if you found Mercury inspecting the Moon from a place in which he has a share or claim, then he will be a master of slaves, and they will be changeable in business and benefit, except that if Mars was in a stake of Mercury (who is the lord of Virgo) so he corrupts Mercury, he will be one who is master of slaves who are bad for his life, and he will not gain good from them, or there will be defects in them, and wickedness and harm for him, and they will seek to kill him. **17** And if you found the Moon in Taurus and you found the Lot of his good Fortune in any of these two signs, then see where you find Venus and whether she inspects the Moon from [Venus's] own house or from a stake of it,[279] and what makes her fortunate and [unclear]: for Venus belongs to his good fortune so that he will be a master of slaves.

---

[273] Sahl seems to mean, "for any Lot."
[274] **E** reads, "or."
[275] **M** reads, "Aquarius," but Sahl's source is interested in the earthy signs.
[276] From here through "lowly," the texts read ungrammatically, mixing genders and mismatching definite and indefinite words; but this seems to be its meaning.
[277] Meaning unclear.
[278] I.e., from Capricorn and Virgo.
[279] Reading as وتد منه, but the poor condition of **E** also makes it look like وتد ملك, "from a stake of a king," which could indicate the tenth.

18 And as for [*uncertain*],[280] so that they are emancipated and wish him well, and follow him and in them is no [wish] to treat him badly, and he will not have evil from them, look at the Moon, if she was in Taurus, where she is from Jupiter. **19** For if you found her in a stake or what follows it, in her own triplicity, and Mars fell away from it, then he will gain many assets from the slaves, and they will be suitable for him, and he will have powerful delights, and much good; and God is more knowledgeable.

[The Lot of slaves: al-Andarzaghar]

20 Then look at the Lot of slaves, which is taken from Mercury to the Moon by day, and[281] by night the reverse of that. **21** So look at the Lot and its lord, for if you found them both made unfortunate, then loss and tribulation will afflict him from slaves, and especially if it was in a convertible sign. **22** Now if the Lot was in a stake and its lord in an excellent position, and they are both looking [at each other] from a trine, then he will have slaves who bend the knee to him, and benefit him, and perhaps they will save him from being killed. **23** And if you found the Lot in an excellent position and its lord in a bad position, not inspecting the Lot, then he will not gain good from them, and harm will enter upon him.

24 Now if you found the Lot opposed to the Moon, and Saturn and Mars with the Moon, then he will have slaves who contend with him and are hostile to him, until they expose him to killing, and there will be many runaways from him.

25 And if you found the Lot in the sixth or twelfth, and you found an infortune with Mercury, and especially if both of the infortunes were looking, then that native will not cease to be in fear for himself from his slaves, and he will keep them with him, in shackles, handcuffs, and confinement, for fear of them.

---

[280] The text seems to read عظماء, which normally would mean "the powerful" but here probably refers to the clientage of freed slaves—in which case, the powerful person is the former master who now has some loyalty and dependence from his former slaves.

[281] Reading for "or." The reversal by night is confirmed by Hephaistion in *Heph.* II.20, and Abū Maʿshar in *Gr. Intr.* VIII.4, **141** also confirms that Theophilus reversed it.

Chapter 7: On marriage
And it has eight topics in it

[al-Andarzaghar][1]

1 The first topic, on marriage: and you will know from it whether he will marry or not, and whether he will get good fortune from his women, or harm, or loss, or something else.

2 The second topic: whether he would marry[2] among the people of his own house, or not.

3 The third topic: on the abundance of his women and their number.

4 The fourth topic: when he will marry.

5 The fifth topic: on the harmony of his women with him.

6 The sixth topic: whether his women would die before him, and when they will die.

7 The seventh topic: whether he would be dissolute, open about [his] adultery.

8 The eighth topic: whether he would desire youths or would be of corrupt morals.[3]

Chapter [7.]1: On the marriage of men & women

[al-Andarzaghar]

1 Look at the lords of the triplicity of Venus, and the goodness of their position, and who is with Venus or looks at her. **2** Then, look at the lords of the triplicity of Venus: are they falling, and do the infortunes make them unfortunate, and are they perhaps under the rays?[4]

---

[1] The following topics are generally found in the eight chapters corresponding to them: topic 1 in Chapter 7.1, and so on.

[2] The word used here (نكح) does have marriage connotations, but especially suggests sexual relations; so it is sometimes unclear what Sahl's sources mean.

[3] **M:** "or would be moral."

[4] This refers to **11** below.

3 And look at the corruption of Venus and her suitability, and her westernness and easternness, and especially if she was in a male sign, and the infortunes look at her.[5]

4 And look at the two lords of the triplicity of Venus, which of the two is more excellent in position, and in the bound and sign of them.[6]

5 And[7] look at the Lot of marriage (and it is from Saturn to Venus) and the condition of its lord, and the planet which is with it, [whether] perhaps it is under the rays, and know the goodness of the planet which is the lord of the Lot. **6** And[8] look at the Lot of women (which you count from Venus to Saturn), and its lord, and the goodness of the lord of the Lot, just as I described to you in the matter of the Lot of men.

7 Then, look at the seventh and its lord, and who is looking at it (of the fortunes and infortunes), and what is the essence of the lord of the seventh.[9]

8 Then, look at the mixture of Venus and Saturn in the places and the bound.[10]

9 Then, look at the Lot of immorality[11] along with the lord of those two Lots which I described to you,[12] and [see if] perhaps you find Venus made unfortunate.[13]

10 Then,[14] look at the Lot which is taken from Venus to the stake of marriage, and its lord, and who is looking at them both (of the fortunes and infortunes).

[Venus and her triplicity lords: al-Andarzaghar]

11 Then,[15] begin with the lord of the triplicity of Venus: for if you found it with Venus in the stakes and what follows them, and it is not under the rays

---

[5] This refers generally to **12-19** below.
[6] Or rather, in *whose* sign and bound they are. See **17**, but generally **12-19** as well.
[7] For this paragraph, cf. *Carmen* II.2, **1-2** and II.3, **1**. For this sentence's topic, see Ch. 7.1, **89-94**.
[8] For this sentence's topic, see Ch. 7.2, **62-69**.
[9] This refers to **75-86** below.
[10] This is only clearly addressed in Ch. 7.1, **82-84** and **64**.
[11] That is, the Lot of *Erōs* or love according to Valens, taken by day from Fortune to Spirit (and reversed at night), and projected from the Ascendant. See **141-42** below.
[12] These are the male and female Lots of marriage, using Saturn and Venus.
[13] This refers to **141-44** below, but see also **87-88** (which is also from *BA*).
[14] Cf. *Carmen* II.5, **4-5**. See below, **145-47**.
[15] Cf. *Carmen* II.1, **2**.

nor retrograde, then judge for him that he will be marry and it will be suitable in his marriage and his women.

12 And[16] if you found the lords of the triplicities falling, made unfortunate, under the rays, and not looking at the Midheaven nor Venus, and Venus also being unfortunate, and especially if she was in a male sign and she is eastern in the position, and you found the Lot of marriage in a cursed house (and that is the sixth and twelfth), then that native will not ever marry.

13 And[17] look at Venus, [to see] if she was with the Moon in the cursed houses (and they are the sixth and twelfth), and Saturn makes her unfortunate by the union or opposition, and Jupiter is not looking, then the passion of men and women will cool, and the pleasure of men from women and the pleasure of women from men will be cut off until they die without passion.

14 But[18] if you found the lords of the triplicities in a bad position, made unfortunate, and Venus with Jupiter, in an excellent position, then he will marry, but because of the corruption of the lords of the triplicities and their misfortune, he will get harm and loss from his women.

15 And if you found Venus in her decline, [but][19] in the stake of Jupiter, and he is the lord of the triplicity of Venus, and he is in a stake, then he will marry a beautiful, magnificent woman. **16** But if you found Venus and Jupiter (he being the lord of her triplicity) both in their falls, falling from the angle, then because of the two fortunes falling and being made unfortunate, he will marry an ugly woman.

17 And[20] if you found the first lord of the triplicity of Venus in an excellent position, and the second in a bad position, falling, and Venus in an excellent place, then he will marry at the beginning of his life, and it will

---

[16] Cf. *Carmen* II.4, **3**.
[17] Cf. *Carmen* II.4, **8**.
[18] Cf. *Carmen* II.1, **4** and **6**.
[19] From here through "and he is in a stake," I have read as a plausible combination of **E** and **M**; there is no sentence quite like this or the next one in *BA* III.7.2, *Carmen*, or Hephaistion. The original **E** reads: "...in a stake of Jupiter (and he is the lord of the triplicity of Venus), in the stake of Jupiter." **M** reads: "in a stake, and Jupiter is the lord of the triplicity of Venus, in the house of his decline, and he is transiting in a stake." The key elements seem to be that although Venus is declining or cadent, she is strongly configured with Jupiter, her triplicity lord, and he is angular.
[20] For this paragraph, cf. *Carmen* II.3, **22**.

worsen with his women at the end of his life, and his condition in women will be difficult.

18 And[21] if you found the lord of the triplicity of Venus in the last degree of the sign, and one of the two infortunes in the house of fathers, in an alien sign, and the infortunes are looking at it,[22] then he will live without marrying until he dies. **19** And likewise, if you found it in its triplicity, then he will delay his marriage until he marries at the end of his life.

[Venus in the places]

20 And if you found Venus by night in the Ascendant, in her own house,[23] bound, or exaltation, and she is not under the rays, and she is inspecting Jupiter, then he will have good fortune from women, and will be happy because of them, and especially if you found Venus eastern. **21** And as she is[24] the indicator of the heat of the woman and of men, then she indicates joy and good for that reason. **22** And if you found Venus in the house or exaltation of Jupiter, then he will marry an eastern woman. **23** And if you found Venus in the house of Mars, it indicates infamy because of women, and especially if he looked at her along with that; and it is worse for that if he makes her unfortunate. **24** Now if Venus was in the house of Saturn, she indicates his marrying an old woman. **25** And if she was in the house of Mercury, she indicates his marrying a woman from the underclass or a servant or slave girl. **26** And if she was in the house of the Moon, it indicates his marrying a woman of the people of his house. **27** And if she was in the house of the Sun she indicates his marrying a woman not suitable for him, and especially if Venus was falling or with the Tail.

28 And if you found Venus in the fifth in nativities of the night, then state good in the matter of women, and[25] the native's marriage will be suitable, in a condition of goodness, in joy and pleasures.

29 And if she was under the earth[26] without the aspect of the infortunes, then say it is like what I mentioned for the fifth.

---

[21] For this paragraph, cf. *Carmen* II.4, **5-6**.
[22] I take "it" to be the triplicity lord.
[23] **E** reads, "in the Ascendant *or* her own house…".
[24] Reading for the more natural (but less coherent) "And if she was" (وإن كانت).
[25] Reading the rest of the sentence somewhat loosely, with **E**. **M** reads almost identically.
[26] I take this to be in the fourth or the IC.

30 And if she was in the third from the Ascendant, it indicates his marrying an appropriate[27] woman.

31 And if she was in the eighth, it indicates benefit from women along with a marriage in slowness and delay, and he will not rejoice in women, and especially if she was with Saturn.

32 And if she was in the sixth, she indicates his marrying a low woman or a sick one, or chronically ill, and by reason of women sorrow and evil will afflict him, and especially if along with that Venus was in her own fall, looking <at> the infortunes.

33 And likewise if she was in the seventh and she was <missing>.

34 <Missing>[28] if she was in her own house, triplicity, or exaltation, going out of the rays, devoid of the aspect of the infortunes, then there is no trust in her in nativities of the day.

35 And[29] if Venus was in the ninth, she is bad in [the matter of] women and he will have little stability with women (and Mars in the ninth is bad for women, because their husbands will not be infatuated with them): because if she was in the ninth she indicates a scarcity of stability with women and the badness of his clashing with them, and he will marry with slowness and delay.

36 And if Venus was in the Ascendant with Jupiter or was looked at by him, then that native will have many women, and especially if it was in a sign having two bodies or a convertible one.

37 And if Venus was <in> the Midheaven, she indicates the fineness of [his] condition, and a livelihood in relation to women, and delights with them, and especially if <neither> Mars <nor> Saturn is looking, and the Tail is not conjoined with her, and Jupiter is looking: because this indicates benefit by reason of females. **38** And if Mercury was with Venus, then he will be wealthy with money because of women, and he will be skilled in things, fortunate in his craft, with many servants,[30] and especially if Venus in addition

---

[27] ملاومة, which does not seem to be quite grammatical: reading as the active participle of Form III (ملائمة). **M** omits this word.

[28] This may be the second place, because it is the only place missing in this list.

[29] For this sentence, cf. *Carmen* II.5, 3 and Rhetorius Ch. 66 (p. 122). This is an example of Sahl having a totally different translation of Dorotheus than *Carmen*, because *Carmen* reads "Mars in the *seventh*."

[30] **E** adds an illegible word.

was in the house of Mercury or in her own house. **39** But if she was associated with Mars and Mercury, she indicates conflict and humiliation, and the badness of the marriage,³¹ and especially if the Moon was with her: because with that it indicates harms in his body; and it is harsher for that if Venus was in the degrees equated with³² marriage; and it is worse for that if Venus was in a male sign and the houses of the infortunes.³³

40 Now if you found Venus in the place of good fortune,³⁴ she indicates that he will marry a suitable woman.

41 And if she was in the twelfth she indicates the love of slave girls and disgrace with them, heavy loss, and tribulation because of them.

42 If Venus was in her fall and Jupiter not looking at her, the native will be of those without pleasure in women and children,³⁵ and especially if Jupiter was not looking at the lord of the triplicity of Venus. **43** If Venus was retrograde she indicates no marriage; while if she was under the rays, she indicates a sickly woman or he will marry in secret.

[More on the triplicity lords of Venus]

44 If you found the lords of the triplicities of Venus in the four stakes or the place of good fortune or in the fifth place, eastern, in one of her own places, then judge for the native the fineness of [his] condition in marriage and women. **45** And if it was the diurnal ones by day and the nocturnal ones by night, then that is easier for marriage. **46** But if you found them in the sixth and twelfth, then make the worst statement in it. **47** And if they were in the eighth, seventh, or second, if they were not made unfortunate and were direct, then say the average of [his] condition. **48** And if they were in the third they indicate affection, and especially if the lord of the triplicity was the Moon (for her joy is in the third).

---

³¹ Or, or sexual activity (النّكاح).

³² الدَرجات المستوية على, reading على for إلى. I take this to be the degrees right around the axis of the Descendant.

³³ M adds the following sentence, which may be a version of **89**: "Then, look at the Lot which is taken by day from <missing> to <missing>, and by night the reverse, and there is added to it the degrees of the Ascendant: for if something of the <illegible> was with it or looked at it from a square, then that Lot will distribute marriage to him, if God wills."

³⁴ That is, the eleventh.

³⁵ That is, *having* children.

[Planets in the seventh]

49 Now if you found [Venus]³⁶ in the seventh place, then it will be good in the matter of marriage, and especially if the sign was convertible or of many children, or had two bodies.

50 But if that planet was Mars, then he will <not> have stability in women, and he will be disgraced in marriage, and it indicates their death in childbirth.

51 Now if Mercury was there, inspecting Mars, it indicates the badness of what Mars indicates, and it indicates conflict and defectiveness in women.

52 Saturn in the seventh indicates coldness in the matter of marriage, and a scarcity of women, and their death, and Saturnian pains.

53 And if it was Jupiter, it indicates a praised woman.

54 And if it was the Moon, it indicates his marrying a woman from his own relatives.

55 And if the Sun was in the seventh, it indicates his marrying a woman who is not suitable for him.³⁷

56 And if the Tail was in the seventh, it indicates discord in marriage.

57 And if you found the lord of the seventh in the sixth or in the twelfth, then he will marry a slave woman or servant, and he will delay the marriage, and will have sex with despicable women. **58** And if you found the lord of the Ascendant in the seventh, then it indicates that he will be desirous of women, and especially if that lord was in a house of Venus or with Venus. **59** Now if you found the lord of the seventh in the seventh, it indicates the suitability of the marriage. **60** And if the seventh was a fixed sign, there will be a divorce³⁸ one time; and [if] having two bodies, twice; and [if] convertible, many times.

61 And if you found the Moon in the house, bound, or exaltation of Venus, or her triplicity, then the native will be eager for women, loving them; and likewise if you found the Sun, Ascendant, meeting, fullness, or the Lot of

---

³⁶ E: "a fortune."
³⁷ This probably means she will be too proud or socially elevated in relation to him, or she will want to be the authority.
³⁸ This should obviously be "marriage."

Fortune in the house, bound, exaltation, and trine[39] of Venus: for he will be desirous of women, eager for them.

62 And the greatest there could be in the nativities of men is if Venus is in the house of a fortune, with Jupiter or looked at by him, devoid of Saturn, and Mars looking at her from a trine or sextile, and Venus is not in the seventh nor under the rays. **63** And it is more excellent if with that she was western, because his women will more obedient to him.

64 And[40] the worst that it would be is if Venus was with Saturn: because the native at that time will be barren, not having sperm, or of few children, and of those not marrying, or likewise he will be a sodomite; so mix the two natures like that, because the nature of Saturn is coldness and dryness, and it dries out the wind of passion as well as the sperm, and his marriage to them will be <free> of the joy of children, for he will marry slave women and the elderly.

65 If Venus was in the house and bound of Mercury, she indicates that he will marry a woman who is younger than him, or a slave girl, or mistress.[41] **66** Now[42] if she was in the house of Saturn and his bound, she indicates that he will have sex with [women] having two teeth,[43] and widows. **67** And[44] if she was in the house and bound of Mars, it indicates that he will be desirous [and] eager for women, or he will marry secretly, or his marriage will be bad. **68** If she was in the house and bound of Jupiter, then he will be sterile[45] [but]

---

[39] This should be understood as "triplicity."
[40] **M** and **E** read their clauses in a different order.
[41] Reading tentatively for this word. **E** reads "impudent women, joker, buffoon."
[42] For this sentence, cf. *Carmen* II.4, **13**.
[43] This is an Arabic expression for someone very old.
[44] For this sentence, cf. *Carmen* II.4, **14**.
[45] This seems to be an error, and perhaps a misread for part of *Carmen* II.4, **14-15**. There, Dorotheus says that Venus in the bound or sign of Mars (with Mars looking) means the *wife* might be sterile because of the presence of *Mars*; but Jupiter and Venus under the rays can show an "unknown" or obscure marriage, especially if the sign is sterile. See **104-05** below.

praised. **69** And[46] if she was in her own house, in her own bound,[47] it indicates that he will have many marriages and women.

ঙ০   ଔ   ଔ

70 If Venus was in a stake, it indicates delights from women, and especially if Jupiter looked at her. **71** And the Moon in some share of Venus indicates his marriage from his relatives, who are older than him in age. **72** And if Mars looked at Venus along with that, it indicates that he will marry a woman in secret or will have sex with low women and slave girls. **73** And if Mercury was with Venus, it indicates that he will marry one whom he buys. **74** And if Mars looked at him, then it indicates conflict because of that; and it is more abundant in sexual intercourse with women, and the native will be desirous of them, if by night Venus was looking <at> Mars by an aspect of trine or sextile.

[The corruption of the marriage: the seventh house: al-Andarzaghar]

75 And[48] look at the house of women and its lord: for if the infortunes were in it and you found its lord falling or made unfortunate by the infortunes, harm and loss will afflict him by reason of a woman. **76** And if Saturn was the lord of marriage, then that loss is in relation to an old conflict or an ugly man or inheritance. **77** And if it was Jupiter, that loss is from a king or from a wealthy man or from the lord of a country or city. **78** And if it was Mercury, then [it is] by reason of conflict and speech and calculation, [and] harms will enter upon him, and perhaps [if] Mercury is in this position then the man will steal a slave girl, so that he will abduct her and marry her. **79** And if it was Mars, then his harm and loss are because of foreigners and travels. **80** And if Mercury was with him, then it is worse because he will kill his woman with his own hands, then he will fall into the hands of the Sultan, [who] will punish him. **81** And if it was Venus, then that harm will indeed be from intoxication and drinking, then he will marry a corrupt woman.

---

[46] For this sentence, cf. *Carmen* II.4, **9**.
[47] **M** is garbled at this point but says that this is when in her own house or *exaltation*. But this contradicts all of the previous sentences.
[48] For this paragraph, cf. *Carmen* II.1, **15-20**.

82 Then, look at Venus: for if she was with Saturn in the Ascendant, and Mars in the <house> of marriage, then he will marry a woman whom he will buy at high value, or heavy loss will afflict him from women.

83 And[49] if Venus was in the bound of Saturn, and Saturn looks at her from the opposition, then it is worse in the matter of women, because he will marry old people or a widow or one chronically ill, or a young girl, or an ugly slave girl of a cheap price. **84** And judge likewise in the nativities of women for their husbands, because they will be corrupted and chilled in sexual intercourse until they are barren, not having children.

85 And[50] if you found Venus in the Ascendant or in the Midheaven,[51] not in anything of her shares, and she is under the rays, and Mars in a stake,[52] then he will marry a foreign, poor woman; but if Mercury looked, he will marry an assistant. **86** Now if you found Mercury with Venus and there is no reception, nor does Jupiter look at them, then he will marry a slave girl or one resembling a slave; and judge likewise in the nativities of women.[53]

87 Now if you found Venus in the house of marriage, and not looking at Jupiter, then he will take[54] slave girls and free ones whom he will marry, they not being suitable for him nor obeying him.

---

[49] For this paragraph, cf. *Carmen* II.4, **13**.

[50] For this paragraph, cf. *Carmen* II.1, **13-14**, and Heph. II.21 (Schmidt p. 70).

[51] *BA* has the seventh, but that may have been a mistake of Hugo's because *Carmen* agrees with the reading here.

[52] *BA* III.7.4 includes his being with the Lot of marriage (probably the Saturn-Venus Lot), as does *Carmen*; but Hephaistion does not. So probably the Lot was added by some of the Persian editions.

[53] Here Sahl omits the next sentence in al-Andarzaghar (*BA* III.7.5, **1**), based on *Carmen* II.1, **11-12**, and partly quoted in Heph. II.21 (Schmidt pp. 69-70). The version in *BA* reads, "However, with Jupiter placed as was already stated, nor Mercury at rest [sc. not in the aspect of Jupiter], or under the regard of Saturn or Mars from any direction, it announces a marriage-bed [with those] more noble than himself; which if they regard the Moon, while however Jupiter would be lingering in that place, they join a lady or one more noble than him, in marriage." *Carmen* reads, "**11** And if Jupiter was with Venus, then state that he will have sex with a praised woman, and especially if Jupiter looked at the Moon: for he will have sex with his own mistress and lady, or the woman of a man of the nobility. **12** And if with that Saturn and Mars looked from <another> region at the Moon (the ruler of the night), then he will have sex with his own mistress or the woman of a man of the nobility; and speak likewise in the nativities of women as well." Hephaistion seems to require that Venus be in the west.

[54] **M** now skips to the eighth house. Reading with **E**'s pointing, but a better verb (spelled almost the same way) would be "is enamored with," though that would require a pronoun which is missing here.

ON NATIVITIES 593

88 And[55] if Venus was in the house of fathers, in a convertible sign, and especially Cancer and Capricorn, then the man will be eager for sexual intercourse until he rejoices in ugly women, prostitutes, and women notorious for fornication.

[The Saturn-Venus Lot of marriage]

89 Then[56] look at the Lot of marriage of men:[57] for if any of the seven is with it or looks at it from a square, then it indicates marriage.[58] 90 And see [if] perhaps the infortunes are with the Lot or the Lot occurs in the sixth or twelfth: for if you found it like that, then he will marry a corrupted, ugly, poor woman.

91 And[59] if you found the lord of the Lot not under the rays, and a fortune looked at it, and [the Lot] is in the stakes or what follows them, rejoicing in its glow, then he will marry a beautiful, virtuous, competent[60] woman, and because of her he will get profit, preference, and powerful rank.

92 And[61] if Jupiter was the lord of the Lot, his preference, profit, and rank will be because of a woman from the nobility. 93 And if Saturn was the lord of the Lot, then he will get many lands and inheritance in connection with his woman.[62]

---

[55] For this sentence, cf. *Carmen* II.4, **11-12**. But in *Carmen*, being under the earth indicates the death of the wife; it is the convertible sign which indicates the sexual proclivities. See also **102** below.
[56] Sentences **89-94** are from al-Andarzaghar. For this paragraph, cf. *Carmen* II.2, **1-4**. This is on the suitability of the marriage.
[57] This is the Saturn-Venus Lot.
[58] Or rather, it is the particular indicator of the marriage (Dorotheus).
[59] For this sentence, cf. *Carmen* II.4, **28**. From **91-94**, this is on the source of benefit or harm in the marriage.
[60] جامعة. This word suggests having a variety of qualities and skills.
[61] For this paragraph, cf. *Carmen* II.4, **29-30**.
[62] *Carmen* II.4, **31-34** lists other lords missing here: Mars, Mercury, and Venus. But *BA* III.7.3 does have them, showing that here *Sahl* has erroneously omitted them. If Mars is the lord of the Lot, the benefit will be because of a foreign man or one who does Martial work, or in relation to the cavalry; if Mercury, due to calculation and speech; if Venus, he will be praised and will benefit from women. Moreover, if the lord (in *Carmen* said to be Mercury) is in a bad place but looked at by fortunes, the wife is good but the native will toil and be unhappy; while if it was in a good place but looked at by infortunes, the toil and unhappiness can be gotten over.

94 And[63] if you found the lord of the Lot in the house of fathers, and the infortunes looked at it, and the lord of the Lot is looking at its own house, then he will marry whores and slave girls.

95 And[64] if you found the Lot of marriage in the seventh, then he will marry a free person. **96** And if the lord of the Lot was Saturn, then he will marry one related to him and a slave girl.[65] **97** And if the lord of the Lot was Mars he will marry in secret, and especially if it was in the west. **98** And if the lord of the Lot was Jupiter, he will marry a wealthy woman <or those> having kinship [with him]. **99** And if the lord of the Lot was Venus, he will marry her and be intoxicated. **100** And if the lord of the Lot was Mercury, then he will marry her in laughter and deception: and if Mars was looking at it,[66] then pain will afflict him in that.

101 Look at the position of the planets in their exaltations or falls, for [if it is] like that you will know with whom women will have sex, nobles or below [that].

[Venus again]

102 And[67] if Venus was in the stake of the earth, it indicates the death of his women; and it is harsher for him if the sign was convertible, and especially Cancer,[68] and it indicates marrying a disgraced woman,[69] and illness will afflict him due to that.

103 And[70] when Venus is with Saturn or in his bound, it indicates a widow, old women, and the underclass, and one with a defect. **104** And if she was like that with Mars, she indicates a strong desire for marriage, what is scandalous, and sorrow about children, and especially if it was her opposi-

---

[63] For this sentence, cf. *Carmen* II.4, **27**.

[64] For this paragraph, cf. *Carmen* II.3, **4-9**. It is on the topic of the type of spouse and activities he is engaged in. But in Dorotheus, this list of lords of the Lot pertains to the Lot of women's marriage, i.e., the types of men a woman will marry. Moreover, *Carmen* combines Sahl's **95-96**, not mentioning being a free person, and also is more extensive in the discussion of Saturn.

[65] In *Carmen*, Saturn only shows a relative if he is in his own sign.

[66] Or perhaps "him," referring to Mercury.

[67] For this sentence, cf. *Carmen* II.4, **11-12**.

[68] *Carmen* adds Capricorn as well.

[69] Reading with *Carmen* for an unknown word (مقعضة).

[70] For this paragraph, cf. *Carmen* II.4, **13-15**.

tion. **105** And if Venus was with Jupiter, both burned in the sign of illness, it indicates old women who will not give birth.

106 And[71] if you found an infortune with Venus or [in] her square or looking at her <from the opposition>,[72] it indicates the separation of what is between men and women, and it is harsher for it if the infortune was Mars, <and> the Moon with that. **107** And if Mercury was with Venus in her sign, made unfortunate,[73] it indicates slave women and the underclass. **108** And if Jupiter was with her, in the aspect of the Moon, it indicates his marrying his mistress or a noble woman.

109 And[74] if she was in the Ascendant or Midheaven by day, burned, and Mars in a stake or with the Moon, it indicates his marrying [someone of] the underclass; now if they looked together at the Moon, they indicate a defective or chronically ill woman.

116 And[75] if Venus was in a sign having two bodies or images, they indicate his marrying not [just one] slave girl.

111 Now[76] if Mercury was with her, they indicate his steadfastness with women, and if with that they were <in> the Midheaven or he looked at her in the Midheaven, they indicate the scarcity of his steadfastness with women. **112** Now if they were both eastern, that will be public; and if they were western, it will be secret. **113** And if Jupiter looked along with that, it indicates her properness afterwards.[77]

---

[71] For this paragraph, cf. *Carmen* II.1, **9-11**.

[72] Adding with *Carmen*.

[73] According to *Carmen*, by Saturn.

[74] For this paragraph, *Carmen* II.1, **13-14**. But note that in *Carmen* this does not involve the Moon, but the Lot of marriage. Moreover, according to *Carmen* the "they" referred to at the end of the sentence are Mercury and Venus.

[75] Cf. *Carmen* II.3, **13**.

[76] This paragraph is based on *Carmen* II.3, **15-18**. However, Sahl's text seems to have it backwards: in *Carmen*, Venus being with Mercury (and Mars) indicates *instability*, while being in the Midheaven means befriending women (and by extension, stability). But the native is befriending the women of other men, so that while it is public, it may not mean there is always approval.

[77] Or rather (per *Carmen*), Jupiter simply makes the problems fewer and improves the situation.

[Various considerations]

114 Then,[78] look at the two lords of the triplicity of Venus: for if they were both not looking at her nor at the Midheaven, they indicate that he will not ever marry.

115 And[79] [it is] likewise whenever Venus opposes the Lot [of marriage], or the Lot opposes the Ascendant, <or is> in a bad place, and Venus in a male sign.

116 And[80] if the lord of the Lot [of marriage] was burned or under the earth, made unfortunate, looking at the Lot, it indicates marrying a disgraced woman or slave girl or a woman whom more than one [man] has married. **117** And if it was the contrary, then make it the contrary; and it is more evident for that[81] if they were both in a stake or what follows a stake.

118 And[82] if the lord of the Lot was in the opposition <of the Lot, and the lord of the opposition of the Lot on the Lot>,[83] it indicates his marrying a woman he had sex with before that.

119 And if the lord of the sign of marriage looked at its own house or exaltation from a triplicity,[84] it indicates the harmony[85] of the women. **120** And if it looked from a square or from the opposite, it indicate the occurrence of evil between him and them. **121** And if the lord of the seventh was in the seventh, it indicates marrying an adoring[86] woman. **122** Now if the lord of the twelfth[87] conjoined with it, then he will marry a servant girl and a low woman; and if with that the lord of the seventh was burned, it indicates old women or marrying [someone of] the underclass.

---

[78] For this sentence, cf. *Carmen* II.4, **3-4** (which also includes the triplicity lord of the Lot of marriage).

[79] For this sentence, cf. *Carmen* II.4, **1**.

[80] For this paragraph, cf. *Carmen* II.4, **27-28**.

[81] I.e., for his benefit, rather than the harm. See **91** above.

[82] See *Carmen* II.4, **36**.

[83] Adding based on *Carmen*.

[84] Reading for "or triplicity," as the rest of the paragraph makes it clear that Sahl means an aspect, not the dignity.

[85] Or, "appropriateness."

[86] Reading عابدة for what seems to be عابرة.

[87] Reading for "second," as in Arabic the word for "twelfth" is "second ten": thus the "ten" must have been omitted. The twelfth is the sixth from the seventh, and also can generally indicate slaves.

123 And if the Head was in the seventh with Saturn and Mercury and Venus, it indicates marrying a non-virgin.[88] **124** And if Venus conjoined with [Mars],[89] then he will marry a blind or old woman. **125** And if Jupiter and Mercury conjoined with it[90] in it, then he will marry a noble woman, and [it indicates] the ruin of the first of his women, and the good will last with them. **126** And if the Tail was in the seventh with an infortune or one looked from a square or opposition, it indicates marrying a low woman suitable for labor. **127** Now if Venus conjoined with it,[91] then [it indicates] marrying a woman whom he loves.[92] **128** And if the Sun conjoined with that,[93] then [it indicates] marrying a blessed, foreign woman.

129 And if the lord of the seventh was <in> the Midheaven, then [it indicates] delights with women. **130** And if it was in the twelfth, then [it indicates] the corruption of the marriage.

131 And when you find the lord of the Lot of marriage in the seventh, and Saturn is making it unfortunate, then his woman will fall, and she will conceal it from the people.

132 And know that Saturn is the lesser of the infortunes in evil:[94] and if he was <in> the west, his works will be for evil, and that [means] that he will perform a work in foul evil, but he will not make them evident.

[The Moon as significator of the wife: Ptolemy]

133 And[95] if the Moon was under the rays and[96] Saturn looked at her, he will not marry except through effort.

---

[88] ثيّب, which is ambiguous as to whether this is a widow or divorcee.
[89] Reading for "it" with al-Rijāl (f. 79rb).
[90] In al-Rijāl, this is Venus (*ibid.*).
[91] In al-Rijāl, this is "them," viz. the Tail as well as the infortunes (*ibid.*).
[92] But al-Rijāl says "marrying a young woman whom he loved at first, but she is [really] an old woman." This makes more astrological sense.
[93] That is Venus (al-Rijāl, *ibid.*).
[94] That is, in relationships.
[95] See *Tet.* IV.5 (Robbins pp. 393-95). Ptolemy then makes similar statements about the Sun to describe a husband.
[96] Reading with Ptolemy for "or."

134 And if the Moon conjoined with the fortunes, he will marry suitable women. **135** And if the Moon conjoined with the infortunes, he will marry stinking women of the underclass, and slave girls, and singers.

136 And if she conjoined with Saturn, he will marry managerial, aged, disobedient[97] women. **137** And if it was Jupiter, he will marry virtuous, managerial women. **138** And if she conjoined with Mars, he will marry rebellious women, persisting in dissent and disagreement with him. **139** Now if Venus conjoined, he will marry beautiful women, flirts, pleasing people. **140** And if Mercury conjoined, he will marry women having services and work [to perform], and composure.[98]

[al-Andarzaghar: two Lots and Venus]

141 Then[99] look at the Lot of passion,[100] which is taken from the Lot of Fortune to the Lot of the Invisible[101] by day. **142** And if you found the Lot of marriage with the Lot of passion, or the Lot of Fortune looking at the Lot of marriage, then the native will fornicate with his woman before he marries her, then he will make her situation public through marriage.[102]

143 And[103] if Venus was under the rays, then it is bad in marriage, and especially if it was in a sterile sign.

144 And[104] look in the nativities of men at Venus: for if Jupiter looked at her, he will get profit and preference; and if it was the nativity of a woman then she will get profit and preference from her husband.

145 And[105] look at the Lot which is calculated from Venus to the house of marriage and is cast out from the Ascendant, and understand its position.

---

[97] Reading عاقات with **E** (since **M** is missing this part of the chapter), but this is a Martial signification; a better reading might be عانقات, "hindering, obstructionist."
[98] Reading رزانة with **E**. But perhaps this should be زراية, "scolding, contempt." Ptolemy has "intelligent and keen."
[99] This paragraph is based on a lost passage of Dorotheus, since we now know from *Excerpt* XVI, **6** that Dorotheus delineated friendship using the Lot of *Erōs* and the Lot of friends. See Ch. 11, **5** and 11.2, **4-6**.
[100] That is, the Lot of *Erōs*.
[101] That is, the Lot of Spirit.
[102] I don't think this means making the fornication public, but making their relationship public and respectable by means of marriage.
[103] For this sentence, cf. perhaps *Carmen* II.5, **6** or II.3, **10**.
[104] For this sentence, cf. *Carmen* II.3, **11-12**.
[105] For this paragraph, cf. *Carmen* II.5, **4-6**.

146 Now if you found an infortune with it or an infortune looked at it, and the fortunes are not looking at it, then judge for him that he will be disgraced in the marriage with that woman. **147** And if you found the lord of the Lot in a bad position and Venus under the rays or made unfortunate, then judge that he will not marry, ever.

༄ ༺ ༻

148 And if Venus was with Mars, he will marry a shameless, adulterous woman, impudent in her manner, not knowledgeable, [and][106] the man will not be eager to marry her; afterwards he will separate from her.

149 Now[107] if Venus was in a sign having one body, he will marry one time; and if she was in one having two bodies or two natures, even if she is conjoining with none of the planets, then it multiplies his marriage and weddings.

[The lord of the Ascendant and lord of the seventh: Māshā'allāh]

150 Māshā'allāh said:[108] look at the lord of the Ascendant and <the lord of> the seventh: for if they looked at each other or one of them connected with the other, it indicates that the native will not remain marriage-less. **151** So look at that time at the one of them accepting the management: for if the acceptor was the lord of the Ascendant and it was in a stake or in its own house or exaltation, then it indicates women's eagerness for him, and he will get rank because of them. **152** And if the acceptor was the lord of the seventh and it is in a stake or in its own house or exaltation, it indicates the native's eagerness for women, and he will get good and exaltation from them and because of them.[109] **153** And [even] if the lord of the Ascendant was falling or in the contrary of its own house or in its fall, it also indicates his eagerness, but he will be ruined because of them and it introduces tribulation upon

---

[106] Reading the rest of this sentence somewhat uncertainly; the Arabic seems to have spelled a word wrong or put two words together.

[107] Cf. *Carmen* II.3, **13**, which may be a truncated version of this sentence.

[108] I believe this material from Māshā'allāh extends through the end of this subsection.

[109] The part about the eagerness makes sense, but it does not seem right to me that the native will benefit no matter which planet is angular. Perhaps in **152** it is the *women* who will benefit because of *him*, since the lord of the seventh is angular or in its own dignity.

him. **154** And if neither of them connects with the other, then look at the lord of the seventh, in which position it is: for if it connected in the third [or] in any of the stakes,[110] then he will marry one of his relatives. **155** And if it was in the eleventh, then he will first have friendly affection, then marry.

156 Then,[111] look at the aspect of the fortunes and infortunes to [the lord of the seventh], and <from> which position it is looked at: for the position is the indication of the manner of the woman's corruption or her properness. **157** Because if the lord of the seventh was in a stake and an infortune looked at it from an opposition or square, it indicates the woman's debauchery; and if they were both in a convertible sign, then what I mentioned will be with not just one [man]. **158** And if it was in the seventh, falling away from the Ascendant[112] and it is made unfortunate, it indicates what I described but it will be hidden, and it is harsher for the concealment of it if the lord of the seventh was not looking at the Ascendant. **159** And if an infortune looked at the lord of the seventh from a trine or sextile, it indicates that the woman will have few children, being [also] corrupt in religion. **160** And if a fortune looked at the lord of the seventh and the lord of the seventh is in at stake, and it is looking from a square or opposition, it indicates the woman's virtuousness and uprightness, and she will be well known for that. **161** And if it looked at it and it is falling, not looking at the Ascendant, then her condition is based on what I described, and not [*uncertain*][113] in that. **162** And if a fortune looked at it from a trine and sextile, it indicates the abundance of her children, and the fineness of her religion. **163** And if an infortune looked, and that infortune was the lord of the eighth and the second, it indicates the death of his women. **164** And likewise, if the lord of the seventh is under the rays and entering into burning, then he will marry in secret.

---

[110] But connects with whom?
[111] I believe the rest of this (from **156-204**) is also Māshā'allāh, but am not yet sure.
[112] But the lord of the seventh cannot both be in the seventh, and be in aversion to it. I see two possibilities. The first is that it should read, "And if *the lord of* the seventh was falling away from the Ascendant," replacing the Arabic "in" with "lord." The second is that it should read, "And if it was in a *decline* [or falling place], falling away from the Ascendant," replacing "seventh" with "declining/falling" (see **161**). Both of these are simple changes in Arabic. In either event, the lord of the seventh is in aversion to the Ascendant.
[113] The text seems to read كر لا تدكر.

165 Then look: for if the lord of the seventh was in a stake or its own house or exaltation, then he will marry a well-known woman who has nobility. **166** And if it was falling and it is in its own fall, he will associate with women who do not have esteem, or a slave girl. **167** And if the lord of the seventh was made unfortunate by Saturn, it indicates the difficulty of his marriage and its delay, or he will marry old women. **168** And if a light star such as Venus, Mercury, and the Moon was in the seventh, it indicates a <missing> woman, and he will have sex with many women. **169** And if the planet was received in its position, he will associate with women suitable for him, [and] celebrated. **170** And if what I mentioned of the planets was in the opposite of the lord of the Ascendant, it will be what I described in the first chapter,[114] and his father[115] will be of those who marry slave girls and those who have defects, and one with no good in him. **171** Now if it was Saturn it is harsher for him, and he will marry old people; and if it was Mars, he will marry harlots. **172** And if as well the lord of the eleventh one of the signs had the eleventh,[116] he will marry a woman he loves. **173** Now if it was in a fixed sign, he will be stable <with> his woman; and if it was convertible, he will not be stable with the woman.

174 Then look at the planets which are in the seventh or oppose the lord of the seventh. **175** For if it was the lord of the Ascendant, the native will be soft, not craving marriage; and if it was the lord of the second he will associate with slave girls and women who do not have social esteem; and if it was the lord of the third he will associate with those having kinship with him, and those who are of the rank of his sister; and if it was the lord of the fourth he will also associate with those having kinship with them, and those who are with them in their rank; and if it was the lord of the fifth he will associate with women younger in years than he is (now if it was a convertible sign, he will associate with many women); and if it was the lord of the sixth he will propose to slave girls or women who have defects from illness; and if it was the lord of the seventh he will associate with women who have equivalency

---

[114] Reference uncertain.
[115] But why the father?
[116] Reading uncertainly for وإن كان أيضًا له بربّ الحادي عشر من البروج الحادي عشر. But perhaps this should simply say that the lord of the seventh is in the eleventh, or that the lords of the eleventh and seventh are well connected.

with[117] the relatives of his mother; and if it was the lord of the eighth or seventh the women will not be changed[118] [while] with him, and he will inherit from them; and if it was the lord of the ninth he will associate with women from abroad, not from his own country; now if it was the lord of the tenth he will associate with well-known women who have esteem from the people of the house of the Sultan; and if it was the lord of the eleventh he will associate with women whom he loves and he will have children from them whom he will be happy with; and if the lord of the twelfth was in the seventh he will associate with and marry women who do not have social esteem nor do they have significance, and he will be desired by them and they will have defects (and it indicates likewise if the opposer was the lord of the Ascendant, for the judgment of it will be based on what I described).

176 Now if the lord of the Ascendant and the lord of the seventh were with the Head and the Tail, opposing the Sun, the native will remain marriage-less.

177 Then, look at the Moon and her position, and the position of the lord of her house. **178** For if she owned the seventh sign from the Ascendant in the distribution [of the signs], and if she was in a strong position, free of the infortunes, and she had testimony, and was received, he will have a suitable woman, abundant in the good, whom he will marry. **179** Now if the lord of the house of the Moon was also in an excellent position, what I mentioned will last and she will not be goaded into separation except by death. **180** Now if the Moon was not received, it indicates the woman's bad character and the abundance of her evil. **181** And if the Moon (she being in a stake) connected with a withdrawing planet, the women will <not> get good from him or they will be ruined at his hands. **182** If the Moon was falling and she is connecting with a planet in a stake, the women will get good from him. **183** And if the Moon and her lord were made unfortunate, he will not be blessed with children from women.

184 Then look at the Lot of marriage (and that is that you calculate from Saturn to Venus), where its position is and who is looking at it: so speak about the twelve signs based on what I have described in the first chapter in this topic[119] (except that in this chapter, if you saw that the women are slave girls, [the signs] do not indicate that they are of the underclass and are bad).

---

[117] This probably means they are either of her clan or of a similar rank.

[118] يتغيّر. This can also mean "corrupted," i.e. to change from one state to another.

[119] I believe this refers to *Nativities* Ch. 1.38, esp. **11-12** and **46-47**.

185 And as for slave girls and others, the indicator for that is the lord of the seventh.[120]

186 Then, look at the lord of the Lot just as you look with the Lot of marriage, concerning the aspect of the fortunes and infortunes to it: for if the fortunes looked at it, then report the suitability of the marriage; and better than that is if the fortune was received, for then with that it indicates the suitability of what is between them; and for the infortunes speak about the corruption of what is between them. **187** Now if the infortune was Saturn, it indicates the long delay of the marriage, and its difficulty, and that he will not marry except after despair. **188** If the infortune was Mars, it indicates the corruption of the woman and the breakdown of what is between them both. **189** Now if the lord of the Lot was corrupted, not looking at its own place, it does not indicate <a good marriage>.[121]

190 Then, after that look at Venus: for if she was free of the infortunes, received, and the lord of her house in an excellent position relative to the Ascendant, then he will marry a woman of significance and rank, and she will have a fine character, with much good, and suitable. **191** But if she was made unfortunate by a square or opposition of Saturn, it indicates that she will be of few children, feeble; if he conjoined with her, she is sterile; and if Saturn looked from a trine, it indicates a scarcity of children, feeble; and if it was from a sextile, she will be of a bad character. **192** And if she was made unfortunate by Mars, it indicates the woman's eagerness for marriage. **193** Now if Venus was not received and she is made unfortunate, she has a defect; and if she was in a stake it will be evident, and if she was falling it will be hidden. **194** And if Venus and Mars were looking at each other and they were both in signs [such that] one of them or both of them together are looking at the Ascendant,[122] then the man will not stand by his woman and the woman will not stand by the man, and she will not be satisfied by marriage.

195 Now if the lord of the Ascendant and of [its] opposite[123] are connecting one to the other from a trine or sextile, it indicates their harmony, their

---

[120] In other words, if the rules here show that the partner is of the lowest type or a slave, then the ranking of the types of signs will not be useful, and we have to look at the seventh alone.

[121] Tentatively adding. But perhaps this should be, "it does not indicate marriage."

[122] This should probably be, "not" looking at the Ascendant.

[123] That is, the lord of the seventh.

affection, and the goodness of their condition. **196** And if they are looking at each other and one of the two is in a stake, then the one in the stake is the indicator, [and] stronger in affection for the other, until that appears and is known.[124] **197** And if there was nothing of them in a stake, then what I mentioned will be kept secret. **198** And if they were looking at each other from a square, their matter will be in the middle, not judged to be apparent until he grows old with her, and he will not love <nor>[125] be passionate about her until that is known from them both. **199** Now if they looked at each other from the opposition, it indicates corruption between the two of them, and their openness [about it],[126] and their disputing, and the scarcity of their agreement, and each will be bored with the other.

200 If Venus or the lord of the Ascendant were made unfortunate in the stakes, then if the native was with wicked people[127] or was of those who live by means of [wickedness], then she is a slave girl, wicked, a lesbian, and impudent or resembling that.

201 And if Venus had testimony in the Ascendant and she was made unfortunate in a stake, it corrupts the native and [*uncertain*][128] something upon him, so speak like that. **202** If Mercury had testimony in the sign and he was made unfortunate (and it is harsher for that if he was in a stake), then it indicates that he will love male youths.

203 And if the lord of the seventh was made unfortunate in the Ascendant, then the native will be despicable, he himself will have sexual relations with a male servant or housemaid.

204 So look into the connection of what I mentioned to you, for if it was empty in course in the sign which it was in, then change it over to the next sign, and the judgment about it will be one.[129]

---

[124] I believe this simply means that that person will be the first to make his or her love known.

[125] Tentatively adding to make the sentence make more sense.

[126] وأبينهما.

[127] Or perhaps simply, "if he was wicked" (بخبثاء).

[128] The text seems to read ودى.

[129] That is, interpret the next connection in the following sign instead of interpreting it in the current one.

[*The lord of the seventh in the houses, according to Māshā'allāh*]

205 Then look at the lord of the seventh: for if it was in the Ascendant, he will have good from women, and he will be successful.[130] **206** The lord of the seventh in the second corrupts his assets because of a contention, and his women will die, and they will have defects. **207** The lord <of the seventh> in the third: the native's brother will marry a woman of his, and he will be hostile to his siblings, or he will marry his relatives, and his marriage will be abroad. **208** The lord of the seventh in the fourth: he will marry a woman from the people of his own house, and she will be well-known [and] virtuous. **209** The lord of the seventh in the fifth: he will marry a woman younger than himself, and she[131] will have compassion [and] goodness of character. **210** The lord of the seventh in the sixth: he will associate with slave girls or women with defects. **211** The lord of the seventh in the seventh: he will marry a well-known woman,[132] an equal match for him, whom he will love. **212** The lord of the seventh in the eighth consumes the inheritance of the women, and he will have a foreign woman. **213** The lord of the seventh in the ninth: he will marry a foreign woman, her brother will give her in marriage, and he[133] will love her. **214** The lord of the seventh in the tenth: he will marry one of the family of the house of the Sultan, a fortunate woman, he will get good from her. **215** The lord of the seventh in the eleventh: he will marry a fertile woman, will love her, and will live in luxury because of her.[134] **216** The lord of the seventh in the twelfth: he will marry a woman who does not have social esteem, [and] will encounter hardship from her, and she will be hostile to him.

217 Look in this topic if the lord of the seventh is[135] free of the infortunes, and the fortunes do not testify.

---

[130] This can also mean "victorious," which suggests it might also be helpful for conflicts.
[131] Reading "she" for Sahl's "he."
[132] Reading معروفة with al-Rijāl for two uncertain words in **M** (ميشومة كبورفة).
[133] I take this to be the native.
[134] Lit., "from her."
[135] Omitting "in the seventh."

[Four Lots]

218 And know that if the lord of the Lot of sexual intercourse[136] occurred in the Ascendant, fifth, tenth, or eleventh, that matter will be with ease from each of the two, for its owner.[137] **219** And if it was in the second, third, fourth, sixth, seventh, eighth, or twelfth, then that matter is in the way of anger or haughtiness.

220 And[138] look in the Lot of men's deception by day and by night from the Sun to Venus, and it is projected from the Ascendant.[139] **221** The Lot of women's deception is taken from by day and by night from the Moon to Mars, and is projected from the Ascendant. **222** So if it and its position were excellent, he will [be able to] deceive as he wishes; and if corrupted, he will not [be able to] deceive in anything.

223 Look[140] at the Lot of marriage and its position in the signs, taken from Saturn to Venus, and it is the Lot of men's marriage. **224** The Lot of women's marriage is taken from Venus to Saturn, and is cast out from the Ascendant.

[The Sun-Venus Lot in the houses, according to Māshā'allāh][141]

225 <Now if> the Lot of women's[142] wedding <was> in the Ascendant and its lord free of the infortunes, in its own glow, his marriage will be with

---

[136] This must be either the Lot of *Erōs*, or the Venus-seventh Lot.

[137] That is, for the person whose nativity it is.

[138] These Lots are defined in Valens, *Anth.* II.38 (Schmidt p. 6), and are related to the "sympathy and illegality" of the marriage; they are attributed to Hermes by al-Rijāl (slide 209, left). They are similar to two other Lots in *Carmen* II.6, which are calculated from the Sun to the Moon, and added to Venus for men, and to Mars for women.

[139] Note that if this were true, then the Lot could only be found in the eleventh through third signs because Venus cannot be more than about 48° from the Sun.

[140] For these calculations, see *Carmen* II.2, **2** and II.3, **1**.

[141] At this point we have a problem, as Sahl seems to have made an error. In what follows Sahl is reporting Māshā'allāh's treatise on Lots virtually verbatim, as we have seen with the other houses. But in the Māshā'allāh text, this Lot is explicitly said to be the *Sun-Venus* Lot mentioned in **220**, *not* the Venus-Saturn Lot which was defined as the Lot of women's marriage. So we must keep in mind that the following delineations, for Māshā'allāh, involve the Sun-Venus Lot (and by extension, the Moon-Mars Lot for women). See Tehran, Dānishgāh, Nafīsī 429 (71a-71b); Majlis 17490 (137-38).

[142] Again, in Māshā'allāh this is only the "Lot of marriage"; and since he is assuming a male native, this should read "men's marriage."

ease, and there will result for him what he seeks due to women; and if it was an infortune, it is harsher. **226** The Lot of wedding (and it is the Lot of marriage) in the second, and its lord free of the infortunes, and it has testimony: its owner will marry slave-girls and those who do not have social esteem, and he will gain from their inheritance. **227** And if it was made unfortunate, there will be furnished on top of that, what is disgraceful from women; and if it was an infortune, it is harsher. **228** The Lot of wedding (and it is the Lot of marriage) in the third: he will marry women who have associated with his brothers <or one who is with him who has the rank of a brother; now if it was made unfortunate or its lord unfortunate, he will associate with his sisters>[143] or one who is with him who has the rank of a sister. **229** The Lot of marriage in the fourth: he will marry from his own relatives, a woman of fine religion, having status according to her ability; now if its lord was made unfortunate, he will mingle with [his] mothers or because of them.[144] **230** The Lot of marriage in the fifth, and it being free of the infortunes, in its own glow: he will marry a woman younger than himself in years, having beauty, soft, of a fine condition; now if <it or its lord> was made unfortunate, he will associate with his own child or one who is with him having the status of a child. **231** The Lot of marriage in the sixth: he will associate with slave girls but they will not have esteem (if it was free of the infortunes); now if it was made unfortunate, they will have defects and because of them he will experience hardship. **232** The Lot of marriage in the seventh indicates what I mentioned about the lord of the Ascendant if it was in the seventh.[145] **233** The Lot of marriage in the eighth: corruption will be feared for him because of women; now if <it or> its lord was made unfortunate, his death will be by reason of them. **234** The Lot of marriage in the ninth: he will marry foreign women; now if its lord was free of the infortunes, they will have faith and he will get good from them, while if it was made unfortunate, it heaps evil upon him and he will experience hardship because of them and evil from

---

[143] Adding with Māshā'allāh, here and throughout the rest of the section.

[144] By "mothers," Māshā'allāh means close female relatives of his mother (such as an aunt).

[145] Māshā'allāh reads: "he will marry a woman [who is] related, well known, he does not love her; and if it was free of the infortunes it allots him harmony. And if the lord of the Ascendant looked at the lord of the seventh with friendship, there will be friendship and love between them."

them.[146] **235** The Lot of marriage in the tenth: he will marry women elevated in significance; now if its lord was free of the infortunes, they will have preeminence, while if it was made unfortunate it announces evil.[147] **236** The Lot of marriage in the eleventh: he will marry women whom he will love before there are children from them, and the majority of them will be maidens:[148] and if it was made unfortunate, it will be what I mentioned, and there will be a corruption of the marriage. **237** The Lot of marriage in the twelfth: he will marry women who have defects, and it introduces sorrows upon him from that, <if it was made unfortunate>.

Chapter [7.]2: On his marrying someone of the people of his house

[al-Andarzaghar]

1 As for marrying one of the people of his house, look at these three items:

2 The first of them [is] the Moon,[149] then Venus, then Jupiter, in whose exaltation they are.[150]

3 And the second [is] the examination of the strength of <the Moon and>[151] Venus in the stakes, or the union, opposition, or square.[152]

4 And the third is that you examine the mixture of Saturn with Venus in the house of Saturn, and the stake of the Ascendant, and how the testimony of Jupiter and his aspect is.[153]

5 So then,[154] look at the Moon, Venus, and Jupiter: for if you found them in the house of the Moon or her exaltation, then the native will marry within the people of his house.

---

[146] Māshā'allāh adds that the wife might run away.

[147] Reading this last phrase with Māshā'allāh, for an uncertain and totally different phrase in Sahl.

[148] This word also has connotations for slaves and maids.

[149] Reading for "Mercury": see **5** below, and *Carmen* II.4, **16**.

[150] This refers to **5** below.

[151] Adding with *BA* III.7.7.

[152] This refers to **6-10** below.

[153] This refers to **11-13** below, but see also **42** and **81-87**.

[154] Reading "the Moon" throughout this sentence for "Mercury," in accordance with *Carmen* II.4, **16**.

6 Now[155] if you found the Moon and Venus (both of them) in a stake, and if one of them looked at the other from a square from the stakes, judge likewise, and especially if with that [the Moon][156] was in her own house or exaltation. **7** And if you found the Moon and Venus in the house of fathers, in [the Moon's] two houses,[157] and[158] Jupiter looked at them, it indicates marrying one for whom it is unlawful. **8** Now if they were both like that in a bad sign, whether the house of the Moon or her exaltation, they indicate harm in his marriage, but no child will be born to him for a long time, [and] then afterwards one will be born to him. **9** And when you find them both together in a stake, they indicate his marrying one not permitted to him.

10 And[159] if you found the Moon with the Lot of marriage or looking at it from a square or opposition, then he will marry the daughter of his paternal uncle, or the daughter of his maternal uncle, or his daughter, or the daughter of his sister or [some other] relation of his.

11 Now if the lord of the Lot was Saturn, then he will marry one of the class of his father and mother. **12** And[160] if Saturn was the lord of the Lot, with Venus, in the house of Saturn in the Ascendant, then he will marry the senior ones of his sisters. **13** And[161] if Jupiter[162] looked from a square, he will marry his maternal aunt.

14 Now if the Moon was in the seventh, it indicates marrying one of his relatives. **15** If you found Venus in the opposition of the Moon, in a male sign, then he will be one of those who have sex with their own sisters and

---

[155] For this paragraph, cf. *Carmen* II.4, **17-18**.
[156] Since in Arabic the Moon is masculine, then between the two planets this and the masculine pronoun (translated "her" in English) must refer to the Moon.
[157] That is, her domicile and exaltation.
[158] Reading with *Carmen* for Sahl's "or."
[159] This sentence seems to be based on *Carmen* II.4, **19**. In *Carmen*, the lord of the Lot is on the Lot, or looking at the Lot, or looking at the Moon (which is so common a set of circumstances as to be useless). Sahl's reading makes more sense, even if it should include the lord of the Lot being on the Lot.
[160] For this sentence, cf. *Carmen* II.4, **20**.
[161] For this sentence, cf. *Carmen* II.4, **20**.
[162] This should be "the Moon," with *Carmen*; but since Sahl is drawing on al-Andarzaghar I will read it his way.

daughters. **16** And if the Moon was in the seventh, it indicates the suitability of the marriage, and he will marry one of the people of his mother, and what is like that. **17** And if you found the lord of the seventh in the triplicity of the Ascendant, then he will marry one of his friends and his sisters; and [it is] likewise if it was the lord of the third[163] and that lord was a fortune.

18 The Moon in the house of Venus or her exaltation, is an indicator for marrying one of the people of his house; and likewise if Venus was in the house <or> exaltation of the Moon, and the Moon is in the exaltation of Venus, and one of them is looking at the other.

19 Now if you found Jupiter and the Moon both in the house of one of them, then speak likewise about his marrying a woman from his relatives and friends.

20 And if you found the lord of the seventh to be Venus, and it[164] was in the third, it indicates his marrying one of his relatives and his friends. **21** And [it is] likewise if you found the lord of the triplicity of Venus with Venus, in the house of marriage.

22 And[165] if Venus and Saturn were in Capricorn or Libra, in the Ascendant or Midheaven, and the Moon was with them, then he will marry his mother and his maternal aunt, and the women of his father. **23** Now if the Sun was looking at these planets and he is in the west, then he will marry his own daughters, or his sister or daughter-in-law, or the daughter of his own daughter.

24 And if you found the lord of the seventh in the third, in one of the stakes,[166] and it connected with the lords of both, then he will marry one of his relatives.

25 And likewise if you found the lord of the third or fourth in the seventh, for then he will marry someone who is[167] with him in the rank of his siblings and the family.

26 And if the lord of the seventh was <in> its place, then he will marry one of his own people and relatives—except that if it was the Midheaven, she will be in a finer condition.

---

[163] Or perhaps, "triplicity." But it is unclear whether we are speaking of one or two planets here, and how. See also **20** and **23** below.
[164] That is, Venus.
[165] For this sentence, cf. *Carmen* II.4, **20**; also *Tet.* IV.5 (Robbins pp. 401-03).
[166] This could only happen if he meant the third sign, with the IC in it.
[167] This should read هي, the feminine form.

The nativities of women

28 And as for the nativities of women, you ought to look at their husbands from Mars just as I described to you about Venus in the nativities of men.[168] **29** If he was in the house or trine[169] of Saturn, it indicates her marrying an old man with defects, [and] inattentive. **30** If he was in the house of Jupiter, then she will marry a praised husband. **31** Now if he was in the house of Mercury, it indicates her husband is a writer, skilled, an artisan, sensible, and one whose work is Mercurial. **32** If he was in the house of Venus, it indicates that her husband is a young man, a lover of amusement. **33** And if he was in the house of the Sun then she will marry a famous man, noted in rank. **34** And if Mars was in the exaltation of the Moon or in her house, then she will marry a sick man, a judge, or something like that, and especially if Jupiter looked at him, if he was in a stake.

35 And likewise look at the lord of the triplicity of Mars: if it was in a fixed sign, <then it indicates her marriage to one man; and if it was in one having two bodies>,[170] then it indicates her marriage is not just to one; and if you found Mars in a convertible sign, and the lord of his triplicity is in what is like that, it indicates her being overwhelmed by husbands and marriage. **36** Now if you found Mars and the lord of his triplicity in one sign, or the exaltation of Venus, then those women are desirous of men. **37** Now if Mars looked at Venus, it will be more for their desire and eagerness.

38 And know that the triplicity of Mars indicates the condition of the husband: so the one you found in a good position, judge delights and the goodness of character and pleasure affecting them[171] from the husband of that woman. **39** And if Jupiter looked at Mars, then say that she will get a gift and benefit from her husband.

40 If[172] Venus and Mars were each of them in the bound of the other, and the one of them looked at the other, then the woman will be deflowered in marriage; and likewise if the Moon was trining the Sun in a male sign, be-

---

[168] Probably Ch. 7.1, **20-27** above.
[169] This must mean, "in a sign which is in trine to" Saturn, which would also be part of the triplicity Saturn is in.
[170] Adding for astrological accuracy.
[171] This is in the feminine plural, meaning multiple women; but the rest of the sentence has one woman.
[172] For the first part of this sentence, cf. *Carmen* II.4, **14**.

cause she will be ignorant. **41** And if Venus looked at the Moon from a square, she indicates that she is pleasant, eager for men.

42 If[173] Saturn was with Venus or in her square or opposition, then she will be sickly or sterile, and especially if the Moon was made unfortunate with Saturn, and Jupiter was not looking at her, or with that Venus was in the house of Saturn.

43 And look at the seventh place, and at its lord, and the essence of the place, and the one looking at it, [and] the planet[s in] that place, [and judge] their [fortune] or misfortune: so speak on the matter of husbands.[174]

44 And[175] look at the Lot of men's marriage (which is taken from Saturn to Venus), and at the Lot of women's marriage (which is taken from Venus to Saturn), where their position is and their lords, for the most excellent it could be is in the houses of the fortunes and being looked at by them both. **45** Now if you found Mars looking at the Lot of marriage from a square or opposition, it indicates their marrying in secret or she will do foul work. **46** And if the Lot was in the house of Jupiter, it indicates virtuousness and uprightness and a good reputation. **47** If Venus was with that, it indicates that he will be pleased in marriage. **48** And if it was with Saturn or[176] he looked at it, then it indicates difficulty in marriage. **49** And if it was with Mercury, it indicates eagerness and desire. **50** And if it was the Moon, it indicates that he will be a master of passions and fickleness.

51 And if Jupiter[177] was with the Sun and not under the rays, he will be esteemed, famous, [and] upright.

52 And if <the lord of> the Lot was Mars, it indicates the marriage of youths—and with the rest of the planets according to their essences.

53 And if you found planets (not just one) in the seventh sign and the sign was convertible, or in it one of the planets, and especially Mars, then it indicates an abundance of husbands and an abundance of sex with more than one [man]. **54** And if Mercury and Venus were there, then it is like that.

55 And if Mars was with Venus <in> the Midheaven, in an alien sign, then she will be a harlot, and especially if Venus was in the sign of an infortune. **56**

---

[173] Cf. *Carmen* II.12, **5-6** and **12**.

[174] Something has gone very wrong in the middle of this sentence, so I have read it rather generically for: "…and the one looking at it the planet due to that place the position or its/their misfortune for it."

[175] For this paragraph, cf. *Carmen* II.2-II.3, **1-9**.

[176] Reading for Sahl's "and."

[177] This is probably if he is the lord of the Lot.

And it is like that if the lord of the triplicity of Venus was with Mars <in> the Midheaven or in the square or opposition of Mars: for then scandal and disgrace will afflict her. 57 And speak likewise in the nativities of men because of women.

58 If Mercury and Mars were both in the house of Mars[178] and Capricorn <in> the Midheaven, Mars is looking, then speak like that about the badness of [the women's] works and their scandal in their sexual unions.

59 And if you found Venus and the Moon in the seventh or the Midheaven, both of them looking <at> Mars, then speak likewise about Aries or Capricorn, for it indicates [women's] eagerness for men, or their affection for them, and especially if Mars looked at them or Mercury looked from the bound of Mars at them both from the square and the opposition: for he does not cease to rule over what is blameworthy in the matter of women.

60 In the matter of women's nativities you ought to look at their Ascendants: for if you found the Ascendant to be a house of the fortunes or a fortune is looking, then make a beautiful statement; and if it was a house of the infortunes and the infortunes looked, then state something else.

61 And[179] when you do not find Venus (in the nativities of women and men) having testimony and an aspect from Mars,[180] then they will be praiseworthy[181] in the matter of marriage,[182] and especially if Venus was in her share, with Jupiter, and her situation is seen by Saturn.

62 And[183] see who is with the Lot of women's marriage or in its square, for that is the indicator. 63 And if Mars was <on or squaring> the Lot,[184] then that woman will live immorally with men equally as with her own husband, and a male servant and disreputable man will live immorally with her. 64

---

[178] This seems to be Aries, according to the next sentence.

[179] This sentence has something missing or distorted in the middle. E seems to have the usual marks showing that something needs to be added or changed after "aspect from Mars" and "they will be."

[180] Omitting the following clause, which E bracketed with marks after "aspect from Mars," and "they will be": "from the square, and Mars [has] testimony from an aspect from Venus."

[181] Reading more grammatically for شيء حمد ("praise a thing"?), part of the awkwardness in the middle of this sentence.

[182] Reading التزويج for E's المرّيخ ("Mars").

[183] For this paragraph, cf. *Carmen* II.3, 2-9. Sentences 62-69 are from al-Andarzaghar.

[184] Reading with *Carmen* for "was the lord of the lord of" the Lot.

And if you found the lord of the Lot to be Saturn, in his house, then that is an old man who is her mother's brother[185] or her paternal uncle, or an old man of her own kind. **65** And if she was young then her first master will live immorally with her. **66** Now if Mars[186] was the lord of the Lot, then the one who lives immorally with her is not known. **67** <But if the lord of the Lot was Jupiter, he is>[187] a noble in her country. **68** And if it was Venus, <then it will be with pleasure and wine>.[188] **69** <And if it was Mercury>, then the one who is immoral with her will deceive her, then his matter will come to litigation with the Sultan, and especially if Mars looked at Mercury.

70 And[189] if she was with Mars, or <in the bound of Mars and>[190] Mars looked at her by an opposition, a woman will have a powerful passion for marriage, a harlot, deflowered, eager for men. **71** And if it was the nativities of men then it is harsher and worse, because his woman will be in this manner.

72 And[191] if Venus was in the house of Mars or[192] his bound, and you find Mars in the house of Venus, or one of them [is like that], she will have a powerful passion for men. **73** And if they were both eastern, that is more public for their passion and their immorality; and if they were both western, it is more secret for them. **74** Now if the Sun looked, their immorality will be public.

75 If[193] you found Mars looking at the Moon from a trine or square or opposition, then judge powerful passion and immorality.

76 If[194] Venus was in the Midheaven and Mercury and Mars looked, and the fortunes are not looking, he will have sex with women just as he has sex with men.[195]

---

[185] Reading more simply and with the sense of *Carmen* for "her brother from her mother."
[186] Reading for "Jupiter" with *Carmen*, as Jupiter belongs with nobility, and Mars with not being known. But see also Ch. 7.1, **97**, for a different interpretation of Mars in this passage. This shows that Sahl's sources were drawn both from 'Umar's transmission (or his Persian source), as well as a different Persian source of Dorotheus.
[187] Adding on the basis of *Carmen*.
[188] Adding here and in the next sentence on the basis of *Carmen*.
[189] For this paragraph, see *Carmen* II.4, **14**; this paragraph is repeated in Ch. 7.7, **9-10** below.
[190] Adding with the sense of *Carmen* II.4, **14** and Ch. 7.7, **9** below.
[191] For this paragraph, see *Carmen* II.4, **23-24**; it is repeated below in Ch. 7.7, **11-13**.
[192] Reading for "and," with *Carmen* II.4, **23** and Ch. 7.7, **11** below. Cf. also *Carmen* II.3, **14**.
[193] See also Ch. 7.7, **14** below. But this seems like too many aspect possibilities.
[194] For this sentence, cf. *Carmen* II.3, **16**.

77 And[196] if you found her in a sign of passion[197] or a convertible sign, and with her was the Moon, then she will have a powerful passion for men, and from her passion it will get to the point that she does business from having sex, and it is worse for that if Saturn was with her.

78 Now[198] if you found the Moon in Taurus, Pisces, Capricorn, or Aries, and you found Mercury with Mars, then they will be harlots, notorious in the marketplaces, and especially if Venus and the luminaries were in the stakes.

79 In the signs which are joined or split[199] she will be a bed for lesbians.

80 And[200] if [each] one of the luminaries trines its associate, it indicates many marriages of men to her.

81 If[201] Venus was with Jupiter and Mercury, and she is looking at the Ascendant, she will be <temperate and pure>.[202] 82 And if <she was with Mercury without Saturn>,[203] she will be elegant, <but> lewd, passionate for men. 83 And if Mars looked at Venus, she will be a shameless harlot. 84 Now if these two planets were in a feminine place, then she will speak to men and joke around with them without marriage[204] taking place; and if it was in a masculine place, there will be [both] marriage and joking. 85 And if Saturn was looking at them both and they were both[205] in a feminine position, that is bad, and especially for marriage; now if the position was eastern, masculine, she will have many [male] friends.[206] 86 And if Jupiter looked at them, it will

---

[195] This may be a reasonable delineation, but *Carmen* and Ch. 7.7, **16** say that he will befriend the women of *other* men, not that he will have sex with men. So perhaps this should be "sex with the women of other men."

[196] Cf. *Carmen* II.4, **22**.

[197] Perhaps the licentious or lecherous signs (Rhetorius Chs. 5 and 76). See Ch. 1.38, **18** above.

[198] For this sentence, cf. *Carmen* II.7, **16**.

[199] I am not sure if this should be connected to the previous sentence or not; but "split" signs might refer to being in aversion.

[200] For this sentence, cf. *Carmen* II.7, **18**.

[201] For this paragraph, cf. *Tet.* IV.5.

[202] Reading with Ptolemy, for an illegible word in **E**.

[203] Reading with the sense of Ptolemy, for "If Mercury was with Saturn."

[204] Or, sexual activity, here and below.

[205] That is, including Saturn as well (Ptolemy).

[206] It is unfortunate that the translator of Ptolemy here seems to be uninterested in the psychology of *Tet.*: there, Saturn indicates either being blameworthy (i.e., licentious) or a lover of censure. But as we know, the loudest moralizers and those most enthusiastic about pun-

be concealed. **87** And if Mercury looked, her matter will be in the open, with legal problems, and she will be masculine, resembling men.

88 And[207] if you found in the nativities of females[208] that Venus was in the seventh, opposing the Moon, she will be a lesbian; and if the native was male, he will be desirous of males, and especially if Venus is in Leo or in Virgo, or in the houses of the infortunes. **89** And if an infortune looked, it will be worse. **90** Now if Venus was under the rays, then it is worse and more wicked.

91 And if Venus was in the opposition of the Moon in a male sign, she will be a lesbian, marrying women.

92 The Moon and Venus in the square of the Ascendant, provokes women to passion.

93 Now[209] as for women who do not get pregnant, or their children follow immediately one upon the other,[210] the worst there could be is if Saturn was in the place of Venus, and Venus in the place of Saturn, if they were both in the Midheaven, or he came to her square; and the worst it could be is if the Moon was looking at them both, and Jupiter is not looking at them: for these are the nativities of sterile women, who do not have children. **94** And if Venus was in the sign of Leo, Capricorn, or Aquarius, it is likewise harsher for women, because they will not have husbands nor children. **95** And men who are examples of this will not have children, nor women; and if they did have women they will die, and perhaps their works will be like the works of women.

96 And[211] if Mars was opposed to Venus in the middle of the day or its quarter, and Jupiter was not looking at her, and Mars in the house of Venus and Venus in the house of Mars, then those women will be harlots, preferring [other] men to their husbands, and corrupting their children and the men. **97** And the men who are born with these nativities will enjoy being in the

---

ishing sexual sin are often themselves the greatest transgressors. So, Ptolemy is pointing to something notable about the dual nature of Saturn that is completely missing in the Arabic.

[207] For this paragraph, see *Carmen* II.7, **7-9**.

[208] Reading with *Carmen*, for "young males."

[209] This paragraph starts out like *Carmen* II.7, **10**, but then in **94-95** seems to reflect *Tet.* IV.5 (Robbins pp. 403-05).

[210] This seems to reflect Ptolemy, that they are overwhelmed by multiple miscarriages, premature births, and abortions.

[211] For this paragraph, cf. *Carmen* II.3, **14-18**. The "middle of the day" has no parallel there, and "its quarter" may mean "her square," as *Carmen* has it.

bed of others' women, and they will fornicate with their women. **98** And if Jupiter looked at them, he will cut off some of this.

The nativities of women and marriage with people of her own house

100 If you found Jupiter in the seventh, her brother will marry her; now if Venus was with Jupiter there, she will live with her husband in a good life. **101** And if Mars was with her, there will not be stability to their union, and the benefit of the union will be [accompanied by] loss, contention, and evil.

102 And[212] if Venus and Mercury were in Capricorn and Libra, she will marry a relative of hers. **103** If they were both in the Ascendant or Midheaven, or the Moon was with them, then her own father will marry her, or her paternal uncle, or the husband of her mother.

104 And[213] if Venus and Saturn were in the Ascendant or Midheaven, or Mars was with them, she will be a madam,[214] a worker in the types of immorality and its ways.

105 And if you found Mars in his own house or exaltation, then the native will marry one of his own relatives.

106 And[215] if you found the Lot <of wedding> with the lord of the Lot, or <the Moon> was looking with it, it indicates her marriage with relatives.

[Chapter 7.3:] The knowledge of the abundance of his women, & how much their number is, in the nativities of men & women

[al-Andarzaghar]

1 Be certain that you work with this[216] if you state the abundance or scarcity of women. **2** So[217] if you found Venus in an excellent place and a

---

[212] For this paragraph, cf. *Tet.* IV.5 (Robbins pp. 401-03). But Ptolemy has Venus with Saturn here, not Mercury.

[213] This sentence is again similar to *Tet.* IV.5 (Robbins pp. 401-03), but Mars is involved later, on Robbins p. 405.

[214] That is, a female pimp.

[215] For this sentence, cf. *Carmen* II.4, **19** and Ch. 7.2, **10** above. Ch. 7.2 has the Moon on, squaring, or opposing the Lot, which makes more sense.

[216] The text reads "it" (referring to the chapter) because the sentence really continues the thought of the title.

convertible sign, and the spear-bearing planets looked at her, and they are good in position, it indicates the abundance of his women.

3 And[218] if you found Venus in a sign having two bodies, then judge that he will marry not one, but two.

4 Now[219] as for the number [of wives], calculate from the Midheaven to Venus, and see how many signs are between them, and make it one women for every sign. **5** And if there were planets <in> those signs, then count one women for every planet, and state that he will marry such-and-such [many]. **6** Then, look with that at the two infortunes: for if they were in excellent positions and the fortunes not looking at them, Saturn chills his passion so it is inactive, and if Mars looked, then it kills.

7 And if you found Venus falling away from the Midheaven, then he will not be stable with women; and judge likewise for women if you found Mars falling away from the Midheaven.[220]

8 In[221] the nativities of women, count from the Midheaven to Mars, for by the number of those signs she will marry according to what I reported to you. **9** Now if Mars was in the Midheaven, then take from the Midheaven to Jupiter, then state that she will marry such-and-such [many] husbands.

[Chapter 7.4:] The knowledge of the <time of the> marriage of men with women

[al-Andarzaghar]

1 Begin[222] by looking at Jupiter, [to see] if he is alighting with the Lot of wedding[223] or looking at it from an opposition or square, or from the position

---

[217] For this sentence, cf. *Carmen* II.4, **10**, which however does not mention spear-bearing planets.
[218] For this sentence, cf. *Carmen* II.3, **13**.
[219] For this paragraph, cf. *Carmen* II.5, **1** and **3**. But note that Sahl is combining the method of counting planets (II.5, **1-3**) with the method of counting signs for the number of children (*Carmen* II.9, **2-4**).
[220] This should actually be "in the ninth," with Rhetorius Ch. 66 (p. 122) and as *BA* has it (III.7.1, **19**). *Carmen* II.5, **3** has Mars in the seventh, which is plausible too, but the confusion probably arose from the similarity of the undotted words "seventh" and "ninth" in Arabic.
[221] For this paragraph, cf. *Carmen* II.5, **2**.
[222] For this paragraph, cf. *Carmen* II.5, **7**.

of Venus in the root of the nativity,²²⁴ and he is in her opposition or in her square—if it was not with Saturn by union <or square or opposition>.²²⁵ **2** Now if Saturn did look at them from a square or opposition, then he will marry, but it chills the love and he will divorce, and that marriage will come to grief, or she will reside with him for three days²²⁶ and they will divorce.

3 And²²⁷ perhaps Jupiter will transit the lord of the sign²²⁸ in which Venus was in the root of the nativity, so he will marry.

4 And²²⁹ if the year made the rounds²³⁰ from the nativity, so that it reached the sign in which the Lot of wedding was, and Saturn is not looking, then he will marry; but if Saturn looked, then he will divorce.

5 And²³¹ if Saturn was strong in the Lot of wedding,²³² and in his course reached the sign in which he was in the root of the nativity,²³³ or he reached the place in which the Lot of wedding was at that time, he will marry a woman [who is] pleasant, agreeable, elevated. **6** And judge likewise for Jupiter too, if he reached the sign in which Venus was, and she looked from the square or opposition, for then he will marry—but she will not have prudence nor right actions.²³⁴

7 And²³⁵ Mars too, if you found him strong in the Lot of wedding,²³⁶ when he reaches Venus in his course or looks at her from a square or opposition:

---

²²³ In *Carmen*, this passage occurs immediately after the definition of the Venus-Descendant Lot described in Ch. 7.1, **10** above (see *Carmen* II.5, **1-2**). So, we should expect that this what Dorotheus means, not the Saturn-Venus Lot. But in Abū Ma'shar's version (*Gr. Intr.* VIII.4), it *is* the Saturn-Venus Lot.

²²⁴ *Carmen* II.5, **7** has the trine, square, or opposition of Venus.

²²⁵ Adding with *Carmen* II.5, **7**.

²²⁶ BP translate this (ثلث) as "thirty," which makes more sense for a trial marriage but the word for "thirty" is longer; nevertheless three days seems short and the word itself means "one-third"—and one-third of a day seems absurd.

²²⁷ For this sentence, cf. *Carmen* II.5, **8**.

²²⁸ In *Carmen* this is only the sign, not the lord of her sign.

²²⁹ Cf. *Carmen* II.5, **9**.

²³⁰ انتقلت. That is, "profects."

²³¹ For this paragraph, cf. *Carmen* II.5, **8-10**.

²³² I.e., he is in a strong place, rules the Lot, and looks at it (*Carmen* II.5, **10**).

²³³ *Carmen* only has him coming to the Lot, not his own place.

²³⁴ This is ambiguous. *Carmen* says that Jupiter helps because he and Venus indicate good wives—so one would expect the signification here to be positive. But Sahl's source must have thought that Saturn would still cause problems.

²³⁵ Cf. *Carmen* II.5, **12**.

then he will marry a women but say he will not remain with her [because] she will die.

8 Now[237] if Jupiter also reached the Lot which is taken from the Sun to the Moon by night and day <and projected from Venus>,[238] or he looked at it from a square or opposition, then with that he will marry a beautiful woman, neat, esteemed, youthful, pure.

9 Then, look at Venus in her easternization or westernization. **10** Now if she was eastern, then the native will marry in his youth; and if she was western, then he will marry in old age. **11** And look at her position in the quarters of the circle, and judge in accordance with that.

12 And look at the one accepting the management of the lord of the Ascendant or the lord of the seventh: for if it was near the Ascendant, that is at the beginning of the time;[239] and likewise in the four stakes.

13 Now as for the marriage of women, if you found Mars eastern, then she will marry in her adolescence and youth. **14** And if he was western, then she will marry after that, being advanced in age.[240] **15** And look at his position in the quarters of the circle as well.

[Ptolemy]

16 And[241] if you found the Sun in what is between the Ascendant and the Midheaven, she will marry in her youth and she will be friendly with young men; and in the other two quarters one looks concerning marriage <in her old age> or she will marry old men. **17** And likewise look for men from the Moon: if she was in the two eastern quarters, in what is between the Ascendant and the Midheaven, and what is opposite that, he will marry in his youth or he will be friendly with young women; and in the two western quarters he

---

[236] See footnote for **5**; but in *Carmen*, Mars is looking at Venus, and has nothing to do with the Lot.

[237] See *Carmen* II.6, **1**. Note that in *Carmen*, the following Lot is reversed by night.

[238] Adding with *Carmen* and BA.

[239] That is, of the lifespan.

[240] حولها في السّنّ.

[241] For this paragraph, cf. *Tet.* IV.5 (Robbins pp. 393-97).

will be late[242] in marriage or will marry a defective woman so that shame will accompany him from her.

18 And[243] if [the Moon] was in a sign having two bodies, he will marry more than one [woman]. **19** And the Sun [in such a sign] indicates that she will marry more than one [man], because the Sun indicates the husbands of women, and the Moon indicates the women of men.

[Chapter 7.5:] The knowledge of how the harmony is, of the woman to her husband & the husband to the woman

[al-Andarzaghar]

1 Look at the Ascendant of each of the two (of the first [person] and the second [person]), which sign it is.[244]

2 Then, look at the luminaries, in which sign you found them both.[245]

3 Third, look at the position of Venus and the Moon and the triplicities of them both, and how each one of them looks at its triplicity lord.[246]

4 Fourth, look at the luminaries and the fortunes, and what kind of places they have in the nativity.[247]

5 Fifth, look at the Lot of wedding: in which sign does it fall?[248]

6 Sixth, look at the luminaries and the infortunes, how they both fall in the nativities of women and their husbands.[249]

☽ ☌ ☋

7 So[250] then, look: for if you found the Ascendants of them both in a single sign, one will not see the erasing of what is between the two who are in agreement, so long as they both live.

---

[242] Reading with the sense of Ptolemy for Sahl's "be radiant with joy."
[243] For this paragraph, cf. *Tet.* IV.5 (Robbins pp. 395-97).
[244] This refers to **7** below.
[245] See broadly **9, 12**, and **14**.
[246] This refers to **8** below.
[247] This refers to **9-10** and **13** below.
[248] This refers to **11** below.
[249] This is not in the table of contents for *BA* III.7.1, **22**, but refers to **14-22** below.
[250] See *Carmen* II.5, **13**.

8 And[251] if you found Venus in the nativity of one of them in the position of the Moon in the nativity of the other, and the Moon in the nativity of one of them in the position of the Venus in the nativity of the other, and especially if the Moons of each of them looked at the other from the trine, one will never see the erasing of what is between the two who are in agreement.

9 Now[252] if you found, in the nativity of one of them, the Sun in the position of a fortune, [and] in the nativity of the other a fortune <in> the place of the Sun, [they are compatible].

10 And[253] judge likewise if you found, in the nativities of them both, the two fortunes in one sign, in a stake.

11 And[254] if you found the Lot of the wedding[255] of both in both of their nativities in one sign, then judge likewise.

12 But[256] if you found the two luminaries, in the nativity of one of them, in a single sign, <and you found> in the nativity of the other an infortune in that position, their matter will not cease to be corrupted until there is evil and tribulation and loss [for] each of the two because of his partner.

13 And if the Venus of one of them was with the other, it indicates harmony.

14 Now[257] if the luminary of one of the two was with an infortune <of the other>, it indicates a scarcity of harmony; and if it was a fortune, then speak of agreement; and likewise if the fortunes of them both were in the stakes.

15 And look:[258] if you found both luminaries in the trine of the Ascendant of one of them, or its sextile, the two natives will be in agreement as well as differ on the very same day, because that is what indicates the length of their union, and especially if the Moon in the nativity of the man fell on the place

---

[251] See *Carmen* II.5, **15**.

[252] See *Carmen* II.5, **16**.

[253] See *Carmen* II.5, **16**.

[254] See *Carmen* II.5, **16**.

[255] In *Carmen* this is the Lot of Spirit.

[256] See *Carmen* II.5, **16**. But *Carmen* does not require the luminaries to be together. This should probably be understood with **9** above, that if the Sun (or maybe the Moon, or preferably both) of one person is on the fortunes of the other, and vice versa, it is good; but if on the infortunes, bad.

[257] See *Carmen* II.5, **15**; also *Tet.* IV.5 (Robbins p. 399).

[258] For this paragraph, cf. *Tet.* IV.5 (pp. 397-99), but note that Ptolemy does not bring the Ascendant into it—rather, he is interested in the relationship of the luminaries to each other. But I do note that in his treatment of friendship, he does include synastry relationships involving the Ascendant. See Ch. 11.4 below.

of the Sun in the nativity of the woman: for that is what adds length in their union. **16** Now if both luminaries occurred in an opposition or square of the Ascendant of one of them, or the place of the luminaries in [that person's] nativity,[259] that is an indicator of the shortness of their union.

17 And[260] if you saw[261] something of the fortunes <in> the places which we mentioned as correspondences [between] the two nativities, they indicate that the woman will be loved, adored, [and] blessed by her husband, sufficiently provided for, abundant in the good, a caretaker for her husband. **18** And if the infortunes looked at them both, that woman will be a harlot, saucy, exasperating to her husband, deprived. **19** And if the fortunes looked at the positions which we mentioned [as being inharmonious],[262] <they will preserve the cohabitation>[263] and the pleasure of their union, and one of them will be sympathetic to the other, and will dissolve the evil, and it indicates that they will return to each other in what there is between them (in terms of disagreement). **20** And if the infortunes looked at that [bad configuration], their breakup will be based on quarreling, and she will be angry, and that is according to the abundance of the partnership which falls between them both. **21** <And if Mercury was with them, it indicates>[264] its evil and its being apparent. **22** And if Venus was with them, the reason for their breakup is debauchery, and what is like that (in terms of foulness).

23 And if one of them was born with Aries and the other with Cancer,[265] they will not be reconciled; Taurus and Leo reconcile, Gemini and Virgo do

---

[259] That is, that the luminaries of one opposed or squared those of the other.

[260] For this paragraph, cf. *Tet.* IV.5 (pp. 397-99). Ptolemy here considers four possibilities involving situations where the luminaries are in signs that (1) are configured by good aspects, suggesting a good union, and (2) anything else: aversion, squares, and oppositions, suggesting a bad one. So, he considers (**17**) benefics affecting a good configuration, and (**18**) malefics affecting it, (**19**) benefics affecting a bad configuration, and (**20**) malefics affecting it.

[261] **E** reads either "And if you saw Venus," or "And if Venus looked," but I have omitted it and read as "And if you saw," because this paragraph continues the thought of Ptolemy on the luminaries.

[262] In Ptolemy, these positions are when the luminaries are in signs that are in aversion to each other, or squaring or opposing each other.

[263] Adding on the basis of Ptolemy. **E** adds a short and largely unreadable phrase in the margin, the first part of which may read, "and it has."

[264] Adding on the basis of Ptolemy, who speaks here of public scandal.

[265] This probably refers to their Ascendants.

not reconcile [when there is] enmity from a stake from these signs, [and] enmity of the two stars of them both: they will not last nor be reconciled.

[Chapter 7.6:] The[266] knowledge of who will die before his partner, the man or the woman

[al-Andarzaghar]

1 Look at the Lot of wedding[267] and the sign it is in, and the aspect of the fortunes and infortunes to it.[268]

2 Second, look at the lord of the triplicity of Venus in the stakes, and its misfortune from the infortunes in the nativities of men; and as for the nativities of women, look at the lord of the triplicity of Mars.[269]

3 Third, look at the misfortune of Venus in the stakes of the nativities of men, and look in the nativities of women at the misfortune of Mars in the four stakes.

4 Fourth, look at the mixture of Venus in the west and east, or in her own places.[270]

5 (And make the indicator of the man in the nativities of women Mars, and in the nativities of men the indicator of their women is Venus.)

6 Then look:[271] for if you found the Lot of wedding[272] in the house of wedding or in the house of fathers, and the infortunes looked at them both, and the fortunes are not looking at them both, then it kills the women or they will die.

7 And[273] likewise if you found the <lord> of the triplicity of Venus in one of the two stakes (the stake of the earth or the stake of the west), and the infortunes made it unfortunate and Jupiter is not looking, then the women will die; and judge likewise <for Mars> in the nativities of women.

---

[266] Omitting "and as for."
[267] In *Carmen* II.6 this seems to be the Sun-Moon-Venus Lot (see **6** below).
[268] This refers to **6** below.
[269] This refers to **7** below.
[270] This refers to **8-10** below.
[271] Cf. *Carmen* II.6, **3**.
[272] Again, in *Carmen* this is from the Sun to the Moon by day (the reverse by night), projected from Venus.
[273] Cf. *Carmen* II.6, **4**.

8 Now[274] if you found Venus in the seventh or in the house of fathers, and the infortunes made her unfortunate and Jupiter is not looking, then his women will die; and judge likewise in the nativities of women if you found Mars thusly and the fortunes are not looking at him, for indeed their husbands will die.

9 And[275] if Venus was western and an infortune looked at her, then his women will die. **10** Now if Venus was in the twelfth and the sixth, and Jupiter looked from the tenth or from the trine,[276] then he will marry but his woman will die in any case, and <he will be sad>.[277]

※   ※   ※

11 Now if the lord of the seventh witnessed the lord of the eighth,[278] it indicates the separation of the husbands by death or divorce. **12** And likewise if the <lord> of the seventh was in the eighth, for it indicates the burial of his women and inheriting from them. **13** And if an infortune looked at it and that infortune was the lord of the eighth and the second, it indicates the death of his women.

14 If the lord of the seventh was under the rays, entering into burning, it indicates the death of the women; <and if Saturn was there, it will be>[279] by Saturnian pains. **15** And if Mars was there, it indicates their death in childbirth or choking.

16 And if you found an infortune with Venus or in her square, or an infortune looked at her, it indicates the separation of men and women; and it is harsher for that if Mars made the Moon unfortunate.

17 And[280] when you found the Lot of wedding or the lord of the triplicity of Venus or Venus in the seventh or fourth, looked at by an infortune, it indi-

---

[274] For this paragraph, cf. *Carmen* II.6, **6-7**.
[275] For this paragraph, cf. *Carmen* II.6, **8-9**.
[276] This is probably the superior square and superior trine.
[277] Adding on the basis of *Carmen*, for **E**'s uncertain (and undotted) phrase.
[278] **E** reads, "And if the lord of the seventh and the lord of the eighth witnessed," but the next sentence suggests this is about the relation between them, not their looking at something else.
[279] Tentatively adding in parallel with **15**.
[280] This paragraph repeats the basic ideas above, from *Carmen* II.6, **3-5**.

cates the death of his women; and likewise in the nativities of women Mars indicates the death of their husbands.

[Chapter 7.7:] The statement on immorality & fornication, & passion & fornication in men & women
And it has six items

[al-Andarzaghar]

1 The first item: look at Venus, Jupiter, and Mars, and the lord of the triplicity of Venus, in the signs.[281]

2 Second, look at Venus and Mars in the bound of each of them, in the nativities of men and women.[282]

3 Third, look at Venus and Mars, how they are exchanged in places, and that is if Venus is in the house of Mars and his bound, and Mars in the house of Venus and her bound, and look at [their being] eastern and western.[283]

4 The fourth item: look at Mars and his position relative to the Moon, and the position of Venus from Mercury and Mars in the nativities of men and women.[284]

5 The fifth item: look at the trine of the Sun[285] <in> the nativities of men and women.[286]

6 The sixth item: look at the Moon in the signs and her union with Mercury, Mars, and Venus.[287]

7 And[288] know that Venus indicates passion from women, and Mars from men: so if they were in the stakes, they indicate <that he is> outrageous in

---

[281] This paragraph is evidently missing in Sahl, because while it is not found here, it does correctly appear as the first paragraph in *BA* III.7.8. So, I have added my summary of it as **9** below.

[282] This refers to **10-11** below.

[283] This refers to **12-14** below.

[284] This refers to **16-19** below.

[285] That is, his trine with the Moon: see **20** below. (This could be read as "triplicity," but I understand it as "trine.")

[286] This refers to **20** below.

[287] See Ch. 7.2, **78**; but cf. also **24-25** below.

[288] Sentences **7-8** are not in *BA*, but see Ch. 7.6, **5** above, and **23** below.

[his] offense regarding women, and likewise if it was in the second image of Pisces. **8** And if they were in what follows the stakes, looking at each other from a trine or square, they indicate good manners and friendship and eagerness for what is virtuous.

[Items 1-5, from al-Andarzaghar]

<**9** If Venus was in the sixth or twelfth, looked at by Jupiter and Mars, or she is with the lord of the Lot in the Midheaven, the woman will be involved in prostitution and abortion, but then they will marry harmoniously.>[289]

10 Now[290] if Venus was with Mars, or she was in the bound of Mars and[291] Mars looked at her from the opposition, the woman will have powerful passion for sex, a harlot, scandalous, eager for men. **11** And if it was the nativity of a man, then it is harsher and worse, because his woman will be in this way.

12 And[292] if Venus and Mars were each of them in the house of its associate, exchanged, so that you find Venus in the house of Mars (or in his bound), and you find Mars in the house of Venus (or her bound), then the native will have powerful passion; and if it was a woman, likewise. **13** And if they were eastern, it is harsher for their passion and their debauchery; and if they were western, his passion will be hidden.[293] **14** And if the Sun looked, his passion will be public (and likewise the woman in all of that).

15 And[294] if you found Mars looking at the Moon from a trine, square, and opposition, then judge powerful passion for him, and likewise [for the nativity of] a woman.

16 And[295] if Venus was with Mercury and Mars in one sign, the native will have much sexual intercourse and fornication. **17** And if they were thus in

---

[289] See footnote to **1** above.
[290] For this paragraph, cf. *Carmen* II.4, **14**; this paragraph also appeared above in Ch. 7.2, **70-71**.
[291] Reading for "or," with *Carmen* II.4, **14**.
[292] For this paragraph, see *Carmen* II.4, **23-24**; it also appeared above in Ch. 7.2, **72-74**.
[293] The Arabic reads, "his passion will be hidden from him," but *Carmen* is clear that the passion of both will be hidden from others.
[294] This sentence also appeared above in Ch. 7.2, **75**. But this seems like too many aspect possibilities.
[295] Cf. *Carmen* II.3, **15-16**. This paragraph is repeated slightly differently in Ch. 7.2, **76**.

the Midheaven,²⁹⁶ then he will be debauched towards the woman of his companion, a female friend. **18** Now if Venus was in the Midheaven and Mercury and Mars looked at her and the fortunes are not looking, then it is likewise.

19 And²⁹⁷ judge concerning Venus being with the Moon in the fourth, that he will have much sexual intercourse and marrying, and it is harsher for that if Mars or Saturn was looking at them both.

20 If²⁹⁸ the Sun and Moon were looking at each other from the trine, then he will have much sexual intercourse with women.

21 If²⁹⁹ Venus and Mercury were at the lowest point of the earth, in a male sign, he will marry a woman <who is not> good.

22 If³⁰⁰ the Lot of Fortune and the Invisible occurred in a sign stimulating sexual intercourse,³⁰¹ then he will associate with many women. **23** The signs of little marriage³⁰² are Aries, <Taurus>,³⁰³ Leo, Capricorn,³⁰⁴ and the middle of Pisces,³⁰⁵ Libra (and that is the rising of "the greedy,"³⁰⁶ rising with it).

---

²⁹⁶ Omitting "and Mercury and Mars looked at them both" or "and Mercury and Mars looked at her." Sahl or his source has redundantly copied this phrase from the next sentence.

²⁹⁷ See Rhetorius Ch. 66, which however has Venus and the Moon in the seventh.

²⁹⁸ See Rhetorius Ch. 66 (p. 121), and *Carmen* II.7, **19**; it appears slightly differently in Ch. 7.2, **80** above. *BA* III.7.8, **9** has these in the house of pleasure and appetite or a convertible sign.

²⁹⁹ Sentences **21-23** are not in the Latin *BA*, but since **21** follows immediately after the previous sentence in Rhetorius (pp. 121-22), they were probably in the original Arabic. Rhetorius does not mention Mercury, and the indication is for women of ill repute.

³⁰⁰ For this paragraph, see Rhetorius Chs. 75-76 (p. 125).

³⁰¹ Reading for "marriage."

³⁰² Again, little marriage but much sexual intercourse.

³⁰³ Adding with Rhetorius.

³⁰⁴ Rhetorius has "part of" Capricorn, probably the goat part.

³⁰⁵ Sahl might be thinking of the middle decan of Pisces, mentioned above.

³⁰⁶ That is, the fixed star Capella, which is near Gemini (Rhetorius says, "the Goat," another name for Capella, which means a she-goat). So when Libra rises, Capella will be near the Midheaven.

[Item 6: The Moon and other planets]

24 And if Venus was in a stake, in a feminine sign, and she is looking at Mars, and he is with[307] Mercury, then he will be of those who <do not> love women.[308]

25 And[309] if Venus was in a desiring sign (and that is Aries, Taurus, Capricorn, and Pisces) with an infortune, burned, she indicates scandals; and it is harsher for him if the other infortune looked down upon them; and likewise if she was burned and an infortune looked down upon her.

ঙ ৫ ৫

26 And[310] likewise if she was in the stake of the west, [in] the opposition of the Moon, and especially if she was in Leo, Virgo, or in the stake[311] of an infortune. **27** Now if the infortune looked along with that, it is harsher for him; and worse if with that she was burned.

28 And[312] if the Sun and Moon were in Aquarius, Pisces, Capricorn, Taurus, or Aries with the Lot of wedding, she indicates scandals.[313] **29** And likewise if Venus was in any of [those signs], made unfortunate, and it is

---

[307] Reading for "leaving."
[308] That is, in a male nativity.
[309] Cf. *Carmen* II.7, **5-6**. But *Carmen* has her first in these signs, under the rays, and with both infortunes (**5**), but secondly in these signs and overcome by one of the infortunes (**6**). A variation on this sentence appears below, Ch. 7.8, **11**. See also Rhetorius Ch. 66 (p. 121), which has a sentence very close to the first scenario mentioned here, and *Carmen* II.7, **5**.
[310] For this paragraph, see *Carmen* II.7, **7-9**. By "likewise," *Carmen* explains that in a female nativity it means lesbianism, and in a male nativity it means male homosexuality.
[311] *Carmen* has, "house."
[312] This sentence is clearly based on *Carmen* II.7, **12-15**. But Sahl's version is both clearer and more ambiguous. *Carmen* begins (**12**) by warning of either both luminaries being in feminine signs, or one of them being there while being looked at by one of the infortunes. But then (**13**) it says that if "it" is in the signs listed here, along with the Lot of *sickliness*, in a feminine sign, then it also indicates homosexuality. So *Carmen* is not clear as to whether the "it" is a luminary or an infortune, and I have my doubts about the Lot of sickliness (probably the Lot of chronic illness): Sahl's Lot of wedding or marriage makes more sense, although I am not sure which one is meant.
[313] Or rather, homosexuality (*Carmen*).

harsher for that if Mercury was made unfortunate along with that. **30** And if Jupiter looked at something of that, he dissolves it.³¹⁴

31 And when you find Mars with Venus or in her house, then state in that [that] the native will love amusement and an abundance of passions. **32** Now if Venus was devoid of Mars, then judge for him the contrary of that.

33 Venus³¹⁵ in the house of Saturn or with Saturn. **34** And if Venus was in the house of Saturn or with Saturn, then he will have sex with disgraced women, and he will be of those who do not take pleasure in women, and he will not cease to be in toil and hardship, along with being of those who do not take pleasure in food, clothing, and what is pleasant. **35** But if Venus was in her own house, eastern, inspecting Jupiter, it multiplies what is pleasant³¹⁶ of works upon him, and he will have a pleasant livelihood.

[Planets in the faces: Rhetorius]

36 The faces which stir up marriage³¹⁷ and lust if one of the planets I will name for you, is in it:

37 If³¹⁸ the Sun was in the third face of Aries, and in the first and second face of Cancer, and in Virgo (the third face), and in Pisces (the third face).

38 And³¹⁹ likewise if the Moon was in the first face and the third of Aries, [it is] with sinfulness and corruption; and in Leo in the third face, in the lowest part of the earth; and in Libra, the first and third face.

39 And³²⁰ likewise Mars in the third face of <Aries, and in the first and third face of Libra.>

40 <And³²¹ likewise Mercury in the first decan of> Libra, and in Capricorn (the first face).

---

³¹⁴ Or, he "makes it lawful" (حلّه).
³¹⁵ For **33-34**, cf. *Carmen* II.4, **13**.
³¹⁶ Tentatively reading for "foul," which does not make astrological sense.
³¹⁷ Again, this should probably be read as "sex."
³¹⁸ For this paragraph, cf. Rhetorius Ch. 69 (p. 124). But Rhetorius's list does not exactly match Sahl's.
³¹⁹ For this paragraph, cf. Rhetorius Ch. 70 (p. 124). But Rhetorius's list does not exactly match Sahl's. Some of this may have gotten mixed up with Rhetorius Ch. 75 (p. 125), on the Ascendant in the faces.
³²⁰ For this paragraph, cf. Rhetorius Ch. 73 (p. 124); the manuscript has blended this with the next sentence regarding Mercury, so I have added the missing material from Rhetorius.
³²¹ See the previous footnote; this is from Rhetorius Ch. 74 (p. 124).

41 And[322] likewise if <Venus>[323] was in <the first face of> Aries, the native will be a lover of scandal, eager for women. **42** And at the beginning[324] of Gemini he will have much gluttonous sex.[325] **43** She being in the first face of Leo, falling or made unfortunate, she indicates he is indecent in [his] eagerness for sex, with the corruption of the marriage. **44** The end of Leo indicates the scandals of women, and distress in that. **45** The first face of Scorpio [indicates] loathing because of women and distress in that. **46** And likewise the first face of Cancer, and the first face of Aquarius. **47** And the third of Pisces indicates that he will be eager for women, having sex with many women.

Chapter [7.]8: The sodomite & the moral person

[al-Andarzaghar]

1 You look in this from five items.
2 First, you look at Venus in the houses of the planets, if she is in a bad place.[326]
3 Second, [look] at the Lot of wedding in the house of Mercury.[327]
4 Third, you look at Mercury and Mars, if they exchanged [places] or they inspected each other from a square or opposition.[328]
5 Fourth, you look at Venus and the Moon in the places, and the position of the infortunes in the stakes, and [if] the luminaries were in the feminine signs.[329]

---

[322] For this paragraph, cf. Rhetorius Ch. 68 (pp. 122-23). Apart from **46** (which are the faces of Venus), the faces in this paragraph are those of the infortunes.
[323] Reading with Rhetorius: the Arabic has "he."
[324] This should be "middle," with Rhetorius.
[325] مع سلا. Rhetorius speaks of being a sodomite, lewd, shameless, and sex-mad. This could also be read as a "group," viz. group sex.
[326] This refers to **8** below.
[327] This refers to **9** below.
[328] This refers to **10** below.
[329] This refers to **11-13** below.

6 The fifth item, in the nativities of women. **7** Look in the nativities of women at Venus and the luminaries, if they were in male signs and the infortunes in the stakes.[330]

[Items 1-4, from al-Andarzaghar]

8 Then,[331] begin by looking at Venus: for if she was in the house of Mercury, bad in position,[332] then judge for him that he is a sodomite.

9 And[333] speak like that if you found the Lot of wedding in the house of Mercury and Mercury was in a male sign, in a stake.

10 And[334] if Mars and Mercury exchanged [houses], each one of them in kinship, judge that he is a sodomite; <and likewise if Mercury looked at Mars from a square or opposition>.[335]

11 And[336] if you found Venus in a desiring sign (and that is Capricorn, Pisces, Aries, and Taurus), and one of the infortunes looked at her, and especially if she was under the rays, then judge for him that he is a sodomite.

12 And[337] if you found Venus in those signs, western or eastern, and Saturn or Mars looked at her, and she looked at them both from the stake of wedding or the house of fathers, or from the sixth, then judge that he is a sodomite. **13** And[338] likewise if Venus was in the eighth from the Ascendant.

---

[330] This refers to **26-29** below.

[331] See *Carmen* II.7, **2**.

[332] **E** reads as though it is Venus in a bad place, but *Carmen* has Mercury in the bad place.

[333] Cf. *Carmen* II.7, **3**.

[334] See *Carmen* II.7, **4**.

[335] Adding with BA and **4** above.

[336] See *Carmen* II.7, **5**. A variation on this sentence appeared above, Ch. 7.7, **24**.

[337] For this paragraph, cf. *Carmen* II.7, **6-10**. But this sentence departs a great deal. For example, the "eastern" and "western" might be a garbled error for II.7, **7**, where Venus is in the west, opposing the Moon in the east. But because it has Venus in the seventh or fourth later in the sentence (which is however similar to *Carmen* II.7, **9**), it might be from somewhere else.

[338] Again, this seems similar to *Carmen* II.7, **10**, which however has "the twelfth." However, this phrase about her in the eighth also appears in *BA* III.7.13, **6**, so the error is Sahl's.

14 If[339] Venus was in the house of Mercury and his bound, and the Moon was in the bound of Mars, then he will be a lover of sodomy. **15** And if he[340] was with Venus, then he will be a lover of males and amusement, and with that he will be eager for women. **16** And it is harsher for that if each of the two was in the bound of the other, or each of them was in the exaltation of one of them, and Jupiter is not looking at them both, and the infortunes are looking. **17** And it is more unfortunate for that if Mars is looking, and more evil if Saturn or[341] Mars are looking. **18** If they were both in the house of Mercury and his bound, and he[342] is looking at Venus, and in a male sign, then it indicates sexual intercourse in the rear. **19** And likewise if the Sun was in the bound of Mercury and especially if Jupiter is not looking; for when he does look, he dissolves that and forgives [him] for it.

20 And[343] likewise if Venus was in the seventh, opposing the Moon: for she indicates that he is desirous of males, and especially if Venus was in Leo and Virgo, or the houses of the infortunes. **21** And if the infortunes looked, then it is harsher. **22** And if Venus was under the rays, then it is worse.

23 And[344] more wicked is if Mercury had testimony in the Ascendant and he was made unfortunate, and it is harsher for that if he was in a stake, for then he is a lover of youths.

24 And if the lord of the seventh was made unfortunate in the Ascendant, then the native will be effeminate,[345] giving himself over to sexual union, be it to a youth or maid.

The knowledge of moral people and the effeminate [from al-Andarzaghar]

26 If[346] Venus was in the sixth and the Moon in the twelfth, in the nativities of men, he will be effeminate, resembling women, and especially if Saturn and Mars looked at Venus.

---

[339] Sentences **14-19** do not appear here in *BA*, so they were probably added by Sahl from another source.
[340] This is probably Mercury, but could be Mars.
[341] This should probably be read as "and."
[342] This may be Mercury.
[343] For this paragraph, cf. *Carmen* II.7, **7-9**. It appears here also in *BA* (in a kind of mixture with **26**).
[344] Sentences **23** and **24** also seem to be inserted by Sahl, as they do not appear here in *BA*.
[345] I would expect it to be the other way around: the lord of the Ascendant in the seventh.

27 And[347] if you found Venus in the sixth and twelfth, and Saturn and Mars in a female sign in a stake, then he will be effeminate,[348] especially if the two luminaries were in a male sign; and if Venus was in a female sign, he will be moral.[349]

[Item 5: Venus and luminaries in female nativities]

28 And if in the nativities of women the luminaries were in a male sign, and if Saturn and Mars looked at them, if they were in the stakes or one of them looked from a stake, from a square or opposition, then judge that she will be a lesbian woman. **29** In the nativities of men, if they were the contrary, and you saw something of what I mentioned, he will be effeminate in manners.

30 And[350] if Venus was in the house of Saturn and Saturn in the house of Venus, in the stake of the west or the stake of the earth, and the sixth and twelfth, then then native will be effeminate, giving himself over to sexual union. **31** And Venus indicates likewise if she was falling or in a bad place, and the infortunes were in the female signs, in a stake: for the native will be soft, effeminate; and it is worse for that if the Sun and Moon were in a feminine sign.
32 If Venus was in the house and bound of the infortunes, in the seventh place, then the native will do the work of women. **33** And likewise if Saturn was in the house of Venus, in the stake of the west, inspecting Venus. **34** And likewise if Venus was with Saturn in the house of Mercury, and Mars looked at them: for then he will be effeminate, corrupt in sexual union.

---

[346] This is similar to *Carmen* II.7, **7-8**.

[347] For this paragraph, cf. *Carmen* II.7, **10-13**. But this is repeated in another way in **30-31** and **35-37** below, as well.

[348] Reading with *Carmen* for "moral."

[349] This last part seems to be the reverse of what *Carmen* says: namely, that if the luminaries are in a feminine sign it will be worse. The same thing goes for the next sentence, which seems likewise switched around.

[350] For this sentence, cf. *Carmen* II.7, **10-11**. It is repeated yet again, starting at **35**.

35 And[351] when you find Venus in the house of Saturn, and Saturn in her house, in the stake of the west, and the stake of the earth, and the sixth and the twelfth, she indicates deviance. **36** And likewise if she was falling or she was in a position not appropriate for her, and an infortune was in a female stake. **37** And it is more wicked for him if with that the luminaries (or one of them) was in a female sign, in the aspect of an infortune.

Courage and the hardness of the soul

39 You[352] see the courage and the hardness of the soul from the advancement of the infortunes, if they were advancing in the circle, safe, and the native is effeminate.[353]

40 And if he was born and <and you found> the Moon and the lord of the Ascendant falling, it resembles the nativities of women; and a woman will be masculine, resembling men.

41 If you found in the nativity when he was born [that] the planets [are] in the masculine region of the quarters of the circle, and the planets male in themselves, the native will be mighty in his soul, [uncertain], powerful in courage, complete, perfect. **42** And if a woman was this way, in the distribution of males, she is strong, masculine, short-lived, similar to men, of bad character, not silent in society, not tall.

43 And if the planet was feminine, in a feminine area of the quarters of the circle, in the nativities of males, the man will [tend] towards weakness, be unhappy, a coward, effeminate in every work he does, not developing properly, and he will do the works of women. **44** And if that was in the nativities of women, she will be a virtuous woman, modest, long-lived, submissive,[354] devoted,[355] well occupied with her husband, of good character, having good sense and knowledge.

---

[351] For this paragraph, see *Carmen* II.7, **9-11**. See the almost identical version above (**30-31**), and a similar version at **27-29**.

[352] For this sentence, see also Ch. 10.3, **17**.

[353] Meaning unclear. But this could also be read as "even if" the native is effeminate: in other words, even if there are other indications of femininity or weakness (مخنّث), the infortunes being like this will still show courage and hardness.

[354] Or, "calm, appeasing."

[355] Tentatively and broadly reading نذرة for what looks like ندرة ("a rarity"). The root I prefer here specifically means to make religious vows or offerings.

45 And indeed that is known from the eastern planets and the western ones, appearing from under the rays: because if the planets were under the rays, they are weak, not having life.

46 And men who are born with nativities like those of women, if the luminaries were in feminine signs, and Jupiter is not looking at them, then those are the natives with whom one acts as one does with women.

Chapter 8: On the causes of death

[Chapter 8.1: Introduction]

1 Look[1] in that from the eighth place from the Ascendant, and know what is the essence of the eighth[2] sign (or [others] besides it),[3] who its lord is, who is in it, and who is looking at it from the opposition.

2 Then,[4] look from the first lord of the triplicity of the <stake> under the earth, and from the lord of the bound of the seventh, and [look] at the Lot of death according to the essence of the place [it is in] and its lord, and the one looking at it—let the judgment in it be in that manner.

Item	Topic	Sahl passage
1	8th and its lord	8.1, **1, 3-17**
2	8th, its lord, aspecting planets	8.4, **1-6**
3	Triplicity lord of IC	8.1, **2**; 8.2, **67**
4	Lot of death	(8.6)
5	8th, its lord, aspecting planets	8.4, **15**
6	Lord 7th and its bound	8.2, **65, 70-73, 92**
7	Moon and infortunes	8.2, **12-13, 82**
8	Lord of pre-natal lunation	8.2, **14-16**
9	Lot of killing	8.2, **17-18**
10	Lot of Fortune, its lord, 8th	8.2, **19**
11	Lords of ASC and Moon	8.2, **85**
12	Lot of Fortune burned	--
13	Fortieth day of birth	8.7, **5-6**
14	Contrary-to-sect infortunes, elongation of Mercury, Venus	8.2, **23-27**
--	Head and Tail	8.2, **20-22**

Figure 62: Sahl's use of al-Andarzaghar in *Nativities* Ch. 8[5]

---

[1] For this sentence, cf. *Carmen* IV.3, **2-3**; also Rhetorius Ch. 77 (pp. 126-27).
[2] Reading for "fifth."
[3] This refers to the essences of other signs as well: see below.
[4] Cf. Rhetorius Ch. 77 (pp. 125-26).
[5] Unlike other chapters, Sahl has pretty much thrown away al-Andarzaghar's organization of this material. The *Book of Aristotle* gives 14 items to examine (and an unnumbered one,

[The eighth and its lord]

3 Now[6] if you found Saturn to be lord of the eighth (and it is the indicator of death), or Saturn was in that sign or looking at it from a square or opposition, and he was made unfortunate <in> what is not his own place, then the death of that native will be outside his country, from moisture and pain of the belly, and from chills and a long illness, and accompanying fever, and paralysis of the body. **4** Now if with that Saturn was in a moist sign, then the native's manner of death will be from his mother's belly, or he will die by drowning in the water, in the bellies of fish. **5** And if Saturn was in a place declining from the stakes, then his manner of death will be from falling from a height or a tree. **6** Now if Saturn was in a mountainous sign, his manner of death will be in the mountains and deserts and other places [like that]. **7** And if the Sun was with Saturn, then he will die from falling from a place raised up high.

8 And[7] if the ruler of the matter of death was Mars,[8] then his manner of death will be in relation to fire or from iron, or wolves and predatory animals, or in burning, blood, or heat, or by robbers or enemies killing him, so that the cause of his death will be from that. **9** Now if Mars was with the Sun (and especially in a house of Jupiter) or the Sun looked at him, and [Mars] is made unfortunate, then his killing will be at the command of kings who are angry with him, so they will kill him or behead him in shackles, or he will be crucified upon a post or his middle cut by a sword, or a lion and a predatory animal will kill him, and especially if that sign was Sagittarius. **10** Now if you found Mars in one of the signs of trees and the airy ones, then likewise say that his death will be by killing or crucifixion, and especially if he was eastern. **11** Now if Mars was in a watery sign, then that death of his will be from blood or the inner corruption of the stomach.

---

involving the Nodes). Most of these are scattered throughout Ch. 8, with the exception of #12 (totally omitted). For #4 Sahl has substituted Māshā'allāh's section on the Lot of death for al-Andarzaghar's, which probably reflected *Carmen* IV.3, **16** and Rhetorius Ch. 77 (p. 125). And we can see why he did so, because those passages simply give the calculation of the Lot and state that one should look at the sign, its lord, and planets looking at it (and if a malefic looks, it signifies a violent death, according to Rhetorius). This table shows the location of the most likely corresponding passages in Sahl for al-Andarzaghar's items.

[6] For this paragraph, cf. *Carmen* IV.3, **4-7** and Rhetorius Ch. 77 (p. 126).

[7] For **8-9**, cf. *Carmen* IV.3, **8-9**.

[8] That is, if he is the lord of the eighth (per *Carmen*).

12 Now[9] if Mercury was the ruler of the matter of death, and he was made unfortunate, then his death will be by reason of a book or knowledge, or his slave will kill him.

13 And[10] if Jupiter was the ruler of the matter of death and he was made unfortunate, then his death will be by the command of kings and their anger at him, or from those comparable to them. **14** But if he was not made unfortunate, then he will die a beautiful death.

15 And[11] if Venus was the ruler of the matter of death and Jupiter was not looking, then his death will be by poison in the drink of women and through relationships with[12] women and from fever.

16 And[13] if the Sun was the ruler of that and he was made unfortunate, falling, then he will die from fevers or something like that, from falling from a place, or being overwhelmed in a mob or drowning in water, or in something of fevers, or the cause of his death will be something like that.

17 And if the Moon was the ruler of the matter of death, then his death will be from illness or because of fathers.

[Chapter 8.2:] On nativities in which their manner of death is by means of iron or something else, from an adversary <or> tribulation

1 When you find Mars in the seventh or eighth, then his death will be from anger or killing. **2** And if you found Mars in the eighth and he is making the lord of the eighth unfortunate, then likewise say that it will be by killing. **3** And when you find Mars in the eighth, in a female sign, and the fortunes not looking at him, then he will be killed by iron, the sword, or something else. **4** And if you found Mars by day in the Midheaven, then say it is an example of that. **5** And if you found Mars looking at the Ascendant and the Moon in a square or opposition, then say that his death will be through a

---

[9] For this paragraph, cf. Rhetorius Ch. 77 (p. 127).
[10] For this paragraph, cf. Rhetorius Ch. 77 (p. 127).
[11] For this paragraph, cf. Rhetorius Ch. 77 (p. 127).
[12] بأسباب. But this could also simply mean "because of" or "through the motives of."
[13] For this paragraph, cf. Rhetorius Ch. 77 (p. 126), which however is rather shorter.

crime; and likewise if you found Mars turned away from[14] the lord of the Ascendant.

6 And if you found various planets in the tenth place, then his death will be in a mob, or [by] toil or drowning or something like that.

7 If you found Saturn under the earth and the Moon in the Midheaven, and Mercury in the stake of the west, then he will be killed by the enmity of groups, and especially if Venus and Jupiter were not in the stakes and not looking at the Moon and the Ascendant. **8** Now if in addition Mars was with Saturn then it is worse and harsher, because cutting or death by fire will afflict him.

9 And[15] if you found the degree of the house of wedding making the Ascendant and its lord unfortunate, and the Moon not looking at the Ascendant, and the fortunes are not looking, then the native will kill himself.

10 Now[16] if the Moon was full of glow in the Midheaven, and you found Mars and the Sun in the house of fathers, and the fortunes not looking, then he will be killed in an ugly way and burned by fire while alive.

11 And[17] if you found the Moon full, in the signs of mutilated limbs, in the house of women, and Mars in the Midheaven, and the fortunes not looking at him, he will die a harsh death through killing in war or robbers will kill him.

12 And[18] look at Mars, Mercury, and Saturn if they were with the Moon in a single degree, for then that native will be killed in an ugly way.

---

[14] That is, in aversion to.

[15] This sentence seems to be based on *Carmen* IV.3, **22**, but is confused here. In *Carmen* it reads: "Now if the seventh and its lord were unfortunate, and the lord of the seventh was looking at the house of life, and the Moon was looking at the house of life, then that native will kill himself with his own hand."

[16] Cf. Rhetorius Ch. 77 (pp. 127-128).

[17] For this paragraph, cf. Rhetorius Ch. 77 (p. 128), but also *Carmen* IV.3, **23**: the Arabic here appears to be a combination of the two. In Rhetorius, the Full Moon is indeed in the mutilated signs without the aspect of the fortunes, but she is dominated by (i.e., overcome by) Mars: if so, then the example is wrong because the Moon in the seventh would overcome Mars rather than he overcoming her (as Rhetorius requires). But in *Carmen*, Mars is in the tenth "but not in the stakes," and the Moon in the seventh (as Sahl has it here), with the infortunes looking at her, but without any mention of the mutilated signs.

[18] For this paragraph, cf. Rhetorius Ch. 77 (pp. 126 and 128). In one sentence (p. 126), the Moon is with both infortunes (but not Mercury) in the same *sign*, whether angular or succeedent. But on p. 128, all three of these planets are with the Moon on the fortieth day after birth (similar to Ch. 8.7, **6** below).

13 And[19] if the Moon was in the house of fathers, in Aries or Scorpio, and the infortunes looked at her, and the fortunes are not looking, then he will be killed in an ugly way.

14 Look[20] at the sign of the meeting and opposition:[21] for if the infortunes looked at the sign of the meeting or opposition, and the fortunes are not looking, then he will be killed in shackles. **15** And likewise, if the lords of those two[22] are not looking at their houses, and the infortunes are looking at them both, then he will be killed in an ugly way.

16 And[23] if you found Mercury looking at the opposition from his unhealthiness[24] or the infortunes looked at him, then he will be killed in shackles.

17 The[25] Lot of killing: then look at the Lot of the killer, which is taken from the lord of the Ascendant to the Moon by day (and by night the reverse), and is cast out from the Ascendant. **18** Now if the Moon alone looked at the lord of the Lot,[26] and especially if it was in a sign with a severed limb, he will be killed in shackles.

19 And[27] look also at the lord of the Lot <of Fortune> and the lord of the eighth: for if each one of them was opposing its associate,[28] then he will be killed in shackles.

20 And[29] look also at the Head of the Dragon and its Tail: for if you found the Head in the eighth and Saturn and Mars and Mercury looking, then he will be killed in an ugly way, whether he will be decapitated, or his eyes will be pierced by iron. **21** Now if the Sun looked at them, he will be chronically ill in his vision or in his legs, but if it was like that and <the fortunes

---

[19] For this paragraph, cf. Rhetorius Ch. 77 (pp. 128-29).
[20] For this paragraph, cf. Rhetorius Ch. 77 (p. 125).
[21] That is, the pre-natal New or Full Moon.
[22] The "two" and "both" here seem to refer to the signs in which the pre-natal meeting or opposition was.
[23] For this paragraph, cf. Rhetorius Ch. 77 (p. 129). There, Mercury is opposing the Full Moon and looked at by the infortunes.
[24] That is, his detriment.
[25] For this paragraph, cf. Rhetorius Ch. 77 (p. 125).
[26] Rhetorius has her looking at the Lot itself, not its lord.
[27] Cf. Rhetorius Ch. 77 (p. 128).
[28] That is, if the lord of one was opposing the lord of the other.
[29] For this paragraph, cf. Rhetorius Ch. 77 (p. 127).

looked>³⁰ while the infortunes are not looking at them, he will die a <fine> death. **22** And if you found the Tail³¹ in the eighth, and you found Jupiter, Venus, and Mars in a stake of that sign, then he will be killed in shackles.

23 And³² if you found Saturn in the Ascendant and Mars in the seventh, predatory animals will eat him. **24** And if you found Saturn in the house of fathers (in a birth of the night) and Mars in the Midheaven, and the fortunes are not looking, then he will be crucified and the birds will eat him.

25 And³³ if you found Mercury going far from the Sun by 24°, then he will be killed in an ugly way. **26** And if the Moon was at the end of her stake (which is 180°), and she had a share in his birth, then he will die a bad death just as the stars indicate if they were at the end of their stake. **27** Now if the distance of Venus from the Sun was 47°, then he will be killed in an ugly way.

28 And if Saturn was made unfortunate in the eighth by Mars, someone who loves him will kill him; now if the Sun witnessed him, [then] likewise say crucifixion or the badness of his killing.

29 And if Mars was in the eighth with the Tail and a fortune together, they indicate his killing by means of injustice, with blood [and] falsehood. **30** Now if he was in it by day, it indicates poverty and diseases; and if he was in it by night, then heat and prostitution along with a sudden death or killing.

31 And³⁴ if the eighth was the house of Mars and a fortune is not looking at the house, and a fortune is not conjoining with him, it indicates a speedy death; now if the Sun witnessed the house, it likewise indicates crucifixion and predatory animals will eat him.

32 And when you find Mars in the eighth, it indicates his killing at the hands of a master of fighting. **33** Now if it was like that and the house was his own house or place, that is in his own country.

34 And when you find Mercury with the Moon in the eighth, they being made unfortunate, they indicate the evil of his killing; and it is harsher for him if, along with that, it is the Ascendant³⁵ and they are both together in

---

³⁰ I have changed some of the words, in line with Rhetorius: **E** originally read that neither the fortunes nor the infortunes were looking.

³¹ In Rhetorius this is the Head, and the three planets mentioned here are actually in the house.

³² For this paragraph, cf. Rhetorius Ch. 77 (p. 128).

³³ For **25** and **27**, cf. Rhetorius Ch. 77 (p. 126).

³⁴ Cf. Rhetorius Ch. 77 (p. 126).

³⁵ إن يكون مع ذلك الطالع, reading مع for من ("from that Ascendant"). Meaning unclear, that this might be an error.

fixed signs: his death will be from the stoning[36] of soldiers or a crowd of people.

35 And[37] if Mars was looking at the Sun and the Moon from what is not his own domain,[38] from a square or opposition, from the signs of people, his death will be in war and fighting; and if Mercury looked, his killing will be at the hands of robbers and cutters[39] and lords of blood. **36** And if [Mars] was in the signs of severed limbs and they arose with Caput Algol, his death will be by decapitation due to the leaders of the people.[40] **37** And if they were in Scorpio or Aquarius,[41] the death will be by fire or cutting or the medicine of doctors. **38** And if they were in the Midheaven or in the stake of the earth, then they will be crucified; and if they were in the seventh sign, it indicates their burning by fire while still alive. **39** And if the Sun[42] was in the signs having four feet, and Mars looked at him, the death will be from being thrown from a riding animal, and a fall from a raised place.

40 And[43] if the two infortunes met together or one of them opposed its associate,[44] the native's death will be due to the place in which they are, and his killing will be based on its nature. **41** And if they both had authority over the killing places, then the native who was born like that will not have his blood-money paid[45] nor be buried, and predatory animals and birds will eat him.

42 If[46] Mars and the Sun combined with the lord of the Ascendant,[47] his death will be by burning.

---

[36] Or perhaps more simply, "abuse" (رجم).
[37] For this paragraph, cf. *Tet.* IV.9 (Robbins pp. 435-37).
[38] "Contrary to sect," according to Ptolemy (Robbins wrongly reads this as "from a sign of the other sect"). So, this must mean a diurnal chart, when Mars is contrary to the sect.
[39] That is, bandits or pirates.
[40] Ptolemy only has decapitation and mutilation, without the reference to the authorities.
[41] Ptolemy has Taurus instead of Aquarius.
[42] In Ptolemy this simply continues the previous thoughts, and does not particularly involve the Sun.
[43] For this paragraph, cf. *Tet.* IV.9 (Robbins p. 437).
[44] In Ptolemy this means that they are together and oppose one of the places responsible for death (such as the fourth, or the position of a killing planet).
[45] That is, in compensation for his death (بوادى); so, this is another way of being forgotten or neglected.
[46] For this sentence, cf. al-Rijāl (slide 213a).
[47] Al-Rijāl adds that either Mars or the Sun must also be the lord of the 8th.

43 And[48] say likewise for the Moon if she was with Mars and the lord of the Ascendant with the Sun:[49] for that is an indicator of the cutting of his limbs.

44 If[50] Mars was in Gemini and the Midheaven, his death will be by crucifixion.

45 And[51] if Mars was the lord of the Ascendant and he is under the rays, kings and the Sultan will kill him. **46** And if the Sun was in Aries or in Leo, then predatory animals will eat him; give a report in the signs based on this.

47 Then, look at the position of the Moon: for if Mars looked at her from a square or opposition or her triplicity,[52] he will die by the sword. **48** Now if it was Aries and its triplicity, he will die under the feet of horses and riding animals, and predatory animals will eat him, and his death will be quick. **49** And if it was in Taurus and its triplicity, black bile will be feared for him. **50** And in the triplicity of water, he will die by submersion and animals of the water will eat him. **51** And if the Moon was as I described in relation to the aspect of Mars, full of glow, or she was with the Sun or the Sun was with the Head or Tail, he will be destroyed in a group of people. **52** And if it was what I described and the lord of the seventh was in the Midheaven, he will fall from a raised place and die.

53 And if the Moon was as I described [but] made unfortunate by Saturn, and Saturn is in Aries and its triplicity, he will fall from a raised place and die. **54** And if he was in Taurus and its triplicity, black bile will overcome him so he will die for that reason. **55** And if he was in Gemini and its triplicity and was <in> the Midheaven, a wall or building will fall upon him, and he will die from it. **56** And if he was in the stake of the earth, he will fall from a raised place. **57** And[53] if Saturn was in Cancer and its triplicity, he will die by submersion or a gastric ailment, unless Saturn is rising up:[54] for if he was going up, he will die by colic.

---

[48] Cf. al-Rijāl (slide 213a).

[49] If, that is, they are also in signs of cut limbs (al-Rijāl).

[50] Cf. al-Rijāl (slide 213a). But in al-Rijāl, the Moon is with Mars in his square or opposition (and he is the lord of the eighth, or perhaps not), and he is in the Midheaven, in Gemini, and especially by day.

[51] In al-Rijāl's version of these two sentences (slide 213a), Mars in Aries indicates being killed by the authorities, and *Mars* in Leo with wild animals; the Sun is not mentioned.

[52] That is, trine. But note that the airy triplicity is not mentioned: perhaps that is what Sahl's source meant.

[53] This sentence is reflected in al-Rijāl, slide 213a.

[54] صاعد. This probably means that he is rising towards the Midheaven by diurnal motion.

58 And if you found the Tail in the eighth with Mercury, in a sign of the types of people, then his death will be before and in the presence of[55] people. **59** And if Venus was looking at that place at the same time, then his death will also be from poison.

60 And[56] if you found Venus in the Ascendant and Saturn in the west, or Saturn in the Ascendant and Venus in the west, then his death will be from the intrigues of women.

61 And if you found Mercury in the west, falling down towards the sixth, and he is looking at the Moon, and the Moon and the Ascendant are both made unfortunate, then his death will be from his children. **62** And if Mars was with Mercury without the aspect of Jupiter, then his killing will be at the hands of his siblings. **63** And if the Lot of friends was with it, then his death will be because of the friends.

64 And if Mars was not in his own share,[57] in the Ascendant, and he looked at the Moon, then if Jupiter was in the eighth, the death will be through the intrigues of servants.

65 And if the Moon was in the seventh,[58] and Mars and the Sun are looking at her (one of them looks at her from the Ascendant and the other from the tenth), then the native will die by fire.

66 And[59] if the infortunes were in the stakes, he will die a bad death.

67 And[60] if the first lord of the triplicity of the stake of the earth was in the fourth and the seventh, then he will die and no one of the people will be made aware of it, nor know how he died.

68 And[61] if the Sun was eclipsed in the seventh, then the native will die in fire or he will die with many people. **69** And judge based on the essence of that sign: if it was water, he will die in water, and likewise the nature of the <other> signs.

---

[55] بالنحرة والحضرة. But نحر also refers specifically to being stabbed in the throat, and means "in front" or "before" only metaphorically. So this could mean that his throat is cut in the presence of others, depriving him of wind or breath (which makes sense for Mercury).

[56] Cf. *Carmen* II.30, **11**; also II.27, **7**.

[57] خظ, which probably means "sect" but could also mean that he is alien or peregrine.

[58] Reading with *Carmen* IV.3, **21**, for "second."

[59] Cf. *Carmen* IV.3, **24**.

[60] Cf. *Carmen* IV.3, **28**.

[61] For this paragraph, cf. *Carmen* IV.3, **35**.

70 Look[62] at the lord of the bound of the degree of marriage: for if it was an infortune and the infortunes looked at it and its bound[63] and you found it in its first slowness, retrograde, then the native will die by a powerful emaciating illness, and the abundance of the doctors' treatments or remedies will kill him. **71** And[64] mix the type of sign which [the lord of the bound] is in: for if it is in the signs of people, that tribulation will be by reason of people (of doctors and others). **72** And if you found it in signs of moisture, then his death will be from phlegm.[65] **73** And if you found it in a sign having four feet, then predatory animals will eat him or he will fall from a raised place.

74 And if you found the lord of the house of marriage in the house of friends, made unfortunate, or the Moon connected with anything of the infortunes and the fortunes do not look at her, then his death will be by reason of friendship. **75** And if Venus was the lord of that place, and she was in the sixth and twelfth, made unfortunate, and the Moon enclosed between the two infortunes, his manner of death will be by reason of women and his own woman.

76 If[66] the lord of the seventh was in a bad place or it was in the tenth, and the Moon was with the infortunes, then he will fall from a high, raised place.

77 And[67] if Venus was in the seventh and the Moon was in an alien place, and the infortunes with [the Moon], then his death will be in relation to a woman who has already had many husbands, [and] then they died. **78** If it was Jupiter instead of Venus, then he will die in relation to children or his own [good] name which is attributed to him. **79** And if it was Mars instead of Venus, then his death will be in relation to his siblings. **80** And if the Sun was like Venus, he will die because of his fathers; and <if the Moon was like Venus>,[68] because of his mother or the woman of his father.

81 Now if Jupiter was the lord of that bound,[69] his death will be at the hands of his children or [because of] envy, since good will be spoken about

---

[62] For this paragraph, cf. Rhetorius Ch. 77 (p. 126).

[63] In this clause, the Arabic refers to "it" with a feminine pronoun, but I am not sure what else it could be referring to besides the lord of the bound.

[64] Cf. *Carmen* IV.3, **32**, which however seems to refer to the seventh sign, not the sign which the bound lord of the Descendant is in. But this is an accurate description of Rhetorius.

[65] In Rhetorius, "water."

[66] For this sentence, cf. *Carmen* IV.3, **36**.

[67] For this paragraph, cf. *Carmen* IV.3, **38-42**.

[68] Adding on the basis of *Carmen* IV.3, **42**.

[69] This must be the bound of the Descendant.

him. **82** And if the Moon was equally with the lord of that bound, and she was enclosed between the two infortunes in the stakes or what follows [them], his manner of death will be ugly, and especially if the Moon was in a convertible sign.

83 And if you found the Moon to be the lord of that house, and she was in the sixth, <missing>.[70] **84** <Missing> then the king and the people of the king will kill him, and especially if he connected with the infortunes.

85 And[71] if both the lord of the Ascendant and the lord of the house of the Moon each looked at its associate[72] from an opposition, then he will die abroad; and if the infortunes looked, then say he is killed.

86 And if the Moon was in the eighth, not flowing away from the degree of the fullness, and Venus conjoined with her, it indicates the corruption of the marriage and death by reason of the spout of water in intercourse,[73] or by reason of a woman. **87** And[74] if Mars was with [the Moon] in the eighth, and Mercury in the opposition of them both, then know that his death will be at the hands of robbers or fearful things. **88** (And know that whether or not a planet was in the eighth sign, it indicates that the reason for death is something like these things.)

89 And[75] if the Head was not in the eighth, it indicates burning with rage,[76] and his manner of death will be bad.

---

[70] In **E**, this and the next sentence run together as one. However, this does not makes sense to me because the "if he connected" in **84** cannot indicate the Moon, and grammatically indicates either a plural (which does not make sense here) or a feminine singular like Venus or the Sun. I take it to be the Sun because of the reference to the king.

[71] For this paragraph, cf. Rhetorius Ch. 77 (p. 128).

[72] That is, at each other.

[73] مصبّ الماء في الجماع, which to me suggests some ethno-biological idea about the dissipation of one's energies in sex, but I cannot find its source. Perhaps it refers to a sexually transmitted disease.

[74] See **91** below, which suggests (as so often) that Sahl was indiscriminately taking from many sources that said the same things.

[75] This sentence very uncertain. First, I doubt that the source really spoke of the Head *not* being in the eighth; second, the "burning with rage" phrase does not make sense without more information. I do note that Rhetorius Ch. 57 (p. 86) has the Head in the eighth, *with* the Sun, Mars, Mercury, or Saturn (or looking at it), which indicates a bad death and short life.

[76] الحمر.

90 And if the Lot of Fortune was with Mars, there will be fighting [and] the spilling of blood, and especially if it was in the eighth or the Midheaven: for truly with that the native will die in war; and it is harsher for that if Mars was looking down upon the Moon.

91 And if the Moon was with Mars in the eighth, and Mercury in the house of assets, then he will die at the hands of his enemies or the hands of robbers.

92 Now[77] if Saturn and Mars are the lord of the seventh, and they make the Ascendant unfortunate, and <the fortunes> are not looking at the Ascendant, then he will kill himself with iron or he will asphyxiate himself, or will fall from a raised place and die.

93 And[78] if you found the lord of the seventh in the sixth or twelfth, or third or ninth, then he will fall from a raised place and die, especially if the Moon was made unfortunate.

[Chapter 8.3: Māshā'allāh on the lord of the Ascendant]

1 Māshā'allāh said: Look at the lord of the Ascendant, for if an infortune connected with it, and that infortune is in the stake of the earth, then no one will be informed of his death. 2 And[79] if the fourth sign was of those having [*uncertain*] in water, and it is harsher for that if the infortune was Saturn. 3 Now, if the lord of the Ascendant was connected with Saturn, and he is in the fourth, in Aries and its triplicity, then he will die from [an illness of] the belly; and it is harsher for that if the lord of the Ascendant was under the rays. 4 And if the infortune which the lord of the Ascendant is connected with was appearing [from out of the rays], he will die publicly. 5 And if the infortune was in the Midheaven, and it is in its fall, and the lord of the Ascendant is connecting with it, then he will die under something which falls on him. 6 And if the lord of the Ascendant was under the rays, he will die from a feverish illness. 7 And if it was at the end of its stake,[80] he will die a bad death because with that, it is in the place of burning.

---

[77] Cf. *Carmen* IV.3, **22**.
[78] This sentence bears a resemblance to *Carmen* IV.3, **36**.
[79] Something is missing from this sentence, or it is a compound of two sentences, but I am not sure where to divide or add to it.
[80] This idiom refers to it being elongated from or opposed to the Sun.

8 Then, look at the infortune which indicates the native's death, [and see] in which position relative to the Ascendant it is, for his death will be by reason of that sign. **9** If it was the Ascendant, an illness will be unleashed[81] upon him in his body; his death will be in it. **10** And if it was in the second, his death will be in relation to assets; and if it was in the third, his death will be on a foreign journey (or by reason of siblings), and likewise the ninth; and <if> the seventh, then by reason of women; or, in the house of the fourth, he will die a mysterious death which will not be evident to his people (except that if the infortune was received, he will die among his people); and likewise in the fifth but it will be feared for him if he has children; and in the sixth it indicates a long illness or by reason of the rabble and slaves; and in the tenth his death will be public; and in the eleventh he will die and it will be in the finest condition it could be; and if the infortune which the lord of the Ascendant connects with was in the twelfth, enemies will kill him.

11 And if the lord of the Ascendant was connecting with a fortune, and that fortune was the lord of the eighth, then he will die a suitable death and many people will witness it. **12** Then, look at the position of that fortune: for if it was in the ninth and third, and it is direct in course, received, then truly the people will bear witness to his piety in his religion. **13** And if it was in the stakes, then it is in relation to his rank among the people and their knowledge of him. **14** And if it was in the eighth or second, then in relation to his assets and his knowledge. **15** And if it was in the sixth or twelfth, then from the compassion of the people towards him, and their mercy towards him.

[Chapter 8.4:] Death abroad

1 And[82] if you wanted to know [if] the death would be abroad or in his own land and country, then look at the lord of the eighth. **2** For if you found it looking at the eighth and it was in its own house, triplicity, or exaltation, it will be in his own land and among his people. **3** Now if you found the lord of

---

[81] The text reads هلاج, which is the Persian word for a cold wind accompanied by rain. This could indicate an illness, but I think it is better related to هيلاج, the word for the longevity releaser: in that case, it seems to mean that an illness will be "unleashed" upon him.

[82] For **1-3**, cf. Rhetorius Ch. 77 (p. 127).

the eighth in exile, he will die abroad; and likewise if it was not in the eighth and not looking at it, for he will die on a journey. **4** And if it was in the eighth, and[83] witnessed it, his death will be in his own home. **5** And if it was in the eighth, made unfortunate, it indicates a death away from home and in contempt. **6** And if the lord of the eighth was falling, it indicates the death is on journeys.

7 And if the lord of the third was in the eighth, he will bury his siblings. **8** And if the lord of the fifth was there, it indicates the burial of the children.

9 And if the lord of the eighth was in the ninth, it indicates his death while away from home.

10 And if the lord of the house of death was strong, the native will not do anything without [death] finding him.

11 And if the lord of the Ascendant connected with an infortune and that infortune was in the seventh, ninth, or third, he will die while away from home. **12** And if Saturn was the infortune, he will die from cold; and if it was Mars, he will die from heat; and if they both met together, he will die from pus and blood.

13 Then,[84] see who of the planets is in the eighth. **14** For if the lord of the third was there, his siblings will die before him; and if the lord of the fourth was there, his father[85] will die quickly; and if the lord of the fifth was there, his children will die before him; and if the lord of the seventh was there, his women will die before him and he will inherit from them.

15 And look at the lord of the eighth, [to see] which sign it is in, and what the essence is: for the native's death will be according to the nature of that sign.

16 And do look at what [kind] of planet the lord of the eighth is connecting with, for the death will be feared for him that is like that nature (the lord of the house of children, and siblings, and fathers), and the manner of the native's death will be based on the nature of the sign which the lord of the eighth is connecting with, or it is in.[86]

---

[83] This should be read as "or."

[84] For this paragraph, cf. Rhetorius Ch. 57 (p. 84), which has a couple of these examples.

[85] **M**: "mother."

[86] This is phrased awkwardly, but I believe this means it could be either the sign of the lord of the eighth, or the other planet's sign.

[Chapter 8.5: The lord of the eighth in the houses, according to Māshā'allāh]

1 Then, look at the lord of the eighth. 2 For if it was in the Ascendant and it is free of the infortunes, he will have a long lifespan, [but] will be frustrated and have difficulty in seeking out [his] necessities.

3 The lord of the eighth in the second: he will be blessed by inheritance and will sometimes be in the steady employ of the Sultan.[87]

4 The lord of the eighth in the third: his siblings will have defects, chronic illness, disease, and they will do the work of slaves, and there will be diminishment in them.

5 The lord of the eighth in the fourth, the fathers will be foreigners, or with defects in them or chronic illness, and their lifespans will be diminished.

6 The lord of the eighth in the fifth: his children will die in their youth, or they will have more power over the people because of the Sultan.

7 The lord of the eighth in the sixth: his calamities will be in slaves and riding animals, and he will not be blessed by them.

8 <The lord of the eighth> in the seventh: he will marry women who have inheritances, he will inherit from them and get their assets from them and because of them, and he will die in exile.

9 The lord of the eighth in the eighth: he will be healthy, and his illness will be insignificant, and his death will be light.

10 The lord of the eighth in the ninth: he will have bad thoughts and work, and he will die in exile.

11 The lord of the eighth in the tenth: his ruin will be because of the Sultan, and at his hands.

12 The lord of the eighth in the eleventh: his friends will be diminished, and it corrupts what is between them, and he will die when his condition is good.

13 The lord of the eighth in the twelfth: it will be feared for him that enemies will kill him, or the foolish will fight him.

---

[87] The second is the sixth from the tenth, so doing labor (6th) for the Sultan (10th).

[Chapter 8.6: The Lot of death, according to Māshā'allāh][88]

1 Then look at the Lot of death: and it is taken by night and day from the Moon to the degree of the eighth place, and cast out from Saturn,[89] and where the number terminates, there is this Lot.

2 Now if this Lot was in the stakes and it is free of the infortunes, he will die in his own country; and if it was made unfortunate, he will die a bad manner of death.

3 And if it was in the third or ninth, he will die while away from home; now if it was made unfortunate, he will die a bad manner of death.

4 And if it was in the fifth or eleventh, the native will die in the finest way there is.

5 When the Lot of death is in the second from the Ascendant, the eighth, sixth, and twelfth, you look at the lord of the eighth and mix [it] with it. **6** And if it was greater in testimony,[90] then [if] it is in the second, he will die because of assets or his assets will kill him. **7** And if it was in the sixth, he will die because of the rabble or a bad illness. **8** And if it was in the twelfth, enemies will kill him or he will die in confinement. **9** And if it was in the eighth, he will die from an illness of its nature.

[Chapter 8.7: Various statements]

1 Nativities of the meeting <and the opposition>. **2** And nativities of the meeting will die at the opposition, and nativities of the opposition will die on[91] the meeting.[92]

3 And count from the lord of the fourth hour, for the lord of the fourth hour is the death of the native, on the day of that planet. **4** An example of that is if the lord of the fourth hour is Mercury, so that the native's death is on Wednesday, and that is the fourth hour[93] from the hour of the birth.

---

[88] Cf. Tehran, Dānishgāh, Nafīsī 429 (71b); Majlis 17490 (138).

[89] Reading with the Māshā'allāh MSS for "Ascendant." This is the Lot as reported by Dorotheus (*Carmen* IV.3, **16**).

[90] The Latin (Vatican, Pal. lat. 1892, 102v) reads, "and if it had many testimonies." The Arabic MSS are all awkward, and I am not quite sure what Māshā'allāh means: perhaps that the Lot has worse planets looking at it, in worse aspects, and so on.

[91] **E**: "before."

[92] That is, people born after a New Moon will die closer to a Full Moon, and vice versa.

[93] For the rest of the sentence, **M** seems to read: مزاحع.

5 A statement of al-Andarzaghar.[94] **6** He said, look at the Moon after the birth by forty nights,[95] for if she connected with the infortunes or the infortunes were with her, he will be killed in shackles.

---

[94] This short paragraph appears only in **M**, in Ch. 8.5 above **3** and **4**, so I have put it here. It is based on Rhetorius Ch. 77 (p. 127), and is mentioned in *BA* III.8.1.

[95] Rhetorius has the third, seventh, and fortieth *day* of the Moon. Rhetorius is undoubtedly counting the nativity as the first day, so for example if the native was born on a Monday (1st day), the 3rd day would be Wednesday, and so on.

Chapter 9: On travels & religion

[al-Andarzaghar]

1 The ninth house,[1] the joy[2] of the Sun, indicates the knowledge of God, and religion, and the matter of the hereafter and the invisible, and it is the area from which you know the native's travels, and what is the reason for his travels, and how they will be, and whether he will return from his travel or not, and in which direction his absence from home and his travel will be. **2** So look in this chapter at eight things:[3]

3 The first item[4] is that you look at the position of the Moon, where she is on the third day from the nativity, and who is looking at her (of the fortunes and infortunes), and in which sign she is, and which bound, and with whom she is connecting and who is looking at her, and how her condition is, and that of her lord.

4 The second item:[5] look at the lord of the Ascendant and the Moon, and the condition of them both, and how their positions and their places are, and who is looking at the Moon, and if she[6] is in a stake or not, and what is the type of sign which she is in, and in which direction she is in.

5 The third item:[7] look at the lords of the triplicities of the luminaries,[8] and whether they look at the luminaries or not.

6 The fourth item:[9] look at the house of travel, who is in it and who its lord is, and how the excellence of its position is, and what is the category of the sign, and how the aspect of the fortunes and infortunes to it is.

7 The fifth item:[10] look at the Lot of Fortune, its opposition, and its square.

---

[1] See also Sahl's *Introduction* Ch. 2, **22-23**.

[2] Reading فرج for برج ("sign").

[3] The following items are all reflected in *BA* (III.9.2), but in a different order of items, and only pertain to travel. For religion, see Ch. 9.5.

[4] This refers to Ch. 9.1, **1-5** below, and Sahl has added **8-11**.

[5] This item is worded differently in the two texts. It refers to Ch. 9.1, **23-25** only (the Moon and the angles), and Sahl has added **6-7** and **32**.

[6] I say "she" here because of the Moon's position in the Midheaven and the fourth below, but this could equally be read as "it," since some rules do involve other planets in various types of signs.

[7] This refers to Ch. 9.1, **28-30** only, but Sahl has apparently added **31** and maybe **32** to this category.

[8] Or rather, the sect light (see below).

[9] This refers to Ch. 9.1, **16-22** only, but see also **33-43**.

8 The sixth item:[11] look at Saturn by night and Mars by day, and how their positions are in the root of the nativity, and who of the fortunes and infortunes is looking at them.

9 The seventh item:[12] look at the Lot of travel, which is taken by night and day from the lord of the ninth to the ninth, and is projected from the Ascendant: see in which sign it is, and who is looking at it.

10 The eighth item:[13] see which planet is stronger in the root of the nativity, and look at which direction the planet is in.

[Chapter 9.1: Whether the native will travel or live abroad]

The first item: [the third day of the Moon]

1 Look[14] at the Moon on the third day from the nativity: for if you found her connected with Mars <by body or>[15] by square or opposition, or she was in the house of Mars, then the native will be a foreigner, traveling, exiled from his country, not settling down in one community, and hardship and fear will afflict him due to that, and his travelling will be in raids and [with] troops. **2** Now if the nativity was by day and Mars was not in his own share, then it is bad, especially if Mars was retrograde. **3** But if (when he was like that) you found Mars in his own house or bound, eastern, or[16] Jupiter looking at him, he will get respect in his traveling, and assets, and much good; but if Mars was in a bad house, and if he was falling, and you found him alien, in a stake of the house,[17] then long tribulation and hardship will afflict him in his traveling. **4** And look at the sign in which Mars is, and what kind it is, and say that that misfortune will strike him from the kind [of thing] that sign is. **5**

---

[10] This refers to Ch. 9.1, **26-27** only.
[11] This refers to Ch. 9.1, **61-62** only, but see also **33-45**.
[12] This refers to Ch. 9.3, **4** only, but Sahl has added Ch. 9.4, **37-45** from Māshā'allāh.
[13] This refers to Ch. 9.3, **1** only.
[14] For this paragraph, cf. Dorotheus *Excerpt* XX, **1-4**, as well as Hephaistion II.24.
[15] Adding with Dorotheus *Excerpt* XX, **1**, for the sake of clarity.
[16] This should be read as "and," with Dorotheus.
[17] This probably means being in the stake of the ninth, but this is not specified in the Dorotheus *Excerpt*.

And if Mars was such, just as I explained to you, and Saturn looked at the Moon,[18] then he will flee from his own land until no trace of him is left in it.

[Item 2: The lord of the Ascendant and the Moon]

6 And[19] if you found the Moon contrary to her own house[20] and the lord of the Ascendant contrary to the Ascendant or to any of its houses,[21] then the native's livelihood will be outside of his parents' country; and likewise if you found them in their falls (which is opposite their exaltations). **7** And[22] if the lord of the Moon was contrary to the Moon, then the native will have travels and exile; and it is worse for that if the planet was an infortune.

[Item 1 again: The third day of the Moon]

8 And if the Moon on the third day is connecting with Mercury, and Mercury is made unfortunate by Mars, then say it is an example of that and resembles that.[23] **9** And if you found the Moon and her lord in the stake of the west, then the native will be a lover of travels. **10** And likewise, if the lord of the Ascendant was in the ninth or the lord of the ninth in the Ascendant, then the native will travel from his own country. **11** And if on the third day you found the Moon connecting with a fortune, and that fortune was eastern, then he will be of those who profit from travels; and if that planet was an infortune and it is eastern, in its own bound and turn,[24] and the fortunes looked at it, then the native will profit from travels.

12 And if you found Mars in the third from the Ascendant, then he will travel while he is a youth; and judge likewise from the ninth house.

---

[18] In Dorotheus it is not clear whether Saturn is looking at the Moon or at Jupiter. But *BA* III.9.2 has the Moon.

[19] For more on these types of configurations, see 9.3, **2-3**.

[20] That is, in her detriment, opposite Cancer.

[21] I.e., the other sign it rules.

[22] For this sentence, compare **24** below.

[23] That is, an example of what Sahl has already described.

[24] دولة. This can also mean "happy condition/state," and has the connotation of rotating or alternating between one thing and another—I believe this is probably a metaphor for "sect," so that the infortune either simply belongs to the sect of the chart, or might even be in a sect-rejoicing condition such as being in its *ḥalb*.

[Item 4: The ninth and its lord]

13 And look at the ninth and its lord: for if you found the ninth place made suitable by the fortunes, then say that the native will be made happy in his travels, and especially if its lord was in a good place with the fortunes. **14** And if the lord of the ninth was in a stake, then the native will be put in charge [and be] powerful in his travelling. **15** And if that planet was Venus, then he will get married on his travels, and will get gold and silver and joy in it; and if it was Jupiter, he will have goodness of action[25] and reputation; and if it was the Sun, then he will be awarded a leadership position; and if it was Mercury, then he will become well known as a scholar; and if it was Saturn and his place was good and Jupiter looked at him, then his profit will be in relation to water and the land; and if it was Mars, then he will be received among cavalry and the nobility,[26] and he will profit from that.

16 And[27] if you found the lord of the ninth[28] in an alien house, and it is in an excellent position, and the fortunes are looking at it, and it is cleansed of the rays, and the sign which it is in is of the signs of people, then he will travel and on his travels he will get respect, a good status, much profit, or he will be acquainted with the nobility, and good will be spoken about him in his travels. **17** And if you found the sign of travel to be bestial and its lord[29] in a bestial sign, and it is cleansed of the rays, then he will get that along with tribulation.

18 And if you found the house of travel and its lord just as I described to you, and its lord was falling from the stake, and the infortunes looked at it, and the fortunes do not look, then judge that powerful tribulation will afflict him in his travels; and it is worse for him if it was in the house of travel, for if it was like that he will not cease to be on that journey, a foreigner, burdened in his travels. **19** And if Venus looked at Jupiter or they were both there, and

---

[25] جمال. **M** reads "completion" or "perfection" (كمال), suggesting the accomplishment or fulfillment of one's actions, which is also astrologically sound.

[26] Traditionally, nobles were also warriors or in charge of armies; normally we would associate the nobility with Jupiter.

[27] For this paragraph, cf. *Excerpt* XXI, **1-4**.

[28] But the lord of Mars, according to *Excerpt* XXI.

[29] Here Sahl does reflect *Excerpt* XXI in speaking about the lord of the ninth rather than the lord of Mars.

the infortunes did not look, then he will get assets and good will be spoken about him.

20 And[30] look too at the Moon: for if you found her in the ninth, and you found Mars with her or he looked at her from a square or opposition, then he will go on a distant[31] journey, and the majority of them are those who do not return from their travels until they are dead.

21 And if you found her in the seventh or in the house of fathers, just as I described to you, then judge that for him. **22** And if the sign was moist, that tribulation will afflict him from water; and if it was of the signs of humans, it will strike him from humans (and that is if the fortunes are not looking).

[Item 2: The Moon and the angles]

23 And if the Moon was in the Midheaven, and especially Sagittarius, and she was just as I described it to you about the infortunes, and the fortunes are not looking at her, then judge likewise for him. **24** And if you found the Moon in the house of fathers, and her lord was opposing her, then he will go on a distant journey.

25 And[32] if you found the Moon along with the Sun[33] in a convertible sign or in the stake, and an infortune is looking at him and the fortunes do not look, then he will travel.

[Item 5: The Lot of Fortune]

26 And look at the Lot of Fortune: for if you found, in what follows[34] the Lot or in its square, Saturn by night and Mars by day, then he will travel.

27 And[35] if you found the Moon on the northern side or the elevated side,[36] then the native will not settle in his own country.

---

[30] For this paragraph, cf. *Excerpt* XXI, 5-6.

[31] Reading with **M** for **E**'s "slow"; *Excerpt* XXI reads "dangerous," and **M** is closer to that.

[32] For this sentence, cf. *Excerpt* XX, 5.

[33] **E** has only "the Sun," but *Excerpt* XX, **5** clearly associates travel with the luminaries being in the tropical (or at least convertible) signs. But the *Excerpt* does *not* say that this has to be at the same time.

[34] يلي. This can also mean "borders on," and would mean the second sign from the Lot. But BA and 7 above confirm that this should be "opposes." But do note that infortunes in the Lot's second house might suggest livelihood (second) gotten through travel (infortunes), or that the native's means of subsistence is unstable enough that he needs to travel.

[Item 3: Triplicity lords of the luminaries]

28 And[37] look at the lords of the triplicity of the luminaries (by day the Sun, and by night the Moon): for if you found them both in their triplicities and they looked at the luminaries, then the native will remain in his own country, and he will not travel. **29** And if you found them both in an alien sign and they looked at the luminaries, then he will make a slow journey, [but] then will return to his family. **30** And if you found the first lord of the triplicity in an alien place and the second one in its own triplicity, and they did not look at the luminaries, then the native will not cease to be on his travels, and tribulation and trouble will afflict him in his travels.

31 And if you found the lord of the triplicity of the glowing one [of the sect] in a stake or in the house of good fortune, or in the fifth or its own place, then the native will not be unhappy in his travels; but if it was falling and not looking at the Ascendant, then the native will be in need in his travels, being humble in his livelihood.

32 And if you found the lord of the Sun[38] not looking at the Sun, and the lord of the Moon not looking at the Moon, and the lord of the Ascendant not looking at the Ascendant, then the native will be a traveler, having trouble, great deprivation, and difficulty.

☊   ☋   ☋

33 And if you found Mars in the third or ninth, then the native will not cease to be deprived, having trouble and travel. **34** And likewise if you found the Lot of travel with Mars, and you find the lord of the Lot contrary to its own house or the lord of the Lot [itself] is Mars, then the native will have illness and tribulation and evil on his travels.

---

[35] I do not know how this relates to the Lot of Fortune, but this sentence appears here in BA.

[36] The "northern" side may be northern ecliptical latitude, and the "elevated" side might be the MC (or perhaps being in the half of her declination circle closer to her apogee).

[37] This paragraph is almost certainly based on Dorotheus, as it uses triplicity lords and is partly reflected in Heph. II.24 (Schmidt p. 75).

[38] This must be if he is the sect light (and likewise the Moon), as apparently confirmed in BA III.9.2, **24-25**.

35 And if you found an infortune in the ninth and the lord of the ninth falling, it indicates deviation,[39] transgression, and misery in his being abroad. **36** And[40] if the Moon was in the ninth with an infortune, it indicates misery in his being abroad, and death by thirst or predatory beasts eating him. **37** And if the Head was in the ninth with the infortune, it indicates leadership and good fortune in travelling, and the gathering of assets, and his generosity in worship. **38** And if there was a fortune in the ninth, it indicates devotion and excellence in his being abroad, and more clearly for that if the lord of the ninth was in its own house or exaltation or in a suitable place, not made unfortunate. **39** And if you found the lord of the ninth in any of its places, in a strong place, not made unfortunate, it indicates good fortune in travels. **40** And if you found the lord of the ninth in the ninth, and it is a fortune, free of the infortunes, then the native will move from his own place in which he was born,[41] and will come to a good[42] place. **41** And if the lord of the ninth was an infortune and it was in it, or you found it in a strong place from the ninth, in the view of the infortunes, the fortunes not looking at it, then the native will move to a bad place, and he will travel to what is harsher than his own place in which he was born; and if he did come to travel, he will experience hardship and tribulation and loss from the journeys. **42** Now if Mars was the one undermining the house of his travel, and he had power over that, then report that his ruin will be in his travels, at the hands of robbers and stranglers, or he will run into an enemy who will take him and he will be killed in the land of his foreign travel, not his own land in which he was born. **43** And if the underminer was Saturn, then his travels will be in a land of waters, and hardship will enter upon him from that, as well as toil which will afflict him, or emaciating illnesses in his journey, and he will not get what he expects or hopes for in his journey, and he will not get good in it, and will not cease to be miserable in his journey, and will do low works, and that is if the fortunes fell away from the position of Mars and Saturn.

44 And if the Moon was weak, it indicates the weakness of his journeys and his slowness in them, if he did travel.

---

[39] This word (فجور) now means "immoral behavior," but that is derivative upon its primary meaning, which is going astray and deviating.

[40] For this sentence, cf. Dorotheus *Excerpt* XXI, **5**.

[41] For the rest of this sentence, **E** reads: "to a quick journey and he will not be established in his own place in which he was born (except a little bit), and he will come to a good place from the place in which he was born."

[42] Reading with **E** for "another."

45 And[43] if you found the Moon between the two infortunes, one of them being in the twelfth from her and the other in the second from her, then the native will travel to a land in which he will get tribulation and trouble, and it will exaggerate the harm upon him, and on the journeys he will not cease to be in hardship from [those] journeys, [both] before he arrives and after he arrives; then misfortune will come to his country and harm will afflict him in it, unless Jupiter was about to inspect the Moon from the stake of the earth (of the stakes), for he breaks the misfortune of the two infortunes which are squeezing the Moon, and will fortify [the native's] strength, and the misfortune will not get him; but the restriction belonging to the place of the two infortunes from the Moon will get him, as well as the restriction of the place of the Moon which she is in.

[Travel according to Ptolemy]

46 And[44] look at the luminaries and the stakes, and especially the Moon: if she was in the seventh or withdrawing from the stakes, then with that it indicates being away from home and moving from place to place. **47** And Mars is like that too when he is in the seventh or withdrawing from the Midheaven, and he is in the opposition of the luminaries or their square. **48** And[45] if Mars occurred with the Lot of Fortune in the sign of travel, then it indicates that their life and their moving about will always be abroad.

49 And if the fortunes looked, they indicate the good and excellence and increase and brilliance; and if the infortunes looked, they indicate the contrary of that. **50** And if the fortunes looked at the sign of travel (even if the Lot of Fortune was not in it in the way I mentioned), the native's return from foreign travel will be quick due to[46] the profit and excellence; and if the infortunes looked, then the contrary of that. **51** And if the fortunes and infortunes

---

[43] This paragraph is based on *Carmen* V.23, **6**. Since this is an inceptional instruction, maybe it only shows these things *if* there are already *other* indications of travel.

[44] This paragraph is based on *Tet.* IV.8 (Robbins pp. 423-27), but sentences **46-48** sound very much like the view attributed to Abraham by Valens in *Anth.* II.29 (which could be the source for Ptolemy).

[45] In *Tet.* this does not involve Mars, but only concerns the Lot of Fortune in the places of travel.

[46] Or perhaps simply, "with" (ب).

were mixed in their looking, then you decree it for them in accordance with their positions.

52 And if Jupiter and Venus were the two authorities over the places of foreign travel,[47] that is safety and attainment and strength [stemming] from the consent of the governors of the countries and their motives.[48] **53** And if Mercury was with them, the native will get gifts from the governors; and if he curried favor, honors.

54 And if the two infortunes were the authority over those places, and the luminaries in those places, and especially if [they] were[49] in the opposition of the luminaries, then the native will fall into major tribulations in his foreign travel. **55** And if they were in moist signs, then the tribulations will be from waves and water. **56** And[50] if they were dry, the tribulations and evil will be from evident matters on which the people in the cities and the nobles[51] agree. **57** And if they were in convertible signs, then the tribulations will afflict him from poverty and need, and pains. **58** And if they were[52] in signs of people, then he will suffer high robbery and be looted. **59** And if they were in dry[53] signs, then the tribulations in his journey will strike him from predatory beasts and earthquakes. **60** And if Mercury was with them, what afflicts him becomes powerful, and it will bring him tribulaistion from [that] evil.

[Item 6: The infortunes contrary to the sect]

61 And[54] if you found Saturn in nativities of the night in an alien sign, in the house of fathers or the house of marriage, and the fortunes do not look at him, then he will travel; and judge likewise <about Mars> for one born by day. **62** And if the fortunes looked at him, then he will return from that journey of his to his own land and people.

---

[47] Ptolemy includes their being lords over the luminaries.
[48] Or more simply, "and because of them" (أسبابهم).
[49] Reading for "it was." Ptolemy seems to mean that the infortunes are opposed to the luminaries, but it is not perfectly clear.
[50] Ptolemy makes this continue the statement about watery places, and says "bad roads or desert places," but clearly Sahl makes more sense—although I am not sure what he means by "evident" things or "agreeing."
[51] Tentatively reading as الأشراف.
[52] Reading with **M**. **E** reads: "And if Mars was with them and it was in...".
[53] Reading with **M**; **E** reads, "fixed." Ptolemy reads "earthy" or "terrestrial."
[54] For this paragraph, cf. Dorotheus *Frag.* I.18 and Hephaistion II.24.

Chapter [9.2]: The knowledge of which direction his travel will be in, & at which time[55]

1 So if you wanted knowledge of that, then look at the luminaries: for if they were in the eastern quadrants, then the majority of the native's foreign journeys away from his own country will be toward the east and the south. **2** And if they were in the western quadrants, then the majority of his foreign travel away from his home will be toward the west and north. **3** And if they were in signs having one body, then the native's foreign travel will be after a long period of time; and if it was in one having two bodies, then his foreign travel will come upon him quickly at all times.

Chapter [9.3]: The knowledge of which direction is better for the native if he travels to it [from al-Andarzaghar]

[Item 8: The direction of travel]

1 Look at which planet is stronger and more excellent by position, and make his journey be toward that direction in which that planet is: for he will benefit from that journey.

[Lords of the planets, again]

2 And if you found the lord of the house of the Sun, Moon, and the Ascendant opposed to their own houses, they indicate travels for the native, and toil, trouble, and fleeing from his land and his fatherland, and especially if that lord was an infortune or made unfortunate.

3 And know that if Mars was in the second, it indicates ruin and flight from his country, and especially if he was in his own fall in a nativity of the day.

[Item 7: The Lot of travel]

4 And[56] as for Antiochus, I have seen him looking into this travel, and he calculates from the lord of the house of travel to the house of travel, and on

---

[55] Again, cf. *Tet.* IV.8.

top of it are added the degrees of the Ascendant, and he judges in the matter of travel from these two things, and this is what bestows the Lot of travel.

[Chapter 9.4: Māshā'allāh on travel]

1 Māshā'allāh said: Begin in this topic by looking at the lord of the ninth and the lord of the Ascendant: for if they were connecting, he will have many travels. **2** And if with that the lord of the Ascendant is looking at the Ascendant, then he will travel much, [but] then will return; and if it is not looking, he will remain away from home. **3** And if the lord of the Ascendant is looking at the lord of the ninth and it is in a stake, then he will not travel far, and will not prolong his journey; now if it was withdrawing [but] looking at the Ascendant, then he will travel [but] will quit and return. **4** And if they were not both looking at each other, then look at the lord of the ninth, in which position it is from the Ascendant: for if it was in the Ascendant and it is a fortune it indicates the piety of the native, and in his youth he will move from the community in which he was born, and his parents will undergo hardship or have a chronic illness.

5 Then, look at the lord of the ninth: for if it was a fortune, and it is direct in course, then what it indicates of piety is without harm, and [with] no deception; and better than that is if it was received, for what he professes is the preferable one of religions. **6** And if it was an infortune and it is in the Ascendant, the native will be wicked in [his] intention and religion, and performs the works of magicians. **7** And if it was retrograde, it is worse, because he will keep company with robbers and have a reputation with them if it was Mars; and if it was Saturn, he will be a companion of chronic illness and his parents will have a chronic illness or defect.

8 The lord of the Ascendant in the ninth, handing over its management or power to a withdrawing planet: he will remain abroad; and if it hands over to a falling planet,[57] then he will travel and not return. **9** Then look at the reason for his remaining on the journey, from the planet which it[58] is handing its management over to: for if it was the lord of the second from the Ascendant,

---

[56] **E** omits this sentence.

[57] Māshā'allāh seems to be distinguishing between a dynamically weak or withdrawing planet, and a planet in a falling or cadent sign; but I do not see what the difference in the interpretation really is.

[58] The lord of the Ascendant.

then he will remain because of assets; and if it was the lord of the third, then he will remain because of siblings; and if it was the lord of the fourth, then in relation to fathers and he is ruined; and if it was the lord of the fifth or eleventh, then from the hope of a livelihood or rank, or a child will be born to him in his foreign journey and it will be by that; and if it was the lord of the sixth or twelfth, then in relation to illness, confinement, or suffering, <or> he will be enslaved and carried off; and if it was the lord of the seventh, then in relation to women or a lawsuit arising from that; and if it was the lord of the eighth then he will be destroyed in his journey; and if it was the lord of the tenth, then in relation to authority.

10 And if you saw that the planet reflecting the light of them both was an infortune or the lord of the sixth or twelfth, then the native will be bought and enslaved, but after that he will become free and his condition will improve, and likewise his affairs. **11** If it was transferring[59] the light from the lord of the Ascendant to the lord of the ninth, and if the one which transferred[60] the light was not the lord of these two places but was in them, then he will be bought and enslaved, but after that he will become free and his condition will improve; and likewise concerning his affairs.

12 Now if it transferred[61] from the lord of the ninth to the lord of the Ascendant, and if the one reflecting the light was the lord of the second or eighth, or it is in them, then he will be bought and sold and enslaved until he dies.

13 And if the one which reflected the light was the lord of the Midheaven, and it is eastern, then he will travel and he will speak[62] in the house of the Sultan.

14 And speak about the remainder of the houses based on their essences.

15 If the lord of the Ascendant was in the ninth or third, and it is connecting with a planet in its exaltation, then the native will devote his time to the nobility in his foreign journey, and he will be known by the one he spends his time with, of the nobles and foreigners (that is, the planet which it is connected to, of the nobles and foreigners).

---

[59] **M**: "bearing."
[60] **M**: "bore."
[61] **M**: "bore."
[62] Reading حدث as حدَّث (Form II); but it seems to me that a better verb would be Form IV, "it will come about in."

16 And if Mars looked at the Ascendant and the lord of the Ascendant was withdrawing, it indicates an abundance of travels, and that will be in war or because of arms. **17** And if Mars was an enemy to the lord of the Ascendant, then from his enmity he will experience fear and hardship, and injuries will afflict him; now if it[63] was in the stakes, killing will be feared for him. **18** And if the lord of the Ascendant was Mars, or he had testimony and he is in the Ascendant, and is connecting with Jupiter, and Jupiter is with the Tail in opposition to the Sun, then stranglers will kill him on the journey. **19** And if it[64] connected with Mars, and Mars was quick in course, and he is in Pisces, and the Moon connects with him, then predatory beasts will eat him. **20** And if the planet was with the Head and Tail, [but] then the Sun was not in its opposition, it does not indicate harms. **21** And that is modified by the Moon, for she crosses the Head and the Tail twice in every month, but there is not a lunar eclipse until the Sun is with one of the two positions; and you look likewise in nativities [in] which the Head and Tail do not have power over corruption except by means of the Sun.[65]

The lord of the ninth in the houses of the circle [according to Māshā'allāh]

23 Look at the lord of the ninth: for if it was in the Ascendant, he will be of fine religion, a good soul, endearing, knowing the Sunnah. **24** The lord of the ninth in the second: he will get assets from a country not his own, and he will be blessed in relation to journeys. **25** The lord of the ninth in the third: his siblings will marry foreign women, and he will transfer from his own country to [another] country. **26** The lord of the ninth in the fourth: his parents will have hidden illnesses, and they will die outside of [their] homeland. **27** The lord of the ninth in the fifth: he will have children in a country not his own, and will marry, and his eye will delight in [the children]. **28** The lord of the ninth in the sixth: he will be blessed with slaves and riding animals, and he will be ill on journeys; and if he was healthy, it corrupts his slaves (and there is no escape from one of the two). **29** The lord of the ninth in the seventh: he will marry a foreign woman, of good character, pleasing; and if it was a fortune, she will be pious. **30** The lord of the ninth in the eighth: he will suffer highway robbery on journeys, and he will be eager in

---

[63] This seems to be Mars, not the lord of the Ascendant.

[64] This may still be Jupiter; it cannot be the Sun, which would be indicated by a feminine verb.

[65] I am not sure what this means.

the accumulation of assets. **31** The lord of the ninth <in> its own place: he will have few journeys, be upright in the religion of [his] fathers, good in intention. **32** The lord of the ninth in the tenth: his siblings will marry women better than themselves, or from the family of the house of the Sultan, and he will be pious. **33** The lord of the ninth in the eleventh: he friends will have piety [and] love him in the religion of God, and his siblings will marry foreign women. **34** The lord of the ninth in the twelfth: he will be wicked in his intention,[66] a corruptor of religion, and will think himself to be in the right. **35** One works in this topic if the ninth and its lord were both free of the infortunes, and the fortunes do not witness.

The Lot of travel [according to Māshā'allāh][67]

37 Then, look at the Lot of travel, and it is that you calculate from the lord of the ninth to the ninth place, and what[ever] there is, project it from the Ascendant, and where it terminates, that is the Lot of travel. **38** So look at this Lot, in which position relative to the Ascendant it is: for if it was in the stakes, it indicates an abundance of travels. **39** And along with it, call upon the lord of the ninth as a witness: for if it was more numerous in its testimony, then the judgment for him [is the same] (and likewise for all topics). **40** If it was in the Midheaven, then he will travel because of the Sultan; then speak about the places based on what I will tell you. **41** (And[68] if it was withdrawing, it is below [that]. **42** And if it was not looking at the Ascendant, this approach is not indicative for him, so look at the lord of the house of the Lot and Mars: for if they both looked at each other, he will have many travels; and if the lord of the Ascendant witnesses them both, he will not be established in his own country.)

---

[66] For the rest of the sentence, following **E**. **M** contains a few more phrases (missing in **E**), but which are smudged; one of them might be a variation of al-Rijāl, who adds here "he will not fear God."

[67] Cf. Tehran, Dānishgāh, Nafīsī 429 (71b-72a); Majlis 17490 (138).

[68] This parenthetical remark must be Sahl's own, as it does not appear in the Māshā'allāh manuscripts nor in this passage in al-Rijāl.

43 If the Lot of travel was in the third, ninth, fifth, or eleventh, then look at the lord of the Ascendant: for if it looked at it, he will travel;[69] and if it did not look at it, he will have few travels. **44** And if it looked at it and it was made unfortunate, he will suffer highway robbery.

45 If the Lot of travel was in the second, sixth, eighth, or twelfth, the lord of the Ascendant looking at it, then his travel will be with the defect which the Lot indicates, and he will experience toil and distress; and if it[70] was made unfortunate, confinement and fetters and illness will afflict him.

Chapter [9.5]: On looking into the matter of religion & fidelity[71]

1 Look at these two places which are the two indicators over that, and they are the third house and the ninth from the Ascendant. **2** So know which sign it is, and who is in it, and who is looking at it from the trine, square, sextile, or opposition, and the lord of the house and of the bound and exaltation, what their positions are.

3 Then, look at the Lot of religion,[72] where is its position and is it in a convertible sign (or in a fixed sign, or in one having two bodies), and is it in a

---

[69] M reads, "And if a fortune looked at it, he will travel and his journey will be profitable." This is something interesting to keep in mind, but is not reflected in the Māshā'allāh Lot texts.

[70] This is probably the Lot, not the lord of the Ascendant.

[71] For this chapter, cf. al-Khayyāt, *JN* Ch. 29 (which however is incomplete in the Latin). Although some sentences may draw on Rhetorius, it does not appear in *BA*. Note that unlike other topics with numerous items, this has three straightforward ones: houses, a Lot, and a natural significator. The terms for "religion" (دين) and "fidelity" or even "loyalty" (وفاء) are important, as is Mercury. "Religion" refers to something one professes, a creed (in Latin, this is sometimes construed as "law," *lex*), and indeed unlike many ancient religions, the Abrahamic and Christian religions are heavy on doctrine, rules, and legal systems. "Fidelity" refers to the level of one's loyalty, and meeting one's obligations. And Mercury is of course a planet of writing, teaching, and interpretation. So a lot of this chapter focuses on the native's relationship to the conventional morality and teachings of his society and legal system, rather than identifying which religion he belongs to, or his personal feelings and devotion.

[72] I believe that Sahl's source is using the Moon-Mercury Lot (projected from the Ascendant, reversed by night), which is identical to Dorotheus's Lot of friendship, and is attested to by Abū Ma'shar (*ITA* VI.2.36 and *Gr. Intr.* VIII.4), al-Rijāl (Ch. IV.10), and Māshā'allāh (unpublished MS) which is identical to Dorotheus's Lot of friendship. By contrast, Abū Bakr (Ch. II.1.10) uses Māshā'allāh's text for the Lot of Spirit or *Daimōn* and refers to it as such: see **73-91**.

stake (or what follows a stake, or falling); and the lord of this Lot, [whether] it is eastern or western, direct or retrograde, is it under the rays or going out of the rays.

4 Then look at Mercury: what is his mixture,[73] and with which of the planets is he greater in participation?

[Sahl's Item 3: Mercury][74]

5 Because if you found Mercury in a house of Jupiter, looked at by him, then the native will be loved, praised, having religion and fidelity, confining himself to the one he is in.[75]

6 And if Mercury was in a house of Saturn and looked at by him, then the native will have assistants and sustenance, being influential in the matters of Fortune and looking into it according to the matters of the world, hating amusements, humble, enduring confinement and difficulty, and especially if along with that Jupiter and Venus were falling, in the bound of Saturn, and they were both not looking at Mercury. **7** And if with this Mars is[76] looking at Mercury, then the native will be skilled at falsehood, a speaker of lies and what is worthless, a liar, criminal, a destroyer of matters in thinking and intentions, [and] unhappy along with that.

8 And if Mercury was in the house and bound of Mars, being looked at by him, and it was from a square or opposition, then he will treat as good what is vain and false, thinking blood is appropriate in it, and lying and anger.[77]

9 And if it was Venus instead of Mars, then it exchanges [that] for pleasures and delights, and generosity, and amusement, and women, and there will be evident good omens. **10** And if Mars looked at him, it will be more fickle and stupid for him.

11 And if Mercury was the governor of that by himself,[78] then he will learn from books, narrate things from them at length, be passionate about books, [and] well reputed in knowledge if Jupiter looked at him.

---

[73] This word (مزج) can also refer to temperament and disposition.
[74] For this subsection, see also Ch. 1.36, **39-51**.
[75] Or perhaps, "confining himself to what is in it."
[76] **E** reads "is not," but I have omitted the "not" because it does not make sense: if Mercury is combined with Mars it does traditionally indicate lying, combativeness, etc., just as described here.
[77] Al-Khayyāt adds that if it was from a good aspect, then the native will compose lies.

12 And if the Sun was the governor of the religion,[79] it indicates that he will be reverent, God-fearing, a lover of invoking God's name,[80] putting little value on himself because of that.

13 And if it was the Moon, then he will be sensible, loving what is appropriate, knowledgeable, actively professing religion,[81] loving[82] books, a worshipper (and especially if the Moon is not unfortunate).

14 And know that if the planet was falling,[83] then the native will be of the devotees and masters of religion and reverence, and especially if Mercury was with the Moon or with Jupiter in the third or ninth place.

15 And if Saturn was with Mercury in either[84] of the two places, then he will be base, [*uncertain*][85] upon him. **16** And if Mars looked at him, then he will be a liar in what he performs of the religion; and if Venus looked at him, then he will preserve[86] his soul in [a state of] innocence;[87] and if Jupiter looked at him, it indicates sincerity and fidelity and love for the other; and if it was the Sun, then he will be a worshipper, calling upon God much,[88] [*two illegible words*].

17 And if the Lot of Fortune[89] was in the bound of the fortunes, then the native will be pure, sensible,[90] especially if the Lot at that time was in a female sign, devoid of the infortunes, and especially from Saturn.

---

[78] That is, in his own sign.
[79] That is, if Mercury is in Leo.
[80] This word (ذكر) can also mean "reputation," which also makes sense for the Sun; but in religious terms it does refer to practices of pronouncing Divine names (especially in Sufism), which seems to make more sense here.
[81] The standard modern lexicon suggests more bland words like "pious" or "religious," but this verb Form (تديّن) means to actively profess religion in one's life.
[82] محبابًا عن, which does not appear in the lexicon but derives from the verb "to love."
[83] This probably means being in the third and ninth.
[84] That is, the third and ninth.
[85] **E** seems to read something like حتفًا (and **M** is missing this passage). My sense is that this should be something like "skeptical," or at any rate not really interested in religion; or perhaps that his intentions are bad. However, Rhetorius Ch. 57 (Holden p. 63) says their being in the third shows revelations from dreams and mysterious things.
[86] محباب, as in **13** above.
[87] Reading tentatively as برينة. Or, "freedom."
[88] See the footnote to **12** above.
[89] This should probably be the Lot of religion or the Lot of Spirit.
[90] This was the same term used for the Moon above (لبيب); note that the Lot of Fortune is especially related to the Moon.

[Sahl's Item 1: The third and the ninth]

18 And if you found the ninth place and its lord in a sign having two bodies, then the native's intention will be in no religion, [he will be] a participant in various religions, and his activity will be in the majority of religions. **19** And speak about his condition and religion according to the planets which are in that place: because if Mars was in the ninth, it indicates that he will leave behind the religion which his parents [raised him] in, and will convert to the worst there could be; and [judge] the rest of the planets based on their essences of fortune and misfortune. **20** And if that place was convertible and its lord in a convertible sign, then he will remain skeptical, changeable, his view not being firm on [one] thought nor action nor religion. **21** And if the sign was fixed, <and its lord in a fixed sign, then the native will be firm>[91] in religion, and especially if the ninth place is not made unfortunate by Mars (and it is worse for that if his misfortune was by day). **22** And if you found the place convertible and its lord in a fixed sign, then he will be skeptical at the beginning of his years, then be religious at the end of his life, based on its lord and the place which it is in.

23 Best is if the lord of the ninth place and the third was in the Ascendant or the Midheaven, if it was not made unfortunate: for then he will be a leader, knowledgeable, loving religion, seeking what is appropriate, and especially if it was with the Sun.[92] **24** Now if it was <eastern, then he will proclaim his religion, and if it was>[93] western then he will relate his religion secretly.

25 If[94] you found the Head of the Dragon by night in the third place, and by day in the ninth place, and Jupiter and Mercury looking at it, then he will be well known by his own name in the religion.

26 And[95] if the lord of the ninth was in its exaltation or triplicity, and it had rulership in the nativity (and equivalent to that is [if] it became the lord of the triplicity of the glowing one),[96] and in addition it is in a stake, in an

---

[91] Adding on the basis of al-Rijāl.
[92] Al-Rijāl and al-Khayyāt both read, "Jupiter." But I could see it both ways.
[93] Adding with the sense of al-Khayyāt.
[94] Cf. Rhetorius Ch. 57 (p. 89), which however lacks any day/night distinction.
[95] Cf. Rhetorius Ch. 57 (p. 87).
[96] That is, if the lord of the ninth is also the primary triplicity lord of the sect light. See also **42** below.

upright position, then he will become a leader in religion or obeyed among the great, being made a chief of them.

27 If Mercury was with the Moon in the ninth place, in his own house or the house of the Moon, and the Lot of religion was with him, then he will be one who is inspired, or he will be effective in insight and knowledge, an interpreter of dreams, and giving voice to spirits. **28** Now if Jupiter was with them or looked at them, then he will be truthful, received[97] due to what he accomplishes, a counselor in the affairs of the powerful.

29 And if the Moon was in the house of Jupiter in the ninth place, in nativities of the night, then he will be an astrologer, knowledgeable, God-fearing.

30 And if you found the lord of the ninth to be Mercury, and in the ninth there was a planet of his share,[98] then he will be a theologian, a judge, and will recite the words of the Book and be devoted to the Book. **31** And likewise if the Ascendant was the house of Mercury or the house of Saturn.

32 And if you found the Moon in the Ascendant, in a sign of the class of people, he will be a lover of morals;[99] and likewise if you found the fortunes in a sign of the class of people (and especially [in] the Midheaven). **33** <And if you found Mars there>,[100] the native will be lethal, committing what is forbidden by the people; and it is worse for that if the Moon was with him. **34** And likewise if you found Saturn in the Ascendant, then he will be hateful to the general populace and [be of] a like viewpoint, and especially if the sign was of the class of people.

35 If you found the Lot of religion with Mars, then he is the worst in the matter of religion. **36** And if it was with Jupiter, then he has fine <religion and speech>.[101] **37** And if it was with Saturn, then he will be <a scholar of ancient things>. **38** <And if it was with Mercury, then he will be> a master of commerce and knowledge. **39** And if it was with the Moon, he will be skillful in professing religion.[102] **40** And if it was with Venus, then he will be a lover

---

[97] That is, received into social circles.

[98] خط. Normally this would mean "sect" or "dignity," but here I take this to really mean a fixed star of the nature of Mercury, not a planet.

[99] Reading as خُلْق; but this could also be read as "humanity" (خَلْق).

[100] Adding on the basis of al-Rijāl, who specifies that Mars should also be in a human sign, but I take this as a given.

[101] **E** reads: "he will be wealthy." I am reading the material in brackets through **38** with al-Rijāl, as both **E** and **M** are confused about or omit parts of **36-38**.

[102] **E**: "A skillful theologian."

of amusement and easy in character. **41** And if it was with the Sun and is not under his rays, then he will be a lover of reputation, knowledgeable.

42 If the ninth place was the exaltation of Jupiter, the exaltation of the Sun, or the exaltation of Venus, and the lord of the exaltation was the lord of the triplicity of the glowing one [of the sect], and its position was good, then his livelihood will be from religion, and in that he will get wealth, he will be praised, and obeyed among the people.

43 Now if the lord of the religion[103] was Mars, and he looked at it, then he corrupts the matter of [the native's] religion. **44** And if it was Jupiter, then the native will be sensible, praised, and especially if Jupiter was in a good place, and not under the rays nor retrograde: because when a planet is retrograde, its signification lies; and if it is under the rays, it is deceptive [and] a failure.[104]

45 Now[105] if a fortune was in the ninth and third, then he will have benefit because of religion, worship, travel, the stars, and dreams, he will get powerful assets from what I mentioned, and especially if the fortunes were in their joys; and likewise if you found the lord of these two places in a good position. **46** And[106] know that the benefit will be from literature and writing, and the praise in them will not occur unless Mercury is with Jupiter or looking at him or in one of his associations.

47 And if Saturn was in the ninth or he was its lord and his position good, then [the native] will have depth and knowledge. **48** And[107] likewise, if he was trining Mercury and each of them was in a share of the other (of the house, bound, exaltation, or image): for the native will be knowledgeable in writing and literature, and after that tribulation will afflict him because of knowledge and literature; and it is worse for that if Mars looked, because perhaps humiliation and ruin will afflict him. **49** And if Saturn was there without an infortune, it indicates worship, dreams, and the knowledge of

---

[103] This could simply be the lord of the ninth, but I have a feeling it is really the triplicity lord of Mercury or the lord of the Lot of religion. It is not reflected in al-Khayyāt.
[104] For these last two adjectives, **E** reads: "ignorant."
[105] For this sentence, see Rhetorius Ch. 57 (pp. 62-63).
[106] For this sentence, cf. Firmicus Maternus III.7, **12-13**; and Ch. 1.36, **51** above.
[107] For this sentence, cf. Rhetorius Ch. 57 (p. 64), which has Saturn and Mercury looking at the *third*.

secrets. **50** Now[108] if that was by day, then say worship and leadership among scholars; and if it was by night, then say worship, dreams, prediction, and augury, and especially if he was in the house of Jupiter; and in every condition he will be wicked in religion and intention, and he will be of those who do not believe and accumulate assets through injustice.

51 And[109] if Jupiter was in the ninth by day, it indicates devoutness and knowledge and secrets, and praise; and if he was in it by night, then say unbelief and the lies of dreams. **52** And if he was in it, burned along with Mercury, it indicates worship, wisdom, books, medicine, and the innovation of marvelous things. **53** And if he was like that [but] appearing, rising [out of the rays] along with Mercury, and [in] the ninth sign, it indicates[110] prediction, the augury of birds, medicine, and perhaps it indicates worship. **54** Now if Jupiter was there with the Sun and he was free of the rays, [the native] will be of those who defend the Sunnah and speak with words of wisdom. **55** And if it was with Saturn and they were appearing from the rays, the native will be of those who collect many assets by reason of religion and knowledge, and he will have many travels.

56 And[111] if Venus was there by day and the sign female, it indicates unbelief and the hypocrisy of the devout, and enemies of knowledge and secrets, and especially if Saturn looked. **57** Now if she was like that by night, it indicates worship and the elegance of knowledge and the building of mosques.

58 And[112] if Mercury was in the ninth [as a morning star],[113] looking at Jupiter, it indicates the stars and the earning of money from it, and he will be

---

[108] For the first half of this sentence, cf. Rhetorius Ch. 57 (p. 89).

[109] For **51** only, see Rhetorius Ch. 57 (p. 89).

[110] Reading for "along with Mercury, and the ninth sign, which indicates…". Otherwise, everything else in the sentence would be parenthetical, and it would end without stating what it indicates.

[111] For this paragraph, cf. Rhetorius Ch. 57 (p. 90), although Sahl's source is misconstruing Rhetorius in the diurnal version. Rather, Venus by day shows someone afflicted by spirits (*daimōns*), or who will go about proclaiming things about the gods and dreams, hairy and in rags, but especially if Saturn looked.

[112] This paragraph bears a resemblance to Rhetorius Ch. 57 (p. 90), but the closest match is Firmicus Maternus (III.7), who uses the same Greek source as Rhetorius. Since the organization of the passages differ (and indeed, Sahl's is more complicated and jumbled), here is Firmicus: "**40** Mercury being established in the ninth place from the Hour-marker, if he were found in this place without the raying of any star, will make argumentative, debating dialecticians, professing to know whatever is suggested to them by no mastery, malicious people, but who are able to fulfill nothing by means of effective thinking. **41** But if he were found as a morning [star] in this place, it will make priests, divine people, haruspices, au-

knowledgeable. **59** And if he was westernizing,[114] without the aspect of Jupiter, he will be knowledgeable [but] unhappy. **60** Now if he was with Saturn there, he will be contentious in religions, and not firm in [one] religion if the sign was convertible. **61** And if it[115] was by night, he will be contentious in religion, a bad man, in conflict with the truth. **62** And if he was with the Sun there, he will be a theologian in making judgments, eloquent, collecting assets for that reason, and he will have many journeys and will gain from foreigners.

63 And if the lord of the Ascendant connected with the lord of the ninth in a strong place, the native will be raised up high because of religion, knowledge, being away from home. **64** And if it was in a bad place such as the twelfth, the native will remain away from home and will experience hardship from enemies and illness. **65** Now if the planet was a fortune, then along with that he will be good in religion and intention, but he will not be raised up high and his livelihood will be with foreigners, and he will be of those who investigate knowledge. **66** And if the lord of the ninth was in the eleventh, the native will be well known, mentioned, a trusted guarantor of the assets of the authorities, an interpreter of dreams.

---

gurs, mathematicians, astrologers, medical doctors, and those from whom the protections of life are sought by means of these arts and practices. **42** But these things will be stronger if he were protected by the raying of a benevolent star, for it will make lucky, blessed, great, powerful people, and those on whom all trappings of luckiness are conferred. **43** But if the malevolent stars regarded a Mercury so put, or if they were found in [his] diameter or in a square, it will make irreligious, sacrilegious people, the despoilers of temples, condemned, condemnable, and those who wander about, fleeing, in foreign places, or who are oppressed by the condemnations of exile. **44** But Mercury being established as an evening [star] in this place will make priests, magicians, medical doctors, artisans, and those for whom the protections of life are prepared from these arts, and people with such cleverness that they teach themselves whatever the teaching of [any] master has not handed down to them."

[113] Adding based on Rhetorius and Firmicus.

[114] مغرّب. Perhaps this means being under the rays; but Firmicus does not have this.

[115] I believe this means, if he is there *with* Saturn by night. This sentence should probably be a parenthetical addition to **60**, but since Sahl's passage differs in many ways from Firmicus, I have left it alone.

[Sahl's Item 2: The Lot of religion][116]

67 Then, look at the Lot of religion: for if Jupiter looked at the Lot, it indicates worship, sincerity, and the native will have suitable dreams, a reporter reporting matters which will exist in the future, and he will speak with the words of prophets and philosophers.[117] **68** And if Mercury was in the Ascendant and looked at the Lot from a sextile, then the native will be of those deceiving the people, and he will work wonders and will get the assets of the people due to the deception, and he will have intelligence, and sense, and [his own] ideas.

69 And[118] if the Lot of Fortune conjoined with the Lot of religion in the third and ninth along with a fortune (or it looked at it), it indicates eloquence in religion. **70** And if the Lot of religion was burned, it does not indicate good in the religion. **71** And the more preferable of its indications is if it is appearing[119] in a stake. **72** Now if the Lot was in Capricorn, it indicates tranquility and dignity; and if it was in Aries, Taurus, Leo, or Scorpio, it indicates stubbornness.[120]

[The Lot of Spirit: Māshā'allāh][121]

73 And[122] if <the Lot of the Invisible> and its lord were both cleansed of the infortunes, <it indicates good for both his inner conscience and the outer practice of his religion>.[123] **74** And if it and its lord were made unfortunate by the infortunes, both being received, it indicates the piety of the native, and

---

[116] Do note **35-41** above, as well. Again, this Lot could easily be the Lot of Spirit, and not the Moon-Mercury Lot.

[117] **E**: "philosophy."

[118] This paragraph is similar to material following Māshā'allāh's treatment of the Lot of Fortune in Ch. 1.37. Sentence **69** is like Ch. 1.37, **33**; sentence **70** is like 1.37, **29**; and sentence **72** is evidently a version of 1.37, **30**.

[119] This probably means, "appearing from under the rays."

[120] Reading with **E**. But **M** reads, "an astrologer."

[121] This subsection on the Lot of Spirit (in Arabic, the Lot of the Invisible) is by Māshā'allāh, as evidenced by Vat. Pal. lat. 1892, ff. 99v-100r. Unfortunately, the Arabic MSS from Tehran omit it. A parallel version can also be found in the Latin Abū Bakr, II.1.10.

[122] What exists of this sentence is from **M**, which then jumps to the middle of **79**. **E** omits all of this sentence and jumps to **74**. In this section, the Lot represents the native's outer practices and behavior (his "openness"), and its lord his inner conscience and thoughts.

[123] Adding very broadly with the astrological logic of this section.

the fineness of [his] conscience,[124] and the praise of the people upon him. **75** And if it was not made unfortunate but its lord was unfortunate, it indicates the fineness of his openness and the badness of his inner soul. **76** Now if it was unfortunate and its lord free of the infortunes, his conscience will be better than his openness.

77 And if the Lot was in the stakes, the native will be firm in [his religion] and there will not be doubt nor uncertainty in it.[125] **78** And if in addition its lord was received and it is looking at its place, what he believes[126] is consistent with reason and the religion of truth. **79** And if its lord was not received (except that the fortunes do[127] look at it, and it is free of the infortunes), then it strengthens good works and he will not do any work except that of reason. **80** And if the lord of the Lot was retrograde, then the native will convert from his own religion to another one. **81** And if the lord of the Lot was contrary to[128] itself, it indicates transgression, foolishness, and slander.

82 And if the Lot was in the ninth, it indicates his piety in his religion. **83** And if along with that its lord was received, looking at the Lot, then it indicates his renunciation and seclusion from the world, and that he will not get involved with anything of the affairs of the world, and he will be self-denying in it, [and] the mentioning of [his] withdrawal from it will grow. **84** And if it was made unfortunate, not received, doubt and corruption will enter upon him in his religion. **85** And speak likewise for the third, except that it is less than what I mentioned, and there will be piety in his siblings.

86 And if the Lot was in the eleventh, it indicates the goodness of the native in the matter of his religion at the end of his life, and it indicates love and superiority. **87** And if its lord was free of the infortunes, looking at its place, it increases the good for him. **88** And if with what I mentioned it was received, he will be good and his inclination in that will conform to the truth and reason; and if it was made unfortunate, it undermines his conscience. **89** And in the fifth, he will have children who have piety in the religion they are in.

---

[124] Reading السريرة with the instances below for السّيرة ("way of life").
[125] The version of this passage in Abū Bakr states that if the Lot or its lord are falling (cadent), the native's piety and so on will fade over time.
[126] Or more literally, "sees" (یری).
[127] Omitting "not."
[128] مضدًا. That is, in its detriment, opposite its sign.

90 And if the Lot was in the second, eighth, sixth, or twelfth, it indicates the badness of the native's openness;[129] but if along with that its lord was corrupted, it indicates the badness of his inner soul along with his openness. **91** And if they not made unfortunate, his openness will be good, from his conscience; and if along with that it was received, his conscience will be powerful in reverence.

---

[129] علانيّة. That is, how he is public and open about his thoughts, as opposed to being secretive.

Chapter 10: [Occupation, authority, & valor]

1 <The tenth> indicates authority, high rank, dignity, and the uprightness of [one's] exertion, and children; and it indicates status, works, occupation,[1] and it is the indicator of the middle of the lifespan, and is in three sections.

2 The first chapter is on work and occupation.

3 The second chapter is on authority and the people of esteem, and the nativities of kings and the nobility.

4 The third chapter is on heroism and valor.[2]

[Chapter 10.1: On work & occupation]

[Chapter 10.1.1: Overview]

[al-Andarzaghar]

1 Now[3] as for work and occupation, begin with an examination of the matter of chronic illness before this chapter, for the reason that if chronic illness afflicts a man, it nullifies work: so you ought to begin with an examination of the topic of chronic illness. **2** Now if you found him to be ill in a limb, you should not judge anything for him in the topic of work. **3** Then, look after that at these nine items:[4]

    4 The first of them: look at the planets which distribute work among the people, and they are Venus, Mars, and Mercury.[5]

    5 Then look also at the Moon: with whom does she connect at the assembly of the meeting or the opposition, and which of the planets is the victor over it?[6]

    6 Third: look at the twelfth-parts of the planets.[7]

---

[1] Or, "craft," "trade" (الصّناعة).

[2] This word (نجدة) also means assistance and help, as in coming to someone's aid.

[3] Cf. Rhetorius Ch. 82 (p. 134). The instruction here to look for chronic illness first, is from Rhetorius's quotation of Anubio.

[4] Sahl has rearranged much of the following material and added from other authors, so I will indicate here in footnotes what sentences correspond to *BA*.

[5] This refers to Ch. 10.1.1, **15-17** and Ch. 10.1.3, **34**; see also the list in Ch. 10.1.5.

[6] This refers to Ch. 10.1.4, **1-14** (and maybe **15-17**), and **26-27**, and Ch. 10.1.6, **6**.

7 Fourth: look at the bound and house of the planet which distributes the work, and who is looking at it (of the fortunes and infortunes).[8]

8 Fifth: look in the easternness of the planets which distribute the work, and their westernness.[9]

9 Sixth: look at the Lot of work.[10]

10 Seventh: how [the Lot's] place is, and its lord.[11]

11 Eighth: look at the essence of the signs in which these planets are.[12]

12 Ninth: look at the more excellent ones of the places: the first of them is the Ascendant, then the Midheaven, the seventh, the house of fathers; then look at the second house from these stakes, and at the sixth sign.[13]

13 So, it is from these nine items that the works of the sons of Adam are known. 14 (The Lot of work is taken from Mercury to Mars by day, and by night the contrary of that.)[14]

15 The sum of what I have mentioned is that you begin by looking at Mercury, Venus, and Mars, and their places, and the houses in which they are, and the bounds and type of signs in which they are, and their easternness and westernness, and who is looking at them (of the fortunes and infortunes), and look at the Lot of work and its lord in the way you looked at these three planets. 16 (And those three things[15] which I described at the top

---

[7] The chapter in *BA* which refers to this (III.10.7) corresponds generally to the occupations in Sahl's Ch. 10.1.5; but only Sahl's sentence 16 actually uses the term.

[8] One reference to bounds and signs occurs in *BA* III.10.7, but the present topic and its source in *BA* III.10.3 corresponds to Ch. 10.1.4, **28-39** below.

[9] That is, the planets which are coming out of the rays within seven days before or after the nativity (Rhetorius). This refers to Ch. 10.1.6, **1-5**.

[10] The single sentence describing this in *BA* III.10.6.1, 1 (from Rhetorius Ch. 83, p. 141), does not correspond exactly to any sentence below, but is close to the end of **15** below and **17**. Instead, Sahl uses Māshā'allāh's Lot in Ch. 10.2.5 (see my commentary there).

[11] See footnote above.

[12] See generally Ch. 10.1.5.

[13] A corresponding passage does not obviously appear in the Latin *BA*, but do see **18-27** below. However, this sentence from *BA* seems to derive from Rhetorius Ch. 82 (p. 134), and is in error. Rhetorius does not use the seventh (and therefore not the eighth), and adds the Lot of Fortune.

[14] This is the Greek Lot of action (*praxis*); see Ch. 10.2.5, which uses several calculations and texts.

[15] The Arabic actually reads "topics" or "chapters" (الأبواب), which suggest the three parts of this whole treatment (i.e., occupation, royal nativities, and heroism); but since this is al-

of the chapter are indeed needed.) **17** And if you looked at these three planets and at the Lot and its lord, and you sought out these things which I have explained to you, then mix the power of the planets distributing the work with the one looking at it, and their places, and the type of sign which the planet is in.

18 And the sum of that is that you take the way of life and work from the second and the Midheaven.

19 Now if you saw the lord of the Ascendant in a position, then he is in need of the essence of that sign and place, so [see what]¹⁶ it grants. **20** But if you saw a star in the Ascendant, then see which house it is the lord of, because [that person] will need him and approach him, and seek what is with him—of siblings, parents, children, women, the Sultan, and what is like that. **21** And if they¹⁷ were in the house of his assets, then likewise they need his assets: so know the meaning of what I have named for you (with respect to the twelve places and their essences), and what I have named for you of the house of life, assets, siblings, fathers, and likewise until the twelve signs are completed for you.

22 And¹⁸ know that the lord of the house of assets indicates profits and work. **23** So look at the lord of the house of assets, where it is: for if it was retreating, then he will have bad work [and] be despised among the people of his work. **24** And if it was advancing,¹⁹ his work will be fine, since he will get the good from it.

25 And²⁰ as for the Midheaven, it indicates authority and status because of the Sultan, and it blends his work with the hands of the Sultan by analogy with the conditions of people:²¹ because the retreating [planet] retreats

---

ready the first part, I think Sahl really means the three *planets* mentioned above: Mercury, Venus and Mars. See also the next sentence.

¹⁶ Reading for what seems to be قبل, "it receives," but this is ungrammatical.

¹⁷ That is, the lords of those houses.

¹⁸ For this paragraph, cf. also Ch. 2.13, **43**.

¹⁹ Ch. 2.13, **43** reads "received" (مقبول), but I believe that is wrong because "advancing" is the proper contrast to retreating.

²⁰ For **25-26**, see another version in Ch. 2.13, **45**.

²¹ See below, **34ff.**

[and] falls, and the advancing one advances [and] indicates every good. **26** And <likewise> in the revolution of years: because if the lord of the house of the Midheaven was in the Ascendant or the house of hope and an excellent position, it indicates strength in authority. **27** And if it was falling, he will not cease to be fallen.

[Action according to Ptolemy]

28 Then,[22] look too at the planet arising in the early mornings, and the planet which is in the Midheaven, and especially if the Moon conjoined with it. **29** Now if you found a planet with these two testimonies (and that is if it is eastern with the Sun, in the Midheaven), then seek the information about the occupation of the native from it and its bound. **30** And if it was not [both] of these two testimonies, and it had one of them, then do also seek information from it about the native's occupation. **31** Now if you found one of the planets arising with the Sun and the other in the Midheaven, and the Moon is with them both,[23] then take them both together as indicators, and you begin the examination and the indication with the more excellent of them by place, and the stronger of them, then you grant this indication to the other one. **32** Now if there was not a planet arising in the early morning nor do you find a planet in the Midheaven, then seek help about the native's occupation from the lord of the Midheaven: and one whose nativity is like that will be idle, except for [certain] ones of them.

33 Now as for the people with an occupation, the knowledge of that is from the natures of the three planets which I described above,[24] and from the signs they are in.

---

[22] For **28-33**, cf. *Tet.* IV.4 (Robbins pp. 381-83).
[23] Ptolemy has the Moon with the planet in the Midheaven, but Sahl or the translator of Ptolemy must have thought this was asymmetrical: for if one planet was making its morning appearance, and the other was *both* in the Midheaven *and* with the Moon, then the latter would be the intuitive victor. So, Sahl's source has made it ambiguous as to whom the Moon is with, so as to compare them.
[24] That is, Mercury, Venus, and Mars.

[Planetary dignities and conditions in professions]

34 And know that the work in everything has three divisions: the higher, the middling, and the lower; and in each one of these are three works according to these ranks which I have explained.

35 So if the planet was in its house, it grants the middling work of the lowest work. **36** Now if it was in its house and its bound or in its house and its face, it grants more preferable works. **37** And if it was in its exaltation, it grants the preferable [and] more elevated of the ranks. **38** Now if it had a share of its own bound or triplicity, it grants the more exalted of works. **39** If it was in its own house and exaltation together, he will have two works together, and it establishes exaltation for him in the work.

40 And if the planet was retrograde, then judge for him half of that work which it establishes for him.

41 And if it was burned under the rays, then it subtracts[25] from that work of his, one-third of it. **42** And you ought to look according to everything which the Sun burns: for if he burned the house of the planets, then subtract one-third of the work from it.

43 And if it was burned [and] retrograde, then he will not have a work nor a name such as when so-and-so is called a coppersmith, and he will come to the market of coppersmiths so he will be in it, and will mix with the people; but he will not work, nor will he get anything.

44 And if the planet of work was in its own fall, it grants the worst of works. **45** Now if in that house it did have a share such as a bound, face, or triplicity, it grants the middle of that lowest work.

46 Now if it was in an alien place, not having a share in it, neither house nor triplicity, it grants a middling work which is below the original rank which there would be if it was in its house: so understand these social classes.

47 And know that the planets have actions: and among them is speech, and the work of the native, and the work of knowledge, and trades, and I will explain that to you.

---

[25] It seems odd that burning would only take away one-third, while retrogradation would take away one-half.

48 And if a planet granted a work and another planet looked at it, it will grant from its own nature.[26] **49** And I will explain to you the matter of Venus and Saturn in the house of knowledge,[27] and I will distinguish the trades for you.

50 And know that in one place the planet will be a scholar, and in another a merchant, or [in] another the master of a work with his own hands. **51** So see which work it is, in relation to the planet which is looking at it or the planet which is with it, and establish [it] for him from the trades according to who is looking at it: because within the explanation of trade and knowledge is the thing one should seek help from. **52** And that is if the lord of the third looked, then it is knowledge; and if the lord of the fifth looked, then it is a trade; and if it looked at a planet from its house, it grants it all the power;[28] and likewise the exaltation too.

[Chapter 10.1.2:] An explanation of the essences of the planets' works, & an enumeration of them & what they grant

1 I will make clear to you the essences of the works of the planets.[29]

2 Know[30] that the Sun is in the middle of the celestial circles, and that there is no authority, nor those who manage the affairs of the Sultan as well as those with command, and a manager in the people such as treasurers, who have power and reason, except from the Sun, and he is the indicator of kings, authority, the masters of alchemy, and the masters of the scholars of religion. **3** Now if Saturn looked at him, the native will be of those who become monks and are seeking religion, and they come to the doors of Sultans and kings, and especially if Saturn was the lord of the ninth; and if he was the lord

---

[26] See Ch. 10.1.2 for an extensive list of combinations.
[27] العلم. Based on **52** below, and 10.1.2, **3**, this is the third.
[28] This is a case of "handing over power": cf. *Introduction* Ch. 3, **70-72**.
[29] Here we can see that Sahl is omitting *BA*'s version of Rhetorius Ch. 83 (*BA* III.10.6), which outlines the combinations of the three trade planets drawn from Ptolemy. Instead, Sahl substitutes a different list of *all* planets.
[30] In what follows, both **E** and **M** have a negative way of stating what belongs to each planet, viz. that "there is no X without planet Y." But each puts it in a slightly different way. I largely follow **E** and will sometimes make no reference to **M**. **M** tends to say, "X comes from planet Y, and it does not come from another."

of the third, he is of those who are conceited in knowledge and seek it.³¹ **4** And if it was something other than that, then they are people weak in their knowledge and their religion. **5** And if Mercury was with the Sun, he will be of those who sculpt the seals for kings, and write in gold, and the masters of alchemy. **6** And if Venus was with him, he will be of those who understand jewels and perfume, and understand entertainment and singing. **7** And if the Moon looked at him, he will be of the great scholars of kings, and of those who traverse [along] the road and water, and what is like that of works. **8** If her aspect is from a weak place, he is of water carriers³² and sailors and like that. **9** And if Mars looked at him, he will be a master of alchemy and will understand mirrors,³³ and like that. **10** And if Jupiter looked at him, he will be of those understanding the reports of kings, and he will converse with them, and will understand conversation. **11** And certainly if Mercury was with the Sun, he will be of the land surveyors of kings, and [their] assessors.

12 *Venus.* As for Venus, from her is singing, poetry, amusement, fun, rapture, laughter, and what is pleasant: and that does not exist without her because the circle of Venus is the indicator over that. **13** Now if Saturn looked at her, it makes him a mourner.³⁴ **14** And if Venus looked at Saturn from the signs of people, she indicates singing.³⁵ **15** And if he looked at her from signs of the earth, it indicates the sale of perfume and aromatic plants. **16** And if she looked at him from signs of water, she indicates the sale of pearls. **17** And if her aspect to him was from her own house or exaltation, <missing>. **18** And if her aspect was from burning or she was retrograde, corrupted, or in a place of exile, he will be of those who launder clothing and what resembles that. **19** And if she looked at him from signs of fire, she grants an occupation <with fire>, and what is like that. **20** And if her aspect was not powerful, she grants the work of a glazier, like bottles and [*uncer-*

---

³¹ What Sahl or his source might mean is that the ninth indicates religion, whereas the third indicates more worldly knowledge. But perhaps this should be read as يتبدّلون, "they are changeable" or "convert."

³² Tentatively reading a much older meaning for what seems to be الفتوح.

³³ Perhaps because metallic mirrors (not to mention the creation of glass) require working with fire.

³⁴ Reading as نَوَّاح. That is, a professional mourner who sings at funerals.

³⁵ Perhaps singing funerary songs? **M** reads "hardship," but that does not really fit the theme here.

tain].³⁶ **21** And if Jupiter looked at her, it makes him be the owner of a hostel,³⁷ and likewise if the lord of the ninth looked at her. **22** Now if Mercury conjoined her or looked at her, he will be a writer of eloquent things. **23** And if the Moon³⁸ looked at her, he will be a master of poetry, sermons, and speech. **24** And if Mars looked at her, he will be of those who rub their bodies with scented oil,³⁹ converse, and scoff. **25** And if she was with the Sun, he will be of those who make kings laugh and offer them stories, songs, pleasure, and amusement.

26 *Mercury.* As for Mercury, there is no writing, wisdom, and commerce except from him, because his celestial circle is an indicator of that. **27** Now if Mercury was in a bad place, instead of writing it indicates knitting (that is, weaving), and there is no knitting except from his aspect from a bad place, nor sewing, darning, or the measuring of clothing except from him—if he was in a bad place. **28** If Venus looked at him, he will be of those who write poems and songs for women. **29** And if Saturn looked at him, he will be of those who write incantations and magic,⁴⁰ medicine, and the work of jesters. **30** And if Jupiter looked at him, he will be of those who write out volumes of the Qur'ān and the Hadith. **31** And if he was with the Sun, he will be of those who write for kings. **32** And if Mars looked at him, he will be of those who write in red [ink] and images.⁴¹ **33** And if the Moon looked at him, he will be of those who write [for] lawsuits.⁴²

34 *The Moon.* Now as for the Moon, there are no messages, lawsuits, and evil eyes of the people toward one another, and haste, and partnership, and the postal service, except from her. **35** If the Sun looked at her,⁴³ he will be an

---

³⁶ **B** seems to read الحرر; **E**: الحرف.

³⁷ Reading as الخان. This could also be الحان, a tavern or bar, but the mention of the 9ᵗʰ (house of travel) suggests a hostel.

³⁸ Reading for "Mercury."

³⁹ Reading as يمرخون, which is the same Arabic root as that of the planet Mars. The text reads يمرحون ("who are cheerful"), but this seems too generic and bland. Still it is unclear to me what is Martial about putting on cologne or scented oil.

⁴⁰ See **44** below.

⁴¹ This probably refers to the Islamic practice of stretching and altering the shapes of the letters to form images with them. But perhaps Mars indicates danger because of the Islamic prohibition on images.

⁴² Or, contentions generally. This probably includes both writing out the legal paperwork, and also recording the proceedings as a stenographer.

⁴³ Reading the rest with **M**. **E**: "he will be in what kings rule, and rulership, and he will manage it."

aide to the king, or a message-carrier. **36** And if Venus looked at her, he will be inventive[44] in the business of women, such as pampering. **37** And if Mercury looked at her, he will be inventive in books. **38** And if Saturn looked at her, he will be a sailor. **39** And if Mars looked at her, he will be one who is inventive in raids, and he will travel, loving fighting and conquests. **40** And if Jupiter looked at her, he will be of those who are sworn to[45] the uprightness of the people, and command with righteousness, and return again to the *hajj*.

41 *Saturn.* As for Saturn, there is no grief, sorrow, wailing, and mourning except from him, along with hardship, poverty, diggers, oppressors,[46] builders, demolition, and suffocation (and what resembles that too) except from him, and that is because his celestial circle is an indicator of that. **42** Now if Venus looked at him, she makes him be wealthy, solitary, and mourning will increase with the wealth. **43** And if Jupiter looked at him, he will be a sorrowful judge.[47] **44** And[48] if Mercury looked at him, he will be of those writing

---

[44] In this and the next few sentences, reading with **M** for **E**'s "he will be in disagreement" (مختلفًا).

[45] Reading somewhat uncertainly as يحتلفون في.

[46] Only **E** has this, and I am reading الجبّارون for what seems to be الغبّارون. The latter root has to do with the past, dust, what is leftover, etc., and I would be tempted to translate it as "relics." But Sahl is listing professions and actions here, so I am following my modified spelling.

[47] Reading as قاضيًا بكّاءً. But perhaps this adjective should be read as some form of ركاء or زكاء, a "righteous" or "clever" judge.

[48] See also **29** above. In this sentence and the next, **M** reads differently enough, and with more implications, than **E**. At the end of this sentence **M** continues: "...sorcerer, *if* he is the lord of the third. 45 And if he was the lord of the ninth, he will be of those who write the Torah." The differences are these. In **E**'s reading, Mercury paired with Saturn automatically suggests sorcery, and the only thing that changes it is Mercury's possible lordship of the third and ninth, which indicate types of knowledge: the third is simply "knowledge," while the ninth is more scholarly knowledge in a religious tradition. But in **M**'s reading, the important point is that the third house itself indicates magic and sorcery, whereas the ninth indicates exoteric, organized religion—they are both religious houses. Deciding between these readings is difficult. On the one hand, (1) the third house *is* a religious house in traditional astrology, and my sense is that it has more to do with folk religion and folk practices (here: sorcery, spells): this favors **M**. And (2) it is hard to believe that the *default* interpretation of Mercury-Saturn is sorcery: again, this favors **M**. But (3) the third house is often taken to be a house of knowledge, whereas the ninth is specifically religious knowledge: this favors **E**. Moreover, (4) the implication of assigning sorcery and magic as a key signification of the third is so striking that my tendency to be conservative in my interpretation again favors **E**.

magical spells, and a sorcerer. **45** And if he was the lord of the third, he will be of those who write knowledge; and if he was the lord of the ninth, he will be of those who write the Torah. **46** And if the Moon looked at him, he will be a [unclear][49] or one who lets his animals of burden out for hire, or <what> resembles that, or <he will be> of those who manage doorways, and he will toil as well as play.[50] **47** And if Mars looked at him and he was the lord of the ninth,[51] he will be of those who seek the *jihād*, and wear wool, and shed false tears.[52] **48** And if the Sun looked at him, he will be of those who come to rulership, and passes judgment <upon> the people, and cries out the cry of hogs, dogs, and roosters, or what resembles that of beasts.[53]

49 *Jupiter.* As for Jupiter, there is no religion, jurisprudence, judgment, knowledge, the Hadith,[54] or faithfulness except from him, because his celestial circle is the indicator of that. **50** Now if Venus looked at him, he will be a singer, singing about[55] the pursuit of women and their matters. **51** And if Mars looked at him, he will be of those who seek the *jihād* and give commands in it. **52** And if Mercury looked at him, he will be of those who write the stipulations [of contracts] for the people, and are consulted in jurisprudence. **53** And if the Moon looked at him, he will be of the ascetics from among whom come exhortations and beautiful sermons, and their words are thought commendable. **54** And if Saturn looked at him, he will be of those who dress in wool and are ridiculed by the people, and are humbled. **55** And if the Sun looked at him, he will be of the companions of the king, who venerate him and are intimately involved with him.[56]

56 *Mars.* Now as for Mars, there is no veterinary medicine, cupping, butchering, and masters of wounds and blood, and robbers, and those who kill people, and cavalrymen, nor does the wisdom of that[57] exist, except from

---

[49] **M** seems to read فنجًا; **E**, فنحًا.
[50] يلعب. If this is correct, then Saturn must be responsible for the toil, and the Moon for play. But I am not sure this is really what the source intends.
[51] I take this "he" to be Mars; but **M** reads, "…looked at him and was his lord."
[52] This combination of jihad, wool, and tears must represent some Islamic symbolism or custom which escapes me.
[53] This is an extraordinary delineation and I do not understand its rationale.
[54] The reason for including the *hadiths* of Muhammad is not simply their religious content, but because they and he are supposed to act as impressive spiritual and moral *exemplars* for the people.
[55] Reading as the standard preposition ب, for في.
[56] This verb can also mean to "meddle," which seems appropriate in the context of politics.
[57] Lit., "nor is there what his wisdom is."

him: because his celestial circle is an indicator of that. **57** And if he was in a bad place, he does cupping and what resembles that. **58** And if Saturn looked at him, he will be a veterinarian (and indeed <the rest> of these works are not an example of what is above).⁵⁸ **59** And if Jupiter looked at him, he will be a butcher, because Jupiter is a fortune and indicates what is [religiously] legitimate.⁵⁹ **60** And if Mercury looked at him, he will be a hunter of birds, and what resembles that. **61** And if the Moon looked at him he will be a cupper, because the Moon belongs to people. **62** And if Venus looked at him, he will be of those who cuts roots.⁶⁰ **63** And if the Sun looked at him, he will be of those who work armaments for the Sultan.

64 And know that every planet granting work, if it was in a sign of fire, it grants work by fire, of the type of that sign: such as an armorer, blacksmith, brass founder, or master of pottery, of those who work with fire. **65** And if it was in a sign of earth, it grants the work of vegetation, and what resembles that of works. **66** And if it was in signs of people, it grants the work of slave dealing,⁶¹ education, and the management of people, and the work of medicine and what resembles that of the fitness of the people, and they indicate animals, because it is in an animal sign. **67** And if it was in the signs of water, he will do works of water, such as a pearl diver, sailor, phlebotomist,⁶² water-carrier, and fisherman.

68 And if the planet of work was moving along in its course and its own management,⁶³ and nothing of the planets looks at it, then this is the condition which I have described.

69 Now if the lord of the work was in a sign, grant him the work of that sign in which the planet is; then after that, add to it from the aspect of the planets to it, and the nature of the sign it⁶⁴ is in. **70** Because if a planet looks at another planet, it grants to it from its own nature, and takes in accordance

---

⁵⁸ Or rather, not all of them; in the next sentence Sahl does mention one of the professions mentioned above.
⁵⁹ *Halāl*, as in halāl meat (or kosher, in Jewish law).
⁶⁰ Or perhaps more broadly, tree-cutters or people who strip vegetation (يقطع العروق).
⁶¹ This word can also mean "cattle dealing" or "driving cattle," showing the parallelism between cattle and slaves in traditional thought.
⁶² Note that phlebotomy deals with blood, not water; but blood is a liquid.
⁶³ Meaning unclear. But Sahl's source seems to mean that the planet is moving direct and is basically unaffected.
⁶⁴ That is, the sign of the planet which is looking.

with its strength; and truly it grants in accordance with its own essence, and the essence of that sign in which it is. **71** And I will explain to you the foundation in the natures of the signs [and] from the inspections of the planets, and the connection of each of them to the other, so understand that.

[Chapter 10.1.3]: The knowledge of the work from the position of the lord of the tenth in the signs, & the natures of every sign[65]

1 Know that if the planet of work was in a sign of vegetation, and a planet looked at it from a sign of vegetation, the native will deal in dried vegetation, such as wheat, barley, walnuts, almonds, and what resembles that. **2** And if it looked at it from a sign of water, he will deal in moist vegetation, such as sweet cucumber, fruit, [other] cucumber, fresh herbs, and what resembles that. **3** And if it looked from a sign of fire, he will trade in lime, birdlime, gypsum, baked brick, plaster,[66] weights, and kohl, and what resembles that, and what is from the fire, earth, and minerals. **4** And if it looked at it from an airy sign, he will trade in woven vegetation.[67]

5 And if the planet of work was in a sign of an animal, and a planet looked at it from the sign of an animal, he will trade in animals. **6** And if that planet was the lord of the eighth, he will trade in animals [both] dead and living. **7** And if the lord of the sixth looked at it, and it was from signs of people, he will trade in people, such as servants and slaves. **8** And if it was in one of four feet, he will trade in riding animals. **9** And if it looked at it from a sign of water, he will trade in water birds. **10** And if it looked at it from a sign of vegetation, he will trade in junk, coffers, and boxes for commerce, because these are leather and cloth.[68] **11** And if it looked at it from signs of fire, he will trade in meat or be a vendor of grilled meat, or a cook or butcher, or one who spills blood; and that is if the one who is looking from this triplicity is Mars, because no planet does this work besides him.

---

[65] This chapter actually describes the planet of work in the signs, not the lord of the tenth. For the lord of the tenth, see Ch. 10.2.4 below.
[66] Tentatively translating from المرد, whose root (مرّد) means "to plaster."
[67] نبات ملحمة. Or perhaps, vegetation used in weaving, and not already woven.
[68] **M**: "and sturdy boxes, because these are [both] vegetation and leather."

12 And if the lord of the action was in a watery sign and a planet looked at it from a sign of water, he will deal in fish and what is in[69] wetlands, except for butchering, for it does not come out from a sign of vegetation, and it is looking at a sign of water. **13** Now if it looked at it from a sign of fire, he will trade in water and fire, such as pearls and gold. **14** And if he was working with his hands, he will be of those who grill fish or heat up the baths, and what resembles that. **15** And if it looked from the signs of fixity,[70] he will deal in adobe brick and building, and what resembles that.

[Happiness and unhappiness in work]

16 And know that the place is corrupted and made suitable relative to the Ascendant: because if the planet of work was in the twelfth, sixth, or eighth, it indicates his lowliness in that work. **17** And if it was in the Midheaven, then his work is distinguished and will increase; and the Ascendant is close to that. **18** And if it was near the Ascendant, then his work will increase. **19** And if it was in the degree of the Ascendant, declining[71] towards the twelfth, then his work will decrease.

20 And concerning the planets in their places, speak with this about delight and joy in the work: because if a planet was in its own sign, he rejoices in that work, and his delight is intensified in it. **21** And if the planet was made unfortunate, in the places in which it has no power, then a man will be contrary to him in it; and if it was made fortunate, then he will have a man wanting him in that work, and indeed he will love the work, with his delight, in the condition of that man.[72] **22** And if the infortune was in a powerful place, then the one who is prejudicial to him is powerful; and if the infortune was in a weak position, then the one prejudicial to him is weak. **23** And if the planet of work was free of the infortune, then he will be stronger than his enemy.

---

[69] Reading the rest of the sentence with **M. E**: "sauce, for it does not come out except from a sign of vegetation and it is looking at a sign of water." Nevertheless it does not quite make sense.

[70] Reading as ثبات, but perhaps this could also be read as نبات, "vegetation."

[71] منحدر. That is, in the rising sign but moving away from the horizon by primary motion. This is normally called "withdrawing."

[72] This probably means, according to the actual social condition he is in.

24 And know that if Saturn looked, it makes his work difficult and breaks him; and if the fortunes were looking at him or received him, they elevate the work and endear him to it.

25 And know that if a planet looked at that planet from a trine, it makes it fortunate and grants to it, and does not make it be corrupted, whether it is a fortune or infortune. **26** And if it looked at it from a square, it undermines it; and if it was a fortune, it will not corrupt it. **27** And if all of the planets looked, they will grant all works, and he will do everything at [some] time.[73] **28** And if the planet of work is receiving a planet, then that work will be more dear to him than another. **29** And if it was not accepting anything of the planets, then he will not accept work and it will not benefit him.

30 And know that if the planet was burned, not accepting anything, then the native will be of those who roam about, who do not accept work. **31** And if Saturn was with it,[74] he will be of those one gives alms to, and he does not accept it.

32 And know that if the Sun was with the planet, he corrupts its work (except with Mercury): for his work will be praised if it was with [the Sun] in [the same] degree.[75]

33 And know that if a planet was looking from the signs having two bodies, they multiply his businesses.

34 Now,[76] look at Mercury, Mars, and Venus: for if you found them all not looking at the Ascendant nor at the Midheaven,[77] they indicate the depriving of the craft, and he will not have work nor a livelihood, and he will be idle.

---

[73] That is, he will have a varied career and do many different things.

[74] **E** reads, "and if [that planet] *was* Saturn."

[75] That is, "in the heart." I am reading this as though (1) Mercury is an exception to being harmed by the Sun, and (2) that any planet is praised when it is in the heart. That Mercury is at least a partial exception to burning, is supported by Ch. 1.13, 7; and most texts would agree with (2). But this could also be read as saying that Mercury himself is the exception to burning *because he in particular* is good when in the heart: but that is not a proper comparison, as it explains burning through being in the heart, when they are separate conditions.

[76] For this paragraph, cf. Rhetorius Ch. 82 and Dorotheus *Excerpt* X.

[77] There is no place from which a planet is in aversion to both of these places (by whole sign).

[Chapter 10.1.4: The meeting & fullness before the nativity]

[al-Andarzaghar?][78]

1 And look at the meeting and the fullness, for it is excellent, strong at the moment when the Moon disengages from the degree and connects with a planet.[79] **2** For the planet which the Moon connects with will be an indicator over the craft and [his] condition, and especially if the lord of the meeting or fullness was in its own exaltation or its house, or the trine of the planet which the Moon is connecting with.

3 And if you found the lord of the bound of the meeting to be Mercury, and the Moon is connecting with him, then the native will be a writer, talkative, eloquent, understanding, knowledgeable, or a merchant. **4** And if with that Mercury was in a stake or in what follows a stake, or [was] with the Lot of religion,[80] or the Lot of craft,[81] or the Lot of exaltation,[82] he will be knowledgeable in religions, a lover of piety, a lord of ideas and conflicts, and he will be reputed for that.

5 And if the connection was with Venus, his livelihood will be from women, and he will be wealthy, a lord of pleasures and women, with a good character, and he will be soft.[83]

6 And if Mars was the one in charge of that, then the native will be excellent,[84] a cavalryman or commander, warlike, reputed, angry, nimble, quick to transform, insolent, making tribulations his business without consideration and without [*uncertain*], and his craft will be by means of fire or iron, and he will do the work of the Sultan—if he was strong. **7** If with that Mars was in his exaltation, in a stake, then he will be the head of the lords of arms and soldiers. **8** And if Jupiter looked at him, and Jupiter was in a good place, the

---

[78] BA III.10.2, **1-5** is very brief but may be a summary by Hugo of the material in **1-14** here.
[79] But notice that the following paragraph assumes that the Moon is connecting with the lord of the bound of the lunation, not just any planet. So perhaps this is a best-case scenario, that she connects with her bound lord. See **15**, where Sahl affirms that the planet might not be the bound lord.
[80] This is probably the Lot of Spirit, not the Moon-Mercury Lot.
[81] This is probably the Lot of work.
[82] M also adds the Lot of Fortune, but this seems too general.
[83] Or perhaps, "comfortable" (ناعم).
[84] Or perhaps more broadly (given the rest of the significations), "capable" (حسن).

native will associate with the powerful, and fine praise will be upon him. **9** And if he was [made unfortunate],[85] he will be a king who is deadly to crowds, destroying cities and countries. **10** And if Venus was with him, he will be sexually active with women, and will be a libertine, lavish. **11** And if Mercury was with him, he will be arrogant, knowledgeable, skilled at lying, corrupting assets, a ruiner of those having established power,[86] and he will have slander and evil from his children and friends.

12 And if Jupiter was the one in charge of that, he will be praised, pleasant, paid honor, and especially by the nobles and the powerful, and the princes and the powerful of the countries. **13** And if Jupiter was in a stake, and in his exaltation, the native will be a chief and king, or judge, a lover of uprightness in religion, followed,[87] fortunate.

14 Now if this planet was Saturn, then he will get that from real estate and the land, and the assets of the dead or inheritances, and slaves, and the rabble, and one who has no repentance,[88] and his good fortune will be in his brother[89] and what is like that, of what his livelihood is from.

15 (And know that if the Moon was not connecting with the lord of the bound of the meeting and fullness[90] afterwards <but> if its position was good, it indicates the fineness of his livelihood and the good.)

16 And if the lord of that bound was eastern, then it is preferable (because that is more well-known and better);[91] and if it was western, then that will be in [his] older years and after youth, and he will be reputed in the crafts and

---

[85] This phrase is uncertain. **M** continues the previous sentence: "…upon him; or, he is a king, deadly to crowds…". **E** reads, "And if it was Mars, he is a king, deadly to crowds…". But **M**'s reading does not match the benefic quality of Jupiter and the goodness of **8**, while **E** is redundant, because we are already dealing with Mars. So I take it that "he" is either Mars or Jupiter, made unfortunate.

[86] **M** reads, "a destroyer of bodies."

[87] But voweled slightly differently, "agreeable" (متابع).

[88] Reading tentatively with what seems to be **M**'s reading (see also **17** below). **E** reads something like "one who is not trusted," which makes sense but contains an extra pronoun that suggests it is a misread for something else.

[89] So **E**, but this does not really make sense. **M** reads two different, undotted words that I cannot decipher.

[90] **M** adds an uncertain word here.

[91] Lit. "superior" as before, but that would be redundant.

will get the good from them. **17** And if it was under the rays of the Sun, he will be despised, weak, not having repentance.

18 And know that the lord of the bound of the meeting by day in the nativities of males is stronger, and the lord of the bound of the fullness in the nativities of females by night is stronger.

19 And you should not neglect the knowledge of the lord of the house of the meeting and fullness: so understand their bodies and their condition, and mix their strength with what I told you of the lord of the bound. **20** For if it was in a house of Jupiter, it indicates praise and appreciation. **21** And if it was in a house of Mars or Saturn, then he will have poverty, leaving the work. **22** And if it was in a house of Mercury, he will be cultured, deceptive. **23** And if it was in the house of the Moon, he will be reasonable, perceptive. **24** And if it was in the house of the Sun, he will be well known. **25** And if Mercury and Jupiter were in its mixture, he will be a writer, knowledgeable in the secrets of the stars and books—and the rest of the planets in accordance with their essences.

[The significator of action again: al-Andarzaghar]

26 Now[92] if the planet with whom the Moon connects after the meeting or fullness has testimony in its position, it will be the indicator of the work just as I described to you. **27** If it was in alien places, then mix with it the power of the lord of its house.

28 For if you found the planet which distributes the work[93] to be in a house of Jupiter, he will be powerful in his work, exalted in [his] craft, [and] good will be spoken about him in his work. **29** Now if you found it in a house of Saturn, his work will be in toil, filthiness, and it will be with the lowness of the craft. **30** And if you found it in a house of Mars, then his work will be by fire or iron or with the work of the Sultan—if he[94] was powerful. **31** And if it was in a house of Venus, then say every craft suitable for women, such as a jeweler, artisan, singers, <and a merchant> of [many] types of

---

[92] For this paragraph, cf. Rhetorius Ch. 82.
[93] In *BA* and Rhetorius, this is the three trade planets alone; but Sahl seems to include all planets playing this role.
[94] This probably means Mars, but it could mean the native—that is, if the native is already of a social class to engage in public or administrative affairs.

stones for rings,[95] and everything suitable for women. **32** And if it was in a house of Mercury, then say writing, commerce, and [what pertains] to scales [for weighing]. **33** And if it was in the house of the Sun, it indicates a [highly] visible craft, <or> by means of fire. **34** And if it was in the house of the Moon, then speak of his innovation, admirable for a craft, and what is invented from himself, and from his own intense searching.

35 And[96] all of this is known from the natures of the signs and the types of the planet which distributes the work, along with the sign in which they are.

[Special Moon-Mercury combinations: al-Andarzaghar]

36 Now[97] if you found the Moon,[98] when she separates from the meeting or fullness, connecting with Mercury in Taurus, Capricorn, or Libra,[99] he will be a soothsayer, a master of spells, summoning, and sorcery. **37** And if you found him in Pisces and Sagittarius, he will be a <summoner of spirits>.[100] **38** And if you found him in Taurus[101] or Scorpio he will be an astrologer, of those who discuss every matter before it comes to be, and those who perceive a matter before it occurs. **39** And if he was in Aries, Leo, and Virgo, he will be an interpreter of dreams.[102]

40 And[103] know that the aspect of the fortunes increases the good, and the infortunes, downfall.

---

[95] This could also be read as "of colors <and> of stones for rings."
[96] For this paragraph, cf. Rhetorius Ch. 82 (itself based on *Tet.* IV.4).
[97] The following material is based on Rhetorius Ch. 82 (again, ultimately from *Tet.* IV.4) and does follow upon the previous sentence, but Rhetorius and Ptolemy themselves include additional sentences in between, about the triplicities and other types of signs.
[98] In Ptolemy-Rhetorius, the Moon in this scenario is also in the house of action.
[99] This ought to be Cancer.
[100] Adding based on Ptolemy-Rhetorius.
[101] This should be Virgo (per Ptolemy-Rhetorius).
[102] Ptolemy-Rhetorius adds: "exorcist."
[103] This sentence is implicit in *BA* but not explicitly stated.

[Chapter 10.1.5: On various occupations, from al-Andarzaghar][104]

1 And[105] if you found Mars, Mercury, and the Moon in the stakes, he will likewise be of those who break into houses and open locks, or a master of talismans.

2 And if you found Saturn in the house of work, in an alien sign, he will be a hunter of wild donkeys, or a farmer of herbs, or a fisherman; and he does not grant work except for work in which there is tribulation and suffering.

3 And if you found Saturn, Mercury,[106] and the Moon in the Ascendant or Midheaven, he will be a philosopher, orator, or knowledgeable in the stars.

4 And[107] if Mercury witnessed Jupiter in the excellent places, and each one of the two was in the bound of his associate, not made unfortunate, visible, they indicate sages and educators.

5 And if the Moon and Mercury were in the Ascendant or Midheaven, it indicates eloquence and the stars.

6 And[108] if you found Mercury in an excellent house (especially if he was in a house of Saturn), in his own bound, not under the rays, and Jupiter, Saturn, and Mars looked at him, he will be knowledgeable in the stars, and having insight into them.

7 And[109] if you found Mercury, Mars, Venus, and the Moon in the stakes, and each of them looked at the other from the stakes, he will be an admirer of machines;[110] and if they were declining from the stakes, he will be of those who juggle.[111]

---

[104] Most of the sentences here are from *BA* III.10.5 and III.10.7, but not all: **1-3, 7-9, 11-14,** maybe **15,** and **18-19.** Therefore I have attributed the whole chapter to al-Andarzaghar and his use of Rhetorius, under the assumption that Hugo garbled some of the sentences, and everything here is in the Arabic version. (In fact Sahl's list here is shorter than what is in *BA*, so Sahl himself might have done some sifting of his own.)

[105] This seems to reflect Rhetorius Ch. 83, but there Rhetorius has Venus instead of the Moon.

[106] Rhetorius has: Mars.

[107] Cf. Rhetorius Ch. 85.

[108] Cf. Rhetorius Ch. 86.

[109] Cf. Rhetorius Ch. 95.

[110] Following Rhetorius, for "wealth" or "singing" (الغناء). Burnett and Pingree (in *BA*) suggest that al-Andarzaghar read the Gr. *mechanikous* as *moichikous*.

[111] Reading with the Greek for "those who play with shovels" (!).

8 And[112] if you found Mercury and Venus in their falls, in their own bounds, each of them in the bound of its associate, he will be idle,[113] and especially if it was in Capricorn due to the fact that in Capricorn there arises the likeness of an ape.[114]

9 And[115] look also at Mars and Mercury if they were both in the house of fathers, for he will play on the strings and singing will please him.

10 And[116] if Venus was in her own house with Mercury, they indicate courtesy and culture, and especially if it was in the stakes.

11 And if Venus and Mercury were in the Ascendant, and the Moon in their bound, it indicates a singer or horn-player, or a master of poetry[117] and amusement.

12 And if you found Venus and Mercury having exchanged their bounds, it indicates a singer of incantations and a master of poems.

13 Mercury[118] and Jupiter, if they exchanged their bounds, and the one of them looked at the other, and they were in suitable places, they indicate a wise man, a master orator.

14 And[119] if you found Saturn and Mercury having exchanged their houses, and each witnessed the other, and they were emerging from the rays, and Jupiter and Mars looked at them, they indicate an astrologer, a sage, a master of crafts and stratagems.

15 And[120] if Mercury and Venus were in their declines,[121] and they exchanged their bounds, they indicate a jester, and especially in Capricorn (because the Ape arises with Capricorn).

16 And[122] if the two infortunes were opposed in a stake, and Mercury conjoined the Moon, and[123] each one of them witnessed the twelfth-part of

---

[112] Cf. Rhetorius Ch. 96.

[113] This should be "mimes" (Rhetorius).

[114] This is a barbaric constellation, *Pithecus* (Rhetorius).

[115] Cf. Rhetorius Ch. 96. But Rhetorius speaks here of rope-walkers and conjurers. See the next sentence; the Persian or Arab author seems to have off-set the correct delineation by one sentence.

[116] Cf. Rhetorius Ch. 96. But Rhetorius speaks here of musicians. See footnote above.

[117] **M**: "the *oud*" (a Middle Eastern stringed instrument).

[118] This seems to be a repetition of **4** above.

[119] This repeats, but in a slightly different way, **6** above.

[120] This repeats **8** above.

[121] That is, in their falls (see **8** above).

[122] Cf. Rhetorius Ch. 92.

the other, it indicates one who kills predatory animals. **17** And if Mercury and the Moon were like that in Virgo, in Sagittarius, or in the first degree of Pisces, it indicates masters of hunting with falcons, and their care.

18 And[124] if Saturn was in the Ascendant and Mars in the west, they indicate a hunter or one who sells wild animals and fights them, and perhaps they will eat him.

19 And if Saturn and the Moon were in the west, in a moist sign, they indicate a sailor or one traveling by sea.[125]

20 So know that and understand it, for you will hit [the target] and not err, God willing.

[Chapter 10.1.6:] The knowledge of the native & his lowness [from al-Andarzaghar]

1 If[126] you wanted to know whether the native would be a chief in that work or an inferior, look at the indicator of that work. **2** For if you found it eastern, in the stakes, then he will be a chief in the work, skilled, masterful in his work, powerful, a chief among his associates. **3** And if it was western, falling, he will be a subordinate, lowly in his work.

4 If[127] the fortunes looked at it, he will be fortunate, powerful, with much profit from that work. **5** And if the infortunes looked at it, he will be declining, poor, suffering, criticized, [with] regret entering upon him from his sad work.

6 And[128] if the planet of the work was in one of its own places, it indicates the exaltation of his craft, in what its sign resembles. **7** If it did not have a share in that sign, then mix its essence with the essence of the lord of its sign.

---

[123] Reading with Rhetorius for "or." The two planets mentioned immediately after must be Mercury and the Moon.
[124] Cf. Rhetorius Ch. 83.
[125] Reading بحر with the sense of Rhetorius Ch. 83 (p. 139) for: "by donkeys" (بحمر).
[126] Cf. Rhetorius Ch. 82.
[127] Cf. Rhetorius Ch. 82.
[128] Cf. Rhetorius Ch. 82.

Chapter [10.2:] On the nativities of kings

[Chapter 10.2.1: Overview]

1 Now as for the nativities of kings and the mighty, look at the luminaries and the honor-guard[129] of the planets for them both. **2** Then look: for if you found the Sun to be eastern, and the Moon western, and Jupiter southern, and Mars northern, all of them being in their exaltations, in the stakes,[130] they indicate the birth of kings, leaders, and the mighty, and especially if that native was in a clime and land matching the lord of the Hundred and the Thousand whose planet is in exaltation, and stronger in the matter of kings.[131]

3 And[132] the utmost of good fortune is if the fixed stars which are of the first and second magnitude are in the Ascendant or Midheaven: for that is more evident for the exaltation and clearer for the good fortune. **4** And likewise, if you found any of them with one of the seven planets, then he will come to something of what there is of their indication; but the Midheaven and the Ascendant are more evident for exaltation,[133] and preferable for that is if the fixed star was with the planet which is the more dominant of the planets in that nativity.

5 And if you found the Head with the fortunes, it is more evident for exaltation and leadership and good fortune, and especially if in addition it was in the Ascendant or Midheaven. **6** And[134] likewise, if you found the Tail by night with Mars, then he will be mighty, a noble, a tyrant, a spiller of blood,[135] a devastator of countries, taking nations prisoner, a waster of assets, and he will be of those who do not have compassion, and especially if the Sun looked at him and they were both[136] in one of the signs of kings or the exaltation of Mars. **7** Now if Mercury witnessed, it is greater for his fervor and his corruption, and the badness of his work. **8** And if you found the Moon with them, it is more corrupting for what I mentioned, because the Moon indicates that the native will be afflicted by the cutting of one of his

---

[129] That is, spear-bearing. See the Glossary and **10ff** below, as well as Ch. 10.2.7.
[130] Meaning unclear. They cannot all be in those areas of the chart while also being exalted.
[131] This last statement about climes has to do with mundane time lords.
[132] For this paragraph, see also Ch. 2.2.
[133] **M** reads: "reputation."
[134] For this sentence, cf. also Ch. 10.3, **18**, and the corresponding sentence in Ch. 2.3, **52**.
[135] **M** adds: "of his companions/lords."
[136] **E**: "and [the Sun] was."

limbs, and the breaking of his limbs, and his manner of death will be bad, and his end a bad end. **9** And likewise if you found the Tail by day with Saturn, then it indicates approximately what I described to you about the gaining[137] of assets, [but] without his losing his mind.[138]

[Spear-bearing according to Ptolemy]

10 Then,[139] look at the luminaries and their positions: for if the luminaries were both in male signs, in the stakes (or one of them), and especially if they were both in their own domain and the planets formed an honor-guard for them (and that is if the planets were eastern from the Sun and western from the Moon), then one whose nativity was like that will be an elevated king, and especially if the planets eastern from the Sun were in the stakes: for if they were like that, he will be a mighty king. **11** And if the eastern planets were in the stakes on the right (of the two which are above the earth),[140] and the luminaries in the stakes, then he will be in this status.

12 And if the Sun was in a male sign and the Moon in a female sign, and one of them is in the stakes, he will be a commander or one of the chiefs of workers, having power over blood and killing.

13 And if there was no honor-guard from the planets to the luminaries and they do not look at them, then he will be a noble man having rank with the Sultan, the people of the village, and the auxiliary forces.

14 And if the luminaries were not in the stakes, and there was an honor-guard (and it is spear-bearing) in the stakes, and they are not looking at them,[141] then the native will be revered, known in the cities.

15 But if you do not find the honor-guard planets in the stakes, nor the luminaries, and the luminaries are also not looking at them, then the native will be below that, without success in his work, and not known, and he will be weak with toil, sinking to the ground.

---

[137] Reading اكتساب with Ch. 2.3, **55**, for كتاب ("book").
[138] Reading حله العقد with Ch. 2.3, **55**, for حلّة. See the footnote in Ch. 2.3.
[139] For this section, cf. *Tet.* IV.3 (Robbins pp. 377-79).
[140] Ptolemy certainly means the Midheaven, but it is unclear whether this other stake is the seventh (less likely) or the Ascendant (more likely). See Ch. 10.2.6, **2**, "the upper posts" (sc. "stakes").
[141] Actually, in this example Ptolemy does allow the spear-bearing planets to be either in a stake or configured to it.

[Chapter 10.2.2:] The statement of Māshā'allāh b. Atharī on the nativities of kings

1 He said:[142] Know that if the luminaries connected together with the lord of the Ascendant, they indicate the nativity of kings. **2** And if the lord of the Ascendant was in the stakes, he will be a powerful king. **3** And if it was withdrawing, he will be a pliable king.

4 If the lords of the stakes of the Ascendant connected with the lord of the Ascendant, they indicate the nativities of kings.

5 And if the lord of the Ascendant and the Moon connected with a planet in its exaltation, and it is in an excellent place from the Ascendant, then the native will reach exaltation; and the utmost of what one reaches [is] from the position of the planet. **6** Now if with what I mentioned the Moon was received, it will be more mighty for his status and easier for his wish, and he will be praised, known for the truth, and good will be reported about him (and that is if the Moon had testimony).

7 Then, begin with the lord of the Ascendant: so see with whom it is connecting, or who is connecting with it. **8** For if it connected with a planet in its exaltation, then the native will associate with nobles and authorities, and he will be mentioned by them. **9** And if the planet accepting [the management] was in a stake, the native will also reach exaltation. **10** And if it was withdrawing [but] looking at the Ascendant, he will be mentioned by them, [but] the native will not reach them until he is assigned to [that] status by the Sultan and kings, and he will be a dependent. **11** And if it was falling away from the Ascendant, then he will get a status, [but] then decline. **12** (And know that the indicator of the native is the lord of the Ascendant, and the planet accept-

---

[142] This chapter can be divided into four parts. (1) Sentences **1-3** refer to the luminaries and the lord of the Ascendant. (2) Sentence **4** refers to the lords of the stakes (most likely, the axial degrees themselves) and the lord of the Ascendant. (3) Sentences **5-6** involve the lord of the Ascendant and the Moon, with an exalted planet. But the most complex scenario is (4) **7-46**, which considers the lord of the Ascendant and another planet, in multiple combinations of angularity and dignities. (4.1) In **7-11**, the lord of the Ascendant connects with an exalted planet. (4.2) In **14-24**, an exalted planet connects with the lord of the Ascendant. (4.3) In **25-30**, the lord of the Ascendant itself is exalted, and considered on its own. (4.4) In **31-34**, this exalted lord of the Ascendant is considered in application with other planets. (4.5) In **35-36** things begin to decline, especially if the lord of the Ascendant is in lower dignities. Finally (4.6) in **37-46** we see types of downfall, as the lord of the Ascendant is mixed up with being in fall, the infortunes, bad aspects, and so on.

ing the management is¹⁴³ the indicator of the man whom he benefits by and is mentioned [by]. **13** So whichever of the two is in a fixed sign or one having two bodies, is fixed in status, getting rank after rank (and that is better if it was in a stake or looking at the Ascendant); and whichever of the two was in a convertible sign, it indicates the ending of his status many times.)

14 And if the lord of the Ascendant is not connecting with a planet, but the planets are connecting to it from exaltation,¹⁴⁴ then the native will be of those whom the masters of authority and the nobles need, and they will seek what he assents to, and they will live at his hands. **15** Then look at the position of the planet which connected with the lord of the Ascendant: for if it was in a stake, it indicates the rank which the native will reach. **16** So if it was in the Midheaven, it indicates a rank in relation to the Sultan, which he will get. **17** And if it was in the Ascendant, then from himself, because of his own insight into matters. **18** And if it was in the seventh, then from women, arguing, and conflict. **19** And if it was in the fourth, then from fathers and the family. **20** And if it was withdrawing [but] looking at the Ascendant, then see in which position it is. **21** Now if it was in the eleventh, then from friends and hope and ambition. **22** And if it was in the ninth, then from knowledge and religion and jurisprudence. **23** And if it was in the fifth, then from children, but it will be at the end of life; and likewise all of the houses. **24** And if it was falling [away from the Ascendant],¹⁴⁵ then in relation to one who does not have nobility, [nor] is known, [nor has] stories [about him]; so speak about the essence of the house which it is in.

25 Now if the lord of the Ascendant was in *its* exaltation and was in the stakes, then the native will have social esteem and will reach exaltation. **26** And if it was withdrawing, he will not have social esteem but he will reach exaltation. **27** Then, see in which position it is: for if it was in the ninth or

---

¹⁴³ Reading فهو for وهو.
¹⁴⁴ Reading with **E**, which implies that these other planets are in their own exaltations, as in **5**. But **M** reads "its exaltation," implying that they are applying from the exaltation of the lord of the Ascendant. For example, let Scorpio be rising, so the lord of the Ascendant is Mars. **E** implies that other, already exalted planets, apply to Mars like exalted people coming to the native (such as Venus in Pisces). But **M** suggests that the other planets are in the exaltation of Mars (such as Venus in Capricorn): this would mean that he is already the exalted lord over the other people, and they apply to him. But I think that **E** is probably right.
¹⁴⁵ Adding in parallel with **11**.

third, it indicates the mind of the native, and his understanding and insight into things. **28** And if it was in the eleventh and the fifth, it indicates his levity and joking around. **29** And if it was falling [away from the Ascendant],[146] then he will get status but not of the chief type, though he will be known in his country and land. **30** Then look at the convertible and the fixed, according to what I explained to you.[147]

31 Then look at the lord of the Ascendant, where it is in its exaltation. **32** For if it connected with a planet, he will be in need of someone else and will be a follower; and if the planets connected with it, then the people will be in need of him, and he will be followed. **33** And if it was received, he is praised among the people and one will commend the good concerning him. **34** And if it was not received, he will be criticized, detested.

35 And if there was not a planet the lord of the Ascendant was connecting with,[148] or the lord of the Ascendant was <not> in its exaltation but it was in its house, then the statement about him will be below what I described to you: because the exaltation is more notable and powerful in rank than the house, so report what is below what I described to you. **36** And if it was also not in its house but it was [only] in its triplicity, then it is below the house; and the bound is below the triplicity.

37 And if the lord of the Ascendant connected with a planet in its fall,[149] it indicates the ruin of the native through himself,[150] and he will not be an earner. **38** And if a planet in its fall connected with the lord <of the Ascendant>, tribulation will come to him in it, and it corrupts his condition in it. **39** Then, look: for if the connection was from a stake, it will be harsher for his condition and more difficult.[151] **40** Then, see in which of the stakes it is: for if the one which the lord of the Ascendant connects with (or the one connecting with the lord of the Ascendant) was in the Midheaven, then his ruin will be at the hands of the Sultan. **41** And if it was in the Ascendant, it will be

---

[146] Tentatively adding in parallel with **11** and **24**.

[147] See **12-13** above.

[148] We might ask why it is bad for the exalted lord of the Ascendant to be without a connection: perhaps it is related to **32**: if an exalted person has no one around to show support, the high position is not worth a lot.

[149] At this point the lord of the Ascendant could be in any dignity, since the other planet in fall represents downfall from wherever the native happens to be.

[150] من سبب نفسه, which read more literally could mean "by reason of his soul."

[151] This is because the disaster will be greater, whether he goes to his own disaster (lord of Ascendant applying to planet in fall), or the disaster comes to him (other planet in fall applying).

illness and tribulation happening to his body. **42** And if it was in the opposite [of the Ascendant], it will be because of women, fighting, and wars. **43** And if it was in the stake of the earth, it will be from fathers and the family. **44** Now if the planet was an infortune, it will pull a wall down upon him, and he will fall from an elevated place.[152] **45** Then, speak about the positions of the signs according to what they indicate, until you reach the twelfth. **46** And if the lord of the Ascendant connected with an infortune from a square or opposition, the native will be weak in combat,[153] a coward; and it is harsher for that if it was not received, and is an enemy to the Ascendant: for with that he will be ill-tempered or a madman.

[Chapter 10.2.3:] On associating with authority & entering into it, according to Māshā'allāh

1 Look at the lord of the Ascendant and the lord of the Midheaven: for if they looked at each other, then his livelihood will be from the Sultan. **2** And if the lord of the Ascendant was the one connecting with the lord of the Midheaven, then he will follow the Sultan and will seek him and be with him. **3** And if the lord of the Midheaven connected with the lord of the Ascendant, the Sultan will seek him and put him in charge, and he will have a fine status, [and the Sultan] will be in need of him. **4** Now if they do not look at each other and a planet reflected the light of them both, he will associate with the Sultan with the help of the people,[154] and they will have graciousness towards him.[155]

5 Then, look after that at the lord of the Ascendant: for if you found it in the stakes of the Ascendant, and the lord of the Midheaven likewise, then he will be of a powerful status [and] a great work; and better than that is if it was the Midheaven and the Ascendant [themselves]. **6** And if the lord of the Ascendant was in the stakes and the lord of the tenth (which is the indicator)

---

[152] Māshā'allāh does mean this literally, but even in the Arabic this falling should probably be taken metaphorically as well, to mean a "position" or "status."
[153] Reading with slightly different spelling (الغلاب) for "conquering" (الغلب), since presumably conquering is not compatible with weakness and cowardice.
[154] M reads, "a slave of the Sultan."
[155] But with different voweling, this same word means "power," i.e. they will have power over him: this ambiguity might be intentional.

falling, then he will be of a powerful rank, known, except that his works will be base. **7** And if the lord of the Ascendant was the one falling, and the lord of the Midheaven in a stake, then he will be unknown but he will get a great work [and] have importance. **8** And if they were both falling, he will not be in [a position of authority] nor will there be good in the work.

9 And if the lord of the Ascendant was in the second and the lord of the Midheaven in the eighth, then he will be of those who kill the people and he will be hostile towards them. **10** Now if the lord of the Ascendant was in the second and the lord of the Midheaven in the sixth, he will be a tax collector, except that he will be oppressive[156] in it. **11** And if the lord of the Midheaven was in the twelfth, he will be the lord of a prison, and of those who imprison the people. **12** And if the lord of the Ascendant was in the third or ninth, and the lord of the Midheaven opposing it, he will be a courier,[157] of those who frequent the Sultan, and he will encounter hardship from [the Sultan]. **13** And speak about all of the houses based on their natures.

14 And if what I described between the lord of the Ascendant and the lord of the Midheaven did not exist, then look at the lord of the Ascendant and the Sun (for [the Sun] is the indicator in the distribution [of authority]).[158] **15** So, see if the lord of the Ascendant is looking at the Sun or one of them is connecting with the other. **16** For if they connected, they indicate that the native will be blessed by the Sultan.[159] **17** And if with that the Sun was in his exaltation, looking at the Ascendant from a powerful place, or he was in the Midheaven and he is received, having testimony, then the native will keep company with kings and those that resemble them. **18** Now if their connection was from a square or opposition, they introduce him into authority, except that the aspect of the opposition indicates that he will encounter hardship from them. **19** If the connection was from the trine or sextile, he will be a friend to them, and he will have good for that reason. **20** And in the

---

[156] This word is somewhat uncertain. The word here for "tax collector" (جلواز) is no longer in used in modern Arabic, and it seems that perhaps the scribes did not know what to make of it, as this phrase is oddly spelled, as if they copied what their source text looked like without understanding the words.

[157] Or specifically, a "mule" used as a messenger (much as we speak of smugglers as mules).

[158] This has a double meaning, for while Sahl's texts do speak of planets "distributing" or doling out a topic of life by being in charge of it, the Sun is also the planet used to predict authority and honors in the predictive technique called "distributions," that is, directing through the bounds.

[159] Or perhaps, "blessed with authority."

assembly and under the rays, he will be intimately involved with them in their secrets and what they conceal from others.

21 If the lord of the Ascendant was in the Midheaven, it indicates that the native is in the houses of the Sultan, or in the house of one who is with the Sultan. **22** If the lord of the Ascendant is opposing the lord of the Midheaven, the native will experience hardship from the Sultan. **23** And in the eighth house, it indicates that he will be killed because of money.

24 If the superior planets were in the Midheaven, they indicate associating with the Sultan and the nobility, and he will be of those who are installed <over> the people. **25** And if the inferior planets were in the Midheaven, he will be of those who work with their hands or of those who has someone above him, using him, and what I have mentioned will be at the beginning of his life.

26 Then look: for if one of the luminaries connects with the lord of the Ascendant, or the lord of the Ascendant connects with one of them, the native will be on intimate terms with kings and the Sultan. **27** Now if it received it, he will get good for that reason, and if it does not receive it, he will not get good from them, and not much benefit. **28** Then, look for the importance of the authority of the one which it connects with, from the position of the luminary: for if the luminary was in its exaltation, he will associate with kings; and if it was in its house it is below that, and likewise the triplicity, and the bound is below that. **29** Then look for the power of the authority and its weakness, from the position of the luminary from the stakes as well as its withdrawing, for from it one may draw conclusions about what I mentioned to you.

[Chapter 10.2.4: The lord of the tenth in the houses, from Māshā'allāh]

1 If the lord of the tenth was in the Ascendant, the native will be an associate[160] of authority, proficient in his work, [and] the Sultan will come to him without [his] seeking [it]. **2** If the lord of the tenth was in the second, the native's livelihood will be from the Sultan and because of him, and he will accumulate assets. **3** The lord of the tenth in the third: he will have few sib-

---

[160] Or perhaps, "master" (صاحب).

lings, and if he did have siblings they will be ruined, and it multiplies travels. **4** The lord of the tenth in the fourth indicates that the parents of the people of the house will be well known at the doors of the Sultan, and hardship will afflict them from the Sultan. **5** The lord of the tenth in the fifth: his children will have a chronic illness or disease, and they will die, and they will experience hardship from the Sultan. **6** The lord of the tenth in the sixth: he will have a short lifespan,[161] he will live by walking,[162] and he will enslave free people, and he will have authority [over them]. **7** The lord of the tenth in the seventh: he will marry a woman more powerful [and] significant than himself, from the people of the house of the Sultan, sensible [and] upright. **8** The lord of the tenth in the eighth: he will get the authority in his younger years, and he will be a follower, and will seek the leadership and be boastful. **9** The lord of the tenth in the ninth: he will get authority in traveling abroad, his leadership will be in it, and he will be offered the good.[163] **10** The lord of the tenth in the tenth: he will be proficient in work, having influence in it, informed in it, and his livelihood will be from it. **11** The lord of the tenth in the eleventh: his friends will get good from him, and his child will inherit assets which he will collect from the Sultan. **12** The lord of the tenth in the twelfth: he will be dispossessed by the authorities,[164] and it introduces griefs and hardship upon him from them.

13 Work in this section if the tenth and its lord were both free of the infortunes and the fortunes did not testify.

---

[161] Al-Rijāl's version reads "assets," probably because of the association between the sixth and poverty; but Māshā'allāh is probably thinking that the sixth is the eighth from the tenth.

[162] I think this means what we would call an "itinerant" or "peripatetic" (lit., "walking around") lifestyle, moving from place to place without a fixed plan or stability.

[163] **M**: "the good will be strengthened."

[164] This could also be read as "he will be deprived of authority," but the use of the plural later in the sentence suggests being dispossessed by them. Still, one should keep an open mind that having authority itself might be the source of misery, and that he will also lose it.

[Chapter 10.2.5:] The Lot of work

[The Lot of expedition or work or authority][165]

1 Calculate by day and night from Saturn to the Moon, and cast it out from the Ascendant, and where it terminates, there is the Lot of work. **2** And look at the position of this Lot from the Ascendant: for if it was in an excellent place from the Ascendant, it indicates the scarcity of the native's leisure time, and better than that if an infortune was not looking at it, and it is looking at the Ascendant. **3** And likewise, look at the lord of the house of the Lot and the lord of the Ascendant: for if they are looking at each other, they indicate the scarcity of the native's leisure time, and better than that is if it was free of the infortunes, looking at the Ascendant.

	Three Lots for work, action, & authority		
Sahl's Nativities	Formula	Old name (Hellenistic)	New name (Persian / Arabic)
10.1.1, 14-17	☿→♂, ASC (R)	Action (Gr. *praxis*)	• Managers, viziers, and Sultans (*Gr. Intr.* VIII.4) • Work (Sahl, *BA*)
10.2.5, 1-3	♄→☽, ASC (R)	Expedition (Gr. *stratia*)	• Authority and what work a native does (*Gr. Intr.* VIII.4) • Work (Sahl)
10.2.5, 4-14	☉→♄, ASC (R)	Father	• Authority, or work and craft (Māshā'allāh, *Treatise on Lots*) • Authority, assistance, and victory (*Gr. Intr.* VIII.4)

Figure 63: Lots of action or work in Sahl's *Nativities*

---

[165] This Saturn-Moon Lot is a military Lot, the Lot of expedition, as found in Dorotheus (quoted in Heph. II.19, Schmidt p. 68), Paul (Ch. 22), and Theophilus (*Labors* Ch. 23). But in this Persian material from Sahl, and later in Abū Ma'shar's *Gr. Intr.* (see *ITA* VI.2.40), it is described as a Lot of "authority, and which work a native does" (*Gr. Intr.* VIII.4). As for its calculation, Paul instructs us to reverse it by night, but Abū Ma'shar says not to. We should follow Paul.

[*A Lot of authority, or work and craft, according to Māshā'allāh*][166]

4 Now if you found this Lot in the stakes, then look at the lord of the Midheaven: for if this Lot was more numerous in testimony, his work will be with the Sultan and because of him. **5** Now if it was free of the infortunes, he will get good in that; and if it was made unfortunate, hardship will afflict him. **6** In this topic, the Midheaven and the Ascendant are better; but as for the opposite [of the Ascendant], they indicate by reason of women, and [in] the stake of the earth because of fathers and the family.

7 If the Lot of work was in the fifth, eleventh, third, and ninth, looking just as I described in the beginning of the section, if it was more numerous in testimony and in the eleventh, his livelihood will be by reason of friends; and the best that it could be for [his] condition is at the beginning of his life. **8** And if it was in the ninth, then in relation to travels and being away from home. **9** And if it was in the third, then in relation to siblings and because of them, and by reason of travels as well. **10** And if it was in the fifth, then in relation to sowing and tilling.

11 If the Lot of work was in the second, it indicates work with his own two hands. **12** And in the eighth it indicates the transfer[167] of the dead and inheritances. **13** And in the sixth, if it was free of the infortunes, it indicates the administering of remedies, and illness; and if it was made unfortunate, it indicates the work of slaves. **14** And in the twelfth he will do the work of villains; and if it was made unfortunate, he will detest work, being lazy.

---

[166] For this section, cf. Tehran, Dānishgāh, Nafīsī 429 (72a); Majlis 17490 (138-39). At this point, Sahl quietly switches to Māshā'allāh's treatise on Lots, so we have a double problem. We were supposed to be discussing the Lot of work (Arabic) or action (Greek), as mentioned above in Ch. 10.1.1, **14**. But Sahl has already substituted the Saturn-Moon Lot of expedition or work or authority instead (**1-3**), and now he is substituting another one without telling us that the formula is different (**7-14**)! For Māshā'allāh refers to *his* Lot as the Lot of "authority," or of "work and craft," or of "work," and defines this in the same way as the *Lot of fathers* (Sun-Saturn)! (Indeed, Abū Ma'shar includes this Lot as well, calling it the Lot of "rulership and authority" or the Lot of "the king and the Sultan".) So we now have three different Lots, ostensibly for the same topic, which I summarize in the table above. The only thing I can say in Sahl's favor is that all of the interpretations do indeed pertain to the general notion of action, craft, and work.

[167] I take this to mean all sorts of work pertaining to corpses, funerals, but especially to the transfer of their property.

[Chapter 10.2.6: Hermes on the nativities of kings]

1 Hermes said: In the nativities of kings and leaders and those having good fortune, and their work, look at the position of the luminaries. **2** For if you found them both in the upper posts,[168] and the Sun by day was in a male sign and the Moon by night in a female sign, or they both happened to be in a masculine sign and each of them was in the position of its companion,[169] then with that they indicate the nativities of kings and the nobles, and commanders who are raised up and are in charge over many peoples, and have authority over death and life; whenever they were <like that>, they are the lords of many crowds and their commands will be carried out in everything. **3** Now if the infortunes looked at them from the seventh or the fourth,[170] they decrease their assets and indicate toil in their lives.

4 If the Sun was with Jupiter, both looking at the Moon, and they are exactly[171] in the Midheaven, the native will be a mighty man, arrogant, the chief of many peoples and cities, and he will have women and children, and his subsistence will be at the doors of power and kings. **5** And if [the Sun] was devoid of the infortunes, all that I have mentioned will be suitable for him.

[Angular combinations of two planets]

6 The Sun in the Ascendant and the Moon in the Midheaven: the native will subjugate peoples and cities, being an authority over life and death: and that is if the infortunes were inclining away from[172] them. **7** The Sun in the

---

[168] See the earlier passage based on Ptolemy (Ch. 10.2.1, **10-11**). Again this probably refers to the area around the Midheaven, and probably in the eastern quadrant moving up towards it. This seems to be a version of spear-bearing.

[169] صاحبه. Normally this phrase would mean "its associate": the Sun in the Moon's house (Cancer) and the Moon in the Sun's house (Leo), but that does not make much sense to me, because they would each be alien and in aversion to their own houses (and not both be in masculine signs, as required).

[170] I take this to be the opposition and square, not the seventh and fourth places.

[171] وهنّ مستويات. But the text uses the plural adjective and pronoun (indicating three or more), and they cannot all be on the Midheaven while *looking at* the Moon.

[172] This seems to mean being in aversion to them. See also **13-14** below. But if the Sun and Moon were in these signs, no planet could be in aversion to both of them at the same time. It could mean "separating" from or "far away from," as **7** and **12** suggest that the fortunes are close to them.

west and the Moon in the Midheaven, devoid of the infortunes, indicates the nativities of kings and nobles and commanders; and if she moved with the fortunes, the native will govern powerful affairs.

8 (The[173] knowledge of what will come to the native of inheritances, is that you look in that at the lord of the second and that of eighth: for if they connected and one of them was in the place of its associate, then the native will have good from the dead, and inheritances because of the dead. **9** And if the lord of the eighth was in the eleventh or fifth, the native will get assets from inheritances. **10** And likewise if you found the fortunes in the eighth, and likewise if you found the lord of the second in the eighth and the lord of the eighth in the second: for then the native will be blessed by inheritances. **11** And if the lord of the eighth was in the seventh, then he will get the inheritances of women, or from their assets and because of them, and his women will die before him.)

12 The Sun in the Midheaven and the Moon in the west, and he[174] being safe from the infortunes: the native will be a king, noble, a commander; now if with that [they] were with the fortunes, he will govern great cities or manage them, and his life will be longer than the life of the people of his house, and he will govern the people of his city, and they will be elevated over many peoples, and he will be raised up. **13** The Moon in the Ascendant and the Sun in the Midheaven: the native will be a king or commander of the army, an authority over death and life, beneficial to one humbling himself before him; and that is if the infortunes were inclining away from them.[175] **14** The Moon in the Ascendant and the Sun in the stake of the earth: the native will be a chief over the people of his countries, and his abilities will be more powerful than the ability of his father and relatives, and his life will increase in joy, if the infortunes were inclining away from them.

15 Saturn in the Ascendant and Jupiter in the Midheaven: the native will be the chief of the people of his house, and he will have assets and respect, and he will be master over the people of his city, and that is if Mars was absent from them. **16** Saturn in the Ascendant and Mars in the Midheaven indicates that the native will be unhappy in his luck, and his death will be in humbleness, and that is if the fortunes were inclining away from them. **17**

---

[173] This paragraph probably did not originally belong here, as it breaks up the combinations of the Sun and Moon, between **7** and **12**.
[174] Or more likely, both of them.
[175] Reading "them" for "it" (meaning the Moon).

Saturn in the Ascendant and the Sun in the Midheaven: the native will get assets, and he will have women and children, and will be master over the people of his house, and that is if Mars was not looking at that place.

18 Mars in the Ascendant and Jupiter in the Midheaven: the native will be established in power, having assets and wealth, and he will be master of the people of his house and his city, and in the middle of his life he will rule over assets and children. **19** The Sun in the Ascendant and Jupiter in the Midheaven indicates that the native will be a king or commander or noble, a conqueror, a chief over peoples and cities, and he will have assets and wealth and children: and that is if the infortunes were inclining <away from them>. **20** Venus in the Ascendant and Jupiter in the Midheaven: the native will have many assets, and women and children, and that is in the houses of the mighty and at the doors of kings, and his life will increase in joy toward the end of his life. **21** The Moon in the Ascendant and Jupiter in the Midheaven, indicates that the native will be wise, having assets and wealth, and he will be known among kings, and will be a chief in religions, and he will have women and children—if the infortunes were inclining <away from them>.

22 Mercury in the Ascendant and Venus in the Midheaven: the native will be wise, venerable, beloved, and he will have respect, and rejoice in his children and women.

23 Mars in the stake of the earth and the Sun in the Midheaven (and more difficult for that is if [the Sun] was looking at the Moon and the fortunes were inclining <away from them>), indicates that the native's death will be by crucifixion while alive, and his corpse will be burned by fire. **24** Mars in the stake of the earth and Venus in the Midheaven: the native will be a chief.

25 Venus under the earth and Jupiter in the Midheaven: the native will be a king or commander, and he will have assets, and will get respect, and he will have children. **26** Now if the infortunes were inclining <away from him>, not looking at him, the native will manage all of his own actions, and complete them. **27** Venus under the earth and Saturn in the Midheaven (and it is greater for that if the Moon looked): the native will be corrupted just as women are corrupted. **28** Now if Jupiter did not have testimony, it indicates fornication and that he will be sterile.

29 Mercury under the earth and Jupiter in the Midheaven, indicates that the native will be[176] a household manager to kings, or the household manager in the houses of God, [appointed] over their assets and the affairs of his city, and he will manage his actions and magnify them: and that is if the infortunes were inclining <away from them>.

30 The Sun in the stake of the earth and Jupiter in the Midheaven, indicates kings and their sons, and he will be master over peoples and cities, and over assets and women[177] and children: and that is if the infortunes were inclining <away from them>.

31 Saturn in the stake of the earth and Jupiter in the Midheaven, indicates kings and the chiefs of cities, and being raised up in his city from [*uncertain*] [but] he will be humbled:[178] and that is if the infortunes were inclining <away from them>.

32 If the Sun was in the Ascendant and Mars looking at the Moon from[179] the seventh or the fourth,[180] the native will be a king or chief, but he will die a bad death and be captured. **33** Now if the Moon was not looking at Mars, but it[181] happened to be in one of the stakes or what follows them, that also indicates kings and chiefs, [but] dying a bad death and being captured. **34** If the Sun happened to be in the post of the Ascendant and Mars in what follows the stakes, and the Moon inclining <away from him>, not looking at him, then the native will be a king.

35 If Jupiter happened to be in one of the posts or in the second [places] from the stakes, and the Moon was with him or in the Ascendant, then the native will be a king, taking the reins of the world, and he will manage many cities.

36 If Jupiter, Mercury, and Venus happened to be in any of the stakes, then the native will be mighty, getting benefit from inheritance, and they[182] will administer in comfort and respect, and in all of their conditions they will be very wealthy. **37** And if Mars was with them or looked at them from a square or opposition, then the native will be thief-like, stealing, and he will die a bad death; now if it was by night, it is an indicator of social esteem.

---

[176] Reading the rest of this sentence largely with **M**.
[177] **E** reads, "the assets *of* women."
[178] Reading tentatively for يضع.
[179] **E** reads "in," as though the Moon is there. But I think **M**'s reading makes more sense.
[180] This might mean, "from the opposition or square."
[181] I cannot tell whether this is the Moon or Mars.
[182] The texts speak in the plural now, perhaps referring to the family of the native.

38 If Saturn was in one of the stakes and in his own house, and he is looking at the Sun, then the native will be the chief of his siblings, and he will be of those entrusted with charitable giving, and he will be raised with a good upbringing.

39 If the Sun was in the Midheaven with Saturn, it indicates that the native will inherit the inheritance of his king or his leadership. **40** Now if Mars happened to be in one of the posts, it indicates as well the rulership and leadership which he will get, but that will be in war, tribulations, and envy.

41 If the Sun was in the Midheaven and Mars in the west, and the Moon in one of the posts or in what follows them, the native will be a king, a chief; but he will die an unpleasant death and be captured. **42** And if Mars was estranged from these places, and Jupiter happened to be in the Ascendant or in the second from it, and the Sun with the Moon in a stake, then the native will be a king, a powerful chief, or the administrator of the authority of the world.

43 If the Sun was in the Midheaven, it indicates that the fathers [of the native] are praised, masters of hypocrisy, making a show before the people, and [unclear] more than that in accordance with the nature of the planet which is with him or which is looking at him.

44 And always, if these planets had equivalent portions,[183] it indicates the elevation of the native and the abundance of his work and his good manners, and that is based on the nature of the planet of the planet which is with it or which is looking at it. **45** And if the Moon happened to be with them,[184] in one of the stakes, it indicates powerful, excellent nativities, abundant in power, the managers of cities and capitals. **46** Now if Mercury happened to be with them, it indicates the abundance of the native's knowledge. **47** And if Saturn happened to be with them, he will be wicked, harsh. **48** And if Saturn happened to be in one of these places in this manner, it indicates the nativities of powerful kings dreaded[185] in the cities and capitals.

---

[183] مستوية الأجزاء. I believe this means that the planets are on (or very close to?) the very degree of the axis—and if connecting to each other by aspect, that the aspect is exact.

[184] Reading for "it." Here and below, there is ambiguity as to which planet Sahl's source means. The feminine ending could indicate the Sun: planets with the Sun. But it could also mean "them," meaning whatever planets (plural) were indicated at the beginning of the paragraph. I will say "them" where indicated in the rest of this paragraph.

[185] Or, inspiring "awe" (مهابة).

49 And[186] know that power and rank among the people is from the stakes from the Ascendant, and the stakes are of the four natures.

50 Now if the native was born, then whether [or not] the heavenly circle was corrupted or suitable at the hour of his coming out from the belly of his mother, it [still] grants the rank which he was born at. **51** For if the planet met with suitability, it raises him up from his station; and if it met with corruption, it takes him down from his station.

52 Because if he was of the children of kings, and the circle corrupted at the hour he was born, it corrupts his position. **53** And if it met with a fortune, the native will meet with what is upright and good. **54** And if the heavenly circle was corrupt, then whenever the circle returns to corruption, his condition is corrupted.

55 And if he was of the children of the poor or those in the middle, and the heavenly circle was suitable, then that is better for [his] condition; now if it met with corruption, it undermines it. **56** And if it was [already] corrupt, so that suitability meets it, the native will meet with the good.

57 And if the degree of the Midheaven withdrew towards the sign of travel, his authority and his work will be scarcely established; and if the sign was convertible, then it is worse. **58** And if the degree was in the sign of the Midheaven, then it is more excellent and he will be in the essence of authority.[187] **59** And if the degree was in the house of hope, then it is more excellent than the house of travel, because it inclines towards the sign of the Midheaven. **60** So emulate that in your work, and emulate the fixed, the convertible, and what has two bodies.

---

[186] This short section first establishes that the social status in the chart is relative to the native's real-life situation: a good or bad chart shows a higher or lower status for the rank he is actually at. (The comment about the stakes in **49** may be part of this: the IC shows lower status than the Midheaven.) But then the text seems to introduce transits or solar revolutions (or perhaps even something like distributions), so that the planets which signify the social status will indicate changes in it as predictive techniques are applied to them. The use of "met with" (استقبل) is intriguing because the root means to confront or meet face-to-face (i.e., it is a kind of oppositional term), and one of the Greek words for a solar revolution is *antigenesis*, a "counter-nativity." So the text seems to say that the annual charts (or again, other techniques like distributions) will show whether his status rises or falls over time.

[187] Or, "the Sultan."

[Chapter 10.2.7: Examples of spear-bearing][188]

1 And [#1] an example of that is a nativity whose Ascendant is Virgo 6°, and he found that the luminaries were paid honor by the planets which are of their domain.[189] **2** As for the Sun, it is from the planets which are eastern[190] in the early mornings, and they are Mercury and Venus. **3** For Mercury was in Libra 4°, and Venus in Virgo 21°, so these two planets come to be in a position of paying honor from the Sun, without a connection from him to them, and without their position being at sunrise except that they are eastern from him.[191] **4** And as for the Moon, she was being paid honor by Venus, who is setting after her: because the Moon is in 6° of Virgo, and Venus in it, 21°, and she is setting after her: so understand this example.[192]

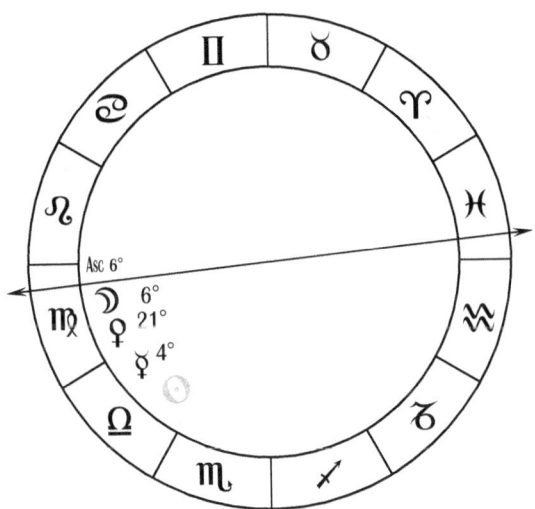

Figure 64: Spear-bearing example #1

---

[188] E puts this section at the end of the whole chapter, but I follow M in inserting it here.
[189] This should probably be reads as "sect."
[190] M reads, "as for the Sun, it is *from Saturn and* the planets which are eastern…". But Saturn plays no other role in the paragraph, and since we do not even know the position of the Sun, the chart is impossible to date. On the other hand, it could be that Saturn *is* rising before the Sun in this chart, just as he is in Examples #2 and #3.
[191] I believe this means that while they rise before him ("eastern"), they are close enough that they do not make a morning rising out of the rays ("without their position being at sunrise").
[192] Lit., something "erected" or a "signpost."

5 Another nativity [#2]: its Ascendant is Aries 19°,[193] an example of a native who was powerful in good fortune, and a king. **6** The planets were paying honor to the Sun (and he is in Aries), because they are in his arising,[194] and his right side. **7** As for Venus, she is in Pisces 8°, Mercury with her 29°, Mars with them both, 24°,[195] Saturn in Capricorn 9°, on [the Sun's] right side, in separation from [Saturn]. **8** So look at these four planets which I have described to you, how they are eastern from the Sun and on his right side, and his honor-guard: for that is an indicator of powerful good fortune and rulership.[196]

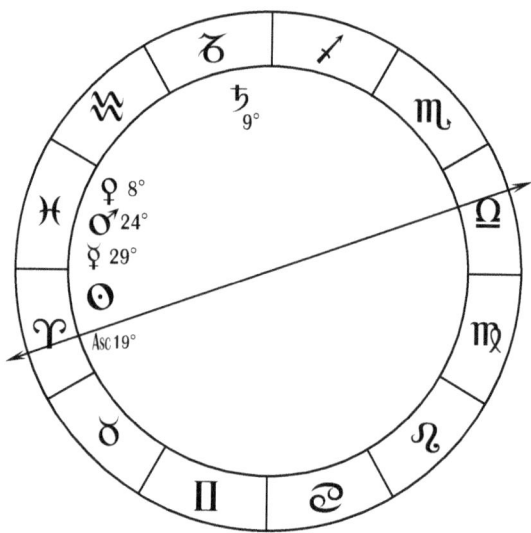

Figure 65: Spear-bearing example #2

---

[193] The rest of this sentence appeared only in **E**, inserted into the middle of the next sentence.
[194] إشراق. Or, perhaps, "radiance."
[195] **M** reads, "twenty-seven" or "twenty-nine."
[196] **M**: "powerful good fortune and assets."

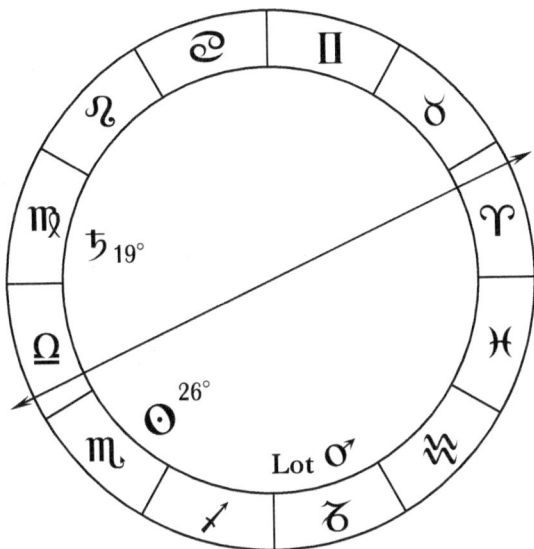

Figure 66: Spear-bearing example #3

9 Another nativity [#3]: his father was elevated. **10** And that is because Saturn is the lord of the Lot of the father, and was in Virgo 19°, and in the trine of the Lot,[197] and in the honor guard of the Sun and his right side, and in [Saturn's] easternization in the early mornings (and the Sun is in Scorpio 26°), indicating the elevation of the father's rank. **11** Since Mercury[198] is the lord of the bound of the Lot, and the Lot is with Mars, and Saturn (the lord of the Lot) in the twelfth,[199] and the good fortune of[200] the Sun with Saturn, it indicates the killing of the father by another.[201]

---

[197] This means that the Lot must be in Capricorn, in the fourth (the Ascendant is Libra, as suggested below).

[198] Actually, **E** reads "Virgo" (العذراء), which is impossible, as signs do not rule bounds), while **M** reads العرى (most likely a sloppy version of the same). However, Mercury does rule Virgo, and his first letter is the same as Virgo's here. But more importantly, the chart is nocturnal, so the Lot of the father is calculated from Saturn to the Sun. There are 67° between Saturn and the Sun. Now we also know that the Lot is in Capricorn, and the Ascendant in Libra. This means that the Lot cannot be more than 7° into Capricorn, or else the Ascendant could not be Libra – and the first 7° of Capricorn are indeed ruled by Mercury. So, the rising degree is within the last 7° of Libra, and the Lot within the first 7° of Capricorn.

[199] This could also be read as, "with Mars *and Saturn*...in the twelfth," so that Mars and Saturn are both in Virgo. But it does mean that Libra is rising.

12 Another nativity [#4]: indicating the elevation of his grandfather and his good fortune. **13** And that is because the Sun was in Aquarius 25°, the degree of the Midheaven,[202] and Jupiter in Aquarius, the first degree, and the Ascendant Taurus 9°.[203] **14** It indicates the goodness of the planets' paying honor to the two glowing ones: Jupiter in his easternization from the Sun, and Saturn and Mercury in their westernization from the Moon. **15** And <the Moon> was in Pisces 9°,[204] and with her Mercury 12°, and Saturn in Aries 13°. **16** And the fall of Saturn (who is the first lord of the triplicity of the Sun) in the twelfth does not harm him at the beginning of his life, and he is not capable of doing violence to him,[205] <because it indicates> an annulment of himself if he happened to be falling, in his own fall if <he was in> the positions which I explained, <in> the Midheaven. **17** And it is certainly necessary for this native that he be in a condition of the planets paying honor to the luminaries: so, understand.

---

[200] حظ. Normally this word is a synonym for "dignity" or "sect," but I take it to refer to the spear-bearing of the Sun here because Saturn.

[201] So in this nativity, Saturn is the spear-bearer for the Sun, which shows eminence; but because Saturn is the lord of the 4th and the Lot, the eminence is connected to his *father*; and because Saturn is in the 12th, it suggests betrayal of the father. So this is indeed like Ptolemy, where the spear-bearing planet tells us something about *why* someone is eminent.

[202] This could also be read as "twenty-five degrees, the Midheaven." So either the Sun is in the Midheaven generally, or he is on the very degree of the Midheaven.

[203] **M** reads: "five." However, these placements for the Ascendant and Midheaven are impossible for any latitude. (1) If the Midheaven is at 25° Aquarius, the Ascendant could be at 9° *Gemini*, at about 22° N latitude. But (2) if the Ascendant must be at 9° Taurus, then there are many possibilities for the Midheaven. If it must be in Aquarius, then it would have to be around 1°, and no more than about 15° N latitude. But the Midheaven could also be at 26° *Capricorn* instead of Aquarius, for a nativity at about 33° N latitude.

[204] **M** seems to read "nine," but may also read يمنه, "on its right."

[205] Here the texts read very differently, seemingly ungrammatically, and without much astrological sense. I have done my best to blend them. **E** reads: "distraction by himself, if he happened to be falling, in his fall, if it was the places which I have mentioned and explained, the Midheaven." **M** reads: "annulment by himself if he happened to be falling, in his own fall, or the Sun was establishing [sic] the planets which I have described, the Midheaven." But **M** does not use the correct gender for these verbs relating to the Sun.

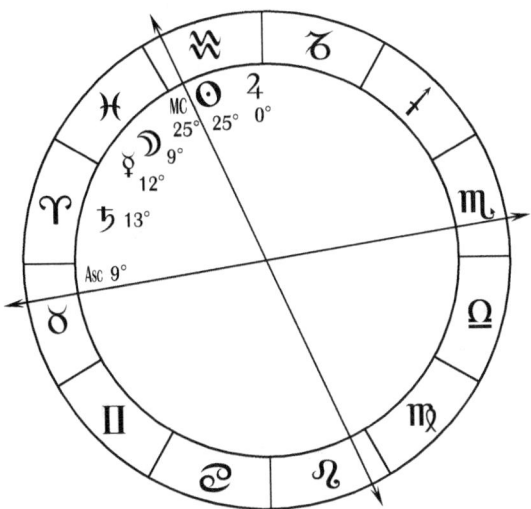

Figure 67: Spear-bearing example #4

18 Another nativity [#5], it is an indication of the might of his power. **19** And the Sun was in Virgo 14°, and Venus in Leo 26°, and the Ascendant Taurus 3°. **20** So his good fortune was the easternization of Venus alone, through a connection,[206] and she does not have a share in the sign she is in.

21 And [#6] in the nativity of a philosopher, an educator of philosophers, the Ascendant was Aries 3°, and the Sun in Aquarius 16°,[207] and Mercury with him, 5°. **22** So look at Mercury, how he is in the honor guard of the Sun and his right side,[208] in his own bound, eastern: and he is the grantor of what I described about this native, concerning philosophy: so understand that, God willing.

---

[206] But a connection with whom? Note also that the Sun is not angular by sign, nor does he seem to be angular by dynamic division.
[207] M reads: "eighteen."
[208] Note that the Sun does not seem to be angular even by dynamic division.

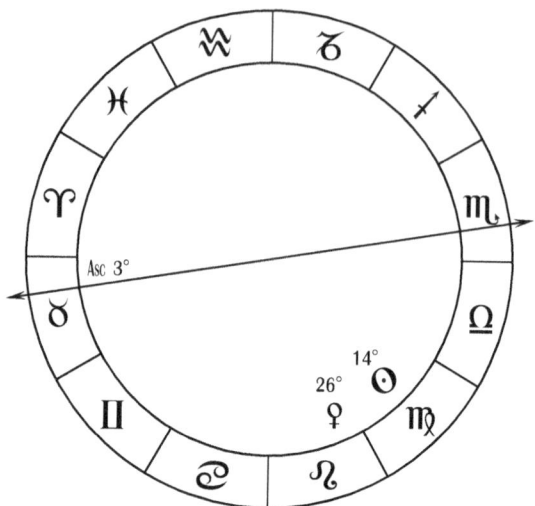

Figure 68: Spear-bearing example #5

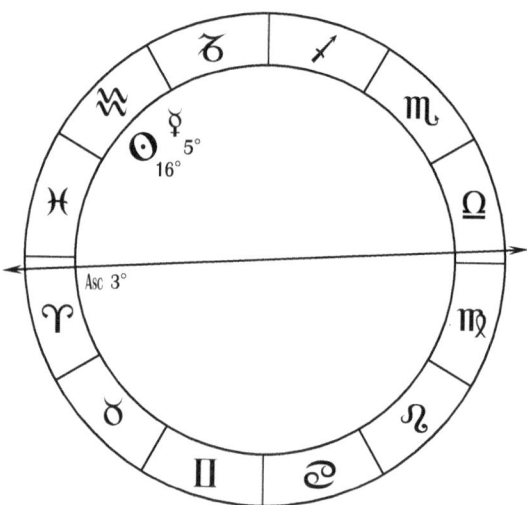

Figure 69: Spear-bearing example #6

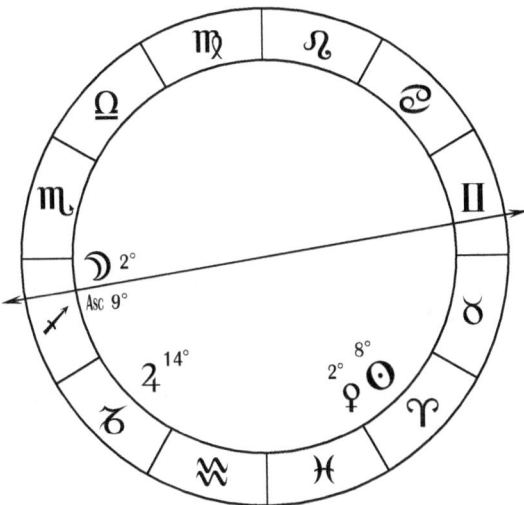

Figure 70: Spear-bearing example #7

23 Another nativity [#7], its Ascendant was Sagittarius 9°, and the Sun in Aries 8°, the Moon in Sagittarius 2°, and the luminaries were being paid honor by the planets. **24** As for the Sun, Venus was paying him honor as well as Jupiter, and they were both in their easternization in the early mornings,[209] and Jupiter in 14° of Capricorn and Venus in 2° of Aries. **25** And as for the Moon, Jupiter paid her honor in his westernization from her, and <it indicates> admiration for this native, how superiority was reported based on him, with uprightness, being well established in reverence, and how he does not gain powerful leadership, a splendid status, and a high reputation.[210] **26** And as for what his father is blessed with (of nobility and love), Jupiter's paying honor to the luminaries indicates good fortune for the native without achievement, because Jupiter (the ease-bringer) was not looking at the Ascendant and at the Moon:[211] so among the mighty he was small, and among the small he was mighty.

---

[209] Only Venus can truly be eastern*izing*, and then only if retrograde. But they are both eastern.
[210] I believe this means that he was greatly respected despite not having official political power: see **26**.
[211] The Moon is the sect light, so being with her or looking at her is important.

[Chapter 10.3:] The lords of horsemanship & valor[212]

1 Now[213] as for nativities which are consistent with what I mentioned of horsemanship, valor, cavalrymen, and those benefiting for that reason, indeed you should look at the Lot of valor,[214] where it is, and who is its lord, and who is looking at it, and what afflicts it in the nativity. **2** Now if this Lot[215] was in a stake, the house of the Moon[216] or the house of the Sun, or in Sagittarius, looked at by Jupiter or Mars, then the native will be a cavalryman. **3** And if Mercury was with the Lot, then he will be a tyrant,[217] [and] tough.

4 And if the Moon was with Mars or with the Sun,[218] and she had a share in the nativity, and she was in the stakes, then he will be a cavalryman.

5 Now if you found the Sun or Moon in the house and triplicity of Mars, looking <at> Mars, then speak likewise.[219]

6 And if you found the Lot of Fortune[220] with Mars and Jupiter, then he will be of the high rank of cavalrymen or their leaders, and the commanders of soldiers.

---

[212] This word (نجدة) also means assistance and help, as in coming to someone's aid.

[213] Much of this chapter is also found in al-Khayyāt, *JN* Ch. 34, and I will refer to it often. It is also reflected in a Latin book of nativities attributed to Māshā'allāh, Paris BNF Lat. 7324, ff. 85r-85v.

[214] نجدة. Note that there seem to be two Lots used here, with a Lot of courage in **8** below. Now, for either of these the author might mean the Hermetic Lot of courage: by day from Mars to the Lot of Fortune (by night the reverse), projected from the Ascendant. And Zarādusht in his book of nativities *does* have that Lot of courage (شجاعة). However, I suspect that one of them—probably the Lot of valor—is originally Dorotheus's Lot of expedition (from Saturn to the Moon, see Ch. 10.2.5 above), because Dorotheus also has combinations of Mars, the luminaries, and angles very similar to this material: see Heph. II.19 (Schmidt p. 68). But I also note that the Latin Māshā'allāh has the Lot of religion, which may be simply the Lot of Spirit.

[215] And its lord, according to al-Khayyāt.

[216] Al-Khayyāt has Mars, which is probably correct and is one of the principles of the Dorotheus passage for the Lot of expedition.

[217] This is an ambiguous word (جبّار), connoting power, a colossus, an oppressor, etc.: that is, someone powerful with the threat of violence.

[218] Al-Khayyāt has the Sun *and* Moon with Mars, which makes more sense.

[219] Al-Khayyāt reads that both luminaries are with Mars or in his house, *or* they look at the Lot of courage (شجاعة) and its lord from the trine: I suspect this is correct.

[220] I would think this is the Lot of courage, but al-Khayyāt has Fortune as well. This may be inspired by Ptolemy: see Ch. 2.12, **5** above.

7 And if you found the Moon in the Midheaven and the Sun in the Ascendant, or that was the other way around, then the native will be a warrior, courageous.²²¹

8 And likewise if you found the <Ascendant and> two glowing ones and <the lord of>²²² the Ascendant in male signs, and Mars in a stake, then the native will be staunch, pushing ahead, a cavalryman, and especially if the Lot of courage²²³ was with Mars or with the Moon in a stake (or what follows a stake): for then the native will be a chief in the cavalry, and a lover of shedding blood. **9** And if you found the Lot with Mars in the ninth and third place, then the native will be shameless, not having mercy. **10** And the native's good fortune in the cavalry will be more excellent if Jupiter looked at its²²⁴ house.

11 If Mars was made unfortunate by Saturn or Saturn was with the Lot of valor,²²⁵ then the native will be pious, averse to horsemanship and the cavalry, weak in it, shrinking away from it. **12** And likewise if you found Mars in a female sign, then there is no good in him, unless he is in the house of Jupiter, or the house of the Sun, and the Moon: because if Mars was in the house of the Sun and Moon, they indicate the native's hatred for the people and his eagerness for their ruin and the shedding of their blood. **13** And if you found Mars²²⁶ under the rays with Mercury and the Moon, then the native will be a robber, a highway bandit, and cavalryman, excited by that. **14** And if he was with Mercury in the Midheaven,²²⁷ then he will be famous for his anger and annoyance.

15 If a planet²²⁸ was eastern, then what it indicates will be well known; and if you found it to be western, then it indicates its essence at the end of [his] years, and especially Mars by day.²²⁹

---

²²¹ See Ch. 10.2.6, **6** and **13**.
²²² Adding the phrases in brackets with the Arabic al-Khayyāt.
²²³ شجاعة, reading with the Arabic al-Khayyāt. E reads "Lot of bitterness" (السّهم مرارة). Both M and al-Rijāl read "Lot of Fortune."
²²⁴ Al-Khayyāt simply has Jupiter looking at *Mars* with an aspect of affection. Maybe Sahl's source means that Jupiter simply looks at the sign which Mars is in (with a good aspect).
²²⁵ Reading with Sahl, but al-Khayyāt has the Lot of courage (شجاعة).
²²⁶ M reads "Jupiter," but my reading agrees with al-Khayyāt.
²²⁷ M omits "with," yielding: "And if Mercury was in the Midheaven."
²²⁸ Lit., "the planet."

16 If you found Mars in a good place, then judge being a cavalryman for the native, and benefit from it.

17 And[230] know that bravery and valor in the soul are from the advancement of the stars, if they were advancing [and] safe.[231]

18 Now[232] if you found Mars by night with the Tail, then he will be powerful, a noble, an oppressor, a shedder of the blood of his lords,[233] a destroyer of countries, a captive[234] of soldiers. **19** And if you found Mars and Mercury in the Ascendant or Midheaven, he will be brave, a lover of weapons or a shedder of blood.

20 [Now as for] the nativities of the lords of courage and valor who are noted for fighting, that is if the Sun and Moon were in a male sign in the stakes, and they are free of the infortunes, and Mars rising,[235] direct, and the fortunes above him, direct, rising.[236] **21** For these natives encounter reputation and fighting, and they are elevated because of their fighting, and no one is given up by them without them killing him; and it is more suitable for that if the luminaries were in charge of the nativity together, and they were both free of the infortunes. **22** And God is more knowledgeable.

---

[229] This is not a proper contrast. This should probably say that if a planet was eastern, it will be (1) well known or happen in youth, while if it is western it will be (2) hidden, or at the end of life.

[230] For this sentence, see also Ch. 7.8, **39**.

[231] The two words used for "advancing" here are near synonyms, so it is unclear what exactly Sahl's source means by them. The first word (إدبار) is always used to mean being angular or pivotal, while the second word (مقبل) tends to mean either this or being in an advancing quarter of the chart (for example, the eastern quarter from the Ascendant to the Midheaven is advancing, while the quarter from the Midheaven to the Descendant is declining or retreating). Because of the heavy emphasis on the Ascendant and Midheaven in this section, Sahl's source probably means that the planet is moving up towards the horizon (the Ascendant) or the Midheaven, being dynamically angular or succeedent and not cadent (falling, withdrawing).

[232] See a very similar passage in Ch. 2.3, **52**; but a closer match is Ch. 10.2.1, **6**.

[233] Or, "companions" (أصحاب).

[234] This should probably read that he is a "captor" of soldiers.

[235] In much of Sahl's work, this word (صعد) refers to being succeedent or at any rate moving towards the angle or pivot. But it is also used in other texts to refer to rising in latitude or rising towards its apogee.

[236] صاعدة. E reads, "suitable" (صالحة).

Chapter 11: On friends & fraternity[1]
And in it are four topics

[al-Andarzaghar][2]

1 The first of them is that you know what [his] friendship will be like, and whom he befriends, and what the condition between them is like.[3]

2 The second: how the friendship is at the beginning of the time, [but] is then corrupted at its end, and how [his] hostility is at first, [but] then he befriends him afterwards.[4]

3 The third: how the man appears to his associate in a friendship which is not from his soul, and how a man is a friend to a man whom he befriends, and how the friend affects his friend.[5]

4 Fourth: which of the friends is more beneficial to his friend, and how the love of a father to his child is known, and the love of a woman to her husband, and the love of a man to his woman, and of two partners, one to his associate.[6]

5 Then, al-Andarzaghar said: look at these five Lots: the first is the Lot of friends (how it is taken <from the Moon to Mercury> by day, and by night the contrary, and is projected from the Ascendant),[7] the second the Lot of Fortune,[8] the third the Lot of Religion,[9] the fourth the Lot of Desire,[10] fifth the Lot of Necessity.[11]

---

[1] E omits "and fraternity" (الإخاء), but Abū Ma'shar confirms brotherhood or fraternity as a signification in *PN4* IX.6, 2 (الإخوان).
[2] The following table of contents (**1-4**) is not as nicely laid out in *BA*, with all of it being crammed into a single sentence, so it is not always clear which item or topic is meant. However, almost every sentence of the contents and instructions *are* found in Sahl. As usual, Sahl rearranges some things.
[3] See generally Ch. 11.1.
[4] See generally Chs. 11.2-11.3.
[5] This does not seem to match any special section below.
[6] See generally Ch. 11.4, but especially Ch. 11.1, **46-49**, and 11.4, **18-29**.
[7] See Ch. 11.1, **29**.
[8] See Ch. 11.3, **15**; 11.4, **2, 4, 10**, and **14**.
[9] That is, the Lot of Spirit or *Daimōn*, later called the Lot of the Invisible or Spirituality. (This is confirmed to be the Lot of Spirit in *BA* III.12.1, 2). See Ch. 11.2, **4-6**.

[Chapter 11.1: What the friendships will be like]

[Well-placed planets and friends analogous to them: al-Andarzaghar][12]

1 And as for what his friendship will be like and whom he will befriend, truly if you found Venus in a stake, in an excellent position, and nothing of the infortunes was with her, nor did they look at her from the square or opposition, and Jupiter is looking at her from an excellent place, and she is in her own exaltation, then the native will befriend women of the nobles and the powerful. **2** And if you found Venus in that position, in a house of Saturn, he will be a friend to old people. **3** Now if she was in a house of Mercury, he will be a friend to a young woman or a housemaid <or> a virgin.

4 And if Mercury was cleansed of the rays, in an excellent place, and the infortunes not looking at him, and a fortune does look at Mercury, he will be a friend to philosophers, sages, and the masters of knowledge. **5** And if at that time Mercury was in a house of Saturn, he will be a friend to sheikhs, while if he was in a house of Mars he will be a friend to warriors on horseback and masters of fighting.[13]

[The lord of the eleventh and the lord of the Ascendant: Māshā'allāh][14]

6 Then, look at the lord of the Ascendant and the lord of the eleventh: for if they looked at each other he will have many friends. **7** Now if the one handing over was the lord of the Ascendant, it indicates the goodness of the native's character and his friendly relations; and if, along with what I men-

---

[10] That is, the Lot of *Erōs*: see Ch. 11.2, **4-6** below.

[11] See Ch. 11.4, **18-20**.

[12] For this subsection, cf. Dorotheus *Excerpts* XVI **1-5**, XIX **3**, and *Frag.* II.F (and *BA* III.12.2). In *BA* III.12.2, **1-8** this is mainly about Venus and Mercury, as Sahl has it here. The Dorotheus *Excerpt* XVI makes it clear that Sahl's **1-5** are about any planet in a good position and condition, not just Venus and Mercury. Indeed, Sahl's **1** seems to be mixing Venus and Jupiter together: Jupiter being well-placed, and not in square or opposition to the infortunes, shows kings and the wealthy as friends; Venus being well-placed, and especially exalted, makes friends of illustrious women. At the end, *Excerpt* XVI, **5** adds that malefics can give occasional friendships when well-placed and in their own dignities, and when configured with benefics—but the friendships are not as firm.

[13] E: "masters from [among] the commanders." *BA* III.12.2, **9** adds that Mercury configured with Jupiter and Venus, and in aversion to the infortunes, indicates that friendship will lead to opportunities and resources.

[14] This is probably from Māshā'allāh, just as in Ch. 12.1, **25-35**, and elsewhere.

tioned the lord of the Ascendant was received, and the lord of the second looked at it, he will get assets from his friends and have enough, and will be in need of them. **8** And if the lord of the eleventh was the one connecting with the lord of the Ascendant, then he will be the one whom his friends need; and if the lord of the eleventh was received, they will have good from him. **9** Then, look at its position relative to the Ascendant: for if they were both in the stakes, then he will be friendly with one adequate to himself; and that one of the two which was corrupted, will have a bad condition. **10** And the one of the two withdrawing from the stakes indicates the corruption of the situation.

11 Then look at Venus, because she has testimony in this place: for if she was in the eleventh and she was received, then the native will mix with women in his friendship, and he will mix often with those [who have] social esteem and importance, based on the social status of the native: so speak. **12** And if she was not received but without being unfortunate, then he will mix with women having social esteem, but they are distinguished by disobedience; and if she was made unfortunate and she is in that place, he mixes with low women, and certainly has sex with more than one of them. **13** And if she was not in this place, while she connects with the lord of this place or it connects with her and they[15] look at the Ascendant and its lord, it also indicates what I explained.

14 And know that if the lord of the twelfth occurred in in the eleventh, or the Lot of friends occurred in the twelfth, the native will experience hardship from his friends. **15** And if the lord of the eleventh was in the Ascendant, and it is received, he will get the things he hopes for, and his friends will multiply, and they will have good from him, and he will see what delights him in his children (if he had children).

[The lord of the eleventh: Māshā'allāh]

16 Then look at the lord of the eleventh: for if it was in the Ascendant, he will be successful, with a good livelihood and condition, [and] be glad. **17** The lord of the eleventh in the second: he will be blessed by his friends, getting assets because of them. **18** The lord of the eleventh in the third: he will

---

[15] E reads the singular "it," referring to the lord of the eleventh only.

have well-known siblings, their conditions good, being blessed in their youth. **19** The lord of the eleventh in the fourth: his father will have a chronic illness, and their lives will be shortened, and it diminishes his condition. **20** The lord of the eleventh in the fifth: he will have delightful children, and they will be blessed with good and comfort, from the first of them to the last of them. **21** The lord of the eleventh in the sixth: he will be of a bad condition in his livelihood, with little good, creating discord. **22** The lord of the eleventh in the seventh: he will have a woman whom he loves, who is lucky, and he will have children from her and will benefit from them. **23** The lord of the eleventh in the eighth: he will not be well known <nor be> of distinguished descent, and he will do low work such as commerce.[16] **24** The lord of the eleventh in the ninth: he will have good fortune and the good when out of the country, and he will be happy until the end of his life. **25** The lord of the eleventh in the tenth: he will have authority in his friendship,[17] and the Sultan of his people will not be hostile.[18] **26** The lord of the eleventh in its own house: he will live a comfortable life, imputed with goodness,[19] with many friends and [much] culture. **27** The lord of the eleventh in the twelfth: he will have little good, be miserable in his way of living, with few friends [and] many enemies. **28** Work in this topic when the eleventh and its lord are both free of the infortunes and fortunes.

[The Lot of friends: general view]

29 Then look at the Lot of friends, and it is that you count by day from the Moon to Mercury (and by night the contrary of that), and on top of it is added the degrees of the Ascendant, and it is cast out from the Ascendant. **30** So see where this Lot falls relative to the Ascendant, and in the house of which planet it occurs, and if the house in which the Lot occurs (from the Ascendant) agrees with the native: so that if it was in the second, he will love assets, and if it falls in the third he will love the siblings. **31** And you consider [it] in all of the signs just as I have explained it.

---

[16] The Latin version in *WSM* reads "it signifies the loss of his neighbors and friends," evidently reading a variant of جار for تجارة. But it is true that "the death of friends" would be a reasonable interpretation for the lord of the eleventh in the eighth.
[17] **E** reads "youth."
[18] Or perhaps, "[his] authority over his family will not be hostile."
[19] ينسب إلى الخير. This might also be understood roughly as "traced to a good lineage."

32 Then, look at the lord of the sign in which the Lot is, what its position is like relative to the lord of the Ascendant. **33** For if they were both looking at each other from friendship, then he will make friends with honor; and if it was from a square, it is in the middle; and if it was from an opposition, it is [with] enmity.

34 And speak likewise about the lord of the Ascendant and the lord of the eleventh if they looked at each other, based on what I explained in [this] part about the lord of the Ascendant and the lord of the Lot.

[The Lot of friends in the houses: Māshā'allāh][20]

35 Then look at this Lot. **36** For if it was in the stakes, his friends will be well known (and if it was in the Midheaven, they will be authorities);[21] and if the lord was also free of the infortunes he will achieve good for this reason, and if its lord was made unfortunate he will have hardship because of them.

37 The Lot of friends in the eleventh, fifth, ninth, and third: he will be firm in affection; and if it was free of the infortunes and was in the ninth and third, he will be friendly with those who are known as being good and who have piety; while if it was made unfortunate, his friends will be of those who do not have piety.

38 The Lot of friends in the second, eighth, sixth, and twelfth: he will befriend the rabble, and if it was made unfortunate it will be harsher because it tells of evil [being] upon him in that.

39 And if you found Jupiter and[22] Venus looking at the Lot of friends, and the infortunes are not looking at it, then the friendship in which he engages will be firm, and because of that friendship he will have good.

[Synastry and inceptions in friendship: Dorotheus, from al-Andarzaghar]

40 Now[23] if you wanted to make friends, then begin and look at the luminaries: for the more excellent friendship and better one is if the luminaries

---

[20] Cf. Tehran, Dānishgāh, Nafīsī 429 (72a-72b); Majlis 17490 (139).

[21] Reading with **E**; the Latin manuscripts agree with this attitude and say the friends will be more powerful and better if in the Midheaven. Both **M** and the Arabic Māshā'allāh manuscripts say that *he* will be an authority over *them*, but this does not make astrological sense.

[22] **M** reads "or."

[23] For this sentence, cf. Dorotheus *Excerpt* XIX, **1**.

were looking at each other from a trine and from <a sextile>, and a fortune is looking at them but the infortunes are not looking: for the friendship which you enter into will be firm, [and] you will have good because of that friendship. **41** And the worst that the root of the friendship could be is if Mars looked at the Sun from an opposition or square, or he was with him. **42** And speak about the Moon if she was in the situation of the Sun and Saturn looked at her, just as I explained to you in the matter of Mars.

43 And[24] make the root of the friendship be when the Moon is in the sign which is the Ascendant of the year in the revolution of years,[25] for that is the most excellent it can be; and [it is also good] if the Moon was in the obeying signs[26] which I mentioned to you above. **44** And more excellent than that is if you look into the situations[27] of the planets: for if you wanted to befriend a chief or powerful person or the head of a city, then use the Sun; and likewise all of the planets based on their essences. **45** If you wanted to befriend a commander, then use Mars; and if you wanted to befriend the king, then use Jupiter; now if you wanted to befriend a distasteful person or the rabble, use Saturn; and for commerce and writing, use Mercury; and if you wanted to befriend women, then use Venus; and if you wanted to befriend noble[28] women, then use the Moon.

46 And[29] as for the benefit of the friendship, and which of the two will be more beneficial to his partner, look at the Midheaven of both nativities. **47** Now if you found the Moon of the other in it, and the Moon of the native in the sixth or twelfth of the other, then that friend will be more beneficial to the native than the native to him. **48** And if you found your Moon in her own house (in Cancer), or in another [sign], and the lord of the Moon of your friend is with your Moon or looking at her from the first trine, or the lord of your Moon and the lord of his Moon is a single planet, and it looks at your

---

[24] For this paragraph, see the original Dorotheus poem in Heph. III.20, **3-4** and **7**; cf. also *Excerpt* XIX, **2-4**.

[25] This is not exactly what the Greek original or the interpretation in *Excerpt* XIX says: rather, the native's profected Ascendant should be on the other person's natal Moon. For example, let the person I want to befriend, have his Moon in Virgo: then I should wait until the year in which my profected Ascendant is in Virgo. Of course, that can only happen every twelve years, so Sahl's source is offering that the native's *solar revolution* Ascendant could be Virgo, too—which would happen more often.

[26] In Dorotheus, these are the hearing and seeing signs.

[27] Lit. "faces," but I take this to be the more analogical meaning of "way, manner, mode."

[28] سيّدة, which is not necessarily nobles, but women who are socially distinguished or higher.

[29] For **47-48**, see *Excerpt* XVII, **3** and Heph. III.9, **24**.

Moon, then the friend will be more beneficial to you than you are to him. **49** And speak likewise about the lords of the Lots—your Lot, and his Lot.

[Chapter 11.2: How friendships change, from al-Andarzaghar]

1 As for the friendship which is suitable at its beginning and dissolves at its end, and enmity which results in friendship at its end, and what the friendship is between two parties. **2** Now if you found the two nativities to be diurnal or nocturnal, then the two of them will become friends, and that friendship will be strong, [but] after a time it will be corrupted or will be converted into enmity. **3** And when the diurnal one is hostile to the nocturnal one, and the nocturnal to the diurnal, then that [initial] enmity will be converted to friendship [later].

4 The Lot of desire.[30] **5** Then, look at the Lot of desire, which is taken by day from the Lot of Fortune to the Lot of Spirituality, and there is added on top of it the degrees of the Ascendant [and it is projected from the Ascendant], and by night the converse of that. **6** If you found Saturn and Mars with this Lot, or in its square or its opposition, then the friendship will be in public, while they will keep the enmity secret.

7 And[31] if the Sun looked at Mars, or Saturn at the Moon, and they were with one of those five Lots which I described to you above, then judge that he is a friend out in the open and an enemy in secret.[32]

8 And if you found, in a nativity of the day or a nativity of the night, the fortunes and infortunes looking at the Sun and the Moon,[33] then at times there will be friendship, and at times enmity.[34]

---

[30] Again, the Lot of *Erōs*. Sentences **4-5** (and probably **6-7**) are from Dorotheus and are briefly referred to in Heph. II.3 (Schmidt p. 73).

[31] For this sentence, cf. Dorotheus *Frag.* II.F.

[32] This seems to mean that even the friend does not know about the enmity—in other words, in **6** they each knew where the other stood, while in **7** the enmity is not known by one of the parties.

[33] The structure of the Arabic suggests that perhaps we are to use only (or perhaps prioritize) the sect light.

[34] Cf. Dorotheus *Frag.* II.E, **2**.

9 Then, look at the Lot of friends and the Lot of enemies:[35] for if they were both in one sign, then judge for him that he will at times be a friend and at times an enemy.

10 And[36] if you found Mars overcoming Mercury, then judge for him that tribulation will afflict him from his friend, and they will never be glad[37] with each other. **11** Now if Mercury overcame the Mars of the other person (and that overcoming is if you found one of them in the Midheaven and the other in the Ascendant),[38] then if you found it like that, then one of them will corrupt the assets of the other, and demolish his house, and their conflict and enmity will become endlessly more intense.

12 And if you found the luminaries in two signs, each looking at its associate from the trine, opposition, square, or sextile, and you do not see them in the obeying signs, then they will become friends but their friendship will not last a long time.

[Chapter 11.3:] The knowledge of when he will be hostile to his friend

[al-Andarzaghar]

1 If[39] you wanted to know when he will be hostile to his friend, then look at the distributor of the time.[40] **2** For if you found the distributor of life to be an infortune, and that infortune already portended evil in the root of the nativity, and you saw it in the Ascendant of your friend's nativity at the revolution of years, then he will abandon his friendship and turn it into enmity.

3 And likewise look for the native and the father, and a woman and her husband, and two partners.

---

[35] See Ch. 12.1, **48-55**.

[36] For this paragraph, cf. Dorotheus *Excerpt* XVII, **1-2**. Part of this first sentence is quoted verbatim from Dorotheus's poem by Hephaistion II.23.

[37] Or more interestingly, "be relaxed with" (سيتريحان).

[38] This is inaccurate (and a common mistake in Arabic and Latin translations), because overcoming is a square relationship between signs, not topical places: see the Glossary.

[39] For this paragraph, cf. Hephaistion III.20, **3-4**; Dorotheus *Frag.* II.F and *Excerpt* XIX, **4**.

[40] The *jārbakhtār*, a Persian word that means "distributor" (see Glossary).

[Times of friendship and enmity according to Ptolemy][41]

4 And[42] if you looked into the transit of the planets of the two nativities, you ought to know in which time period there will be misfortune for those places, and which places of the waystations[43] their transit goes through, because in their transit in these places there will be enmity and separation based on what I will tell you.

5 So as for Saturn and Jupiter, if one of them transited the place of his associate, then it brings about courtesy, associating, and friendliness between the two natives, in agriculture and inheritance and what resembles that. **6** And as for Saturn and Mars, if one of them transited the place of his associate, then it brings about fraternal relations and quick clashing between the two natives that does not last long. **7** And as for Saturn and Venus, if one of them transited the place of its associate, then it brings about friendship and courtesy between the two natives by reason of relatives[44] and females, or piety and devotion. **8** And as for Saturn and Mercury, if one of them transited the place of the other, then it brings about partnership between the two, and the goodness of the friendship, and taking and giving.

9 And as for Jupiter and Mars, if one of them transited the place of the other, then it brings about friendship and courtesy between the two natives by reason of devotion and the masters of armies, conquest, and violence.[45] **10** And as for Jupiter and Venus, if one of them transited the place of its associate, then it brings about friendship and courtesy between the two natives by

---

[41] For this section, cf. *Tet.* IV.7 (Robbins pp. 413-21).

[42] This paragraph is a very condensed version of certain instructions by Ptolemy. Here, Ptolemy looks at fortunes and infortunes which transit through—it seems—the configurations between the two charts. These configurations involve the mutual relationships of the natives' luminaries, Ascendants, and Lots of Fortune. But Ptolemy is also interested in the primary direction of a planet in one nativity, to a planet in the other nativity: so, in the following paragraph, he will look at the Saturn of one chart being directed to the Jupiter of the other chart, and so on. In practice this would involve putting the other's Jupiter into the chart of the first person and then performing the direction, because they may have been born at different latitudes, with different semi-arcs, and so on.

[43] Reading the plural for the singular in the MSS; I take this word to refer to the signs, but it can also mean the lunar mansions (although I am not sure how to apply them here).

[44] Reading as الأنسباء with Ptolemy, for the similarly-spelled النّساء ("women").

[45] But Ptolemy has: dignities and household management (or the management of property).

reason of women, babies, piety, and devotion. **11** As for Jupiter and Mercury, if one of them transited the place of his partner, then it brings about friendship between the two natives in relation to logic[46] and knowledge.

12 As for Mars and Venus, if one of them transited the place of its associate it brings about associations and agreement between the two natives by means of fornication and passion, but [with] separation [later]. **13** As for Mars and Mercury, if one of them transited the place of his partner, it brings about hostility and evil between the two natives, and fighting and conflict, by reason of documents and lying, and hostility in this respect. **14** And as for Venus and Mercury, if one of them transited the place of its associate, it brings about the good and friendship between the two natives, and strong emotions,[47] and freedom from want <because of writing>, and affection in this respect.

15 And as for increase and decrease and the future outlook of enmity, understand that from the four places which I described to you in the indication of agreement between the two natives, or their disagreement (and they are the two luminaries, the Ascendant, and the Lot of Fortune): because if the Lot of Fortune and the two luminaries are in the stakes, and the infortunes end up at[48] their positions, they make hostility appear and be known; while if they were not in the stakes, the enmity will be light, with nothing hinging on it.[49]

16 And as for slaves and their harm to their masters, and their hostility, that is known from the sign of enemies and from the planets looking at that place on the day of the nativity. **17** And harsher for that is the planet which is in that sign.[50]

---

[46] This can also refer to eloquence and the use of reason generally (المنطق).
[47] Or, "cohabitation" (Ptolemy). This is a tentative reading from **E**, as it is smudged and **M** omits this sentence.
[48] The text uses the verb normally reserved for profections, but this probably means transits and primary directions; Ptolemy does not specify a method in his version of this sentence.
[49] بغير معلق بها. Or as Ptolemy puts it, "inconspicuous." In other words, planets that are dynamically cadent or falling will have less of an effect on friendship. As for the Arabic, I believe there might be an error, since the text uses معلق, when مغلق would mean "obscure" or "ambiguous" (more in line with Ptolemy); but that would require omitting the بغير.
[50] In Ptolemy, this includes transits in the sign *and opposite* it.

[Chapter 11.4: Benefit & love between people]

[Synastry in friendship: Dorotheus, from al-Andarzaghar][51]

1 Now as for a beneficial friendship, look in the nativity of two men, or the nativity of a man and his woman, or the nativity of two women, if you wanted an examination of them both.

2 Now if:

[1] their Moons were in one [and the same] sign, and if:

[2] the Moon of this nativity was in the place of a fortune in the other nativity, and if:

[3] the two fortunes in both nativities were looking [at each other] from a trine, and if:

[4] the Lot of Fortune in both nativities was in one [and the same] sign, and if:

[5] the Lot of Fortune in one of the nativities was in the house of the Moon [of the other], and the Moon of the other nativity was in the place of the Lot of Fortune [of the first one], and if:

[6] the Moon and the Lot of Fortune in both nativities were trining, and if:

[7] the Sun in both nativities was in one [and the same] sign, and if:

[8] you saw the luminaries in both nativities having exchanged places, and if:

[9] you saw the two Moons in the Midheaven, and if:

[10] you found the two Moons in the two nativities in the sixth and twelfth, or the Moon in the nativity in one of them was in the sixth, and in the nativity of the other in the twelfth, and if:

[11] you found the competition (and it is the opposition)[52] in both nativities in one [and the same] place, and if:

[12] you found the luminaries in both nativities looking each one at its associate in the obeying signs (and they are the signs which, if the

---

[51] For the following long list of possibilities, cf. Dorotheus *Excerpts* XVII, **3** and XVIII, **1-6** and XIX, **1** (see also Hephaistion III.20, **5**); Dorotheus *Frags.* II.E and II.F; cf. also *Tet.* IV.7.

[52] That is, the Full Moon before birth. But perhaps the source would include the pre-natal New Moon, for natives with that?

Sun alighted in one of them, the day decreases in them, so that they are obedient to the signs in which day increases),[53] and if:

[13] you found the luminaries in a sign which is obedient to its associate,

—then judge that their friendship will be lasting, until death separates them.

[*Principles of synastry according to Ptolemy*][54]

3 And[55] when your Ascendant agrees with his Ascendant, and your Sun with his Sun, and your Moon with his Moon, you will associate with him.

4 Then, look at the place of the Sun, Moon, Ascendant, and the Lot of Fortune: for if they were all in [something] other than their own signs and places, or the majority of them were likewise in [something] other than their places,[56] then it indicates that there will be enmity between them, tribulation, [and] offense, and [with] no initiating [of friendship] from the native, and he will not concern himself with that. **5** And if it was by a contrast and opposition, one of them to the other, then it indicates powerful hostility and conflict, and they will loathe each other for a long time. **6** And if it was by a trine or sextile, one of them to the other, it diminishes the hostility and there will be a truce. **7** And if the fortunes transited over these places which we mentioned, then after their enmity there will be a reconsideration and a return to friendship.

---

[53] According to Heph. II.23 (Schmidt p. 73), this should include signs like Aquarius commanding Sagittarius, Pisces commanding Scorpio, Aries commanding Libra, Taurus commanding Virgo, and Libra commanding Leo. This leaves Capricorn and Cancer out, but Hephaistion also says that Aries and Libra are left out of the scheme of hearing signs. The example of Taurus-Virgo is confirmed in **29** below.

[54] Again, cf. *Tet.* IV.7.

[55] This sentence is not exactly reflected in Ptolemy, but it is not in the existing Dorotheus sources either. In *Tet.* IV.7, Ptolemy associates the luminaries with what Aristotle called (roughly) friendship based on character and choice, whereas a relationship based on Ascendants indicates friendships based on pleasure and pain. See also the next subsection below.

[56] This makes some astrological sense but is not an accurate representation of Ptolemy. Ptolemy means that if the relevant points are in signs that are *in aversion to each other* in each other's nativities, there will be enmity. So for instance, if the Sun of one person is in aversion to the Sun of the other.

[Three kinds of friendship, according to Ptolemy][57]

8 Know that <friendship and> enmity is of three types. **9** One of them is a disagreement having enmity and a scarcity of agreement between them in their preferences.[58] **10** The second, for benefit and harm. **11** The third, for joy or sorrow.[59] **12** Now if these places which we have described before generally coincided with each other, then it indicates agreement;[60] and if it was contrary to that, it indicates hostile treatment, in the manner which the nativities indicate. **13** So if the disagreement or agreement in the two nativities was from the place of the luminaries only, it indicates enmity and hatred and grudges—or friendly relations and affection and sincerity—and the agreement and disagreement they indicate will be lasting [and] firm. **14** And if the agreement or disagreement in the two nativities was from the position of the Lot of Fortune, that indicates that the benefit or harm is from one of them to the other. **15** And if the disagreement or agreement in the two nativities was from the Ascendant, that indicates that they will rejoice or be sad, one with the other.

16 And it is that you should understand the places in a more powerful position and their strength, and the aspect of the planets in the nativities, and the signs which arise after these places, adjacent to them: for truly they indicate the confirmation of friendliness. **17** And know that if the fortunes looked at them, that is an increase in fraternizing and friendliness, and a component of friendship, and that is with the transiting of those planets in those places; and likewise enmity and consternation in that position when the infortunes look at them or transit them.

---

[57] Again, cf. *Tet.* IV.7.
[58] In Aristotle this is called "complete" friendship, based on shared values and life choices.
[59] In *Tet.* IV.7 (Robbins pp. 415-17), the first type involves the relationship between the friends' luminaries; the second involves their Lots of Fortune; the third, their Ascendants. This is reflected below in **13-15**, respectively.
[60] Or rather, if all or most of the coincide or correspond in the way stated above, the friendship will also have characteristics of each type; now Sahl (Ptolemy) will identify which indicators support which type of friendship.

[Synastry in other relationships: al-Andarzaghar][61]

18 Now as for the love of a father for his child (or his hatred towards him), and of a woman to her husband, or one of two partners to his companion, look at the Lot of necessity[62] in your nativity and his nativity. **19** For if they were both in one sign, or each one of them was in the house of the other, then the two people will be hostile and do harm, each one of them to his partner. **20** And if they were not both in one sign and they were in the sign of a single planet, then likewise judge enmity for them.

21 Now as for a child and a father, look at the Lot of fathers. **22** For if you found it in one of the signs, and that sign was the Ascendant of the child, then the child will love his father. **23** And if it was not [the child's] Ascendant, and you found the Lot of children in the sign in which the Lot of fathers was,[63] then the child will love his father. **24** And if you did not find the Lot in anything of what I described to you, then the child will not love his father, and the father[64] will experience tribulation from his child. **25** And judge likewise for the mother and child from the Moon and the Lot of mothers.

26 Now as for a woman and her husband, look at the Lot of marriage of the woman and the Lot of marriage of the man. **27** For if they both occurred in the obeying signs which I have described to you,[65] then they will both remain loving to each other, forever. **28** And if you found an infortune with the two Lots, it indicates an abundance of shouting and evil between them; and likewise if they were both with the Tail, and likewise if the infortune looked from a square or opposition: for with that, they will separate (and if the infortune looked from a trine or sextile, then it changes that hostility [to something less]); and truly he will have that in it if the two infortunes were rulers of the Sun, and they were both in a bad place: for then he will divorce her or they will separate. **29** And see if perhaps you find the Lot of marriage

---

[61] This material seems to be based on Dorotheus, not only because all of the sentences can be found in *BA*, but Heph. II.23 and *Excerpt* XVIII also refer to the family and sign relationships. But in **21-29** Hephaistion makes it seem like we are speaking of the Lots of *Erōs* for each person being in these signs, and the *Excerpt* makes it seem like the Moon.

[62] This is the opposite of the Lot of *Erōs*: by day from the Lot of Spirit to the Lot of Fortune (and by night the reverse), projected from the Ascendant.

[63] This probably means, "the Lot of children in the *father's* chart, is in the same sign as the Lot of fathers in the *child's* chart."

[64] Here and in the next sentence, **E** begins to read "parents" and "mother and father" instead of "mother and child."

[65] See the footnote to Ch. 11.4, **2** above.

of the man in Taurus, and the Lot of marriage of the woman in Virgo: for if you found them to be thus, then the man will be obedient towards his woman; and if you found the Lot of marriage of the woman in Taurus and the Lot of marriage of the man in Virgo, the woman will be obedient to her husband and love him.[66]

---

[66] See also Hephaistion III.23, who connects not only this statement about Virgo-Taurus to synastry, but also the Lot of *Erōs* and the statements about parents and children and wives and husbands. So these paragraphs are probably from Dorotheus.

Chapter 12: On enemies & suffering
And in it are two topics:
One of them on the abundance of enemies and their scarcity, and the second on riding animals and livestock

[Chapter 12.1: Enemies]

1 In the matter of enemies, look at the twelfth sign: is it fixed, convertible, or having two bodies?[1]

2 Then look: does it belong to an infortune or a fortune, and where is its lord in the signs, and does it look [at it] or not?

[Planets in the house of enemies]

3 Now if you found a fortune in the twelfth, and it has testimony and a claim, then it breaks every evil in accordance with what you see of its power, and his enemies will be few, and it diminishes the suffering upon him from the people, and slander towards him; and if one of his enemies treated him in a hostile manner, [the enemy] will be weakened and he will not gain what he seeks from him, and especially if that fortune was Jupiter: [because] he will strengthen [the native] and break the evil from the infortunes and the wickedness of the enemy and of enemies generally, unless you find Jupiter retrograde or made unfortunate or in his own fall, or he is burned or conjoined with an infortune.

4 And if you found an infortune in the twelfth and it had power in that place, and the fortunes fell away from it, then his enemies will multiply and become more powerful over him, and they will not cease to stir up calamities against him, and not one of them will be good for him, and they will harbor hostile feelings towards him.

5 Now if that infortune was Mars, [and he was] in this manner and power, then the native will be harmed[2] by some of his enemies (and the enemies are

---

[1] See **10** below.

[2] **E**: بلاه. Reading the rest of this sentence with **E**. **M** reads: "he will be ruined in the land of the enemy, taken prisoner in fighting, and no friends will save or receive him in the country in which he was born, so wounds and beatings by iron will kill him, or burning by fire will afflict him, unless that infortune was in an alien sign, not having a claim in the Ascendant: then you will say that he will be ruined by enemies while abroad."

in the country in which he was born), by wounds and beatings with iron, and burning by fire will afflict him; or, [if] the infortune was in an alien sign, not having a claim in the Ascendant, then you will say that he will be ruined by hostility and enemies while abroad. **6** And if Mars had a claim in the Ascendant, then he will be ruined in the place he was born in. **7** And if you found a fortune which Mars was inspecting, with the fortune being strong in its own place and one of the stakes,³ then his enemies will harass him with calamities and will seek evil for him, [but] then they will be broken by him and he will get revenge upon them in speech, enmity, evil, and lawsuits, and they will not gain what they want from him due to the position of the fortune which you found in the stake of Mars: for it breaks the enmity and the power which belongs to Mars.

8 And if Saturn was the infortune, in the condition which I described to you about Mars, being free of the aspect of the fortunes, then his enemies will deceive him with prisons and confinements, witnesses, falsehood,⁴ the seeking of calamities, evil, and betrayal,⁵ and double-dealing in that, until he dies in their enmity; and they will not part from him unless you find Jupiter inspecting him based on what I described to you about Mars: for he will be rescued from their enmity and their evil due to Jupiter breaking the misfortune of Saturn—though there is no escaping the harshness in the enmity due to the condition of Saturn and what I described to you of his misfortune.

9 And if you found the lord of the twelfth to be an infortune,⁶ and it was falling away from it, and the twelfth was clear, not a planet in it, then report that his enemies will not get anything from him except through their tongues; but due to the fact that the lord of the twelfth is an infortune, the native will still be hated, [and] evil will be said about him, and ugly speech about him will be abundant from his enemies, without his being present or [their having] shame about it, nor will they reveal it to him.

10 And if the sign was fixed, of the straight signs, then that one of them⁷ will never refrain from speaking about him. **11** And if it was of the converti-

---

³ Below the text says that this is one of the stakes of Mars, but I am not so sure this would be required.
⁴ This should probably be understood better as "false witnesses."
⁵ **M**: "stratagems" or "ruses."
⁶ Reading with **M. E**: "And if Saturn was the lord of the twelfth...".
⁷ This is awkward; perhaps Sahl means the people described by its lord.

ble signs, then they will make a show, from softness and restraint, of what is not in their hearts. **12** And if it was a sign having two bodies, then they will [act] towards him sometimes with restraint, and sometimes with enmity.

13 And if the lord of the twelfth was a fortune, and fell away from its own house, and the house was purified of the infortunes or their inspection, then his enemies will sometimes meet with him and sometimes disagree with him, but will not give up their friendship with him, and they will envy him in something which has no reason and no calamity, and he will gain from them.

14 And know that if you found the degree of the house of enemies strong and you found the degree of the house of friends weak in the root of the nativity, then his friends will become few and it weakens them, and it strengthens his enemies and multiplies them, and reinforces their power over him; now if you found the degree of friends to be stronger, then his enemies are weak and his friends strong, and it multiplies them. **15** For these two degrees are witnesses for what you find of the condition of the native in friends and enemies.

16 And look at the Moon and what her condition is at her fullness in the two degrees: so speak about that based on what you see of the Moon's inclination towards one of the two degrees.[8]

17 And if you found a planet in the opposition of the luminaries or the Ascendant, and especially if it was an infortune, then the native will have enemies and will quarrel. **18** Now if it was Jupiter in this opposition, it indicates something like this, but it will be a great matter and a matter of the Sultan, and it turns his affliction and harm around.

19 And know that if the lords of the house of suffering[9] (and [houses] other than it) were not looking at those houses, and they passed through their own positions,[10] he will rejoice in those regions and be safe from them.

20 And if Mars was in the Ascendant, then the native will be foul in [his] speech, very angry at enemies, and especially by day. **21** And if the Moon looked at him, then pains and breaking and beating will afflict the native.

22 And likewise if Mercury was in the seventh, and he is made unfortunate, then he is bad, because it makes speech about him bad, and he will be

---

[8] This may refers to the cusps of the eleventh and twelfth just mentioned.
[9] That is, the twelfth.
[10] I think this means that the lords are in aversion to their own place *or* they have already passed their natal position or aspect *by transit*.

unlucky in [his] expression.[11] **23** And if a fortune looked, it will set [things] aright and repel that.

[The lord of the Ascendant and lord of the twelfth: Māshā'allāh]

24 And Māshā'allāh b. Atharī of Basrah[12] said: Look at the lord of the Ascendant and the lord of the twelfth: for if they looked at each other or connected one to the other, then the native will be unhappy, and with many enemies. **25** Now if it[13] was received, and the lord of the Ascendant strengthened by the lord of the twelfth, he will not be unhappy but hardship and sorrow will afflict him. **26** And if it was not received, and the lord of the Ascendant was in a stake and the lord of the twelfth withdrawing, then he will be victorious over his enemies and have power over them. **27** And if the lord of the twelfth was strong and the lord of the Ascendant was withdrawing, then his enemies will have power over him. **28** And if they were both in stakes, then the one greater in testimony in its own place will be stronger. **29** And if the lord of the twelfth was in its own exaltation or in the Midheaven, then his enemies will be from the Sultan; and likewise if the lord of the Ascendant was in the Midheaven, it indicates the power of the native over the enemies and victory over them.

30 And if the two indicators did not look at each other, the one of them to its associate, then look at the place of the lord of the twelfth: for if it does not look at the Ascendant, it will not be harmful to the native. **31** And if there was an aspect, then see from which place it is looking: for truly the enemies of the native will be of the essence of the sign which it is in. **32** If the lord of the twelfth was in the Ascendant, then the native will have a bad character; and if it was in the second, then his assistants; and if it was in the third he will be hostile to his siblings; and speak in this manner for all of the places.

33 If the lord of the twelfth was Saturn, old men will be hostile to him; and if it was Mars, the masters of wars will be hostile to him, and one who works with fire and blood, and likewise the essence of [all of] the planets. **34** And if it was the Moon, then look at her position relative to the Ascendant, and the position of the one looking at her, and judge based on both of those.

---

[11] مقال. This can mean both speech as well as written works.
[12] Reading البصري more accurately for المصري ("Egyptian").
[13] I believe this is the lord of the twelfth.

[The lord of the twelfth in the houses: Māshā'allāh]

35 Then, look at the lord of the twelfth: for if it was in the Ascendant, he will be unhappy, his enemies will multiply, and they will be victorious over him, and he will experience tribulations and will be belligerent. 36 And if it was in the second, he will do a work which he is embarrassed about, and he will have a bad character, a bad livelihood, with deception in it. 37 And in the third, his siblings will be hostile towards him, and he will experience hardship and the badness of their condition from them. 38 And in the fourth the parents and family will be hostile towards him, and they will quarrel with him, and he will destroy the home he was born in and move from it. 39 And in the fifth his children will disobey him and be hostile towards him, and there will be defects in them, and their condition bad. 40 And in the sixth he will be saddened by his slaves and riding animals, and they will have no good in them. 41 And in the seventh he will mix with low women with defects in them, and they will be hostile towards him. 42 And in the eighth he will have few enemies and many of his slaves will die. 43 And in the ninth his siblings will experience hardship from enemies, and if he travels he will experience hardship from enemies, and he will have bad religion. 44 And in the tenth, the Sultan will be hostile towards him, and those who wield power over him, and his sorrow and griefs will last a long time. 45 And in the eleventh he will leave the goodness of friends and they will return to his enmity, and he will be unhappy. 46 And in the twelfth his enemies will be few and will not appear to him, and he will be safe from their evil. 47 Operate in this topic when the twelfth and its lord are both free of the infortunes, and the fortunes do not bear witness.

[The Lot of enemies: Māshā'allāh][14]

48 And[15] know that Mercury has testimony in this topic: so count from him to the Lot of the Moon, and cast it out from the Ascendant, and where it

---

[14] Cf. Tehran, Dānishgāh, Nafīsī 429 (72b); Majlis 17490 (139).

[15] This paragraph presents several problems. It and the formula for the Lot of enemies do not appear in the Arabic versions of Māshā'allāh's full *Treatise on Lots* (Tehran, see footnote above), while a Latin version of it (Vat. Pal. lat. 1892, f. 103r) and both Sahl manumanuscripts contain three different versions of the formula. (1) I have used **M** here, which adopts the "Hermetic" Lot of necessity (from Mercury to Fortune or "the Lot of the Moon," reversed by night). This Lot *does* have to do with enmity, but the problem is that the end of **48** equates it with the Lot of slaves, and that is not true: the Lot of slaves is from

terminates, there is the Lot of enemies (and it is the Lot of slaves). **49** So look at the position of this Lot and the position of its lord relative to the Ascendant, and speak about it just as I have explained it to you in the topic of friends.

Treatise on Lots	Formula	Real name
M: Sahl, *Nativities* Ch. 12.1, **48**	☿ → ⊗	Necessity
E: Sahl, *Nativities* Ch. 12.1, **49**	☿ → ☽	Slaves
Vat. Pal. Lat. 1892, f. 103r	Lord 12th → 12th	Enemies (Hermes)

Figure 71: Three versions of Māshā'allāh's Lot of enemies

50 Now if the Lot was in the stakes, and it is free of the infortunes, well-known people who have importance will be hostile to him, and they will do hostile things to him, and he will experience hardship; and that is harsher if it was made unfortunate, because one who makes his enmity known will be hostile to him, and will struggle against him. **51** And if the lord of the Ascendant was made unfortunate along with what I mentioned, he will die at the hands of his enemies.

52 If the Lot was in the eleventh, third, fifth, and ninth, his enemies will not have strength, and he will have few enemies, <and he will be of a good

---

Mercury to the *Moon*, not the *Lot of* the Moon (Fortune). Then (2) the more jumbled version in **E** has the formula for the Lot of slaves and so is internally consistent, but slaves are not the same as enemies, even though they overlap in some hostility. Then (3) the Latin version gives a formula attributed to Hermes by many people: from the lord of the twelfth to the twelfth. (Actually, the Latin measures from the lord of the twelfth to the sixth, and then subtracts the twelfth, which does not make sense and is obviously some kind of error.) On the other hand, the main argument for using a Lot of slaves (Mercury-Moon) as the Lot of enemies, is that all three texts imply something about slavery: **M** explicitly makes the comparison, **E** uses the Lot of slaves and contains the odd phrase "and it is this," as though it means to equate it with the Lot of slaves just like the end of **48**; and the Latin has the unusual calculation using the sixth. So it is just possible that Māshā'allāh *did* use the Mercury-Moon Lot. Hopefully we will get other texts in the future. In the meantime, I use **M** here because **E** is more jumbled and awkward. (Incidentally, I should also mention that I have a copy of an uncatalogued manuscript from a private collector, which purports to be by Māshā'allāh, and which gives the Lot of enemies as the Saturn-Mars calculation, which is Valens's Lot of accusation, and also mentioned by Abū Ma'shar and al-Rijāl. But I am not yet very certain about its authenticity.)

religion>.¹⁶ **53** <If the Lot was in the ninth and the third, free of the infortunes, then his enemies will have> reasonable minds and piety; while if it was made unfortunate, masters of sorcery will be hostile to him, as well as those accused of magic. **54** And in the eleventh, if it was made unfortunate, his own friends will be hostile to him; and in the fifth, his children will be hostile to him.

55 The Lot of enemies in the second, eighth, sixth, and twelfth: he will have few enemies, [and] his enemies will not harm him—<but>¹⁷ if the lord of the Lot of enemies was an infortune, and it is making the lord of the Ascendant unfortunate, and is looking at the Lot, then if it was according to what I have described to you, the hostility will be from the essence of the sign which the Lot is in: if it was in the second, then by reason of assets; and if it was in the eighth, by reason of death; and in the sixth, by reason of slaves; and in the twelfth, by reason of one whom he already knows through enmity.

[Chapter 12.2: Riding animals & livestock]¹⁸

1 Now as for what the native has of riding animals and livestock, look in that from the twelfth place, and from Mars, and what kind of place he has. **2** For the best thing in the matter of riding animals is if Mars is eastern, in a sign having four feet, and especially if he was in one of the signs of kings, in the highest stake (that is, in the Midheaven), or in the place of good fortune:¹⁹ because if he was found in this condition, and Jupiter and the Sun were looking, then the native will have many riding animals, much livestock, and especially if Mars was in his own bound. **3** Now if with that you found Mars with the Lot of Fortune, then the native will desire horses and weapons, and places for training horses. **4** And if the Moon was with him or Mars

---

¹⁶ Adding with the Arabic Māshā'allāh, here and below.
¹⁷ Adding based on Māshā'allāh, who clearly connects this condition and what follows to these four houses, not to just any affliction of the lord of the Lot.
¹⁸ This whole chapter is very close to one attributed to Māshā'allāh in the Latin Paris BNF lat. 7324, f. 80v, and is virtually identical to al-Khayyāt's Ch. 23. I do have an Arabic manuscript attributed to Māshā'allāh which contains a Lot of riding animals: by day and night from the Sun to Saturn, and projected from the Ascendant.
¹⁹ That is, the eleventh.

was the lord of the Ascendant and the lord of the meeting,[20] and his place is good, inspecting the fortunes, then the native will have many horses, many riding animals, [and] be really interested in that.

5 And likewise, if you found the lord of the twelfth in a sign having four feet, along with a fortune, then he will profit from riding animals, along with what I mentioned; but if that sign was fixed,[21] and in it was Saturn, then evil and tribulation and sorrow will afflict the native because of riding animals, and especially if that sign was not a house of Mars or a house of Jupiter: because if it happened to be that Mars was in a good place, in Aries and its triplicity, the native will have riding animals [consisting] of types [such as] horses, camels, and powerful and large cattle, especially if Jupiter looked at him.

6 If Mars happened to be in Taurus and its triplicity, then the native will have a mixture of riding animals, livestock, cows, horses, and sheep, and the rest of that; and speak likewise for the rest of the signs, and speak about the benefit in that class [of animal] based on their essences.

7 And if you found the Ascendant to be Sagittarius or any of these signs appropriate for riding animals, and its lord was with Mars or looking at Mars, then the native will love riding animals [themselves], more so than the riding of them. **8** And likewise the Moon if she happened to be in any of these places.

9 The book of Sahl b. Bishr the Israelite on nativities is finished, with praise to God and His help.

---

[20] **M, E**, and al-Rijāl all give different combinations of whether this should read "and" or "or" for Mars's role here; clearly if he was all of these at once, the judgment would be even more certain.

[21] **M** reads: "watery."

APPENDIX A:
THE SECTIONS ON ASCENDANTS
& THE JUDGMENTS OF NATIVITIES

Comment by Dykes. This short set of 66 statements appears in two manuscripts mentioned by Sezgin (p. 127, #5). The following is based on Nuruosmaniye 2785/3, 13a-15a; the other manuscript (not yet seen by me) is Cairo, Tal'at 139/4, 62a-65a. They cover all areas of traditional astrology: questions, inceptions, nativities, and mundane.

It so happens that every one of these is reflected in the famous *Propositions of al-Mansūr*, one of several centiloquies popularized in the Latin Middle Ages. In some cases, the Latin helps clarify some readings in **N**. I have prefaced each of the sections with a "Sahl number" [S] and an "al-Mansūr number" [M] so that they may be compared.

ಬಿ   ಞ   ಞ

*In the name of God, the Merciful, the Compassionate,
and His blessing be upon our master Muhammad, the seal of the prophets, and
upon his family.*

The Sections
by Sahl b. Bishr the Israelite
and it is in 66 sections

1 [S1/M20] *The first section*: He will not save up on provisions except one whose lord of the Ascendant and lord of the fourth are a single planet, just as one will not take on rank and assets and a pension except one whose lord of the Ascendant and lord of the tenth are a single planet.

2 [S2/M23] For one going to meet the king while the Moon is in Aquarius, he will not heed him; and if he went to meet him while she is in Pisces, he will turn his face away from him.

3 [S3/M24] Bloodletting[1] is detested with the Moon in Gemini, just as cupping is detested with the Moon in Taurus.

---

[1] Cf. *Carmen* V.40, **1** and **8** (as Gemini rules the arms and Taurus is specifically warned against).

4 [S4/M26] The most preferable of the signs for entering into a partnership are the fiery ones: and the most praiseworthy[2] of them is Leo, and the most blameworthy of them is Aries.

5 [S5/M30] If the heavy planets were westernizing from the Sun, they grant the native good fortune at the end of his lifespan.[3]

6 [S6/M31] One[4] who buys something with the Moon from the beginning of Cancer to the end of Sagittarius, buys it at an expensive price and sells at a cheap one; and it is the contrary if he buys with the Moon from the beginning of Capricorn to the end of Gemini.

7 [S7/M32] Circumcision is detested with the Moon in Scorpio, just as medical treatment[5] is detested when she is in Leo.

8 [S8/M35] If the Moon is made unfortunate in the root of the nativity, and the first lord of the triplicity of the Ascendant is falling, and the stakes harmed,[6] then judge for the native the shortness of his survival.

9 [S9/M37] If all of the lords of the triplicities[7] were falling, and in one of the stakes was [one of the] fixed stars which are of the first and second magnitude, of the complexion of the lords of the triplicities, the upbringing will be completed and the years will be passed by.[8]

10 [S10/M42] The alighting of Saturn in the fixed signs produces infectious disease as well as expensiveness in the region which is of the division of that sign.[9]

11 [S11/M46] Mars[10] does not harm travelers on the sea, just as Saturn does not harm travelers on land.

---

[2] Reading وأحمدها for وأخمدها ("calm"?).

[3] The Latin al-Manṣūr adds, "and conversely": that is, if easternizing they will indicate it earlier in life.

[4] Cf. *Carmen* V.44, **1-2**, which however states the contrary of this.

[5] The Latin al-Manṣūr reads, "vomiting," suggesting an emetic.

[6] Reading اجترمت for احترمت ("honored"). The Latin al-Manṣūr reads it that there is an infortune in the angle, so probably an infortune is harming the angle by being in it.

[7] This must be all of the triplicity lords of *the Ascendant*, which are the lords indicating upbringing.

[8] Put better, *the native* will pass beyond those years.

[9] That is, the countries and landscapes indicated by that sign. This is a mundane consideration.

[10] See *Choices* Ch. 9, **28**.

12 [S12/M47] <In journeys>,¹¹ the convertible signs are loved, and the fixed ones detested.

13 [S13/M53] Every planet, when it parts from the Sun, speeds up its course; and if it goes <toward him>,¹² it slows its course down.

14 [S14/M54] The testimonies of the connection of the Moon with a planet are stronger in the Ascendant or the Midheaven.

15 [S15/M55] Cancer indicates many, active waters; Scorpio indicates the waters running in rivers; and Pisces indicates waters gathered together.¹³

16 [S16/M56-57] Every¹⁴ thing which occurs quickly and corrupts quickly, that is from the indication of Mars; and if it happened slowly and is slow in corruption, that is from the indication of Saturn.

17 [S17/M59] One whose Moon in the root of his nativity is found in the minute of [her] exaltation, and the Sun in Leo on the horizon of the east, will reach a powerful rank.

18 [S18/M60] What occurs in the world is sought from the power of the indicator and its superiority;¹⁵ now if it was not like that, then let it be sought from the power of the planet which collects the power of the [other] planets.

19 [S19/M61] If a planet in the root indicated something, then when the management and the distribution passes over to it, its indication will be brought to light, be it good or bad.

20 [S20/M62] One whose lord of the Ascendant is connected to the lord of his tenth, will be received by his employer; and one whose lord of his tenth is separated from the lord of his Ascendant,¹⁶ will in no way be received by his employer.

21 [S21/M62] If the Moon and Ascendant were in signs of the fortunes, and the two fortunes were also like that, and one of the two looked at the other, the native will have strong exaltedness¹⁷ and ability.

---

[11] Adding with the Latin al-Mansūr.
[12] Adding with the Latin al-Mansūr.
[13] الجامعة. The Latin al-Mansūr adds, "namely lakes and wells." In *Gr. Intr.* VI.24, Abū Ma'shar has "stagnant" water (راكد). Nevertheless this seems wrong to me: I would expect the fixed sign Scorpio, with connotations of crawling animals, to indicate stagnant waters.
[14] Cf. **54** below.
[15] استعلائه. Or, "elevation." This occasionally means that one planet is elevated in latitude over another, or is in or near its apogee; I am not sure exactly what Sahl means here.
[16] The Latin al-Mansūr makes this be by retrogradation.
[17] Or perhaps, "pride" (العظمة).

22 [S22/M64] He will gain good fortune and power and a good condition, whose year of his revolution resembles the root and the celestial circle, according to the image of the matter which he gains from that year.[18]

23 [S23/M65] The condition of the native day by day is taken from the direction of the lord of the sign the year terminates at, to the bounds explained before.

24 [S24/M66] If Saturn is rising to the peak of the circle of his apogee or his epicycle, and the Moon is departing from the Sun at the beginning of the [lunar] month and connects with [Saturn], it indicates the rising[19] of what that sign indicates by its nature.

25 [S25/M67] If a planet alights on the minute of the east, and conjoins with the Moon in it, then the indication of that planet will appear in the world, be it good or bad.

26 [S26/M68] If one of the planets governs one of the years of the world [while] in the degree of its exaltation, its indication will appear and the king will move to its region and its cities which belong to it.

27 [S27/M69] The[20] misfortune of Mercury by Saturn necessitates a knot in the native's tongue; and harsher for that is the assembly.

28 [S28/M70] What makes the fear for a sick person greater, is when the two luminaries are under the earth at [the time of] the question about him.

29 [S29/M71] One whose nativity has each one of the luminaries in the degree of its exaltation, safe from the infortunes, [that] native will rule the world and [his seed will inherit his lands, and will occupy][21] them for a long time.

---

[18] This sentence seems to say two things: (1) if the solar revolution is similar to or reinforces what is promised in the nativity, then he will get it; (2) but the exact nature of this effect will depend on the precise details of the solar revolution chart. What I do not understand is why Sahl frames this only in terms of good fortune rather than effects in general: for surely if the solar revolution reinforced negative qualities in the nativity, they would manifest as well? The Latin al-Manṣūr reads unevenly and uncertainly in the second part of this section, so is not very helpful.

[19] صعود. I take this to mean that it will manifest and be strong (the Latin al-Manṣūr says "increase"). But this word also has older connotations of difficulty, as ascending a steep hill.

[20] See *Nativities* Ch. 6.3.6, **1**, and *Carmen* II.16, **12**.

[21] Reading with the Latin al-Manṣūr for an uncertain and partly undotted phrase.

30 [S30/M72] If the Ascendant of the nativity was the Midheaven of the world,[22] and it is a convertible sign, Aries or Cancer (or Gemini, which is in the line of the Midheaven), and the portion of the Sun and the portion of the exaltation[23] belonging to the Sun or Jupiter, his command will be known in the world, and his name will become powerful.

31 [S31/M74] From the lord of the exaltation, and the distributor and the ray,[24] and the lord of the year, and the shifting of the planets in the places, and substitution,[25] and [their] inspection [of each other], you will know the conditions of the world in the revolution of their years.

32 [S32/M77] If the lord of the fourth is made unfortunate by the lord of the Ascendant, it is feared for the parents of the native; and if the lord of the Ascendant is made unfortunate by the lord of the fourth, it is feared for the native.[26]

33 [S33/M80] If Mars came to be with the Sun in the northern signs, the heat will be intensified; and likewise [the Sun's] course with Saturn in the southern signs the cold will be intensified; and the contrary.

34 [S34/M82] The ominous events which will be in the conjunctions, truly they are from the terminating of the years at the bodies of the infortunes, a year for every sign.[27]

35 [S35/M86] The connection of the Moon with Mars is detested from the houses of Venus, [nor with Jupiter from the houses of Mercury, nor with the Sun from the houses of Saturn].[28]

---

[22] This probably means the Midheaven of the mundane ingress chart for the year of his birth.

[23] This probably refers to the degree of the Sun and of the Lot of exaltation, so that the Sun and Jupiter are their lords.

[24] That is, the partnering planet in distributions.

[25] البدل. This could mean the planet being in each other's places, such as a mutual reception by sign. The Latin al-Mansūr omits this.

[26] Probably from his parents, rather than in general.

[27] This is a mundane profection.

[28] I have read this in an astrologically more appropriate way: namely, that we don't want the Moon to connect with a planet from the signs which are opposite that planet's signs: Mars-Venus, Jupiter-Mercury, and Sun-Saturn. The Arabic and Latin versions each make some unusual pairs which can be explained by accidentally skipping and mismatching some clauses. For example, the Latin is close to mine but pairs Jupiter with both Saturn and Mercury, while the Arabic pairs Jupiter with Saturn and the Sun.

36 [S36/M91] The inception of a powerful, important matter is detested in the half [of the month] in which the lord of the [preceding] meeting or opposition is made unfortunate: so let him beware of that and watch out.

37 [S37/N95] The[29] strongest of the indications for the father is the first child born to him, and what follows after that becomes a partner.

38 [S38/M99] If the lord of the Ascendant was in the bound of the fortunes in nativities, and a praiseworthy place, and the lord of the bound in a good condition, attached to it,[30] then it grants benefit and leadership and goodness of conduct.

39 [S39/M101] The reasons for good fortune are the alighting of the lord of the house of the Sun, and the lord of the house of the Moon, and the lord of the Ascendant, in their own domain,[31] in the stakes, looking at each other from a trine or sextile.

40 [S40/M102] The most powerful status which one's Sun can have is in the Midheaven, in a fiery sign, and the Moon looking at him from a trine or sextile, she being on the left of him.[32]

41 [S41/M103] The most powerful king is one whose lord of the second is in its exaltation, house, or its *halb*,[33] connecting with the lord of the Ascendant, and especially if it was Jupiter.

42 [S42/M105] If the fortunes were the lords of the destructive places, they will sever [matters] just as the infortunes sever when they connect with the indicator[34] or it connects with them.[35]

---

[29] This seems to mean that indications for children in someone's nativity, will primarily refer to the first child. To me this makes sense. But see *Nativities* Ch. 4.1, **1-2**, which says that the *following* children will be more indicative in the father's nativity.

[30] مرتبط به. This unusual word suggests that Sahl is drawing from an older author who was translating the Greek *kollēsis*, a conjunction within 3°. Normally, Arabic authors use اتّصال, "connection."

[31] حيّزهم. This probably means they are of the sect of the chart, but could mean that they are in this sect-related rejoicing condition (see "domain" in the Glossary).

[32] In this case she would be waxing in light as well.

[33] Tentatively reading for جلبه or حلبه. If my reading is correct, this is a sect-related condition: see the Glossary. (The Latin al-Mansūr omits.)

[34] This is probably the Moon.

[35] The Latin al-Mansūr reads differently enough: "If a fortune were in the places of Mars, and the significator came toward it (or it towards the significator), it will sever just as the infortunes do." This most likely refers to longevity techniques, in which one directs an indicator of life by primary directions.

43 [S43/M106] Do not take a look at a chart[36] when Mars is in the stakes, especially if the Ascendant was Scorpio.

44 [S44/M107] One eager for the extraction of something[37] with the indicator looking at Saturn [will find] the extraction of it difficult.

45 [S45/M109] If a warrior or the king is departing, it is detested that he should travel with the lord of the Ascendant in the eighth, even if it was its house or its exaltation.

46 [S46/M112] What is most powerful for [what a sign] is responsible for, is a sign in which there alights a planet whose fall is that sign, or it is retrograde in it, or one in a bad condition relative to the Sun.

47 [S47/M113] The[38] places of the planets in the circle, and in relation to the Sun and in themselves, indicate coming-to-be and corruption.

48 [S48/M116] A[39] sound report is one presented with the stakes being fixed,[40] and the Moon and Mercury in fixed signs, and the Moon separating from the fortunes, and in one of the stakes is a fortune: for then it will definitely not be invalid.

49 [S49/M118] One whose lord of the Ascendant is right-siding the Sun and has spear-bearing, and is superior to [the Sun], and its easternization is accomplished, is of those who associates with kings and the powerful, and he will have eminence and rank.

50 [S50/M121] One who has the two infortunes in the fourth sign, in one bound,[41] the native will certainly be contemptible, disreputable.

51 [S51/M122] Pertaining to evident marks of distinction[42] is the alighting of the planets in the stakes.

52 [S52/M123] One who has the stakes of his Ascendant as convertible [signs], and the two infortunes in the stakes, will fall down low within his lifespan.[43]

---

[36] Reading زائجة for زائحة.

[37] This could mean the literal extraction of something from the ground, but could also refer to the extraction or drawing out of the client's intention—i.e., thought-interpretation (see Hermann of Carinthia, *The Search of the Heart*).

[38] Cf. *On Times* Ch. 1. The Latin al-Manṣūr prefaces this with the following: "The signs signify bodies, but the planets [signify] what moves bodies."

[39] Cf. *Questions* Ch. 14, **11** and **16**.

[40] This means being in fixed signs.

[41] The Latin al-Manṣūr reads, "in the degree of the fourth house, and in the same bound."

[42] That is, people who are famous or eminent.

[43] ساقطًا دون عمره.

53 [S53/M124] If the Moon was in the stakes, her indication will be sound, especially if she had <missing> in her claims.[44]

54 [S54/M125] There[45] will not be speed except from Mars, just as there is no steadiness except from Saturn.

55 [S55/M126] The passing of a people from good to bad or from bad to good, is through the shifting of the signs and the movement of the planets indicating them, [going] either from rising to falling or from declining to a height or the contrary of that.[46]

56 [S56/M132, 134] If the two infortunes met and the Moon and Saturn conjoined in latitude, then it will produce famine and epidemic; and if it was with Mars it will produce civil unrest, and the rousing of war and the shedding of blood, and the moving [away] of the chiefs, and civil war in what the sign indicates, and it will definitely not fail to appear. **57** If the two fortunes united and the Moon conjoined with Jupiter in latitude, it will produce justice, gentleness, and fertility; and if it was Venus she will produce justice, joy, delights, strength, and the health of bodies.

58 [S57/M133] From the conjunction of Saturn and Jupiter in the convertible signs, you will know the transformation of the world's conditions; and from their union in the fixed ones, the contrary of that.

59 [S58/M135] If Venus and Mars were [in the] heart with the Sun, degree by degree, in the places of Venus and her shares, the speech of the native will be received by all the people, [his] decisions not rejected.

60 [S59/M136] The worshipper who is close to prophethood is one whose Jupiter and Venus are [in the] heart in his nativity.

61 [S60/M137] Those who are celebrated in leadership and the effectiveness of their matters are those whose Jupiter and Moon are in one degree, rising up to the cycles of their spheres.[47]

62 [S61/M138] One harsh in power and mighty in force is one who has the Sun in the Midheaven with Saturn, in a male sign, easternizing.

---

[44] That is, in her dignities. The Latin al-Mansūr reads, "especially if she had authority in the Ascendant."

[45] Cf. **16** above.

[46] This probably means both (1) entering exaltation or fall, and (2) their relation to their apogee. See *On Times* Ch. 1.

[47] This probably means rising up toward the apogee of their deferent circles.

63 [S62/M139] If the Moon and the indicators are withdrawing, the matter will not be completed unless the question was about travel.

64 [S63/M140] If there was no connection [by] aspect between the indicator and one of the planets but they were both in one [and the same] of the circles parallel to the meridian of the day or in a corresponding path,[48] then it is the most preferable aspect.

65 [S64/M143] [For] the inception of the noble person, he will be praised in it if the two luminaries are in the bounds of fortunes, looking at each other, and if the lords of the bounds are harmonious and suitable to the nature of the inception.

66 [S65/M145] Neither good nor evil will be introduced into one of the regions except through the alteration of the figures[49] of the signs and the planets indicating it by nature.[50]

67 [S66/M148] The harm of the Nodes to the inferior planets is more powerful than their harm to the superior planets.

Praise to God Alone

---

[48] This sounds like being in the same declination, but I would expect a different word for that; perhaps it means that they are each equidistant from the meridian in right ascension?

[49] Or, "form, appearance, manner" (أشكال). This probably refers to things like being a human or watery sign.

[50] The Latin al-Manṣūr is different enough: "No good nor bad will befall anyone, unless the nature or figure of the triplicity (of the signs of the planets which are the significators of that place), is changed."

APPENDIX B:
THE CONNECTIONS OF THE LORD OF THE ASCENDANT

Comment by Dykes. This short piece gives easy, cook-book style interpretations for connections between the lord of the Ascendant and the lords of other houses. The author focuses on the following principles of interpretation:

1. Whether the lord of the Ascendant hands the management over to the other lord, or *vice versa*.
2. Out of which house the management is handed over (i.e., where the applying planet is).
3. Whether the planet being handed over to (or applied to) is a fortune or infortune.

ಭ ಞ ಞ

Secret[1] sections apart from this topic:

2 Look: for the lord of the Ascendant and the lord of the second indicate acquisition through their light. **3** Now if that management was [coming] from the third sign from the Ascendant, then what he gets will be because of siblings. **4** And if it was handed over from the ninth, the assets will reach him from another country; and if the manager was a fortune, it indicates that it will reach him in relation to uprightness, religion, and virtuousness. **5** And if the management was from the fourth sign, then in relation to sowing and the land. **6** And if it was from the fifth sign, then from a place he had not given a thought to, [or] from friends; and likewise [if] it was in the eleventh, what there is will be like what I mentioned for the fifth. **7** And if it was from the sixth house and the sign was of the images of people, then in relation to illness and slaves; and if it had four feet, then from the yields of animals and their profit. **8** And if the management was from the seventh sign, then look: for if the sign was female, then in relation to women and because of them; and if it was male, then in relation to contention, hardship, and hostility. **9**

---

[1] Reading الخفيّة for الحبه.

And if it was from the eighth, then in relation to something entrusted [to someone] and the dead, and the assets of women. **10** And if the management was from the tenth sign, then in relation to authority or the secret of technical expertise. **11** And if the management was from the eleventh, then in relation to what I mentioned in the fifth. **12** And if the management was from the twelfth sign, then in relation to prisons and enemies, or the matter which <missing>. **13** And if the management was in the Ascendant and the one handing over was the lord of the Ascendant, to the lord of the second, it indicates benefit and the production of dirhams in the ways which we set forth [and] a mention of which is in the chapter on acquisition;[2] and if the lord of the second handed over the management to the lord of the Ascendant in the Ascendant, then in relation to speech, singing, poetry, and the work of his own hands.

14 *A section: the lord of the Ascendant and the lord of the third.* **15** If the lord of the Ascendant handed over its management to the lord of the third, it indicates riding and outings, and encountering siblings, and what resembles that. **16** And if it accepted the management from the lord of the third, and the lord of the third is a fortune, it indicates the activity which he hopes for a fee[3] [from], is from God; and if it was an infortune, a report will reach him which will distress him, and he will encounter some of his friends and siblings, and whatever there will be from them will be what the light of the planet indicates. **17** For if it connected from a sextile or trine, it will be what he longs for and he will see what he loves; and the square is middling except that the square of the third indicates that between him and his siblings and friends there will be words and reprimands.

18 *A section: the lord of the Ascendant and the lord of the fourth.* **19** So look into the aspect of one of them to the other when the management is handed over, and their aspect to the Ascendant, and their positions relative to the Ascendant. **20** If the lord of the Ascendant handed over its management to the lord of the fourth, it indicates the home and deeds[4] with the family; if the planet was a fortune, the deeds are in what he has responsibility for and

---

[2] This may refer to *Questions* Ch. 2, **8-9**.

[3] Reading as الأجر, but this could also be الأخر, "other." I do not see how fees or payments relate here, but I do not see how "other" makes sense either.

[4] الحديث, which properly means *reports* or *accounts* of deeds, but mere reports does not seem appropriate here.

yearns for; and if it was an infortune, it is reprimands and [*uncertain*].⁵ **21** And if it accepted the management from the lord of the fourth, he should beware of some of his family.⁶ **22** Now if the lord of the fourth was accepting the management or handing over management, then if it managed from the square, what comes to him will be from corruption. **23** And if it was in the fifth, it will be from children; and if it was in the sixth or twelfth, it will be from slaves; and if it was in the seventh or the Ascendant, it will be from his woman; and if it was from the eighth and second, it will be from the powerful and slaves (and there will not be joy in their souls,⁷ but they will hope for it); and if it was from the ninth or third, it will come to him from a country he is not in; and if it was from the tenth, it will come to him from one more excellent than he in the family (and if he was fit to be an authority, it is the Sultan—and that is if the planet was received in its management). **24** <So>⁸ take this topic into account, and speak in it according to the positions [as] to who the important people [are], or the placement of what I have explained to you, and take a lesson from it, for if you alter it, it will prolong the doing of the things, one to the other; and understand the matter which he believes will be, its manner and from where [the management] is, and to where⁹ it goes.

25 *A section: the lord of the Ascendant and the lord of the fifth.* **26** If the lord of the Ascendant handed over the management to the lord of the fifth, and the lord of the fifth is a fortune, he will work at what he hopes for and¹⁰ reckons it as being in religion, such as piety and something he hopes to profit him, as well as sexual intercourse. **27** And if it accepted the management from the lord of the fifth, he will be successful in some of what he hoped for: for if he had a woman or servant girl, wanting her childbirth, it will be in that management; or if he had an absent child, hoping for [the child's] arrival. **28**

---

⁵ The text seems to read منار, "lighthouse."
⁶ This is probably from the square and opposition.
⁷ Reading نفوسهم somewhat confidently for بفنهم or بقنهم.
⁸ This is a difficult sentence, with many uncertain and unpointed words. The second half sounds like it is part of instructions for a question chart.
⁹ Reading for "from where."
¹⁰ This should probably be read as "or."

And work in the topics just as I have explained to you in the places of the management, and as I have mentioned it in the fourth house.[11]

29 *A section: the lord of the Ascendant and the lord of the sixth.* **30** If the lord of the Ascendant handed over its management to the lord of the sixth house, he will be extravagant in his eating until his stomach becomes thick, and his body will become heavy from that so that it kills him. **31** If it was in the root, it indicates illness and no good in the drinking of a medication and remedy in that management. **32** And if it accepted the management from the lord of the sixth, spoils[12] [and] comfort will appear to him, without an ailment.[13] **33** And if it was in the root, it indicates the buying of livestock; now if the sign was one having four feet, he will buy beasts; and if it was of the images of people he will buy slaves; and if it was neither of these two types it will be what I mentioned of heaviness. **34** And work in all of the topics according to what I explained to you in the fourth house. **35** And I am making clear to you that if the management was from the sixth house and the twelfth, what I described to you will be from illness and other things. **36** And if it was from the seventh and the Ascendant, it will not be because of food and medications, but it will be because of sexual intercourse and corruption, and a scarcity of eating. **37** And if it was from the eighth house and the second, it will be an illness if it was made unfortunate, and it will be buying and selling, and the taking and giving of inheritances <if it was made fortunate>. **38** And if it was from the third house and the ninth, and it was buying and selling, it will be milk from other than the land and area he is in (and if the one which manages is a fortune, it will be days of charity, fasting, and a matter of beneficence). **39** And if it was from the fourth and tenth (in which there is authority), it indicates the agility of the slaves and animals; and if it indicated illness, then [it is] from the essence of the sign and it will do damage until he makes a sacrifice and scatters the camels in it;[14] and the fourth sign is below what I mentioned. **40** And if it was in the eleventh or the fifth, distress will enter upon him in relation to friends and children, and one he wants a promise [from]. **41** Work in these topics according to what I explained to you, and take heed, and seek the matters, one to the other, for indeed what I have mentioned in this book is an example; and if I had wanted to judge [*unclear*],

---

[11] Lit., "fourth section" (باب).
[12] Reading somewhat uncertainly for what seems to be نعل.
[13] This must be if the lord of the Ascendant is a fortune.
[14] For this clause about sacrifice and scattering, reading uncertainly as يفاد ويشمع به الإبل.

I would not turn down anything needed for reaching that [*unclear*], but the active [student] should take heed and be satisfied with what is lesser and greater: so understand this and take heed.

42 *A section on the lord of the Ascendant and the lord of the seventh.* **43** If the lord of the Ascendant handed over its management to the lord of the seventh, if Venus looked [*illegible*], it indicates sexual intercourse,[15] and he will be pleased with women, and better than that if its management was from its own place, for then it indicates [someone from his own] family.[16] **44** Now if it was from the sixth, second, eighth, and twelfth, it indicates affliction and what he is embarrassed by with women. **45** And as for the stakes, they indicate [a woman] who has social esteem, [*uncertain*],[17] or she is an equal. **46** And if it was from the third, the eleventh, the fifth, and the ninth, then it indicates that he is courting her or she him (and that is love): keep these topics in mind and stick to them. **47** If the lord of the Ascendant accepted the management from the lord of the seventh, it will prepare sexual intercourse for him <without> [his] seeking it. **48** And if the owner of the question did not have a woman or one to have sex with, there will be words and conflict from women, and because of them, and it will come to him from his reputation in [his] rank and [*uncertain*].[18]

49 *A section on the lord of the Ascendant and the lord of the eighth.* **50** If the lord of the Ascendant accepted the management from the lord of the eighth, it indicates gaining from a source one had not hoped for. **51** And if [the lord of the Ascendant] handed over the management to it, and it was in the revolution of the year, it indicates his death: he will die in that management. **52** The place of the affliction is known from the place of the light: if the light was in the second and eighth, it is from where I explained; and if it was in the ninth and third, the gain will be from travels (and if it was death, it is in a country other than his own); and if it was from the tenth or fourth, the gain will be because of the Sultan and lands (and if it was death, it will be in his own country and with his family, but if it was in the Midheaven, he will die

---

[15] This can also mean marriage (النّكاح), but Sahl tends to use it to mean sex.
[16] Perhaps this should be understood as something more like "people" or "clan."
[17] The texts seems to read مثله.
[18] The text seems to read محلّه, which in this context could mean something like "residence."

because of the Sultan), or he will have authority if it was a fortune. **53** Take heed of these things and understand them.

54 *A section on the lord of the Ascendant and the lord of the ninth.* **55** If the lord of the Ascendant accepted the management from the lord of the ninth, and the Sun looks at it, those days indicate piety and charity, and what he hopes for in repentance from God, if the planet was a fortune; and if it was an infortune, he will work with the corruption of this thought and ugly things will be related about him. **56** And reports will come to him in that management: if it was a fortune, then [it is] what delights him; and if it was an infortune, what saddens and infuriates him. **57** And if it handed over its management to the lord of the ninth, he will travel or move from one place to another place, and in the days of passing.[19]

58 *A section on the lord of the Ascendant and the lord of the tenth from the Ascendant.* **59** That indicates that they[20] will rejoice or be sad with one another: and it is that one [should] know the positions of the stakes[21] and their power, and the aspect of the planets in nativities and the signs which rise after these strong places of them: for they indicate the stability of the friendship. **60** And know that if the fortunes looked at them, that is an increase in affection and its extension to friendship, and that will be due to[22] those planets in those places. **61** And likewise [it indicates] enmity and restraint in that social status if the infortunes looked them or squared them.

62 *A section on the lord of the Ascendant and the lord of the eleventh.* **63** If the lord of the Ascendant accepted the management from the lord of the eleventh from a powerful position, their owners[23] will be powerful, well known. **64** And if the position was middling, they will be well known [but] will not have that strength. **65** And if the position is falling, they will be worthless, not known. **66** And if [the lord of the eleventh] accepted the management from the lord of the Ascendant, his siblings and friends will have good from him, and will mourn him, and will wish him well; and his condition and importance is known from the position of the management.

---

[19] انتقال, which normally means "transfer" or "shift," but according to Wehr also refers to the passage of the Sun in the zodiac: so Sahl probably means that it indicates this in the revolution of years and not simply in the nativity.

[20] This is probably the querent and the authority figure.

[21] Reading الأوتاد for what seems to be الاحداد. This probably refers to "upright" stakes.

[22] Reading somewhat broadly for ممن عنده.

[23] That is, the people indicated by them.

67 Then look: for if they were looking with the management[24] or the lord of the Ascendant is looking at the position of the eleventh, then they will have good from him and will live in his protection; and if it is not looking at that position nor at their lords, they will be deceived by him.

68 *A section on the lord of the Ascendant and the lord of the twelfth.* **69** If the lord of the Ascendant was handing over its management to the lord of the twelfth, griefs will enter upon him, and that will be from his own action, and what he brings upon himself; and from what direction it is, is known from the position of the management. **70** If the management was from the Ascendant, it indicates the situation of his own hands, and the distress is for that reason; now if it was in the second, because of assets; and if it was in the third, because of siblings; and in the fourth, in relation to family and the land of the parents; and if it was in the fifth, then because of children and from a joy he hopes for; and in the sixth, in relation to the underclass and slaves; and in the seventh, then from contrary people or from husbands. **71** And investigate the falling [place] and the stake: for a falling [place] is indicative of his condition, and [as for] the withdrawing place, it is better.[25]

72 So take heed of what I have given to you as an example in the houses set forth, [and] you will find what you want, if God wills.

---

[24] Meaning unclear, but perhaps this means they are conjoined in the same place. But see **43** and **55**, which seem to want other planets like the natural significators to look at the place. So maybe they are both configured to the eleventh place.

[25] Meaning unclear.

APPENDIX C: RELATION BETWEEN SAHL'S *NATIVITIES* & *THE BOOK OF ARISTOTLE*

BA	Sahl	BA	Sahl
Miscellaneous			
I.1, **3-11**	1.33, **43-52**	II.1, **10-19**	1.22, **1-6**
I.1, **21-24**	1.33, **17-20**		
Survival, upbringing, longevity			
III.1.2, **1-7**	1.25, **8-14**	III.1.7, **1**	1.32, **1-3**[1]
III.1.2, **8-25**	1.29, **15-23**	III.1.7, **4**	1.32, **4**
III.1.3, **1-17**	1.30, **36-50**	III.1.7, **6-13**[2]	1.32, **5-10**[3]
III.1.3, **26-27**	1.30, **36-38**	III.1.7, **31-35**	1.32, **11-14**
III.1.4, **1-5**	1.30, **66-67**	III.1.9, **3-16**	1.16, **1-6**
III.1.6, **13-17**	1.32, **14-18**[4]	III.1.9, **25-30**	1.16, **7-11**
Eminence, finances			
III.2.0, **1-8**	2.1, **1-9**	III.2.2, **12-13**	2.17, **13, 11**
III.2.1, **1-4**	2.2, **1, 5-6**	III.2.2, **14**	2.17, **10**
III.2.1, **6-42**	2.2, **8-72**	III.2.2, **16**	2.17, **14**
III.2.1, **44-49, 51-54**	2.3, **1-11**	III.2.3, **1-6**	2.16, **1-6**
III.2.1, **55**	2.3, **15**	III.2.4, **1-9**	2.19, **1-9**
III.2.1, **56-57**	2.3, **12**	III.2.5, **1-7**	2.20, **1-6**
III.2.1, **58**	2.3, **13-14**	III.2.6, **1-3**	2.22, **1-2**
III.2.1, **59**	2.5, **1**	III.2.6, **4**	2.21, **1**
III.2.2, **1-9**	2.17, **1-9**	III.2.6, **5**	2.22, **3**
Siblings			
III.3.0, **1-6**	3, **1-8**	III.3.3, **24**	3.2, **2-3**?
III.3.2, **1**	3, **9**	III.3.4, **1-13**	3.2, **17-31** (and 3.1, **11**)
III.3.2, **2-5**	3.11, **1-4**	III.3.4, **14**	3.5, **14-15**
III.3.2, **6**	3, **10**	III.3.5, **1-3**	3.3, **1-2**
III.3.3, **1-8**	3.1, **1-7**	III.3.5, **4-6**	3.13, **14-18**
III.3.3, **14-16**	3.1, **8-10**	III.3.5, **7-9**	3.3, **3-5**

---

[1] Sahl's list of items for longevity omits one of them found in *BA*.
[2] *BA* omits Sahl's **6**, which must be an error by Hugo.
[3] Sahl's **9-10** are more abbreviated, and do not include the Persian transliterations which Hugo retains (so I suspect Sahl has edited his version).
[4] This is a little speculative, but matches rather well.

APPENDIX C: COMPARISON OF SAHL AND BA

BA	Sahl	BA	Sahl
Siblings contd.			
III.3.3, **18-20**	3.2, **12-13**	III.3.6, **1**	3.4, **1**
III.3.3, **22-23**	3.2, **14-16**	III.3.7, **1-5**	3.8, **1-2, 4-5**
Parents			
III.4.1, **1-2** (first part)	4.2, **1**	III.4.6, **1-6**	4.20, **16-21**
III.4.1, **23**	4.20, **27**	III.4.6, **7-10**	4.20, **3-6**
III.4.2, **1-4**	4.1, **4-5**	III.4.6, **11**	4.20, **2**
III.4.3, **1-6**	4.2, **4-9**	III.4.6, **12-13**	4.20, **14-15**
III.4.3, **7**	4.2, **2**	III.4.6, **14**	4.20, **1**
III.4.3, **8-12**	4.15, **1-6**	III.4.6, **15-16**	4.20, **7-8**
III.4.3, **13-15** (first part)	4.15, **7-8**	III.4.7, **1**	4.19, **1**
III.4.3, **17**	4.16, **19**	III.4.7, **2-6**	4.20, **22-30**
III.4.3, **18-19**	4.5, **5-6, 9-10**[5]	III.4.8, **1-6**	4.18, **1-6**
III.4.3, **20-21**	4.5, **11-12, 22-24**	III.4.9, **1-2**	4.19, **17**
III.4.3, **22-24**	4.7, **15**	III.4.9, **3-4**	4.19, **2-3**
III.4.3, **27-28**	4.5, **14-15**	III.4.9, **5-6**	4.19, **20-21**
III.4.4, **1-2, 4**	4.16, **5-7**	III.4.9, **7-15**	4.19, **5-15**
III.4.4, **5**	4.16, **17**	III.4.9, **16-18**	4.19, **18-19**
III.4.5, **1-9**	4.17, **1-9**		
Children			
III.5.0, **1-6**	5, **1-6**	III.5.4, **1-8**	5.6, **1-13**[6] (and prob. **14-16**)
III.5.1, **1-3**	5.2, **1-2**	III.5.4, **9-12**	5.6, **17-18**
III.5.1, **4-9**	5.1, **1-5**	III.5.4, **14-15**	5.6, **20**
III.5.1, **10-11**	5.3, **1**	III.5.5, **1-3**	5.6, **19-20**
III.5.1, **15-16**	5.3, **2-3**	III.5.5, **4-5**	5.3, **8**
III.5.1, **18-19**	5.3, **15**	III.5.5, **7** (first part)	5.3, **9**
III.5.1, **20-22**	5.4, **1**; 5.3, **16**	III.5.5, **7** (middle)	5.3, **3**
III.5.2, **1**	5.5, **1-2**	III.5.5, **8-9**	5.5, **3-4**

---

[5] These sentences in Sahl match somewhat loosely, but are part of a passage that is closely parallel in *Carmen*, Rhetorius, and *BA*.

[6] Sahl's sentence **10** is an expansion of what is found in *BA*, but was probably in the original.

BA	Sahl	BA	Sahl
\multicolumn{4}{c}{Children contd.}			
III.5.3, **1-4**	5.1, **9-16**	III.5.5, **10** (first part)	5.5, **5**
III.5.3, **5-13**	5.1, **33-41, 91**	III.5.5, **10** (second part)	5.5, **13**
III.5.3, **14-15**	5.1, **46-47**	III.5.5, **11**	5.5, 6 (and **15**?)
III.5.3, **16**	5.1, **51-52**	III.5.5, **12**	5.4, **13**
III.5.3, **17**	5.1, **58-59**; 5.3, **6-7**	III.5.5, **13-18**	5.3, **16-21**
\multicolumn{4}{c}{*Illness and injury*}			
III.6.0, **1-8**	6, **2-9**	III.6.3, **22**	6.3.10, **15**?
III.6.1, **1-6**	6.2, **1-6**	III.6.3, **23**	6.3.4, **7**?
III.6.1, **7**	6.4, **1-2**	III.6.3, **24**	6.3.10, **5**
III.6.1, **8-12** (first part)	6.3.1, **1-7**	III.6.3, **27**	6.3.9, **1-2**
III.6.1, **13-17**	6.6, **1-6**	III.6.3, **28**	6.3.9, **1**?
III.6.2, **1-5**	6.2, **11-12, 14**	III.6.4, **1-6**	6.6, **7-11, 14-15**
III.6.2, **6-11**	6.2, **15-19, 21**	III.6.4, **7-8**	6.6, **26-27**
III.6.2, **12**	6.2, **7**	III.6.4, **9**	6.6, **13**?
III.6.2, **13-16**	6.2, **48-57**	III.6.4, **10-12** (first part)	6.6, **17-19**
III.6.3, **1-2**	6.2, **13**	III.6.4, **13**	6.6, **28-29**
III.6.3, **3-11**	6.3.1, **8-15**	III.6.5, **1-3**	6.7, **1-6**
III.6.3, **12-13**	6.3.4, **1-4**?	III.6.6, **1-4**	6.8, **1-5**[7]
III.6.3, **14-20**	6.3.1, **16-24**	III.6.7, **1**	6.9, **1-2** (and **3**?)
III.6.3, **21**	6.3.8, **3**	III.6.8, **1-3**	6.5, **1-2**
\multicolumn{4}{c}{*Marriage*}			
III.7.0, **1-13**	7, **1-8**	III.7.6, **2-3**	7.1, **87-88**
III.7.1, **1-7**	7.1, **1-10**	III.7.6, **4**	7.1, **35**
III.7.1, **8**	7.2, **1-4**	III.7.6, **5-11**	7.1, **141-47**
III.7.1, **9-15**	7.7, **1-6**	III.7.7, **1-7**	7.2, **5-13**
III.7.1, **22**	7.5, **1-5**	III.7.8, **1-10**	7.7, **9-20**
III.7.1, **23**	7.6, **1-4**	III.7.8, **11**	7.2, **78**
III.7.1, **24**	7.8, **1-7**	III.7.9, **1-9**	7.3, **1-9**

---

[7] Sentence **4** repeats material here.

APPENDIX C: COMPARISON OF SAHL AND BA

BA	Sahl	BA	Sahl
Marriage contd.			
III.7.2, **1**	7.1, **11**	III.7.10, **1-8**	7.4, **1-8**
III.7.2, **3-10**	7.1, **12-19**	III.7.11, **1-4**	7.5, **8-10, 12-13**
III.7.3, **1-6**	7.1, **89-94**	III.7.12, **1-6**	7.6, **6-10**
III.7.4, **1-4**	7.2, **62-69**	III.7.13, **1-4**	7.8, **8-12**
III.7.4, **5-13**	7.1, **75-86**	III.7.13, **5-7**	7.8, **13, 26-29**
Death			
III.8.0, **2, 4**[8]	8.1, **1, 2**	III.8.1, **16**	8.2, **82** (maybe **12-13**)
III.8.1, **1-6**	8.1, **3-4, 6-8**	III.8.1, **17**	8.2, **14-15**
III.8.1, **7**	8.1, **15**	III.8.1, **18-19**	8.2, **17-18**
III.8.1, **8-9**	8.1, **12-13**	III.8.1, **20**	8.2, **19**
III.8.1, **10**	8.2, **16**	III.8.1, **21-22**	8.2, **85**
III.8.1, **11**	8.4, **1-3**	III.8.1, **25-27**	8.2, **20-22**
III.8.1, **12**	8.2, **67**	III.8.1, **28**	8.7, **5-6**
III.8.1, **14**	8.4, **15**	III.8.1, **29-31**	8.2, **23-25, 27**
III.8.1, **15**	8.2, **65, 70-73, 92**		
Travel			
III.9.0, **1-2, 4-10**	9, **1-10**	III.9.1, **9-24**	9.1, **16-30**
III.9.1, **1-5**	9.1, **1-5**	III.9.1, **25-26**	9.1, **61-62**
III.9.1, **6**	9.1, **25**	III.9.1, **27**	9.3, **1**
III.9.1, **7-8**	9.1, **12**	III.9.1, **28-29**	9.3, **4**
Profession			
III.10.0, **1-10**	10.1.1, **1-13**	III.10.4, **1-3**	10.1.6, **1-5**
III.10.1, **1-3**	10.1.1, **15-17**	III.10.5, **28-30**	10.1.5, **1-3**
III.10.1, **4**	10.1.3, **34**	III.10.5, **32-33**	10.1.5, **18-19**
III.10.2, **1-4**	10.1.4, **1-14**	III.10.6, **1**	10.1.1, **15** (last part)
III.10.2, **5**	10.1.4, **26-27**; 10.1.6, **6**	III.10.7, **4-6**	10.1.5, **11-14**
III.10.3, **1-9**	10.1.4, **28-35**	III.10.7, **22-24**	10.1.5, **7-9** (and see **15**)
III.10.3, **11**	10.1.4, **36-39**		

---

[8] Since much of the material on death is missing in *BA*, I cannot be absolutely sure what material Sahl includes.

BA	Sahl	BA	Sahl
Friends, enemies, slaves			
III.11.1, **2** (first half)	6.10, **20**	III.12.4, **1-3**	11.1, **46-49**
III.11.1, **6-9**	6.10, **21-25**	III.12.5, **1-2**	11.4, **18-20**
III.12.1, **1-2**	11, **5**	III.12.6, **1-2**	11.3, **1-2**
III.12.1, **4**	11, **1-4**	III.12.7, **1-8**	11.4, **21-29**
III.12.1, **5-9**	11.4, **1-2**	III.12.8, **1-2**	11.1, **40-42**
III.12.2, **1-8**	11.1, **1-5**	III.12.9, **1-2**	11.1, **43-45**
III.12.3, **1-10**	11.2, **1-12**		

Glossary

This Glossary contains terms from all branches of traditional astrology, from all of my translations. Most entries also provide the Greek, Latin, and Arabic source words. Boldface terms in the definitions and descriptions indicate that the Glossary also contains that word.

- **Absent from** (Ar. غائب عن). See **Aversion**.
- **Accident** (Lat. *accidens*, Ar. عرض, حادث). An event which "befalls" or "happens" to someone, though not necessarily something bad.
- **Adding in course.** See **Course**.
- **Advancement, advancing** (إقبال \ مقبل; Lat. *accedens*). Refers to being (1) dynamically **angular** or **succeedent**, i.e. moving by **primary motion** toward an **axial** degree. (But occasionally might refer to angular or succeedent **whole signs**). Its two antonyms are **retreat/retreating**, and **withdrawal/withdrawing**. It can also refer to (2) the **eastern quadrants**.
- **Advantageous places.** One of two schemes of **houses** which indicate affairs/planets which are more busy or good in the context of the chart. The seven-place scheme according to Timaeus and reported in *Carmen* includes only certain signs which **look at** the **Ascendant** by **whole-sign**, and suggests that these places are advantageous for the *native* because they look at the Ascendant. The eight-place scheme according to Nechepso lists all of the **angular** and **succeedent** places, suggesting places which are stimulating and advantageous for a planet *in itself*.
- **Ages of Man** (Ar. أسنان الإنسان). Ptolemy's division of a typical human life span into periods ruled by planets as **time lords**.
- **Agreeing signs.** Groups of signs which share some kind of harmonious quality. Sometimes planets are said to agree with one another, although this meaning must be taken in context.
- *Alcochoden.* Latin transliteration for *kadkhudhāh*, the **House-master**.
- **Alien** (Lat. *alienus*, Ar. غريب). Lit., "a stranger, foreigner." When a planet is not in one of its five **dignities**. In later astrology in English this is often called "peregrine," from Lat. *peregrinus* ("foreigner, pilgrim").
- *Almuten.* A Latin transliteration for Ar. *mubtazz*: see **Victor**.
- **Angles, succeedents, cadents.** A division of houses into three groups which show how powerfully and directly a planet acts. The angles are the 1st, 10th, 7th and 4th; the succeedents are the 2nd, 11th, 8th and 5th; the cadents

are the 12th, 9th, 6th and 3rd. But the exact regions in question will depend upon whether and how one uses **whole-sign** and **quadrant houses**, especially since traditional texts refer to an angle or pivot (Gr. *kentron*, Ar. وتد) as either (1) equivalent to the **whole-sign** angles from the **Ascendant**, or (2) the **axial degrees** of the **Ascendant-Midheaven** themselves, or (3) **quadrant houses** (and their associated strengths) as measured from the degrees of the axes.

- **Antiscia** (sing. *antiscion*), Greek for "throwing shadows." Refers to a degree mirrored across an axis drawn from 0° Capricorn to 0° Cancer. For example, 10° Cancer has 20° Gemini as its antiscion.
- **Apogee of eccentric/deferent** (Ar. أوج). The point on a planet's **deferent circle** that is farthest away from the earth; as seen from earth, it points to some degree of the zodiac.
- **Applying, application** (Lat. *applicatio*). When a planet is in a state of **connection**, moving so as to make the connection exact. Planets **assembled** together or **looked at** by sign, but not yet connecting by the relevant degrees, are only "wanting" to be connected.
- **Apsides, apsidal line.** In geocentric astronomy, the line passing through the center of the earth, which points at one end to the **apogee** of a planet's **deferent**, and at the other end to its **perigee**.
- **Arisings** (Lat. *orientia*). See **Ascensions**.
- **Ascendant.** Usually the entire rising sign, but often specified as the exact degree on the horizon (the **axial degree**). In **quadrant houses**, a space following the exact rising degree up to the cusp of the 2nd house.
- **Ascensions** (Ar. مطالع, Lat. *ascensiones*). Degrees on the celestial **equator**, measured in terms of how many degrees pass the **meridian** as an entire sign or **bound** (or other spans of zodiacal degrees) passes across the horizon. They are often used in the predictive technique of ascensional times, sometimes as an approximation of primary **directions**.
- **Aspect** (Lat. *aspectus*, Ar. نظر). For the verb, see **look at**. As a noun, a **configuration** between two things (such as two planets or a planet and a sign): see **sextile, trine, square,** and **opposition**. See also **Connection** and **Assembly**
- **Assembly** (Lat. *conventus*, Ar. مقارنة). When two or more planets are in the same sign, and more intensely if within 15°. (It is occasionally used in Arabic to indicate the conjunction of the Sun and Moon at the New Moon, but the more common word for that is **meeting**).

- **Aversion.** Being in the second, sixth, eighth, or twelfth sign from a place, as a planet in Gemini is in the twelfth from, and therefore in aversion to, Cancer. Such places are not **configured** and so cannot **look at** or see each other by the classical scheme of **aspects**.
- **Axial degree, axis.** The degree of the **zodiac** which the horizon or **meridian**: the **Ascendant, Midheaven, Descendant,** and *Imum Caeli/IC*.
- **Ayanamsha.** In sidereal astrology, a point or degree which acts as the beginning of the zodiac. The **equinoctial point** acts as the ayanamsha in the tropical **zodiac**.
- *Azamene.* Equivalent to **Chronic illness.**
- **Bad ones.** See Fortune/Infortune.
- **Barring.** See **Blocking.**
- **Bearing** (Lat. *habitudo*). Hugo's term for any of the many possible planetary conditions and relationships.
- **Benefic:** see **Fortune/Infortune.**
- **Benevolent.** See **Fortune/Infortune.**
- **Besieging** (Lat. *obsido*). Equivalent to **Enclosure.**
- **Bicorporeal signs.** Equivalent to "common" signs. See **Quadruplicity.**
- **Blocking** (Lat. *prohibitio*, Ar. منع), sometimes called "prohibition." When a planet blocks another planet from completing a **connection**, either through its own body or **ray**. This may happen in several ways: see Sahl's *Introduction* Ch. 3, **31-48**.
- **Body** (Lat. *corpus*, Ar. جرم). Normally, a planet considered by itself, in the degree where it is located. But in **aspect** theory, also equivalent to an **orb**.
- **Bodyguarding.** See **Spear-bearing.**
- **Bound, bounds** (Gr. *horion*, Lat. *terminus*, Ar. حدّ). Unequal divisions of the zodiac in each sign, each bound being ruled by one of the five non-**luminaries**. Sometimes called "terms," they are one of the five classical **dignities.**
- **Bright, smoky, empty, dark degrees.** Certain degrees of the zodiac said to affect how conspicuous or obscure the significations of planets or the Ascendant are.
- **Burned up, burning** (Lat. *combustus, combustio;* Ar. محترق, احتراق). Normally, when a planet is between about 1° and 7.5° away from the Sun. See also **In the heart.**

- **Burnt path** (Lat. *via combusta*). A span of degrees in Libra and Scorpio in which a planet (especially the Moon) is considered to be harmed or less able to effect its significations. Some astrologers identify it as between 15° Libra and 15° Scorpio; others between the exact degree of the **fall** of the Sun in 19° Libra and the exact degree of the fall of the Moon in 3° Scorpio.
- **Bust**. Certain hours measured from the New Moon, in which it is considered favorable or unfavorable to undertake an action or perform an **election**.
- **Busy places**. Equivalent to the **Advantageous places**.
- **Cadent** (Lat. *cadens*, "falling"; Ar. ساقط). Typically, when a planet is one of the following **whole sign** or **quadrant houses** (called "cadent/falling" from the **angles**): 3rd, 6th, 9th, 12th. But see also **falling away from**, which is equivalent to **Aversion**.
- **Cardinal**. Equivalent to "movable" or "convertible" signs. See **Quadruplicity**.
- **Cardine**. Equivalent to **Angle**.
- **Cazimi**: see **In the heart**.
- **Centers of the Moon**. Also called the "posts" or "foundations" of the Moon. Angular distances between the Sun and Moon throughout the lunar month, indicating possible times of weather changes and rain.
- **Choice**. See **Election**.
- **Choleric**. See **Humor**.
- **Chronic illness (degrees of)**. Sometimes called the "azamene" degrees, which are especially said to indicate chronic illness, due to their association with certain fixed stars.
- **Claim** (Ar. مزاعمة). See **Dignity**.
- **Cleansed** (Ar. نقيّ, Lat. *mundus*). Ideally, when a planet is in **aversion** to the **infortunes** (but certainly not in an **assembly**, **square**, or **opposition** to them.
- **Clothed**. Equivalent to one planet being in an **assembly** or **aspect** with another, and therefore partaking in (being "clothed in") the other planet's characteristics.
- **Collection** (Lat. *collectio*, Ar. جمع). When two planets **aspecting** each other but not in an applying **connection**, each **apply to** a third planet.
- **Combust** (Lat. *combustus*). See **Burned up**.
- **Commanding/obeying**. A division of the signs into those which command or obey each other (used sometimes in **synastry**).

- **Common signs.** See **Quadruplicity**.
- **Complexion.** Primarily, a mixture of elements and their qualities so as to indicate or produce some effect. Secondarily it refers to planetary combinations, following the naturalistic theory that planets have elemental qualities with causal power, which can interact with each other.
- **Confer.** See **Handing over**.
- **Configuration.** A geometrical relationship, figure, or **aspect** between signs, which allows things to **look at** each other or **connect**.
- **Configured.** To be in an **aspect** by **whole-sign** (though not necessarily **connecting** by degree).
- **Conjunction** (Lat. *conjunctio*, Ar. قران). As a relationship of planets, normally equivalent to **assembly** and **connecting** by body. In mundane astrology it refers to the **mean** conjunction (normally, of Saturn and Jupiter).
- **Conjunction/prevention.** The position of the New (conjunction) or Full (prevention) Moon most immediately prior to a **nativity** or other chart. For the prevention, some astrologers use the degree of the Moon, others the degree of the luminary which was above the earth at the time of the prevention.
- **Connection** (Lat. *continuatio*, Ar. اتّصال). When a planet **applies** to another planet (by body in the same sign, or by **ray** in **configured** signs), within a particular number of degrees up to exactness.
- **Conquer** (Lat. *vinco*). Normally, the equivalent of being a **victor**, which comes from the same Latin verb.
- **Convertible** (Lat. *conversivus*, Ar. منقلب). See **Quadruplicity**. But sometimes planets (especially Mercury) are called convertible because their **gender** is affected by their placement in the chart.
- **Convey.** See **Handing over**.
- **Corruption.** Normally, the harming of a planet, such as being in a **square** with an **infortune**. But sometimes, equivalent to **Detriment**.
- **Counsel** (Lat. *consilium*). See **Management**.
- **Counting** (Ar. عدد). In the context of **house** theory, it refers to **whole-sign** houses (namely, assigning the house numbers by counting each sign); it is opposed to **quadrant houses** (by **division** or **equation**).
- **Course, increasing/decreasing in.** For practical purposes, this means a planet is quicker than average in motion. But in geometric astronomy, it re-

fers to what **sector** of the **deferent** the center of a planet's **epicycle** is. (The planet's position within the four sectors of the epicycle itself will also affect its apparent speed.) In the two sectors that are closest to the planet's **perigee**, the planet will apparently be moving faster; in the two sectors closest to the **apogee**, it will apparently be moving slower.

- **Crooked/straight.** A division of the signs into those which rise quickly and are more parallel to the horizon (crooked), and those which arise more slowly and closer to a right angle from the horizon (straight or direct). In the northern hemisphere, the signs from Capricorn to Gemini are crooked (but in the southern one, straight); those from Cancer to Sagittarius are straight (but in the southern one, crooked).
- **Crossing over** (Gr. *parallagē*). When a planet begins to **separate** from an exact **connection**. See also **Right/left**.
- **Cutting of light** (Ar. قطع النّور). Any of several ways in which a **connection** is prevented, such as by **blocking**.
- *Darījān*. An alternative **face** system attributed to the Indians.
- **Dastūriyyah** (دستوريّة). See **Spear-bearing**.
- **Decan** (Lat. *decanus*). A division of the **zodiac** into 36 divisions or **faces** of 10° each.
- **Decimation.** A form of **overcoming**, specifically from the superior **square** (i.e., the tenth sign from something else).
- **Declination.** The equivalent on the celestial **equator**, of geographical latitude. The signs of northern declination (Aries through Virgo) stretch northward of the **ecliptic**, while those of southern declination (Libra through Pisces) stretch southward.
- **Decline, declining** (Gr. *apoklima*, Ar. سقط, حدر). Equivalent to **cadence** or **falling** by whole sign, but perhaps in some Arabic texts referring rather to cadence by **quadrant house** divisions.
- **Decreasing in number.** See **Increasing/decreasing in number**.
- **Deferent.** The large circle which is off-center or **eccentric** to the earth, on which a planet's system rotates.
- **Degrees of equality** (سواء), **equal degrees**. Degrees of the zodiac, as opposed to degrees of **ascensions** or measured on the celestial **equator**.
- **Descension** (Lat. *descensio*). Equivalent to **fall**.
- **Detriment** (Lat. *detrimentum*, Ar. ضدّ, وبال). The sign opposite a planet's **domicile**. For example, Libra is the detriment of Mars.
- **Dexter.** "Right": see **Right/left**.

- **Diameter.** Equivalent to **Opposition**.
- **Dignity** (Lat. *dignitas*, Ar. مزاعمة, نصيب, حظّ). Any of (typically) five ways of assigning rulership or responsibility to a planet (or sometimes, to a **Node**) over some portion of the zodiac. They are often listed in the following order: **domicile, exaltation, triplicity, bound, face/decan**. The opposite of domicile is **detriment**, the opposite of exaltation is **fall**.
- **Directions, directing** (Ar. تسيير, Lat. *directio*). A predictive technique in which a point in the chart (the significator) is considered as stationary, and other planets and their **connections** by degree (or even the **bounds**) are sent forth (**promittors**) as though by **primary motion** until they come to the significator. The degrees between the significator and promittor are converted into years of life. This is the method used in **distributions**. An astronomically less accurate version is done by **ascensions**. Some astrologers also allow "converse" directions, in which points may be directed contrary to primary motion.
- **Disregard.** Equivalent to **Separation**.
- **Distribution** (Lat. *partitio, divisio*; Ar. قسمة). The primary **direction** of a **releaser** (often the degree of the **Ascendant**) through the **bounds**. The bound **lord** of the distribution is the **distributor**, and any body or **ray** which the **releaser** encounters is the **partner**.
- **Distributor** (Lat. *divisor*, Ar. قاسم). The **bound lord** of a **directed releaser**. See **Distribution**.
- **Diurnal.** See **Sect**.
- **Division** (Ar. قسمة, تسويّة). In the context of **house** theory, it refers to any **quadrant house** system, as these are derived by dividing each of the the **quarters** by three. Synonymous with houses by **equation**, and opposed to **whole-sign** houses by **counting**.
- **Domain** (حيّز). Sometimes, a synonym for **sect**. But also used for a specific sect and **gender**-based planetary condition, in which a planet is in a sign of its own gender and also in its preferred hemisphere relative to the Sun (for example, Jupiter being in a male sign and above or below the horizon, wherever the Sun is).
- **Domicile.** One of the five **dignities**. A sign of the **zodiac**, insofar as it is owned or managed by one of the planets. For example, Aries is the domicile of Mars, and so Mars is its domicile **lord**.
- **Doryphory** (Gr. *doruphoria*). Equivalent to **Spear-bearing**.

- **Double-bodied.** Equivalent to the common signs. See **Quadruplicity.**
- **Dragon:** see **Node.**
- **Drawn back** (Lat. *reductus*). Equivalent to being **cadent** from an **angle.**
- **Dodecametorion.** Equivalent to **Twelfth-part.**
- **Duodecima.** Equivalent to **Twelfth-part.**
- **Dustoria** (Lat. transliteration of Ar. *dastūriyyah*). See **Spear-bearing.**
- **East** (Lat. *oriens*). The **Ascendant.**
- **Eastern** (Lat. *orientalis*, Ar. شرقيّ) and **western** (Lat. *occidentalis*, Ar. غربيّ). Four primary meanings: (1) when a planet rises before the Sun or Moon in an earlier zodiacal degree (eastern), or setting after it in a later degree (western); (2) to be outside the **Sun's rays** and visible (eastern) or under them and invisible (western). See also **Easternize, easternization.** (3) When a planet is in an eastern/diurnal or western/nocturnal **quadrant** of the chart: the eastern quadrants are from the horizon/Ascendant to the **meridian**/Midheaven, and from the Descendant to the IC; the western quadrants are the opposite. (4) In an eastern or western quadrant relative to the Sun: eastern is to be in the 90° span of the zodiac which precede the Sun, and the opposite 90°; the other two are western.
- **Easternize, easternization** (شرّق \ تشريق), and **westernize, westernization** (غرّب \ تغريب). Two meanings: (1) when a planet is coming out of or going under the **Sun's rays**, with different distances for different planets (normally around 15° from the Sun); (2) when a planet is close enough to the Sun that *within 7 or 9 days* it will come out of our go under the rays. **Superior planets** easternize and westernize when rising before or setting after the Sun, respectively. The **inferior planets** Venus and Mercury are ambiguous, since each can come out of or go under the rays on either side. See **Eastern and western.**
- **Eccentric.** As an adjective, it describes circles that are "off-center" to the earth; it is also a synonym for the **deferent circle,** the larger circle in a planetary model (which is likewise eccentric or off-center).
- **Ecliptic.** The path defined by the Sun's motion through the **zodiac,** defined as having 0° ecliptical latitude. In tropical astrology, the ecliptic (and therefore the zodiacal signs) begins at the intersection of the ecliptic and the celestial **equator** (the **equinoctial point**).
- **Election** (Lat. *electio*, Ar. اختيار). Literally, "choice": the deliberate choosing of an appropriate time to undertake an action (called an **inception**), or avoid something unwanted.

- **Element** (Lat. *elementum*, Ar. أصل, طبيعة). One of the four basic bodies or qualities (fire, air, water, earth) describing how matter and energy operate, and used to describe the significations and operations of planets and signs. They are usually described by pairs of four other basic qualities (hot, cold, wet, dry). For example, Aries is a fiery sign, and hot and dry; Mercury is typically treated as cold and dry (earthy).
- **Emptiness in course** (Lat. *vacuum cursu*, Ar. خلاء السَّير, Gr. *kenodromia*). Medievally, when a planet does not complete a **connection** for as long as it is in its current sign. In Hellenistic astrology, when a planet does not complete a connection within the next 30°.
- **Enclosure** (Gr. *perischesis, emperischesis*; Lat. *obsido*; Ar. احتوى, حصر, ضغط). When a planet has the rays or bodies of the **infortunes** (or alternatively, the **fortunes**) on either side of it, by degree or sign.
- **Epicycle.** A circle on the **deferent**, on which a planet turns.
- **Equant.** In Ptolemaic astronomy, a mathematical point in outer space from which measurements are made. At the equant, planetary motion is seen as virtually constant and unchanging in speed.
- **Equation, Equate.** (1) In astronomical theory, a correction that is made to the **mean motion/position** of a planet, in order to convert its idealized or **mean** position to its **true motion/position**. Equations are found in a table of equations calculated individually for each planet. (2) In **house** theory, it refers to any **quadrant house** system, where house divisions are derived by exact calculation or equation (Ar. التَّسوية); synonymous with house division by **division**, and **whole-sign** houses by **counting**.
- **Equation of the center (planetary theory).** The angular difference between where the center of a planet's **epicycle** is, as seen from the **equant** (also known as its **mean position**), and its **true position** as seen from earth.
- **Equation of the center (solar theory).** The angular difference between the **mean Sun** (where we expect it to be) and the **true Sun** (where we observe it to be).
- **Equator (celestial).** The projection of the earth's equator into space, forming a great circle. Its equivalent of latitude is called **declination**, while its equivalent of longitude is called **right ascension** (and is measured from the beginning of Aries, from the intersection of it and the **ecliptic**).

- **Equinoctial point, equinox.** The point where the circles of the **ecliptic** and celestial **equator** cross, which defines the beginning of spring (and 0° Aries, in the tropical **zodiac**) or beginning of autumn (and 0° Libra).
- **Escape** (Ar. فوت, Lat. *frustratio, evasio*). When a planet wants to **connect** with a second one, but the second one moves into the next sign before it is completed, and the first planet makes a **connection** with a different, unrelated one instead.
- **Essence** (Lat. *substantia*, Ar. جوهر). Deriving ultimately from Aristotelian philosophy, the fundamental nature or character of a planet or sign, which allows it to indicate or cause certain phenomena (such as the essence of Mars being responsible for indicating fire, iron, war, *etc.*). This word has often been translated as "substance," which is a less accurate term.
- **Essential/accidental.** A common way of distinguishing a planet's conditions, usually according to **dignity** (essential) and some other condition such as its **configurations** or **connections** or rulership (accidental).
- **Exaltation** (Lat. *exaltatio*, Ar. شرف). One of the five **dignities**. A sign in which a planet (or sometimes, a **Node**) signifies its matter in a particularly authoritative and refined way. The exaltation is sometimes identified with a particular degree in that sign.
- **Excellent place** (Ar. مكان جيّد). Includes several of the **advantageous places**, among which the Ascendant, Midheaven, and eleventh are consistently mentioned. (These may be the only excellent places.)
- **Exile** (Ar. غربة) In Arabic astrology, an **alien** (or "peregrine") planet. But in some later Latin astrology (Lat. *exilium*), it denotes being in **detriment**.
- **Face** (Lat. *facies*, Ar. وجه). One of the five **dignities**. The **zodiac** is divided into 36 faces of 10° each, starting with the beginning of Aries. Each division is equivalent to a **decan**.
- **Facing** (Ar. مواجهه). See **Proper face**.
- **Fall** (Gr. *hupsōma*, Ar. هبوط, Lat. *casus, descensio*). The sign opposite a planet's **exaltation**; sometimes called "descension."
- **Falling** (Lat. *cadens*, Ar. ساقط). Refers to being **cadent**, but sometimes ambiguous as to whether dynamically by **quadrant division** or by **whole sign** (which is also called **declining**). When understood dynamically, it is equivalent to **retreating** and **withdrawing**.
- **Fall away from** (Ar. سقط عن). See **Aversion**.
- **Familiar** (Lat. *familiaris*). A hard-to-define term which suggests a sense of belonging and close relationship. (1) Sometimes it is contrasted with be-

ing **alien**, suggesting that a familiar planet is one which is a **lord** over a degree or **place** (that is, it has a **dignity** in it): for a dignity suggests belonging. (2) At other times, it refers to a familiar **configuration** or **connection** (and probably the **sextile** or **trine** in particular): all of the family houses in a chart have a **whole-sign** aspect to the **Ascendant**.

- *Firdāriyyah*. See *fardār*.
- **Feminine**. See **Gender**.
- **Feral** (Ar. وحشيّ, Lat. *feralis*). Equivalent to **Wildness**.
- **Figure** (Lat. *figura*). One of several polygons implied by a **configuration**. For example, a planet in Aries and one in Capricorn do not actually form a **square**, but they imply one because Aries and Capricorn, together with Libra and Cancer, form a square amongst themselves.
- **Fardār, firdāriyyah** (Ar. فردار, فرداريّة). A **time lord** method in which planets rule different periods of life, with each period broken down into sub-periods (there are also mundane versions).
- **Firm**. In terms of signs, the **fixed** signs: see **Quadruplicity**. For houses, equivalent to the **Angles**.
- **Fixed**. See **Quadruplicity**.
- **Fixing** (Gr. *pēxis*). See **Root**.
- **Flow away** (Lat. *defluo*, Ar. انصبّ). See **Separation**.
- **Foreign** (Lat. *extraneus*, Ar. غريب). Usually equivalent to **Peregrine**.
- **Fortunate, made fortunate** (Lat. *fortunatus*, Ar. مسعود). A planet whose condition is made better, often by a **trine** or **sextile** from a **fortune**.
- **Fortune/Infortune** (Ar. سعد \ نحس, Lat. *fortuna / infortuna*). A division of the planets into groups that cause or signify typically "good" things (Jupiter, Venus, usually the Sun and Moon) or "bad" things (Mars, Saturn). Mercury is considered variable.
- **Foundations of the Moon**. See **Centers of the Moon**.
- **Free** (Ar. بري, Lat. *liber*). Sometimes, being **cleansed** of the **infortunes**; at other times, being out of the **Sun's rays**.
- **Gender**. The division of signs, degrees, planets and hours into masculine and feminine groups.
- **Glow** (Ar. ضوء). This has three primary meanings: (1) a planet in "its own glow" is of the **sect** of the chart, or in some sect-related rejoicing condition; (2) the Moon increases and decreases in her light or glow by waxing

and waning; (3) a planet can be "in its own glow" when it is out of the **Sun's rays** so as to be visible.
- **Good ones.** See **Fortune/Infortune**.
- **Good places.** Equivalent to **Advantageous places**.
- **Governor** (Ar. المستولي \ الوالي). Normally a generic term referring to a **victor** over a place, such as the Ptolemaic victor (by rulership and **aspect**). Sometimes used to denote the **house-master** or a **time lord**.
- **Greater, middle, lesser years.** See **Planetary years**.
- **Halb** (Ar. حلب). Probably Pahlavi for **sect**, but normally describes a special sect-related rejoicing condition. For **diurnal** planets, when they are in the same hemisphere as the Sun (upper or lower); for **nocturnal** planets, when they are in the hemisphere opposite the Sun. For example, if Saturn during the day is above the earth (where the Sun by definition also is).
- **Handing over** (دفع إلى) When a planet applies by **connection** to another, it hands over its **management**.
- **Harm.** A broad category of conditions by which a planet may be made **unfortunate**.
- **Hayyiz.** (Ar. حيّز). Arabic for **domain**, technically equivalent to *halb*, except that the planet is also in a sign of its own **gender**. But sometimes this term simply means **sect**.
- **Head (of the Dragon).** See **Node**.
- **Hexagon.** See **Sextile**.
- **Hīlāj** (Ar. هيلاج, from the Pahlavi for "releaser"). Equivalent to **releaser**.
- **Hold onto.** Hugo's synonym for a planet being in or **transiting** a **sign**.
- **Honor guard, paying honor** (تكرمة). A synonym for **Spear-bearing**.
- **Horary astrology.** A late historical designation for **questions**.
- **Hours (planetary).** The assigning of rulership over hours of the day and night to planets. The hours of daylight (and night, respectively) are divided by 12, and each period is ruled first by the planet ruling that day, then the rest in descending planetary order. For example, on Sunday the Sun rules the first planetary "hour" from daybreak, then Venus, then Mercury, the Moon, Saturn, and so on.
- **House** (Gr. *oikos*, Lat. *domus*, Ar. بيت). A twelve-fold spatial division of a chart, in which each house signifies one or more areas of life. Two basic schemes are (1) **whole-sign** houses, in which the **signs** are equivalent to the houses, and (2) **quadrant houses**. But in the context of dignities and

rulerships, "house" is the equivalent of **domicile**: so, Aries is the house of Mars.

- **House-master** (Gr. *oikodespotēs*, Ar. كدخداه). Often called the *alcochoden* in Latin, from the Arabic transliteration of a Persian word (*kadkhudhāh*). One of the **lords** of the longevity **releaser**, preferably the **bound lord**. But the Greek word is also used in a general way to mean simply any **lord**, or even a **victor**.
- **Humor** (Lat. *humor*, Ar. خلط). Any one of four mixtures or substances in the body (according to traditional medicine), the balance between which determines one's health and **temperament** (outlook and energy level). Choler or yellow bile is associated with fire and the choleric temperament; blood is associated with air and the sanguine temperament; phlegm is associated with water and the phlegmatic temperament; black bile is associated with earth and the melancholic temperament.
- **Hundred, Hundreds** (الألف). A Persian mundane **time lord**, which rules the world for a period of 100 years.
- **Hyleg**. See *Hīlāj* and **Releaser**.
- **IC**. See *Imum Caeli*.
- **Imum Caeli** (Lat. "lowest part of heaven"). The **axial degree** or degree of the zodiac on which the lower half of the **meridian** circle falls; in **quadrant house** systems, it marks the beginning of the fourth **house**.
- **In the heart**. Often called *cazimi* in English texts, from the Ar. كصميمي. A planet is in the heart of the Sun when it is either in the same degree as the Sun (according to Sahl b. Bishr and Rhetorius), or within 16' of longitude from him.
- **Inception** (Lat. *inceptio*, Ar. ابتداء). See **Election**.
- **Increasing/decreasing in calculation**. A planet is increasing in calculation when its **equation** is added to the **mean motion/position**, because the **true motion/position** is farther ahead in the zodiac than the mean one. It is decreasing in calculation when the equation is subtracted.
- **Increasing/decreasing in number**. When the daily speed of a planet (or at least the speed of the center of its **epicycle**) is seen to speed up (or slow down). When moving from its **perigee** to its **apogee**, it slows down or decreases in number, because it is moving farther away from the earth; when moving from the apogee to the perigee, it speeds up or increases in number because it is coming closer to the earth.

- **Indicator.** A generic term synonymous with **significator**. See also *namūdār*.
- **Inferior** (Lat. *inferior*, Ar. سفليّ). The planets lower than the Sun: Venus, Mercury, and sometimes the Moon.
- **Infortunes.** See **Fortune/Infortune**.
- **Inspection** (مناظرة). Equivalent to an **aspect**, but might specifically refer to a degree-based **connection** from another sign.
- *'Ittisāl* (Ar. اتّصال). Equivalent to **Connection**.
- **Joy** (Lat. *gaudium*, Ar. فرح). Signs or hosues in which the planets are said to "rejoice" in acting or signifying their natures.
- *Jārbakhtār* (Ar. جاربختار, from the Pahlavi for "distributor of time"). Equivalent to **Distributor**; see **Distribution**.
- *Kadkhudhāh* (كدخذاه). An Arabic transliteration from Pahlavi or Middle Persian for the **House-master**, often called the *alcochoden* in Latin transliteration.
- *Kardaja* (Ar. كردجة, from Sansk. *kramajyā*). The numerical interval used in rows of an astronomical table, when entering an **argument** and then finding the result in the relevant column (and therefore sometimes seems to refer to portions of the astronomical circles themselves). Ptolemy's tables often used intervals of 6°, while Indian tables often used 3° 45', which is 1/24 of 90°.
- *Kasmīmī* (Ar. كصميمي). See **In the heart**.
- **Kingdom.** See **Exaltation**.
- **Largesse and recompense** (Ar. نعمة والمكافاة). A reciprocal relation in which one planet is rescued from being in its own **fall** or a **well**, and then returns the favor when the other planet is in its fall or well.
- **Leader** (Lat. *dux*). Equivalent to a **significator** for some topic. The Arabic word for "significator" means to indicate something by pointing the way toward something: thus the significator for a topic or matter "leads" the astrologer to some answer. Used by some less popular Latin translators (such as Hugo of Santalla and Hermann of Carinthia).
- **Linger in** (Lat. *commoror*). Hugo's synonym for a planet being in or **transiting** through a **sign**.
- **Lodging-place** (Lat. *hospitium*). Hugo's synonym for a **house**, particularly the **sign** which occupies a house.
- **Look at** (Lat. *aspicio*, Ar. نظر). Two things may look at each other if they are in signs which are **configured** or in **aspect** to each other by a **sextile**,

square, trine, or **opposition**. See also **Whole signs**. Places and planets which cannot see or look at each other, are in **aversion**.
- **Look down upon** (Ar. أشرف). A synonym for **overcoming**, and in particular **decimation**.
- **Lord of the year.** Usually, the **domicile lord** of a **profection**, namely where the profection **terminates**. But in mundane astrology it can also refer to a kind of **victor**, the planet in the chart which is the most powerful and sums up the meaning of the year.
- **Lord.** A designation for the planet which has a particular **dignity**, but when used alone it usually means the **domicile** lord. For example, Mars is the lord of Aries.
- **Lord of the orb.** See **Orb**.
- **Lord of the question.** See **Owner**.
- **Lord of the year.** In mundane ingress charts, the planet that is the **victor** over the chart, indicating the general meanings of the year. But in **profections**, the lord of the sign of the **terminal point**.
- **Lot** (Gr. *klēros*, Lat. *pars, sors*, Ar. قرعة, سهم). Sometimes called "Parts." A place (often treated as equivalent to an entire sign) expressing a ratio derived from the position of three other parts of a chart. Normally, the distance between two places is measured in zodiacal order from one to the other, and this distance is projected forward from some other place (usually the Ascendant): where the counting stops, is the Lot.
- **Lucky/unlucky.** See **Fortune/Infortune**.
- **Luminary** (Lat. *luminarium*, Ar. نيّر). The Sun or Moon.
- **Lunation.** See **Conjunction/prevention**.
- **Malefic.** See **Fortune/Infortune**.
- **Malevolent.** See **Fortune/Infortune**.
- **Management** (Ar. تدبير). A generic term referring to how a planet "manages" a topic by signifying it. Typically, planets **hand over** and "accept" management to and from each other, simply by **applying** to one another.
- **Manager** (Ar. المدبّر). Sometimes, the planetary **partner** in **distributions**; sometimes a term for the longevity **releaser**. But also a generic name for planets which have any kind of **management**.
- **Masculine.** See **Gender**.

- **Maximum equation.** In solar theory, the greatest angular amount of the **equation of the center**, which occurs when the **mean Sun** is perpendicular to the **apsidal line**.
- **Mean motion/position.** The motion or position of a planet as measured from the **equant**, namely assuming a constant rate of speed. To be contrasted with **True motion/position**.
- **Mean Sun.** A fictitious point which revolves around the earth in exactly one year, in a line parallel with the **true Sun**. The mean Sun represents where we would expect the Sun to be, if it traveled in a perfect circle around the earth. It coincides with the true Sun at the Sun's **apogee** and **perigee**.
- **Meeting** (Ar. اجتماع). The **conjunction** of the Sun and Moon at the New Moon, which makes it a **connection** by body. See **Conjunction/prevention**.
- **Melancholic.** See **Humor**.
- **Meridian.** The great circle which has its center at the middle of the earth, and points north-south relative to the horizon. The degree which intersects the **ecliptic** (or **axial degree**) is called the degree of the **Midheaven** or *Imum Caeli/IC*.
- **Midheaven.** Either the tenth sign from the **Ascendant**, or the **axial degree** on which the celestial **meridian** falls.
- **Minister.** A synonym for **Governor**.
- **Movable signs.** See **Quadruplicity**.
- *Mubtazz* (Ar. مبتزّ). See **Victor**.
- **Mutable signs.** Equivalent to "common" signs. See **Quadruplicity**.
- *Namūdār.* (Ar. نمودار) Persian for "indicator," a special way of determining the moment of conception or the nativity (if they are known only approximately).
- **Native** (Lat. *natus*, Ar. مولود, مولد). The person whose birth chart it is.
- **Nativity.** Technically, a birth itself, but used by astrologers to describe the chart cast for the moment of a birth.
- **Ninth-parts.** Divisions of each sign into 9 equal parts of 3° 20' apiece, each ruled by a planet. Used predictively by some astrologers as part of the suite of **revolution** techniques.
- **Nobility.** Equivalent to **Exaltation**.
- **Nocturnal.** See **Sect**.

- **Node** (Lat. *nodus*, Ar. عقدة), lit. "knot." The point on the ecliptic where a planet passes into northward latitude (its North Node or Head of the Dragon) or into southern latitude (its South Node or Tail of the Dragon). Normally only the Moon's Nodes are considered.
- **Northern/southern.** Either planets in northern or southern latitude in the **zodiac** relative to the ecliptic, or in northern or southern **declination** relative to the celestial **equator**.
- **Not-reception** (Ar. غير مقبول). When an **applying** planet is in the **fall** of the planet being applied to, or applies from a place in which the other planet has no **dignity**.
- **Number** (Ar. عدد). For house theory, see **counting**. For its use in calculating planetary positions, see **Increasing/decreasing in number**.
- **Oblique ascensions.** The **ascensions** used in making predictions by ascensional times or primary **directions**.
- **Obstruction.** See **Resistance**.
- **Occidental, occidentality.** See **Eastern and western**.
- **Opening of the portals/doors.** Times of likely weather changes and rain, determined by certain **transits**.
- **Opposition** (Lat. *oppositio, oppositum*; Ar. مقابلة, استقبال. A **configuration** or **aspect** either by **whole sign** or degree, in which the signs have a 180° relation to each other: for example, a planet in Aries is opposed to one in Libra.
- **Optimal place** (Lat. *optimus*). See **Excellent place**.
- **Orb** (Ar. دور, Lat. *orbis*), **lord of the orb**. Denotes a natal **time lord** technique; this same word is the basis of **Turn** (a mundane technique), and sometimes **Turning** (see **Profections**).
- **Orbs/bodies** (Lat. *orbis*, Ar. جرم). A space of power or influence on each side of a planet's **body** or position, used to determine the intensity of interaction between different planets.
- **Oriental, orientality.** See **Eastern and western**.
- **Overcoming.** When a planet is in the eleventh, tenth, or ninth sign from another planet (i.e., in a superior **sextile**, **square**, or **trine**); being in the tenth sign is considered **decimation**, a more domineering or even harmful position.
- **Overlord** (Ar. المسلّط). Refers to a **victor** over a place, but often used to designate the primary **triplicity lord**.

- **Own light** (Ar. ضوءه, Lat. *lumen suum*). See **Glow**.
- **Owner** (صاحب). The person who "owns" or is the subject of a chart: the **native** is the owner of a nativity, the **querent** is the owner of the question chart, etc.
- **Part.** See **Lot**.
- **Partner** (Ar. شريك, Lat. *particeps*). The body or **ray** of any planet which a **directed releaser** encounters while being **distributed** through the **bounds**.
- **Peregrine** (Lat. *peregrinus*, Ar. غريب), lit. "a stranger, foreigner." See **Alien**.
- **Perigee (of eccentric/deferent).** The point on a planet's **deferent circle** that is closest to the earth; as seen from earth, it points to some degree of the zodiac. It is opposite the **apogee**.
- **Perverse** (Lat. *perversus*). Hugo's occasional term for (1) the **infortunes**, and (2) **places** in **aversion** to the **Ascendant** by **whole-sign**: definitely the twelfth and sixth, probably the eighth, and possibly the second.
- **Phlegmatic.** See **Humor**.
- **Pitted degrees.** Equivalent to **Welled degrees**.
- **Pivot** (Lat. *cardo*). Equivalent to **Angle**.
- **Place.** Equivalent to a **house**, and more often (and more anciently) a **whole-sign** house, namely a **sign**.
- **Planetary years.** Periods of years (or, other units of time) which the planets signify according to various conditions.
- **Portion** (Ar. جزء, Lat. *pars, portio*). Normally, refers to either (1) a specific zodiacal degree, especially the degree of the Ascendant or the degree where a **ray** falls, or (2) the degrees within a particular **bound**: especially, the bound in which the Ascendant falls.
- **Possess.** Hugo's synonym for a planet being in or **transiting** a **sign**.
- **Post** (Ar. مركز). A **stake** or **angle**. (The Arabic verb is virtually equivalent to Ar. *watada*, used for a stake.) Sometimes translated as **center**, as in the centers of the Moon.
- **Posts of the Moon.** See **Centers of the Moon**.
- **Prevention.** See **Conjunction/prevention**.
- **Predominator** (Gr. *epikratētōr*). See **Victor**.
- **Primary directions.** See **Directions**.
- **Primary motion.** The clockwise or east-to-west motion of the heavens. See **secondary motion**.

- **Profection** (Lat. *profectio*, "advancement, setting out"). A predictive technique in which some part of a chart (usually the **Ascendant**) is advanced either by an entire sign or in 30° increments for each year of life.
- **Prohibition.** Equivalent to **Blocking**.
- **Promittor** (lit., something "sent forward"). A point which is **directed** by **primary motion** to a **significator**, or to which a significator is **released** or directed (depending on how one views the mechanics of directions).
- **Proper face** (Gr. *idioprosōpos*). A relationship between a planet and a **luminary**, so that the **signs** the occupy have the same relationship as the **domiciles** they rule. For example, Leo (ruled by the Sun) is two signs to the **right** of Libra (ruled by Venus): so whenever Venus is **western** and two signs away from the Sun, she will be in the proper face of the Sun.
- **Pushing.** See **Handing over**.
- **Qāsim/qismah** (Ar. قاسم, قسمة) See **distributor** and **distribution**.
- **Quadrant.** A division of the heavens into four parts, defined by the circles of the horizon and **meridian**, marked out by the **axial degrees** of the **Ascendant-Descendant**, and **Midheaven-IC**.
- **Quadrant houses.** A division of the heavens or local space into twelve spaces which overlap the **whole signs**, and are assigned topics of life and ways of measuring strength (such as Porphyry, Alchabitius Semi-Arc, or Regiomontanus houses). For example, if the degree of the **Midheaven** fell into the eleventh sign, the space between the Midheaven and the Ascendant would be divided into sections that overlap with, and are not coincident with the signs.
- **Quadruplicity.** A "fourfold" group of signs indicating certain shared patterns of behavior. The movable (or cardinal or convertible) signs are those through which new states of being are quickly formed (including the seasons): Aries, Cancer, Libra, Capricorn. The fixed (sometimes "firm") signs are those through which matters are fixed and lasting in their character: Taurus, Leo, Scorpio, Aquarius. The common (or mutable or bicorporeal) signs are those which make a transition and partake both of quick change and fixed qualities: Gemini, Virgo, Sagittarius, Pisces.
- **Quaesited/quesited.** In **horary** astrology, the matter asked about.
- **Querent.** In **horary** astrology, the person asking the question (or the person on behalf of whom one asks).

- **Questions**. The branch of astrology dealing with inquiries about individual matters, for which a chart is cast.
- **Ray, raying** (Lat. *radius, radiatio*; Ar. شعاع). An imaginary line which represents an exact **aspect** cast from a planet to the corresponding degree in another sign, such as if a planet is in 15° Gemini and casts a **square** ray to 15° Virgo. See also **Sun's rays**.
- **Receive, reception** (Lat. *recipio*, Ar. قبل). What one planet does when another planet **hands over** or **applies** to it, and especially when they are related by **dignity**, or by a **trine** or **sextile** from an **agreeing** sign of various types. For example, if the Moon applies to Mars, Mars will accept her application; and if he rules the sign in which she is, he will receive her (an intensified condition).
- **Reflection** (Ar. رد, Lat. *redditus*). When two planets are in **aversion** to each other, but a third planet either **collects** or **transfers** their light. If it collects, it reflects the light elsewhere.
- **Refrenation**. See **Revoking**.
- **Regard** (Lat. *respectus*). Equivalent to **looking at** or an **aspect**.
- **Releaser** (Ar. هيلاج). The point which is the focus of a **direction**, often one of a standard set of five (the luminaries, **Ascendant**, **Lot** of Fortune, and the prenatal **lunation**. In determining longevity, it is the **victor** among a set of possible points, which often includes the five just mentioned.
- **Remote** (Lat. *remotus*, prob. a translation of Ar. زائل). Equivalent to **cadent**: see **Angle**. But see also *Judges* §7.73, where al-Tabarī (or Hugo) distinguishes being **cadent** from being **remote**, probably translating the Ar. زائل and ساقط (**withdrawing** and **falling**).
- **Render**. When a planet **hands over** to another planet or place.
- **Resistance** (Ar. اعتراض). When one planet is moving towards a second (wanting to be **connected** to it), but a third one in a later degrees goes **retrograde**, connects with the second one, and then with the first one.
- **Retreat, retreating** (Ar. إدبار \ مدبر). Refers to being (2) dynamically **cadent**, i.e. moving by **primary motion** away from an **axial** degree. (But occasionally might refer to being cadent by **whole signs**.) A near synonym to **withdrawal**. Its antonym is **Advancement**. It may also refer to (2) the **western** quadrants.
- **Retrograde, retrogradation** (Lat. *retrogradus*, Ar. راجع). When a planet seems to move backwards in its **secondary motion**.
- **Return, Solar/Lunar**. Equivalent to **Revolution**.

- **Returning** (Ar. رَدّ, Lat. *redditus, reditio*). What a **burned** or **retrograde** planet does when another planet **hands over** to it.
- **Revoking** (Ar. انتكاث, Lat. *refrenatio*). When a planet making an applying **connection** stations and turns **retrograde**, not completing the connection.
- **Revolution** (Lat. *revolutio*, Ar. تحويل). Sometimes called the "cycle" or "transfer" or "change-over" of a year. Technically, the **transiting** position of planets and the **Ascendant** at the moment the Sun returns to a particular place in the zodiac: in the case of nativities, when he returns to his exact natal position; in mundane astrology, usually when he makes his ingress into 0° Aries. But the revolution is also understood to involve an entire suite of predictive techniques, including **distribution**, **profections**, and *fardārs*.
- **Right ascensions.** Degrees on the celestial **equator** (its equivalent of geographical longitude), particularly those which move across the **meridian** when calculating arcs for **ascensions** and **directions**.
- **Right/left.** Right (or "dexter") degrees and **configurations** or **aspects** are those earlier in the zodiac relative to a planet or sign, up to the **opposition**; left (or "sinister") degrees and configurations are those later in the zodiac. For example, if a planet is in Capricorn, its right aspects will be towards Scorpio, Libra, and Virgo; its left aspects will be towards Pisces, Aries, and Taurus.
- **Right-siding, being on the right, right-sidedness** (ميمنة \ تنامن). A synonym for **Spear-bearing**.
- **Root** (Gr. *pēxis*, Lat. *radix*, Ar. أصل). A chart used as a basis for another chart; a root particularly describes something considered to have concrete being of its own. For example, a **nativity** acts as a root for an **election**, so that when planning an election one must make it harmonize with the nativity.
- **Safe** (Ar. سليم). When a planet is not being harmed, particularly by an **assembly** or **square** or **opposition** with the **infortunes**. See **Cleansed**.
- *Sālkhuday / sālkhudāh* (Ar. سالخدى \ سالخداه, from Pahlavi, "lord of the year"). Equivalent to the **lord of the year** in a **profection**.
- **Sanguine.** See **Humor**.
- **Scorched** (Lat. *adustus*). See **Burned up**.

- **Secondary motion.** The motion of planets forward in the zodiac, rather than the **primary motion** of the heavens around the earth.
- **Sect** (Gr. *hairēsis*). A division of charts, planets, and signs into "diurnal/day" and "nocturnal/night." For similar terms, see **Glow, Share,** and **Domain.**
- **Sector** (Ar. نطاق). A division of the **deferent** circle or **epicycle** into four parts, used to determine the position, speed, visibility, and other features of a planet.
- **See.** See **Look at.**
- **Seeing, hearing, listening signs.** A way of associating signs similar to **commanding/obeying.**
- **Separation** (Lat. *separatio*, Ar. انصراف). When planets have completed a **connection** by **assembly** or **aspect**, and move away from one another.
- **Sextile** (Lat. *sextilis*, Ar. تسديس). A **configuration** or **aspect** either by **whole sign** or degree, in which the signs have a 60° relation to each other: for example, Aries and Gemini.
- **Share** (Ar. حظّ, but sometimes نصيب, or حصّة, "allotment, share"). Often equivalent to **dignity,** but sometimes used to mean **sect** (where it is synonymous with and perhaps confused with **domain** (Ar. حيّز).
- **Shift.** (1) Equivalent to **sect** (Ar. نوبة), referring not only to the alternation between day and night, but also to the period of night or day itself. The Sun is the lord of the diurnal shift or sect, and the Moon is the lord of the nocturnal shift or sect. (2) In mundane astrology, it refers to the shift (Ar. انتقال, Lat. *mutatio*) of the Saturn-Jupiter conjunctions from one **triplicity** to another about every 200 (tropical zodiac) or 220 (sidereal zodiac) years.
- **Sign.** One of the twelve 30° divisions of the **ecliptic** or **zodiac**, named after the constellations which they used to be roughly congruent to.
- **Significator** (Lat. *significator*, Ar. دليل). Either (1) a planet or point in a chart which indicates or signifies something for a topic (either through its own character, or house position, or rulerships, *etc.*), or (2) the stationary point in primary **directions.**
- **Significator of the king.** In mundane ingress charts, the **victor** planet which indicates the king or government.
- **Sinister.** "Left": see **Right/left.**
- **Slavery.** In Hugo of Santalla's Latin, equivalent to **Fall.**
- **Sought matter, sought thing** (Ar. حاجة). See **Quaesited.**

- **Sovereignty** (Lat. *regnum*). In Hugo of Santalla's Latin, equivalent to **Exaltation**.
- **Spear-bearing** (Ar. دستوريّة, Lat. *dustoria*, Gr. *doruphoria*). A special configuration in a chart showing eminence and prosperity, of which there were several types and definitions. Spear-bearing requires that there be a royal planet (usually, a **luminary**), which is accompanied by a spear-bearing planet.
- **Square**. A **configuration** or **aspect** either by **whole sign** or degree, in which the signs have a 90° relation to each other: for example, Aries and Cancer.
- **Stake** (Ar. وتد). Equivalent to **Angle**.
- **Sublunar world**. The world of the four **elements** below the sphere of the Moon, in classical cosmology.
- **Substance** (Lat. *substantia*). Sometimes, indicating the real **essence** of a planet or sign. But often it refers to financial assets (perhaps because coins are physical objects indicating real value).
- **Succeedent**. See **Angle**.
- **Suitable, suitability** (Ar. صالح \ صلاح). For **places** of the chart, equivalent to the schemes of **advantageous places**. Otherwise, a general term for the good or bad condition of a planet.
- **Sun's rays** (or Sun's beams). In earlier astrology, equivalent to a regularized distance of 15° away from the Sun, so that a planet under the rays is not visible at dawn or dusk. But a later distinction was made between being **burned up** (about 1° - 7.5° away from the Sun) and merely being under the rays (about 7.5° - 15° away).
- **Superior** (Lat. *superior*, Ar. علوي). The planets higher than the Sun: Saturn, Jupiter, Mars.
- **Supremacy** (Lat. *regnum*). Hugo's word for **exaltation**, sometimes used in translations by Dykes instead of the slightly more accurate Latin **sovereignty**.
- **Synastry**. The comparison of two or more charts to determine compatibility, usually in romantic relationships or friendships.
- **Tail (of the Dragon)**. See **Node**.
- *Tasyir* (Ar. تسيير, "dispatching, sending out"). Equivalent to primary **directions**.

- **Temperament** (Lat. *temperamentum*, Ar. مزاج). The particular mixture (sometimes, "complexion") of **elements** or **humors** which determines a person's or planet's typical behavior, outlook, energy level, and health.
- **Terminal point, terminate** (Ar. انتهاء). The sign or degree which a **profection** comes to, at a particular day or time.
- **Testimony** (Lat. *testimonium*, Ar. شهادة). From Arabic astrology onwards, a little-defined term which can mean (1) the planets which have **dignity** in a place or degree, or (2) the number of dignities a planet has in its own place (or as compared with other planets), or (3) a planet's **assembly** or **aspect** to a place of interest, or (4) generally *any* way in which planets may make themselves relevant to the inquiry at hand. For example, a planet which is the **exalted** lord of the **Ascendant** but also **looks at** it, maby be said to present two testimonies supporting its relevance to an inquiry about the Ascendant.
- **Tetragon.** See **Square**.
- **Thought-interpretation.** The practice of identifying a theme or topic in a **querent's** mind, often using a **victor**, before answering the specific **question**. Called the "extraction of the heart" in Arabic (استخراج الضمير), it was sometimes used to identify an object in the hand prior to a consultation.
- **Thousand, Thousands** (المائة). A Persian mundane **time lord**, which rules the world for a period of 1000 years.
- **Time lord.** A planet or sign ruling over some period of time according to one of the classical predictive techniques. For example, the **lord of the year** in nativities is the time lord over a **profection**.
- **Transfer** (Lat. *translatio*, Ar. نقل) When one planet **separates** from one planet, and **connects** to another. Not to be confused with a **shift** of triplicities in Saturn-Jupiter conjunctions, or annual **revolutions**, either mundane or natal.
- **Transit** (Lat. *transio*, Ar. مرّ). The passing of one planet across a planet or point (by body or **aspect** by exact degree), or even through a particular sign.
- **Translation** (Lat. *translatio*). Equivalent to **Transfer**.
- **Traverse** (Lat. *discurro*). Hugo's synonym for a planet being in or **transiting** through a **sign**.
- **Triangle.** Normally, equivalent to **trine**, but sometimes **triplicity**.
- **Trigon.** Normally, equivalent to **trine**, but sometimes **triplicity**.

GLOSSARY

- **Trine** (Lat. *trinus*, Ar. تثليث). A **configuration** or **aspect** either by **whole sign** or degree, in which the signs have a 120° relation to each other: for example, Aries and Leo.
- **Triplicity** (Ar. مثلثة, Lat. *triplicitas*). A set of three signs which form a triangle, such as Aries-Leo-Sagittarius. (Arabic texts sometimes use the plural "triplicities" when they mean the singular.)
- **Triplicity lords.** A set of three planets which jointly rule a **triplicity** as a whole. One planet is primary by day, another by night, and the third lord always acts as their partner. For example, the Sun, Jupiter, and Saturn are the triplicity lords of Aries-Leo-Sagittarius: the Sun is primary by day, Jupiter by night, and Saturn is always the last, partnering lord.
- **True motion/position.** The motion or position of a planet as measured from the earth, once its **mean motion/position** has been adjusted or corrected by various types of **equations.**
- **True Sun.** The zodiacal position of the Sun, as seen from the earth, after its **mean** position has been **equated** or corrected.
- **Turn** (Ar. دور). A predictive technique in which responsibilities for being a **time lord** rotates among different planets. It may also refer to other methods in which cycles through the planets, assigning them roles as **time lords.** See **Lord of the orb.**
- **Turned away from** (Gr. *apostrophē*). See **Aversion.**
- **Turning** (Ar. إدوار \ دور). See **Profection.**
- **Turning signs** (Lat. *tropicus*). Normally, equivalent to **movable** or **convertible** signs. See **Quadruplicity.** But sometimes refers to the tropical signs Cancer and Capricorn, in which the Sun turns back from his most extreme **declinations.**
- **Twelfth-part** (Lat. *duodecatemorion, duodecima*; Ar. اثنى عشريّة). Signs of the zodiac defined by 2.5° divisions of other signs. For example, the twelfth-part corresponding to 4° Gemini is Cancer.
- **Two-parted signs.** Equivalent to the double-bodied or common signs: see **Quadruplicity.**
- **Under the rays.** See **Sun's rays.**
- **Underground.** Equivalent to *Imum caeli/IC.*
- **Unfortunate** (Lat. *infortunatus*, Ar. منحوس). When a planet's condition is made more difficult, usually by **assembly, square,** or **opposition** with the **infortunes.**

- **Unhealthiness** (Ar. وبال). Equivalent to **Detriment**.
- **Union** (Ar. اقتران). Usually, any **conjunction** of planets by body; but sometimes, a **mean** conjunction or even the New Moon (see **Conjunction/prevention**).
- **Unlucky**. See **Fortune/Infortune**.
- **Upright** (Ar. قائم). Describes the axis of the MC-IC, when it falls into the tenth and fourth signs, rather than the eleventh-fifth, or ninth-third.
- *Via combusta*. See **Burnt path**.
- **Victor** (Ar. مبتزّ). A planet or point identified as the most authoritative over a particular topic, **place** or **house**, or for a chart as a whole. Dykes distinguishes procedures that find victor "over" several places at once, and a victor "among" several candidate victors, usually on a ranked list.
- **Void in course**. See **Emptiness in course**.
- **Well, welled degrees** (Lat. *puteum*, Ar. بئر). A degree in which a planet is said to be more obscure in its operation. In later, English-speaking astrology, sometimes called the "pitted" degrees.
- **Western**. See **Eastern and western**.
- **Westernize, westernization** (تغريب \ غرّب). See **Easternize, easternization**.
- **Whole signs**. The oldest system of assigning house topics and **aspects**. The entire sign on the horizon (the **Ascendant**) is the first house, the entire second sign is the second house, and so on. Likewise, aspects are considered first of all according to signs: planets in Aries **look at** planets in Gemini, even if aspects which **connect** by degree are more intense.
- **Wildness** (Ar. وحشيّة, Lat. *feralitas*). When a planet is not **looked at** by any other planet.
- **Withdrawal, withdrawing** (زائل \ زوال; in some Latin translations, *recedens*). Refers to being (1) dynamically **cadent**, i.e. moving by **primary motion** away from an **axial** degree. (But occasionally might refer to being cadent by **whole signs**.) A near synonym to **retreat**. Its antonym is **Advancement**. It may also refer to (2) the **western** quadrants.
- *Zīj* (Ar. زيج). The Arabic for a Persian word meaning a set of astronomical tables for calculating planetary positions and other things. Ptolemy's *Almagest* can be considered a *zīj*.
- **Zodiac**. Three ways of dividing the **ecliptic** into signs. The "constellational" zodiac uses the actual constellations, which are of different sizes. The "sidereal" zodiac divides the ecliptic into twelve equal divisions, starting

from some fixed star which acts as the **ayanamsha**. The "tropical" zodiac also uses equal divisions, but starts from the **equinoctial point**.

BIBLIOGRAPHY

Abū Bakr, *On Nativities*, in Dykes 2010 (*Persian Nativities II*)
Abū Ma'shar, *Persian Nativities IV: On the Revolutions of the Years of Nativities*, Benjamin N. Dykes trans. and ed. (Minneapolis, MN: The Cazimi Press, 2019)
Allen, Richard Hinckley, *Star Names: Their Lore and Meaning* (New York: Dover Publications Inc., 1963)
Al-Bīrūnī, Muhammad, trans. Mohammad Saffouri and Adnan Ifram, *Al-Bīrūnī on Transits* (American University of Beirut: 1959)
Brennan, Chris, *Hellenistic Astrology: The Study of Fate and Fortune* (Denver, CO: Amor Fati Publications, 2017)
Burnett, Charles and Ahmed al-Hamdi, "Zādānfarrūkh al-Andarzaghar on Anniversary Horoscopes," *Zeitschrift für Geschichte der Arabisch-Islamischen Wissenschaften*, Vol. 7, 1991/1992, pp. 294-400.
Burnett, Charles, and David Pingree eds., *The Liber Aristotilis of Hugo of Santalla* (London: The Warburg Institute, 1997)
Dorotheus of Sidon, *Carmen Astrologicum*, trans. and ed. Benjamin N. Dykes (Minneapolis, MN: The Cazimi Press, 2017)
Dorotheus of Sidon, *Carmen Astrologicum*, trans. David Pingree (Abingdon, MD: The Astrology Center of America, 2005)
Dykes, Benjamin trans. and ed., *Works of Sahl & Māshā'allāh* (Golden Valley, MN: The Cazimi Press, 2008)
Dykes, Benjamin, trans. and ed., *Persian Nativities I: Māshā'allāh & Abū 'Ali* (Minneapolis, MN: The Cazimi Press, 2009)
Dykes, Benjamin, trans. and ed., *Persian Nativities II: 'Umar al-Tabarī & Abū Bakr* (Minneapolis, MN: The Cazimi Press, 2010)
Dykes, Benjamin trans. and ed., *Introductions to Traditional Astrology: Abū Ma'shar & al-Qabīsī* (Minneapolis, MN: The Cazimi Press, 2010)
Dykes, Benjamin, trans. and ed., *Astrology of the World I: The Ptolemaic Inheritance* (Minneapolis, MN: The Cazimi Press, 2013)
Dykes, Benjamin, trans. and ed., *Astrology of the World II: Revolutions & History* (Minneapolis, MN: The Cazimi Press, 2014
Dykes, Benjamin, "Planetary Magic among the Harrānian Sābians," in *The Celestial Art: Essays on Astrological Magic*, Austin Coppock and Daniel A. Schulke eds. (Three Hands Press, 2018)

Firmicus Maternus, *Mathesis*, ed. P. Monat (Paris: Les Belles Lettres, 1992-1997)

Firmicus Maternus, *Mathesis*, trans. and ed. Benjamin N. Dykes (forthcoming)

Hava, J.G., *Arabic-English Dictionary for Advanced Learners* (New Delhi: Goodword Books, 2011)

Hephaistio of Thebes, *Apotelesmatics* vols. I-II, trans. and ed. Robert H. Schmidt (Cumberland, MD: The Golden Hind Press, 1994 and 1998)

Hephaistion of Thebes, *Apotelesmatics Book III: On Inceptions*, trans. Eduardo Gramaglia and ed. Benjamin N. Dykes (Minneapolis, MN: The Cazimi Press, 2013)

Hermann of Carinthia, Benjamin Dykes trans. and ed., *The Search of the Heart* (Minneapolis, MN: The Cazimi Press, 2011)

Holden, James H., *Porphyry the Philosopher: Introduction to the Tetrabiblos and Serapio of Alexandria: Astrological Definitions* (Tempe, AZ: American Federation of Astrologers, Inc., 2009)

Hoyland, Robert G., *In God's Path: The Arab Conquests and the Creation of an Islamic Empire* (New York, NY: Oxford University Press, 2015)

Kennedy, Hugh, *The Prophet and the Age of the Caliphates* (Harlow, Great Britain: Pearson Education Limited, 2004)

Kennedy, Hugh, *When Baghdad Ruled the Muslim World: The Rise and Fall of Islam's Greatest Dynasty* (Cambridge, MA: Da Capo Press, 2005)

Kunitzsch, Paul and Tim Smart, *A Dictionary of Modern Star Names* (Cambridge, MA: New Track Media, 2006)

Lane, Edward, *An Arabic-English Lexicon* (Beirut: Librairie du Liban, 1968)

Leopold of Austria, *A Compilation on the Science of the Stars*, trans. and ed. Benjamin N. Dykes (Minneapolis, MN: The Cazimi Press, 2015)

"Al-Manṣūr," *Almansoris astrologi propositiones, ad Saracenorum regem*, tr. Plato of Tivoli and Abraham Bar Hiyya (Basel: Iohannes Hervagius, 1533).

Māshā'allāh b. Atharī, *Book on Reception*, in Dykes 2008.

Al-Nadīm, Muhammad b. Ishāq b., ed. and trans. Bayard Dodge, *The Fihrist of al-Nadīm*, 2 vols. (New York & London, Columbia University Press, 1970)

Paul of Alexandria, *Late Classical Astrology: Paulus Alexandrinus and Olympiodorus*, trans. Dorian Gieseler Greenbaum, ed. Robert Hand (Reston, VA: ARHAT Publications, 2001)

Pingree, David, "Antiochus and Rhetorius," *Classical Philology*, v. 2 no. 3 (July 1977), pp. 203-23.

Pingree, David, "Classical and Byzantine Astrology in Sassanian Persia," Dumbarton Oaks Papers, v. 43 (1989), pp. 227-239.

Pingree, David, "Māshā'allāh's (?) Arabic Translation of Dorotheus," in *La Science des Cieux. Sages, mages, astrologues*, Res Orientales Vol. XII, 1999 (pp. 191-209)

Pingree, David, "The Byzantine Translations of Māshā'allāh on Interrogational Astrology," in Magdalino, Paul and Maria Mavroudi, eds., *The Occult Sciences in Byzantium* (Geneva: La Pomme d'or, 2006)

Ptolemy, Claudius, *Tetrabiblos*, trans. F.E. Robbins (Cambridge and London: Harvard University Press, 1940)

Ptolemy, Claudius, *Ptolemy's Almagest*, trans. and ed. G.J. Toomer (Princeton, NJ: Princeton University Press, 1998)

Al-Qabīsī, *The Introduction to Astrology*, eds. Charles Burnett, Keiji Yamamoto, Michio Yano (London and Turin: The Warburg Institute, 2004)

Rhetorius of Egypt, *Astrological Compendium*, trans. and ed. James H. Holden (Tempe, AZ: American Federation of Astrologers, Inc., 2009)

Al-Rijāl, Abū al-Hasan 'Alī b. Abī, *Kitāb al-Bāri'* (The Book of the Skilled), in London, BL Add. 23399.

Sahl b. Bishr, *Introductorium, Praecipua Iudicia, De Questionibus, De Electionibus*, and *De Significatione Temporis* in *Tetrabiblos*, ed. Girolamo Salio (Venice: Bonetus Locatellus, 1493)

Sarton, George, "Notes & Correspondence," in *Isis* vol. 14 (1950), pp. 420-22.

Sezgin, Fuat, *Geschichte des Arabischen Schrifttums* vol. 7 (Leiden: E.J. Brill, 1979)

Stegemann, Viktor, *Dorotheus von Sidon und das sogenannte Introductorium des Sahl ibn Bišr* (Prague: 1942, Orientalisches Institut in Prag)

Al-Tabarī, Abū Ja'far Muhammad b. Jarīr, *The History of al-Tabarī Vols. 31-34* (Albany, NY: SUNY Press, 1987-1992)

Theophilus of Edessa, trans. Eduardo Gramaglia and ed. Benjamin Dykes, *Astrological Works of Theophilus of Edessa* (Minneapolis, MN: The Cazimi Press, 2017)

Valens, Vettius, *The Anthology*, vols. I-VII, ed. Robert Hand, trans. Robert Schmidt (Berkeley Springs, WV: The Golden Hind Press, 1993-2001)

INDEX

'Abbāsid Caliphate...... 2-5, 7, 9, 15
Abraham/Abram (legendary astrologer) 661
Abū Bakr ... 22, 31, 352, 424, 459, 668, 676-77
Abū Ma'shar ... 1, 8-10, 14-16, 19, 31, 54, 63, 71, 257-58, 283, 312, 315, 319, 418, 451, 521, 582, 619, 668, 709-10, 727, 747, 752
Abū Sinīna (astrologer) 10, 287
Abū Sufyān (astrologer) ... 10, 282
Advancing ... 33-34, 52, 66, 69, 90, 201, 315, 333-34, 369, 406, 410, 413, 635, 681-82, 726
Ages of Man................ 257-58, 337
al-Abakh, al-Hasan (astrologer) 10, 280
al-Amīn (Caliph) 4-5
al-Andarzaghar, Zādānfarrūkh .. 2, 7-9, 20-21, 24-32, 38, 290, 323, 331, 345, 351-52, 355, 379-84, 386-93, 399, 421-22, 424-27, 429-30, 432, 438, 440, 444, 446, 451, 456, 459, 462, 495, 497, 499-501, 503-04, 512, 525-26, 528-30, 532, 538, 542-44, 548-49, 552, 561, 570, 572, 574, 576, 578-79, 582-84, 591-93, 598, 608-09, 613, 617-18, 621, 624, 626-27, 631-33, 637-38, 653-54, 663, 679, 693, 695-97, 699, 727-28, 731, 733-34, 737, 740
al-Bīrūnī...........26, 302-03, 305-06
al-Dāmaghānī (astrologer) 9, 29

al-Fadl b. Sahl 4-6, 8
al-Hādī (Caliph) 3, 5
al-Hasan b. Sahl............... 4, 6-8, 10
Alien (peregrine) planets... ..... 62, 68, 81, 83, 86, 121, 142, 149, 160, 164, 170-71, 175, 191, 298-99, 321-22, 395, 436, 456, 463, 468-69, 477, 491, 505, 537, 586, 612, 645-46, 650, 655, 657, 659, 662, 683, 685, 695, 697, 711, 742, 743
al-Khayyāt, Abū 'Alī ... 10, 16-19, 22-23, 30, 178, 235, 331, 396, 409-11, 431, 460, 489, 508, 668, 671, 673, 724-25, 748
al-Khurāsānī, Muhammad b. Bishr (astrologer) 10, 441
al-Ma'mūn (Caliph) ...4-6, 10, 280
al-Mahdī (Caliph) 3, 9
al-Mansūr (Caliph) ... 9-10, 21, 750-58
al-Nadīm (historian) ... 3, 6-8, 10-13, 15-16, 19, 280
al-Qabīsī (Alchabitius)......... 9, 175
al-Rijāl, 'Alī b. Abī (Abenragel).. 8, 16, 18, 20, 119, 165, 178, 198, 222, 237, 373, 597, 605-06, 643-44, 667-68, 671-72, 708, 725, 747, 749
al-Tabarī, 'Umar ... 3-4, 25-26, 298-300, 302, 790
Anonymous of 379 392
Antiochus (astrologer) ... 13, 400, 663
Anubio 259, 679

Apogee... 206, 228, 273, 276-77, 359, 564, 659, 726, 752-53, 757
Apollinarius 324
Aristotle 738
Ascensions, ascensional times.. 19, 87, 240, 252-53, 262, 274, 280-84, 290, 295, 308, 323, 332, 337, 346, 347, 393, 403, 413, 421, 427-28, 447
Aspects
   first and second 50
   general definition 49
   right and left 50
Aversion... 14, 45, 47, 49-51, 54, 56, 63-64, 66-67, 69, 71, 78, 81, 83-84, 88, 102, 104-06, 108-09, 111, 118, 121, 125-29, 132, 134-37, 139-40, 148-49, 151-58, 160-61, 164, 169, 171, 178, 183-84, 186-89, 200-01, 205-07, 221, 226, 228-29, 236, 247, 249, 271, 288-90, 295-96, 298, 309-10, 316, 324-26, 339-44, 347, 350, 352, 363-64, 370-74, 376, 394-95, 398, 409-11, 413, 415-17, 420, 422-23, 425-27, 438, 440, 442, 447, 452, 457, 459-61, 464, 467-69, 472, 482-84, 487, 492, 497, 499, 501, 504, 508, 515-17, 523-24, 533, 537, 543-44, 546, 553-54, 563-65, 567, 571, 574-78, 581-82, 585, 587-88, 590, 592, 596, 599-600, 603, 612, 614-16, 618-19, 623-25, 628, 630, 633, 636, 639-42, 646, 648, 650, 657-60, 662, 664, 667-670, 692, 701-05, 709, 711-14, 723, 728, 731-32, 738, 742-45, 765

Baghdad 2-7, 9-10, 27-28, 32
Besieging... 31, 67, 69-70, 72-73, 211, 291, 317, 323, 340, 542-43, 567, 569, 575, 577, 646-47, 661
Bizidaj... 8, 20, 23-28, 31, 271, 373, 435, 454-55, 465-66, 551
Blocking
   cutting the light. 56-59, 84, 115
   intervention 56-57, 59
   nullification........... 13, 56-59, 80
Bonatti, Guido................... 1, 16, 98
Bounds... 35-36, 47, 60-61, 66, 70, 73, 82, 84, 128-29, 132-33, 140, 166, 175-77, 200, 207, 216, 223, 240, 246, 263-65, 288-90, 294-96, 298, 301, 311, 314, 316, 319-22, 338, 340, 362, 365, 381, 394, 396, 398, 400, 404, 407, 425-26, 433, 435, 449-50, 459-60, 463, 468, 472-73, 489-91, 497-99, 503, 507-08, 511, 513-14, 530, 535, 548, 553, 565, 567, 579, 584, 586, 589-92, 594, 611, 613-14, 626-27, 633-34, 637, 646-47, 654-56, 668-70, 673, 680, 682-83, 693-95, 697-98, 704, 706-07, 719, 721, 748, 753, 755-56, 758
Būrān (astrologer) 4
Burned path (*via combusta*) 42, 70, 200, 203, 375
Burnett, Charles... 1, 9, 14, 29, 32, 381, 391-92, 697

INDEX

Burning (combustion)...19, 70, 76, 81-82, 91-92, 95, 100, 104, 108-09, 111, 122-25, 137, 147-48, 153, 156, 168-69, 190, 199, 203, 206, 208, 218, 241-42, 249-53, 286, 289, 291-92, 299, 301-02, 307-10, 330, 342, 348-50, 356, 370, 372, 410, 420, 424, 436-37, 466-67, 469, 471, 504, 508, 514, 524, 529, 546, 549, 552-53, 557, 595-96, 600, 625, 629, 637-38, 643, 647-48, 674, 676, 683, 685, 692, 742-43

Buzurjmihr...8, 20, 23-24, 26, 31, 459

Collection of light...13, 52, 55-56, 92-93, 142, 158-60, 460, 752

Days of the Moon...325, 331, 337-38, 403, 640, 653-56

Deferent............564, 757

Detriment...48, 68-69, 88, 170, 200, 306, 463, 469, 516, 577-78, 641, 656, 677

Distributions...195, 288, 294-97, 304, 308, 312-14, 317, 319-22, 421, 427-28, 448, 452, 466, 468, 489, 490, 508, 706, 716, 734, 752, 754

Domain (*hayyiz*)...36, 218, 408, 643, 701, 717, 755

Dorotheus of Sidon...1-2, 8-9, 13, 15-17, 20, 23-26, 29, 37, 110, 199, 202-03, 215, 217, 225, 228, 284, 288, 297, 303, 323, 328, 355, 379, 393, 399, 414, 418, 426, 432, 435, 438, 444, 451, 506, 527, 532-33, 535, 550, 587, 590, 593-94, 598, 614, 619, 652, 655-56, 659-60, 662, 668, 692, 709, 724, 728, 731-34, 737-38, 740-41

Eastern/western planets...18, 36, 66, 68-69, 75, 80, 86, 102, 105, 107, 109, 117, 130, 141, 143, 164, 166, 176, 207, 208, 210, 215, 228, 232, 239, 241, 245, 247, 253, 265, 298-305, 322, 327, 331, 353-54, 359, 361, 363-65, 382, 394-96, 407, 421, 425, 431-32, 435, 437, 440, 444, 461, 464-65, 471, 474, 483, 491, 505-06, 513, 515, 517, 525-26, 540, 543-44, 546, 570, 572, 580, 584-86, 588, 590, 595, 614-15, 620, 625-27, 630, 632, 636, 638, 655-56, 665, 669, 671, 680, 682, 694, 699-701, 717-18, 721, 723, 725-26, 748

Easternization, westernization 35, 84, 85, 86, 109, 117, 133, 150, 234, 299, 300, 302, 303, 304, 305, 306, 355, 362, 407, 418, 464, 503, 543, 587, 620, 636, 648, 669, 674, 675, 680, 682, 717, 719, 720, 721, 723, 751, 756, 757

Eclipses...200, 336, 476, 565, 645, 666

Emptiness in course...52, 61, 63, 71, 78, 99, 151, 162, 170, 181,

201, 229, 323, 335, 414, 502, 604
Epicycle 234, 564, 753
Escape 16, 61, 79, 80
Exaltation... 36, 47, 60-62, 64-66, 68, 73, 77, 80-84, 86, 92, 94, 112, 129, 140, 159, 164, 175-77, 205, 207, 217, 219, 249-50, 259, 265, 281, 288-90, 294, 298, 300, 311, 330, 365, 368, 378, 387, 394, 396-401,407, 420, 427, 436, 438, 441, 459, 462, 464, 466, 469, 472, 475, 479, 495, 514-15, 528-29, 534-36, 580, 586-87, 589-91, 594, 596, 599, 601, 608-11, 617, 633, 649, 656, 660, 665, 668, 671, 673, 683-85, 693-94, 699-700, 702-04, 706-07, 728, 745, 752-57
Faces... 47, 66, 73, 84, 128-29, 140, 175-77, 224-25, 281, 288, 351-52, 375, 404, 449, 630-31, 683, 732
Fall (contrary of exaltation) ... 61-62, 66-67, 69-70, 78, 94, 111, 140-41, 147-48, 153, 168-71, 175, 177-78, 210, 300, 315, 317, 331, 363, 368, 397, 399, 407, 425, 433, 437, 460, 463, 469, 514, 516, 529-30, 534, 579, 585, 587-88, 599, 601, 648, 656, 663, 683, 698, 704, 720, 742
Firmicus Maternus 13, 673-75
Fixed stars... 21, 27, 31, 256, 374, 380-93, 543, 546-51, 559, 628, 643, 672, 700, 751

Glow
  as sect 35, 66, 73, 83, 311
  out of rays ... 35, 73, 361, 492, 521-23, 606-07
Good/suitable places ... 37, 47-49, 66, 69, 83, 86, 104-06, 109, 117, 137, 141, 165, 167-68, 176, 218, 222, 226-27, 229, 247, 345, 351, 369, 393-94, 397, 410, 417, 421-22, 424, 445, 456, 463, 466, 495, 515, 517-18, 521, 534, 585, 617, 660, 697-98, 702, 709, 728
7-place system 48-49, 397
8-place system 14, 47, 48
Governor
  as general victor... 35, 218, 265, 327-28, 353, 362-63, 467, 481
  as house-master... 299, 301, 307-10, 317-18
  as lord of sign 669-70
  as time lord........................... 514
Handing over... 14, 22, 37, 58, 62-65, 77, 80, 83, 116, 120, 123, 136, 138-39, 164, 237-38, 258-59, 292, 315, 319, 358, 664, 684, 728, 759-60
  management... 22, 58, 64-65, 77, 80, 105, 109, 154, 157, 159-60, 168-71, 182, 230, 252-53, 258, 291-93, 315, 321, 349-50, 357, 413, 545, 581, 664, 759-65
  management and nature........65
  management and power....... 65, 159-60, 161, 411
  power....... 64-65, 164, 566, 664

Harthama b. A'yan............... 5, 6
Hārūn al-Rashīd (Caliph) 3-5
Head of the Dragon ... 68, 70, 139, 165, 200, 203, 213, 288, 291, 301, 317, 395, 397, 439, 465, 476, 552, 565, 567, 569-70, 597, 602, 638, 641-42, 647, 660, 666, 671, 700, 758
Hephaistion of Thebes ... 24, 26, 31, 37, 85, 191, 204, 206, 209-10, 217, 225, 228, 231, 260, 265-70, 273, 303, 323-24, 527, 582, 585, 592, 655, 662, 734, 737-38, 740-41
Hermes ... 8-9, 18, 243-45, 260-61, 266, 272-74, 278-79, 451, 521-32, 606, 711, 747
House-master ... 241, 287-88, 290, 294, 296-304, 307-08, 310, 315, 317, 319, 336, 339, 343, 345, 346, 423
Hugo of Santalla ... 1-2, 9, 16, 21, 145, 147-48, 150, 178, 381, 384-85, 390, 422, 424, 496, 538, 592, 693, 697, 766
ibn Hibintā................................8, 26
In the heart (*cazimi*) ... 67, 69, 85, 302, 692, 757
John of Spain 16
Joys/rejoicing ... 66, 84, 217, 477, 673
  by gender................... 74, 75
  by place ... 48-49, 73-74, 555, 588, 654
  by sect ... 74, 311, 444, 528, 593, 656, 755
  by sign 73-74

halb 73, 656, 755
Khurrazādh b. Dārshād................ 8
Khusrau I (Sasanian Shah).......... 8
Leopold of Austria 278
Lots
  7th house (Venus-DESC) 584, 598
  accusation 747
  action 680, 709
  assets ... 394, 403, 407, 410-11, 416-19, 426, 495
  authority.............................. 710
  children ... 20, 347, 418, 512, 515, 518-19, 521-23, 525, 527, 530, 533, 535, 740
  chronic illness ... 22, 538, 540, 552, 561, 563-66, 629
  courage 724-25
  craft.................................... 693
  death........................ 637-38, 652
  enemies................... 734, 746-48
  Erōs ... 456, 584, 598, 606, 728, 733, 740-41
  exaltation 459-60, 693, 754
  expedition 244, 709, 724
  father ... 358, 447, 459-62, 467, 469, 472, 477, 481, 484-85, 490-92, 495-96, 498-502, 504-05, 507, 509, 710, 719, 740
  female children 526-28, 531
  Fortune ... 127, 130, 148, 161, 201, 204-05, 218, 240, 243-44, 288-89, 293, 296, 311, 325, 331-32, 335-36, 338, 345-46, 353, 369-70, 372-74, 376, 393-94, 396, 404,

407-08, 410-12, 419-28, 439-42, 446, 456-57, 459, 495, 552, 554, 568, 573-75, 577, 581, 590, 598, 628, 637, 641, 648, 654, 658-59, 661, 670, 676, 680, 693, 724-25, 727, 733, 736-40, 746, 748
friends... 438, 456, 598, 645, 668, 727, 729-30, 731, 734
killing 641
livelihood 418, 419
male children 526-28, 531
marriage (Saturn-Venus) . 493, 584-85, 592-98, 602-03, 606, 609, 612-13, 621, 629, 631-32, 740-41
marriage (Sun-Moon-Venus) 620, 624-25
marriage (Sun-Venus) .. 606-08
marriage (uncertain) 618-19, 622, 629
men's deception 606
mother... 358, 461, 472-73, 475, 490, 493-94, 501-02, 508
necessity 727, 740, 746
number of siblings 446, 451
religion... 244, 372, 668, 670, 672-73, 676, 693, 724, 727
riding animals 748
siblings... 432, 437-42, 445-47, 451-53, 456-57
slaves 580, 582, 746, 747
Spirit/the Invisible ... 22, 335, 369, 372, 376, 428, 568, 575-78, 598, 622, 628, 668, 670, 676, 693, 724, 727, 733, 740
timing of children 525
travel... 655, 659, 663-64, 667-68
valor 724-25
women's deception 606
work 680, 693, 709, 710
Lunation (esp. pre-natal)... ......30, 240, 262-70, 272, 282, 287-88, 290-91, 296, 325-26, 340, 343, 345, 353, 404, 423, 425, 465, 474, 496, 499, 502-03, 545-46, 574-76, 589, 641, 652, 679, 693-96, 749, 755
Manethō 31, 323
Māshā'allāh b. Atharī... 1-4, 9-10, 12, 15-23, 25, 27-30, 32, 48, 54, 61, 73, 76, 81, 84, 98, 101, 103, 135, 155-56, 165, 172, 177-79, 181, 183-85, 197, 201, 206-13, 221, 228, 233, 235, 241, 245, 247-48, 251, 253, 283, 293, 300, 307-08, 310-16, 319-20, 331-32, 336, 347, 348-49, 368-72, 379, 409, 411, 415-18, 421, 432, 436-37, 450, 452-54, 468, 475, 482, 486, 488, 491-93, 495, 508-09, 511, 518-24, 526, 528, 540, 542-43, 551-52, 560-63, 599-600, 605-08, 638, 648, 651-52, 655, 664, 666-68, 676, 680, 702, 705, 707-10, 724, 728-29, 731, 745-48
Midpoints 240

Moon
  waning... 71, 202, 209-11, 213-14, 227, 340, 362, 544-45, 549, 566-67, 577
  waxing... 71, 108, 117, 204, 206, 208, 212-13, 215, 220, 227-28, 330, 362, 411, 474, 544, 549, 569, 576
Namūdār... 263, 272-73, 283-85, 287
Nawbakht al-Hakīm ("The Persian")... 3, 9, 25, 287, 335-37, 347, 540, 551
Non-reception.... 52, 60-62, 94, 96
Overcoming... 51, 82, 143, 165, 217, 367, 377, 464, 475, 479-82, 499, 503-05, 566, 578, 629, 640, 648, 734
Overlord
  lord of sign 35, 408
  primary triplicity lord... 35, 402
Paul of Alexandria 709
Petosiris 273, 516
Pingree, David... 1, 9, 17, 24, 26-29, 32, 303, 381, 391-92, 482, 697
Planetary years... 18, 237-38, 241, 247, 250-51, 298-02, 319, 343, 373, 402, 428, 506, 548, 573
Planets
  diurnal/nocturnal... 66, 69, 72-74, 83, 192, 293, 298-99, 311, 333, 345, 377, 394, 400, 424, 444, 491, 588

female/feminine... 66-67, 75, 107, 298, 311, 358, 377, 446, 462, 503, 539, 635
male/masculine... 66-67, 75, 288, 298, 311, 328, 358, 377, 446, 457, 462, 503, 527
Orbs or bodies 53
Primary directions... 19, 235, 241, 246, 253, 288, 296, 307-08, 310-14, 316, 318, 321, 337, 427, 466-67, 489-90, 495, 501, 505-09, 511, 753
Profections... 18, 37, 171-72, 220, 250-53, 308-09, 311-14, 316, 318-22, 334, 336-37, 427-28, 489, 506, 511, 619, 736, 754
Ptolemy, Claudius... 1, 8, 20, 24, 38-39, 87, 164, 257, 260, 264, 273, 278, 295, 324, 326-29, 341-42, 352-55, 357, 359-60, 379, 408, 420, 474, 505, 546-47, 597-98, 615-17, 620-23, 643, 661-62, 682, 684, 696, 701, 711, 720, 724, 735-36, 738-39
Quadrants... 18, 67, 69, 74, 124, 164, 233, 244-45, 280-82, 313, 327, 333, 352, 355, 404, 427, 443, 449, 457, 616, 620, 635, 663, 711, 726
Reception... 15, 23, 52, 60-62, 65-67, 69, 76-77, 80-81, 94-95, 105-06, 108, 112, 116, 120, 136-37, 150, 153, 159-62, 164, 168, 171-73, 177, 180-81, 185, 198, 203, 207, 218, 226, 228,

241, 250-52, 291-94, 301, 308, 311, 315-18, 333, 336, 348-50, 359, 361-62, 368, 370-72, 411-13, 415-17, 436-37, 446, 453, 466, 468-69, 470-71, 475, 487-88, 491, 498, 508, 519, 528, 592, 601-03, 649, 664, 672, 676-78, 681, 692, 702, 704, 706-07, 729, 745, 752, 754, 761

perfect 60

planets not received 109, 150, 159-60, 162, 169, 171, 177, 181, 349, 415, 437, 488, 491, 509, 528, 602-03, 677, 704, 705, 729, 745

with minor dignities 60

Reflecting light ... 15, 54, 104, 109, 122, 127, 142, 148, 158, 411, 665, 705

Releaser ... 240-41, 286-91, 294-95, 297-98, 307-08, 310, 314-18, 338-39, 343, 345-47, 649

Retreating ... 33-34, 52, 69, 91, 99, 315, 413, 681, 726

Retrogradation ... 14, 18, 23, 63, 67, 69, 76, 79-81, 84, 87, 92-93, 95-96, 101-02, 108, 110, 117, 120-21, 123, 133, 136-37, 139-42, 147, 152-53, 157, 170, 181, 185, 204, 210-11, 222, 228, 231, 234-35, 239, 247, 251, 286, 291-94, 299-302, 305-06, 317, 323, 330, 345, 348-50, 355, 362-64, 367, 371-72, 437, 446, 457, 475, 485, 487, 489, 505, 508, 514, 562, 580, 585, 588, 646, 655, 664, 669, 673, 677, 683, 685, 723, 742, 752, 756

Returning light 63-64, 80

Rhetorius of Egypt ... 1-2, 7-8, 14, 20, 24-29, 31-32, 392-93, 550, 630

Sasanian Persians ... 2, 5, 8, 13, 16, 24, 28

Sect of chart .. 43-44, 66, 71-74, 83, 165, 198, 219, 249-50, 253, 260-64, 272, 280-82, 287-88, 292-93, 298-99, 311, 315-16, 322, 330-33, 336, 345, 347, 358, 367, 369, 377-78, 383-84, 386-88, 393-94, 396-99, 400, 402, 412, 418-19, 422, 424-26, 431, 435, 440, 444, 451, 457, 459, 462, 464-68, 471, 473, 476, 478-79, 481, 483, 485, 489-91, 493, 497, 499-500, 502, 504, 507, 511, 513, 515, 521, 523-24, 528, 530-31, 539, 543, 545, 547-48, 551, 561, 563, 572, 574, 576, 582, 584, 586-88, 591, 595, 598, 606, 620, 624, 639, 641-44, 652, 655, 658-59, 662-63, 668, 671-72, 674-75, 680, 695, 700-01, 709, 711, 714, 724-27, 730, 733, 740, 744, 746, 748

Sezgin, Fuat ... 3-4, 8-12, 19, 21-23, 27, 280, 460, 750

Shapūr I (Persian Shah) 24

Sibārmahnar 9, 381

Signs

accumulating and squandering 378

INDEX

airy... 42-43, 102, 131-33, 151, 187, 207, 229, 355, 375, 418, 533, 567, 569, 638, 644, 690
and terrain............43, 102, 131
bestial.................. 214, 644, 657
character traits............ 376, 377
convertible (movable)...42, 69, 87, 106, 109, 117-18, 135, 138, 140-41, 155, 165, 169-71, 173, 181, 183, 188, 196-97, 208, 213-16, 229, 235-36, 241, 245, 250, 315, 359, 400, 411, 423, 445, 497-98, 543, 562, 569, 580, 582, 589, 593-94, 600-01, 611-12, 615, 618, 628, 647, 658, 662, 668, 671, 675, 703, 716, 744, 752, 754, 757
dark.............................42, 375
defective/cut limbs... ....566, 570, 640-41, 643-44
degrees of high rank............ 377
diurnal/nocturnal... 41, 72-73, 198
double-bodied (common) ..42, 87, 94, 102, 106, 109, 117-18, 122, 129, 135, 140-41, 143, 155, 171-73, 188-89, 191-92, 197, 203, 205, 208, 213-17, 228-29, 236, 241, 245, 250, 328-29, 360, 400, 408, 423, 444-46, 455, 515-17, 523, 527, 532-33, 562, 579-80, 587, 589, 595, 599, 611, 618, 621, 663, 668, 671, 692, 703, 716, 742, 744

earthy... 42-43, 102, 124, 131-33, 187, 212-13, 224, 356, 375, 404-05, 473, 533, 569, 580-81, 644, 662, 685, 689, 749
female/feminine... 41, 67, 71-72, 99, 106-07, 209-10, 214, 222, 281, 285, 288, 311, 322-23, 331, 340, 358, 377, 398, 402, 406, 445, 451, 452, 456-57, 461, 463, 465, 472, 482, 485, 502, 510, 524, 526, 555, 572, 581, 629, 631, 634-36, 639, 670, 701, 711, 725, 759
fertile/sterile... 43, 375, 429, 513
fiery... 42-43, 102, 131-33, 198, 229, 356-57, 418-19, 513, 533, 567, 569, 644, 648, 685, 689-91, 749, 751, 755
fixed... 42, 66, 69, 87, 94, 109, 117-18, 135, 138, 140-41, 150, 155, 165, 171, 173, 183, 188-89, 197, 208, 212, 215-16, 220, 226, 228, 235, 241, 245, 250, 263, 314, 360, 423, 445, 516, 562, 587, 589, 601, 611, 643, 668, 671, 703-04, 716, 742-43, 749, 751-52, 756-57
four-footed... 42, 99, 325-26, 338, 374, 404, 482, 581, 643, 646, 690, 748-49, 759, 762
giving and taking 378

human/of people ... 43, 99, 151, 325-26, 375, 405, 643, 645-46, 657-58, 662, 672, 685, 689-90, 758-59, 762
lecherous/licentious 375-76, 615
male/masculine ... 41, 67, 71-72, 99, 106-07, 209, 222, 281, 285, 311, 322-24, 328, 331, 340, 358, 364, 377, 402, 406, 445-46, 451-52, 456-57, 461-62, 478-79, 485, 502, 510, 526-27, 531, 553, 581, 584-85, 588, 596, 609, 611, 616, 628, 632-34, 701, 711, 725-26, 757, 759
obeying/commanding 732, 734, 737, 740
of animals 689, 690
of anxiety 375
of pleasures 375
of predatory animals .. 325, 326
of sexual intercourse 376
of trees 638
of vegetation ... 42-43, 151, 448, 690-91
powerful 375
rational 378
royal ... 198, 397, 404, 406, 447, 700, 748
social classes ... 375, 378, 403, 473, 580
straight/crooked ... 31, 41, 87, 197, 198, 201-02, 204, 210, 218, 322-24, 743
tranquil 375
various illnesses 375-77
voiced/unvoiced 42, 375-76

watery ... 42-44, 102, 131, 133, 151, 187, 190, 198, 207-08, 217, 223-24, 229-30, 356-57, 372, 376, 404, 418, 429, 448, 482, 513, 533, 539, 568-69, 638, 644-46, 658, 662, 685, 689-691, 699, 749, 758
Slow planets ... 71, 79, 110, 197, 200, 222, 239, 245
Solar revolutions ... 11, 19, 23, 194, 220, 249-53, 258, 286, 288-89, 296, 307-09, 312, 314, 319, 337, 413, 438, 447, 450, 458-59, 506, 508-09, 682, 716, 732, 734, 753-54, 763-64
Spear-bearing ... 36, 400-01, 496, 618, 700-01, 711, 717-18, 720, 723, 756
Stations, stationary planet..76, 79, 87, 96, 123, 133, 152, 234, 251, 294, 349, 355, 364, 446, 452, 503, 646
Stegemann, Viktor 1, 66
Stephanus (associate of Theophilus) 27
Sulaymān 'Uthmān (unknown astrologer) 168
Ṭāhir b. al-Husayn 4-7
Tail of the Dragon..68, 70, 98, 139, 142, 165-66, 191, 200, 203, 205-06, 216, 226, 286, 291, 297, 301-02, 317, 397-98, 463, 465, 472, 476, 478, 510, 514, 516, 539, 570, 580, 586-87, 589, 597, 602, 642, 644-45, 666, 700-01, 726, 740, 758

Thayūghūrs (unknown book or astrologer) 10, 282
Theophilus of Edessa ... 2-3, 8-10, 15, 17-18, 24-25, 27-28, 31, 76, 79, 82-83, 86, 107, 141-46, 148, 152, 154, 165, 196-97, 224, 243, 245, 248, 282, 358, 395, 401, 406, 434, 439, 441-42, 459, 521, 539, 546-47, 575, 582, 709
Transfer of light ... 15, 52, 54, 61, 77, 92-93, 99, 101, 108, 113-16, 120, 123, 127, 142, 148, 158, 164, 237, 248, 359, 460, 665
Transits ... 78, 96, 139, 159-60, 169, 172, 217, 234, 237, 244, 246, 249, 251, 253, 288, 309, 345-46, 395, 402, 409, 427, 489-90, 495, 504, 506-09, 525-26, 540, 542, 560, 585, 619, 666, 716, 735-36, 738-39, 744, 754, 757
Triplicity lords 43
  of Ascendant ... 258, 287, 311, 330-35, 337-38, 340-41, 343-45, 350, 430, 435, 440, 497, 751
  of IC 552-53, 637, 645
  of Jupiter ... 512, 514-15, 518, 524, 532-33, 535
  of Lot of assets or livelihood 419
  of Lot of Fortune 332, 426-427
  of Mars ... 432, 435, 444, 447, 611, 624
  of Moon 316, 399, 412, 447
  of sect light .. 331-32, 362, 393-95, 400, 402, 404, 406-07, 412-13, 421-22, 424-25, 574, 576, 654, 659, 671, 673
  of Sun .. 316, 412, 447, 462-63, 465, 477, 499, 503
  of the second place 399
  of Venus ... 447, 583-86, 588, 596, 610, 613, 624-26
  of pre-natal lunation 331
Twelfth-parts ... 200, 218, 243, 325, 328, 401-02, 464, 473, 485, 496, 548, 679, 698
Under the rays ... 63, 67-68, 82-85, 104-05, 108, 111, 117, 123-25, 127, 143, 156, 203, 208, 211, 220, 222, 224, 226, 230, 290, 297-300, 303-305, 330, 333, 341, 344-46, 348, 355, 361-64, 367, 369-71, 377, 407, 410, 432, 436, 446, 459-60, 464, 470-71, 490, 492, 503, 505, 508, 512, 514, 515, 529, 531, 540, 553, 557, 570, 577, 580, 583-86, 588, 590, 592-93, 597-600, 612, 616, 625, 629, 632-33, 636, 644, 648, 669, 673, 675-76, 683, 695, 697, 707, 725
Valens, Vettius ... 2, 8, 20, 24, 26, 31, 79, 266, 271-72, 283, 308, 335, 373, 427, 451, 493, 516, 554, 573, 584, 606, 661, 747
Victors .. 35, 98, 236, 240-41, 264, 328, 337, 353, 408, 679, 682
Whole signs (discussion) 32
Wildness 63, 71, 515

Withdrawing... 33-34, 91, 170, 177, 190, 249, 286, 311, 315, 331, 409-10, 423, 469-71, 475-77, 479, 481, 484, 602, 661, 664, 666-67, 691, 702-03, 707, 716, 726, 729, 745, 758, 765

Zarādusht (astrologer)........9, 724

Zoroastrians, Zoroastrianism .4, 6

www.ingramcontent.com/pod-product-compliance
Lightning Source LLC
Chambersburg PA
CBHW060356230426
43663CB00008B/1291